Financial
Institutions and
Markets in a
Changing World

Financial Institutions and Markets in a Changing World

Third Edition

Edited by
Donald R. Fraser
Peter S. Rose
Both of Texas A&M University

1987

BUSINESS PUBLICATIONS, INC.
Plano, Texas   75075

© Business Publications, Inc., 1980, 1984, and 1987

ISBN 0-256-03695-0

Library of Congress Catalog Card No. 86–61850

Printed in the United States of America

1 2 3 4 5 6 7 8 9 0 K 4 3 2 1 0 9 8 7

Preface

As *Financial Institutions and Markets* enters its third edition, it is appropriate to look at the tremendous—many would say revolutionary—changes that have reshaped the financial marketplace in recent years. The menu of financial services and financial instruments available to the public has broadened so greatly that businesses and consumers often seem bewildered and confused about what their financial options really are, and on what finance and investment alternatives best suit their needs today. At least part of the reason for the confusion lies in the genius of modern technology. Computers, automated service delivery systems, and satellite and wire communications have improved so much today that they are applied to an increasingly broad range of financial tasks. Moreover, the cost of electronic information processing has declined so significantly that the newest technology is now economically available to millions of businesses and households, permitting faster, more convenient, and more accurate interaction between financial firms and the customers they serve.

Deregulation of the financial sector, especially for banks, credit unions, savings and loans, and other depository institutions, has also spurred the recent revolution in new financial services and new financial instruments. Passage of such landmark federal laws as the Depository Institutions Deregulation and Monetary Control Act of 1980 and the Garn-St Germain Depository Institutions Act of 1982 have loosened the chains which for so long restricted the creativity of providers of financial services. The ensuing creative revolution has given birth to a rapidly lengthening list of new financial instruments—futures, options, collateralized mortgage obligations (CMOs), Super NOWs, flexible-rate and checkable money market deposits (MMDAs), STRIPs, interest-rate SWAPs, to name but a few. Not surprisingly, deregulation, the proliferation of financial services and instruments, the accelerating pace of technological change, and other forces within and without the financial sector have not been unmixed blessings. Indeed, economics and finance teach us that nothing is really "free." Every new idea captured by the marketplace has a cost in terms of using resources, in upsetting established institutions and destabilizing existing relationships, and in posing risks to profits and long-run survival for many businesses. Today's financial market revolution is certainly no exception to this fundamental principle. Banks, savings and loans, credit unions, and other financial institutions have failed in numbers not seen since the 1920s and 1930s. Buffeted by economic turmoil in agricultural and other commodity markets, in international credit and currency markets, in basic manufacturing, energy, and high-tech industries, today's financial institution faces more uncertainty in the cost and availability of the funds it needs to operate and in the profitability and risk of its loans and investments than at any time in the past half century.

The turmoil and uncertainty of today's changing financial marketplace has significant implications for each of us. Recent developments present us with both a *challenge* and an *opportunity*. The challenge is that we must all know and understand so much *more* today about financial institutions and their markets in a rapidly changing world. We must learn how to assemble, process, and sort financial information more quickly and learn how to make consistently sound financial decisions based on quality information, careful analysis, and well-schooled judgment. For the marketplace within which those decisions will be hammered out is so much more competitive and less forgiving of our ignorance and of our mistakes than ever before. But, there is also greater *opportunity* today to develop new financial ideas and to test them in a more responsive financial marketplace where increased risk, fortunately, is balanced by greater potential rewards.

The challenge and the opportunity in today's financial system is what this book is about. This third edition is designed to present the most important ongoing changes in financial institutions and markets from the perspective of both management decision makers and consumers of financial services. Both managers and consumers of financial services have a critical stake in the workings of the financial system, especially in how it operates and where that system seems to be headed. But, while the emphasis in the pages that follow is on *new* financial developments and recent changes, this third edition, like the two previous editions, also addresses the fundamentals of the financial marketplace—timeless factors that must be considered in every financial decision and transaction. It is hoped that the conscientious reader of this book will emerge from the long journey through its pages with a deeper understanding of the forces that shape the return and risk of financial transactions and the opportunity costs of every financial decision.

The authors have chosen readings which stress again and again the fundamental contributions that financial markets and institutions make to our standard of living, to solving basic problems, and to fulfilling basic needs. Each one of us—regardless of income, social status, or profession—must continually interact within the financial system to secure any or all of the following services:

1. *Attractive outlets for our savings,* so those savings will grow to meet our future needs (e.g., purchase of an automobile, a home, an education, a comfortable retirement, and the like).
2. *Sources of credit* to support potentially profitable investment ideas and to fund the level of consumption of goods and services that fits our chosen lifestyle.
3. *Channels for making payments* via checks, currency, credit cards, and so on for the goods and services we choose to buy.

4. *Instruments in which to store liquidity* (purchasing power) that pay a satisfactory rate of return but assure us that our investment can readily be rolled over into cash at the moment cash is needed with little risk of loss.

5. *Sources of risk protection* to safeguard against loss of property or income through the purchase of insurance policies, financial instruments to store precautionary funds, and financial contracts to hedge against fluctuating interest rates and security prices.

Moreover, from the perspective of the whole economy and nation, the financial system is an essential conduit today for government economic policies designed to achieve society's broad economic goals of high employment, low inflation, sustainable economic growth, and a stable balance of international payments. As students and as customers of financial institutions and markets, we must understand how and why the nation's financial system provides these services and what our role can be in accessing that system and working to improve it. The goal of better understanding is, of course, the key objective of this book.

The readings in this edition fall into seven parts—the same grouping of articles as appeared in the second edition. But, there are many *new* articles in this edition (31 new articles in all) which appear more relevant to current financial problems and issues. Each article in the book touches upon one or another of the fundamental services and tasks performed by the nation's financial system—savings, credit, payments, liquidity, risk protection, and public policy.

Parts One and Two—"Financial Institutions: Management and Regulation" and "Deregulation of Financial Institutions"—are concerned with the problems of managing and regulating key financial institutions (particularly banks and thrifts) in today's volatile economic and financial environment. The articles in these two sections focus on such issues as how to protect a financial institution's earnings and net worth against the ravages of fluctuating interest rates, the development of new financial services, and the appearance of new competition. The implications of recent federal deregulation legislation are viewed from the point of view of both financial institutions' management and from the perspective of regulators who must supervise and examine these institutions. A key issue here is how to structure government regulation of the financial sector in an age of deregulation in order to encourage competition and promote equity but to avoid damaging the public's confidence in our most important financial institutions.

Part Three—"Determination of Interest Rates and Stock Prices"—looks at the markets within which financial institutions must sell their services. The principal focus of this section is on *financial prices*—interest rates (the "price" of credit) and the market value of equity securities (stock). What causes these prices to change? Obviously, answering such a question is vital to the managers of financial institutions, the public, and the regulatory community because changing financial prices affect both the cost and availability of financial services, the profits of financial institutions, and the net worth of thousands of individual and institutional investors. Among the key causal factors considered in this portion of the book are inflation, market expectations, the availability of new information, and the changing needs of borrowers and lenders of funds.

Part Four—"Instruments of the Money and Capital Markets"—examines a number of the most popular and newer securities and loans developed in the financial markets in recent years. Examples include the new options markets for government and other high-grade securities and financial futures contracts and the growing use of zero-coupon and other deeply discounted bonds. There is also an analysis of recently troubled securities markets, such as the market for repurchase agreements (RPs) where increased lender risk has become a key consideration. This portion of the book also looks in some detail at several traditional financial instruments—for example, federal funds, commercial paper, and bankers' acceptances—whose markets have experienced both rapid growth and structural change in recent years.

Part Five—"International Finance"—looks beyond the domestic marketplace to the problems of financing international trade in today's increasingly interdependent but tumultuous world. The reader is introduced to the methods by which foreign currencies are priced and traded and to the institutions that literally make the currency markets "go." Here, too, innovation in the form of new financial instruments has appeared, and one of the most important of these—foreign currency options—is discussed in detail. This section of the book also devotes considerable space to international banking and its recent problems, especially the difficulties associated with international loans to lesser-developed countries and to energy producers and commodity traders. These problems are related to domestic banking and to the perennial issues of how to control and supervise U.S. bank expansion overseas and the entry of foreign banks into the United States.

What happens to financial markets and institutions is profoundly affected by government economic and financial policies. As Part Six—"Macroeconomic and Financial Policy"—brings out, government policies significantly influence the interest rates paid by borrowers of funds, the value of securities traded in the financial markets, and the volume and growth of saving, borrowing, and spending. These policies generally fall into three categories:

1. Money and credit (or monetary) policies set by the Federal Reserve System.
2. Government spending, taxing, and borrowing policies set by Congress and the President but carried out by the Treasury (known as fiscal policy).
3. Management of the huge federal debt by the U.S. Treasury Department (referred to as debt-management policy).

All three of these forms of government policy are considered in this section of the book, with special emphasis upon the unique problems of government policy in the 1980s—lower inflation, but sluggish economic growth that is still volatile and highly uncertain. The size and effects of the massive federal debt and government budget deficits are singled out for careful analysis in this portion of the book.

Finally, no book focusing upon today's financial system would be comlete without a look at the process of *financial innovation* itself—the steps that lead to the development of new financial services and new financial instruments. Current trends in key financial markets and institutions have spawned a welter of new services and securities—products of creative men and women responding to the challenging problems of today with new and better financial tools. Part Seven looks at this innovative trend both in the United States and abroad and at some of the key services and credit instruments it has created. Examples include interest-rate SWAPs and the electronic processing and transfer of financial information.

Each innovation and innovative process is presented against the backdrop of today's problems. Why was the new service or new instrument needed? What problems does it attempt to solve? What risks does innovation present to individuals and institutions?—and how can we best deal with those risks? What legal and technological barriers still lie ahead as our financial markets and institutions come to grips with the challenge and the uncertainty of today and tomorrow. These and other critical issues that surround the process of financial innovation are explored from a private and public perspective in the concluding section of the book.

As with the earlier editions, the authors believe that this edition of *Financial Markets and Institutions* is suitable for a wide variety of courses in economics and finance. It has particular application to courses dealing with money and banking, financial institutions, the money and capital markets, and commercial bank management. In addition, practitioners in industry and other individuals who desire to update their knowledge of recent innovations and policy issues in the financial sector will find the book a useful guide.

The authors wish to express their deep gratitude to those who wrote the articles included in this edition. We hope their thoughts and ideas will reach an even larger audience through the medium of this book. In addition, we would like to acknowledge the cooperation of the publishers of the articles included whose support made this book possible. A special thanks is due to our families who, as before, endured the demands of time and not infrequent frustration in putting this new edition together. Without their encouragement and understanding, this project could not have been completed.

Donald R. Fraser
Peter S. Rose

Contents

PART ONE

Financial Institutions: Management and Regulation

A revolution is taking place in the banking and financial system in the United States and, indeed, of the entire world. This revolution is market-driven, encompasses the attempts of new competitors to enter the financial service industry, and is heavily influenced by the spread of new technology that has to a considerable extent made distance irrelevant in the delivery of financial services. It is also, though, affected greatly by the rising instability in the economy and in financial markets that has characterized the 1980s. Financial deregulation—encompassing the virtual elimination of deposit-rate ceilings, the spread of interstate banking, and the extension of new products and services to depository institutions—is an important part of the significant changes occurring in the financial system. However, the growth of financial conglomerates and financial supermarkets play an equally important role.

The revolution in the banking and financial services industry has markedly affected the way in which financial institutions are managed. Growing competition that has placed downward pressure on profit margins has made the management of risk even more critical to the viability of financial institutions. The management of interest rate and credit risk thus takes on new significance in a world of shrinking profits. Interest-sensitive portfolio positions must be monitored and managed. Similarly, the degree of credit risk involved in the extension of loans must be estimated before the credit decision is reached and monitored during the life of the loan.

Bank management of interest-rate risk conventionally focuses on the "gap" position. In this analytical technique, a bank's assets are dichotomized into those which are interest-rate sensitive (i.e., allowing repricing within a specified period) and those which are not interest-rate sensitive. As Brewer points out in the first article in this section, "Bank Gap Management and the Use of Financial Futures," the gap is the difference between the volume of fixed-rate assets and fixed-rate liabilities. A bank (or other depository institution) which has less fixed-rate assets than fixed-rate liabilities would have a negative gap and would find that its net interest margin (the difference between interest revenue and interest expense) would fall if interest rates rose and would rise if interest rates fell. While useful as a first approximation in monitoring the effects of interest rate movements, this "basic" gap model may be misleading in some respects. Brewer points out the necessary modifications needed in this basic gap model, including the concept of "duration gap" and also shows how banks may make use of financial futures in managing their interest sensitivity.

One of the most significant developments in the financial system has been the entry into financial services of firms whose primary orientation has been nonfinancial. Attracted by the relatively stable profits available in financial services and by the ability to diversify their income sources many retailers, manufacturers and other nonfinancial firms have made major inroads into financial services. In the second article in this section, "Banks and Nonbanks: The Horse Race Continues," Pavel and Rosenblum consider the dimensions of this phenomenon. As shown in that article, large nonfinancial firms offer a wide range of services, including commercial finance, consumer finance, real estate, insurance, leasing, investment services, and other finance-related services. Moreover, nonfinancial firms have been quite successful in acquiring market share and in gaining profits. Pavel and Rosenblum consider the importance of these activities and their implications for the future of the banking industry.

In the third article in this section, "A Deregulated Rerun: Banking in the Eighties," Merris and Wood consider the recent changes in the banking industry from a longer-term perspective. They point out that many of the developments of recent years are not unprecedented. In fact, in many respects, these changes represent a return to practices that were well established by the 1920s. In their view, the increase in competition in banking that has characterized the 1980s has merely placed commercial banks back on the path that was blocked by the legislation of the 1930s.

Fortier and Phillis, in "Bank and Thrift Performance since DIDMCA," consider the effects of deregulation on the financial performance of banks and thrifts. They compare the financial position of these financial institutions in the 1975–79 period (prior to passage of the Depository Institutions Deregulation and Monetary Control Act of 1980) and in the 1980–84 period (after the passage of DIDMCA). Although they point out that the effects of deregulation on banks and thrifts cannot be separated from other factors, they conclude that the effects have generally been beneficial, especially for consumers of financial services.

In "Recent Developments in The Credit Union Industry," Pearce considers some of the major changes at one of the smallest of the nation's financial institutions (through a rapidly growing part of the financial-services industry). As Pearce points out, although credit unions have shown rapid growth, their expansion has been uneven. High interest rates combined with deposit and loan interest-rate ceilings have affected their ability to compete effectively with other financial institutions. The future of credit unions in an increasingly deregulated financial environment is somewhat uncertain.

The last two articles in this section deal with the regulation of financial institutions, a topic of increasing difficulty and complexity as financial institutions become less specialized and as the traditional distinctions between different institutions lose their meaning. George Benston raises the basic philosophic issue of why banks and other depository institutions should be regulated. As he points out, many of the historical reasons for bank regulation may no longer be relevant. In particular, Benston argues that using banks as a means of raising government revenue, prevention of centralized power, assurance of bank services, and achieving a socially desirable allocation of banking services and credit are no longer relevant reasons for bank regulation. Indeed, following Benston's views, there would be very little regulation of commercial banks beyond the regulation relevant to all business corporations. In a related article, "Reorganization of the Federal Regulatory Agencies," Paul Horvitz argues that deregulation has produced a need for substantial changes in the structure of regulatory agencies. He proposes bringing banks and thrifts under the same regulator and removing the regulatory (but not the monetary policy) functions of the Federal Reserve.

1

Bank Gap Management and the Use of Financial Futures

Elijah Brewer

Interest-rate "gap" management has become an increasingly important part of bank funds management over the past decade. This mangement technique matches liabilities to assets of similar maturity lengths and risk classes.

As interest rates have become more volatile and have climbed to historically unprecedented high levels, the degree to which variable-rate assets are different from variable-rate liabilities (or, in other words, the amount of variable-rate assets supported by fixed-rate funds) has caused concern. This gap—really an imbalance—measures the exposure of bank net interest margin (i.e., interest income less interest expense) to unexpected changes in market interest rates.

Such changes can result in gains or losses in a bank's portfolio. Losses result if the bank finances its fixed-rate long-term loans with relatively short-term funds and market interest rates rise. Losses also occur if relatively fixed-rate longer-term funds are used and lending rates fall. Gains can be made if interest rates move in the other direction. A bank, then, is exposed to interest-rate risk whenever there is a quantitative imbalance between its fixed-rate liabilities and its fixed-rate assets of the same maturity.

Bankers have recognized the importance of gap management in reducing interest-rate risk and achieving acceptable bank performance.[1] Furthermore, bank regulators are paying increased attention to a bank's gap position. They are concerned that exposed asset and liability positions could threaten the profitability of some banks and, therefore, their capital positions if interest rates should move adversely. Controlling the size of the gap is an important function of bank funds management and managers are now using financial futures contracts to hedge exposed asset and liability positions.

To what extent can bank profits be stabilized by trading financial futures? To what extent are bank futures trading decisions constrained by the regulatory

From *Economic Perspectives,* Federal Reserve Bank of Chicago, March/April 1985, pp. 12–21.

Elijah Brewer is an economist at the Federal Reserve Bank of Chicago.

5

requirement that futures positions represent bona fide hedges of interest-rate exposure? This paper provides some insight into how financial futures can be used as vehicles for reducing interest-rate exposure and managing the gap position, and may aid regulators in their supervision of bank use of these instruments.

THE BASIC FUNDS GAP CONCEPT

In a typical gap management process, bank management is asked to dichotomize all items, both assets and liabilities, on the balance sheet according to interest-rate sensitivity. An asset or liability with an interest rate subject to change within a year is considered variable. One that cannot change for more than a year is considered fixed. The imbalance between fixed-rate liabilities and fixed-rate assets is a gap that can be expressed either as dollars or as a percentage of total earning assets. If fixed-rate liabilities exceed fixed-rate assets, the bank has a positive gap. Under rising short-term interest rates, this positive gap would increase net interest margin. But declining short-term interest rates, with a positive gap, would exert downward pressure on net interest margin.

If fixed-rate liabilities are less than fixed-rate assets, there would be a negative gap. With a negative gap, net interest margin would decline if short-term interest rates rose and increase if short-term interest rates fell.

Table 1 presents the gap positions (the difference between rate-sensitive assets and rate-sensitive liabilities divided by total assets) in the fourth quarter of 1983 and the first three quarters of 1984 for 20 large domestic banks in the United States. During the December–September period, the 20-bank sample became generally more liability-sensitive. The rate sensitivity gap as a percent of total assets in the third quarter of 1984 ranged from − 12.1 percent at Bank of America to 4.2 percent at Mellon Bank, compared with a range between − 11.4 percent at Bank of America and 9.0 percent at Chase Manhattan Bank in the fourth quarter of 1983.

Controlling the size of gaps such as those in Table 1 is an important function of bank funds management. To keep from relying too much on short-term funds, banks set a limit on the use of variable-rate liabilities to finance fixed-rate long term assets. Thus, while federal funds are a constant source of funds for some banks, their use to finance fixed-rate long-term assets—with their potential for exposing banks to interest rate risk—is limited to a permissible range by, say, the ratio of variable-rate assets to variable-rate liabilities.

The size of the gap has a major influence on the volatility of earnings. If, for example, all variable interest rates changed 1 percent, a 30 percent gap would have a $6 million effect on pretax earnings of a bank with $2 billion in assets. The acceptable size of the gap, then, varies with a bank's interest rate expectations.

The tendency, of course, is for banks expecting higher interest rates to accept large positive gaps, with the plan being to reverse the gap before interest rates turn down. But because demand for short-term loans is usually heaviest when interest rates are highest, most banks cannot close large gaps when they want to. For banks expecting lower interest rates, the appropriate strategy would involve accepting negative gaps.

The gap, then, indicates the extent to which banks have used fixed-rate liabilities to fund variable-rate assets. The larger this imbalance the more exposed

TABLE 1
Rate Sensitivity Gap as a Percentage of Total Assets* (20 large banks)

	1983	1984		
	Fourth quarter	First quarter	Second quarter	Third quarter
Bank of America	−11.4	−10.5	−13.8	−12.1
Bank of New York	6.6	7.2	5.8	0.8
Bankers Trust Company	3.9	5.9	−1.1	1.7
Chase Manhattan Bank	9.0	−2.7	−3.5	−5.0
Chemical Bank	1.9	2.2	−2.8	−1.0
Citibank	−1.8	−3.1	−2.9	−3.6
First Interstate Bank, California	−1.8	−1.8	−0.3	−0.2
First National Bank of Boston	−0.9	−2.5	−1.1	−0.4
First National Bank of Chicago	−4.1	−9.0	−6.9	−8.6
Interfirst Bank, Dallas	−4.2	−5.3	−2.5	−5.0
Irving Trust Company	−4.0	2.5	4.7	2.0
Manufacturers Hanover Trust Company	5.9	5.4	4.6	2.7
Marine Midland Bank	−1.9	−7.5	−5.8	−4.2
Mellon Bank	−3.2	2.0	4.3	4.2
Morgan Guaranty Trust Company	−2.4	−1.4	−0.7	−4.0
National Bank of Detroit	0.8	−0.2	0.7	1.0
North Carolina National Bank	−2.1	3.2	2.2	2.2
RepublicBank, Dallas	2.4	3.6	1.2	2.1
Security Pacific National Bank	−4.1	−4.7	−4.6	−6.8
Wells Fargo Bank	−1.9	−5.7	−5.9	−4.9
Average	−0.3	−1.1	−1.4	−1.9

* One-year rate-sensitivity gap.
   Rate-sensitive assets include all assets repricing or maturing within one year and comprise loans and leases, debt security, and other interest-bearing assets.
   Rate-sensitive liabilities are all those liabilities scheduled to reprice or mature within one year and include domestic time certificates of deposits of $100,000 or more, all other domestic time deposits, total deposits in foreign offices, money market deposit accounts, Super NOWs, and demand notes issued to the U.S. Treasury.
   Source: Salomon Brothers, "Bank Analysts Rate Sensitivity Quarterly Handbook First Quarter 1984," July 27, 1984, and "Bank Analysts Quarterly Handbook Third Quarter 1984," January 29, 1985. The use of these figures does not constitute an endorsement of these estimates or the underlying methodology by the Federal Reserve System.

the bank is to interest-rate risk; the closer to zero this imbalance, the better off the bank is with regard to interest rate risk. Such a gap, however, shows nothing of a bank's assets and liabilities that are repriced within the gapping period.[2] All that matters with the "basic" gap approach is that repricing occurs during the gapping period; it does not matter when during the period the repricing occurs. For example, suppose the gapping period is one year and all the rate-sensitive assets are repriced on day 1, while all the rate-sensitive liabilities are repriced on the last day of the year. If variable-rate assets equal variable-rate liabilities, the gap measurement would show incorrectly that the bank portfolio is hedged against unexpected changes in market interest rates.

MATURITY BUCKET APPROACH

The maturity bucket approach attempts to solve the intraperiod problem by measuring the gap for each of several subintervals of the gapping period. Balance sheet items are grouped in a number of maturity "buckets"; for example, one day, one to three months, three to twelve months, one to five years and so on. Balance, or maturity, gaps are computed for each bucket. These separate dollar gap values are called "incremental gaps" and they algebraically sum to the total that is measured by the basic funds gap model.

Asset and liability positions can be hedged by setting each incremental gap equal to zero. If rates are expected to rise, positive gaps should be put into place; the opposite holds for expected rate declines. The use of incremental gap, rather than the basic funds gap model, increases the probability that net earnings will turn out to be as expected.

One of the drawbacks of this technique, as well as of the basic funds gap concept, is that it assumes interest-rate changes for assets and liabilities of all maturities are of the same magnitude. There is overwhelming evidence that interest-rate changes occur in varying magnitude.[3] The gap literature has handled this issue of different interest-rate change magnitudes by assuming that the volatility of the interest rates in question is in constant proportion to the volatility of some standard interest rate.

THE STANDARDIZED GAP

The standardized gap is a concept that adjusts for the relative volatilities of various instruments. A more volatile interest-rate financial instrument has a greater impact on income when it is reset, so it should contribute more to the standardized gap than other, less volatile, interest-rate financial instruments. In the gap literature, historical interest-rate change data on various rate-sensitive assets and liabilities are used to estimate interest-rate change proportionalities. These proportional factors measure the rate volatility of rate-sensitive assets and liabilities relative to a standard of account. Consider, for example, the bank depicted in Figure 1. If the rate-sensitive liabilities are $500 and the rate-sensitive assets are $200, there is a naive gap of −$300. But suppose the rate-sensitive liabilities are treated as $500 in 90-day large certificates of deposit (CDs) and the rate-sensitive assets as $200 in 30-day commercial paper and the 90-day large CD rate is 105 percent as volatile as the yield of 90-day Treasury bill futures while the 30-day commercial paper rate is 31 percent as volatile.[4] Then the standardized gap is −$463. (The $500 in 90-day large CDs is equivalent to the volatility of $1.05 \times \$500 = \$525$ in 90-day Treasury bill futures. The $200 in 30-day commercial paper is equivalent to the volatility of $0.31 \times \$200 = \$62$ in 90-day Treasury bill futures. The standardized gap position is $\$200 \times 0.31 - (\$500 \times 1.05 = \$463$).)[5]

Now let the rate-sensitive liabilities be six-month money market certificates of deposits (MMCs). Dew has estimated that the yield of six-month MMCs was 185 percent as volatile as the yield of 90-day Treasury bill futures contracts. The standardized gap of the above bank whose rate-sensitive liabilities are six-month MMCs is −$863. The naive gap, in both cases, remains −$300.

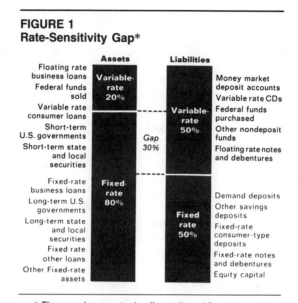

FIGURE 1
Rate-Sensitivity Gap*

* There can be some trade-off maturity and fix versus variable-rate instruments on bank balance sheets.

Therefore, a bank that has more variable-rate liabilities than variable-rate assets and whose variable rate liabilities are, say, 90-day large CDs, has a different exposure to rising rates than one whose variable-rate liabilities are six-month MMCs. This is because various assets and liabilities of different maturity have different sensitivities to changes in interest rates. By taking into account relative interest-rate volatilities, the standardized gap increases the probability that net earnings will turn out to be as expected.

THE BEST BENCHMARK

There are several factors to consider in choosing the benchmark to use in estimating the effective contribution of money market instruments to the standardized gap. First, the relationship between the benchmark rate and other interest rates affecting the net interest margin of the institution should not vary substantially with the passage of time, since the contribution of other instruments to the rate exposure of the firm has been based on the historical relationship between the benchmark rate and those other interest rates.

One property that would make a benchmark rate desirable from this point of view is that it should have a maturity as close as possible to the average maturity of all other instruments affecting the incremental gap position. This will minimize the impact of shifts in the slope of the yield curve on the accuracy of the estimated relationship between the benchmark rate and the other interest rates affecting the standardized gap.

A second way to assure the reliability of estimates of the standardized gap is to choose a benchmark rate that is market-determined. Administered rates may change their relationships to predominantly market-determined interest rates found on the balance sheets of financial institutions. Therefore, it seems reasonable to avoid the prime rate, the Federal Reserve discount rate, and perhaps the federal funds rate, in choosing a benchmark. The current gap literature recommends that financial futures contracts be used as benchmark instruments, because futures rates are market-determined and the contracts themselves are useful in adjusting the gap position in the direction desired by the bank. If the calculation of the standardized gap yields a positive number for a given month, the firm is asset-sensitive[6] and therefore should go long in, say, 90-day Treasury bill futures for delivery in that month or the month nearest it. If the calculation yields a negative number, the firm is liability-sensitive and therefore should go short in 90-day Treasury bill futures.

In interpreting the standardized gap concept, as well as the other gap concepts, it is important to remember that it does not measure the interest-rate risk resulting from the effect of changes in interest rates on present values of cash flows and periodic principal payments of assets and liabilities.

DURATION GAP MODEL

Duration, a concept first introduced by Frederick R. Macaulay, has recently been used in the gap literature to measure interest-rate risk resulting from the effect of changes in interest rates on present values of cash flows and periodic principal payments of assets and liabilities. Duration is defined as the period of time that elapses before a stream of payments generates one half of its present value.

Conceptually, duration is computed by weighting the present value of each future cash flow by the number of periods until receipt of payment and then dividing by the current price of the security, or

$$D = \frac{\sum\limits_{t=1}^{N} t \, PV(F_t)}{\sum\limits_{t=1}^{N} PV(F_t)} \tag{1}$$

where D is duration, t is length of time (number of months, years, etc.) to the date of payment, $PV(F_t)$ represents the present value of payment (F) made at t, or $\frac{F_t}{(1+i)^t}$; i represents the appropriate discount rate, and $\sum\limits_{t=1}^{N}$ is the summation from the first to the last payment (N).

Duration is an important measure of the average life of a security, because it recognizes that not all the cash flow from a typical security occurs at its maturity. Duration of a stream of positive payments is always less than the time until the last payment or maturity, unless the security is a zero-coupon issue, in which case duration is equal to maturity. Duration expresses also the elasticity of a security's price relative to changes in the interest rate and measures a security's responsiveness to changes in market conditions.

Consider the extreme case of two banks, each holding loans with 10-year terms to maturity and with identical yields to maturity. Bank A loans make no interest payments during the term of the contract and return their face value at the end of the 10-year period. Bank B loans make 6 percent interest payments per year for each of the 10 years. Further, assume that the two banks purchased the loans

TABLE 2
Analysis of Bank Exposure to Interest-rate Risk

Bank A

Assets	Liabilities
Duration of the ten-year maturity loan is ten years since it is a zero-coupon instrument.	Duration of the 7.50-year zero-coupon deposit is 7.50 years.

Because the duration of its assets is greater than that of its liabilities, Bank A is exposed to gains or losses from unexpected changes in interest rates. That is, when interest rates move, capital value of the loan will move more than that of the deposit.

Bank B

Assets	Liabilities
Duration of the ten-year 6 percent coupon loan is 7.45 years.	• Duration of the 7.50-year zero-coupon deposit is 7.50 years.

Since the duration of the loan is approximately equal to the duration of the deposit, Bank B is protected against unexpected movements in interest rates.

during a period when the yield curve was rising and the loans are funded with 7½ year zero-coupon deposits. Thus, the interest rate on the financing is lower than the interest rate on the loans. A summary of these conditions and an analysis of the banks' exposure to interest rate risk are presented in Table 2.

Bank A is more exposed to interest-rate risk than Bank B. The average term-to-maturity per dollar of payment stream for the interest-payment loan is approximately equal to that for the deposit. That is, the duration or the "true" term to maturity of Bank B's interest-payment loan is less than 10 years because the bank is getting its funds back faster with the interest-payment loan. Fisher and Weil estimate the duration of the 6 percent loan to be 7.45 years.[7] Since the duration equals maturity for zero-coupon instruments, the duration of 7.50 years for Bank B's deposit is approximately equal to the duration of the loan so the bank is hedged against unexpected changes in interest rates. On the other hand, the term to maturity and duration are 10 years for Bank A's noninterest-payment loan. As a result, Bank A is exposed to gains or losses from unexpected changes in interest rates because the duration of its assets is greater than the duration of its liabilities.

Banks, then, can hedge against uncertain fluctuations in the prices and yields of financial instruments by so managing their loans and investments that the duration composition of their asset portfolio matches the duration composition of their liabilities. Because of the typically short duration of banks' liabilities and the traditional emphasis on liquidity, they often prefer to hold short-duration to medium-duration assets.

If a bank accepts a liability, say, a deposit of short duration, it can offset that liability by lending for the same duration. In theory, cash flows from the asset can be used to pay off the debt coming due at the same time. The bank is, presumably, content to make its profit on the spread between the interest rate paid on the liability and the rate charged on the loan.

To the extent, however, that banks try to match the duration of an asset with the duration of a liability, they may give up opportunities for profits, because asset duration does not fit into the duration structure of the existing portfolio. Although the duration of the loan may initially be equal to that of the liability, it may not remain so over the life of the loan. As the loan ages, its duration may change at a different rate than that of the liability funding it. So the bank will be exposed to interest rate risk.

Furthermore, duration will be accurate only if the yield curve is presumed to shift in a parallel fashion (i.e., where the slope of the curve remains flat). The assumption of a stable yield and slope is unrealistic since normal interest-rate movements involve greater fluctuations in short-term than in longer-term interest rates. Despite these shortcomings, the application of duration analysis to gap management helps improve bank understanding of interest-rate risk.

In a typical gap management process, the bank attempts to protect net interest income against unexpected changes in interest rates over some gapping period. One year is usually chosen for this gapping period. Expected net interest income over the gapping period can be expressed as

$$NII = RSA \left[(1 + Y_{rsa})^{T_{rsa}} (1 + K_{rsa})^{(1-T_{rsa})} - 1 \right] \\ - RSL \left[(1 + Y_{rsi})^{T_{rsi}} (1 + K_{rsi})^{(1-T_{rsi})} - 1 \right] \qquad (2)$$

where $T_{rsa}(T_{rsi})$ is the length of time (fraction of a year) to the date of payment of the rate-sensitive asset (liability); RSA (RSL) is the rate-sensitive asset (liability) book value at the beginning of the year of a single cash inflow (outflow) that will occur at time $T_{rsa}(T_{rsi})$; $Y_{rsa}(Y_{rsi})$ is the rate-sensitive asset (liability) contractual interest rate; and $K_{rsa}(K_{rsi})$ is the rate-sensitive asset (liability) expected interest rate upon any repricing during the gapping period.

It can be inferred from equation (2) that net interest income will be protected against unexpected changes in interest rates provided that the weighted market value of the rate-sensitive asset equals the weighted market value of the rate-sensitive liability where the weights are equal to the fraction of the year from repricing to the end of the year.[8] Since both the asset and liability are single-payment instruments, duration is equal to maturity expressed as fractions of a year. The duration of the rate-sensitive asset, D_{rsa}, is T_{rsa} and that of the rate-sensitive liability, D_{rsi}, is T_{rsi}.

The duration gap (DG) that measures the exposure of net interest income to unexpected changes in interest rates can be defined most simply as the difference between the present value of rate-sensitive assets times one minus their duration and the present value of rate-sensitive liabilities times one minus their duration[9], or

$$DG = MVRSA(1 - D_{rsa}) - MVRSL(1 - D_{rsi}) \qquad (3)$$

where $MVRSA$ and $MVRSL$ are the present values of rate-sensitive assets and liabilities, respectively.

The sign of DG indicates the type of rate risk to which the bank is currently exposed. The larger DG is in absolute value, the greater is the risk. If the calculation of DG yields a positive number, then the bank is asset-sensitive and exposed to falling interest rates. If the calculation yields a negative number, then the bank is liability-sensitive and exposed to rising interest rates. The duration gap thus defined yields a single-valued risk index that is not only convenient but at least as accurate an indicator of risk as the risk level derived from the maturity bucket approach.

FINANCIAL FUTURES REDUCE BANK EXPOSURE

Financial futures markets give banks a chance to hedge exposed asset and liability positions. The primary function of futures markets is to transfer the risk of commodity price changes to speculators who are willing to take the risks. Financial futures provide protection against losses from unexpected adverse price changes by enabling participants to lock into a future price, currently quoted in the futures market.

A futures contract is a standardized contract which establishes, in advance, the purchase (and sale) price of a commodity for delivery and settlement at a fixed future time. The futures price embodies the market's expectations of the spot price of the item that will prevail at the time of delivery.[10]

Hedging involves taking a position in the futures market that is equal and opposite to a current or a planned future position in the spot or cash market. Therefore, regardless of the movement in prices, losses in one market will be offset by gains in the other. A successful hedge requires that cash market prices and futures market prices move in the same direction. The difference between the prices in the two markets is called "the basis."

The hedge would be perfect if the basis did not change—that is, if the futures and cash prices moved in the same direction by the same amount. In real life, the basis rarely remains constant.[11] Hedgers watch for changes in basis risk—that is, in the relationship between futures and cash prices that could expose them to a loss or gain.

A bank can hedge the interest-rate risk caused by the mismatch in the duration of the firm's assets and liabilities. When a negative duration gap exists, a normal bank response would be to extend the duration of liabilities or to reduce the duration of the assets. But alternatively, financial futures could be sold to hedge this exposure. When a positive duration gap exists, a normal bank response would be to extend the duration of the assets or to reduce the duration of the liabilities. But a banker also can hedge this asset-sensitivity by buying financial futures.

Consider the case of a bank whose net asset and liability positions are shown in Table 3. It has initially extended loans with face values of $500, $600, $1,000, and $1,400 to be repaid in a single payment at the end of 90 days, 180 days, 270 days, and 360 days, respectively. For simplicity, loans that mature at the end of 90 days, 180 days, 270 days, and 360 days are assumed to be rolled over for 360 days, 270 days, 180 days, and 90 days, respectively. The interest rate for any loan account is 12 percent.[12] The present value of these loans, and, therefore the total value of the loan portfolio, is $3,221.50 $(= \$500.00/(1.12)^{0.25} + \$600.00/(1.12)^{0.50} + \$1,000.00/(1.12)^{0.75} + \$1,400.00/(1.12))$. To finance the loan portfolio, the bank borrows $3,221.50 in 90-day large certificates of deposits (CDs) at 10 percent interest. The two percentage-point spread is the return earned by the bank for employing its specialized capital in intermediating between borrowers and lenders. This will be the spread bank funds management is content to make over the planning period.

The amount that the bank will owe in 90 days is $3,299.18 $(= \$3,221.50 (1.10)^{0.25})$, which it plans to pay by borrowing this amount for another 90 days.

TABLE 3
Interest-Sensitive Assets and Liabilities

Days	Assets	Liabilities
90	$ 500	$3,299.18
180	600	
270	1,000	
360	1,400	

TABLE 4
Current Value of Assets and Liabilities

Days	Assets	Liability	Net interest income
0	$3,221.50	$3,221.50	$ 0.00
90	3,314.08	3,299.18	14.90
180	3,409.31	3,378.74	30.57
270	3,507.28	3,460.21	47.07
360	3,608.08	3,543.65	64.43

Return on assets = $64.43/$3,221.50 = 2.0 percent

The bank anticipates being able to roll the large CDs over every 90 days at the same interest rate.

A summary of the present value of the asset and liability positions and the corresponding net interest income in each of the 90-day periods is presented in Table 4. As that table reveals, the net interest income on the initial investment of $3,221.50 yields a return of 2 percent ($64.63/$3,221.50).

In this example, the bank is subject to considerable interest-rate risk because its fixed-rate loans mature at various times during the year while all of its deposit liabilities must be rolled over every 90 days. The duration of the large CDs is 0.25 years—the duration of a single payment is always the time to the payment date. The duration of the loan portfolio is 0.73 years $(0.25(\$486.03/\$3,221.50) + 0.50(\$566.95)/\$3221.50) + 0.75(\$918.52)/\$3,221.50) + (\$1,250.00/\$3,221.50))$. The duration gap ($DG$) is negative and equals $-\$1,514$ $(\$3,221.50(1.00 - 0.73) - \$3,221.50(1.00 - 0.25))$.[13] As a practical matter, the assets' longer duration implies that a given change in interest rates will change the present value of the assets more than it will affect the present value of the liabilities. The difference, of course, will change the value of the bank's equity. By appropriately structuring a hedge, the bank can effectively insure that net interest income will turn out to be as expected—yielding the 2 percent return.

TABLE 5
Portfolio Characteristics
for the Duration
Analysis

D_p	=	.25 years
D_{rsa}	=	.73 years
D_f	=	.25 years
FP	=	$97.21
V_{rsa}	=	$3,221.50

The financial futures market can be used in at least two ways to remove this duration imbalance: (1) to shorten the duration of the assets to 0.25 years or (2) to lengthen the duration of the liabilities to 0.73 years. Since this bank is net long (i.e., the duration of its assets is longer than the duration of its liabilities), the appropriate futures positions for a hedge will always be short (i.e., it will involve the sale of futures contracts). Suppose, to hedge its exposure to interest-rate risk, the bank decides to form a "loan-with-futures" portfolio consisting of both cash loans and futures contracts. The duration of a portfolio containing cash loans and futures contracts is given most simply by[14]:

$$D_p = D_{rsa} + D_f \frac{N_f FP}{V_{rsa}} \tag{4}$$

where D_p is the duration of the entire portfolio; D_{rsa} is the duration of the cash loan portfolio; D_d is the duration of the deliverable securities involved in the hypothetical futures contract from the delivery date; V_{rsa} is the market value of the cash loan portfolio; N_f is the number of futures contracts, and FP is the futures price.

Since the goal is to shorten the asset duration to 0.25 years, it must be that $D_p = 0.25$ years. Table 5 summarizes the relevant data. The price of each future contract is $100.00/(1.12)^{0.25} = 97.21$. These (hypothetical) contracts call for delivery of $100 face value of Treasury bills having 90 days remaining until maturity. Since Treasury bills are pure discount instruments, their duration will always be equal to the number of years to maturity, which is 90 days or 0.25 years.[15]

Solving the above equation for the number of futures contracts yields -64, which indicates that the number of Treasury bills futures contracts to sell short at the beginning of the planning period is 64. Because no cash changes hands at the time the futures contracts are originated and no deliveres are made, the future contracts per se do not change the current cash value of the portfolio, which remains $3,221.50.[16] However, as time passes and interest rates change, the futures contracts must be marked to market and any changes in the price settled in cash on the day they occur. Thus, changes in the value of the futures contracts change the cash value of the portfolio.

TABLE 6
Effects of a 200-Basis Point Increase in Yields on Realized Interest-Rate Spread (with futures)

	Assets	Liabilities
Original portfolio value	$3,221.50	$3,221.50
New portfolio value	3,180.31	3,207.02
Gain/loss on futures	27.52	0.00
Total portfolio change	(13.67)	(14.48)
Beginning portfolio value	3,207.83	3,207.02
Value of all accounts at day = 360	3,656.92	3,591.86
Annualized yield spread over 360 days	$\dfrac{\$3{,}656.92 - \$3{,}591.86}{\$3{,}221.50}$ $= \dfrac{\$65.06}{\$3{,}221.50} = 2.0\%$	

TABLE 7
Effects of a 200-basis Point Increase in Yields on Realized Interest-Rate Spread (without futures)

	Assets	Liabilities
Original portfolio value	$3,221.50	$3,221.50
New portfolio value	3,180.31	3,207.02
Total portfolio change	(41.19)	(14.48)
Beginning portfolio value	3,180.31	3,207.02
Value of all accounts at day = 360	3,625.55	3,591.86
Annualized yield spread over 360 days	$\dfrac{\$3{,}625.55 - \$3{,}591.86}{\$3{,}221.50}$ $= \dfrac{\$33.71}{\$3{,}221.50} = 1.05\%$	

Suppose the bank sells 64 (hypothetical) 90-day Treasury bills futures contracts at a price of 97.21 to hedge its net interest-rate exposure. Now assume that interest rates rise unexpectedly by 200 basis points immediately following this transaction and remain 200 basis points higher indefinitely.[17] Assume also that all cash flow receipts during the 360-day planning period can be reinvested at 14 percent.[18] Table 6 presents the effect of the interest-rate shift on asset and liability values, the futures contracts, and the asset and liability values at the end of the planning period (360 days). Table 7 presents the same result without financial futures. As Table 6 reveals, the bank was able to earn 14 percent on the asset portfolio and paid 12 percent on its large CDs. The unexepected increase in interest rates causes the present value of the loans to fall more ($41.19) than the

TABLE 8
Effects of a 200-Basis Point Decrease in
Yields on Realized Interest-Rate Spread
(with futures)

	Assets	Liabilities
Original portfolio value	$3,221.50	$3,221.50
New portfolio value	3,264.05	3,236.31
Gain/loss on futures	(28.16)	0.00
Total portfolio change	(14.39)	(14.81)
Beginning portfolio value	3,235.89	3,236.31
Value of all accounts at day = 360	3,559.48	3,495.21

Annualized yield spread over 360 days	$\dfrac{\$3,559.48 - \$3,495.21}{\$3,221.50}$
	$= \dfrac{\$64.07}{\$3,221.50} = 2.0\%$

present value of the liabilities ($14.48). By itself, this would cause a reduction in the bank's equity and in the spread between the rate earned on the loan portfolio and the rate paid on the large CDs (see Table 7). At the same time, however, the increase in interest rates generates a gain of $27.52 from the futures contracts. Other things the same, this causes equity to rise, and allows the bank to maintain its 2 percent spread between the rate earned on assets and the rate paid on large CDs. The effects of a 200-basis-point decline in yields on realized interest rate spread are summarized in Table 8.[19]

Thus, the use of financial futures enables the bank to eliminate its exposure to interest-rate risk. The formulation of a bank futures position in light of its entire mix of assets and liabilities helps to balance the interest sensitivity of duration-mismatched assets and liabilities. These macro financial futures hedges are an effective means for banks to reduce the variability of net interest margin and improve the stability of bank profits.

While macro hedges are important gap management tools, they must be used with a great deal of care and attention. Due to the nature of banks' assets and liabilities, gap positions can change rapidly. Therefore, the size of the interest-sensitive gap being hedged may also vary significantly from day to day. Because of this, when a macro hedge is employed, it must be monitored continuously and sometimes modified, if a target gap or interest sensitivity is to be maintained. The value of the futures contracts employed in macro hedges is also marked to market and the associated income or expense shown on the income statement in each reporting period.

In managing its asset and liability positions in the financial futures markets, a bank is limited by federal guidelines to transactions related to the bank's business needs and its capacity to meet its obligations. By taking a position in the futures market, a bank should reduce its exposure to loss through interest-rate changes affecting its investment portfolio.

Accounting rules and futures contracts

Current accounting procedures for futures contracts are set out in a uniform policy on bank contract activity issued by the Federal Reserve Board, the Federal Deposit Insurance Corporation, and the Comptroller of the Currency on November 15, 1979, revised March 12, 1980. Federal regulations give banks the option of carrying futures contracts on a mark-to-market or lower-of-cost-or-market basis. Other rules require all open contract positions be reviewed at least monthly, at which time market values are determined. Futures contracts are valued on either the market or lower-of-cost and market method, at the option of the bank, except that the accounting for trading account contracts and cash positions should be consistent. Underlying securities commitments relating to open futures contracts are not reported on the balance sheet; the only entries are for margin deposits, unrealized losses and, in certain instances, unrealized gains related to the contracts. In addition, banks must maintain general ledger memorandum accounts or commitment registers to identify and control all commitments to make or take delivery of securities. Following monthly contract valuation, unrealized losses would be recognized as a current expense item, and banks that value contracts on a market basis would also recognize unrealized gains as current income. Acquisition of securities under futures contracts are recorded on a basis consistent with that applied to the contracts, either market or lower-of-cost-or-market.

The Financial Accounting Standards Board (FASB), in its ruling effective December 31, 1984, introduced new guidelines for futures contracts. The new rules allow firms to use hedge accounting for future transactions.* In hedge accounting, a futures position is defined as a hedging transaction if it can be linked directly with an underlying asset or liability and if the price of the futures contracts is highly correlated with the price of the underlying cash position. If these conditions are met, and if the underlying cash position is not carried at market, futures gains or losses can be *deferred* until the position is closed out. The gains or losses can then become part of the accounting basis of the underlying cash position, to be *amortized* over the remaining life of the asset or liability, and therefore taken into income gradually.

The FASB standards require that banks and other firms formulate their hedged positions in light of their entire mix of assets and liabilities so that macro interest rate exposure is reduced by micro hedges. By insisting that all futures hedges be linked to an identifiable instrument "or group of instruments, such as loans that have similar terms" to qualify for hedge accounting, the FASB is encouraging banks to analyze thoroughly their overall exposure to interest rate risk as well as the components that make up that risk. The FASB standards, however, do not allow hedge accounting for the macro hedging of an overall gap on a bank's balance sheet that cannot be identified with a specific item.

The FASB statements call for the classification of deferred gains and losses as an adjustment to the carrying amount of the hedged items. Bankers should be aware that if such an adjustment is made to appropriate general ledger accounts, the computation of average daily balances for the purpose of determining average yields will be distorted unless special provisions are made. In addition, other FASB statements require that the amortization of the deferred futures gains or losses to interest income or expense start no later than the date that a particular contract is closed out. Profits or losses from the futures position must be taken into the income stream over that time period when the bank expected an adverse impact from interest rates.

---

*Bank regulators reactions to FASB statement, if any, are yet to be determined. As a result, banks futures transactions are still governed by federal banking regulations.

CONCLUSIONS

The recent increases and broad fluctuations in interest rates have led many banks to a better understanding of interest-rate risk and how to manage it. The use of gap management can be particularly important to bank funds management as a technique to manage interest-rate risk. A bank can reduce the risk of loss due to unfavorable changes in interest rates by hedging its duration gap. The use of financial futures and the duration approach to gap management enables the bank to maintain a predetermined spread and to lock in an anticipated rate of return.

NOTES

[1] See Sanford Rose, "Dark Days Ahead for Banks," *Fortune,* June 30, 1980, pp. 86–90.

[2] The length of time over which net interest margin is to be managed.

[3] See Paul L. Kasriel, "Interest Rate Volatility in 1980," *Economic Perspectives,* Federal Reserve Bank of Chicago, January/February 1981, pp. 8–17.

[4] These numbers were taken from James Kurt Dew, "The Effective Gap II: Two Ways to Measure Interest Rates Risk," *American Banker,* September 18, 1981, p. 4.

[5] The historical volatility of an entire spectrum of assets and liabilities relative to a benchmark financial instrument can be calculated using regression analysis. Dew (1981) shows how such calculations are made.

[6] This means that, when interest rates change, interest income changes more than interest expense.

[7] See Lawrence Fisher and R. Weil, "Coping with the Risk of Interest Rate Fluctuations: Returns to Bondholders from Naive and Optimal Strategies," *Journal of Business,* October 1971.

[8] The market value of a contractual flow of $RSA(1 + Y_{rsa})^{T_{rsa}}$ dollars T_{rsa} periods from now is $RSA(1 + Y_{rsa})^{T_{rsa}}/(1 + K_{rsa})^{T_{rsa}}$. Similarly, the market value of a contractual flow of $RSL(1 + Y_{rsi})^{T_{rsi}}$ dollars T_{rsi} periods from now is $RSL(1 + Y_{rsi})^{T_{rsi}}/(1 + K_{rsi})^{T_{rsi}}$. It is assumed that all asset and liability interest rates are affected equally when any movement in rates occurs.

[9] See Alden Toevs, "Gap Management: Managing Interest Rate Risk in Banks and Thrifts," *Economic Review,* Federal Reserve Bank of San Francisco, Spring 1983, pp. 20–35.

[10] For a discussion of this point, see Albert E. Burger, Richard W. Lang, and Robert H. Rasche, "The Treasury Bill Futures Market and Market Expectations of Interest Rates," *Review,* Federal Reserve Bank of St. Louis, June 1977, pp. 2–9.

[11] As a futures contract moves toward maturity, the futures price and cash price tend to converge. Therefore, basis narrows predictably over time.

[12] A flat yield curve is assumed for ease of exposition.

[13] See Alden Toevs, "Gap Management."

[14] For further details, see G. O. Bierwag, George G. Kaufman, and Alden Toevs, "Duration: Its Development and Use in Bond Portfolio Management," *Financial Analysts Journal,* July–August 1983, pp. 15–35; and Gerald D. Gay and Robert W. Kolb, "Interest-Rate Futures as a Tool for Immunization," *The Journal of Portfolio Management,* Fall 1983, pp. 65–70.

[15] G. O. Bierwag, George G. Kaufman, and Alden Toevs, "Duration."

[16] A cash or liquid security margin requirement is generally maintained.

[17] Zero-basis risk is assumed.

[18] Actually the reinvestment rate is not certain. However, the assumption of a 14-percent reinvestment rate simplifies the example with no loss in generality.

[19] It is interesting to note that if a bank were to engage in the type of hedge in these examples when it was exposed to loss from increases in interest rates, it would not only limit the potential rise in bank costs from unfavorable shifts in interest rates but agree implicitly to limit the potential of its lower costs from favorable shifts in interest rates. The bank must be content with the usual profits from lending.

2

Banks and Nonbanks:
The Horse Race Continues

Christine Pavel and Harvey Rosenblum

Financial services have been provided by individuals and commercial enterprises at least since Biblical times. During the last few centuries, some business firms began to specialize by providing only financial services. Until recently, the specialization tended to be very narrow; some firms provided insurance, others home mortgage lending, and still others consumer lending. Even commercial banks, which now serve a wide range of commercial, household, and government customers by intermediating across a wide range of financial products, for many years restricted themselves to commercial lending.

During the last decade, several trends have reshaped the financial services industry. Many specialized financial firms have sought to diversify themselves and have begun to offer a wider range of financial products than they had offered previously. For example, S&Ls and mutual savings banks now offer commercial and consumer credit in addition to their more traditional product, home mortgages, and credit unions have begun to offer home mortgages in addition to their traditional product, consumer credit. Further, all three of these depository institutions have begun to offer a wider range of deposit instruments, particularly transaction accounts, that they had not offered previously. In addition to depository institutions, many other financial firms have sought to increase the breadth of their product array. For example, insurance companies have acquired securities companies, consumer finance companies, and banks.

Also over the last decade, firms whose primary orientation has been nonfinancial have become much more heavily involved in financial services, both related and unrelated to their primary product lines. Not only have these firms been making inroads into the market share of banks with some of the products they

Economic Perspectives, Federal Reserve Bank of Chicago, May/June 1985, pp. 3–17.

Christine Pavel is an associate economist at the Federal Reserve Bank of Chicago, and Harvey Rosenblum is vice president and associate director of research. Helpful research assistance was provided by Dorothy Robinson, who was a summer intern at the bank during 1984.

TABLE 1
Financial Services Offered by Selected Nonfinancial Companies

	General Motors	Ford	ITT	General Electric	Control Data	Borg-Warner	Westing-house	Sears	Marcor	J. C. Penney
Commercial finance:										
Commercial lending	1944	1960	1954-5	1965	1968	*	1961		1966	
Factoring					1968					
A/R and inventory finance	1919	1959	1971	1932	1968	1950	1954			
Venture capital				1970	1971					
Consumer finance:										
Sales finance	1919	1959	1964	1964	1968	1953	1959	1911	1917	1958
Personal finance		1966	1964	1965	1968	1969		1962	1966	1970
Credit card			1983		1983			*	1957	1958
Real estate:										
Mortgage banking			1983	1981	1982	1982		1972		1970
Residential first mortgages				1981	1982	1982		1961		1981
Residential second mortgages		1972	1965		1979		1969	1961	1966	
Real estate development		1969	1970	1960	1972	1969	1969	1960	1970	1970
Real estate sales & management				1983	1981			1960	1970	1970
Commercial real estate & finance		1960	1980	1963			1969	1961	1966	1970
Insurance:										
Credit life insurance	1975	1962	1964	1973	1968	1970		1960	1966	1970
Regular life insurance		1974	1964	1973	1968			1957	1966	1970
Property & casualty insurance	1925	1959	1964	1970	1968	1970		1931		1970
Accident & health insurance			1964	1973	1968			1958	1968	1967
Leasing:										
Equipment and personal property	1981	1966	1968	1963	1968	1968	1968			
Real property leasing								1960	1970	1970
Lease brokerage		1982	1982					1981		
Investment services:										
Investment management			1966					1969		
Mutual fund sales		1982	1966					1969		1970
Corporate trust & agency										
Custodial services										
Business and personal services:										
Travel services		1978						1961	1971	
Cash management services								1981		
Tax preparation services									1966-70	1969
Financial data processing services			1965			1968	1970			1982
Credit card management services				1965			1969			

* Entry date unavailable.
Source: Cleveland A. Christophe, *Competition in Financial Services* (New York: First National City Corporation, 1974), company annual reports, and phone conversations with company spokesmen.

offer, but the pace of these new competitive thrusts seems to have accelerated during the last five years (see Table 1).

The list of bank competitors now includes not only depository institutions—commercial banks, savings and loan associations, mutual savings banks, and credit unions—but well-known nondeposit-based competitors, such as American Express, Merrill Lynch, and Sears, as well as lesser-known nonbank competitors, such as National Steel, J. C. Penney, and Westinghouse. Some of these nonbank firms have been more successful than others in providing financial services. Some firms are retrenching, while others are integrating and regrouping, after recently acquiring or establishing financial services operations.

This article examines competition in financial services over the past few years and analyzes how the financial services operations of nondeposit-based firms have fared relative to banking firms and relative to each other. The article is the third annual review of this subject by the authors and differs from the previous studies in that it is able to distinguish a few emerging trends that were not available in the prior ''snap-shot,'' cross-sectional analyses. In addition, the use of 1983 and some 1984 data allows us to speculate on deregulation's impact upon

---

TABLE 2
List of 30 Nonbank Firms and 15 Largest
BHCs Ranked by Assets

NONBANKS:

Retailers:
Sears
J.C. Penney
Montgomery Ward

Industrials:
General Motors
Ford Motor
Chrysler
IBM
General Electric
Westinghouse
Borg-Warner
Gulf & Western
Control Data
Greyhound
Dana Corp.
Armco Corp.
National Intergroup
ITT Corp.

Diversified Financials:
American Express
Merrill Lynch
E.F. Hutton
Household International
Beneficial Corp.
Avco Corp.
Loews Corp.
Transamerica

Insurance companies:
Prudential
Equitable Life Assurance
Aetna Life & Casualty
American General Corp.
The Travelers

BANK HOLDING COMPANIES

Citicorp
BankAmerica Corp.
Chase Manhattan Corp.
Manufacturers Hanover Corp.
Continental Illinois Corp.
Chemical New York Corp.
J.P. Morgan & Co.
First Interstate Bancorp
Security Pacific Corp.
Bankers Trust New York Corp.
First Chicago Corp.
Wells Fargo & Co.
Crocker National Corp.
Marine Midland Banks, Inc.
Mellon National Corp.

---

the ability of commercial banks to deal with the nondeposit-based rivals. The financial services activities of 30 nonbank companies, classified into four groups—retailers, industrial-based companies, diversified financial firms, and insurance-based companies—are examined along with publicly available accounting data for the 30 firms, the 15 largest bank holding companies, and all insured, domestic commercial banks. (For a list of the nonbank companies in each group and the 15 largest bank holding companies, see Table 2.)

Most of the data are for the years 1981, the first year for which information on the individual companies was gathered, and 1983, the last year for which annual report information was readily available. When available, however, 1984 data are used. Unless stated otherwise, total consumer lending includes consumer installment and one-to-four family residential mortgages; commercial lending includes commercial and industrial (C&I) loans and commercial mortgages; and total finance receivables include consumer loans, commercial loans, and lease finance receivables.

OVERVIEW AND BACKGROUND

In 1972, at least 10 nonfinancial firms had significant financial services earnings,[1] and by 1981 this list had grown over threefold.[2] Further, in 1981, these nonbank companies posed a competitive threat to banks and other depository institutions in a number of their traditional product lines.

In the area of consumer lending, nonbank firms seemed to have dominated in 1981. Of the 15 largest consumer installment lenders, 10 were nonbank firms, and General Motors topped the list with over $31 billion in consumer finance receivables. These 10 firms accounted for 24 percent of all consumer installment credit outstanding.[3] This is quite impressive since the remaining 76 percent was accounted for by over 15,000 commercial banks, 3,100 savings and loan associations, 400 mutual savings banks, 3,100 credit unions, as well as numerous other nondeposit-based companies, primarily finance companies. Nevertheless, market shares in consumer installment lending are quite fluid: the new business volume accounted for by any supplier changes drastically with changes in the economy.

By 1981, nonbank firms had also encroached on commercial banks' prime turf—business lending—although commercial banks were, and still are, the dominant commercial lenders. At year-end 1981, the top 15 bank holding companies had nearly $300 billion in C&I loans outstanding worldwide, while the selected 30 nonbank companies had less than one third of that total. However, 14 selected industrial-based firms did outweigh the bank holding companies in lease financing, and a mere 5 insurance-based firms bested the bank holding companies in commercial mortgage lending.

Throughout 1982, nonbank competitors continued to make inroads in the financial services industry. Sears, for example, opened its first in-store financial service center, and several securities-based firms and a furniture store acquired "nonbank banks." Nevertheless, commercial banks were beginning to regain some of the market share that they had lost, mostly in consumer lending, over the previous four or five years. By 1983, the entire banking industry was reacting vigorously to the competitive threats posed by the nonbanks, aided in part by the virtual demise of Regulation Q and the creation (in December 1982) of the Money Market Deposit Account. Banks of all sizes and locations began to offer new services, such as discount brokerage, and to find other ways to compete more effectively in a new and changing environment.[4]

During 1983, the nonbanks continued to increase their financial services earnings (Table 3). The profits from financial activities of 30 selected nonbank companies increased 19 percent between 1981 and 1983, exceeding the earnings growth of the 15 largest bank holding companies and all domestic, insured commercial banks. At year-end 1983, the 30 nonbank firms' profits from financial activities were $8 billion, more than half of the combined profits of the nation's 15,000 commercial banks.

Over the 1981–83 period, the nonbanks increased their total finance receivables as well. The combined finance receivables of the 30 nonbank firms increased 16 percent from 1981 to 1983, slightly faster than the top 15 bank holding companies, but slower than all commercial banks.[5]

All nonbank firms are clearly not alike in providing financial services. They do not offer all of the same financial products and services, and they do not target the same markets. Some nonbank firms primarily target consumers, while some do

TABLE 3
Financial Services at a Glance: 1981–1983 (dollars in billions)

	Total finance receivables		Consumer loans		Commercial loans		Lease financing		Financial services earnings	
	1983	% change 1981-83	1982	% change 1981-83	1983	% change 1981-83	1983	% change 1981-83	1983	% change 1981-83
3 retailers	26.4	38	26.4	38	--	--	—	—	0.9	50
14 industrial-based firms	133.3	16	72.0	14	43.8	17	17.5	22	2.2	57
8 diversified financial firms	38.7	8	29.7	9	7.4	14	1.6	26	1.6	18
5 insurance-based firms	63.3	13	14.4	18	48.3	13	0.6	-33	3.3	3
Total, 30 nonbanks	262.3	16	142.5	17	99.5	15	19.7	18	8.0	19
Top 15 bank holding companies (domestic)	295.5	14	104.4	26	175.1	8	16.0	12	3.6	0
All domestic, insured commercial banks	1,136.5	21	383.8	13	563.7	24	14.2	8	15.7	6

Source: Company annual reports and *Federal Reserve Bulletin*, various issues.

not provide financial services to consumers at all. Also, some nonbank firms have outperformed other nonbanks as well as banks, whereas others have struggled to earn a profit.

To gain more insight into these nonbank competitors and, therefore, competition in the financial services industry, it is helpful to classify the nonbanks into groups based on each firm's primary line of business and then analyze each group in relation to traditional suppliers of financial services—banks and bank holding companies—before examining them in relation to one another.

RETAILERS

Retailers compete with banks and other financial services providers primarily in consumer-oriented product lines. Retailers' concentration in consumer-oriented financial services should not be surprising, because many of them entered the financial services industry by offering credit in conjunction with retail purchases. Sears, perhaps the most famous and aggressive of the retailers that provide financial services, began offering retail credit in 1910. Similarly, J. C. Penney and Montgomery Ward became involved in financial services by financing their retail sales.

Retailers, however, offer many financial products and services besides retail credit. Some offer many of the same financial products and services to consumers that banks do. In addition, they offer insurance products and maintain offices across state lines.

One explanation for the retailers' foray into financial services can be found in the retail trade. Retailing has undergone several changes over the last few years. Such retailers as Sears, J. C. Penney, and Montgomery Ward have been faced with stiff competition from the new discount stores and the specialty stores. Furthermore, according to *Moody's Industry Outlook,* only moderate growth in retailing is expected over the next five years, and the retailers that will "show some growth are off-price retail[ers] and some companies in the upscale discounting and specialty fields.''[6]

Such an environment has sent retailers like Sears searching for ways to capitalize on their extensive distribution networks, large customer bases, and solid reputations. Together these three retailers operate over 2,600 stores nationwide, giving them the underlying basis for a retail branching network that banks, at least for the time being, are prohibited from duplicating. In addition, Sears, Penney, and Wards combined have 50 million credit customers, many of whom utilize these stores on a regular basis.

Given their experience in credit operations and, for some, their experience in providing insurance, retailers seem particularly well-suited to expand their activities in financial services. In addition, these retailers are getting closer and closer to providing one-stop financial shopping. A consumer can obtain many of his financial services at some Sears or Penney stores, and shop for clothes, furniture, or hardware at the same location.

Business Volume.   Some retailers have been very aggressive in providing financial services, including installment credit, to consumers.[7] In 1981, the three retailers had combined consumer installment receivables of $16 billion. By 1983, the three retailers increased their total consumer installment credit almost 40 percent to $23 billion. Sears alone in 1981 held nearly $10 billion in consumer installment credit, and by 1983 had increased its holdings of such debt 45 percent to $14 billion.

In comparison, over the same two years, all insured, domestic commercial banks increased their installment credit by 17 percent; but the 15 largest bank holding companies' installment credit outstanding jumped 35 percent. Citicorp, perhaps the most aggressive of the top 15 bank holding companies in consumer financial services, increased its consumer installment credit 61 percent over the 1981–83 period.

Although there are banks like Citibank, which are aggressively pursuing the consumer market, the commercial banking industry as a whole has neither gained nor lost market share in consumer installment lending. Commercial banks held about 44 percent of consumer installment debt in 1981 and in 1983. And even though a few retailers are very actively offering financial services to consumers, retailers have not increased their share of consumer credit outstanding, holding about 9 percent of all consumer installment credit since 1978. The 15 largest bank holding companies, however, increased their share of consumer installment credit outstanding nearly 2 percentage points, from 13.0 percent to 14.9 percent, over the 1981–83 period, while Sears, Wards, and Penney increased their combined share from 5.4 percent to 5.8 percent.

Credit Cards.   Retailers' consumer finance receivables are mostly credit card receivables. In this narrow area of consumer lending, the retailers seem to be more successful than the banks, although banks have come a long way since 1972. Since that year, the number of bank cards outstanding has more than doubled, and annual customer charge volume has grown nearly eightfold.

In credit card operations, however, the retailers still have the edge. At year-end 1983, all retailers had over $46 billion in credit card receivables, while banks held $38 billion in Visa and MasterCard credit card receivables. No individual bank had more customer account balances outstanding at that time than Sears, and on the basis of customer charge volume and cards issued, no individual bank came close to Sears in 1983. In fact, Sears had more customer charge volume than the two largest issuers of bank cards (Bank of America and Citibank) combined.[8]

The Sears credit card, of course, is only accepted in Sears stores, but has achieved widespread acceptance and usage in spite of this disadvantage largely because of the size of Sears relative to other retailers. Visa, MasterCard, and American Express cards are, at least to their users, reasonably good substitutes for money in conducting many day-to-day transactions. Because of its drastically more limited acceptance (it can be used in only about 800 locations), the Sears card is almost useless as a money substitute. In order to overcome this disadvantage, Sears announced plans in February 1985 to introduce a universal credit card that would compete directly with Visa, MasterCard, and American Express.

Profitability.   The financial services operations of the retailers mentioned above are profitable. In 1981, Sears, Wards, and Penney had combined financial services earnings of nearly $600 million, and, in 1983, the financial earnings of these three retailers had increased more than 50 percent to $927 million. This is about equal to the total 1983 earnings of Bank-America, Chemical New York, and Manufacturers Hanover, the fourth, fifth, and sixth largest bank holding companies ranked by earnings. Also, by 1983, the three retailers had a combined ROE of 12 percent from financial services activities, higher than their combined ROE from retailing and higher than the ROE for all commercial banks.

Furthermore, in 1981 and 1983, financial services earnings represented a significant portion of total earnings for these retailers. For Sears, financial services account for more than half of its total profits. And were it not for its finance subsidiary, Wards would have shown a net loss in 1983, as it did for 1981.

Long-run Impact.   It is probably too soon to conclusively assess the impact that the retailers have, or could have, on the competitive position of commercial banks and other depository institutions. So far only a few retailers have significant financial services operations, and only recently has Sears, the predominant financial services provider among the retailers, committed to becoming a major supplier of financial services. Penney and Wards are still "experimenting" with financial services. Yet the retailers are making money from their financial businesses; they are increasing their finance receivables; they are expanding their financial operations; and the number of retailers that offer financial services in their stores is increasing. K mart and Kroger are offering various financial products and services in their retail outlets in conjunction with depository institutions and insurance companies. It appears, therefore, that the financial businesses of retailers have met with success—so far.

The success of a few retailers, however, does not imply the demise of over 15,000 commercial banks as providers of financial services to consumers. In October 1982, *ABA Banking Journal* asked bankers in the eight cities where Sears had launched its financial network whether the in-store centers posed a threat.[9] At that time, none of the bankers thought Sears threatened their competitive positions. One year later, *ABA Banking Journal* repeated its survey and found:

> In general, community bankers in cities where in-store centers have opened can't imagine ever feeling seriously threatened by Sears—no matter how numerous nor generally accepted such centers might become.[10]

INDUSTRIAL-BASED FIRMS

Industrial-based firms provide a variety of financial services through subsidiaries. At least 14 industrial firms have significant financial services operations (see Table 2). Four of these are captive finance subsidiaries of their manufacturer-parents (General Motors Acceptance Corporation, Ford Motor Credit Company, Chrysler Financial Corporation, and IBM Credit Corporation), and three were captive subsidiaries but have become independent providers of financial services (General Electric Credit, Westinghouse Credit, and Borg-Warner Acceptance Corporation). The other seven have always been independent of their parents.

The captive finance subsidiaries of the auto companies were originally formed to bolster the sales of their parents' products, especially when demand is weak or other lenders, such as banks and independent finance companies, are decreasing their auto lending. Thus, in a period, such as the 1978–82 period, which was characterized by a decrease in domestic car sales, liberalized bankruptcy laws, soaring costs of funds, and interest-rate volatility, the captive finance companies of the U.S. automakers offered below-market-rate financing to support the sale of their parents' automobiles. During this period, the auto captive finance companies increased their share of auto loans outstanding and greatly increased their share of new auto lending volume (see Figure 1).[11]

Even though their primary mission remains to support the sale of their parents' products, some of these captives are expanding into other areas of financial services. For example, in March 1985, General Motors announced plans to purchase two mortgage banking subsidiaries. Also, Chrysler is considering expanding its financing operations to include nonautomobile financing.

Some captive finance companies have become independent providers of financial services. These finance companies have the advantage of once having been

FIGURE 1
Shares of Auto Loans Outstanding

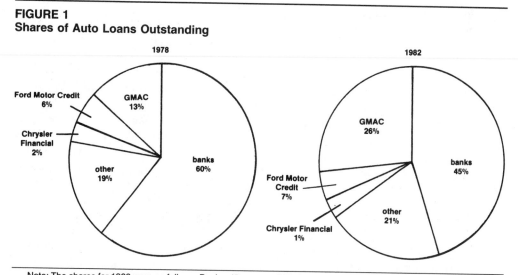

Note: The shares for 1983 were as follows: Banks, 47 percent; GMAC, 26 percent; Ford Motor Credit, 8 percent; Chrysler Financial, 1 percent; and other, 18 percent.
Source: *Federal Reserve Bulletin* and company annual reports.

under their parents' wings. Borg-Warner Acceptance Corporation, for example, gained experience *and* customers by offering inventory financing to dealers of Borg-Warner products. Today, BWAC provides this service for some of the same customers, but it finances the inventories of products from other manufacturers.

One disadvantage, however, that the finance subsidiaries of industrial-based firms have is that financial services is very different from their parents' traditional lines of business. To some extent this has been overcome by the captives and the once-captives, as financial services activities developed as a complement to their parents' manufacturing operations. For at least one of the independents, this disadvantage could not be overcome. As a result of its huge losses in financial services, Armco sold its insurance operations in 1983. As stated in the 1983 Armco *Annual Report,* "This change in strategic direction reflects a renewed emphasis on the businesses and market niches we know best."[12]

Business Volume.   The industrial-based firms, as a group, provide financial services to consumers as well as to businesses. Ten of the 14 industrial firms provide consumer financing; these 10 companies held over $72 billion in consumer credit outstanding at year-end 1983, nearly all of which was consumer installment credit (Table 3). These 10 industrial firms held nearly 16 percent of all consumer installment credit outstanding, while the top 15 bank holding companies held 15 percent. Further, in 1983, GMAC alone held over $40 billion, more than the combined consumer installment credit held at the four largest bank holding companies.

Consumer finance receivables held by the 10 industrial firms grew by 14 percent over the 1981–83 period, yet they did not keep pace with the bank holding companies. Similarly, in consumer installment lending the 10 industrial companies increased their outstandings 19 percent over the two-year period, but again they did not keep pace with the top 15 bank holding companies.

Each of the 14 selected industrial firms offers commercial financing or lease financing. At year-end 1983, these 14 industrial firms held nearly $44 billion in commercial loans (C&I loans and commercial mortgages); C&I loans account for nearly all of this amount. Nevertheless, the 14 industrial firms accounted for about 8 percent of all C&I loans outstanding at the end of 1983, while the top 15 bank holding companies accounted for 31 percent. GMAC, however, held $11.4 billion in C&I loans, roughly equal to the domestic C&I loans of Chase Manhattan Corporation, the third largest bank holding company.

The industrial-based companies increased their C&I loans 14 percent between 1981 and 1983, outpacing the bank holding companies but not all commercial banks, which increased their C&I loans by 25 percent. Borg-Warner and Commercial Credit Corporation led the industrial firms, increasing their C&I loans 43 percent each.[13]

The 14 industrial firms increased their commercial mortgage receivables 74 percent from 1981 to 1983, much faster than the top 15 bank holding companies and all insured domestic commercial banks. The industrial firms, however, have only $3.4 billion in commercial mortgages, less than one percent of all commercial mortgages outstanding in 1983, and only 6 of the 14 industrials make commercial real estate loans.

Lease financing is the area in which the industrial companies shine. At year-end 1983, they had a combined $17.5 billion in lease receivables, more than the 15 largest bank holding companies and more than all domestic commercial banks. Further, the industrial firms increased their lease receivables 22 percent over the 1981–83 period. Bank holding companies increased their lease receivables only 12 percent and banks 8 percent during this period.

One reason for the industrial firms' success in leasing is that such companies as GECC and Westinghouse, which have parents with large and growing profit bases, gain a competitive advantage by exploiting an opportunity in the tax laws. In their leasing activities, the finance subsidiaries retain ownership of the equipment they lease; therefore, their parents get to apply the depreciation, investment tax credits, and, in some cases, energy credits to their taxable income (since the finance subsidiaries are consolidated with the parent and other subsidiaries for tax purposes). These tax savings can then be passed on to the finance subsidiaries' customers in the form of lower leasing rates, thus allowing the finance subsidiaries to undercut the competition. Banks and bank holding companies have the same opportunity to use leasing to shelter income from taxes. But from 1981–83 the net income of banks and bank holding companies grew very slowly, providing comparatively little incentive to banks to expand their leasing operations.

Only 5 of the 14 industrial-based firms take deposits, and each of these 4 owns depository institutions. As of year-end 1983, these firms—Dana, National Steel, ITT, Control Data—had $8.4 billion in deposits, 3 percent of the deposits of the five largest bank holding company based on deposits.

Profitability.   Financial services have been profitable for most of the selected 14 industrial-based firms. The combined financial services earnings of the 14 companies was $2.2 billion in 1983, nearly two thirds as much as the earnings of the top 15 bank holding companies. GMAC was by far the biggest money-maker among the finance subsidiaries of the industrial-based firms, with 1983 earnings over $1 billion. All other finance subsidiaries earned less than half as much as GMAC, and only one financial services subsidiary posted a net loss for 1983.

The industrial-based firms' financial services earnings grew rapidly (57 percent) over the 1981–83 period, while the total earnings of the top 15 bank holding companies were virtually unchanged over this same period. On an individual basis, however, earnings growth among the manufacturers was mixed. For five industrial companies, financial services earnings fell, while financial services earnings more than doubled for four others.

Returns on equity (ROEs) for the industrial firms' financial operations exceeded those of their nonfinancial operations in 1981, but the reverse was true in 1983. In 1983 their nonfinancial operations returned 20 percent on equity, outperforming their financial operations by nearly 5 percentage points. Nonetheless, the financial operations of the manufacturers, as a group, experienced a higher ROE in 1983 than did the top 15 bank holding companies or all domestic commercial banks. To some extent, these differences reflect cyclical behavior. The earnings of retailers and manufacturers tend to be coincident with the business cycle; 1981 and 1982 were recession years while 1983 was a year of strong economic rebound. Bank performance tends to lag behind the general economy. Clearly, several more years of profitability data are necessary before conclusions can be drawn regarding the changing comparative profitability of banks and nonbanks.

Long-run Impact.   In some business lines, these industrial companies are formidable competitors of commercial banks. Furthermore, if changing technology provides any basis for economies of scale in offering consumer lending, some of these industrial companies may be even more formidable competitors in the future.

Prior to 1985, none of the industrial firms seem to have posed a competitive threat to banks in commercial or consumer mortgage lending. However, a few, such as General Electric and Borg-Warner, have made aggressive moves into mortgage banking.[14] And as mentioned earlier, General Motors has proposed to acquire two mortgage banking firms. If there are economies of scope in mortgage banking or, more importantly, if these industrial firms *perceive* that there are economies of scope, then certain industrial firms do pose some competitive threat to banks, particularly since Regulation Q no longer confers a cost-of-funds advantage to banks.[15]

In areas in which banks and the industrial firms do compete, the industrial firms' results have been mixed. Some industrial companies have increased their finance receivables in the various lending categories faster than banking organizations, while others have actually decreased their receivables over the 1981–83 period. Of course, some firms in the latter group, such as General Electric and Westinghouse, have intentionally decreased their holdings of certain receivables to devote their attention and resources to other financial services areas. Also, some industrial firms have maintained highly profitable financial services operations, but the financial earnings of other firms' plummeted over the 1981–83 period.

DIVERSIFIED FINANCIALS

Eight diversified financial firms have been identified as having a significant presence in the financial services industry (see Table 2). American Express, Merrill Lynch, and E. F. Hutton are large national distribution companies; they have many offices throughout the country and the world; and they offer a wide array of financial services to both consumers and commercial customers. Beneficial and Household are primarily consumer finance companies, and the remaining three firms are truly diversified, having financial as well as nonfinancial operations.

These diversified financial firms compete with banking firms; and it seems that some, but not all, may pose competitive threats to banking firms in providing financial services to consumers as well as to business customers. These eight firms compete with banks in most product areas, and they offer a few services that banks are prohibited from offering, such as life and property-casualty insurance.

The diversified financials have extensive distribution networks. These networks give them a nationwide presence, allow them to deliver their services to millions of customers, and enable them to experiment with new products and services at a lower cost than would be possible without their existing distribution networks. These networks, however, may be laden with a history, culture, and tradition that preclude these firms from fully exploiting their advantages.

For example, while Merrill Lynch's delivery network is one of its major strengths, it is also one of its major weaknesses. Indeed, Merrill Lynch's extensive nationwide branch network of over 400 branches, employing nearly 9,000 brokers, is the primary reason that it generates huge sales volume. But because its brokers get a cut of all they sell and are motivated primarily by commission income incentives, this approach has tended to be a high-cost distribution system. Furthermore, this type of product delivery system has an inherent inflexibility that makes Merrill Lynch vulnerable at a time when discount brokering and other low-cost distribution methods are gaining market share.[16] The fact that Merrill Lynch operates essentially as a brokerage house also stymies its innovations. At first, Merrill Lynch's Cash Management Account met with much opposition from the brokers because it pays no commission.[17]

Like Merrill Lynch, other diversified financials have found the need to change as more and more financial services concerns are moving toward becoming financial conglomerates; these diversified financial firms are finding change difficult but necessary. American Express, for instance, was until 1981 essentially a travel services company. In 1981, American Express began an acquisition campaign in order to become a major diversified financial services competitor. These acquisitions did allow American Express to enter new markets, including securities brokerage (Shearson), middle-market investment products distribution (Investors Diversified Services) and investment banking (Lehman Brothers), and target new customer bases; but the company is now faced with the delicate task of integrating and managing its recently acquired financial businesses. And the success of American Express in these endeavors is not a foregone conclusion; in the early 1970s, American Express entered the brokerage business by acquiring a 25 percent interest in Donaldson, Lufkin, Jennrette, but divested it a few years later.

A characteristic among the diversified financials, which some (especially bankers who want to enter the industry) view as an advantage, is their ability to underwrite and market insurance. Whether insurance products really confer an advantage, however, is open to serious question because the property-casualty insurance industry has suffered losses recently, losing money every year since 1978, and 1983 was the worst year ever.[18] Income from investments, which saved the industry from losses in the past, did not keep pace with underwriting losses. Also, fierce price competition in this industry has contributed to the problem.

Business Volume. The eight diversified financial firms engage in both consumer and commercial lending. At year-end 1983, they had about $30 billion of consumer finance receivables outstanding, of which over three quarters was installment credit (see Table 3). In fact, almost all of the mortgage loans of the diversified financials are second mortgages and could, therefore, be classified as installment lending as well. This $30 billion represented a 9 percent increase over 1981, but a smaller increase than those of all commercial banks and the top 15 bank holding companies.

The range of growth in consumer receivables among the diversified financial firms is quite large. Loews' consumer finance receivables fell 58 percent, while E. F. Hutton's consumer receivables grew 37 percent over the two-year period. Loews' drop in consumer loans reflects the sale of its consumer finance subsidiary in 1983, and Hutton's growth reflects more margin lending. American Express and Merrill Lynch also increased their margin account lending quite rapidly over this period because of the bull market that began in late 1982 and ran through much of 1983. Since bull markets come and go, this high rate of consumer credit expansion is probably not sustainable.

All eight diversified financial firms engage in some form of commercial lending. Over the 1981–83 period, the eight diversified financials increased their holdings of commercial loans faster than the top 15 bank holding companies but slower than the growth rate for all commercial banks. As with the growth of consumer loans, however, the range of commercial loan growth among the eight firms was quite wide. Merrill Lynch increased its outstandings 152 percent, while Household *decreased* its outstandings 44 percent. Furthermore, the absolute size of the combined commercial loan portfolio of the eight diversified financial firms is small—only $7.4 billion, 1 percent of all C&I loans outstanding at year-end 1983. In contrast, the eight largest bank holding companies accounted for over 20 percent of all C&I loans at that time.

The diversified financial firms are weak, relative to the banking firms, in C&I lending but are somewhat stronger in lease financing and commercial mortgage lending. At year-end 1983, the eight diversified financials held only 3 percent of the C&I loans held by the top 15 bank holding companies, but they held 11 percent of the lease receivables and 16 percent of the commercial mortgage loans of the bank holding companies.

Deposit Substitutes. The diversified financial firms offer products that compete with bank deposits as well as the lending products just reviewed. Four of the diversified financial firms managed money market funds. At year-end 1984, these four had money fund assets of about $67 billion. Merrill Lynch alone managed more than $39 billion, which is roughly equivalent to the deposits of Chemical New York Corporation, the sixth largest bank holding company. In addition, six of the eight diversified financial firms own depository institutions, which combined had over $15 billion in deposits at year-end 1983.

The ownership of money market funds by the diversified financials and others may have represented a competitive threat to banks in the past; but the threat in the current environment seems minimal because money market funds (MMFs) have become a less attractive substitute for money or bank deposits. The Garn-St Germain Act of 1982 granted banks and thrifts the right to offer a money market deposit account (MMDA) that is directly competitive with MMFs. MMDAs were an instant success, growing from zero to more than $350 billion in just a few months. Over this same period, MMF balances declined by more than 20 percent. By year-end 1984, MMF balances had grown to $236 billion, about the same level as they were when MMDAs were first introduced. Nonetheless, general purpose MMFs declined from 9.2 percent of M2 (the Federal Reserve's broadly defined money supply) in December 1982 to 7.1 percent in December 1984.

There are several reasons for this decline: (1) MMDAs are covered by federal deposit insurance while MMFs are not; (2) MMDAs can pay the same market rates as MMFs; and (3) MMDAs allow a depositor to maintain an account directly competitive with MMFs at the same depository institution where he conducts the rest of his deposit business, thus affording the convenience of one-stop shopping.

MMFs, however, do have some advantages over MMDAs. MMFs generally allow a greater number of checks to be written than MMDAs, although they usually impose a high minimum denomination on each check. Also, many MMFs are part of a "family" of mutual funds and allow convenient shifting among members of the mutual fund family, a service that banks cannot match.

Nevertheless, banks can apparently compete very well against their less regulated competitors—such as those diversified financial firms that offer MMFs—when regulatory barriers are relaxed sufficiently for them to compete on a roughly equal footing.

Profitability. Financial services seem to be quite profitable for the diversified financial firms. In 1983, the combined eight firms earned more than $1.6 billion from financial operations, 18 percent more than they earned two years earlier. In comparison, the 15 largest bank holding companies earned $41 million less than they earned in 1981; however, the top eight bank holding companies earned 16 percent more than they earned in 1981 and twice as much as the eight diversified financial firms. American Express earned $515 million, the highest 1983 net earnings of the diversified financials and more than any bank holding company except Citicorp (the largest).

All of the diversified financial firms' product lines are not necessarily profitable. Five of the selected eight diversified financial firms have been hurt recently by problems that have plagued the property-casualty insurance industry. Also, some of these firms have recently exited certain financial businesses. Further, two diversified financial companies, Baldwin-United and Walter E. Heller International, which were included in the Chicago Fed's two previous studies, have fallen on bad times and were removed from the sample.

Long-run Impact. The financial services operations of the diversified financial firms seem to be in a state of flux, so whether or not, as a group, they are a significant threat to traditional suppliers is uncertain.

In consumer finance, the combination of the eight diversified financial firms did not do as well as the 15 largest bank holding companies. None of the diversified financials pose any kind of threat in making residential first mortgage loans: almost all of the diversified financial firms' residential mortgages are second mortgages. Only four of the diversified financials "take deposits" through money market funds, but six own nonbank banks or have savings and loan subsidiaries.

Some diversified financial firms are expanding their offerings of financial products and services to businesses. Yet even those diversified financial firms that have growing commercial operations accounted at the end of 1983 for too small of a share of total commercial lending and deposit-taking to pose a serious threat to commercial banking firms in these product areas in the near future.

INSURANCE-BASED COMPANIES

Insurance companies compete with commercial banks and other depository institutions primarily through their investment portfolios. Some insurance companies also compete in the financial services industry through other means. Five of these insurance-based firms are Prudential, Equitable Life Assurance, Aetna Life & Casualty, American General, and Travelers. Among the noninsurance activities of these five firms are mutual funds, brokerage, cash management, mortgage banking, leasing, and consumer finance.

Business Volume. At year-end 1983, life insurance companies held $69.5 billion in consumer loans, over three fourths of which was consumer installment credit (policy loans). The five insurance-based companies mentioned above held $12.3 billion, or about 3 percent, of all consumer installment loans outstanding.

But installment credit held at the 15 largest bank holding companies grew almost three times as fast over the 1981–83 period as installment credit at these five insurance companies. This is what would be expected as interest rates decline, since the demand for policy loans increases when interest rates rise.

In consumer mortgage lending, insurance companies are dwarfed by commercial banks. At year-end 1983, life insurance companies held less than one tenth of the consumer mortgages held by all commercial banks. Moreover, only two of the selected five insurance-based firms had consumer mortgages on their books in 1983; however, one (Equitable) increased its holdings 24 percent, faster than all commercial banks and faster than the top 15 bank holding companies.

In commercial lending, insurance-based firms are only significant in mortgage lending. In 1983, the five insurance companies held 8 percent of all commercial mortgage loans outstanding—more than the top 15 bank holding companies and about one third that of all insured commercial banks. Commercial mortgages, however, grew at a faster pace over the 1981–83 period at commercial banks than they did at insurance companies.

Profitability.   Total earnings for the five insurance-based firms exceeded $3.3 billion, nearly as much as the worldwide earnings of the top 15 bank holding companies. Over the 1981–83 period, however, the combined earnings of the five insurance firms increased only 3 percent, and for three of the firms, earnings fell.

Long-run Impact.   Insurance companies do not seem to be a threat to banking firms. In fact, banks have certain attributes that would contribute to their success in offering insurance. These include their image as providers of financial services, their existing customer base, and their existing distribution networks. Consequently, the insurance industry has expressed more concern about banks invading the turf of insurance companies than vice versa.

HOW THEY ALL STACK UP

All nonbank firms do not compete with all banking firms or with each other. The retailers offer financial products and services, almost exclusively, to consumers, while many of the industrial-based companies devote a greater proportion of their financial services activities to commercial customers than to consumers. Also, of those firms that provide financial services to consumers, not all target the same ones. Some, like Merrill Lynch and American Express, target the "upscale" customer, while others, especially the retailers, target "middle America."

Also, as would be expected, each group of nonbank competitors has not been as successful as other groups in providing financial services, and, within the groups, some companies have not done as well as others. Furthermore, banks and bank holding companies have been more successful than the nonbanks in some areas.

In 1983, the nonbank firms held about $262 billion in finance receivables, almost as much as that held by the top 15 bank holding companies. The industrial firms accounted for over half of this amount; however, the retailers led the nonbanks in receivables growth over the 1981–83 period, while the diversified financial firms brought up the rear.

In the consumer finance area, the 30 nonbank firms accounted for over 30 percent of all consumer installment credit outstanding in 1983. At that time, seven nondeposit-based firms each held over 1 percent of all consumer installment credit

---

TABLE 4
Top 10 Consumer Installment Lenders: 1983

	1983		1981	
	$ bil	Market* share	$ bil	Market* share
General Motors	$40.2	10.2%	$31.1	9.3%
Citicorp	15.4	3.9	9.6	2.9
Sears	13.8	3.5	9.5	2.8
Ford Motor	11.9	3.0	11.9	3.5
BankAmerica Corp	11.4	2.9	9.7	2.9
American Express	7.7	1.9	5.0	1.5
Prudential	6.7	1.7	5.1	1.5
Merrill Lynch	6.1	1.5	4.7	1.4
J.C. Penney	5.5	1.4	4.4	1.3
Security Pacific	5.5	1.4	3.8	1.1
	124.2	31.4	94.8	28.2

---

* Market shares for the nonbank firms are slightly understated because second mortgages are excluded from consumer installment credit for these companies.
    Source: Company annual reports and *Flow of Funds Accounts, Assets and Liabilities Outstanding 1960–83,* Board of Governors of the Federal Reserve System.

(see Table 4). An industrial firm, General Motors, held over 10 percent, and a retailer, Sears, held 3.5 percent. In contrast, Citicorp, the largest consumer installment lender among the bank holding companies, held about 4 percent.

In commercial financing, the only relevant nonbank groups (so far) are the industrial firms and the insurance companies. The retailers do not engage in commercial financing, and the eight diversified financials held less than 1 percent of all commercial loans in 1983.

The insurance-based firms and the industrial-based firms each had about a 4 percent share of all commercial receivables at year-end 1983, with $48.3 billion and $43.8 billion, respectively. General Motors and IBM had the largest shares of C&I loans among the nonbanks, with 2.3 percent and 1.5 percent, respectively. In contrast, BankAmerica, the largest C&I lender among the bank holding companies had a 4.1 percent share. In commercial mortgage lending, Prudential and Equitable had the largest shares, each with about 2 percent. Citicorp held less than 1 percent of all commercial mortgage loans outstanding in 1983.

In lease financing, the only significant group of nonbank firms is the industrial-based companies. They held almost 90 percent of the lease receivables held by the 30 nonbank firms in 1983. Over the 1981–83 period, however, the diversified financial firms increased their lease financing receivables 26 percent, a faster pace than the industrial firms' 22 percent increase. The industrial firms that dominate this lending category are General Electric, General Motors, Ford, Greyhound, and Control Data. Each held over $1 billion in lease receivables at year-end 1983.

The 30 nonbank firms reported $8 billion in earnings from financial services in 1983. The five insurance companies accounted for the largest share of these earnings. The insurance companies, however, although appearing strong in absolute earnings, lag the other nonbank firms in earnings growth. Over the 1981–83 period, the 14 industrial-based firms increased their financial services earnings 57 percent, while the earnings of the insurance companies grew only 3 percent. Five nonbank firms had both high financial services earnings in 1983 and high earnings growth over the 1981-83 period. Three are industrial-based firms—General Motors, Ford, and General Electric. The other two are Sears and American General. No diversified financial firm made this list.

CONCLUSIONS

When attention began to be focused on nonbank competitors—such as Sears, American Express, General Motors, Prudential, and Merrill Lynch—early in the 1980s, their new competitive thrusts seemed to represent a real and immediate danger to the banking industry. With the benefit of hindsight and the research discussed in this and our previous studies, we conclude those fears are unwarranted, although some nonbank firms have gained substantial market shares in some product lines and are increasing their presence at a very fast pace.

The environment at the beginning of the 1980s must be kept in mind. The banking industry was still reeling from three unanticipated forces: (1) deregulation brought on by the Depository Institutions Deregulation and Monetary Control Act passed in March 1980, which opened up a new era in price competition by phasing out Regulation Q ceilings; (2) prolonged downward sloping yield curves containing record level interest rates all along the maturity spectrum; and (3) record high volatility, or lack of predictability of interest rates. If this were not enough, these events were followed by the steepest recession of the post-World War II period; an international debt crisis; a period of disinflation that undermined the value of tangible assets, such as real estate and commodities; and an oil glut. To sort out the separate impact of each of these simultaneous events on the performance of banks would be nearly impossible. To evaluate the impact on bank performance resulting from increased nonbank competition during a period when banks were being buffeted by these other events is even more difficult, if not impossible. Despite these caveats, and the fact that only three or four years of data have been analyzed extensively, we offer a few tentative conclusions on financial industry competition.

By far the safest observation that can be made from our analysis is that the banking industry has shown an amazing degree of resiliency in the face of these changes. Small banks gained market share in commercial lending relative to large banks and nonbanks. Large banks gained market share in consumer lending relative to small banks and all nonbanks except retailers. In this hostile macroeconomic environment, bank profitability suffered relative to nonbanks. Yet, in those areas where banks were deregulated in recent years, they have fared quite well against their nonbank competitors. The MMDA versus MMF battle is a case in point.

Prior to 1980, banks were subject to price regulation (Regulation Q and usury ceilings), product restrictions, and geographic restrictions. To be sure, banks do have federal deposit insurance while nonbank competitors do not, but nonbank competitors were subject only to usury ceilings. Since 1980, the driving force behind the contentiousness of banks and nonbanks has shifted to such issues as the Glass-Steagall Act, and the McFadden Act and the Douglas Amendment to the Bank Holding Company Act.

The nonbanks increased their emphasis on the financial services and products offered by banks because they saw profitable opportunities to be exploited in going against competitors like banks that were not free to adjust their price, product, and geographical mix. Many of these nonbank competitors at the time were not doing particularly well in their own primary product lines where they faced competition that had equal price, product, and geographical freedom.

They also recognized some synergies between their primary lines of business and financial services. For the retailers, financial services allows them to take advantage of their extensive distribution networks, large customer bases, and years of credit experience. Similarly, industrial firms can capitalize on their captive financing experience and, in some cases, their distribution systems. Diversified financials and insurance companies also have extensive distribution systems, and are recognized as suppliers of financial services.

This is not to say that all nonbanks will do well in financial services. Some will do well, others will not. Our research to date does not indicate any particular nonbank firm or group of firms that seems destined to outperform their banking and nonbank competitors. By the same token, no particular bank or group of banks seems destined for success or extinction. However, the limited evidence we have reviewed suggests that banks will improve their chances of competing successfully against their nonbank competitors as geographic and product restrictions are relaxed. That is, many of the regulations designed to protect banks from one another have hurt them by limiting their ability to formulate strategies and actions to deal effectively with their nonbank competitors.

NOTES

[1] Cleveland A. Christophe, *Competition in Financial Services* (New York: First National City Corporation, 1974).

[2] Harvey Rosenblum and Diane Siegel, *Competition in Financial Services: The Impact of Nonbank Entry*, Staff Study 83-1, Federal Reserve Bank of Chicago, May 1983; and Harvey Rosenblum and Christine Pavel, *Financial Services in Transition: The Effects of Nonbank Competitors*, Staff Memo 84-1, Federal Reserve Bank of Chicago, 1984.

[3] Consumer installment credit for the nonbank firms is slightly understated because it excludes second mortgages, which, for the nonbanks, were grouped with consumer first mortgages.

[4] Harvey Rosenblum and Christine Pavel, "1983: The Year in Review," *Commercial West* 165 (December 31, 1983), pp. 10–11.

[5] Bank assets expanded at a fast rate during the 1981–83 period partly because of a vigorous economic expansion, accompanied by an easier monetary policy beginning in July 1982.

[6] *Moody's Industry Outlook Retail Industry* (New York: Moody's Investors Service, August 24, 1984), p. 4.

[7] Mortgage loans are excluded here because only Sears makes mortgage loans, through Sears Savings Bank in California.

[8] *Nilson Report,* no. 337 (August 1984), p. 4, and no. 338 (August 1984), p. 3.

[9] "The only thing we have to fear is Sears itself," *ABA Banking Journal,* October 1983, pp. 58–60.

[10] Ibid., p. 58.

[11] For a variety of reasons, this increased market share was purchased through vigorous price-cutting. For detailed discussion see Harvey Rosenblum and Christine Pavel, "Banking Services in Transition," *Handbook for Banking Strategy* (1984), pp. 219–26; and Donna Vandenbrink, "Did usury ceilings hold down auto sales?" *Economic Perspectives,* September/October 1984, pp. 24–30.

[12] Armco *Annual Report, 1983,* p. 102.

[13] While it is difficult to provide a definitive interpretation, these findings are consistent with recent trends that show the larger banks emphasizing middle-market lending and noncredit services because of the shrinking profitability of lending to large companies that have access to national or global money and credit markets. Smaller and medium-size banks have always confined their commercial lending to small and medium-size customers which, because of their limited access to the national money markets, are forced to maintain their credit relationships with banks and suppliers of trade credit. These data suggest that the larger banks and bank holding companies have a long way to go in luring so-called middle-market customers away from their relationships with local and regional banks, trade credit suppliers, and commercial finance companies. When combined with the evidence on consumer lending, these data suggest a significant change in the perceived relative opportunities and profitability of commercial versus consumer lending.

[14] Since 1981, GECC has engaged in mortgage banking through two subsidiaries, General Electric Mortgage Corporation, and General Electric Mortgage Securities Corporation. Control Data has engaged in mortgage banking since 1982 through a subsidiary of Commercial Credit Corporation.

[15] Economies of scope result when there is a cost advantage to producing two products simultaneously, rather than each separately.

[16] "Merrill Lynch's Big Dilemma," *Business Week,* January 16, 1984, pp. 63–67.

[17] In 1984, Merrill Lynch responded to this apparent disadvantage by adopting a reorganization plan designed to transform the company from a sales-oriented firm into a marketing one.

[18] "Insurers' Mounting Troubles," *New York Times,* 14 February 1984, sec. D, pp. 1, 17.

3

A Deregulated Rerun:
Banking in the Eighties

Randall C. Merris and John Wood

The story of commercial banking during the past 25 years has been one of rapid and sometimes radical change. The more significant changes include the shift from demand deposit sources of funds toward interest-sensitive money market liabilities, such as federal funds and certificates of deposit; the payment of interest on checking accounts; the growth of variable-rate loans and the shortening of loan maturities; the decline of the prime rate convention; the growth of consumer and real estate lending; the development of automatic transfer services between different types of accounts; the rapid growth of branch banking and bank holding companies both within and between states; and the infringement of traditional commercial banking functions, such as the creation and servicing of checking accounts, by nonbank institutions, accompanied by infringements in the opposite direction, such as underwriting and brokerage activities by banks, with complaints on both sides. The legality of many of these innovations has been questioned, but they have for the most part been accommodated by the regulators, courts, and Congress.

All these developments are important and the publicity they have received is deserved. But they are not unprecedented. Almost entirely they represent returns to practices that were well established by the 1920s or the resumption of trends that were underway in that decade but were interrupted by the Great Depression and World War II. The similarities between the years since 1960 and those preceding 1930 are not difficult to understand and may be explained in terms of interactions between the profitable lending opportunities that go with high interest

From *Economic Perspectives*, Federal *Reserve* Bureau Bank of Chicago, September/October 1985, pp. 69–79.

Randall C. Merris is a research economist at the Federal Reserve Bank of Chicago, currently on leave of absence and serving as research advisor, Bank Negara Malaysia, in Kuala Lumpur under the Technical Assistance Program of the International Monetary Fund. John Wood, a visiting scholar at the Federal Reserve Bank of Chicago, is professor of finance at Northwestern University. He recently accepted an appointment at Wake Forest University.

rates and the restrictive regulatory framework that has long been imposed on the American banking system.

The most severe of these restrictions, especially when compared with the nationwide branch-banking systems of Canada and Great Britain, are the limitations on branching. Branching across state lines has been almost completely prohibited and most states either prohibit or severely limit branching within their boundaries. For many years national banks (i.e., banks chartered by the Comptroller of the Currency under the National Bank Act of 1863[1]) were limited to a single office. Americans have denied themselves the principal means by which in other countries funds are sent from net lending to net borrowing sections of the country—that is, between branches of truly national banks. The portfolio diversification, the protection against excessive reliance upon the fortunes of particular sections, that naturally arises in such a national system has also been impeded by the American system of small, geographically concentrated banks.

Other restrictions that have in various times and degrees been imposed on commercial banks include prohibitions or severe limits on real estate loans, interest payable on deposits, and brokerage, underwriting, investment advisory, and trust services. But rules are made to be broken, and frequently have been in the financial sphere, where there appears to be no natural separation of functions, no obvious criteria governing who should lend in what form to whom. In a prosperous and expanding economy with abundant profit opportunities it is inevitable that many firms and individuals will seek to extend their activities in a variety of directions, even into areas that by tradition or law had been reserved to others or prohibited altogether.

Recent innovations in banking are widely known and have been discussed in many places.[2] The purposes of this paper are to document the innovations of the 1920s and previously and, along the way, to indicate the similarities between old and new banking trends. Before proceeding to our list of pre-1930 developments it may be worthwhile to look at the interregnum that lasted from the early 1930s until well into the 1950s. The Great Depression halted and reversed nearly all extensions of financial institutions into new areas for the simple reason that profit opportunities had virtually been extinguished. In a world of massive industrial and financial failures the overriding thought was not expansion but survival, principally by retrenchment.

Although the Great Depression's trough is usually dated in 1933, a strong recovery was not mounted until World War II and the entire decade of the 1930s was characterized by deep depression. The unemployment rate, which had risen from 3 percent to 25 percent between 1929 and 1933, was still 17 percent in 1939. Industrial production and real per capita gross national product remained lower in 1939 than in 1929, and real gross private domestic investment in 1939 was only 61 percent of its value 10 years earlier. Interest rates fell throughout the decade, and the average yield on corporate Aaa bonds was 2.92 percent in June 1939, compared with 4.73 percent in June 1929. The rate on four- to six-month prime commercial paper fell from 6.00 percent to 0.56 percent during the same period. (Changes in the commercial paper rate are compared with developments in banking in Figures 1 to 3). This decade of bank failures and depressed loan demands and interest rates saw member bank excess reserves as a percentage of deposits rise from one tenth of one percent to 10 percent, a hundredfold increase. Loans fell from 69 percent to 29 percent of deposits.

The demand for bank credit picked up during the war, but almost entirely in the form of government borrowing, which the Federal Reserve enabled the banks to finance by supplying unlimited reserves through open market purchases of government securities that were designed through an agreement with the Treasury to maintain stable and low interest rates—three-eighths of 1 percent on Treasury bills and about 2 percent on long-term Treasury bonds. This pegging operation continued until mid-1947, and the Federal Reserve did not cease active support of bond prices until 1953. Private investment and loan demands had begun to rise immediately upon the end of the war but interest rates did not return to pre-1930 levels until the 1960s. Now let us compare developments during the earlier period with those of today.

COMMERCIAL BANK LOANS, INVESTMENTS, AND RESERVES

In 1914, commercial bank loans made up 78 percent of bank earning assets—that is, of total loans and investments. (See Figure 1.) U.S. government securities constituted only 5 percent of bank earning assets. Bank securities purchases reduced the loan-to-earning-asset percentage to 70 and raised the percentage for U.S. securities to 16 by the end of World War I. There was some movement toward the pre-war figures during the 1919–1920 expansion, and again during 1928–29, but loans were only 73 percent of earning assets in 1929, after which there was a dramatic decline in loans (which fell 56 percent between 1929 and 1936) and an equally dramatic rise in bank holdings of U.S. securities (which more than tripled between 1929 and 1936). Loans and U.S. securities each made up about 40 percent of bank earning assets in 1936. These proportions were fairly stable between 1936 and 1941. Large-scale purchases of U.S. securities during World War II, accompanied by only a slight rise in loans, resulted by 1945 in banking earning assets consisting of 73 percent U.S. securities and 21 percent loans. Perhaps the most striking feature of bank portfolios during the past 40 years has been their strong and almost continuous movement toward the loan/investment ratio that existed before World War I. Loans as a percentage of earning assets rose from 21 percent in 1945 to 61 percent in 1960, 70 percent in 1970, 73 percent in 1980, and in 1984 to 78 percent, which is where we came in.

Commercial bank excess reserves have varied inversely with profit opportunities and the availability of liquid, low-risk sources of reserves. It is convenient to express the excess reserves of Federal Reserve member banks as a percentage of their required reserves, as in Figure 1. Beginning in 1929, the first year for which data on excess reserves are available, excess reserves were 1.8 percent of required reserves. Excess reserves rose sixtyfold between 1929 and 1936, to become 90 percent as large as required reserves.

Excess reserves were reduced by administrative action to 14 percent of required reserves when the Federal Reserve doubled reserve requirement ratios in a series of steps between August 1936 and May 1937. But nearly all additions to reserves during the next three years were kept as excess reserves and by 1940 excess reserves were 97 percent of required reserves. That is, by the end of the 1930s nearly one half of member bank reserves were in excess of legal requirements. Although interest rates remained low during World War II, the Fed's bond support program meant that banks could convert their excess reserves into highly liquid short-term governments without fear of loss and excess reserves had fallen below 10 percent by 1945. Rising interest rates induced further economies in

FIGURE 1
Loans and Investments, Excess Reserves, and the Commercial Paper Rate

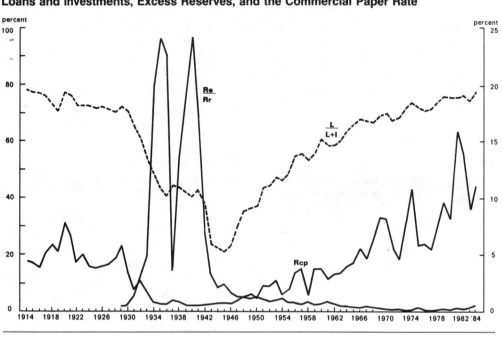

Definitions:

$\dfrac{L}{L+I}$: Loans as a proportion of loans and investments, all commercial banks, end of June.

$\dfrac{R_e}{R_r}$: Member bank excess reserves as a proportion of required reserves, average of daily figures for June.

R_{cp}: Four–six month prime commercial paper rate (1914–79) or average of three- and six-month prime commercial paper rates (1980–84), average of daily figures for June.

Note: Some of these series (particularly those pertaining to commercial bank assets and liabilities) have been revised from time to time, so the data are not perfectly comparable over time. However, the revisions have not been so great as to affect the principal movements shown in the charts and discussed in the text.

Sources: *Banking and Monetary Statistics, 1914–41 and 1941–70,* and various issues of *Annual Statistical Digest* and *Federal Reserve Bulletin,* all published by the Board of Governors of the Federal Reserve System, Washington, D.C.

reserves during the postwar period and excess reserves as a percentage of required reserves fell below 3 percent in 1956, below 2 percent in 1963 (returning to their 1929 relation), and below 1 percent in 1970.

LIABILITY MANAGEMENT

In the 1920s, most of the liabilities of large banks paid interest that varied closely with other money market rates. Of vital importance to the money center banks and to their correspondents in outlying areas was interbank lending in the form of bankers' balances, either as time or demand deposits. Competition for these interbank deposits was one of the most important means by which funds were induced to flow from surplus to deficit regions of the country. During the 1920s, about 20 percent of the deposits of New York City and Chicago banks consisted of balances owed to other banks, principally interest-bearing demand deposits. Federal funds and repurchase agreements were also significant sources of funds for the more aggressive banks.[3] In 1922, for example, the average daily purchases of fed funds in New York City were about 6 percent as large as the interbank deposit liabilities of New York City banks, a figure that rose to 12 percent in 1925 and 18 percent in 1928.[4] The fed funds market virtually disappeared during the 1930s and 1940s in the face of low interest rates, massive excess reserves, and easy Federal Reserve credit.

However, the prohibition of interest on demand deposits by the Banking Act of 1933[5] meant that renewed competition for reserves in the form of interbank lending in the 1950s and afterward had to shift its emphasis from bankers' balances to federal funds. By the 1980s, the liabilities of New York City banks in the forms of federal funds and repurchase agreements were more than seven times as large as their interbank deposit liabilities and about 45 percent as large as their total deposits. The competition for nondeposit funds that was resumed in the 1950s has gone far beyond the point at which it was interrupted in 1930. Again, rising interest rates, and the resulting increased cost of idle reserves helped induce this behavior.

Until the 1930s, many banks also paid interest on the demand deposits of their nonbank customers, with the minimum required balance for interest-earning demand deposits ranging from $100 to $10,000.[6] Interestingly, service charges on deposits, which had not been common before the 1920s, became widely used during that decade. A 1929 survey by the New York State Bankers Association showed that about 35 percent of banks imposed service charges on small accounts.[7] High interest rates and the growing competition for funds had resulted in greater cost consciousness and a desire to set prices of services in line with costs.[8]

The competition for funds in the 1920s was also reflected in increasing interest rates on time and savings accounts, a development that was stimulated by reductions in reserve requirements on those accounts. The National Bank Act had not distinguished between types of accounts in setting reserves requirements, and the same was true of the laws under which most state banks operated. But in 1913 the Federal Reserve Act reduced the reserve requirement ratios on time and savings deposits to less than one half of those on demand deposits, and most states followed suit in order that state banks would be placed at a competitive disadvantage.[9] The resulting reduction in the marginal cost of time and savings accounts, in combination with generally rising interest rates and growing competition for funds, led to increases in time and savings accounts as a percentage of total national bank deposits from 19 percent in 1914 to 23 percent in 1919 and 41 percent in 1929. The percentages for all commercial banks in these three years were 31, 33, and 46, respectively. (See Figure 2.)

Savings and loan associations and mutual savings banks, supported by their regulators, complained about the growing competition from commercial banks. Time and savings accounts in S&Ls and MSBs as a percentage of those in commercial banks fell from 77 percent in 1915 to 43 percent in 1925. In New York, Massachusetts, and Connecticut, the strongholds of mutual savings banks, commercial bank time and savings deposits grew from less than one fifth to more than one half of those in mutual savings banks.[10] The Commissioner of Banks of Massachusetts and the Superintendent of Banks of New York both wrote the following in their reports for 1918:

> If in any state there has been created a great system of mutual savings banks, in that state the national banks, although not mutual but operated for the profit of shareholders, will be authorized to call their interest departments savings departments, and so appropriate a word which has for a generation or more been syn-

FIGURE 2
Time and Savings Deposits as a Percentage of Total Bank Deposits, and the Commercial Paper Rate

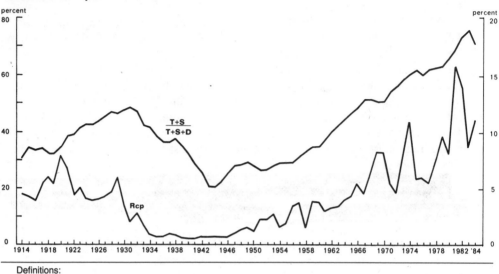

Definitions:

$\dfrac{T + S}{T + S + D}$: Time and savings deposits as a proportion of total commercial bank deposits, end of June.

R_{cp}: See Figure 1.
Note: See Figure 1.
Sources: See Figure 1.

onymous in this State with mutual institutions created under State laws. These deposits, moreover, will not be segregated, nor will the entire net income from investments be distributed among the depositors.[11]

The New York Superintendent also wrote:

It is not surprising, in view of the extension of Federal control over various classes of business and industry as a result of the necessities of the war, that the attention of the advocates of centralization and Federal domination should be attracted by the prosperity and success of State banking institutions. In their desire to bring under Federal control all classes of banking institutions, they seem, in the first instance, to have conceived the idea of conferring all the multifarious powers of the different classes of State institutions in all the States upon National Banks and to create a Federal system of department banks into which all banking institutions would ultimately be driven. Such a bank would closely resemble one of our great department stores. . . . Instead of having a uniform system of National Banks consisting of strictly commercial banking institutions and needing no other definition than the name, we would have heterogeneous varieties of hybrid institutions of as many kinds perhaps as there are States or possibly of as many types as there are classes of State banking institutions in all the States.

Later the Federal Reserve Board expressed concern over the growing tendencies of banks to provide automatic transfers between savings and demand deposits and to allow depositors to draw checks against savings deposits.[12] The Federal Advisory Council (a citizens advisory group) recommended to the board that

Regulation D, which governs reserve requirements, "might be amplified to pre-vent some of the abuses which have developed, such as the withdrawal by check of savings and time deposits and the lack of a clear distinction between demand and time deposits."[13] Savings associations also allowed drafts, or checks, to be drawn against savings accounts.[14]

These trends were reversed by the great decline in interest rates and the virtual disappearance of bank competition for funds in the 1930s and 1940s. Time and savings deposits as a percentage of total commercial bank deposits in the United States fell from 46 percent in 1929 to 36 percent in 1939 and 20 percent in 1944, which was the low point, well below the 1914 figure of 31 percent. Postwar prosperity and rising rates saw the figure rise to 47 percent (about the 1929 figure) in 1965, 62 percent in 1975, and 75 percent in 1983.

The resumption of interest-rate competition for funds was eventually also reflected in the effective resumption of interest payments on checking accounts and the ability to write checks on savings accounts. Congress had attempted to end these practices by the banking laws of the 1930s, but as soon as they once again became profitable, financial institutions, accommodated by their regulators or the courts, found ways of implementing them—including repurchase agree-ments and automatic transfer services by commercial banks, negotiable order of withdrawal (NOW) accounts by New England savings institutions, and share draft accounts by credit unions. However, in 1979 the last three practices were enjoined by a U.S. Court of Appeals.[15] The court expressed the following views in its ruling on suits filed by the American Bankers Association (with the Tioga State Bank) against the National Credit Union Administration, the Independent Bank-ers Association against the Federal Home Loan Bank Board, and the U.S. League of Savings Associations against the Federal Reserve Board:

> It appears to the court that the development of fund transfers . . . utilized by . . . commercial banks with "Automatic Fund Transfers," savings and loan associations with "Remote Service Units," and federal credit unions with "Share Drafts," in each instance represents the use of a device or technique which was not and is not recognized by the relevant statutes, although permitted by regulations of the respective institutions' regulatory agencies.[16]

The court pointed out that these procedures amounted to "the practical equiv-alent of checks drawn on . . . interest-bearing time deposits" in violation of laws governing the institutions concerned.

> The history of the development of these modern transfer techniques reveals each type of financial institution securing the permission of its appropriate regulatory agency to install these devices in order to gain a competitive advantage, or at least competitive equality, with financial institutions of a different type in services offered to the public. The net result has been that three separate and distinct types of financial institutions created by Congressional enactment to serve different public needs have now become, or are rapidly becoming, three separate but homogeneous types of financial institutions offering virtually identical services to the public, all without the benefit of Congressional consideration and statutory enactment.

The court recognized that the statutes had been rendered obsolete by events and also appreciated that "enormous investments" had been made in the new technology. The court also recognized the disruptions that would result from the sudden withdrawal of these services, upon which the financial community had "rapidly grown to rely." Therefore, about seven months, until January 1, 1980, were allowed for compliance with the court's ruling. The lag would also give Congress time to decide whether it wanted to override the court by changing the law. Spurred to action, Congress began hearings in June, enacted legislation in December that temporarily authorized the devices found illegal by the court, and granted those devices statutory approval in the Depository Institutions Deregulation and Monetary Control Act of 1980. And financial institutions were thereby enabled to continue to compete for funds in the 1980s in much the same way as in the 1920s.

RISK MANAGEMENT

The liquidity and interest-rate risks to which banks were exposed by their short-term, interest-sensitive liabilities were offset in the 1920s, as in the 1980s, by the use of these liabilities to fund short-term and variable-rate loans. During the earlier period, between 25 and 30 percent of the loans of large banks were call loans, mainly to brokers and dealers in securities, with rates that were subject to daily revision. About 45 percent of the loans of large New York City banks were call loans. Most of the remaining loans were business loans with maturities less than 90 days.[17] Although the liquidity of many of these loans was doubtful because they were repeatedly renewed as parts of long-term customer relationships,[18] their short-term contractual nature permitted the frequent adjustment of loan rates in line with the costs of funds.

However, these characteristics of bank loans, which had evolved in response to volatile interest rates and increasingly competitive conditions over several decades, were greatly modified by the events of the 1930s and 1940s—especially by the low and stable interest rates, enormous excess reserves, and easy Federal Reserve credit (discussed above). Short-term loans were no longer necessary for liquidity purposes, which were met by excess reserves and large holdings of short-term government securities, or to hedge interest-rate risk, which was virtually nonexistent. Furthermore, the great decline in stock market activity greatly reduced the demand for call loans. One of the consequences of this combination of events was the increased use of explicit long-term loans. Business loans with maturity of one year or more (term loans) rose from almost nothing in 1929 to nearly one third of business loans in 1940, a trend that continued until well into the 1950s.[19]

The high and volatile interest rates, very low excess reserves, and more volatile money stock changes in recent years have induced a return to the loan practices of the 1920s. For example the Federal Reserve's *Survey of Terms of Bank Lending* indicates that during the six years following 1977 (the first year of the survey in its present form) term loans fell from 16 percent to 9 percent of commercial and industrial loans, the percentage of term loans with floating rates rose from 49 to 73 percent, and the average maturity of short-term loans fell from 2.2 months to 1.1 months.[20] Recent data on bank loan rates show that these rates have become as variable as, perhaps more variable than, rates on short-term money market instruments such as commercial paper.[21] Apparently, "sticky" loan rates were peculiar to the 1930s to 1960s.

INVESTMENT BANKING BY COMMERCIAL BANKS

The so-called tradition of the separation of commercial banking and investment banking functions, including the idea that the former's credit ought to be limited to short-term, self-liquidating commercial loans, is unique to the English-speaking peoples and even there the tradition has been honored more in the breach than the observance. The Bank of England, the First and Second Banks of the United States, and most early state banks were chartered with the express goal of helping to float government debt. Commercial banks were especially active in underwriting government bonds during the Civil War and World War I, and had become heavily involved in corporate issues during the nineteenth century. It is likely that commercial banks first "became partners in underwriting syndicates . . . in order to obtain newly issued bonds at favorable prices. Acquisition of securities for the bank's own portfolio led to purchases on behalf of customers, particularly correspondent banks. In a few cases, that eventuated in a full range of investment banking activities."[22]

In 1902, the Comptroller of the Currency ruled that commercial banks were prohibited by the National Bank Act from underwriting or distributing equities. But the First National Bank of Chicago organized a state bank, owned by the same shareholders as First National, to carry on its securities activities. The First National Bank of New York and the National City Bank of New York soon followed suit.[23] Later, in the 1920s, official hostility toward securities underwriting by commercial banks changed to support, or at least acquiescence, in order to prevent defections from the national banking system, and the McFadden Act of 1927 legalized a wide range of securities activities by national banks. "For all practical purposes, adoption of the McFadden Act represented an abandonment of traditional banking theories and a recognition of a natural economic development. By the end of the decade, there was no longer any institutional separation of banking functions."[24] In 1929, 591 commercial banks were underwriting securities directly or through affiliates. These institutions originated 45 percent of all new bond issues in 1929, up from 22 percent in 1927.[25]

Commercial bank performance of what some people thought were not proper commercial banking functions did not prevent these firms from complaining about the invasions of their turf by others. Private investment banking houses paid interest on deposit liabilities and, in 1912, the largest house, J. P. Morgan, had deposits of $160 million, compared with $252 million in National City Bank, the largest commercial bank.[26]

Trust companies had also become major competitors of commercial banks. Trust companies originally specialized in the management of property for others, but by 1900 "the range of financial services they offered increased until, apart from their fiduciary function, they became indistinguishable from commercial banks"[27]—except, as bankers bitterly pointed out, in their virtual freedom from regulation, including legal reserve requirements. However New York State and some other states began to subject trust companies to reserve requirements during the early years of this century, and commercial banks received a further equalizing concession in 1913, when the Federal Reserve Act extended trust powers to national banks. In 1910, a trust officer forecast that "we shall have but one kind of financial institution, which will combine all the functions of the commercial bank, savings bank, and trust company."[28] He might also have included "investment bank," but perhaps he meant that function to be comprehended by "commercial bank."

The banking laws of the 1930s attempted to turn back the clock by divorcing commercial banking and investment banking and in other ways separating financial activities between different types of institutions.[29] But the hands have resumed their forward motion as banks have increased their involvement in the securities business and securities firms have reentered the deposit business, so that it has once again become difficult to answer the question "What is a bank?"[30]

GROUP AND BRANCH BANKING

Branch banking has from time to time been prohibited or severely restricted in most states, and national banks were not allowed to open branches until well into the 20th century. These restrictions gave rise to a variety of evasive devices during the 30 years of rapid bank expansion preceding the Great Depression, when the number of bank offices grew from about 9,000 (in 1900) to about 27,000 (in 1929).[31] Chief among these evasions was the exchange of national for state charters in those states in which branching was permitted. Another device was the bank holding company. Virgil Willit described the future of banking as the proponents of branching saw it in 1930:

> Group banking is simply the result of the introduction into the banking field of the holding company device, which has been long known and much used in other businesses. Through the holding company a number of banks can be operated as practically one institution. Such an institution is very closely akin to a branch bank. Indeed, the opponents of group banking maintain that it is simply a device for evading the legal restrictions on branch banking.
>
> In spite of much criticism and opposition, group banking is developing with amazing rapidity. At the present time group banks control one-fifth of the bank resources of the country. The movement is not localized, for groups are found throughout the country. A few states have attempted to check it by legislation but as yet no adequate means have been found to stop its growth. Thus group banking constitutes a greater menace to the unit system than does branch banking, which is easily amenable to legislative control. This situation has fortified the advocates of branch banking with a new and powerful argument. Unit banking, they contend, is doomed. The question no longer is whether we shall have unit or branch banking; the issue lies, rather, between group and branch banking.[32]

Between 1900 and 1929, the number of banks operating branches rose from 87 to 764, the number of branches rose from 119 to 3,533, and the assets of banks with branches rose from 2 percent to 43 percent of total bank assets. In 1921, "to meet the challenge of state branch banks" the Comptroller of the Currency "authorized national banks to open tellers windows limited to accepting deposits and cashing checks where a state permitted its banks to branch."[33] The National Bank Consolidation Act of 1918 had earlier made full-service branching by national banks a little easier by allowing them to keep the offices of the state banks that they acquired.[34] Further moves "designed to place the national banks on a more equal competitive plane with the state banks,"[35] or in the parlance of the

FIGURE 3
Commercial Bank Branches and the Commercial Paper Rate

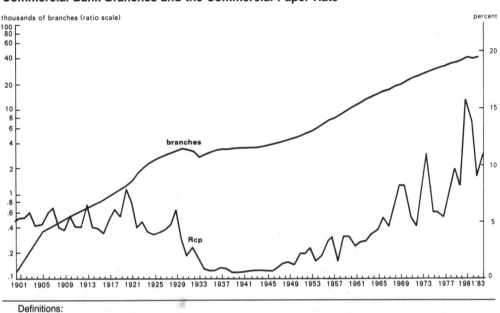

thousands of branches (ratio scale)

Definitions:
   Branches: Number of commercial bank branches, ratio scale, end of year. Before 1920, data are available only for
        selected years.
   R_{cp}: Same as Figure 1, but note the longer time span.
Sources: See Figure 1.

1980s, to "level the playing field," came in the McFadden Act, which relaxed restrictions on the real estate lending of national banks[36] and allowed them to open full-service branches. However, these branches were confined to the head-office city in states that allowed branching by state banks.

The number of branches fell 20 percent between 1929 and 1933, to 2,784. But unit banks declined even more rapidly, so, by 1933, the assets of branch systems made up 50 percent of total bank assets. Political opposition to branch banking declined markedly during the early 1930s, when the number of unit banking states was reduced from 22 to 10 and the Banking Act of 1933 permitted national banks to open branches on the same geographical basis as state banks. However the onerous capital requirements imposed on Fed member banks that opened branches outside their head-office cities retarded branching by those banks until 1952, when their capital requirements were reduced to the same level as those of nonmember competitors.[37]

Branching resumed its growth after 1933. But this growth was for a while much slower than during the first 30 years of the century. By 1940, the number of branches had recovered their 1929 level of about 3,500, and then rose to about 4,700 in 1950. But during the next decade the number of branches more than doubled, reaching 10,200 in 1960, again more than doubled to 21,400 by 1970, and rose to 38,400 in 1980. Group banking has not been left far behind. The proportion of all commercial bank deposits in multibank holding companies rose from about

10 percent in the mid-1950s to 16 percent in 1970 and 34 percent in 1980. It seems that, after some delay, the forecast of the banking industry offered by Professor Willit in 1930 is about to be realized.

CONCLUDING COMMENT

The financial services industry, including commercial banking, is once again on the expansive and competitive path that was temporarily blocked in the 1930s and 1940s—and regulation and legislation, as during the early years of this century, have accommodated the profit-seeking goals of financial firms and their clients. Branching, bank holding companies, interest on checking accounts, and securities activities by banks are responses to profit opportunities, which constitute the only effective deregulatory force. As in the 1920s, de jure deregulations—new legislation and new interpretations of existing laws—merely follow de facto deregulations that have already been instituted by the public in search of the most efficient means of carrying on financial transactions.

NOTES

[1] Actually the 1863 law that provided for national bank charters was called the National Currency Act. That act was amended and renamed the National Bank Act in 1864. For the history of these acts see Ross M. Robertson, *The Comptroller and Bank Supervision: A Historical Appraisal* (Washington, D.C.: Comptroller of the Currency, 1968).

[2] For example, see discussions of the events leading to the Depository Institutions Deregulation and Monetary Control Act of 1980 and the Garn-St Germain Act of 1982 in *Leveling the Playing Field: A Review of the DIDMCA of 1980 and the Garn-St Germain Depository Institution Act of 1982* (Chicago: Federal Reserve Bank, Chicago, 1983); and also in Federal Reserve Bank of Chicago, *Proceedings of a Conference on Bank Structure and Competition, April 12–14, 1982* (Chicago; 1982).

[3] For discussions of bank transactions in federal funds and repurchase agreements before 1930, see Parker B. Willis, *The Federal Funds Market: Its Origin and Development,* 4th ed. (Boston: Federal Reserve Bank of Boston, 1970), pp. 3–13; and H. G. Moulton, "Commercial Banking and Capital Formation," *Journal of Political Economy* 26 (July 1918), pp. 705–31.

[4] These percentages are based on estimates in Willis, *The Federal Funds Market,* p. 12.

[5] This prohibition is still in force for demand deposits. However, a number of alternative interest-bearing personal transactional accounts have been introduced. Historically, including the 1920s, over 90 percent of interbank deposits have been demand deposits.

[6] See James M. Boughton and Elmus R. Wicker, "The Behavior of the Currency-Deposit Ratio during the Great Depression," *Journal of Money Credit and Banking* 10 (November 1970), pp. 405–18.

[7] Ibid., p. 408.

[8] Service charges were retained and generally increased when interest rates fell during the 1930s. Total annual service charges grew 80 percent between 1929 and 1933 even though total deposits fell 40 percent and demand deposits fell 36 percent. (Ibid.)

[9] These changes are discussed by Charles M. Linke, "The Evolution of Interest Rate Regulation on Commercial Bank Deposits in the United States," *The National Banking Review,* June 1966, pp. 449–69; and Eugene N. White, *The Regulation and Reform of the American Banking System, 1900–1929* (Princeton: Princeton University Press, 1983), pp. 27–33, 98–102.

[10] Weldon Welfling, *Mutual Savings Banks: The Evolution of a Financial Intermediary* (Cleveland: Case Western Reserve University Press, 1968) p. 77.

[11] This and the next quotation are from Welfing, *Mutual Savings Banks,* pp. 78–79.

[12] See the discussions and references in Milton Friedman and Anna J. Schwartz, *A Monetary History of the United States, 1867–1960* (Princeton: Princeton University Press, 1963), p. 277; and Benjamin J. Klebaner, *Commercial Banking in the United States: A History* (Hinsdale, Ill: Dryden Press, 1974), p. 123.

[13] Federal Reserve Board, *Annual Report, 1928,* p. 228.

[14] See William H. Kniffen, *The Savings Bank and its Practical Work* (New York: Bankers Publishing Company, 1928), p. 258.

[15] The following discussion is taken from John H. Wood and Norma L. Wood, *Financial Markets* (New York: Harcourt Brace Jovanovich, 1985), pp. 61–63.

[16] This and the following quotation are from United States Court of Appeals for the District of Columbia Circuit, September term 1978, nos. 78–1337, 78–1849, 78–2206.

[17] For summaries of bank loans during the 1920s and recently, see John H. Wood, "Familiar Developments in Bank Loan Markets," *Economic Review,* Federal Reserve Bank of Dallas, November 1983, pp. 1–13.

[18] For a discussion of customer relationships before the 1930s, see Davis R. Dewey and Martin J. Shugrue, *Banking and Credit* (New York: Ronald Press, 1922), pp. 176–78.

[19] See Neil H. Jacoby and Raymond Saulnier, *Term Lending to Business* (New York: National Bureau of Economic Research, 1942); and George S. Moore, "Term Loans and Interim Financing," in *Business Loans of American Commercial Banks,* ed. Benjamin H. Beckhart (New York: Ronald Press, 1959).

[20] See Wood, "Familiar Developments," table 3. For a discussion of the growth of variable-rate loans during the 1970s, see Randall C. Merris, "Business Loans at Large Commercial Banks: Policies and Practices," *Economic Perspectives,* Federal Reserve Bank of Chicago, November/December 1979, pp. 15–23.

[21] See Wood, "Familiar Developments," table 2.

[22] Klebaner, *Commercial Banking,* p. 82.

[23] For accounts of this and other early episodes of investment banking by commercial banks, see Klebaner, *Commercial Banking,* pp. 80–84; and Larry R. Mote, "Banks and the Securities Markets: The Controversy," *Economic Perspectives,* Federal Reserve Bank of Chicago, March/April 1979, pp. 14–20.

[24] Edward J. Kelly, "Legislative History of the Glass-Steagall Act," in *Deregulating Wall Street: Commercial Bank Penetration of the Corporate Securities Market,* ed. Ingo Walter (New York: John Wiley & Sons, 1985).

[25] Mark J. Flannery, "An Economic Evaluation of Bank Securities Activities before 1933," in *Deregulating Wall Street,* ed. Walter.

[26] Klebaner, *Commercial Banking,* p. 82.

[27] Klebaner, *Commercial Banking,* p. 83. Also see White, *Regulation and Reform,* pp. 38–42, for a discussion of the banking activities of trusts during this period.

[28] Quoted from Klebaner, *Commercial Banking,* p. 84.

[29] In fact, commercial banks were never completely forced out of the securities business. The Banking Act of 1933 expressly authorized them to buy and sell securities for customer accounts, to purchase some types of securities for their own accounts, and to underwrite Treasury issues and general obligation municipal bonds. (See Mote, "Banks and the Securities Market," p. 17.)

[30] John J. Di Clemente, "What is a Bank?" *Economic Perspectives,* Federal Reserve Bank of Chicago, January/February 1983, pp. 20–31. Also see Walter H. Wriston, "Bank 'n' Burger" *Euromoney,* October 1981, pp. 53–54; and Jean M. Lovati, "The Growing Similarity among Financial Institutions," *Review,* Federal Reserve Bank of St. Louis, October 1977, pp. 2–11.

[31] The peak number of offices (above 31,000) actually occurred in 1922, before widespread failures of banks in agricultural areas.

[32] Virgil Willit, "Introductory Note," in *Chain, Group and Branch Banking,* ed. Willit (New York: H. W. Wilson, 1930), pp. 10–11.

[33] Klebaner, *Commercial Banking,* p. 126.

[34] The number of national bank branches rose from 26 in 1915 to 318 in 1925. (White, *Regulation and Reform,* p. 161.) The 26 branches existing in 1915 were possible because in the early years of the National Bank Act the Comptroller of the Currency had allowed newly chartered national banks to keep their branches, a policy reversed after 1870.

[35] Virgil Willit, "The Rise of Multiple Banking in the United States," in Willit, *Chain, Group and Branch Banking,* p. 102.

[36] The comptroller's office had in the preceding years adopted an increasingly lenient attitude toward national bank evasions of restrictions on their real estate loans, prompting the following analysis and criticism by the deputy comptroller, as excerpted here:

> Banking today is conducted upon widely different lines to what it was when the Bank Act of 1864 was enacted, and the law has not kept pace with the constantly changing conditions.

Competition with trust companies and other banking institutions operating under State authority, more liberal in the scope of corporate powers conferred, forced many competing national associations doing business in the same locality into undertakings not contemplated by the national banking laws and foreign to the legitimate functions of a commercial bank. The powers conferred upon trust companies and savings banks to make loans upon real estate security, induced many national associations to make loans upon like security by resorting to indirect methods to evade the restrictions of the statute. . . .

While the national banking laws should be construed as broadly and as liberally as possible consistent with the intent and spirit of the statutes, it is the sworn duty of an administrative officer to enforce an observance of the law as it exists and not endeavor to twist it out of shape either to meet his own views or the wishes of bankers as to what it should be.

Excerpt is from Thomas P. Kane, *The Romance and Tragedy of Banking* (New York: The Bankers Publishing Company, 1922), p 90.

[37] For histories of legislation and regulations affecting branch banking and bank holding companies, see Klebaner, *Commercial Banking;* and Gerald C. Fischer, *American Banking Structure* (New York: Columbia University Press, 1968).

4

Bank and Thrift Performance since DIDMCA

Diana Fortier and Dave Phillis

The financial services industry has changed dramatically over the past five years. The consumer, the regulatory agencies, and the financial services industry have influenced and been influenced by these changes. However, it is unclear how much of this change is attributable to the new laws and how much to other economic and technological factors. The liberalization of FHLBB policies on advances and adjustable mortgage instruments, the decline in interest and inflation rates, technological developments, and the generally improved economy may have contributed as much, if not more, to the current status and future prospects of the financial services industry.[1]

The changes initiated by the acts have affected the source and cost of funds, the asset powers and use of funds, and hence the growth and profitability of banks and thrifts. This article examines the acts' impact on these factors for commercial banks and thrifts by looking at their performance during selected pre-(1975–79) and post-(1980–84) legislation periods. Are these institutions net winners or losers in the changing game of deregulation? Is size an important determinant of an organization's ability to adjust and react to the changing and more competitive financial services industry in the post-legislative period?

SOURCES OF FUNDS

Designed to promote competitive equality among depository institutions, the acts authorized depository organizations throughout the nation to offer interest-bearing transaction accounts, and to expand their deposit offerings and servicing capabilities. As short-term interest rates continued to rise in the late 1970s and

From *Economic Perspectives,* Federal Reserve Bank of Chicago, September/October 1985, pp. 58–68.

Diana Fortier and Dave Phillis are regulatory economists at the Federal Reserve Bank of Chicago. They thank Herbert Baer, Douglas Evanoff, and John Di Clemente for their helpful comments, and Frederic Wells for his research assistance.

TABLE 1
Source of Funds: Percentage of Total Deposits by Institution Type

Banks

Year	Demand deposits	Transaction				Nontransaction				
		Other checkable deposits				Savings	MMDA	Small time	Large time	Total deposits
		Except Super NOW	Super NOW	Total						
1975	33.9	.04	NA	33.9	24.0	NA	21.5	20.6	623.5
1980	28.4	1.8	NA	30.2	20.1	NA	28.5	21.2	929.8
1982	21.1	6.5	NA	27.6	14.5	.2	33.9	23.8	1107.5
1984	18.4	5.4	2.2	26.0	9.5	18.4	27.6	18.5	1342.2

Thrifts

1975	*	.1	NA	.1	53.6	NA	44.7	1.5	403.2
1980	*	.8	NA	.8	31.9	NA	61.6	5.7	683.9
1982	*	2.5	NA	2.5	25.1	.2	64.2	8.0	752.3
1984	*	2.8	1.2	4.0	17.9	15.6	48.9	13.6	954.5

* Demand deposits for thrifts are not available separately and are included in other checkable deposits.
Note: Percentages may not add to 100 percent due to rounding.
Source: Federal Reserve Board H.6 Release, various years.

FIGURE 1
Deposit Components at Commercial Banks
(post-legislation period)

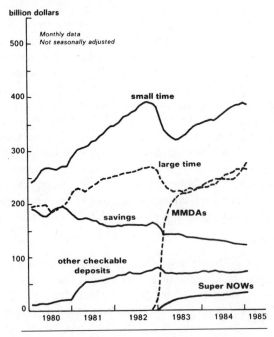

FIGURE 2
Degit Components at Thrifts (post-legislation period)

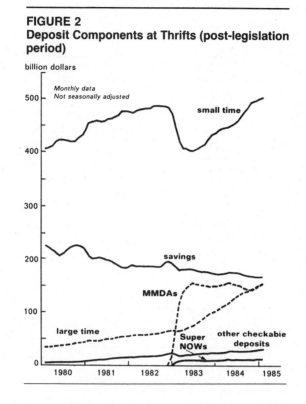

Regulation Q became more and more binding, pressures mounted for a consumer deposit instrument at depository institutions that, like the money market mutual fund (MMMF), yielded a market rate of return. This led Congress, in 1980, to legislate a phase-out of Regulation Q. This process was accelerated with the introduction of the money market deposit account (MMDA) in December 1982. The MMDA was created to bring competitive equality to banks, thrifts, and nondepository financial institutions. This savings instrument, along with the NOW and Super NOW accounts, although not significantly altering the growth rate of total deposits, altered the composition of the liability portfolio of both banks and thrifts in the post-legislation period. (See Table 1 and Figures 1 and 2.)

BANKS

The deposit-to-asset ratio for banks, on average, and for all but the largest banks, has remained approximately the same or risen only slightly from 1975 to 1984.[2] (See Table 2.) Looking at the types of deposit liabilities held by banks, transaction deposits since 1975 have gradually become less significant as a source of funds. However, one component of transaction deposits, other checkable deposits, has become increasingly important. (See Table 1.) The introduction of the automatic transfer savings (ATS) account in 1978 and the negotiable order of withdrawal (NOW) account in 1980 contributed to this transition. By 1983–84 a significant

TABLE 2
Assets and Liabilities of Banks and Thrifts (in percent of total assets)

	Banks			Thrifts		
	1975	1980	1984	1975	1980	1984
Assets						
Cash	10.5	9.5	8.3	1.7	1.6	2.0
Investments[1]	36.7	35.5	34.8	12.9	14.6	23.1
Loans	49.8	53.5	54.0	81.8	80.1	67.1
Residential mortgages	*9.3*	*10.4*	*10.1*	*66.8*	*66.2*	*52.9*
Commercial mortgages	*6.6*	*8.2*	*8.1*	*12.8*	*10.5*	*9.6*
Consumer loans	*14.1*	*14.2*	*12.2*	*2.1*	*3.2*	*3.8*
Commercial loans	*10.4*	*11.5*	*13.2*	*0.1*	*0.1*	*0.8*
Other loans[2]	*9.4*	*9.2*	*10.4*	*NA*	*NA*	*NA*
Subsidiaries	0.0	0.0	0.0	0.2	0.3	0.6
Other	3.0	2.0	2.9	3.4	3.4	7.2
Total assets	100.0	100.0	100.0	100.0	100.0	100.0
Liabilities						
Total deposits	87.7	87.9	87.4	87.5	85.9	87.7
transaction	*33.4*	*27.7*	*23.9*	*0.1*	*0.5*	*NA*
savings	*20.2*	*15.6*	*19.1*	*40.0*	*19.8*	*NA*
time	*34.1*	*44.7*	*44.4*	*48.5*	*65.6*	*NA*
Borrowed funds[3]	0.8	1.7	1.9	3.3	5.0	5.6
Other liabilities	2.1	1.2	1.5	2.8	2.6	1.5
Total liabilities	90.6	90.8	90.8	93.6	93.5	94.8
Capital						
Subordinated debt	0.2	0.2	0.1	0.0	0.0	0.0
equity[4]	8.5	9.0	9.2	6.4	6.5	5.1
Total capital	8.7	9.2	9.3	6.4	6.5	5.1

[1] Mortgage-backed securities held by thrifts were: 1975 = 3.0 percent, 1980 = 3.6 percent, 1985 = 9.0 percent.

[2] Other loans by thrifts are included in commercial loans.

[3] Federal Home Loan Bank advances used by thrifts were: 1975 = 4.5 percent, 1980 = 3.2 percent, 1984 = 3.7 percent.

[4] Regulatory equity provided to thrifts was 0.2 percent in 1984.

Source: Report of condition and semiannual financial reports as of December 31, 1985, December 31, 1980, and June 30, 1984.

shift is apparent with Super NOWs making up approximately one quarter of other checkable deposits.

Commercial bank funding from savings accounts also decreased continuously over the past decade due to below market rates on savings. This trend corresponded with a continual increase in banks' reliance on small and large time deposits as a source of funds. This trend was reversed by the introduction of the MMDA. The increasing reliance on small and large time deposits had been in large measure driven by the changing structure of interest-rate ceilings. These shifts in funding sources (particularly from 1979 to 1982) also reflected the flow of retail funds away from banks to MMMFs and other savings instruments bearing market rates of return.

The introduction of the MMDA at banks significantly decreased the percentage of banks' total deposits from small and large time deposits, from 57.7 percent in 1982 to 46.1 percent in 1984. Initially, banks experienced substantial and rapid growth of MMDAs. They regained direct access to the retail deposit market that had been lost to the MMMFs. Yet a significant portion of the funds flowing into these new accounts were simply shifted from small time deposits within the banking system and large CDs held by MMMFs. (See Figure 2.)

In the pre-legislation period, banks' savings account deposits were a greater share of total deposits than were small time deposits. This trend was reversed in the post-legislation period and remained so until the introduction of the MMDA. For 1983 and 1984, MMDA deposits plus traditional savings deposits accounted for 28 percent of funding, approximately the same percentage of banks' overall funding as savings deposits provided prior to the acts (1976–78). They accounted for approximately one half of the nontransaction funds from accounts under $100,000 (i.e., savings, MMDAs, and small time deposits).

The introduction of the MMDA has led to a rapid decline in the share of large time deposits at banks. Large time deposits as a percentage of total deposits at banks declined by 5.4 percentage points from 1982 to 1983 but changed only minimally from 1983 to 1984. With the renewed ability to compete aggressively for retail deposits, banks, particularly the largest ones, were able to rely less on the more costly and less stable wholesale deposits.

The period following the acts not only saw an overall reduction in the use of uninsured domestic deposits (i.e.; large time deposits over $100,000, excluding Eurodollars) by banks, but also saw a shift in the share of uninsured deposits from money center banks to other banks.[3]

THRIFTS

The ratio of total deposits-to-assets for thrifts has approximately equaled that for banks and has also remained relatively stable over the pre- and post-legislation periods. (See Table 2.) However, the two types of institutions differ in that borrowed funds have been a greater percentage of assets for thrifts and continue to grow more rapidly at thrifts than at banks.[4] This primarily reflects differing FHLBB and Fed lending policies. FHLBB advances, especially in the post-legislation period, has come to be viewed as a legitimate funding source and liability management tool, particularly for the restructuring and lengthening of liability portfolios. (For example, an adjustable rate advance was developed for thrifts to match with adjustable-rate loans.)[5]

The availability of consumer transaction accounts at thrifts gave them the opportunity to increase their core deposit base by providing a more complete array of deposit services that were previously only available at banks. After the acts, transaction deposits increased substantially as a proportion of total thrift deposits, particularly in 1983 and 1984 when Super NOWs became available. (See Table 1 and Figure 2.) Moreover, after a slow start in 1980 and 1981, other checkable deposits have grown faster at thrifts than at banks. This was primarily attributable to the more rapid growth rate of NOWs at thrifts than at banks, in spite of the removal of the traditional 25-basis-point interest-rate differential.

NOWs filled the need for an unlimited transaction (interest bearing) account at thrifts. For banks, the attractiveness of NOWs over noninterest-bearing demand deposits led to a decline in demand deposits outstanding in 1981 and 1982. But the net growth of NOW and demand deposit balances at banks was substantially less than the growth of NOWs alone at thrifts.

However, the growth of NOWs at thrifts and banks declined significantly with the introduction of the $2,500 minimum balance Super NOW account. (This minimum balance was lowered to $1,000 on January 1, 1985.) The absence of an interest ceiling on the unlimited transaction Super NOW proved to be its drawing card at both banks and thrifts, but especially at banks where Super NOWs grew nearly twice as fast as they did at thrifts. Although still falling short of the comparable commercial bank percentage (7.6) by almost one half, thrifts' ratio of total deposits in transaction accounts increased (at a decreasing rate) in a four-year period from 0.8 percent to 4.0 percent. (See Table 1.)

Although savings deposits have historically been a more significant part of thrifts' total liabilities than of commercial banks, the relative importance of the savings and small time components of nontransaction funds of thrifts paralleled that of banks over the pre- and post-legislation periods. For thrifts this trend is, in part, a result of account shifting occurring with the introduction of various money market certificates.

Thrifts most closely resembled banks in their ability, at least in the first year, to attract MMDAs. (See Figure 2.) MMDAs at thrifts amounted to 16.6 percent of total deposits and at banks to 16.3 percent in 1983. But in the second year (1984) the growth rate of MMDAs at banks was three times that at thrifts and MMDAs decreased as a percentage of thrifts' deposits. This reduction may have been a result of an attempt by thrifts to hold back the growth of short-term (market rate) liabilities.

The growth of MMDAs affected thrifts' liability portfolios somewhat differently than banks'. Thrifts' percentage of deposits from small time deposits decreased more rapidly than at banks. In contrast to banks, thrifts' reliance on large time deposits continued to increase, despite the worsening condition of the industry. The MMDA experience at thrifts and banks is further differentiated in that thrifts appear to have gained a smaller proportion of their MMDA deposits from new accounts (rather than from account shifting).

In contrast to the experience at banks, thrifts' reliance on large time deposits was minimal in the pre-legislation period and has increased significantly since then, rising from 3.6 percent in 1979 to 13.6 percent of total deposits in 1984. FSLIC-insured S&Ls' reliance on managed liabilities (large time deposits, FHLBB advances, and other borrowings) has risen continuously and significantly in the post-legislation period from 16.7 percent in 1980 to 24.6 percent of assets in 1984. Moreover, large time deposits have become a greater proportion of this funding—38.3 percent in 1980 and 46.3 percent in 1984.[6]

Thrifts, on average, have made little progress in lengthening the maturity of their liability portfolio. The introduction of the NOW, Super NOW, and MMDA has increased thrifts' core deposits but has not aided in lengthening the maturity of their liability portfolio. As of 1979, 38.8 percent of thrifts' total deposits were in transaction and savings accounts. As of June 1984, that category stood at 25.9 percent and, including deposits in MMDAs, equaled 37.5 percent.[7]

As the data indicate, the MMDA did prove to be a competitive substitute for MMMFs in the eyes of the consumer, who benefited from market competitive rates of return on insured funds at local depository institutions. Additionally, the higher yielding and functionally similar NOW and Super NOW accounts proved to be preferable to the consumer than the traditional demand deposit account. The attraction for consumers of NOWs and Super NOWs was the reduced opportunity costs of holding funds as checkable deposits. Seventy-five percent of funds initially deposited in NOWs were previously noninterest-paying transaction balances.[8]

COST OF FUNDS

Two major elements of an institution's use and cost of funds—reserve requirements and interest expenses—were also influenced by the acts. When combined with the changes in liability portfolios this had the potential to alter significantly an institution's cost of funds.

RESERVE REQUIREMENTS

Title I of DIDMCA was intended to improve monetary control and equalize its cost among all depository institutions. A major element in accomplishing this goal was the imposition of uniform reserve requirements on transaction and nonpersonal time and savings deposits at all depository institutions. The expansion of the reserve base and the equalization of the reserve burden was to be accomplished over a transitional period of four years for member banks and eight years for nonmember banks and thrifts. The transitional period for member banks was completed in February 1984, while for nonmember banks and thrifts the transitional period ends in 1987. However, reserve requirements on new accounts (introduced after April 1, 1980), such as NOWs, Super NOWs, and MMDAs, were not included in the transitional period.[9]

Using data from reports filed with the Fed, reserve costs (deposits held on reserve multiplied by the Fed funds rate) and reserve ratios (reserves as a percentage of total deposits) were calculated by institution size. (See Table 3.) The effect of changes in reserve requirements were separated from changes in the distribution of deposit liabilities. In that reserves are calculated based on net transaction deposits, any change in the amount of items deducted from transaction accounts, namely demand balances due from depository institutions and cash items in the process of collection, would also play an important role in altering the distribution of reservable liabilities and hence the cost of reserves.

The DIDMCA-induced changes in reserve requirements reduced the reserve burden the most—by 76 percent—for small member banks. In comparison, reserve requirements for large member banks fell by 55 percent. This significant disparity primarily results from the reduced number of steps in the reserve requirement schedule (from five to two) and the 3.00 percent versus the old 7.00 to 11.75 percent requirement applied to the lowest deposit interval, the threshold of which was increased from $2.0 million to $28.9 million. This effect combined with deposit shifts led to a reduction in large and small member bank reserves by approximately 4 percent and 2 percent, respectively. The institutions losing the most from the change in reserve requirements were the large nonmember banks, which are now required to hold reserves against their sizeable deposit bases.

At the end of the transition period, only bank size will significantly influence reserve requirement costs among banks; large banks will continue to carry a greater reserve burden than small banks. The relative reserve burden prior to DIDMCA was 14 percent higher for large member banks than small member banks, whereas in the post-legislation period (as of June 1984) that burden is 100 percent higher.

The impact of the varying distribution of deposit liabilities—the larger percentage of transaction deposits held by banks than thrifts—is apparent in the differing reserve burdens for nonmember banks and thrifts. As a result of DIDMCA, thrifts

TABLE 3
Impact of DIDMCA on Reserve Requirements of Banks and Thrifts

Reserves as a percentage of total deposits	Large institutions			Small institutions		
	Banks			Banks		
	Member (n=167)	Nonmember (n=89)	Thrifts (n=27)	Member (n=673)	Nonmember (n=925)	Thrifts (n=36)
Pre-DIDMCA reserves (12/80) (%)	4.66	0.00	0.00	4.08	0.00	0.00
Effect (as of 6/84) from:						
Change in reserve requirements (%)	−2.67	.86	.10	−3.11	.58	.10
Shifts in deposits (%)	−.18	.08	.05	−.07	.09	.08
Post-DIDMCA reserves (6.84) (%)	1.81	.94	.15	.90	.76	.18
Complete phase-in (%)	1.81	1.32	.18	.90	.88	.23
Reserve cost for average institutions ($mil)						
Pre-DIDMCA (12/80)	$4.963	$0.0	$0.0	$.292	$0.0	$0.0
DIDMCA requirements (12/80)	$4.370	$0.061	$0.009	$.218	$0.038	$0.002
DIDMCA requirements (6/84)	$1.732	$0.224	$0.054	$.050	$0.089	$0.014
Institution size ($mil)						
Average total deposits (12/80)	$515.540	$156.230	$193.822	$36.123	35.429	$59.807
Average total deposits (6/84)	$587.335	$199.797	$327.737	$49.031	$48.065	$76.950

[1] Includes reporting banks and thrifts in the 7th Federal District. Small institutions are those with total deposits of less than $100 million and large institutions are those with deposits equal to or greater than $100 million. Data do not take into account the Garn-St Germain reserve calculation exemption (currently $2.4 million).

gained direct access to the payments mechanism and gained new asset powers to become more banklike. But as long as thrifts' net transaction deposits remain relatively low they will continue to bear the smallest reserve burden, particularly the smallest thrifts.

INTEREST EXPENSE

Garn-St Germain's introduction of the noninterest-ceiling MMDA and Super NOW account was an immediate move toward the ultimate goal of the elimination of all depository-rate ceilings by 1986. Currently, only corporate demand deposits, savings deposits, MMDAs and NOWs less than $1,000, and 7-day to 31-day time deposit accounts of less than $1,000 are subject to interest-rate ceilings.

To control costs associated with reserve requirements (i.e., foregone income), banks and thrifts have priced their deposit instruments relative to the instrument's reserve requirements. For example, banks' interest rates on Super NOWs have consistently been lower than MMDAs by approximately 12 percent of the rate paid on MMDAs. This serves to compensate for the reserve requirements, and any additional costs associated with the unlimited transaction nature of the Super NOW.[10]

Liability adjustments in the post-legislation period have left banks and thrifts with significantly more funds in market-rate-bearing accounts. As of December 1984, 84 percent of the nontransaction component of M2 was in interest-ceiling-free accounts. The institutions benefit from this composition through the increased stability associated with the nontransaction market-rate accounts. That is, the availability of competitive market rates of return on bank and thrift nontransaction accounts has decreased the interest-rate sensitivity of M2.[11] Indeed, subsequent to the short-term interest sensitivity exhibited with respect to its own rates and the rates of substitute assets (e.g., MMMFs) in its initiation period, the MMDA has stabilized with a relatively low long-run interest-rate sensitivity.[12]

TABLE 4
Composition of Operating Ratios for Banks and Thrifts

	Operating income to total assets				Operating expense to total assets				
	Loans	Investments	Other	Total*	Salary	Deposit interest	Other	Total*	Net income to total assets
	(%)	(%)	(%)	(¢/$)	(%)	(%)	(%)	(¢/$)	(¢/$)
Banks									
1975	61	32	8	6.84	24	49	26	5.89	.78
1980	62	31	7	9.87	20	57	23	8.41	1.09
1984	59	34	7	11.25	16	61	23	10.10	.90
Thrifts									
1975	87	9	4	7.57	10	76	15	6.89	.50
1980	81	17	2	9.43	8	78	14	9.28	.11
1984	74	23	3	11.21	8	77	15	10.73	.31

* Total refers to the ratio of operating income (expense) to total assets in cents per dollar of assets.
Source: Reports of condition and semiannual financial reports for periods ending December 31, 1975, December 31, 1980, and June 30, 1984.

EFFECT ON TOTAL EXPENSES

Recent studies on the implicit and explicit cost of savings deposits have shown that under binding interest-rate ceilings, depository organizations have paid implicit rates of return that move with the rate on MMMFs and three-month T-bills, both in periods of rising and falling interest rates. The implicit component of interest rates was highest in periods when Regulation Q was most binding. With the removal of binding interest-rate ceilings, institutions would not need to substitute implicit interest payments in the forms of increased convenience, service, and other means of non-price competition for explicit interest.[13] Thus, the removal of binding interest-rate ceilings would not only benefit the consumer with competitive market yields but may not decrease depository institutions' profitability, because the increase in explicit interest cost may be partially or completely offset by lower operating expenses.

The recent behavior of banks and thrifts substantiates this analysis. Banks have in fact contained salary and other expenses since 1980.[14] However, despite the fact that salary expenses remained stable and market rates fell, the ratio of banks' total operating expenses to assets rose by 20 percent between 1980 and 1984. Although thrifts' deposit interest expense has been consistently higher than that at banks, by controlling interest expenses substantially better than banks, thrifts have been better able in the post-legislation period to slow the growth of total expenses, which rose 15 percent from 1980 to 1984. This suggests that the acts have had a more adverse impact on total operating expenses of banks than thrifts. Nonetheless, total operating expenses of thrifts are, on average, still greater than banks at all size classes. (See Table 4.)

However, salary and other expenses grew faster at thrifts than at banks.[15] Thrifts' inability to contain salary expenses may have been influenced by thrifts' need to develop expertise in the provision of new products (e.g., commercial loans) and the restructuring of asset/liability portfolios to diminish the previous maturity mismatch. The increasing other expenses of thrifts basically represent the increased use of FHLBB advances and other borrowed funds.

Technological developments and the substitution of explicit for implicit interest have contributed to a significant decline in branch offices in the post-legislation period. The rate of growth in bank and thrift branch offices in the pre-legislation period was seven times as high as in the post-legislation period. The number of new branch offices established by banks and thrifts across all branching status categories (statewide and limited branching and unit banking states) fell dramatically in the post-legislation period—17,120 branch offices were established in the pre-legislation period, while only 3,350 have been established in the past five years. Even statewide-branching and unit-banking states, each of which had the greatest growth in number of banks in the post-legislation period, experienced a substantial drop in the number of branches opened from 1980 to 1984. Despite this decreased growth rate of branch offices, customer convenience as measured by population per branch office has not been diminished. Rather, population per branch office for banks and thrifts combined has declined across all branching categories from 1975 to 1984.

However, this decline may not simply be the result of the elimination of interest-rate ceilings. It may also reflect changes in banking technology. As the growth in branch offices has declined, the number of automated teller machines (ATMs), shared ATM networks, and the number of ATM transactions have all increased significantly in the past few years. From 1982 to 1984, the number of ATMs nationwide grew by 80.3 percent to 39,921. They are operated by 7 national networks, 211 shared regional networks, and 389 proprietary regional networks. Although legally not branches unless established (owned or rented) by a bank, ATMs may be viewed as improved branch substitutes. ATMs may be operated free of federal branching restrictions to provide consumers convenient regional or nationwide access to deposits. ATMs, particularly shared networks, provide more efficient and less costly direct access to retail deposit markets and establish the technological framework for future direct linkage among networks and point of sale terminals, which will further reduce transaction costs. Merchants, especially supermarket chains and oil companies, as well as depository institutions, will benefit from the reduced check, credit card, and cash handling costs associated with such networks.[16]

NEW ASSET POWERS AND USE OF FUNDS FOR THRIFTS

Title IV of DIDMCA and portions of Garn-St Germain also focused on the expansion of federally chartered S&Ls' asset powers. The expansion of such powers was intended to aid the return to profitability of the thrift industry by expanding opportunities to increase the interest-rate sensitivity of their asset yields, and thus, reduce the maturity mismatch associated with their predominantly long-term asset portfolios (primarily fixed-rate mortgage loans) and short-term liability portfolios.[17]

Thrifts still maintain their traditional character, even though mortgage loans as a percentage of total loans has decreased from 97.3 percent in 1975 to 93.4 percent in 1984. Although thrifts' portion of assets in investments has increased as their loan-to-asset ratio has fallen, much of the increase in investments are mortgage-backed securities.[18] This provides thrifts with more liquidity without their significantly diversifying out of the mortgage market.

Balance sheet data indicate that, in absolute terms, the growth of nontraditional lending at thrifts has been impressive. However, taking into account the growth of total assets, thrifts have a relatively small percentage of assets in nontraditional

TABLE 5
Percentage of Consumer Installment Credit by Institution Type* (1975–1984)

Total credit	1975	1976	1977	1978	1979	1980	1981	1982	1983	1984
Amount outstanding	$164.9	$185.5	$230.8	$275.6	$311.1	$314.9	$335.7	$355.8	$396.1	$460.5
Commercial banks	47.7	48.3	48.7	49.4	48.1	46.7	44.0	43.0	43.4	44.5
Thrifts	NA	NA	4.1	4.0	4.1	4.4	4.9	4.7	7.0	8.4
Credit unions	15.6	16.4	16.3	16.7	15.4	14.0	13.7	13.3	13.5	14.2
Other	32.7	31.1	30.9	29.9	32.4	34.9	37.4	38.0	36.1	32.9

* "Other" includes finance companies, retailers, auto dealers, and gasoline companies for the years 1977–84. For 1975 and 1976, "other" includes finance companies and retailers (except 30-day charge credit). Amounts of credit outstanding are at end of period and are in billions of dollars.
  Source: *Federal Reserve Bulletins*, Domestic Financial Statistics-Consumer Installment Credit, various issues.

lending and are far below the maximum allowable percentages for all classes of nontraditional lending. (See Table 2.)

The extent to which individual thrifts are using their new asset powers varies widely. Besides financial factors, size and location (i.e., the influence of liberalized asset powers of state-chartered thrifts, which has occurred primarily in the South and West) seem to have an important influence on the aggressiveness of thrift institutions in expanding into nontraditional lending.[19]

Survey results of S&Ls in Illinois and Wisconsin indicate that few S&Ls, mostly the largest ones, are willing to take the associated risks and are able to surmount the start-up costs of entering the business of commercial lending.[20] Only 41.8 percent of thrifts held commercial and industrial (C&I) loans as of June 1984, and 30.6 percent of total C & I loans at these thrifts were held by the top 10 institutions. This contrasts with the same concentration measure for total thrift assets—13.8 percent and traditional thrift assets—residential mortgages 14.1 percent and commercial mortgages 14.8 percent.

In becoming providers of banklike services, thrifts are more likely to enter the business of consumer lending, which, unlike commercial lending, has fewer barriers to entry for thrifts (i.e., it is more familiar and less costly to enter). In fact, the smallest thrifts (under $100 million total assets), which account for 52.8 percent of all thrifts, win the honors for growth of consumer loans. Their consumer loan-to-asset ratio increased from 2.1 percent in 1975 to 4.0 percent in 1984 and is the highest ratio of all thrift size classes. (See note 20.)

In contrast with the limited participation in commercial lending, 88.6 percent of all thrifts made consumer loans in 1984 and 17.0 percent of the total consumer loans made by thrifts were held by the top 10 thrifts. Moreover, thrifts as a group have made significant inroads in the consumer loan market, particularly in the submarket for mobile home loans. Such moves are reflected in decreased market shares for commercial banks. (See Table 5.)

The most dramatic change in thrifts' asset portfolio in the post-legislation period has not been their use of new asset powers but rather the increased flexibility in yields on their most prominent asset—mortgages. The FHLBB's authorization (April 1981) of adjustable mortgage loans (under regulatory limitations) and the standardization of AMLs by Freddie Mac has increased the availability and market acceptance of flexible mortgage instruments—particularly, adjustable-rate mortgages (ARMs).[21]

In January 1985, ARMs, balloons, and other adjustable mortgages accounted for 71 percent of thrift mortgage originations. These mortgages also made up 37.9 percent of thrifts' mortgage portfolios. Also, almost all S&Ls (91.4 percent as of December 1984) offered ARMs.

The improved economy and increased mortgage demand, and thrifts' ability to offer new types of mortgage instruments, especially ARMs, has diminished their need to turn to new, unfamiliar, and nontraditional lending powers to alter their asset portfolio. With 22.0 percent of their assets in variable-rate mortgage instruments (as opposed to 1.4 percent in 1980), thrifts have substantially increased their ability to reduce interest-rate risk exposure.

IMPACT ON INCOME

The rate of growth in total operating income was lower in the post- than the pre-legislation period for both banks and thrifts, only more so for banks. For all bank and thrift size categories, the percentage of income attributed to loans and the rate of growth of loan income declined in the post-legislation period. The decline in income share from loans was twice as great for thrifts as for banks. (Unlike banks, thrifts had experienced a similar decline in the pre-legislation period.) But thrifts still obtain, on average, 15 percent more of their income from loans than do banks.

The growth of bank and thrift investment and loan income varied in relation to changes in interest rates in the pre- and post-legislation periods. The differing maturities of bank and thrift loan portfolios is reflected by the fact that the rate of growth of loan income fell much more dramatically for banks (40.0 percentage points) than for thrifts (7.3 percentage points) from the pre- to the post-legislation period. However, the rate of growth in investment income fell for both thrifts and banks, although more for thrifts, in the years 1980 to 1984. Also offsetting the declining share of income from loans was an increased proportion of income from "other" income, except for the smallest banks and the largest thrifts.

The Final Score: Net Income

In an environment of deregulation, on average, banks in every size class, except the smallest (less than $100 million), were able to maintain their 1980 level of net income. However, this smallest size group accounts for 83.9 percent of all banks. Thus, banks as a whole had a lower level of net income at the end than at the beginning of the post-legislation.

Although thrifts continued to post substantial losses in the years following the acts, on average, thrifts in each size class experienced significant increases in net income levels by June 1984. Interestingly, on average, the rate of increase in net income for thrifts was approximately equal to the rate of decrease in net income for banks from 1980 and 1984. Despite these gains, 833 thrifts or 24 percent of all thrifts experienced losses in the first half of 1984. This compares favorably to the 34.3 percent of thrifts that had negative net income in 1980.

The net worth of thrifts as a group worsens only marginally (for 1984) when regulatory net worth (income capital certificates, Garn St Germain net worth certificates, and appraised equity capital) is eliminated. The impact of regulatory net worth is substantial for the largest thrifts, for it was these thrifts that had, and still have, the lowest levels of net income and were the heaviest users of these methods of net worth enhancement.[22] As with banks, the smallest thrifts gained the least with respect to improved performance in the post-legislation period. This size category composes over half (52.8 percent) of all thrifts. The improved levels of net income were most significant for the larger size categories of thrifts—the over $1 billion group (6.0 percent of all thrifts) and the $100–$500 million size group (34.9 percent of all thrifts).

CONCLUSION

The effect of the acts on bank and thrift performance cannot be quantified separately from other factors. Declining interest and inflation rates and the generally improved economy, and more liberal FHLBB policies (e.g., on advances and flexible mortgage instruments) may be attributed equal, if not more, importance than the acts themselves for the current status and future prospects of the financial services industry. Managerial expertise and institution size have also played a large role in the ability of and manner in which institutions have reacted to the deregulated environment. Well-managed institutions performing well in the more regulated environment are likely to perform well in the less regulated environment. Regulatory and statutory restrictions which had imposed inherent differences in the balance sheets of thrifts and banks also can not be overlooked in the ability of these institutions to react to the more level playing field.

Nonetheless, an analysis of average bank and thrift balance sheets and income statements across size classes for the pre- and post-legislation periods gives an indication of the absolute and relative impact of the acts on banks and thrifts, and the influence of size on the manner in which an institution adjusts to the new environment.

The consumer of financial services has gained from the more competitive environment created by the acts. There are increased alternatives for commercial and consumer loans and insured deposit instruments with competitive market rates of return. As a whole, reregulation resulting from the acts has thus far had a positive or, at worst, neutral impact on all parties, except perhaps the smallest banks. Further deregulation of product lines and geographic barriers, if adequately monitored, should be viewed favorably.

NOTES

[1] Throughout the article thrifts refer to savings and loan associations (S&Ls) and mutual savings banks (MSBs). Ratios for banks and thrifts presented in this article were derived by calculating ratios at the institution level, summing those ratios and dividing by the appropriate number of observations for each size class.

[2] Deposit-to-asset ratios for banks by size group:

	All Banks	Assets < $100 mil.	Assets $100 to $500 mil.	Assets $500 mil-$1 bil.	Assets > $1 bil.
1975	87.7	88.0	86.0	81.8	78.4
1980	87.9	88.4	85.6	81.6	73.9
1984	87.4	87.8	86.8	83.3	75.8

[3] Large time deposits as a percentage of total large time deposits, by size group and year for banks:

	Assets < $100 mil.	Assets $100 to $500 mil.	Assets $500 mil-$1 bil.	Assets > $1 bil.
1980	13.7%	14.8%	7.0%	64.4%
1984	15.2%	16.9%	6.4%	61.5%

[4] The use of borrowings is particularly important for the largest thrifts and varies directly with thrift size. Listed are borrowings-to-asset ratios:

	All Thrifts	Assets < $100 mil.	Assets $100-$500 mil.	Assets $500 mil-$1 bil.	Assets > $1 bil.
1975	3.3	2.9	4.7	5.2	5.2
1980	5.0	3.8	6.6	9.1	9.8
1984	5.6	3.2	6.9	11.7	13.5

[5] M. Kulczycky, "Advances Grow for Old and New Uses," *Savings Institutions,* April 1985. For recent major FHLBB regulatory changes per thrifts, see *Savings Institution Sourcebook,* U.S. League of Savings Institutions 1981, 1982, 1983, and 1984.

[6] P. Mahoney, A. White, and D. Goodman, "The Thrift Industry in Transition, 71 *Federal Reserve Bulletin* (137), March 1985. (Also see note 4.)

[7] Maturity structure of liabilities of FSLIC insured S&Ls and thrifts for 1981 and 1984, respectively. (Percentage of total deposits.)

	Large CDs	Accounts with No Fixed Term MMDAs, Passbook Savings, Other	Small Denomination CDs Term 1 yr. or less	Small Denomination CDs Term over 1 yr.
July 1981	8.9	19.4	39.7	31.6
Dec. 1984	14.8	24.8	29.0	31.3

[8] B. Higgins and J. Faust, "NOWs and Super NOWs: Implications for Defining and Measuring Money," *Economic Review,* Federal Reserve Bank of Kansas City, January 1983.

[9] For detail on changes in reserve requirements, see: 70 *Federal Reserve Bulletin,* Table A6 1.15, "Reserve Requirements of Depository Institutions," December 1984.

[10] *Bank Rate Monitor,* Advertising News Service, Inc., Miami Beach, Florida.

[11] H. Roth, "Lasting Effects of Deregulation on Monetary Policy," *Economic Review,* Federal Reserve Bank of Kansas City, March 1985.

[12] L. Wall and H. Ford, "Money Market Account Competition," *Economic Review,* Federal Reserve Bank of Atlanta, December 1984; and M. Keeley and G. Zimmerman, "Competition for Money Market Deposits Accounts," *Economic Review,* Federal Reserve Bank of San Francisco, Spring 1985.

[13] Elijah Brewer, unpublished paper, "Cost of Savings Deposits: The evidence from Illinois and Wisconsin Savings and Loan Associations," Federal Reserve Bank of Chicago; and John P. Judd and John L. Scadding, "Financial Change and Monetary Targeting in the United States," Asilomar Conference Proceedings, Federal Reserve Bank of San Francisco, November 28–30, 1982.

[14] Percentage change in expense categories for banks for pre- and post-legislation periods. Other expenses include the purchase of Fed funds, provisions for loan losses, and occupancy expenses.

Expenses:

	1975–1980			
	Salary	Deposit Interest	Other	Total
All banks	14.6	66.3	26.3	42.8
Assets < $100 mil.	14.5	65.4	24.2	42.1
Assets $100 to $500 mil.	10.0	65.4	23.2	40.0
Assets $500 mil. to $1 bil.	10.1	75.9	34.5	45.8
Assets > $1 bil.	16.8	102.4	58.2	66.8

	1980–1984			
	Salary	Deposit Interest	Other	Total
All banks	.6	28.6	15.7	20.1
Assets < $100 mil.	.6	29.9	16.8	21.1
Assets $100 to $500 mil.	2.6	23.2	2.6	14.1
Assets $500 mil. to $1 bil.	3.7	19.5	1.6	10.8
Assets > $1 bil.	16.3	10.2	4.6	9.1

[15] Percentage change in expenses for thrifts.

Expenses:

	1975–1980			
	Salary	Deposit Interest	Other	Total
All thrifts	11.8	38.1	31.0	34.7
Assets < $100 mil.	15.7	38.9	29.2	34.9
Assets $100 to $500 mil.	15.3	39.5	24.1	34.7
Assets $500 mil. to $1 bil.	16.4	35.7	30.7	33.0
Assets > $1 bil.	13.5	41.2	28.6	36.6

	1980–1984			
	Salary	Deposit Interest	Other	Total
All thrifts	11.8	15.0	20.6	15.6
Assets < $100 mil.	13.6	16.9	13.7	16.2
Assets $100 to $500 mil.	16.2	15.0	15.8	15.3
Assets $500 mil. to $1 bil.	20.3	12.1	30.7	16.0
Assets > $1 bil.	16.9	9.3	35.7	14.8

[16] S. Fedgram, "From ATM to POS Networks: Branching Access, and Pricing," *New England Economic Review,* Federal Reserve Bank of Boston, May/June 1985.

[17] For a summary of new S&L powers granted by state and federal legislation, see: R. Goudreau, S&L Use of New Powers: "A Comparative Study of State- and Federal-Chartered Associations," *Economic Review,* Federal Reserve Bank of Atlanta, October 1984.

[18] Percentage of thrift assets in investments by size group and year.

	All Thrifts	Assets < $100 mil.	Assets $100 to $500 mil.	Assets $500 mil-$1 bil.	Assets > $1 bil.
1975	12.9	12.4	14.3	18.4	19.3
1980	14.6	14.5	14.0	17.7	18.7
1984	23.1	22.8	22.5	25.3	26.6

Percentage of thrift assets in mortgage-backed securities by size group and year.

1975	3.0	2.9	3.0	13.6	12.2
1980	3.6	3.3	4.0	5.8	4.9
1984	9.0	7.7	9.9	11.8	13.3

[19] Commercial and consumer loans as a percentage of assets for thrifts by size group (June 30, 1984).

	All Banks	Assets < $100 mil.	Assets $100-$500 mil.	Assets $500 mil-$1 bil.	Assets > $1 bil.
Consumer	3.8	4.0	3.7	3.8	3.3
Commercial	0.8	0.6	0.8	1.3	1.3

[20] C. Pavel and D. Phillis, "Cautious Play Marks S&L Approach to Commercial Lending," *Economic Perspectives,* Federal Reserve Bank of Chicago, May/June 1985.

[21] The national average for ARMs as a percentage of the number of total conventional home mortgages closed for S&Ls since 1982:1982Q4 = 39.3%, 1983Q4 = 61.3% and 1984Q4 = 66.0%. *FHLB News,* May 7, 1985, and January 10, 1984.

[22] Net income for thrifts.

	All Banks	Assets < $100 mil.	Assets $100-$500 mil.	Assets $500 mil-$1 bil.	Assets > $1 bil.
1975	0.50	0.50	0.47	0.47	0.40
1980	0.11	0.14	0.09	0.02	(.06)
1984	0.31	0.34	0.30	0.33	0.17

5

Recent Developments in the Credit Union Industry

Douglas K. Pearce

Less than a decade ago, U.S. depository institutions could be clearly distinguished from each other. Banks made commercial loans and offered checkable deposits. Savings and loan associations and mutual savings banks made residential mortgage loans and offered fixed-rate passbook savings accounts. Credit unions made consumer installment loans and offered dividend-paying share accounts. In recent years, however, financial deregulation and high and volatile interest rates have led to a substantial blurring of these differences as each type of intermediary has broadened its range of activities in an effort to become a "financial supermarket."

Changes in the structure and behavior of the credit union industry have been particularly striking. Since 1977, regulatory changes have relaxed many of the traditional restrictions on credit unions. While these changes have improved the prospects for growth of the credit union industry, similar deregulation of other depository institutions has exposed credit unions to more intense competition. Moreover, because ceilings on deposit and loan rates were still in effect when short-term interest rates rose sharply in the late 1970s, growth of credit unions slowed substantially from 1979 to 1981. The credit union industry responded by making significant balance sheet adjustments and expanding the roles of their trade associations.

This article argues that credit unions adapted well to the new financial environment and that they are likely to continue to compete effectively in unregulated markets. The first section reviews the distinctive features of credit unions, the regulatory framework in 1976 before deregulation, and the performance of credit

From *Economic Review*, Federal Reserve Bank of Kansas City, June 1984, pp. 3–19.

Douglas K. Pearce is an associate professor of economics at the University of Missouri–Columbia and a visiting scholar at the Federal Reserve Bank of Kansas City. The author thanks Terry Fitzgerald for research assistance and Walter L. Johnson for helpful comments. The views expressed here are those of the author and do not necessarily reflect the opinions of the Federal Reserve Bank of Kansas City or the Federal Reserve System.

unions from 1961 to 1976. The second section describes the restructuring of the credit union industry with respect to the regulatory framework and functions of the trade associations. The third section examines the performance of credit unions from 1977 to 1983. The fourth section looks at the prospects for credit unions in the near term.

STRUCTURE AND PERFORMANCE OF CREDIT UNIONS BEFORE 1976

Distinctive Features of Credit Unions

Credit unions are nonprofit, cooperative organizations composed of individuals with a "common bond" who borrow from and lend to each other.[1] As credit unions are mutual organizations, owned by their members, deposits are considered shares and interest payments on deposits are considered dividends.[2] Officers of credit unions are usually unpaid volunteers elected from the membership.[3] The unique feature of credit unions is their common bond requirement for membership. The bond is usually the place of employment or the occupation of members, but it can also be based on association ties, such as church or union membership, or, more rarely, on area of residence. Credit unions often receive subsidies, such as free office space, from their sponsoring organization. Unlike other mutual depository institutions, federally chartered and most state-chartered credit unions are not subject to federal or state income taxes.

These characteristics have given credit unions both advantages and disadvantages relative to other depository institutions in competing for household savings and consumer loans. On the plus side, volunteer help and sponsors' subsidies lower operating costs. The common bond feature of credit unions probably keeps down consumer loan rates by lowering administrative costs. In particular, occupation-based credit unions are well positioned to obtain low-cost information on the income and job security of prospective borrowers. Moreover, loan repayments can be processed inexpensively through payroll deductions. The common bond may also make borrowers more reluctant to default on loans, and the lower default rates allow credit unions to charge lower loan rates. Payroll deduction plans for saving at credit unions are convenient for depositors, and the common bond may make them loyal to their credit union, reducing the interest sensitivity of depositors. The cooperative, nonprofit nature of credit unions combines with the common bond requirements to keep credit unions from viewing themselves as competitors. This has led to extensive pooling of resources through trade associations that allows individual credit unions to obtain some economies of scale that their small size would not otherwise permit.

The mutual organization and nontaxable status of credit unions also give them potential advantages. The capital of a credit union consists basically of reserves against loan losses, reserves built up by retaining part of the income generated in the past. This capital need not be paid a return, as is the case of such stock intermediaries as commercial banks. Therefore, if a credit union has enough capital, it can use all its income in excess of operating costs to pay depositors more or give borrowers refunds. A growing credit union generally needs to increase its capital. If credit union income were taxed in the same way as, say, mutual savings and loans, a credit union would have to generate more pre-tax income to make the desired addition to its capital. The tax-free status allows credit unions to charge less for loans or pay more on deposits given any desired addition to their capital. The taxation of credit unions is a controversial issue discussed in more detail later.

Some credit union characteristics also have negative aspects. Volunteer help may lack the incentive or the expertise to operate the credit union efficiently. A narrowly defined common bond—and this is the traditional bond—inherently limits the growth potential of a credit union. A common bond based on employment further restricts the asset growth of a credit union to the growth of its sponsoring firm. The common bond requirement also keeps credit unions from achieving much diversification across both depositors and borrowers. Thus, sudden plant closings or substantial layoffs can create severe liquidity problems for credit unions and sometimes force them into liquidation. A disadvantage to the mutual organization of credit unions is that the only source of funds is deposits. Credit unions cannot raise capital for expansion by selling equity.

The cooperative or mutual nature of credit unions presents problems in analyzing the industry. First, the objective of individual credit unions is not clear. While stock institutions, such as banks, may seek to maximize profits, the goals of credit unions are less well defined. Since members can be primarily savers or primarily borrowers, a conflict of interest arises when credit unions decide the rates to pay savers and charge borrowers.[4] A decision to pay higher rates on deposits, all else equal, means a decision to charge higher loan rates. Refunds to borrowers or lower loan rates, on the other hand, imply lower dividends to saving members. This internal conflict exists as long as external competition does not force both loan rates and deposit rates to their market values. In other words, any "profit" a credit union makes is divided among borrowers and savers, but the division can vary across credit unions.

A second problem is measuring industry performance. This article follows the custom of the credit union movement and takes asset growth as the measure of success. Since the traditional goal of credit unions has been to promote thrift among members and provide them with low-cost consumer credit, asset growth seems a reasonable proxy for this goal, particularly if most assets are consumer loans. As noted above, however, the officers of individual credit unions have no pecuniary interest in growth and may even prefer the ease of operating a small institution. On the other hand, the cadre of professionals in the credit union trade associations and managers of large credit unions have a clear interest in industry growth.

Regulatory Framework in 1976

Credit unions can obtain either federal or state charters. Since regulations governing state-chartered credit unions vary across states, this article concentrates on the regulations imposed on federal credit unions.[5] The regulatory agency for federal credit unions is the National Credit Union Administration (NCUA), which is responsible for chartering and supervision. Since 1971, the NCUA has also administered share insurance for federal and many state credit unions through the National Credit Union Share Insurance Fund (NCUSIF).

In 1976, federal credit unions faced several restrictions on their lending activities and on the types of accounts they could offer. They could not charge more than 12 percent a year on loans, inclusive of all charges. The size of loans was limited, maximum maturities were 5 years on unsecured loans and 10 years on secured loans, and loans had to be approved by a loan committee.[6] These constraints effectively excluded credit unions from making loans through credit card programs and severely limited their ability to initiate residential mortgage loans. Consumer installment loans for relatively small amounts made up most of the loan portfolio of credit unions. Funds not loaned to members could be invested in U.S. government and agency securities, deposits at insured savings and loans or mutual savings banks, or in loans to or shares at other credit unions.[7]

Federal credit unions also faced restrictions on the accounts they could offer. Each share had a legislated par value of $5 so that a member with as little as a $5 deposit qualified for voting on credit union policy. The NCUA placed a 7 percent ceiling on share account dividend rates. Since this exceeded the Regulation Q ceiling deposit rates at banks and savings and loan associations, credit unions enjoyed a competitive advantage over other depositories when market rates were high enough to make their competitors' ceilings effective. Federal credit unions were not formally authorized to offer shares that resembled checkable deposits. The NCUA, however, had given temporary permission to some credit unions to offer share drafts. Because these accounts were essentially interest-earning demand deposits, their introduction subsequently led to legal challenges from banks.

Unlike banks, credit unions did not have to keep a specific ratio of cash assets to shares, although the needs of members necessitated that a small proportion of assets be held in cash. However, credit unions were required to maintain a reserve against possible loan losses. Gross income had to be allocated to maintain this ratio, analogous to a capital-asset ratio requirement, at 10 percent of their risky assets.[8]

Credit Union Performance, 1961–76

Credit unions grew rapidly throughout the 1961–76 period. Assets at credit unions rose at an annual rate of 12.8 percent, compared with 11.2 percent at savings and loans and 8.6 percent at commercial banks. Credit union deposits also grew an average of 13.7 percent a year, compared with 11.1 percent at savings and loans and 11.6 percent for passbook and small time deposits at banks. As a result of this more rapid growth, credit unions' share of total household savings deposits rose from 3.0 percent in 1961 to 4.4 percent in 1976. Over this same period, credit unions increased their share of total consumer installment credit from 9.3 percent to 16.1 percent.[9] While the number of credit unions did not increase substantially over this period, membership almost tripled, reaching close to 34 million members by 1976.

Despite substantial growth, the credit union industry remained small, compared with other depository institutions. Although total credit union assets exceeded $45 billion by 1976, this was only about 5 percent of commercial bank assets and 11 percent of savings and loan assets. Most of the 22,533 credit unions operating in 1976 were small. Four out of five credit unions had assets of less than $2 million. Together these institutions held only 18.5 percent of total credit union assets. The 60 largest credit unions held 14.5 percent of all credit union assets.[10] Thus, the credit union industry was characterized by a large proportion of small institutions and few large ones.[11]

Table 1 summarizes the balance sheets of credit unions at the end of 1976. Loans to members made up 76 percent of the assets. These loans were mainly for durable goods purchases (about 48 percent) and personal loans (32 percent). The

TABLE 1
Balance Sheet for All Credit Unions, 1976

Total Assets, $100,156 million

Distribution of Assets	Percent
Loans to members	57.4
Cash	2.4
Investments	37.7
Other	2.5
Distribution of Liabilities and Capital	
Members' savings	90.5
Reserves and undistributed earnings	6.1
Notes payable and other	3.4

Source: NCUA, 1976 Annual Report on State-Chartered Credit Unions.

restriction on maximum loan maturity kept residential mortgage loans to less than 5 percent of all loans. Investments were divided among U.S. government or agency securities (45 percent), common trust investments (21 percent), deposits at savings and loans (19 percent), and loans to or shares in other credit unions (15 percent).[12] On the liability and capital side, members' savings accounted for 86.6 percent. These were almost all in the form of regular share accounts since share drafts and other types of shares were uncommon.

CREDIT UNION RESTRUCTURING, 1977-1983

Three major developments affected the credit union industry over the 1977–83 period. First, the general movement toward financial deregulation eliminated many of the previous constraints on credit unions but also exposed credit unions to more competition. Second, changes in the regulatory structure provided the credit union industry with new sources of liquidity. Third, expansion of the services offered by credit union trade associations helped credit unions broaden their range of financial services and gave credit unions more convenient access to money markets.

Deregulation of Credit Unions

Of all the regulatory changes in the U.S. financial sector from 1977 to 1983, the most dramatic changes may have been in the credit union industry. Many of the restrictions on credit unions were removed either by legislation or administrative ruling, enabling credit unions to compete across a broad range of financial services. Some of these changes, however, have also eliminated or reduced competitive advantages of credit unions. Table 2 chronicles the major regulatory changes affecting federal credit unions since 1976.[13]

The lending powers of credit unions have been significantly enlarged. First, credit unions can now make residential mortgage loans of any size or maturity. They can also sell the mortgages they originate in the secondary mortgage market.[14] Second, the NCUA can temporarily increase the interest ceiling on loans if

TABLE 2
Credit Union Regulatory Changes, 1977–1983

1977 Amendments to Federal Credit Union Act
    Increased loan maturities on nonresidential loans to 12 years.
    Allowed 30-year residential mortgage loans and 15-year mobile home and home-improvement loans.
    Permitted self-replenishing lines of credit.
    Permitted participation loans with other financial institutions.
    Permitted government-insured or guaranteed loans.
    Lowered reserve formula for larger credit unions.
    Allowed different types of share accounts, including share certificates.

1978 Financial Institutions Regulatory and Interest Rate Control Act
    Restructured NCUA into three-member board.
    Established Central Liquidity Facility under NCUA.
  NCUA regulations
    Permitted sale of mortgages to FNMA, FHLMC, or GNMA.
    Set maximum rate on small share certificates at 8 percent.
    Permitted market rates on large share certificates ($100,000 or more).
    Permitted six-month, $10,000 certificates paying 1/4 percent above the six-month Treasury bill rate.

1979 Congress
    Gave 90-day authorization (starting December 28) for credit unions to offer share drafts.
    NCUA regulations required credit unions with over $2 million in assets or offering share drafts to hold 5 percent of member accounts plus notes payable in liquid assets.

1980 Depository Institutions Deregulation and Monetary Control Act
    Classified credit unions as depository institutions.
    Gave permanent authority for share drafts.
    Set required reserves on share drafts.
    Established timetable for phasing out interest ceilings.
    Raised loan rate ceiling to 15 percent and authorized NCUA to increase
    this ceiling.
    Required Federal Reserve System to price its services.
  NCUA regulations raised loan ceiling to 21 percent for nine-month period (starting December 3).

1981 NCUA regulations
    Extended 21 percent ceiling on loan interest rate to June 1982.
    Allowed credit unions to make variable interest rate consumer and mortgage loans

1982 Garn-St Germain Depository Institutions Act
    Freed credit unions to set par value of shares and to determine internal organization.
    Eliminated limits on size and maturity of mortgage loans, allowed refinancing of first mortgages, and extended maturity limit on second mortgages.
    Excluded credit unions with less than $2 million in reservable accounts from reserve requirements.
    Permitted Central Liquidity Facility (CLF) to lend to the National Credit Union Share Insurance Fund (NCUSIF) and also made CLF an agent of the Federal Reserve System.
  NCUA regulations
    Allowed credit unions to determine the kinds of shares offered and the dividend rates paid.
    Repealed fixed liquidity requirement on federally insured credit unions.
    Permitted credit unions greater flexibility in the kinds of services they can offer and the joint sharing of activities with other credit unions.

1983 NCUA regulations expanded definition of ''family member'' in common bond requirement.

warranted by economic conditions.[15] Third, credit unions can now establish self-replenishing lines of credit for members. These latter two changes removed the barriers to credit union participation in credit card programs.

Regulatory changes have also increased the ability of credit unions to attract deposits. Credit unions can offer members a wide variety of share accounts, including accounts similar to money market deposit accounts, with no restrictions on the interest they can pay. Since the interest rates banks and savings and loan associations can offer on some accounts are still restricted, credit unions continue to have a competitive advantage. The Depository Institutions Deregulation and Monetary Control Act (DIDMCA) of 1980 gave credit unions permanent authority to offer share drafts (checkable accounts). This provision was coupled at first with the stipulation that credit unions must meet the same reserve requirements as other depository institutions. The Garn-St Germain Depository Institutions Act of 1982, however, excluded from the reserve requirement credit unions and other depository institutions with less than $2 million in checkable deposits (about 95 percent of all credit unions).

Two other changes that may benefit credit unions are the less restrictive interpretation of the common bond requirement and the wider access of depository institutions to Federal Reserve services. The NCUA and state regulators have relaxed substantially the common bond aspect of credit union membership.[16] This increases the potential membership for credit unions and allows more mergers between credit unions. The DIDMCA provided for the pricing of Federal Reserve services, such as wire transfers, and permitted the credit union industry to access such services directly rather than indirectly through correspondent relationships with member banks. This may reduce the costs of such services to some credit unions.

Financial deregulation also increased the range of activities of competing depository institutions. Savings and loan associations and mutual savings banks can now compete actively in the consumer loan market. While commercial banks, savings banks, and savings and loans are still legally constrained on the interest rates they can offer on some accounts, they can offer any rate on many of their deposit options and the remaining limits are being phased out. Thus, the traditional advantage of credit unions—the ability to offer higher deposit rates—is dissipating. Another earlier advantage for large credit unions has been eliminated by the requirement that they maintain noninterest earning reserves with the Federal Reserve based on the amount of their share drafts.[17]

Changes in the Regulatory Structure

Several important changes in the credit union regulatory structure were made between 1977 and 1983. The NCUA was reorganized more along the lines of the Federal Home Loan Bank Board and the Board of Governors of the Federal Reserve. Up to 1978, the NCUA was run by an administrator counseled by an advisory board. The Financial Institutions Regulatory and Interest Rate Control Act of 1978 replaced this structure with a three-member board headed by a chairman. Members of the board are appointed by the President, confirmed by the Senate, and serve staggered six-year terms.[18]

Perhaps a more significant change, also due to the 1978 legislation, was the establishment of the Central Liquidity Facility (CLF), under the administration of the NCUA. Until the creation of the CLF, credit unions had no access to a "lender of last resort," such as the Federal Reserve.[19] The CLF fills this gap. Both federal and state-chartered credit unions can join the CLF by subscribing 0.5 percent of their unimpaired capital. The CLF generally makes short-term loans to member credit unions having unexpected liquidity problems. The CLF raises most of its funds by borrowing through the Federal Financing Bank and can, if the need arises, borrow directly from the U.S. Treasury. In addition to lending to individual credit unions, the CLF can lend to the NCUSIF.

The relationship between the credit union industry and the Federal Reserve System also changed considerably over this period. Not only can credit unions now buy Federal Reserve services directly, as large credit unions must hold reserves with the Federal Reserve, these credit unions also have legal access to the discount window. They do not really have the choice between borrowing from the CLF or the Federal Reserve, however, since the Federal Reserve requires that credit unions first approach the CLF. One difference between the CLF and the discount window is that the CLF always sets a penalty interest rate on its loans— that is, a rate slightly above market rates.[20]

Expanded Role of Trade Associations

While regulatory changes have greatly increased the services that credit unions can offer, credit unions have had to turn to their trade associations for help in competing in these new areas. Credit unions have always relied heavily on services provided through trade associations.[21] They rely even more now because of the competitive disadvantages they face in a deregulated environment where competition is vigorous and financial innovation rapid. The small size of most credit unions keeps them from realizing any economies of scale in such areas as data processing and investment. Moreover, the unpaid volunteers who make the investment decisions for most credit unions usually do not have the expertise in portfolio management that their counterparts in the banking or savings and loan industries have. These disadvantages have been largely offset, however, by the credit union trade associations having essentially integrated most credit unions into one financial network. The cooperative nature of credit unions and the common bond requirement encourage such integration since credit unions do not generally consider one another as competitors and their nonprofit status avoids antitrust problems.

By far the largest and most influential of the credit union trade associations is the Credit Union National Association (CUNA). CUNA, as the major spokesman and lobbyist for the credit union industry, is the umbrella organization for several companies providing services to credit unions. There are also trade associations at the state level. Known as credit union leagues, most of them are also affiliated with CUNA so that about 90 percent of all credit unions are connected with CUNA.

CUNA provides services to credit unions through the CUNA Service Group, Inc., and the Corporate Credit Union Network. The Service Group has several subsidiaries. ICU Services, Inc., sells to credit unions financial services, such as investment trusts in U.S. government securities, automatic teller machine (ATM) and electronic funds transfer (EFT) systems, credit card programs, and IRA/ Keogh plans. CUNA Mortgage Corporation buys mortgages originated by credit unions and sells pools of these mortgages on the secondary mortgage market. CUNA Supply, Inc., wholesales operational and promotional supplies to credit unions. Credit Union Internet provides credit unions with computer services and allows credit unions to be linked to an on-line telecommunications network. These service companies, catering only to credit unions, make it possible for the industry to compete more effectively by gaining the benefits of economies of scale.

Since it was started in the mid-1970s, the Corporate Credit Union Network has grown rapidly, probably in response to the volatility of interest rates. The network provides liquidity and investment expertise for the credit union industry. It has a pyramid structure with about 17,500 individual credit unions at the bottom, 42 corporate central credit unions in the middle, and the U.S. Central Credit Union at the top. A corporate central credit union, owned by its member credit unions through capital subscriptions, acts as a credit union for credit unions. Corporate centrals provide an outlet for credit union investments by offering a variety of shares and deposits. They also make loans to member credit unions needing liquidity. U.S. Central, in turn, acts as a credit union for the corporate centrals. It offers investment instruments ranging in maturity from overnight to three years and makes loans to corporate centrals with liquidity needs.[22] Essentially, the Corporate Credit Union Network allows credit unions to channel investment funds through the corporate centrals to one portfolio run by U.S. Central. In this way, individual credit unions do not need financial expertise to obtain competitive rates on their investments. Moreover, the Internet system permits the Corporate Network to be so linked electronically that instructions and information can be transmitted quickly and inexpensively.

In addition to providing liquidity and investment expertise, the Corporate Network also provides credit unions with services traditionally acquired through correspondent relationships with commercial banks. This is accomplished by U.S. Central, which, through the corporate centrals, serves as the credit unions' main link to the Federal Reserve System. U.S. Central can provide such correspondent services as wire transfers, share draft settlements, federal funds trading, coin and currency delivery, and corporate share drafts. Corporate share drafts are essentially NOW accounts for corporate centrals, a replacement for the correspondent balance accounts at banks. The corporate centrals can also hold the required reserves of credit unions on a pass-through basis. The ultimate goal of the Corporate Network is to supply all the services that credit unions have traditionally acquired through correspondent relationships with banks and savings and loans.

The dominant role of CUNA and its subsidiaries makes the credit union industry resemble in some respects one large financial entity. The individual credit unions collect deposits and orginate loans. They buy their office supplies, computer services, and investment advice within the industry. Funds in excess of loans can be funneled into one pool to be managed by professionals or loaned to other credit unions. Thus, in analyzing the competitiveness of credit unions relative to other depository institutions, it may be more realistic to view the credit union industry as one financial network with thousands of branches rather than thousands of small imtermediaries.[23]

CREDIT UNION PERFORMANCE, 1977–1983

The performance of the credit union industry between 1977 and 1983 reflected both economic conditions and regulatory changes. This section examines the growth of credit unions, the changes in their assets and liabilities, and the rise of the Corporate Credit Union Network over this period.

Growth

Total assets at credit unions more than doubled during the 1977–83 period, rising at an annual rate of 12 percent. While this growth rate was slightly less than in the

1961–76 period, it still exceeded asset growth rates at banks (9.9 percent) and savings and loan associations (11.4 percent).[24] Deposits at credit unions grew slightly faster than assets at an annual rate of 12.7 percent. In contrast, deposits at banks grew an average of 9.2 percent a year and deposits at savings and loans grew an average of 9.5 percent. As a result of better deposit performance, the share of total household deposits (including money market shares) held at credit unions rose to 4.9 percent in 1978. With the dramatic rise in money market funds beginning in 1979, however, this share fell to about 4.4 percent in 1983.

While credit union membership rose to over 48 million by the end of 1983, the number of credit unions declined by over 3,300, falling to 19,205 by December 1983. The size distribution of credit unions, however, did not change radically. Credit unions with less than $2 million in assets still made up more than 70 percent of all credit unions and held about 10 percent of all assets. The 60 largest credit unions still held about 14 percent of all assets.[25]

Growth in assets and deposits varied considerably from 1977 to 1983. Charts 1 and 2 show the annual growth rates in assets and deposits at credit unions, banks, and savings and loans. As these charts indicate, credit union growth was relatively rapid in 1977 and 1978, considerably slower from 1979 through 1981, and then rapid again in 1982 and 1983. The growth pattern was similar for savings and loans while bank growth fluctuated moderately.

The pattern of credit union growth reflects a combination of regulatory and economic conditions. Up until the end of 1980, there was a ceiling on the rates most credit unions could pay on small certificates of deposit and other accounts. When short-term interest rates began rising sharply in 1978, credit unions found it difficult to pay competitive rates. At first, the difference between the rates paid by

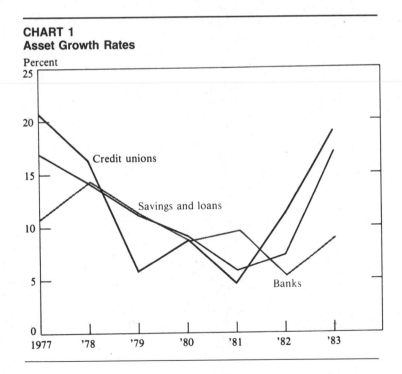

CHART 1
Asset Growth Rates

Percent

CHART 2
Deposit Growth Rates

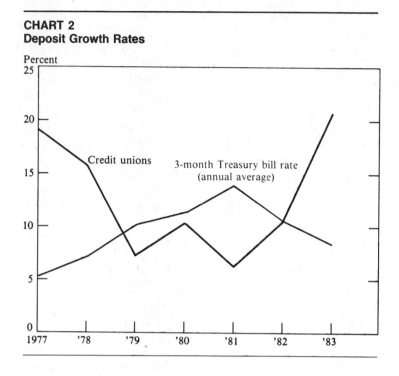

Percent

Credit unions

3-month Treasury bill rate
(annual average)

1977 '78 '79 '80 '81 '82 '83

CHART 3
Deposit Growth and Interest Rates

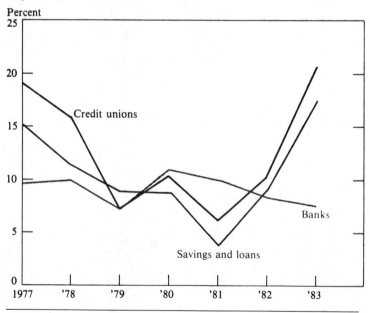

Percent

Credit unions

Banks

Savings and loans

1977 '78 '79 '80 '81 '82 '83

credit unions and the ceiling rates paid by banks and savings and loans gave credit unions a competitive advantage. This advantage was largely offset, however, by the surge in money market funds, which had no interest rate ceilings. The competitive advantage of money market funds caused slower growth in deposits and assets at credit unions as well as other depository institutions throughout the 1979–81 period.

Chart 3, which plots deposit growth at credit unions and the interest rate on three-month Treasury bills, supports the argument that high money market rates had a significantly negative effect on credit union growth. The relatively high rate of unemployment over much of this period also was probably detrimental to growth. Since many credit union members make deposits through payroll deductions, high unemployment could have more adverse effects on credit unions than other depository institutions.

Deposit growth at credit unions began to increase after April 1982, when the NCUA lifted all restrictions on the rates and maturities of federal credit union deposits. Since this preceded by about eight months the authorization for banks and savings and loans to offer money market deposit accounts, credit unions had a head start in offering accounts with money market rates. The general decline in interest rates may have reduced the attractiveness of money market funds to the point where the convenience and insurance of credit union deposits outweighed the interest differential. The exceptionally rapid growth in 1983 probably reflected the lower short-term interest rates and the rapid recovery from the 1982 recession.

Balance Sheet Composition

The composition of both assets and liabilities of credit unions changed substantially over the 1977–83 period. Table 3 presents the balance sheet for credit unions in 1983. A comparison of Table 3 with Table 1 shows that the proportion of loans to total assets dropped abruptly from 76 percent at the end of 1976 to 57 percent at the end of 1983. Several factors account for this decline. First, interest rate differentials often favored investments over loans. Until late 1980, the maximum interest rate many credit unions could charge on loans was 12 percent. When interest rates on short-term investments, such as Treasury bills, rose above this ceiling, as they often did between late 1979 and late 1980, loans became unattractive assets. Second, the expansion of the Corporate Credit Union Network made money market investing easier for small credit unions. Third, the riskiness of consumer loans was increased by swings in interest rates and unemployment rates in the 1977–83 period. Fourth, as discussed below, credit union deposits became more sensitive to market interest rates. As a result, the share of consumer installment loans held by credit unions peaked in 1978 at 16.7 percent. By the end of 1983 they had fallen to 13.8 percent.[26]

Not only did the distribution between loans and investments change between 1976 and 1983, the composition of investments held by credit unions also changed considerably. These changes represented a move toward short-term money market assets. The percentage of investments held in U.S. government or agency securities fell from 45 percent in 1976 to 22 percent in 1983, while the percentage in common trust investments fell from 21 percent to under 2 percent. Over the same period, investments in the form of deposits at corporate central credit unions rose from essentially 0 to 34 percent. Investments in the form of deposits at banks

---

TABLE 3
Balance Sheet for All Credit Unions, 1983

Total Assets, $45,225 million

Distribution of Assets	Percent
Loans to members	76.0
Cash	2.6
Investments	19.1
Other	2.3

Distribution of Liabilities and Capital	
Members' savings	86.6
Reserves and undistributed earnings	8.4
Notes payable and other	5.0

---

and savings and loans, mostly large certificates of deposit, rose from 19 to 37 percent. This last trend partly reflects credit union use of money brokers who direct the deposits to banks and savings and loans offering the highest yields.[27]

The changing composition of credit union deposits also caused credit unions to hold more of their assets in money market investments so they could match the characteristics of their assets and liabilities more closely. At the beginning of 1977, almost all deposits were regular share accounts similar to passbook savings accounts at banks. By November 1983, however, share accounts comprised only 45.4 percent of all deposits. Share drafts, money market accounts, and fixed-rate certificates—all of which pay market-related rates—comprised 8.3, 9.0, and 37.3 percent of deposits, respectively.[28] Deposit growth was also faster in large accounts. The rapid shift in deposit composition at credit unions suggests that depositors at credit unions are quite sensitive to the rates on alternative assets. Volatile interest rates thus required that credit unions, to offer competitive rates on deposits, hold assets with yields that moved with market rates.

Corporate Credit Union Growth and Balance Sheets

The growth of the Corporate Credit Union Network over the 1977–83 period was extraordinary. Because of the large increase in deposits from member credit unions, total assets at corporate centrals rose from under $1 billion to about $7.9 billion. The composition of corporate centrals' assets reflected the needs of their members. The percentage of deposits loaned to member credit unions requiring liquidity was high at first, peaking at 89 percent at the end of 1978. This percentage dropped quickly, however, to 5 percent by 1983. About 77 percent of corporate centrals' assets are deposits at U.S. Central with the rest in U.S. government and agency securities, shares at the CLF, and other assets. About 90 percent of the corporate centrals' funds come from deposits by member credit unions.

Growth of the corporate centrals brought similar growth at U.S. Central, which had assets of $7.2 billion by the end of 1983. Most (85 percent) of U.S. Central's assets are funded by the deposits of corporate centrals, while the rest are funded largely through the issue of commercial paper (2.7 percent) and the sale of government securities under repurchase agreements (7.3 percent). The composition of U.S. Central's assets reflects the needs of the corporate centrals. Depending on market conditions and the maturities of their own liabilities, corporate centrals choose from a variety of deposit options, ranging from regular deposits available on demand to fixed-rate, fixed-maturity certificates of deposit. In 1983, corporate centrals held about 56 percent of their deposits in regular deposits and 44 percent in certificates. U.S. Central, in turn, makes investments that closely match the maturity composition of its deposits. In 1983, U.S. Central held about 46 percent of its investment portfolio in federal funds, 40 percent in repurchase agreements, and the rest in a variety of money market securities.[29]

PROSPECTS FOR CREDIT UNIONS

While the credit union industry seems to have adapted well to changing financial markets, the future growth and structure of the industry are uncertain. One trend likely to continue is the softening of the common bond requirement for membership. Traditionally, only a credit union member's immediate family was eligible for membership in the union. Eligibility requirements have now been diluted to where a credit union can allow anyone to join who is related by blood or marriage to a current member, substantially increasing potential membership. In addition, the NCUA has promoted mergers between healthy and weak credit unions, regardless of differences in their common bonds. These rulings will allow more diversification across borrowers and depositors as ties to specific employers are weakened.

There are, however, drawbacks for credit unions to a weaker common bond requirement. To the extent that the common bond kept default rates on loans relatively low, default rates should rise as the common bond requirement fades. Weaker common bonds also imply less of an advantage on information regarding borrowers. The disintegration of the common bond further reduces the distinction between credit unions and other depository institutions, making it more difficult for the credit union industry to argue for the continuation of their nontaxable status.

A second trend that is likely to continue is the expansion of financial services offered by credit unions. At present, there are considerable differences in the services offered by large credit unions (over $5 million in assets) and small credit unions. Many large credit unions have taken advantage of financial deregulation and now offer money market accounts, first and second home mortgages, credit cards, and share drafts. Most small credit unions, however, have yet to offer these services, maybe because of lack of expertise or incentives of their volunteer officers or inadequate capital to acquire the necessary equipment.[30] The Corporate Credit Union Network is trying to provide the support necessary for more small credit unions to expand their services, particularly in the areas of share drafts and credit cards. Recently, CUNA started CUNA Brokerage, which gives credit union members access to discount stock brokerage through their credit union. This development is clearly a response to similar services now offered by banks and such "nonbank banks" as Sears. Some state-chartered credit unions have even begun making commercial loans.[31]

It is not clear whether the trend toward smaller consumer loan-asset ratios will continue. Credit unions will have a greater incentive to increase loan-asset ratios, if money market interest rates do not return to the high and variable levels of 1979–81 and if the interest ceiling on loans does not become binding. Consumer lending should also rise if credit unions' credit card programs become more widespread. On the other hand, the competition for consumer lending is increasing now that savings and loans are in the market and large banks are aggressively seeking to expand their share of the market by starting so-called consumer banks. In addition, the volunteers running smaller credit unions may have become accustomed to the ease of investing funds instead of making loans, particularly given the convenience of investing through the Corporate Credit Union Network.

Complete deregulation of deposit rates could force credit unions to focus more on consumer lending if they want to continue their rapid growth. Consumer loans may generate higher returns than investments, given credit unions' expertise, lower information costs, and comparatively low default rates. These higher returns will be required to maintain rapid deposit growth in the face of unrestricted competition for deposits from other depository institutions. Moreover, since the FDIC and FSLIC are requesting legislation to eliminate insurance on the deposits of institutions, credit unions may soon be unable to make insured deposits at risky institutions that offer high rates. Thus, credit unions may be forced to return to their previous practice of loaning out most of their deposits if they want to maintain growth. This strategy will be successful, however, only if interest rates are relatively stable.

An issue with potentially important implications for the growth of credit unions is their tax-exempt status. There have been many challenges to this status, the latest being the report of the Grace Commission.[32] The traditional argument for the nontaxable status of credit unions is that they are restricted in membership and exist only to promote thrift and provide low-cost credit to their members. As credit unions expand their services and phase out the common bond requirement, competitors will argue strongly for the taxation of credit unions.

The effects of taxation on credit unions would depend on the specific legislation. If credit unions were treated like mutual savings and loans or mutual savings banks, they could deduct the interest they pay on deposits, even though it is formally a payment of dividends. They could also deduct at least some of the income set aside for possible loan losses. If credit unions could add without limit to their loan loss reserves, they would never have to pay any tax. Presumably, therefore, some limit would be placed on the ratio of loan loss reserves to assets. It would seem that the only case in which credit unions would be signficantly affected by such tax provisions is if they wanted to build up their capital beyond the tax-free maximum. If they are satisfied with the maximum ratio, they can adjust their loan rates and deposit rates and invest in tax-preferred investments, such as state and local securities, to keep their tax liability negligible. If, however, credit unions wanted to increase their capital more rapidly, maybe in the anticipation of higher costs arising from complete deregulation or in anticipation of additional expenditures required to expand services, taxation would retard their growth. This is because credit unions would have to raise loan rates or lower deposit rates to generate enough after-tax income to meet their capital needs. In this case, taxation would reduce the competitiveness of credit unions and slow their growth.

CONCLUSIONS

Volatile economic conditions and financial deregulation have caused considerable change in credit unions since 1977. While credit unions have maintained their position as the fastest growing depository institutions, their growth has been uneven. The high interest rates of 1979–81 combined with interest ceilings on loans and deposits and high unemployment rates to slow credit union growth substantially. With the subsequent removal of the ceiling restrictions, the fall in market interest rates, and the revival of the economy, credit unions resumed their rapid growth in 1982 and 1983.

The most dramatic change in credit union portfolios was the relative decline in consumer loans from about 80 percent of assets in 1976 to below 60 percent in 1983. This decline reflected both the more attractive returns on money market investments and the changing composition of credit union deposits from passbook accounts to more interest-sensitive accounts. Another important development was the expansion of services provided by credit union trade associations. The trade association connection allows credit unions economies of scale that are not available to most individual credit unions due to their small size. As a result, credit unions have greatly broadened the financial services they offer. In addition, credit union liquidity has been substantially increased by the creation of the Central Liquidity Facility and the growth of the Corporate Credit Union Network.

The prospects for future credit union growth are uncertain. Complete deregulation of interest rates by 1986 will eliminate the deposit rate advantage they have had. Credit unions should be able to compete successfully, however, if they retain their tax-free status and renew their emphasis on consumer lending.

NOTES

[1] For more background on credit unions before 1977, see Peggy Brockschmidt, "Credit Union Growth in Perspective," *Monthly Review,* Federal Reserve Bank of Kansas City, February 1977, pp. 3–13; Mark J. Flannery, "An Economic Evaluation of Credit Unions," *Federal Reserve Bank of Boston Research Report No. 54,* 1974; and Donald J. Melvin, Raymond N. Davis, and Gerald C. Fischer, *Credit Unions and the Credit Union Industry* (New York Institute of Finance, 1977).

[2] Some state-chartered credit unions accept deposits, but these are often treated as equity capital. Since credit union shares are equity, they represent a residual claim on credit union assets, unlike the claim of bank depositors. Because credit unions are considered depository institutions, this article will use the terms shares and deposits interchangeably.

[3] No officer except the treasurer can receive compensation. Most credit unions have paid clerical help, and larger credit unions employ professional managers. Officers of credit unions affiliated with large business firms may receive implicit payments from the firm for their services to the credit union.

[4] Flannery, "An Economic Evaluation of Credit Unions," analyzed a 1972 sample of federal credit unions and found that most credit unions appear to balance the goals of savers and borrowers or to be dominated by savers. He reported that credit unions with a residential bond are more likely to be saver dominated. This issue is also discussed in Donald J. Smith, Thomas F. Cargill, and Robert A. Meyer, "An Economic Theory of a Credit Union," *Journal of Finance,* May 1981, pp. 519–28.

[5] Differences between state regulations are given in issues of *Comparative Digest of Credit Union Acts,* Credit Union National Association, Inc.

[6] The maximum unsecured loan was $2,500 while the maximum secured loan was 10 percent of the credit union's capital.

[7] Many states allowed state-chartered credit unions more investment choices.

[8] Risky assets are essentially loans that are not guaranteed by the government or secured by the borrower's shares.

[9] All data are from *Flow of Funds Accounts, Assets and Liabilities Outstanding, 1959–82,* Board of Governors of the Federal Reserve System, August 1983.

[10] The largest credit union was the Navy Federal Credit Union in Washington, D.C., with $568 million in assets. The 60th largest credit union had about $56 million in assets in 1976.

[11] The size distribution of other depository institutions are also skewed. For example, in 1976, commercial banks with assets under $50 million comprised 83.0 percent of all insured banks but held only 19.8 percent of all insured bank assets, while the 18 largest banks held 26.3 percent of all assets (*Annual Report of the Federal Deposit Insurance Corporation 1976,* table 104, p. 227).

[12] Common trust investments are NCUA-approved mutual funds that invest in securities approved for credit unions. They are often run by credit union trade associations.

[13] See issues of *Comparative Digest of Credit Union Acts* for how these changes affected state-chartered credit unions.

[14] Initially, credit unions were restricted to 30-year loans on homes that were less than 150 percent of the median house price in their area.

[15] The NCUA can raise the ceiling (15 percent) for up to 18 months if it can demonstrate that growth, liquidity, capital, and earnings have been adversely affected and that interest rates have been rising in the last six months. The NCUA must inform Congress before raising the ceiling.

[16] For a discussion of this change, see *1983 Annual Report,* NCUA, pp. 9–11.

[17] The NCUA had required larger credit unions to keep a 5 percent ratio of liquid assets to deposits beginning in 1979, but this requirement was removed in 1982. The reserve requirements for credit unions are being phased in over time. By September 1987, credit unions will face the same reserve requirements as do member banks.

[18] The NCUA divides the United States into six administrative regions, each with its own regional office.

[19] For a discussion of previous recommendations for such a facility, see Flannery, "An Economic Evaluation of Credit Unions," pp. 162–64.

[20] As discussed later, credit unions can also borrow from other credit unions through the Corporate Credit Union Network. The CLF sets its rate just above the average rate charged by corporate central credit unions.

[21] For background on the trade associations, see Melvin, Davis, and Fischer, *Credit Unions and the Credit Union Industry,* chap. 3.

[22] U.S. Central belongs to the CLF and thus its member credit unions also have access to the CLF.

[23] Large credit unions are much less dependent on trade associations.

[24] All assets are at book value. Since savings and loans had assets with much longer maturities than banks or credit unions, the market value of their assets fell considerably when interest rates rose unexpectedly in 1979. The source of all data is *Flow of Funds,* Board of Governors.

[25] The asset distribution of commercial banks became somewhat more skewed over the same period. Banks with less than $50 million in assets comprised 66 percent of all insured banks and held about 9 percent of all bank assets. The largest 18 banks held 37.6 percent of all bank assets at the end of 1983.

[26] Commercial banks' share of the consumer installment market also fell from 48.3 percent in 1976 to 45.7 percent in 1983. The share of savings and loans and mutual savings banks combined rose from 3.9 percent to 5.7 percent over this period and the share of nondepository institutions also increased.

[27] Institutions offering exceptionally high interest rates are likely to be more risky. While deposit insurance eliminates the risk for deposits up to $100,000, credit unions often made uninsured deposits. For example, when the Penn Square Bank failed in July 1982, 139 credit unions held a total of $111.5 million in uninsured deposits in the bank (*Annual Report 1982,* NCUA, p. 6).

[28] Other depository institutions experienced similar changes in the composition of their deposits. Passbook savings accounts at banks as a percentage of total bank deposits fell from 23.7 percent in 1976 to 8.9 percent in 1983, while such accounts at savings and loans declined from 40.4 percent of all deposits in 1976 to 19.9 percent in 1982.

[29] The composition of U.S. Central's portfolio is for February 29, 1984.

[30] For a breakdown of credit union services by asset size, see *Credit Union Magazine,* December 1983, p. 23.

[31] Credit unions in 23 states were making commercial loans in 1983, although the volume was quite small. See *Credit Union Magazine,* January 1984, pp. 60–61.

[32] *President's Private Sector Survey on Cost Control,* U.S. Government Printing Office, January 1984. Also, Flannery, "An Economic Evaluation of Credit Unions," pp. 155–57, argues for the taxation of credit unions and discusses past recommendations.

6

Federal Regulation of Banking:
Analysis and Policy Recommendations

George J. Benston

Banking is and has been one of the most regulated of industries. In almost all countries and at all times since the establishment of banking, governments have imposed controls on the institutions, even when most other businesses were free to operate, subject only to the statutes and other general rules of law. In the United States, the extent of regulation has ranged from the free entry banking period of the 1800s, when banks still were supervised and required to maintain specified reserves against the notes they issued, to the extensive controls imposed in the 1930s. The Depository Institutions Deregulation and Monetary Control Act of 1980 removed some regulatory restrictions (e.g., allowing thrift institutions to make consumer and business loans) while imposing others (e.g., requiring noninterest-bearing reserves for all chartered institutions' demand and similar deposits). But as increased nominal interest rates raised the opportunity cost of holding money as deposits at the regulated, chartered financial institutions and as the cost of electronic and telephonic fund transfers declined, the development of products and services designed to avoid the regulations and competition by unregulated providers of financial services increased. It is imperative, therefore, to determine whether the present regulatory structure best serves the public interest and should be extended to all providers of financial services (the level playing field simile), whether regulations should be removed from all providers (perhaps a free-for-all would be a parallel simile), or whether some other restructuring and/or consolidation of the regulations and regulators would be desirable.

However, before changes in the existing order are recommended, the reasons for the past and present regulatory situation should be delineated and analyzed. In this regard, two considerations are likely to be important. First, there were reasons for regulating financial intermediaries more than almost any other industry; should some regulations be removed, the conditions that gave rise to them might reoccur, to the detriment of some people. It is best if the lessons of history

Reprinted with permission from the *Journal of Bank Research*, published by Bank Administration Institute, Winter 1983, pp. 216–44.

are not relearned. Second, the present situation in the United States may make previously relevant regulations no longer applicable or useful. These vestigial regulations impose burdens on society without any compensating benefits. The bulk of the paper is directed toward identifying the antecedents and contemporary relevance of the present set of regulations and regulatory agencies.

The analysis presented in the next section leads to the conclusion that most of the historical reasons for regulating financial institutions are no longer relevant (if they ever were) to our society. These reasons (which are discussed below) include taxation of banks as monopoly suppliers of money, the prevention of centralized power, bank solvency and the effects of failures on the economy, the provision of banking services as a social goal, support of housing and other attempts to allocate credit as social goals, and the prevention of invidious discrimination and unfair dealing against persons. What is needed, therefore, is abolition of most federal regulation. Indeed, with the exception of deposit insurance, the only currently meaningful reason for regulating financial institutions is to control the money supply and to protect some suppliers of financial services from competition. Assuming that the last reason is not considered to be desirable and can be overcome politically, almost all restrictions on entry (including intra- and inter-state branching and the offering of all financial products), prices, and the restructuring of organizations should be removed. With the exception noted below, financial intermediaries should be treated the same as other corporations.[1]

Consequently, almost all of the *raison d'être* of the federal regulatory agencies would be obviated. In particular the Office of the Comptroller of the Currency (OCC), the Federal Home Loan Bank Board (FHLBB), and the National Credit Union Administration (NCUA) would serve simply as chartering agencies for depository institutions. Because mutuals are not owned by investors who put their resources at risk, the FHLBB and the NCUA would have to act as the ultimate authority that could remove incompetent or dishonest managers. Stockholder-owned institutions, though, would be regulated no differently than other corporations. Charters would be granted to depository institutions if they had deposit insurance provided by an insurer that was approved by the OCC, the FHLBB, or the NCUA. The existing deposit insurance agencies—the FDIC, the FSLIC, and FCUSIF—would be so authorized to provide insurance to any depository institutions that there would be some competition among insurors. (Therefore, it is important that they not be merged into a single agency as has been proposed.) In addition, nongovernment insurers (such as major insurance companies) and banks could be recognized by the chartering agencies and could offer their services to the depository institutions. Because they bear the risk of failures, the insurers would impose whatever restrictions on the activities of the depository institutions that they felt useful, subject to the same sort of mutual agreement that insurance companies exercise with their other clients.

The Federal Reserve Board would cease to have any responsibilities for bank supervision. The payments facilities would be divested and set up as a separate corporation with shares held privately. Reserves probably would continue to be required of depository institutions. And the Fed would lend reserves and provide currency at market rates that were consistent with its mandate to conduct monetary policy.[2] In the further interest of equity and efficiency, the taxes imposed on depository institutions would be the same as those imposed on other corporations.

This would require the Fed paying interest on the required reserves and the Congress removing tax subsidies.

In short, it is time that we recognized that financial institutions are simply businesses with only a few special features that require regulation. The following analysis provides the reasoning and evidence on which this conclusion and the recommendations are based.

BASIC REASONS FOR REGULATING BANKING

Taxation

The Historical Record.   Perhaps the oldest reason for regulating banking was to enhance the ability of those who had political power, be they monarchs or legislatures, to raise revenues (tax). Before the advent of central banking taxation took two forms: seigniorage from the production of money, and loans at lower than risk-adjusted market rates.

Seigniorage is the difference between the accepted and the commodity value of money. When the government could maintain a monopoly over the money supply, it could require people to use the designated money at its token value by declaring it to be legal tender. Since money costs considerably less to produce than its accepted or token value, the producer (the government) benefits. Even when people could substitute among other forms of money, the convenience over commodities (e.g., gold) of money that was backed by the power of the government to punish forgers enabled governments to obtain seigniorage from the production of money. However, because governments often abused their power to produce legal tender by debasing the currency and printing paper money with apparent abandon, people tended to prefer bank notes produced by private banks. Hence, governments tended to regulate banks for two reasons. One was to restrain the banks' interference with the government's gains from seigniorage. The second was to permit banks to produce money but tax them by requiring them to lend money to the government at favorable rates and/or to give an ownership share to those who controlled the government (e.g., the monarch and his associates).

Government regulation, therefore, took the form of restricting people from the money creation aspects of banking by requiring governmentally granted charters. Needless to say, relatively few charters were granted, since competition among money suppliers would reduce the profits from money creation, profits that could be garnered by government directly, through seigniorage, or indirectly, via loans from and ownership shares in the chartered banks that would be subsidized by the monopoly profits earned with the aid of regulations that restricted their competition.

Loans at less than market rates (net of an allowance for risk) were a favored means by which monarchs and other governmental officials taxed banks. (More accurately, the tax was imposed on the users of bank money, who were prevented from benefiting from competition among banks.) Unfortunately, but predictably, the governments tended to use this form of taxation for revenue to finance extravagances and wars, which led them to enhance further the possibility of the banks achieving monopoly profits that could be taxed additionally (fattening the calf). Sometimes the governments overdid it: loans were defaulted and banks failed (killing the golden goose). Thus a cause of major banking failures was overtaxation by government.

Central banking grew out of the use of banks as a source of governmental revenue.[3] As the bank that served as a revenue source for the government was given more complete monopoly powers and served as the government's primary source of loans, it became an instrument of government—the central bank (e. g., the Bank of England). The existence of a central bank permitted the government to enhance its revenue from seigniorage, since the notes of the bank tended to become the only legal tender (they were the only notes accepted in payment of taxes). Occasionally this led to extreme excesses, as in the case of the monopoly given to John Law in 1716 for his Banque Generale, which issued notes with such abandon that the bank failed within five years, bringing the economy of France down with it. But most often, the central bank used its monopoly powers effectively, which included restraining excess production of notes and using the power of government to prohibit or control the issue of notes and deposit services by competitors.

Probably because of their experiences with the near-monopoly powers of the Bank of England,[4] the U.S. founding fathers generally were against the establishment of a central bank, whether privately or governmentally controlled. For this reason, together with the preeminence of states' rights and the desire of existing banks to avoid the dominance of a strong national bank, banking was regulated by the states until 1863, with the exception of the First and Second Banks of the United States, whose 20-year charters were not renewed when they expired. Prior to the National Currency Act of 1863 and the National Banking Act of 1864 (which established federal chartering), state-chartered banks often were required to hold state bond issues as backing for their notes.[5] The national banks (the notes of which supplanted the state banks' notes when the National Banking Act of 1864 imposed a prohibitory tax on them) were required to keep U. S. obligations as collateral. While concern for the note holders was an important reason for this requirement, it also benefited the governments involved. State and federal reserve requirements on demand deposits similarly reflected the government's interests.

The creation of the Federal Reserve in 1913 gave the United States its first central bank. By requiring member banks to hold reserves with the Federal Reserve or (since 1960) in vault cash, neither of which bears interest, the federal government imposed a tax on these banks and on their customers. When the reserve requirements were extended to all suppliers of third-party transfers (checking accounts and equivalents) by the Depository Institutions Deregulation and Monetary Control Act of 1980, this tax was imposed generally (though still not evenly).[6] Since the Federal Reserve remits 90 percent of earnings on its investments in U. S. government obligations to the U. S. Treasury, in effect the tax is collected by the Treasury.

The Present Situation.   Though regulation of and limitations on bank charters were instituted as a means of maximizing the amount of tax (direct and indirect) that could be imposed on banks and users of bank money, this type of regulation is no longer meaningful in the United States. Neither state nor federally chartered banks are required to invest in state or federal obligations or lend to the governments at favorable rates. But, by imposing reserve requirements on all providers of third-party transfers, the Federal Reserve can and does impose a tax on users of bank money. Indeed, the amount of this tax and the efficiency with which it is collected is reduced by regulations other than reserve requirements that might be imposed on financial institutions. Limitations on charters or any other restrictions that impose costs on users of bank money reduce the value of this asset to users and, therefore, reduce the amount of tax that can be imposed. Therefore, assuming that a tax on users of bank money is desirable (an assumption that is questioned below), other banking regulations than reserve requirements on all money providers should be repealed.

Prevention of Centralized Power

The Historical Record.   As noted above, the United States has a history of concern for and aversion toward centralized power. This concern was reflected in part by the refusal of Congress to renew the charter of the First Bank of the United States in 1811, and President Jackson's veto of the charter of the Second Bank of the United States in 1832. One argument against these banks was that they were too powerful (although many scholars believe that the discipline imposed by the banks on their state-chartered rivals was a more important reason for their demise).[7]

The prohibitions against intrastate branch banking enacted by several of the states also may be considered to be a reflection of a basic bias against bigness. But the record does not support this as a general interpretation of branch banking legislation. While the branching activities of the Second Bank of the United States, in particular, were objected to by the state bankers with whom the bank competed, by the end of the 19th century 20 states permitted branch banking. However, though the number of branches had increased somewhat from 1834 to 1900 (from 100 to 119), the increase in the number of banks over this period was so great (from 406 to 12,423) that the percentage of branches to banks declined from 24.5 percent to 0.0.[8] As the automobile increased mobility in the 1920s, branching increased steadily to 785 branches operated by 397 banks in 1915 to 3,005 branches operated by 724 banks in 1934.[9]

The increasing technological desirability of branching gave rise to two developments. One was the adoption of the McFadden-Pepper Act of 1927, which conceded to national banks limited power to branch in their home cities, subject to state legislation. (The home city restriction was removed in 1934). The second was increased attempts by local bankers to have laws enacted that would restrain competition from larger banks. This often successful attempt linked branching with the underlying popular fear of centralized power. In this regard, an early observation by H. Parker Willis, the most influential U.S. banking academic of his time (or perhaps any time) is instructive and still pertinent. He states that the owners of small banks assert that branching ". . . would result in building up a money power which would crush the small banks out of existence. A more absurd reversal of the actual facts in the case could scarcely be imagined. What the establishment of branches would actually do would be to destroy the local money power which now practically stifles many forms of legitimate industry by a pressure of excessive interest rates, and by other even less justifiable means.[10]

Perhaps because the validity of Parker's remarks was recognized, or possibly because the bankers in some states saw the advantages of branching, only a third of the states in the later 1920s prohibited banks from operating branches, a third permitted limited branching, and a third allowed statewide branching. Presently, only 12 states prohibit branching, 15 allow limited branching, and 23 statewide branching. Thus, a prohibition against branching neither was nor is the rule in the United States, and it is difficult to view the restrictions placed on this type of banking organization as a manifestation of a general fear of centralized power. Though the fact that interstate branching and nationwide banking has been prohibited argues in favor of the hypothesis that fear of large banks is a continuing feature of U. S. banking regulation, an alternative, or perhaps supplementary, explanation is that the restrictions have been based more on the local bankers' desire to protect themselves from competition. This is discussed below.

It also is important to distinguish the particular aspects of banking toward which the concern about centralized power was directed. Principally, centralization of the power to grant loans and make investments was the object of the founding fathers' fear. The centralization of note issuance also was important when bank notes were the most important circulating medium. Once demand deposit banking developed, there appeared to be relatively little concern about the centralization of this banking product. Nor was the centralized offering of collateral banking services ever considered much of an issue.

The Present Situation.   Fear of centralized note issue is meaningful but irrelevant for bank regulation; the Federal Reserve now controls or can control the money supply.[11]

Fear of the provision of centralized depository services has been stated as an important issue by bankers who oppose intra- and inter-state branching. Without these restrictions they assert that large branch banks would come to dominate the country and local communities. In large measure, their concern is based on the assumption that there are considerable economies of scale in banking operations, such that banking is akin to a natural monopoly. However, empirical studies have not found this to be the situation. Earlier studies (using data from the 1960s) found some economies of scale with respect to operating costs (with output defined as the number of accounts processed and average dollar size of accounts), but higher costs of branching. These effects were offsetting for larger branch banks.[12] A recent study that uses nationwide data for 1975 through 1978 found diseconomies of scale and very similar average costs for branch and unit banks when all variables were held constant (including the average size of accounts), except for numbers of accounts and branches. Most importantly for the present question, a small unit bank had slightly lower operating costs than a similar branch of a branch bank, all other things held constant.[13] Therefore, there is no reason to believe that smaller unit banks and small banks generally have a cost-disadvantage, such that they could not compete with large banks. Consistent with this conclusion is the experience in New York State when statewide branching was permitted and several New York City banks opened offices in out-of-city locations. They were unable to take much business away from the existing banks.

Because banking does not appear to be subject to economies of scale, the removal of restrictions on entry can only serve to decrease the centralization of banking services, particularly in local communities that are served by few banks.[14]

Loans to large and to many middle-sized borrowers, at the present time, are made nationwide, indeed worldwide, by banks. Loans and other sources of capital, such as direct and publicly placed bonds and equity shares, also are available from a very large number of non-banking services. Thus, most business borrowers can look to commercial banks in all states and in other countries, to insurance companies, to pension funds, to venture capital companies, and to underwriters for short and long-term capital. Trade credit is another source of funds for businesses. Government agencies also supply loans. Consumers can borrow from and through commercial banks, thrift institutions, mortgage bankers, consumer finance companies, sales finance companies, life insurance companies, and retailers, among others.

Since enactment of the "Garn-St Germain Depository Institutions Act of 1982," which removed most of the restrictions in thrift institutions' lending to business, the principal constraint on people's opportunities for obtaining financing from banks is the Glass-Steagall Act's provisions. These prohibit commercial banks from underwriting and dealing in corporate bonds and equity securities and from investing in equities. Similarly, underwriters are forbidden from offering depository services. Presently, this prohibition is supported by reference to fears of banks controlling loan and equity sources of funds. But were banks allowed to offer customers funds packaged as securities as well as loans, this would hardly result in a concentration of power, as long as the customers have the alternative of obtaining funds and services from insurance companies, pension funds, investment companies, underwriters, and others. Another frequently expressed fear concerns the possibility of banks abusing their fiduciary responsibilities. In particular, they might use information gathered in the course of lending to trade in a corporation's equities. Or they might attempt to "bail out" of a bad loan by selling equities to the public, the proceeds of which would be used to repay the bank. If these fears are valid, though, they apply equally to underwriters, since they hold, buy, and sell the corporate obligations. It also is important to note that, though these fears presently are expressed, they were not given as argument for the Glass-Steagall Act. Rather, Senator Glass (who, prior to the bank failures that triggered the act, had attempted to legally separate investment from commercial banking) believed as a matter of banking theory that the loans and investments of depository institutions should be limited to self-liquidity obligations (the real-bills doctrine).

Restrictions on interstate banking and branching also limit, somewhat, the numbers of potential sources for loans for people living in less-populated states and communities and in communities that straddle state borders. At the least, these restrictions tend to raise the price of loans to borrowers. Again, considering the multitude of sources for loans that are now available, there seems no reason to believe that any fear of centralized power can justify continuing these restrictions.

Avoidance of Competition

The Historical Record.   Bankers are not unique in wanting to foreclose or limit competition. As is discussed above, such limitations served the interests of monarchs and other governmental authorities and were the source of such regulations as restrictive chartering. In the United States, where, compared to Europe, many more banks were chartered, such restrictions on competition also took (and still take) the form of limiting or prohibiting branching. While these prohibitions often were (and still are) justified as a means of limiting centralized power, the reasoning and evidence given above is contrary to this rationale.

Limitations on the right of nonbanks to offer banking services also were used to restrain competition. Until recently, thrift associations were prohibited from offering checking accounts to their customers. In most states, they also were prohibited from offering consumer loans, other than those related to real estate and a few types of specialty loans (such as education loans). Nor could they offer checking accounts and loans to businesses. The prohibition against dealings with business were justified on the grounds of potential self-dealing by the officers of mutual associations and their charge to look to the needs of individual consumers. But these restrictions were maintained long after the thrift associations had changed from small, charitable institutions to large-scale lenders to real estate related enterprises as well as individuals.

Since banking was a regulated industry, the power of government also was used by the banks' competitors to constrain competition by banks (e. g., the Glass-Steagall Act, which prohibits banks from offering securities underwriting services). Direct investments in companies not considered by the regulations to offer banklike (congeneric) services also were prohibited. The arguments for these constraints were couched in terms of concern for the safety and soundness of the banks or fear of centralized power by the banks. But the Glass-Steagall Act's prohibitions were not based on empirical findings demonstrating that the provision of securities services by banks contributed to failures or to cheating of customers.[15] Rather, the evidence supports the belief that the investment bankers and underwriters were concerned about severe competition from banks and bank affiliates and sought (successfully in 1933) to eliminate these competitors.[16] Similarly, such businesses as travel agencies and computer service companies have sought to keep banks from providing services on the grounds that this would exceed the banks' legally granted powers. Thus, regulation has worked both ways with respect to banks, though in either instance the cost was borne by customers.

The Present Situation.   The desire and possibly the power of business people to restrain their competition is still with us. Commercial bankers do not want to face competition for business loans and deposits from thrift associations. Bankers who run small unit banks fear having to compete with the branch managers of large banks. Bankers in some states do not want to compete with bankers in neighboring or any other states. Brokers want to offer checking accounts but do not want bankers to offer brokerage services. And so forth.

But the ability of people in and at the periphery of the financial services industry to prevent others from competing for their customers is increasingly being eroded by technological change fueled by the opportunity cost of high nominal interest rates and the advantages of avoiding restrictive regulations. Three (of many) specific examples illustrate this situation:

- The transfer of funds by check first was offered by thrift institutions by means of negotiable orders of withdrawal and by credit unions with share drafts. Both forms of transfers look like checks, can be used as checks, but are legally not called checks. Better yet (for the consumer), interest is paid at the savings rate which, while constrained by Regulation Q, is still greater than the rate of zero permitted on regular demand deposits.
- Stockbrokers offer their customers de facto checking accounts on which interest is paid at market rates. Furthermore, they are not constrained by geographic limitations but operate nationwide. And they simultaneously

can offer clients a wide range of investment alternatives, including direct ownership of stocks and bonds and participation in funds.

- Offices that solicit and service business and consumer loans are operated by major banks directly and as holding company affiliates in major cities throughout the country. Unregulated mortgage bankers and sales finance companies offer consumer loans throughout the country.

Thus, the present set of regulations serve bankers who want to constrain competition primarily with respect to services provided on the local level, particularly deposit services where the depositor wants personally to deposit and withdraw funds. On the other hand, the regulations prevent bankers from organizing their operations in whatever way is most efficient for a given market and set of products and also prohibit them from directly offering a full range of services to their customers.

Bank Solvency and the Effects of Failures on the Economy

The Historical Record. Bank failures were not always considered to be horrendous occurrences to be avoided at all costs. All enterprises that involve risk may be sufficiently unsuccessful, poorly managed, fraudulently run, or the victims of bad luck. Banks are no exception. And the record shows that banks regularly failed throughout history. Many of the more spectacular bank failures were due to overly rapacious taxation by monarchs and other government officials. In these cases, regulation served to increase the ability of the rulers to overuse their power to the detriment of the banks' other customers, owners and employees, and often of the state. While it is true that many banks failed because their operators acted incompetently or fraudulently, it appears that failures were more often the consequence of governmental interference or incompetence.

The experience of the United States, which (together with Scotland) was one of the few countries that permitted competitive banking, is particularly instructive.[17] Prior to 1837, bank charters had to be obtained by special acts of the state legislatures. In part to avoid the corruption that tended to accompany the granting of these quasi-monopolies, and in part because of the public demand for more banking facilities and a sentiment toward unrestricted enterprise, Michigan in 1837 and New York and Georgia in 1838 enacted free bank chartering laws. These laws permitted anyone to open a bank who provided a minimum amount of capital and deposited with a state agent a specified amount of bonds that could be sold to repay the holders of bank notes (which served as hand-to-hand currency) should the bank fail to redeem the notes as promised. By 1860, 18 of the 32 states had passed such laws (Michigan twice).[18]

Because some of the state laws were drawn so as to permit the bankers to issue notes with face values in excess of the market values of the bonds, and because the public was led to believe that the bonds provided adequate security for the notes, "wildcat" banking was profitable in some of the states. Wildcat banking occurs when bankers issue many more notes than they can redeem and, if the notes stay in circulation long enough (whence the term, *wildcat banking,* which refers to establishing redemption offices in areas populated primarily by wildcats), the issuers can profit even if they later become bankrupt. In these states, there were many bank failures. Michigan, in particular, suffered such a rash of failures (the typical life span of a free bank was no more than six months) that the legislature suspended the law after about a year, in April 1838. The reason for this bad experience was that the notes issued by the Michigan banks did not have to be redeemed in specie and could be backed by mortgages. Consequently, Rockoff explains, people would "create a mortgage on a worthless piece of property, have it certified as being valuable by some friends, and then transfer it to a wildcat bank in exchange for a mass of bank notes. . . . Other [currency issues] were simply frauds which operated in violation of the free banking law."[19]

Nevertheless, the losses suffered by the public as a consequence of holding worthless or depreciated bank notes were not great. Including the $1 million lost by holders of Michigan bank notes and $394,700 lost in the first years of New York free banking (after which losses were negligible), estimated losses in the 18 states through 1860 totaled only $1,852,900, or less than 2 percent of the money stock.[20] Indeed, despite its bad experience, Michigan reinstated free banking in 1857. On the other side of the ledger, free banking resulted in increased banking services and lower profits to banks (and, hence, lower costs to consumers). Furthermore, private regulatory arrangements, such as the Suffolk system in Boston and the New York clearinghouse, virtually eliminated the member banks' failures to redeem their notes for specie.

The national banking system, created in 1863, represented a continuation of free banking, since entrepreneurs were able to obtain bank charters without having to get special bills passed by state legislatures. However, they did have to put up more capital than was generally required for state charters, maintain specified reserves against their deposits, and could issue bank notes only in amounts that did not exceed the lesser of 90 percent of the market value or 100 percent of the par value of registered U. S. bonds which had to be deposited with the U. S. Treasurer. Even then there were many bank failures for reasons which included actions by the U. S. Treasury that reduced the amount of bonds available for backing note issues, and a prohibition of branch banking that was not relaxed somewhat until 1927.

Even after 1927 (indeed to this day) banks are restricted from branching within many states and across state lines by state-enacted laws. These laws restrain banks from efficiently diversifying their operations geographically. Hence, they are more liable to local and area economic failures and depressions. This is borne out by the data, which show that from 1921 through 1931, when 8,916 banks were suspended, only 7 were banks with more than 10 branches; of these, only 3 operated branches outside the city of the head office.[21] It should be noted, however, that permission to branch intrastate is unlikely to have benefited most of the banks that failed. As is described further below, the largest group of failures were among small banks in agricultural states. But, had interstate branching been permitted, these banks could have diversified sufficiently, as did the Canadian banks, where nationwide banking was permitted and only one bank (in 1923) failed.

The data on bank suspensions since about the turn of the century might, by contemporary standards, appear descriptive of a total banking collapse. Between 1890 and 1899, 1,084 banks were suspended, 1,789 were suspended between 1900 and 1920, and 5,712 between 1921 and 1929.[22] Expressed as annual percentages of active banks, the suspensions in each of the periods are 1.50 percent, 0.34

percent, and 2.30 percent. As annual percentages of the deposits of active banks the deposits of the suspended banks are 0.10 percent for the 1900–1920 period and 0.24 percent for the 1921–29 period. And in the period of the largest number of suspensions, 1921–29, the average annual losses borne by depositors as a percentage of deposits are only 0.15 percent. Thus, in the decade before the debacle of the Great Depression, the losses to depositors were not very great. Perhaps this is the reason that, despite the large number of suspensions, there were no successful moves to "reform" the system. Nor did the bank suspensions adversely affect the economy in general. In fact the overall growth of the economy was particularly great in the 1920s, the period of the greatest number of suspensions. To the contrary, the principal cause of the suspensions appears to have been adverse local economic conditions, particularly those in the agricultural regions of the western grain states (where 47 percent of the suspensions during 1921–29 occurred) and of the southeastern and southwestern states (with 18 percent and 11 percent of the suspensions).

The Great Depression saw 9,096 bank suspensions between 1930 and 1933. These are 11.29 percent per year of the active banks; they held 4.14 percent of the deposits. Between 1930 and 1933, the average annual losses borne by depositors as a percentage of deposits averaged 0.81 percent, 5.4 times the loss rate of 0.15 percent experienced in the 1920s. While the great number of bank failures undoubtedly affected the economy negatively, most scholars agree that the banks were primarily the victims, rather than the cause, of the Great Depression.[23]

However, it should be noted that bank runs played an important role in the Great Depression and in previous financial collapses. "Black Thursday" 1873 saw the failure of Jay Cooke's banking house and the first closing of the New York Stock Exchange. It was followed (perhaps causally) by six years of depression. The failure in 1884 of former President Grant's firm, Grant & Ward, and of the Marine National Bank sparked runs and the consequent failure of numerous banks and brokerage houses. The Panic of 1893 was touched off by the 1890 failure of the London banking firm of Baring Brothers, which specialized in financing U.S. enterprises. Baring's European creditors demanded that Americans pay their debts in gold. As a consequence, the base money supply was depleted and a multiple contraction resulted, and 1891 saw a mini-panic. During the following 1893 panic, over 600 banks and 13 of every 1,000 businesses failed in perhaps the second deepest depression (after the depression of 1837) in the nation's history before 1930. The New York Clearing House suspended convertibility to specie, which ended the run. The situation also was helped by J. P. Morgan's negotiation of a sale in Europe of a $100 million U.S. bond issue. Panic struck again in 1907, when New York City and several corporations were unable to sell high-yielding bond issues. The Knickerbocker Trust Company failed (largely as a consequence of speculation with depositors' funds) and several major banks experienced severe runs. Again, the New York Clearing House suspended convertibility to specie and J. P. Morgan later helped increase reserves with European loans and U.S. Treasury deposits.

The creation of the Federal Reserve in 1913 was supposed to rid the country of these recurring collapses. As the lender of last resort, with great resources and the power of the printing press, it should have been able to better the New York Clearing House's and J. P. Morgan's record. But, when the Bank of the United

States collapsed in 1930, runs were made on other banks. And the Fed did not prevent the collapse of a third of the banks during the next several years. Though the losses to depositors and others as a consequence of the panics that preceded the Federal Reserve were considerable, the costs absorbed by the public after the creation of the central bank appear to be greater. The sharp and relatively short depressions of 1837, 1873, 1893, and 1907 should be compared with the Great Depression of the 1930s. The recession of 1920–21 should be contrasted with the sharper recession of 1937–38 (when the Fed doubled the required reserves ratios) and the relatively small post-World War II recessions, and the present recession. And the cost of losses in purchasing power absorbed by depositors because of the nonwartime inflations of 1916–17 and the 1970s to the present should be compared to the losses depositors took because of bank failures at all times, including the 1930s. The record may not give one faith in regulation by a central bank as a means of protecting depositors and maintaining the solvency of the banking system and the economic well-being of the nation.

The creation of the Federal Deposit Insurance Corporation in 1933 was a salutatory innovation. Since most depositors no longer need fear that their funds will be lost should a bank fail, runs have largely become a relic of the past. The word *largely* is used because uninsured depositors (those with over $100,000 in an account) have reason to fear loss of their funds, particularly if the FDIC closes the bank, rather than arranges for its assumption by another bank. Furthermore, the event of a bank failure gives large depositors reason to question the safety of their funds in other banks where the assets held and operating procedures appear to be similar to those of the failed bank. For example, when the Penn Square and Abilene National banks failed in 1982, other banks faced the problem of convincing depositors that their funds were safe. However, the snowballing effect of pre-FDIC runs did not occur. Nor did banks that were unconnected to the failed banks experience difficulties.[24]

The question to be considered, then, is whether bank failures or even the possibility of limited bank runs are presently a matter for concern more than the failure of any nonregulated enterprise.

The Present Situation.   With the possibility of a bank failure causing runs on other banks largely a concern of the past, and with protection of bank note holders no longer meaningful since the currency is provided and guaranteed by the Federal Reserve, what reasons can be adduced for governmental concern about the solvency of banks? This question can be answered by considering the costs to the principal persons who would be affected by a bank failure: owners, employees, borrowers, depositors, and users of other banking services.

The owners (stocks and bondholders) clearly are hurt by failures. But their position is no different than that of the owners of other enterprises. In fact, because banks use little if any specialized assets, the owners tend to lose less than had they owned the shares of most other types of businesses. Mutual banking organizations—mutual savings banks, savings and loan associations, and credit unions—are an important exception. The mutual form was adopted for these institutions because they began as charitable or fraternal nonprofit organizations. Most of them are constrained by competition in the marketplace to operate as efficiently as do stockholder-owned institutions. But, unlike the situation for stockholder-owned enterprises, monitoring by stockholders and the securities market is not present. Consequently, should a mutual institution be operated inefficiently or fraudulently, there is a need for a supervisory government agency to step in to protect the equity in the assets that, in effect, belong to the community.

Employees of banks also would be adversely affected by the failure of their employers. But, because so many banks operate similarly, bank employees have skills that are readily transferable, unlike the employees of most other enterprises. In addition, a failed bank is likely to be absorbed into another bank, rather than dissolved. Hence, bank employees are less in need of governmental concern than are other workers.

Borrowers would lose the value of their contacts with the officers of a failed bank and the officers' knowledge of them. But if the failed bank is taken over by another organization, the cost is likely to be small. Depositors whose accounts are fully insured suffer, at most, a short delay and some inconvenience until their accounts are paid off or transferred to another bank. Uninsured depositors might lose. But, since they are holders of large accounts (currently over $100,000), it seems likely that they are capable of assessing the risks and obtaining sufficient compensation, *ex ante,* for the risks. In any event, the historical record suggests that the expected losses are relatively small. Nor are the users of other bank services likely to be seriously inconvenienced, since, if entry were not restrained by regulation, there are likely to be many competing sources of services available.

This leaves only the owners and others associated with banks that might experience runs because an apparently similar bank failed. To the extent that these banks are misperceived as offering greater risks to uninsured depositors, they will bear unfairly imposed costs. But, the possibility of runs also gives banks a salutary incentive to conduct their affairs to engender confidence among their large depositors. The complete removal of this concern by depositors and of the banks about depositors' fears is likely to lead to greater than optimal risk-taking by banks. In the following section, some changes in the present institutional arrangements are suggested that should lead to a better balance between these conflicting concerns.

To summarize, in today's environment with FDIC insurance, the effect of a failure of a bank on employees and customers (and hence on communities) and even on owners is likely to be less than for most other types of enterprises. With bank runs virtually not a problem, the possibility of failure is no longer a valid reason to subject banks to special regulations other than deposit insurance requirements. (The interests of the deposit insurance agency and of the banks with respect to deposit insurance are considered next.) Indeed, there is reason to believe that many of the regulations imposed on banking increase the possibility of failure. In particular, regulations restricting branching reduce the banks' ability to diversify their deposits geographically. Restrictions on the types and maturities of the products that they can offer their customers similarly restrict their ability to diversify their portfolios. (Witness the current situation of thrift institutions because of past regulations.) Hence, they are more vulnerable to unexpected changes in local economies, the fortunes of specific industries (e. g., housing), and interest rates. The regulations also reduce the alternatives available to customers should a bank fail. Therefore, if concern for bank failures is an important issue, these restrictive regulations should be removed. The only supervising function that might be justified from a concern with failures is the ultimate supervision of mutual institutions.

Deposit Insurance

The Historical Record.   Federal deposit insurance, established in 1933, came about as a consequence of the very large number of bank failures of the early 1930s. These were primarily the consequence of the joint effect of a major sustained decline in the money supply and the U.S. fractionalized banking system, where interstate branching was not allowed and many states prohibited or restricted branching.[25] Consequently, the portfolios of a large number of banks were not diversified geographically or across many types of businesses. Hence, they were inordinately subject to the effects of local economic collapses and to a rapid decline in the money supply. The banks in other countries did not suffer similar failures, because they were able to meet deposit drains with funds drawn from other areas. While the U.S. banks had established relationships with other banks from whom, presumably, they could borrow funds, these express or implied contracts apparently did not hold up in the generally adverse conditions of the early 1930s.[26]

Following the collapse between 1930 and 1933 of 9,096 commercial banks (36.4 percent of those operating in 1929), 526 savings and loan associations (4.4 percent of the total in 1930), and 10 mutual savings banks (1.7 percent of the number in 1930), some reform was politically, if not economically, necessary. The smaller unit banks opposed branch banking and, considering that in 1930–31, 93 percent of the suspended banks had total loans and investments of under $2 million (70 percent were under $500,000), they reasonably feared both gradually lost deposits and runs as depositors sought the safety of larger banks. The large banks wanted to eliminate the payment of interest on demand deposits, since they had been unable to sustain repeated agreements to limit competition among themselves for the deposits of correspondent banks and large nonbank depositors.[27] The apparently politically acceptable compromise was a liberalization of the branch-limiting McFadden Act to permit national banks to branch to the extent that state banks could branch (but not permission to branch regardless of state law either within states or nationally), the legal prohibition of interest payments on demand deposits, and the establishment of the Federal Deposit Insurance Corporation. Although the FDIC insured individual deposit accounts only to a maximum of $2,500 (raised the next year to $5,000), assessments were imposed on a bank's total deposits. Thus, the larger bank that held largely uninsured deposit accounts subsidized the small banks. But, as Carter Golembe estimated, this cost was almost exactly offset by their savings of interest payments on demand deposits.[28]

Federal deposit insurance not only has benefited smaller and particularly unit banks, it has made bank runs no longer a serious problem. Banks are unlike all other enterprises in being subject to the externality of runs. For example, if someone is a bondholder of General Motors Corporation and believes that the company has or is about to absorb large losses, the best that person can do is sell the bond to someone else before the buyer learns of the bad news. The bondholder cannot successfully get General Motors to repay the bond until it is legally due. But, if someone is a demand depositor in a bank and believes that the bank is in financial difficulties, funds can be removed by the person simply by writing a check or personally making a withdrawal. Since a rapid withdrawal of funds by depositors may force the bank to sell assets at distress prices or to borrow at high rates, this may result in losses that exceed the stockholders' investment—losses that will have to be absorbed by the remaining depositors. Therefore, even if the bank is paying depositors interest that compensates them for the risk they take, the depositors are well advised to remove their funds if the possibility of a failure times the deposit balance exceeds the cost of making another banking arrangement plus any interest that might be foregone if it were credited on a delayed basis. With deposit insurance, those depositors whose balances do not exceed the insured amount need not fear a bank failure. While depositors with uninsured balances face potential losses should the bank fail, they need not fear a panic by the presumably uninformed holders of smaller accounts. Furthermore, depositors' experience with the FDIC gives them reason to believe that the deposit liabilities of most banks (especially very large ones) will be assumed by other banks without loss to the depositors. Hence, while they are not completely shielded from loss, the risk is very small and the incentive for panic withdrawals is concomitantly small.

But, because federal deposit insurance saves insured depositors (and, to a large extent, uninsured depositors as well) the cost of learning about the operation of banks, it also serves to free the banks from the discipline of those depositors' concerns. In this situation, the banker has an incentive to put the depositors' funds into risky assets. Should the events turn out well, the banks' stockholders reap the benefits. Should events turn out badly, the FDIC pays off the depositors. While the stockholders also are likely to lose their investments, in the absence of a sufficient risk premium or other costs imposed by the FDIC, the expected gains from risk-taking exceed the expected losses.[29]

Previous (prior to the FDIC) U.S. history bears out this expectation and also provides lessons that should be useful today. Prior to the National Banking Act of 1863, deposit guarantee systems were established in New York (1828), Vermont (1831), Indiana (1834), Ohio (1845), and Iowa (1858).[30] The New York and Vermont systems were state run and the others were based on mutual agreements among the participating banks. Their systems operated successfully, largely because they included the authority of the plan officials to monitor operations of the participating banks and control excessive risk-taking.[31] A second wave of deposit guarantee plans for state banks occurred after 1908. With one exception (Mississippi), the plans did not include effective supervision and they failed. These included the compulsory plans of Oklahoma (1908), Nebraska (1909), and South Dakota (1916), and the voluntary plans of Kansas (1909), Texas (1910), and Washington (1917). Since depositors were told that their money was safe, there was a great incentive for unscrupulous operators to take excessive risks. Indeed, the record shows greater failure rates of guaranteed banks than among similar nonguaranteed banks operating in the same areas. The Mississippi plan (1915), which included supervision and bank examinations, continued until 1930.

Thus, a cost of deposit guarantee represents effective supervision by the insurance company or other authorities and/or the charging of risk-adjusted rates. While fees that reflect the risk could be charged by the FDIC, Federal Savings and Loan Insurance Corporation (FSLIC), and National Credit Union Share Insurance Fund (NCUSIF), they have opted instead to impose costs in the form of onsite examinations on the insured institutions. When the operations of the institutions are considered to be unsafe, the institutions are subject to more frequent and more extensive examinations. The cost of these examinations include per diem fees (levied by some agencies) and the cost of disruption. Restrictions on the institution's right to expand and required infusions of capital also are imposed. More severe penalties include cease and desist orders, the removal of the institution's officers, and its closing or merger with another institution. The extent to which these costs exceed the benefits from deposit guarantees and alternatives to the present system are considered next.

The Present Situation.   Given the past history of bank runs, together with the fractionalized banking system that makes stopping runs difficult, it appears to be necessary to continue deposit insurance. It is possible that the necessity for mandatory deposit insurance would be obviated if the Federal Reserve could be counted on to provide the reserves required to offset runs and if the removal of regulations made it possible for banks to offer depositors an acceptable mix of interest payments, diversified portfolios, and private insurance. But, considering the almost universal expectation by depositors with smaller account balances that they need not acquire information about the riskiness and management of bank assets, continuation of deposit insurance appears to be unavoidable. Also, considering the cost to these borrowers of assessing risks, an insurance system would seem to be cost-effective.

The present system though suffers from three important defects. One is that the procedure of charging depository institutions a flat fee against their total deposit liabilities gives the institutions an incentive to hold riskier assets. At the same time, the insurance agencies (FDIC, FSLIC, and NCUSIF) have a complementary incentive to over-regulate the institutions, since the agencies lose should a failure occur but do not garner the gains from a risk taken. There is no reason to believe that the outcome is reasonably close to optimal, particularly with respect to the efficient allocation of capital. Second, bank runs still can be a problem, since uninsured depositors have a considerable incentive to remove their funds if they believe a bank will fail and not be assumed. Probably because of this expectation, very large banks (which hold relatively large amounts of uninsured deposits) have been loaned large sums of money by the Federal Reserve to keep them from failing and, when they failed, assumptions rather than payments were arranged by the FDIC. Consequently, depositors in such banks are, de facto, 100 percent insured and they no longer serve as monitors of the banks' activities. Collaterally, banks that are thought to be subjected to the payout procedure are placed at a competitive disadvantage. Third, the methods of examination and supervision employed by the agencies are unlikely to be efficient, since each is in a monopoly position with respect to its institutions—for example, national banks cannot elect to be examined by the FDIC, rather than by the Comptroller of the Currency. Although the agencies have made some attempts to improve their supervisory methods in recent years. Flannery and Guttentag (among others) find the techniques used to "fall well short of the state of art."[32] As long as the agencies have a clientele that has no alternatives, they need not be too concerned with the costs of inefficient examinations and oversupervision.

The flat fee compared to variable risk-fee defect could be corrected by requiring the insurance agencies to charge risk-related fees. One might ask, though, why they have failed to adopt this procedure, even though it has been suggested by most writers on the subject and is used by most private companies. The answers might be that the assessment of banking risk is too difficult, would engage the agencies in too great an involvement in banking activities (since risk-related fees have the effect of directing a bank's allocation of resources), or that there presently is no incentive for the agencies to change established procedures. While there is some validity in each explanation, I prefer the last, which implies that, unless the present legal arrangements are altered, the flat-fee system will remain.

The remaining possibility of bank runs could be eliminated and the monitoring by depositors enhanced by the following change. All deposits transferable on demand (including savings deposits for which the 30-day waiting period is almost never invoked) would be completely insured. But, all time deposits over, say, $10,000, would not be insured at all unless a bank wished to purchase the insurance. Under this regime, runs could not occur because the time deposits could not be withdrawn until maturity. But, if a bank was thought to be operated in a manner that might result in a failure, the expectation would be reflected in the interest rates it would have to offer on its time deposits and certificates.

Finally, the defects of inefficient examination and supervision and the charging of inappropriate insurance fees can be cured, or at least reduced, by introducing competition among insurers for the business of financial institutions. Competition can be introduced first by permitting any depository institution to be insured by any of the three federal agencies. The agencies would be permitted to levy the types (e. g., variable rates) and levels of charges and monitoring mechanisms (e. g., examinations) that they felt desirable, and the institutions could switch among the agencies much as any person can choose insurance companies. Then, to introduce even more competition into the market for deposit insurance, depository institutions should be permitted to purchase insurance from private companies or from other banks, as long as these companies and banks were approved by the chartering agency (about which more is said below). The private insurance can be in place of or supplementary to government agency insurance. So that the public is not misinformed, the depository institutions would have to prominently state the insurer they use, much as they now must state "Member Federal Deposit Insurance Corporation."

One should consider the concern that competition among insurers might lead to "agency shopping" by badly or fraudulently run banks wanting to escape regulation. Two factors argue against this possibility. One is the evidence of switches in bank charters. During the years 1960 to 1966, when Comptroller of the Currency James Saxon liberalized regulations, state banks had an incentive to convert to national charters. In the years since the late 1960s, when the opportunity cost of required reserves increased considerably, banks had an incentive to switch to nonmember bank status. But the number of state banks adopting national charters from 1960 through 1977 relative to the number at year-end 1977 was only 5.9 percent. In the same 18-year period, 6.3 percent of the national banks became nonmembers.[33] A detailed study of these (and other) changes revealed that "some, but not many, bankers abuse the forum shopping principle of choice."[34] The second, more important, factor is that a depository institution cannot change to another insurer unless that insurer accepts the institution. Since the insurer bears the cost of a failure, it has a strong incentive to refuse to accept institutions that are badly or fraudulently run.

Control of the Money Supply

Even those economists who do not declare that control of the supply of money is essential believe it to be desirable. The Federal Reserve can effect this control in several ways. As is the procedure in many countries, the central bank could issue and withdraw legal tender by buying and selling securities (open market operations) and by printing currency. The demand deposits' (which hereafter includes such close substitutes as NOW accounts) portion of the money supply then could be controlled via the substitution by money users of currency for deposits and vice versa. The principal problems with this procedure are that demand deposits comprise the bulk of the money supply, the link between deposits and currency is inexact, and there are real resource costs in not permitting the public to have the amount of currency required for day-to-day transactions. Most of these problems can be avoided by using required reserves against demand deposits to control the money supply. The central bank can determine the amount of reserves that banks (hereafter denoting all suppliers of demand deposits) hold with one or a combination of three methods: Adjusting the required reserve ratio, open market operations, and/or controlling borrowing from the central bank. Changes in reserves that result from changes in float, foreign transactions, Treasury operations, shifts among deposits against which different reserve ratios are required (if this practice is followed), and changes in the banks' and the public's desired holdings of excess reserves and currency can be offset with open market operations.

For the effective control of the money supply via reserves, the central bank must have information on the banks' reserve balances and be reasonably assured that the relationship between the reserves and the money supply is stable or, at least, predictable—for example, there will not be unexpected shifts of deposits for money substitutes that it cannot effectively offset. For this purpose it is desirable (but not necessary) that the providers of demand deposits be subject to specified reserve requirements and that they be known to and possibly report to the Federal Reserve. (Reporting would not be necessary if the Fed could adequately estimate the needed data with sampling.)

Monetary policy would be more effective if velocity were more predictable. For this reason, and as an aid to identifying the assets that are used by the public as money, it would be desirable if the opportunity value to nonbanks of providing money substitutes were minimized. For these purposes (and for reasons of equity and the efficient allocation of resources), bank-provided money should not be taxed at a higher rate than other forms of money. This leads to the conclusion that the Federal Reserve should pay interest on the required reserves it holds against demand deposits. The rate of interest should offset the opportunity loss to the banks of the funds required to be held as reserves. With no other regulations imposed on banks (other than required deposit insurance) competition would ensure that the demand deposits, rather than the banks, would benefit from the removal of this tax on their funds. While the government would lose this source of revenue, the public would gain from the Federal Reserve's more effective control of the money supply and from a more efficient allocation of resources. At the same time, tax subsidies to banks should be removed, such as their right to earn tax-free interest on state and municipal bonds while being allowed to deduct against taxable income the cost of funds used to purchase the bonds.

The Furtherance of Social Goals—The Provision of Banking Services

Three general types of social goals are distinguished: (1) the provision of the banking services of loans, fund transfers, and savings; (2) support of housing and other attempts to allocate credit; and (3) prevention of individual discrimination and unfair dealing against individuals. Each is described and analyzed individually in the following sections.

The Historical Record.   Until recently, commercial banks were expected to further social welfare primarily by providing businesses and consumers with an efficient means of making transactions (bank notes and checking) and borrowing and lending assets (loans and savings). The banks also served as a vehicle for collecting taxes (as is discussed above). The additional goal of unrestricted access to these facilities was characteristic of the United States. Hence a powerful, national quasi-monopoly bank, such as the Bank of England, was not permitted to develop until the Federal Reserve was created in 1913; and, for most of the nation's history, bank charters were not difficult to obtain.

It is important to note that the Federal Reserve was not conceived of as a central bank but as a bank for and by bankers. Its function was to facilitate check clearing and to provide other banking services for its members. After it was converted into a central bank by Senator Glass and President Wilson, a principal social purpose still was the development of an efficient nationwide clearing system, as well as a vehicle for eliminating panics and providing the nation with an "elastic" currency. The cost of the system was borne by the members with the noninterest-bearing reserves they were required to keep at the Federal Reserve banks. With the passage of the Depository Institutions Deregulation and Monetary Control Act of 1980, the Fed was directed to charge users of its services for the full cost of those services. By this action, the social desirability of publicly supporting a national payments system was recognized as being no longer a concern of the present.

The United States developed specialized financial institutions in large measure to serve perceived social goals. Mutual savings banks (MSBs) were established (the first in 1816) for the social purpose of providing a place where the working poor could save with safety.[35] These institutions were founded as mutuals, because the costs of providing these services exceeded the revenues derived therefrom; hence, space and personal services often were donated, and the institutions were not taxed. The MSBs were established primarily in the Northeast, where they dominated the market for savings. They did not develop much in other areas of the country, for two reasons. One is that the mutual form of organization made establishment of a new bank difficult, particularly when the charitable desire to help the poor in this way was not as strong as it was in the Northeast. The second is the newly established banks in the other, newer states were not averse to serving the less affluent individuals shunned by the well-established northeastern banks. Because their principal stated goal was service to the working poor, and as a consequence of some failures during the panic of 1873, the MSBs were legally prohibited from investing these peoples' savings in such risky and potentially fraudulent assets as business loans. Consequently, they tended to hold bonds. By 1910, though, about half of their portfolios were in mortgages. The percentage declined after the 1930s and did not get up to about 60 to 70 percent until the 1960s.

Savings and Loan Associations (S&Ls) were established principally to make mortgage loans. They developed from mutual building and loan societies. In the early years of the Great Depression federal chartering of mutual S&Ls was established with the goal of helping the housing industry recover. Thus, although the financial statements of the S&Ls and MSBs now look very similar, they were initially established to serve different social goals.

Consumer finance companies and credit unions also were established for a social purpose. Consumer finance companies were licensed by states (the first in 1916) to make small loans at gross rates that greatly exceeded the states' usury ceilings. The small loan laws were passed when it became clear that the urban population was prevented by the usury statutes from obtaining loans legally; those who were unable to borrow from friends and relatives had to turn to loan sharks. Credit unions similarly were established to provide a source of small loans to individuals. Churches, fraternal groups, and businesses supported their development with donations of space and labor, since they made loans to members of these groups. Their growth also was helped by exemption from taxation.

The Present Situation.   The laws and regulations that first forbade and now constrain thrift associations from serving their clients have had a negative social impact. As consumers' demands changed from wanting a safe haven for savings and for mortgage loans to also wanting a wide range of financial services (particularly checking accounts and consumer loans), the institutions should have been free to offer the products demanded. Furthermore, the institutions were prevented from offering business loans and other services that would have benefited their communities. Similarly, restraints on commercial banks (e. g., the Glass-Steagall Act) that prevent them from offering a full range of services and geographical constraints in the form of prohibitions against intra- and interstate branching have kept them from meeting the social goal of service to consumers. Laws that limit payments to savers—the prohibition of interest on demand deposits and Regulation Q—obviously are contrary to the social goal of not hurting consumers, particularly since these limitations affect mostly the depositors who are ignorant of such alternatives as money market funds or who hold balances that do not meet the funds' minimum requirements. Indeed, it is difficult to find any of the laws and regulations that prohibit or constrain banks or any enterprises from offering their services to the public as operating to further social goals as these usually are expressed. While these constraints may have been imposed to reduce the incidence of bank failure (although that motivation and the effectiveness of the laws and regulations for that purpose are very doubtful in many instances), the advent of deposit guarantees should have eliminated this concern.

The continued provision of payments clearance and other banking services by the Federal Reserve also is no longer relevant for advancing the social concern of improved banking services. Alternative and supplementary services have been offered by nongovernment organizations for some time. Now that all depository institutions that offer third-party transfers are required to maintain reserves with the Federal Reserve banks and all can obtain Federal Reserve services at a price, there seems no reason for these services to be provided by a government agency. Rather, this aspect of the Federal Reserve's operations should be split off into a separate corporation. A method for achieving this transformation is offered in the last section of this article.

Support of Housing and Other Attempts to Allocate Credit as Social Goals

The Historical Record. Housing was adopted as a social goal in the 1930s, when federal chartering of S&Ls and federal guarantees of home mortgage loans were established. This goal was furthered by the creation of the Federal Home Loan Bank Board as a regulatory agency, and the Federal Home Loan Banks, the Government National Mortgage Association, and the Federal Savings and Loan Insurance Corporation as vehicles for diverting funds into home mortgages. The extension of Regulation Q ceilings to thrift associations in 1966 and their continuation at a level below market rates on the savings deposits of all insured depository institutions were justified as means of keeping funds flowing into mortgages. Other means of supporting home ownership were restrictions on the nonmortgage assets in which thrift institutions can invest and the granting of tax benefits if mortgages are above a given percentage of total assets. Most recently, the Home Mortgage Disclosure Act of 1975 and the Community Reinvestment Act of 1977 were enacted to encourage (or force) chartered financial institutions located in older urban areas to make mortgage and other loans in those areas. The former act is simply a disclosure statute that requires the institutions to identify publicly the volume and type of mortgages made by census tract. The Community Reinvestment Act requires institutions to demonstrate they have adequately served their local communities, particularly when they request permission to open or close branches.

Other attempts to allocate credit that can be mentioned include the Federal Reserve's down payment and maturity requirements for consumer cash loans that have been imposed at various times, margin requirements on loans secured by securities, and moral suasion (or threats) by the Federal Reserve Board designed to get banks to forbear from lending for what the authorities consider to be socially undeserving projects.[36]

The Present Situation. Whether housing should be subsidized, while a valid question, need not be addressed here, since the laws and regulations designed to support this industry have not achieved this goal. Indeed there is reason to believe that these constraints have had the opposite effect. These conclusions are based on considerations of the availability and cost of funds for house purchases.

Availability has two dimensions. One is the effect that the number and type of sources have on the quantity (or level) of funds that flow into mortgages. The second is the effect of the variation of the fund flows on house purchases. With respect to the quantity of funds, there is no reason to believe that the required specialization in mortgage lending by a particular set of institutions is either necessary or desirable for funds to flow freely into mortgages. Money is the most fungible of all assets. Mortgage lending requires skills, but there are no barriers or great costs that prevent people from acquiring them or lenders from hiring people who have these skills. As long as there are no constraints on the yields that can be earned by lenders, demands for mortgages will be met by a large number of sources. Even now, people obtain mortgages from mortgage companies and private parties as well as from chartered financial institutions.[37] In addition, people can use their own funds and obtain purchase money mortgages and land sales contracts from the seller (which often are not recorded as mortgages). Furthermore, all of these sources for mortgage funds are available to home buyers in most markets.

Not only are mortgage funds available from many sources, but the evidence does not support the essential assumption that there is a direct and necessary linkage between mortgages and home buying. Mortgages are but one of many means of borrowing money. A house can serve as collateral for funds that are used to purchase other assets. Thus, Dwight Jaffee, who reviewed the relationship between mortgage finance and housing, concludes: "The main effect of developed policies [subsidies and interventions in the mortgage market] has been to extend greatly the use of mortgage debt in the U.S., but without any appreciable payoff in terms of housing investment."[38] From his review of several studies, Allan Meltzer similarly finds "no evidence that the availability of the particular type of credit has any important or lasting effect on the type of assets individuals acquire. If the housing market is the market in which 'availability matters' or matters most, there appears to be very little if any empirical basis for the conjecture on the public policies based on it."[39]

Variation in the amount of funds available for mortgages, though, is likely to be an important short-run deterrent to house purchases. If a mortgage cannot be obtained, at virtually any price, houses can be purchased by very few people. This situation can occur when thrift institutions dominate mortgage lending in an area because laws and regulations give them a comparative advantage over other lenders. (These advantages may be positive, in the form of tax breaks and other subsidies, or negative, in the form of penalties that other lenders can avoid.) Then, when an event such as an unexpected increase in interest rates results in a reduced flow of funds to the thrift institutions, because they are unable to offer the market rate for deposits, a major source of mortgages is cut off. Unexpected increases in interest rates also can result in the failure of the specialized thrift institutions, since they are unable to match the maturity (or duration) of their assets and liabilities. Consequently, they are subjected to capital losses when the value of their assets (mortgages) decreases, but they must pay the market rate on their liabilities (time deposits) or face disintermediation. Such failures obviously reduce the flow of funds to mortgages, at least until other lenders obtain the required skills to meet the demand.

Expected variations in fund flows also tend to reduce the flow of funds to mortgages. In this situation, lenders usually find it desirable to maintain assets that can be sold and purchased at relatively low transaction costs. Nonspecialized lenders can hold a mix of assets and liabilities where the expected fund flows tend to offset each other. Since, until recently, thrift institutions generally were not permitted to invest in consumer and business loans and to obtain checking account deposits, they tended to hold bonds as a buffer stock (secondary reserve). In those states (such as Connecticut) where the mutual savings banks could hold consumer loans, the institutions tended to hold relatively fewer bonds and more mortgages.[40] Hence, enforced specialization tended to reduce the flow of funds to mortgages.

Turning now to the cost of mortgage funds, it is obvious that the greater the number of lenders vying to make mortgages, the lower the cost to mortgagors. And, the greater the variation of funds to lenders and borrowers, the greater the costs to both. Therefore, laws and regulations that restrict entry into the mortgage market and that require financial institutions to specialize in mortgages tend to increase the cost of mortgages.

A final question that should be considered is whether subsidies to thrift institutions in return for their specializing in mortgage lending are likely to be supportive of housing (whether these subsidies are otherwise justified). The subsidies take the form of lower taxes and legally imposed limits on the amounts that can be offered to depositors (Regulation Q). As is discussed above, the first form of subsidy is likely to increase the variation and reduce the flow of funds available for mortgages, because of the enforced specialization of the institutions in mortgages and the reduced incentives of other lenders to make this type of loan (witness the virtual withdrawal of life insurance companies from one to four family unit mortgages). The second is only temporarily useful, even if one assumes that the lower interest rates paid to depositors are passed on to home buyers. As we have seen in the past and are witnessing today, when market interest rates are above the Regulation Q ceilings, disintermediation occurs. The enormous growth of money market mutual funds is due entirely to the desire and ability of savers and entrepreneurs to get and offer the best return on funds. But, unfortunately for those who want to obtain mortgages, the savers who take their money out of the thrift institutions that specialize in the mortgages and purchase money market mutual funds' shares are actually redepositing their funds principally in commercial banks and are financing corporate and government borrowing. The money market mutual funds tend to hold commercial paper, U. S. treasury issues, and the certificates of deposit (CDs) of large commercial banks. They hold these CDs because only CDs over $100,000 can bear market rates of interest, and CDs of these amounts are not guaranteed by the FDIC. Hence, the funds would be foolish to risk investment in the CDs of thrift institutions, many of which are in danger of bankruptcy, or of smaller commercial banks, about which information is more expensive to obtain and which are more likely to be permitted by the FDIC to fail than are the very large banks.

The effectiveness of directing credit by regulation toward other specified assets and borrowers has also been found to be slight and often dysfunctional. A number of these studies are surveyed by Thomas Mayer, who concludes: "As the above has shown, credit allocation is not an efficient system. The shifts in the distribution of credit which it tried to bring about are of doubtful value, and, in any case, credit allocation would be ineffective in the long run."[41] When the controls are effective (in the short run), they cause borrowers and lenders to incur the costs of complying with and attempting to avoid the controls. While some borrowers are advantaged and some set of social goals advanced, the effect, at best, is temporary. At worst, the benefits do not flow to those who are presumed to be aided, but to others who are more adept at using regulations to their advantage.

With such credit allocation laws as the Community Reinvestment Act of 1977, harm rather than good is likely to be done to those for whom the law presumably is directed. The law requires chartered financial institutions to direct loans to mortgages on local houses and businesses, particularly if these are in older, blighted areas. If lenders would make these loans without the law, compliance costs are needlessly imposed. If these loans would not be made because the risks exceed the interest rates that can be charged (given institutional or legal constraints), the law encourages institutions to leave the area and discourages others who are similarly regulated from opening branches in the area. In either event, while the volume of loans flowing into the area may be increased initially, the funds will tend to be directed toward the least risky borrowers. As lenders can adjust to the situation, consumers in the area will find fewer sources of funds and other banking services.[42] The law will benefit consumers only if bankers had been discriminating against borrowers for noneconomic reasons and, as a consequence of the law, they were led or forced to give up their taste for discrimination. With respect to mortgages particularly, almost all of the empirical studies find no evidence of discrimination against persons or areas (redlining).[43]

Prevention of Invidious Discrimination and Unfair Dealing against Persons

The Historical Record.   Laws that explicitly prohibit invidious discrimination in the provision of banking services (especially loans) were first enacted in 1968.[44] The Fair Housing Act of 1968 prohibited banks and other lenders from denying mortgages or home improvement loans on account of a person's race, color, religion, sex, or national origin. The Equal Credit Opportunity Act (Title VII of the Consumer Protection Act—CCPA—of 1968), enacted in 1974 and amended in 1976, added prohibitions against all credit discrimination on the grounds of age, race, religion, national origin, receipt of public welfare benefits, and exercise of rights under the CCPA. The Federal Reserve's Regulation B supplements the law. Regulations written under the dictates of the Community Reinvestment Act of 1977 forbid the alleged practice of denying mortgage and home improvement loans on properties solely because they are old or are located in older areas (redlining).

Several laws are directed at providing borrowers with complete information and forbidding certain practices in the belief that without these laws borrowers would be victimized. The Truth-in-Lending Act of 1968 (Title I of the CCPA) requires disclosure of credit costs and terms on consumer loans and long-term leases of consumer goods. It also regulates the content of credit advertising and regulates credit card distribution, terms, and liabilities. The provisions of the act are implemented by the Federal Reserve's detailed and lengthy Regulation Z. The Electronic Fund Transfer Act (Title IX of the CCPA), enacted in 1978, requires disclosure of account terms, documentation of transfers and prompt error resolution, limits the consumer's liability for unauthorized transfers, and imposes liability for unauthorized transfers by financial institutions. The Real Estate Settlement Procedures Act, adopted in 1974 and amended in 1976, requires mortgage lenders to provide borrowers with a statement of actual charges, forbids kickbacks of settlement fees and tie-ins of sales of title insurance, and limits escrows for taxes and insurance. The Right to Financial Privacy Act of 1978 restricts the right of government agencies to gain access to a consumer's banking records.

Finally, some lending and collection practices of creditors are constrained or prohibited by various laws. The Fair Credit Reporting Act (Title VI of the CCPA), passed in 1970, regulates the content, accuracy, and disclosure of credit and investigative reports furnished to creditors, employers, and insurers in connection with consumer transactions. Title III of the CCPA establishes a minimum level of wages that are exempted from garnishment and prohibits an employer from firing an employee because of a single garnishment. The Fair Debt Collections Act (Title VIII of the CCPA), enacted in 1977, prohibits abusive and coercive collection practices and requires bill collectors to provide debtors with certain information. It applies to banks only insofar as they collect the debts of other lenders. In addition, the Federal Trade Commission's holder-in-due-course rule, issued in 1975, effectively abolished this protection for banks which discounted consumers' notes made to retailers.

In addition, the states have enacted laws that similarly regulate credit practices. Some of these parallel the federal Truth-in-Lending and Equal Credit Opportunity Acts. In several states, notably California, the anti-redlining regulations are more severe than the federal regulations. Most states have usury statutes that stipulate the maximum interest rate that can be charged on various types of loans. These laws are quite diverse and complex. The Uniform Consumer Credit Code, promulgated in 1969, has been adopted by only six states, and they changed various provisions. (In contrast, the Uniform Commercial Code has been adopted virtually intact by almost all states.) Finally, the laws of various states restrict creditors' collection remedies more severely than do the federal statutes. These restrictions on contractual provisions include prohibitions against confession of judgment clauses or cognovit notes, restrictions on collateral available as security, restrictions on deficiency judgments following repossession, and limitations on cosigner agreements.

The Present Situation.   Assuming (as I do, as an ethical value) that invidious discrimination against individuals should not be permitted as a matter of social policy, two questions related to the laws and regulations should be considered. First, are these laws effective in eliminating or reducing invidious discrimination at a cost that is not excessive? Second, is the particular way in which these laws are enforced preferable relative to alternatives? While answers to these questions appear to require value-based assumptions about the meaning of the words *excessive* and *preferable,* important aspects of the answers need not await agreement about their operational meaning.

A preliminary question, though, is whether invidious discrimination by financial institutions was a serious problem before the laws were enacted. If such were not the case, the laws simply impose costs on the institutions and their customers without yielding benefits to those whom the laws purport to help. Passage of the Equal Credit Opportunity Act was supported by testimony before the National Commission on Consumer Finance and before Congressional committees that described incidents of invidious discrimination in lending to women.[45] However, any activity, including credit granting, is conducted with some error and insensitivity. When these occur to women, blacks, or other persons who have experienced invidious discrimination in other situations, the refusal of credit is likely to appear to have been deliberate and unfair. Since testimony by men and whites who were turned down for loans was not heard, it is not possible to know whether the lenders systematically practiced discrimination.

Several studies have been conducted since the hearings that find no evidence of invidious discrimination against women. Chandler and Ewert examined the records of slightly over 2,000 credit card applicants at a large metropolitan bank, drawn from applications made between 1971 through early 1974, prior to the passage of the Equal Credit Opportunity Act (ECOA).[46] They constructed credit scoring models to determine the effect of using or not using an applicant's gender as a variable in rejecting or accepting applicants and, if the applicant was accepted, whether the person would be predicted to be a good or bad (loss) payer. They found that, when the applicant's gender was included as a variable, 22 percent more females would be accepted, compared to excluding gender as is required by the ECOA. Among those accepted, use of gender would have identified 19 percent more good payers and the same number of bad payers.[47] Thus, if these data are typical, the ECOA regulations tended to make credit cards more difficult to obtain for females and to have imposed greater losses on lenders.

The question of whether commercial banks discriminated against female small loan borrowers before enactment of the ECOA was studied with data obtained by the Federal Reserve from 30 banks in five regions, each consisting of a major metropolitan area plus surrounding environs.[48] Randomly selected data from the pre-ECOA period of 1966–71 included 3,000 charged-off, 12,000 good paid-off, and 13,500 new direct consumer loans. These were analyzed with a well-specified model to see if commercial banks systematically discriminated against one sex or another in granting consumer credit by oversecuring loans, thereby reducing loss ratios and probabilities, credit-rationing to reduce loss probabilities, or charging higher rates to certain borrowers based on sex. The study found: "Overall, the tests provided extensive evidence that commercial banks did not discriminate against potential borrowers based on their sex before ECOA (Equal Credit Opportunities Act) was passed."[49] The only other studies of which I am aware consider possible invidious discrimination in mortgage lending related to the area in which the home is located (redlining) or the race or other personal characteristics of the actual or potential mortgagor. With one exception, all of these find no evidence of invidious discrimination in the denials of loan applications, the types of loans made or the terms charged.[50]

Thus, the empirical analyses do not find evidence of discrimination in lending by financial institutions in the years before or after the laws prohibiting such discrimination were enacted. This result is not surprising if one views lenders as people who prefer to maximize their wealth. If they are bigots and if they and their shareholders are willing to accept lower rewards (and it is likely that some are, considering that more than a few people speak and act in this way), it seems unlikely that they would indulge this taste on people with whom their principal contact is a loan agreement and the receipt of repayments (usually by mail).

While the benefits to those who are supposed to be protected by the anti-discrimination acts at best appear to be negligible (and possibly are negative), the costs to financial institutions (and, therefore, to their customers) are substantial. James Smith estimated these for compliance with the Federal Reserve's Regulation B that implemented the antidiscrimination provisions of the ECOA.[51] He included the nonrecurring costs of legal fees, training, and obsolete form removal and the additional costs of printing and mailing notices, changing systems, and handling responses due to the requirements that women be informed that they can establish separate credit records. These costs are estimated to be $88.6 million for financial institutions (commercial banks, thrift associations, credit unions, and finance companies) and $78.8 million for merchants (retailers, oil companies, and other credit card issuers). Recurring costs include increased losses, collection expense, and record retention costs. These annual costs are estimated to be $68.8 million for financial institutions and $58.7 million for merchants.

Chartered depository institutions are subjected to additional costs in the form of compliance examinations. Rohner reports that, in the fiscal year ended June 1978, 9,117 compliance examinations were conducted and $7.1 million was spent by the federal banking agencies (FDIC, Federal Reserve, and Comptroller of the Currency).[52] Additional examinations and expenditures were made by state agencies. In addition, the banks incurred additional costs related to the examinations, including the cost of special computer runs, time spent with examiners, and the opportunity cost of constraints on banking operations that examiners might question. Indeed, bankers are reported to find these examinations particularly costly and of very limited benefit to consumers. In a study of the opinions of banks, regulators, and consumer specialists toward federal and state regulation, Gloria Elhat elicited opinions on the following aspects of consumer protection: credit discrimination, disclosure, community reinvestment, creditor practices and remedies, and regulation of loan terms (interest rates, maturities, and amounts).[53] She reports most (from 70 to 90 percent) of the bankers saying that compliance with the consumer protection laws are "very or quite" costly and were not important in protecting consumers.[54] The regulators and examiners interviewed tended to agree with the bankers (though they were not as strongly negative, particularly with respect to the importance of the limitations on creditor practices). Not surprisingly, the professional consumer advocates were of the opposite opinion. Thus, all except the consumer advocates believe that the consumer protection laws as administered are considerably more costly than beneficial. Assuming, though, that these laws are not repealed, it seems clear that they can be administered in a more efficient and more equitable manner than by compliance examinations. This issue is considered further below.

CONTEMPORARY REASONS FOR AND METHODS OF REGULATING BANKING—A RECAPITULATION

No Longer Relevant Reasons

Taxation.   Restriction of entry as a means of enhancing taxes, the initial reason for bank regulation, is no longer relevant. (The effect of differential taxation of depository institutions compared to other suppliers of banking services is discussed below.)

Prevention of Centralized Power.   Restriction of entry for this purpose also is no longer relevant, if it ever was. In particular, there is no reason to believe that the removal of all restrictions on branching or holding companies would result in the demise of small locally owned banks. Indeed, if further decentralization of banking services is desired, all legal restrictions on entry and the provision of services, by banks as well as other enterprises, should be removed.

Bank Solvency and the Effects of Failures on the Economy.   The requirement of deposit insurance has eliminated concerns about bank runs and the consequent effects on the economy. While bank failures, as such, are not desirable, they now are likely to be somewhat less disruptive on employees, customers, and local economies than are the failures of most other types of enterprises. Therefore, special government supervision of financial institutions (with the possible exception of mutuals) is no longer justified for this reason.

The Social Goal of Available Banking Services.   Regulations that prevent or impede organizations from providing services to the public violate this social goal. Consequently, such constraints as limitations on the banking services that thrift institutions can provide, securities services that commercial banks can offer, and interest that can be offered to depositors are undesirable. There also no longer is any reason to subsidize the payments mechanism by maintaining it as a Federal Reserve operation.

Support of Housing and Other Attempts to Allocate Credit.   It is unlikely that enforced specialization of thrift institutions as providers of mortgages benefits the production and sale of houses. To the contrary, such specialization tends to increase the variance of fund flows into mortgages, which works a temporary hardship to those who want to buy and sell houses. Interest-rate ceilings on deposits and mortgages also restrict the flow of funds to mortgages. Credit-directing legislation, particularly the Community Reinvestment Act, raises the cost of lending and is unlikely actually to direct a greater flow of funds to the presumably favored borrowers, except perhaps in the very short run. Such legislation, though, tends to raise costs to bank customers and allocate resources inefficiently. Consequently, if support of the housing market is a social goal, the existing regulations on lenders and prices should be removed.

Possibly Relevant Reasons

Taxation.   If the government wants to levy a tax on bank-supplied money, it can do so efficiently by requiring all enterprises that supply this product to maintain a given percentage of the relevant deposits as noninterest-bearing reserves with the Federal Reserve. With the exception of equality of reserve ratios among enterprises (larger banks are required to hold higher percentages than smaller banks), this procedure is presently being followed. Any regulation on entry, products supplied, interest paid or charged, and so on would either be unnecessary or counter productive, since anything that impeded or made more costly the supply of bank money would favor nontaxed substitutes, such as credit cards.

Money Supply Control.   The Federal Reserve can exercise control over the money supply by requiring all suppliers of third-party transfers (demand deposits and close substitutes) to maintain reserves and, possibly, to report statistics. Alternatively, the Federal Reserve could control the money supply simply by predicting the effect of open market operations, on the assumption that the relationship between voluntarily held reserves and money is predictable. In either event, unexpected changes in the money supply and velocity can be reduced by making substitutes for specified third-party transfers less desirable. This can be accomplished by removing the tax on required reserves represented by the opportunity loss on these presently noninterest-bearing funds. At the same time, tax subsidies to banks should be removed.

Avoidance of Competition.   Regulations that restrict entry are particularly beneficial to those providing a product or service. Thus, the present requirement that those who would open banks must obtain a charter, the granting of which is not automatic even if some basic qualifications are fulfilled (such as the obtaining of deposit insurance), provides an opportunity for existing bankers or other competitors to raise objections. Restrictions on interstate and intrastate branching also serve to reduce competition. Competition is reduced further by laws and regulations that restrict thrift associations from providing a wide range of banking services (most of which have now been removed or reduced), prevent commercial banks from providing securities services, impose interest rate ceilings on deposit accounts, and restrain nonchartered enterprises from providing depository banking services. Indeed, restraining competition is a very relevant past and contemporary reason for regulation. However, as the advantages from avoiding restrictions grow and as technological change and innovations reduce the cost of avoiding the laws and regulations, the constraints serve predominantly to raise costs to consumers with fewer and fewer benefits to the increasingly less-protected producers.

The Protection of Depositors and Bank Solvency. Since the creation of the FDIC and the other federal deposit insurance agencies, this concern is relevant only insofar as the requirement of deposit insurance tends to restrict competition and innovation and to increase the cost to consumers of credit and other banking services. Solvency, as such, is a currently relevant regulatory problem only for mutual associations—and then only because there are no stockholders and securities market to discipline wayward managers.

Prevention of Invidious Discrimination and Unfair Dealing against Persons. The legislative history indicates that this concern is currently relevant, even though there is no scientifically acceptable evidence that supports the underlying belief that financial institutions invidiously discriminated, at least in recent times. The present procedure of compliance examinations, though, is neither cost-effective nor fair. Further discussion and an alternative method are presented below.

RECOMMENDATIONS

Regulatory Agencies

Comptroller of the Currency. Other than as a means of allowing existing suppliers to avoid competition, there is almost no purpose served by requiring those who would provide banking services and banks which would provide other services to obtain regulatory permission. But, since state laws require banks to have charters, and since depository insurance is desirable to protect banks from runs and depositors from losses, the Comptroller of the Currency (and the Federal Home Loan Bank Board) should be directed to provide charters to any corporation that offers demand deposit or similar services to the public as long as it has obtained satisfactory insurance. The Comptroller (or the FHLBB) also would issue permits to foreign banks to have offices in the United States. The only conditions imposed on these banks would be that they have deposit insurance comparable to that required of U. S. banks. The comptroller also would be responsible for getting foreign countries to accept U. S. banks' offices. The principal function of the comptroller, then, would be to evaluate and approve a list of insurance companies and be assured that coverage is maintained. Examination and other supervisory functions are the concern only of the insurers.

Federal Home Loan Bank Board.   The functions of this agency are similar to those of the Comptroller of the Currency. Its continued existence is justified for two reasons. First, it provides potential and present federally chartered deposit providers with an alternative to the Comptroller of the Currency. The ability of banks to switch to another chartering agency, even if seldom exercised, constrains the agencies somewhat from attempting to expand their control. Second, the FHLBB administrators have experience in dealing with thrifts and with mutual associations. Therefore, until this situation changes, the FHLBB would charter mutual savings and loan associations and mutual savings banks. If these institutions should wish to convert to stockholder status, this agency would be charged with seeing that the public was not cheated. This could be accomplished by supervising the sale of stock by the mutual institutions, the proceeds of which would be returned to the U. S. Treasury (since a large portion of the equity in the associations is due to favorable tax laws and protective regulations).[55] For those institutions that remain mutuals, the FHLBB would provide residual authoritative control, should it be necessary to remove or discipline incompetent or dishonest officers.

Federal Home Loan Banks.   These institutions already operate as if they were privately owned banks. They should be considered as such, with ownership transferred entirely to the member associations in the form of marketable stock. At this point, there is no reason for them to be treated differently than other banks, particularly with respect to taxation and Treasury guarantees of their debt obligations.

National Credit Union Administration.   Since credit unions are mutuals and often operate as charitable or fraternal organizations, some chartering and residual administration is likely to be necessary. These services would be provided much as they are now.

The Federal Reserve Board.   The Fed should function solely as a central bank that is concerned only with control of the money supply and the collection of statistics that are considered necessary for this and other governmental tasks. Membership in the Federal Reserve has been an anachronism for some time (roughly not long after the Fed was founded as a government bank, rather than as the originally intended bankers' bank). With the passage of the Depository Institutions Deregulation and Monetary Control Act of 1980, which required reserves of all depository institutions and allowed them access to the Fed's services, membership now has almost no meaning. Hence, the Fed should forego its examination and supervision of state member banks.[56] Since there is no present purpose (other than restrictions on competition) of bank holding company legislation, and since there is no reason to treat bank mergers as different than any other type of mergers, these aspects of Federal Reserve bank supervision are not required.[57]

The Federal Reserve's payments system should be set up as a private corporation, with the marketable stock distributed to the member banks in exchange for their stock in the Federal Reserve. The Fed's related buildings, equipment, other assets, liabilities, and personnel should be ceded to this new corporation.

Since it controls base money, the Fed would continue to be the "lender of last resort." Its borrowing facilities would be available to all institutions that maintained reserves with it. Should an institution wish to borrow reserves, it could do so only at a penalty rate. Furthermore, the institution's deposit insurance company would have to be notified and its objections (if any) would have to be considered since the insurer bears the cost of a failure.

The Federal Reserve, then, would only maintain the reserves of providers of third-party transfers, transfer balances upon request by the newly private payments system corporation and banks that have reserves at the Fed, issue currency (at a fee) to banks and others, continue to collect statistics, and serve as the lender of last resort. This reduction in responsibility would free it to improve its management of the money supply.

Depositors' Insurance

All institutions that offered funds transferred on demand would be required to have depositors' insurance. The insurance companies would have the responsibility of estimating the risk assumed and setting the insurance fees. By agreement with the institutions in which depositors' accounts are insured, the companies might conduct field examinations and maintain the power to remove officers, issue cease and desist orders, and have the institutions' stockholders increase their investments. The deposit insurers' powers and responsibilities would be similar to those of other insurance companies, with the practices employed tailored to the risks undertaken.

To control the insurers' power and work toward greater monitoring efficiency, depository institutions should be permitted to purchase insurance from any company approved by their chartering agency. These companies would include the FDIC, FSLIC, and NCUSIF. They would remain government agencies, at least for the present. But other private companies, including banks, could enter the market. As a consequence of competition, the insurers have an incentive to set the fees charged and conduct examinations in an efficient manner. If they conduct unnecessary or inefficient examinations and fail to adopt cost-effective procedures for assessing risk and keeping the insured institutions from engaging in overly risky and potentially fraudulent behavior, the institutions have an incentive to get insurance from another agency or company. But if the insurers do not institute effective controls, they bear the costs of failures and frauds. Given this incentive there is no role for the Office of the Comptroller of the Currency, the Federal Reserve Board, the Federal Home Loan Bank Board, or the National Credit Union Administration to play (except as noted above for mutuals).

Bank Holding Company Regulation

Bank holding companies presently are regulated by the Federal Reserve. Since the affiliated banks may be chartered by states and by the Comptroller of the Currency, this regulatory structure is subject to interagency conflicts and inadequate supervision.[58] In addition, the Federal Reserve has the responsibility of approving multibank holding company acquisitions but not the authority to grant charters or approve branches, both of which could offset the possible anticompetitive effects of a reduced number of independent banking firms.

If the recommendations set forth here are adopted, these problems will disappear. Entry will be essentially unrestricted and banks will no longer be supervised, except by their insurance agency or company and by the same authorities that are concerned with other enterprises (e.g., the SEC and the Justice Department). The deposit insurer, which is concerned that the insured bank does not waste its assets, may look to the bank's arrangements with its parent (if it is a subsidiary corporation) and with related corporations. (Similarly, the insurer would be concerned about any arrangements that are likely to be conducted at less than arm's length.) Furthermore, the insurer probably would want the distinction between the insured bank and noninsured related companies to be clear to the public, perhaps by insisting on quite different names. In any event, neither the Federal Reserve nor any other banking agency would have a role to play.

Anti-Discrimination and Other Consumer Protection Laws

Economic reasoning and evidence supports the conclusion that consumers are protected best by competition among suppliers for the consumers' trade. Therefore, the social objective of benefiting consumers will be served by removing legal barriers to entry and inefficiencies that raise costs to consumers, as is recommended above. Laws that make invidious discrimination against consumers illegal and that specify how credit terms are to be stated and which specify collection practices may not be required additionally.

But the antidiscrimination laws serve a symbolic function as well as provide a basis for the legal authorities to investigate and act on consumer complaints. And the credit practice laws may be justified as protecting ignorant and powerless consumers from a relatively few unscrupulous suppliers (though such scoundrels usually are quite willing to break the law). However, if the laws are to be effective and fair, they should apply to all suppliers of credit and other banking services. Financial institutions clearly are not the sole suppliers of these services, and, if the recommendations made herein are adopted, they will be even less so. Indeed, more consumer credit is supplied by retail stores, mortgage bankers, consumer finance companies, and sales finance companies than by depository institutions.

The present difference in the application of antidiscrimination and credit practices laws among suppliers of credit is that only the depository institutions are subjected to compliance field examinations. Not only is this difference in administration unfairly burdensome to a subset of credit suppliers, but there is no reason to believe that the result is beneficial to consumers. The costs of the examinations are considerable both for the examining agencies and for the institutions examined. Furthermore, because depository institutions tend to serve more highly educated and wealthier individuals than do other suppliers of credit, laws designed toward protecting the ignorant and powerless should not be applied more stringently to them than to other suppliers. On the possible benefits side, studies have found no evidence of discrimination in credit granting by banks before the laws were enacted nor (to my knowledge) have studies been publicly released that show improvements. Furthermore, the use of field examinations to determine whether a law has been violated is contrary to most U.S. legal practice. The only other similar instances of which I am aware are field examinations for violations of health laws. These are justified as preventing damage to consumers for which compensating damages would not be adequate. But such is not the case of violations of antidiscrimination laws. Therefore, field compliance examinations of depository institutions should no longer be conducted. The authority and responsibility for enforcing the antidiscrimination and other consumer protection laws should be vested in the Justice Department or the Federal Trade Commission.

Taxation

Resources tend to be inefficiently allocated when alternative suppliers of goods are subjected to different degrees of taxation. This is the situation for suppliers of deposit services. Because the reserves required against deposits held by the Federal Reserve banks do not bear interest, the suppliers and thus the users of bank money are subjected to a special tax. This tax could be removed by having the Federal Reserve pay interest on the reserves.[59] However, two other important differences in taxation should be mentioned and considered. One is that hand-to-hand currency does not, and in practice cannot, bear interest. Furthermore, if the government chooses to tax with inflation, there is no reason to give part of this tax to the suppliers of bank money via the multiple expansion of deposits. Therefore, some tax on bank money is equitable and efficient. Second, present tax laws permit banks, and only banks, to deduct against taxable income the full cost of funds used to purchase interest tax-free state and municipal bonds. (These costs include the operations costs of processing demand deposits less fees charged plus explicit interest payments and implicit payments in the form of lower loan and other charges to depositors.) A careful study of the incidence of these taxes and benefits is beyond the scope of this paper. But if taxes on all suppliers of banking services are to be equalized, such a study is necessary (though given political reality, unlikely to be sufficient).

Repeal of Laws

A number of laws should be repealed or suitably amended to remove federal restrictions from financial institutions, as specified above. These laws include the McFadden-Douglas Act, the Banking Act of 1933 as it pertains to bank regulation, the Bank Holding Company Act, and the Community Reinvestment Act. Regulations that set ceilings on interest payments and charges (either on demand or time deposits on loans) and that call for compliance field examinations also should be rescinded.

The effect of the changes suggested above on the dual banking system should be mentioned. The states will have the power to charter banks. They also might choose to examine and otherwise regulate them, but that would be a waste of resources since there is no public interest in this activity. Rather, the states' principal role will be to assure the residents that, if the Comptroller of the Currency ever limits the institutions that would serve the state, there is an alternative source of charters. In addition, the states could impose regulations and taxes on banks, much as they do on other companies that do business in their jurisdictions.

CONCLUSION

The suggested removal of almost all legal restrictions that especially constrain financial institutions is based on the underlying assumption that the purpose of regulation is to benefit consumers, rather than producers. The historical analysis presented above shows that most of the reasons for regulating banking are no longer relevant. Furthermore, credit is supplied by a very large number of other enterprises, including retail stores, gas stations, mortgage bankers, security brokers, commercial paper dealers, pension funds, and insurance companies. Except for the possibility of runs and the propensity of financial intermediaries to be defrauded, banks are no different from other businesses. Consequently, only the requirement that providers of third-party transfers (checking accounts) have deposit insurance should be imposed. Also, the laws forbidding invidious discrimination against individuals and protection to consumers should be reconsidered and, at the least, applied equally to all credit suppliers, and taxes imposed on all suppliers should be equal. Only those suppliers that benefit from keeping the constraints on competition and regulators whose domains would be reduced should object.

NOTES

[1] The principal regulators for banks would be the state banking commissions and the Securities Exchange Commission (SEC). For an analysis of the disclosure regulations of the SEC and proposals for reform, see my essay, "Security for Investors," in *Instead of Regulation: Alternatives to Federal Regulatory Agencies,* ed. Robert W. Poole, Jr. (Lexington, Mass.: Lexington Books, D. C. Heath, 1982), pp. 169–205.

[2] Alternatives to the present system are not considered herein.

[3] See Vera C. Smith, *The Rationale of Central Banking* (London: P. S. King and Son, Ltd., 1936).

[4] The Bank of England did not have a complete monopoly. A few smaller banks of issue were permitted to operate outside of London, and entry was essentially unlimited in Scotland.

[5] See Hugh Rockoff, "The Free Banking Era; A Reexamination," *Journal of Money, Credit and Banking* VI (May 1974), pp. 141–67.

[6] For estimates of the tax imposed, see George J. Benston, *Federal Reserve Membership: Consequences, Costs, Benefits and Alternatives.* A Study Prepared for the Trustees of the Banking Research Fund of the Association of Reserve City Bankers, Chicago, 1978, chap. III.

[7] See Deane Carson and Paul H. Cootner, "The Structure of Competition in Commercial Banking in the United States," Research Study Two in *Private Financial Institutions.* Prepared for the Commission on Money and Credit (Englewood Cliffs, N. J.: Prentice-Hall, 1963), pp. 56–59. They give three reasons for the limited lives of the two federally-chartered banks: (1) concerns by agrarian and small business borrowers with concentrated banking power; (2) sentiment for unit banking (the U.S. banks were establishing branches); and (3) desire for inflation (the U.S. banks were conservative note issuers).

[8] Carson and Cootner, p. 65.

[9] Ibid., p. 73.

[10] H. Parker Willis, "The Demand for Centralized Banking," *Sound Currency* 8 (March 1902), pages 23–24.

[11] While there is reason to believe that this centralized power should be restrained, perhaps by repealing the legal tender laws and allowing alternative currencies and other means of payment to be used, the issue presently is moot.

[12] For a review of these studies, see George J. Benston, "Economies of Scale in Banking," *Journal of Money, Credit and Banking* IV (May 1972), pages 312–41; and George J. Benston, Gerald A. Hanweck, and David H. Humphrey, "Operating Costs in Commercial Banks," *Economic Review,* (Federal Reserve Bank of Atlanta), November 1982.

[13] George J. Benston, Gerald Hanweck, and David H. Humphrey, "Scale Economies in Banking: A Restructuring and Reinterpretation," *Journal of Money, Credit and Banking* XIV (November 1982).

[14] Even if banking were characterized by economies of scale, consumers still would benefit by the removal of organizational constraints as long as entry were unrestricted. In this event, should a bank drive out its competitors by underpricing them, it could not subsequently raise its charges without inviting in new competitors or reviving the old ones. Considering that there are few physical, capital, or technological barriers to entry, predatory pricing would seem to be a foolish practice, but one that is beneficial to consumers if it is practiced.

[15] The most comprehensive work on the legislation lists the alleged abuses but does not cite any evidence of their occurrence. See W. Nelson Peach, *The Security Affiliates of National Banks* (Baltimore: Johns Hopkins Press, 1941).

[16] Between 1927 and 1930, the participation of banks in bond issues grew from 36.8 percent to 61.2 percent. Ibid., p. 110.

[17] The Scottish experience is one of stable banking, much more so than the experience of England with its central bank and restrictions on entry and competition.

[18] See Rockoff, "The Free Banking Era," from which this account is drawn.

[19] Ibid., p. 146.

[20] Ibid., pp. 150–51.

[21] George J. Benston, "Bank Examination," *The Bulletin* of the Institute of Finance, Graduate School of Business Administration, New York University, nos. 89–90, May 1973, table 11, p. 12.

[22] Ibid., table 11, p. 12.

[23] Clark Warburton carefully studied the relationship between bank failures by county and the 1930s depression. He concludes: "There was a massive contraction of deposits nationally during the early 1930s, relative to the rate of growth during the 1920s, of which less than one fourth was accounted for by deposits in suspended banks. This indicated that the depression of the 1930s could not be explained by the impact of balances of payment resulting from adverse conditions in particular industries or areas, but was due to, or at least associated with, some potent force operating on a national scale." *Depression, Inflation and Monetary Policy, Selected Papers: 1945–1953* (Baltimore: Johns Hopkins Press, 1966), p. 2.

[24] An exception is the small run on the Franklin Savings Bank when the Franklin National Bank (an unrelated institution) failed.

[25] Note Warburton's study referenced above, the concentration of suspensions among small banks (noted below), particularly those in the agricultural areas, and the very few failures of branch banks noted above.

[26] The only important exception is the mutual savings banks. Apparently because of a fraternity derived from shared mutualism, they provided each other with the currency needed to pay off anxious depositors and, then, stem incipient runs. They also benefited from not practicing reserve banking and from their concentration in long-maturity assets, the present values of which increased when interest rates declined unexpectedly.

[27] See Carter Golembe, "Memorandum re: Interest on Demand Deposits," Carter H. Golembe Associates, Inc., vol. 1975–10 for an excellent review of the legislative maneuvering.

[28] Ibid., p. 7.

[29] If entry into banking is not constrained (as is suggested in this paper), the gains to shareholders from risk-taking will be greater, *cet. par.,* since they will no longer face the loss of rent from restricted entry.

[30] This narrative is derived from George J. Benston, "Bank Examination," *The Bulletin* of the Institute of Finance, Graduate School of Business Administration, New York University, nos. 89–99, May 1973, pp. 50–52.

[31] However, it should be noted that the New York state system was phased out as bank charters were granted and renewed under the free (entry) banking law. As banks left the insurance system, the premiums went up considerably.

[32] Mark J. Flannery and Jack M. Guttentag, "Problem Banks: Examination, Identification and Supervision," in *State and Federal Regulation of Commercial Banks,* Leonard Lapidus et al., Federal Deposit Insurance Corporation, Washington, D.C., 1980, vol. 11, p. 218.

[33] Randall J. Miller, "An Analysis of Chartering and Conversions, 1960–1977," in *State and Federal Regulation of Commercial Banks,* Leonard Lapidus et al., Federal Deposit Insurance Corporation, Washington, D.C.: 1980. vol. 11. pp. 495–96.

[34] Ibid., p. 492.

[35] See George J. Benston, "Savings Banking and the Public Interest," *The Journal of Money, Credit and Banking* IV, part II (February 1972), chap. II.

[36] Subsidies to borrowers are a much more important means of allocating credit. These extensive (and expensive) programs include the FHA 221 ((d)(2) and 235 programs that provide low interest rate, low down payment loans to lower-income persons and other house buyers in declining urban areas, education loans, farm loans, and small business loans. The cost of these programs in terms of the difference between market rates of interest and the rates charged to the borrowers has been very great and no doubt has resulted in the shifting of resources to those assets and activities that would qualify for the subsidies. An additional cost is the nonrepayment of the loans. Since these allocations of credit and their associated costs are not an aspect of banking regulation, as such, they are not considered further here.

[37] As an indication of this fact, note that the $1,503 billion of total mortgages and $992 billion of one to four family mortgages outstanding as of June 30, 1981, were held by the following:

	All	1 to 4 Family (percent)
Commercial banks	18.3%	16.8%
Mutual savings banks	6.6	6.6
Savings and loan associations	34.2	43.3
Life insurance companies	9.0	1.8
Federal and related agencies	7.9	6.3
Mortgage pools or trusts	10.1	13.0
Individuals and others	13.8	12.2
Total	99.9%	100.0%

[38] Dwight M. Jaffee, "Housing Finance and Mortgage Market Policy," in *Government Credit Allocation,* Institute for Contemporary Studies, San Francisco, 1975, p. 119.

[39] Allan H. Meltzer, "Credit Availability and Economic Decisions: Some Evidence from the Mortgage and Housing Markets," in *Government Credit Allocation*, Institute for Contemporary Studies, San Francisco, 1975, p. 149.

[40] See George J. Benston, "Savings Banks and Public Interest," pp. 174–76.

[41] Thomas Mayer, "Credit Allocation: A Critical View," in *Government Credit Allocation,* Institute for Contemporary Studies, San Francisco, 1975, p. 91.

[42] For a further analysis, see George J. Benston, *The Anti-Redlining Rules: An Analysis of the Federal Home Loan Bank Board's Proposed Nondiscriminatory Requirements,* Law & Economics Center, University of Miami School of Law, Miami, 1978.

[43] See George J. Benston, "Mortgage Redlining Research: A Review and Critical Analysis," in *The Regulation of Financial Institutions,* Conference Series no. 21, October 1979, Federal Reserve Bank of Boston, pp. 144–95, and *Journal of Bank Research* 12 (Spring 1981), pp. 8–23.

[44] See Ralph J. Rohner, "Problems of Federalism in the Regulation of Consumer Financial Services Offered by Commercial Banks," in *State and Federal Regulation of Commercial Banks,* vol. II, Leonard Lapidus et al., Federal Deposit Insurance Corporation, 1980, pp. 1–168, especially 16–75 for a good description of the federal and state laws and regulations.

[45] National Commission on Consumer Finance, *Consumer Credit in the United States: Report of the National Commission on Consumer Finance,* Superintendent of Documents, U.S. Government Printing Office, Washington, D.C., 1972, pp. 153–56.

[46] Gary G. Chandler and David C. Ewert, "Discrimination on the Basis of Sex under the Equal Credit Opportunity Act," Working Paper no. 8, Credit Research Center, Krannert Graduate School of Management, Purdue University, 1976.

[47] Ibid., table 6, p. 16. The figures are for a 0.75 cutoff score (a number that determines how stringently credit is granted). At higher cutoff scores (to 0.80), relatively more applicants are accepted (including bads that should have been rejected). At lower cutoff scores (to 0.55) the relative differences decline, but even then more rejected female applicants would be accepted, and more good and bad applicants identified.

[48] Richard L. Peterson, "An Investigation of Sex Discrimination in Commercial Banks Direct Consumer Lending," *The Bell Journal of Economics* 12 (Autumn 1981) pp. 547–61.

[49] Ibid., p. 560.

[50] George J. Benston, "Mortgage Redlining Research: A Review and Critical Analysis."

[51] James F. Smith, "The Equal Credit Opportunity Act of 1974: A Cost/Benefit Analysis," *Journal of Finance* XXXII (May 1977), pp. 609–22.

[52] Ralph J. Rohner, "Problems of Federalism," p. 107.

[53] Gloria A. Elhat, "The State and Federal Regulation of Banks: Interpretive Analysis and Principal Findings of a Survey of Bankers, Regulators and Consumer Specialists," in *State and Federal Regulation of Commercial Banks,* Leonard Lapidus et al., Federal Deposit Insurance Corporation, Washington, D.C., 1980, pp. 406–24, 492–502, 542–57.

[54] Similar findings are provided by a "representative nationwide sample of 1,585 chief executive officers of national, state member and state nonmember banks" conducted in 1979 by the FDIC. An

average of 91 percent said these examinations were "very or quite costly." Randall J. Miller, "On the Cost of Double Supervision for Insured State Chartered Banks," in *State and Federal Regulation of Commercial Banks,* Leonard Lapidus et al., pp. 379–80.

[55] Some compensation in the form of founders' stock also should be awarded to the officers of the mutuals whose efforts were responsible for a portion of the equity and who would lose if control of their associations passed to stockholders.

[56] For an analysis that concludes that bank supervision and examination is unrelated to money supply, interest rate, or credit control, see George J. Benston and John Tepper Marlin, "Bank Examiners' Evaluation of Credit: An Analysis of the Usefulness of Substandard Loan Data," *Journal of Money, Credit and Banking* VI (February 1974), pp. 23–44.

[57] See Merton H. Miller and Richard A. Posner, "An Approach to the Regulation of Bank Holding Companies," *Journal of Business* 51 (1978), pp. 379–411, for a review of the law and the arguments for and against special regulation.

[58] These problems and some case studies are reviewed by Bernard Shull, "Federal and State Supervision of Bank Holding Companies," in *State and Federal Regulation of Commercial Banks,* vol. 11 Leonard Lapidus et al., Federal Deposit Insurance Corporation, Washington, D.C., 1980, 11, 271–374.

[59] Alternatively, the Fed could allocate its portfolio of interest-bearing Treasury obligations to the reserves, which is equivalent to paying interest on the balances and may be more acceptable politically.

7

Reorganization of the Financial Regulatory Agencies

Paul M. Horvitz

The United States has an extremely complicated structure of governmental agencies involved in the regulation of financial institutions. Such regulation is virtually the full-time activity of the Federal Home Loan Bank Board (FHLBB), the National Credit Union Administration (NCUA), the Federal Deposit Insurance Corporation (FDIC), and the Office of the Comptroller of the Currency (OCC), while such activity comprises a major part of the responsibilities of the Federal Reserve System (FRS) and a significant fraction of the responsibilities of the Securities and Exchange Commission (SEC) and the Antitrust Division of the Justice Department. Each of the 50 states has at least one agency responsible for supervision of financial institutions.

It has long been recognized that this complicated structure gives rise to inefficiencies, duplication, and overlap, and creates opportunities for conflicts that might be reduced by a simplification of the regulatory agency structure. The only legislation in recent years designed to resolve the problems posed by this structure has in fact created additional regulatory organizations—the Depository Institutions Deregulation Committee (DIDC) and the Financial Institutions Examinations Council (FIEC).

It has become traditional to describe the growth in the complexity of U.S. supervisory agency structure as accidental or ad hoc, rather than the result of reasoned policy judgments,[1] but this is an inaccurate way to view the evolution of our agency structure to its current position. In fact, the agency structure reflects the scope and complexity of regulation of financial institutions—virtually every facet of the operations of financial institutions is subject to government regulation and supervision, and the nature of the regulation itself reflects several different and conflicting objectives. Each time the Congress has enacted legislation which relates to financial institution regulation it has considered the issue of agency structure and the merits of divided responsibility versus centralization. In

Reprinted with permission from *Journal of Bank Research,* published by Bank Administration Institute, Winter 1983, pp. 245–61.

each such case a conscious decision has been made by the Congress as to the desired agency structure. Obviously, not everyone would agree with those decisions, and even their strongest supporters would concede that the decisions reflected some compromises necessary to achieve political support. In many cases the conditions leading to a decision have changed so that the result is no longer appropriate. Nevertheless, it is misleading to view those decisions as "accidents."

While all observers agree that the present system does not look neat on paper, and nearly all agree that it is not the system they would design if they were starting with a clean slate, there are at least three distinguishable views as to the appropriate course of action from our present position:

1. Some argue that the disadvantages of the present system are substantial, and that some consolidation of the agency structure is necessary to eliminate conflicts and inequities, and/or to achieve operating economies.

2. A large group supports the view that, while the present system has disadvantages and appears illogical, nevertheless the system works reasonably well. They point to evidence that the cost savings from consolidation would probably be small, and note that agency heads are usually men of good will who are able to resolve differences amicably despite unclear or conflicting lines of authority. Their position (which is the one that has prevailed up to now), is best summed up in the dictum of former OMB director Bert Lance, "if it ain't broke, don't fix it." They further point out that there are substantial costs in managing the transition to a new system, and very large political costs in obtaining agreement on any particular solution. Those who do advocate change are far from united as to the solution they seek.

3. A smaller group argues that the present system, despite its apparent complexity, has substantial advantages as compared to a more uniform system headed by a single agency. They see the possibilities for innovation and experimentation inherent in divided supervisory responsibility as outweighing the extra costs involved. This group, like the preceding one, would deal with intolerable conflicts or problems by ad hoc legislation or through the functioning of a coordinating committee designed to moderate and resolve differences among the agencies.

This overview of various positions is, of course, an oversimplification. There are many differing points of view included in each of these categories. There are many who believe that the present system is satisfactory except for one or two specific problems that they believe require correction.

The congressional decisions over the years on matters of financial institution regulation exhibit several perennial themes and concern about some long-lived conflicts. The dominant theme has been the American distrust of concentration of financial power. This is a tradition that runs deep in the roots of American history, and it is a mistake to view it as merely a holdover from the populism of past decades. This theme affects decisions relating to the centralization of regulatory power and conflicts regarding the role of the states versus that of the federal government.

A different type of continuing theme that runs through most congressional considerations of regulatory issues is the conflict between safety and competition.

Financial institutions have been deemed to require some regulation to assure that their operations do not involve too great a degree of risk.[2] But our system still relies on a healthy dose of competition to help assure that consumers of financial services receive good service and equitable prices. While competition is restricted in the provision of financial services, competition is still viewed as desirable. The task of regulation is clearly more difficult than it would be in a system in which all competition is eliminated. In such a system the regulatory agency structure would also be simpler to design. Congress has frequently dealt with conflicting objectives in regulation by assigning conflicting responsibilities to different agencies. Thus, certain conflicts that are inherent in our regulatory structure appear as conflicts among agencies; in a consolidated regulatory agency the conflicts would still exist but they would have to be resolved within the single agency. It is not obvious which approach is superior.

To illustrate the purposeful, rather than accidental, nature of the U.S. regulatory agency structure, it may be helpful to examine a few examples of the way in which these themes and conflicts have been dealt with by the Congress. These examples are not intended to demonstrate that all congressional decisions in these matters have been optimal or wise, but only that they were based on reasonable considerations.

The structure of the Federal Reserve System itself is an instructive example. The system comprises a Board of Governors, 12 regional Federal Reserve banks (each with its own board of directors), and has its most important function—open market operations—carried out by a committee consisting of membership from both the Board of Governors and the banks. That is not the way one would think to organize a central bank today. But that structure emerged from sharp disagreements as to whether a centralized monetary authority was necessary in the United States, and it reflected the fear of concentrated financial power that we have already noted. In the early 20th century, the U.S. economy was mainly agrarian, and money markets were regional rather than national. In that context a decentralized regional structure for the Federal Reserve System made some sense. Moves toward centralization took place at several times in the system's history, so that now there is no doubt that the power rests with the Board of Governors, but the trappings of a regional system still exist. The perpetuation of regional Federal Reserve banks makes the system structure look more complex, and results in some organizational oddities (Federal Reserve bank presidents receive higher salaries than governors), but it is hard to argue that it results in less effective monetary policy than if the Federal Reserve banks did not exist.

A similar concern over concentration of financial power shows up in state laws restricting branch banking and the deference of federal law to state law in this area. While there are many aspects to the debate over branch banking in the United States, it is clear that much of the original antagonism to the concept of branching by commercial banks was concern from rural areas that branching would lead to domination of financial power by big city interests that might not be sympathetic to the needs of the small farmer, rancher, or merchant.

Public policy toward bank mergers evolved gradually over the years, exhibiting a continual balancing of the conflicting objectives of increasing competition and minimizing risk. During the 1950s, a wave of mergers among large banks led to an increase in concentration in many banking markets. Congress enacted the Bank Merger Act of 1960 to deal with this situation while under the impression that existing antitrust law could not be effective (Sherman Act violations are hard to prove, and it was generally believed that the Clayton Act did not apply to bank mergers). The Bank Merger Act included standard antitrust concepts and language, but also recognized that banking was different from other industries, and provided that the banking agencies could approve mergers under certain circumstances even if the merger had adverse effects on competition.

The picture was clouded in 1963, when the Justice Department won a case under the Clayton Act against the proposed merger of Philadelphia National Bank and Girard Trust Company. The possibility that bank mergers might have to be undone years after the merger had been approved by the appropriate banking agency was of grave concern to the Congress (and also to several banks that had Clayton Act cases pending against them). This led to a new rebalancing of competitive and banking factors in the 1966 Amendments to the Bank Merger Act.

The Bank Merger Act divides responsibility for approval or rejection of bank merger proposals among the federal banking agencies, depending on whether the surviving bank is a national bank, a state member bank, or an insured nonmember bank. In the interest of achieving uniformity in administration, the act requires the agency making the decision to obtain an advisory opinion on the competitive factors involved in the merger from each of the other banking agencies, and also from the Justice Department. But Congress was not willing to rely totally on the judgment of the banking agencies in this area because of concern that the banking agencies, in view of their supervisory responsibilities, would tend to give too little weight to competitive factors. Thus, the Justice Department was authorized to continue to bring antitrust suits against mergers after they had been approved by the appropriate banking agency. (In the interest of avoiding an unscrambling of a consummated merger, the Justice Department must act within 30 days of approval; and if it does bring suit, the merger cannot be consummated until the case is resolved by a final court decision.)

This is certainly a cumbersome system, but it is not arbitrary or accidental. It represents a serious attempt to balance conflicting objectives and recognizes that the banking agencies have basic responsibilities different from those of the Justice Department. The law is an attempt to see that both competitive and banking factors receive appropriate weight.

The system has not worked quite as planned by the Congress. Despite the advisory opinions, there have been differences in merger policy among the banking agencies. Agency policy has differed over time as the personality heading the agency has changed, and the Comptroller of the Currency has consistently followed a more liberal merger policy than the Federal Reserve or the FDIC.[3] This lesson was not lost on the Congress when it was faced with determining analogous approval authority over bank holding company acquisitions in the Bank Holding Company Act of 1970. There the Congressional solution was delegation of approval authority over all holding company acquisitions to the Federal Reserve. The delegation of holding company supervisory authority to the Federal Reserve, while responsibility for the subsidiary banks is divided among the three federal agencies, has led to some serious problems in bank supervision. These difficulties have been documented in several studies, and have led the comptroller and the chairman of the FDIC to call for division of holding company responsibilities among the agencies in a manner similar to bank supervision.[4]

Regulatory agency responsibility for bank chartering decisions is divided among agencies in a complicated manner, but one that reflects concern that too liberal an entry policy can lead to excessive risk of bank failure, while too restrictive a policy inhibits competition and leads to excessive concentration of financial power. A bank charter can be obtained from either the state or the OCC. The dual source of charters keeps either federal or state authorities from preventing new entry. State decisions are subject to review by a federal agency if the newly chartered bank is seeking federal deposit insurance (as nearly all new banks are). This "checks and balances" approach to bank entry may not be the most efficient design possible, but it is an understandable solution to the conflicting objectives involved in entry decisions.

Regulation of financial disclosure by banks is subject to divided responsibility analogous to that of bank mergers. The Securities and Exchange Commission is the federal agency with the expertise in this area and with responsibility for regulation of disclosure by all companies in the country except banks. Again Congress recognized that banks are different, and that disclosure as complete as that required of nonbanks might interfere with the supervisory responsibilities of the banking agencies. The resulting division of responsibilities is complicated, but it represents an attempt to balance conflicting objectives and reflects doubts about the ability of one agency to resolve such conflicts internally.

A final example is the separate regulatory structure for the savings and loan industry. Federal regulation of savings and loans is vested in the Federal Home Loan Bank Board, but the FHLBB is not simply a regulatory agency; it is charged with promoting the savings and loan industry. The supervisory duties of the FHLBB are similar to those of the banking agencies, and if supervision were its only function it could logically be combined with a bank supervisory agency. But none of the banking agencies is a promoter of the institutions it supervises. This distinction has led to conflicts over various matters, particularly the setting of interest-rate ceilings on deposits. Until the establishment of the Depository Institutions Deregulatory Committtee, decisions on ceilings were made by the Federal Reserve Board (for member banks), the FDIC (for nonmember insured banks and mutual savings banks), and the FHLBB (for savings and loans). Consultation among the agencies was frequent but not binding on the individual agencies. Now the DIDC decisions are based on a vote of its members and are binding on all institutions (except credit unions). But even this procedure may not be sufficient to produce uniformity.

The lesson to be drawn from this discussion of regulation and regulatory structure is that in building a supervisory agency structure we must follow the architectural dictum that form follows function. Our present agency structure developed from the policy considerations behind the congressional decisions on regulation. Agency structure was not simply tacked on to the regulatory framework in an arbitrary manner, and it cannot be changed without considering the objectives of regulation.

We are now considering some major steps toward deregulation of the financial services business. The existing agency structure is designed for regulation as it exists now. This is, of course, not the same as saying that the existing structure is optimal for our existing scope and nature of regulation, but it was designed for the regulation that exists. If we change the scope of regulation, the existing structure is no longer entitled to a presumption of relevance. If we change regulation, we must investigate what sort of change in the regulatory agency structure is appropriate for the new environment. The importance of this consideration is that even those who favor the present agency structure, or those who believe it works well enough, should recognize that if the function of the agencies changes, it may be appropriate to change the form as well.

Some aspects of the present regulatory agency framework are described in Section I, along with an evaluation of how well it fits the present regulatory functions. Section II describes the deregulation that is likely to occur over the next several years and an analysis of the regulation that will remain. Section III attempts to demonstrate that the present agency structure will be inappropriate for the environment after deregulation (even if one believes that it is appropriate for today). My proposals for an improved agency structure for this new environment are spelled out in Section IV. Since deregulation will not occur overnight, this section also suggests a framework for gradual change in the agency structure that moves toward the final outcome in step with the pace of deregulation.

I. THE CURRENT REGULATORY SYSTEM

Depository institutions are subject to a variety of regulations and restrictions. Entry into the business is restricted, as is branch expansion by existing institutions. There are limitations on the types of activities that can be engaged in, with even financial activities limited. Commercial banks, mutual savings banks, and savings and loan associations are limited in the rate they can pay on most types of deposits, and banks can not pay interest on demand deposits. Balance sheets are subject to constraints on financial ratios—capital and liquidity, and the size of individual loans is limited to some fraction of capital. A variety of laws, most of them of recent vintage, are designed to protect consumers in their dealings with financial institutions. While most of the regulations exist to reduce the risk of failure, some regulations are designed to affect the allocation of resources in a particular way (most important are those aimed at stimulating the housing industry).

These regulations evolved historically from real or perceived economic needs and were influenced by the value systems of the population or the legislatures that enacted them. Laws are rarely self-enforcing. Each piece of legislation required the designation of some governmental agency or official to oversee its enforcement. For reasons we have discussed, in the United States this process took the form of creation of a number of different government agencies to carry out the regulatory effect. The Antitrust Division of the Justice Department has a direct involvement in bank mergers, and other agencies play their normal roles with respect to financial institutions (the FTC is concerned with trade practices, and OSHA is concerned with occupational safety in financial institutions). Each state has at least one agency, usually more than one, to supervise state-chartered financial institutions.

The previous brief description of principal regulatory responsibilities is inadequate—the situation is much more complex than a listing of agencies and principal regulated institutions would imply. The FDIC insures deposits in all insured commercial banks, regardless of their source of charter or Federal Reserve membership. The Federal Reserve is a source of liquidity to all listed institutions.

The Federal Home Loan Bank System supervises state-chartered savings and loans as well as chartering and supervising federal savings and loans. A number of state-chartered mutual savings banks are members of the Federal Home Loan Bank System (as are a few insurance companies). Financial disclosure by banks and bank holding companies is subject to regulation by the SEC as well as the banking agencies. Some consumer protection regulations for all banks are promulgated by the Federal Reserve.

The multiplicity of agencies is partly due to duality, whereby both the federal government and state governments charter financial institutions, and partly to the specialized nature of financial institutions. Since commercial banks, savings and loans, and credit unions are perceived as performing separate and distinct functions, with different needs for supervision and regulation, the approach has been to establish separate regulatory agencies for each institution (except that mutual savings banks are regulated by either the FDIC or the FHLBB).

There were reasons (though not necessarily good reasons) for the original decisions on the allocation of responsibilities among the agencies. There are reasons now why the continued separation of responsibilities is maintained. These reasons are partly philosophical (such as concern that consolidation of the federal banking agencies will be detrimental to the dual banking system) and partly based on interests of the constituency (such as concern that a "banking" agency would not adequately "promote" the savings and loan business).

There are three basic reasons for concern about the existing structure of regulation: first, the multiplicity of agencies may be unnecessarily costly or inefficient; second, there may be gaps in the regulatory structure that could result in safety and soundness problems being overlooked or missed; third, the overlapping responsibilities may give rise to conflicting rulings that are difficult to resolve or that treat similar institutions inequitably.

It is only recently that attempts have been made to determine the cost implications of the current agency structure, and those attempts have been limited to measuring the potential savings from consolidation of the banking agencies. While it appears that there is some potential for cost-saving from agency consolidation, the savings are relatively modest. The principal economy would seem to be in examiner travel time and expense. Some examiners, particularly Federal Reserve examiners, must travel long distances between institutions being examined. If one agency were responsible for examination of all financial institutions, it could set up a system of regional offices that would reduce travel costs. There may be some modest savings from combining computer facilities and from reducing the number of agency heads.[5] While there are many proponents of some form of agency consolidation, no one has based the justification for such a change primarily on the cost savings.

The possibility that there are gaps in the coverage of the present regulatory system is important, because the potential social losses due to the existence of such gaps is greater than the operating cost issue or, indeed, than the cost of duplication and overlap. The problem of gaps is simply that the complicated structure of regulation may lead to some problem or abuse not being detected, because a particular agency believes that the problem lies in some other agency's bailiwick.

The only significant example of this type of problem concerns the regulation of bank holding companies and their subsidiary banks. The Federal Reserve is responsible for supervision of holding companies, even if their subsidiary banks are national or nonmember banks (as they usually are). It is possible for each agency to meet its responsibilities, yet have a problem develop because of the relationship between the holding company and the subsidiary bank. The most significant example of this was the experience of the Hamilton National Bank with its parent and affiliated mortgage banking company. It appears that, since this experience, the Federal Reserve has stepped up its monitoring activity with regard to holding companies, so that a repetition is unlikely.

Some would argue that a gap may exist with respect to supervision of money market funds resulting from the differences in supervisory approach between the SEC and the banking agencies. SEC regulation of mutual funds is oriented toward disclosure—the SEC does not care how risky the policy of a mutual fund is, as long as the prospectus discloses the risks. The banking agencies do limit the risk taken by the institutions they regulate. The money market fund is selling an instrument not very different from that issued by a bank or savings institution. Some would argue that buyers of money market funds do not read prospectuses, and that a gap in the regulatory framework exists here. It is probably more appropriate to view this issue as part of the problem of conflicts or differences in treatment of different institutions.

It is clear that the present regulatory structure provides many instances of overlapping responsibilities, with many opportunities for the same regulation or law to be applied unevenly to different institutions, and with a waste of time and money when several agencies must pass on the same application.

It must be recognized that not all inequities or differences in treatment are the result of the regulatory framework. Many, if not most, are the result of laws that treat similar institutions differently. The differential in interest-rate ceilings between commercial banks and thrift institutions is statutory. Commercial banks complain about the differential now that it is administered by the Depository Institutions Deregulation Committee just as much as when the ceilings were administered by separate agencies for banks and savings and loans. Federal savings and loans have broader branching powers than national banks in many states because of differences in the law. If branch applications for savings and loans and national banks were passed on by the same agency, these differences would persist.

Of course, conflicting decisions by the agencies do occur. If these differences were random, they would not be a cause of great concern. The concern is that conflicts may be systematic and reflect a "competition in laxity," as one agency or another seeks to benefit its "constituency" or gain converts by adopting a permissive regulatory posture. Former Federal Reserve chairman Arthur Burns has argued that "the present system is conducive to subtle competition among regulatory authorities, sometimes to relax constraints, sometimes to delay constructive measures."[6]

Related to this concern that permissiveness might lead to a banking system that is excessively risky is the concern that decisions by an aggressive Comptroller of the Currency could upset the balance between state and national banks, and thereby destroy or weaken the dual banking system. Conversely, an excessively restrictive posture by the comptroller could put the national banking system at a disadvantage, compared with state banks. It should be noted that the initiative is with the comptroller, because a permissive posture by a state supervisor (or even by all state supervisors) would not be effective unless supported by the federal supervisors of state banks (FDIC and Federal Reserve).

The potential in the system for conflicting regulatory postures among the agencies became a reality during the administration of James Saxon as comptroller. Saxon made a number of decisions that broadened the operating authority of national banks, and also took a liberal attitude with respect to new charters and branching by national banks. On a number of occasions the comptroller issued rulings applying liberally the same provisions of federal law that the Federal Reserve and the FDIC applied more restrictively to state-chartered banks. In addition, the comptroller issued other rulings or adopted policies which gave national banks an advantage over state-chartered banks that did not involve positions conflicting with the other federal agencies. The comptroller issued several rulings permitting national banks to engage in activities previously regarded as prohibited.

The policies adopted by comptroller Saxon certainly did shatter the image of cooperation among the state and federal banking agencies that had existed previously. The policies adopted also led to an expansion in the number and size of national banks relative to state-chartered banks. In particular, several large banks converted to national charters during this period.

It is not the task of this paper to determine who was right in conflicts of the past. The question is whether conflict is necessarily bad, or whether allowing such conflicts to surface can lead to an improvement in financial regulation. The existence of more than one agency to pass on issues that arise may increase the chances of correct decisions. A single agency may be less inclined to consider change on its merits.

The most recent example of conflicting interpretations by the supervisory agencies did not involve the comptroller, but rather the Federal Reserve and the FHLBB in a dispute over regulations about who was entitled to have a NOW account. Both agencies were empowered to issue regulations—the Federal Reserve for commercial banks and the FHLBB for savings and loans—under the same law. The FHLBB adopted a more liberal regulation, allowing more entities to have NOW accounts with savings and loans than the Federal Reserve regulation allowed for commercial banks. Either interpretation could be justified on the basis of the law, and both positions were the preferred ones from the point of view of the agencies' constituents—savings and loans wanted more potential holders of NOW accounts, and the commercial banks wanted to discourage holders of demand deposit accounts from switching to NOW accounts. If there were a single agency making the decision, we would save the large costs involved in resolving this dispute in the courts, and the public squabbling between the agencies would have been avoided, but the quality of the resolution would not necessarily have been any better.

Criticism of the multiple-agency nature of our regulatory system is not based solely on the possibility of conflicts among the agencies but is also concerned about the need for duplicative administrative processes. A state-chartered bank's application of anything needing supervisory approval (a branch, for example) must be approved at the state level and also by a federal agency. Expansion by a bank holding company frequently requires approval by the agency supervising the bank subsidiary as well as by the Federal Reserve. The delays involved in this process are costly to the banks involved. This problem is less serious for national banks, and this has been a force favoring the growth of the national system. This force has been more than offset in the past by the requirement for Federal Reserve membership that goes with the national charter; but now that all banks must meet Federal Reserve reserve requirements, it can be expected to lead to a gradual shift toward the national charter.

Given the nature of our present regulation of financial institutions,[7] there are both advantages and disadvantages to having the multiple-agency structure that exists today. There have been proposals for change in the agency structure for 50 years. The best summary of the arguments for the present system and for consolidation was put forth by Frank Wille in testimony before the House Banking Committee in 1975.[8] He listed several arguments in favor of consolidation:

1. Simplification of administration.
2. Elimination of conflicting goals (particularly the Federal Reserve responsibility for both bank supervision and monetary policy).
3. Cost savings from combining the legal research, data processing, and training activities of the separate agencies.
4. Elimination of policy conflicts.
5. Facilitation of the handling of failing banks.[9]
6. Improved regulation of bank holding companies, better coordinating supervision of the holding company and its subsidiary banks.
7. Benefits to bank customers from more uniform rules applying to all institutions.
8. Greater flexibility and ability to adjust to change in the environment.

The arguments against consolidation include:

1. The present system has worked reasonably well (and the costs of adjusting to a new system would offset many of the benefits).
2. Differences within each agency are as great as interagency differences. Consolidation would not resolve this problem, and perhaps interagency coordination might accomplish much of what consolidation could.
3. Concentration on regulatory power. The present system allows for criticism from within the regulatory structure and not just from the regulated institutions, as in other industries.
4. Benefits of diversity. There may be a greater tendency to experiment and a greater receptivity to change with several agencies than with only one.

Weighing these pros and cons is a difficult task. Wille came to the conclusion that "it would be a grave mistake to consolidate." Wille believes that there are only two serious areas of interagency conflict and operating problems: merger policy and holding company regulation. We have already noted that differences among the banking agencies with respect to merger applications have been well documented. On occasion these differences have led to conversions of banks to national charters in order to benefit from the comptroller's more liberal policy on mergers. The holding company problem will be discussed in Section III.

II. THE DEREGULATED FINANCIAL SYSTEM

There is a clear trend toward deregulation in our financial system that is supported by nearly all participants and observers. When a system is as overregulated as U.S. financial markets, it is relatively easy to see that change should be in the direction of deregulation. It is much more difficult to be precise on just how far deregulation should proceed. This is not an exercise in pure economic theory; appropriate weight must be given to American history, traditions, and culture.

There is general agreement that certain major types of restriction on financial institutions should be and will be eliminated in the future. Interest-rate ceilings on deposits are now being phased out under the direction of the DIDC. There is room for debate about how rapid this phaseout should be, but no doubt that eventually we will have a system without rate ceilings. There is almost as clear agreement that geographic restrictions on financial institutions will be eliminated. Here the process is still in question, with debate on whether removal of the barriers should begin with repeal of the Douglas Amendment or by change in the McFadden Act. In either case, there are various means of adjusting to the change gradually, as with the various proposals for allowing regional interstate activity as a first step. Similarly, restrictions on branching within states will be eliminated, both with respect to traditional brick-and-mortar manned facilities and electronic facilities. There remains strong opposition to wider branching by commercial banks, both within states and across state lines, that will not be overcome easily or quickly; but the long-run prospect is that all geographic restrictions will eventually be eliminated.

There is also general agreement that modification of the Glass-Steagall Act is inevitable, with many arguing in favor of complete repeal of the restrictions on investment banking activity by commercial banks. At the very least, commercial banks will be allowed to underwrite municipal revenue bonds as well as full-faith-and-credit obligations, and will be allowed to operate mutual funds and to engage in brokerage activities. Repeal or amendment can remove the present inconsistency that prohibits links between securities firms and member banks, but not nonmember banks.

The legal distinctions between commercial banks and thrift institutions (at least savings and loans and mutual savings banks) will disappear as these institutions gain full commercial bank powers. Most thrift institutions will continue to specialize in mortgage finance and in providing financial services to households, because they have built up expertise in that business. But this specialization also characterizes some comercial banks. The point is that savings institutions will be able to offer a full range of commercial services, and hence there will no longer be any basis (if there is one now) to restrict consolidations between commercial banks and savings institutions.

This latter point has relevance to the issue of interstate banking. If a savings and loan can be a subsidiary of a bank holding company under section 4(c)(8), then there are no geographic restrictions on that activity. This may be the means by which interstate banking comes about, rather than by change in the Douglas

Amendment or the McFadden Act. Note also that, in many states, savings and loans have broader branching powers than commercial banks.

Remaining Regulations

When these desirable and inevitable changes take place there will still remain a great deal of regulation of financial institutions. Some of the other types of regulation will be modified and generally reduced in scope, but it is probably desirable that much regulation remain.

Most important, we will continue to have a Federal Reserve System with responsibility for monetary policy. In one sense, government control of the money supply is a major form of regulation; this implies government determination of the aggregate amount of some liabilities of financial institutions, whereas there is no government control over the aggregate amount of steel, wheat, or other commodities produced in the economy. From the point of view of individual financial institutions, however, this aggregate control of the money supply is not a meaningful restriction on their operations or opportunity to compete.

For the purposes of this paper, the important point is not whether monetary policy continues to exist, as it clearly will, but whether that implies some additional role for the Federal Reserve in the regulation of financial institutions. We will return to that issue later.

A second major element of our present financial system that will remain after deregulation is deposit insurance. Theoretical arguments can be made about whether the federal deposit insurance system should be retained in a competitive financial system, and there are many suggestions for change in the way in which deposit insurance is operated and premiums assessed. Nevertheless, it is reasonable to assume that deposit insurance will continue to be a federal responsibility. Once we accept federal deposit insurance, much additional regulation becomes necessary to protect the insurance fund. Federal deposit insurance allows an institution to attract deposits regardless of its financial condition or risk exposure, as depositors rely primarily on deposit insurance for their protection. This provides the owners of the institution with an incentive toward excessive risk-taking, as any gains are reaped by stockholders and, if failure results, the losses are primarily borne by the insurance system. While there are many possible ways of dealing with this problem, such as insurance premiums based on risk, or coinsurance, we have historically dealt with this by restrictions on the activities of the institution, capital requirements, bank examination, and scrutiny of the character of new entrants into the business.[10]

While most regulation of financial institutions has traditionally been oriented toward protecting the safety and soundness of the financial system, in recent years we have seen an explosive growth of legislation designed to protect consumers in credit transactions. This began with enactment of the Truth-in-Lending law in 1968, but that has been followed by the Fair Credit Reporting Act, the Fair Credit Billing Act, the Real Estate Settlement Procedures Act, the Federal Trade Commission Improvement Act, the Home Mortgage Disclosure Act, the Consumer Leasing Act, the Fair Debt Collection Practices Act, the Equal Credit Opportunities Act, the Community Reinvestment Act, and the Electronic Funds Transfer Act. All of this legislation grew out of evidence of real abuses (though it is not clear whether the abuses were isolated or widespread), and much of it has produced real benefits to consumers. None of these benefits have been produced without cost, however, and it is not clear whether the benefits to some consumers from the legislation outweighs the cost to all credit transactions that has resulted from administration and enforcement of the new legislation. In at least two cases—Truth-in-Lending and RESPA—the burdens on lenders were found to be great enough to require amendment and simplification of the original legislation. It is likely that such legislation will continue even after deregulation of other aspects of the financial structure. It should be noted, however, that such consumer protection is, in theory, less necessary in a competitive environment than when lenders have monopoly power. Attention can be given to simplification or elimination of such legislation as is found not to be cost effective.

As deregulation proceeds along these lines, there will be a major consolidation of the financial structure. Allowing broader branching, as well as interstate activity, will lead to many bank mergers and many bank holding company acquisitions. Similarly, allowing for commercial bank/savings and loan combinations will result in a number of such mergers. Virtually everyone agrees that such consolidations should face scrutiny under the antitrust laws, though there is disagreement as to the mechanism of that review.

We have already noted that bank mergers are treated differently than other mergers under the antitrust laws. Bank mergers (and holding company acquisitions) first must gain approval from a federal banking regulatory agency, and then can be challenged in the courts by the Justice Department. The volume of merger and holding company applications that are likely to result from the deregulation discussed here is likely to swamp the processing resources of the agencies (and the Justice Department). Many of the cases will involve difficult issues of potential competition on which the Supreme Court has yet to give solid guidance. A good argument can be made for reliance on the antitrust laws, without the requirement of supervisory agency approval. This issue is discussed in the following section of the paper.

Areas of Disagreement

With respect to the areas of regulation discussed so far in this section, there is a great deal of general agreement in the literature. The most significant area of disagreement concerns the separation of banking and commerce. The allowable activities of commercial banks, as corporate entitites, are severely restricted by the National Bank Act, state laws, and other federal legislation. There is little argument over the general restriction of banks to financial activities. Under the Bank Holding Company Act, as amended in 1970, there is also a severe restriction on the affiliates of commercial banks. The history of such restrictions is a strange one, and there are inconsistencies in the law that must be resolved, but it is not clear how that will be done.

Before the 1970 amendments to the Bank Holding Company Act, there were no restrictions on the allowable activities of nonbank affiliates of those bank holding companies that controlled only one bank. Restrictions did exist on the activities of affiliates of bank holding companies that controlled more than one bank (the so-called multibank holding companies). There was never any logic in using the number of banks controlled as the determining factor in limiting the activities of nonbank affiliates of a holding company, and that distinction was eliminated by the 1970 amendments. Now all bank holding companies are subject to section 4(c)(8) of the act, which delegates to the Federal Reserve the authority to determine allowable activities of bank holding companies. The Federal Reserve must find that an allowable activity is "so closely related to banking . . . as to be a proper incident thereto," and must also determine whether the performance of this activity "can reasonably be expected to produce benefits to the public."

There are some anomolies in the present law. First of all, there are no parallel restrictions on the allowable activities of affiliates of savings and loan holding companies. Thus Sears Roebuck and National Steel own savings and loan associations and engage in a variety of nonfinancial activities. As savings and loans become virtually identical in powers to commercial banks, it will not be feasible to maintain this distinction indefinitely. Second, the Bank Holding Company Act includes its own definition of a bank, which is not the same definition of a bank used in other federal legislation. Under the Bank Holding Company Act, a bank is an institution that accepts demand deposits and lends to businesses. An institution that avoids business lending is not a "bank" for Bank Holding Company Act purposes, even though it has a charter from the Comptroller of the Currency as a national bank and is insured as a bank by the FDIC.

One way to resolve these problems would be to eliminate all restrictions on activities of bank holding companies, while keeping appropriate restrictions on the activities of banks themselves. This would allow a firm in any line of business to become a bank holding company by acquiring a bank, or would allow a bank holding company to engage in any line of business by creating a subsidiary separate from the bank. This would resolve the problem of disparate treatment of bank and savings and loan holding companies, and the problem of defining a bank for holding company purposes. It would return us to the situation that existed prior to 1970, in which many companies (Goodyear, Tenneco, and others) owned banks and engaged in both banking and industrial activities. The issue was debated at great length in connection with the 1970 amendments and the traditional separation of banking and commerce was upheld. There are at least three different issues involved here.

Foremost in the minds of many is the traditional American concern with concentration of financial power. The giant conglomerate, with industrial subsidiaries intertwined with a captive bank, in the nature of the Japanese *zaibatsu*, was viewed as a potentially unfair competitor and a threat to the concept of a decentralized economic system. There was also the problem of whether a relationship with nonbank affiliates which would be engaged in risky activities could pose a threat to the safety of the bank. Some argued that the bank could be insulated from the fortunes of the nonbank affiliates, and that regulation could be concerned solely with the bank. Others argued that the fortunes of a bank subsidiary were inevitably tied up with those of its parent and affiliates, and that even in a legal sense, insulation of the bank was impossible. The question of the possibility that the courts would seek to "pierce the corporate veil" in case of difficulty of affiliates was debated heatedly. And as a practical matter, when the issue was debated in 1970, commercial banks had little enthusiasm for a breakdown of the separation of commerce and banking, because of fear that elimination of restrictions could lead to unfriendly takeover attempts by aggressive industrial concerns.

These considerations still exist, and make it unlikely that a major lowering of the barrier between banking and commerce will occur in the near future. But even with existing law, many believe that administration of the Bank Holding Company Act by the Federal Reserve has been overly restrictive. In the 12 years since enactment of the 1970 amendments, the Federal Reserve has not allowed bank holding companies to engage in any significant activities not already allowable to national banks directly. This raises the issue of what the role of the Federal Reserve should be in the regulation of financial institutions. We return to this matter in the following section.

III. THE NEED FOR AGENCY CONSOLIDATION

We have noted that the debate over agency consolidation has gone on for many years, with many different proposals being advanced. The only action of recent years has been the creation of two coordinating committees: the Federal Financial Institutions Examination Council and the Depository Institutions Deregulation Committee. While some saw these committees as a means of producing the uniformity, or at least the coordination, that might otherwise require consolidation of the agencies, others argue that the committtees themselves have simply become additional regulatory agencies.[11]

The failure to take action to bring about definitive consolidation reflected the view (prevalent until recently) that the system works well enough and has such advantages that the potential benefits of consolidation are not great enough to warrant action. For reasons discussed in Section I, that has been a reasonable decision up to now. However, as regulatory distinctions among institutions are reduced or eliminated, and as regulatory restrictions on all institutions are eased, the existing regulatory structure will not be a defensible one. This section describes the problems that the current agency structure will have in dealing with the deregulated environment of the future.

Future Problems of the Current Agency Structure

While several problems have long called out for a solution by means of change in agency structure, several recent changes in the regulatory system will play a role in the future change in agency structure. Most important will be the grant of full commercial bank powers to thrift institutions. It appears that this change toward deregulation will occur sooner than thought just a few years ago. Also important in requiring change in the agency structure are the changes included in the Monetary Control Act of 1980, and the elimination of barriers to interstate operations.

Additional Powers for Savings Institutions. A separate supervisory agency for savings and loan associations was appropriate when savings and loans had limited powers and were viewed as an instrument for increasing the availability of housing by improving the flow of funds into the mortgage market. Future deregulation will result in savings and loans having full commercial bank powers. As these institutions become full competitors with commercial banks, there is no reason to continue a separate supervisory arrangement for institutions subject to similar regulations, let alone the perpetuation of a regulatory agency charged with promotion of the industry.

In addition to supervisory differences, we now have separate insurance funds and agencies for commercial banks, savings and loans, and credit unions. There are now some differences in the statutes concerning FDIC and FSLIC procedures that should be changed, but consolidation of the insurance agencies is a better approach. The FDIC is financially better able to meet the potential calls upon it than is the FSLIC. Consolidation not only makes long-run sense in terms of agency structure but helps to resolve short-run problems of the savings and loan industry.

Differences in Branching.   At the present time, branching powers of savings and loans are considerably more liberal than those of commercial banks. This arises from two sources: *first,* many states provide broader branching powers for state-chartered savings and loans than for state-chartered commercial banks; *second,* state laws with respect to branching are binding on federally chartered commercial banks but not federally chartered savings and loans. That distinction cannot be allowed to continue as savings and loans gain broader powers. It may be resolved by action at the state level to liberalize commercial bank branching restrictions, or it may be resolved through federal legislation on branching powers for commercial banks. Federal legislation easing geographical restraints on commercial banks will eventually allow interstate banking as well.

The implication of this is that the role of the states in determining banking structure will be diminished or eliminated. The Monetary Control Act has already moved us in that direction. The requirement that all banks, regardless of source of charter, maintain reserves in accord with Federal Reserve requirements, removes the major incentive to a state charter—the opportunity to operate as a nonmember bank. Interstate banking also produces a trend toward national charters for banks. A state-chartered bank operating in several states is going to be subject to supervision by each state in which it operates, and this is likely to be intolerable to the bank. No state is likely to have the resources to supervise the interstate operations of banks chartered within the state. The only reasonable outcome is that banks that operate in more than one state will do so with a national charter.

One solution to this is to completely eliminate the role of states in the chartering and supervision of depository financial institutions. This could be done by making federal deposit insurance only available to institutions with federal charters. A more logical approach is for federal law to set branching powers for federally chartered institutions on the basis of congressional consideration of the advantages and disadvantages. Such federal law would take precedence over state law. Unlimited branching for national banks need not mean the end of the dual banking system, as this would likely lead the states to change their law to accord equal privileges to state-chartered banks. In one sense, broader intrastate branching powers for national banks would not affect the choice of charter, assuming state laws conformed, since such branching laws are now uniform for national and state banks. We have already noted, however, that interstate branching powers will tend to favor the national charter for those banks that will seek to operate in more than one state.

The Commercial Banking Agencies.   Despite the frequently expressed concern that the present divided structure of commercial bank supervision leads to a "competition in laxity," it has not been easy to move back and forth from one supervisor to another. A commercial bank may have a preference for supervision by a different agency, but a change, while possible, involves a number of problems. In the past, while many banks could see an advantage in dealing with one supervisor, rather than with a state and federal supervisor (and many have believed that the comptroller has been a more sympathetic supervisor than the Federal Reserve or the FDIC), conversion to a national charter involved mandatory Federal Reserve membership. This requirement has been sufficient to discourage many banks from making such a conversion. In addition, there are some aspects of state charters that present advantages, such as (in many states) more liberal lending limits. Conversion from national to state charter has nearly always been because of the opportunity to escape Federal Reserve requirements, rather than reflecting a choice of supervisor. Similarly, movements of state-chartered banks from federal supervision by the FDIC to supervision by the Federal Reserve, or vice versa, has usually been dominated by considerations of Federal Reserve membership, rather than supervisory considerations.

The regulatory changes that have taken place (the Monetary Control Act), and those that are likely, change this picture. The advantages of dealing with one supervisor, the elimination of Federal Reserve membership as a consideration, and the advantages of federal supervision to a bank operating in more than one state will produce a substantial trend toward national charters for commercial banks. Inertia plays a very important role in bank decisions in these matters, and change will not occur overnight. Nevertheless, the direction of change is clear. In particular, there will be little reason for larger banks to remain with state charters, and none to remain as nonmember banks.

Even at the present time, there is good reason to remove the Federal Reserve from bank supervision. On the basis of efficiency considerations, the Federal Reserve supervises too few banks to justify continuation of this role. The number of bank examiners that can be efficiently employed in most Federal Reserve districts, and the unnecessary travel costs involved in arranging examiner schedules, suggest that the supervisory task could be performed more efficiently by another agency.

More important, and despite the arguments of the Federal Reserve, there is no good reason for combining the task of monetary policy management with the job of individual bank supervision, while there are reasons to see a conflict in such a combination of duties. There are several arguments involved in this issue.

At one time it was argued that there are benefits from combining monetary policy and bank supervision, in that pressure on banks to adopt liberal or tight lending policies can be transmitted through the examination process in accord with the counter-cyclical objectives of monetary policy. That argument has now disappeared, and virtually no one argues in favor of using bank supervision as a tool of macroeconomic policy. Nevertheless, the Federal Reserve has often argued that the information obtained in the course of bank examination is useful to the Federal Reserve in making monetary policy decisions. In a 1977 study of this issue, Manferd Peterson concluded that, "There is no evidence that data from bank examinations have been used in the formulation of open market policy. The meager evidence suggests that examination data are not very useful for monetary policy."[12] It would seem that the burden of proof on this matter rests with the Federal Reserve; and, apart from frequent assertion, the Federal Reserve has not been able to demonstrate how any useful information is obtained from the supervisory process that could not be obtained with another agency doing the supervision.[13]

The potential for conflict in Federal Reserve involvement in supervision is twofold. First is a conflict in time. Monetary policy is an important responsibility which must absorb the major part of the attention of board members. Supervisory issues are likely to get less attention from board members (and that is as it should be). Former board governor Robertson has stated that board members spend as much time on supervisory matters and applications as on monetary policy. While this is less likely to be true of board members with less interest in supervision than governor Robertson, it means that board members do face a conflict in allocation of time.

The more important conflict, however, involves the need to make choices in policy objectives. Both monetary policy and financial regulation involve political controversy. The Federal Reserve has always defended its authority to make its own decisions on monetary policy, though the political criticism of the Federal Reserve has often been intense. Its desire to protect its "independence" has led the Federal Reserve to seek to avoid generating criticism emanating from what it sees as peripheral issues. Carter Golembe has argued that regulatory policy is "held hostage to monetary policy objectives" of the Federal Reserve in certain situations. He notes that "at a time when bold innovative action might be called for in the regulation . . . of depository institutions, the political side effects of adopting such a course of action . . . might well, and quite understandably, lead the central bank to defer taking needed regulatory actions." In recent years the political sensitivities have been such as to make deregulation more likely to generate controversy than resisting change. It is not coincidental that the Federal Reserve has been the most conservative and least innovative of the federal banking agencies.

These considerations lead to the conclusion that, apart from any other change in the structure of financial regulation, the Federal Reserve should be removed from that responsibility. That is, even if no other changes were to be made, it would be appropriate to transfer the bank and bank holding company supervisory responsibilities of the Federal Reserve to the FDIC and/or the Comptroller of the Currency.

Mergers.   The major current difference in policy among the agencies relates to mergers and holding company acquisitions. Differences with respect to mergers have been documented among the agencies, but we should also note that there have been significant changes in policy related to the individual agency heads. Although the comptroller has generally been viewed as having a more permissive attitude toward mergers than the Federal Reserve or FDIC, that has depended on the individual comptroller. The merger policy of the FDIC was more restrictive during the term of Frank Wille as chairman than before or since. And the policies of the Federal Reserve on holding company acquisitions are impossible to explain on any consistent basis that does not recognize changes in the composition of the board of governors.

These inconsistencies have caused problems in the existing regulatory framework. But we have noted that deregulation will lead to an increase in the number of mergers and holding company acquisitions. It will be intolerable to have differing policies at the different agencies. Differences will create substantial inequities and will lead to shifts among supervisory agencies as banks seek out the most permissive. As we have noted, such changes, including charter conversions, will be easier in the future. There are two reasonable solutions. Consolidation of the agencies could put the authority to pass on applications for all mergers and holding company acquisitions with the single agency. Alternatively, whether agency consolidation takes place or not, the merger process could be so changed that no agency approval is required. Bank mergers would then be treated under the antitrust laws just like all other mergers. Unless agency decisions are given some special status in court (i.e., overturned only on grounds of being arbitrary and capricious), there seems to be little value to going through the agency approval process, as at present. This has become clearer as decisions have limited the agencies' ability to deny merger applications on competitive grounds that do not reach the level of antitrust violations.

The principal advantage of the present system for handling bank mergers is a combination of the short statute of limitations and the automatic injunction against consummation of a merger against which the Justice Department has filed suit. This prevents the possible need for a divestiture if the ultimate court decision goes against the merger. This benefit is a significant one in the case of mergers, though it is less important in the case of holding company acquisitions. Of course, holding company acquisitions are not subject to a divided regulatory process, since the Federal Reserve is the responsible agency regardless of the bank involved. Recently, however, several cases that basically represent a holding company expansion have been structured as mergers involving a subsidiary bank so as to have the decision made by the comptroller, rather than the Federal Reserve.

Holding Company Regulation.   There are now substantial differences between the regulation of bank holding companies and savings and loan holding companies. The major difference is that one-association savings and loan holding companies are not subject to any restrictions on their nonfinancial activities, while one-bank holding companies are subject to the same very restrictive restrictions on their nonbanking activities as multibank holding companies. This difference in treatment creates no serious problem if the business of commercial banking is separate and distinct from the savings and loan business. But as savings institutions gain powers that make them indistinguishable from commercial banks, the difference will create both serious inequities and administrative problems.

A one-association savings and loan holding company must meet a definitional standard in order to receive this favorable treatment. However, the definition of a qualifying savings and loan association is not very difficult to meet. It requires that 60 percent of assets be held in qualifying assets, which include not only mortgages and housing-related securities, but also U.S. government securities and bank deposits. Not only do virtually all savings and loans meet this standard, but also many commercial banks now have portfolios which would qualify, and many more could easily make changes to meet the standard. Thus many commercial banks could convert to savings and loans and gain the power to operate any nonfinancial business they care to. Alternatively, the converted institution could be sold to a firm in any line of business. As distinct from the "nonbank banks" that have been acquired by holding companies, these savings and loans could continue to accept demand deposits and make commercial loans. Moreover, in several nonbranching states (such as Texas, Illinois, Colorado), the converted institution could establish branches, whereas as a commercial bank it could not.

This difference in rules must be resolved, but it is not clear how to accomplish that. Prior to 1970, there were no limitations on the nonbanking activity of one-bank holding companies, but in that year the Bank Holding Company Act was amended. The change was traumatic for many such holding companies, with widespread divestiture required. Presumably something of that sort could be done with respect to one-association savings and loan holding companies, but there is one added complication now. In recent months the FHLBB has been urging industrial companies to acquire savings and loans that are in danger of failure. It would be strange public policy to urge nonfinancial firms to perform a public service by taking on an ailing savings institution, and then, a few months or years later, to require divestiture of the acquired institution.

It should be stressed that the distinction between one-association holding companies and those owning more than one savings and loan will disappear when barriers to interstate branching are eliminated. In that case, all subsidiaries could be merged into one, including interstate operations.

In any case, regardless of the form of the resolution of this problem, equity and consistency in administration is going to require that a single regulatory agency supervise bank holding companies. We have discussed earlier in this section the reasons for believing that the Federal Reserve should be out of the supervisory business.

IV. RECOMMENDATIONS

The considerations discussed in the previous section of this paper lead to the conclusion that the regulatory agency structure that exists today is not appropriate for the financial system that will exist when the deregulation process now underway is completed. At that time thrift institutions will have virtually the same powers as commercial banks, the distinction between member banks and non-members will be meaningless (as it nearly is now as a result of the Monetary Control Act of 1980), and geographic restrictions on depository institutions will be eliminated. The optimal approach to this situation is a single regulatory agency at the federal level with responsibility for commercial banks, mutual savings banks, savings and loan associations, and credit unions. If regulation of bank and savings and loan holding companies continues, this consolidated agency should have supervisory responsibilities for the holding companies as well.

The single agency would represent a consolidation of the functions of the Office of Comptroller of the Currency, the Federal Home Loan Bank Board, the Credit Union National Administration, the FDIC, and the supervisory and regulatory functions of the Federal Reserve System. It is not clear whether continuation of the Federal Home Loan Bank System and the Credit Union Central Liquidity Facility is appropriate. Savings and loans and credit unions now have access to the Federal Reserve discount window for liquidity problems, and that could eliminate need for the separate specialized industry facilities. However, Home Loan Bank advances are not simply designed to provide for temporary liquidity needs, as are loans from the Federal Reserve, but represent a long-term source of funds to be used for financing housing. Further, administration of the discount function by the Federal Reserve is more complicated when the borrowing institution is not supervised by the Federal Reserve. Of course, that situation already exists, and means must be developed for the Federal Reserve to receive information on the financial status of discount window loan applicants, whether they be commercial banks or thrift institutions.

A consolidated agency at the federal level does not necessarily mean the end of the dual banking system, though state supervisory officials have frequently contended that it will. The states will still be able to charter and supervise banks and thrift institutions, though any such institutions that want federal deposit insurance will have to subject themselves to regulation by the federal regulatory commission. It should be noted that a dual chartering system exists in the savings and loan industry, even though there is just one regulatory agency at the federal level. The Federal Home Loan Board now both charters federal savings and loans and regulates state-chartered institutions.

There are several possible approaches to the design of the new consolidated federal regulatory agency. There are sound arguments in favor of a single administrator and in favor of a multimember commission. I see considerable merit in a plan proposed by an advisory committee to the Comptroller of the Currency in 1962, which would have had a single administrator heading a bureau of the Treasury Department. The Secretary of the Treasury is the chief financial officer of the government, and it is logical that supervision of the federally insured depository institutions fall in his bailiwick. This approach would probably stir up considerable opposition—both from those who oppose the single administrator concept and those who would prefer an independent agency rather than a location in the Treasury.[14]

The most palatable approach to a consolidated agency would involve an "independent" agency headed by a commission appointed by the President for fixed terms. My preference is for as small a commission as possible; the fewer the members, the greater the prestige and status, and the easier to get first-rate people to serve. On the other hand, three members often turns out to be too few for smooth personal relationships. This suggests a commission of five members. Because there may be concern about the elimination of the bank supervisory role of the Federal Reserve, it would be appropriate to have a member of the Board of Governors as a member of the financial institution regulatory commission. This could be on a nonvoting basis or as a regular member of the commission. My preference would be for the former.

The commission would administer the deposit insurance responsibilities that now rest with the FDIC, FSLIC, and the Credit Union Share Insurance Fund, but there is no compelling reason to continue the deposit insurance funds. It would be preferable to make deposit insurance a direct guarantee of the U. S. Treasury. There are several reasons for such a change (which has merit even in the absence of any other changes in the regulatory agency framework).

In recent months the problems of the thrift institutions have led to questions concerning the solvency of the insurance funds and their ability to meet the losses they may be faced with in the future. In the past it was very easy to dismiss such questions, but that is no longer true. The efficiency of the financial system would be adversely affected if depositors became more reluctant to rely on the security of deposit insurance. It should be noted that while a good argument can be advanced in favor of leaving some degree of risk in the banking system (so that uninsured depositors choose among institutions on the basis of their soundness and conservatism), there is no comparable benefit to leaving risk in the deposit insurance system itself.

A change from our present system of divided responsibility for supervision of financial institutions to the consolidated agency I have described will be rather traumatic, and will involve rather substantial adjustment costs. It is appropriate, therefore, to seek a means of phasing into the consolidated system over time. An intermediate plan proposed by Frank Wille several years ago may be appropriate as a means of moving toward eventual full consolidation.[15]

Under that plan, the Office of the Comptroller of the Currency would continue with little change in function. The examination and supervisory responsibilities of the FDIC and the Federal Reserve would be combined in a new office, headed by a single administrator (the "Federal Supervisor of State Banks"). Wille's plan calls for the creation of a five-member Federal Banking Board, which would have direct responsibility for passing on merger and bank holding company acquisitions, would administer Section 4(c)(8) of the Bank Holding Company Act, would administer the deposit insurance system, and would be responsible for serving in a general coordinating role (as is now played by the Federal Financial Institutions Examination Council). The banking board would also be responsible for promulgation of regulations for all banks in those areas (particularly consumer protection) in which Congress has delegated responsibility to the Federal Reserve, and would be responsible for collecting data and reports from all institutions on a uniform basis.

Under Wille's plan, the comptroller, the federal supervisor of state banks, and a governor of the Federal Reserve System would serve as ex officio members of the Federal Banking Board, while the two remaining members would be appointed by the President (with one of them designated as chairman).

It is easy to modify this proposal to include the functions I have proposed for the consolidated depository institutions commission. The board could also have responsibility for merger and holding company acquisitions and credit unions, and would administer their deposit insurance systems. It could also assume the responsibility for financial disclosure by such institutions that now rests with the SEC. The chairman of the Federal Home Loan Bank Board and the Credit Union national administrator could be added to the board (the board could be established with seven members, or preferably, the Federal Reserve representative would be a nonvoting member).

The attraction of a plan of this sort is that it does not require a drastic reshuffling of existing agency responsibilities, yet does provide for centralized decision making in certain areas where the present system leads to differences in policy—particularly mergers and holding company acquisitions and activities—which will become more of a problem in the future. Also, the framework proposed here provides for an easy evolution toward full consolidation. That is, it would be possible to move to a system in which the board absorbs the separate agencies, perhaps as divisions of the consolidated commissions. In this case the comptroller, the federal supervisor of state banks, CUNA, and the FHLBB all become a formal part of the consolidated commission.

This plan could have some political appeal both to those who prefer to keep the separate agency system we now have, but recognize the need for improved coordination, and to those who see it as a significant step towards full consolidation.

SUMMARY

The basic point of this paper is rather simple: While it may be argued that the present regulatory agency structure works rather well under our present regulatory framework, that agency structure is not appropriate for the financial environment that will exist as deregulation proceeds. Several conflicts or inequities that are tolerable now will become major stumbling blocks to an efficiently operating financial system. The movement towards deregulation is desirable and should continue, but it will call for some consolidation among the financial regulatory agencies.

This paper sets forth a regulatory structure that should be adequate to handle the problems. The plan set forth here has some nice features, particularly an adaptability to being phased in over time, but a number of variations on the consolidated agency approach are possible. An acceptable plan, however, must have certain characteristics: bringing commercial banks and thrift institutions under the same regulator; all merger and holding company acquisitions decided by the same regulator; elimination of the Federal Reserve as a regulatory agency (though preserving Federal Reserve access to whatever information generated in the process of supervision that is useful for monetary policy); assuring confidence in the soundness of the deposit insurance system; allowing for a continued role for the states in chartering financial institutions (though assuring that all insured institutions operate with some federal supervision and that state laws do not interfere with the national character of financial markets). It would be nice if operating economies were to result from the consolidated agency structure, but that should not be a major criterion in choosing among plans and, in any case, such economies are likely to be small.

At many times in our history a consolidation of the supervisory agency structure would have been desirable. In the future it will be necessary.

NOTES

[1] Bernard Shull has written: "The current distribution of responsibilities and authority among agencies regulating depository institutions is not the result of a master plan. It developed on an *ad hoc* basis over a long period of time . . .", in *Financial Institutions and Markets,* 2nd ed., eds. Murray E. Polakoff and Thomas A. Durkin (Boston: Houghton Mifflin Company, 1981). George Kaufman states, "The existing regulatory structure was developed in bits and pieces on an *ad hoc* basis in response to . . . crises. . . . The changes . . . were not part of a . . . well-considered overall blueprint." *The U.S. Financial System* (Englewood Cliffs, N. J.: Prentice Hall, 1980), p. 267.

[2] See, for example, Robert A. Eisenbeis, "Differences in Federal Regulatory Agencies' Bank Merger Policies," *Journal of Money, Credit and Banking,* 1975.

[3] Ibid.

[4] See Bernard Shull, "Federal and State Supervision of Bank Holding Companies," in *State and Federal Regulation of Commercial Banks,* vol. 2 (Washington, D.C.: FDIC, 1980).

[5] The best attempt to quantify the potential savings has been done by the FDIC. In a March 26, 1979, letter to Senator Proxmire, the FDIC's chief financial officer, James A. Davis, reported that "consolidation of the [banking] agencies . . . could possibly save about $700 thousand per year." Mr. Davis went on to note that, "These savings would be realized only after initial consolidation costs and the costs of phasing personnel and procedures into the consolidated organization."

[6] "Maintaining the Soundness of our Banking System," speech to the American Bankers Association, October 21, 1974, pp. 18–19.

[7] The crucial elements here are a system of dual chartering of depository institutions, but with state-chartered institutions subject to federal law and regulation, and federally chartered institutions

subject to some elements of state law; bank holding companies with subsidiary banks of various clases, but not with savings and loan subsidiaries; nonbank depository institutions limited in powers, compared with commercial banks; a separation of commercial banking and investment banking. Until recently, we have also had a central bank with voluntary membership and participation in its reserve requirements, and separate deposit insurance systems with different rules of operation for different institutions.

[8] "Comments on Bank Regulatory Reform," hearings before the Subcommittee on Financial Institutions, Committee on Banking, Currency and Housing, U.S. House of Representatives, July 21, 1975.

[9] Handling large bank failures involves much agency cooperation. The Franklin National Bank failure could only be resolved through a purchase and assumption transaction facilitated by FDIC funds. But working out this solution took time, during which the Federal Reserve was the only source of liquidity to keep the bank afloat; and when the deal was arranged, only the comptroller could close the bank to put the deal into effect. Nevertheless, Wille argues that a different agency structure would not have prevented any of the large bank failures of recent years.

[10] For a good exposition of this issue, see John Kareken, "Deregulating Commercial Banks," *Quarterly Review,* Federal Reserve Bank of Minneapolis, Spring–Summer 1981.

[11] The FIEC has consumed large amounts of staff time among the agencies without much to show in terms of improved coordination. The DIDC has not prevented differing interpretations of the same law by the FHLBB and the FRB. The NCUA has not been abided by the passbook ceilings determined by the committee for banks and savings and loans.

[12] "Conflicts between Monetary Policy and Bank Supervision," *Issues in Bank Regulation,* Autumn 1977, p. 34.

[13] For example, in recent testimony on this issue, Federal Reserve Governor J. Charles Partee argued that "the board is convinced that bank supervision and monetary policy are closely and inevitably linked, and that supervisory policy and monetary policy should not be determined in isolation. . . . In the board's judgment, breaking this link could at times impair the Federal Reserve's ability to carry out monetary policy effectively." Governor Partee's testimony included no evidence or examples to support this contention. Hearings before the Committee on Banking, Housing and Urban Affairs, U.S. Senate, February 28, 1979.

[14] It is interesting to observe that both proponents and opponents of a single administrator point to the term of James Saxon as comptroller in support of their position. They are probably correct that a three or five member commission is very unlikely to take the innovative steps that Saxon was able to.

[15] "Centralization Which Preserves a Regulatory Choice," speech before the Association of Registered Bank Holding Companies, Palm Beach, Florida, November 17, 1975.

PART TWO

Deregulation of Financial Institutions

Deregulation has three principal components: (1) deposit-rate deregulation, which involves the lifting of ceilings on the maximum rates that commercial banks (and other depository institutions) may pay to attract deposits; (2) product deregulation, which involves reducing the restrictions on the types of services that may be offered by commercial banks (and other depository institutions), with particular reference to entry into investment banking, insurance, real estate, and underwriting; and (3) geographical deregulation, which encompasses the reduction of barriers to intrastate and interstate banking and focuses particularly on the issue of "nationwide" banking.

Deposit-rate deregulation occurred to a limited extent in the 1970s through the administrative actions of the bank regulatory authorities. However, most deposit-rate deregulation took place in the early and mid-1980s following congressional passage of the Depository Institutions Deregulation and Monetary Control Act of 1980 and the Garn-St Germain Depository Institutions Act of 1982. By April 1986, the only remaining deposit-rate ceiling was the statutory prohibition against the payment of interest on demand deposit accounts.

In contrast to the substantial degree of deposit-rate deregulation in the early and mid-1980s, the amount of product deregulation has been relatively slight for commercial banks. DIDMCA in 1980 and Garn-St Germain in 1982 did extend substantial additional powers to federally chartered savings and loans and credit unions. However, through early 1986, the U.S. Congress had taken no action about allowing banks to expand their activities into securities underwriting, insurance, real estate, and other areas now prohibited by the Glass-Steagall Act of 1933.

Action on the federal level to bring about geographic deregulation has been most notable by its absence, though substantial action has taken place at the state level. Banking organizations have been able to expand interstate through their nonbank subsidiaries. In addition, many states have responded aggressively to the lack of federal action on interstate banking and have taken a variety of actions to expand the geographical areas over which banking organizations could operate. For example, Massachusetts permits depository institution holding companies located in other New England states to acquire Massachusetts depository institutions on a reciprocal basis. In addition, Arizona allows out-of-state bank holding companies to acquire Arizona banking organizations without requiring any reciprocity. While the future of interstate banking through state initiatives had been subject to legal questions, a decision by the U.S. Supreme Court in June 1985 affirmed the constitutionality of these state actions.

Since deposit-rate deregulation has been occurring for an extended period and is essentially complete, the readings in this section concentrate on product and geographical deregulation. In addition, the focus of these articles is on the potential effects of further product and geographical deregulation, rather than on the existing status of these restrictions on banking organizations.

In the first article in this section, "Risk Considerations in Deregulating Bank Activities," Larry Wall and Robert Eisenbeis explore the potential effects on the riskiness of banking organizations of allowing banks to expand their product offerings. They point out that the effects of expanding activities at banking organizations on their risk level depends not only on the risk of the activity itself but also on the manner in which the risk of the new activity affects the risk of the entire organization (determined by the correlation coefficient between the earnings of the new activity and the existing bank products). Examining the evidence on the risk (variability) of different activities, they find that some activities (such as insurance agency operations) are *less* risky than banking but others (such as security and commodity broker/dealers) are *more* risky than banking. However, while security broker/dealers are more risky than banking, their earnings move inversely to those in banking, suggesting that allowing banks to move into securities activities may not, in fact, increase risk at banking organizations.

The second article in this section, "Securities Activities of Commercial Banks," by Anthony Saunders focuses more narrowly on one possible new activity proposed for commercial banking, that of underwriting corporate securities, an activity prohibited since 1933 by the Glass-Steagall Act. In addition, the article focuses upon one particular concern about allowing banking organizations to underwrite corporate securities, that of conflict of interest between the investment and commercial banking parts of these organizations. Saunders evaluates the various arguments that compromise the conflict-of-interest issue, and discusses the existing controls that are designed to reduce the significance of this problem. He concludes that "positive social benefits may well accrue" from allowing banks into securities underwriting.

The two articles in this section that deal with interstate banking focus on different dimensions of this issue. In "The Competitive Effects of Interstate Banking," Charles Morris explores the potential effects of interstate banking on competition. Many of those who oppose interstate banking argue that the authorization of nationwide banking would produce an increase in the concentration of banking resources and a diminution of competition. Morris evaluates this argument, as well as the argument that interstate banking would actually increase competition. He also reviews the extensive evidence of previous studies that looked at the effects on bank performance of changes in market concentration. Morris concludes that interstate banking is unlikely to increase concentration and that, even if it did, there would most likely be no significant effects on bank performance.

While Morris deals with the potential effects of interstate banking on concentration and competition, David Whitehead in "Interstate Banking: Probability or Reality?" deals with the existing evidence on the extent of interstate banking. As Whitehead points out, despite the existing laws that restrict a banking organization in expanding interstate through adding additional banks or branches, these organizations have found numerous other ways to operate interstate. For example, at the end of 1982, banking organizations operated over 5,000 interstate offices of their nonbank subsidiaries. These subsidiaries made consumer loans, originated mortgages, leased equipment, and engaged in a number of other bank-like activities.

The final article in this section, "The Regulation of Bank Entry," by Michael Keeley, deals with a less-discussed dimension of regulation and deregulation—the effects of legal restrictions on bank entry, with particular reference to the banking industry. He also attempts to determine if entry constraints in banking have been reduced in recent years. He finds that bank entry has been relatively unrestricted since the early 1960s and particularly during the 1980s.

8

Risk Considerations in Deregulating Bank Activities

Larry D. Wall and Robert A. Eisenbeis

Easing restrictions on bank products may carry risks if an institution's activities are poorly managed, but perpetuating those limitations poses dangers as well. Here's a look at the arguments on both sides of the dilemma.

Bank activities have long been heavily regulated, not only because of concern over potential conflicts of interest, unfair competition, and undue concentration of resources, but, more important, for safety and soundness reasons.[1] Safety and soundness regulations limit banking organizations' asset and liability portfolios, provide for examinations, provide deposit insurance, and offer access to the discount window at the Federal Reserve.

Proponents of deregulation argue that continued regulation of activities adds nothing to the system protecting bank safety and soundness. They further contend that regulation places banks at a competitive disadvantage and will allow less-regulated nonbank competitors to assume banks' role in our financial system. Advocates of continued regulation argue that deregulation would strain the rest of the safety and soundness system and could even undermine the banking system.

We have reviewed the argument that continued regulation jeopardizes banks' competitive position and then considered the risks of allowing new activities. Our conclusion is that deregulation poses no threat to the stability of the financial system but that failure to deregulate does pose such a threat. The risks inherent in deregulation arise because the deposit insurance agency and the discount window bear much of the costs of bank failure. We have examined three regulatory reforms suggested as substitutes for activity deregulation but found significant problems with each.

We then considered the effect on bank risk of allowing banks to expand into currently prohibited financial activities. Our findings suggest that, had banking organizations been passive owners of some prohibited activities, their earnings might have been less volatile during the 1970s. But their earnings might have been

From *Economic Review*, Federal Reserve Bank of Atlanta, May 1984, pp. 6–19.

The authors wish to thank Felicia Bellows and Rebel Cole for their research assistance.

more volatile had they been passive owners of some other activities. We also found no evidence to indicate that the bond market anticipates significant changes in the riskiness of acquirers of various financial firms.

RISKS OF CONTINUED REGULATION

The system set up to maintain bank safety and soundness exists in large part because banks' deposit-taking activities play such an important role in the economy. Banks traditionally have dominated payments services, and we learned during the 1800s and early 1900s that protecting bank safety was critical to a smoothly functioning economy. This dominance is being challenged, however, by competitors from outside the banking industry.[2] These competitors generally are not sheltered by the protective system covering banks. Thus, regulation that weakens banks' competitive position—even if it strengthens bank safety—can weaken the economy by increasing the growth rate of institutions that offer liabilities serving as money but that lack access to federal deposit insurance or the discount window.

Some proponents of deregulation, such as Charles S. Sanford, Jr., of Bankers Trust Company, argue that regulation threatens banks' competitive position. Sanford (1984) contends that commercial and investment banking are becoming indistinguishable. He also argues that current restrictions increase banks' riskiness by limiting their ability to employ risk-management techniques, such as selling off credit risk. Other banks point to the growing list of retail products offered by Merrill Lynch, Sears, Prudential, and others as evidence that they need to expand into new activities to compete effectively.

Given current regulation, the threat nonbank challengers pose to commercial banks' competitive position depends on consumer preferences and the ability of less-regulated firms to generate synergies between different financial services. Regardless of the conclusions drawn from available evidence, the risk of regulating commercial banks and unknowingly affecting the structure of the financial system must be considered. Maintaining the soundness of individual banks is only a means to an end; the ultimate goal is a safe and sound financial system.

THE RISK RATIONALE FOR ACTIVITY RESTRICTIONS

Two major types of restrictions on the affiliation of commercial banks with other firms have been imposed at different times for different reasons. Specific restrictions barring commercial banks from affiliating with investment banking were adopted shortly after the banking crisis of 1933 and were in part a reaction to that crisis. The general restrictions on commercial bank affiliations with other banks and nonbanking firms are based on the 1956 Bank Holding Company Act and its 1970 amendments. These restrictions appear to have been justified primarily by a desire to prevent concentration of financial power and conflicts of interest. Risk considerations played a less significant role.

Advocates of continued activity regulation frequently argue that commercial and investment banking were separated by the Glass-Steagall Act in 1933 to protect commercial banks' safety. A review of the record suggests, however, that conflict of interest considerations played a larger role in the separation. During the late 1920s and early 1930s, commercial bank affiliates could engage in investment banking. During this period some investment banking affiliates engaged in operations that appeared unethical (though they were legal at that time).[3]

Furthermore, commercial banks were making loans for securities purchases, and some people believe the banks were feeding the " . . . speculative fever of the late 1920s."[4] The fever ended with a stock market crash in 1929. The early 1930s saw a wave of bank failures, culminating in a 1933 panic that struck both strong and weak banks. That panic forced President Roosevelt to declare a nationwide bank holiday shortly after he was inaugurated. Congress responded to the collapse by passing a series of banking laws, including the Glass-Steagall Act, which prohibits commercial banks and their affiliates from engaging in investment banking.

The 1930s collapse of the banking system was tragic, but it did not prove that the safety and soundness of the current banking system depends on activity regulation. Many contemporary analysts doubt that the 1933 collapse was due to banks' affiliation with securities firms.[5] Most banks that failed during the 1920s and early 1930s were small and had no large securities affiliates.[6] The prominent commercial banks whose affiliates' unethical behavior had upset Congress remained in business.

Another reason for doubting a current safety-activity regulation connection is the development of deposit insurance and the more active role taken by the discount window since 1933. The 1933 banking crisis occurred because even sound banks became illiquid when the public lost confidence and withdrew deposits. The creation of deposit insurance reduced the incentives for people to withdraw money if they think a bank will fail. Furthermore, as a consequence of changes in Federal Reserve policies for administering the discount window, the Fed now provides sound banks with the resources they need to survive a liquidity crisis.

Federal deposit insurance and strengthening the Federal Reserve discount window have reduced the probability of a banking system collapse, but they have created new problems. As Edward Kane (1983 and 1984) points out, the government now bears much of the risk of bank failures. If banks are allowed to engage in new activities that increase bank risk, then the government will bear those risks.

One problem with the government's bearing the risk of bank failure is the effect on competition between firms. If the market believes that banking organizations' liabilities all have implicit government backing, then it will charge lower risk premiums on those liabilities. This will give banking organizations a competitive advantage over firms not associated with a commercial bank.[7]

Fear of concentration of power and conflicts of interest were far more responsible for the Bank Holding Company Act of 1956 and its 1970 amendments than was the financial risk of nonbanking activities.[8] Prior to 1956, BHCs could acquire banks outside their home state and commercial firms without obtaining permission from the state of the acquiring bank. Some BHCs were building interstate networks of banks and commercial firms. For example, William Upshaw (1968) notes that Transamerica held 38 percent of all commercial bank deposits in five western states in 1946. In 1956, following the Supreme Court's refusal to uphold the Federal Reserve's attempt to force a divestiture of Transamerica's interstate holdings, Congress turned its attention to BHC activities. It found some BHCs building a conglomeration of bank and nonbank firms that raised concerns about the concentration of financial power. A Senate Banking and Currency Committee report on the proposed act makes it clear that the primary rationale for restricting BHCs was a fear of concentrated power:

> It is not the committee's contention that bank holding companies are evil of themselves. However, because of the importance of the banking system to the national economy, adequate safeguards should be provided against undue concentration of control of banking activities.

Further support for the concentration of power theory is given by the fact that the act covered only multibank holding companies. If the primary concern had been bank safety, one would expect the controls also would have been placed on one-bank holding companies, but no such restrictions were placed on them. The Senate report justified this by arguing that:

> Your committee did not deem it necessary to include within the scope of this bill any company which manages or controls no more than a single bank. It is possible to conjure up visions of monopolistic control of banking in a given area through ownership of a single bank with many and widespread branches. However, in the opinion of your committee no present danger of such control through the bank holding company device threatens to a degree sufficient to warrant inclusion of such a company within the scope of this bill.

Starting in early 1968, many large banks began to form one-bank holding companies to exploit the potential diversification opportunities. This alarmed many observers, including then Federal Reserve chairman William Martin, who argued in 1969 that: " . . . if we allow the line between banking and commerce to be eased, we run the risk of cartelizing our economy."[9] This concern dealt more with the potential for problems than the reality of any problems. As the Senate Banking Committee's report on the 1970 BHC act amendments notes:

> In making this decision, the committee wishes to note its agreement with all of the government regulatory agencies who testified that there have been no major abuses effectuated through the one-bank holding company device. It is clearly understood that the legislation is to prevent possible future problems rather than to solve existing ones.

Essentially, the one-bank holding company movement exposed a major loophole in the 1956 restrictions and Congress wanted to extend the restrictions to prevent undue concentration of power. This interpretation of the 1970 amendments is further bolstered by the statement of the House managers in the conference committee report on the amendments. The report details its concerns with the concentration of economic resources and power, decreased or unfair competition, adverse competitive effects, and tie-ins. It then says that the Federal Reserve Board also should consider potential conflicts of interest and unsound banking practices when it authorizes a new activity. Congress was concerned about bank safety and soundness when it passed the 1970 amendments, but these appear to have been secondary concerns.

Thus, safety and soundness considerations do not appear to have been the primary factor behind either the Glass-Steagall restrictions or the BHC act's activity restrictions. Furthermore, the development of deposit insurance and the revision of discount window administration minimized the risk of a banking system collapse. The real problem with removing activity restrictions is that it could shift risks to the government. Such a shift could strain the safety and soundness system and give banks a competitive advantage in their nonbanking endeavors.

The potential problem of allowing traditional banking organizations to enter into currently prohibited activities is not one-dimensional. Firms currently operating in activities prohibited to banks are acquiring savings and loans and nonbank banks.[10] These thrifts and nonbank institutions can provide most of the asset and liability services, such as transaction accounts and commercial loans, that have in the past made banks uniquely important in our financial system. Furthermore, nonbank institutions can be insured by the federal government and can gain access to the discount window, so their problems can also impose costs on the system designed to protect traditional banking organizations. These nonbank bank acquisitions raise the same fundamental questions posed by proposals to expand permissible bank activities. The conclusions drawn below, therefore, apply to acquirers of thrifts and nonbank banks.[11]

OTHER METHODS OF MAINTAINING BANK SAFETY

The above analysis argues that, given deposit insurance and the discount window, activity restraints are not necessary to protect the banking system from collapse— but they may have a role in limiting the risks borne by the government safety and soundness programs when insurance is not properly priced.[12] This suggests that reform of the safety and soundness system could substitute for activity regulation.[13] Possible reforms include proposals to deregulate the activities of BHC nonbank subsidiaries, proposals to reform deposit insurance so that banks are charged risk-based premiums, and proposals to increase the risk borne by private creditors of banks.

One proposal to allow activity deregulation through expanding the permissible activities of BHC subsidiaries was made by the Treasury Department a couple of years ago.[14] It attempts to ensure safety and soundness by restricting transactions between bank and nonbank subsidiaries to insulate banks from the risks borne by their affiliates. It assumes that individual nonbank subsidiaries within a BHC could fail without affecting the health of the banking subsidiaries.

This proposal is attractive because it claims to eliminate the safety and soundness problems associated with expanded BHC activity. Unfortunately, as Robert Eisenbeis (1983) points out, subsidiary banks' risk exposure can be independent of the exposure of its affiliates only if the BHC is run as a passive mutual fund. If the BHC controls or coordinates the activities of its subsidiaries to maximize joint (or consolidated) profit, then BHC affiliates' problems will inevitably affect the bank subsidiaries. Furthermore, existing evidence suggests that BHCs operate as integrated entities.[15]

An important problem is that BHCs have shown a tendency to draw on all of their resources to help troubled subsidiaries. For example, BHCs risked substantial losses in the 1970s to prevent the real estate investment trusts they sponsored from failing, even though the BHCs did not even have substantial ownership interest in those REITs. The primary stake to individual BHCs in an REIT failure was their reputation. BHCs logically would do at least as much for units they own, especially if those units generate important synergies with the BHCs' banking subsidiaries. The Treasury Department argues that regulations can be developed to prevent BHCs from using banks to help nonbank subsidiaries. Eisenbeis argues, however, that such regulation imposes costs on the BHC and will induce it to shift activities from subsidiary banks to nonbank affiliates. These shifts would increase bank dependence on nonbank affiliates for customer services and operational support. Thus, attempting to isolate banks from their subsidiaries could increase their dependence on subsidiaries.

The risk borne by the government if a bank or an affiliate is allowed to engage in a new activity could be controlled by charging the bank a variable-rate insurance premium based on risk exposure. The government bears some of the cost of a failure because it fails to charge premiums based on the banking organization's risk. Thus, individual banks are in a position to take large gambles knowing that the bank can keep its earnings if the risk pays off and that the government will cover the losses if it fails. Furthermore, even banks not inclined to gamble have less of an incentive to control their risk exposure than they would if they were charged for the risks they take. As Mark Flannery (1982) notes: "FDIC's fixed-rate premium structure is unusual and this constitutes the *raison d' être* for other bank regulations."

Variable-rate insurance may work well in some theoretical models, but risk-based premiums would be difficult to implement. In its report to Congress, for example, the FDIC said that an "ideal system" with premiums closely tied to (commercial bank) risk "is simply not feasible." If relating insurance premiums to risk for banks is difficult, it must be even more difficult within a holding company framework.[16]

A third way of deregulating while limiting the risk exposure of government is to shift more of the risk exposure to the private sector. The FDIC recently began experimenting with this approach by limiting full payment on deposits to $100,000 per depositor for selected bank failures.[17] Other possible ways of transferring the risk to the private sector include substituting private for government insurance, and requiring banking organizations to use more equity and subordinated debt funding.

Before the government can shift more risk to the private sector, several problems must be addressed. One is that shifting risk to depositors and private deposit insurers means that uninsured depositors will be more likely to panic when bank solvency becomes a question.[18] As noted above, the banking collapse of 1933 was due in part to a loss of public confidence in the system. Deposit insurance was created in part to prevent bank runs, and it (along with the discount window) has prevented the reoccurrence of widespread runs. Thus, reducing deposit insurance coverage to limit bank risk would create an anomalous situation. We imposed deposit insurance to prevent such panics, but now are considering reimposing market discipline through the threat of runs to limit the risk exposure of the insurance system.[19]

A second problem with shifting risk is that in order to do so the government must be perceived as willing, and must in fact be willing, to let troubled banking organizations fail.[20] The private sector will not control bank risk exposure effectively if it believes the government may not allow banks to fail.[21] The FDIC report notes that, at present, many large depositors doubt that multi-billion dollar institutions will be closed.[22] The public's view of large bank failures is represented in a recent article by Robert A. Bennett in the *New York Times*. Bennett states that "big banks . . . are too important to be allowed to collapse. Public policy has for decades affirmed this doctrine by keeping banks from going far afield into other businesses and by propping them up when they get in trouble."

Each of the three methods of minimizing the government's exposure to potential losses from expanded banking activities would be desirable if they worked as intended. Unfortunately, each of the three has problems. The separate subsidiary approach can work only if BHCs operate as passive mutual funds or if regulations are imposed to force them to operate that way. The FDIC has difficulty measuring bank risk now, and these problems would be increased as banks expanded into new activities. Finally, greater reliance on the public sector may be possible, but the issues of bank runs and the closing of very large banks must be addressed first.

ANALYZING THE RISKINESS OF PROHIBITED ACTIVITIES

There is reason, then, to be concerned about the riskiness of currently prohibited activities. Ideally, these concerns would be reduced by reforming the safety and soundness system. Unfortunately, no reform proposal appears both workable and easy to implement. Furthermore, the financial services industry is evolving too fast to allow us to take several years to reform the system. As an interim measure, we could permit banking organizations to engage in financial activities that seem unlikely to increase significantly the risk of failure. Limiting the range of permitted activities to financial activities would allow banks to compete with the aspiring financial supermarkets, while limiting the types of risks borne by the government. Prohibiting acquisition of activities likely to increase banking organizations' risk would further limit the government's exposure.

If risk is to be a criterion for activity reform, then some method of measurement is needed. A naive approach would be to compare each activity's variability of earnings and failure rate with those of banks. A more sophisticated approach is suggested by David Meinster and Rodney Johnson (1979). Their approach looks at the effect of diversification on banking organizations' cash flow. It is clearly superior to the naive approach because it recognizes that some "risky" activities can actually curtail risk by reducing the variability of a combined organization's cash flow. For example, a risky activity could produce most of its cash flow when bank cash flow is weak but produce little when the bank's cash flow is strong. The variations in flow from the risky activity would offset variations in the bank's flow and their combined cash flow would be less variable than either of their individual flows.

While Meinster and Johnson's approach is an improvement, it still has some weaknesses. Their focus on liquidity, rather than solvency, is inappropriate for most larger banking organizations. These organizations rely on liability management for their liquidity, rather than cash flows from operations. Another weakness is the authors' concern about the combined organization's capitalization. Bank regulators can offset any attempt to undercapitalize the new activities by imposing capital standards on the bank or BHC. Thus, capitalization appears irrelevant in deciding whether to allow banking organizations to perform a particular activity.[23]

The Meinster and Johnson study's focus on the effects of diversification is an appropriate first step in reviewing the risks of allowing banks to expand into new activities. One way to analyze the diversification effects is to look at the level and variance of earnings of banking and other activities, and then look at the correlation between those earnings. Nonbanking activities can reduce the riskiness of banking organizations if either (1) the earnings from a nonbank activity are less volatile than in banking or (2) earnings from the nonbanking activity are negatively correlated with those in banking (i.e., if nonbanking profitability is highest when bank profits are at their lowest and vice versa). A banking organization's risk could increase if it acquires financial activities that have more volatile earnings than banking and whose returns are highly correlated with banking.

Analysis of those diversification effects are important, but they are not the sole criteria on which a decision should be based. The way an activity is managed can also affect its risk significantly. Cautious managers can turn a risky activity into a safe one, while an aggressive or inept management can jeopardize a safe activity. Banks already can take huge undiversified risks by speculating on interest rate and foreign exchange movements, but few banks have failed for these reasons. This suggests that regulators should scrutinize a bank's management when considering whether to let it expand into new activities. Some activities that may be too risky for banks in general could be acceptable for a bank that has a plan for maintaining reasonable risk levels. In other cases, a bank with weak management might not be permitted to perform an activity allowed to most other banks.[24]

RISKINESS OF NEW ACTIVITIES: PRIOR STUDIES

Two types of studies may shed some light on the effect on bank risk of expanding permitted activities. One type uses accounting data to study the riskiness of selected activities by themselves and their riskiness in combination with a banking organization. These studies typically have assumed that the bank and its prospective nonbank affiliates were held by a passive holding company that did not interfere in their operations. The evidence from these studies suggests that allowing banks to engage in additional activities may reduce their riskiness. The other type of study examines stock market reactions to the changing activity restrictions and to mergers of bank and nonbank firms. Studies of stock market reactions are useful because of their prospective nature. The market evaluates a company's expected future earnings and risk, taking account of any anticipated operating changes. These studies have found evidence that stock returns increase when a BHC can undertake geographic diversification, but that stocks neither gain nor lose on product diversification.

One of the earliest studies comparing the risks of banking and nonbanking organizations was conducted by Arnold Heggestad (1975). Heggestad used industry data to examine a variety of activities that one-bank holding companies engaged in prior to 1970.[25] He noted that one weakness of using industry data is that it captures only cyclical variations in profitability and not firm specific variations in profits. Heggestad found that commercial banking is one of the most risky activities when risk is measured as the coefficient of variation in profits. He also found that the returns to some activities (including real estate agents, brokers and managers, and insurance brokers and agents) are negatively correlated with banking. These findings suggest that banks could reduce their risk exposure by diversifying into new activities.

Johnson and Meinster (1974) also used industry data and reached conclusions similar to Heggestad's. They also simulated various portfolio combinations and found that BHCs that expand into nonbank activities can be less risky than BHCs that confine their activities to banking.

Peter Eisemann (1976) looked at a small sample of firms in different industry groupings and concluded that banking is one of the lowest risk activities based on profit variability. John Rose (1978b) reexamined Eisemann's results and concluded that banks were more risky, taking into account both profit levels and variability (using coefficient of variation in profits). Interestingly, Eisemann's simulation found that insurance brokerage was in the simulated portfolio that gave the highest return for low- and medium-risk organizations.

Michael Jessee and Steven Seelig (1977) compared the coefficient of variation of profits for selected BHCs and independent banks to determine whether BHCs were less risky and whether differences in diversification across BHCs reduced risk. They found that risk is not lower in BHCs than independent banks nor is it lower in BHCs that have a greater share of nonbanking assets. Rose (1978b) argued, however, that Jessee and Seelig's results may reflect econometric problems with their model. Rose also argued that the reduction in risk due to the BHC diversification may be offset by increased risk-taking by the bank and its nonbanking affiliates.

Roger Stover (1982) examined the effect on a BHC's value of establishing a portfolio of banks and assorted nonbank subsidiaries. He began by determining the debt capacity of a portfolio of bank and nonbank assets given a fixed probability of failure. He then assumed that an organization's value increases as its debt capacity increases. His results also have implications for the portfolio's risk. In his model, an increase in debt capacity would imply a decrease in the riskiness of the firm with leverage held constant. The model was estimated using both industry average data and data from specific firms. Stover found that BHC diversification outside of banking increased the organization's value. His analysis of companies found that fire and casualty insurance, investment banking, land development, and savings and loan companies should be included in a portfolio along with banking organizations because they increase its debt capacity and, by implication, lower its risk given constant leverage.

John Boyd, Gerald Hanweck, and Pipat Pithyachariyakul (1980) point out an important problem with using industry data when analyzing risk. Their study uses data on existing BHC subsidiaries. They found that the risk is almost always underestimated when one uses industry data, rather than data for individual companies. They also found that the correlations of returns can even change signs when one uses individual company data, rather than industry data. Their results suggest that we should not read too much into analysis using industry-wide data.

The effect of one-bank holding company formations (and the impact of the 1970 amendments to the Bank Holding Company Act) on bank stock returns is examined by Robert Eisenbeis, Robert Harris, and Josef Lakonishok (1982). Prior to the 1970 amendments, a one-bank holding company could engage in any activity except investment banking. Thus, the stock market's reaction to holding company formation during the sample period would reflect the market's opinion of the value of diversification. The researchers found that the stock market valued the potential for one-bank holding companies to provide for geographic diversification, but they found little evidence that the stock market valued product diversification.

The effect on the stock price of nonbank organizations acquiring so-called nonbank banks is examined by Jeffery Born, Robert Eisenbeis, and Robert Harris (1983). Presumably, if banking is less risky than nonbank activities, then acquiring nonbank banks should lower a nonbank organization's risk. That study found positive, but statistically insignificant, returns to the shares of nonbank organizations.

These studies of stock market returns provide some information on change in the firms' value. The results, however, are ambiguous concerning the perceived change in risk of an acquiring firm. Stock prices can increase even if the combined organization is more risky, provided the firm's expected returns also increase. Conversely, stock prices can fall for the acquirer even if the combined organization is less risky, provided the combined organization's expected returns are lower.

Studies that examine earnings data often find that banking is one of the riskiest activities and that banks' risk exposure would be reduced if they diversified. These studies use the best available data, but they must be interpreted with caution. Boyd, Hanweck, and Pithyachariyakul demonstrate the problems with using industry data and the studies that used data from individual companies relied on small samples. Studies that looked at stock market returns have found no evidence to demonstrate that banks will become either more or less risky.

EVIDENCE ON RISK: ANALYSIS OF EARNINGS

Table 1 provides a detailed look at the variability of returns from the *Corporate Source Book of Income* similar to those examined by Heggestad.[26] Heggestad's data covered the 1953–67 period, prior to passage of the 1970 amendments to the BHC Act. He examined the variability of both the ratio of average profits to capital and the ratio of net income to total assets. Given what has subsequently proved to be a significant difference in the capitalization of BHC subsidiaries, compared to independent firms and the widespread use of double leverage by holding companies, only the variability of net income to assets from nonbanking activities is examined in Table 1.[27] The 1970–80 data allow a comparison with those of Heggestad of any differences that may have occurred over a period of rapid change in the banking industry. These expanded tabulations also permit a preliminary examination of securities, insurance, and related activities now being considered as possible permissible activities for bank holding companies.

Several observations are worth noting. First, if the coefficient of variation is used as a risk measure then we conclude that banking (whether looking only at banks or at bank holding companies) is neither the most- nor least-risky activity. Second, conclusions about risk are influenced by the period under investigation. For example, using these same measures, Heggestad found that "lessors of railroad property" were among the riskiest firms investigated, while the present

TABLE 1
Coefficients of Variation and Determination for Selected Banking Activities (1970–1980)

	Coefficient Variation	Coefficient Determination
Banking	0.173503	0.622278
Mutual Savings Banks	0.296098	−0.43451
Banks and Trusts Except Mutual Savings Banks	0.211527	1
Credit Agencies Other than Banks	0.229455	−0.26771
Savings and Loans	0.337307	−0.20784
Personal Credit Agencies	0.326252	−0.49144
Business Credit Agencies	0.253581	0.586265
Other Credit Agencies and Finance Companies Not Allocable	0.146301	−0.05962
Security and Commodity Brokers, Dealers, etc.	0.350792	−0.16108
Security Brokers, Dealers, etc.	0.406553	−0.17821
Commodity Brokers, Dealers, etc.	0.213660	0.431596
Insurance	0.183474	0.167736
Life Insurance	0.100957	−0.163621
Mutual Insurance	0.487323	0.095143
Other Insurance Companies	0.427181	0.202264
Insurance Agents, Brokers, Service	0.118640	0.487375
Real Estate	0.216494	0.605346
Real Estate Operators, Lessors of Buildings	0.200242	0.645042
Lessors of Mining, Oil, etc.	0.434163	0.370005
Lessors of RR Property, Other Property Not Allocable	0.124316	−0.36543
Condominium Management, Co-op Housing Associations	0.542500	0.928662
Subdividers and Developers	0.306568	0.560607
Other Real Estate	0.184351	0.310724
Holding and Other Investment Companies	0.259857	0.792789
Regulated Investment Companies	0.247479	0.599360
Real Estate Investment Trusts	0.609843	0.421816
Small Business Investment Companies	0.627969	0.808927
Other Holding and Investment Companies Except BHCs	0.156598	0.686523
General Merchandise Stores	0.385963	−0.24442
Food Stores	0.106876	0.456074
Bank Holding Companies	0.198433	0.621591

The coefficient of variation is a measure of risk of the activity by itself. The coefficient of determination is a measure of the correlation of earnings of the firms with banking.

results suggest they are among the least risky. Third, many of the activities presently under consideration, such as securities, insurance, and certain real estate activities are more risky than banking. On the other hand, these activities appear somewhat less risky than other activities (such as consumer and commercial finance, operating small business investment corporations, and owning S&Ls), already permissible to banking organizations, which have not necessarily caused substantial problems. Examination of the coefficients of determination, however, reveals that several activities that appear more risky than banking (S&Ls, personal credit agencies, security brokerages and dealers, life insurance, and general merchandise) have returns that are negatively correlated with those of banking. This would suggest that such activities would be risk-reducing and imply the potential for beneficial diversification.

As Heggestad noted, we must exercise care in interpreting these data. They look only at cyclical variability of returns without weighing any synergies that may accrue; the fact that bank holding companies (not controlling for size) seem to have a smaller coefficient of variation than commercial banks alone suggests that such synergies may exist, possibly because certain risk-reducing activities have been authorized. Nor do the data imply anything about the riskiness of specific acquisitions. Finally, no attention is paid to cash flows. Rather, those data raise more questions than they answer concerning, for example, the stability of such measures over time. Also, the importance of negative correlation among banking and various nonbanking activities deserves further investigation.

EVIDENCE ON RISK: BOND MARKET REACTIONS

What about the return on bonds of firms that have recently acquired a financial services firm? Can it provide additional information on the riskiness of different financial services? The bond markets, in determining the price of a company's bonds, consider the factors that can influence its riskiness. Thus, the market will provide information on the expected effect of management on the riskiness of the new combination.[28] If the bond markets expect the new firm to be more risky, after considering all factors including management, then the price of the firm's bonds will fall. If the new firm is expected to be less risky, prices will rise.[29]

Unfortunately, most of the cases where one firm entered a new aspect of the financial services industry did not involve banking organization acquisitions. Therefore, most of the acquiring organizations we looked at are nonbank financial firms and nonfinancial firms. This analysis should shed some light on which combinations of services in the financial services industry are the most risky, and whether the financial services industry is less risky than some nonfinancial industries.

For this study we used the monthly returns on the bonds of 11 companies.[30] We separated the sample into four groups based on the characteristics of the acquiring and acquired firms. The composition of the four groups and the merger dates are given in Table 2.

The returns on a company's bonds normally fluctuate, so we needed some method to distinguish abnormally large fluctuations due to a merger from random fluctuations. We utilized the comparison period returns approach that Stephen Brown and Jerold Warner (1980) used in analyzing changes in stock returns.[31] This method compares fluctuations in returns during a control period with their fluctuations at the time of acquisitions. If the fluctuations are significantly larger at the time of acquisition than during the comparison period, the acquisition is assumed to have had a significant effect on bond prices. The control period extends from six months prior to the acquisition to two months prior and from one month after to six months after. The abnormal returns are measured over the month before and month of the acquisition.

Some of the abnormal bond returns in Table 3 are quantitatively large, but all are statistically insignificant. Neither were the abnormal returns of the individual acquiring firms significant. The large size of some of the abnormal returns appears to reflect volatility in long-term rates during this period. The insignificance of the abnormal returns suggests that bondholders did not perceive the acquisitions to have a significant effect on the acquiring firm's risk position.

TABLE 2
List of Firms in Bond Study by Characteristics of Acquired and Acquiring Company

Group	Acquiring Company	Acquired Company	Announcement Date	Bond Rating
Nonfinancial firms acquiring financial firms	American Can	Associated Madison Co.	1/8/82	Baa
	Sears, Roebuck & Co.	Dean Witter Reynolds	10/8/81	Aa
	Dana Corp.	General Ohio S&L Corp.	1/2/81	Aa
	Xerox	Crum & Foster	9/22/82	Aaa
Banks acquiring discount brokers	United Jersey Banks	Richard Blackman & Co.	9/29/82	N/A
	Bank America	Charles Schwab & Co.	11/25/81	Aaa
Financial firm acquiring another financial firm	American General	Credithrift Financial Inc.	9/21/81	A
Financial firms acquiring a nonbank bank	Household International	Valley National Bank	7/13/81	Aa
	Aetna Life & Casualty	Samuel Montagu & Co.	7/23/82	Aaa
	Walter E. Heller Intl. Corp.	American National Bank & Trust	7/14/72	N/A
	National Steel Corp.	United Financial Corp.	3/7/79	Aa

TABLE 3
Mean Abnormal Bond Returns of Firms Acquiring a New Financial Activity

Group	Annualized Return (t-statistic)
Nonfinancial firm acquiring a financial firm	−.00202 (−.104)
Banks acquiring a discount broker	−.19737 −.70289
Financial firm acquiring another financial firm	.25844 (.24117)
Financial firm acquiring a nonbank bank	−.19089 (−.48717)

CONCLUSION

Bank activity regulation is part of a larger system designed to protect the stability of the U.S. financial system. The threat that activity deregulation will destabilize the financial system is minimal, given the rest of the safety and soundness system, especially deposit insurance and discount-window access. The problem with activity deregulation is that the government now bears much of the risk of bank failure. Thus, the government will bear additional risk to the extent that deregulation increases the riskiness of banks. We cannot avoid all risks, however, by maintaining existing activity regulations. Banks are regulated to protect the financial system. Regulation may allow important bank functions to be assumed by institutions whose safety is less protected. If this happens, we would defeat the very purpose of regulating and protecting banks.

One alternative to regulating activities is to so reform the safety and soundness system that the private sector, and not the government, bears the risks of new ventures. Each of the three reforms under consideration have important problems that must be resolved. The first reform we considered would allow the new activities to be performed in BHC nonbank subsidiaries, and then use regulations to insulate the banking subsidiaries from their nonbank affiliates. Unfortunately, the health of the banking subsidiaries necessarily will depend on the health of their nonbank affiliates so long as the BHC uses its control over subsidiaries to maximize synergies and profits.

Another possible reform would charge risk-based premiums for government deposit insurance. The problem is that the FDIC says it cannot link premiums closely to risk for traditional banks, and the task is certain to be more difficult as the range of covered activities expands. A third possible reform would be to transfer more of the risk of bank failure to the private sector. This may have some merit, but first we must consider what to do about dealing with bank runs and about allowing very large banks to fail.

Since the decision to maintain existing regulations and the decision to reduce activity regulation both carry risks, one possible interim measure would be to allow banking organizations to offer additional financial services that are unlikely to increase their risk significantly. We explored this possibility by looking at the evidence on the effect of deregulation on risk. The evidence, based on historical earnings data, suggests that banking organizations' risk would have been lower in the 1970s had they been passive owners of some activities, but it would have increased for other activities.

This evidence is incomplete, however, because management can have a significant effect on risk. Cautious bank managers can make a risky activity relatively safe, but aggressive or inept managers can make a safe activity become risky. An analysis of bond market reactions to the acquisition of financial firms suggests that the bond market doubts that these acquisitions significantly change the risk exposure of the acquiring firm. This evidence also is incomplete, however, because examples of banks acquiring firms performing prohibited activities are, by definition, unavailable.

NOTES

[1] See Rose (1984) for an overview of the rationale for bank activity regulation.

[2] For example, banks lost substantial consumer deposits to the money market funds when bank deposit rates were limited by Regulation Q.

[3] For example, an affiliate of National City Bank sold Peruvian bonds without notifying the public that its agents had reported that Peru was a bad credit risk. The value of these bonds fell from 96½ with a spread of 5.03 points when issued in 1927 to 7 in February 1933. See Kennedy (1973), especially Chapter 5, for a discussion of the unethical behavior.

[4] The Supreme Court commenting on the reasons for the passage of Glass-Steagall in *I.C.I.* v. *Camp* decision, 91 S. Ct. 1091 (1971).

[5] Benston (1982), for example, argues that the primary purpose behind the legislation was to restrict competition.

[6] Kennedy notes that the overwhelming majority of small banks were small, rural, and located in unit banking states.

[7] Sanford argues that commercial banks are charged a lower-risk premium than other firms because regulation reduces their risk.

[8] Some restrictions on bank holding company affiliates were passed in the 1933 banking act, but these restrictions were weak. They only limited BHC affiliation with an investment banking firm and limited BHCs' ability to vote the shares of any Federal Reserve member banks.

[9] Senate Banking Committee's 1970 report.

[10] The Bank Holding Company Act of 1956, as amended, defines a bank as an institution that accepts demand deposits and makes commercial loans. A nonbank bank is an insured and regulated commercial bank, but it does not offer either demand deposits or commercial loans. It does not, therefore, meet the legal definition of a bank for the purposes of the Bank Holding Company Act.

[11] See Eisenbeis (1984) for a further discussion of the issues raised by nonbank banks.

[12] See also Kareken and Wallace (1978).

[13] Ignoring for the moment the concentration of financial power and conflict of interest problems.

[14] Chase and Waage (1983) also argue that banking subsidiaries can be protected from the problems of their nonbank affiliates.

[15] See Walen (1982a, b), Rose (1978), and Murray (1978).

[16] See Wall (1984a) for a review of the FDIC report and Wall (1984b) for further discussion of the problems with a risk-based insurance premium scheme run by the government.

[17] The first failure to be handled with the modified purchase and assumption method that exposes depositors to risk was the failure of Seminole State Bank. See Murray and Paltrow (1984).

[18] Private deposit insurance will not stop bank runs unless the solvency and liquidity of the private insurer are guaranteed by someone with unquestionable solvency and liquidity. See Leff and Park (1977) for discussion of the collapse of the Mississippi savings and loan insurance fund.

[19] Wall (1984b) discusses the potential for overcoming the problem by requiring banks to issue additional subordinated debt. Subordinated debt holders can redeem their claims only when the debt matures and they are, therefore, unable to participate in bank runs. He also points out, however, that the amount of subordinated debt that can be issued in the short run (and perhaps in the long run) will be limited due to practical problems.

[20] Mayer (1975) and Longstreth (1983) both discuss reasons why the government may not want to let large organizations fail.

[21] See Wall (1984b) for a further discussion of the issues involved in shifting the risk of loss to the private sector.

[22] Even if depositors, private insurers, or other parties are nominally at risk, the government can prevent a bank from failing if it wishes. The Federal Reserve can keep an illiquid bank open by providing loans to the bank, but this will result in a subsidy by the government to the extent the rates on the loans are below those the market would charge the bank.

[23] This concern is obviously relevant to the agencies, however, when they modify current standards.

[24] This suggestion would effectively extend current restrictions on BHC expansion to BHC expansion into new activities.

[25] The activities of one-bank holding companies were not restricted prior to the passage of the 1970 amendments to the Bank Holding Company Act except for the Glass-Steagall restrictions on investment banking.

[26] Source: Internal Revenue Service, various years 1970–1980.

[27] See, for example, the studies reviewed in *The Bank Holding Company Movement to 1978: A Compendium,* a study by the staff of the Board of Governors of the Federal Reserve System, Washington, D.C., 1978.

²⁸ The effect of management on risk could also be examined by looking at the earnings of the combined firms after the acquisition. This is not done in this study because the mergers being analyzed have taken place since 1979, which is too recent to have produced enough information on earnings.

²⁹ The unambiguous effect of risk on bond prices contrasts with the ambiguous effect of risk on stock prices. If an increase in the risk of a stock is more than offset by an increase in expected return, then the price of a stock will go up, and vice versa for a decrease in risk. In contrast, the maximum return on bonds is fixed, so bondholders concentrate on risk and can ignore changes in expected returns.

³⁰ An initial list of companies was obtained from Rosenblum and Siegel, Information Access Corporation, Trade and Industry Index (DIALOG ONLINE FILE 148), and Born, Eisenbeis, and Harris. The list was then pared down to those acquisitions involving a new entry or dramatic increase in current position of the acquiring firm in some aspect of the financial services industry. The firms actually used are those in the reduced sample with publicly traded bonds that were listed in Moody's Bond Guide.

³¹ Masulis and Woolridge also use this method to examine bond returns.

REFERENCES

Bennett, Robert A. "A Banking Puzzle: Mixing Freedom and Protection." *The New York Times* (February 19, 1984), pp. F1, F12–F13.

Benston, George J. "Why Did Congress Pass New Financial Service Laws in the 1930s? An Alternative Opinion." *Economic Review*. Federal Reserve Bank of Atlanta, 67 (April 1982), pp. 7–10.

Born, Jeffery, Robert A. Eisenbeis, and Robert S. Harris. "The Benefits of Geographical and Product Expansion in the Financial Services Industry." Paper Presented to the Financial Management Association Meeting in Atlanta, October 1983.

Boyd, John H., Gerald A. Hanweck, and Pipat Pithyachariyakul. "Bank Holding Company Diversification." *Proceedings of Conference On Bank Structure and Competition,* Federal Reserve Bank of Chicago (1980), pp. 105–121.

Brown, Stephen J., and Jerold B. Warner. "Measuring Security Price Performance." *Journal of Financial Economics* 8 (1980), pp. 205–58.

Chase, Samuel, and Donn L. Waage. "Corporate Separateness as a Tool of Bank Supervision." Samuel Chase and Company, Washington, D.C., 1983.

Eisemann, Peter C. "Diversification and the Congeneric Bank Holding Company." *Journal of Bank Research,* 7 (Spring 1976), p. 68–77.

Eisenbeis, Robert A. "How Should Bank Holding Companies Be Regulated?" *Economic Review,* Federal Reserve Bank of Atlanta, 68 (January 1983), pp. 42–47.

Eisenbeis, Robert A. "Policy Issues Raised by the Expansion of Nonbank Banks." Mimeo, 1984.

Eisenbeis, Robert A., Robert S. Harris, and Josef Lakonishok. "Benefits of Bank Diversification: The Evidence from Shareholder Returns." University of North Carolina School of Business Administration, (forthcoming in *Journal of Finance),* October 1982.

Federal Deposit Insurance Corporation. *Deposit Insurance in a Changing Environment.* A Study Submitted to Congress by the Federal Deposit Insurance Corporation, Washington, D.C. (April 1983).

Flannery, Mark J. "Deposit Insurance Creates a Need for Bank Regulation." *Business Review,* Federal Reserve Bank of Philadelphia, January–February 1982, pp. 17–27.

Hayes III, Samuel L. "Commercial Banking Inroads into Investment Banking." *Economic Review.* Federal Reserve Bank of Atlanta, 89 (May 1984).

Heggestad, Arnold A. "Riskiness of Investments in Nonbank Activities by Bank Holding Companies." *Journal of Economics and Business,* 27 (Spring 1975), pp. 219–23.

Jessee, Michael A., and Steven A. Seelig, *Bank Holding Companies and the Public Interest: An Economic Analysis.* Lexington, Mass.: D. C. Heath, 1977.

Johnson, Rodney D., and David R. Meinster. "Bank Holding Companies: Diversification Opportunities in Nonbank Activities." *Eastern Economic Journal,* 1 (October 1974), pp. 1453–65.

Kane, Edmund J. "Role of Government in Thrift Industries' Net Worth Crisis." In *Financial Services: The Changing Institutions and Government Policy,* ed. George Benston, Englewood Cliffs, N.J.: Prentice-Hall/Crest, 1983.

Kane, Edmund J. *Gathering Crisis in Federal Deposit Insurance: Origins, Evaluation and Possible Reforms*. Book in progress, 1984.

Kareken, John H., and Neil Wallace. "Deposit Insurance and Bank Regulation: A Partial-Equilibrium Exposition." *Journal of Business* (July 1978), pp. 413–38.

Kennedy, Susan Estabrook. *The Banking Crisis of 1933*. Lexington: University Press of Kentucky, 1973.

Leff, Gary, and James W. Park. "The Mississippi Deposit Insurance Crisis." *Bankers Magazine*. 160 (Summer 1977), pp. 74–80.

Longstreth, Bevis. "In Search of a Safety Net for the Financial Services Industry." *Bankers Magazine*. 166 (July–August 1983), pp. 27–34.

Masulis, Ronald W. "The Effects of Capital Structure Change on Security Prices: A Study of Exchange Offers." *Journal of Financial Economics* 8 (1980), pp. 139–78.

Mayer, Thomas. "Should Large Banks Be Allowed to Fail?" *Journal of Financial and Quantitative Analysis* 10 (November 1975), pp. 603–10.

Meinster, David R., and Rodney D. Johnson. "Bank Holding Company Diversification and the Risk of Capital Impairment." *The Bell Journal of Economics*. 10 (Autumn 1979), pp. 683–94.

Murray, William. "Bank Holding Company Centralization Policies," prepared for the Association of Registered Bank Holding Companies, Golembe Associates, Inc., February 1978.

Rose, John T. "Bank Holding Companies as Operational Single Entities." In *Bank Holding Company Movement to 1978: A Compendium*. Washington: Board of Governors of the Federal Reserve System, 1978a, pp. 69–93.

Rose, John T. "The Effect of the Bank Holding Company Movement on Bank Safety and Soundness." In *The Bank Holding Company Movement to 1978: A Compendium*. Washington: Board of Governors of the Federal Reserve System, Septembr 1978b, pp. 137–84.

Rose, John T. "Government Restrictions on Bank Activities: Rationale for Regulation and Possibilities for Deregulation." (forthcoming in *Bank Regulation)*, January 1984.

Stover, Roger D. "A Reexamination of Bank Holding Company Acquisitions." *Journal of Bank Research*. 13 (Summer 1982), pp. 101–08.

Sanford, Charles S., Jr. "Should the Glass-Steagall Act be Repealed? Two Views: Pro." *American Banker* (March 8, 1984), pp. 4, 7, 9, 12–14.

U. S. Congress. Conference Report (to accompany H. R. 6778). Bank Holding Company Act Amendments, House Report 1747. 91 Cong. 2 Sess. Washington: Government Printing Office, 1970.

U. S. Congress. Senate Committee on Banking and Currency. Bank Holding Company Act Amendments of 1970. Senate Report 1084. 91 Cong. 2 Sess. Washington: Government Printing Office, 1970.

U. S. Congress. Committee on Banking and Currency. Bank Holding Company Act of 1955. Senate Report 609.84 Cong. 1 Sess. Washington: Government Printing Office, 1955.

Upshaw, William F. "Federal Regulation of Bank Holding Companies—I." *Monthly Review*. Federal Reserve Bank of Richmond, October 1968, pp. 2–5.

Wall, Larry D. "Deposit Insurance Reform: The Insuring Agencies' Proposals." *Economic Review*. Federal Reserve Bank of Atlanta, 89 (January 1984a), pp. 43–57.

Wall, Larry D. "The Future of Deposit Insurance: An Analysis of the Insuring Agencies' Proposals." *Economic Review*. Federal Reserve Bank of Atlanta, 89 (March 1984b), pp. 26–39.

Whalen, Gary. "Multibank Holding Company Organizational Structure and Performance." Working Paper 8201, Federal Reserve Bank of Cleveland, March 1982a.

Whalen, Gary. "Operational Policies of Multibank Holding Companies." *Economic Review*. Federal Reserve Bank of Cleveland (Winter 1981–1982b), pp. 20–31.

Woolridge, J. Randall. "Dividend Changes and Security Prices." *Journal of Finance*. 38 (1983), pp. 1607–15.

9

Securities Activities
of Commercial Banks:
The Problem of Conflicts of Interest

Anthony Saunders

The 1980s have witnessed an increasing trend towards bank deregulation. One important aspect of this trend has been the growth in the securities activities of banks and bank holding companies. These activities have taken several forms, including operating discount brokerage houses, selling commingled IRAs, and acting as advisors to closed-end mutual funds. However, one activity which banks are still expressly prohibited from entering (under the 1933 Glass-Steagell Act) is underwriting and dealing in corporate securities—stocks or bonds. Despite this, many large banks are vigorously lobbying Congress to be allowed back into securities underwriting (and, therefore, for the abolition of the Glass-Steagall Act).

Allowing banks to engage once again in corporate securities underwriting may well have important social benefits. First, it would probably ease the access of small firms into the capital market; commissions on the initial public offerings of these firms would decline, since increased competition would likely lower the very high underwriting fees. Indeed, a number of studies have shown that existing underwriters have persistently underpriced new offerings by small firms and have charged fees and commissions exceeding 10 percent of the gross revenues from the issue.[1] Second, allowing bank holding companies' subsidiaries to underwrite securities may enhance their ability to diversify, which could significantly help stabilize bank holding companies' earnings.[2]

These benefits are sufficient to warrant a serious look at relaxing restrictions on corporate securities underwriting, particularly in today's financial environment. Indeed, banks and bank holding companies contend that advances in management controls and information technology can mitigate the problems of conflict of

From *Business Review,* Federal Reserve Bank of Philadelphia, July/August 1985, pp. 17–27.

Anthony Saunders is a visiting scholar in the research department of the Federal Reserve Bank of Philadelphia, and associate professor of finance, New York University.

interest that, in part, gave rise to the restrictions. Regulators, however, remain
concerned that allowing banks into securities underwriting raises questions regarding bank safety and soundness and heightens the potential for conflicts of
interest. While potential conflicts of interest are present in virtually all buyer/
seller relationships, they may be particularly acute problems in the context of a
multiproduct (or multiactivity) bank or bank holding company with a great diversity of customers.[3] Indeed, in the period leading up to the 1929 stock market
crash, conflicts of interest in the securities activities of several major banks
received considerable publicity and were a major factor prompting the restrictive
Glass-Steagall provisions.

A BRIEF HISTORY AND BACKGROUND OF BANK SECURITIES ACTIVITIES

Prior to 1933, large banks were heavily engaged in securities underwriting. Although under the 1864 National Bank Act national banks were not authorized to
underwrite securities directly, they avoided this restriction by establishing state-
chartered securities affiliates. These affiliates played a major role in underwriting
bonds issued by large railroad and industrial companies in the late 19th and early
20th centuries, as well as in helping distribute government bonds, called Liberty
Loans, in World War I. In 1927, the McFadden Act was passed. While this act is
perhaps best known for its prohibitions on interstate banking, it also legalized
national banks' underwriting activities by giving the Comptroller of the Currency
the right to define approved securities. As a result, between 1927 and 1929 the
share of national banks and their affiliates involved in new bond underwritings
more than doubled, from 22 percent in 1927 to 46 percent in 1929.[4]

The financial panic and great stock market crash of 1929, after which large
numbers of banks failed or froze the convertibility of deposits (nearly 10,000 in the
1929–33 period alone), led to a number of contemporary investigations into its
causes. One of the most influential of these investigations was undertaken in 1933
by the Senate Banking and Currency Committee and its counsel, Ferdinand
Pecora. Pecora documented a considerable number of abuses that had occurred
between large banks and their securities affiliates and customers in the pre-1929
period. For example, banks had made loans to purchasers of securities to help
artificially fix securities prices; they had dumped "bad" securities with correspondents or in trust accounts; and they had engaged in insider trading. Indeed,
publicity surrounding the Pecora hearings created an environment in which it was
widely felt that greedy bankers were in part to blame for the crash, and that a
sound banking system would result only if commercial banking activities were
rigidly separated from investment banking activities.[5]

The Glass-Steagall Act, passed in 1933, made it a felony for an organization
that receives deposits to engage at the same time "in the business of issuing,
underwriting, selling or distributing of stocks, bonds, debentures or other securities." The act did allow four exceptions: municipal general obligation bonds,
U.S. government bonds, private placements, and real estate loans.

For some 30 years commercial banks appeared content to accede to the
restrictive intent of the Glass-Steagall Act. But, by the beginning of the 1960s,
banks perceived they were earning a declining proportion of profits from traditional bank activities, compared to their permitted nonbank activities. Moreover,
they were often at the frontier in the computerization of financial products. These

---

LITIGATION HIGHLIGHTS

The legal battles over securities underwriting are too numerous to document fully, but the trends in the arguments and in the courts' decisions can be seen from looking at a few of the highlights. In 1963, following a ruling by the Comptroller of the Currency, a number of banks began underwriting municipal revenue bonds (in addition to the permitted general obligation bonds). The major argument here was that municipal *revenue* bonds barely existed at the time of the Act's passage (only approximately 3 percent of all municipal bonds issued in 1933 were revenue bonds) so that the Act did not apply to these instruments. However, in the case of Baker, Watts and Co. vs. Saxon in 1966, this underwriting activity was expressly prohibited as being contrary to the intent of Glass-Steagall. Similarly, in 1962 Citibank began selling shares in an open-ended mutual fund managed by the bank. This was challenged by the securities industry, arguing that Citibank had a direct "salesman's stake" in such a fund and that this was contrary to the intent of Glass-Steagall. In 1971, in Investment Company Institute vs. Camp, this activity was also declared illegal. In more recent legal disputes, commercial banks have had greater success, especially where it has been easier to establish that the bank has been providing an "agency function," rather than dispensing advice in the activity concerned. Thus banks were allowed to establish *automatic* investment services in 1977 and banks and bank holding companies were authorized to acquire discount brokerage houses in 1984. Although commercial paper was ruled a security in 1983, the district court, in A.G. Becker and the Securities Industry Association vs. the Federal Reserve Board, asked the Fed to make an initial determination of whether certain commercial paper activities constitute underwriting or whether they are permissible for bank holding companies. In June 1985, the Board decided that Bankers Trust's assistance to commercial paper issuers in private placement did not constitute underwriting so long as the bank did not promote the issue widely, take an ownership interest in the issue, or extend credit directly or indirectly to the issuer to compensate for unsold amounts. The court will review the Fed's opinion.

---

features of a changing financial environment led a group of large banks to challenge "gray areas" in the Glass-Steagall Act. This, in turn, brought them into conflict with the securities industry. As a result, the last 20 years have witnessed an almost continuous state of legal combat between commercial banks and their securities industry adversaries regarding the permissible securities activities of commercial banks (see Litigation Highlights exhibit).

Today, commercial banks legally can undertake a whole variety of agency functions on behalf of individual clients. These include buying and selling stocks, safekeeping securities, providing quotes on prices of securities, and switching funds between bank accounts and stock accounts. In addition, they continue to underwrite municipal general obligation bonds, as well as U.S. government bonds and Eurobonds (bonds issued outside of the United States). Thus, along with open-ended mutual funds and revenue bonds, underwriting and dealing in corporate securities remains the last major bastion of the securities industry.[6]

WHY SO MUCH CONCERN ABOUT CONFLICTS OF INTEREST?

Any further advances banks make into securities activities and, in particular, into securities underwriting will hinge largely on the answer to a crucial question: if banks are allowed to engage in such activities, will the types of abuse and conflicts observed in the 1930s reemerge and will they be as extensive? Any serious evaluation of this question has to look at the incentives and disincentives in *today's* legal, economic, and regulatory environment, and not that of the 1930s. An example of one change is that a whole body of securities laws and regulations has been passed since 1933 (e.g., the Securities Act of 1934, which established the

Securities and Exchange Commission). And today, the technology of disseminating and monitoring information is vastly superior to that of the 1930s.

But, even given these improvements in regulation and surveillance, serious problems could still ensue if conflicts of interest are exploited. First, public disclosure of a conflict of interest might lead to a loss of confidence in the bank and its management, resulting in an erosion of deposits (and revenue) which ultimately affects a bank's stability or safety and soundness. In the extreme, a loss of confidence by depositors could result in a run on the bank and lead to its eventual demise—even if the bank were "solvent" before the adverse information was publicly disclosed. Realistically, however, it seems likely that only pervasive and widespread abuses that were extensively publicized would lead to catastrophic runs. Second, exploitation of certain conflicts, such as unsound inter-company loans between a bank and its securities subsidiary, for example, could work directly to weaken the bank irrespective of any indirect confidence or disclosure effects. Third, conflict exploitation raises important questions of equity. Specifically, small less-sophisticated firms, correspondent banks, investors, and uninsured depositors appear to be more susceptible to exploitation through conflicts of interest than larger ones. In a sense, these concerns are closely linked to regulators' interest in protecting the welfare and savings of small investors, especially since small investors often have less access to information than larger investors and are unable to switch assets without bearing relatively high transaction costs, such as service fees. Of course, the more accurate, cheap, and widely disseminated information is, and the more competitive financial and banking markets are, the less easy it becomes to exploit smaller firms, and the less weight should be attached to this "equity" issue.

TYPES OF POTENTIAL CONFLICTS

The lobbying by commercial banks to be allowed back into securities underwriting, and their expansion into other securities activities, has helped improve our understanding of the types of potential conflicts of interest that might arise. The nine potential conflicts discussed below either have been raised at congressional hearings leading up to the Glass-Steagall Act in the early 1930s or have been suggested more recently by industry observers or by the securities industry in opposing bank involvement in private debt placements, open- and close-end mutual funds, and other securities-related activities[7] Although it is difficult to classify the conflicts precisely, a unifying theme among them is that each conflict is related to problems of asymmetric information (where one party has more information than the other), or the abuse of monopoly power, or both.

The Conflict between the Promotional Role of the Investment Banker and the Commercial Banker's Obligation to Provide Disinterested Advice to Depositors.   When a commercial bank affiliate underwrites securities, bankers may have incentives to encourage depositors or other customers (such as correspondent banks) to buy these securities. As a result, bankers may play a promotional role on behalf of the securities affiliate, a role which is in conflict with the best interests of its customers. For example, a customer might have chosen an alternative investment, with a superior risk-return trade-off, had a banker proffered "disinterested" advice. This potential conflict, it should be noted, is not confined solely to securities underwriting but pertains to all "nonbank" activities undertaken by a bank holding company.

Using the Bank's Securities Affiliate to Issue New Securities to Repay Unprofitable Loans.   A bank may use the underwriting ability of its securities affiliate to transfer risk from itself to the bondholders (or equity holders) of a corporate loan customer. The scenario usually conjured up is that of a bank holding a partly collateralized risky loan. To avoid an expected loss on the loan, the bank may induce a loan customer to issue new bonds (or equity) through the bank's securities affiliate and use the cash proceeds to pay off the loan. Thus, the bank eliminates its default risk exposure, and its affiliate earns a fee on the underwriting.

It is not clear that this potential conflict is very likely to materialize. For example, why would any but a highly risk-averse bank prefer this arrangement to simply restructuring loan repayments? Further, it is not obvious that any incentives exist for the risky loan customer to take part in such a scheme, particularly since either its stockholders or bondholders (or conceivably both) stand to lose.

Economic Tie-ins of Different Holding Company Products.   A bank may use its potential leverage over customers—through its lending function and as a guarantor (e.g., via standby letters of credit)—to coerce them into buying other products. Specifically, threats of credit rationing, curtailing or refusing to renew credit lines, and increasing the cost of loans could all be used to "tie" existing customers to other products of the holding company, such as securities underwritings by its affiliate.[8]

Placing Unsold Securities in the Bank's Trust Accounts.   This potential conflict might arise if the securities affiliate of a bank holding company has securities in its inventory that can only be sold off at a loss to outside investors. To avoid such losses, the affiliate may seek to place the securities, at prices favorable to the affiliate, in other parts of the holding company—for example, with the trust accounts of the affiliated bank. This conflict is unlikely to occur with large institutional trust or pension fund accounts, since owners of these accounts monitor their performance closely; however, this monitoring may be absent in the management of smaller personal trusts over which banks, as trustees, have considerable discretionary power.

Director Interlocks between Bank Holding Companies and Nonfinancial Firms.   With the ability of bank securities affiliates to underwrite debt and equity issues, the potential conflicts arising from director interlocks between banks and other firms (when a bank director also serves on the boards of nonfinancial corporations) may become more important. The combination of director interlocks and large holdings of corporate stock in bank trust departments, together with the ability of a bank holding company affiliate to offer underwriting services, may increase the potential for conflicts of interest. For example, decisions made in the boardroom, such as whether to finance with loans or bond issues, bonds or equity, and which underwriter to choose, may all be influenced either directly or indirectly by the presence and voting powers of bank directors.

Bank Loans to Support the Price of a Security.   In acting as an underwriter, the securities affiliate may want its underwriting effort to be seen to be as successful as possible. This may be especially true for new entrants into the underwriting business. As a result, bank loans may be made at relatively favorable rates to third-party investors on the understanding that part, or all, of these funds would be used to purchase certain new issues underwritten by the affiliate and its syndicates. In such a case, bank loans could be used to support the prices of those securities, sending favorable but misleading signals to the market regarding the true performance of the underwriter. Further, such a cheap loan policy might undermine bank profits, and thereby the safety and security of its uninsured depositors and the FDIC, which backs the insured depositors.

Imprudent Loans to Issuers of Securities Underwritten by the Affiliate.   In this case a new issue of bonds is underwritten by a bank affiliate and subsequently either the investment projects financed by the proceeds fail or there is some other negative impact on the issuing firm's (customer's) cash flow which serves to increase its default risk. As a result, the bank may make new loans to the firm to keep it from failing, and thus avoid possible litigation costs arising from bondholders' claims against the securities affiliate and holding company (relating to information disclosure and lack of due diligence in the original underwriting prospectus). If the new loans of the bank are subordinated (i.e., junior—paid off last in the event of default) to the claims of existing bondholders, the market value of the firm's bonds—including those just issued—will tend to rise. This is because the assets of the firm have expanded, while the stock of senior or unsubordinated bonds remains unchanged.[9] Implicitly, bank management is subsidizing the risky claims of the issuing firm's bondholders in conflict with the best interests of its depositors and the FDIC by threatening the bank's safety and soundness through imprudent loans.

The Bank May Make Direct Loans to Its Securities Affiliate.   If the securities affiliate is separately capitalized, it might seek to increase leverage through loans from the banking arm of the holding company. Although direct loans from a bank to its affiliate are subject to a ceiling of 10 percent of bank capital (like loans to any unaffiliated firm or individual), and must be backed by more than 100 percent collateral, it is still possible that such loans could be made at less than an appropriate risk-adjusted interest rate. In such a case, the protection of bank depositors, via earnings, would be weakened. Or, loans could be made to a third party (such as another bank) and re-lent by the third party to the securities affiliate—perhaps for a direct fee or an increase in compensating balances held with the third party—in order to circumvent the 10 percent-of-capital loan ceiling.

Informational Advantages Regarding Competitors.   As bank holding companies and other financial and nonfinancial firms cross traditional market and product boundaries, they encounter increasing competition. Since bank-affiliated underwriters may become privy to inside information regarding firms whose securities they underwrite, this information could be disseminated to other affiliates of the holding company, including the bank, in order to generate a competitive advantage in lending, leasing, and so forth.

CONFLICT CONTROL

The potential conflicts of interest that have been identified suggest that conflicts of interest would be pervasive if banks were allowed back into securities underwriting. But several "controls" exist which would limit the exploitation of potential conflicts. These controls have three dimensions: economic, regulatory, and legal.

Economic Controls

The Structure of Financial Compensation Schemes in Bank Holding Companies.   Most of the conflicts described require some form of collusion or coalition between the managers of the bank and the securities affiliate. In addition, most involve a probable trade-off between short-run and long-run profits for the holding company. Thus, a crucial question is: what are the economic incentives (salary or compensation structures) that make managerial collusion more or less likely? There is a growing recognition that managerial interest may diverge from those of stockholders.[10] One reason is that managers' short tenure, relative to the expected life of the firm, may make them overly concerned with short-run profits. By contrast, stockholders will be more concerned with the long-run value of the firm, or with the value of the firm as a going concern. Under such conditions, managers may have greater incentives to exploit conflicts for short-run opportunities than if they shared the long-run profit interests of shareholders.

This short-run outlook of managers suggests that the structure of managerial compensation schemes could be very important for conflict control. Specifically, a compensation scheme in which financial rewards for managers in the bank and the securities affiliate were kept separate—such as in separate profit centers—and in which stock or equity bonuses played a significant part, would work toward reducing the incentives for bank and securities affiliate managers to form coalitions. In turn, such a scheme would better align managerial interest with those of stockholders. By comparison, a salary scheme that linked bank and securities affiliate managers' compensation to the *consolidated* current profits of the holding company would both accentuate the different time horizons between managers' and stockholders' interests and create incentives for bank and securities affiliate managers to create coalitions to ensure that the current consolidated profits of the holding company are maximized.[11] Under this scheme, any collective bank-securities affiliate activity, such as product or service "tie-ins," which produce an increase in holding company profits, would directly benefit both managerial teams. In sum, by creating separate profit centers and linking compensation partly to the long-run performance of the holding company—for example, through stock bonus schemes—stockholders can impose a degree of *internal* control over managerial incentives to exploit conflicts of interest. It also might be noted that stock bonus plans now play an increasingly important role in both investment and commercial bank compensation packages.

When there are no *internal* controls (or "carrots") which limit managers' incentives to exploit conflicts, or if those controls are weak, there are at least three *external* "market" control mechanisms (or "sticks") that limit managers from diverging too far from maximizing long-run holding company profits through conflict exploitation for short-run gains. These are: the market for corporate control, the market for bank and securities affiliates' products and services, and the monitoring role of bond-rating agencies.

The Market for Corporate Control.[12]   The idea underlying the market for corporate control is that the current managers of the banking and securities affiliate arms of the holding company are just two of many potential teams in the professional labor market offering their managerial services to the holding company's shareholders. Should existing managers overtly pursue short-run profits by exploiting conflicts, thereby adversely affecting or damaging the reputation of the enterprise, then shareholders will have an incentive to replace them with managers whose objectives are more closely aligned with their own long-run objectives. In addition, stockholders are increasingly seeking financial recourse in the courts against errant managers. For example, both Bank of America and Chase Manhattan are taking legal action against officers involved in, respectively, bad international loans and the failure of Drysdale Securities. Nevertheless, managerial change will only occur when the perceived benefits of managerial reorganization outweigh the expected costs involved. Often only a major crisis will cause managerial reorganization, although less dramatic personnel shifts can have the same effect.

The Market for Bank and Securities Affiliates' Products and Services. The ability of managers to exploit certain conflicts of interest is further limited by the degree of market power the bank or its affiliate managers have over customers—such as depositors, borrowers, and issuing firms. For example, tie-ins can only be exploited if the bank has a substantial degree of market power over the issuing firm in the provision of loans or other services. If a firm has a number of potential lenders and credit lines available, it is less likely to accede to bank pressure in that direction. Smaller firms or large firms in financial distress are likely to be the most susceptible to this type of pressure. Similar arguments can be made regarding the pressure to restructure debt. However, the deregulation of the financial system, together with the technological and information revolutions currently under way, imply that even smaller firms eventually will be able to escape or at least mitigate tie-ins and similar pressures. Indeed, in a fully competitive market in which all participants are fully informed, it would be impossible for any seller to exploit a potential conflict of interest that harms the buyer, since the buyer would be immediately aware of the situation and could switch to a competitor.

Bond Rating Agencies. The role of bond-rating agencies such as Moody's and Standard & Poor's is to monitor externally and independently the financial performance of firms that issue bonds, and to provide investors with information regarding the default risk attached to those bonds. If carried out successfully, this monitoring would make it difficult for a bank-affiliated underwriter to unload a new issue of debt so an issuing firm could pay off "bad" bank loans.

A critical question is how successful bond rating agencies are in detecting the default risk of firms issuing securities prior to the offering date. As there have been relatively few bond defaults in the last 40 years, studies of the default prediction ability of bond-rating agencies have been unable to provide conclusive results.[13] However, when the sample period is extended back to incorporate the pre-World War II period, studies have shown that an inverse relationship exists between changes in bond ratings and default rates; that is, a higher bond rating is usually associated with a lower default rate.[14] Moreover, since bond-rating agencies have to maintain a reputation—so their evaluations remain credible—they have to be correct on average. Thus, rating agencies provide the crucial function of improving the quality and increasing the quantity of information available to investors, which makes it more costly for banks or their affiliates to exploit conflicts.

The Value of Reputation and Long-term Profit Maximization.   So far, the controls have implicitly assumed that it is in the best interests of bank holding company stockholders to avoid conflicts of interest, and have concentrated on factors that discipline managers. It is also important to analyze the role of market reputation in disciplining stockholders.

Given that stockholders, through boards of directors, want to maximize long-term profits, they will be vitally concerned with building and maintaining a good long-run reputation with their customers. Thus, reputation, or the stock of "goodwill," can be viewed as an asset of the firm which has real value to existing shareholders and is reflected in bindng commitments or implicit contracts with its customers.[15] In this view, banking and securities underwriting activities undertaken by a holding company with its customers are similar to economic games which take place in a repeated, or dynamic, market setting. While the holding company may earn a net profit in the short run from exploiting a conflict with a given customer, such as promoting the sale of tainted securities or tie-ins, in the long run the exploitation of conflicts, or breach of the implicit contract, may eventually impair the reputation of the holding company and its various affiliates and damage its future growth and profit prospects.

Specifically, the customer who feels he has been exploited will seek to move his business to another institution, while adverse publicity will tend to deter new customers from forming permanent relationships with the bank or its securities affiliate. In particular, the greater the flow of information among customers, the higher will be the costs to holding company shareholders from conflict exploitation.

Regulatory Controls

In addition to economic disincentives, regulatory controls constitute a major restraint on exploiting conflicts of interest. Margin requirements and collateral requirements on loans to affiliates, combined with direct monitoring and examination by regulatory authorities, each impose *external* nonmarket constraints on conflict exploitation. Currently, margin requirements on securities purchases substantially limit the amount of credit (bank loans) that investors and brokers or dealers can use to purchase securities. Therefore, high margin requirements also substantially limit banks' ability to support the price of securities underwritten by their affiliates with third-party loans to individual investors. As noted earlier, direct bank loans to affiliates are subject to a ceiling of 10 percent of capital and must be backed by at least 100 percent collateral. Violation of these restrictions would lead to costly penalties being imposed on managers and shareholders if discovered by the SEC, the Federal Reserve, the FDIC, or other regulatory agencies with examination authority. Regulatory examination and surveillance thus provides an additional disincentive to exploit conflicts. The more efficient are bank examiners, the higher is the expected cost of exploiting a potential conflict—with potential costs or penalties ranging from fines and criminal prosecution of bank officers to bank charter revocations.

As an external mechanism of conflict control, examination and surveillance would probably be most efficient if there were coordination between those examining the bank, its trust department, and the securities affiliate. This suggests that optimal surveillance might be achieved when each part of the holding company is examined by a single regulatory authority. If different regulatory agencies had examination powers and took an adversarial (rather than cooperative) stance over interagency information exchange, regulatory disincentives might be significantly weakened.[16]

Legal Recourse.   Bank and securities affiliate customers also have the option of turning to the courts in the event of a conflict exploitation, although the costs of legal action may often be prohibitive for the small investor, and the outcome far from certain. Such recourse has often been taken with respect to the trust activities of banks, when a customer (trustee) felt that the bank had violated its fiduciary responsibilities.[17] Also, class action suits in the courts are becoming more frequent in cases where investors feel that underwriters failed to exercise due diligence, such as in fully disclosing information prior to a new issue. This might be particularly pertinent in the case where banks are tempted to induce a firm to pay off its loans through a new issue. The bad publicity surrounding such court cases acts as a clear disincentive for securities firms to exploit conflicts, apart from the legal costs involved in defending such cases. An example of a class action suit is the one currently outstanding against Merrill Lynch and Salomon Brothers, alleging failure to show due diligence over issues of Washington Public Power Supply System bonds in 1982–83.

SUMMARY AND OUTLOOK

As part of the trend toward bank deregulation, banks are lobbying to be allowed to underwrite corporate securities—an activity they are expressly prohibited from by the Glass-Steagall Act of 1933. The major source of this prohibition, both 50 years ago and today, is concern about possible conflicts of interest. In the debate about this issue, several potential conflicts of interest have been identified. Although they seem to suggest that the potential for conflict is fairly formidable, there are a number of economic, regulatory, and legal controls in place which create strong disincentives to conflict exploitation. This is especially so given *today's* security laws, regulatory structure, and improvements in information technology.[18] Moreover, regulatory and legal controls could always be strengthened if there were genuine concern that the current set of disincentives is not sufficiently strong. For example, new "Chinese walls" could be established between the securities affiliate and the bank, and between the securities affiliate and the bank's trust department. Thus, it seems that, suitably regulated, bank holding companies might be allowed to expand into corporate securities underwriting. Indeed, by allowing banks into securities underwriting, positive social benefits may well accrue. These benefits would include the ability of bank holding companies to diversify their earnings in a more optimal fashion, thereby enhancing bank safety and soundness. In addition, securities markets may become more efficient and competitive, with smaller firms finding access easier.

The current prospects for the abolition of Glass-Steagall are unclear. In recent sessions of Congress, numerous draft bills have been debated. These bills have incorporated provisions allowing banks to offer open-ended mutual funds and to underwrite both municipal revenue bonds and mortgage-backed securities, proposals which represent significant modifications of Glass-Steagall. However, no serious proposal has been made to allow banks back into domestic corporate securities underwriting, despite the apparent success of large U.S. banks in underwriting corporate (dollar-denominated) Eurobonds. Nevertheless, there is little doubt that this difficult issue will remain at the center of the "deregulation" debate.

NOTES

[1] See, for example, the study by Stoll (1976).

[2] See the studies by Wall and Eisenbeis, and by Saunders (1983).

[3] This organizational structure, in which a separately capitalized bank is linked to a separately capitalized securities underwriting affiliate through a holding company, appears to be the most likely format should any future deregulation take place.

[4] See Flannery (References: forthcoming).

[5] More recent evidence on the causes of the crash, however, have centered blame on the Federal Reserve's restrictive monetary policies (see Friedman and Schwartz (1971)). For a more extensive discussion of commercial banks' securities activities before 1933, see Flannery (forthcoming) and Sametz et al. (1979).

[6] In June 1985, the Federal Reserve Board concluded that Bankers Trust could continue to act as an agent and advisor to corporations in the private placement of commercial paper with a small group of institutional investors. If this position is accepted by the courts, banks will be able to participate in the limited distribution of commercial paper without violating the Glass-Steagall prohibition on underwriting corporate securities.

[7] See, for example, Investment Company Institute (1979), New York Clearing House Association (1977), and Securities Industry Association (1977).

[8] However, as Posner (1976) has argued, the market conditions under which a monopolist would rationally exploit a tie-in are quite restrictive.

[9] Although the aggregate of junior plus senior debt has increased.

[10] See Jensen and Meckling (1976), for example.

[11] For example, an incentive may exist for bank management to make subsidized loans to the securities affiliate or a third party if the net profit generated by the affiliate's activities more than compensates for any loss in bank revenues or profit.

[12] See Jensen and Meckling (1976), and Jensen and Ruback (1983) for more detailed discussion.

[13] Although there has been a widely observed negative relationship between bond rating changes and bond yields.

[14] See West (1973) for a review of these studies.

[15] This view is developed in Bull (1983), Klein and Leffler (1981), and Telser (1980). As Bull has noted: "authors have suggested that concern by the firm for its reputation or brand name . . . may lead the employer [principal] to fulfill his part of the contract. In other words, an appeal is made to a third party, here the market rather than the court for enforcement" (p. 659).

[16] The Bush Task Force has proposed combining the federal bank regulators into a single entity, the new Federal Banking Agency, and transferring the regulation of securities activities of bank holding companies, and thus the securities affiliate, to the SEC—see *Inside the Administration* (1983).

[17] See Schotland (1980).

[18] The quality and quantity of corporate financial information available to outside investors is likely to be increased considerably in 1985 when the SEC puts its EDGAR System (Electronic Data Gathering and Retrieval System) into effect. Under this system, companies will electronically file quarterly and annual reports with the SEC while investors, brokers, and dealers will gain direct access to those files through their own office (or home) computer terminals. Thus information should be disseminated in a far more timely fashion and be available to a much wider audience.

REFERENCES

Bull, C. "Implicit Contracts in the Absence of Enforcement and Risk Aversion." *American Economic Review*, 1983, pp. 658–71.

Flannery, Mark J. "An Economic Evaluation of Bank Securities Activities before 1933." In *Commercial Bank Penetration of the Corporate Securities Market,* ed. Ingo Walter. New York: John Wiley & Sons, forthcoming.

Friedman, Milton, and Anna Schwartz. *A Monetary History of the United States, 1867–1960.* Princeton, N.J.: Princeton University Press, 1971.

Inside the Administration. Vol. 2, no. 25, December 16, 1983.

Investment Company Institute. *Misadventures in Banking: Bank Promotion of Pooled Investment Funds.* Washington, D.C., 1979.

Jensen, M. C., and W. H. Meckling. "Theory of the Firm: Managerial Behavior, Agency Costs and Ownership Structure." *Journal of Financial Economics,* 1976, pp. 305–60.

Jensen, M. C., and R. S. Ruback. "The Market for Corporate Control: The Scientific Evidence." *Journal of Financial Economics,* 1983, pp. 5–50.

Klein, B., and K. Leffler. "The Role of Market Forces in Assuring Contractual Performance." *Journal of Political Economy,* 1981, pp. 615–41.

New York Clearing House Association, *Commercial Bank Private Placement Advisory Services.* April 1977.

Posner, Richard A. *Antitrust Law: An Economic Perspective.* Chicago: University of Chicago Press, 1976.

Sametz, A., M. Keenan, E. Block, and L. Goldberg. "Securities Activities of Commercial Banks: An Evaluation of Current Developments and Regulatory Issues. "*Journal of Comparative Law & Securities Regulation,* 1979, pp. 155–94.

Saunders, A. "An Economic Perspective on Bank Uniqueness and Corporate Securities Activities." New York University working paper, 1983.

Schotland, R. A. Introductory chapter to *Abuse on Wall Street: Conflicts of Interest in the Securities Markets.* Westport, Conn.: Quorum Books, 1980.

Securities Industry Association. *Private Placement Activities of Commercial Banks.* Memorandum to the Federal Reserve Board of Governors, May 1977.

Stoll, Hans R. "The Pricing of Underwritten Offerings of Listed Common Stocks and the Compensation of Underwriters." *Journal of Economics and Business* 28 (Winter, 1976), pp. 96–103.

Telser, L. "A Theory of Self-Enforcing Agreements." *Journal of Business,* 1980, pp. 27–44.

Wall, L., and R. A. Eisenbeis. "Bank Holding Company Nonbanking Activities and Risk." Paper presented to the Conference on Bank Structure and Competition, Federal Reserve Bank of Chicago, 1984.

West, R. "Bond Ratings, Bond Yields, and Financial Regulation: Some Findings." *Journal of Law and Economics,* 1973, pp. 159–68.

10

The Competitive Effects of Interstate Banking

Charles Morris

The prohibitions against interstate banking have emerged in recent years as a policy issue. Although federal law prohibits branch banking and bank holding company control of banks across state lines, the demand for interstate financial services has increased as state economies have become more integrated with one another. And because there are profits to be made by providing the goods and services that society wants, financial institutions have been extremely innovative in finding ways around the restrictions on interstate banking. As a result of these natural market forces, many bank and banklike services are now provided on an interstate basis. Bank holding companies can cross state lines and own loan production offices, Edge corporations, and nonbank subsidiaries that provide services closely related to banking. Nonbank institutions, such as thrifts, brokerage houses, and retailers, also offer many financial services on an interstate basis.

It is often argued that the laws should be changed to allow interstate banking because many financial services are already provided on an interstate basis, but in an excessively costly and inequitable way. Not only do financial institutions spend resources finding ways around current laws but they also often provide interstate banking services in a more costly way than if interstate banking were allowed. Major corporations and wealthy individuals can easily make financial transactions across state lines, but small businesses and households cannot easily make such transactions. Also, traditionally defined banks cannot compete with other financial institutions on an equal basis.

Before legislators decide whether to change the laws, however, several other factors should be considered. These include the effect of interstate banking on the safety and soundness of the banking system, the flow of credit between regions, the viability of small banks, and the competitiveness of the banking system.

From *Economic Review,* Federal Reserve Bank of Kansas City, November 1984, pp. 3–16.

Charles Morris is an economist in the economic research department at the Federal Reserve Bank of Kansas City.

Although all of these factors are important, the impact of interstate banking on competition is of major importance.[1] The reason is that social welfare is usually greatest when firms in an industry actively compete against each other. Competition among firms in an industry results not only in larger levels of output than would otherwise be produced but also in lower prices and higher quality products. To remain competitive, firms must also meet the demands of consumers and produce at the lowest possible cost.

This article argues that interstate banking will result in a more competitive banking system. Thus, the current prohibitions against interstate banking cannot be justified on the basis that interstate banking would adversely affect the competitiveness of the banking system. A brief discussion of the legislative history of restrictions on interstate banking is presented in the first section. This is followed by a theoretical discussion of the competitive effects of interstate banking. Empirical evidence on the competitive effects is discussed in the third section. Concluding remarks are presented in the final section.

LEGISLATIVE HISTORY

Geographic restrictions on expansion by state and national banks, particularly across state lines, have long been part of the U.S. banking system. State banks can operate only in the state that charters them. If a state bank wants to operate in another state, it must apply for a charter in that state. National banks are also prohibited from crossing state lines. A system of national banks, chartered and regulated by the Comptroller of the Currency, was created by the Currency Act of 1863, later revised as the National Bank Act of 1864. Although neither act mentioned branches, early comptrollers interpreted the law as meaning that national banks could not branch at all, either within a state or across state lines. The current prohibition against interstate branching by national banks was adopted in a provision of the Banking Act of 1933 that amended the McFadden Act of 1927. According to the McFadden Act as amended in 1933, national banks can branch in any state within the geographic limits specified by the laws of that state. Thus, the issue of branching was deferred to the states.

Restrictions on branching were often overcome through the use of bank holding companies.[2] If restrictions on branching kept a bank from operating a multioffice system, the bank could achieve the same end by forming a holding company that owned more than one bank. Multibank holding companies, used to circumvent restrictions against branching in unit-banking states, were also used to set up interstate banking networks. By 1956, seven domestically owned and five foreign owned bank holding companies owned banks in more than one state. As a result, interstate banking had come into existence even though the McFadden Act prohibited interstate branching.

The Douglas Amendment to the Bank Holding Company Act of 1956 prevented any further use of this "loophole" in the McFadden Act by limiting the interest that a bank holding company could acquire in an out-of-state bank to 5 percent of the voting stock.[3] Apparently, to avoid a conflict with states' rights, the Douglas amendment allows a bank holding company to acquire an out-of-state bank if such acquisitions are specifically allowed by the laws of the state where the bank to be acquired is located.

Although the 12 companies that already owned banks in more than one state were allowed to continue their interstate operations, the Douglas amendment, for the most part, prevented any further expansion of bank holding companies across state lines. In recent years, however, holding companies have used provisions of new and old laws to expand across state lines.

The Garn-St Germain Act, passed in 1982 primarily to help regulators aid distressed institutions, created a way for banks to expand interstate by allowing failing institutions to be acquired by institutions from out of state. For example, the two largest bank holding companies in the United States, Citicorp and Bank-America Corporation, have used this act to extend their interstate operations.

Still more recently, the so-called nonbank bank loophole has given bank holding companies a means of crossing state lines. The Bank Holding Company Act as amended in 1970 defines a bank as an institution that accepts demand deposits and makes commercial loans. A nonbank bank is an institution that has a bank charter and offers many banklike services, but either does not accept demand deposits or does not make commercial loans. Because nonbank banks do not meet the definition of a bank, bank holding companies can establish nonbank banks in any state without violating the Douglas amendment. Over 40 major bank holding companies have applied for charters for more than 300 nonbank banks. The future of nonbank banks depends, however, on pending national legislation that redefines a bank for purposes of the Bank Holding Company Act. Depending on the outcome of this legislation, the nonbank bank movement will be halted or it will not.[4]

Several states have taken advantage of the clause in the Bank Holding Company Act that allows bank holding companies to acquire out-of-state banks if explicitly allowed by outside states. Twelve states have authorized entry by out-of-state bank holding companies. The constitutionality of some of these state laws is being challenged, however, leaving the future of the laws uncertain.

Although the trend in recent legislation has been to provide ways for banks to offer traditional services across state lines within the spirit of the law, some would like to reverse that trend. These opponents of interstate banking give many reasons for their opposition. One of the main reasons is that they believe interstate banking will result in a less competitive banking system.

INTERSTATE BANKING AND COMPETITION: THEORY

At a theoretical level, there is great debate over the competitive effects of interstate banking. Some argue that interstate banking would be anticompetitive in that it would result in a less-competitive banking system, while others counter that interstate banking would not be anticompetitive. Still others argue that interstate banking would result in a more competitive banking system.

The Anticompetitive Argument . . .

The anticompetitive argument is usually framed within the context of the concentration-conduct-performance hypothesis. According to this hypothesis, market *concentration* in an industry influences firm conduct, which, in turn, affects industry performance. The concentration of a market is measured as the percentage of an industry's output that is produced by the largest firms in the industry.

FIGURE 1

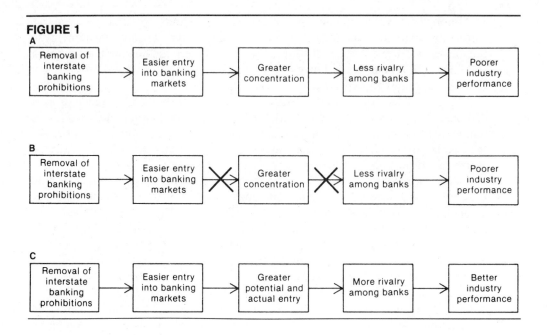

Conduct refers to the degree of rivalry among competing firms in a market or to the extent to which they engage in competitive activities. And industry *performance* refers to the closeness of industry output and price to their competitive levels.

Figure 1A illustrates the argument that interstate banking would result in a less competitive banking system. Removal of the interstate banking prohibitions, it is argued, would make it easier for out-of-state banking organizations to enter new banking markets either by opening new banks or by acquiring existing banks. These newly opened or acquired banks would then expand their market share at the expense of other banks, making local markets more concentrated.[5] As concentration increased, the banks in a market would explicitly or tacitly agree to reduce the degree of rivalry among themselves. They might, for example, refrain from raising deposit rates or from lowering loan rates. The result would be a deterioration of industry performance as banks restricted ouput below the competitive level and provided lower-quality services in their efforts to raise prices and profits. For example, the volume of deposits and loans might be held below competitive levels. This argument is used by many as a reason for not removing the prohibitions against interstate banking.

. . . and the Counterarguments

Arguments that interstate banking would not result in a less competitive banking system are illustrated in Figure 1B. One of these counterarguments is that easier conditions of entry would not cause concentration to increase. A second counterargument is that even if greater concentration were to occur it would not cause a reduction in the degree of rivalry among firms. A variation of the second counterargument is that greater concentration might initially result in a lesser degree of rivalry among firms, but it would not cause a reduction in the degree of rivalry in the long run. If any of these counterarguments are correct, interstate banking would not result in a less competitive and poorer performing industry.

Some critics of the anticompetitive argument say that easier conditions of entry would not cause concentration to increase. Local market concentration would increase as out-of-state banking organizations entered new markets only if the market share of newly opened or acquired banks increased at the expense of other banks. But these critics argue that the market share of the new banks, whether newly opened or acquired, would increase only if they could produce more output at a lower additional cost than banks of similar size that were not part of a banking network. A newly acquired bank's market share would increase, for example, only if it could attract more deposits or make more loans at a lower additional cost than before it was acquired.[6] Because these critics do not believe there are significant cost advantages to affiliating with banking networks, they argue that entry would not cause concentration to increase. They conclude that, regardless of the link between concentration and conduct, interstate banking would not be anticompetitive because it would not cause concentration to increase.[7]

Other critics of the anticompetitive argument say that, even if interstate banking resulted in greater local market concentration, there would not be a reduction in the degree of rivalry among banks. Even if there are only two banks in a market, they say, there are strong incentives for each bank to engage in competitive activities. Each bank would still have an incentive to compete with the other bank for a larger market share, for example, by offering higher deposit rates or a more attractive mix of deposit services. Output and prices, therefore, will be the same whether there are 2 banks or 100 banks in a market. These critics conclude that although the degree of rivalry does influence performance, there is no connection between concentration and the degree of rivalry. There is no connection, therefore, between concentration and performance.

A variation of this argument is that even if concentration increased and banks explicitly agreed to refrain from rivalry, there would be no effect on the competitive activities of banks in the long run. These critics argue that explicit collusive agreements are inherently unstable and, therefore, often unsuccessful. Because every bank in the colluding group has an incentive to produce more than its share of output, successful collusion requires the colluding group to police the behavior of group members and enforce the production quotas. Effective enforcement of such agreements, always difficult, is even more difficult because collusive agreements to restrict output and raise prices are illegal in the United States. Without effective enforcement, such agreements would not be successful so that output would rise and prices and profits would fall to competitive levels.[8] These critics conclude that, even if interstate banking led to high concentration and explicit agreements that prevented rivalry initially, rivalrous behavior would still result in the long run.

The Procompetitive Argument

The procompetitive argument, illustrated in Figure 1C, is that interstate banking would result in more competitive banking markets because easier entry results directly in banks engaging in more competitive activities. Because current prohibitions against interstate banking make market entry more difficult, they have resulted in many markets with only a few banks. It is argued that there is little rivalry among banks in these markets. Moreover, the banks in these markets are protected not only from actual competition but also from the threat of competition from banks ready to enter a market where profits are above competitive levels. If the prohibitions against interstate banking were removed, entry would be easier. The threat of competition from potential entrants would increase immediately in all banking markets, bringing output, quality, prices, and profits to competitive levels in many previously protected markets. Even in many one-bank markets, the increased threat of competition would prevent the single bank from earning excess profits by restricting output and charging noncompetitive prices. Where banks continued to maintain noncompetitive conditions, high profits would lead to actual entry by new banks that would eventually force output, quality, prices, and profits to competitive levels. This argument is used by many as a reason for removing the prohibitions against interstate banking.

INTERSTATE BANKING AND COMPETITION: EVIDENCE

Because the competitive effects of interstate banking cannot be determined at a theoretical level, it is an empirical question. The competitive effects of interstate banking depend on the resolution of several issues discussed in the previous section. Does less restriction on geographic expansion by banks result in more concentrated banking markets? If so, does concentration affect bank conduct and performance? And what is the direct effect of easier entry on bank conduct and performance? Evidence from studies that look at these questions will be presented. Further evidence on the competitive effects of interstate banking will be presented from studies that do not test a particular theory but look directly at the relationship between branching laws and bank performance. Overall, the evidence supports the view that interstate banking would result in more competitive markets.

Interstate Banking and Concentration

The effect of interstate banking on market concentration depends on how interstate banking is implemented. If the Douglas amendment is changed to allow *bank holding companies* to cross state lines, the effect of bank holding company expansion on market concentration must be determined. On the other hand, if the McFadden Act is changed to allow national banks to *branch* across state lines, the effect of branching on concentration must be determined.

Holding Company Expansion and Concentration.   There are two ways to infer the effect of bank holding company expansion on concentration. One way, which is based on the claim that the market share of banks affiliated with a holding company would increase only if they had lower marginal production costs than unaffiliated banks, is to determine whether such costs are lower for affiliated banks.[9] Another way is to see how past holding company expansion has affected concentration.

Two recent studies indicate that the marginal costs of banks affiliated with a multibank holding company are greater than or equal to those of banks that are not affiliated. A study by George Benston, Gerald Hanweck, and David Humphrey showed that holding company affiliation had no effect on state branch or unit bank costs.[10] A later study by Benston, Hanweck, Humphrey, and Allen Berger showed that marginal production costs are greater at affiliated state unit banks than at unaffiliated state unit banks.[11] Holding company affiliation had no effect on the costs of state branch banks. Because these studies do not find a cost advantage to bank holding company affiliation, they suggest that interstate banking in the form of bank holding company expansion across state lines is not likely to result in more concentrated banking markets.

The implications of the cost studies for banking concentration must be viewed with caution, however, because they do not use data from banks with more than $1 billion of deposits. While this would not ordinarily be a problem, it becomes a serious shortcoming if these studies are used to determine the likely effect of holding company expansion across state lines on concentration. If there are cost advantages to these large banks affiliating with a holding company, and if these are the banks that would become affiliated if the Douglas amendment was amended, interstate banking could result in more concentrated markets.

As would be expected from the evidence in the cost studies, most studies of the effect of past intrastate bank holding company expansion on banking market concentration have found that holding company expansion had little effect on concentration. These studies have generally looked at changes over time in local banking market concentration after holding companies had expanded in those markets. Cynthia Glassman and Robert Eisenbeis reviewed several studies, conducted in the 1970s, of trends in banking concentration and concluded that bank holding company expansion has not significantly increased local market concentration, where market output is measured as the value of deposits.[12] In another survey of the effect of bank holding company expansion on concentration, Stephen Rhoades looked at seven studies and concluded that bank holding companies had no effect on concentration.[13] Rhoades also examined the results from four other studies and concluded that bank holding company acquisitions had no systematic effect on the market share of the acquired banks. A more recent study by John Rose and Donald Savage shows that, when bank holding companies open new banks in rural and small metropolitan area markets, significant decreases in concentration follow.[14] In another study, Rose found that bank holding company entry into local markets had little effect on the market share of the acquired bank.[15]

Although these studies would seem to indicate that removal of the prohibition against interstate expansion by bank holding companies would not increase banking concentration, these results must also be viewed with caution. One reason is that some of the earlier studies attribute all changes in concentration to bank holding company expansion and thereby neglect other factors that could be responsible for the changes in concentration. Another is that many of the studies looked at the change in concentration for only a short period after bank holding companies expanded. If the effect of holding company expansion was not complete in that time, the evidence from these studies could be misleading.

Branching and Concentration.   Because there is no evidence on whether bank branches have lower marginal production costs than similar-sized unit banks, the only way to infer the effect of branching on banking concentration is to see how past intrastate branching has affected concentration. Instead of looking at how a change in state branching laws has affected market concentration over time, most analysts have looked at how concentration varies across states with different branching laws.[16]

The evidence on the effect of branching on local market concentration seems to indicate that local markets are slightly more concentrated in branching states than in unit banking states. Defining a local banking market as a standard metropolitan statistical area (SMSA), in June 1982 the largest bank's local market share averaged 32.5 percent in SMSAs in statewide branching states, 33.0 percent in SMSAs in limited branching states, and 29.0 percent in SMSAs in unit banking states.[17] The average local five-firm concentration ratios were 82.3 percent in SMSAs in statewide branching states, 82.9 percent in SMSAs in limited branching states, and 76.0 percent in SMSAs in unit banking states. While the quantitative differences across states are not large, the evidence seems to imply that branching is related to greater local market concentration. On the other hand—from a comparison of the 1982 concentration ratios with 1970 concentration ratios that were reported in a study by Donald Savage—it appears that concentration tends to decline over time at about the same pace in branching states as in unit banking states.[18]

The evidence based on comparisons of concentration ratios between markets may be misleading, however, as such comparisons are meaningful only if the markets are correctly defined. A market is an area in which the action of one firm has an effect on another firm. While the SMSA may be the relevant market in states that allow branching throughout the SMSA, the area may be too wide in unit banking states. The relevant market for many retail deposits and small loans is probably smaller than the SMSA. Where branching is allowed throughout an SMSA, all the banks in the SMSA can have an effect on each other because they can compete for these retail deposits and small loans by branching throughout the area. But in unit banking states, a bank competes for these retail deposits and small loans mostly in the small area around its location. Because the size of the relevant market is overstated in unit banking states, the number of banks and value of deposits in the market are overstated. The concentration ratio, therefore, is understated. Although the average concentration ratio in SMSAs is greater in branching states than in unit banking states, the difference in the ratios may be overstated. If the correct market was used to determine concentration in unit banking states, markets in branching states might even be found to be less concentrated than markets in unit banking states.[19]

Overall, the evidence does not support the view that interstate banking would increase market concentration. First, evidence from the cost studies, though limited, suggests that interstate banking in the form of holding company expansion would not cause greater concentration. Second, evidence on the effect of past bank holding company expansion on concentration is consistent with the evidence from the cost studies and shows that bank holding company expansion has not affected market concentration. Finally, while the evidence on branching suggests that SMSAs are slightly more concentrated in branching states than in unit banking states, the difference might be reduced or even reversed if the relevant market in unit banking states was correctly defined. Moreover, concentration tends to decline over time at about the same pace in branching states as in unit banking states.

Concentration-Performance Studies in Banking

Studies of the competitive effects of greater concentration usually focus only on the relationship between concentration and performance. Although the competitive effects of greater concentration depend on the relationship between concentration and conduct in banking, conduct is difficult to measure. Therefore, conduct is usually ignored in empirical studies of the concentration-conduct-performance hypothesis.

Most studies use statistical techniques, such as multiple regression or correlation analysis, to determine the relationship between concentration and performance in state or local markets. Although concentration ratios are usually used in these studies, other measures of market structure are also used, such as the number of banks in the same market, or the Herfindahl index.[20] Performance refers to the closeness of output and price to their competitive levels, but these measures are not available. Thus, performance is measured by average bank profits in the market or by the price of bank services, such as interest rates on loans.

Most empirical studies of the concentration-performance hypothesis in banking show a definite but only slight relationship between concentration and performance. Stephen Rhoades reported that, of 39 studies conducted between 1960 and September 1977, 30 showed a positive but small relationship between concentration and performance in banking.[21] In other words, increases in concentration are associated with small increases in bank profits or prices of bank services. The relationship was generally less than that found in concentration-performance studies of other industries. In a follow-up survey of 26 studies performed between October 1977 and June 1982, Rhoades found that 23 studies found a positive but small relationship between concentration and performance.[22]

The evidence in support of the concentration-performance hypothesis is not as strong as it first appears, however. First, Rhoades noted that many of the studies that used prices as a measure of performance did not account for the effect of costs on prices. Higher prices due to higher costs is not an indication of poorer industry performance. In the first survey, for example, Rhoades found that 31 studies used prices to measure performance but only 12 accounted for costs. Of the 31 studies that used prices, 27 found a positive relationship between concentration and price. But of those 12 that accounted for costs, only 8 found a positive relationship between concentration and price. Rhoades also noted that while 13 of 20 studies found a positive relationship between concentration and profits, these studies usually used profits from a single year, rather than profits averaged over a few years. The problem with using profits for a single year is that good business conditions in that year could raise profits. Profits averaged over a few years, however, gives a better indication of the long-run profit rate in a particular market.

A more fundamental problem with studies that use profits instead of prices as a measure of performance is that high profits do not necessarily indicate less competitive performance. High profits are seen not only in noncompetitive industries where output is restricted but also in highly competitive industries where some firms produce at a lower cost than others. Thus, a positive relationship between concentration and profits does not necessarily mean that increases in concentration cause poorer industry performance.

There is good reason, in fact, for believing that a positive relationship between concentration and profits reflects superior performance. Harold Demsetz argues that the superior performance of some firms causes both concentration and profits to rise together.[23] He argues that it is the potential increase in profits that provides firms with the incentive to lower costs and improve their product. If firms that are more efficient or that produce a better quality product are not rewarded at least temporarily with higher profits, they have no incentive to perform better. And if firms are more efficient, it is the resulting lower costs of production, rather than the higher prices caused by collusion, that produce larger profits. Superior performing firms not only earn greater profits but also expand their market share as they successfully compete with less-able firms. Because superior performance causes profits and market shares to rise together, a positive relationship between concentration and profits is to be expected in industries where some firms are more efficient than others. Using data from almost 100 industries, Demsetz presents empirical evidence in support of this view.

Although the evidence on the relationship between concentration and performance suggests that increases in concentration reduce performance, the evidence must be interpreted with caution. First, the effect is small. Second, many studies failed to control for other factors that affect prices and profits. Finally, studies that found a positive relationship between concentration and profits may have found such a relationship only because superior performance by some banks causes both concentration and profits to rise together.[24]

The Effect of Entry on Bank Performance

There have been several studies of the direct effect of entry on bank performance. These studies usually looked at new bank entry into unit banking markets with relatively few banks and compared the pre-entry and post-entry performance of banks in entry markets with the performance of banks in non-entry markets. Better performance was measured not only by decreases in prices and profits as in other studies but also often by increases in loan to asset ratios and interest-bearing to non-interest-bearing deposit ratios. The studies found that entry substantially improved unit bank performance.

Robert Chandross examined the effect of new bank entry on unit bank performance in 98 previously one-bank towns.[25] For the three years before the new entry, these banks earned significantly above-average profits and had significantly below-average loan to asset ratios. In the three years after entry, their earnings fell significantly but not below the average for large groups of banks in the same state. Their loan to asset ratios also rose significantly.

In another study, Donald Fraser and Peter Rose compared the pre-entry and post-entry performance of banks in markets previously served by one, two, or three independent unit banks with the performance of a control group of banks of similar size in a similar environment except that there was no entry.[26] Before entry, the loan to asset ratios and time deposit to total deposit ratios were lower in the entry markets than in the nonentry markets. Profit rates were the same in both markets. After entry, both the loan to asset ratios and time deposit to total deposit ratios rose in the entry markets to the same levels as in the nonentry markets, without an increase in prices or a decrease in profitability or growth.

Alan McCall and Manferd Peterson also compared the pre-entry and post-entry performance of banks in markets previously served by one, two, or three unit banks with the performance of a control group of similar banks in markets where there was no entry.[27] They found the net benefits of entry substantial in number and magnitude. Before entry, the sample banks in entry markets had greater earnings on assets than banks in the nonentry markets. They also had lower loan to asset ratios and smaller interest-bearing to total deposit ratios. They paid lower interest rates on time and savings accounts and had a greater proportion of expenses due to officer and employee expense. In the year after entry, the banks in the entry markets raised the interest rates paid on deposits. Their loan to asset ratios rose, as did the time and savings deposit to total deposit ratios. The proportion of expenses due to officers and employees declined. Except for the change in the loan to asset ratio, which was not affected consistently after the first post-entry year, all these changes persisted throughout the five-year period after entry that was studied. Although profit rates declined significantly over the five-year period, they did not fall below the levels at the control banks, so that entry did not have an adverse impact on the viability of the banks that existed before entry.

These studies indicate that, to the extent interstate banking leads to entry into small banking markets with only a few banks, the markets would become more competitive. If interstate banking led mostly to entry into large banking markets, however, the competitive effects are less clear. And while these studies provide evidence on the competitive benefits of actual entry, they give no evidence on the competitive effects of potential entry.

The Effect of Branching Laws on Bank Performance

The difference in performance between banks in unit banking states and banks in branch banking states provides direct evidence on whether interstate banking would result in markets that were more competitive or less competitive. If easier entry due to less-restrictive branching laws results in more competitive markets, bank performance should be better in branching states than in unit banking states. But if less-restrictive branching laws result in less-competitive markets, bank performance should be worse in branching states than in unit banking states.

In their study of the effect of bank entry on performance, McCall and Peterson also found that the effect of entry on performance in branching states was significantly different from the effect in unit banking states.[28] In branching states, pre-entry profit levels, deposit interest rates, operating costs, and asset structures were the same at banks in entry markets as at banks in nonentry markets. The only difference was that banks in entry markets had higher service charges on demand deposits than banks in the nonentry markets. Over a five-year period after entry, the only change was that service charges on demand deposits fell in the entry markets in all five years. In unit banking markets, however, there was a substantial difference between banks in entry markets and the control banks before entry, and that difference was largely eliminated after entry. Also, before entry, banks in branch entry markets performed better than banks in unit entry markets. Entry in branching areas apparently had little effect, because the ability to branch resulted in either actual or potential competition that made bank performance better from the start.

In another test of the effect of branching laws on competition, Donald Savage and Stephen Rhoades compared the performance of unit banks in unit banking states with the performance of unit banks in branching states.[29] Unit banks in statewide branching states earned a lower rate of return on assets and paid higher interest rates on time and savings deposits than unit banks in unit banking states.

Service charges on demand deposits were the same in both groups. Unit banks in limited branching states earned a lower rate of return on assets than unit banks in unit banking states. They also charged lower interest rates on loans, charged lower service charges on demand deposits, and paid higher interest rates on time and savings accounts.

In a similar study, Mark Flannery found that unit banking restrictions result in significant price inefficiencies.[30] Flannery estimated that unit banks in unit banking states earn 17.5 to 23.0 percent higher profits than unit banks in branching states. He attributed the difference to unit banks in unit banking states being able to charge higher prices—as opposed to producing banking services at a lower cost.

The evidence suggests that interstate banking would likely result in a more-competitive banking system. The evidence is consistent with the hypothesis that less-restrictive branching laws result in more-competitive banking markets. Banks in unit banking states are apparently protected to some extent from competition. Whether due to potential or actual competition, bank performance is better in branching states than in unit banking states. Because intrastate branching increases competition, it can be inferred that interstate banking would also increase competition.

CONCLUSION

Many financial institutions have found ways of providing bank and banklike services on an interstate basis. Along with the growth of interstate financial services, there has been an increasing demand for removal of the prohibitions against interstate banking so traditionally defined banks can participate in providing these services. Many issues must be settled, however, before legislators decide to remove the prohibitions.

One issue is the competitive effects of interstate banking. This article discusses the theoretical aspects of this issue and empirical evidence. The evidence suggests that interstate banking would likely result in a more competitive banking system. The evidence indicates that interstate banking is not likely to result in more-concentrated banking markets. And even if concentration increased, the evidence from concentration-performance studies suggests that there would be little effect on bank performance. The evidence from studies of the effect of entry suggests that the removal of prohibitions against interstate banking would, in fact, result in substantial benefits if it led to new banks being opened in protected local markets. Finally, comparisons of bank performance in branching states with performance in unit banking states are consistent with the view that the benefits from removing the prohibitions against interstate banking could be large.

Although interstate banking should result in more competitive banking markets, other questions have to be answered before legislators and regulators will support interstate banking legislation. These questions include the effect of interstate banking on the cost efficiency of the financial services industry, the safety and soundness of the banking system, the viability of small banking institutions, and the flow of credit between regions. Furthermore, decisions would have to be made about the best way to implement interstate banking. Some analysts favor repeal of the Douglas amendment, while others favor amendment of the McFadden Act. Some recommend a gradual movement toward full interstate banking, while others recommend immediate removal of all geographic restrictions in banking. Thus, many issues other than the competitive effects of interstate banking still must be resolved before any legislative action is taken.

NOTES

[1] Many analysts dismiss the argument that interstate banking would lead to a less competitive banking system as irrelevant to the issue. They argue that the antitrust laws are sufficient to prevent anticompetitive behavior.

[2] Restrictions on branching also were overcome in other ways. For example, chain banking was often used as a way to avoid branching restrictions.

[3] The Douglas amendment does not prevent bank holding companies from owning subsidiaries that provide banklike services across state lines. Bank holding companies can establish an interstate presence by owning, say, mortgage banking, factoring, or finance companies in other states.

[4] For a more detailed discussion of the nonbank bank issue, see Charles Morris, "Nonbank Banks and Interstate Banking," *Financial Letter,* Federal Reserve Bank of Kansas City, September 1984.

[5] Even if the market share of newly opened banks increases, there could still be a net decline in market concentration. This is because concentration initially declines when a new bank is opened.

[6] Because marginal costs must be lower, a decrease in fixed costs will not affect the newly affiliated bank's market share, although it will affect the bank's profits. Affiliation with a banking network could allow a bank to increase its market share without a reduction in marginal costs, however, if affiliation was accompanied by an increase in the demand for bank services. This could happen, for example, if affiliation led to the introduction of a new product that other banks in the market could not copy.

[7] To the extent that such cost advantages are responsible for more concentrated markets, society still may be better off with interstate banking than without it. The savings in production costs may be greater than other costs associated with interstate banking.

[8] Successful collusion is even more difficult because it requires not only that group members successfully enforce output quotas but that they prevent all forms of rivalry—price and nonprice.

[9] There are some methodological problems with cost studies in general. They use historical accounting costs, rather than opportunity costs, they implicitly assume that all firms choose from the same set of technologies, they never take risk into account, and they cannot account for unquantifiable aspects of output, such as service differences among banks. Also, older studies may no longer be relevant because of changes in banking technology and the regulatory environment.

[10] George J. Benston, Gerald A. Hanweck, and David B. Humphrey, "Scale Economies in Banking: A Restructuring and Reassessment," *Journal of Money, Credit, and Banking,* November 1982, pp. 435–56.

[11] George J. Benston, Allen N. Berger, Gerald A. Hanweck, and David B. Humphrey, "Economies of Scale and Scope in Banking," *Proceedings of a Conference on Bank Structure and Competition,* Federal Reserve Bank of Chicago, 1983, pp. 432–55.

[12] Cynthia A. Glassman and Robert A. Eisenbeis, "Bank Holding Companies and Concentration of Banking and Financial Resources," *The Bank Holding Company Movement to 1978: A Compendium,* Board of Governors of the Federal Reserve System, September 1978, pp. 209–61. Banking industry output is measured in most studies as the value of deposits. Throughout the remainder of this article, unless specified otherwise, the value of deposits is the measure of output used in calculating market shares and concentration ratios.

[13] Stephen A. Rhoades, "The Effect of Bank Holding Companies on Competition," *The Bank Holding Company Movement,* pp. 185–207.

[14] John T. Rose and Donald T. Savage, "Bank Holding Company *De Novo* Entry and Banking Market Deconcentration," *Journal of Bank Research,* Summer 1982, pp. 96–100.

[15] John T. Rose, "Bank Holding Company Affiliation and Market Share Performance," *Journal of Monetary Economics,* January 1982, p. 118.

[16] A 1972 study by Bernard Shull examines the change in concentration in Virginia banking markets after a 1962 change in Virginia law that allowed banks to branch statewide by merger. Shull reports, however, that the change in the law encouraged statewide expansion through the bank holding company mechanism. Thus, the Virginia case cannot be used for evidence on the relationship between branching and concentration. See Bernard Shull, "Multiple-Office Banking and the Structure of Banking Markets: The New York and Virginia Experience," *Proceedings of a Conference on Bank Structure and Competition,* Federal Reserve Bank of Chicago, 1972, pp. 30–43.

[17] Donald T. Savage of the Board of Governors of the Federal Reserve System kindly provided these data. The average concentration ratios exclude multistate SMSA data and were computed from *Summary of Deposits,* 1982.

[18] Donald T. Savage, "Developments in Banking Structure, 1970–81," *Federal Reserve Bulletin,* Board of Governors of the Federal Reserve System, Washington, D.C., February 1982, pp. 77–85. Savage also reports average state five-firm concentration ratios for different types of state branching laws. He notes, however, that because states are not banking markets this evidence is of limited value.

[19] There is some empirical evidence that an SMSA in a unit banking state is not a single market for banking services. According to the law of one price, all firms that sell exactly the same good and operate in the same market will charge the same price. In one study, Larry Mote reports that the prices of banking services across banks are more variable in SMSAs in unit banking states than in branching states. He also reports that in branching states prices of banking services in the suburbs of SMSAs are not significantly different from prices in the central city, but in the largest unit banking SMSAs there are significant price differences between the suburbs and the central city. Because the variation in prices for essentially the same good is greater in SMSAs in unit banking states that in SMSAs in branching states, SMSAs in unit banking states are more likely to be composed of several markets than are SMSAs in branching states. See Larry Mote, "The Perennial Issue: Branch Banking," *Compendium of Issues Relating to Branching by Financial Institutions,* Subcommittee on Financial Institutions, Committee on Banking, Housing, and Urban Affairs, U.S. Senate, U.S. Government Printing Office, 1976, p. 446.

[20] The Herfindahl index is defined as the sum of the squared market shares of all firms in the same market. Whereas the concentration ratio reflects only the size of the largest firms in an industry relative to the other firms, the Herfindahl index reflects the number of firms in the industry and the size distribution of all firms.

[21] Stephen A. Rhoades, "Structure-Performance Studies in Banking: A Summary and Evaluation," Staff Economic Studies no. 92, Board of Governors of the Federal Reserve System, 1977.

[22] Stephen A. Rhoades, "Structure-Performance Studies in Banking: An Updated Summary and Evaluation," Staff Studies no. 119, Board of Governors of the Federal Reserve System, 1982.

[23] See Harold Demsetz, *The Market Concentration Doctrine,* American Enterprise Institute–Hoover Institution Policy Studies, August 1973.

[24] There are also reasons for believing that the estimated relationship between concentration and performance is biased. First, if the relevant market is not correctly defined, the results will be upwardly biased. Second, the effect of risk on the measures of performance is usually not taken into account. For a discussion of other problems with concentration-performance studies, see George J. Benston, "The Optimal Banking Structure: Theory and Evidence," *Journal of Bank Research,* Winter 1973, pp. 220–37.

[25] Robert H. Chandross, "The Impact of New Bank Entry on Unit Banks in One Bank Towns," *Journal of Bank Research,* Autumn 1971, pp. 22–30.

[26] Donald R. Fraser and Peter S. Rose, "Bank Entry and Bank Performance," *Journal of Finance,* March 1972, pp. 65–78.

[27] Alan S. McCall and Manferd O. Peterson, "The Impact of *De Novo* Commercial Bank Entry," *Compendium of Issues,* pp. 499–521.

[28] McCall and Peterson, "The Impact."

[29] Donald T. Savage and Stephen A. Rhoades, "The Effect of Branch Banking on Pricing, Profits, and Efficiency of Unit Banks," *"Proceedings of a Conference on Bank Structure and Competition,* Federal Reserve Bank of Chicago, 1979, pp. 187–96.

[30] Mark J. Flannery, "The Social Costs of Unit Banking Restrictions," *Journal of Monetary Economics,* March 1984, pp. 237–49.

11

Interstate Banking: Probability or Reality?

David D. Whitehead

Though interstate banking is restricted legally, banks and holding companies have abundant opportunities for providing banking-type services across state lines, as this inventory shows.

The McFadden Act limits branching by a national bank to a single state, while the Douglas Amendment to the Bank Holding Company Act restricts holding companies from acquiring banks across state lines. But, in fact, banks and holding companies are providing financial services across state lines and doing so legally. Interstate banking is a reality today in everything except name.

The word *bank* is the key to determining which institutions fall under the prohibitions against interstate banking. For purposes of the Bank Holding Company Act, a bank is defined as "any institution which (1) accepts deposits that the depositor has a legal right to withdraw on demand and (2) engages in the business of making commercial loans." Therefore, any organization offering both demand deposits and commercial loans may be defined as a commercial bank and thus becomes subject to the interstate banking restrictions.

Federal laws limit the ability of a formal banking entity to offer both demand deposits and commercial loans at a single location—that is, to function as a bank—in more than one state. But no other type of organization providing financial services is prohibited by federal law from interstate activities. Whereas a chartered bank may not branch interstate and a holding company may not acquire a "bank" across state lines, an individual is free to own banks in several states. Moreover, despite the branching restrictions, banks may sell CDs nationwide; they may send out calling officers or establish loan production offices and Edge Act offices; they may advertise across the country for deposits or loans; they may offer credit cards throughout the nation and tie these to unified demand and time

From *Economic Review*, Federal Reserve Bank of Atlanta, March 1985, pp. 6–19.

The author is a research officer who heads the financial institutions and payments research team at the Federal Reserve Bank of Atlanta.

accounts accessible by mail or telephone. A bank holding company may skirt restrictions by establishing nonbank subsidiaries capable of engaging in almost any type of financial service activity that a bank does; and as long as the subsidiary does not offer both demand deposits and commercial loans, it may provide its services on an interstate basis.

The purpose of my presentation is to point out the avenues banking organizations have taken to establish an interstate brick-and-mortar presence. I will present six of these avenues and, where possible, the number of interstate offices maintained. This review should give a realistic picture of the extent to which interstate banking is in fact a reality today.

GRANDFATHERED ACTIVITIES

Quite often, banking organizations initiate an activity and legislators react to the evolving market circumstances. In some cases, it is detrimental or impossible to require an organization to cease that activity, even though a general prohibition is thought desirable. One equitable means of dealing with such a situation is to allow organizations already so engaged to continue but to prohibit them from expanding the activity. A clause written into legislation for this purpose is termed a *grandfather provision.*

A number of banking organizations, both domestic and international, enjoy grandfather provisions in the interstate banking context. Table 1 shows which organizations operate banks across state lines under grandfather provisions, their state of residence, and the number of interstate banking subsidiaries they are operating. Each is a banking office, not limited just to certain activities banks may perform. In total, 9 domestic banking organizations control 139 banks and 1,137 branch offices in 21 states. Seven international banking organizations also have grandfathered status and control 138 interstate offices. Fifteen foreign organizations control 15 interstate banks with 214 branches. If we include the foreign banking organizations controlling branch banks, Edge Act offices, and agency offices, the number grows to 103 organizations controlling 254 interstate offices (see Table 2).

LOAN PRODUCTION OFFICES AND EDGE ACT CORPORATIONS

Domestic banking organizations may also establish loan production offices and Edge Act corporations on an interstate basis. Loan production offices can do little more than calling offices, yet they are useful in establishing a wholesale brick-and-mortar presence. Edge Act offices likewise are aimed at wholesale customers but are limited to servicing organizations engaged in international trade. A survey by the Federal Reserve Bank of Atlanta in December 1982 identified 44 banking organizations controlling 202 loan production offices spread over 34 states (see Table 3). In addition, we were able to identify 143 interstate Edge Act offices, largely concentrated in New York, Florida, California, and Texas, maintained by 49 domestic banking organizations. Obviously, these banking organizations were following their international customers (see Table 4).

4(c)8 SUBSIDIARIES

Another avenue for a bank holding company wishing to establish a physical presence across state lines is the acquisition or creation of so-called 4(c)8 subsidi-

TABLE 1
Grandfathered Bank Holding Companies with Subsidiary Banks in More Than One State

Bank Holding Company	Home State	Number of States	States in Which Banks Are Located	Number of Interstate Offices
First Interstate Bancorporation	CA	11	AZ, CA, CO, ID, MT, NM, OR, NV, WA, WY, UT	626
Norwest Corporation	MN	7	IA, MN, MT, NE, ND, SD, WI	140
First Bank System	MN	5	MN, MT, ND, SD, WI	89
First American Bancshares Corporation	DC	5	DC, MD, NY, TN, VA	131
Bremer Financial Corporation	MN	3	MN, ND, WI	31
General Bancshares Corporation	MO	3	IL, MO, TN	25
First Security Corporation	UT	3	ID, WY, UT	71
NCNB Corporation [1]	NC	2	FL, NC	159
Northern Trust Corporation	IL	2	FL, IL	4
Bank of Montreal*	NY	2	CA, NY	3
Canadian Imperial Bank of Commerce*	NY	2	CA, NY	23
The Bank of Tokyo Ltd.*	NY	2	CA, NY	4
The Sumitomo Bank Ltd.*	CA	2	CA, HI	16
Barclays Bank Ltd.*	NY	2	CA, NY	58
The Royal Bank of Canada*	NY	2	NY, PR	17
Banco Central, S.A.*	NY	2	NY, PR	17
Total				1,414

[1]Includes the February 1984 acquisition of Ellis Banking Corporation.
*Foreign Banking Organizations.
Source: Federal Reserve Board of Governors, data as of December 31, 1983.

TABLE 2
Foreign Banking Organizations Controlling Interstate Offices

State	Number of Foreign Banking Organizations Controlling Interstate Offices by State of Residence	Number and Type of Interstate Office Locations by Type of Office				Total Number of Interstate Offices Controlled by Foreign Banking Organizations Headquartered Outside the State***
		Banks	Branches	Edge Acts	Agencies	
California	26	8	2	2	63	75
District of Columbia	—	—	1	—	—	1
Florida	1	—	—	6	22	28
Georgia	—	—	—	—	10	10
Hawaii	—	1	—	—	2	3
Illinois	1	1	36	3	—	40
Louisiana	—	—	—	—	1	1
Massachusetts	1	—	4	—	—	4
New York	58	3	37	2	18	60
Oregon	—	—	7	—	—	7
Pennsylvania	—	—	6	—	—	6
Texas	—	—	—	9	—	9
Washington	—	—	10	—	—	10
Total	103*	13**	103	22	116	254

*16 of these organizations that have offices in more than one state are international organizations having no residence state—i.e., agency offices of international banks.
**Two additional banks are located in Puerto Rico.
***Excludes branches of foreign-owned U.S. banks.
Source: Federal Reserve Bank of New York, data as of June 30, 1982.

TABLE 3
Interstate Loan Production Offices

Parent State	Number of Organizations Establishing Loan Production Offices	Number of Interstate Loan Production Offices Maintained	Number of States Entered by LPOs
California	5	36[a]	14
District of Columbia	1	7	7
Florida	1	1	1
Illinois	4	31	13
Kentucky	2	8	7
Maryland	1	3	3
Massachusetts	3	14	12
Michigan	1	1	1
Minnesota	2	5	5
Missouri	2	22[b]	6
New Jersey	1	2	2
New York	8	31[c]	13
North Carolina	2	4	2
Oklahoma	1	1	1
Pennsylvania	2	4	2
Rhode Island	2	6	5
Texas	2	5	3
Virginia	2	12	5
Washington	2	9	7
Total	44	202	34[d]

Notes: [a] Only 3 LPOs from California are in New York.
[b] General Bancshares Corporation of St. Louis, MO has full service banks in Missouri, Illinois, and Tennessee. They have 13 LPOs in Tennessee and 4 LPOs in Illinois.
[c] 10 of the 31 are in California.
[d] A total of 34 different states contain interstate LPOs.

Source: Federal Reserve Bank of Atlanta, Survey of Largest 200 Banking Organizations, data as of December 31, 1982.

aries. In its Section 4(c)8, the Bank Holding Company Act as amended in 1970 provides that holding companies may engage in certain nonbank activities. Bank holding companies may acquire "shares of any company the activity of which the Board after due notice and opportunity for hearing has determined (by order or regulation) to be so closely related to banking or managing or controlling banks as to be a proper incident thereto."

Table 5 lists the 4(c)8 activities permitted by regulation (generally approved for all holding companies), activities permitted by order (case-by-case approval by the Board of Governors because of special circumstances); and activities denied by the board as of November 1984. The 4(c)8 subsidiaries are not banks, and so once established they may open offices in any number of states. Since the vast majority of approved nonbank activities are those in which banks may engage—activities "closely related to banking or managing or controlling banks"—the 4(c)8 provisions effectively allow holding companies to provide financial services similar to those banks offer, but on an interstate basis.

The survey by the Federal Reserve Bank of Atlanta identified 139 holding companies that controlled a total of 382 4(c)8 subsidiaries with at least one interstate office. The holding companies' geographic distribution is portrayed in Map 1. Map 2 shows the number of 4(c)8 subsidiaries controlling interstate

TABLE 4
Interstate Edge Act Corporations of Domestic
Banking Organizations

Parent State	Number of Organizations with Edge Act Corporations	Number of Edge Act Offices
Alaska	1	1
California	5	27
Connecticut	1	1
District of Columbia	3	3
Georgia	1	2
Illinois	4	19
Maryland	1	1
Massachusetts	4	4
Minnesota	2	3
Missouri	1	1
New York	9	54
North Carolina	3	3
Ohio	1	1
Pennsylvania	5	9
Rhode Island	1	1
Tennessee	1	1
Texas	3	4
Washington	2	3
Wisconsin	1	1
Total	49	143

Source: Federal Reserve Bank of New York, data as of June 30, 1982.

offices. The number in each state represents the interstate 4(c)8 subsidiaries established by holding companies residing within the state; for example, holding companies in New York have established 96 such subsidiaries with at least one interstate office.

The number of interstate 4(c)8 offices controlled by holding companies in various states is displayed on Map 3. Bank holding companies in New York have been most active in establishing 4(c)8 subsidiaries that have opened interstate offices. Map 4 shows the number of interstate offices of 4(c)8 subsidiaries controlled by non-resident bank holding companies. Each office is providing at least one type of financial service allowed under the Bank Holding Company Act outside the state where its parent holding company resides.

In total, the survey uncovered more than 5,500 interstate offices, each providing a financial service across state lines and each ultimately controlled by its parent holding company. These findings lend substantial support to the reality of interstate banking.

RECIPROCAL AND NONRECIPROCAL INTERSTATE BANKING LAWS

Recent legislation adopted by a number of states to allow entry by out-of-state banking organizations represents a less-traditional avenue for interstate expan-

TABLE 5
Permissible Nonbank Activities for Bank Holding Companies under Section 4(c)8 of Regulation Y, November 1984

Activities Permitted by Regulation	Activities Permitted by Order	Activities Denied by the Board

1. Extensions of credit[2]
   Mortgage banking
   Finance companies:
     consumer, sales,
     and commercial
   Credit cards
   Factoring
2. Industrial bank, Morris
   Plan banks, industrial loan
   company
3. Servicing loans and other
   extensions of credit[2]
4. Trust company[2]
5. Investment or financial
   advising[2]
6. Full-payout leasing of
   personal or real property[2]
7. Investments in community
   welfare projects[2]
8. Providing bookkeeping or
   data processing services[2]
9. Acting as insurance agent
   or broker primarily in
   connection with credit
   extensions[2]
10. Underwriting credit life,
    accident, and health
    insurance
11. Providing courier services[2]
12. Management consulting to
    all depository institutions
13. Sale at retail of money
    orders with a face value of
    not more than $1000,
    travelers checks, and
    savings bonds [1, 2, 7]
14. Performing appraisals of
    real estate[1]
15. Issuance and sale of
    travelers checks
16. Arranging commercial real
    estate equity financing
17. Securities brokerage
18. Underwriting and dealing
    in government obligations
    and money market
    instruments
19. Foreign exchange advisory
    and transactional services
20. Futures commission
    merchant
21. Options on financial
    futures
22. Advice on options on
    bullion and foreign
    exchange
	1. Issuance and sale of travelers
	   checks[2, 6]
	2. Buying and selling gold and silver
	   bullion and silver coin[2, 4]
	3. Issuing money orders and general-
	   purpose variable denominated
	   payment instruments[1, 2, 4]
	4. Futures commission merchant to
	   cover gold and silver bullion and
	   coins[1, 2]
	5. Underwriting certain federal, state,
	   and municipal securities[1, 2]
	6. Check verification[1, 2, 4]
	7. Financial advice to consumers[1, 2]
	8. Issuance of small denomination
	   debt instruments[1]
	9. Arranging for equity financing of
	   real estate
	10. Acting as futures commissions
	    merchant
	11. Discount brokerage
	12. Operating a distressed savings and
	    loan association
	13. Operating an Article XII
	    Investment Company
	14. Executing foreign banking
	    unsolicited purchases and sales of
	    securities
	15. Engaging in commercial banking
	    activities abroad through a limited
	    purpose Delaware bank
	16. Performing appraisal of real estate
	    and real estate advisor and real
	    estate brokerage on nonresidential
	    properties
	17. Operating a Pool Reserve Plan for
	    loss reserves of banks for loans to
	    small businesses
	18. Operating a thrift institution in
	    Rhode Island
	19. Operating a guarantee savings bank
	    in New Hampshire
	20. Offering informational advice and
	    transactional services for foreign
	    exchange services
		1. Insurance premium funding
		   (combined sales of mutual
		   funds and insurance)
		2. Underwriting life insurance
		   not related to credit
		   extension
		3. Sale of level-term credit
		   life
		4. Real estate brokerage
		   (residential)
		5. Armored car
		6. Land development
		7. Real estate syndication
		8. General management
		   consulting
		9. Property management
		10. Computer output
		    microfilm services
		11. Underwriting mortgage
		    guaranty insurance[3]
		12. Operating a savings and
		    loan association[1, 5]
		13. Operating a travel
		    agency[1, 2]
		14. Underwriting property and
		    casualty insurance[1]
		15. Underwriting home loan
		    life mortgage insurance[1]
		16. Investment note issue with
		    transactional character-
		    istics
		17. Real estate advisory
		    services

[1] Added to list since January 1, 1975.
[2] Activities permissible to national banks.
[3] Board orders found these activities closely related to banking but denied proposed
acquisitions as part of its "go slow" policy.
[4] To be decided on a case-by-case basis.
[5] Operating a thrift institution has been permitted by order in Rhode Island, Ohio, New
Hampshire, and California.
[6] Subsequently permitted by regulation.
[7] The amount subsequently was changed to $10,000.

Source: Federal Reserve Board.

Map 1
Resident State of Bank Holding Companies Controlling
Interstate 4(c)8 Subsidiaries

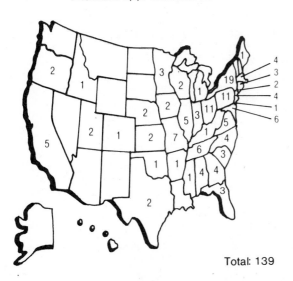

Total: 139

Map 2
Number of Interstate 4(c) 8 Subsidiaries of Holding
Companies Home-Officed in State

Total: 382

Map 3
Number of Interstate 4(c)8 Offices Established by
Nonbank Subsidiaries of
Holding Companies Home-Officed in State

Total: 5,500

Map 4
Total Number of Offices in State,
by Primary Activity of
Interstate 4(c)8 Subsidiaries

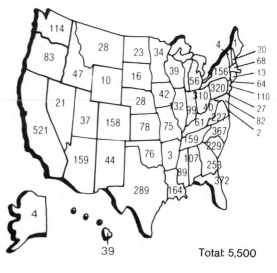

Total: 5,500

Source: All maps, Federal Reserve Bank of Atlanta, data as of 12/82.

TABLE 6
States with Out-of-State Banking Laws as of December 1984

State	Year Passed	Provisions
Alaska	1984	*De novo*-No *Acquisition of existing banks*-Yes, in business for 3 years *Branching into state*-Not explicitly stated *Acquisition SB (savings bank), S&L and Trust company*-Trust companies only *Reciprocal agreement*-No *Miscellaneous provision*-Unrestricted, permits out-of-state bank holding companies to acquire in-state banks.
Connecticut	1983	*De novo*-Not explicitly stated *Acquisition of existing banks*-Yes *Branching into state*-Not explicitly stated *Acquisition SB, S&L, and Trust*-Yes, other than trust companies (variety of other restrictions) *Reciprocal agreement*-New England only and anti-leapfrogging provision (non-NE to Maine and then Connecticut, Massachusetts, and/or Rhode Island)
Delaware	1981	*De novo*-Yes, if 1. Minimum capital stock and paid-in-surplus is at least $10 million, with 1 year to reach $25 million 2. Employ at least 100 persons 3. Not likely to attract customers from general public *Acquisition of existing banks*-Not explicitly stated *Branching into state*-Not explicitly stated *Acquisition SB, S&L, and Trust*-Not explicitly stated *Reciprocal agreement*-Not explicitly stated *Miscellaneous provision*-No interest rate ceiling on credit cards
	1983	*De novo*-Yes, if above 3 conditions are met and bank holding company was present under 1981 law. May also charter de novo bank although capital requirements for consumer credit banks may be different (initial capital requirement different if affiliated with credit card bank). *Acquisition of existing banks*-Not explicitly stated *Branching into state*-Not explicitly stated *Acquisition SB, S&L, and Trust*-Not explicitly stated *Reciprocal agreement*-Not explicitly stated *Miscellaneous provision*-Bank may only accept deposits other than demand deposits and make loans to natural persons for noncommercial uses.
Florida	1984	*De novo*-No *Acquisition of existing banks*-Yes, in-state bank must have been in existence at least five years *Branching into state*-Not explicitly stated *Acquisition SB, S&L, and Trust*-Not explicitly stated *Reciprocal agreement*-Yes, but only by holding companies located in Alabama, Arkansas, Georgia, Louisiana, Maryland, Mississippi, North Carolina, South Carolina, Tennessee, Virginia, West Virginia, and the District of Columbia *Miscellaneous provision*-The law takes effect on July 1, 1985.
Georgia	1984	*De novo*-No *Acquisition of existing banks*-Yes, in-state bank must have been in existence at least five years *Branching into state*-Not explicitly stated *Acquisition SB, S&L, and Trust*-Not explicitly stated *Reciprocal agreement*-Yes, but only by holding companies located in Alabama, Arkansas, Florida, Louisiana, Maryland, Mississippi, North Carolina, South Carolina, Tennessee, Virginia, West Virginia, and the District of Columbia *Miscellaneous provision*-The law takes effect on July 1, 1985.

TABLE 6 (*continued*)

State	Year Passed	Provisions
Illinois	1981	*De novo*-Not explicitly stated *Acquisition of existing banks*-Only grandfathered interstate bank holding companies under Bank Holding Company Act of 1956 *Branching into state*-Not explicitly stated *Acquisition SB, S&L, and Trust*-Not explicitly stated *Reciprocal agreement*-Not explicitly stated
	1984	*Miscellaneous provision*-Permits an out-of-state banking organization to acquire an in-state institution with liquidity problems and more than $1 billion in assets.
Iowa	1972	*De novo*-Not explicitly stated *Acquisition of existing banks*-Yes, if on 1-1-71 bank holding company was registered as a bank holding corporation and owned 2 banks in Iowa *Branching into state*-Not explicitly stated *Acquisition SB, S&L, and Trust*-Not explicitly stated *Reciprocal agreement*-Not explicitly stated
Kentucky	1984	*De novo*-No *Acquisition of existing banks*-Yes, in-state bank must have been in existence for at least five years *Branching into state*-Not explicitly stated *Acquisition SB, S&L, and Trust*-Not explicitly stated *Reciprocal agreement*-Yes, only with contiguous states *Miscellaneous provisions*-The contiguous state limitation will be dropped in two years.
Maine	1984	*De novo*-no *Acquisition of existing banks*-Yes *Branching into state*-Not explicitly stated *Acquisition SB, S&L, and Trust*-Not explicitly stated *Reciprocal agreement*-No *Miscellaneous provision*-Unrestricted, permits out-of-state bank holding companies to acquire in-state banks.
Maryland	1983	*De novo*-Yes, if 1. Minimum capital stock and paid-in-surplus of $10 million, rising to $25 million in 1 year 2. Employ at least 100 persons 3. Not likely to attract customers from general public *Acquisition of existing banks*-Not explicitly stated *Branching into state*-Not explicitly stated *Acquisition SB, S&L, and Trust*-Not explicitly stated *Reciprocal agreement*-Not explicitly stated *Miscellaneous provision*-24% interest rate ceiling on credit cards
Massachusetts	1982	*De novo*-Yes *Acquisition of existing banks*-Yes *Branching into state*-Yes *Acquisition SB, S&L, and Trust*-Yes *Reciprocal agreement*-Yes, New England only and anti-leapfrogging provision

TABLE 6 (*continued*)

State	Year Passed	Provisions
Nebraska	1983	*De novo*-Yes, if 1. Limited to one office 2. Minimum capital stock and paid-in-surplus is at least $2.5 million 3. Employ at least 50 state residents within one year 4. Operate in a manner not likely to attract customers from the general public *Acquisition of existing banks*-Not explicitly stated *Branching into state*-Not explicitly stated *Acquisition SB, S&L, and Trust*-Not explicitly stated *Reciprocal agreement*-Not explicitly stated *Miscellaneous provision*-No interest rate ceiling on credit cards
	1983	*De novo*-Not explicitly stated *Acquisition of existing banks*-Yes, if on 3-12-63 the bank owned at least 2 banks in state *Branching into state*-Not explicitly stated *Acquisition SB, S&L, and Trust*-Not explicitly stated *Reciprocal agreement*-Not explicitly stated
Nevada	1984	*De novo*-Yes, limited purpose wholesale-oriented, single-office banks *Acquisiton of existing banks*-Not explicitly stated *Branching into state*-Not explicitly stated *Acquisition of SB, S&L, and Trust*-Not explicitly stated *Reciprocal agreement*-Not explicitly stated
New York	1982	*De novo*-Yes *Acquisition of existing banks*-Yes *Branching into state*-Not explicitly stated *Acquisition SB, S&L, and Trust*-No *Reciprocal Agreement*-Yes
North Carolina	1984	*De novo*-No *Acquisition of existing banks*-Yes *Branching into state*-Not explicitly stated *Acquisition SB, S&L, and Trust*-Not explicitly stated *Reciprocal agreement*-Yes, only by holding companies located in Alabama, Arkansas, Florida, Georgia, Kentucky, Louisiana, Maryland, Mississippi, South Carolina, Tennessee, Virginia, West Virginia, and the District of Columbia *Miscellaneous provision*-The law becomes effective January 1, 1985.
Oregon	1983	*De novo*-No *Acquisition of existing banks*-Yes, but of mutual savings banks only *Branching into state*-No *Acquisition SB, S&L, and Trust*-Mutual savings banks only *Reciprocal agreement*-No
Rhode Island	1983	*De novo*-Not explicitly stated *Acquisition of existing banks*-Yes *Branching into state*-Not explicitly stated *Acquisition SB, S&L, and Trust*-Yes, but not trust companies *Reciprocal agreement*-Yes, New England states only; after 7-1-86, nationwide *Miscellaneous provision*-Law does not take effect until 7-1-84.

TABLE 6 (*concluded*)

State	Year Passed	Provisions
South Carolina	1984	*De novo* -No *Acquisition of existing banks*-Yes, in-state bank must have been in existence at least five years *Branching into state*-Not explicitly stated *Acquisition SB, S&L, and Trust*-Not explicitly stated *Reciprocal agreement*-Yes, only by holding companies located in Alabama, Arkansas, Florida, Georgia, Kentucky, Louisiana, Maryland, Mississippi, North Carolina, Tennessee, Virginia, West Virginia, and the District of Columbia *Miscellaneous provision*-The law takes effect on July 1, 1986.

South Dakota	1983	*De novo*-Yes, if
		  1. Minimum capital of $5 million
		  2. Operated in manner not likely to attract the general public
		  3. Limited to one banking office
		Acquisition of existing banks-Yes, but must not be for acquisiton of additional offices
		Branching into state-Not explicitly stated
		Acquisition SB, S&L, and Trust-Not explicitly stated
		Reciprocal agreement-Not explicitly stated
		Miscellaneous provision-State-chartered banks may engage in all facets of insurance business.

Utah	1984	*De novo*-No *Acquisition of existing banks*-Yes *Branching into state*-Not explicitly stated *Acquisition SB, S&L, and Trust*-Yes *Reciprocal agreement*-Yes, only by bank holding companies located in Alaska, Arizona, Colorado, Hawaii, Idaho, Montana, Nevada, New Mexico, Oregon, Washington, and Wyoming *Miscellaneous provision*-Permits out-of-state banking organizations to acquire failing in-state institutions.

Virginia	1983	*De novo*-Yes, if
		  1. Minimum capital and paid-in-surplus of $5 million
		  2. Employ at least 40 state residents
		  3. Operate in manner that is not likely to attract the general public
		Acquisition of existing banks-Not explicitly stated
		Branching into state-Not explicitly stated
		Acquisition SB, S&L, and Trust-Not explicitly stated
		Reciprocal agreement-Not explicitly stated
		Miscellaneous provision-No interest rate ceilings on credit cards

Washington	1983	*De novo*-Not explicitly stated *Acquisition of existing banks*-Yes, but bank must be in danger of closing and there must be no in-state institution willing to acquire it *Branching into state*-Not explicitly stated *Acquisition SB, S&L, and Trust*-Trust companies only *Reciprocal agreement*-Not explicitly stated

Source: *Banking Expansion Reporter,* vol. 3 (August 20, 1984), and B. Frank King, "Interstate Banking: Issues and Evidence," *Economic Review,* Federal Reserve Bank of Atlanta, vol. 69 (April 1984), pp. 38-39.

sion. To date, 22 states have adopted such legislation, either on a reciprocal or nonreciprocal basis (see Table 6). Alaska and Maine passed the most liberal measures, permitting any out-of-state banking organization to enter without requiring reciprocal treatment, and they were followed closely by New York, which will reciprocate with any state. Nine additional states passed regional reciprocal interstate banking laws—Connecticut, Rhode Island, Massachusetts, Utah, North Carolina, South Carolina, Florida, Georgia, and Kentucky. The first of the regional compacts was established by four New England states approximately two years ago. However, no regional mergers or acquisitions have been consummated, largely because of court actions initiated by Citicorp and the Northeast Bancorp of New Haven, Connecticut. These banks seek to outlaw the regional reciprocal limitations, which would mean that each of the four New England states must reciprocate with any other state wishing to reciprocate. The U.S. Supreme Court probably will resolve the constitutional issue by midyear.

NONBANK BANKS

An even more recent means of expanding interstate is through the creation of nonbank banks. "Nonbanks" are chartered as banks but engage in only one of the two activities that define a bank, either accepting demand deposits or making commercial loans. Three basic types of nonbanks exist—special-purpose banks, consumer banks, and commercial lending banks. Special-purpose banks are the creation of state legislation that enables out-of-state institutions to establish a bank limited to certain operations. For example, an out-of-state bank holding company may set up a single office to engage in wholesale banking or credit card operations. To date, South Dakota, Delaware, Virginia, Maryland, Nebraska, and Nevada have adopted such special-purpose provisions. Table 7 shows the organizations using state laws to establish special-purpose banks.

Both the consumer-oriented and commercial-oriented nonbank banks grew out of the Bank Holding Company Act's definition of a commercial bank as an institution that accepts demand deposits and makes commercial loans. Because the nonbank bank does not engage in both activities, it does not meet the definition and therefore is not subject to interstate restrictions. Nonbank banks may be established as either state-chartered or nationally chartered institutions.

As of early 1985, fully 55 applicants had filed with the Office of the Comptroller of the Currency to establish 360 nationally chartered nonbank banks. Most of these applications (218) are for consumer-oriented nonbank banks, which will offer demand deposits but not commercial loans. The remaining 142 applications are for the commercial-oriented type of nonbank institution, offering commercial loans but not demand deposits. Commercial-oriented nonbanks may offer deposit accounts, such as time certificates and savings accounts, which are not classified as demand deposits.

The proposed locations of nonbank banks by state are depicted in Table 8. Seven states—Colorado, Connecticut, Florida, Maryland, New Jersey, North Carolina, and Pennsylvania—have enacted legislation barring nonbank banks, and more states are expected to follow. This may slow geographic expansion via the nonbank avenue. Interestingly, applications that have been filed for nonbank banks generally follow the same geographic patterns as the spread of interstate

TABLE 7
Bank Holding Companies with Limited Purpose Banks in Other States

Bank Holding Company	Home State	Number of States	Other States in Which Banks Are Located
Citicorp	NY	3	DE, SD
J. P. Morgan & Company	NY	2	DE
Mellon National Corporation	PA	2	DE
Chase Manhattan Corporation	NY	2	DE
PNC Financial Corporation	PA	2	DE
Maryland National Corporation	MD	2	DE
Philadelphia National Corporation	PA	2	DE
First Maryland Bancorp	MD	2	DE
Equitable Bancorporation	MD	2	DE
Chemical New York Corporation	NY	2	DE
Manufacturers Hanover Corporation	NY	2	DE
NCNB	NC	2	VA

Source: Federal Reserve Bank of Atlanta.

TABLE 8
Nonbank Bank Applications Filed with Office of the Comptroller of the Currency after March 31, 1984 (as of January 11, 1985)

Alabama	6	Mississippi	3
Arkansas	3	Missouri	3
Arizona	11	Nevada	2
California	14	New Hampshire	3
Colorado	8	New Jersey	12
Connecticut	10	New Mexico	6
Delaware	5*	New York	10
DC	9*	North Carolina	9
Florida	42	Ohio	9*
Georgia	22	Oklahoma	5
Hawaii	3	Oregon	6
Idaho	2	Pennsylvania	17
Indiana	4	South Carolina	8
Illinois	10	Tennessee	14
Kansas	1	Texas	28
Louisiana	8	Utah	4
Maryland	14	Vermont	2
Massachusetts	11	Virginia	19
Michigan	1	Washington	11
Minnesota	4	West Virginia	1
Total			360*

*Total includes 3 applications for Delaware, DC, and Ohio that were withdrawn.

Source: Office of the Comptroller of the Currency.

TABLE 9
Summary of Interstate Activity

| Location | Grandfathered (as of 12/83) | | | | | | Foreign Banks (as of 6/82) | | |
| | Domestic | | | Foreign[A] | | | | | |
	Holding Companies*	Banks	Branches	Holding Companies*	Banks	Branches	Agency	Edge	Branch
Alabama									
Alaska									
Arizona	1	1	171						
Arkansas									
California				8	8	135	63	2	2
Colorado	1	3	5						
Connecticut									
Delaware									
District of Columbia									1
Florida	2	22	141				22	6	
Georgia							10		
Hawaii				1	1	15	2		
Idaho	2	2	103						
Illinois	1	6	5	1	1	0		3	36
Indiana									
Iowa	1	11	32						
Kansas									
Kentucky									
Louisiana							1		
Maine									
Maryland	1	2	28						
Massachusetts									4
Michigan									
Minnesota									
Mississippi									
Missouri									
Montana	3	25	18						
Nebraska	1	5	11						
Nevada	1	1	72						
New Hampshire									
New Jersey									
New Mexico	1	5	29						
New York	1	1	8	3	3	32	18	2	37
North Carolina									
North Dakota	3	32	40						
Ohio									
Oklahoma									
Oregon	1	1	164						7
Pennsylvania									6
Puerto Rico				2	2	32			
Rhode Island									
South Carolina									
South Dakota	2	6	72						
Tennessee	2	2	24						
Texas									
Utah	1	1	38					9	
Vermont									
Virginia	1	2	78						
Washington	1	1	91						10
West Virginia									
Wisconsin	3	6	7						
Wyoming	2	4	0						
Totals		139	1137		15	214	116	22	103

*The columns are not included in total number of offices per state.
U - Allow unrestricted entry.
F - Allow out-of-state acquisition of a failing bank.
R - Reciprocal agreements.
O - Allow entry of limited purpose banks.
□ - Allow expansion of grandfathered banks.
M - Allow acquisition of mutual savings banks.
A - Six of the foreign bank holding companies own only one U.S. bank, but the bank is located outside the home state of the foreign banking organization.

Source: Federal Reserve Bank of Atlanta.

TABLE 9 (concluded)

Limited Purpose Banks* (as of 12/84)	States with Interstate Banking Provisions* (as of 12/84)	Preferred Stock Deals Filed with Board* (as of 3/83)	Interstate S&Ls* (as of 9/83)	Offices of 4(c)8 Subsidiaries (as of 12/82)	Loan Production Offices (as of 12/82)	Edge Act Corporations (as of 10/82)	Total Offices per State
		1	1	107	1		108
	U			4	1		5
				159			331
				3			3
			2	521	22	23	776
			1	158	14		180
	R	1		64	1		65
11	O			27	3	5	35
			2	2	3		6
	R	1	7	372	6	25	594
	R	1	2	253	8	5	276
			2	39	*		57
			2	47			152
	□F		1	132	21	11	215
				99	1		100
	□	1		42	2		87
			1	78			78
	R		1	61			61
				164	4	1	170
	U	1		1			1
	O		3	82	7		119
	R	2	1	68	6	3	81
				56	2		58
		1		34	5	4	43
				89			89
			1	75	6	2	83
			2	28	1		72
	O□			28	2		46
	O		1	21			94
				20	1		21
				110	2		112
				44			78
	R	4	5	156	16	31	304
	R			367	3		370
				23	1		96
		2		310	8	4	322
		1		76	3		79
	M		4	83	7	3	265
		2		320	7	2	335
							34
	R			13			13
	R	1		229			229
1	O			16			94
				159	14		199
		1	6	289	19	17	334
	RF		1	37	1		77
				4			4
1	O		2	227	1		308
	F		2	114	3	6	225
				40			40
				39		1	53
			1	10			14
13	22	20	51	5500	202	143	7591

4(c)8 subsidiaries across the country. There are 42 applications pending for nonbank banks in Florida, the most popular location; 28 in Texas; and 22 in Georgia.

CONCLUSION

Given all the avenues open to banks or holding companies for providing banking-type financial services across state lines, it is hard to deny that interstate banking is a reality today. Though somewhat dated, Table 9 gives a good overview of the extent to which banking organizations already are providing interstate financial services. Since its numbers count only the brick-and-mortar locations of these organizations, the table generally understates the level of services provided. In every way except name, then, interstate banking is here today, and its proponents are urging legislators to lift remaining interstate restrictions.

12

The Regulation of Bank Entry

Michael C. Keeley

This paper analyzes the regulation of entry into banking through government chartering. Entry regulations are shown to be necessary for other anticompetitive regulations to succeed in raising industry profits to above-normal levels. Empirically, we find that although regulation reduced entry during the 1936–62 period, entry restrictions appear to have been relaxed since then. If entry has been unrestricted for some time, the deregulation of deposit rates or other forms of banking deregulation are unlikely to affect the aggregate profits of the banking industry, at least in the long run.

Commercial banking in the United States is a highly regulated industry. Banking regulations pervade almost every aspect of the business, including whether, how, and where a bank can do business. Ostensibly, the primary rationale for banking regulation is to protect and promote the safety and soundness of the financial system. Indeed, recently, as bank failures have mounted, some have called for increased regulation.

As a legacy of the 1930s, many banking regulations were implemented that did not deal directly with safety and soundness issues, but, instead, restricted competition among banks themselves and between banks and other financial institutions. For example, various restrictions on entry, such as government control of chartering, geographic restrictions on branching, and product-line restrictions, at least have the potential to reduce competition.

Other regulations that do not deal with entry, such as consumer deposit rate ceilings, also have the potential to lessen competition. In fact, some economists have argued that the regulation of entry as well as other anticompetitive measures reflect the "capture" of the regulators by the regulated firms. Since banks as a group have an interest in restricting competition (and thereby generating economic rents), they would promote regulations that would eliminate or reduce

From *Economic Review,* Federal Reserve Bank of San Francisco, Summer 1985, pp. 5–13.

Michael C. Keeley is senior economist, Federal Reserve Bank of San Francisco. Comments from Fred Furlong, Gary Zimmerman, and the editorial committee, and research assistance from Joni Whitmore are appreciated.

interbank competition or reduce competition from nonbank firms that provide substitute services.

Currently, many of these restrictions on bank competition are breaking down. Deposit-rate ceilings essentially have been eliminated on all but business checking accounts. Geographic restrictions are diminishing through the liberalization of branching laws and through regional interstate compacts. They are also being evaded through various legal loopholes, such as "nonbank" banks.[1] Product-line distinctions between banks and nondepository financial firms are also blurring. What will be the impacts of these changes? Is banking becoming more competitive and less profitable, and will bank failures consequently mount as profits decline?[2] Or, will deregulation merely change the way banks compete with each other, rather than increase the overall degree of competition?

The answers to these questions depend in large part on how effective entry regulations have been in actually reducing entry.[3] In general, anticompetitive regulations that fix prices would be effective in reducing the degree of competition only if entry also were restricted. This is because, if entry is not limited, the regulation of prices will not be able to suppress nonprice competition by new entrants. Conversely, if entry is restricted, the degree of competition generally will be reduced even without other anticompetitive restrictions.

PURPOSE AND ORGANIZATION

The objectives of this paper are threefold. First, we analyze, in general, the effects of the government regulation of entry into an industry and the interaction of entry regulation with other types of regulation. We show that, without entry restrictions, other regulations seeking to limit competition will be ineffective in the creation of economic rents. However, anticompetitive regulations may very well alter the form of competition. Conversely, effective entry regulations generally will limit competition and thereby create economic rents even in the absence of other anticompetitive restrictions. Second, we apply this general analytic framework to the banking industry. We analyze empirically how regulation has affected the rate of entry into banking and whether entry restrictions have been relaxed recently. Finally, the implications of the current deregulatory trend in banking are explored in light of our findings about the regulation of bank entry.

Section I examines how entry restrictions alone or in conjunction with other regulations in theory would affect competition in banking. Then, in Section II, data on bank entry are analyzed to assess whether actual entry has been limited. Section III presents the summary and conclusions.

I. THE THEORY OF ENTRY AND COMPETITION

Entry plays a prominent role in the economic theory of competition. Free entry is the key economic force that ensures that there are an optimal number of firms (from society's viewpoint) in a particular industry and that individual firms charge competitive prices and operate at optimum scales.[4]

In an industry in which individual firms operate independently (i.e., they do not collude), the short-run supply curve is the (horizontal) sum of the marginal cost curves of the firms in the industry (at a particular moment in time). If, at the price determined by supply and demand, price is above each firm's average cost (because individual firms have increasing marginal costs), new firms will be attracted to the industry until price is forced down to equal average cost. Thus, in long-run equilibrium, the entry of new firms ensures that price equals (minimum) average cost (which also equals marginal cost), that an optimal number of firms are in the industry, and that profits are normal.

If, however, entry were restricted at less than the socially optimal number of firms, firms would produce at levels above their minimum average costs, prices would exceed average costs, and firms would enjoy above-normal profits (even in the absence of collusion) unless firms were able to produce at constant costs. If firms would produce at constant costs, so marginal and average costs were equal, then restrictions on the number of firms in an industry would have no effects on prices or profits as long as the firms did not collude. Thus, constant costs of production are equivalent in a sense to unrestricted entry.

Although there is an empirical literature that suggests banking is characterized by constant costs, at least for banks above some miminum size, these econometric results are inconsistent with a wide range of other evidence.[5] First, the new theory of firm size, developed by Rosen (1982), Oi (1983), and others, argues that each firm may have a U-shaped cost function even though firms of widely differing sizes appear to have similar measured average costs.[6] According to this theory, any given firm will be subject to increasing average (and marginal) costs if it expands output beyond its equilibrium level, holding managerial talent constant. The apparent equality of average costs of firms of different sizes is due to higher levels of managerial talent at larger firms and greater compensation of more able managers.

Second, there is anecdotal evidence that there are very strong economic forces propelling the nation toward interstate banking. This suggests there must be important scale economies, at least in banking. Finally, if banking were characterized by constant costs, it seems unlikely that such a wide variety of regulations regarding the scale of their operations, such as merger regulation, chartering, and geographic restrictions, would exist since such regulations would have no effect on competition, interest rates, or the pricing of bank services. Thus, it seems likely that, in banking, firms do have U-shaped cost functions.

Entry and the threat of entry are also strong forces that tend to eliminate cartels. For example, if the firms in an originally competitive industry (where price equaled average cost) succeeded in forming a successful cartel that restricted industry output by allocating output to members (and consequently raising prices), new firms would have a strong incentive to enter because of the above-normal profits to be earned. Now firms would continue to enter until price equalled average cost and profits returned to normal levels. Since potential cartel members are aware of the incentives for entry caused by a cartel, cartels rarely form if entry is unrestricted. Thus, restrictions on entry are a necessary precondition for other restrictions on competition to succeed in raising firms' profits to above-competitive levels.

Regulation and Entry Restrictions

A large number of government regulations are either intended to restrict competition and thereby raise the regulated firms' profits or have that effect. However, just as private restrictions on competition (e.g., cartels) will be unsuccessful in restricting competition unless entry is limited, so will government regulations.

Despite the much stronger enforcement tools at the government's disposal, competition can take place along so many dimensions that it is virtually impossible to prevent it by regulation.

For example, suppose the government attempts to restrict competition in an industry by imposing a minimum price above the competitive level. Such an above-competitive price (relative to costs) would make an industry highly profitable and thus attractive to enter. If price cutting were permitted, new firms would enter and force down prices and profits to competitive levels by increasing the quantity of the product and cutting prices.

However, even if price cutting were prohibited, new firms would still enter and compete along various nonprice dimensions. As George Stigler stressed in his classic (1968a) article: "When a uniform price is imposed upon, or agreed to by, an industry, some or all of the other terms of sale are left unregulated." For example, competition through quality, advertising, convenience, and by providing additional nonpriced or underpriced services may all be viable forms of nonprice competition.

Unless nonprice competition is also fully prohibited, something virtually impossible to do without assuming full control of an industry (e.g., nationalizing it), new firms will enter and existing firms will expand their level of nonprice competition until average costs are driven up to equal price. Thus, without entry restrictions, firms will compete away any potential economic rents due to regulation through nonprice competition. With entry restrictions, however, things are much different.

First, consider the effects of entry restrictions alone. If there were fewer than the socially optimal number of firms in an industry, then firms would price competitively (price would equal marginal cost), but price would exceed average cost and the firms would earn above-normal profits. If a regulation, such as a minimum price, were then imposed on the industry (set to equate industry marginal revenue with industry marginal cost), then the industry would have the potential to earn even larger (above-normal) profits depending on whether the potential economic rents were entirely competed away through nonprice competition. Thus, regulation has the potential to reduce competition and increase profits only in an industry in which entry is restricted.

But will economic rents be competed away through nonprice competition even in an industry in which entry is restricted?

With restricted entry, only existing firms would expand the level of nonpriced services (and goods). Assuming such firms face increasing marginal costs of nonprice competition (as is likely), existing firms would expand output to the point where the total marginal cost of the product plus the nonpriced services equals demand. Thus, with entry restrictions, above-normal profits would not be competed away unless nonprice competition can occur at constant costs—something that seems highly unlikely. Thus, regulation has the potential to increase the profits of the regulated firms to above-normal levels, but only if entry is also limited. Moreover, nonprice competition alone is unlikely to lead to competitive profit levels.

Entry and Deposit Ceilings

As an example of how entry restrictions interact with other regulations, consider the effects of the regulation of deposit interest rates on consumer accounts.

Initially, if a deposit-rate ceiling were imposed below the market rate, existing banks would earn supranormal profits by having lower costs of deposits. This above-normal level of profits would provide strong incentives for both new banks to enter and existing banks to increase levels of convenience or nonpriced services until (average) deposit costs were bid up to competitive levels and profits returned to normal levels. The effects of the ceilings, however, would differ if entry also were restricted.

First, consider the case where entry is unrestricted. As long as new banks could enter at no cost disadvantage to existing banks, any excess profits would be eliminated in the long run. This is because firms would continue to enter and provide various forms of underpriced conveniences until any excess profits were eliminated. However, such nonpriced services would be expanded beyond the level they would have attained in the absence of regulation and, consequently, average (and marginal) deposit costs would be higher because consumers value these services at less than their costs (i.e., from a consumer's viewpoint, services and interest are not perfect substitutes).[7]

If existing banks could not provide such services and conveniences at constant costs (i.e., if existing firms face increasing marginal costs of expanding the provision of such services so that marginal costs exceed average costs), new firms would be attracted to such a regulated industry. Thus, binding deposit ceilings, as well as other forms of anticompetitive restrictions, may attract new entrants. Counterbalancing this force would be the overall decline in the industry caused by its increased costs, compared to industries providing substitute products that are not subject to regulation. With unrestricted entry, deposit ceilings may affect the type of competition and the number of firms, but they will not affect the degree of competition or the profitability (aggregate economic rent) of the industry.

The effects of deposit interest ceilings generally will be very different with restricted entry. First, entry restrictions alone reduce the demand for deposits so that rates paid on deposits would be below levels that would prevail in the absence of entry restrictions. Thus, if the number of banks were limited by entry restrictions, this alone would cause deposit costs to be lower, loan rates to be higher and, consequently, profits to be higher than normal. Second, if binding ceilings were then imposed on such an industry, limiting deposit rates to below the (already low) levels the firms would set through competition with one another, the existing banks would then expand nonpriced services up to the point where interest plus marginal service costs of deposits equaled their marginal revenue products.

If individual banks faced increasing marginal costs of providing nonpriced services, additional services would be provided up to the point where marginal deposit costs equaled the value of deposits' marginal products, but average deposit costs would be less. Thus, with entry restrictions, consumer deposit ceilings may confer economic rents on existing banks.

Since the effects of (nonentry) regulation and hence deregulation on industry profitability depend in large degree on whether entry was limited, we now turn to an empirical analysis of the effects of chartering regulation on entry into banking.

II.   EMPIRICAL ANALYSIS OF CHARTERING RESTRICTIONS

The United States has a "dual" banking system. Currently, persons wishing to start a bank can apply for a federal charter from the Comptroller of the Currency or apply to the appropriate state banking agency for a state charter. However, to obtain federal deposit insurance, newly chartered state banks must either receive approval directly from the Federal Deposit Insurance Corporation (FDIC) or become members of the Federal Reserve System. (Federally chartered banks are all members of the Federal Reserve System and all have federal deposit insurance.)

In general, competition among chartering agencies would seem to limit any single agency's power to restrict entry. This is because, if one agency restricted entry severely, firms seeking charters would go to another agency. Over time, an agency with an overly restrictive chartering policy would find itself with few firms to regulate.

Prior to the creation of the FDIC and the passage of the Banking Act of 1935, which set up a federally administered "needs" criteria for chartering federally insured banks, there was active competition between the states and the federal government for chartering banks. However, with the creation of the FDIC, the competition for the chartering of *insured* banks was probably reduced since the owners of state-chartered banks had to apply either to the FDIC or the Federal Reserve to obtain federal deposit insurance. Thus, the federal government could control the number of (federally) insured banks, although the power to do so was diffused through three agencies.

As thrifts have gained more bank powers recently, thrift charters may be becoming good substitutes for bank charters. If so, competition from the Federal Home Loan Bank Board (FHLBB), which controls the chartering of federally insured savings and loans, may be introducing a new element of competition among federal agencies for the chartering of depository institutions.

Although the diffusion of chartering powers through several federal agencies may have introduced a significant degree of interagency competition and made entry regulation relatively ineffective in actually restricting entry, it is an empirical question whether and/or to what degree entry has been limited.

Previous Studies

In a classic study (1965) dealing with the effects of chartering on the rate of bank entry, Sam Peltzman concluded that chartering reduced the rate of bank entry by at least 50 percent compared to what would have occurred without such restrictions. His finding is based on a comparison of the rate of entry prior to the passage of the Banking Act of 1935 and the creation of the FDIC, which he characterizes as the "free-banking" era, to the 1936–62 period, during which he argues federal-state competition for the chartering of insured banks was effectively eliminated.

In conducting a study to determine what the effects of the 1935 Banking Act were, ideally one would want to control for all factors other than the passage of the act that might affect entry. Especially important would be the profitability of the industry, because increased profitability would lead to greater entry (and lower profitability would lead to less entry), all other things equal. However, to control for variations in profitability properly is difficult, because profitability itself depends on entry restrictions (i.e., it is endogenous). (In fact, the whole point of entry restrictions is to increase profitability.)

Although Peltzman included profitability as a control variable, he ignored its endogeneity. Thus, his estimates may have been less reliable than estimates that ignored potential (exogenous) changes in profitability altogether. By neglecting the fact that limited entry itself would increase profitability, he likely overestimated the effect of the act on deterring entry.

A more recent (1974) reanalysis of Peltzman's data by Linda and Franklin Edwards tries to address the endogeneity of profitability.[8] They argue that, although Peltzman overstated the effects of chartering restrictions, his conclusion that chartering restrictions substantially limited the rate of entry is valid.

Below, I take another look at these data and extend the analysis from 1962 through 1983, the last year for which complete data are currently available. I do not attempt to control for the effects of varying profitability on entry because of the difficulty in properly controlling (statistically) for the effect of regulation on profitability.

A Further Analysis

Although the Banking Act of 1935 did apparently substantially lessen state-federal competition for the chartering of insured banks during the 1936–62 period, there was still interagency competition between the FDIC, the comptroller, and the Federal Reserve.[9]

More recently, as S&Ls have gained more and more banklike powers, the FHLBB may have increased the degree of competition among federal agencies for chartering. Because of this actual and potential competition among chartering agencies, it may well be that chartering would become a less and less *effective* restriction to entry over time. Below, we look at entry rates during the post-1962 period in addition to those during the 1921–62 period analyzed by Peltzman to see whether entry rates have remained low or increased.

Entry rates (the number of banks opening in year t divided by the number of existing banks at year t-1) are plotted in Chart 1. The sources of the data used to calculate entry rates are the same as those used by Peltzman and are described in the Data Appendix. For the free-banking period, 1921–35, it is somewhat difficult to define entry properly, because of the relatively large number of reopenings of previously suspended banks and the difficulty in distinguishing new openings from reopenings. The reopenings of suspended banks was especially high during the 1931–35 period before FDIC insurance reduced the number of bank failures.

I have chosen to define *entry* as simply the number of banks opening, regardless of whether they were new openings or reopenings, partly because this is the only consistent definition in the published data across the whole 1921–83 period, and partly because reopenings also represent a new source of competition. Because entry rates might be somewhat overstated by this procedure, especially during 1933 and 1934 when the number of reopenings was very large, I have excluded data for these years from the analysis. This has the effect of reducing the average entry rate during the free-banking period.

For the period 1921–35, the average rate of entry was about 1.7 percent per year. In contrast, during the 1936–62 period, the average rate of entry declined to only 0.7 percent a year, a statistically significant decline (see Chart 1). This decline of approximately 50 percent is approximately the same magnitude found by Peltzman using his more complex but flawed statistical procedure. Thus, the evidence supports the notion that there was a significant decline in the rate of bank entry during the period following the passage of the Banking Act of 1935 until 1962.

CHART 1
Entry Rates for Commercial Banks, 1921–1983

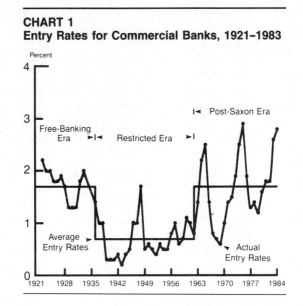

On November 15, 1961, James Saxon was appointed Comptroller of the Currency. He was widely regarded as a proponent of the national banking system and was viewed as being much more liberal than his predecessors in his chartering policies. The data in Chart 1 suggest that initially his policies did have a significant effect on raising entry rates. However, by the last year of his tenure, 1966, entry rates had fallen back to the pre-Saxon levels. Then, beginning in 1968, entry rates again began a sharp upward rise and continued to follow a cyclical pattern unique to the post-1962 period.

Looking at the 1962–83 period as a whole, entry rates averaged essentially the same as during the 1921–35 period. Thus, it appears that Saxon began an era where entry into banking was no more difficult than during the "free-banking" era. If correct, this means that banking has been a more competitive industry, at least since 1962.[10] However, another interpretation of the data in Chart 1 would be that entry restrictions were gradually relaxed, beginning perhaps as early as 1950, since the data would not be inconsistent with an upward trend in entry rates starting then. In either event, entry now does not appear to be significantly restricted, at least compared to the free-banking era.

Looking at entry in banking only in terms of entry by new banking organizations probably understates entry because of the possibility of entry through branching, entry by S&Ls, and increased competition by nondepository institutions (such as Merrill Lynch). For example, although the total number of banking and S&L offices was relatively constant from 1934 to the early 1950s, the number of offices has almost tripled since then (see Chart 2), and the number of offices per real deposit dollar has shown an upward trend since 1962 (although it has not reached anywhere near the level of the 1920s and 1930s).

The recent deregulation of banking, specifically the removal of consumer deposit-rate ceilings, appears to be taking place in an environment in which entry

CHART 2
Total Banking and Savings Association Offices,
1920–1982

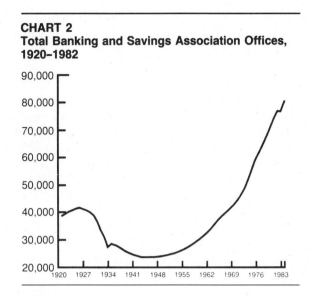

restrictions have been effectively eliminated or at least have been substantially relaxed. If so, deposit-rate deregulation should have little or no long-run effects on the profitability of the banking industry as a whole, because free entry ensures that, in the long run, profitability will be at normal, competitive levels.

However, individual banks may have different experiences as they make the transition from nonprice to price competition.[11] Further, if entry restrictions had been effectively removed prior to deregulation, then deregulation, by eliminating the inefficiencies inherent in nonprice competition, should have led to an expansion of the banking industry relative to its nonbank competitors and this, in turn, would increase incentives for entry. The effects of deregulation may explain the very high entry rates of the last few years, shown in Chart 1. They are also consistent with anecdotal evidence that there has been a recent surge in new bank start-ups (see Brannigan, 1985).

III. CONCLUSIONS

The data on bank entry suggest that the regulation of entry through chartering has been much less restrictive in the post-Saxon era. Since 1962, entry rates have on average been equal to those before 1936, a period during which, it is argued, entry was relatively unrestricted.

If, in fact, bank entry has been unrestricted since 1962, then various anticompetitive regulations, such as deposit rate ceilings, would not have been effective in reducing the degree of competition in banking. (They would, however, have made the banking industry less efficient.) This, in turn, means that bank profits were not enhanced (or at least are not currently being enhanced) by these anticompetitive restrictions.

If the degree of competition and banking profits have been at the level they would have been without entry restrictions, then deregulation of consumer deposit rates is unlikely to affect banking profits or the degree of competition, at least in the long run. Thus, the current calls to reregulate banking—to reduce competition and bolster bank profits—to stem the recent spate of bank failures are not focusing on the real causes of these failures.

DATA APPENDIX

All commercial banking data except those so noted, including the number of banks and branches[12] in existence in a given year, the number of new "primary" organizations, and the total deposits data[13] come from publications of the Board of Governors (BOG) of the Federal Reserve System (FRS).

Series for the 1921–40 period[14] come from the U.S. BOG of the FRS. *Supplement to Banking and Monetary Statistics,* Section I, 1962. (*Note*: This supplement was originally released in Sections in 1943 as a revised version of available data from the period 1914–41. It was published in 1962.)

The *1941–1970* series are from the U.S. BOG of the FRS. *Banking and Monetary Statistics,* 1941–1970, 1976.

Data for the *1970–1979* period were taken from the *Annual Statistical Digest,* 1970–1979, published in 1981 by the BOG.

Since 1979, the *Annual Statistical Digest* has been published yearly, and they were used on a yearly basis from 1980 through 1982.

Data for 1983 for commercial banks, branches, new openings, and total deposits were obtained directly from the BOG; 1983 data on savings and loans were obtained directly from the FHLBB.

Although these data are from several different publications (of primarily the same sources), all series are consistently defined, with the exception of those indicated.

NOTES

[1] The legal status of nonbank banks was unclear at the time this article went to press.

[2] Failures are less likely in an industry where firms are earning above normal profits (economic rents). In such industries, it takes a larger random shock to reduce demand or increase costs to make earnings (or net worth) negative and drive the firm out of business.

[3] Chartering regulation, branching restrictions, and product-line regulation are all forms of entry regulation.

[4] Throughout this paper, I use the definition of a barrier to entry that was first formulated by George Stigler (1968b): "A barrier to entry may be defined as a cost of producing (at some or every rate of output) which must be borne by a firm which seeks to enter an industry but is not borne by firms already in the industry."

Free or unrestricted entry means there are no barriers to entry. This concept of a barrier to entry contrasts sharply with the view that any cost of doing business is a cost of entry. That is, I do not view capital requirements (or land or labor requirements for that matter) as costs of entry per se, as opposed to costs of doing business.

[5] See Gilbert (1984) for a review of this literature.

[6] See Keeley (1984) for evidence supporting this notion.

[7] See Keeley and Zimmerman (1985) for an elaboration of this argument.

[8] However, they do not employ a simultaneous equations technique. Thus, one may also question the validity of their estimates.

[9] See Kenneth Scott (1979).

[10] An alternative hypothesis consistent with these data is that some other force, such as an exogenous increase in banking profitability, caused the rate of entry to increase during these years. However, it seems unlikely that an increase in profitability would persist over a 20-year period.

[11] It is conceivable that deregulation might have a short-run negative effect on profitability as

specific capital used to support nonprice competition depreciates in value. However, this factor would have no lasting effect if entry had been unrestricted prior to deregulation.

[12] Commercial bank branch data for the year 1920–34 were obtained from the *Historical Statistics of the United States, Colonial Times to 1970,* part 2, U.S. Department of Commerce, Bureau of the Census, 1975.

Branch data for thrifts was collected from the *Savings and Home Financing Source Book,* 1952–1955, U.S. Federal Home Loan Bank Board; and the *Savings and Loan Fact Book,* 1962, 1965, 1980, U.S. League of Savings Association, and represent total insured (federal- and state-chartered) savings and loan associations.

[13] *Total deposits* data for savings and loan associations were taken from the *Source Book* (see above citing), 1955, Federal Home Loan Bank Board, for the years prior to 1955. Citibase was used from *1955 to 1983* (actually from BOG FRB Table 1.7).

Total real deposits were calculated using an *implicit price deflator* (wholesale) from the *Historical Statistics of the United States, Colonial Times to 1957* (see above).

Total offices per real deposit dollar was calculated by dividing total bank and thrift offices by the sum of their total real deposits.

[14] The *1921–1940* portion of the total number of commercial banks in existence (at year-end) series was multiplied by a factor of 1.003919373 to correct for a change in the series definition from "All Incorporated" to "All Commercial" banks after 1940.

REFERENCES

Brannigan, Martha. "Deregulation Spawns a Wealth of Small Banks." *The Wall Street Journal,* vol. CXII, no. 88, May 6, 1985.

Dwyer, Gerald P., Jr. "The Effects of the Banking Acts of 1933 and 1935 on Capital Investment in Commercial Banking." *Journal of Money, Credit and Banking,* vol. 13, no. 2, May 1981.

Edwards, Linda N., and Franklin R. Edwards. "Measuring the Effectiveness of Regulation: The Case of Bank Entry Regulation." *Journal of Law and Economics,* vol. 17, no. 2, October 1974.

Gilbert, R. Alton. "Bank Market Structure and Competition." *Journal of Money, Credit and Banking,* vol. XVI, no. 4, pt. 2, November 1984.

Keeley, Michael C. "The Economics of Firm Size: Implications from Labor Market Studies." *Economic Review.* Federal Reserve Bank of San Francisco, Winter 1984.

Keeley, Michael C., and Gary C. Zimmerman. "Competition for Money Market Deposit Accounts." *Economic Review,* Federal Reserve Bank of San Francisco, Spring 1985.

Oi, Walter. "Heterogeneous Firms and the Organization of Production." *Economic Inquiry,* vol. XXI, no. 2, April 1983.

Peltzman, Sam. "Entry into Commercial Banking." *Journal of Law and Economics,* vol. 8, no. 11, October 1965.

—————. "Capital Investment in Commercial Banking and Its Relationship to Portfolio Regulation." *Journal of Political Economy,* vol. 78, no. 1, January/February 1970.

—————. "Bank Entry Regulation: Its Impact and Purpose." *The National Banking Review,* vol. 3, no. 1, September 1965.

Rosen, Sherwin. "Authority, Control and the Distribution of Earnings." *Bell Journal of Economics,* vol. 13, no. 2, Autumn 1982.

Scott, Kenneth. "Bureaucratic Competition and the Structure of Bank Regulation", in *Issues in Financial Regulation,* ed. Franklin R. Edwards. New York: McGraw-Hill, 1979.

Stigler, George. "Price and Nonprice Competition." *Journal of Political Economy,* vol. LXXII, No. 1, February 1968a.

—————. *The Organization of Industry.* Homewood, Ill.: Richard D. Irwin, 1968b.

Throop, Adrian W. "Capital Investment and Entry in Commercial Banking." *Journal of Money, Credit and Banking,* vol. 7, May 1975.

PART THREE

Determination of Interest Rates and Stock Prices

Financial markets have experienced great volatility throughout the 1970s and through the mid-1980s. Interest rates on both short- and long-term financial instruments reached record levels in the early 1980s, then declined appreciably from 1982 through early 1986. Similar volatility was experienced in stock prices, with most major stock indices at low levels in 1981 and early 1982, only to move upward sharply and reaching new record levels (in nominal terms) in early 1986.

The volatility in financial markets reflects volatility in the economy as well as in the rate of inflation. From 1980 to 1982, the economy experienced its sharpest contraction since the Great Depression of the 1930s. Unemployment rates reached levels not experienced in the post-World War II era. Business bankruptcies increased markedly which, in turn, added to interest-rate levels on corporate securities through the addition of a default-risk premium. The rate of inflation, one of the principal determinants of nominal yields on securities, fluctuated dramatically with a rising trend through the early 1980s, though inflation rates declined sharply after 1982.

Three readings in this section deal with the important topic of inflation and its effect on financial markets. As Irving Fisher argued, the nominal yield on a security may be thought of as being composed of two elements: the expected real rate and a premium for the expected rate of inflation. Assuming a constant expected real rate, then, changes in nominal interest rates are determined by changes in the expected rate of inflation. A similar argument could be made relating expected inflation and returns on common stocks, although the connection is more complex for such financial instruments as common stocks, whose cash flows are variable.

As Herbert Taylor points out in "Interest Rates: How Much Does Expected Inflation Matter?" the connection between inflation and interest rates for fixed-income securities, such as bonds, is also rather complex. For one thing, changes in the expected inflation rate may produce changes in the expected real rate of interest. Also, Fisher's theory ignored income taxes. Taking into account taxes and the fact that income taxes are levied on nominal income, rather than real income, the nominal interest rate must include more than expected inflation in order to leave the real after-tax rate of return to the lender constant. How much does the nominal interest rate actually change in response to changes in expected inflation? While no one can be certain, Taylor concludes that changes in inflationary expectations produce a change in interest rates almost equal, though slightly smaller, than the change in inflationary expectations.

Basic to understanding the effects of expectated inflation is knowledge of the real rate. Yet the expected real rate is not directly observable. In "Revealing Real Interest Rates: Let The Market Do It," Donald Mullineaux and Aris Protopapadakis argue that the real rate could be estimated if the U.S. Treasury offered inflation-indexed bonds. Holders of these index-linked bonds would be protected from the currency depreciation that comes with inflation. They would also be free of default risk. As such, the yield on the bonds would be "the real rate, pure and simple." Moreover, market-revealed real interest rates would provide a useful indicator of the thrust of monetary policy. Mullineaux and Protopapadakis argue that there would be substantial demand for such an instrument and that the U.S. Treasury should consider the desirability of offering these index-linked bonds.

The third article concentrates on the effects of inflation on stock prices. In "The Impact of Inflation on Stock Prices," Douglas Pearce explores the effects of inflation on equity values since the late 1960s. At the beginning of that period, it was often thought that common stocks were a hedge against inflation, because they represented a claim against real and tangible assets, whose prices would rise with inflation. However, rising inflation rates during the 1970s and into the early 1980s were associated with falling (or at best stagnant) stock prices. Pearce discusses the various arguments that have been put forth to explain the negative empirical association between inflation and stock prices. These include the argument that inflation reduces after-tax profits by raising the corporate tax burden and that inflation causes shareholders to raise the required rate of return. In contrast, however, the impact of inflation on the real value of corporate debt might be expected to raise the value of equities. On balance, Pearce finds that the higher required rate of return associated with inflation was the dominant factor in the stagnation of the equity market in the 1970s and early 1980s.

The final article in this section deals with the prime rate charged on business loans, a rate that is administratively determined by commercial banks, rather than determined in a competitive market by the interplay of supply and demand. The prime rate does respond to market rates, especially rates that reflect the cost of bank funds, though often with a lag. Also, the prime rate is highly visible and, therefore, is sometimes subject to political pressures. In "When Is the Prime Rate Second Choice?" Brian Gendreau deals with one of the most interesting developments relating to the prime rate—the growing tendency for banks to make loans below prime. In fact, as pointed out in the article, in November 1982 over 90 percent of all business loans made by 48 of the largest banks in the United States were made at rates below prime. Gendreau discusses the causes of this phenomenon as well at its implications.

13

Interest Rates: How Much Does Expected Inflation Matter?

Herbert Taylor

Many business analysts blame today's high interest rates on the public's anticipation of continued high inflation. Policymakers seem to share this view. The Reagan administration contends that, once people realize that its programs will reduce inflation, interest rates will drop. The Federal Reserve argues that its restrictive monetary policy will ultimately lower interest rates by demonstrating the Fed's resolve to maintain noninflationary money growth in the future. What is the nature of the link between interest rates and expected inflation? Is a decline in the expected rate of inflation likely to produce substantial reductions in interest rates?

According to one popular rule of thumb, market interest rates respond point for point to changes in the expected rate of inflation. So if everyone became convinced that inflation would decline from, say, 10 percent to 6 percent next year, interest rates on one-year securities would drop by four percentage points. But many analysts suspect that the relation of inflation expectations to interest rates is not that simple. Some argue that any change in the expected inflation rate works through the Federal income tax structure to change interest rates by even more. Others maintain that business taxes and other economic forces so blunt the impact of inflation expectations on interest rates that the change in interest rates is smaller than the change in the expected inflation rate.

Economists have examined the link between interest rates and expected future inflation using many different methods, and their estimates of interest rates' responsiveness to changes in the expected rate of inflation vary. On balance, though, the evidence suggests that interest rates rise and fall by somewhat less than changes in the expected inflation rate.

RECENT EXPERIENCE

Interest rates have been rising steadily since the late 1950s. Though both long-term and short-term rates have declined during recessions (see Figure 1), each

From *Business Review*, Federal Reserve Bank of Philadelphia, July–August 1982, pp. 3–12.

FIGURE 1
Interest Rates

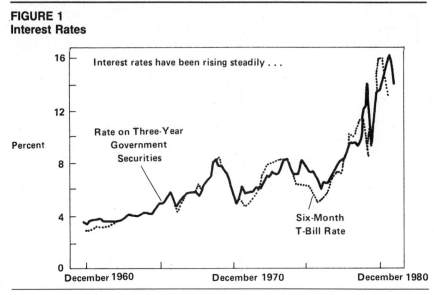

Source: Average six-month-ahead CPI inflation forecast from the Livingston Surveys, compiled at the Federal Reserve Bank of Philadelphia.

subsequent expansion has carried them to still higher levels. Economists have often attributed the secular rise in interest rates to rising inflation expectations. Confirming the influence of inflation expectations on interest rates is difficult because the public's expectations are not directly observed. But available data do support a direct relation between interest rates and expected inflation: interest rates have risen in tandem with measures of expected inflation.

FIGURE 2
Inflation Expectations

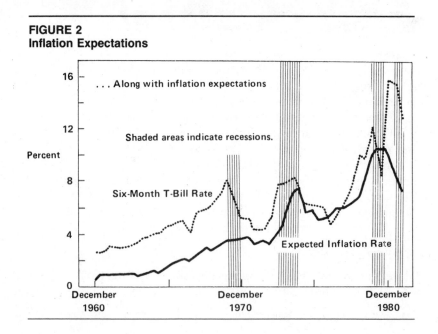

One widely used measure of the expected rate of future inflation is provided by Joseph A. Livingston, business columnist for the *Philadelphia Inquirer*. Every June and December, Livingston surveys a group of about 50 economists for their forecasts of inflation. The average of economists' six-month-ahead inflation forecasts shows a close correlation with the average interest rate on six-month Treasury bills for the survey month (see Figure 2). The six-month Treasury bill rate has been more volatile than Livingston's expected inflation measure, but the two have risen together over the last 20 years.[1]

The evidence suggests that changes in inflation expectations are at least partly responsible for movements in interest rates. But economists have used the tools of economic theory and statistical analysis to assess this linkage more precisely. In doing so, they have built upon the work of Irving Fisher, an American economist of the early 20th century. Fisher clarified the basic link of interest rates to inflation expectations by distinguishing nominal from real rates of interest.[2]

NOMINAL AND REAL RATES

Almost everybody borrows at one time or another. When consumers buy new homes, they borrow the money by taking mortgages. When a business decides to purchase more modern equipment, it may issue notes or bonds to raise the money. When the federal government's expenses outrun its tax revenues, the Treasury obtains the funds by selling securities.

Financial instruments, such as Treasury bonds, commercial paper, and home mortgages, are evidences of loans to the issuers of the securities. The borrower agrees to pay specified amounts of money later in exchange for use of the lender's money today. The nominal, or market, interest rate on these instruments states the rate at which the borrower must pay future dollars to get the current dollars. For instance, a corporation marketing one-year notes with a 15 percent interest rate is agreeing to pay $115 after one year for every $100 that the note-buying public lends it now.

But people are not as concerned about dollars, present or future, as they are about the goods and services those dollars command. Inflation erodes the purchasing power of money. Each percentage point of inflation means one percentage point less in goods and services that lenders will be able to purchase when a loan bearing a particular nominal interest rate matures. Consequently, lenders consider not only an asset's nominal rate of interest but also the rate of inflation likely to prevail over the loan's term to maturity.

Fisher put the matter succinctly. He said that, in evaluating a loan, people do not consider the nominal rate of interest—the rate at which current future dollars are exchanged. They consider the expected real rate of interest—the rate at which they expect to exchange current for future *goods* and *services*. The nominal rate of interest that an asset promises can be decomposed into the real rate of interest lenders expect plus an adjustment for the rate of inflation they expect over the asset's term to maturity.[3]

Nominal rate of interest	=	Expected real rate of interest	+	Expected future rate of inflation

If, for example, everyone expects 10 percent annual inflation, then the corporation's 15 percent one-year notes carry an expected real interest rate of 5 percent. Both the borrowing business and the lending public view the notes as offering roughly the same opportunity to exchange present for future goods as would notes with a 5 percent nominal interest rate were no inflation expected.

Fisher's argument underlies the view that nominal interest rates adjust point for point to changes in the expected rate of inflation. For when the public revises its inflation expectations, only an identical revision in prevailing nominal interest rates can preserve the expected real interest rate, *provided* that the revised inflation expectations affect neither the willingness to borrow nor the willingness to lend at that expected real rate.

THE MARKET-CLEARING REAL RATE

The role of the financial markets is to settle on the expected real rate of interest at which the amount that savers are willing to lend is exactly equal to the amount that investors find worthwhile to borrow. Economists call this rate the *market-clearing* expected real rate of interest. The nominal rate of interest at which the loans are actually made, in turn, reflects this market-clearing real rate and the expected rate of inflation. For example, suppose that at an expected real rate of 5 percent savers are willing to lend, and investors are willing to borrow, $400 billion. If inflation is expected to run at 10 percent, the nominal interest rate will settle at 15 percent. This establishes the 5 percent expected real rate at which the $400 billion will be exchanged.

What happens when inflation expectations change? Suppose that the public suddenly anticipates a decline in the future rate of inflation from 10 percent to 9 percent. If the nominal rate stays at 15 percent, the expected real rate of interest on loans jumps from 5 percent to 6 percent. At a 6 percent expected real rate, lenders would want to lend more than $400 billion, but borrowers would want to take down less than they did at 5 percent. The excess supply of loanable funds puts downward pressure on the nominal rate of interest. In order to make loans, some potential lenders accepted lower interest rates and nominal rates begin to slip below 15 percent. If the change in inflation expectations has not changed people's willingness to borrow and lend $400 billion at the 5 percent expected real interest rate, then the nominal rate settles at 14 percent. This restores the expected real rate to 5 percent (14 percent minus 9 percent) and eliminates the excess supply of loanable funds. Generally, any change in the expected rate of future inflation would result in an equal change in the current nominal interest rate, provided the market-clearing expected real interest rate remains the same.

What complicates the relationship between nominal interest rates and inflation expectations is that, when inflation expectations change, the market-clearing expected real interest rate is not likely to remain unchanged. People's willingness to borrow and lend at any particular expected real interest rate depends on many factors, such as savers' income and wealth, the potential productivity of investment projects, taxes, and uncertainty. If a change in expected inflation were to alter any of these factors, the expected real rate, which at first had equated the supply and demand for loanable funds, might no longer do so. The expected real rate would have to change in order to reestablish consistency between the plans of borrowers and lenders. Nominal interest rates would then have to adjust both for the change in expected inflation itself and for the movement in the market-clearing expected real rate that it induced. So nominal interest rates would no longer move one for one with changes in the expected inflation rate.

Since Fisher's early work, economists have discerned several channels through which a change in the expected rate of inflation affects the market-clearing expected real rate of interest. They have found that a change in the expected rate of inflation alters economic agents' willingness to borow and lend at the original expected real rate, both because the change in expectations leads to changes in savers' income and wealth and because of tax laws.[4]

Changes in Income and Wealth

When the public's inflation expectations change, economic factors other than interest rates also adjust. Several economists have investigated how these adjustments could ultimately influence people's income and wealth, thereby affecting the expected real rate of interest.[5] They have shown that, if a decrease in the expected rate of inflation were to lower real income or raise real (inflation-adjusted) wealth, the market-clearing expected real interest rate would rise. Nominal rates, therefore, would wind up falling by less than the decrease in expected inflation.

How do these income and wealth effects arise? Initially, a percentage point decline in the expected rate of inflation increases the expected real rate of interest associated with the original nominal rate. Savers are suddenly willing to lend more funds than investors want to borrow. In the financial market example, the nominal interest rate was the only variable that changed. Thus, the nominal interest rate had to decline by a full percentage point to restore the original market-clearing expected real rate and to close the gap between the amount of funds demanded and supplied. But a change in inflation expectations also opens up a gap between the volume of goods and services demanded and supplied at the original interest rate. Depending on how the economy adjusts to close this gap, there could be changes in other determinants of borrowing and lending.

When anticipated inflation dips and the expected real rate rises at first, households want to increase their net supply of loanable funds: they would do that by economizing on their own purchases of goods and services. At the higher expected real interest rate, businesses want to cut back on their demand for funds, so they trim their expansion plans and, likewise, purchase fewer goods and services. In short, when the expected inflation rate falls, the excess supply of loanable funds at current nominal interest rates is accompanied by an excess supply of both consumption and investment items at current levels of output. Just as the excess supply of loanable funds puts downward pressure on interest rates, the excess supply of goods and services puts downward pressure on the output and prices of those goods and services. Suppliers of goods and services must choose between selling less of their products and lowering the prices they charge for them.[6]

Many economists argue that, at least in the short run, businesses tend to stand their ground on prices and cut their output. Workers' hours are shortened, overtime is eliminated, and, if sales decline enough, some workers are laid off. Production facilities are used less intensively as second or third shifts are dropped, and perhaps some plants are shut down completely. As a result, the purchasing power that flows from businesses to households in the form of wages, rents, and profits falls. Faced with a reduction in income and unwilling to reduce current consumption by an equal amount, households reduce saving. In other words, they make smaller amounts of funds available for loans at any expected real rate of interest. Consequently, the expected real rate of interest need not drop back to its original level to choke off the excess supply of loanable funds. A higher expected real rate of interest now clears the market. Therefore, nominal interest rates decline by less than the drop in the expected inflation rate.

Of course, when faced with a drop in demand for their products, businesses could choose to maintain their output of goods and services by lowering prices or, at least, by reducing the rate at which their prices increase. Indeed, this is the response economists predict more businesses would make in the long run, once they have had a chance to adjust to a less inflationary environment. At that point, the reduction in expected inflation would leave real output, and hence real income, relatively unchanged, so the income effect would be smaller. But there could be a wealth effect on interest rates associated with the decline in actual inflation.

Lower prices for goods and services increase the purchasing power of money and, therefore, may make people already holding money in their portfolios feel substantially wealthier. The greater an individual's wealth, the less incentive he or she has to accumulate still more by buying securities or making loans. So increased wealth, like decreased income, reduces the supply of loanable funds at any expected real rate of interest. And the reduced supply of funds raises the market-clearing expected real interest rate. If the wealth effect is significant, a decline in the expected rate of inflation would be associated with a rise in the prevailing expected real rate of interest even if real income did not change. So nominal rates still would fall by less than the expected rate of inflation does.

In sum, a decline in the expected rate of inflation, to the extent that it reduces income or raises real wealth, tends to increase the market-clearing expected real rate of interest. With the expected real interest rate rising as the expected inflation rate falls, the nominal interest rate—the sum of the two—winds up declining less than point for point with expected inflation.

The Tax Angle

In this era of supply-side economics, we routinely hear about the complicated maze of economic incentives and disincentives that the Federal tax code creates. So it comes as little surprise that changes in expected inflation work through the tax structure to alter the decisions of borrowers and lenders. But sorting out the role of taxes is no simple task. Different provisions of the tax system have contrary effects on the relation of interest rates to expected inflation. While federal tax treatment of interest income and expenses tends to amplify the impact of changes in inflation expectations on nominal interest rates, for example, the tax treatment of depreciation on business plant and equipment tends to dampen this impact.

Because interest income is taxed, lenders are concerned about the expected real rate of interest after taxes.[7] But when the expected rate of inflation rises, an equal increase in the nominal rate preserves only the before-tax expected real rate of interest. That increase will not be sufficient to preserve the expected real rate of interest after taxes because part of the increase in the nominal interest income will

FIGURE 3

Inflation and the After-Tax Real Rate of Interest

Since nominal interest income is taxed, a lender's expected real rate of interest after taxes is roughly

$$
\begin{array}{c}
\text{expected} \\
\text{real rate} \\
\text{of interest} \\
\text{after taxes}
\end{array}
=
(1 - \text{tax rate})
\times
\begin{array}{c}
\text{nominal} \\
\text{rate of} \\
\text{interest}
\end{array}
-
\begin{array}{c}
\text{expected} \\
\text{rate of} \\
\text{inflation}
\end{array}
$$

where the tax rate is the percentage of his income that he would have to pay in taxes.* Consider the individual earning 15-percent nominal interest on a loan and anticipating 10-percent inflation, so that he expects to earn a 5-percent real rate before taxes. If he is in the 20-percent tax bracket, his expected real return after taxes is 2 percent [= (1 - .2) x 15 percent - 10 percent].

Suppose that his view of the future changes and he expects 11-percent rather than 10-percent inflation. Now a loan bearing a 16-percent nominal interest rate would offer him the same 5-percent expected real rate before taxes but it would provide only 1.8-percent [= (1 - .2) x 16 percent - 11 percent] after taxes. In order to maintain his original 2-percent after-tax real return, the individual would have to make a loan with a 16.25-percent nominal interest rate.

On the other hand, suppose that the individual's inflation expectations fall and he anticipates 9-percent rather than 10-percent inflation. A loan with a 14-percent nominal yield would offer him the same 5-percent expected before-tax real return that a 15-percent nominal yield did previously, but it would offer a higher real return after taxes at 2.2 percent [= (1 - .2) x 14 percent - 9 percent]. In fact, this saver could settle for a loan bearing only a 13.75-percent nominal yield, and still maintain his original expected after-tax real rate of interest at 2 percent [= (1 - .2) x 13.75 percent - 9 percent].

In short, maintaining expected after-tax real interest rates in the face of changing inflation expectations requires more than equal changes in nominal interest rates.

---

*When deciding on the purchase of an asset, the lender must consider his marginal tax rate, that is, the additional tax liability as a percentage of the additional interest income. How much of his interest income a taxpayer must surrender at the margin depends upon the precise source of the income and his overall income level, among other factors. The present discussion assumes that the saver does not expect inflation to alter his marginal tax rate. In reality, of course, higher inflation raises nominal income and hence pushes people into higher tax brackets. Allowing for so-called bracket creep would only reinforce the argument presented here.

be taxed away. The nominal rate would have to rise by more than any increase in expected inflation to keep the after-tax real rate unchanged. Conversely, when the expected rate of inflation falls, an equal decrease in nominal rates would preserve the lender's expected real rate of interest before taxes. Nominal rates would have to fall by more than the drop in expected inflation to keep the after-tax rate unchanged. In other words, lenders have to lose in interest what they gain in smaller tax liabilities if their expected after-tax real rate is to remain the same when expected inflation falls (see Figure 3).

To summarize: taxes on lenders' interest incomes tend to amplify the size of changes in nominal rates associated with changes in expected inflation.[8]

Other tax laws, particularly those concerning depreciation, dampen nominal rates' response to changes in expected inflation, however. Historical cost depreciation rules reduce businesses' incentives to invest and hence, tend to depress expected real interest rates when the expected rate of inflation rises.

A profit-seeking business undertakes only those investment projects when the

---

FIGURE 4

Inflation And Depreciation

The firm's net return from an investment project is the increased sales revenue that it generates less the increased production costs it creates. The net real revenues from the project would not be affected by a general inflation; both sale and production costs would rise at the same rate. Theoretically, with a fixed tax rate, real net revenues after taxes would grow at the rate of inflation. But, in fact, inflation does reduce real net revenues after taxes because the depreciation laws preclude the firm from fully adjusting its production costs for inflation when computing its tax bill.

As a piece of capital—such as a new machine, a new truck, a new plant—is being used, its ability to produce is being run down (depreciated) and, ultimately, will be exhausted. The cost to the firm of using up the capital's stream of productive services is the price it will have to pay to replace the capital when it has worn out completely. But in computing its taxable income, the business is allowed to deduct an amount based on the original purchase price of the capital. If inflation is high over the course of the capital's useful life, its replacement cost will be high relative to its original or historical purchase price, so the taxable income from the project will be overstated and the project's after-tax real return will be cut. If inflation is low, capital's replacement cost will be closer to its historical purchase price and depreciation rules will not distort after-tax return as much. So, the higher the rate of inflation a business expects, the lower the after-tax real rate of return it expects on any particular project, and, consequently, the lower the expected after-tax real rate of interest it is willing to pay for financing.

after-tax real returns are expected to exceed the after-tax real rate of interest it must pay for financing. Increases in the expected inflation rate work through depreciation laws to reduce the after-tax real return expected on each potential investment project (see Figure 4). That lower expected after-tax return reduces the incentive to finance the acquisition of new plant and equipment by borrowing at any particular expected real rate of interest. And the reduced willingness to borrow puts downward pressure on the market-clearing expected real rate of interest. With the expected inflation rate higher but the prevailing expected real rate lowered by the decreased demand for funds, nominal interest rates wind up rising by less than the expected rate of inflation. Conversely, a decrease in expected inflation raises the after-tax real return on investments through this depreciation channel. This, in turn, increases businesses' willingness to borrow and raises the market-clearing real rate. As a result, nominal interest rates fall by less than the decline in the expected rate of inflation.[9]

In short, historical cost depreciation rules for tax computations tend to push expected inflation and the market-clearing expected interest rate in opposite directions. So depreciation rules, by themselves, imply less than a point-for-point adjustment of nominal rates to changes in expected inflation. On balance, the tax system may, as some argue, foster a more than point-for-point response of nominal rates to changes in expected inflation. Because of depreciation rules, however, the response is not as great as the income tax rules alone imply.

HOW MUCH INFLUENCE DO INFLATION EXPECTATIONS HAVE ON INTEREST RATES?

When the public expects a decline in the future rate of inflation, federal income tax provisions work toward a more than equal reduction in nominal rates. On the other hand, income and wealth effects and the tax laws concerning depreciation work toward less than equal reduction in nominal interest rates. What is the net result? According to most empirical studies, the latter set of forces dominates.

Economists have made many attempts to estimate just how much of an impact changes in the expected inflation rate have on interest rates. Some investigators have found that inflation expectations have a substantial impact. For example, a 1979 study by John Carlson suggests that each percentage point change in the expected rate of inflation alters nominal interest rates by as much as 1.3 percentage points. In a 1975 study, Eugene Fama found that nominal rates respond point for point to changes in inflation expectations. Most often, though, analysts have found that nominal interest rates respond less than point for point to changes in the expected rate of inflation. According to investigations by Tanzi, by Yohe and Karnosky, and by Anderson and others, for example, each percentage-point change in the expected inflation rate generates a change in nominal rates between 0.8 and 0.9 of a percentage point. Benjamin Friedman reports in a 1980 study that a percentage-point change in expected inflation produces as little as a 0.65 percentage-point change in nominal interest rates.[10]

These findings support the view that, when the expected rate of inflation changes, the income, wealth, and depreciation effects of the change dominate the income tax effects, and, as a result, the expected real rate of interest changes in the opposite direction. So, when the expected rate of inflation falls, the expected real rate of interest rises at least for a while. The nominal rate, the sum of the expected real interest rate and the expected inflation rate, falls, but not by as much as expected inflation.

CONCLUSION

Everyone would like to see lower interest rates. Both the administration and the Federal Reserve have attempted to formulate policies which will reduce current inflation and hence people's expectations about future inflation. Lower inflation expectations, it is hoped, will mean lower interest rates.

The path to lower interest rates is not necessarily short or direct. Expectations of high inflation have been building up for 20 years and may not change quickly. Moreover, policy actions do not affect interest rates only by affecting inflation expectations. Monetary and fiscal policy can directly affect the market-clearing real interest rate, too. In fact, many argue that the current mix of fiscal and monetary policies, while intended to lower inflation and inflation expectations over the long run, has driven up market-clearing real interest rates, at least in the short run.

Nonetheless, both economic theory and statistical evidence give reason to believe that interest rates are closely related to inflation expectations. When the expected rate of inflation is revised downward by a percentage point, interest rates should fall by nearly a percentage point. So if the public comes to expect inflation of 5 percent instead of 10 percent—and if other factors do not drive up real interest rates—nominal interest rates should decline by about 4.0 or 4.5 percentage points. Compared to the level of interest rates in 1981 and early 1982, that would be a welcome change.

NOTES

[1] The simple correlation between the six-month Treasury bill rate and Livingston's six-month-ahead inflation forecast is 0.9.

[2] This discussion of Fisher is based on his book, *The Theory of Interest* (New York: Macmillan, 1930).

[3] This breakdown of an instrument's nominal return allows for the impact of inflation on the value of the principal but not on the value of the interest. To be precise, a $1 security bearing nominal rate n over a time when the inflation rate is expected to be p^e has an expected real return of r^e where:

$$1 + r^e = (1 + n)/(1 + p^e)$$

This can be rearranged to:

$$n = r^e + p^e + r^e p^e$$

Since the product of two rate items is relatively small, $r^e p^e$ is usually dropped.

[4] In this section, and throughout the article, the impact of changes in the expected future rate of inflation is discussed without any explanation of what changes people's inflation expectations. Two important issues should be mentioned in this regard.

First, people consider a diverse set of factors when they try to predict future inflation. Among these factors, the expected future course of monetary and fiscal policy is likely to play an important role in people's forecasts. The current stance of government economic policy, in turn, is likely to provide them a strong signal about the future direction of that policy. But the precise linkage between current policy actions and expected future inflation is not examined here.

Second, current policy actions do not affect current interest rates *only* by affecting inflation expectations. Shifts in policy can affect the market-clearing real interest rate, too, by altering the desired amount of private borrowing and lending at any particular real rate of interest. A complete analysis of the impact of monetary and fiscal policy on interest rates requires an analysis of policies' direct effects on interest rates as well as their expectations-related effects. Only the expectations-related changes in nominal rates are discussed here.

[5] The possibility of a wealth effect on expected real rates of interest was demonstrated by Robert A. Mundell, "Inflation and Real Interest," *Journal of Political Economy* 71 (June 1963), pp. 280–82. The conditions under which an income effect could arise have been clearly laid out by Thomas J. Sargent. See Thomas J. Sargent, "Rational Expectations, the Real Rate of Interest, and the Natural Rate of Unemployment," *Brookings Papers on Economic Activity* (1973:3), pp. 429–72, especially pp. 430 and 437–38; and also see "Anticipated Inflation and the Nominal Rate of Interest," *Quarterly Journal of Economics* 86 (May 1972), pp. 212–25, especially pp. 220–25. The process of adjustment of the economy to a change in expected inflation is also discussed in Martin J. Bailey, *National Income and the Price Level: A Study in Macrotheory,* 2nd ed. (New York: McGraw-Hill, 1971), especially pp. 74–82.

[6] The precise combination in which nominal interest rates, the prices of goods and services, and the output of goods and services adjust to changes in the expected inflation rate also depends on how economic agents decide how much of their funds to hold in the form of money. For either the income or wealth effects to occur, the public's demand for money must be sensitive to nominal interest rates. We assume that this is the case here.

[7] The importance of the distinction between savers' expected real rate of interest before and after taxes was emphasized by Michael Darby, "The Financial and Tax Effects of Monetary Policy on Interest Rates," *Economic Inquiry* 85 (June 1975), pp. 266–76.

[8] Of course, what the expected real rate and the volume of lending will be when expectations change also depends on how borrowers are affected. But the income tax effects on borrowers complement those on lenders. The interest that lenders count as taxable income, borrowers count as a tax-deductible expense. So if, for example, borrowers and lenders are subject to the same tax rate, the after-tax real rate of interest that lenders earn is equal to the after-tax real interest rate that borrowers pay. In that case, when the expected inflation rate rises, borrowers are willing to pay the more than proportionate increase in nominal rates that lenders require to maintain their original level of lending. When the expected rate of inflation falls, lenders are willing to accept precisely the lower expected real rate that borrowers require to maintain their original level of borrowing. If borrowers and lenders are subject to different tax rates, then, whatever the expected before-tax real rate of interest, each faces a different expected after-tax real rate. Nonetheless, the tax provisions for interest income and expense allow borrowers to pay a higher real rate of interest when expected inflation rises and allow lenders to accept a lower real rate when expected inflation declines.

For a detailed discussion, see Niels Christian Nielson, "Inflation and Taxation," *Journal of Monetary Economics* 7 (1981), pp. 261–70.

[9] Some of the ways in which inflation affects investment via tax rules are discussed by Richard W. Kopcke, "Why Interest Rates Are So Low," *New England Economic Review,* July/August 1980, pp. 24–33.

[10] References in this section are to:
    Paul A. Anderson, Thomas Sargent, and Carol Thistlethwaite, "The Response of Interest Rates to Expected Inflation in the MPS Model," *Journal of Monetary Economics* 1 (1975), pp. 111–15.

SUGGESTED READINGS

Carlson, John A. "Expected Inflation and Interest Rates." *Economic Inquiry* 89 (October 1979), pp. 597–608.

Fama, Eugene F. "Short-Term Interest Rates as Predictions of Inflation." *American Economic Review* 65 (June 1975), pp. 269–82.

Friedman, Benjamin M. "Price Inflation, Portfolio Choice, and Nominal Interest Rates." *American Economic Review* 70 (March 1980), pp. 12–21.

Tanzi, Vito. "Inflationary Expectations, Economic Activity, Taxes and Interest Rates." *American Economic Review* 70 (March 1980), pp. 12–21.

Yohe, William P., and Denis S. Karnosky. "Interest Rates and Price Level Changes, 1952–1969." *Review.* Federal Reserve Bank of St. Louis, December 1969, pp. 18–39.

14

Revealing Real Interest Rates: Let the Market Do It

Donald J. Mullineaux and Aris Protopapadakis

> When money and goods change with reference to each other—in other words, when the money standard appreciates or depreciates in value in terms of goods—the numbers expressing the two rates of interest, one reckoned in terms of money and the other reckoned in terms of goods, will be quite different. Moreover, the money rate, the *only rate quoted in the market,* will be influenced by the appreciation or depreciation.
>
> —Irving Fisher, *The Theory of Interest* (1930)

Most Americans today would view as commonplace the notion that inflation (what Professor Fisher calls a "depreciation of the monetary standard") affects interest rates. Living through the great inflation of the late 1960s and 1970s made the link between accelerating inflation and rising interest rates painfully obvious. Many would also recognize that inflation can drive a substantial wedge between the money interest rate and the so-called real rate of interest (what Fisher labels the rate "reckoned in terms of goods"). But few, if any, people could give a precise answer to the following seemingly simple question: "What is the real rate of interest on Treasury bills this week?

Fisher hints at one reason why. Only money rates are "quoted" by brokers and dealers and published in the financial press. No one can look in *The Wall Street Journal* or call his or her bank to find out the real rate. People instead are forced to make an estimate—an educated guess—about the level of real interest rates. And policymakers, who presumably care about interest rates at least as much as the rest of us, must do the same. That we are left with an error-prone estimation procedure to gauge real rates seems anomalous, since economists claim that real rates are more important than money rates for explaining many kinds of behavior.

From *Business Review*, Federal Reserve Bank of Philadelphia, March/April 1984, pp. 3–8.

Donald J. Mullineaux is senior vice president and chief economist of the Federal Reserve Bank of Philadelphia. Aris Protopapadakis is research officer and economist of the Federal Reserve Bank of Philadelphia.

It is possible to structure a means for markets to "reveal" real rates of interest, however. If some substantial borrower—the federal government, for example—issued bonds with interest and principal tied to some index of the general price level, then brokers who traded such bonds would be quoting a real rate of interest, rather than a money rate. The yield on indexed Treasury securities, for example, would represent a real rate of interest based on a particular index.[1] Movements in the "quoted" real rates on indexed Treasury bonds could prove valuable to households, businesses, and policymakers.

WHY REAL INTEREST RATES MATTER . . .

To say that interest rates are important is like saying that kids like ice cream—few people will disagree with either suggestion. Crucial decisions—whether to consume or save, for example, whether to buy a car, whether to build a new plant, whether to pump oil from the ground or leave it there—all depend on the level of interest rates. Indeed, any decision that involves looking into the future—and almost all do—involves taking account of interest rates.

. . . to Households. Households, for instance, must decide whether to consume today or at some point in the future. A decision to postpone consumption is, by definition, a decision to save. The expected real interest rate is the reward for saving, or, to put it another way, it is the amount of extra future consumption households expect to get by refraining from consuming today. Therefore, the higher this rate, the stronger the incentive to save.

When people decide to save, however, they typically do not set aside goods, such as groceries or tennis shoes, nor do they receive interest payments in goods. Rather, they set aside money (they lend the money) and they are paid back in money. The distinction between receiving interest in the form of goods or in money is not important in a world where there is no inflation. In such a case, one dollar can be exchanged for the same basket of goods whether it's today or tomorrow. The money rate of interest (sometimes called the "nominal rate") therefore would be the same as the rate of interest expressed in terms of goods (the "real rate of interest"). An interest rate of 5 percent, for example, means that lending $1,000 gets you back $1,050 a year hence. But, since prices are unchanged, it also means that you can buy 5 percent *more* goods next year than you can buy today. With no possibility of inflation, the expected real interest rate and the nominal interest rate are one and the same.

If there is some inflation, however, then it takes more money "tomorrow" than today to buy the *same* basket of goods. Therefore, if people expect to get extra goods by postponing consumption, the nominal (money) interest rate must include not just the expected real rate but also a component that reflects the amount of anticipated inflation between today and tomorrow. This component, which is intended to preserve the consumer's purchasing power, is referred to as an inflation premium. For example, if the inflation premium is 5 percent and the nominal rate is 10 percent, then lending $1,000 gets you back $1,100 one year hence, but it only buys $1,050 worth of goods in this year's prices. In other words, the reward for saving is identical to that when nominal rates are 5 percent and there is no expected inflation. So, there is no incentive to consume less today simply because nominal rates are high. It would take a rise in the real rate to induce postponing more consumption.

. . . **to Business.**   Similarly, it is the expected real rate which firms must consider in deciding whether to build a new plant or install some new equipment. New equipment will benefit the stockholders of a corporation if the amount of extra goods which can be produced with the new machine adds more to the company's revenues than the costs of owning and operating the new equipment. The interest rate is an important component of those costs, because a firm must borrow the capital necessary to finance such purchases.[2]

When the company borrows to buy equipment, it pays the nominal rate on those borrowings. However, it is the size of the real rate component of that nominal rate that influences the firm's decision. The real rate reflects the cost (in percentage form) of financing *in terms of the good produced*. A 5 percent annual real rate, for example, suggests that if a widget firm borrows an amount equivalent to 100 widgets for one year, it would expect to repay 105 widgets-worth at year's end. Thus, the expected real interest rate allows for an easy comparison with the number of extra widgets that investment in new equipment would yield. If the new machine yields 100 widgets, then it's a good deal. The lower the real cost of borrowing (the real interest rate), the stronger the incentive for a business to buy new equipment or to build a new plant.

If there is no significant inflation underway, then there is no reason to emphasize the distinction between real and nominal interest rates in making investment decisions. When inflation is high, however, nominal interest rates will also be high. But high nominal interest rates need not discourage investment if the real rate is low. The reason is simple: though higher inflation increases borrowing costs, it also raises revenue flows because a firm's product will sell at higher prices. A business will look through the impact of inflation on its profits to assess the "real" gains from investment, and the real interest rate serves as the standard against which those gains are compared.[3]

The expected real rate is a useful indicator of the amount of investment businesses are likely to undertake in any one year, because of its role in the way businesses make decisions. Increases in this rate tend to discourage investment, and conversely, declines in the expected real rate tend to encourage investment.

. . . **and to Policymakers.**   The importance of the real rate of interest has not been lost on monetary policymakers. Indeed, the short-run impact of changes in monetary policy is transmitted to the economy largely through changes in the real interest rate. If the Fed unexpectedly reduces the rate of money growth, for example, people try to make up for the "shortage" of money by selling various kinds of financial assets. This makes both nominal and real interest rates rise. Nominal rates rise because the sale of these assets depresses their prices. The real rate rises because the inflation premium adjusts slowly to changes in money growth.[4] Therefore, the expected real rate—namely, the difference between the nominal rate and the inflation premium—increases.

Consumers react to the rise in expected real rates by postponing purchases of new homes and automobiles, and firms react by cutting back on plans to build new plants and to buy equipment. Inventories are also likely to be trimmed, since a higher real rate makes them more expensive to finance. These reactions to an increase in real rates reduce the overall demand for goods and services in the economy, and the growth rate of real GNP is likely to decline. Alternatively, if the Fed provides more money to the economy unexpectedly, then the real rate falls, at least temporarily, and economic growth accelerates for awhile.

The expected real rate of interest is one of the channels through which monetary policy influences the economy. In principle, therefore, the Fed can judge how its policy actions are influencing the economy by monitoring what is happening to the real rate of interest. A rising real rate would signal a more restrictive monetary policy, while a declining real rate would suggest some monetary ease, other things being equal. In practice, the Fed has a difficult time using the real rate as an indicator of the thrust of monetary policy, because it, like everyone else in the economy, lacks adequate knowledge of what the real rate is. There is no asset available in the financial markets which pays just a real rate. Instead, the real rate must be estimated in some fashion or other. Unfortunately, none of the procedures used to gauge the expected real rate offers much promise of yielding good estimates.

THE REAL RATE MUST BE ESTIMATED

Analysts have a useful starting point for estimating the expected real rate, namely, today's nominal interest rate in the market. The expected real rate is embedded in the nominal rate, so one way to get at it is to separate the expected real rate from the other components that make up the nominal rate. One of these is the inflation premium; to identify that component in nominal rates, analysts must have some means of estimating the *anticipated* rate of inflation. Anticipated inflation is not the only "premium" which gets built into nominal interest rates. Lenders also will want some protection from the risk that their inflation forecast is likely to be wrong. If actual inflation exceeds what lenders and borrowers expected over the life of a loan contract, for instance, then lenders will unexpectedly lose purchasing power and borrowers will gain. Borrowers will repay lenders with "cheaper" dollars in terms of purchasing power. Should inflation fall short of expectations, lenders gain and borrowers lose. Inflation is indeed imperfectly predictable, so credit market participants find their future purchasing power at risk over the horizon of a loan. Since people typically are averse to risky situations, financial markets build a *risk premium* component into nominal interest rates to induce lenders to take on these risks. The more uncertain the outlook for inflation, the larger this risk premium is likely to be.

If good information is available on the size of the inflation premium and the risk premium, then these components can be "netted out" of the nominal interest rate.[5] What's left is the expected real rate the compensation lenders require for postponing consumption when there is no inflation expected and no risk concerning the inflation outlook.[6] Calculating the expected real rate sounds like simple arithmetic: just subtract the inflation premium and the risk premium from the nominal rate.

THE REAL RATE ARITHMETIC HAS DIFFICULTIES . . .

Unfortunately, information about the expected inflation and risk premium components of interest rates is very hard to come by. How do we know, for example, what credit market participants expect inflation to be? One way is to ask them. But there are no comprehensive surveys of the inflation forecasts of borrowers and lenders, presumably because no one has strong incentives to collect such information. Furthermore, it is not obvious that borrowers and lenders have the incentives to be as careful in responding to surveys as they are in investing their money. There are surveys of professional economists' forecasts of inflation (well-known examples are surveys by Joseph Livingston and Robert Eggert), but it is far from obvious that the average of such forecasts coincided with the average sentiment of credit market participants. Another shortcoming of such surveys is that they seldom contain inflation predictions for more than one year ahead. This makes it impossible to use the surveys to gauge long-term real rates of interest. Yet it is long-term real rates that probably matter most for certain key decisions, such as whether to build a new plant or to buy a house.

An alternative to extracting an average expected inflation from survey information is to forecast inflation using econometric models. But this method also has some difficulties. For one thing, the various forecasting models commercially available do not agree closely in their predictions of inflation, particularly over periods longer than a year. Furthermore, these longer-term forecasts have not been very accurate, which raises the question of whether inflation is inherently unpredictable or whether the models are not very good. In sum, while there are available measures of inflation expectations, they are of limited scope and doubtful quality.

While information on anticipated inflation is flawed, data on risk premia are virtually nonexistent. There is no way to measure in any direct way the size of the risk premium. Nor has anyone developed a reliable technique for estimating the risk premium. Some analysts have tried to avoid this difficulty by assuming that the risk premium is zero (there is no risk premium), but there is no strong evidence to support that presumption. That neither the inflation premium nor the risk premium can be measured with much precision makes it very difficult to use the arithmetic procedure to determine the expected real rate of interest.

. . . AND SO DO ALTERNATIVE APPROACHES

The difficulties with the real rate arithmetic have prompted some economists to try an alternative method for estimating the expected real rate. They note that it is easy to calculate an "after-the-fact" or ex post real rate by simply subtracting the actual inflation rate over the horizon of a loan from the nominal rate on the loan.

If economists can uncover a set of factors—an econometric model—which explains the ex post real rate, then it should be possible to use that model to estimate the expected real rate. Factors that have been used to explain ex post real rates include the behavior of real GNP, investment, federal deficits, money growth, and inflation.

There are several difficulties with this approach to estimating expected real rates, however. First, the statistical methodology assumes that market expectations of inflation *were correct on average* over the horizon of the interest rate in question. While this may be a valid view over long periods of time and during periods of relatively stable policy, it probably doesn't hold over shorter periods or when the policy environment is changing. A second difficulty is that this approach fails to take account of the behavior of the risk premium. If the economy is characterized by changing risk premia, the ex post rate approach will mismeasure the expected real rate of interest. Thus, both the arithmetic and ex post rate approaches to estimating expected real rates seem unsatisfactory.

CAN THE MARKET REVEAL REAL RATES OF INTEREST?

Markets frequently are touted as sources of cheap information. By relying on prices to convey information about relative demands and supplies, for example, both buyers and sellers can avoid collecting huge amounts of data to help them decide how to behave. Unfortunately, no market currently conveys direct information about the real rate of interest. But it may be possible to create such a market.

The prospect, which has been suggested on a number of occasions in recent years, is for the U.S. Treasury to offer bonds that are indexed to a measure of the price level. The amount of interest and principal paid on indexed bonds (the yield) is adjusted in line with movements in the designated price index.[7] If inflation increases during the second year of a two-year security, for instance, the yield to the bond holder automatically rises, while if inflation falls, the yield falls.[8] One of the advantages these bonds offer is that the interest rate quoted on them in the financial press would be the expected real rate of interest on these securities. In other words, now you can open *The Wall Street Journal* and answer the question we posed earlier: What's the real rate of interest on Treasury bills this week?

The market reveals a real rate because holders of index-linked securities will be compensated for whatever inflation occurs over the life of a loan contract, so they need not build any inflation forecast into the rate they require for lending. Moreover, the yield on index-linked bonds need contain no "risk premium" against unexpected future inflation, since inflation will not erode future purchasing power. The quoted yield on an indexed security is the real rate, pure and simple.

Treasury issues of indexed securities would, of course, provide direct information only about real rates on government bonds. It would still be necessary for people and businesses to estimate real rates on other kinds of assets.[9] However, the changes in the yields on indexed securities would provide valuable information as indicators of probable changes in other real rates. These other rates would be expected to change when indexed-bond yields change, because investors can choose to hold either kind of security in their portfolios. A rise in yields on indexed bonds would therefore require a rise in other real rates to make those other assets as attractive as index-linked securities.

From the viewpoint of monetary policymaking, indexed bonds would fill a crucial need. Fed decisionmakers would have a very important indicator of the economic impact of monetary policy, which could alert them that a particular policy course may have run "too far." From a monetary policy standpoint, it would be most useful to have indexed Treasury bonds in a series of maturities. Information about changes in short-term real rates could then be distinguished from changes in long-term real rates. Such a distinction is important, because the movement of real rates at different maturity classes yields information about different aspects of real economic activity. Short-term real rates generally affect working capital and inventory decisions, for example, while long rates affect the outcomes for housing and for investment in plant and equipment.

Indexed bonds are likely to answer certain needs for consumers and businesses even beyond providing valuable information. Investors cannot presently purchase insurance against unexpected inflation in the form of indexed securities; nor is it easy to think of a way for investors to combine purchases and sales of other assets that will guarantee preservation of purchasing power against inflation. Consequently, indexed bonds would have to make at least some investors better off.

The ramifications of having indexed bonds are, in fact, even broader. In a world without indexed bonds, the government can end up, in a sense, defaulting on some of its debt if inflation is in excess of what people expect. Suppose people purchasing Treasury securities anticipate 6 percent inflation, but government policies produce a 10 percent rise in the price level. Then each dollar of debt the government repays yields 4 percent less purchasing power than people expected when they bought the bonds. The government has repaid its nominal debt but has "defaulted" in terms of purchasing power. Many economists believe that this possibility of defaulting weakens the government's incentives to prevent surprise inflations.[10] With indexed bonds, however, the government simply cannot "default" on its debt in purchasing power terms.

CONCLUSION

There is much to be said in favor of proposals for the U.S. Treasury to begin issuing index-linked securities. Policymakers would benefit from the availability of improved information, and, if better information produced better policies, then everyone would be better off. In addition, investors are likely to gain from the existence of such bonds. Financial markets have fostered a large number of innovations in recent years which provide more information and allow investors to better manage risks, including a wide range of financial futures contracts, options, and even options on futures. The substantial growth in the volume of these new assets suggests there is a large demand for securities which allow investors to manage risks better and which reveal information. Indexed-linked securities would make a welcome addition to the menu of such assets.

NOTES

[1] The "real" rate quoted on an indexed bond is in reference to a particular price index. The same bond tied to a different index could carry a different real rate. The expectation is that real rates with respect to a variety of indices will move together, enabling policymakers, households, and businesses to use the quoted real rates as indicators of the real rates not quoted.

[2] Borrowing in this context should be broadly conceived. It includes borrowing from financial institutions, issuing commercial paper, selling long-term bonds, using retained earnings, and floating new stock issues.

[3] We are not claiming here that inflation is "neutral" in the sense that it has no impact on real economic activity. Inflation can have an impact on relative prices of goods and on corporate profits. Rather, we claim that, since an individual corporation's investment decisions have no measurable impact on inflation, a corporation can calculate the real demand for its products as well as the costs of production in terms of its output, without reference to the trend growth in the prices of all the goods.

[4] Empirical evidence shows that inflation adjusts slowly to money growth; hence, expected inflation—that is, the inflation premium—also adjusts slowly.

[5] For a more complete analysis of these concepts, see Simon Benninga and Aris Protopapadakis, "Real and Nominal Interest Rates Under Uncertainty: The Fisher Theorem and the Term Structure," *Journal of Political Economy* 91 (October 1983).

[6] If there is some prospect of default on repayment of interest on principal, still another kind of premium gets built into a security's yield—a default risk premium. The securities we discuss in what follows—Treasury issues—are presumed to be free of default risk.

[7] There are two possible types of indexing. One is to add the amount of actual inflation to the agreed-upon coupon payment. Thus, if inflation turns out to be 6 percent and the agreed-upon coupon rate is 2 percent, the total interest paid would be 8 percent. An alternative method is to pay the agreed-upon coupon rate but to increase the face value of the nominal bond by the inflation rate. In the example above, the coupon payment would be only 2 percent, but the face value of the bond would increase by 6 percent. Since both methods of indexing insure the purchasing power of the owner of the bond against inflation, the agreed-upon coupon rate is the real rate of interest.

[8] There are, of course, a number of details that would need to be specified in an indexed-bond contract, including the specific price index to be used, the frequency of adjustment, procedures for

handling issues, such as possible revisions in the index and the tax treatment of the index-related compensation. In a highly developed market for such securities, bonds indexed to different price-level indices might well be available, just as options on several different stock market indices are now available.

[9] The private sector's failure to provide index-linked securities has been a puzzle to financial economists. Some have argued that risk considerations militate against the use of indexed bonds by businesses. In particular, since actual inflation is unpredictable, corporations issuing indexed securities commit to an unknown stream of future interest payments. And there is no guarantee that the price of its own products will match up well with the rate of inflation. The real interest rate *in terms of its own products* is therefore uncertain if it issues indexed bonds.

[10] See T. Sargent and N. Wallace, "Some Unpleasant Monetarist Arithmetic," *Quarterly Review*. Federal Reserve Bank of Minneapolis, Fall 1981, pp. 1–18.

15

The Impact of Inflation on Stock Prices

Douglas K. Pearce

The rapid and variable inflation experienced since the late 1960s has caused wealthholders to seek to protect themselves against increases in the general price level. At the beginning of this period of inflation, it is likely that common stock—which represents a claim on real capital—was recommended as such a hedge. However, those who followed such advice and placed funds in a broad portfolio of stocks in 1968 have seen the real value of their holdings fall by about 50 percent. This surprising result has spurred considerable research on the relationship between inflation and the stock market. While no consensus has yet emerged on the theoretical nexus between inflation and equity prices, several empirical studies have confirmed that inflation and stock returns have been negatively related in the postwar period.[1]

It is important to investigate the reasons for this anomalous finding given the significance of the stock market. Movements in share prices are viewed as a prime indicator of the private sector's evaluation of current and future business conditions. Moreover, the stock market is thought to have a substantial influence on the consumption behavior of households and the investment decisions of business firms.[2] A fall in the real value of stocks is likely to reduce consumption demand since households hold about one sixth of their net worth in common stock.[3] Lower stock prices should also discourage investment spending because they signal firms that the market places a lower value on their capital stock and, thus, should encourage mergers, rather than the purchase of new capital equipment and structures.[4] If there is a negative, causal relationship running from inflation to stock prices, inflation will reduce the growth of the corporate capital stock and, thus, have direct, adverse effects on productivity and output.

The purpose of this article is to analyze the possible connections between stock prices and inflation to see if such a causal link exists. The first section briefly reviews the traditional model of stock price determination. The second section

From *Economic Review,* Federal Reserve Bank of Kansas City, March 1982, pp. 3–18.

Douglas K. Pearce is an associate professor of economics at the University of Missouri-Columbia and a visiting scholar at the Federal Reserve Bank of Kansas City. Research assistance was provided by Dan Vrabac, a research assistant with the bank.

presents the historical record of stock prices, stock returns, and inflation. The third section surveys the major alternative hypotheses which have been put forth to explain the negative relationship between equity prices and inflation. The fourth section investigates the plausibility of these explanations by examining how well they accord with the empirical evidence. The final section summarizes the findings of the article.

INFLATION AND THE PRESENT VALUE MODEL OF STOCK PRICES

The effect of inflation on stock prices and stock yields can be analyzed using the traditional model for asset prices, the present value model. This model asserts that the price of a share of stock is the discounted, or present value of all future dividends. For simplicity, it is assumed that all corporate profits are paid out so that the terms *profits, earnings,* and *dividends* are interchangeable. If real dividends are expected to be constant and inflation is zero, the stock price of a debt-free (unlevered) corporation can be computed using a simple formula:[5]

$$S_t = \frac{D^e}{r} \qquad (1)$$

where: S_t = the price of the stock at the beginning of period t.
D_e = the expected dividend to be received at the end of each period.
r = the real rate of return required by stockholders.

For example, if the required real rate of return is 5 percent and the corporation is expected to earn $5 per share every year, the stock should sell for ($5/0.05), or $100. Stock price movements, according to this model, reflect some combination of changes in the expected dividend stream or the required rate of return. This required rate is assumed to equal the real interest rate on a default-free security plus a risk premium, due to the uncertainty of dividend payments. The one-period yield on the stock is defined as:

$$\text{Stock yield t} = \frac{D^e + S_{t+1}}{S_t} - 1 \qquad (2)$$

and thus the expected yield is r, the required rate of return.[6]

In this model, inflation will cause nominal stock prices to rise at the same rate as the general price level, leaving real stock prices constant, unless inflation changes expected real dividends or the required rate of return. If inflation is neutral, in the sense that all prices rise at the same rate, firms will see their revenues and costs increasing at this same rate so nominal profits and dividends also rise at the rate of inflation. When inflation is at rate p (and is fully anticipated), the equation for the nominal price of stock becomes:[7]

$$S_t = \frac{D^e(1 + p)^t}{r} \qquad (3)$$

Thus, for the example above, if inflation is 10 percent per year, nominal dividends would be expected to be $5.50 at the end of the first year, $6.05 at the end of the second year, and so on. The initial stock price, S_0, would still be $100, but the price at the beginning of the next year, S_1, would be ($5.50/0.05), or $110, and S_2 would be ($6.05/0.05), or $121. The real price of the stock would remain unchanged, since the nominal stock price increases just match the increases in the general price level. The nominal one-period yield on the stock would be approximately r + p, leaving the real yield unaltered.[8] Hence, inflation has no real effects on stock prices or yields unless it changes the real profitability of the corporation's capital, D_e, or the return demanded by shareholders, r.

This analysis assumes a firm which has no debt. If the firm raised some of its funds through issuing bonds or other debt, inflation might raise real equity prices. While inflation should not change the real market value of the firm—that is, the real value of all claims on the firm—if it is unexpected it will benefit shareholders (debtors) and hurt bondholders (creditors), thus raising share prices in real terms.[9] Again, this prediction is based on the assumption that inflation neither affects the profitability of capital nor raises the required rate of return.

It should be noted that the validity of the present value model is not unquestioned. Keynes, for example, considered this model of share prices only a convention.[10] Doubting that movements in stock prices were dominated by the long-run expectations embedded in equation (1), he considered short-run speculation to be the primary force. Speculators in the stock market, Keynes asserted, spend the majority of their time guessing the preference of other speculators instead of evaluating the future earnings of firms. While other critiques of the model have also appeared, the present value model remains the predominant tool for analyzing stock prices.[11]

THE HISTORICAL PERFORMANCE OF COMMON STOCKS

The history of nominal stock prices is presented in Chart 1 along with the general price level for the 1901–80 period. The stock price index employed is Standard & Poor's Composite Index of 500 (S&P 500) of the largest stocks (measured by their market value) with the weights of each stock corresponding to the relative market value of the stock. The general price level is measured by the consumer price index (CPI). While the two series are not closely related, they moved broadly together until the mid-1960s. From then on, however, the general price level has spurted sharply upward while nominal stock prices remained roughly constant. Chart 2 dramatizes this recent divergency by plotting the real value of stocks over the last 30 years.

As mentioned previously, the constant purchasing power value of common stock peaked around 1968 and has since fallen to about 50 percent of that level. It is this dramatic plunge in real equity prices which has puzzled analysts.

The pattern of real stock prices is mirrored by the behavior of stock yields. Table 1 reports the nominal and real yields on the S&P 500 portfolio and the inflation rate for 1926–80 and subperiods. Over the entire period, investors enjoyed a 9.4 percent nominal yield and a 6.5 percent real yield on this portfolio. While similar yields occurred during the last 30 years, the last two columns of Table 1 indicate that there were two distinct eras. From 1951 to 1965, stocks earned high nominal returns while inflation averaged less than 2 percent per year. However, from 1966 to 1980, the nominal yield was well below the historical mean while inflation was rapid, producing real returns that were negative. Thus, these data also suggest that recent inflation has had a substantial, adverse effect on the stock market.

CHART 1
Stock Prices and the General Price Level

CPI, S&P 500 Index

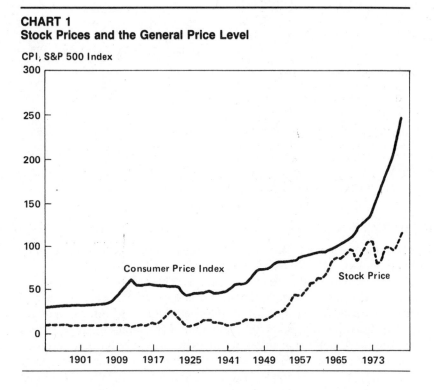

CHART 2
Real Stock Prices

Real Stock Price Index

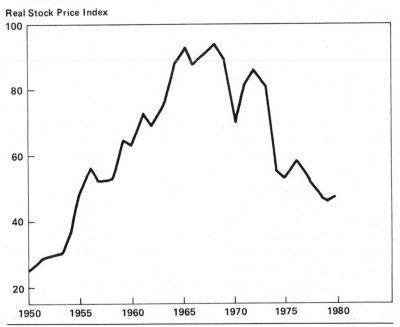

TABLE 1
Nominal and Real Yields on Common Stocks (amounts in percent)

	1926–80	1926–50	1951–80	1951–65	1966–80
Nominal compound yield on Standard & Poor's 500 Stock Portfolio	9.4	7.7	10.9	15.2	6.7
Inflation rate (CPI)	2.9	1.3	4.2	1.6	6.9
Real yield on Standard & Poor's 500 Stock Portfolio	6.5	6.4	6.7	13.6	−0.2

Note: the yields are computed assuming all dividends are reinvested and that the portfolio was held for each period.
Source: R. G. Ibbotson and R. A. Sinquefield, *Stocks, Bonds, Bills and Inflation: Historical Returns (1926–1978)*, Financial Analysts Research Foundation, 1979. Updated to 1980 by the authors.

WHY INFLATION HAS HURT THE STOCK MARKET: ALTERNATIVE VIEWS

The failure of stock prices to rise with the general price level and nominal yields to keep up with inflation during the last 15 years has stimulated several researchers to seek an explanation for this anomaly. The present value model indicates that the fall in real stock prices signals a reduction in expected real earnings and thus real dividends, or an increase in the required rate of return on stock.

This section reviews two arguments why inflation might reduce expected earnings—namely, that inflation raises the real tax burden on corporate capital and that inflation causes investors to underestimate the returns to shareholders. Following this discussion is an examination of why inflation might raise the rate of return required by stockholders by either increasing returns on alternative assets, increasing perceived risk, or confusing investors into misapplying the present value model.[12]

Inflation and Expected Corporate Earnings

Tax Effects. Much of the discussion concerning the poor performance of stocks during periods of inflation has centered on the role of taxes. Several researchers believe that inflation substantially increases the real tax rate on corporate profits and, therefore, that expected inflation causes investors to revise downward their forecasts of real after-tax corporate earnings.[13]

Inflation is thought to raise the effective tax rate faced by corporate capital because of the tax treatment of depreciation charges and inventory changes. When computing its taxable profits, a corporation deducts the amount of depreciation of its physical assets. This deduction helps the firm to maintain its capital stock. During inflation, however, the replacement cost of equipment and structures rises with the general price level. Because the depreciation deductions are based on the historical cost of the assets, they no longer reflect the amount required to keep the capital stock intact. Since inflation swells nominal revenues but does not increase the depreciation charges, nominal profits rise and overstate the true profits of an ongoing firm. With taxes based on nominal income, the real tax burden on the corporation is enlarged and real after-tax earnings are reduced.

A similar argument is relevant to the treatment of inventories. During an inflationary period, firms selling goods from inventory realize nominal gains which are taxed as ordinary income. These gains arise because the firm can only

TABLE 2
Effect of Inflation on Accounting Profits

		Initial conditions of firm:		Equity = $1,000 Debt = $1,000			
		Initial economic conditions:		Nominal interest rate (i) = 0.05			
				Inflation (p) = 0			

Period	Revenue	Labor Cost	Interest Cost	Accounting Profit	Dividends	Change in Debt	True Profits
0 (p = 0)	200	100	50	50	50	0	50
1 (p = 100)	400	200	1,100	− 900	100	1,000	100
2 (p = 100)	800	400	2,200	−1,800	200	2,000	200
3 (p = 0)	800	400	200	200	0	0	200

Note: when expected inflation is 100 percent, the nominal interest rate rises from 5 percent to 110 percent in order for the real interest rate to be unaffected. The equation for this relationship is $i = 4 + p + r \cdot p$ where i is the nominal interest rate, r is the real interest rate, and p is inflation.

deduct the original cost of buying goods, rather than the current cost of replenishing the inventory. Again, an ongoing firm has made no real gains, but its real tax bill has increased. This problem is exacerbated by the still prevalent use of the first-in, first-out (FIFO) accounting method.[14] A rise in inflation will thus raise taxable profits and therefore taxes, even when real profits have not increased, with the result that after-tax earnings fall.

Gains from Debt. It has been argued that inflation reduces real corporate debt and that such gains offset much or all of the impact of taxes on corporate earnings. However, some economists believe that shareholders ignore the gain from debt in evaluating their equity and thus underestimate true profits and undervalue the supporting stocks. This argument assumes a kind of money illusion on the part of investors because they fail to adjust reported profits adequately for all the effects of inflation.[15]

Table 2 illustrates why gains from debt should be added. Assume a firm initially has a net worth of $1,000 and debt of $1,000. The debt is in the form of one-period bonds paying 5 percent. Inflation is known to be zero, there are no taxes, and equity also yields a real return of 5 percent. Line one gives the initial revenues, costs, and profits, with all profits distributed as dividends. Line two shows the effects of 100 percent inflation, completely anticipated. Revenues and labor costs double, but interest expense rises to $1,100 because the nominal interest rate fully reflects expected inflation. Accounting or book profits are now negative (− $900), but the firm can still pay the same real dividend and cover the increased interest expense by borrowing $1,000. All the firm is doing is maintaining the same real debt. Thus, accounting profits provide a misleading guide to the true picture of the firm since inflation is actually neutral. There are no effects on real dividends, real debt, or the debt-equity ratio. The correct measure of profits in the last column equals accounting profit plus the gain on real debt—that is, the inflation rate times nominal debt.

Inflation and the Required Rate of Return on Stocks

Even if it had no effect on expected profits, inflation would cause real stock prices to fall if it raised the required rate of return on stocks. This might occur if inflation increased the after-tax real returns on alternative assets or if investors believed that stocks had become riskier, because of inflation, and thus demanded a higher risk premium. Also, investors might mistakenly use the nominal interest rate, which moves with inflation, to discount real earnings.

Return on Alternative Assets.   Some analysts have attributed much of the fall in real stock prices to the exceptionally high real returns that owner-occupied housing has provided during recent inflationary times.[16] This asset enjoys two tax advantages when the general price level rises. The main return is the rental services of the house for which the owner, in effect, pays himself. Since this imputed return rises with inflation but is not taxed, the real, after-tax earnings of the house rises relative to other assets. Second, unlike common stock, realized nominal capital gains largely can be avoided by reinvestment in houses until age 55. The adjustment of portfolios by wealthholders results in housing prices being bid up and in stock prices falling, so that comparable real after-tax returns might be reestablished.

Greater Risk.   An alternative reason for a rise in the required rate of return is a rise in the perceived riskiness of corporate profits. If increases in the risk premium for stocks are associated with higher inflation rates, inflation would reduce share prices even if it left expected earnings unaffected. It has been argued that much of the decline in stock prices can be attributed to added uncertainty about corporate earnings and that inflation is a primary cause of this uncertainty.[17]

There are several reasons why inflation might make corporate profits less predictable. There is evidence that a rise in the level of inflation is accompanied by an increase in both the variability and the dispersion of relative price movements.[18] Either of these factors will tend to make the profits of any firm less certain. For example, an unpredictable inflation rate imposes real efficiency losses as economic agents scramble to protect themselves by using shorter contracts. In addition, a volatile inflation rate makes it more difficult to distinguish relative price movements from changes in the overall price level, possibly resulting in incorrect allocation decisions.

A higher level of inflation, even without more variability, may also cause corporate earnings to be less certain if agents anticipate corrective measures by the government. Investors may fear the imposition of wage-price controls with their inherently arbitrary effects on profits. Similarly, rapid inflation is likely to bring on some form of restrictive monetary or fiscal policy which may not only dampen profit expectations but, given the unknown nature of the exact policies that will be undertaken, make planning an even more hazardous task.

Finally, energy-related inflationary jumps may add to the unpredictability of profits. Over the 1970s, the two largest jumps reflected steep increases in energy prices. Uncertainty about future energy prices and supplies coupled with the existence of production techniques and capital equipment geared to low energy prices is likely to have reduced the perceived stability of corporate earnings. Thus, the inflation rate may serve as a proxy for the riskiness assigned to returns to corporate capital. Therefore, increases in inflation may lead investors to require higher returns on stock.

Incorrect Discount Rate.   A third reason why inflation could raise the required rate of return on stocks is the use by investors of a nominal interest rate, rather than a real interest rate, to discount future real profits.[19] This is roughly equivalent to shareholders comparing the earnings-price ratio of stocks to the nominal interest rate on bonds when making portfolio decisions. As discussed earlier in the paper, inflation should raise earnings and the price of stocks at the same rate, leaving the earnings-price ratio unchanged. In other words, the earnings-price ratio is a real yield. Thus, the correct comparison is the earnings-price ratio to the real rate of interest, the nominal rate less expected inflation. If investors do commit the error of looking at nominal interest rates, then as inflation pushes up nominal interest rates, stock prices would have to fall to provide comparable yields.

EMPIRICAL EVIDENCE ON STOCK PRICES AND INFLATION

This section reviews empirical evidence on the possible connections between inflation and stock prices. The first part examines both whether inflation has reduced the expected profitability of corporate capital through raising effective tax rates and the impact of ignoring the gains from debt on the return on equity. The second part of the section investigates the proposition that inflation has raised the required return on stock which, if true, would force stock prices down.

Inflation and Expected Corporate Earnings

Tax Effects.   The tax effects hypothesis asserts that inflation reduces real after-tax corporate profits because it raises the effective tax rate. This view implies that the after-tax profitability of corporate capital should be inversely related to inflation and that the before-tax profitability should be unrelated to inflation. If inflation has little or no impact on real after-tax profitability, the tax effects theory would not account for the fall in real stock prices.

The before-tax rate of return on nonfinancial corporate capital (BTROR) is defined here as the ratio of profits plus net interest paid to the replacement cost of the nonfinancial corporate stock. The after-tax rate of return (ATROR) is similarly defined but with corporate income taxes subtracted from the numerator. The profits in both measures are adjusted for the effect of inflation on inventory and depreciation charges.[20]

Chart 3 plots the BTROR and the ATROR for the last 30 years. The series follow a similar pattern, peaking in 1965 and dropping sharply to lower levels thereafter. Since the difference between the two measures, which reflects corporate income taxes, narrowed over the whole period, it would seem that inflation has not raised the tax burden on capital. However, the impression from Chart 3 may be misleading since other factors, such as fluctuations in the economy, also affect tax liabilities.

To isolate the effect of inflation on the rates of return, a model was estimated in which the rate of return depends on inflation and the level of economic activity as measured by the percentage gap of actual real GNP from full employment real GNP.[21] As expected, both the BTROR and the ATROR were found to be sensitive to movements in the real economy with the before-tax rate falling about 0.30 percent and the after-tax return about 0.17 percent for every 1.00 percent rise in the GNP gap. The estimated impacts of inflation on the rates of return give weak support for the tax effects theory. No statistically significant relationship was found between the BTROR and inflation, but inflation was found to have a negative effect on the ATROR, although the level of statistical significance is

CHART 3
Before and After-Tax Returns on Corporate Capital

somewhat low. While the results are consistent with the tax effects view, the estimated reduction in the ATROR is only 0.1 percent for a 1.0 percent rise in inflation. Since the ATROR has fallen about three percentage points since 1965, while inflation has risen about eight percentage points, inflation accounts for only 0.8 percentage points of the drop in the ATROR.[22]

Gains from Debt.   To evaluate the proposition that inflation causes investors to underestimate the returns on equity by ignoring the gains from debt, it is necessary to look at the rate of return on stockholders' equity, with and without these gains. The rate on stockholders' equity is defined as adjusted profits divided by the net worth of the corporation (the replacement cost of the capital stock less the value of net debt). Chart 4 gives two measures of the return on equity. One is the after-tax return (ATROE), which includes an adjustment of profits for the effects of inflation on inventory and depreciation charges but ignores gains from debt due to inflation. The other measure is the after-tax rate of return (ATROED), which includes gains from debt. The latter measure assumes investors make all relevant adjustments for inflation while the former assumes that investors do not recognize the full effects of inflation on corporate earnings.

As Chart 4 illustrates, the ATROE has fallen dramatically to less than half its 1965 peak. The ATROED has also decreased substantially, but the drop is about 25 to 30 percent from the peak return. To assess the contribution of inflation to these decreases, the same model employed above for the return on capital was estimated.[23] While both measures of the return on equity fall significantly when the economy weakens, the impact of inflation on these returns differs. As pre-

CHART 4
Rates of Return on Stockholders' Equity

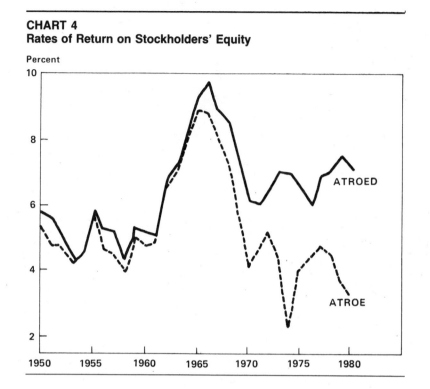

dicted by the tax effects theory, inflation has a negative effect on the ATROE, similar to that found above for the ATROR. The ATROED, however, is positively related to inflation, which suggests that the benefits inflation produces by reducing real debt outweigh the costs coming from higher taxes. If investors ignore these benefits, inflation does appear to decrease the return on equity, although the size of this effect can account for only a small portion of the observed total decline.

To sum up, the rate of return on both corporate capital and stockholders' equity was substantially lower in the 1970s compared with the mid-1960s. The poor performance of capital does not, however, appear to be due primarily to inflation, since empirical evidence indicates that the tax effects hypothesis cannot account for most of the fall in the after-tax return on capital. The fall in the return on stockholders' equity, the return relevant to the determination of stock prices, can account for a little over one half of the decrease in real stock prices, but this lower rate of return cannot be attributed to inflation if investors correctly compute this return.[24]

The Required Rate of Return on Stocks and Inflation

The analysis above suggests that inflation has not caused real stock prices to fall by lowering the return on equity if shareholders include the gains from debt in this return. Nevertheless, inflation may have depressed real share prices by increasing the required rate of return on stocks. This argument is supported by the pattern of the earnings-price ratio given in Chart 5. As discussed in the beginning of the

CHART 5
Earnings-Price Ratio and Inflation

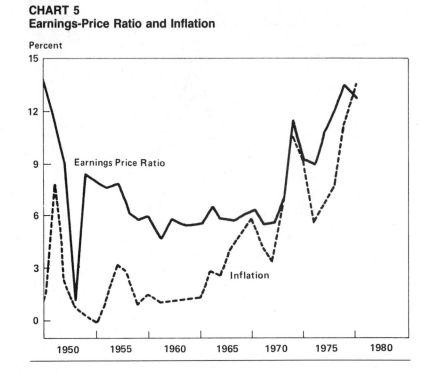

paper, if inflation does not raise the required rate of return on stocks, earnings and the price of stocks should both rise at the inflation rate, leaving the earnings-price ratio unaffected. However, as Chart 5 illustrates, the earnings-price ratio for the S & P 500 rose substantially as inflation worsened.[25] Assuming that the gains from debt are taken into account by investors, the required rate of return on stocks has increased. This section considers evidence on the three alternative factors mentioned earlier by which inflation may have caused a rise in the required rate: higher returns on alternative assets, higher perceived risk on stock returns, and the incorrect use of the nominal interest rate to discount real earnings.

Return on Alternative Assets.   Because fixed-income financial assets exhibited negative real returns over the last 15 years, they seem unlikely candidates for attracting investors away from stocks.[26] A more plausible possibility is owner-occupied housing. Imputed nominal rents rise with inflation but are untaxed, and the tax liability on nominal capital gains can generally be avoided. Hence, inflation should increase the relative return to houses, and investors should react to higher inflation by bidding up housing prices. It has been estimated that the escalating inflation rate of the 1970s reduced the real rental cost of owner-occupied housing to close to zero for higher-income families and that much of the fall in real stock prices can be attributed to investors reacting to this low real cost of housing by diverting funds from the stock market to the housing market.[27] Additional support for this view comes from the finding that the return to housing, unlike that for corporate equity, rises with expected inflation.[28] This hypothesis is also consistent with the rise in the median price of existing homes by 9.8 percent

TABLE 3
Variability of Profits and Macroeconomic Activity

Variable	Standard Deviations* of Time Period					
	1951–55	1956–60	1961–65	1966–70	1971–75	1976–80
Percentage change in real book profits	20.5	16.3	8.5	9.9	12.5	11.2
Percentage change in adjusted real profits (IVA + CCA)	20.1	19.9	9.8	11.8	39.9	15.1
Percentage change in adjusted real profits including gains from debt	21.3	17.9	11.7	9.8	11.4	11.1
Percentage growth in real GNP	3.6	2.3	1.4	2.3	3.3	2.4
Inflation (CPI)	3.3	1.0	0.2	1.4	3.3	3.3

* Standard deviation for a variable x is defined as:

$$S.D. = \left[\frac{1}{n-1} \sum_{i=1}^{n} (x - \bar{x})^2 \right]^{1/2}$$

where n = number of observations
$\bar{x}$ = arithmetic mean of x.

per year for the 1969–80 period—over 2.0 percent more than inflation—which occurred while stock prices fell relative to the general price level.

Greater Risk. The second factor which may have raised the required rate of return on stocks is higher perceived risk. If corporate profits are less predictable in an inflationary environment, risk-averse wealthholders will place a lower value on them. Past work has found a statistically significant negative effect of risk on the market value of firms, although the size of the effect was generally small.[29]

Was the decade of the 1970s a period of increasing risk to investment in corporate capital? One traditional measure of risk is the actual variability experienced. Table 3 reports one gauge of variation: the standard deviation for the annual growth rates of three real profit measures, real GNP, and the CPI for five-year intervals, 1951–80. These data indicate that variation in these variables generally declined over the first 15 years and then rose again over the last 15. However, the only dramatic rise in variability of profits was for adjusted profits excluding gains from debt for the 1971–75 interval. Moreover, the last half of the 1970s exhibited less variability than the first half, and yet real stock prices continued to fall. Thus, these data suggest that rising variability in the economy may have contributed to lowering real share values, but it cannot be the whole story.

On the other hand, actual variability may be a poor measure of perceived risk. Another suggested measure of the change in risk is the differential between medium-grade bonds and U.S. government bonds.[30] More uncertainty about corporate earnings is expected to raise this differential, which has grown substantially from an average of just under 1.00 percent for 1951–65 to about 1.65 percent for 1966–80. If higher expected inflation is an important contributor to higher risk, the interest differential should be positively related to expected inflation. This proposition is supported by the data, using lagged inflation to proxy expected inflation, with a one percentage point increase in expected inflation being associated with an increased differential of about 0.16 percentage points.[31] While this evidence is supportive of the risk hypothesis, the differential, while higher in the 1970s, does not trend upward and thus cannot explain the downward trend in real share prices.

Incorrect Discount Rate.   A third possible reason for a higher required rate is the comparison by investors of the earnings-price ratio with the current nominal interest rate on bonds. Since the correct comparison is with the real interest rate, use of the nominal interest rate, which rises roughly with inflation, means stock prices have to fall steeply, relative to earnings, in order for the earnings-price ratio to rise.

This hypothesis is difficult to test directly. One study of it employed a model in which stock prices depended mainly on expected earnings and the real interest rate.[32] The latter variable was measured by the nominal interest rate and expected inflation proxied by lagged inflation. Accordingly, if investors did not suffer from money illusion and thus used the real interest rate to discount real earnings, the coefficients on the nominal interest rate and expected inflation should have summed to zero. However, it was found that the coefficient on expected inflation was negative in sign and statistically insignificant from zero, which was interpreted as evidence of money illusion. Other investigators reported results which also can be construed as consistent with this view. It has been calculated that the discount rate required to equate the present value of future earnings to the market value of firms roughly doubled from 1968 to 1977.[33] This latter result is also consistent with rising risk. The unanswered question is why investors would confuse nominal and real rates of return. Since evidence suggests that bondholders demand compensation for inflation and households see the inflation-induced benefits of homeownership, it is puzzling why investors would be confused by inflation only in the stockmarket.[34]

SUMMARY AND CONCLUSIONS

Over the last 15 years, the real value of common stock has fallen about 50 percent, coincident with a generally rising inflation rate. If inflation is to blame for the dismal performance of stocks, then it must reduce expected real corporate profits or raise the required rate of return on stocks, according to the traditional model of stock prices. This paper has examined several arguments as to why inflation may have had these consequences.

One prominent theory asserts that inflation reduces expected profits by raising the real tax burden on corporate earnings through nonindexation of inventory and depreciation charges. An alternative proposal is that inflation confuses investors, causing them to undervalue corporate profits by failing to take account of the inflation-induced fall in the real debt of corporations. On the other hand, it has been argued that inflation may have increased the required rate of return on stock by missing the return on owner-occupied housing, by creating more uncertainty about corporate profits, or by misleading investors into using too high a discount rate.

The analysis of this article indicates that the crucial issue is whether investors take into account the gains from debt which accrue to corporations when inflation occurs. The rate of return on stockholder equity when these gains are ignored has dropped by about half since the mid-1960s, consistent with the belief that lower stock prices reflect lower earnings. However, this decline in returns seems to have been due primarily to the low return on corporate capital, before as well as after taxes, reflecting perhaps the rise in energy costs and regulatory activity which characterized the period. Rising real tax burdens on corporate capital could not account for this fall in the rate of return.

Assuming investors correctly include the gains from debt when estimating corporate profits, the fall in real stock prices was caused in part by a higher rate of return required by stockholders. This conclusion is supported by the observed rise in the earnings-price ratio. Evidence indicates that inflation has been an important determinant of the increase in the required rate by producing large returns on homeownership, by increasing the perceived risk attached to stock, and by deceiving stockholders into using the nominal rather than the real interest rate to discount earnings. Thus, while inflation cannot account for all of the decrease in real stock prices which has occurred in the last 15 years, it has been a significant factor in the decline.

APPENDIX

TABLE A
Estimated Rate of Return Equations: 1951–1980 (rate of return measure)

	BTROR	ATROR	ATROE	ATROED
Constant	.102	.040	.046	.034
	(10.623)	(6.130)	(4.442)	(4.380)
PCGAP	−.338	−.149	−.153	−.228
	(−4.149)	(−2.683)	(−2.228)	(−4.856)
Inflation	−0.43	−.100	−.173	.123
	(−.460)	(−1.556)	(−2.177)	(2.255)
Time	.0007	.002	.002	.003
	(.793)	(3.171)	(1.900)	(3.959)
Time · D66	−.002	−.003	−.003	−.004
	(−1.15)	(−2.217)	(−1.767)	(−3.037)
D66	.019	.034	.045	.055
	(.809)	(1.836)	(1.599)	(2.665)
R^2	.582	.534	.509	.623
SEE	.0087	.0059	.0074	.0051
DW	1.80	1.87	1.83	1.63
p	.541	.548	.685	.725

Notes: PCGAP = (Full employment real GNP-actual real GNP)/Actual real GNP
Inflation = Rate of change in the CPI
Time = time trend with 1951 = 1
D66 = 0 for 1951–65
1 for 1966–80
SEE = standard error of estimate
DW = Durbin-Watson statistic
p = estimated autocorrelation coefficient

NOTES

[1] Studies reporting a negative relationship between returns and inflation include John Lintner, "Inflation and Common Stock Prices in a Cyclical Context." *NBER 53rd Annual Report,* September 1973; Zvi Brodie, "Common Stocks as a Hedge Against Inflation, *Journal of Finance,* May 1976, pp. 459–70; Jeffrey F. Jaffe and Gershon Mandelker, "The 'Fisher Effect' for Risky Assets: An Empirical Investigation." *Journal of Finance,* May 1976, pp. 447–58; Charles R. Nelson, "Inflation and Rates of

Return on Common Stocks," *Journal of Finance,* May 1976, pp. 471–83; and Eugene F. Fama and G. William Schwert, "Asset Returns and Inflation," *Journal of Financial Economics,* November 1977, pp. 115–46.

[2] For a detailed discussion of the stock market and the economy, see Barry Bosworth, "The Stock Market and the Economy," *Brookings Papers on Economic Activity,* 1975:2, pp. 257–90.

[3] The role of wealth in the consumption function is stressed in the influential life-cycle hypothesis of saving. See Franco Modigliani and Richard Brumberg, "Utility Analysis and the Consumption Function," in *Post-Keynesian Economics,* ed. Kenneth K. Kurihara (New Brunswick, N.J.: Rutgers University Press, 1954), and Albert Ando and Franco Modigliani, "The 'Life Cycle' Hypothesis of Savings: Aggregate Implications and Tests," *American Economic Review,* March 1963, pp. 55–84.

[4] James Tobin has emphasized the ratio of the market value of a firm to the replacement cost of its capital stock, the q ratio, as the primary determinant of investment spending. See James Tobin, "A General Equilibrium Approach to Monetary Theory," *Journal of Money, Credit, and Banking,* February 1969, pp. 15–29. A more recent paper, which finds that a model emphasizing stock prices yielded forecasts superior to those from several alternative frameworks, is Robert F. Engle and Duncan K. Foley, "An Asset Price Model of Aggregate Investment," *International Economic Review,* October 1975, pp. 625–47.

[5] The present value model for share prices is generally associated with John Burr Williams, *The Theory of Investment Value* (Cambridge: Harvard University Press, 1938). The general expression for the present value of dividends is:

$$S_t = \sum_{i=0}^{\overline{}} \frac{D_{t+1}^e}{(1+r)^{i+1}}$$

which can be expressed as equation (1) when all dividends are assumed to be equal.

[6] If D^e is constant

$$\text{Stock yield } t = \frac{D^e + \dfrac{D^e}{r}}{\dfrac{D^e}{r}} - 1$$

$$= r$$

[7] To see this result, note that:

$$S_0 = \frac{D^e(1+p)}{(1+r)(1+p)} + \frac{D^e(1+p)^2}{(1+r)^2(1+p)^2} + \cdots$$

and

$$S_1 = \frac{D^e(1+p)^2}{(1+r)(1+p)} + \frac{D^e(1+p)^3}{(1+r)^2(1+p)^2} + \cdots$$

thus

$$S^1 = (1+p)S_0 = \frac{(1+p)D^e}{r}$$

A similar development would show $S_2 = (1+p)^2 S_0$ and so on.

[8] The actual nominal yield is $r + p + rp$, but the last term is generally negligible.

[9] For a more detailed discussion of this argument, see Lintner. Support for the hypothesis that inflation raised the stock prices of net debtor firms was found by Reuben A. Kessel, "Inflation-Caused Wealth Redistribution. A Test of a Hypothesis," *American Economic Review,* March 1956, pp. 128–41.

[10] John Maynard Keynes, *The General Theory of Employment, Interest and Money* (New York: Harcourt Brace Jovanovich, 1936), p. 152.

[11] For recent applications of this model, see Roger E. Brinner and Stephen H. Brooks, "Stock Prices," in *How Taxes Affect Behavior,* eds. Henry J. Aaron and Joseph A. Pechman (Washington, D.C.: Brookings Institution, 1981); and William C. Brainard, John B. Shoven, and Laurence Weiss, "The Financial Valuation of the Return to Capital," *Brookings Papers on Economic Activity,* 1980:2, pp. 453–502. For critiques of the model based on its apparent inability to account for the volatility of stock prices, see Stephen F. LeRoy and Richard D. Porter, "The Present Value Relation: Tests Based on Implied Variance Bounds," *Econometrica,* May 1981, pp. 555–74; and Robert J. Shiller, "Do Stock Prices Move too Much to be Justified by Subsequent Changes in Dividends?" *American Economic Review,* June 1981, pp. 421–36.

[12] A recent paper by Eugene F. Fama, "Stock Returns, Real Activity, Inflation and Money," *American Economic Review,* September 1981, pp. 545–54, gives a fourth explanation for the negative correlation between stock returns and inflation. Fama argues that this finding is really the result of omitting the effects of real activity from the analysis. He contends that stock returns are positively related to expected real activity, while inflation is negatively related to expected real activity. This

produces the negative contemporaneous correlation between stock returns and inflation. A key assumption of his model, which many analysts may question, is that commodity prices are flexible enough to keep the money market in equilibrium even when the period of analysis is monthly.

- [13] Richard Kopcke, "Are Stocks a Bargain?" *New England Economic Review*, May–June 1979, pp. 5–24; and Martin Feldstein, "Inflation and the Stock Market," *American Economic Review*, December 1980, pp. 839–47.

[14] Firms could reduce their tax liability (assuming inflation continues) by switching to the last-in, first-out (LIFO) method, yet only about one quarter of inventories were under LIFO accounting in 1977. See Martha S. Scanlon, "Postwar Trends in Corporate Rates of Return," in *Public Policy and Capital Formation*, Board of Governors of the Federal Reserve System, 1981, pp. 75–87.

[15] The money illusion argument is made by Franco Modigliani and Richard A. Cohn, "Inflation, Rational Valuation and the Market," *Financial Analysts Journal*, March–April 1979, pp. 24–44.

[16] Patric H. Hendershott and Sheng Cheng Hu, "Inflation and Extraordinary Returns on Owner-Occupied Housing: Some Implications for Capital Allocation and Productivity Growth," *Journal of Macroeconomics*, Spring 1981, pp. 177–203; and Lawrence H. Summers, "Inflation, the Stock Market and Owner-Occupied Housing," *American Economic Review*, May 1981, pp. 429–34.

[17] See Burton G. Malkiel, "The Capital Formation Problem in the United States," *Journal of Finance*, May 1979, pp. 291–306. Increased risk has also been emphasized by William Fellner, "Corporate Asset-Liability Decisions in View of the Low Market Valuation of Equity," in *Contemporary Economic Problems 1980* (Washington, D.C.: American Enterprise Institute, 1980).

[18] For a review of this literature, see John B. Taylor, "On the Relation Between the Variability of Inflation and the Average Inflation Rate," in *The Costs and Consequences of Inflation*, Carnegie-Rochester Conference Series on Public Policy, eds. Karl Brunner and Allan H. Meltzer (Amsterdam, Netherlands: North-Holland, 1981).

[19] This is the second part of the money illusion theory of Modigliani and Cohn.

[20] The correction for the understatement of inventory costs is the inventory valuation adjustment (IVA), which essentially removes the distortion arising from firms using FIFO accounting. The impact of inflation on depreciation allowances is measured by the capital consumption adjustment (CCA), which converts reported depreciation into true depreciation by taking into account both the accelerated depreciation allowed by tax laws, which overstates depreciation, and the difference between replacement cost and historic cost. For a detailed discussion of these adjustments, see John B. Shoven and Jeremy I. Bulow, "Inflation Accounting and Nonfinancial Corporate Profits: Physical Assets," *Brookings Papers on Economic Activity*, 1975:3, pp. 557–98; and Philip Cagan and Robert E. Lipsey, *The Financial Effects of Inflation*, National Bureau of Economic Research (Cambridge, Mass.: Ballinger, 1978).

[21] The estimated models are reported in Table A of the Appendix. The models allow for the intercept and time trend to differ for 1951–65 and 1966–80, following the study by Richard W. Kopcke, "The Decline in Corporate Profitability," *New England Economic Review*, May–June 1978, pp. 36–60.

[22] Nicholas J. Gonedes also found little support for the tax effects hypothesis. See his "Evidence on the 'Tax Effects' of Inflation under Historical Cost Accounting Methods," *Journal of Business*, April 1981, pp. 227–70.

[23] The estimated models are given in Table A of the Appendix.

[24] A major negative effect of inflation is found by Richard Kopcke, "Are Stocks a Bargain?" while a smaller impact is reported by Marcelle Arak, "Inflation and Stock Values: Is our Tax Structure the Villain?" *Quarterly Review*, Federal Reserve Bank of New York, Winter 1980–81, pp. 3–13.

[25] Since the earnings figure in this ratio is reported after-tax profits unadjusted for any effects of inflation, the higher ratios may have resulted from investors correcting these earnings for inflation distortions. This conjecture is not supported by a comparison of reported earnings to earnings, which incorporate the IVA, CCA, and gains from debt, since the two series move together quite closely, generally differing by less than $5 billion in the post-1965 period. In those years, when the difference was greater, adjusted profits were greater than book profits, so earnings-price ratios should have fallen rather than increased.

[26] From 1966 to 1980, the real yield on U.S. government long-term bonds was −4.3 percent, while U.S. Treasury bills had a real yield of −0.5 percent. R. G. Ibbotson and R. A. Sinquefield, *Stocks, Bonds, Bills, and Inflation: Historical Returns (1926–1978)*, Financial Analysts Foundation, 1979.

[27] See Hendershott and Hu.

[28] See Summers.

[29] Brainard, Shoven, and Weiss.

[30] Malkiel. The use by Malkiel of a bond series which included low-yielding "flower" bonds was criticized by Patric H. Hendershott, "The Decline in Aggregate Share Values: Taxation, Valuation Errors, Risk, and Profitability," *American Economic Review,* December 1981, pp. 909–22.

[31] The estimated relationship was:

$$\text{Interest differential } t = 0.077 + 0.156\, I_{t-1}$$
$$\qquad\qquad\qquad (4.633)\quad (5.978)$$

$$R^2 = 0.59 \qquad SEE = 0.0028 \qquad DW = 1.82 \qquad \hat{p} = 0.554$$

Time period 1954–1980 annual observations

where I_{t-1} = inflation rate lagged one period

p = estimated autocorrelation coefficient

t-statistics in parentheses.

Additional lagged inflation rates do not alter the results.

[32] Modigliani and Cohn. For an alternative explanation of these results, namely, that the lagged inflation rates are an inadequate proxy for expected inflation and are really picking up the negative tax effects of inflation, see Arak.

[33] Brainard, Shoven, and Weiss.

[34] Hendershott, "The Decline in Aggregate Share Values," argues that the inflation illusion argument of Modigliani and Cohn implies lower nominal interest rates when inflation occurs, rather than lower share values, an implication which does not accord with experience.

16

When Is the Prime Rate Second Choice?

Brian C. Gendreau

Not long ago, little controversy surrounded the prime rate convention. The prime rate was understood to be the rate banks charged on loans to their most creditworthy corporate customers. Other corporate borrowers paid a rate marked up over the prime. Though prime-related loans were generally floating-rate loans—such that borrowers' loan rates changed with the prime—the prime rate usually rose and fell gradually, giving customers a measure of stability in their borrowing costs.

Banks still post prime rates, and changes in the prime continue to be reported on national newscasts and greeted by bursts of trading activity in securities markets. But now the prime seems to change faster in response to market interest rate movements. Moreover, many loans are being made at rates below the prime. According to a Federal Reserve Board survey of the terms of all short-term business loans granted by 48 of the nation's largest banks, in the first week of November 1982, over 92 percent were at rates below the prime.

Consequently, many commentators now doubt that the prime is a useful benchmark loan rate. After the staff of the House Banking Committee studied lending practices at 10 large banks in early 1981, chairman Ferdinand St Germain concluded that "the prime rate has been so often misused, abused, and tortured in recent years that the phrase now seems beyond repair." Secretary of the Treasury Donald Regan concurs that the prime rate no longer reflects loan costs accurately, and recently proposed creating in its stead a "watch rate" set at half a percentage point above the commercial paper rate—the interest rate firms pay on short-term notes sold in money markets. Why have bank lending practices changed? What kinds of loans are being made below prime? What does the prime rate mean today? The answers depend in part on the characteristics of the prime, and especially on the manner in which prime rate changes are determined.

From *Business Review,* Federal Reserve Bank of Philadelphia, May/June 1983, pp. 13–23.

Brian C. Gendreau is an associate economist in the banking section of the research department of the Federal Reserve Bank of Philadelphia.

THE PRIME: A CURIOUSLY STICKY RATE

Popular definitions of the prime rate usually distinguish it from other rates by the credit quality of the underlying loan. The prime rate also differs importantly from other interest rates, however, in the way it reacts to changes in credit market conditions. While rates on money market instruments, such as Treasury bills and commercial paper, change with trading throughout each day, the prime rate changes less frequently. In past years, when interest rates were more stable, the prime rate did not change for months or even years on end. Now the prime rate changes more often, but it still lags changes in market rates.

The stickiness in the prime rate is easily seen in Figure 1, which compares the movements of the prime rate, the three-month commercial paper rate, and their difference from 1972 through 1982. The prime rate adjusts fully to short-term interest rate movements, but only after a substantial lag. When short-term rates rise, the prime rate initially does not keep pace, and the spread between the prime and short-term rates narrows and occasionally becomes negative. Conversely, when interest rates fall, the prime rate lags behind, and the spread between the prime and market rates widens appreciably.

The stickiness in the prime rate can be traced to a corresponding stickiness in banks' cost of attracting new funds from so-called *core deposits*—demand deposits and those time deposits subject to binding interest rate ceilings. Since Congress prohibited the payment of interest on demand deposits and authorized the Federal Reserve to limit the rates paid on time deposits in the Banking Act of 1933, banks have competed for core deposits by paying implicit interest in the form of services provided below cost. These services, which are provided on core deposits to this

FIGURE 1
The Prime Rate Responds Slowly to Changes in Market Interest Rates

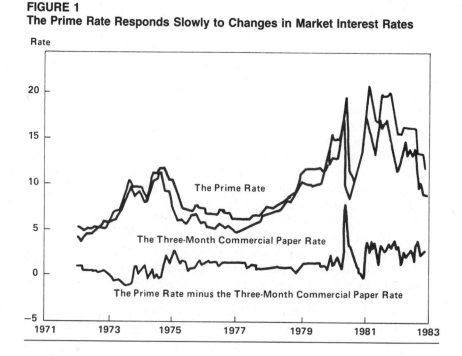

NONRATE COMPETITION AND THE PRIME

An industry-wide prime rate first emerged in 1934, shortly after Congress prohibited the payment of interest on demand deposits. Banks having suffered three consecutive years of losses (in the aggregate) by 1934, welcomed the legal restrictions against deposit rate competition and began to compete for deposits by paying implicit interest in services, as they do to this day. The timing of the inception of the prime rate suggests that the prime is closely connected to nonrate deposit competition. But why would banks prefer nonrate to rate competition? And how is the prime linked to nonrate competition?

When banks engage in interest rate competition for deposits, they must pay the competitive rate on all deposits. This rate is highly visible, and can be compared with other banks' rates with ease. In contrast, with nonrate competition customers must undertake a costly search among banks to find the best loan and deposit service bundles. Once interest rate competition is prohibited, banks can take advantage of the imperfect information customers have about each other's services to reduce services below the competitive level. Moreover, by competing for deposits with services banks are able to reduce their costs by offering less in services to customers who are relatively insensitive to the return on their deposits than to more return-sensitive customers.

The prime rate is connected with nonrate deposit competition because many bank depositors are also borrowers. The most effective way to pay implicit interest to depositor-borrower customers is through loan rate concessions. Widespread loan rate concessions, however, would have wiped out the benefits of nonrate competition provided by deposit rate ceilings. Hence banks attempted to preserve nonrate competition by adopting a uniform rate for loans to their best customers—the prime rate—that served as a floor rate for industry-wide loan pricing.

---

day, include check clearing, gifts, the convenience of a multitude of bank branches, extended hours, credit lines, and, for firms, payroll and cash management systems (see Nonrate Competition and the Prime).

Banks Adjust Implicit Deposit Rates Slowly . . .

When interest rates are low and stable, banks have little difficulty in attracting core deposits by paying implicit interest. But when interest rates move higher and become more variable, bank deposit and loan pricing becomes more complicated. The problem is that implicit interest payments cannot be changed quickly in response to interest rate movements. It takes time to build new branches, to run or pull advertising campaigns, to mail out notices of changes in service charges (and to decide to do these things). Banks cannot hope to match frequent fluctuations in short-term interest rates with costly, cumbersome changes in services. Nonetheless, banks that fail to adjust their implicit interest payments to meet a permanent change in market rates risk losing customers.

FIGURE 2
Estimates of the Implicit Interest on Demand Deposits

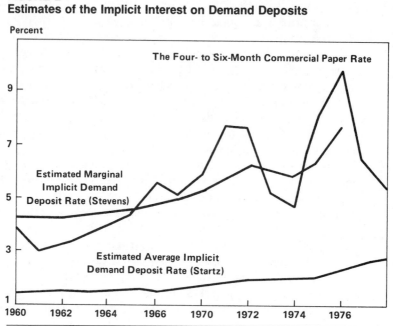

Unable to change services quickly, yet compelled by competition to match eventually a sustained change in market rates, banks have little choice but to adjust implicit interest payments gradually to changes in market interest rates. Economists' estimates of the implicit interest rates paid by banks are consistent with this kind of rate setting behavior. Two estimated implicit interest rate series are presented in Figure 2. These estimates show that implicit rates respond to changes in market rates, but do not adjust on a one-to-one basis with changes in current period, short-term interest rates.[1]

. . . Making the Prime Rate Sticky

In seeking to maximize profits, banks adjust their loan rates to reflect changes in their costs in raising new funds. As long as some of these funds are obtained by paying implicit interest on core deposits, banks' costs in attracting additional funds will change only gradually in response to market rate movements. Since loans are priced as a markup over these costs, loan rates will also change gradually.[2]

In the process of adjusting their loan rates, banks use the prime rate as an industry-wide pricing guide. Because there is no objective indicator of when bank costs have changed permanently, banks are likely to disagree over when the prime rate should change. But once a large money center bank has signaled its judgment that a given level of interest rates will be sustained by changing its prime rate, and other banks have ratified that change, a new guideline exists for loan pricing.

WHY IS THE PRIME RATE CONVENTION CHANGING?

Throughout the postwar period, the critical ingredient in banks' slow deposit and loan rate adjustment was their ability to attract core deposits when market rates were rising relative to implicit interest rates, and to retain loan customers when money market rates were falling relative to the prime rate. Though banks could not adjust services quickly to short-term interest rate fluctuations, they did attempt to attract deposits by offering a stable level of services that was attractive, on average, over the interest rate cycle. In some periods—particularly when interest rates were rising—implicit interest rates on core deposits fell below short-term market rates. But in periods of falling interest rates, implicit interest payments remained high relative to short-term money market returns.[3] Similarly, because the stickiness in implicit deposit rates was reflected in the prime, banks gave prime borrowers rates that were competitive with market rates, on average, over the interest rate cycle; borrowers' relatively high bank loan rates in periods of falling market rates were followed by comparatively low loan rates in periods of rising market rates.

When interest rates were low and stable, banks' strategy of competing for customers by offering deposit and loan products that were attractive on average relative to market rates was successful. Temporarily uncompetitive rates relative to market rates on bank deposits or loans were likely to be offset by more than competitive rates in the future, and the differences were not large enough to customers to search for more attractive rates in money markets.

Volatile Interest Rates Brought Competition from Money Markets

As interest rate swings became sharper and wider in the 1970s, however, more and more customers became dissatisfied with the slow rate adjustment on core deposits and on prime-related loans. Increasingly, customers bypassed banks to borrow and lend directly in money markets.

On the deposit side, customers shifted out of core deposits into money market instruments, such as commercial paper, with each big swing in short-term market rates above the implicit deposit rate. These shifts can be seen in Figure 3, where the ratio of commercial paper to demand deposits outstanding together with the spread between the four-to-six month commercial paper rate and estimates of the implicit rate paid on demand deposits have been graphed from 1960 to 1976. Initially, most of these shifts were by corporations. The rapid growth of money market mutual funds after the mid-1970s, however, facilitated households' shifts out of core deposits by opening the money markets to small investors previously unable to buy large denomination financial instruments. Once investors overcame costs involved in placing their funds in money markets, they never went back to holding as much of their assets in the form of core deposits, as reflected in the steady decline in the share of core deposits among large bank liabilities visible in Figure 4.

On the loan side, the sluggish prime and the commercial paper rate widened to several hundred basis points during declines in market rates in the 1970s and 1980s, motivating large firms to incur the start-up costs necessary to tap the money markets. About 500 new companies began to issue commercial paper in the

FIGURE 3
Favorable Returns Have Encouraged the Growth of Commercial Paper Relative to Demand deposits.

Percent

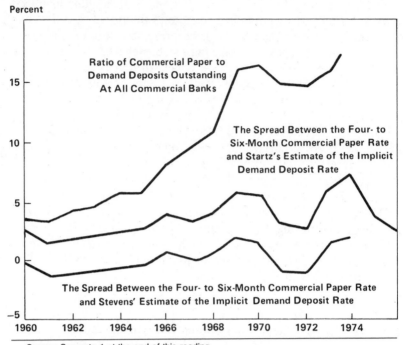

Source: See note 1 at the end of this reading.

FIGURE 4
Demand and Savings Deposits Have Fallen Relative to Interest-Sensitive Funds in Large Banks' Liabilities (percent of total liabilities)

Date	Demand and savings deposits	Interest-sensitive funds[a]	Other liabilities
1972	52.3	28.8	18.9
1973	45.9	38.3	15.8
1974	40.9	45.3	13.8
1975	41.7	44.1	14.2
1976	46.7	39.0	14.3
1977	45.4	40.0	14.6
1978	42.3	43.7	14.0
1979	39.1	47.2	13.7
1980	36.1	48.2	15.7
1981	33.1	50.9	16.0
1982	28.6	53.8	17.6

Note: data are for Large Weekly Reporting Banks with assets of $2 billion or more in 1972 dollars as of June of each year.
  [a] Interest-sensitive funds are defined as the sum of federal funds purchased, time deposits in accounts of $100,000 or more, and other borrowings (including liabilities to foreign branches as a proxy for Eurodollar borrowings).
  Source: Weekly Report of Assets and Liabilities for Large Banks, Board of Governors, Federal Reserve System.

years after 1974, boosting the amount of paper outstanding in that market from $50 billion in 1974 to almost $180 billion by mid-year 1982.[4]

Banks Responded by Moving towards Market Rate Pricing

To replace the core deposits that could no longer be relied upon as their principal source of loanable funds, banks issued liabilities carrying market rates of interest such as domestic and Eurodollar certificates of deposit (CD's), money market certificates, and federal funds. By 1981, large banks were raising more than half their funds from interest-sensitive liabilities. As banks attracted fewer funds from the core deposits that were responsible for the sluggishness in deposit costs, they changed their loan rates faster in response to fluctuations in market interest rates. The average lag in the response of the prime rate to money market rates fell markedly between 1970 and 1982, from over eight weeks in the early 1970s to slightly over four weeks in the 1979–82 period (see the Technical Appendix).

In addition to speeding up the pace of prime rate changes, banks hastened their move towards market rate loan pricing by offering loans tied to money market rates to customers with the ability to draw on the commercial paper market. These new loans—called money market loans—are typically for short maturities (one month or less), and are matched by the bank to the size, rate, and maturity of a specific liability. A bank may, for example, issue a 30-day CD and use the funds to make a 30-day loan to a customer at a fixed rate over the CD rate. By matching the loan to a specific liability with the same maturity, bank earnings on the transaction are unaffected by interest-rate fluctuations over the life of the loan. When the loan matures, the liability matures, too, and a new transaction can be made at the new market rates.[5] Money market lending is often carried out in close cooperation with the bank's financial instrument trading desk to ensure that the pricing and maturity matching on the transaction are precise. Because the rate on money market loans must be close to money market rates to be competitive, bank profit margins are small, and large transactions are necessary to cover the costs of arranging the loan.

WHAT ACCOUNTS FOR BELOW–PRIME LENDING?

In experimenting with money market lending in recent years, banks have offered corporate customers with good credit standing a choice between a variety of short-term credits tied to money market rates as well as prime-related loans with longer maturities. Given the stickiness in the prime rate, it was inevitable that rates on short-term loans tied to money market rates would fall below the prime when interest rates declined. In those periods, firms tried to reduce their borrowing costs by taking fixed-rate, short-term credits instead of prime-related loans. The responsiveness of fixed-rate borrowing to the spread between the prime and the 30-day commercial paper rate can be seen in Figure 5. The peaks in the proportion of large loans made with fixed rates occurred when the commercial paper rate fell below the prime. The peaks in fixed-rate lending in Figure 5 also mark periods of widespread below-prime lending. In both the first weeks of May 1980 and November 1981, for example, the weighted average rate on all commercial loans at surveyed banks was below the ruling prime rate. In those weeks the prime rate was over 800 basis points and 330 basis points, respectively, above the 30-day commercial paper rate. Given these cost differences, it should not be

FIGURE 5
**Below-Prime Lending and Fixed-Rate Lending Varies with the Ratio
of the Prime to Money Market Rates**

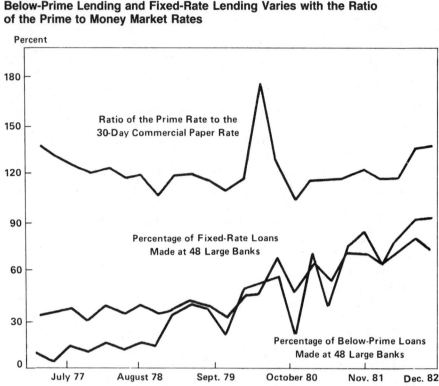

Source: *Federal Reserve Bulletin* and unpublished portions of the Survey of Terms of Bank Lending.

surprising that customers with the ability to take out loans at money market rates did so.

The recent episodes of fixed-rate lending and below-prime lending cannot be dismissed as mere aberrations from normal prime-related lending patterns. Since late 1979, as Figure 5 shows, a trend towards more below-prime lending developed at large banks, reflecting the trend toward more fixed-rate lending in large credits. Yet it would be premature to conclude that the prime rate is not more than an artifact of past lending practices. Assuming that the majority of floating-rate loans are prime-related, and that most large fixed-rate loans represent money market credits, Figure 5 shows that in many periods large banks make more floating-rate loans (in dollars of credit extended) than money market loans, and that even in periods of massive fixed-rate lending large banks still make some prime-related loans.[6] Data collected in the Federal Reserve's Survey of the Terms of Bank Lending indicate, moreover, that fixed-rate lending and below-prime lending are not as widespread at small and medium-sized banks as at large banks.

The reason prime-related loans coexist with money market loans is that not all loan customers can substitute money market loans for prime-related credits, and those who can do not find them to be perfect substitutes. Prime-related loans today, as in past years, are generally floating-rate loans, usually repaid in 60 to 90 days, that are used as working capital by businesses.[7] A firm will not substitute money market loans or commercial paper for prime-related loans if its funding needs are small, because only large money market credits and commercial paper issues will overcome the fixed costs of going to the market. If a firm's credit is less than impeccable, it will not be able to sell its commercial paper, and it will have little power in bargaining for a money market loan from its bank. Even firms with funding needs and a credit standing allowing them to obtain money market loans will not always do so, because it is not always clear that a string of short-term credits at market rates will be less expensive than a single prime-related loan. If interest rates were to take an unexpected upturn over the firm's borrowing horizon, for example, the rate increases on market-related credits could outstrip the more slowly changing costs of prime-related credit.

For these reasons, small firms without access to the commercial paper market and larger firms with less than flawless credit are likely to find prime-related loans attractive. Large creditworthy firms, furthermore, can be expected to continue to bargain with banks for money market loans when interest rates are falling rapidly, and to try to switch back into prime-related loans when rates are rising or expected to remain unchanged.

CONCLUSIONS

The distinguishing feature of the prime rate has always been its stickiness in comparison with money market interest rates. The prime has never been closely related to any specific current short-term rates but instead has been priced as a markup over banks' cost of raising new funds from all sources. A substantial portion of these funds have been from deposits subject to interest rate ceilings, and have been paid for by banks with implicit interest in the form of services. Because these implicit interest payments were difficult and slow to adjust, banks' cost of funds, and hence their loan rates, were slow to adjust to fluctuations in market rates.

As interest rates became higher and more volatile in the past 15 years, the incentive for customers to bypass banks and borrow and lend directly in money markets strengthened. Banks responded by issuing liabilities carrying market rates of interest to finance their loans, by speeding up changes in the prime rate, and by offering customers loans with rates tied to the rates on money market instruments. Much of the below-prime lending in recent years occurred when the rates on these money market loans fell below the more slowly moving prime during a decline in interest rates.

With the advent of a large quantity of below-prime lending, the prime no longer represents the lowest rate at which banks are extending credit. But prime-related lending is far from gone. Firms without the credit standing or funding needs to tap money markets are likely to receive prime-related loans for some time in the future. And even those firms with the ability to issue their own paper in the market are likely to find prime-related loans attractive when interest rates are unchanged or rising.

As deposit-rate ceilings are phased out and demand and savings deposits are replaced by banks' new money market accounts, bank loan rates will move more closely with market rates. Banks and their customers are likely to find a reference rate for the cost of short-term credit like the prime useful in the future, but it will probably be a faster moving, more closely market-related rate than today's prime.

TECHNICAL APPENDIX: Has the Way the Prime Is Priced Changed?

Bankers' formulas for pricing loans and economists' models of setting loan rates are often based on regressions of the prime on current and past money market rates. These regressions contain estimates of the average lag of adjustments of the prime rate to market rates. By estimating these regressions over different periods and comparing the average lags, we can tell whether the speed of adjustment of the prime has changed over time.

Changes in the source of funds used to make loans in turn change the speed with which the prime adjusts to market rates. Consider, for example, the simple case of banks that raise in any period t, a portion α of their loanable funds from liabilities by paying a market rate of interest RCD_t and the rest $(1 - \alpha)$ from demand deposits by paying implicit interest in the form of services at the rate RDD_t. The banks will set their prime rate PR_t as a markup γ over the weighted cost of raising extra funds from both sources, as:

(1)
$$PR_t = \gamma + \alpha RCD_t + (1 - \alpha)RDD_t$$
$$0 \leq \gamma, 0 < \alpha < 1$$

If banks paid a competitive, market rate of interest at all times on demand deposits, then $RDD_t = RCD_t$, and the prime would be set simply as a markup on current market rates:

(2)
$$PR_t = \gamma + RCD_t$$

Banks, however, generally adjust the services they pay on demand deposits incompletely to changes in current market rates. The inability to adjust services quickly, uncertainty about whether market rate changes are permanent or transitory, and avoidance of interest-rate risk will contribute to a gradual adjustment of implicit interest rates to market rates. Assuming for expository purposes that all adjustment takes place within two periods, this process can be represented as:

(3)
$$RDD_t = \beta_1 RCD_t + \beta_2 RCD_{t-1}$$
$$0 < \beta_1 \beta_2 < 1$$

Substituting equation (3) into equation (1) gives an expression for the prime as a function of current and past market rates:

(4)
$$PR_t = \gamma + \theta_1 RCD_t + \theta_2 RCD_{t-1}$$

where: $\theta = (\alpha + \beta_1 - \alpha\beta_1)$

and $\theta_2 = (\beta_2 - \alpha\beta_2)$.

In equation (4) it is easy to see that as the proportion of funds from interest-sensitive liabilities α increases, current rates will get a larger weight in setting the prime. If all bank funds are interest sensitive ($\alpha = 1$), the prime rate will be a markup over current rates alone. If instead banks attract all their funds from demand deposits ($\alpha = 0$), the prime rate will be a markup of the relation of implicit interest rates to market rates as given in equation (3). Changes in the sources of bank funds should be reflected in different coefficient estimates over time in a regression of the prime against current and past market rates as specified in equation (4).

Adjustment Lag Estimates.   To measure the changes in the adjustment lag of the prime to market rates, the prime was regressed against a distributed lag of current and past three-month CD rates, using weekly data for each of the four three-year periods between November 4, 1970, and September 29, 1982. The three-month CD rate was taken to be representative of rates on banks' interest-sensitive liabilities. A geometrically declining pattern of weights extending indefinitely into the past was specified for each regression, under the assumption that banks place progressively less weight on market rates further in the past in setting the prime.[8] (Reasonable values of α and the β_1 coefficients in a regression of equation (4) with lags extending further into the past will produce a geometric lag distribution like the one used here in estimation.)

The estimated weights on the current and past CD rates from the regressions are shown in the following figure. The estimated average lag in adjustment of the prime rate to changes in CD rates has changed significantly over the four periods, and it has generally been getting shorter over time, as can be seen in the table. By these estimates, the prime was adjusted twice as fast over the 10/10/79 to 9/29/82 period as it was between 11/4/70 and 10/24/73. This quicker adjustment speed is

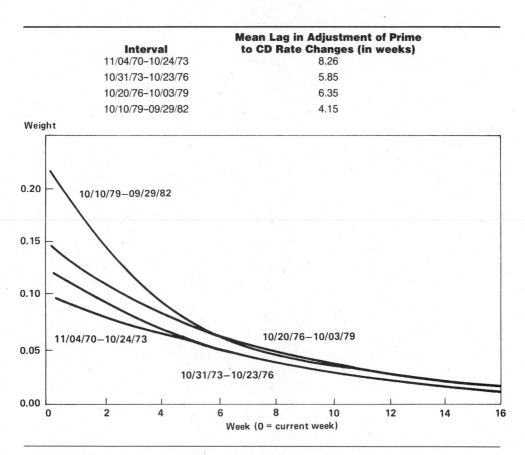

Interval	Mean Lag in Adjustment of Prime to CD Rate Changes (in weeks)
11/04/70–10/24/73	8.26
10/31/73–10/23/76	5.85
10/20/76–10/03/79	6.35
10/10/79–09/29/82	4.15

Weights are from regressions of the prime rate on an infinite geometric distributed lag of current and past three-month CD rates.

Estimated weights placed on current and past weeks' three-month CD rates by banks in setting the prime rate, 1970–82.

reflected in the visibly steeper pattern of estimated weights in the following figure, indicating that banks have placed heavier weights on current and recent weeks' CD rates in setting the prime in more recent years.[9]

NOTES

[1] See Richard Startz, "Implicit Interest on Demand Deposits," *Journal of Monetary Economics* 5 (1979), pp. 515–34, and Edward J. Stevens, "Measuring the Service Return on Demand Deposits," Federal Reserve Bank of Cleveland Working Paper no. 7601 (December 1976). Startz's series is an estimate of the average implicit interest rate paid on all demand deposits, and is available through 1976. Stevens' series is an estimate of the implicit rates paid to attract extra (marginal) demand deposits, calculated under the assumption of perfect competition, and is available through 1974.

[2] An added benefit to banks in making loan rates more in tandem with their costs of raising new funds from all sources is that by following such a strategy bank earnings will be unaffected by interest rate movements. Slow loan and deposit rate adjustment, moreover, is consistent with empirical evidence that, on the whole, bank profits are not very responsive to changes in market interest rates. See Mark J. Flannery, "How Do Changes in Market Interest Rates Affect Bank Profits?" *Business Review,* Federal Reserve Bank of Philadelphia, September–October 1980, pp. 13–22.

[3] Twice in the 1970s money market rates fell below passbook savings account rates. Because banks also paid implicit interest on savings deposits, these deposits must have been quite attractive to customers in these periods. For an analysis reconciling temporarily high core deposit costs with bank profit maximization, see Mark J. Flannery, "Retail Bank Deposits as Quasi-Fixed Factors of Production," *American Economic Review* 72, (June 1982), pp. 527–36.

[4] See Evelyn M. Hurley, "The Commercial Paper Market Since the Mid-Seventies," *Federal Reserve Bulletin,* June 1982.

[5] Not all money market loans are fixed-rate credits. Indeed, banks are now offering large customers an exotic variety of loans, pegged to different short-term rates and adjustable (repriced) at different intervals. For example, some banks are making five-day loans with rates pegged to the daily federal funds rate. Others are making one-year loans priced as a markup over the three-month Treasury bill rate, but repriced quarterly. These hybrid credits are likely close substitutes for and have rates highly correlated with those on the more numerous fixed-rate, short-term credits. No distinction is made in the text among the varieties of money market loans.

[6] No data are available on the quantities of prime-related and money market loans. Conversations with bankers, however, indicate that most floating-rate loans are tied to the prime rate. Though not all fixed-rate credits are short-term money market loans, the fixed-rate credits of $ 1 million or more graphed in Figure 5 generally had average maturities of one month or less, and thus may be considered money market loans.

[7] Prime-related loans are commonly made with a variety of fixed maturities, as well as on demand. A precise average maturity for prime-related loans thus cannot be provided. Survey data and conversations with bankers, though, indicate that 60 to 90 days is a reasonable approximation of the normal effective maturity of prime-related loans.

[8] The weights were estimated by applying a Koyck transformation to the geometric distributed lag relationship, regressing the prime rate on the prime rate lagged one week, and the current week's CD rate. For a discussion of the estimation of geometric distributed lag models, see Jan Kmenta, *Elements of Econometrics* (New York: Macmillan, 1971), pp. 474–75.

[9] For an alternative interpretation of regression of the prime rate on a distributed lag of current and past CD rates, in which the prime rate reflects the cost of previously issued but still outstanding CDs as well as current CD rates, see Michael A. Goldberg, "The Pricing of the Prime Rate," *Journal of Banking and Finance* 6 (June 1982), pp. 277–96. In Goldberg's study, the prime rate is linked to banks' average cost of funds, rather than their marginal cost of raising funds from all sources as described in the article.

PART FOUR

Instruments of the Money and Capital Markets

In the preceding parts of this book we have traced through the great changes in financial institutions and markets that have occurred in recent years. These changes reflect the powerful impact on the financial system of wide swings in economic conditions, the pressures of inflation and soaring production costs, the development of new technological methods to store and transfer financial information, and deregulation of the financial sector. Each of these powerful economic, technological, and regulatory trends has, in turn, reshaped our financial institutions and the services they offer the public. The result has been a refashioning of old and familiar types of securities and loans—financial instruments—traded in the financial system and the development of many new instruments, more responsive to today's problems and needs.

In this section of the book we look first in detail at several of the more-important and familiar financial instruments traded in our money and capital markets. Examples include federal funds, repurchase agreements, commercial paper, bankers' acceptances, Eurodollars, and federal agency securities. Following a review of recent developments in the market for these instruments we swing to an appraisal of newer and more innovative forms of loans and securities, including discount and zero coupon bonds, financial futures, adjustable-rate home mortgages and consumer loans, and security options. In each article describing these financial instruments the reader will see the pervasive effects of the sweeping, often tumultuous, changes that have impacted the nation's economy and financial system, transforming both in profound ways.

The section begins with Seth Maerowitz's history and analysis of the workings of the *federal funds market*. As he notes, federal funds are the most liquid and one of the most actively traded of all financial instruments. Fed funds are simply "immediately available money"—deposits at banks and nonbank thrift institutions that can be transferred from lender to borrower the same day. Typically, this rapid transfer of loanable funds takes play via wire or through a simple telephone call. The majority of federal funds loans are overnight or over the weekend, with the funds returned to the lender the next business day. Among the most important uses of fed funds are the meeting of legal reserve requirements on deposits held by banks and thrift institutions and aiding security dealers in financing purchases of securities for their portfolios. Seth Maerowitz traces the long history of this market from its beginnings in the 1920s among a handful of major money-center banks to today's market, where thousands of smaller banks, thrifts, and their largest depositors loan funds daily through the nation's financial network to large banks, thrifts, corporations, and security dealers. As Maerowitz notes, the rapid growth of the fed funds market in recent years is traceable to the aggressive use of liability management by financial institutions, to relatively high interest rates that encourage intensive use of surplus funds, and to the increasing sophistication of money managers.

Closely connected to the federal funds market is the U.S. government securities market—the largest, most important, and probably the most efficient financial market anywhere on earth. It is through the workings and channels of this huge security market that the U.S. Treasury borrows billions of dollars every week, the Federal Reserve conducts most of its monetary policy operations, and scores of individuals and institutions inside the United States and abroad find a relatively safe haven for their investible funds and a ready source of liquidity.

For decades, traders in the government securities markets have prided themselves on the smoothness and efficiency with which this market operates and its relative freedom from regulation. Unfortunately, storm clouds appeared over the horizon in the 1980s as several government security dealer houses collapsed and a number of investors (including banks, thrifts, and state and local units of government) experienced serious losses. Most of the problem centered on a prominent type of loan—the *repurchase agreement, or RP*—used to support the purchase of many government securities. In two very important and carefully researched articles in this section, Sheila L. Tschinkel and Richard Syron take a close look at the nature and problems of RPs and of the larger U.S. government securities market in which they are used. Additional information on these two markets is provided by Lisa Rockoff and A. E. Martin, III—all associated with the Federal Reserve Bank of Atlanta. Their analysis of how government security dealers are organized and operate, and especially how they fund their operations, is particularly enlightening. Sheila L. Tschinkel offers some useful suggestions on how investors in this market, particularly users of repurchase agreements, can reduce their risk exposure.

Many corporations today use RPs to borrow and lend money. An even more important market for corporate IOUs, however, is the *commercial paper market*. An excellent overview of this market—one of the oldest and today one of the most rapidly growing markets in the American financial system—is provided by Peter A. Abken. As Abken relates, commercial paper consists of short-term corporate notes that are unsecured—that is, no specific company asset is pledged to pay off any notes issued. Instead, commercial paper depends for its quality on the earning power and borrowing capacity of the issuing corporation. Because of this lack of specific security, only large and top-credit-rated borrowers can easily tap this market for funds.

One of the most interesting commercial-paper trends in recent years has been the entry of scores of smaller domestic firms, foreign companies, and even municipal governments into this market. These smaller borrowers have entered with the aid of money-center banks that frequently issue letters of credit guaranteeing repayment of the notes if the issuer cannot pay. As Abken notes, the future of the commercial paper market is very optimistic at this point, due to growing corporate borrowing demands associated with rising business operating expenses, to regulatory and practical limits on other sources of credit, and to relatively low interest rates on commercial paper compared to other sources of credit (such as bank loans).

In addition to commercial paper, many corporations today, especially those purchasing goods and services in international markets or trading commodities, tap another old and well-established market for short-term credit—the *bankers' acceptance* market. Bankers' acceptances are simply pledges made by a bank—usually a large money-center banking institution—to pay a specific sum of money on a specific date to the holder of the acceptance. Because a bank's promise to pay is considered a high-quality commitment, acceptances are readily salable to money market investors and may change hands many times before they reach maturity. Their safety and popularity is reflected by the fact that they typically bear one of the lowest interest rates in the money market. Acceptances are especially popular in international trade, with all of its special risks, because a trader or exporter of goods usually feels he or she can ship goods or provide services with little fear of loss once a bank has given its unconditional commitment (acceptance) to pay on behalf of one of its customers. In a most useful article, Frederick H. Jensen and Patrick M. Parkinson explore the intricacies of the bankers' acceptance market and explain why it grew so rapidly over the past two decades. They carefully illustrate how acceptances are created and why the creation of acceptances is limited by federal regulation. Jensen and Parkinson predict that dollar-denominated acceptances are likely to grow more slowly in future years, due to the appearance of innovative alternative financing instruments and financial deregulation in many countries.

The international financial system in which most acceptances are created is also the setting for the creation and destruction of *Eurodollars*—one of the largest of all short-term financial markets. By definition, Eurodollars are dollar-dominated deposits placed in a bank or bank branch located outside the borders of the United States. These dollar deposits, whose rapid growth first occurred in the 1960s, have proven to be a major source of short-term financing for large multinational corporations, governments, commercial banks, and other financial institutions. Indeed, during periods of tight credit and limited availability of loanable funds inside the United States, domestic banks and corporations stepped up their borrowings of these overseas dollar deposits to supplement whatever funds were available in the home market. Marvin Goodfriend's outstanding piece on the growth, character, uses, and problems of the Eurodollar market is an important component of this section of the book. He carefully traces through the principal sources of Eurodollars, including the growth of world trade, U.S. balance-of-payments deficits, and overseas activities of U.S. banks.

While all the instruments we have focused upon to this point have been money market or short-term financial instruments, the capital or long-term market has experienced its share of dramatic changes and innovations in recent years. Indeed, the capital market, because of the long-term character of the bonds, notes, stocks, and other instruments traded there, has been subject to even more turmoil and change than the money market. Inflation, high interest rates, changes in Federal Reserve monetary policy, and deregulation of financial institutions have all exerted potent effects on how and where long-term funds flow in search of the highest returns.

The capital market has been especially sensitive to the impact of *inflation,* which repeatedly over the past two decades has driven the cost of long-term borrowing to lofty, historically unprecedented highs. Moreover, the inflation factor, coupled with a shifting money and credit policy by the Federal Reserve System, resulted in not only higher interest rates but also more volatile and unpredictable rates. Financial market participants responded creatively to this challenge with the development of new financial instruments designed either to take advantage of the tendency for interest rates to periodically soar to new heights or to protect (hedge) against the damage such rate changes might bring to both borrowers and lenders.

The articles on the capital market, then, fall into two groups—those tracing how long-term financial instruments have become more flexible and responsive to inflation and interest-rate changes and those discussing relatively new devices to protect or hedge against the ravages of unpredictable rate changes. For example, Andrew Silver presents the brief history and the advantages and disadvantages of *discount and zero coupon bonds.* Large-scale offerings of discount bonds—so-called because they sell for prices well below their face or par value and generally appreciate in value as maturity approaches—are products of the decade of the 1980s. As Silver observes, much of their growth and acceptance among capital market borrowers and investors stems from their generally low after-tax borrowing cost and low risk of being called in advance of their maturity.

Perhaps nowhere else in the financial system is the response to inflation and high and rising interest rates more profound and more widely felt by the public than in the market for *home mortgage loans and other forms of household credit.* As John L. Goodman, Jr., and Charles A. Luckett relate, the desire of consumer lending institutions to get out from under the risk of fluctuating interest rates spawned the development of adjustable-rate home mortgage loans (ARMs) and shorter-term, multipurpose adjustable-rate consumer credit. So rapid has been the rise of ARMs since their emergence in the late 1970s that today nearly half of all long-term loans made to buyers of new homes and about one fifth of shorter-term consumer loans are made with floating or periodically adjustable interest rates. Goodman and Luckett carefully analyze the forces and factors which led to the widespread adoption of flexible-rate loans and then compare the home mortgage and consumer credit markets for their important similarities and differences.

Adjustable-rate loans shift the risk of interest-rate changes to the borrower and away from the lender. Lenders and borrowers have developed still other ways to deal with interest-rate risk in recent years—devices to *hedge* against rate changes by undertaking related transactions in more than one financial market. The two most familiar examples of such *hedging* methods are the financial futures markets, which appeared during the mid-1970s, and a welter of new security option markets centered around the stock market, the U.S. government securities market, and the market for the world's most widely recognized currencies. Mark Drabenstott and Anne O'Mara McDonley take us through the history and the fundamental principles of hedging using *financial futures contracts.* They explain why hedging with futures can work to *shift* interest-rate risk from a security trader, lender, or borrower to someone willing to bear that risk in the hope of greater gain. Drabenstott and McDonley provide a number of helpful guidelines on what types of futures hedges should be used, depending on whether interest rates are expected to rise or fall, and how investors can decide how many futures contracts or what dollar volume of contracts would help most to achieve the desired result—protection against interest-rate risk. They also provide a balanced analysis of the principal risks and dangers of using futures and how government regulations and accounting rules have affected the growth of the futures market. The article concludes with a useful appendix of key terms most frequently used in futures trading.

Interest-rate hedging is also attainable today through the use of security *options* on common stock, selected debt securities, and major national currencies. As Laurie S. Goodman notes in her informative and detailed article on security options, most of these markets and instruments are quite new. Indeed, prior to 1982 there were no organized markets for financial instruments other than common stock. However, the damaging effects of wide swings in market interest rates and bond prices, as well as shifting currency exchange rates in international markets, led to an explosion in new put and call option contracts.

By definition, an option contract grants the *buyer* of that contract the right to buy or sell certain assets at a specific price during a designated time period. In corresponding fashion, the *writer* (seller) of the option contract is obligated to buy or sell the asset at the contract buyer's request on or before the expiration date.

Option contracts may be either *puts* or *calls*. A *put* option grants the right to the contract purchaser to *sell* a security or other designated asset to the option writer before a certain date at the contracted price. A *call* option, on the other hand, allows the contract purchaser to *buy* or "call away" a security or other asset from the option writer on or before a specific day and at a guaranteed price. As Laurie Goodman explains, put options provide protection against falling security prices and rising interest rates, while call options can be used to offset falling interest rates and take advantage of rising asset prices. She describes what option contracts are now available, some of the key problems in the development of these markets, the features of newer option agreements, and the factors that influence the market price of an option contract (known as its *premium*).

Finally, no account of recent changes in the financial markets would be complete without a survey of the rapidly growing federal credit agencies. These institutions (such as Fannie Mae and Sallie Mae) have become familiar even to the general public, and today they are major borrowers and lenders of funds in both national and international markets. Acting like private financial intermediaries, these agencies have provided billions of dollars in credit to the home mortgage market, to the farming sector, and to students in search of a college education. Michael J. Moran, a member of the staff of the Federal Reserve Board, provides an excellent overview of these important credit market institutions and, especially, of five government agencies that account for most of the borrowing and lending done by this sector. He sees an uncertain future for these institutions, with continuing deregulation of the financial sector, and he questions whether they are really the most efficient way to direct credit to high-priority sectors of the economy. Moran draws our attention to a public policy issue that touches each one of us and is not likely to go away in the foreseeable future.

17

The Market for Federal Funds

Seth P. Maerowitz

The market for the most liquid of money market instruments—federal funds—
evolved as borrowers and lenders sought to exploit opportunities through trading
in reserve deposit funds. Trading in federal funds began in the 1920s and involved
only a few Federal Reserve member banks located in New York City. Today, the
market includes over 14,000 commercial banks and a wide range of nonbank
financial institutions.[1] The characteristics of federal funds as well as the mechanics of their purchase and sale reflect the needs of today's market participants.

WHAT ARE FEDERAL FUNDS?[2]

Federal funds are short-term loans of immediately available funds (i.e, funds that
can be transferred or withdrawn during one business day). Such immediately
available funds include deposits at Federal Reserve banks and collected liabilities
of commercial banks and other depository institutions. Federal funds are exempt
from reserve requirements and the vast majority are unsecured. Most federal
funds are "overnight money"—funds lent out on one day and repaid the following
morning. Loans of longer maturity, known as "term federal funds," are not
uncommon, however.

The law requires, for purposes of monetary control, that all depository institutions maintain reserves as prescribed by the Federal Reserve System. Federal
Reserve Regulation D delineates specific classes of liabilities which are subject to
Federal Reserve requirements. Commercial banks, thrift institutions, U.S.
branches and agencies of foreign banks, and Edge Act corporations must hold set
percentages of these liabilities in a combination of vault cash and noninterest-
earning reserve balances at a Federal Reserve bank. The opportunity cost of
holding reserve balances, which yield no return, provides the incentive to depository institutions to minimize their holdings of excess reserves. The federal funds
market provides the primary avenue for doing so.

Ordinary banking activities give rise to variations in a bank's asset and liability

---

Reprinted from *Economic Review*, Federal Reserve Bank of Richmond, July/August 1981.

This article was written for *Instruments of the Money Market*, 5th ed., Federal Reserve Bank of
Richmond.

holdings. These changes in the balance sheet result in corresponding fluctuations in a bank's reserve position. Consequently, on any given day some institutions hold reserves above their desired reserve position while others are below their desired position. An institution holding excess reserves can earn interest on its funds by loaning them to others in need of reserves. Such a transaction is considered a federal funds purchase by the borrowing institution, and a federal funds sale by the lending institution.

THE MECHANICS OF FEDERAL FUNDS TRANSACTIONS

Federal funds transactions can be initiated by either a funds lender or a funds borrower. An institution wishing to sell (buy) federal funds locates a buyer (seller) either directly through an existing banking relationship or indirectly through a federal funds broker located in New York City. Federal funds brokers maintain frequent telephone contact with active buyers and sellers of federal funds. Brokers match federal funds purchase and sale orders in return for a commission on each completed transaction.

At the center of the federal funds market are financial institutions that maintain reserve accounts at Federal Reserve banks. These institutions use the Federal Reserve communications system, or Fedwire, to carry out rapid transfer of funds nationwide. The Federal Reserve communications system links all Federal Reserve banks and branches. Private financial institutions and government agencies are able to gain access to the wire network either through direct (online) links to Federal Reserve computers or through telephone or telegraph (offline) contact with their Federal Reserve bank.

When transfers are conducted within a Federal Reserve district, the institution transferring funds authorizes the district Federal Reserve bank to debit its reserve account and to credit the reserve account of the receiving institution. Interdistrict transactions are only slightly more complicated but are best clarified by an example. Suppose a thrift institution in Richmond (the Fifth Federal Reserve District) wishes to transfer funds to a bank in New York (the Second Federal Reserve District). The thrift initiates the transaction. The Federal Reserve Bank of Richmond debits the account of the thrift and credits the account of the Federal Reserve Bank of New York. Finally, the Federal Reserve Bank of New York debits its own account and credits the reserve account of the receiving commercial bank. This series of accounting entries is carried out instantaneously.

OVERNIGHT FEDERAL FUNDS

In a typical federal funds transaction, the lending institution with reserve funds in excess of its reserve requirements authorizes a transfer from its reserve account to the reserve account of the borrowing institution. The following day, the transaction is reversed. The borrower pays back the loan through a transfer of funds from its reserve account to the lender's reserve account for an amount equal to the value of the original loan plus an interest payment. The size of the interest payment is determined by market conditions at the time the loan is initiated.

Numerous institutions that buy and sell federal funds do not maintain accounts at the Federal Reserve. Instead, these institutions buy and sell funds through a correspondent bank. Correspondent banks will often agree to purchase on a continuing basis all federal funds that a respondent has available to sell. Typically, the respondent institution holds a demand deposit account with the correspondent. To initiate a federal funds sale, the respondent bank simply notifies the correspondent by telephone of its intentions. The correspondent purchases funds from the respondent by classifying the respondent's liability from a demand deposit to federal funds purchased. Upon maturity of the contract, the respondent's demand deposit account is credited for the total value of the loan plus an interest payment for use of the funds. The rate paid to respondents on federal funds is usually based on the nationwide effective federal funds rate for the day.

ALTERNATIVES TO OVERNIGHT FEDERAL FUNDS

The different needs of participants in the fed funds market and the wide range of financial environments in which they operate have resulted in the development of alternatives to overnight federal funds. These alternatives include term and continuing contract federal funds. According to the results of a 1977 survey, approximately 7.5 percent of all federal funds transactions have maturities longer than overnight.[3] Banks contract for term federal funds when they foresee their borrowing needs lasting for several days and/or believe that the cost of overnight federal funds may rise in the immediate future. Like overnight fed funds, term fed funds are not subject to reserve requirements. For this reason, term fed funds are often preferred to other purchased liabilities of comparable maturity. The majority of term federal funds sold have maturities of 90 days or less, but term federal funds of much longer maturity are purchased occasionally.

Federal funds sold through a correspondent banking relationship are sometimes transacted under a continuing contract. *Continuing contract federal funds* are overnight federal funds that are automatically renewed unless terminated by either a fund's lender or borrower. In a typical continuing contract arrangement, a correspondent will purchase overnight federal funds from a respondent institution. Unless notified by the respondent, the correspondent will continually roll over overnight federal funds, creating a longer-term instrument of open maturity. The interest payments on continuing contract federal funds are computed from a formula based on each day's federal funds quotations. The specific formula used varies from contract to contract.

SECURED AND UNSECURED FEDERAL FUNDS

Most federal funds transactions are unsecured (i.e., the lender does not receive collateral to insure him against the risk of default by the borrower). In some cases, however, federal funds transactions are secured. In a secured transaction, the purchaser places government securities in a custody account for the seller as collateral to support the loan. The purchaser retains title to the securities, however.[4] Upon completion of the federal funds contract, custody of the securities is returned to the owner. Secured federal funds transactions are sometimes requested by the lending institution, or encouraged by state regulations requiring collateralization of federal funds sales.

THE HISTORY AND EVOLUTION OF MARKET STRUCTURE

The federal funds market of the 1920s developed out of the common interests of a few Federal Reserve member banks operating in New York City that often found themselves with temporary shortages or surpluses of reserves. Before the emergence of the federal funds market, banks having a deficiency of reserves had to borrow from the discount window, while banks with a surplus of reserves had no profitable use for their excess reserve deposits. A market in reserve deposits was formed that benefited both deficient reserve and surplus reserve institutions. Banks that borrowed in the new market found federal funds to be an inexpensive substitute for this discount window, while banks that lent funds were pleased to receive a liquid earning asset to replace their nonearning excess reserve balances.

By 1929, the daily trading volume in federal funds had expanded to over $250 million, but with the stock market crash of October 1929 and the economic contraction that followed, the federal funds market disintegrated.[5] The contraction and the large number of bank and industrial failures that accompanied it led to great uncertainty about the safety of most earning assets except U.S. government securities. It resulted in a market preference for cash, reflected in the large increase in excess reserve balances maintained by commercial banks in the period. The disinterest in federal funds trading by potential lenders was matched by the diminished needs of potential borrowers. Weak loan demand and large gold inflows throughout most of the early and mid-30s left few institutions in need of borrowings to meet their reserve requirements.

The market revived briefly in 1941, in response to financial pressures resulting from World War II.[6] The revival was short-lived, however; Federal Reserve pegging of Treasury bill prices from 1942 to 1951 rendered the funds market superfluous. With the price of Treasury bills fixed, banks made adjustments in their reserve balances through trading Treasury bills free of market risk. The funds market remained dormant until securities prices were unpegged by the Treasury–Federal Reserve Accord of 1951. Since trading in Treasury bills was now subject to the risk of securities price fluctuations, federal funds trading became the preferred mode of reserve adjustment. Furthermore, the higher market rates of interest prevailing after the Treasury–Federal Reserve Accord increased the opportunity cost of holding sterile balances, making more frequent reserve adjustments desirable. Consequently, the volume of aggregate trading in federal funds grew sharply. Improvements in banking technology and the growth of correspondent banking during the 1960s brought about important changes in the nature of federal funds trading. Large correspondent banks intentionally began to run down their reserve positions, substituting federal funds as a new source of loanable funds. Smaller regional banks specializing in retail banking, with a large inflow of deposits but few lending opportunities, sold federal funds to the larger institutions. Such banking relationships developed that large correspondents stood ready to purchase all the funds that their smaller respondent banks had available to sell.

In this environment, the federal funds market took on a broader role, beyond that of reserve adjustment borrowing. Large banks began to depend on federal funds as a semipermanent source of nondeposit funds, while smaller respondents recognized fed funds to be a profitable, liquid investment. In 1963, the Comptroller of the Currency eliminated capital adequacy restrictions on federal funds purchases and sales, and, in 1964, the Federal Reserve Board ruled that member banks could purchase federal funds from nonmember respondents. These two rulings increased the supply of federal funds to the purchasing banks, further augmenting market growth.

THE FEDERAL FUNDS RATE AND THE DISCOUNT RATE

The Federal Reserve limits most borrowing at the discount window to banks facing temporary shortages of reserves. Prior to the mid-1960s, the federal funds rate rarely rose above the discount rate. Federal funds were viewed primarily as a substitute for discount window borrowing. Since banks only used the discount window occasionally, they were generally not constrained by Federal Reserve discount window policies. Temporary borrowing needs were easily met at the discount window, leaving little incentive to purchase funds at a rate exceeding the discount rate.

By late 1964, the practice of liabilities management had become widespread. In this environment, incentives existed for banks practicing liabilities management to borrow from the discount window on a continuing basis. Discount window administration policies, however, remained oriented toward providing funds to banks facing temporary reserve deficiencies, thus preventing banks from using the window as a continual source of funds. Since access to the discount window was limited, banks in need of additional funds were willing to pay a premium above the discount rate for federal funds. In late 1964, the federal funds rate rose above the discount rate, reflecting a demand for overnight funds exceeding the supply available at the discount window.

During the "credit crunch" of 1966, regional banking institutions without well-developed networks of funds suppliers often found federal funds difficult to obtain.[7] Problems of funds availability soon subsided, however, and the funds market continued to grow rapidly throughout the late 1970s. Banks willing to purchase federal funds at the market rate found them to be expensive, but readily available. The federal funds rate rose rapidly towards the end of the 196us and reached a peak of 9.2 percent in August of 1969. Many banks were squeezed in the short run by the rapid increase in the cost of funds. Over the long run, however, they adjusted by developing flexible asset management and loan pricing policies in order to deal more effectively with variation in the cost of nondeposit funds.

In 1970, approximately 60 percent of all member banks were active buyers or sellers of federal funds.[8] Despite questions of funds price and availability, the federal funds market has grown dramatically throughout the 60s. In 1960, daily average gross interbank federal funds purchases of 46 money market banks were $1.1 billion.[9] By 1970, daily average purchases of this group had soared to $8.3 billion.[10] The rapid growth in federal funds trading throughout this period reflected the expanded role of the federal funds market as a source of purchased liabilities, as well as its value as a tool of member bank reserve adjustment.

THE MARKET IN RECENT YEARS[11]

The federal funds market of the 1970s was characterized by further growth spurred on by regulatory change. Prior to 1970, borrowings from nonbank financial institutions were subject to reserve requirements, and, consequently, nonbanks were not active in the federal funds market. In 1970, an amendment to Regulation D exempted borrowings from savings and loan associations, mutual savings banks, and U.S. government agencies from reserve requirements. Following the 1970 ruling, the nonbank institutions assumed a role in the federal funds market very similar to that of small commercial banks. Savings and loan associations and mutual savings banks found sales of federal funds to be a profitable and liquid alternative to purchases of Treasury securities. In recent years, nonbank depository institutions supplied 35 percent of the federal funds purchased by the 45 large weekly reporting banks.[12]

The funds market of the 1970s continued to reflect the patterns of growth which had developed in earlier years. During periods of high short-term interest rates, the federal funds market expanded as small financial institutions sought to economize on their cash and reserve balances, while large banks practicing liabilities management demanded federal funds to meet the needs of their loan customers. In times of low short-term interest rates and slack loan demand, growth in the federal funds market was less rapid. The federal funds market, however, was not subject to large declines in trading volume, as were other markets for purchased liabilities such as large certificates of deposit.[13]

THE FEDERAL FUNDS MARKET AND MONETARY POLICY

The Federal Reserve exerts control over the money supply primarily by influencing the level of nonborrowed reserves available to the banking system. The federal funds rate reflects the cost of interbank borrowing, in essence the price of nonborrowed reserve deposit funds. If the supply of nonborrowed reserves is reduced, the immediate effect will be an increase in the federal funds rate; conversely, an increase in the supply of nonborrowed reserves will bring about a fall in the funds rate. Following a rise in the funds rate, banks will slow the growth of their loan portfolios and/or increase the rates charged on new loans to reflect the higher cost of nondeposit funds. Hence, the federal funds market acts as an integral part of the transmission process for monetary policy.

Throughout the 1970s, the Federal Reserve used the federal funds rate as its principal operating target of monetary policy. When money growth was above the desired growth path, the federal funds rate target was raised. The Open Market Desk was directed to sell government securities and drain reserves from the banking system until the desired funds rate target was met. If more rapid monetary growth was desired, the funds rate target was lowered, and reserves were added to the banking system. Funds traders formed their expectations of the funds rate based on what they believed the Federal Reserve's target rate to be; under usual procedures, whenever the funds rate rose ⅛ to ³⁄₁₆ percentage points above its target level, the Federal Reserve provided reserves through the purchase of government securities (via overnight RPs), and whenever the rate dropped ⅛ to ³⁄₁₆ points below target, the Federal Reserve absorbed reserves through the sale of securities. Market participants soon came to depend on such signals of Federal Reserve intentions, which provided important information for forecasting federal funds rate movements.

The inflation of recent years and the tendency of the Federal Reserve to overshoot its money supply targets raised serious questions about the efficacy of the federal funds rate as an operating target for monetary policy. On October 6, 1979, a major policy shift was announced. The Federal Reserve would now focus more attention on nonborrowed reserves and less attention on day-to-day fluctuations in the federal funds rate.

The impact of the new policy on the market was immediate and dramatic. Variation in the funds rate increased from a daily trading band of approximately 2 percentage points during the month preceding October 6 to a daily trading band of approximately 5 percentage points during the month following October 6.[14] Despite greater variation in the funds rate, trading volume continues to be strong, reflecting the importance of federal funds as a short-term money market instrument.

CONCLUSION

The federal funds market of today is the evolutionary result of changes in general economic conditions, federal and state regulations, and financial innovation. From its beginnings as a market limited to the purchase and sale of excess reserve deposits among member banks, the federal funds market has undergone tremendous expansion. Active liability management practices of the past two decades created new demand for federal funds, and less restrictive regulations brought the funds market to a new group of financial institutions. Today, federal funds are an important purchased liability for large banks, a profitable liquid investment for a wide range of market participants, and a valuable reserve adjustment tool.

NOTES

[1] Thomas D. Simpson, *The Market for Federal Funds and Repurchase Agreements* (Washington: Board of Governors of the Federal Reserve System, 1979), p. 20.

[2] The term *federal funds* is occasionally used in a broader sense than that described in this article. Sometimes, members of the financial community will consider all funds which are immediately available and not subject to reserve requirements to be federal funds. Repurchase agreements, included under this broad definition, are excluded from this discussion.

[3] Board of Governors, *Repurchase Agreements and Other Nonreservable Borrowings in Immediately Available Funds,* report giving results of a 1977 survey, 1978, p. 4.

[4] The crucial difference between a secured federal funds transaction and a repurchase agreement is that in a federal funds transaction title to the security is not transferred. RPs are available to a wider range of market participants than federal funds.

[5] Marcos T. Jones, Charles M. Lucas, and Thom B. Thurston, "Federal Funds and Repurchase Agreements," Federal Reserve Bank of New York, *Quarterly Review,* Summer 1977, p. 39.

[6] Parker B. Willis, *The Federal Funds Market, Its Origin and Development* (Boston: Federal Reserve Bank of Boston, 1970), p. 15.

[7] S. M. Duckworth, *Problems in Liability Management: Case Studies of Attitudes at Seven Banks* (Boston: Federal Reserve Bank of Boston, 1974), pp. 20–22. This discussion is drawn from interviews of bankers in the First Federal Reserve District.

[8] Willis, *The Federal Funds Market,* p. 52.

[9] *Federal Reserve Bulletin,* August 1964, table, "Basic Reserve Position, and Federal Funds and Related Transactions of 46 Major Reserve City Banks," p. 954; same table in various issues of 1970, 1971.

[10] Ibid.

[11] The analysis of the federal funds market of the 1970s and '80s is complicated by the development of the repurchase agreement. Repurchase agreements gained rapid acceptance by bankers as a near perfect substitute for federal funds. Data on federal funds sales and purchases were, and continue to be, reported in aggregate with data on repurchase agreements. According to studies by the Federal Reserve Board of federal funds and RPs supplied to 45 large member banks, federal funds accounted for 89.4 percent of gross nonreservable borrowings of immediately available funds from depository institutions and U.S. government agencies on December 7, 1977. Since federal funds have remained the predominant money market instrument for borrowing immediately available funds among banking institutions, an analysis of the federal funds market in the '70s can still be made on the basis of the available data.

[12] Board of Governors, *Repurchase Agreements and Other Nonreservable Borrowings,* p. 4. A data series consisting of 46 large banks was begun by the Federal Reserve System in 1964. In March 1980, the sample group was expanded to include 121 large member banks. The figure is based upon a special survey of the original 46 bank group, conducted on December 7, 1977.

[13] CDs were subject to a rapid runoff in 1975 and 1977. (See Summers, "Negotiable Certificates.")

[14] Federal Reserve Bank of New York, "Composite Closing Quotations for U.S. Government Securities," September 4, 1979–November 9, 1979.

REFERENCES

Board of Governors of the Federal Reserve System, *Repurchase Agreements and Other Nonreservable Borrowings in Immediately Available Funds*. Washington, D.C., 1978.

Board of Governors of the Federal Reserve System. *Selected Interest Rates and Bond Prices*. Washington, D.C., 1969.

Brandt, Harry. "The Discount Rate Under the Federal Reserve's New Operating Strategy." *Economic Review,* pp. 6–15. Federal Reserve Bank of Atlanta. March/April 1980.

Depamphilis, Donald Michael. *A Microeconomic Econometric Analysis of the Short-term Commercial Bank Adjustment Process*. Federal Reserve Bank of Boston, 1974.

Duckworth, S. M. *Problems in Liability Management: Case Studies of Attitudes at Seven Banks*. Federal Reserve Bank of Boston, 1974.

Federal Reserve Bank of New York. "Monetary Policy and Open Market Operations in 1979." *Quarterly Review,* Summer 1980, pp. 50–64.

Fieldhouse, Richard C. "The Federal Funds Market." *Money Market Memo*. New York: Garvin, Bantel & Co., October/November 1964.

Gambs, Carl M., and Ralph C. Kimball. "Small Banks and the Federal Funds Market." *Economic Review*. Federal Reserve Bank of Kansas City, November 1979, pp. 3–12.

Jones, Marcos T.; Charles M. Lucas; and Thom B. Thurston. "Federal Funds and Repurchase Agreements." *Quarterly Review*. Federal Reserve Bank of New York, Summer 1977, pp. 33–48.

Kaufman, Herbert M., and Raymond E. Lombra. "Commercial Banks and the Federal Funds Market: Recent Developments and Implications." *Economic Inquiry,* October 1978.

Kimball, Ralph C. "Wire Transfer and the Demand for Money." *New England Economic Review*. Federal Reserve Bank of Boston, March/April 1980, pp. 5–22.

Monhollon, Jimmie R. "Federal Funds." In *Instruments of the Money Market,* 4th ed., ed. Timothy Q. Cook. Richmond: Federal Reserve Bank of Richmond, 1977.

Simpson, Thomas D. *The Market for Federal Funds and Repurchase Agreements*. Washington, D.C.: Board of Governors of the Federal Reserve System, 1979.

Stigum, Marcia. *The Money Market Myth, Reality, and Practice*. Homewood, Ill.: Dow Jones-Irwin, 1978.

Summers, Bruce J. "Negotiable Certificates of Deposit." *Economic Review*. Federal Reserve Bank of Richmond, July/August 1980, pp. 8–19.

Willis, Parker B. *The Federal Funds Market, Its Origin and Development*. Federal Reserve Bank of Boston, 1970.

18

Overview of Repurchase Agreements

Sheila L. Tschinkel

Repurchase agreements against government securities can be a safe, effective method of raising short-term funds and of earning a return on surplus funds available for a brief time. However, problems have arisen involving the use of repurchase agreements, or "repos." Since the beginning of the year, the failure of two firms—ESM Government Securities and Bevill, Bresler, and Schulman—has cost customers more than $500 million. Losses associated with ESM triggered the temporary closing of 70 privately insured savings and loan associations in Ohio.[1] Although some problems were associated with allegedly fraudulent practices by government securities dealers, customers could have avoided or greatly limited losses by following certain procedures and prudent management practices.

This overview of current issues involving repos describes the mechanics of repurchase agreements and the market in which these transactions occur; summarizes how various customers, including state and local governments as well as banks and thrifts, find repos useful money market instruments; reviews recent problems; and outlines how customers can minimize associated risks. Subsequent articles consider these topics in greater depth.

Our discussion of government securities used in repurchase agreements refers primarily to direct obligations of the U.S. Treasury—bills, notes, and bonds. Only a few examples are provided of repos against federal agency issues, such as those of the Government National Mortgage Association (GNMAs). However, in both instances the principles essentially are the same. Their application in the case of repos against federal agency issues might be more complex than for Treasuries, but the fundamental points—such as abiding by a master repo contract, evaluating collateral carefully, establishing control over collateral, and monitoring the value of collateral and interest accruals during the term of a repo—remain the same. In fact, many of these procedures can be used whenever a transaction is outstanding for some time period, and one party's exposure to another is linked to an instrument that is traded in a market. Thus, they are relevant to collateralized deposits, for example.

From *Economic Review,* Federal Reserve Bank of Atlanta, September 1985, pp. 5–9.

The author is senior vice president and director of research at the Federal Reserve Bank of Atlanta.

THE GOVERNMENT SECURITIES MARKET

Repurchase agreements are money market transactions in which one party sells securities to another while agreeing to repurchase those securities at a later date. Interest payments are an essential part of the transaction, since the seller of the securities has use of the buyer's funds during the term of the repo. (For more detailed information on repurchase agreements, see Exhibit 1.)

State and local governments use repos to earn extra income on idle cash they have on hand for short periods.[2] Their earnings from repos help hold down taxes while maintaining a given level of public services. Many banks and thrifts also use repos to raise needed cash. Since such institutions often hold government securities in their portfolios, they can use them to obtain funds, usually on a short-term basis, at a rate generally below the fed funds rate. Dealers often use repos to finance their positions in securities, from which they earn a major portion of their profits, as discussed below. Since repurchase transactions figure importantly in the financing of government securities holdings, we must know how the government securities market and dealers participating in it work to understand both the importance of repos and how recent problems developed.[3]

The U.S. Treasury is the preeminent issuer of short and long-term debt securities on a regular basis. The Treasury auctions bills, notes, and bonds to meet U.S. government financing requirements.[4] The majority of these securities are issued and held in book-entry form, basically as messages or data stored in a computer.[5] They are transferred over a wire system, called "Fedwire," operated by the Federal Reserve in much the same way that money is transferred from one depository to another. The Fed, as the U.S. Treasury's fiscal agent, maintains the securities for the Treasury on the Fed's computerized book-entry system and issues new securities to investors on the Treasury's behalf. In addition, the Fed buys and sells Treasury issues in the market, dealing with some 36 firms, including banks, diversified investment houses, and specialty firms. These transactions are an essential part of the Fed's conduct of monetary policy.

The firms with which the Fed transacts are known popularly as primary dealers. Many other firms of all sizes and types trade government securities on a routine basis, and dealers are serviced by a number of brokers and clearing banks. The final tier of the market is the array of customers in government securities—banks, thrifts, state and local governments, pension funds, and individuals, among others.

Anyone—or any firm—can become a government securities dealer. There are no uniform or comprehensive margin or capital requirements with which all dealers must comply. A dealer's inventory of securities usually is financed with a small amount of capital combined with funds raised in the market—often through the use of repurchase agreements. Capital can, at times, be as low as 1 percent of securities holdings.

There is, of course, regulation of many types of dealers. Dealers related to banks are supervised by one of three federal banking regulators—the Fed, the Federal Deposit Insurance Corporation (FDIC), or the Office of the Comptroller of the Currency (OCC). Other firms may be subject to regulation by the Securities and Exchange Commission (SEC) or the Commodities Futures Trading Commission (CFTC), according to the type of instruments in which they deal. However,

EXHIBIT 1

What is a Repo?

A repurchase agreement, or "repo," is the sale of securities on a temporary basis, involving the seller's agreement to repurchase the same or similar securities at a later date. The other party has a corresponding obligation to sell them back. The repurchase price can include an interest component, or the sale and repurchase prices can be the same with interest paid separately for the use of the acquired funds. Usually a "margin" is taken to protect the buyer should the seller later default. As a result, the amount of the funds transferred (sale price) is less than the market value of the securities transferred. This arrangement, though cast in terms of a purchase and sale, is in concept similar to a collateralized loan. Many parties in repos are legally constrained to treat repos as purchases and sales, while others can treat them as secured lending. Because of this situation, much of the popular terminology associated with repos is borrowed from the latter though those terms are not of controlling legal significance in the repo context. Securities, for example, are often called collateral.

A reverse repo is simply the same transaction viewed from the perspective of the other party. For example, a dealer may wish to buy securities from a customer, often a bank or a thrift, in order to make delivery to another customer interested in that particular security at that particular time. The dealer buys securities from a customer under an agreement to resell the same securities at the same price on some future date. Every repurchase agreement is composed of a repo on one side and a reverse repo on the other. However, the terms are sometimes used inconsistently. Usually both parties to a repurchase agreement use the dealer's perspective. Thus, for example, when a customer delivers securities to the dealer, the transaction is often termed a reverse repo by both parties.

Repos can be done on an overnight basis, on a term basis for a specified number of days, or on a continuing contract basis. Term repos rarely extend over 30 days because both parties may be unnecessarily constrained by such longer time spans. Repos are sometimes done under continuing contracts, whereby a new interest rate or the amount of funds invested may change from day to day. This permits an investor to manage cash while minimizing the interest rate risk that would arise with a longer term repo or security.

Repurchase agreements typically involve relatively large transfers of funds, short maturities, and thus a small volume of earnings per transaction relative to potential changes in value in the underlying securities. The return to any investor is calculated by the following basic formula:

Earnings = funds transferred x interest x (number of days/360)

Funds Transferred = (par amount of securities x market price) + accrued interest - margin

The denominator is 360 because calculating interest on the basis of a 360 day year is typical money market practice. Assuming an investor has $1 million in surplus funds to invest overnight and the best rate he can get is 7 1/2 percent, he would earn:

$$\frac{(\$1,000,000 \times .075)}{360} \text{ or } \$208.33$$

If the investor held this surplus for 5 days and entered into a continuing contract, his earnings might look like this:

Day	Rate	Calculation	Earnings
Monday	7 5/8	($1,000,000 x .07625)/360	211.81
Tuesday	7 1/2	($1,000,000 x .07500)/360	208.33
Wednesday	7 3/4	($1,000,000 x .07750)/360	215.28
Thursday	7 5/8	($1,000,000 x .07625)/360	211.81
Friday	7 3/4	($1,000,000 x .07750)/360	215.28
Total Interest			$1,062.51

Interest rates on repurchase agreements are generally lower than those on federal funds or deposits because the agreements are collateralized by government securities. Thus, if a depository institution owns eligible securities, it can use them to raise money cheaply. Since repurchase agreements can be written with tailor-made maturities, they provide these institutions with flexibility in asset-liability management. Similarly, investors with surplus cash can invest for short periods of time while keeping interest rate risk at a minimum.

NOTE

[1] For example, the SEC defines repos and reverse repos from the dealer's perspective, but the Government Accounting Standards Board uses an inverted definition for municipal investors.

firms that deal only in government or other exempt securities are free from comprehensive oversight or regulation.[6] This can also be the case for subsidiaries of otherwise regulated firms, often called Government Securities, Inc. (GSIs), which are themselves not subject to regulation.

The free entry that characterizes the market adds to its efficiency, since the large number of firms able to provide these services minimizes costs to those using them. Customers can compare the prices of several dealers by telephoning them or by subscribing to a service that reports such information continuously via computer. Thus, transactions usually can be executed at the best price. The market's intense competitiveness also reduces the Treasury's cost of issuing debt, and the liquidity that results from an efficient market makes the securities attractive to a variety of investors.

Although the market is characterized by highly favorable features, including liquidity, efficiency, innovation, and a good safety record, free entry can allow problems to go undetected unless customers adhere to prudent business practices and respect the rule of caveat emptor—let the buyer beware. Transactions involving government securities can involve significant risk, even if the securities themselves are free of default risk. To understand better how problems can develop, consider some common patterns that appeared in recent losses.

COMMON ELEMENTS IN RECENT PROBLEMS

In recent cases where dealers failed and customers lost money, some common patterns were apparent. Had all of the customers involved exercised judicious management and followed certain procedures, they could have avoided such losses. Some customers assumed they were dealing with one counterparty, or dealer firm, only to find they had been dealing with an affiliate, often an insolvent one whose earlier losses had been masked by various transactions. Certain investors failed to gain control of the securities used as collateral during the life of the repurchase agreement. Others, who held control, did not require securities whose market value exceeded the cash they had provided in an amount sufficient to protect themselves against fluctuations in the market value of those securities. Many customers failed to monitor the value of their securities to see that they continued to have sufficient coverage. Even though some dealers who failed were allegedly engaging in fraud, losses could have been avoided or greatly limited if customers had followed specific procedures. In fact, many customers who did business with the failed firms did not lose money.

As noted previously, some of the customers who suffered losses failed to follow the old adage of good business, "Know your counterparty." Customers should investigate the history, financial condition, business practices, and regulatory status of their dealer.[7] Some investors had not even obtained an up-to-date audited financial statement. While such a statement is not a guarantee of a firm's condition at any time, it is an essential part of the process of finding out about one's counterparty.

A second and related pattern in recent losses involved collateral risk. Insolvent firms could continue raising funds because customers had not taken the necessary steps to evaluate collateral or had not established sufficient control over the securities used in repos. Because the dealer and not the customer controlled the securities, the dealer could raise funds using the same securities twice or as many times as there were customers willing to leave the securities with the dealer. When the dealer defaulted and investors tried to recover the securities underlying the repos, they found their securities had been used as collateral for other repos or did not exist at all.

Generally speaking, risk associated with custodial arrangements is best minimized by taking the securities out of the control of the dealer. Legal reasons may exist for doing so.[8] In addition, should a dispute arise over the terms of the agreement or should the dealer become insolvent, the customer is in a more desirable position if the securities are in the customer's (or the customer's custodian's) control or with an independent custodian responsible to both the customer and dealer. The first type of arrangement is known as a "delivery repo"; the second a "three-party repo" or "tri-party repo." The safety of these arrangements entails the added costs of transfer fees and paperwork by the external parties.

In a third type of custodial arrangement involved in recent losses, called a "letter repo," the dealer retains control over the customer's securities. The securities remain with the dealer or his clearing bank. This type of arrangement is inexpensive, since delivery fees are unnecessary and generally no costly contractual arrangements need to be drawn up. However, this obviously can be much riskier for the customer. Making the proper arrangements for custody of the securities is a critical safeguard against losses, even if it costs money and lowers an investor's rate of return.

Another pattern in recent losses entails market or interest-rate risk. Once customers have taken steps to gain control of their collateral, they still must protect themselves against fluctuations in prices of government securities that occur whenever interest rates change. Investors providing funds to a dealer should start by valuing the securities at their current market price, rather than at their par value. Then they should protect themselves against changes in the market prices of securities they receive by requiring a package of securities whose total market value exceeds the value of cash they exchange. This process is called "taking margin" and is especially important the longer the maturities of the securities and the longer the term of the repurchase agreement.

In addition, since interest rates can fluctuate substantially during the life of a repo, no matter how short, customers need to assess frequently whether the collateral remains of sufficient value to protect their interest. This process of monitoring the value of securities is called "marking to market." It should be done at least daily. When the market value of the securities being held as collateral slips below the preestablished margin, a margin call should be made on the dealer. Of course, a dealer also may ask for margin calls when the margin grows too large.

Customers who have raised funds by selling securities from their portfolio must follow these procedures as well. However, in their case, they need to determine whether the margin given the dealer is appropriate, and they should not let it grow too large if interest rates decline. The margin given when an investor borrows using repos is equivalent to an unsecured loan of securities to the dealer.

One problem in earlier losses was a failure to account properly for interest that was accruing on a coupon of a note or bond. The funds that can be obtained by selling a security increase each day as a result of interest accruing. Controlling for this type of risk is especially important for those using their securities to raise funds in the repo market, since they stand to lose from ignoring this feature of government securities.[9]

HOW TO PREVENT FUTURE LOSSES

Losses can be limited in doing repos, if not avoided entirely, by following four basic rules: (1) operate under the terms of a clearly specified and executed master repurchase agreement; (2) properly assess counterparties, including their corporate structure and capital strength; (3) use appropriate procedures for obtaining control of securities; and (4) evaluate securities appropriately and monitor them regularly, making margin calls when necessary.

The Federal Reserve and other regulatory and industry groups will continue to work toward developing better systems to curb abuse. The Fed's approach at this time is twofold. One part is an extensive educational effort to inform investors and other market participants of the risks involved in repos and of these four ways to minimize the chance of losses. The other is the development of a voluntary capital adequacy guideline that customers can use to help them evaluate the credit-worthiness of dealers with whom they transact.

The Federal Reserve's voluntary capital adequacy guideline is designed for those who do not already comply with some standards, such as bank capital ratios or the SEC's Uniform Net Capital Rule. The guideline calls for dealers to comply voluntarily with a minimum ratio of liquid capital to risk at any point in time of 1.2 to 1.0. That is, dealers are asked to make sure their ready capital exceeds their risk by 20 percent. The measurement of risk takes into consideration various aspects of dealer operations. Dealers complying with these guidelines are to certify their compliance in each of three ways: a general letter from the dealer to the customer, audited financial statements, and a letter from the dealer's certified public accountant indicating that there are no material weaknesses in the dealer's internal procedures for compliance.

These standards will not be enforced by any federal regulatory agency. Rather, their effectiveness will depend on primary dealers, clearing banks, and customers, all of whom should request the relevant certifications and then trade only with those dealers that provide them.

In addition, the Federal Reserve regards as desirable some form of minimum regulation, including registration, inspection, and financial standards. That approach, however, requires congressional action. Currently, several bills are before Congress that would subject the market to additional regulation. Whether or not the government securities market becomes subject to additional regulation, market participants need to work together to preserve the generally good record of safety. The customer shares responsibility for safety, not only by requiring capital adequacy from his counterparty but also by implementing proper internal procedures, controls, and contractual arrangements. Prudent management practices can go a long way toward preventing fraud.

NOTES

[1] The Bevill, Bresler and Schulman failure triggered the failures of several small securities firms in the Midwest. Recently some smaller failures have occurred, such as Parr Securities. Earlier failures included the Lion Capital Group and RTD in 1984 and Drysdale Government Securities in 1982.

[2] See Bobbie H. McCrackin, A. E. Martin III, and William B. Estes, III, "State and Local Governments Use of Repos: A Southeastern Perspective," *Economic Review*, Federal Reserve Bank of Atlanta, September, 1985.

[3] See Richard Syron and Sheila L. Tschinkel, "The Government Securities Market: Playing Field for Repos," Reading 19 in this book.

[4] For more information on government securities, see Exhibit 1, Reading 19, in Syron and Tschinkel.

[5] See Exhibit 2 in Syron and Tschinkel, Reading 19.

[6] Transactions in certain securities have traditionally been exempt from regulation. These include Treasury and agency issues, bankers' acceptances, commercial paper, and CDs.

[7] See Gary Haberman and Catherine Piche, "Controlling Credit Risk Associated with Repos: Know Your Counterparty," *Economic Review*, Federal Reserve Bank of Atlanta, September 1985.

[8] See Don Ringsmuth, "Custodial Arrangements and Other Contractual Considerations," *Economic Review*, Federal Reserve Bank of Atlanta, September 1985.

[9] See Sheila L. Tschinkel, "Identifying and Controlling Market Risk," *Economic Review*, Federal Reserve Bank of Atlanta, September 1985.

19

The Government Securities Market: Playing Field for Repos

Richard Syron and Sheila L. Tschinkel

Our nation's government securities market is characterized by its huge volume, its efficiency, and its lack of comprehensive regulation. Here is a look at how the market operates and why it has grown so rapidly.

Repurchase agreements are important transactions in the U.S. government securities market, the world's largest and most liquid capital market—having absorbed over $1 trillion in gross new issues in 1984 to raise close to $200 billion in new funds and to refinance maturing debt.

The market has grown substantially in recent years because of the rapid expansion of Treasury debt. Trading in the secondary market has grown at an even faster pace. One salient characteristic of this market is its lack of comprehensive regulation. This freedom has encouraged rapid entry into the market by many types of firms, keen competition, and extraordinary innovation.

Understanding the market's structure and functions is essential to gaining a sound understanding of repurchase agreements, including recent problems involving their use and the procedures necessary to avoid loss. This article describes the market's structure, the organization and operations of major participants, and its performance.

THE MARKET'S STRUCTURE

The government securities market consists of five broad categories of participants: the U.S. Treasury Department, the Federal Reserve System, primary securities dealers, other dealers, and a wide array of investors. The fount of this market is the Treasury Department, the preeminent issuer of short and long-term

From *Economic Review,* Federal Reserve Bank of Atlanta, September 1985, pp. 10–19.

The authors are senior vice president and advisor at the Federal Reserve Bank of Boston and senior vice president and director of research at the Federal Reserve Bank of Atlanta, respectively. This article also draws from work done by Edward Geng, senior vice president of the Federal Reserve Bank of New York.

debt securities on a regular basis. The Treasury auctions bills, notes, and bonds to finance new U.S. government debt as well as maturing securities (See Exhibit 1). Several government-sponsored agencies also issue securities. Government and agency securities have a wide variety of maturities, and this along with particular characteristics and the level of interest rates determines their market values.

The Treasury does not market its securities directly but relies on the Federal Reserve to serve as its fiscal agent. The Fed's fiscal agency role has several aspects. The Fed issues most new securities on behalf of the Treasury through a computerized book-entry system (see Exhibit 2). Most Treasury securities no longer are issued in a tangible form as engraved certificates that can be kept in a vault, technically referred to as "definitive securities," and the issuance of definitive securities soon will be discontinued altogether. The Fed transfers most securities between depository institutions over its own wire system, called the "Fedwire," in much the same way money is transferred electronically among depository institutions. The Fed not only maintains and transfers securities but also handles the initial sale of the securities. The Fed conducts auctions of new Treasury securities by collecting and processing competitive and noncompetitive bids from dealers, banks, individuals, and others.

Although the Fed serves as fiscal agent for the Treasury, it does not buy securities directly from the Treasury (except to roll over maturing holdings). Rather, if the system wishes to change its own holdings of Treasury securities for monetary policy reasons, it does so by transactions in the open secondary market. Thus, the Federal Reserve has a key interest in the government securities market because of its responsibility for implementing monetary policy as well as executing investments for foreign central banks. The New York Fed's trading desk purchases and sells government securities to implement the directives of the Federal Open Market Committee.[1] The Fed's open market operations—or transactions in government securities—influence the pace of monetary expansion. The New York Fed often uses repos and a transaction similar to reverse repos to provide or absorb bank reserves on a temporary basis. Last year the aggregate gross volume of open market transactions including repurchase agreements and transactions similar to reverse repos exceeded $200 billion, in addition to Fed market transactions on behalf of 150 foreign central banks and other foreign official institutions.

In its market operations the Fed transacts only with certain dealers, known as primary dealers. Among these primary dealers, currently, are banks or bank subsidiaries, diversified investment houses, and specialty firms. There are now about 36 of these so-called primary dealers. Ten years ago there were about 25. No formal limit governs their number.

Primary dealers serve two crucial functions in the market: they help distribute the Treasury debt and they stand ready to "make markets," or buy and sell securities for customers. Their selection by the Fed as counterparties revolves around their ability to fulfill these two functions. Besides their ability to meet the needs of the Fed, criteria for being a primary dealer include volume of activity and participation in Treasury auctions, breadth of customer base, ability and commitment to buy and sell securities for customers even when market conditions are unfavorable, financial strength, depth of experience of management, and commitment to fulfilling this role over the long term.

EXHIBIT 1

Treasury Securities
Lisa Rockoff

The market for Treasury securities has grown rapidly in recent years largely in response to the federal government's expanding financial requirements. In addition to the growth in new issue activity, trading in the secondary market also has increased even more rapidly, attracting new dealers and greater customer participation.

What Are Treasury Securities?

The U.S. Treasury provides for the federal government's financial needs. In this capacity the Treasury is responsible for debt management, which includes borrowing funds to cover any shortfall between outlays and revenues and arranging for the refinancing, servicing, and repayment of maturing debt.[1] To meet this responsibility the Treasury issues debt securities in a wide variety of initial maturities. The best-known Treasury securities are bills, notes, and bonds. Bills are short-term, one year or less; notes are medium-term, one to 10 years; and bonds are long-term issues, greater than 10 years. Currently, the Treasury issues three-month, six- month, and one-year bills in minimum denominations of $10,000, with multiples of $5,000; two- through 10-year notes; and 20- and 30-year bonds in denominations of $1,000, $5,000, $10,000, $100,000, and $1 million. Occasionally, the Treasury issues very short-term cash management bills, with minimum denominations of $1 million, to bridge gaps when its cash balances are temporarily low.

The increasing size of the federal budget deficit in recent years has enlarged the volume of debt that the Treasury needs to sell. Because the timing and amount of its offerings can have a substantial impact on the financial markets, the Treasury has adopted a practice of issuing specific maturities on a regular schedule in order to facilitate absorption of its marketable debt with minimal disturbance. Quarterly Treasury announcements of the major mid-quarter refundings provide information on the exact amounts of each maturity to be offered, the amount of new cash to be raised by the operation, and the amount being refinanced. It also indicates the total amount of financing remaining to be done in that quarter and a range of financing likely to be done in the following quarter. Other auctions generally are announced about a week before they are held. The public can determine when an issue is forthcoming by consulting the financial sections of major daily newspapers or the 24-hour information lines on scheduled auctions at all 12 Federal Reserve Banks. In addition, customers may request that their names be added to any Federal Reserve Bank's mailing list for note and bond circulars.

How Are Treasury Securities Marketed?

Aside from nonmarketable securities, such as savings bonds, most Treasury securities can be bought in two ways—at Treasury auctions when they initially are offered or in the secondary market through a dealer. Initial interest rates on marketable, or negotiable, Treasury securities (and the coupons on coupon-bearing notes and bonds) are established at auction.

Bids are made on both a competitive and a noncompetitive basis. A competitive bidder submits a tender for the amount of securities he or she wishes to purchase at a specified rate carried out to two decimal places. The Treasury generally limits competitive tenders to 35 percent of the amount offered to the public in each auction per single bidder. A noncompetitive bidder specifies the amount of securities he wishes to purchase but agrees to accept the average rate (and price) established through competitive bidding. The Treasury limits noncompetitive tenders, except those of the Federal Reserve System and its customers, to $1 million per bidder. Therefore, most noncompetitive bids come from smaller investors.

On the day of the auction, all Federal Reserve Banks receive tenders until a specified time, usually 1 p.m. Eastern time. Subsequently, these are wired to the Treasury. After all timely bids have been received, the volume of noncompetitive tenders is subtracted from the total amount to be issued. Allowable noncompetitive tenders are accepted in full. The remainder of the issue is allocated to competitive bidders, beginning with those who bid the lowest rate. After filling the bids at the lowest rate, the Treasury awards issues at the next higher rate and so on until all of the issue has been awarded. A partial award may be made at the highest accepted rate (the stop-out rate) in order to come as close as possible to the exact amount the Treasury plans to sell. Once the stop-out bid is reached, a weighted average rate is computed from all accepted competitive bids. Noncompetitive bidders are awarded their securities at a price based on the established average rate. Competitive bidders whose tenders have been accepted pay the price equivalent to the rate they specified. Auction results can be found in the financial sections of many major daily newspapers on the day following the auction.

In most respects, auctions for bills are conducted in a manner similar to those for notes and bonds. There are a few key differences, though, largely due to differences in the way the two types of Treasury securities are priced, discussed below.[2]

How Are Prices and Rates of Return on Treasury Securities Determined?

Treasury Bills. Treasury bills, or T-bills, are non-interest bearing securities issued at a discount. That is, Treasury sells the bills at a price that is below their face value—or at a discount—and redeems them at face value. Thus, the return to the investor is determined by the discount at which the securities are bought and the length of time until maturity. The Treasury computes the price per $100 face value of discount securities using the following formula:

EXHIBIT 1 *(continued)*

$$P = \left(1 - \frac{r_d \times D}{360}\right) \times 100$$

where

P = price per $100 face amount,

r_d = interest rate on a discount basis decimalized (e.g. 7.36% = 0.736),

D = days to maturity.

For example, assume six-month (182-day) bills are purchased at a 7 percent discount rate. The price of the bill is calculated as follows:

$$P = \left(1 - \frac{0.07 \times 182}{360}\right) \times 100$$

=96.4611112

The Treasury rounds the price to three decimal places, so $96.461 is the price per $100 face value of securities. Thus, the purchase price of $1 million of these bills would be $964,610.00.

Rates quoted on a discount basis do not reflect the fact that the amount invested is less than the face value of the securities. In addition, Treasury bill rates are calculated on a 360-day basis, whereas interest on longer-maturity Treasury securities is computed on a 365-day basis. To allow rate comparisons, bill rates are often converted into bond-equivalent yields (BEY). The BEY on a discount instrument with a maturity of six months or less is derived as follows:

$$BEY = 100 \times \left[\frac{(100 - P) \times 365}{P \times D}\right]$$

Using our earlier example, the bond-equivalent yield on a six-month bill with a 7 percent discount rate is found as follows:

$$BEY = 100 \times \left[\frac{(100 - 96.461) \times 365}{96.461 \times 182}\right]$$

= 7.36%

For a bill with a maturity of six months or more, the BEY calculation must reflect the approximate return that would have been obtained if interest had been paid at the end of six months (since interest payments on securities with interest coupons are made every six months). The formula is complex but similar in principle to deriving the yield on coupon securities in the case where the coupon is set at zero.

Treasury notes and bonds. Unlike bills, notes and bonds pay separate interest every six months. They carry a fixed interest payment, the coupon rate, and, hence, are also called coupon securities. The coupon rate is established at auction.[4] Bidding on coupon issues is based on yields, not prices. After an issue has been awarded at auction, the Treasury establishes a fixed coupon, rounded down to the nearest eighth of one percent, based on the weighted average of the accepted competitive yields.

The price charged to competitive bidders is set at or rounded down to slightly below par. At the time of issue, prices are expressed as a percentage of par, par equaling 100.

In the secondary market, fractional prices are expressed in 32nds. Securities that trade below par are said to be at a discount, while those trading above par are said to be at a premium. For example, the price of a coupon security trading below par might be expressed as 99 12/32, often shown as 99.12. This figure represents a price of $993.75 for a $1,000 bond. A bond trading above par might be quoted at 102 5/32, or 102.5, implying a price of $1,021.56 for a $1,000 bond.

The coupon rate established on any note or bond represents the simple annual interest rate the Treasury pays to the investor on the face value. Since the Treasury pays interest semiannually, the interest payment each six months is represented by the formula:

$$i = \frac{\text{Coupon Rate} \times \text{Face Value}}{2}$$

The rate of return on notes and bonds held to maturity when both the present value of the future interest payments and the redemption value of the security are taken into account is called the yield to maturity. The present value may be viewed as the amount one is willing to pay now for the stream of coupon payments plus the face value received at maturity. The higher (or lower) the yield, the less (or more) one is willing to pay to receive any specified payment in the future. Thus, price varies inversely with yield.

The longer the maturity of the security, the greater the number of payments. Also, the further away a payment is in time, the more its present value changes in response to any change in yield. Thus, for any given yield change the size of the resulting price change—or volatility—varies directly with maturity.

Finally, price changes depend on the coupon. The lower the coupon, the larger the share that the present value of the final payment represents in the calculation of present value or price. Since that payment is furthest in the future—and so is most sensitive to a yield change—the more the price of the entire security will change to reflect a given change in yield. Thus, price volatility varies inversely with the coupon rate. Some investors use a measure known as duration in figuring yield. While the computation of this measure is too complex to describe succinctly, duration essentially recognizes both the relative importance of coupons and the final maturity of a bond or note. Therefore, the price volatility of debt securities varies directly with both their duration and the volatility of interest rates.

In calculating yield to maturity one assumes coupon payments are reinvested every six months at the same yield, specifically the yield to maturity. Although using a current interest rate as a proxy for future rates is somewhat arbitrary, alternative methods involve estimating expected rates in the future, an extremely complex and equally unrealistic process.

After-tax yield calculations need to take into account any capital gain or loss arising from the difference between a security's purchase price and its face value at redemption. For example, if an investor purchases

EXHIBIT 1 *(concluded)*

notes and bonds at slightly below par, say, at 99.120 (or $993.75 for a $1,000 bond) and redeems it at face value (or $1,000), the investor receives a capital gain of $6.25.

Most outstanding 30-year bonds have 25-year call provisions, which allow the Treasury to redeem the bonds at par after 25 years. Technically, the Treasury might exercise this option if interest rates 25 years after issue are below the coupon on the bond. Valuation of

callable bonds can be complex, but they typically behave as if they have a 25-year maturity when interest rates are significantly below their coupons and a 30-year maturity when the opposite holds.

The author is an analyst in the Research Department of the Federal Reserve Bank of Atlanta.

NOTES

[1] Treasury borrowing constitutes only one part—albeit the largest—of total government-related borrowing. Federally sponsored agencies set up by Congress to make credit available to specific sectors of the economy also borrow. Agencies financing in the open market include the Federal National Mortgage Association (FNMA), the Farm Credit Banks, the Federal Home Loan Banks, and the Government National Mortgage Association (GNMA). There are differences between Treasury and agency borrowing. First, whereas the Treasury borrows to finance the federal deficit, agencies act more as financial intermediaries. Second, while some agency debt is guaranteed as to principal and interest by the U.S. government or has the full faith backing of the U.S. government, other agency debt does not have this backing.
[2] Another difference pertains to tenders by the Fed. Fed tenders typically are noncompetitive. On three- and six-month T-bills the amount tendered by the Fed is subtracted from the total. In contrast, the amount tendered by the Fed on one-year T-bills, notes, and bonds is not subtracted from the

total since the Fed is issued securities in addition to the amount offered to the public.
[3] The bill price formula illustrates that price varies inversely with interest rate. It also reflects the fact that, for any given rate change, the size of price movements varies directly with the maturity of the bill. That is, the farther away in time a customer receives the face amount, the less he is willing to pay now for the bill.
[4] Under the public debt statutes there is a 4 1/4 percent interest-rate limit on bonds. When interest rates were low, the Treasury had no problem issuing bonds under this constraint. As interest rates rose, though, this limit forced the Treasury to concentrate debt issuance in short- to intermediate-term issues. Therefore, in the early 1970s Congress granted a partial exemption from this ceiling for a specified dollar amount (face) of bonds and has since raised these amounts several times. Congress also responded to the problem by extending the maturity of notes (which are not subject to the rate ceiling) from a maximum of five years to seven and later to ten years.

In addition to primary dealers, many other firms routinely trade in U.S. government securities. These also include a mix of depository institutions, diversified securities firms, and specialty firms. Some participating firms are as large as primary dealers but have elected not to seek designation as such. Others service clients in a particular region. Still others may specialize in small transactions or odd lots.

This diversity is advantageous to investors because it provides them a greater choice of firms and services. Of course, these investors in government securities make up the largest sector of the market, and they include individuals; insurance, financial, and other corporations; funds; state and local governments and authorities; banks and savings institutions; and foreign investors.

HOW GOVERNMENT SECURITIES DEALERS OPERATE

Government securities dealers perform three interrelated activities. First, they make markets for customers and provide information, analysis, and advice to encourage transactions and customer loyalty. Second, to meet customer needs, they generally maintain an inventory of securities. The composition of this inventory is structured to allow dealers to sell securities at a higher price than they bought them. Third, they manage their positions, speculating on market trends with a view to profiting from swings in interest rates.

When a dealer makes a bid or an offer to a customer, the dealer is buying or selling securities for its position. That is, the dealer is acting as principal and not as agent. When a dealer finances his holdings of securities, he is also acting as a principal. Thus, dealers are distinct from brokers. The latter earn a profit by acting as go-betweens, matching parties with complementary needs and charging a commission for their services.

EXHIBIT 2

The Book-Entry System for Treasury Securities[1]
A. E. Martin III

An important aspect of the government securities market is understanding how a book-entry system for recording ownership of and interests in securities operates. In contrast to "definitive" securities (those represented by a physical certificate), an interest in book-entry securities is reflected by an entry, often computerized, in the accounts of a book-entry custodian indicating the party for whom it holds the securities. The following discussion provides a brief overview of the book-entry system for U.S. Treasury securities. U.S. Treasury bills are issued exclusively in book-entry form; Treasury notes and bonds, although available in

definitive form as well, are held mainly in book-entry. Moreover, the Treasury Department has announced its plans to offer new issues of Treasury notes and bonds exclusively in book-entry form beginning some time in 1986.

The book-entry system for Treasury securities is governed by Treasury regulations, which facilitate the establishment of a "tiered" custodial system whereby the ownership of securities is represented by entries on the books of a series of custodians. This system extends from the Treasury itself through the Federal Reserve Banks, depository institutions, and brokers

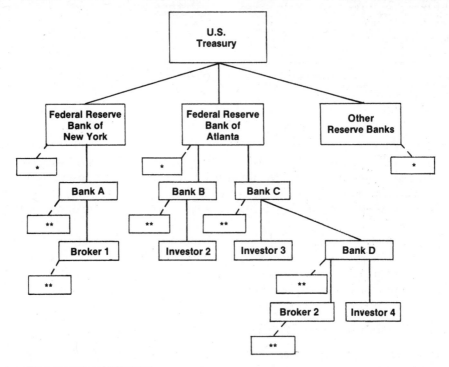

*Other depository institutions.
**Other custodians (depository institutions, brokers/dealers, etc.) or ultimate investors.

EXHIBIT 2 *(concluded)*

or dealers to the ultimate owner or party in interest.[2] The Treasury's records reflect the total amount of an issue of securities outstanding and the portion held by each Federal Reserve Bank. In turn, each Reserve Bank's entries establish how much of the issue is held by the depository institutions in its district that maintain book-entry accounts with it.[3]

A depository institution's records further divide the amount it holds at its Reserve Bank, reflecting how much it holds for itself, for other depository institutions (including those that do not maintain accounts at the Federal Reserve), for brokers and dealers, and for the ultimate investors. Thus, the custodial chain may include only the Treasury, a Reserve Bank, and a depository institution, or additional custodians such as other depository institutions and broker/dealers. Payments of principal at maturity as well as interest payments on Treasury notes and bonds are made through the crediting of funds by the Treasury down through the custodial tiers.

Under Treasury regulations and the operating circulars of the Reserve Banks, only depository institutions may have book-entry accounts at a Reserve Bank.[4] Other parties must have their holdings reflected on the books of a depository institution or other "depositary" that in turn holds through a depository institution.[5] In certain limited instances, such as the pledge of securities by a depository institution to secure the deposits of state or local government funds, a third party's interest in book-entry securities may be noted at the Reserve Bank level. However, securities acquired under a repurchase agreement are not held to secure deposits and are not eligible for such treatment.

Transfers and pledges of book-entry securities are effected by making appropriate entries, according to the instructions of the parties involved in the transaction, on the records of the custodian(s) involved. Under Treasury regulations, making such an entry renders the custodian a "bailee," or legal custodian, with respect to the party for whom it holds.[6] Referring to the chart, a transfer from Broker 1 to Investor 2 would involve not only the ultimate making of an entry on Bank B's books, reflecting the transfer to Investor 2, and on Broker 1's books, decreasing its own holdings, but also entries on the books of Banks A and B, both Federal Reserve Banks, and the Treasury. A transfer from Investor 2 to Investor 3 would entail entries on the books of Banks B and C and the Atlanta Reserve Bank but not the Treasury. At the other extreme, a transfer from Broker 2 to Investor 4 would involve only an entry on the books of Bank D, reallocating a portion of the amount it held through its Reserve Bank between Broker 2 and Investor 4. No revision of entries on the books of the Reserve Bank or the Treasury would be involved.

Under Treasury regulations, a transfer or pledge of book-entry securities is accomplished by means that would be effective under applicable law a transfer or perfect a pledge of definitive securities in bearer form. No filing or recording with a public recording office or officer is required. A transferee, or pledgee, may obtain from its custodian acknowledgment that securities are held for it. A Reserve Bank, however, deals exclusively with the depository institutions for which it holds book-entry accounts and does not accept notices or instructions from remote parties holding through depository institutions regarding their interests in securities.

Procedurally, transactions are effected by instructions transmitted by and through the parties and custodians involved. If a transaction involves entries on the books of a Reserve Bank or several Reserve Banks (and the Treasury), then the Fedwire (the Federal Reserve's wire transfer system) is used to transmit instructions electronically.[7] For transactions that do not reach the Reserve Bank level in the custodial chain, no specific mode of communication is required for the transfer. This distinction has implications for repurchase transactions of small amounts or short duration.

Don Ringsmuth's article in this issue discusses several types of delivery and custodial arrangements that can be used in a repo transaction. The foregoing summary of the mechanics of the book-entry system for Treasury securities is designed to provide only a brief structural overview of the system. There are additional issues and factors that require expertise or the advice of experienced counsel to engage in repo transactions.

The author is an attorney in the Legal Department of the Federal Reserve Bank of Atlanta.

NOTES

[1]This box discusses only the book-entry system for Treasury securities, although similar systems exist for other types of securities that are also used in repo transactions, including some securities issued by federal agencies and handled by the Federal Reserve.

[2]Subpart O of 31 C.F.R. Part 306 - The General Regulations Governing United States Securities ("Treasury regulations") governs the book-entry system for Treasury securities. Virtually identical rules with respect to Treasury bills held in book-entry through the Federal Reserve are contained in Subpart D of 31 C.F.R. Part 350. Subpart C of these Treasury bill regulations also establishes a system whereby Treasury bills may be held in book-entry accounts maintained by the Treasury itself. Transactions in bills so held, however, require that the bills be transferred into the tiered system described in this article.

[3]Prior to the Monetary Control Act of 1980, only member banks of the Federal Reserve System could maintain book-entry accounts with the Federal Reserve. Now any depository institution may do so.

[4]Section 306.117 of the Treasury regulations; each of the Federal Reserve Banks has issued an operating circular, letter, or bulletin containing additional provisions governing the maintenance of book-entry securities accounts at the Federal Reserve. See, e.g., Operating Circular No. 21 of the Federal Reserve Bank of Atlanta.

[5]Under the Treasury's regulations (section 306.118(b)), a "depositary" is defined as a bank, banking institution, financial firm, or similar party, which regularly accepts in the course of its business Treasury securities as a custodial service for customers and maintains accounts in the names of such customers reflecting ownership of or interest in such securities. In this box, the term "custodian" is used rather than "depositary" to avoid confusion with the term "depository institution," which is one type of depositary.

[6]Section 306.118(b) of the Treasury regulations.

[7]Each of the Federal Reserve Banks also has issued an operating letter or circular regarding the wire transfer of book-entry securities, such as Operating Circular No. 20 of the Federal Reserve Bank of Atlanta.

Securities dealers absorb and distribute a large share of the U.S. government debt when it is sold at auction. They also buy and sell existing securities in the secondary market. The price at which a dealer is willing to buy a security is called a "bid"; the price at which he is willing to sell is an "offer." A dealer firm tries to earn the spread between the bid and offer prices on customer transactions.

Dealers also position securities to reflect their assessment of likely changes in interest rates. If a dealer expects interest rates to fall and hence prices of debt securities to rise, he will typically "take a long position" in these issues. If he expects rates to rise, he will "go short," selling securities he does not own in the expectation of buying the securities back later at a lower price. Long and short positions generally are highly leveraged, or supported with borrowed funds, at times to over 99 percent. Thus, position management is a major source of variation in profit and capital in either direction.

As explained earlier, in a repo the dealer agrees to sell a security at a specified price for a specified period, after which he agrees to repurchase the security, usually at the agreed-upon price. In return for the security, the dealer receives funds to finance its positions in government securities. Since the dealer has use of the customer's money while the repurchase agreement is outstanding, the dealer agrees to pay interest to the customer.

Dealers often use reverse repos, whereby they provide money and take in customer securities, to obtain the securities they have sold short—those they have sold without owning and need to deliver. When one party is executing a repo, the counterparty must be executing a reverse repo.

Some dealers also arrange repos and reverse repos at the same time, operating what is called a "matched book," to earn income from the spreads between what they receive from one type of transaction and pay for the other. Such dealers are acting as a principal and are intermediating, or raising funds from one customer and providing funds to another.

Matched books also may be used to speculate on the direction of short-term interest rates. If a dealer expects short-term rates to rise, he will arrange repos with a longer maturity than the reverse repos in his matched book. That is, he will raise funds for a longer period than he provides them, expecting that rates on the rollover of the reverse repo will rise relative to the rate set on the repo.

TYPES OF DEALER ORGANIZATION

The way that a government securities operation fits into a firm's overall organizational structure determines whether the operation is subject to the oversight and capital rules of the SEC. Four forms of organization are widely used by government securities dealers. The simplest is a single firm, where the government securities dealer is a department in the overall securities firm or bank. In two cases the dealer operation is a separate subsidiary in a holding company; in the other, the dealer is a commonly owned affiliate. Securities firms of all sizes use the holding company structure. In many instances, the holding company is a shell with activity transacted through its subsidiaries (see Chart 1).

Government securities may be traded in the same entity which also trades nonexempt securities. In this case, the whole entity, including its government securities operations, is subject to SEC rules. However, many organizations using a holding company structure conduct regulated activities through their principal

CHART 1
Common Holding Company Structure

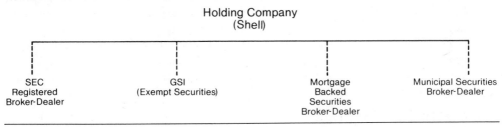

Holding Company
(Shell)

| SEC Registered Broker-Dealer | GSI (Exempt Securities) | Mortgage Backed Securities Broker-Dealer | Municipal Securities Broker-Dealer |

subsidiary, a broker-dealer registered with the Securities and Exchange Commission, while government and other exempt security activity is transacted through another subsidiary known as a Government Securities, Inc. (GSI). The GSI is not constrained by the SEC's capital or custodial rules.

The separation of exempt and nonexempt securities activities increases the firm's overall flexibility. For example, less capital must be devoted to the GSI than would be the case if the business were SEC regulated. Similarly, an organization may use other subsidiaries to separate management authority or legal liability for other activities, such as mortgage-backed or municipal bond trading.

Using another organizational structure, many smaller specialty firms concentrate their government and other exempt securities trading in the parent company while setting up a small SEC-registered broker/dealer subsidiary to trade in regulated markets (see Chart 2). A fourth form of organization involves affiliation of multiple firms through common ownership (see Chart 3).

CHART 2
Common Specialty Firm Structure

Parent
(Exempt Securities)

| SEC Registered Broker-Dealer | Municipal Securities Broker-Dealer | Other Sales |

CHART 3
Common Holding Company Structure

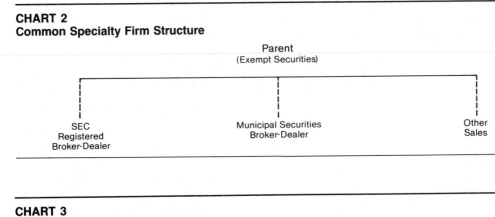

Common Ownership

SEC Registered Broker-Dealer – – – – – – – – – Municipal Securities Broker-Dealer – – – – – – – – – GSI (Exempt Securities) – – – – – – – – – Other Entities

Customers should be careful to review financial statements for the specific subsidiary with which they are dealing. In some cases, financial statements for holding companies with multiple subsidiaries are prepared for the consolidated firm only. In these consolidated holding company financial statements, the footnotes concerning "excess capital" under the SEC's rules refer only to the SEC-regulated affiliates. Furthermore, common ownership or affiliation may or may not be reported in financial statements or disclosed by the firm. If there are substantial transactions with affiliates, customers should ask for financial statements on any such affiliated entities.

REGULATORY FRAMEWORK

Whether a particular dealer firm is subject to official oversight depends on the markets in which the firm participates and on its individual characteristics and organization. Most diversified securities houses, for example, deal in corporate issues and municipal securities as well as U.S. government securities. Since the Securities and Exchange Commission regulates corporate issues, these firms are subject to SEC regulation. The SEC, in turn, delegates some of its supervisory responsibilities to the various stock exchanges, the National Association of Securities Dealers, and the Municipal Securities Rule-Making Board. Some small government securities dealers that participate in the financial futures exchanges are regulated by the Commodities Futures Trading Commission (CFTC). Because of their corporate affiliation, dealer departments of banks are subject to examination by federal and state bank regulatory authorities such as the Fed, the Office of the Comptroller of the Currency (OCC), and the Federal Deposit Insurance Corporation (FDIC). Primary dealers also are subject to oversight by the Fed. The New York Fed scrutinizes the primary dealers with which it transacts as part of its business relationship with them and its concern for the health of the markets. The Fed, however, has no statutory authority to regulate these firms.

Some government securities dealers are free from any form of federal supervision or regulation. Dealers in this group trade only exempt securities—U.S. government and agency securities, certificates of deposit, bankers' acceptances, and commercial paper—and are not subject to examination by the SEC, the Fed, or any federal banking regulator. Furthermore, there is no federal regulation of GSI subsidiaries or affiliates of seemingly "regulated" firms.

ADVANTAGES AND DISADVANTAGES OF UNRESTRICTED ENTRY

The government securities market, in many respects, exemplifies the free markets described in classical economics. No formal barriers restrict entry. Dealers must meet no licensing requirements, for example. Anyone can become a government securities dealer, and the diversity among secondary dealers demonstrates that many different kinds of businesses enter the market. Once a firm is in the market, no uniform capital requirements or standards for custodial control or sales practices apply. Furthermore, there are no margin requirements; dealers can and often do finance over 99 percent of the purchase cost of most Treasury securities.

The resultant structure of the securities market has produced competition, efficiency, and innovation. The profusion of competitors helps narrow the spread between the prices at which a dealer buys securities from a customer and the prices at which a dealer sells securities to a customer. This clearly is advantageous to customers. Customers also benefit by being able to compare the prices offered by several dealers over the telephone or through dedicated telecommunications services that report such information continually. The availability of information enables customers to transact at the best price. The market's intense competitiveness also reduces the Treasury's cost of issuing debt. Finally, free entry has enabled all kinds and sizes of customers to obtain service from the myriad firms in the market.

However, the lack of uniform supervision has permitted abuses to go undetected longer than they probably would have under a more regulated regime. The wide scope of these problems became apparent earlier this year when defaults by several government securities dealers resulted in costly losses for a number of local governments and thrift institutions. Given the problems that have appeared in the repo market, many people, including members of Congress, have questioned whether the government securities market should remain under its current incomplete and diverse regulatory framework. Several bills have been introduced in Congress to address this issue.

The Federal Reserve favors some form of minimum regulation involving registration, capital and operating standards, and inspection. To help protect investors in the interim or in the absence of full-scale regulation, the Federal Reserve has developed a voluntary capital adequacy guideline for government securities dealers not already subject to some regulation.[2] The guideline, along with the Fed's efforts to educate investors regarding proper procedures to use with repurchase agreements, is designed to help guard against abuses while minimizing inefficiencies and additional costs and preserving the strength and dynamism of the market.

CONCLUSION

The government securities market enjoys a favorable record characterized by efficiency, competitiveness, and innovation. While the recent spate of losses involving investors in repurchase agreements is disturbing, failures and defaults have been rare exceptions. The liquidity and other positive characteristics provided by the market have contributed to its growth and attractiveness to a broad array of investors and made the market a vital part of our nation's financial markets.

NOTES

[1] The FOMC consists of the seven members of the Board of Governors, including the chairman, the president of the Federal Reserve Bank of New York, and presidents of the other 11 district banks, serving on a rotating basis.

[2] This is discussed in Gary Haberman and Catherine Piche, "Controlling Credit Risk Associated with Repos: Know Your Counterparty," *Economic Review,* Federal Reserve Bank of Atlanta, September 1985.

20

Commercial Paper

Peter A. Abken

Commercial paper is a short-term unsecured promissory note that is generally sold by large corporations on a discount basis to institutional investors and to other corporations. Since commercial paper is unsecured and bears only the name of the issuer, the market has generally been dominated by large corporations with the highest credit ratings. In recent years, commercial paper has attracted much attention because of its rapid growth and its use as an alternative to short-term bank loans. The number of firms issuing commercial paper rose from slightly over 300 in 1965 to about 1,000 in 1980. Moreover, the outstanding volume of commercial paper increased at an annual rate of 12.4 percent during the 1970s to a level of $123 billion in June 1980. This article describes the commercial paper market, focusing primarily on the 1970s, the period of greatest change and growth.

MARKET CHARACTERISTICS

The principal issuers of commercial paper include finance companies, nonfinancial companies, and bank holding companies. These issuers participate in the market for different reasons and in different ways. Finance companies raise funds on a more or less continuous basis in the commercial paper market to support their consumer and business lending. These commercial paper sales in part provide interim financing between issues of long-term debentures. Nonfinancial companies issue commercial paper at less frequent intervals than do finance companies. These firms issue paper to meet their funding requirements for short-term or seasonal expenditures such as inventories, payrolls, and tax liabilities. Bank holding companies use the commercial paper market to finance primarily banking-related activities, such as leasing, mortgage banking, and consumer finance.

Denominations and Maturities

Like other instruments of the money market, commercial paper is sold to raise large sums of money quickly and for short periods. Although sometimes issued in denominations as small as $25,000 or $50,000, most commercial paper offerings

---

From *Instruments of the Money Market*, 5th ed., Federal Reserve Bank of Richmond.

are in multiples of $100,000. The average purchase size of commercial paper is about $2 million. The average issuer has $120 million in outstanding commercial paper; some of the largest issuers individually have several billion dollars in outstanding paper.

Exemption from registration requirements with the Securities and Exchange Commission reduces the time and expense of readying an issue of commercial paper for sale. Almost all outstanding commercial paper meets the conditions for exemption, namely: (1) that it have an original maturity of no greater than 270 days and (2) that the proceeds be used to finance current transactions. The average maturity of outstanding commercial paper is under 30 days, with most paper falling within the 20- to 45-day range.

Placement

Issuers place commercial paper with investors either directly using their own sales force or indirectly using commercial paper dealers. The method of placement depends primarily on the transaction costs of these alternatives. Dealers generally charge a one eighth of one percent commission on face value for placing paper. Therefore, if a firm places $100 million in commercial paper using the intermediary services of a dealer, commissions would cost $125 thousand. There are six major commercial paper dealers.

Firms with an average amount of outstanding commercial paper of several hundred million dollars or more generally find it less costly to maintain a sales force and market their commercial paper directly. Almost all direct issuers are large finance companies. The short-term credit demands of nonfinancial companies are usually seasonal or cyclical in nature, which lessens the attractiveness of establishing a permanent commercial paper sales staff. Consequently, almost all nonfinancial companies, including large ones, rely on dealers to distribute heir paper.

There is no active secondary market in commercial paper. Dealers and direct issuers may redeem commercial paper before maturity, if an investor has an urgent demand for funds. However, dealers and direct issuers discourage this practice. Early redemptions of commercial paper rarely occur primarily because the average maturity of commercial paper is so short. One major commercial paper dealer estimates that only 2 percent of their outstanding commercial paper is redeemed prior to maturity.

Quality Ratings

The one thousand or so firms issuing paper obtain ratings from at least one of three services, and most obtain two ratings. The three rating companies that grade commercial paper borrowers are Moody's Investors Service, Standard & Poor's Corporation, and Fitch Investor Service. Table 1 shows the number of companies rated by Moody's, classified by industry. This table, covering 881 issues, gives a good indication of the industry grouping of issuers. Moody's describes its ratings procedure as follows:

> Moody's evaluates the salient features that affect a commercial paper issuer's financial and competitive position. Our appraisal includes, but is not limited to the review of factors such as: quality of management, industry strengths and risks, vulnerability to business cycles, competitive position, liquidity measurements, debt structure,

TABLE 1
Industry Grouping of Commercial Paper Issuers Rated by Moody's (November 3, 1980)

Industry Grouping	Number of Firms Rated	Percentage of Total Firms Rated
Industrial.................	370	42.0%
Public utilities	193	21.9
Finance	155	17.6
Bank holding	119	13.6
Mortgage finance	9	1.0
Insurance	25	2.8
Transportation	10	1.1
Total	881	100.0

Source: Moody's Bond Survey, Annual Review.

operating trends, and access to capital markets. Differing weights are applied to these factors as deemed appropriate for indiviual situations.[1]

The other rating services use similar criteria in evaluating issuers. From highest to lowest quality, paper ratings run: P-1, P-2, P-3 for Moody's; A-1, A-2, A-3 for Fitch. For all rating services as of mid-1980, the average distribution of outstanding commercial paper for the three quality gradations was about 75 percent for grade 1, 24 percent for grade 2, and 1 percent for grade 3. As will be discussed below, the difference in ratings can translate into considerable differences in rates, particularly during periods of financial stress.

The multifaceted rating system used by Moody's reflects the heterogeneous financial characteristics of commercial paper. Paper of different issuers, even with the same quality rating, is not readily substitutable. Consequently, commercial paper tends to be difficult to trade, and bid-asked spreads on paper of a particular grade and maturity run a wide ⅛ of a percentage point.

Backup Lines of Credit

In most cases, issuers back their paper 100 percent with lines of credit from commercial banks. Even though its average maturity is very short, commercial paper still poses the risk that an issuer might not be able to pay off or roll over maturing paper. Consequently, issuers use a variety of backup lines as insurance against periods of financial stress or tight money. These credit lines are contractual agreements that are tailored to issuers' needs. Standard credit line agreements allow commercial paper issuers to borrow under a 90-day note. Swing lines provide funds over very short periods, often to cover a shortfall in the actual proceeds of paper issued on a particular day. Revolving lines of credit establish credit sources that are available over longer periods of time, usually several years.

Noninterest Costs of Issuing Commercial Paper

There are three major noninterest costs associated with commercial paper: (1) backup lines of credit, (2) fees to commercial banks, and (3) rating services fees. Payment for backup lines is usually made in the form of compensating balances, which generally equal about 10 percent of total credit lines extended plus 20 percent of credit lines activated. Instead of compensating balances, issuers sometimes pay straight fees ranging from 3/8 to 3/4 percent of the line of credit; this explicit pricing procedure has been gaining acceptance in recent years. Another cost associated with issuing commercial paper is fees paid to the large commercial banks that act as issuing and paying agents for the paper issuers. These commercial banks handle the paperwork involved in issuing commercial paper and collect the proceeds from an issue to pay off or roll over a maturing issue. Finally, rating services charge fees ranging from $5,000 to $25,000 per year to provide ratings for issuers. Foreign issuers pay from $3,500 to $10,000 per year more for ratings, depending on the rating service.

Investors

Investors in commercial paper include money center banks, nonfinancial firms, investment firms, state and local governments, private pension funds, foundations, and individuals. In addition, savings and loan associations and mutual savings banks have recently been granted authority to invest up to 20 percent of their assets in commercial paper. These groups may buy commercial paper from dealers or directly from issuers, or they may buy shares in short-term investment pools that include commercial paper. Except for scattered statistics, the distribution of commercial paper held by the various investor groups is not precisely known. At year-end 1979, all manufacturing, mining, and trade corporations held outright over $11 billion in commercial paper. A substantial but undocumented amount is held by utilities, communications, and service companies. Commercial banks held approximately $5 billion in their loan portfolios, while insurance companies had about $9 billion. Much commercial paper, about one third of the total amount outstanding, or $40 billion, is held indirectly through short-term investment pools, such as money market funds and short-term investment funds operated by bank trust departments. At year-end 1979, short-term investment pools held 32.5 percent of all outstanding commercial paper.

History of Commercial Paper

Commercial paper has a history that extends back to colonial times, prior to the existence of a banking system in America. The precursor of commercial paper was the domestic bill of exchange, which was used to finance trade as early as the beginning of the 18th century.[2] Bills of exchange allowed the safe and convenient transfer of funds and provided a short-term loan between the time of purchase and payment for goods. As financial intermediation evolved, banks and paper brokers began discounting paper. The supply of negotiable paper was held by commercial banks or by entrepreneurs investing surplus funds.

In marked contrast to today's commercial paper market, firms that relied upon commercial paper in earlier times were usually inferior credit risks that could not obtain bank credit. Reflecting this difference in credit risk, commercial paper rates in the early 19th century were much higher than bank lending rates. Another basic difference between the early and contemporary commercial paper markets is the type of obligation commercial paper represented. Up until the mid-19th century, paper bore both the names of the buyer of goods (the commercial paper issuer) and the seller of goods (the commercial paper drawee), and was issued in odd denominations according to the value of the underlying transaction being financed. Hence, commercial paper was called two-name because, if the issuer failed to pay an investor upon maturity of his outstanding paper, it became the obligation of the drawee. As trade and financing practices changed after the Civil

War, commercial paper began to be issued extensively as one-name paper (i.e, paper was only the issuer's obligation).[3] Also, the face value of the paper was unrelated to a specific purchase or shipment of goods and was instead issued in round lot denominations.

From the last quarter of the 19th century until the early 20th, commercial paper allowed borrowers and investors to take advantage of substantial seasonal and more persistent interest rate differentials that existed in different regions of the country. Because of the decentralized banking system that restricted individual banks to particular states and even localities, banks could not readily exploit regional interest rate differentials. However, commercial paper was marketed throughout the country. Commercial banks were able to invest in commercial paper issued in high interest rate areas. Similarly, firms could obtain funds more cheaply by selling commercial paper to banks in low interest rate areas instead of relying entirely on local bank loans.[4]

In the 1920s, commercial paper borrowers included manufacturers, wholesalers, and retailers in a wide variety of product lines. There were about 4,400 firms borrowing in the commercial paper market as a seasonal supplement to bank credit, which was the primary source of funds. Virtually all paper was handled by dealers. Finance companies emerged as major commercial paper borrowers as the automobile industry, sales finance, and small-loan companies grew in importance. In 1920, the largest sales-finance company, General Motors Acceptance Corporation, began to place its paper directly with investors and set maturities specified by investors. Other large finance companies began direct placement about a decade later.

Commercial banks held by far the largest portion of commercial paper outstanding, which served as a secondary reserve asset. Although no secondary market existed in commercial paper, banks nonetheless regarded paper as highly liquid because the impersonal nature of the credit usually meant there would be no requests for extensions or renewals. Moreover, paper provided banks with an opportunity to diversify their portfolios by industry and geographical area. After 1914, some categories of paper became eligible for discount by the Federal Reserve, which further increased commercial paper's liquidity.

Although the volume of directly placed paper increased during the 1920s, the total volume of paper outstanding declined. The outstanding volume of commercial paper fell precipitously between 1929 and 1932, from $420 million to $94 million, as the demand for business credit fell sharply in the Great Depression. In addition, the number of issuers diminished from several thousand to several hundred. From 1933 to the outbreak of World War II, the amount of commercial paper outstanding increased fairly steadily to $840 million, reflecting improvement in the general economy, the growing role of consumer credit in financing consumer durables, and the rapid rise of finance companies. Consequently, by 1941 commercial paper outstanding had returned to the levels of the first half of the 1920s. There was a decline in outstanding commercial paper from 1941 to 1945, however.

The immediate postwar period brought a resurgence in the commercial paper market and by 1951 the market recovered almost to its 1920 peak. The market had changed substantially, however. On the issuer side of the market, directly placed paper, predominantly paper issued by the three largest finance companies, rose to about two thirds of all paper outstanding by the early 1950s from about only one fifth at the trough of the Great Depression. On the investor side, nonfinancial corporations were now beginning to invest liquid assets in commercial paper instead of placing them strictly in demand deposit accounts. Banks were simultaneously relying to a much greater extent on Treasury securities as secondary reserve assets and were no longer the principal purchasers of commercial paper.

DEVELOPMENTS SINCE THE MID-1960s

Two events stimulated growth in commercial paper in the 1960s. First, during the last three quarters of 1966, interest rates rose above Regulation Q ceilings on bank negotiable certificates of deposit (CDs), making it difficult for banks to raise funds to meet the strong corporate loan demand existing at that time. Without sufficient funds to lend, banks encouraged their financially strongest customers to issue commercial paper and offered backup lines of credit. Many potential commercial paper borrowers who formerly relied exclusively on bank short-term credit now turned to the commercial paper market. Consequently, the annual growth rate of total outstanding commercial paper rose from 7.8 percent in 1965 to 46.6 percent in 1966.

Second, credit market tightness recurred in 1969 as open market interest rates rose above Regulation Q ceilings, again boosting growth in commercial paper. Financial innovation by banks contributed to this growth. The banking system sold commercial paper through bank holding companies, which used the funds to purchase part of their subsidiary banks' loan portfolios. This method of financing new loans resulted in rapid growth in bank-related commercial paper during late 1969 and early 1970, as is seen in Chart 1. The annual growth rate of total outstanding commercial paper more than doubled, to 54.7 percent in 1969. In August 1970, the Federal Reserve System imposed a reserve requirement on funds raised in the commercial paper market and channeled to a member bank by a bank holding company, or any of its affiliates or subsidiaries. As a result, bank-related commercial paper outstanding plummeted late in 1970 and early in 1971. This episode, however, marked only the beginning of bank use of commercial paper, which would regain prominence by the mid-1970s.

The Penn Central Crisis

The commercial paper market grew steadily during the 1960s. Only five defaults occurred during this decade, the largest of which amounted to $35 million. In 1970, however, the commercial paper market was rocked by Penn Central's default on $82 million of its outstanding commercial paper. The default caused investors to become wary of commercial paper issuers and more concerned about their creditworthiness. In the aftermath of the Penn Central default, many corporations experienced difficulty refinancing their maturing commercial paper. Financial disruption was lessened due to a Federal Reserve action, which removed Regulation Q interest-rate ceilings on 30-day to 89-day CDs and temporarily liberalized the discount policy for member banks. These actions insured that funds were available from commercial banks to provide alternative financing for corporations having difficulty rolling over commercial paper.

After the Penn Central episode, investors became more conscious of creditworthiness and more selective in their commercial paper purchases. During this

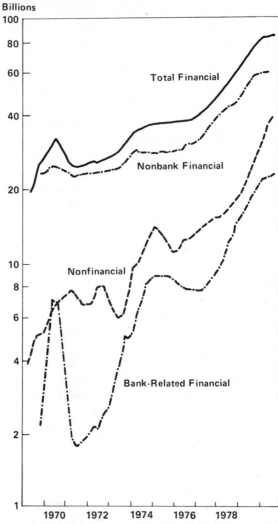

CHART 1
Outstanding Commercial Paper

Source: Board of Governors of the Federal Reserve System.

period, the heightened concern over creditworthiness was evidenced by a widening rate spread between the financially strongest and weakest paper issuers. Although some paper had been rated long before the Penn Central crisis, paper was now rated on a widespread basis.

Interest-Rate Controls

Wage and price controls imposed during the early 1970s dampened the growth of the commercial paper market. On October 15, 1971, the Committee on Interest and Dividends (CID) established voluntary restraints on "administered" rates, such as the prime rate. No restraints were placed on open market rates, however.

This policy triggered flows of funds between controlled and uncontrolled credit markets as the relationship between administered rates and market rates changed. As interest rates rose in 1972, banks came under pressure from the CID to moderate their prime-rate increases. By early 1973, the prime rate was held artificially below the commercial paper rate as a consequence of CID policy. Nonfinancial firms substituted short-term bank credit for funds raised through commercial paper issues. Consequently the volume of nonfinancial commercial paper outstanding fell sharply during the first and second quarters of 1973, as is seen in Chart 1. In April of 1973, the CID tried to stem the exodus from the commercial paper market by establishing a dual prime rate. One rate for large firms moved with open market rates, while the other for smaller firms was controlled. Despite these measures, the spread between commercial paper rates and the prime rate persisted and substitution out of paper continued. In the fourth quarter of 1973, CID controls were removed and the commercial paper rate dropped below the prime rate, causing substantial growth in commercial paper. This growth continued throughout 1975.

The 1973–75 Period

The recession of 1973–75 strained the paper market as investors became increasingly concerned about the financial strength of commercial paper issuers. Reflecting this concern, the quality-rate spread (the difference between the inter-

CHART 2
Yields and Spreads on 30-day Commercial Paper

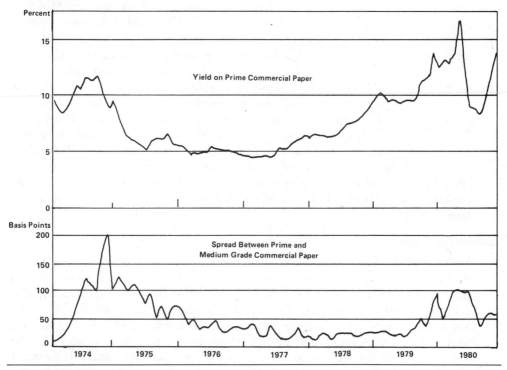

Source: Salomon Brothers.

est rates on highest-quality paper and medium-quality paper) rose from about 12 basis points in January 1974 to 200 basis points in November of that year. Chart 2 shows movements in the quality spread from 1974 to 1980. Utility companies experienced problems selling commercial paper as their ratings were downgraded. Real Estate Investment Trusts (REITs) were another group to encounter problems in the commercial paper market. Loan defaults and foreclosure proceedings early in the recession led to financial difficulties and resulted in a downgrading of REIT paper. As a result, many REITs and utilities were forced to turn to bank credit.

Bank holding companies also experienced difficulty issuing commercial paper in the spring of 1974. The failure of Franklin National Bank caused widespread concern about the strength of other banking organizations. As a consequence, smaller bank holding companies in particular found it hard to place their paper. Nonetheless, the aggregate volume of outstanding bank-related commercial paper remained relatively unchanged during this period of uncertainty. In general, the strongest paper issuers with prime ratings sold their paper without problems during the 1973–75 recession, although less financially sound issuers had to pay a premium to acquire funds in the commercial paper market.

The Late 1970s

After the 1973–75 recession, the commercial paper market grew rapidly. The volume of outstanding nonfinancial commercial paper expanded at a 31.9 percent compound annual rate from the first quarter of 1980. Over the same period, nonbank financial paper grew at a 20.1 percent compound annual rate and bank-related paper at a 27.9 percent annual rate. The number of commercial paper issuers increased substantially as well. For example, issuers rated by Moody's Investor Service increased from 516 at year-end 1975 to 881 at year-end 1980.

The recent rapid growth in the commercial paper market owes much to the secular substitution of short-term for long-term debt, which accelerated because of the high rate of inflation in the late 1970s. Volatile interest rates due to uncertainty about the future rate of inflation make firms hesitant to structure their balance sheets with long-term, fixed-rate assets and liabilities. In addition, because of inflation's debilitating effects on equity markets, debt has grown more than twice as fast as equity during the past decade. On the demand side, investors also have become wary of long-term, fixed-rate securities because of the uncertainty about the real rate of return on such commitments of funds. Therefore, funds have tended to flow away from the capital markets and into the money markets. A large share of these funds have been channeled into the commercial paper market.

Nonfinancial Paper

As nonfinancial firms acquired familiarity with open market finance during the 1970s, they gradually reduced their reliance on short-term bank loans. This is understandable since use of open market funds offers the potential for substantial savings to corporate borrowers compared to the cost of bank credit. Large commercial banks' primary source of funds for financing loans is the CD market, where interest rates are roughly equal to commercial paper rates. In addition, the cost of funds to commercial banks includes reserve requirements.[5] Noninterest expenses associated with lending also add to the cost of bank operations. These various costs drive a wedge between open market and bank lending rates, and the spread between the prime rate and the commercial paper rate is a good proxy for the difference in financing costs facing companies that need funds.

Large financially sound nonfinancial firms, therefore, have relied to an increasing extent on the commercial paper market for short-term credit. The ratio of nonfinancial commercial paper to commercial and industrial (C&I) loans at large commercial banks, rose from about 11 percent in the mid-1970s to almost 25 percent in 1980. Chart 3 shows the movements in the ratio of paper to loans from 1972 to 1980.

Banks reacted to this loss of market share by becoming more aggressive in pricing loans. Since 1979, for example, some banks have begun making loans below the prime rate. In a Federal Reserve Board survey of 48 large banks, the percentage of below-prime loans rose from about 20 percent of all commercial loan extensions in the fourth quarter of 1978 to about 60 percent by the second quarter of 1980. Most of these loans were extended at rates determined by cost-of-funds formulas. In addition, the average maturity of loans over $1 million, which make up almost half of all C&I loans in volume, fell from about 3.0 months in 1977 to a low of 1.2 months in August 1980. Loans below prime had an average maturity of well under one month. These below-prime loans were in the same maturity range as the average maturity for commercial paper.

Aside from becoming more competitive with the commercial paper market, banks have tried at the same time to provide services to support their customers' commercial paper issues. Some banks have offered customers more flexible short-term borrowing arrangements to allow commercial paper issuers to adjust the timing of their paper sales. Morgan Guaranty Trust Company, which originated

CHART 3
Ratio of Nonfinancial CP* to C&I Loans of Large
Weekly Reporting Commercial Banks

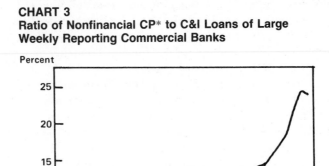

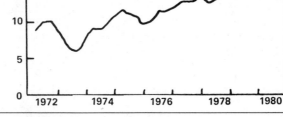

* Commercial paper.
Source: Board of Governors of the Federal Reserve System.

this service, calls its open line of credit a "Commercial Paper Adjustment Facility" and prices the service below the prime rate. Commercial banks also provide backup lines of credit and act as issuing agents, as discussed previously.

In summary, competition with the commercial paper market is changing the lending practices of commercial banks. Although banks still extend a large volume of short-term business loans, the profitability of loans to their largest customers has been reduced partly because of competition with the commercial paper market, and some commercial bank activity now focuses on supporting the issuance of their customer's commercial paper.

Financial Paper

Since the 1920s, finance companies have been important participants in the commercial paper market. They provide much of the credit used to finance consumer purchases. Historically, around 20 percent of outstanding consumer credit has come from finance companies. Finance companies also supply a large and growing amount of business credit, such as wholesale and retail financing of inventory, receivables financing, and commercial and leasing financing. About half of all the credit extended by finance companies goes to businesses, predominantly to small and medium-sized firms.

The primary source of short-term funds for finance companies is sales of commercial paper. In fact, the outstanding commercial paper liabilities of finance companies were about five times as large as their bank loans in the late 1970s. Like nonfinancial companies, finance companies since the mid-1960s gradually increased the proportion of borrowing in the commercial paper market, compared to short-term borrowing from commercial banks.

As seen in Chart 1, nonbank financial paper constitutes the largest proportion of outstanding commercial paper. Sixty percent of all commercial paper is directly placed and the greatest proportion of this is finance company paper. Finance company paper, however, is issued by only a small fraction of the total number of finance companies. According to the Federal Reserve Board's *Survey of Finance Companies, 1975,* 88 of the largest finance companies out of a total of about 3,400 such firms issued 97 percent of all finance company paper and extended 90 percent of total finance company credit.

The outstanding volume of bank-related financial paper has been extremely volatile compared to nonbank financial paper. As mentioned before, this market received a major jolt when the Federal Reserve imposed reserve requirements on bank-related commercial paper issues in August 1970. Growth in outstanding bank-related commercial paper resumed by mid-1971, however. This growth corresponded with record acquisitions of nonbank firms by bank holding companies, which peaked at 332 nonbank firms acquired in 1973 and 264 firms in 1974. Some of the primary activities of these newly acquired subsidiaries are commercial finance, factoring, and leasing. The 1973–75 recession curtailed the growth in bank paper, but growth resumed its upward trend by 1976 and has continued strongly since.

NEW DIRECTIONS FOR THE COMMERCIAL PAPER MARKET

Recently several new groups of issuers have entered the commercial paper market. These include foreign banks, multinational corporations, and public utilities; thrift institutions; second-tier issuers relying on guarantees from supporting entities; and tax-exempt issuers. These issuers have found the commercial paper market to be a flexible and attractive way to borrow short-term funds.

Foreign Issuers

Foreign participation in the commercial paper market has been growing and will probably continue to be an important source of new growth. As of year-end 1980, Moody's rated 70 foreign issuers, which collectively had about $7 billion in outstanding commercial paper. These issuers fall into three categories: foreign-based multinational corporations, nationalized utilities, and banks. Some large foreign multinational corporations issue paper to finance their operations in the United States. Others borrow to support a variety of activities that require dollar payments for goods and services. Nationalized utilities have been major borrowers in the commercial paper market largely because their purchases of oil require payment in dollars. Finally, foreign banks raise funds for their banking activity or act as guarantors for the commercial paper of their clients by issuing letters of credit. These banks have been among the most recent entrants into the market.

The commercial paper market is often the cheapest source of dollars for foreign issuers. A major alternative source of dollar borrowing is the Eurodollar market, in which rates are generally linked to the London Interbank Offered Rate (LIBOR). Many foreign banks, for example, obtain funds in the commercial paper market for 0.25 percent or more below LIBOR. Aside from cost considerations, another important motivation behind foreign participation in the commercial paper market is foreign issuers' interest in obtaining ratings and gaining acceptance with the American financial community. The exposure from selling paper helps to broaden a foreign issuer's investor base and prepares the way for entering the bond and equity markets.

Two obstacles to foreign participation in the commercial paper market are obtaining prime credit ratings and coping with foreign withholding taxes on interest paid to investors outside the country. Ratings below top quality wipe out the cost advantage of raising short-term funds in the commercial paper market. To date, for example, no foreign banks have issued paper with less than top ratings.

Withholding taxes on interest paid to investors outside the country also may eliminate commercial paper's cost advantage over the Eurodollar market. These taxes are intended to curtail short-term capital outflows and are used in France, Belgium, Australia, Canada, and other countries. For foreign issuers' commercial paper to be marketable, the issuer must bear the cost of the withholding tax. The tax, therefore, raises the cost of acquiring funds using commercial paper.

By taking advantage of loopholes and technicalities in the withholding tax laws, foreign issuers often circumvent these laws. For example, the nationalized French electric company, Electricite de France, one of the largest foreign or domestic issuers, has its commercial paper classified as long-term debt, which is not subject to France's 15 percent withholding tax on interest. The reason for this classification is that the utility backs its paper with a 10-year revolving credit facility from its banks that establishes the commercial paper borrowing as long-term debt. French banks use a different approach to take advantage of a withholding tax exemption on short-term time deposits, like CDs. They set up U.S. subsidiaries to sell commercial paper and then transfer the proceeds to the French parent banks by issuing CDs to their U.S. subsidiaries.

In general, foreign issuers pay more to borrow in the commercial paper market than domestic issuers for two reasons. First, almost all foreign commercial paper issues have a sovereign risk associated with the issuer that results from additional uncertainty in the investor's mind about the probability of default on commercial paper because of government intervention, political turmoil, economic disruption, and the like. This uncertainty creates a risk premium which increases the interest rate on foreign issues relative to domestic issues. The size of the premium depends on the issuer, the country, and the level of interest rates. A second source of additional costs arises when foreign issuers pay to establish and operate U.S. subsidiaries to issue paper and, in the case of foreign banks, incur reserve requirement costs on commercial paper issues. In addition, rating service fees are higher for foreign issuers than for domestic issuers, as mentioned earlier. Nevertheless, the commercial paper market is proving to be the least expensive source of short-term dollar funds for an increasing number of foreign borrowers.

Thrift Commercial Paper

Both savings and loan associations and mutual savings banks have recently been allowed to borrow funds in the commercial paper market. Mutual savings banks (MSBs) had the authority to issue commercial paper, but faced restrictions on advertising, interest payments, and minimum maturity that effectively prevented them from issuing commercial paper. On March 3, 1980, the Federal Deposit Insurance Corporation (FDIC) removed the restrictions and thereby cleared the way for MSB participation in the commercial paper market. The FDIC ruled that MSB commercial paper must be unsecured, have a maximum maturity of nine months, sell at a minimum price of $100,000, state that it is uninsured by FDIC, and bear a notice that the instrument will pay no interest after maturity. Despite the relaxation of restrictions, as of early 1981 no MSBs have issued paper. The failure of MSBs to issue commercial paper has been largely due to impaired MSB earnings, which make it difficult to obtain the high credit ratings necessary to realize the cost advantage in borrowing in the commercial paper market.

Savings and loan associations have had access to the commercial paper market since January 1979, when the Federal Home Loan Bank Board approved the first applications for S&Ls to issue commercial paper and short-term notes secured by mortgage loans. S&Ls use commercial paper principally to finance seasonal surges in loan demand and to finance secondary mortgage market operations. Commercial paper allows greater flexibility for S&Ls in managing liquidity because they can borrow large amounts of cash quickly and for periods as short as five days. Relatively few S&Ls carry commercial paper ratings. Of the 60 or so large S&Ls expected to participate in the market after the FHLBB approved the first applications, only 12 had ratings from Moody's as of mid-1980, though all were P-1. These S&Ls collectively had $327 million in outstanding commercial paper as of mid-1980.

The attractiveness of commercial paper for S&Ls and MSBs has been sharply diminished as a result of the Monetary Control Act of 1980. Under the act, commercial paper is considered a reservable liability, except when issued to certain exempt investors, such as depository institutions. S&Ls and MSBs have to hold reserves in the ratio of 3 percent against outstanding commercial paper, which is classified as a nonpersonal time deposit. Reserve requirements increase the cost of funds raised through commercial paper and consequently reduce the incentive for S&Ls and MSBs to issue paper.

Support Arrangements

Many lesser-known firms gain access to the commercial paper market through financial support arrangements obtained from firms with the highest credit ratings. Second-tier issuers frequently issue paper by obtaining a letter of credit from a commercial bank. This procedure substitutes the credit of a bank for that of the issuer and thereby reduces the cost of issuing commercial paper. This kind of support arrangement is known as "commercial paper supported by letter of credit" and resembles bankers' acceptance financing except that the issuance of commercial paper is not associated with the shipment of goods. Because the letter of credit is appended to the commercial paper note, commercial paper supported by letter of credit is alternatively referred to as a "documented discount note." Typically, letters of credit are valid for a specific term or are subject to termination upon written notice by either party. To have a commercial bank stand ready to back up an issue of paper, an issuer must pay a fee that ranges from one quarter to three quarters of a percentage point.

Although commercial paper with letter of credit support reached an outstanding volume of about $2 billion by mid-1980, this segment of the market is still comparatively small. Many issuers of letter of credit commercial paper are subsidiaries of larger corporate entities. These second-tier issuers include firms involved in pipeline construction, vehicle leasing, nuclear fuel supply, and power plant construction. Other commercial paper issuers also have acquired letter of credit support from commercial banks, particularly during the period of restricted credit growth in early 1980. Issuers whose ratings were downgraded faced difficulty selling their paper and paid substantial premiums over high-grade paper. Buying a letter of credit from a commercial bank reduced their borrowing costs in the commercial paper market and still offered a cheaper alternative to short-term bank loans.

Other supporting entities that provide guarantees or endorsements are insurance companies, governments for government-owned companies, and parent companies for their subsidiaries. For example, the commercial paper of the nationalized French utilities, such as Electricite de France, carries the guarantee of the Republic of France. Guarantees or endorsements by parent companies for their subsidiaries are the most prevalent form of support arrangement.

Tax-Exempt Paper

One of the most recent innovations in the commercial paper market is tax-exempt paper. Except for its tax-exempt feature, this paper differs little from other commercial paper. To qualify for tax-exempt status the paper must be issued by state or municipal governments, or by qualified nonprofit organizations. Like taxable commercial paper, tax-exempt paper is also exempt from Securities and Exchange Commission registration, provided the paper matures within 270 days. Most tax-exempt paper matures within 15 to 90 days. These short-term debt obligations are alternatively known as short-term revenue bonds or short-term interim certificates.

The outstanding volume of tax-exempt paper has grown rapidly, rising from an insignificant amount in 1979 to about $500 million in 1980. It will probably exceed $1 billion in 1981. Much of the demand for tax-exempt paper comes from short-term tax-exempt funds, which had assets of $1.5 billion in mid-1980, and from bank trust departments. Many mutual fund groups are setting up tax-exempt money market funds in response to the apparent increasing demand for this type of investment. A current shortage of tax-exempt commercial paper has depressed the yields on outstanding issues, making this instrument especially attractive to tax-exempt issuers. However, constraints on public agency use of short-term debt in some states may continue to limit the supply of tax-exempt commercial paper.

CONCLUSION

The commercial paper market has served the short-term financing needs of several groups of borrowers to an increasing degree in recent years. Many nonfinancial companies, especially large firms, have substituted commercial paper for short-term bank loans to satisfy their working capital requirements. Commercial paper has generally been a less-costly financing alternative than bank short-term credit for these firms. Finance companies have relied to a greater extent on commercial paper than nonfinancial companies for short-term financing and have issued the greatest proportion of outstanding commercial paper. Most large finance companies realize economies of scale by placing commercial paper directly with investors. Bank holding companies also have depended on the paper market to finance their banking-related activities, which increased in size and scope during the 1970s.

Other types of issuers have been recently attracted to the commercial paper market because of the potential saving in interest costs over alternative ways of borrowing short-term funds. Foreign issuers have sold a substantial amount of commercial paper since entering the market in the mid-1970s. Foreign and domestic issuers who lack sufficient financial strength to offer commercial paper on their own have gained access to the market via support arrangements with stronger financial or corporate entities. Tax-exempt issuers are expected to increase in number and generate larger supplies of tax-exempt paper. Thrift institutions, on the other hand, probably will not make much use of the market in the future because recently imposed reserve requirements on commercial paper have reduced its cost advantage over other sources of short-term credit.

Many investors find commercial paper to be an attractive short-term financial instrument. Although corporations and other institutional investors held most outstanding commercial paper in the past, financial intermediation by money market funds and other short-term investment pooling arrangements has given many new investors, especially individuals, indirect access to commercial paper.

NOTES

[1] Sumner N. Levine, ed., *The 1979 Dow Jones-Irwin Business Almanac* (Homewood, Ill.: Dow Jones-Irwin, 1979), pp. 256–57.

[2] A bill of exchange is an order written by a seller instructing a buyer to pay the seller a specified sum of money on a specified date.

[3] For an extensive account of commercial paper's early history, see Albert O. Greef, *The Commercial Paper House in the United States* (Cambridge, Mass.: Harvard University Press, 1938), pp. 3–114.

[4] Greef, pp. 46, 55, 412–14.

[5] The following example illustrates how reserve requirements on CDs increase the cost of funds to

banks. Suppose the reserve requirement against CDs is 3 percent and bank's CDs offer a 12 percent yield. Then for every dollar obtained through a CD, only 97 cents are available to lend. The funds idled as reserves increase the effective cost of funds raised by issuing a CD. In this example, the additional cost imposed by the reserve requirement is 37 basis points (i.e., $12.00 \div 0.97 = 12.37$).

REFERENCES

"A Way to Upgrade Corporate IOUs." *Business Week,* March 31, 1980.

Board of Governors of the Federal Reserve System, "Short-Term Business Lending at Rates Below the Prime Rate." *Federal Monetary Policy and Its Effect on Small Business, Part 3. Hearings before a Subcommittee on Access to Equity Capital and Business Opportunities of the House Committee on Small Business.* U.S. Congress, House. Committee on Small Business, 96th Cong., 2nd sess., 1980, pp. 318–27.

Chell, Gretchen. "Tax-Exempt Commercial Paper Beginning to Catch on as an Investment Medium." *The Money Manager,* July 21, 1980.

"Domestic Financial Statistics." *Federal Reserve Bulletin,* various issues.

"FDIC Eases Curbs on Mutuals Issuing Commercial Paper." *American Banker,* February 7, 1980.

Grant, James. "Crowding Out Chrysler . . . News in Commercial Paper." *Barron's,* August 4, 1980.

Greef, Albert O. *The Commercial Paper House in the United States.* Cambridge, Mass.: Harvard University Press, 1938.

Hildebrand, James L. "Enter Euro-Commercial Paper." *Euromoney,* July 1980.

Hurley, Evelyn M. "Survey of Finance Companies, 1975." *Federal Reserve Bulletin,* March 1976.

———. "The Commercial Paper Market." *Federal Reserve Bulletin,* June 1977.

Judd, John P. "Competition Between the Commercial Paper Market and Commercial Banks." *Economic Review,* Federal Reserve Bank of San Francisco, Winter 1979.

Levine, Sumner N., ed. *The 1979 Dow Jones-Irwin Business Almanac.* Homewood, Ill.: Dow Jones-Irwin, 1979.

McKenzie, Joseph A. "Commercial Paper: Plugging into a New and Stable Source of Financing." *Federal Home Loan Bank Board Journal,* March 1979, pp. 2–5.

Moody's Commercial Paper Record. Monthly Statistical Supplement. Moody's Investors Service, Inc., November 1980.

Moody's Commercial Paper Record. Quarterly Reference Edition. Moody's Investors Service, Inc., Fall 1980.

Nevins, Baxter D. *The Commercial Paper Market.* Boston: The Bankers Publishing Company, 1966.

Puglisi, Donald J. "Commercial Paper: A Primer." *Federal Home Loan Bank Board Journal,* December 1980, pp. 4–10.

Quint, Michael. "Short-Term, Below-Prime Rates to Big Customers Seem Permanent." *American Banker,* May 2, 1978.

———. "Banks Give Paper Issuers New Backup." *American Banker,* September 27, 1978.

"Selling Paper Abroad to Skirt a Ratings Cut." *Business Week,* September 22, 1980.

Stigum, Marcia. *The Money Market: Myth, Reality, and Practice.* Homewood, Ill.: Dow Jones-Irwin, 1978.

"The New Dynamics of the Market for Business Credit." *The Morgan Guaranty Survey.* March 1978, pp. 6–11.

"The Rush Into U.S. Paper." *Business Week,* January 26, 1981.

21

Recent Developments
in the Banker's Acceptance Market

Frederick H. Jensen and Patrick M. Parkinson

The market for dollar-denominated bankers' acceptances grew rapidly throughout the 1970s and into the early 1980s. The expanding dollar value of U.S. and world trade, and sharp increases in the price of oil and other commodities whose shipment frequently is financed with acceptances, stimulated the growth of the market through this period. In addition, the surge in market interest rates during the late 1970s greatly increased the value of the exemption of certain types of acceptances from reserve requirements. As a result, the proportions of U.S. and world trade that were financed with dollar acceptances rose substantially. By the early 1980s, however, many major accepting banks were unable to accommodate further increases in demand for acceptance credit because they had reached statutory limits on the amount of acceptances they could create. As a result, regional banks and U.S. agencies and branches of foreign banks were able to expand their presence in this market, but not enough to keep the growth of the market from slowing or fees charged by accepting banks from rising significantly.

This restriction on supply spawned proposals for remedial legislation, and in October 1982, the Congress passed the Bank Export Services Act, which effectively doubled the statutory limits on acceptances. As anticipated, immediately following passage of this legislation the volume of acceptance financing swelled and fees declined substantially, as the major accepting banks attempted to regain their market share. In early 1983, however, the acceptance market began to contract in a trend that continued, on balance, through September 1985. Over this latter period, total dollar acceptances declined about $11 billion, or 15 percent.

Many analysts have pointed to the stagnation of international trade and sharp declines in commodity prices as the primary reasons for the shrinkage of the market for bankers' acceptances. Although these factors undoubtedly have

From *Federal Reserve Bulletin,* January 1986, pp. 1–12.

The authors are with the Board of Governors of the Federal Reserve System, Division of Research and Statistics. Chinhui Juhn provided research assistance.

played a role, the substitution of alternative sources of credit appears to have been more important. The shrinkage of the banker's acceptance market is symptomatic of the declining role of U.S. banks as direct providers of short-term credit to foreign banks and multinational nonfinancial corporations. More and more, such borrowers have obtained funding directly from domestic and foreign nonbank investors in the U.S. commercial paper market and in the Eurodollar markets. In addition, sharp declines in market interest rates since mid-1982 have reduced the cost of reserve requirements, thereby allowing bank loans to be priced more competitively with acceptance credit.

THE INSTRUMENT AND ITS MARKET

A banker's acceptance is a time draft drawn on a bank, usually to finance the shipment or temporary storage of goods. By "accepting" the draft, the bank makes an unconditional promise to pay the holder of the draft a stated amount at a specified date. Thus, the bank effectively substitutes its own credit for that of a borrower and, in the process, creates a negotiable instrument that may be freely traded.

Creating an Acceptance

In a typical transaction, a buyer of goods will seek credit to finance the purchase until the goods can be resold. If the seller knows the buyer and does not need cash, the seller may be willing to extend open trade credit. But this is infrequently the case with the financing of international trade, so the buyer often turns to its bank, which is better acquainted with the buyer's business and is a specialist in evaluating and diversifying credit risk. The buyer could borrow the funds directly from the bank, although for reasons outlined below, acceptance financing is frequently less costly.

When a bank agrees to provide acceptance credit to a buyer, it often notifies the seller (perhaps through the seller's bank) that a letter of credit has been issued authorizing the seller to draw a time draft on the bank for the amount of the transaction. The letter of credit also specifies any conditions that must be met before the draft will be accepted. These terms may require that documents be attached to the draft that verify shipment of the goods and that provide the bank assurance that the underlying transaction meets certain regulatory requirements. When the draft is presented to the bank with the proper documents, it is stamped "accepted" on its face, information about the nature of the underlying transaction is inscribed, and the draft is endorsed by an appropriate bank officer.

By accepting the draft, the bank has acquired an unconditional obligation to pay at maturity a specified amount, either to the seller or, more frequently, to the holder of the instrument. The drawer of the draft, in this case the seller, remains secondarily liable to the holder in the event of default by the bank. The bank's customer—here, the buyer—has an obligation to pay the bank the same amount at or just before the maturity date. The seller may choose to hold the draft until maturity, but typically chooses to receive immediate payment by selling the acceptance at a discount, usually to the accepting bank itself. If the accepting bank purchases (discounts) the acceptance, it may elect to hold it in its own portfolio. In this event, it is recorded as a loan to the borrower, the buyer of the goods in this example, and must be funded like any other loan. More commonly, however, the bank will elect to replenish its funds by selling (rediscounting) the acceptance into the secondary market, either directly or through a dealer. If the acceptance is not held in portfolio, the bank records its obligation as an "acceptance liability outstanding" and the corresponding asset, a claim on the borrower, as a "customer's liability on acceptance outstanding."

Other types of transactions also are common. The acceptance may not involve a letter of credit: such "clean" acceptances are typically authorized by prior arrangement between the buyer's bank and the seller's bank. Moreover, the draft may be drawn on the seller's bank or some other bank, particularly if the buyer's bank is small and its acceptances are not traded widely. In this case, the buyer's bank may arrange for another bank—perhaps a larger correspondent—to accept the draft and agree to indemnify the accepting bank against any losses that it might suffer in the event of a default. Alternatively, the smaller bank could accept the draft but arrange for a better-known bank to endorse it. By so doing, the buyer's bank retains the credit risk but can offer the buyer access to acceptance financing at a lower cost than if it issued an acceptance on its own.

In other cases, the buyer may wish to pay the seller immediately upon shipment. Under these circumstances, the bank can extend short-term credit to the buyer to finance the purchase, then accept and discount a time draft drawn on it by the buyer and apply the proceeds to pay off the short-term credit used to finance the purchase. The buyer retains an obligation to repay the bank at or before the maturity of the acceptance.

Some acceptances do not arise from the shipment or storage of goods. For example, a firm may draw a draft on its bank for acceptance in order to borrow funds for working capital purposes. Such acceptances are termed *finance bills*.

In all cases, the accepting bank charges a fee, or "commission," for accepting the draft that varies depending on the maturity of the draft as well as the creditworthiness of the borrower. Commissions are quoted in terms of basis points, calculated on an annual basis. The bank also may receive a fee if a letter of credit is involved and may hope to realize a difference in the price, comparable to a bid/asked spread, if it purchases the acceptance for subsequent resale. Of course, if it holds the acceptance in its loan portfolio to maturity, the bank also earns a return equal to the original discount. The costs of the financing typically are borne by the borrower; in the example above, the buyer. Even when, through negotiation, the seller agrees to bear some of the costs, these likely will be reflected in the sales price of the goods.

Types of Acceptances

Virtually all acceptances traded in the United States are denominated in dollars, and only a very small amount of dollar-denominated acceptances are traded elsewhere. Thus the U.S. market for acceptances has been almost synonymous with the market for dollar-denominated acceptances. The U.S. market is principally one for "eligible" acceptances—that is, those that are of the type that are eligible for sale at a discount at Federal Reserve Banks. As a matter of practice, the Federal Reserve has discontinued discounting assets and instead provides funds to depositories through collateralized advances. Consequently, the only practical significance of the eligibility criteria is that eligible acceptances are not subject to reserve requirements: under Federal Reserve regulations, acceptances that are of the type specified in section 13(7) of the Federal Reserve Act not only are eligible for discount, as specified in section 13(6), but also are exempt from reserve requirements. According to these regulations, eligible acceptances must grow out of the import or export of goods, the temporary storage of readily marketable staples, or the domestic shipment of goods. In addition, eligible acceptances must have an original maturity—or "tenor"—of six months or less.

The reserve status of ineligible acceptances is an important factor that affects their issuance. For example, until 1973, all acceptance liabilities, ineligible as well as eligible, were exempt from reserve requirements. During periods of tight credit, when below-market Regulation Q ceilings on rates payable on certificates of deposit (CDs) restricted their issuance, banks created a substantial volume of finance bills in order to provide funds to their corporate customers. Even after the removal of interest rate ceilings on large CDs in mid-1970, banks continued to issue sizable amounts of finance bills to take advantage of the exemption from reserve requirements. Concerned that such issuance enabled banks to avoid reserve requirements on CDs or other sources of funds, in mid-1973 the Federal Reserve imposed reserve requirements on ineligible acceptances, and their issuance declined precipitously. Today, few ineligible acceptances trade in the secondary market.

There are three main types of eligible acceptances. The *first,* acceptances that finance the domestic shipment and storage of goods, historically has accounted for only a small amount of total acceptances in the marketplace. The popularity of open trade credit in the United States, where buyers and sellers are more likely to be accustomed to doing business with each other, is probably an important reason. The higher cost of documentation relative to other types of acceptances may be another factor: domestic-storage acceptances must be secured with a warehouse receipt, and, until 1982, title documents had to be attached to acceptances used to finance domestic shipments. The *second* type of acceptance finances U.S. imports and exports of goods. Before the 1960s, this was by far the dominant category, but now it accounts for less than half of total acceptance financing. The *third,* and now the largest, category is "third-country" acceptances, which arise from the shipment of goods between foreign countries.

Third-country acceptances became increasingly popular in the 1970s as foreign borrowers found the U.S. acceptance market a highly attractive source of short-term financing. The majority of third-country acceptances are of the type known as "refinance bills." These bills typically originate with drafts drawn on a foreign bank by one or more of its customers. Because the foreign bank may not be well known to U.S. investors and its own acceptances would require a larger discount, it often will hold the acceptances drawn on it in its loan portfolio and refinance these acceptances by drawing a draft on a U.S. bank for acceptance. The U.S. bank accepts the draft and advances funds to the foreign bank to finance the extension of credit by the foreign bank to its own customers. Because the foreign bank is the borrower in this transaction, the market for refinance bills is an interbank market.

The Market for Acceptances

The amount of dollar-denominated acceptances outstanding depends on a variety of factors. An obvious one is the dollar value of transactions suitable for financing with eligible acceptances. Currently, more than 20 percent of U.S. imports and exports and more than 10 percent of third-country shipments are funded in the U.S. acceptance market. Equally important are the cost and availability of alternative sources of credit in the United States and elsewhere.

From the point of view of the bank, acceptance financing is the functional equivalent of funding a loan with a deposit liability, such as a CD. In either case, the bank has an unconditional obligation to pay the holder of the instrument at maturity as well as a claim on the borrower. Because acceptances are not subject to an assessment for deposit insurance and eligible acceptances are exempt from reserve requirements, acceptance liabilities are a less-costly source of funds than deposits. Moreover, because the acceptance commission is a front-end fee and is not refundable, or is refundable only with a penalty, the customer may be less likely to prepay an acceptance borrowing than certain other types of bank credit, particularly revolving loans with pricing tied to the prime rate. And because the maturities of the acceptance liability and the corresponding asset are automatically matched, acceptances carry none of the risk inherent in funding loans with deposits with different maturities or repricing schedules.

For an investor, a banker's acceptance is a close substitute for other bank liabilities such as CDs. Consequently, bankers' acceptances trade at rates very close to those on CDs (see Chart 1); in recent years, yields on bankers' acceptances have consistently been within 10 basis points of those on CDs. Although bankers' acceptances are not federally insured, many investors view them as one of the most secure money market instruments because their historical default rate is very low. Also, some investors may feel that the likelihood of repayment is increased by the secondary obligation of the drawer to pay the holder at maturity if the accepting bank does not (though as a rule, investors do not know the identity of the drawer). The principal investors are institutions: money market mutual funds, trust departments, state and local governments, insurance companies and other corporations, pension funds, foreign central banks, and commercial banks. Smaller-denomination acceptances may be placed directly with individuals by the accepting bank.

CHART 1
Yields on Bankers' Acceptances and Certificates of Deposit

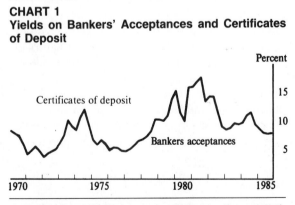

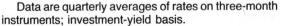

Data are quarterly averages of rates on three-month instruments; investment-yield basis.

The market for acceptances also offers advantages to many borrowers. With the bank as its intermediary, a borrower with eligible transactions gains access to the nation's money markets. And, because the cost to the bank of financing eligible acceptances is lower than that of a direct loan funded with a deposit subject to reserve requirements, the bank may be able to offer the financing at a lower "all in" rate (one including the discount plus fees and commissions) than that on a direct loan.

Like the market for CDs, the acceptance market is an over-the-counter market. The market is highly liquid and is supported by around 30 dealers and a dozen brokers. Dealers quote bid and asked prices for round lots of $5 million. If the transaction to be financed is larger, several drafts of $5 million each will be drawn. For smaller transactions, a number of drafts of similar maturities drawn on the same bank will be packaged to trade as a round lot. Typical maturities are one, three, and six months, with the average reportedly around three months.

GROWTH OF THE MARKET

During the 1970s, the U.S. acceptance market expanded rapidly. From 1973 to 1979, total eligible acceptances increased more than fivefold, from $7 billion to $43 billion, while, by comparison, total loans at U.S. banking offices roughly doubled. Several factors seem to have been at work. The oil price hikes of 1973–74 and 1978–80 boosted the dollar value of oil imports and world trade and had a particularly pronounced impact on the demand for financing of third-country acceptances (see Chart 2).

CHART 2
Total U.S. Dollar Acceptances, by Type of Acceptance

Billions of dollars

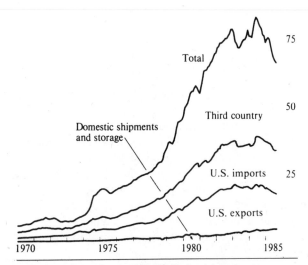

Source: Monthly Survey of Eligible Bankers' Acceptances.

CHART 3
Total World Trade, U.S. and Third Country, and Proportions Financed by U.S. Dollar Acceptances

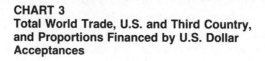

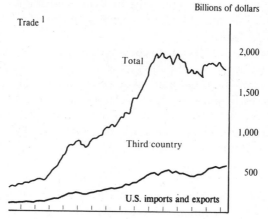

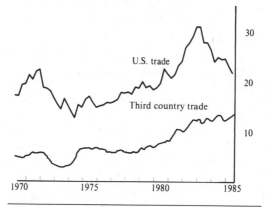

[1] Data are annualized quarterly flows.
[2] Shares financed assume an average acceptance maturity of 90 days.
Sources: *International Financial Statistics* and Monthly Survey of Eligible Bankers' Acceptances, selected issues.

However, the importance of the growth of trade as an influence on the growth of the acceptance market is often overstated. The proportions of U.S. and third-country trade financed in the U.S. acceptance market are relatively small and are far from constant (see Chart 3). Inasmuch as acceptances are free from reserve requirements and the opportunity cost of those requirements varies proportionately with interest rates, the cost advantage of acceptances over other forms of bank credit widens as interest rates rise. Hence, the general uptrend in interest rates during the 1970s contributed importantly to the rapid expansion in acceptance financing.

The increasing use of refinance bills also facilitated the financing of a greater share of third-country trade in the U.S. acceptance market. The largest borrowers in this market reportedly were Japanese, Korean, and Latin American banks. Third-country acceptances grew especially rapidly during the 1970s, increasing from 45 percent of the total market to 53 percent over the decade.

Development of Supply Constraints

In addition to setting eligibility criteria, section 13(7) of the Federal Reserve Act limits the amount of eligible acceptances that an individual bank can create. Before 1982, these limits applied only to member banks and were set at 50 percent of the bank's paid-up capital and surplus, or 100 percent with permission of the Federal Reserve Board. Although most banks had long since been granted the higher limit, the rapid growth of acceptances brought many accepting banks near their ceilings.

Throughout the 1970s, the market for acceptances was dominated by the largest U.S. banks. For one thing, these banks have had the most extensive international operations among U.S. institutions and naturally tend to attract a large share of international trade financing. In addition, these banks generally can market their acceptances at lower yields than smaller banks can. The discount at which an individual bank's acceptance will trade depends on the size and recognition of the bank by investors as well as on its overall creditworthiness. Dealers quote a range of acceptance rates and normally trade the liabilities of the top-tier banks, generally the largest 9 or 10 U.S. money-center banks, "on the run"—that is, interchangeably—quoting rates for them at the lower end of the range. Quotes on the second tier, comprising 20 or so of the largest regional banks and some of the largest foreign banks, tend to be toward the top of the range. Rates offered on acceptances of smaller U.S. banks and on most foreign banks tend to be above— in some cases well above—this range.

During the 1970s, the top-tier domestic banks held around 45 percent of the total dollar acceptance market and the second tier of domestic banks had another 17 to 18 percent. With the rapid growth of this market, acceptance liabilities of these groups expanded apace. By 1980, however, almost all of the top-tier banks and many of the larger regional banks were at or near the statutory limits on their creation of eligible acceptances.

Because bank capital was growing relatively slowly, these ceilings effectively constrained the supply of eligible acceptance financing available at the larger banks. Acceptance commissions reportedly increased to around 100 to 150 basis points at the larger banks, and growth in the volume of their acceptances slowed markedly. The rise in commissions at the largest banks enabled the smaller regional banks and U.S. agencies and branches of foreign banks to price their acceptances more competitively. Moreover, the U.S. agencies and branches were not subject to capital limits, and most of the smaller regional banks were well below their ceilings. This combination enabled the smaller domestic issuers and the U.S. agencies and branches to increase significantly their share of the total acceptance market, principally at the expense of the largest banks; by the end of 1981, the share of the market held by the top-tier banks had declined to less than 35 percent (see Chart 4).

To some extent, the top-tier banks were able to channel their acceptance activity to their Edge Act corporation subsidiaries. These subsidiaries, which are

CHART 4
Percentage of Total Acceptance Liabilities Outstanding Issued by Various Institutions

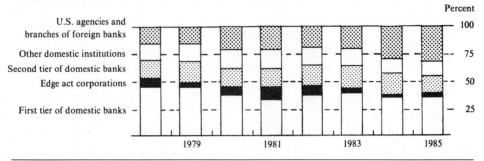

Source: Quarterly Reports of Condition (Call Reports). December data are used for 1978–84 and June data for 1985.

First-tier domestic banks are the nine largest U.S.-chartered banks. Second-tier domestic banks are the next 20 largest U.S.-chartered banks.

restricted by charter to a banking business that is international in character, are subject to less stringent restrictions on their volume of acceptance liabilities. Edge corporations may create eligible acceptances up to 200 percent of paid-up capital and surplus, and even in excess of this limit so long as the acceptances are secured by another bank. In effect, an Edge corporation can issue acceptances without limit by acquiring an indemnification agreement from a bank that protects it against loss in the event of borrower default. By contrast, the regulations in effect at the time did not allow member banks to use such "risk participations" to issue eligible acceptances in excess of their limit.

By channeling some of their acceptance activity through their Edge subsidiaries, the largest member banks were able to retain a portion of their market share: the market share of top-tier banks plus their Edge subsidiaries declined 9 percentage points from 1978 to 1981, while the share of the top-tier banks shrank 12 percentage points. The retention of market share was not without cost, however, because the participating banks receive a share of the acceptance commission in exchange for the indemnification agreement.

Legislative Relief

As many of the largest member banks approached the limits on eligible acceptances, they began to seek legislative relief. These efforts reached fruition with the passage by the Congress of the Bank Export Services Act (BESA), effective October 8, 1982. Section 207 of the act raised the limits on the aggregate amount of eligible acceptances that may be issued by an individual member bank to 150 percent of capital (200 percent with board permission). The act included three other important provisions. *First,* it applied these same limits to U.S. agencies and branches of any foreign bank whose parent bank has more than $1 billion in worldwide consolidated bank assets or is controlled by a foreign company that has such assets. *Second,* it clarified the treatment of participations in acceptances by providing that in cases in which a member bank or a branch or agency covered by the BESA limits sells a participation to another covered bank, the portion sold will be applied to the purchaser's limit, not the seller's. *Third,* it eased the eligibility requirements for acceptances financing domestic shipments of goods by eliminating the need to attach documents conveying or securing title at the time of origination.

The Federal Reserve Board, to which the Congress delegated the authority to define the terms used in section 207, subsequently clarified the application of the limits to U.S. agencies and branches of foreign banks and to participations in three ways.

First, with regard to foreign bank capital, the board decided that for purposes of calculating limits on eligible acceptances, the foreign parent should be defined as the bank entity that owns the agency or branch most directly, capital should be measured in accordance with accounting standards in the parent bank's home country, and conversion to the dollar equivalent should be made at least quarterly.

Second, with regard to participations in which a noncovered bank (e.g., a nonmember bank or an Edge act corporation) is a party, the board concluded that the Congress had intended to place a limit on the total amount of eligible acceptances that may be created by all covered banks. Accordingly, the board ruled that an eligible acceptance issued by a covered bank and sold through a participation agreement to a noncovered bank will still be applied to the covered bank's limit, and the same treatment will apply to an eligible acceptance issued by a noncovered bank and purchased by a covered bank through a participation agreement.

Finally, the board established two minimum requirements that a participation must satisfy for purposes of the BESA limits: (1) the selling and the purchasing banks must enter into a written agreement under which the latter acquires the former's claim against the borrower in the amount of the participation that is enforceable if the borrower fails to perform under the acceptance; and (2) the agreement must provide that the selling bank obtains a claim against the purchasing bank in the amount of the participation that is enforceable if the borrower fails to perform. The board did not require the purchasing bank to be obligated to pay the holder of the acceptance at the time it is presented for payment, although such a provision would be acceptable. Thus, the board defined a participation to include both "traditional" participations, under which both the obligation to pay the holder and the claim on the borrower are transferred from the seller to the purchaser, and "risk" participations, in which the selling bank retains the obligation to pay the holder but is indemnified by the participant bank against a share of the default risk of the borrower. This definition also repealed a requirement that the names or interests of the purchasing banks appear on the acceptance, which the board had set forth in an interpretation issued in 1979.

Developments since the BESA

Immediately following passage of the BESA, growth in bankers' acceptances accelerated: Total acceptances increased $3 billion in the fourth quarter of 1982, an annual rate of growth of about 17 percent. Acceptance commissions also reportedly dropped considerably, especially for prime customers.

In the first quarter of 1983, however, the acceptance market began to contract.

Over the first two quarters of that year, acceptances outstanding declined about $7 billion, or 18 percent at an annual rate. The market rebounded in the second half of 1983 and surged in the summer of 1984, achieving a new peak of $82 billion in June 1984. Since that time, the market has contracted steadily, falling nearly 20 percent from the peak, to $66 billion in September 1985. The sharpest declines have been registered in third-country and U.S. export acceptances; only domestic-shipment acceptances have increased. Informal reports by bankers indicate that commissions have narrowed a bit further, to around 50 basis points on average.

FORCES UNDERLYING THE CONTRACTION

In part, the contraction of the banker's acceptance market since early 1983 has resulted from a reversal of the trends that had spurred the market's rapid growth in earlier years: the dollar value of eligible global international trade has been virtually flat, on balance, since the beginning of the decade; and market interest rates have declined sharply from the historic peaks reached early in the decade, thereby reducing the value of the exemption of eligible acceptances from reserve requirements. But the shrinkage of the acceptance market also reflects fundamental changes in the market for short-term credit for major nonfinancial corporations and foreign banks. Changes in investors' perceptions of risk have allowed such borrowers to meet an increasing share of their short-term financing requirements in the U.S. commercial paper market and the Eurodollar markets. To a degree, banks have responded to stiffer competition from these markets by pricing business loans and acceptances more competitively. However, some large domestic banks appear increasingly reluctant to accept the narrow commissions now available in the acceptance market, in part because of pressures to improve capital/asset ratios. Over the past year, the willingness of domestic banks to extend acceptance credit appears to have depended importantly on whether the asset can be removed from the balance sheet of the parent holding company, and thus from the computation of its capital/asset ratio, through sale of a risk participation.

The Dollar Value of Eligible Transactions

After rising at an annual rate of about 20 percent in the 1970s, the dollar value of global international trade actually declined in 1981–82 and, on balance, was about unchanged in the first four years of this decade (see the top panel of Chart 3). This turnaround resulted largely from declines in the dollar prices of internationally traded goods owing to both the rising foreign exchange value of the dollar and the slowing of world inflation. Dollar-denominated commodity prices fell more than 20 percent between 1980 and 1984, and the physical volume of world trade also decelerated significantly—both depressed by the global recession early in the decade and the emergence of financing difficulties in many developing countries.

As noted earlier, the correlation between the dollar value of international trade and the amount of acceptance financing of such trade is far from perfect. The acceptance market outpaced international trade throughout the 1970s and early 1980s, and the recent contraction of the market occurred despite some recovery in international trade (see Chart 3). Nonetheless, disaggregated data on acceptances suggest that the value of eligible transactions does affect the amount of acceptances. For example, with the dollar value of U.S. imports increasing rapidly in the past two years, acceptances financing U.S. imports have declined much less than acceptances financing third-country trade or U.S. exports.

Alternative Sources of Credit

To a large extent, the U.S. banker's acceptance market is an interbank market. As noted earlier, many foreign banks, especially Japanese and other Asian banks, have relied heavily on U.S. banks to refinance their own acceptances. Indeed, at the end of March 1985 such refinancings accounted for roughly 60 percent of the outstanding acceptances created by U.S. banks, according to the Senior Loan Officer Opinion Survey on Bank Lending Practices. Discussions with U.S. bankers suggest that this share has declined during the past two years, as the volume of refinance bills has fallen especially rapidly. In part, this decline has occurred because Japanese banks have issued a larger amount of their own acceptance liabilities through their U.S. agencies and branches. By itself, this development would not have resulted in a decline in the total size of the market; however, at the same time, Japanese banks and other foreign banks apparently also have funded an increasing share of their customers' eligible transactions by issuing Eurodollar CDs and borrowing in the Eurodollar interbank markets.

Between December 1982 and June 1985, acceptance liabilities outstanding at U.S. agencies and branches of Japanese banks increased $8.5 billion, thereby nearly doubling their market share, from 14 percent to 27 percent. Over the same period, Eurodollar CDs outstanding at London branches of Japanese and other foreign banks rose about $13.5 billion, raising their market share from 46 percent to 63 percent (see Table 1). Apparently, investors in these markets, primarily nonbanks, have come to view more favorably the risks associated with holding dollar-denominated claims on Japanese banks. Rate spreads between liabilities of large Japanese banks and of large American banks have narrowed signficantly in the secondary markets for acceptances and Eurodollar CDs. In each market, liabilities of 12 large Japanese banks now trade on a "no name" (interchangeable) basis at rates as little as 5 basis points above the liabilities of U.S. money center banks, whereas several years ago these banks reportedly paid a premium of as much as 50 or 60 basis points.

Only relatively few large foreign banks from the major industrialized countries have been able to issue any significant volume of their own liabilities in the banker's acceptance market or in the Eurodollar CD market. For most foreign banks, borrowing in the Eurodollar interbank markets is the primary alternative to refinancing in the acceptance market. Such substitution has been encouraged by a marked narrowing of the spread between the London interbank offered rate (LIBOR) and the rate on acceptance liabilities (see Chart 5), which can be traced in part to declining costs of reserve requirements. (Efforts by large U.S. banks to minimize their cost of funds tend to place a floor under LIBOR equal to the domestic CD rate, adjusted for the cost of reserve requirements. See, for example, the study by Lawrence L. Kreicher in the summer 1982 issue of the Federal Reserve Bank of New York's *Quarterly Review*.) For foreign banks that can obtain funds at LIBOR, this spread places a ceiling on the commission the bank is willing to pay for refinancing its acceptances. If the commission quoted is larger,

TABLE 1
Eurodollar CDs Outstanding at London Offices of Commercial Banks

Billions of dollars

Date	Total	Type of bank		
		U.S.	Japa-nese	Other
1978				
December............	27.9	15.5	4.8	7.6
1979				
December............	43.3	26.0	7.7	9.6
1980				
December............	49.0	26.9	8.9	13.2
1981				
December............	77.7	44.7	12.1	20.9
1982				
December............	92.3	50.2	18.9	23.2
1983				
March	90.4	45.0	22.3	23.1
June.................	93.5	45.9	24.3	23.3
September	95.0	45.7	25.9	23.4
December............	100.2	46.1	29.3	24.8
1984				
March	100.0	44.1	30.6	25.3
June.................	97.6	38.1	32.8	26.7
September	98.9	35.2	33.6	30.1
December............	95.8	34.2	33.7	27.9
1985				
March	95.7	35.6	30.5	29.6
June.................	88.0	32.2	27.6	28.2
September	92.9	33.8	29.4	29.7

Source: Bank of England.

CHART 5
Spread between LIBOR and the Yield on Prime Bankers' Acceptances

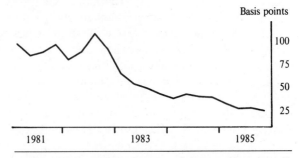

Data are quarterly averages of rates on three-month instruments; investment-yield basis.

those foreign banks will borrow in the Eurodollar market, rather than draw a refinance bill. Since U.S. banks reportedly have been reluctant to accept commissions of 25 basis points or less, the most creditworthy foreign banks have greatly reduced their use of refinance bills.

The demand for acceptance credit by nonfinancial corporations also has diminished in recent years, for much the same reasons that demand by foreign banks has fallen off. One factor has been the increased availability of funding from nonbank investors in the U.S. commercial paper market: from March 1983 through September 1985, outstanding nonfinancial commercial paper increased from $46 billion to $75 billion. Prime commercial paper generally trades at rates near those on acceptance liabilities of prime banks; and for firms with access to this market, the overall cost, including placement fees charged by dealers and fees for backup lines of credit, usually is below the all-in cost of acceptance credit.

Another factor that has depressed the demand for acceptance credit by nonfinancial corporations has been the diminishing role of the prime rate as a benchmark for the pricing of business loans (see, for example, the study by Thomas F. Brady in the January 1985 issue of the *Federal Reserve Bulletin*.)

Whereas acceptance credit once was virtually the only source of financing at rates below the prime rate, competition from the commercial paper market and from foreign banks has induced U.S. banks to offer other below-prime pricing options to an increasing number of nonfinancial corporations. For example, revolving credit facilities now typically offer a choice among pricing off the prime rate, LIBOR, or rates on domestic CDs (usually adjusted explicitly for the cost of reserve requirements). As such arrangements have spread and declining interest rates have reduced the cost of reserve requirements, the cost of business loans has declined significantly relative to rates on acceptance liabilities. Although a paucity of data on acceptance commissions precludes precise comparisons of the cost of acceptance credit and the cost of business loans, discussions with bankers suggest that rates on bank loans priced off LIBOR or other money market rates now are not significantly higher than the all-in rates quoted for acceptance credit.

Several other factors have tended to reduce the attractiveness of acceptance credit. First, banker's acceptance pricing is seldom available to nonfinancial corporations under loan commitments. If the corporation pays a fee on the unused portion of the loan commitment, it incurs an opportunity cost when it uses acceptance credit, rather than drawing on a loan commitment. The exclusion of a banker's acceptance pricing option from most loan commitments probably is a legacy of the period when the statutory limits on eligible acceptances were a binding constraint on many member banks. With the new limits now generally well in excess of outstanding acceptances, banks may offer an acceptance pricing option in loan commitments more frequently. Second, the eligibility requirements for domestic- and foreign-storage acceptances continue to impose additional documentation costs. Documentation costs can significantly reduce the attractiveness of acceptances, as evidenced by the growth of domestic-shipment acceptances since BESA removed the requirement that documents conveying title be attached at the time of acceptance. While other eligible acceptances outstanding have declined 15 percent since the passage of BESA, domestic-shipment acceptances have increased nearly 500 percent, albeit from a very low base.

Willingness to Extend Acceptance Credit

The decline in acceptance commissions over the past several years suggests that the contraction of the market has resulted primarily from a reduction in the demand for acceptance credit, rather than in the supply of acceptance credit. Nevertheless, a decrease in the willingness of certain large U.S. banks to supply acceptance credit may have contributed to the contraction in both the overall size of the market and the market share of U.S. banks. Since the early 1980s, both federal banking regulators and investors have pressured large U.S. banks to boost their capital/asset ratios. Some banks are believed to have responded to this pressure in part by reducing their acceptance credits and other low-yielding, low-risk assets.

The influence of concern about capital adequacy on the willingness to extend acceptance credit has been evident in data on sales of risk participations in acceptances. The sale of a risk participation has had implications for capital/asset ratios because in some cases it has allowed the seller to reduce its reported assets by the amount of the participation. Federal banking regulators have not allowed banks to follow this accounting practice on their quarterly reports of condition (Call Reports), which are used by the federal regulatory agencies to assess the capital adequacy of commercial banks. Until recently, however, the absence of generally accepted accounting principles has allowed some banks to deduct risk participations from the balance sheet in other public financial statements. In particular, some banks have deducted risk participations from the balance sheets reported quarterly as part of the Bank Holding Company Financial Supplement (Form FR Y-9), which the Federal Reserve uses to compute capital ratios for use in administering capital-adequacy guidelines for bank holding companies. Public accounting firms, which strongly influence the accounting practices of banks on public financial statements, have expressed divergent views on the appropriate treatment of risk participations.

Decisions to sell risk participations have not been based solely on the implications for capital/asset ratios. Banks have sold participations to limit their credit exposure to particular customers or countries and to direct business to banks with which they have correspondent relationships. Discussions with bankers and comparisons of Call Reports with other public financial statements suggest, however, that capital considerations have been paramount. Banks that have been active sellers of risk participations generally have deducted participations from other financial statements, whereas banks that have sold only small amounts often have not claimed a reduction. In turn, the willingness to extend acceptance credit has clearly been related to the sale of risk participations. A number of banks have sold risk participations quite actively: at the end of September 1985, 14 U.S. banks had sold risk participations in 20 percent or more of their outstanding eligible acceptances. In the previous 11 months, these 14 banks expanded their share of the acceptance market about 3 percentage points, while the market share of other U.S. banks declined 9 percentage points (see Chart 6).

Both federal regulators and accounting industry groups recently have addressed the divergent practices in accounting for risk participations in acceptances. In November 1985, the Federal Reserve announced that, beginning in

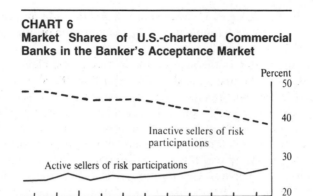

CHART 6
Market Shares of U.S.-chartered Commercial Banks in the Banker's Acceptance Market

Source: Monthly Survey of Eligible Bankers' Acceptances.

Monthly data; active sellers are those that as of September 1985 had sold participations in 20 percent or more of their outstanding acceptances.

March 1986, it will collect data on sales of risk participations in acceptances on the Y-9 and use these data to adjust upward the reported assets of banks that deduct risk participations from the balance sheet. At the same time, the Emerging Issues Task Force of the Financial Accounting Standards Board considered appropriate practices for such transactions. A clear majority of the task force members concluded that the sale of a risk participation in an acceptance does not allow the selling bank to remove the amount sold from its balance sheet. On the basis of the task force's discussion, the Securities and Exchange Commission announced that it believes that material amounts of acceptances should not be removed from an accepting bank's balance sheet after the sale of risk participations. In light of these actions, such sales no longer will significantly affect capital/asset ratios.

OUTLOOK

The market for dollar-denominated acceptances appears unlikely to resume rapid growth in the near future and may well continue to contract. Even if the dollar value of world trade continues to expand, the demand for acceptance financing will probably remain weak. Attractive substitutes for dollar-denominated acceptance financing continue to proliferate as a result of financial innovation and deregulation. Within the past two years, for example, markets for short-term dollar-denominated notes have evolved in London—Euronotes, issued under note-issuance facilities, and Euro-commercial paper—that in many ways resemble the U.S. commercial paper market. Although to date only a relatively small amount of notes appears to have been distributed in these markets, many borrowers, including many borrowers based in the United States, have arranged such facilities, and both commercial and investment banks appear to be devoting substantial resources to enlarging their distribution capacity. Meanwhile, deregulation abroad likely will foster greater use of foreign currencies to finance world trade. For example, the deregulation of the Japanese financial markets may facilitate the financing of a larger share of Asian trade and other world trade in yen. A noteworthy development was the inauguration on June 1, 1985, of a market in bankers' acceptances denominated in yen.

On the supply side of the market, the picture is less clear. The recent decisions by the federal regulators regarding the reporting of risk participations in acceptances may cause those banks that have been active sellers of participations to become more reluctant to extend acceptance credit. On the other hand, the Federal Reserve is carefully considering proposals for quantifying a risk-adjusted capital measure to supplement the present approach to the measurement of capital adequacy. One objective of this effort is to temper the present incentives for U.S. banks to reduce their low-yielding, low-risk assets, such as acceptance credits. Meanwhile, Japanese banks likely will remain an important source of dollar-denominated acceptance credit.

22

Eurodollars

Marvin Goodfriend

THE NATURE OF THE EURODOLLAR

Eurodollars are deposit liabilities, denominated in United States dollars, of banks located outside the United States.[1] Eurodollar deposits may be owned by individuals, corporations, or governments from anywhere in the world. The term *Eurodollar* dates from an earlier period when the market was located primarily in Europe. Although the bulk of Eurodollar deposits are still held in Europe, today dollar-denominated deposits are held in such places as the Bahamas, Bahrain, Canada, the Cayman Islands, Hong Kong, Japan, Panama, and Singapore, as well as in European financial centers.[2] Nevertheless, dollar-denominated deposits located anywhere in the world outside the United States are still referred to as Eurodollars.

Banks in the Eurodollar market and banks located in the United States compete to attract dollar-denominated funds worldwide. Since the Eurodollar market is relatively free of regulation, banks in the Eurodollar market can operate on narrower margins or spreads between dollar borrowing and lending rates than can banks in the United States. This allows Eurodollar deposits to compete effectively with deposits issued by banks located in the United States. In short, the Eurodollar market has grown up as a means of separating the United States dollar from the country of jurisdiction or responsibility for that currency, the United States. It has done so largely to reduce the regulatory costs involved in dollar-denominated financial intermediation.

THE SIZE OF THE EURODOLLAR MARKET

Measuring the size of the Eurodollar market involves looking at the volume of dollar-denominated loans and deposits on the books of banks located outside the United States. However, dollar-denominated loans and deposits may not match.

This article was written for *Instruments of the Money Market,* 5th ed., Federal Reserve Bank of Richmond. The focus is on Eurodollar instruments per se rather than on the economics of the Eurodollar market. The author is a research officer at the Federal Reserve Bank of Richmond.

Consequently, a decision must be made whether to measure the volume of Eurodollars from the asset or liability side of the bank balance sheet.

A liability-side measure may be too broad, since it may include foreign currency liabilities incurred to fund loans to domestic residents denominated in domestic currency. Strictly speaking, this is a traditional type of international financial intermediation. Measuring Eurodollar market volume from dollar-denominated assets, however, may also overstate the size of Eurodollar volume, since these assets may reflect nothing more than traditional foreign lending funded with domestic currency-denominated deposits supplied by domestic residents.

In practice, Eurodollar volume is measured as the dollar-denominated deposit liabilities of banks located outside the United States. For example, the Bank for International Settlements (BIS) defines and measures Eurodollars as dollars that have "been acquired by a bank outside the United States and used directly or after conversion into another currency for lending to a nonbank customer, perhaps after one or more redeposits from one bank to another."[3]

Under a liability-side measure, such as the one used by the BIS, the sum of all dollar-denominated liabilities of banks outside the United States measures the gross size of the Eurodollar market. For some purposes, it is useful to net part of interbank deposits out of the gross to arrive at an estimate of Eurodollar deposits held by original suppliers to the Eurodollar market. Roughly speaking, to construct the net size measure, deposits owned by banks in the Eurodollar market are netted out. But deposits owned by banks located outside of the Eurodollar market area are not netted out because these banks are considered to be original suppliers of funds to the Eurodollar market. For still other purposes, such as comparing the volume of deposits created in the Eurodollar market with the United States monetary aggregates, it is useful to further net out all bank-owned Eurodollar deposits. Doing so leaves only the nonbank portion of the net size measure, or what might be called the "net-net size" of the Eurodollar market.

The most readily accessible estimates of the size of the Eurodollar market are compiled by Morgan Guaranty Trust Company of New York and reported in its monthly bank letter, *World Financial Markets*.[4] Morgan's estimates are based on a liability-side measure and include data compiled by the BIS. However, Morgan's estimates are somewhat more comprehensive. Morgan reports estimates of the size of the entire Eurocurrency market based roughly on all foreign-currency liabilities and claims of banks in major European countries and eight other market areas.

As of mid-1980, Morgan estimated the gross size of the Eurocurrency market at $1,310 billion.[5] The net size was put at $670 billion.[6] Morgan also reports that Eurodollars made up 72 percent of gross Eurocurrency liabilities, putting the gross size of the Eurodollar market at $943 billion.[7] No net Eurodollar market size is given. However, 72 percent of the net size of the Eurocurrency market yields $482 billion as an approximate measure of the net size of the Eurodollar market. Finally, Morgan reports Eurodollar deposits held by nonbanks at $200 billion, and those held by United States nonbank residents as less than $50 billion.[8]

M2 is the narrowest United States monetary aggregate that includes Eurodollar deposits. M2 includes overnight Eurodollar deposits held by United States nonbank residents at Caribbean branches of Federal Reserve member banks. As of June 1980, M2 measured $1,587 billion; its Eurodollar component was $2.9 billion.[9]

Even though it is conceptually appropriate to include term Eurodollar deposits held by United States nonbank residents in M3, they are only included in L, the broadest measure of money and liquid assets reported by the Federal Reserve, because the data used to estimate their volume is available with a long lag relative to other data in M3. M3 was approximately $1,846 billion in June 1980; the Eurodollar component of L was $51.8 billion.[10] Eurodollar deposits owned by United States nonbank residents continue to grow rapidly, but these comparisons show clearly that such Eurodollar deposits still account for a relatively small portion of United States nonbank resident holdings of money and liquid assets.

INCENTIVES FOR DEVELOPMENT OF THE EURODOLLAR MARKET[11]

By accepting deposits and making loans denominated in United States dollars outside the United States, banks can avoid many United States banking regulations. In particular, banks located outside the United States are not required to keep noninterest-bearing reserves against Eurodollar deposits. These foreign banks hold balances with United States banks for clearing purposes only. Moreover, there is no required Federal Deposit Insurance Corporation insurance assessment associated with Eurodollar deposits. Virtually no restrictions exist for interest rates payable on Eurodollar deposits or charged on Eurodollar loans; and there are few restrictions on the types of assets allowed in portfolio.

In most Eurodollar financial centers, entry into Eurodollar banking is virtually free of regulatory impediments. In addition, banks intending to do Eurodollar business can set up in locations where tax rates are low. For example, Eurodollar deposits and loans negotiated in London or elsewhere are often booked in such locations as Nassau and the Cayman Islands to obtain more favorable tax treatment.

Foreign monetary authorities are generally reluctant to regulate Eurodollar business because to do so would drive the business away, denying the host country income, tax revenue, and jobs. Even if the United States monetary authorities could induce a group of foreign countries to participate in a plan to regulate their Euromarkets, such a plan would be ineffective unless every country agreed not to host unregulated Eurodollar business. In practice, competition for this business had been fierce, so, even if a consensus should develop in the United States to regulate Eurodollar business, it would be extremely difficult to impose regulations on the entire Eurodollar market.

INSTRUMENTS OF THE EURODOLLAR MARKET[12]

The overwhelming majority of money in the Eurodollar market is held in fixed-rate time deposits (TDs). The maturities of Eurodollar TDs range from overnight to several years, with most of the money held in the one-week to six-month maturity range. Eurodollar time deposits are intrinsically different from dollar deposits held at banks in the United States only in that the former are liabilities of financial institutions located outside the United States. The bulk of Eurodollar time deposits are interbank liabilities. They pay a rate of return which, although fixed for the term of the deposit, is initially competitively determined.[13]

From their introduction in 1966, the volume of negotiable Eurodollar certificates of deposit (CDs) outstanding reached roughly $50 billion at the beginning of 1980.[14] Essentially, a Eurodollar CD is a negotiable receipt for a dollar deposit at a bank located outside the United States.

On average over the past seven years, fixed-rate three-month Eurodollar CDs have yielded approximately 30 basis points below the three-month time deposit London Interbank Offer Rate (LIBOR).[15] LIBOR is the rate at which major international banks are willing to offer term Eurodollar deposits to each other.

An active secondary market allows investors to sell Eurodollar CDs before the deposits mature. Secondary market makers' spreads for short-term fixed-rate CDs are usually 5 or 10 basis points.[16]

Eurodollar CDs are issued by banks to "tap" the market for funds. Consequently, they have come to be called "Tap CDs." Such Tap CDs are commonly issued in denominations of from $250,000 to $5 million. Some large Eurodollar CD issues are marketed in several portions in order to satisfy investors with preferences for smaller instruments. These are known as Tranche CDs. Tranche CDs are issued in aggregate amounts of $10 million to $30 million and offered to individual investors in $10,000 certificates, with each certificate having the same interest rate, issue date, interest payment dates, and maturity.

In recent years. Eurodollar floating rate CDs (FRCDs) and Eurodollar floating rate notes (FRNs) have come into use as a means of protecting both borrower and lender against interest-rate risk. Specifically, these "floaters" shift the burden of risk from the principal value of the paper to its coupon.

Eurodollar FRDCs and FRNs are both negotiable bearer paper. The coupon or interest rate on these instruments is reset periodically, typically every three or six months, at a small spread above the corresponding LIBOR. Eurodollar FRCDs yield, depending on maturity, between 1/8 and 1/4 percent over six-month LIBOR.[17] They are an attractive alternative to placing six-month time deposits at the London Interbank bid rate. Eurodollar FRN issues have usually been brought to market with a margin of 1/8 to 1/4 percent over either the three- or six-month LIBOR or the mean of the London Interbank bid and offer rates.[18] To determine LIBOR for Eurodollar FRNs, "the issuer chooses an agent bank who in turn polls three or four Reference Banks—generally, the London offices of major international banks. Rates are those prevailing at 11 A.M. London time two business days prior to the commencement of the next coupon period."[19]

Eurodollar FRDCs have been issued in maturities from 1.5 to 5.0 years and are employed as an alternative to short-term money market instruments. Eurodollar FRNs have been issued in maturities from 4 to 20 years, with the maturity of issues concentrated in the 5-year to 7-year range. Eurodollar FRNs tend to be seen as an alternative to straight fixed-interest bonds, but they can in principle be used like FRCDs. Eurodollar FRNs have been issued primarily, but not exclusively, by banks.

A secondary market exists in Eurodollar FRCDs and FRNs, although dealer spreads are quite large. Secondary market makers' spreads for FRCDs are normally 0.25 percent of principal value.[20] The spread quoted on FRNs in the secondary market is generally 0.5 percent of principal value.[21]

INTEREST-RATE RELATIONSHIPS BETWEEN EURODOLLAR DEPOSITS AND DEPOSITS AT BANKS IN THE UNITED STATES

Arbitrage keeps interest rates closely aligned between Eurodollar deposits and deposits with roughly comparable characteristics at banks located in the United States. This is illustrated in Charts 1 and 2. Chart 1 shows yields on federal funds

CHART 1
Yields on Federal Funds and Overnight Eurodollar Deposits
(monthly average)

Percent per annum

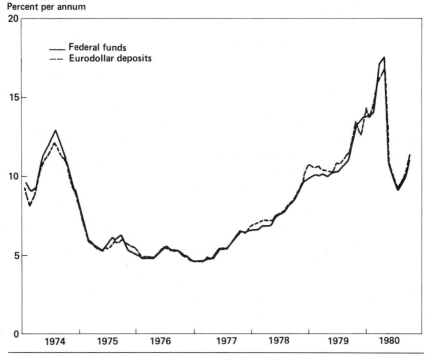

Source: Morgan Guaranty Trust Company of New York, *World Financial Markets*.

and overnight Eurodollar deposits. Chart 2 shows yields on Eurodollar CDs and
CDs issued by banks located in the United States.

THE RELATIVE RISKINESS OF EURODOLLAR DEPOSITS
AND DOLLAR DEPOSITS HELD IN THE UNITED STATES[22]

There are three basic sources of risk associated with holding Eurodollars. The
first concerns the chance that authorities where a Eurodollar deposit is held may
interfere in the movement or repatriation of interest or principal of the deposit.
But this risk factor does not necessarily imply that Eurodollar deposits are riskier
than dollar deposits held in the United States. The riskiness of a Eurodollar
deposit relative to a dollar deposit held in the United States can depend on the
deposit holder's residence. For United States residents, Eurodollars may appear
riskier than domestic deposits because of the possibility that authorities in the
foreign country where the deposit is located may interfere in the movement of
repatriation of the interest or principal of the deposit. Foreign residents—Iranians
for example—may feel that the United States government is more likely to block
their deposits than the British government. Consequently, Iranians may perceive
greater risk from potential government interference by holding dollar deposits in
the United States than by holding Eurodollar deposits in London.

CHART 2
Yields on United States and Eurodollar Three-month Certificates of Deposit
(at or near the first of the month)

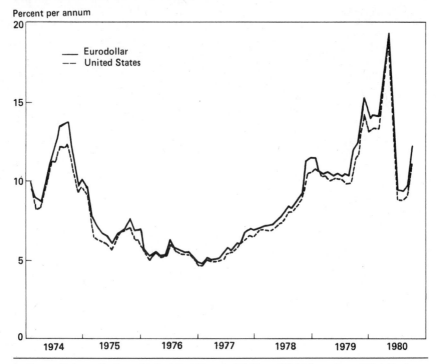

Percent per annum

Source: Salomon Brothers, *An Analytical Record of Yields and Yield Spreads,* part IV, table 2.

A *second* element of risk associated with Eurodollars concerns the potential for international jurisdictional legal disputes. For example, uncertainty surrounding interaction between United States and foreign legal systems compounds the difficulty in assessing the likelihood and timing of Eurodollar deposit payments in the event of a Eurodollar issuing bank's failure.

A *third* type of risk associated with holding Eurodollars concerns the relative soundness per se of foreign banks compared to banks located in the United States. Specifically, it has been argued that Eurodollars are absolutely riskier than deposits held in the United States because deposits held in the United States generally carry deposit insurance of some kind while Eurodollar deposits generally do not. In addition, it has been argued that in the event of a financial crisis banks located in the United States are more likely to be supported by the Federal Reserve System, whereas neither Federal Reserve support nor the support of foreign central banks for Eurodollar banking activities in their jurisdiction is certain.

A related factor compounding the three basic risk factors identified above is the greater cost of evaluating foreign investments compared with domestic investments. Acquiring information on the soundness of foreign banks is generally more costly than assessing the soundness of more well-known domestic banks. This means that, for a given level of expenditure on information acquisition, investors must generally accept more ignorance about the soundness of a foreign bank than a domestic bank.

Two comments on this argument are relevant here. *First,* the fact that it is more costly to evaluate foreign than domestic investments does not imply that Eurodollar deposits are inherently riskier than deposits held in the United States. If a depositor resides in the United States, the argument implies that a given expenditure on research will generally yield more information about the safety of deposits located in the United States than in the Eurodollar market. But if the depositor resides outside the United States, the reverse may be true.

Having said this, it must be pointed out that the amount of financial disclosure required by regulatory authorities abroad is generally not as great as in the United States. This fact may make it more difficult to evaluate the soundness of non-U.S. banks than U.S. banks for any depositor, regardless of his or her residence.

Second, to a large extent assessing the safety of Eurodollar deposits relative to deposits in banks located in the United States is made easier by the fact that many banks in the Eurodollar market are affiliated with and bear the name of a bank whose home office is in the United States. For example, a London branch of a United States bank is as closely associated with its home office as a branch located in the United States.

However, foreign offices bearing the name of a United States bank, usually in a slightly altered form, have been set up as subsidiaries. Under most legal systems, a branch can not fail unless its head office fails; but a subsidiary can fail even if its parent institution remains in business. Technically, a foreign office can bear the name of a United States bank in some form, and yet the parent institution may not be legally bound to stand fully behind the obligations of its foreign office. This suggests that a foreign office named after a parent United States bank may not be as sound as its namesake, although the parent bank, unquestionably, has great incentive to aid the foreign office in meeting its obligations in order to preserve confidence in the bank's name.

On the whole, it is difficult to assess the relative riskiness of Eurodollar deposits and dollar deposits held in the United States. Some factors affecting relative risk can be identified, but their importance is difficult to measure. What is more, perceived relative riskiness can depend on the residence of the depositor. The extent to which risk-related factors affect the interest-rate relationship between Eurodollar deposits and comparable deposits at banks in the United States remains unclear.

SUMMARY

From the depositor's point of view, Eurodollar deposits are relatively close substitutes for dollar deposits at banks located in the United States. Eurodollar deposits are able to compete effectively with deposits offered by banks located in the United States, because Eurodollar deposits are free of reserve requirements and most other regulatory burdens imposed by the United States monetary authorities on banks located in the United States. In fact, the tremendous growth of the Eurodollar market in the last two decades has largely been the result of efforts to move dollar financial intermediation outside the regulatory jurisdiction of the United States monetary authorities.

Host countries have competed eagerly for Eurodollar business by promising relatively few regulations, low taxes, and other incentives to attract a portion of the Eurodollar banking industry. Financial intermediation in United States dollars is likely to continue to move abroad as long as incentives exist for it to do so. Since these incentives are not likely to disappear soon, the Eurodollar market's share of world dollar financial intermediation is likely to continue growing.

NOTES

[1] Dollar-denominated deposits at a bank located outside the United States are Eurodollars, even if the bank is affiliated with a bank whose home office is in the United States.

[2] See Ashby (1978 and 1979) for discussions of Europe's declining share of the global Eurocurrency market. The Eurocurrency market includes, along with Eurodollars, foreign currency-denominated deposits held at banks located outside a currency's home country.

[3] Bank for International Settlements, *1964 Annual Report,* p. 127.

[4] See Morgan Guaranty Trust Company of New York, *World Financial Markets,* January 1979, pp. 9–13, for a discussion of Morgan's method of measuring the size of the Eurodollar market. Other useful discussions of issues involved in measuring the Eurodollar market's size are found in Dufey and Giddy (1978, pp. 21–34) and Mayer (1976).

[5] Morgan Guaranty, December 1980, p. 15. Most of the growth of the Eurocurrency market has occurred in the last two decades. For instance, Dufey and Giddy (1978, p. 22) report Morgan's earliest estimate of the gross size of the Eurocurrency market as only $20 billion in 1964. See Dufey and Giddy (1978, chap. 3) for a discussion of the growth of the Eurocurrency market.

[6] Morgan Guaranty, December 1980, p. 15.

[7] Ibid.

[8] Ibid., p. 4.

[9] Board of Governors of the Federal Reserve System. H.6 statistical release, "Money Stock Measures and Liquid Assets," February 20, 1981, pp. 1, 4.

[10] Ibid., pp. 1, 5. The figure for U.S. nonbank resident Eurodollar holdings given by the Federal Reserve exceeds that reported by Morgan because the Federal Reserve includes in its figure Eurodollar CDs held in the name of U.S. banks that are being held for the beneficial interest of U.S. nonbank residents.

Eurodollar deposits included in L are those held by U.S. nonbank residents at all banks in the United Kingdom, Canada, and at branches of U.S. banks in other countries. These account for nearly all U.S. nonbank resident Eurodollar holdings. Some overnight Eurodollar deposits issued to U.S. nonbank residents by other banks than Caribbean branches of member banks are only included in L because current data do not separate these overnight Eurodollars from term Eurodollars.

At present, Eurodollars held by non-U.S. residents are not included in any of the U.S. monetary aggregates. As improved data sources become available, the possible inclusion of Eurodollars held by non-U.S. residents, other than banks and official institutions, could be reviewed. See Board of Governors of the Federal Reserve System, *Federal Reserve Bulletin,* February 1980, p. 98.

[11] See Dufey and Giddy (1978, pp. 110–12) for more discussion of the conditions that made large-scale Eurodollar market growth possible.

[12] Dobbs-Higginson (1980, pp. 55–61), Dufey and Giddy (1978, pp. 228–32), and Stigum (1978, chaps. 15 and 16) contain useful surveys of Eurodollar instruments.

[13] See Stigum (1978, p. 433) and Dufey and Giddy (1978, p. 227) for discussions of Eurodollar deposit rate tiering according to perceived issuing bank creditworthiness.

[14] Bank of England, Financial Statistics Division, International Banking Group. This data only include London dollar CDs. But until recently, virtually all Eurodollar CDs have been issued in London. See "Out-of-Towners," *The Economist,* July 12, 1980, p. 89.

[15] This spread was calculated from data in Salomon Brothers, *An Analytical Record of Yields and Yield Spreads* 1980.

[16] Dobbs-Higginson (1980, p. 59).

[17] Credit Suisse First Boston Limited, "A Description of the London Dollar Negotiable Certificate of Deposit Market," January 1980, p. 3.

[18] Salomon Brothers, *Eurodollar Floating Rate Notes: A Guide to the Market,* 1980, p. 3. The spread between interbank bid and offer rates is normally ⅛ percent, so an issue priced at ¼ percent over the mean of the bid and offer rates would return ³⁄₁₆ percent over LIBOR.

[19] Ibid., p. 7.

[20] Dobbs-Higginson (1980, p. 59).

[21] Ibid., p. 56.

[22] See Dufey and Giddy (1978, pp. 187–90) and Tyson (1980) for more discussion of the riskiness of Eurodollars.

REFERENCES

Ashby, David F. V. "Challenge from the New Euro-Centres." *The Banker,* January 1978, pp. 53–61.

———. "Changing Patterns in the $800 Billion Super-Dollar Market." *The Banker,* March 1979, pp. 21–23.

Bank of England. Personal correspondence, Financial Statistics Division, International Banking Group, April 28, 1980.

Bank for International Settlements. *1964 Annual Report.* Basle, Switzerland.

Board of Governors of the Federal Reserve System. *Federal Reserve Bulletin,* February 1980.

———. H.6 statistical release, "Money Stock Measures and Liquid Assets." February 20, 1981.

Credit Suisse First Boston Limited. "A Description of the London Dollar Negotiable Certificate of Deposit Market," January 1980.

Dobbs-Higginson, M. S. *Investment Manual for Fixed Income Securities in the International and Major Domestic Capital Markets.* London: Credit Suisse First Boston Limited, 1980.

Dufey, Gunter, and Ian H. Giddy. *The International Money Market.* Englewood Cliffs, N.J.: Prentice-Hall, 1978.

"The London Dollar Certificate of Deposit." *Quarterly Bulletin,* Bank of England, 13, no. 4 (December 1973): 446–52.

Mayer, Helmut W. "The BIS Concept of the Eurocurrency Market." *Euromoney,* May 1976, pp. 60–66.

Morgan Guaranty Trust Company of New York. *World Financial Markets.* Various issues.

"Out-of-Towners." *The Economist,* July 12, 1980, p. 89.

Salomon Brothers. *An Analytical Record of Yields and Yield Spreads.* New York: Salomon Brothers, 1980.

———. *Eurodollar Floating Rate Notes: A Guide to the Market.* New York: Salomon Brothers, 1980.

Stigum, Marcia. *The Money Market: Myth, Reality, and Practice.* Homewood, Ill.: Dow Jones-Irwin, 1978.

Tyson, David O. "Fund Managers Wary of Risks in Non Domestic CDs." *The Money Manager,* July 14, 1980, pp. 3–4.

23

Original Issue Deep Discount Bonds

Andrew Silver

In response to the high and volatile levels of interest rates experienced in the United States during the past two years, borrowers in the corporate bond market have increasingly experimented with alternatives to the traditional fixed-rate long-term bond as a means of raising funds. These alternatives include bonds with warrants, variable rates, links to commodities prices, and stock convertibility features (Box 1). Another such innovation, which has been heavily used since the spring of 1981, is the original issue deep discount bond (henceforth referred to as a discount bond). When issued, discount bonds offer coupon payments well below the market rate of return and, therefore, must be sold at a substantial discount from par. Thus, in general, the return on a discount bond held to maturity consists of both coupon payments and the appreciation from the discounted issue price to par value at maturity. However, in the extreme, a bond sold at a discount may offer no coupon (a zero coupon bond) and provide a return solely through its appreciation from the discounted value to par.

Discount bonds offer both advantages and disadvantages to borrowers and investors when compared with current coupon bonds (hereafter referred to as conventional bonds).[1] While it is difficult to place precise monetary values on the different characteristics of the bonds, it is probably true that the advantages outweigh the disadvantages for participants on both sides of the market. For investors, the (implicitly) increased call protection and lower reinvestment risk are attractive features of discount bonds, while the potentially large tax disadvantage is of no consequence to a significant group of buyers—nontaxable entities and foreign investors. Borrowers benefit greatly from the tax treatment of these bonds, so they, too, prefer them to conventional bonds. Therefore, investors would be willing to accept lower yields on discount bonds than on conventional bonds, and borrowers would be willing to pay higher yields. Since discount bonds have actually been sold at effective rates below those on comparable conventional bonds, issuers have definitely benefited by offering these innovative bonds. Investors also may have gained, to the extent that the market rates have exceeded

From *Quarterly Review*, Federal Reserve Bank of New York, Winter 1981–82.

Box 1: Other Unconventional Bonds

A number of bonds that have been issued over the past year have offered investors some combination of the characteristics of conventional bonds and those of instruments of other markets. By combining features of different markets in such "hybrid" instruments, borrowers have sought to attract investors at lower costs than with conventional bonds. A few of the types of unconventional bonds, and examples of their uses, are described below.

Variable rate bonds are bonds that periodically adjust interest payments to reflect market rates. Therefore, in contrast to fixed-rate bonds, if interest rates rise during the term of the bond, investors will not earn below-market rates for any extended period of time. Furthermore, since variable rate bonds earn approximately the market rate of interest, their prices should not vary much from par; consequently, investors have little risk of incurring capital losses if interest rates have risen and they sell the bonds before maturity. Of course, with variable rate bonds, investors give up the opportunity, for the most part, to "lock in" current rates and to earn capital gains should interest rates fall in the future. In these respects, purchasing variable rate bonds is similar to buying a series of short-term investments, such as commercial paper.

As is the case with issuing commercial paper and then turning it over repeatedly, issuers are not sure of their future borrowing costs with variable rate bonds. However, variable rate bonds offer borrowers a long-term commitment for funds, unlike a commercial paper offering and, in this respect, are similar to conventional bonds.

Variable rate bonds have been used rarely in the United States corporate bond market, though they are seen frequently in the Eurobond market. One of the few examples of a domestically issued variable rate bond is a twenty-year issue offered in February 1981 by General Felt Industries, Inc. The interest payments are adjusted quarterly and set at 133 percent of a 20-day average of the constant maturity yields on 20-year Treasury bonds.

Commodity linked bonds are another type of unconventional security. The principal of these bonds is convertible, at the option of the buyer, into a fixed quantity of some commodity. To the extent that the price of the commodity tracks the general level of prices in the economy, commodity linked bonds provide protection against unexpected increases in the rate of inflation.

In effect, a commodity linked bond is similar to a combination of a conventional bond and an options contract for the linked commodity. The major difference is that, in the hybrid instrument, exercise of the option also terminates the bond contract. If the conventional bond and option were purchased separately, the option could be exercised but the bond retained.

HMW Industries, Inc., issued an example of this type of bond, a silver-indexed bond with 8 percent coupons. Starting May 1, 1983, investors may redeem each $1,000 principal amount for cash equal to the market price of 43 ounces of silver, or for the quantity of silver itself. However, since the value of 43 ounces of silver was $472.57 at the time of the bond offering, the convertibility option would provide value to the investor only after a very considerable increase in the price of silver.

A more common alternative to conventional bonds is the *convertible bond,* which may be converted into a fixed number of shares of common stock at a set price. Typically, that price represents a premium of 10 to 20 percent over the current share price. For instance, in August 1981, Toys "R" Us, Inc., issued a bond at par, which, for each $1,000 principal amount, was convertible into 31.01 shares of common stock. Therefore the initial conversion price, or minimum price at which investors would profit by converting the bond principal into stock, was $32.25 (*i.e.,* the $1,000 principal amount divided by 31.01 shares). Since the price of Toys "R" Us stock was $29.95 at the time of the offering, the conversion price represented a 10.3 percent premium.

In the past year, there also have been a number of bond issues with *warrants* attached. Warrants are options to purchase either shares of stock at a set price or other bonds with a fixed coupon, at some future date (*i.e.,* they are essentially options contracts). When the warrants represent options to buy stock, they provide protection similar to that of convertible bonds; if the price of the corporation's stock rises above the price specified by the warrant, then investors holding bonds with warrants can purchase the stock at a discount. However, warrants are different from convertible bonds in that they are essentially separate from the bond itself; if the warrant option is exercised, the investor still retains the bond.

As an example, consider the offering by Unifi, Inc., in June 1981. The company offered notes in denominations of $1,000, each with 45 warrants. Each warrant represents a right to purchase a share of common stock at $17.625 until maturity (July 1, 1988). Since Unifi's stock was selling in the $17 to $18 range at the time of the offering, any price appreciation could be converted into an immediate gain by investors holding warrants.

Warrants representing options to buy bonds provide a different kind of potential benefit to investors. These warrants reinforce the benefits of holding long-term bonds when interest rates *fall,* since they entitle the holder to purchase another bond yielding a higher return. For instance, the warrant on the ten-year bond with 13 3/8 percent coupon issued by Beneficial Corporation in January 1981 entitled the holder to purchase another 13 3/8 percent bond, at par, any time before June 30, 1981. The warrants were allowed to trade separately from the bonds. If bond yields had dropped below 13 3/8 percent before June

30, the bonds with coupons of 13 3/8 percent would have sold at a premium. Therefore, investors would have been able to realize a capital gain on the original bond, as well as on the bond purchased with the warrant.

Of the different types of unconventional bonds mentioned, only convertible issues were used with any frequency in the past year. However, even those bonds have not comprised a major share of the total volume of funds raised in the bond market. The major reason that none of these alternative types of bonds have become very popular is that, although they offer certain advantages to investors, they also present corresponding disadvantages to borrowers. Only when the value placed on the advantage by the investor is larger than the value placed on the disadvantage by the borrower, will the borrower choose to issue the unconventional bond instead of the traditional, fixed-rate bond.

the minimum rate at which they would buy discount bonds instead of conventional bonds.

This article examines how original issue discount bonds provide the various advantages and disadvantages to borrowers and lenders, with special attention being paid to the tax considerations. It also shows how the value of some of the bonds' characteristics are accentuated by high and/or volatile interest rates, thus offering a possible explanation for the fact that discount bonds have only recently become a popular means of raising funds in the bond market.

BACKGROUND

The first publicly placed discount bond by a highly rated United States corporation was issued in early March 1981 by Martin Marietta Corporation. Prior to that time, these bonds had been issued only by companies with low credit ratings or by higher-rated companies through private placements. Following the Martin Marietta issue, other major corporations followed in quick succession, and by the end of July there had been 21 publicly placed discount issues, raising funds totaling $2 billion. Although the pace slowed somewhat from August through October (both on a dollar-volume basis and as a percentage of total funds raised with corporate bonds), it picked up considerably in November, when discount bonds accounted for more than 24 percent of the total funds raised publicly in the domestic bond market. For the entire March through November period, the comparable figure was approximately 14 percent (Table 1).

The discount bonds issued in 1981 (from March through November) varied widely with respect to coupons, prices, yields, credit ratings, and terms to maturity. Coupons ranged from 16 percent to zero, and prices from $85.50 to $25.25. The Martin Marietta issue and a recent Security Pacific Corporation offering (rated A and Aa, respectively, by Moody's Investors Service, Inc.) both had the lowest yield to maturity of any discount bond to date—13.25 percent—while another recent offer, by Lorimar (rated B), was priced to yield 20.01 percent (Box 2 explains how yields to maturity are calculated.) In the March through May

TABLE 1
Publicly Placed Corporate Bonds (total funds raised and funds raised with original issue discount bonds)

1981	All Bonds (millions of dollars)	Discount Bonds (millions of dollars)	Discount Bonds as a Percentage of All Bonds
March	$ 3,778	$ 256	6.8%
April	3,668	781	21.3
May	2,520	269	6.7
June	4,603	490	10.6
July	1,925	327	17.0
August	905	78	8.6
September	2,198	168	7.6
October	2,582	107	4.1
November	6,560	1,601	24.4
March–November	28,739	3,977	13.8

period, most discount bonds that were issued had 30 years to maturity; the weighted average term to maturity for that period was 28 years, compared with approximately 20 years for conventional bonds. However, in the subsequent five months (through October), the weighted average term to maturity for discount bonds was similar to that for conventional issues, approximately 18 years.

Bonds sell at more of a discount the lower the coupon and, as long as the coupon is below the market rate, the longer the term to maturity (Box 2). While some discount bonds have been issued with zero coupons and others have had very long maturities (30 years), there has been neither a zero coupon bond issue with maturity of longer than 10 years nor a 30-year bond with a coupon of less than 6 percent. Thus, by combining a zero coupon bond with a 30-year maturity, there is the potential for bonds to be issued at even deeper discounts than the market has heretofore seen. As will be shown in the following sections, such bonds would tend to accentuate most of the advantages and disadvantages of discount bonds.

TAX ADVANTAGE TO BORROWER

Discount bonds that pay the same yield to maturity as conventional bonds provide distinct tax advantages to taxable borrowers. This is because of special provisions in the tax laws which apply to the treatment of the original issue discount amount. Discounts on original issue discount bonds are "deductible as interest and shall be prorated or amortized over the life of the obligation."[2] With a straight-line prorating procedure, borrowing firms realize a tax advantage with discount bonds vis-à-vis conventional bonds because the present value of the deductible interest expenses is higher with the discount bonds.

This tax advantage can be illustrated with a simple example. Consider, first, a two-year $100 conventional bond with a 10 percent coupon paid annually, thus providing the following pre-tax cash flows to the borrower:

Period	0	1	2
Cash flow ...	$100	−$10	−$110 (i.e., $100 principal repayment plus $10 coupon)

Box 2: The Yield to Maturity Calculation

Bond purchases generally involve an initial cash outlay (the price of the bond), some periodic cash inflows (the coupon payments), and a large cash inflow at maturity (the principal repayment). When the price of the bond is equal to the principal repayment, the coupon rate provides a good measure of the bond's rate of return. However, when comparing the returns on bonds, some of which may be purchased at prices other than par, one should take into account the price appreciation or depreciation that will occur on the bonds. One way to do that is to calculate the bond's current yield, or the coupon payment divided by the bond price. However, the current yield does not take into account the length of time over which that appreciation or depreciation is to occur. For example, it does not differentiate between a one-year bond with 10 percent coupons that sells for $90 and a two-year bond with the same coupons and price; the current yield on both bonds is 11.11 percent. While both bonds appreciate $10 in value, the one-year bond does so in half the time and, in that sense, is better from the investor's point of view.

The yield to maturity takes into account all these factors—the coupon payments, the price appreciation or depreciation, and the period of time over which that appreciation or depreciation takes place. Implicit in the yield calculation is the assumption that all periodic payments are reinvested at the same rate; the yield to maturity represents the rate at which the initial price of the bond would have to grow so that, at maturity, it equaled the sum of the principal repayment and the value of the coupon payments (after reinvestment). In algebraic terms, the yield to maturity is the rate that satisfies the equation:

$$(1) \quad P = \frac{C_1}{(1 + r/2)^1} + \frac{C_2}{(1 + 4/2)^2}$$

$$+ \ldots + \frac{C_{2n}}{(1 + r/2)^{2n}} + \frac{F}{(1 + r/2)^{2n}}$$

or

$$(2) \quad P = \sum_{i=1}^{2n} \frac{C_1}{(1 + r/2)^1} + \frac{F}{(1 + r/2)^{2n}}$$

where P is the initial price of the bond, C_1 is the periodic cash flow, F is the principal repayment, and n is the number of years to maturity.*

The complexity of equation (1), or (2), does not allow one to solve explicitly for the yield, given specific values for the parameters P, F, and C_1. Instead, one must resort to a trial and error procedure, where different values of r are tested to see if they are consistent with the other given parameters. (A computer simulation program is often used to shorten the time necessary to do all the required calculations.) For example, to calculate the yield to maturity for a twenty-year bond with a coupon rate of 14 percent selling at a price of $88.08, one would try different values of r until the following equation was satisfied:

$$88.08 = \frac{7}{(1+r/2)^1} + \frac{7}{(1+r/2)^2} + \frac{7}{(1+r/2)^3} + \cdots$$
$$+ \frac{7}{(1+r/2)^{40}} + \frac{100}{(1+r/2)^{40}}$$

The yield to maturity for this bond is 16 percent.

From equation (1), or (2), it is obvious that, given a yield to maturity, the lower the coupon payments, the lower the price at which the bond can be sold; the borrower must offer some price appreciation in exchange for the lower coupon payments. For example, a 20-year bond with 12 percent coupons would sell at only $76.51 to yield 16 percent to maturity. Furthermore, the longer the period of time investors are to be paid below-market coupons, the lower the price the investor is willing to pay for the bond. Changing the term to maturity in the preceding example to thirty years, for instance, reduces the investor's offering price to $75.25. Therefore, bonds with the lowest coupons and longest maturities would sell at the deepest discounts and thus would present the most extreme examples of original issue discount bonds.

---

*By convention, yields to maturity on bonds are calculated assuming semi-annual compounding—that is, the yield is calculated on a seminanual basis and then doubled to get an annual yield to maturity. Therefore, a conventional bond bought at par with a coupon yield of 16 percent also has a yield to maturity of 16 percent; this is true despite the fact that the coupons are paid in semiannual instalments of $8 each, and thus offer the potential for reinvestment and a compound-interest effect on an annual basis.

The pre-tax yield to maturity (and cost to the borrower) of this bond is obviously 10 percent. For tax purposes, the borrower is allowed to deduct the $10 coupon payments as interest expense.

Now consider an alternative way of raising $100: a bond offering no coupon payments. To provide the investor with the same pre-tax yield to maturity as the conventional bond (and thus, to provide the borrower with the same pre-tax cost), this zero coupon bond must repay a par value of $121 at the end of the second year; this is because the value of the conventional bond's coupon payments at the end of year 2, compounded at a 10 percent rate, is $21. The pre-tax cash flow for the zero coupon bond is therefore:

Period	0	1	2
Cash flow ...	$100	0	−$121 (i.e., $100 return of principal plus $21 discount)

For tax purposes, however, the $21 discount may be prorated between the two

TABLE 2
Comparison of Tax Deductions
on Zero-Coupon Bonds and
Current-Coupon Bonds (in dollars)

Bonds	Period 1	Period 2
Zero-coupon bonds	10.50	10.50
Current-coupon bonds	10.00	10.00

years (i.e., $10.50 may be deducted each year by the borrowing firm as interest expense). Thus, while the pre-tax payment streams of the two bonds are equivalent (on a present-value basis), the annual tax deductions generated by the zero coupon bond are higher than on a conventional bond, making the zero coupon bond a more desirable instrument for any taxable borrower (Table 2). A taxable borrower, therefore, would be willing to offer a *higher* pre-tax yield to maturity on a zero coupon bond than on a conventional bond; on bonds with equal yields to maturity, zero coupon bonds (and, in fact, all discount bonds) result in lower after-tax costs to the borrower.

The cost savings to the borrower because of this tax advantage can be very large on discount bonds with characteristics (i.e., yields, coupons, maturities, and the like) similar to those issued in recent months. Consider, for instance, two hypothetical 20-year bonds yielding 16 percent to maturity—one is a conventional bond with a coupon rate of 16 percent, the other a discount bond with a coupon rate of 7 percent. Both bonds pay $100 at maturity. With market rates at 16 percent, the discount bond would sell at a price of $46.34; the conventional bond, of course, would sell at $100. For a corporate borrower in the 46 percent tax bracket, the after-tax cost of the 16 percent conventional bond is 8.64 percent. However, the after-tax cost of the discount bond yielding the same 16 percent would be only 7.95 percent; this is equal to the after-tax cost of a conventional bond yielding 14.72 percent before taxes. Thus, by issuing a bond with a 7 percent coupon instead of a 16 percent coupon, the issuer in effect could save 128 basis points before taxes, or 69 basis points after taxes—the difference between 8.64 percent and 7.95 percent (Table 3).

The amount of the tax saving available at a given market rate of interest depends on the amount of the discount, which in turn, depends on the coupon payments and the term to maturity. As illustrated in Table 4, lower coupons and longer terms to maturity increase the discount and the tax saving. The table shows the potential tax saving is huge—with a zero coupon 30-year issue, borrowing costs would be 47 percent lower than on a comparable conventional bond. However, as noted earlier, borrowers have not yet fully exploited this potential tax advantage, since bonds with the longest maturities have not had the lowest coupons (i.e., zero).

The size of the potential tax saving also depends on the market rate of interest; higher rates raise the potential advantage. With market rates at 10 percent (Table 4), a 30-year zero coupon bond could save only 263 basis points, far less than the 748 basis point saving for a similar bond when the market rate is 16 percent. This relationship between the tax saving and the market rate of interest may account

TABLE 3
Comparison of Borrowing Costs on Current-Coupon Bonds and Original Issue Discount Bonds Yielding 16 Percent to Maturity

Item	Current Coupon Bonds	Discount Bonds
(1) Term to maturity	20 years	20 years
(2) Original price	$100	$46.34
(3) Pre-tax yield to maturity	16%	16%
(4) Pre-tax coupon payments	$16.00	$7.00
(5) After-tax coupon payments*	$8.64	$3.78
(6) Income deduction due to prorated discount†	—	$2.68
(7) Tax saving due to income deduction‡	—	$1.23
(8) Periodic cash outflows§	$8.64	$2.55
(9) Principal repayment at maturity	$100	$100
(10) After-tax yield to maturity	8.64%	7.95%
(11) Pre-tax current-coupon bond equivalent yield to maturity ‖	16%	14.72%
(12) Pre-tax savings on issuing 7% discount bonds instead of 16% current-coupon bonds	—	128 basis points

  * After-tax coupon payments are equal to $Cx(1-t)$, where C is the pre-tax coupon payments (line 4) and t is the borrower's marginal tax rate, 46 percent.
  † Income deduction due to prorated discount amount is equal to $(100-P)/n$, where P is the original price, $46.34 (line 2), and n is the term to maturity, 20 years (line 1).
  ‡ Tax saving is equal to txI, where I is the income deduction (line 6).
  § Periodic cash outflow is equal to the after-tax coupon payment (line 5) minus the tax saving due to the income deduction (line 7).
  ‖ Pre-tax current-coupon bond-equivalent yield to maturity is the pre-tax rate a current coupon bond would need to pay to obtain the after-tax yield to maturity on line 10, or $Y/(1-t)$, where Y is the after-tax yield to maturity.

TABLE 4
Comparison of Borrowing Costs on Current-Coupon Bonds and Original Issue Discount Bonds (bonds issued at various coupons, terms to maturity, and under different market rates of return)

Market Rate of Interest (percent)	Coupon Rate (percent)	Term to Maturity (years)	Current-Coupon Bond-Equivalent Cost (percent)	Basis Point Saving over Current-Coupon Bonds
16%	7%	20	14.72%	128
16	7	30	14.30	170
16	0	20	11.44	456
16	0	30	8.52	748
10	7	20	9.80	20
10	7	30	9.68	31
10	0	20	8.67	133
10	0	30	7.37	263

for the fact that borrowers have turned to discount bonds only recently, in a period in which interest rates have reached record highs.

The borrower's marginal tax rate also plays a major role in determining the size of the tax saving, due to issuing discount bonds instead of conventional bonds. Higher tax rates imply larger savings. For instance, if the marginal tax rate were 40 percent instead of 46 percent, the tax saving of a 30-year zero coupon bond yielding 16 percent (compared with a similar conventional bond) would fall to 712 basis points from 748 basis points (before taxes).

The fact that discount bonds result in a tax savings to issuers implies that borrowers should be willing to offer these bonds at higher pre-tax rates than comparable conventional bonds. But, paradoxically, market analysts have estimated that borrowers have been issuing discount bonds at yields to maturity 40 to 100 basis points *lower* than on comparable conventional bonds. This is because certain investors have been willing to sacrifice yield in exchange for other advantages offered by discount bonds (explained in the next section).

CALL PROTECTION

Most conventional bonds can be called after a 5- to 10-year (nonrefundable) period. That is, the borrower has the option, any time after the end of the nonrefundable period, to buy back all or part of the original bond issue at par or, as is more frequently the case, at a premium.[3] Thus, if interest rates fall between the time a bond is issued and sometime after the end of the noncall period, the corporation may call the bond and refinance its activities at lower interest rates. Similarly the investor must reinvest the refunded funds at the lower market rates. Therefore, the investor's yield to maturity on a callable bond is not assured. If the bond is called, the series of investments consisting of the original bond (to call) and a new lower-yielding bond will produce an overall yield to maturity less than that of the original bond (if held to maturity).

For example, consider a 20-year conventional bond issued at par with 16 percent coupons, callable after 10 years at a price of $110. At the end of 10 years, the borrower is faced with the choice of continuing its financing for another 10 years with the 10-year-old conventional bond or calling that bond and issuing a new conventional bond with 10 years to maturity. If interest rates on 10-year debt have fallen, say to 12 percent, then the corporation can certainly reduce its borrowing costs by calling the bond. However, in doing so, it reduces the 20-year yield to maturity for the investor, from the expected 16.00 percent to just 15.64 percent (even with the 10.00 percent call premium).

The risk to the investor of an original issue discount bond being called, however, is far less than with a conventional bond, despite the fact that discount bonds are generally callable at par at any time. Because of the very low coupon payments associated with discount bonds, market rates would need to fall very substantially for the borrower to find it profitable to call the bonds. For example, a discount bond with 7 percent coupons would not be called unless interest rates fell to approximately 7 percent.[4]

The call protection advantage to the investor provided by a discount bond is associated with a corresponding *disadvantage* to the borrower. Should interest rates fall, the corporation can no longer reduce its cost by calling the bond. Thus, *ceteris paribus,* the conventional bond is preferable to the discount bond from the borrower's perspective, given the possibility that rates may decline enough to make the call provision on the conventional bond (but not the discount bond) important. Hence, without the tax considerations discussed above, the corporation would issue a discount bond only if it could do so at a lower rate than a conventional bond. While investors might be willing to accept lower yields, because of the increased call protection, it is not clear a priori that the differential acceptable to investors is enough to compensate borrowers. Furthermore, if the call protection characteristics are the reason that discount bonds have become popular, there is no obvious reason that a completely noncallable (but otherwise) conventional bond would not be just as popular. Thus, one is led to believe that the call protection characteristics form, at best, only part of the explanation for the popularity of discount bonds.

REINVESTMENT RISK

As mentioned previously, the return on a new conventional bond held to maturity is derived solely from coupon payments. The standard calculation of the yield to maturity of this type of bond assumes that the coupons can be reinvested at the same rate, thus achieving a compound interest effect. But the rates at which investors will be able to reinvest the future coupon payments are not known with certainty at the time the bond is purchased. Therefore, when buying conventional bonds, investors incur some reinvestment risk.

For a given yield to maturity, however, there is less reinvestment risk on a discount bond than on a conventional bond. This is because less of the return on a discount bond is due to coupon payments and more is due to the price appreciation of the original investment. The growth of the price of the original investment takes place at an *assured* (implicit) rate, thus reducing the number of dollars which must be reinvested at uncertain future rates. An extreme example is the zero coupon bond, on which the yield to maturity represents the implicit compounded rate at which the original dollar investment grows to par; no coupons need be reinvested, resulting in zero reinvestment risk during the life of the investment.

Table 5 illustrates the point in the following hypothetical situation: reinvestment rates for the coupons of 20-year bonds (originally priced to yield 16 percent) are 16 percent for the first 10 years and then drop to 12 percent for the final 10 years. As the table shows, the lower the discount bond coupon rate, the higher the realized 20-year yield. Furthermore, the relationship between changes in coupon rates and changes in realized yields is highly nonlinear; the effect of a one percentage point change in coupon rates is much larger at lower levels of coupon rates. Finally, it should be noted that the zero coupon bond provides the ultimate protection against reinvestment risk, guaranteeing the 16 percent return and thereby providing 175 basis points more yield than the conventional bond, if rates should fall to 12 percent.

However, the advantage reaped by the investor in reducing reinvestment risk may result in either an advantage or disadvantage to the borrower. The effect depends on the cash flows generated by the investment project for which the corporation has borrowed funds. In general, the corporation can reduce its reinvestment risk by attempting to match the investment project's cash inflows to the firm's outflows of bond payments. Hence, if the investment project generates funds throughout the life of the bond, a conventional bond would result in a lower reinvestment risk to the firm—a discount bond would require that the firm save funds for the large payout at maturity by reinvesting those cash flows at uncertain future rates. Alternatively, a firm which expects not to receive any cash flows until the very end of the project would need to raise funds at uncertain future rates to pay the coupons on a conventional bond; a discount bond would be less risky in this situation. Therefore, depending on their cash flow positions, borrowing firms may be willing to offer either lower or higher yields on discount bonds than on conventional bonds.

TABLE 5
Realized Yield to Maturity for 20-year Bonds with Various Coupons (when reinvestment rates drop from 16 percent to 12 percent after 10 years)

Coupon (in dollars)	Realized Yield to Maturity (in percent)
$16	14.248
15	14.254
14	14.261
13	14.270
12	14.279
11	14.290
10	14.303
9	14.319
8	14.338
7	14.362
6	14.392
5	14.435
4	14.493
3	14.581
2	14.728
1	15.019
0	16.000

TAX CONSIDERATIONS FOR INVESTORS

While the call protection and reinvestment risk characteristics of discount bonds are attractive to certain investors, the tax treatment of these bonds makes them less appealing when compared with conventional bonds. This is due to the fact that investors must prorate the discount on a straight-line basis and treat this amortization as interest income each year.[5] Therefore, just as the present value of the tax deductions for the borrower is higher on a discount bond than a comparable conventional bond, the present value of the tax *liabilities* of the investor is larger, creating a tax *disadvantage*.

Nontaxable investors, however, are not subject to the negative tax implications of discount bonds. Furthermore, some of these investors are particularly attracted by the nonpecuniary advantages of discount bonds—increased call protection and lower reinvestment risk. As a result, nontaxable investors, such as pension funds, have become the principal buyers of discount bonds.

Another group of investors on whom the negative tax consequences of discount bonds would have little impact is foreign investors. As a result, these investors have also shown some interest in purchasing discount bonds. Foreign investors are subject to a 30 percent withholding tax on interest payments from United States corporate bonds. While the withholding tax applies to both the coupon payments and the prorated discount amount, the sum withheld cannot exceed the amount of the coupon. Any excess liability would be withheld from the principal repayment at maturity, if the bond were still held by the same owner. Thus, with deeply discounted bonds, foreign owners can at least delay some of their tax liabilities (until maturity), reducing the present value of those payments. Furthermore, since only the issuing corporation is required to withhold taxes, and on the earnings only of the current holder of the bond, the foreign investor can avoid the excess tax withholding liability entirely by selling the bond shortly before maturity. For example, on a zero coupon bond, no taxes can be withheld until the principal repayment. If the original holder sells the bond just before maturity, the corporation withholds (from the principal repayment) the tax liability incurred during the relatively short time the bond is held by the new owner (and only if the. new owner is also a foreign investor). The original holder, in this case, would not have *any* tax withheld on the interest earned on the zero coupon bond.

OTHER CONSIDERATIONS

Although discount bonds "guarantee" a larger portion of their returns than do conventional bonds if held to maturity, investors may also be interested in comparing the volatility of realized yields for other holding periods, given that interest rates may fluctuate and investors may decide to sell the bonds before maturity, thereby earning capital gains or losses. For a given interest-rate change, deeply discounted bonds (whether or not issued originally at a discount) exhibit more volatility in holding period yields than do current-coupon bonds. This is because a relatively large portion of the yield on discount bonds is paid late in the life of the bond (in the form of price appreciation); a change in interest rates affects the present value of a stream of payments that includes a large distant payment more than it does a smooth stream that includes only coupon payments (as for a conventional bond). Therefore, a discount bond's price is relatively more volatile than that of a conventional bond and, as a result, discount bond holding period yields vary over a wider range than do conventional bond yields.

The greater volatility of discount bond yields may be regarded either as an advantage or a disadvantage, depending on investors' views on the future direction of interest rates and the appropriateness (to the investor) of risk-taking. If investors believe that interest rates will decline, they will probably prefer discount bonds to conventional bonds, to take advantage of the higher potential holding period yields. Similarly, if they think that interest rates will rise, they will prefer conventional bonds.[6] When investors have a "neutral" interest-rate outlook— when they feel that interest rates have as much of a chance of rising as they do of falling—investors will choose the conventional bonds if they are "risk averse" (i.e., if they prefer less yield volatility to more, all else being equal); otherwise, they will choose the discount bond.

Another consideration in evaluating the choice between conventional and discount bonds is that the latter generally have more "credit risk" (i.e., the risk that the borrower may default on all or part of the coupon and principal payments). The risk is higher with discount bonds because they "pay out" more slowly than conventional bonds, since the return on discount bonds relies less on coupons (paid periodically) and more on price appreciation (realized at maturity). Therefore, investors get their return "earlier" with conventional bonds and stand to lose less if the borrower defaults. Consequently, investors to whom this risk is very important would prefer conventional bonds to discount bonds. However, this disadvantage is probably not a major consideration in judging the merits of a highly rated company's discount bond.

SUMMARY

The many advantages and disadvantages of discount bonds relative to conventional bonds are summarized in Table 6. In deciding which type of bond to issue

TABLE 6
Summary of Advantages and Disadvantages of Original Issue Discount Bonds
Relative to Current-Coupon Bonds

Feature	Impact on Borrower	Impact on Investor
Tax treatment	Advantage	Disadvantage for taxable investor; of no consequence to nontaxable investor
Call protection	Disadvantage	Advantage
Reinvestment risk protection	Can be advantage, disadvantage, or of no consequence, depending on cash flows	Advantage
Intermediate holding period yield volatility	Of no consequence	Can be advantage or disadvantage, depending on investors' expectations of future interest rate movements and views on rate volatility
Credit risk	Of no consequence	Disadvantage

(invest in), borrowers (investors) must place a value, positive or negative, on each of the features which differentiate the two types of bonds. If the net result is positive (i.e., if the positively valued features of discount bonds outweigh the negatively valued features), then these bonds are the appropriate instrument. Obviously, given the relatively large volume of discount bond issues since March, many market participants have come to that conclusion.

Of all the characteristics of discount bonds which differentiate them from conventional bonds, the tax treatment is undoubtedly the most important. The potential savings in borrowing costs is tremendous and tends to swamp the potential disadvantages that the call protection and reinvestment risk characteristics pose to the issuer. This is true for two reasons. *First,* the call protection and reinvestment risk features are disadvantages only if interest rates decline, which may or may not happen; the tax advantage of discount bonds is effective regardless of the future course of rates. *Second,* even if interest rates decline substantially during the term of the bond, the total after tax cost of issuing a conventional bond, calling it, and then issuing a new lower-yielding conventional bond, would probably still be higher than the cost of borrowing with a single-discount bond for the entire term. For example, the after tax cost of a 30-year zero coupon bond yielding 16.0 percent to maturity is only 4.6 percent (for an issuer in the 46.0 percent marginal tax bracket). If, instead, the borrower originally issued a 16.0 percent conventional bond, called it after 15 years (at par), and then issued a 15-year conventional bond at, say, 6.0 percent, the average after tax cost over the 30 years would be approximately 5.9 percent. Therefore, even with a decline in rates from 16 percent to 6 percent, the discount bond would be less costly.

If borrowers prefer the characteristics of discount bonds to those of conventional bonds, why have discount bonds been issued at lower yields? One necessary reason is that investors also value the relative advantages of discount bonds more than their disadvantages. But this is not a sufficient condition, because the combination of preferences for discount bonds by both issuers and investors suggests only that there is a *range* of rates at which a discount bond could sell, a range which includes the rate on a comparable conventional bond.

There are a number of factors that determine where within the range the actual market rate will fall. Included in these factors are the negotiating powers of the market participants and the levels of competition among buyers and sellers. Since discount bonds are relatively new instruments, it is conceivable that not all investors and borrowers have been fully aware of the value of each of the advantages and disadvantages of the bonds. As a more complete understanding becomes widespread with the passage of time, the supply of, and demand for, these securities may shift, altering the yield at which the bonds are sold.

NOTES

[1] The term *current-coupon bonds* refers to bonds issued at or near par, with coupons reflecting the current level of market interest rates. For example, if the current level of market yields is 15 percent, then a current-coupon bond would promise coupon payments of $15 per year per $100 of face value.

[2] *Treasury Regulations,* Section 1.163-4(a), 1971. Borrowers are allowed to prorate the discount and take it as an interest expense deduction regardless of the size of the original issue discount. However, in the tax treatment of investors, an original issue discount bond is defined as one that is sold at an original issue discount greater than or equal to 0.25 percent of the redemption price at maturity multiplied by the number of complete years to maturity. Therefore, a 20-year bond would be considered an original issue discount bond if it were sold at a price of less than or equal to $95.

[3] This premium has recently ranged from zero (i.e., the bond is callable at par) to as high as 18.75 percent (i.e., the bond is callable at $118.75). Frequently, the premium is scheduled to decline gradually to zero sometime before maturity.

[4] While one's first guess might be that interest rates would need to fall at least to the coupon rate for the refunding to be undertaken by the corporation, this is not quite the case, due to tax considerations. Firms are allowed to deduct from taxable income the difference between the bond's redemption value and its amortized value (to be discussed later), reducing the after-tax price of the bond being refunded. Thus, firms would be willing to call bonds even when the market yields are slightly above the coupon rate.

[5] The treatment of an original issue discount is in contrast to the treatment of the discount on a bond issued at par but bought in the secondary market below par; the latter discount is treated as a capital gain.

[6] This analysis only examines the choice between discount bonds and conventional bonds. In reality, investors can also choose a third type of financial investment, a sequence of short-term instruments. The conclusions reached in the text depend on the implicit assumption that the conventional bond rates are set at a level which makes investors indifferent between those bonds and a sequence of short-term investments of the same total term.

24

Adjustable-Rate Financing in Mortgage and Consumer Credit Markets

John L. Goodman, Jr., and Charles A. Luckett

The variability of interest rates in recent years and the trend toward deregulation in financial markets have spawned a number of innovations in lending practices. Among the more prominent of these changes is the use of adjustable-rate loans in the home mortgage and consumer credit markets, where the fixed-rate, fixed-term contract had long been the dominant credit instrument.

Lenders have embraced the adjustable-rate loan as a means of shifting to borrowers part of the sharply increased risk to which higher and more widely fluctuating interest rates have exposed them. That risk was particularly acute in the mortgage market—mortgage loans were typically written with 25-year to 30-year maturities, while for most creditors the cost of obtaining loanable funds was tied to liabilities with much shorter terms. Borrowers, meanwhile, have found that adjustable-rate loans possess several attractive features that can compensate for sharing the risk of higher interest costs. These features include the opportunity to benefit from possibly lower interest rates in the future, without resort to costly refinancing, as well as access to initial interest rates that are generally lower than prevailing fixed rates.

Adjustable-rate loans currently account for almost half of the home mortgages and perhaps as much as 20 percent of the consumer loans being made. This article describes the forces underlying the development of adjustable-rate lending in mortgage and consumer credit markets and compares typical lending practices in the two markets.

HOME MORTGAGE CREDIT

The emergence of the adjustable-rate mortgage (ARM) as a major form of home financing is one of the most significant developments in the residential mortgage

---

From the *Federal Reserve Bulletin,* November 1985, pp. 828–35.

The authors are with the Federal Reserve Board's Division of Research and Statistics.

market since the long-term, self-amortizing, fixed-rate loan was introduced in the 1930s. The share of ARMs in the market has grown from a negligible portion as recently as 1980 to approximately half of all home loans originated today. The sharply increased flow of these loans pushed their share of all home mortgage debt outstanding to almost one fifth by mid-1985.

With ARMs, the U.S. housing credit market has been moving in the same direction as the market for commercial and industrial loans, in which the trend over the years has been toward variable rates (as discussed by Thomas Brady in a new Federal Reserve staff study[1]). And though ARMs are a fairly recent arrival on the U.S. home mortgage scene, mortgages with adjustable interest charges have long been the standard in some other industrialized countries, including Australia, Canada, and the United Kingdom.

Reasons for the Expansion of ARM Lending

The high and volatile interest rates of the late 1970s and early 1980s sparked the development of ARMs. Thrift institutions, the largest single source of home mortgage credit, were especially harmed by the unanticipated rise in interest rates during that period. The higher rates raised costs of relatively short-term deposits for those institutions more quickly than it increased returns on their portfolios of long-term, fixed-rate mortgage assets.

Before 1979, only state-chartered institutions in a handful of states were permitted to make adjustable-rate home loans; California accounted for most of such lending. But, by 1981, federally chartered savings and loan associations and savings banks, as well as national banks, were allowed to make adjustable-rate home loans. Unlike the earlier variable-rate loans, which were subject to state regulation, the ARMs authorized by the federal enabling laws and regulatory changes in 1981 carried few restrictions. In particular, a wide range of index rates and schemes for periodic rate adjustments were permitted.

The easing of regulations was an essential condition for ARM lending to grow, but did not guarantee that consumers would accept such loans. In principle, several kinds of homebuyers are apt to find ARMs an attractive alternative to fixed-rate mortgages. One group includes consumers who expect interest charges (and thus their loan payments) to be lower in the future with an ARM than with a fixed-rate loan. To be sure, ARMs have caught the attention of many consumers because initial interest rates typically have been below rates available on fixed-rate mortgages. But the relevant cost measure for borrowers is the average interest rate that they expect to pay over the entire term of indebtedness—an expectation dependent on changes in interest rates as well as on the duration of the indebtedness. A borrower likely will require a lower expected average rate on an ARM than on a fixed-rate loan to compensate for the risk of rate increases.

Others who may find ARMs attractive are homebuyers who expect to reside in their new home for only a short time. A low initial interest rate on an ARM, especially if combined with limits on periodic rate adjustments, can often guarantee a relatively low average rate for someone planning to move again within, say, three years. ARMs may also appeal to those who expect their incomes, and therefore their ability to make mortgage payments, to move closely in step with any rise in interest rates. Borrowers constrained by the income requirement for a fixed-rate loan also may find the ARM attractive because practices in loan underwriting have typically permitted homebuyers to qualify for a larger loan with an ARM than with a fixed-rate mortgage.

ARM Features and Pricing

The interest rate on an adjustable-rate home loan is subject to changes that can result in higher or lower monthly mortgage payments. Some other types of mortgages, notably the graduated-payment mortgage, also have a variable monthly payment; however, an ARM differs from the graduated-payment mortgage in that increases or decreases in future payments are not scheduled or known in advance. The ARM is thus characterized by the transfer, from lenders to borrowers, of some of the risk of changes in market interest rates.

Several features govern the interest rates on ARMs:

- The *index* is the base rate from which the ARM rate is calculated. Typically, indexes are widely available measures not under the control of any single lender, such as interest rates on Treasury securities or the cost of funds at federally insured thrift institutions.
- The *adjustment period* is the length of time that the interest rate or loan payment on an ARM is scheduled to remain unchanged; at the end of this interval, the rate is reset and usually the monthly loan payment is recalculated accordingly.
- The *margin* is the markup that, when added to the index, establishes the scheduled rate, called the "program" rate, at each adjustment interval.
- *Initial discounts* are the interest-rate concessions offered on the first year or more of the loan that reduce the interest rate below the program rate (i.e., the index plus margin). Initial discounts are often offered as marketing aids on ARMs.
- *Caps* are limits on the extent to which either the interest rate or the monthly payment can be changed at the end of each adjustment period or over the life of the loan.

The mix of ARM features has varied considerably since 1981 as creditors have gained experience and consumer preferences have changed. Industry surveys indicate that immediately after ARMs were authorized nationally, they often featured either three- or five-year interest-rate adjustment periods. By early 1985, however, the adjustment interval of the typical ARM had been cut to one year. As the interval has been reduced, more market-sensitive measures have been chosen as indexes. Formerly, among the most common indexes were the cost of funds at federally insured thrift institutions nationwide or in the home loan bank district covering California, Arizona, and Nevada (Chart 1); now the more variable one-year U.S. Treasury borrowing rate is more widely used.

Two other important changes in the past few years relate to the magnitude of the initial rate discounts and the caps on adjustments to the interest rate. During 1983 and early 1984, some lenders were offering large promotional "teaser" discounts—3 to 6 percentage points below the scheduled ARM rate—in the initial period. In the case of new homes, the cost of the discount often was paid by the builder, who "bought down" the interest rate and added the cost back into the purchase price of the house. Recently, lenders and insurers have come to realize that large discounts usually render the loans unprofitable; also, lenders perceive

CHART 1
Commonly Used ARM Indexes

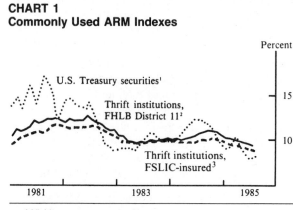

¹ Yields on one-year securities.
² Average cost of funds at thrift institutions in FHLB District 11 (California, Arizona, and Nevada).
³ Median cost of funds at FSLIC-insured thrift institutions.

the threat of regulation in reaction to consumer complaints of misleading lending practices. As a result, considerably fewer offerings of loans with large discounts seem to have been made during late 1984 and 1985. At the same time and for some of the same reasons, caps on annual and life-of-loan adjustments to interest rates have become more common. In early 1985, more than 95 percent of ARMs originated at thrift institutions featured annual or lifetime caps or both.

ARM lenders have faced several marketing questions in determining the combination of ARM features and rates that will maximize the profitability of their mortgage lending. Presumably, a lender will set ARM rates and terms to generate the same expected revenue as a fixed-rate mortgage over the anticipated life of the loan, except for a concession in the ARM rate for lessened interest-rate risk. In practice, a given expected yield can be generated from any one of several sets of ARM features. For example, the potential cost to a lender of setting caps on periodic adjustments to the interest rate can be offset by reducing the initial discounts, by raising margins, or both.

The variety of design options consequently has spurred a proliferation of ARM types. By one count, more than 400 distinct kinds of ARMs were being originated early in 1984. More recently, trade reports indicate some consolidation in the variety of ARMs, partly because trading in the secondary market requires a more standardized product. The most common type has become an ARM with annual interest rate adjustments tied to the yield on one-year Treasury securities; the adjustments are capped at 2 percentage points annually and at 5 to 7 percentage points over the life of the loan.

Changes over time in the average initial interest rate on ARM loans have been affected by the evolving mix of ARM features. As shown in Chart 2, the spread between ARMs and fixed-rate mortgages has varied considerably during the past four years. At first, when short-term interest rates in general were unusually high relative to longer-term rates, the average adjustable rate actually exceeded the fixed rate; later the two rates occasionally moved in opposite directions. Generally, however, they have followed similar patterns of change.

CHART 2
Effective Initial Interest Rate on Conventional
Home Mortgages Closed (monthly data)

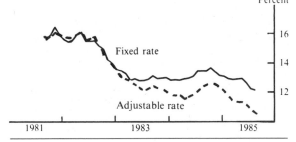

Source: Federal Home Loan Bank Board.

CHART 3
Selected Interest-Rate Spreads

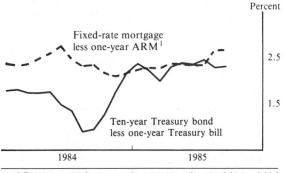

[1] Rates on new loan commitments at savings and loans; initial rates in the case of ARMs.

Much of the first-year rate advantage of ARMs in 1984 apparently reflected special initial discounts because neither the index values nor the other features of ARMs being written at that time imply the relatively low initial rates. In 1985, by contrast, the initial interest rate advantage on ARMs appears to have reflected mainly the fact that rates on short-term securities in general were low relative to long rates. Throughout the first half of 1985, the spread between initial rates on one-year ARMs and rates on fixed-rate loans with an expected life of roughly 10 years has approximated the spread between Treasury securities of comparable maturities, as shown in Chart 3.

Determinants of ARM Market Share

The volume of adjustable-rate mortgages in the marketplace demonstrates that many consumers have found them preferable to fixed-rate mortgages. The market share of ARMs, however, has varied substantially (see Chart 4). Two factors that explain statistically much of the change in share are the general level of mortgage interest rates and the initial rate advantage on ARMs.

CHART 4
ARM Share of Home Loan Originations
(quarterly data)

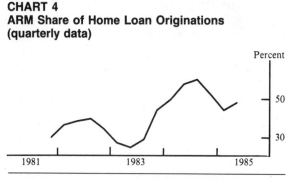

Sources: Federal Home Loan Bank Board, Federal Housing Administration, Veterans Administration.

Other things equal, the ARM share of all home loan originations—including conventional loans as well as federally insured or guaranteed mortgages—has tended to be high during periods of relatively high interest rates and lower at other times. Of secondary importance is the initial rate advantage on ARMs—that is, for any given general level of rates, the ARM share usually has been higher when the initial rate advantage on ARMs has been larger. This pattern is consistent with a choice by consumers of a fixed-rate loan when interest rates are low enough for them to have both the security offered by the fixed rate and the house they want. But even at low fixed rates, some homebuyers can be won over to adjustable rates by larger initial rate advantages.

The consumers who used ARMs to borrow during the first half of 1982 and those who borrowed with ARMs in 1984 may have had different reasons. Housing activity was low in 1982 because of the high interest rates, reduced incomes, and lowered consumer confidence accompanying the business recession that continued through the end of the year. Mortgage borrowers in 1982, many of whom presumably had little flexibility in the timing of their changes of residence, were faced with an unattractive choice: a fixed-rate loan at an unusually high interest rate, or an ARM with an equally high initial rate but at least the possibility of a subsequent downward adjustment. More than one third chose an ARM despite the lack of any initial rate advantage.

By 1984, total home mortgage lending was more than double the volume of 1982, and the ARM share rose further in the first half of the year. By that time, interest rates on fixed-rate loans had declined more than 2 percentage points from their 1982 peaks; but the initial rate on one-year ARMs had fallen twice as much, and these loans were widely available at first-year rates of 11 percent or less, compared with 13 percent or more for fixed-rate mortgages. Consumers were apt to be attracted to ARMs if they expected the ARM rate not to rise significantly— whether because of their expectations of market developments, caps on their rate adjustments, or inadequate understanding of the terms of their loans. Also likely to choose an ARM during this period were homebuyers with short expected durations of residence or with a desire for a mortgage larger than the amount for which they could qualify with fixed-rate financing.

TABLE 1
Home Mortgage Originations, by Lender Type, 1984[1] (percent of total dollar volume)

Type of Lender	All Home Loan Originations	ARM Originations
Savings and loan associations	48	60
Mortgage companies	24	14
Commercial banks	20	13
Savings banks	6	8
Other institutional lenders	3	6
Total	100	100

[1] Data exclude home loans provided by individuals.
Note: Components do not add to totals because of rounding.
Sources: U.S. Department of Housing and Urban Development, Federal Home Loan Bank Board, Federal Reserve Board.

Impact of ARMs on Financial Institutions

A variety of institutions offer home mortgage loans. Thrift institutions (savings and loan associations and savings banks) originated more than half of the total dollar volume in 1984, a fairly typical year in this respect. Commercial banks and mortgage companies accounted for most of the rest (Table 1). By last year, thrift institutions had become specialists in ARM lending. Savings and loans issued a disproportionately large share of all ARMs; their incentive to make ARMs has been greater than that for other lenders because of the wider gap between the average maturity of assets and liabilities at savings and loans. The largest of these institutions have shown the greatest tendency to make ARMs, and some of these institutions report that they no longer even offer fixed-rate home loans.

Although more than half of all conventional home loans made by thrift institutions since late 1981 have been ARMs, most of the mortgage holdings of these institutions carry the fixed rates prevalent in earlier years. Furthermore, some of the ARM holdings are not particularly rate-sensitive, compared with deposits and borrowings at thrift institutions. Sluggish indexes of the cost of funds and caps on rate adjustments keep returns on a portfolio of ARMs from adjusting fully to market rates, even annually. To date, therefore, the reduction in the exposure of savings and loans to interest rate risk has been limited.

Commercial banks, too, have increased their ARM lending. These institutions have had less incentive than their thrift counterparts to enhance the interest-rate sensitivity of their assets because they have held relatively more short-term or variable-rate loans of other types.

Mortgage companies have continued to concentrate on fixed-rate lending. One reason is that, more than other lenders, they specialize in home loans that are insured by the Federal Housing Administration (FHA) or guaranteed by the Veterans Administration (VA). FHA and VA loans accounted for approximately 15 percent of the total dollar volume of home loans originated in 1984, but such loans made up nearly half of the volume originated by mortgage companies. Not until late 1984 did the FHA begin to insure adjustable-rate mortgages, and the volume of ARMs it has underwritten to date has been insignificant. The VA has no guaranty program for ARMs.

The Secondary Market for ARMs

A second reason for the relatively few ARMs originated by mortgage companies is that these companies usually sell the mortgages that they originate, rather than hold them, and there have been relatively few buyers of ARMs. Mortgage companies have, however, sold some ARMs to thrift institutions that want to increase the proportion of ARMs in their portfolios.

The Federal National Mortgage Association (FNMA) has been the other major purchaser of ARMs from mortgage companies and other loan originators. FNMA has carried out its functions of enhancing the liquidity and stability of the mortgage and housing markets largely by buying mortgage loans from originators; it finances these purchases by issuing debt. FNMA suffered from the runup of interest rates in the late 1970s and early 1980s because, like the thrift institutions, it had a portfolio of mortgage loans with an average maturity longer than that of its liabilities. In an attempt to reduce its maturity gap as well as to generate fee income on its purchases, FNMA bought more than $9 billion of ARMs in 1983–84, roughly 5 percent of all ARMs originated during that period.

Few secondary market outlets for ARMs have emerged other than FNMA and thrift institutions. A market for pass-through securities issued against pools of adjustable-rate mortgages has developed only slowly. This is one reason that the Federal Home Loan Mortgage Corporation (FHLMC), a major issuer of fixed-rate mortgage pass-throughs, has not purchased a large volume of ARMs so far. The lack of ARM-backed securities stands in sharp contrast to the situation in the fixed-rate mortgage market, where "securitization" of mortgages mainly through the issuance of pass-throughs by FHLMC and FNMA or guarantees by the Government National Mortgage Association (GNMA) has been a prime source of capital for mortgage lending.

The slow pace at which ARM-backed mortgage securities have developed is in part a consequence of the diversity of the product. First, the variations in ARMs make it difficult to create a large pool of such loans with similar features, as traditionally required to back a marketable security issue. Second, potential investors in an ARM pass-through security can turn to alternative outlets that have many of the desirable traits of ARM pass-throughs but none of the uncertainty regarding the duration of the investment or the possibility that caps will limit interest-rate increases. In this connection, the weak secondary market to date for the FHA-insured ARM in particular is attributable to investor coolness toward the comparatively restrictive annual cap of 1 percent on interest-rate adjustments on these loans. Because most FHA-insured and VA-guaranteed loans are originated for sale in the secondary market via GNMA-guaranteed pass-through securities, the lack of investor demand for GNMA ARM securities has effectively blocked origination of FHA-insured ARMs in the primary market.

A final constraint on the growth of ARM-backed mortgage securities has been the inclination of many thrift institutions to hold ARM loans in their portfolios in order to narrow the maturity gap between their assets and liabilities. Because thrift institutions have been originating roughly 60 percent of all ARMs since the beginning of 1984, their retention of ARMs has significantly limited the potential flow of these instruments to the secondary market.

Underwriting and Insuring ARMs

The potential with adjustable-rate mortgages for increases in interest rates and, therefore, in monthly payments, raises the chances that some homeowners will be unable to meet the payments on their ARM loans. Thus, while ARMs relieve lenders of some interest-rate risk, they may expose lenders to greater credit risk— that is, the risk that borrowers will default on the loans.

Although a homeowner's cash flow difficulties can lead to delinquency on mortgage payments, an owner's equity in his or her house is the most important determinant of default and eventual foreclosure on a loan. As long as the market value of a house exceeds the loan balance, an owner has an incentive to sell the property or to borrow additional funds needed to meet the payments, rather than default. The possibility that ARMs will generate low or even negative owner's equity is, therefore, the prime reason for concern about increased risk of default with these loans. The average loan-to-value ratio on ARMs has been comparatively high: on conventional ARM home loans originated between January 1984 and July 1985, it was 78 percent; on conventional fixed-rate mortgages, it was 74 percent.

Another source of concern about owner's equity with ARMs is the scheduled or potential negative amortization on some of these loans. Graduated-payment ARMs and ARMs with caps on increases on loan payments but not on the underlying interest rate can cause the loan balance to build up over time, further shrinking the owner's equity; this can occur if the scheduled interest payment goes up more than the maximum allowable increase in payment. The resulting increase in loan principal may be repaid by higher future monthly payments or by extending the life of the loan. These forms of ARMs have accounted for only a small percentage of ARMs originated recently but were more common before this year.

Because ARMs are still new and because rates on which the ARM indexes are based have been falling during much of the period since 1981, reliable evidence has yet to emerge about the delinquencies and defaults on these loans. Experience with fixed-rate mortgages suggests that home loans are most likely to go bad in the third year after origination, and most ARMs are not yet that old. Delinquency and default rates on fixed-rate mortgages have reached postwar highs in the past year as the average annual rate of increase in property values slowed from 12 percent in the last half of the 1970s to about 3 percent since 1981. (In some locales, house prices have even been declining.) By restricting the buildup of equity, slower appreciation in prices may be expected to increase default rates for ARMs as well.

Private mortgage insurance companies have a heavy stake in the incidence of default on home loans whether with fixed or adjustable rates. These firms have insured roughly 30 percent of all home loans originated in recent years and a somewhat larger share of adjustable-rate loans. Insurance, usually required by lenders for all conventional mortgages with initial loan-to-value ratios greater than 80 percent, typically covers the top 20 to 25 percent of the mortgage amount. Private mortgage insurers have already decided that their risks of insuring ARMs exceed their risks on traditional fixed-rate business. In mid-1984, these companies raised their premiums on ARMs to a third or more above the premiums for fixed-rate mortgages and raised the ratio of income to initial loan payments required of new ARM borrowers.

The private mortgage insurance companies are not alone in their attempts to limit the potential for default on ARMs. Recently, the Federal Home Loan Bank Board, its subsidiary, the Federal Home Loan Mortgage Corporation, and the Federal National Mortgage Association have all taken steps to restrict the origination and trading of those ARMs with the highest probability of default. These measures were taken in response both to market forces and to the threat of renewed regulation motivated by concerns for consumer protection.

The multitude of ARM forms and their novelty have made it difficult for consumers to assess the advantages and the risks of all the alternative kinds of loans available to them. Without adequate information, consumers face greater chances of entering credit agreements with more interest rate risk than they are prepared to bear. Since early 1984, a variety of private and public actions have been taken to educate mortgage borrowers about ARMs, including joint publication by the Federal Reserve Board and the Federal Home Loan Bank Board of a congressionally mandated booklet on ARMs, which is widely distributed to prospective mortgage borrowers. And, in cooperation with lender and consumer groups, the Federal Reserve Board continues to refine the information on rates required by law to be disclosed on certain mortgage contracts.

Effects of ARMs on Housing Demand

In theory, the availability of ARMs might have stimulated aggregate housing demand during the past two years. That is, if the many home mortgage borrowers who chose ARMs viewed them as a less expensive alternative to fixed-rate financing, the perceived savings in credit costs might have been reflected in stronger housing demand than would have existed otherwise, as well as in the selection of ARMs over fixed-rate mortgages.

Furthermore, during much of the past three years, an individual or family could qualify for a larger mortgage if the loan carried an adjustable rate instead of a fixed rate. That was the case because qualifications were set with reference to the initial loan payment, which is typically lower on an ARM than on the corresponding fixed-rate loan.

Somewhat surprisingly, recent studies indicate that ARMs have generated little, if any, added housing demand (see, for example, the study by Howard Esaki and Judy A. Wachtenheim in the Winter 1984–85 issue of the Federal Reserve Bank of New York's *Quarterly Review*). This research has suggested that the strong expansion of single-family housing construction since the recessionary low of late 1981 has coincided with the emergence of ARMs but has not resulted from it. Other factors—notably lower interest rates on fixed-rate mortgage loans, the larger number of potential homebuyers, and sustained growth in income and consumer confidence—explain most of the rise. Although conclusions can be only tentative at this early date, the anticipated savings with ARMs have apparently been sufficient to persuade consumers to switch forms of financing but not to alter substantially their choices of housing.

TABLE 2
Consumer Lending Programs with Adjustable Rates at Commercial Banks,
by Size of Bank (percent of respondents)

Size of Bank (deposits in millions of dollars)	Currently Offering Adjustable-Rate Lending				Planning to Offer Adjustable-Rate Lending			
	1981	1982	1983	1984	1981	1982	1983	1984
Less than 25	4.3	4.0	13.8	24.0	24.3	17.8	3.1	12.0
25–50	4.5	4.0	14.0	29.6	28.0	40.0	11.3	15.2
50–100	4.2	4.5	14.1	29.5	40.4	34.3	17.9	15.5
100–500	5.1	12.4	17.3	31.4	51.8	46.9	38.7	30.2
More than 500	10.3	17.8	34.7	42.6	64.1	63.2	40.0	35.0

Source: American Bankers Association, *Retail Bank Credit Report,* 1982, 1983, 1984, and 1985 editions.

From another perspective, there is little evidence that ARMs have affected the degree to which housing production is sensitive to interest rates. Because of ARMs, the mode of home financing may now vary with the general level of interest rates, but the volume of mortgage borrowing and housing demand appears to vary inversely with interest rates about as much as it has in the past.

CONSUMER CREDIT

The movement toward adjustable-rate lending is less well documented in the consumer credit market than it is in the mortgage market. Adjustable-rate instruments for consumer loans clearly were developed later than the mortgage type and have spread more slowly. As a result, the ratio of adjustable-rate to fixed-rate loans made today is much smaller for consumer lending than for mortgage lending.

Among commercial banks with deposits of more than $500 million, which account for 60 percent of all consumer loans, fewer than half were making adjustable-rate consumer loans by the end of last year, according to the American Bankers Association, although as many as one third reportedly planned to offer adjustable rates at some point (see Table 2). Only about one fourth of the smaller banks made adjustable-rate loans, and fewer than that expressed any intention to do so. At other financial institutions that lend to consumers, principally credit unions and thrift institutions, the incidence of adjustable-rate lending apparently is lower than it is at banks.

The Limited Appeal of Adjustable-Rate Consumer Loans

Multiyear fixed-rate lending in the consumer market, like that in the mortgage market, began to entail greater risks to lenders during the 1970s as market rates of interest rose to unprecedented levels and became more volatile as well. With the maturities of their liabilities typically shorter than those of their consumer loan assets, lenders faced an increasing risk that net yields on their consumer loan portfolios would shrink. In addition, the looser regulation of interest rates paid on consumer deposits and growing competition for funds among bank and nonbank entities intensified the risks to profitability associated with fixed-rate consumer lending by depository institutions. On the other side of the transaction, the availability of various adjustable-rate plans enabled credit seekers of widely differing expectations and risk tolerances to select loans tailored to their own specific tastes.

Nevertheless, the movement toward adjustable-rate lending has been much less rapid for consumer loans than for home mortgages. Although the same basic stimulants to adjustable-rate lending have operated in both markets, they appear to be generally less critical in consumer lending for both creditors and borrowers.

To Creditors. From the viewpoint of the credit grantor, adjustable-rate consumer loans may be less appealing than ARMs because the interest rate risk is less acute on loans with two- to four-year maturities—the typical term for the bulk of consumer loans—than it is on mortgages with terms of 25 to 30 years. With the more rapid turnover of consumer loan portfolios and the ability of lenders to match maturities on at least some of their consumer loans with maturities on longer-term certificates of deposit or similar liabilities, net yields on consumer lending are simply less vulnerable than on mortgages to adverse movements in market interest rates. Also, the cost of making an adjustment, such as notifying the borrower of the change, is greater relative to the amount outstanding for a consumer loan than for a mortgage loan.

In addition, the leading suppliers of consumer credit (commercial banks) have been much less exposed to the risks of fixed-rate lending than have the leading suppliers of mortgage credit (savings and loan associations). Historically, long-term, fixed-rate mortgages have constituted the bulk of credit extended by savings and loans, whereas consumer loans typically have made up less than 20 percent of commercial bank loan portfolios. Moreover, a sizable portion of the assets of commercial banks, other than consumer loans, already carry adjustable rates (or were written for very short terms), and the broader asset powers of banks permit them to channel funds away from consumer loans as an alternative to establishing variable rates for such loans. Thus, commercial banks may have felt less incentive to adopt adjustable-rate financing than did their counterparts in the mortgage market.

On the other hand, originators of consumer loans do not enjoy the same access to a well-developed secondary market that mortgage originators do. For instance, the ability to package loans for sale through mortgage-backed securities allow mortgage originators to lighten their exposure to interest-rate movements. In contrast, development of a market for securities backed by consumer loans is at a very early stage, limited so far to a few private placements. Although lenders sometimes sell portions of their consumer portfolios directly to other institutions, and some major consumer creditors have sold "participations" in consumer credit accounts on an ad hoc basis, regular channels for secondary market trans- actions in consumer loans are largely lacking—a situation that in itself may reflect the lesser vulnerability of consumer lenders to interest rate risk.

On balance, the forces motivating institutions to make adjustable-rate loans appear less compelling in the consumer market than in the mortgage market.

To Borrowers. From a credit seeker's point of view, the lower initial interest rates generally available under adjustable-rate plans afford smaller benefits on consumer loans than on mortgage loans. This situation reflects the smaller prin- cipal amounts typically involved in a consumer loan and the smaller proportion of

TABLE 3
Impact of Interest Rates on Monthly Payments for Typical Loans
(dollars except as noted)

Item	48-Month New-Car Loan for $10,000	360-Month Home Mortgage Loan for $80,000
At 14 percent[1]:		
Principal	10,000	80,000
Total interest	3,117	261,240
Total obligation	13,117	341,240
Monthly payment	273	948
At 13 percent[1]:		
Principal	10,000	80,000
Total interest	2,877	238,584
Total obligation	12,877	318,584
Monthly payment	268	885
Difference in monthy payment between loans at 13 and 14 percent	−5.0	−63.0
Expressed in percent	−1.8	−6.6

[1] Annual percentage rate.

the total payment that interest constitutes because of the much shorter amortization period. At current interest rate levels, for instance, an initial discount of 1 percentage point on a four-year, $10,000 new-car loan would reduce the monthly payment $5; a 1 point concession on a 30-year, $80,000 home mortgage would lower the monthly payment $63 (Table 3).

The potential impact of future rate adjustments on monthly and lifetime payments is likewise smaller for consumer loans than for mortgages. Expectations of future rate movements thus seem less crucial to borrowers contemplating an adjustable-rate consumer loan than to potential users of adjustable-rate mortgage credit. If borrowers expected rates to rise, they would tend to resist taking on adjustable-rate mortgages without a sizable rate concession or the anticipation of near-term liquidation. Accordingly, the much higher proportion of adjustable-rate lending observed in the mortgage market could, to some extent, reflect borrower expectations in recent years that rates will fall; or it could reflect stronger efforts by mortgage lenders than by consumer lenders to promote adjustable-rate loans through such inducements as annual or lifetime caps on rate movements and limits on payment increases.

Another consideration that pertains less critically to the consumer market than to the mortgage market is a borrower's ability to qualify for a loan. With a mortgage, the impact on the monthly payment of the difference between the prevailing fixed rate and the initially lower adjustable rate can be a crucial factor in determining whether a prospective homebuyer qualifies for a mortgage of given size. In contrast, because of the smaller impact of interest-rate differentials on the size of monthly payments for consumer loans, the difference between fixed and adjustable rates is less likely to be a pivotal factor in a borrower's qualification for that type of loan.

Volume of Adjustable-Rate Lending

The proportion of banks making adjustable-rate consumer loans, according to a 1984 survey by the American Bankers Association, ranged from 25 percent for smaller banks to a bit more than 40 percent for the largest banks. A recent survey of large banks and thrift institutions by the Trans Data Corporation had similar results: 45 percent of respondents offered adjustable-rate consumer loans in mid-1985. This survey also found that, on average, about one fifth of the loans held by institutions offering such plans actually carried an adjustable rate.

Pricing of Adjustable-Rate Loans

The terms that characterize consumer and mortgage loans differ in several ways. For instance, rate caps of some kind, now almost universally applicable to mortgage loans, are apparently a feature of only a little more than half of the adjustable-rate consumer loans originated recently.

The Index and the Initial Rate.   According to the mid-1985 Trans Data survey, interest rates on Treasury bills are the most common base to which adjustable-rate consumer loans are indexed (Table 4). In this they resemble ARMs. But the prime rate on business loans—hardly ever used as a reference rate for ARMs—is frequently employed in consumer lending. In fact, on consumer surveys sponsored by the Federal Reserve in 1983 and 1984, respondents having adjustable-rate loans cited the prime rate far more often than any other as their index. In some cases an institution will use a measure of its own cost of funds as an index rate.

Initial rates on adjustable-rate consumer loans appear to range between 0.5 and 1.5 percentage points below the corresponding fixed rate offered, with 1 point perhaps the most common differential.

Adjustment Period.   Nearly half the lenders making adjustable-rate consumer loans specify monthly adjustments. Quarterly adjustments are also common. Fewer than 5 percent of the institutions making adjustable-rate consumer loans reprice them annually—the most widely followed practice in the mortgage market.

Adjustment Method.   The most common method of accommodating a change in the interest rate on an outstanding consumer loan is to maintain a fixed size of payment and extend the maturity of the loan. When interest rates rise, this method generates extra loan payments at the end of the scheduled term: when interest rates fall, it reduces the number of scheduled payments. But rarely will such a method result in more than a couple of additional payments; for instance, even in the unusually adverse event that the rate on a three-year loan jumped immediately after it was made from 15 to 20 percent and remained at that level, only about three and one half additional monthly payments would be required.

Maturities on mortgage loans seldom are extended in this manner. Given the high proportion of interest to principal in the early stages of repayment on a mortgage, upward rate adjustments of as little as 1 percentage point can create negative amortization when caps on annual increases in mortgage payments are employed, as is often the case. At some point the entire loan is rescheduled, usually with the original maturity date retained.

TABLE 4
Features of Adjustable-Rate Consumer Loans at Commercial Banks and Thrift Institutions

Feature	Percent of Institutions
Index rate:	
Rate on Treasury bills	39.7%
Prime rate	31.0
Own cost of funds	10.3
Federal Reserve discount rate	1.7
Other	26.7
Adjustment period:	
Monthly	45.8
Quarterly	32.5
Semiannual	10.0
Annual	4.2
Other	20.0
Adjustment method:	
Maturity change	79.0
Payment change	33.6
Balloon payment	22.7
Interest rate caps:	
Lifetime	44.0
Annual	32.1
None	36.7
Memo: Lifetime floor	31.2

Source: Trans Data Corporation, 1985. Percentages do not add to 100 because some respondents provided more than one answer.

Rate Caps.   Of the financial institutions making adjustable-rate consumer loans, nearly 40 percent provide no contractual limit on the extent to which interest rates may rise if an increase is warranted by the indexing formula. (In some cases, however, state laws establish ceiling rates for various types of consumer loans.) About 45 percent of the institutions specify caps on rate increases over the life of the loan, and about one third place caps on the increase that can be made in any one year. (Some among these provide both types of caps.) Nearly one third of the lenders in the Trans Data survey establish a floor for rate declines.

Economic Impact of Adjustable-Rate Consumer Loans

The innovation of adjustable-rate consumer lending could conceivably affect the overall supply of consumer credit and the quality of loan portfolios of lending institutions. Aggregate demand for consumer credit could be augmented by the availability of a wider choice of loan types.

Total Supply of Credit.   The spread between the gross yield on a consumer loan portfolio and the cost of funds undoubtedly can be made more stable if adjustable rates are used, and this prospect may have expanded the aggregate supply of consumer credit somewhat in recent years. Still, as noted above, the mismatching of maturities on assets and liabilities is much less severe in consumer lending than in mortgage lending, so the potential boost to the supply of consumer credit from adjustable-rate programs is probably quite limited.

The willingness of lenders to extend consumer credit has increased since the early 1980s, a trend that seems attributable more reasonably to other factors than adjustable rates. The widespread raising or removal of state ceilings on consumer interest rates was likely an important stimulant to supply. In 1979, when the sharp rise in market interest rates began, as many as 35 states were mandating ceilings of 13 percent or lower on new-car loans. Commercial banks, the largest suppliers of auto credit, retreated sharply from the auto loan market during the following three years. More recently with the various rate ceilings liberalized, average auto loan rates at banks have fluctuated between 13 and 17 percent, and banks have returned in full force to the auto loan market.

Consumer credit supply, whether through adjustable-rate or fixed-rate lending, has also been augmented by the removal of barriers to the participation of savings and loan associations in consumer credit markets. These institutions have been the fastest-growing segment of the market since 1982. Savings and loan portfolios have expanded at rates of 30 to 45 percent per year, advancing from an industry total of $16 billion at the end of 1982 to $36 billion by mid-1985. While some of this expansion undoubtedly represents substitution for other sources of credit, it seems likely that the presence of a new and aggressive entrant into the market has added to the overall supply of consumer credit.

Loan Quality.   In the shifting of some portion of interest-rate risk from lender to borrower through adjustable-rate lending, the lender may take on increased credit risk: the risk that the borrower may be unable or unwilling to make loan payments should the interest rate on the loan be adjusted upward.

Little information is available on delinquencies or defaults on adjustable-rate consumer loans. Collection experience on such loans has not been tested by a prolonged period of sharply rising interest rates. However, in view of the relatively small effect that even large rate changes would have on the size or the number of monthly payments, a high incidence of delinquencies due solely to adjustable rates does not seem likely. At the margin, a few borrowers may be unable to handle an increased loan payment, and slower amortization of a loan collateralized by a depreciating asset may lead a few borrowers with negative equity to stop repaying a loan. But defaults that hinge on the small changes in payments stemming from interest-rate adjustments should be rare.

Rates of delinquency on consumer loans dropped during the current economic upswing to their lowest levels in more than 10 years, though they retraced part of their decline in the first half of 1985. However, the overall downtrend in delinquencies seems attributable mainly to the generally buoyant economic conditions since 1982 and to an unusually low level of consumer debt entering the recovery period, rather than to any favorable impact of interest-rate adjustments in a period of gradually declining rates.

Credit Demands.   Adjustable-rate financing probably has had a minimal effect on credit demand as well. Some econometric studies have identified consumer interest rates as a factor of statistical significance in explaining observed levels of consumer credit, but the average effect of a change of 1 percentage point in rates—about the amount of the initial rate concession on an adjustable loan—generally is estimated to be rather small. Presumably, the chance to benefit from future rate reductions with an adjustable-rate loan could make individuals less reluctant to borrow at high rates; adjustable rates are, however, probably seldom the decisive factor behind a consumer's decision to borrow.

OUTLOOK

Largely in response to the higher levels and greater volatility of interest rates in the late 1970s and early 1980s, adjustable-rate credit is appearing more often on the menu of financing choices available to households. Having become established, adjustable-rate credit arrangements now seem likely to retain a significant position in both home mortgage and consumer financing. There always will be some borrowers and lenders whose needs and preferences can be met best by adjustable-rate financing. At the same time, competitive pressures will continue to work toward maintaining the availability of fixed-rate credit, because other borrowers will always be willing to pay what lenders require to provide the security of fixed-rate financing.

The shares of adjustable-rate and fixed-rate credit in the marketplace are likely to continue to change in response to the level and fluctuations in short-term and long-term interest rates, much as the ARM share of home mortgages has varied during the past three years. And as lenders acquire more experience and sophistication with adjustable-rate financing, they may modify their pricing of these loans, even in the absence of any change in market interest rates. Consumers, too, can be expected to become more knowledgeable about adjustable-rate lending and therefore more fully informed in their choices. A greater number of informed borrowers will benefit both households and lenders by helping them avoid ill-advised financing decisions.

So far, adjustable-rate credit appears to have had more impact on the composition of household balance sheets than on aggregate demand for housing and consumer goods. As pointed out earlier, the favorable initial price of adjustable-rate credit appears to have had only a small impact on total demand. Rate adjustments as well have probably had only a small aggregate effect on demand, although the ability of a household sector with substantial adjustable-rate debts to maintain expenditure levels or to avoid financial strains during periods of rising interest rates has yet to be seriously tested. The household sector lends more than it borrows, however, and a sizable share of the sector's assets are in adjustable-rate instruments, such as money market deposit accounts and money market mutual funds. Any detrimental impact of rising interest rates on the sector as a whole should, therefore, be quite limited, although individual borrowers with relatively few financial assets—such as some first-time home buyers using ARMs—may experience difficulty.

Plainly, adjustable-rate credit enhances the ability of the financial system to accommodate large changes in market conditions. And finally, it should be noted that the growing prevalence of adjustable-rate financing is producing a broader constituency of consumers with a direct and immediate concern about financial market developments that affect interest rates.

NOTE

[1] *Federal Reserve Bulletin,* November 1985.

25

Futures Markets:
A Primer for Financial Institutions

Mark Drabenstott and Anne O'Mara McDonley

Volatile interest rates and deregulation in recent years have highlighted the interest-rate risk of financial institutions. Because most financial institutions are highly leveraged, improperly managed interest-rate risk can reduce earnings or even result in losses that jeopardize the firm's financial stability. As a result, the new interest-rate environment has forced institutions to rethink and reemphasize strategies to manage their interest-rate risk.

In examining strategies, financial institutions are looking to both old and new risk-management techniques. Banks and thrift institutions traditionally have reduced interest-rate risk by matching maturities of interest-sensitive assets and liabilities and by pricing loans with variable rates. But with the advent of new futures contracts, hedging in futures markets has become a viable technique for managing risk.

This article describes how futures markets work and how they can be used by financial institutions. A brief history of futures markets is provided, followed by a discussion of how futures markets operate. The article then discusses how financial institutions can hedge interest-rate risk by using futures markets. Finally, the article considers broad issues that will determine whether futures markets will be widely used by financial institutions.

THE HISTORY OF FUTURES MARKETS

Futures markets arose from the need to reduce price risk in commodity trading. Commodity price risk became evident during the mid-1800s in the grain market center of Chicago. In the fall of each year, large numbers of farmers hauled their harvested grain to Chicago, resulting in a glut of grain that inevitably dampened prices. In the spring, a shortage of grain pushed prices to high levels. These wide

From *Economic Review,* Federal Reserve Bank of Kansas City, November 1984, pp. 17–33.

Mark Drabenstott is a senior economist in the research department at the Federal Reserve Bank of Kansas City, and Anne O'Mara McDonley was formerly an assistant economist in the research department at the Federal Reserve Bank of Kansas City.

price swings created price uncertainties for producers that sold grain and processors that bought grain.

Futures markets emerged as a means for buyers and sellers to reduce price risk.
The Chicago Board of Trade was organized in 1848 as a place of grain trade, both
for immediate cash delivery or for delivery in the future. As a central market, the
Board of Trade allowed buyers and sellers to enter into a contract that guaranteed
a price at a future date. Prices confirmed in the futures markets allowed the price
uncertainty of the spot market to be avoided.

Commodity futures trading became popular, both as a price protection device
for grain buyers and sellers and as a new market for speculators. Grain producers
and buyers could legitimately "hedge" price risk. Speculators, those that bought
or sold contracts without owning or intending to buy grain, found a new arena for
profit. Such traders, though seeking quick profits, serve a useful purpose. They
add liquidity to the markets, making hedging transactions easier to accomplish.

As the Chicago Board of Trade grew, so did other futures exchanges. The New
York and New Orleans Cotton Exchanges became well established and served a
vital role in exporting cotton. The Butter and Egg Board, forerunner to the
Chicago Mercantile Exchange, came into being because of seasonal variations and
problems of storing perishable commodities, a risk different from the risk of grain
marketing. And, as the number of exchanges grew so did the number of successful
futures contracts. These new contracts allowed the prices of more and more types
of commodities to be hedged.

By the early 1970s, futures markets had proven their value as risk-shifting
mechanisms. But in the late 1970s and early 1980s—with higher rates of inflation,
deregulated financial markets, and changing macroeconomic policies—interest
rates were increasingly volatile and of major concern to the financial economy.
Fluctuating interest rates became one of the most prominent risks facing financial
institutions.

Because interest-rate risk is just another form of commodity price risk, futures
markets quickly developed new contracts that allowed hedging. A contract based
on Government National Mortgage Association (GNMA) bonds began trading in
1975. After its success, numerous contracts followed. Nine interest-rate futures
contracts are actively traded today on three exchanges in the United States, with
additional contracts traded in London and Singapore. Thus, with the evolution of
successful financial futures contracts, futures markets have become a tool that
financial institutions can use to manage interest-rate risk.

HOW FUTURES MARKETS WORK

The economic functions of futures markets are to provide a competitive market
price discovery mechanism, a hedging mechanism for price risk, and a means to
improve market efficiency. The price of a futures contract for a commodity or
financial instrument represents the expectations of a large number of buyers and
sellers concerning the current and prospective effect of all market influence. As
events shape the current situation, the expected changes are reflected in the form
of changing prices for futures contracts. In short, futures markets provide a
current consensus of knowledgeable opinions about the future price of commodities or financial instruments. Futures markets improve market efficiency by
providing a central marketplace where price offers are known and compared. This

free flow of information defuses attempted monopoly positions. Futures markets enhance competition by allowing the free flow of information relative to prices, volume, and market expectations. Thus, futures markets help eliminate market imperfections and contribute to more efficient economic activity.[1]

A number of unique terms are associated with futures markets. To aid in understanding this terminology, a glossary is included in the Appendix. Some basic terms, however, require discussion.

Futures contracts, simply stated, are a promise between two persons to exchange a commodity at a specified time and place in the future for a stated price. As a commitment between a buyer and a seller, a futures contract specifies precisely the commodity being traded and the terms of delivery. The clearinghouse of the commodity exchange, made up of exchange members, guarantees contract performance by both parties. Individual traders cease to deal with each other and instead become obligated to the clearinghouse, which becomes the guarantor of performance of all futures contracts traded on a particular exchange. At the close of every trading day, the clearinghouse matches buy and sell contracts for the day and informs every exchange member of their net settlement status.

Financial futures contracts are no different from commodity futures contracts, except that the item delivered is a financial instrument, rather than a commodity, such as wheat or cattle. Financial futures include contracts not only for debt instruments but also for precious metals, foreign currencies, and stock indexes. Futures in precious metals, such as gold, silver, and platinum, allow manufacturers using these metals to hedge price risk. Currency futures, based on specific foreign currencies, allow various commercial interests to hedge against fluctuations in exchange rates. A recent innovation is stock index futures. Based on the performance of a group of stocks, these futures allow investors to protect a portfolio of stocks from a decline in value.[2] The narrower term *interest-rate futures* refers to specific contracts for interest-sensitive financial instruments.

The Mechanics of Interest-Rate Futures

Interest-rate futures are based on long and short-term, fixed-income financial debt instruments with prices that vary inversely to their interest rates. For example, U.S. Treasury bills are sold on a discount basis and then redeemed at maturity at face value. The difference between the face value and the discounted selling price equals the amount of interest earned.[3] Similarly, the price of a futures contract is inversely related to the interest rate of the underlying debt instruments.

Participants in futures markets can take one of two positions in the market. A *buyer* of a futures contract takes a *long* position in the market. This is true because the buyer owns a contract that can be sold at any time. To profit from a long position, he must sell the contract for a price higher than the purchase price. In the case of an interest-rate futures contract, such as a Treasury-bill contract, a long position profits from a decline in interest rates. A lower interest rate means a higher contract price, since the two are inversely related. Thus, a long position in a Treasury bill futures contract can be sold at a profit when interest rates fall. An increase in interest rates, on the other hand, produces a loss in a long position.

A *seller* of a futures contract takes a *short* position in the market. That is true because the seller sells a contract that is a promise to deliver on a specified date a commodity or financial asset, even though he may not currently own that asset. To profit from a short position, he must buy the contract at a price lower than the selling price. In the Treasury bill futures contract example, a short position profits from an increase in interest rates, because the contract price then declines, allowing the contract to be bought at a profit. A decline in interest rates produces a loss in a short position.

Only rarely do buyers and sellers of futures contracts ever make or accept delivery of the actual instrument. Rather, most participants offset their positions by taking a market position opposite to the original one. For instance, if the original position was to buy a March Treasury bill contract, the position would be offset by subsequently selling a March Treasury bill contract. When futures positions are offset this way, the final result is a profit or loss, not an exchange of securities. Only 2 percent of all futures contracts are believed to result in actual delivery of the financial instrument or commodity involved. Most market participants prefer to offset futures positions, rather than to make actual delivery, for many reasons. The most common reason, however, is that the market is used primarily for either risk management or speculation, and neither purpose requires delivery.

Essential Concepts of Hedging

Hedging in futures markets is synonymous with shifting risk. A hedge is placed by taking a futures position opposite to the position held in the cash market, and exactly equivalent in value. For example, a banker who expects to invest $1 million in a Treasury bill in three months needs to protect himself against a decline in interest rates. A decline would lower his interest income. To hedge, he buys a Treasury bill futures contract, thus taking a long position. Later, when he actually invests the $1 million, he offsets his futures position by selling a Treasury bill futures contract. Such a strategy protects the banker against the risk of an adverse movement in interest rates, because reduced yields in the cash market resulting from lower interest rates are offset by profits in the futures position. Example 1 illustrates the mechanics of a banker placing a perfect hedge.

There are few perfect hedges in the real world. This is because of basis risk. Basis is defined as the difference between the futures market price and the cash market price. Basis is both stable and predictable, because of the tendency of the cash and futures prices of a financial instrument to move together. Three market forces operate to assure similar price movements. First, arbitrage between the cash and futures markets help remove distortions in the basis. Second, changes in economic and financial market conditions influence cash and futures prices simultaneously. Third, the possible delivery of the cash instrument forces cash and futures prices to converge as the delivery date approaches.

Basis risk refers to unexpected changes in the cash-futures price relationship. These unexpected changes can arise for a number of reasons. In essence, however, to the extent that futures prices correctly anticipate impending movements in cash market interest rates, basis risk will be minimized. And while swings in the basis at times can be large, they are generally less than price movements in the cash or futures markets alone.

EXAMPLE 1

A bank investment manager learns from his current cash flow report in January that $1 million will be available for investment in March. He knows the $1 million will be invested in a 90-day Treasury bill. The investment manager expects interest rates to decline between January and March, lowering his rate of return when the $1 million is actually invested. To preserve the current rate until the cash becomes available to invest, he hedges in the futures market. By buying a Treasury bill futures contract—by taking a long position—he stands to profit in the futures market if interest rates decline. In January, his cash and futures markets positions are as below:

January

Cash Market	Futures Market
Notified of cash flow situation. Can purchase a 90-day T-bill at a price of 92.40, which implies a 7.60 percent interest rate.	Buys one T-bill contract for March delivery at a price of 91.90, which implies an 8.10 percent interest rate.

March

Cash Market	Futures Market
Invests $1 million in a 90-day T-bill at a price of 93.20, which implies a 6.80 percent rate of return.	Sells one T-bill contract for March delivery at a price of 92.70, which implies a 7.30 percent interest rate.

Final Result

Cash Market	Futures Market
92.40 Target price	92.70 Selling price
93.20 Current price	91.90 Purchase price
0.80 Net loss	0.80 Net profit
Or, 80 basis points at $25 per basis point = $2,000 loss	Or, 80 basis points at $25 per basis point = $2,000 profit

In March, the $1 million becomes available to invest, but interest rates have declined. The cash and futures markets positions are then as shown.

The final outcome, as shown, is a futures market profit that offsets the cash market loss.

The profit made in the futures market exactly offsets the loss in the cash market. The investment manager effectively locked in the interest rate that prevailed in January by hedging in the futures market. In this example, the hedge worked perfectly because basis risk was zero. In most cases, basis risk will make the hedge less effective.

Many factors interact to influence the basis. Changing economic conditions can cause interest rates in cash and futures markets to fluctuate differently. When a cross hedge—hedging with a similar but not identical futures contract—is placed, the relationship between the prices of the cash instrument and the futures contract may be more volatile than expected. If the cash instrument bears an administered rate while the futures instrument bears a free market rate, the basis can be affected by changing market conditions. Of greatest importance, changing expectations about future interest rates, particularly the future shape of the yield curve, can cause wide basis swings. On balance, however, basis risk remains less volatile and more manageable than cash market risk.

Other important hedging concepts are margin requirements and leverage. The initial margin requirement on a futures transaction is simply a good-faith deposit to ensure performance according to the terms of the futures contract. For example, an investor might purchase a $1 million 90-day Treasury bill contract and be required to deposit $1,500 margin money, less than 1 percent of the face value of the contract. Daily settlements are made relative to each trader's profits and losses—that is, futures positions are marked-to-market daily. A trader that suffers a loss on a futures contract is required to post additional margin money to maintain the original margin level. A trader that profits from the futures transaction on a particular day has any excess margin money added to the account, and it can be withdrawn.

Margin requirements ensure the performance of both parties to a futures contract. They also provide traders with substantial leverage. A position can be taken in the futures market with less capital than in the stock market, which requires that a much higher percentage be deposited in a margin account with the broker.

A complete analysis of the many intricacies of futures markets and the factors that affect their function cannot be presented here. A list of selected readings discussing the detailed underpinnings of futures markets appears at the end of the article.

MANAGING INTEREST-RATE RISK

This section outlines how financial institutions can use financial futures in managing interest-rate risk. The section also examines other potential uses for futures.

Assessing Interest-Rate Risk

Interest-rate risk must be understood and fully assessed before it can be managed. For the financial institution, interest-rate risk is the risk that—because of a mismatch of rate-sensitive assets and liabilities—fluctuations in interest rates will adversely affect net interest margin. The risk arises naturally from an institution's portfolio. For example, when the portfolio mix is such that rate-sensitive liabilities outweigh rate-sensitive assets, the institution's net worth will decline if interest rates rise.

Interest-sensitivity analysis provides a technique for assessing an institution's interest-rate risk. The analysis is an effort to determine how net interest margin is affected by changes in interest rates. Interest-sensitivity analysis entails a number of steps. First, the institution must separate its fixed-rate and rate-sensitive assets and its fixed-rate, rate-sensitive, and nonpayment liabilities. Following this separation, the portfolio can be examined at successive categories of maturities by comparing the volume of rate-sensitive assets and rate-sensitive liabilities. The difference, or gap, provides a measure of interest-rate risk. The size of the gap will be influenced by the current balance sheet position and also by any expected balance sheet changes. A negative gap, greater volume of liabilities than assets, is vulnerable to rising interest rates and a positive gap is vulnerable to declining interest rates.

The gap provides a measure of interest-rate risk that serves as the foundation for an institution's business plan. In constructing its plan, an institution has two choices. It can accept this cash market risk or set out to reduce the risk. In accepting the risk, it is also endorsing an interest-rate forecast. If it accepts a negative gap, it accepts a forecast that interest rates will decline, for only in that outcome can it earn profits. If it accepts a positive gap, it accepts a forecast that interest rates will rise.

In setting out to reduce the risk, an institution can use traditional asset/liability techniques that include restructuring rate-sensitive assets to match the maturities of rate-sensitive liabilities more closely. This may be difficult in the short run, either because the institution lacks experience in making loans of the proper maturity or because it faces resistance in shortening maturities of existing loans. The institution can also make more of its assets rate-sensitive by making more loans with variable rates. A final alternative is to reduce the risk by hedging with futures contracts.

Before the use of futures is discussed, it should be noted that assessing interest-rate risk has taken on a new meaning in the last couple of years as duration analysis has gained support. Duration analysis goes beyond gap analysis to focus on the pattern of the cash flow associated with assets and liabilities.[4] While duration analysis has the benefit of considering the timing of cash flow, not just the maturity, it remains a new and somewhat controversial technique for financial institutions.

Hedging with Futures Contracts

Presently, commercial banks can use either of two hedge strategies to reduce interest-rate risk—the short hedge or the long hedge. Thrift institutions are restricted to making short hedges to reduce risk.

Institutions can take a short position in the futures market to hedge the risk of rising interest rates in the cash markets—a *short hedge*. By selling interest-sensitive futures contracts, an institution stands to profit should interest rates rise. A bank that will issue a CD in three months, for instance, faces the risk of higher interest rates if the CD is not matched by an asset that either matures or is repriced then. To hedge this risk, the bank could sell a CD or Treasury bill futures contract. If interest rates rise, the higher cost of issuing the CD would be offset by profits in the futures position. The size of futures markets profits, of course, will depend on the amount of basis risk encountered. Similarly, a short hedge can be used to protect the value of a pool of mortgages against rising interest rates before the mortgages are discounted to a national purchaser.

Alternatively, banks can take a long position in the futures market to hedge the risk of falling interest rates in the cash market—a *long hedge*. By buying an interest-sensitive futures contract, an institution will profit when interest rates decline. For example, a bank that will invest $1 million in three months faces the risk of reduced income if interest rates fall. To hedge this risk, the bank can buy a Treasury bill futures contract. If interest rates decline, the lower yield in the cash market will be augmented by the profits made when the futures position is offset. Similarly, a long hedge can be used to preserve the value of currently held assets.

When hedging, an institution should first take a macro perspective and determine its overall interest-rate exposure through some form of interest-sensitivity analysis. By identifying individual or groups of assets or liabilities responsible for this exposure, it can then develop hedging strategies and place specific hedges, using a short hedge for a negative gap and a long hedge for a positive gap. While the firm will be making hedges on specific balance sheet items—microhedges—it will be done within a broader context of lowering total balance sheet risk. Although there is controversy about the application of microhedging, regulatory guidelines do allow banks to use financial futures in situations that reduce overall interest-rate exposure. If only one balance sheet item is hedged, it must be done to reduce overall balance sheet interest-rate risk.

Successful hedging involves a series of steps. The following is a general description of the steps to be taken. A more detailed description appears in Example 2.

The first step is to assess total interest-rate risk. Having determined the dollar volume of the risk, the institution must decide how much of the risk it is willing to accept. Management can decide to accept all the exposure or only a part of it.

The second step is to select a futures contract for the hedge. To hold basis risk to a minimum, the contract should have a price that correlates highly with the price for the asset or liability category being hedged. Some of the hedges can be made with contracts for the same financial instruments as the instrument being hedged. In many situations, however, cross-hedging with similar instruments is the only alternative. One consideration in selecting the appropriate contract is the liquidity of trading in that contract. Even though one contract might not correlate as well as some other contract in terms of the pattern of interest rate movements, greater trading volume—and therefore, greater ease in placing and lifting the hedge—could make it the better hedging vehicle.

The third step is to determine the number of contracts needed to hedge the dollar volume at risk. This determination depends on four factors: the dollar amount to be hedged, the face value of the futures contract, the maturity of the asset or liability in question, and the correlation between cash and futures prices. Expressed as a formula, or hedge ratio, the number of contracts can be stated as follows:

$$N = \frac{V}{F} \cdot \frac{M}{M} \cdot b$$

where N = number of contracts needed.
      V = value of asset or liability to be hedged.
      F = face value of the futures contract instrument (usually $1 million).
      M = maturity of asset or liability to be hedged.
      M = maturity of futures contract instrument.
      b = correlation coefficient of cash and futures interest rates.

For example, to hedge a $1 million six-month Treasury bill with a 90-day Treasury bill futures contract, and assuming perfect correlation, two contracts are needed.

$$\frac{\$1 \text{ million}}{\$1 \text{ million}} \cdot \frac{180 \text{ days}}{90 \text{ days}} \cdot 1 = 2 \text{ contracts}$$

The fourth step is to determine the length of time the hedge will extend and the number of contracts needed in each period of the hedge. This amounts to spreading the number of contracts over the life of the hedge. Ideally, the contracts will be put together in a "strip" consisting of equally sized pieces that extend over the life of the hedge.[5] One problem with this approach is that contracts are listed for

EXAMPLE 2

Step 1. *Determine total interest-rate risk.*   In March, a financial institution issues a $1 million six-month money market certificate of deposit (MMCD). The institution knows it will roll over the MMCD in September. Through interest-sensitivity analysis, the institution concludes that it will have a negative gap in September because no assets are repriced then. Because the MMCD rollover accounts for most of the gap, the institution decides to hedge the MMCD portion of its negative gap against the risk of higher interest rates.

Step 2. *Select a futures contract.*   The institution selects the 90-day Treasury-bill futures contract as the hedging medium because price movements between Treasury bills and MMCD's are closely correlated. Technically, the hedge is a cross hedge. It is used because the volume of trading is heavier in Treasury-bill futures contracts than in the CD futures contracts.

Step 3. *Determine the number of contracts needed.*   The institution calculates the hedge ratio as below:

$$\frac{180 \text{ days}}{90 \text{ days}} \cdot \frac{\$1,000,000}{\$1,000,000} \cdot 1 = 2 \text{ contracts}$$

For the purpose of this example, MMCD and Treasury bill interest rates are assumed to be perfectly correlated.

Step 4. *Determine the length of hedge.*   The length of the hedge is six months, to correspond with the rollover of the six-month MMCD.

Step 5. *Place the hedge.*   The institution places the hedge by selling two 90-day Treasury bill contracts for September delivery. The cash and futures markets positions in March are as shown.

Step 6. *Monitor the hedge.*   A realistic hedging strategy requires that the hedge be closely monitored to determine basis risk and the direction that risk takes. In this example, basis risk is assumed to be zero.

Step 7. *Lift the hedge.*   Interest rates have risen since March. In September, the institution rolls over the MMCD at a rate of 11.64 percent, an increase of 191 basis points. The hedge is offset by buying two 90-day Treasury bill contracts for September delivery. The cash and futures market positions then are as shown.

trading only about two years in the future. If the hedge extends longer than two years, the necessary number of contracts must be "stacked" on the available contract months.

The stacking approach has two drawbacks. First, it requires that more contracts be purchased and sold, because the contracts must be rolled forward—that is, they must be offset and replaced as new contract months are listed. This raises transaction costs. Second, stacking creates new uncertainty, because the cost of the rollover is uncertain. If the basis moves against the hedger, the cost of rolling the hedges forward can be high. Because of these drawbacks, institutions may choose to hedge only the part of the cash instrument's maturity that can be covered by contracts that are being currently traded.

The fifth step in a successful hedge is to monitor the hedge. Once a futures position is undertaken, it has to be watched in much the same way that investment managers monitor cash investments. Of primary concern are movements in the basis and changes in expectations for future interest rates. In short, the institution must manage basis risk. While unnecessary placing and lifting of futures positions can amount to speculation, placing a hedge and forgetting it in the face of fundamental changes in the basis can amount to imprudent hedging.

EXAMPLE 2 (*concluded*)

Thus, hedging in the futures market produced a profit to offset the cash market loss, as shown.

The net result also can be examined in terms of annual interest expense. The total MMCD interest expense for March and September issues is $106,850 ($48,650 plus $58,200). Subtracting the $2,950 profit made in the futures market lowers the total expense in $103,900. Thus, hedging lowered the institution's annual interest expense from 10.69 percent to 10.39 percent.

March

Cash Market	Futures Market
Issues six-month MMCD at a rate of 9.73 percent. Interest expense for six months is $48.650.	Sells two 90-day T-bill contracts for September delivery at a price of 90.87, which implies an interest rate of 9.13 percent

September

Cash Market	Futures Market
Rolls over six-month MMCD at a rate of 11.64 percent. Interest expense for six months is $58,200.	Buys the 90-day T-bill contracts for September delivery at a price of 89.69, which implies an interest rate of 10.31 percent.

Final Result

Cash Market		Futures Market	
$48,650	March interest expense	90.87	Selling price
−$58,200	September interest expense	89.69	Purchase price
$(9,500)	Net loss	1.18	Net profit
			Or, 118 basis points at $25 per basis point = $2,950 net profit

In sum, a successful hedge begins with the proper assessment of interest-rate exposure. It includes selecting the appropriate futures contract and the right number of contracts. The contracts must then be spread out over available contract months for the life of the hedge. Finally, the hedge must be monitored.

For the profit-maximizing financial institution, hedging contains a paradox. If an institution decides to hedge only part of its overall interest-rate risk, it should not be surprised to find its hedging program reporting losses. The reason is that, by hedging only part of the risk, the financial institution accepts some cash market risk and effectively endorses an interest-rate forecast. If this forecast for the cash market is correct, net interest margin will be positive. But by definition, profits in the cash market position mean losses in the futures market. Thus, losses in the futures market, when only part of the risk is hedged, probably mean that the business plan embodied in the cash position was the correct one.

Options Markets

One drawback of hedging with futures contracts is that, if interest rates move favorably in the cash market, profits will be foregone. For instance, if a financial institution hedges a negative gap in its portfolio by selling futures contracts and then interest rates decline, the increased profits in the cash market are negated by losses in the futures market. One way of capturing these potential profits is through options markets.[6]

Combining the use of options markets and futures markets gives a firm additional flexibility in managing its interest-rate risk. The institution that hedged a negative gap by selling futures contracts could have preserved its potential cash market profits by buying an option contract when it placed the short hedge.[7] Then, when interest rates declined, the institution could have exercised its option, offset its futures position without loss, and thereby preserved its cash market profit.

Options markets are very recent innovations. Few financial institutions are likely to become involved in the potentially complex strategies that combine futures contracts and options. Moreover, the high cost of the option premium deters the use of options. But as options markets develop, institutions may begin adding options in their complement of risk-management techniques.

Other Uses for Futures

Although hedging interest-rate risk is the primary use made of futures markets, financial institutions can make use of them in other situations. Synthetic fixed-rate loans, investment trading, and hedging exchange rates are three situations where hedges can be used.

Many financial institutions pass interest-rate risk on to borrowers through variable-rate loans. However, this strategy can lead to increased risk of loan default. And beyond that consideration, many borrowers prefer fixed-rate loans. To avoid the problems of variable-rate loans, lenders can make a fixed-rate loan and then hedge the interest-rate risk in the futures market, a strategy limited primarily to short-term loans. These "synthetic fixed-rate loans" effectively insulate the institution from interest-rate risk while providing the borrower a fixed loan rate.[8] Used in this way, futures may be more a tool for marketing financial services than for managing the institution's interest-rate risk.

Financial institutions can also look to futures contracts for investment trading purposes. Because interest-rate futures contracts are based on a deliverable financial instrument, institutions can view the futures market as an alternative to the cash market for purchasing investment securities. A financial institution can buy a futures contract, let the contract expire, and take delivery of a financial instrument, rather than buy it in the cash market. Naturally, this strategy entails basis risk. But depending on the similarity of the movements in the cash market and futures markets, basis risk may be minimal.

An institution might choose this futures market alternative for any of three reasons. First, the implied rate of return in the futures market may be higher than in the cash market. In other words, there may be opportunity for arbitrage between the cash and futures markets. Second, the futures market may be more liquid than the available cash market. The institution may find the range between the bid and ask prices lower in the futures market than the available cash market, reducing transaction costs. Third, the financial institution may want to use futures contracts for tax reasons.

Financial institutions with large foreign currency positions can use foreign currency futures contracts to hedge their exposure to fluctuations in exchange rates. Such fluctuations could adversely affect their income and equity in the same way as fluctuating interest rates. Exchange-rate risk is hedged in much the same way as interest-rate risk. For instance, a U.S. commercial bank with large Deutsche mark holdings faces the risk of a decline in the exchange rate between marks and dollars. To reduce this risk, the bank can sell Deutsche mark futures contracts. Then, if the mark weakened, the dollar value loss in the cash position is offset by gains in the futures position.

THE POTENTIAL FOR FUTURES

Because financial futures can be highly effective as a tool for managing interest-rate risk, the real question is whether their potential will be realized. Several issues will determine the use of financial futures as a risk-management device.

THE INTEREST-RATE ENVIRONMENT

The future interest-rate environment could be a major issue encouraging wider use of financial futures. Deregulation and macroeconomic policies will remain critically important in determining the interest-rate environment.

Deregulation has intensified competition among financial institutions and forced institutions to pay market rates for deposits and charge market rates on loans. The resulting squeeze on bank margins places a premium on interest-rate risk management. Institutions that cannot manage this risk effectively will go the route of merger, acquisition, or closing. The institutions that take their places will likely use more sophisticated tools in crafting their business. The result will be more financial institutions that understand interest-rate risk and consider hedging in their strategy to manage risk.

Huge prospective federal budget deficits create a large element of uncertainty about future interest rates, as well. Financial markets worry that the sheer size of federal borrowings, relative to the pool of investable funds, will keep upward pressure on rates. Whether these deficits can be funded without excessive growth in the money supply creates additional uncertainty about future rates. The uncertainty and potential volatility in interest rates that result from the current mix of economic policies will encourage more financial institutions to manage interest-rate risk.

Acceptance and Access

One of the main barriers to wide use of hedging by financial institutions is their general acceptance of the concept. For many, the distinction between hedging and speculating is nebulous. A survey of agricultural banks in 1981 showed that about a third of the banks cited skepticism or lack of understanding about futures markets as primary reasons for not hedging.[9] Obviously, education on the workings of futures markets and their uses for financial institutions is the antidote for this constraint.[10]

Whether financial institutions make full use of financial futures will depend to some extent on their access to broadly developed and liquid markets. Given the rapid development of financial futures trading, both in number of contracts and in volume of trading, this constraint would not appear to be a factor in the future. Nevertheless, the thin liquidity of outlying contracts is a concern to institutions that want to hedge interest rates one year out or more. The lack of liquidity in the contract that matures then forces hedgers to use near-term contracts and roll their hedges over as succeeding contracts mature. However, this is a more costly approach. Thus, institutions that can hedge most efficiently by using outlying contracts may have to decide whether they are willing instead to pay the added cost of using near-term contracts.

Regulations and Accounting

The use of futures markets by financial institutions is circumscribed by the guidelines of regulatory agencies, guidelines that vary across regulators. The Comptroller of the Currency, which regulates national banks, allows the use of financial futures for activities deemed to be "incidental to banking." The comptroller's policy allows hedging to reduce a bank's overall interest-rate exposure. The Federal Home Loan Bank Board, regulator for federal savings and loan associations, allows associations to hedge when the hedging is used to reduce overall interest rate exposure.

One regulatory issue of current importance is macrohedging as against microhedging. Regulators tend to favor macrohedging and have become concerned over the use of microhedging. Until the controversy surrounding the use of macro and microhedges is resolved, an appropriate strategy for financial institutions may be to determine the optimal overall macrohedge position and then implement this strategy by a series of microhedges tied to individual assets.

Controversy has surrounded the accounting treatment of financial futures since financial institutions began using them. The controversy centers essentially on two issues. First, what types of futures positions are hedges and what types are speculative? Second, should futures positions be accounted for in financial statements by marking-to-market or by deferring gains and losses? Regulators, wanting to discourage speculation, have required institutions to mark-to-market all futures contract positions.[11] Financial institutions, on the other hand, favor deferral accounting—deferring gains and losses until the hedge is offset or the underlying cash position is changed.

The Financial Accounting Standards Board (FASB) recently came out with the long-awaited statement on the accounting for futures contracts. The new guidelines take effect for futures contracts entered into after December 31, 1984. The new rules allow the use of deferral accounting for futures transactions that meet the following hedge criteria. First, the asset or liability to be hedged exposes the institution to price or interest-rate risk. And second, the futures contract selected reduces the interest-rate exposure of the institution, is specifically designated as a hedge, and its price is highly correlated with the cash item being hedged. Futures transactions not meeting these criteria will be accounted for by marking-to-market.

Although thrift regulators already allow deferral accounting, bank regulators do not. Their reaction to the FASB statement, if any, is yet to be determined.

Potential Pitfalls

Although hedging interest-rate risk in futures markets may be straightforward in theory, in practice it holds many potential pitfalls. Financial institutions that decide to hedge must recognize that imprudent use of futures can only worsen their financial position. The recent experiences of some institutions who incurred large futures market losses serve as a reminder of the problems that can be encountered.[12] Thus, financial institutions need to exercise caution both in considering and in implementing hedging programs.

Financial institutions should consider using financial futures only after they have been studied and can be integrated into a thorough, ongoing asset liability management program. A hedging program will never fully replace other risk-reducing techniques, it will augment them. Some financial institutions, and particularly the smallest institutions, may find that more traditional risk-management techniques are adequate. But those institutions that can use futures markets prudently and effectively will have a broader range of tools to manage interest-rate risk.

CONCLUSIONS

The more volatile interest-rate environment of the 1980s has led many financial institutions to a better understanding of interest-rate risk and how to manage it. The rapid increase in trading of financial futures contracts over the past decade has made hedging a viable means of managing this risk. Money-center financial institutions now use futures markets daily in managing interest-rate risk. Small and medium-sized institutions, however, have been much slower to adopt hedging.

As futures markets and their applications for the financial services industry become better understood, more financial institutions will view hedging the same way they view more traditional risk-managing devices. Although human resources may always constrain small institutions, a steadily emerging supply of advisory services can probably be expected to make futures a part of asset/liability management for more financial institutions. While the cost of using financial futures may be low, some financial institutions will continue to view traditional risk-management techniques as adequate.

Use of futures markets holds benefits for both financial institutions and their customers. Hedging can enable a financial institution to keep the portfolio it wants while reducing the risk of doing so. And the financial institution that properly manages interest-rate risk will be in a better position to meet the financial services needs of all its customers.

APPENDIX: A GLOSSARY

Basis: The difference between the price of a futures contract and the price of underlying cash instrument or commodity. The cash price minus the futures price equals the basis.

Cash market: A market (a public place where buying and selling takes place) in which transactions for the purchase or sale of physical commodities or financial instruments are conducted at agreed-on prices and terms. The cash market is sometimes referred to as the spot market, an outgrowth of the phrase "on the spot," meaning commodities available for immediate delivery.

Cross hedge: Hedging a cash market instrument (commodity) with a futures contract whose deliverable instrument (commodity) is similar but not identical to the cash instrument (commodity).

Futures contract: A transferable written agreement to make or take delivery of a standard amount of a commodity or financial instrument in a particular month at a specific price.

Futures market: A market in which contracts for the future delivery of a commodity or financial instrument are bought and sold on a designated futures exchange.

Hedging: A method of reducing risk by taking a position in the futures market that is intended as a temporary substitute for either the sale or purchase of the actual commodity or financial instrument. A hedge in the futures market is a market position that is equal in value but opposite to a position in the cash market.

Interest-rate Risk: The risk that fluctuations in interest rates will adversely affect net interest margin due to a mismatch of rate-sensitive assets and liabilities.

Long hedge: To buy a futures contract in anticipation of a future purchase of a cash commodity or financial instrument as protection against the risk of an increase in the cash price.

Margin: An amount of money deposited by both buyers and sellers of futures contracts to ensure the performance of the terms of the contract.

Margin call: Additional margin money required by a clearinghouse or brokerage firm from a trader when the market has moved against the trader's position.

Open interest: The number of futures contract positions that are not yet offset for a specific contract month. For each contract counted as open there will be one short position and one long position.

Price risk: The potential that the value of an asset or commodity may decline from the seller's perspective or rise from the buyer's perspective.

Risk: The potential for losses or foregone profits due to adverse price or interest-rate fluctuations.

Short hedge: To sell a futures contract in anticipation of the future sale of a cash commodity or financial instrument as protection against the risk of a decline in the cash price.

Speculator: An individual who tries to anticipate commodity or financial instrument price changes and profit through the sale or purchase of futures contracts or of the actual physical commodity.

Spread: Four applications: (1) differences between bid and offer prices on a commodity or financial instrument, (2) differences between yields or prices of two cash instruments, (3) difference between the two prices of futures contracts, and (4) the profit margin of a dealer in a transaction.

Volume: The number of transactions that have taken place during a specific trading session.

NOTES

[1] For a more detailed discussion, see Mark Powers and David Vogel, *Inside the Financial Futures Markets,* 2nd ed., (New York: John Wiley & Sons, 1984), pp. 5–13.

[2] Stock index futures contracts are based on cash settlement, rather than delivery of a commodity or financial instrument.

[3] The dollar price or discount value of a Treasury bill is calculated by the following formula:

$$\text{Discount value} = \text{Face value} - \frac{(\text{Days to maturity} \times \text{Yield} \times \text{face value})}{360}$$

For example, a \$1 million Treasury bill yielding 10.01 percent and maturing in 91 days would have a discounted value of \$974,697.

$$\$1,000,000 - \frac{(91 \times 10.01 \times \$1,000,000)}{360} = \$974,697$$

[4] Duration determines the average life of an asset or liability by applying present value weights to the cash flow of the asset or liability. The duration of an institution's assets, therefore, is found by multiplying the time until receipt of each prospective cash flow by the present value of the cash flow, adding the weighted present values, and dividing by the current asset price. If the duration of liabilities is less than the duration of assets, net worth declines if interest rates increase.

For a discussion of duration analysis, see Sanford Rose, "Once More, with Feeling," *American Banker,* July 3, 1984. Also see Ingersoll, Skelton, and Weil, "Duration Forty Years Later," *Journal of Financial and Quantitative Analysis,* November 1978, pp. 627–50.

[5] The term *strip* hedge can carry two meanings. In this case, it simply refers to a chain of futures contracts joined together for the life of the hedge. Frequently, a strip hedge refers to a strategy of purchasing a series of futures contracts to secure a higher rate of return than is currently available in the cash market. In effect, this type of strip hedge simply takes advantage of yield curve relationships.

[6] Basically, an option is a contract that gives the buyer the right but not the obligation to complete a transaction according to specified terms. Options can be written on actual commodities or on futures contracts. Similar to the short and long positions in the futures markets, two opposite positions can be taken in the options market. The buyer of a "call option" has the right but not the obligation to execute a long futures position at a predetermined price. The buyer of a "put option" has the right but not the obligation to execute a short position at a predetermined price. Buyers of call or put options pay a price conceptually similar to an insurance premium. And in many respects, using options can be compared with buying insurance against price movements.

[7] In this case, the institution would buy a call option. By exercising the call option, it would offset its short futures position with a long position that has a price determined by the option contract. Alternatively, it could sell a put option on a financial instrument.

[8] The synthetic fixed-rate loan can be set up in a variety of ways, but important issues center on picking a loan rate that corresponds to an available futures contract and determining who places the hedge: the borrower or lender. For further discussion, see James Kurt Dew and Terrence F. Martel, "Treasury Bill Futures, Commercial Lending, and the Synthetic Fixed-Rate Loan," *Journal of Commercial Lending,* June 1981, pp. 17–38.

[9] See Drabenstott and McDonley, "The Impact of Financial Futures in Agricultural Banks," *Economic Review,* Federal Reserve Bank of Kansas City, May 1982, pp. 19–30.

[10] For individual financial institutions, the board of directors' lack of approval of a hedging program can be a very real constraint to wider use of futures. Regulators require that the board of directors authorize all financial futures trading and assume final responsibility. Thus, the most important educational task within an institution is often convincing a reluctant board of directors that hedging can be in their best interest.

[11] Federal Home Loan Bank Board regulations allow savings and loan institutions to use deferrel accounting.

[12] For example, see "Norwest Ousts Chief of Its Mortgage Unit Due to Big Write-Off," *The Wall Street Journal,* August 31, 1984, p. 10.

SELECTED READINGS

Textbooks

Fabozzi, Frank J., and Frank G. Zarb. *Handbook of Financial Markets: Securities, Options, and Future.* Homewood, Ill.: Dow Jones-Irwin, 1981.

Loosigian, Allan M. *Interest Rate Future.* Homewood, Ill.: Dow Jones-Irwin, 1980.

Powers, Mark, and David Vogel. *Inside the Financial Futures Markets,* 2nd ed., New York: John Wiley & Sons, 1984.

Rothstein, Nancy H., and James M. Little. *The Handbook of Financial Futures.* New York: McGraw-Hill, 1984.

Accounting

Arthur Andersen & Co. *Accounting for Interest Rate Futures: An Explanation of the Proposed FASB Statement,* 1983.

Financial Accounting Standards Board. *Accounting for Futures Contracts.* Statement of Financial Accounting Standards Number 80, August 1984.

Asset/Liability Management

Dew, James Kurt. "The Effective Gap." *American Banker.* Three-part series, June 10, September 18, and December 9, 1981, beginning on p. 4.

McCabe, George M., and Robert W. McLeod. "The Use of Financial Futures in Banking." *The Journal of Commercial Bank Lending,* August 1983, pp. 6–21.

Olson, Ronald L., and Donald G. Simonson. "Gap Management and Market Rate Sensitivity in Banks." *Journal of Bank Research,* Spring 1982, pp. 53–58.

Picou, Glenn. "Managing Interest Rate Risk with Interest Rate Futures." *The Bankers Magazine,* May–June, 1981, pp. 76–81.

Simonson, Donald G.; Carl W. Allendoerter; and George H. Hempel. "Improving Gap Management for Controlling Interest Rate Risk." *Journal of Bank Research,* Summer 1982, pp. 109–15.

Bank Strategies

Edwards, Franklin R. "The Clearing Association in Futures Markets: Guarantor and Regulator." *The Journal of Futures Markets,* vol. 3, no. 4, 1983, pp. 370–92.

Gammill, James F., Jr., and James M. Stone. "Options, Futures, and Business Risk." *The Journal of Futures Markets,* vol. 2, no. 2, 1982, pp. 141–49.

Laudeman, Mark L. "An Application of Financial Futures to Fixed-Rate Lending." *The Journal of Commercial Bank Lending,* August 1983, pp. 23–35.

Potter, Howard. "Hedging Money-Market Deposit Accounts." *ABA Banking Journal,* October 1983, pp. 179–83.

Thayer, Charles J. "The Financial Futures Market." *Bankers Desk Reference: New Topics,* 1983, pp. 134–48.

Options Market

Bankers Research. "Futures Options." *Bankers Research,* February 11, 1983, pp. 4–8.

Goodman, Laurie S. "New Options Markets." Federal Reserve Bank of New York. Quarterly Review, Autumn 1983, pp. 35–47.

Hartzog, Jerry. "Options: A New Tool for Managing Risk." *Savings and Loan News,* November 1982, pp. 56–60.

Regulation

Comptroller of the Currency. "National Bank Participation in the Financial Futures and Forward Placement Markets." *Banking Circular BC-79* (3rd rev.)., April 19, 1983.

Edwards, Franklin R. "The Regulation of Futures and Forward Trading by Depository Institutions: A Legal and Economic Analysis." *The Journal of Futures Markets,* vol. 1, no. 2, 1981, pp. 201–23.

Stone, James M. "Principles of the Regulation of Futures Market." *The Journal of Futures Markets,* vol. 1, no. 2, 1981, pp. 177–91.

26

New Options Markets

Laurie S. Goodman

Wide price swings have been a hallmark of financial markets in recent years. This greater volatility subjected market participants holding traditional assets to unaccustomed risks and increased their demands for instruments designed to shift risk to those better able or more willing to bear it.

This atmosphere has fostered the development of new options markets to reallocate risk. These markets offer options on Treasury bonds, notes, and bills, Treasury bond futures, gold futures, foreign currencies, stock indexes, and stock index futures. These newly established options markets, while very small at present, are potentially important. They create more flexibility in risk management than is available with existing cash and futures markets. They also provide market participants with a more efficient hedge against some contingencies that they assume in the normal course of their operations.

This article surveys the new options markets—why they have arisen, who is using them, and what purposes they serve. It also discusses how these instruments differ from conventional equity options in terms of pricing and other financial characteristics.

RISK-RETURN CHARACTERISTICS OF OPTIONS

An option is an agreement between two parties in which one party grants the other the *right* to buy or sell an asset under specified conditions while the counterparty assumes an obligation to sell or buy that asset. The party who must decide whether to exercise the option is termed the *option buyer*, since he must pay for the privilege. The party granting the right to buy or sell an asset is called the *option seller* or *writer of the option*. There are two basic types of options: calls and puts.

A *call option* gives the buyer the right to purchase, or "call away" a specified amount of the underlying security at a specified price up to a specified date. The price at which the security may be bought is the *exercise price* or the *striking*

From *Quarterly Review*, Federal Reserve Bank of New York, Autumn 1983, pp. 35–47.

price. The last date on which the option may be exercised is called the *expiration date* or the *maturity date*. The price of this option contract is its *premium*.

A call option can best be described by means of a simple example. A December call option on Treasury bonds gives the holder of the option the right to purchase $100,000 par value of specified Treasury bonds at a price of $90,000 on or before the expiration date in December.[1] The price of these bonds on September 19, 1983, was $90,500. The price of the call option on that date was $2,094. If the market value of the bonds is greater than $90,000 on the expiration date, the option will be exercised. The rationale is that, even if the buyer does not want to hold the bonds, they can be resold at the market price. If the market value of the Treasury bonds is less than $90,000 at expiration, the option will not be exercised because the buyer can purchase the bonds at a lower cost in the market.

The price of an option consists of two components—*intrinsic value* and *time value*. The price of an option, if exercised immediately, is the maximum of either zero or the market price minus the exercise price. This is called the "intrinsic value" of the option. In the example above, the intrinsic value of the option is the $90,500 market price less the $90,000 exercise current price, or $500. An option must always sell for at least its intrinsic value or there will be arbitrage opportunities. Market practitioners call an option with a positive intrinsic value an "in-the-money" option. Similarly, an option with zero intrinsic value is known as an "out-of-the-money" option.

The time value of an option is the difference between the premium on the option and its intrinsic value. This is the seller's compensation for the possibility that the option will be worth more at the end of its life than if exercised immediately. In the example, the time value of the option is the difference between the total price of $2,094 and the intrinsic value, or $1,594.

A *put option* is the right to sell, or "put to" the writer, a given amount of the underlying security at a given price on or before a specific date. In the example above, the Treasury bond December/90 put option gives the buyer the right to sell $100,000 par value of Treasury bonds at a price of $90,000 on or before the expiration date. If the market value of the Treasury bonds is greater than $90,000, the buyer will not exercise the offer, as the bonds can be sold in the open market. If the market value of the bonds is less than $90,000 at expiration, the option to sell the bonds at that price is valuable.

Some market participants purchase options for much the same reason people purchase insurance—they feel the protection they are receiving against adverse developments is worth more to them than the option premium. In the case of the call option example, the buyer of the option is purchasing protection against the price of the bonds rising above $90,000. In the case of the put option, the buyer is purchasing protection against the price of the bonds dropping below $90,000.

Other market participants purchase options as a way to speculate on asset price movements. Consider an investor who owns a Treasury bond and buys a call on a Treasury bond future. This investor is using the options market to compound his bet that interest rates will fall (bond prices will rise). Similarly, a financial institution which has liabilities of a shorter repricing period than its assets will be favorably affected if interest rates fall and unfavorably affected if interest rates rise. If this institution bought a put option on a debt security, it would clearly be hedging. If it purchased a call option, it would be compounding its current interest-rate mismatch.

Why do investors write options? Their gain is limited by the premium, while their potential loss is much larger. Options writers believe that the premium is adequate compensation for their potential loss. In fact, the premium is the equilibrating price variable, equating the quantity of options supplied with the quantity of options demanded. If the option premium were too low to compensate the writer for the risk, there would be more buyers than sellers, forcing the premium to rise.

It is important to realize that option writing need not be speculative. An investor who writes call options on an equity (covered call writing) may perceive himself as hedging, as the option increases his returns in periods of poor and moderately good stock returns and reduces it in periods of very good stock returns. Similarly, if a bank that has liabilities with a shorter repricing period than its assets writes a call option on a bond or bond future, it is actually reducing its interest rate sensitivity. If interest rates rise, the option cushions the portfolio loss as the bank receives the option premium. If interest rates fall, the bank receives the premium but trades away some of its potential gain.

NEW OPTIONS MARKETS

Prior to 1982, organized markets existed only for options on common stock. These equity options are traded on four exchanges: the Chicago Board Options Exchange (CBOE), the American Stock Exchange (Amex), the Philadelphia Stock Exchange, and the Pacific Stock Exchange. Put options on the securities of the Government National Mortgage Association were traded on an over-the-counter basis.

Since the last quarter of 1982, many new options markets have opened; others are in the final planning stages (Table 1). These new options are written on four types of financial instruments:

- Options on stock indexes.
- Options on debt instruments.
- Options on foreign currencies.
- Options on gold.

The new contracts take two basic forms:

- Options on so-called physicals (i.e., actual commodities, securities, or indexes).
- Options on futures contracts.

Market Participants

Since these markets are very new, it is difficult to assess who will eventually constitute the customer base. Institutions that are more conservative and less inclined to enter new markets may well turn out to be very large customers once the markets become better established.

Nevertheless, preliminary evidence indicates that the options on stock indexes and stock index futures are dominated by individuals, rather than institutions. They are using the market as a method to wager bets on aggregate market movements, rather than focusing attention on particular securities. Broker/dealer firms are relatively small users of options on stock indexes for their own account. Institutional money managers are just beginning to enter the market on the buy

TABLE 1
The New Options Markets

Instrument	Options on Physicals	Options on Futures Contracts
Stock indexes	**Chicago Board Options Exchange:** S&P 100 (formerly CBOE 100) S&P 500 S&P integrated international oil group S&P Computer and Business Equipment Index	**Chicago Mercantile Exchange:** S&P 500
	American Stock Exchange: Amex Major Market Index Amex Market Value Index Oil and Gas Index Computer Technology Index	**New York Futures Exchange:** NYSE Composite
	New York Stock Exchange: NYSE Composite Index	
U.S. government debt	**American Stock Exchange:** Treasury bills Treasury notes	**Chicago Board of Trade:** Treasury bonds
	Chicago Board Options Exchange: Treasury bonds	
Foreign exchange	**Philadelphia Stock Exchange:** Various currencies*	
Precious metals		**The Commodity Exchange:** Gold
		Mid-American Exchange: Gold†

S&P: Standard & Poor's Corporation.
* Canadian dollars, German marks, Japanese yen, Swiss francs, and pound sterling.
† Approved, not traded.

side as a hedging vehicle for their portfolio and on the sell side as a source of fee income.

By contrast, options on debt instruments appear to be dominated by institutions. Conversations with exchange officials indicate that well over half the business is generated by broker/dealer firms for their own account. The wholesale nature of the market is corroborated by evidence that almost all the transactions in the most popular of the instruments—the options on bond futures—are for 10, 20, or 50 contracts, rather than for 1 or 2. The face value of the contracts is $100,000. Other users of options on debt instruments include savings and loan associations, commercial banks, and commodities houses.

Options on foreign currencies traded on the Philadelphia Stock Exchange appear to have generated substantial interest abroad, with more than half the business coming from Europe. Broker/dealers in the United States and abroad account for an estimated 30 percent of the business. Corporate treasurers are believed to be the largest customer group. Several banks and some professional money managers are also using the market. The contracts have also attracted some retail interest.

Options Versus Futures as a Hedging Tool

There are established futures markets in the same instruments as the new options markets.[2] However, since options and futures have different profit profiles, options contracts can be better hedges than futures contracts for some important kinds of risk exposure. Options are ideally suited to hedge the risks of a potential transaction that is not certain to take place. Consider, for example, a U.S. firm that must submit a competitive bid in a foreign currency to provide a product but is unsure that its bid will be accepted. Here the normal business risks of competitive bidding are compounded by exchange risks. The rate of exchange is a substantial cost element in the bid price of the contract, but the firm will be reluctant to lock in these costs at the time it submits its bid—by selling its potential foreign currency receipts forward, for example—because it is uncertain about the outcome of the bidding process. However, the firm can create a perfect hedge against the contingent receivable by buying a put option in the foreign currency. If the firm's bid wins, the foreign currency can be "put" to the option seller. If the bid fails, the firm will simply not exercise the option.

In a similar vein, a bank can use options to hedge its fixed-rate loan commitments to businesses. These lines are attractive to the borrowers. If interest rates go up, the borrower will generally utilize the commitment; if rates fall, the borrower will let the commitment lapse. The bank has essentially written a put option. Banks may desire to provide this service to keep valuable customers, but they may not be so anxious to bear the full interest-rate risk on their contingent liability. The bank can hedge this contingent liability by purchasing a put option on interest rates for an appropriate maturity, say, a Treasury note contract.

There are situations in which options and futures can serve similar hedging purposes. Consider a bank with a longer repricing period on its assets than on its liabilities. This institution should gain from falling interest rates and lose from rising rates. If the bank management believes that interest rates will rise more than accounted for by the term structure of interest rates, it can hedge via either futures or options. Both instruments would be attractive, since the option premium and the futures prices will look cheap in terms of the protection they provide to the bank. The choice between the two will depend on the cost of the option premium, how certain management is of their prediction of future interest rates, and the risk-return trade-off preferred by management. The use of options for such a transaction is examined in Appendix 1.

Market Mechanics: Margins and Delivery Provisions

Margin requirements are a necessary protection for the clearinghouse members. On options contracts, the buyer pays the entire premium up front and is not subject to margin calls.[3] The seller of an uncovered option is subject to an initial margin requirement. If the market moves against him, he is also subject to additional or variation margin. A specific example of margin requirements on options and their calculation is given in Appendix 2.

For options on futures contracts, it is customary to hold interest- bearing assets in margin accounts. Consequently, initial margin requirements do not usually represent foregone interest for these contracts. For options on physicals, initial margin requirements must be posted in cash. Alternatively, a security position can be held in lieu of the margin. For example, for an options contract on Treasury bills, Treasury bills with a par value equal to the par value on the contract can be posted instead of the margin. This is customarily done for options on debt securities. Variation margin must, in all cases, be posted in cash.

The terms of delivery for the new options contracts include cash settlement and physical delivery. Options on futures contracts require delivery of the underlying futures contracts. Options on stock indexes require cash settlement—that is, the securities which comprise the Standard & Poor's (S&P) 100, for example, do not actually have to be delivered. Rather, the difference between the exercise price and the current price must be settled in cash. Foreign currency options require delivery of a specified amount of foreign currency.

But options on debt instruments present a unique deliverability problem that arises because of the limited life of the underlying security. Other options (equities, stock indexes, foreign exchange) are written on physicals that have an infinite life and thus are not directly affected in their characteristics by the passage of time. But debt instruments get closer to maturity as the option gets closer to expiration. This feature of debt instruments requires that options on them take one of two forms: fixed deliverable or variable deliverable.

Fixed deliverable options require that a debt instrument with specified characteristics be delivered when the option is exercised. For example, a three-month call option on a six-month Treasury bill would require that a Treasury bill with six months remaining to maturity be delivered. Contracts for fixed delivery allow for the possibility that the optioned security could have a shorter lifetime than the option itself. That is, a nine-month option on a three-month Treasury bill is possible; when the option is exercised, a three-month bill is delivered. Treasury bills on the Amex are traded on a fixed deliverable basis.

A variable deliverable option specifies the existing debt issue that is deliverable against exercise. This has been adopted for Treasury notes and bonds. For example, a 1-year option on a 10-year bond spells out the specific 10-year bond to be delivered. At the expiration of the option, the bond will have nine years to maturity. Thus, the maturity date of the bond must be later than the option expiration date for variable deliverable options.[4]

Market Development

Why the sudden emergence of these new markets? Increased use of futures contracts and existing equity options indicated to the management of the stock and commodities exchanges that the public desired new instruments which could serve a risk transfer function. Proposals on some of these new options contracts were submitted as early as 1980. However, questions about the division of regulatory authority between the Commodity Futures Trading Commission (CFTC) and the Securities and Exchange Commission delayed the approval process, allowing other exchanges time to design similar, slightly differentiated products. The ultimate agreement, signed into law by President Reagan in October 1982, gave the SEC jurisdiction over options contracts on physical securities traded on organized securities and commodities exchanges, and options on foreign currency when traded on a national securities exchange. The CFTC has jurisdiction over options on financial futures.

The exchanges are well aware that the first to begin trading a product has a real advantage. Liquidity will tend to develop in that market. If a second exchange enters with a similar product, even if it is slightly superior in design, it must compete with a market which has already developed liquidity. Trades can be executed with greater ease in the first market, and hence gravitate there. It is extremely difficult for the second market to develop liquidity, and it generally fails. Consequently, the competitive pressure between the exchanges induces the submission of numerous proposals on similar instruments.

Yet, if there were a demand for these products, why did over-the-counter markets not develop? Regulatory approval only is necessary for options to be traded on organized exchanges. The answer is in part that the use of an organized exchange avoids the potential for abuse that is inherent in an options contract. Otherwise, the option buyer, who pays the premium up front, has very limited recourse if the writer does not uphold his obligations at the end of the contract.

Trading of standardized contracts on an organized exchange overcomes this problem because it allows for the development of a clearinghouse. On securities exchanges the clearinghouse assumes any credit risk. Thus, the option really consists of two contracts: one between the buyer and the clearinghouse and the other between the seller and the clearinghouse. On commodities exchanges, the clearinghouse member which handles the writer's account assumes the credit risk. Consequently, a buyer of an exchange-traded option does not have to pass judgment on the creditworthiness of the seller.[5]

While the clearinghouse or a clearing member thus assumes the credit risk in the contract, they can protect themselves against the risk by marking the contracts to market on a daily basis and assessing additional margin requirements as required by price movements. If the margin calls are not met, the clearinghouse can move quickly to liquidate the contracts. Two other reasons for the importance of an organized exchange is contract standardization, which allows for the development of liquidity, and a reported price, which gives option buyers and writers information on the price of the last actual trade. This information can be used to evaluate returns better on the anticipated option strategy. Since trading on an organized exchange is preferable to trading on an over-the-counter basis, regulatory approval was a crucial ingredient for market creation.

Will All These New Options Markets Survive?

There are four possible markets for any instrument: a cash market, a futures market, an option on the cash market, and an option on the futures market. But, generally, the existence of all four markets on one instrument is redundant. A cash market, a futures market, and one options market will usually be sufficient to fulfill all risk-transfer possibilities, since the option on the cash market and the option on the futures market serve very similar functions.[6]

If there is room for only one options market, what determines whether the option on the cash instrument or the option on the future wins out? Since there were only small differences in the start-up times of the various markets, technical or operational differences will make one market more desirable than the other. For example, if the cash market is more liquid than the futures market, or has lower transactions costs, an option on the cash market would be preferred. In the case of a commodity like gold, an option on the physical would involve the costs of assaying and delivery. Consequently, for gold the options market has developed on the futures contract. In the case of foreign exchange, spot markets are much deeper than the forward exchange markets.[7] The futures market is smaller still. In this case, options are written on the spot currency contract.

Options on both cash instruments and futures currently coexist in markets

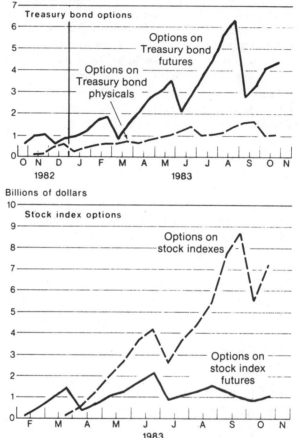

CHART 1
The Options Contract Race

Total open interest

Billions of dollars

Treasury bond options

Options on Treasury bond futures

Options on Treasury bond physicals

O N D | J F M A M J J A S O N
1982 | 1983

Billions of dollars

Stock index options

Options on stock indexes

Options on stock index futures

F M A M J J A S O N
1983

Sources: *The Wall Street Journal,* various dates, and information provided by the exchanges.

where the reasons to prefer one type of option over the other are not so clear-cut. But signs are already emerging to show which options will dominate. Options on Treasury bond futures appear to be generating more business than options on Treasury bond physicals. By contrast, the options market for stock indexes is more active than the market in options on stock index futures (Chart 1).

Many market participants believe that the contract design of options on Treasury bond futures is slightly superior, for three reasons. For one, options on futures have no coupon or dividend payments. By contrast, with an options contract on a bond or note, the buyer of a call or seller of a put must compensate the other party for accrued interest when exercise occurs. Furthermore, options on bond futures are also believed to be "cleaner" instruments because of the reduced possibility of delivery squeezes. Options on bonds are written on particular issues. Since the supply of any particular issue is fixed after the date of issuance, there is always the chance of a squeeze developing that could artificially raise the price of that bond. Options on bond futures, however, are written on the underlying futures contract, which, in turn, is written not on a particular bond issue but rather on a bond with particular characteristics. One bond (usually a high-coupon bond) will always be cheapest to deliver against the futures contract. But, if there were a squeeze on this bond, other deliverable bonds would be available.[8] Consequently, the deliverable supply of Treasury bond futures will always prove more than adequate. Third, it is easier to learn the price of an underlying bond future, rather than the bond itself. For option pricing purposes, it is crucial to know the price of the underlying security. The price of the last bond futures trade is easily accessible, as bond futures and options on bond futures are traded on the same floor. This saves the investor the trouble of canvassing dealers to obtain a price on the security itself.

Options on stock indexes appear to be more popular than options on stock index futures. Of the four markets on stock indexes, the two most successful are the S&P 100 followed by the Amex Major Market. These two markets have attracted substantial retail interest because the contract sizes on these options are much smaller than those for options on the S&P 500, the Amex Market Value, or the stock index futures. Moreover, options on stock index futures can be sold only by a CFTC-registered representative. Options on stock indexes can be sold by any registered representative. Thus, a stockbroker who services retail portfolios can market the S&P 100 and the Amex Major Market Index, but not the options on the futures contracts.[9]

While options on the Treasury bond futures and options on the S&P 100 appear to be doing somewhat better than their competitors, the contract race is not yet over. The markets are all relatively new, and the emergence of one contract over another takes time. But weaker markets face the threat of gradually losing liquidity through a loss of customers. Participants who remain in those markets will find over time that their trades cannot be executed promptly enough or that bid/ask spreads are too wide.

FINANCIAL CHARACTERISTICS OF THE NEW OPTIONS

The new options, particularly on debt instruments, have financial characteristics that are quite different from those of the more familiar equity options. An equity is the instrument with the same characteristics over the life of the option. Unlike equities, debt instruments have finite lives and their effective maturity shortens as time passes. This creates the distinction between fixed deliverable options and variable deliverable options, as discussed above. Both fixed deliverable and variable deliverable instruments attempt to capture some of the characteristics of options on equities. A fixed deliverable option tries to preserve the characteristics of a debt instrument (i.e., its sensitivity to changes in interest rates) but must move from security to security to avoid the aging problem. The variable deliverable bond option stays with a single issue, but the characteristics of the issue age over time as the bond moves to maturity.

The other major difference between the new options and traditional equity options concerns the effects of financial variables—such as the level of interest rates—on the price of the options contract. The standard theory of options pricing

TABLE 2
Effects of Changes in Financial Factors on Pricing of New Options Instruments

Call Options on Instruments	Security Price (S)	Exercise Price (E)	Volatility of Security Price (s)	Time to Expiration (T)	Factor Level of Interest Rates (r)
Conventional equity or stock index	+	−	+	+	+
Foreign currency	+	−	+	+	?
Fixed deliverable debt instrument	+	−	+	?	−
Variable deliverable debt instrument	+	−	+	+	−
Futures contract	+	−	+	?	−

This table should be read as follows: a plus sign indicates that an increase in the value of a factor will increase the value of a call option on an instrument, a minus sign indicates a decrease in the option value, and a question mark indicates an ambiguous effect.

holds that changes in certain financial variables, including the level of interest rates, will have definite effects on the price of an equity option. For the new options, however, in some cases the effects of such factors may be ambiguous or even may go in the opposite direction to that predicted by traditional options pricing theory.

Valuation of New Options Instruments

In 1973, Black and Scholes described a formula for calculating the value of a call option on a stock.[10] This model, which has received wide recognition and attention, shows that the price of a call option depends on five factors: the price of the underlying security (S), the strike or exercise price of the option (E), the volatility of the price of the underlying security (s), the time remaining to maturity (T), and the level of interest rates (r).[11] It is useful to explore the extent to which the same factors are important in the pricing of the new options markets.[12] (The results of this section are summarized in Table 2, and the relationship between put and call prices is discussed in Appendix 3.)

The effect of changes in the underlying security price or the exercise price are unambiguous. For all call options, as the price of the underlying security increases or the exercise price decreases, the price of the option must increase because the intrinsic value is higher. The effect of increased volatility is similar for conventional equity options and new options instruments, as described below. However, the analysis of changes in the time to expiration and the level of interest rates is different for new options instruments than for conventional equity options.

Volatility

For all options, the more volatile the underlying security price, the greater the value of the option. Consider the extreme case in which there are two securities, A and B. Security A is riskless and Security B is risky, but its mean return is the same as the sure value of Security A. Assume further that the exercise price of the option is the same as the value of Security A at expiration. Hence, an option on Security A will be worthless, as the exercise price is the same as its current value.

Security B has a probability of one half of expiring worthless, and a probability of one half of expiring with value. Its current price will reflect this, and consequently will be positive. Consider now two risky securities with the same mean value. Security B is riskier than Security A. The argument easily generalizes, as Security B will have a greater probability of a higher value at expiration than Security A. It also has a greater probability of a lower value but, since the option cuts off the lower tail of the distribution, this does not matter. Thus, the value of options on more volatile securities, holding all other factors constant, will generally be greater.

Time to Expiration

In the Black-Scholes model, an option with a longer time to expiration will be worth at least as much as another option with the same exercise price and a shorter time to expiration. The intuition is that an option with a longer time to expiration has all the attributes of an option with a shorter exercise date, as the longer option may be exercised before maturity. Once the shorter-run option has expired, the longer-term option can still be exercised. This is true for options on foreign currencies, options on stock indexes, and options on variable deliverable debt instruments as well.

This pricing property does not necessarily hold for options on futures and fixed deliverable options, although it will generally be the case. By way of illustration, consider the September and December call options on a futures contract. The time value of an option on a December future will, of course, be higher than that on a September future. But the September future is a different contract from the December future. Consequently, it is possible—if interest rates are currently very low and expected to rise sharply between September and December—for the option on the September future to have a positive intrinsic value, while the option on the December future has a zero intrinsic value. Thus, depending on the relative magnitudes of the time values and the intrinsic values, the option on the December future could conceivably be less valuable than the option on the September future.

Interest Rates

The Black-Scholes formula shows that, as interest rates rise, the value of a call option must rise.[13] To understand this, note that holding a call option and holding the stock itself are alternative ways for an investor to capture any gain on the security price. Consequently, as rates rise, the cost of carry on the underlying security will rise and the call option will appear more attractive vis-à-vis the underlying stock.[14] And what holds for an option on a single equity will hold for an option on a stock price index, which is just a basket of many individual equities.

For options on stock index *futures*—and on futures contracts generally—there is no opportunity cost associated with holding a futures contract, as no funds need be expended until expiration. Consequently, the interest-rate effect will be negative although very small.[15] This can best be described by considering a riskless world. The option buyer would be charged an amount equal to the present discounted value of the difference between the value of the futures contract at expiration and the exercise price. (In a risky world, this difference would be higher by the amount of an implicit insurance premium.) Then, as interest rates go up, this present discounted value, which is the price of the call option, would decline. Essentially, the purchaser of the call is forfeiting interest until contract expiration on the original call price, for which cash must be put up front. However, since the futures price and the exercise price are expected to be relatively close when the option is originally purchased, interest-rate variations are only a second-order effect in the price changes of these contracts.

Assuming that the price of the underlying security is independent of the level of interest rates is a reasonable simplification in the case of equity options. However, it is an absurd assumption to make for options on debt instruments or on currencies. Major movements in the prices of debt instruments and exchange rates will occur *because* of changes in interest rates. For debt instruments, as interest rates rise, any cost-of-carry considerations will be dwarfed by the fall in the price of the underlying security.[16]

Interest-rate increases as a rule will have a negative impact on the price of options on bond futures, as a rise in interest rates will most likely cause a fall in the price of the underlying futures contract. And this loss is compounded by the negative effect of higher interest rates on the opportunity cost of the call premium.

The effect of interest-rate changes on the value of a foreign currency option will generally be ambiguous. For simplicity, consider the case where foreign interest rates are constant while dollar interest rates rise. The theory of interest-rate parity holds that the forward premium or discount on foreign exchange should equal the differential between domestic and foreign interest rates. Then, as dollar interest rates rise, the forward exchange rate (expressed as dollars per unit of foreign currency) must rise relative to the spot rate. The interest-rate parity linkage allows the value of the options contract to be written equivalently in terms of either the spot or the forward exchange rate.[17] And this equivalence in the valuation formulas for the option can be used to deduce the effect of interest rate changes on the option price. There are three cases:

- If the spot rate is unaffected by a rise in domestic interest rates, option values will rise; as in the case of a typical equity option, the cost-of-carry effect will dominate.
- If the forward rate is unaffected by a rise in domestic rates, option values will fall. Intuitively, one can think of the option as being written on a futures contract that expires on the same date as the option. In this instance, the negative relationship existing between options on futures and interest rates will prevail.
- If both the spot and forward rates change when domestic interest rates rise, the effect on option values cannot be determined without precise knowledge of how much either exchange rate moves.

Since the third case represents the typical adjustment, the effect of interest-rate changes on foreign currency options values is indeterminate.

To summarize, there are three interest-rate effects at work. There is a negative effect, which relates to the cost of carry on the option premium—the call premium is paid when the contract is entered into and no proceeds are received until maturity or exercise. There is a positive effect, which relates to the cost of carry on the underlying security. Finally, there is a negative effect of interest rates on the security price. The second effect dominates the first, and the third effect generally dominates the second. For options on futures, only the first effect is present. For options on conventional equities and equity indexes, the first two effects are present, and the impact of interest rates is positive. For options on debt instruments, all three effects are present, and the third effect dominates. For foreign currencies, the extent to which the third effect is present depends on the relative movements of spot and forward exchange rates, thus the effect of interest rates is indeterminant.

OPTIONS IN THE BROADER FINANCIAL CONTEXT

As risk in the financial environment has increased, many of the traditional risk-bearers are no longer willing to play that role to so large an extent. Banking institutions have moved away from their conventional activity of borrowing short and lending long; instead, they are confining the calculated interest-rate risks they take to the short end of the maturity spectrum. Portfolio managers who feel they have a particular expertise in picking stocks now wish to remove the market component of their risk. Corporations are looking for ways to eliminate exchange-rate risk that they had normally assumed in the course of their business. Consequently, changes have emerged in the financial system that enrich the menu of risk-management techniques. The new options markets are one such example. These markets allow traditional risk-bearers to lay off unwanted risks and provide alternative outlets for their customers.

It must be borne in mind that, while options provide real opportunities for market participants to lay off unwanted risk, and for sophisticated market participants to earn a return by accepting these risks, they also create the potential for unsophisticated writers of options to expose themselves to much larger risks than is prudent. The bank regulatory authorities are monitoring bank participation in these markets in an effort to assess what types of activities commercial banks should be able to engage in and what limits should be placed on these activities.

The interest in these markets from the Federal Reserve System's point of view goes well beyond regulatory rules for banks. The existence of these markets may well alter the risk-taking behavior of financial intermediaries and real sector participants. If the markets become very important, they could affect the response of the economic system to real and monetary disturbances. However, it is still too early to tell even which option markets will succeed in establishing themselves and how large they will become. Time and careful study will allow us to determine the full implications for the behavior of market participants.

Appendix 1: An Illustrative Trade

To appreciate fully the flexibility of option instruments, it is useful to work out an illustrative example. Let us consider a depository institution—a bank, for instance—and examine how it could use options in asset-liability management. Let us assume that the financial institutions believe that interest rates will rise more than is expected in the current term structure. The bank has some long-term fixed rate commercial loans and mortgages and is funded by shorter term instruments. To hedge itself the bank wants to buy a put option on a bond future. If interest rates rise, the bank's higher funding costs will be offset or nearly offset by the gain on the options contract.

Meanwhile, a professional money manager across town has very different interest rate expectations. He believes that interest rates will fall more than is expected in the current term structure. He would like to collect the fee income from writing a put option on a bond future.* There is clearly room for a trade between the financial institution and the money manager.

We assume that it is December, the market price of a March futures is 70-00, and the strike price on the option is 70. The premium is $2,000 for $100,000 face value of bonds. The bank thinks there is a 75 percent probability the futures price in March will be 65 and there is a 25 percent probability the price will go up to 72. If the price goes above 70, the bank will not exercise the contract. Thus, the bank perceives this contract as having a positive expected value, as it has a 75 percent chance of making $5,000 and a 25 percent chance of making nothing. Thus, the expected value of the contract is $3,750 and its cost is $2,000.†

Meanwhile the money manager believes that there is a 25 percent probability the futures price in March will be 65 and a 75 percent probability the futures price in March will be 72. The expected cost of this contract to the money manager is $1,250, and he will receive the $2,000 premium. Thus, his expected profit is $750. Let us look at four scenarios at expiration (table).

Note that, while in scenario 1 the bank has lost the $2,000 option premium, interest rates have fallen or held steady. Consequently, the bank will have a gain on its portfolio. Therefore, while the bank would have been better off not buying the option, the hedge worked as it was supposed to. That is, the hedge provided insurance against rising interest rates while preserving the value of the bank's portfolio should interest rates fall.

In the example described above, the money manager writing the put leaves himself with an unlimited exposure if interest rates rise (bond prices fall). If the money manager has interest rate expectations as described above but wants to limit his downside risk, he could write a put option at 70 and buy a put option at 65. If the bond futures contract price comes in below 65, the money manager could exercise the March/65 put. The initial cost of the March/65 put is low, as it is fairly far out of the money; say it costs $250. The money manager would then collect $1,750 in net premium income but would have limited his possible loss to $5,000 on the option. This strategy is called a "bull put spread" (meaning the investor is bullish on bond prices).

The money manager may also have written the put option as part of a straddle. In a straddle, the writer anticipates that interest rates and bond prices will be relatively flat. Writing a straddle involves writing a put and a call option at the same exercise price for the same expiration. If the premium on a March/70 call option is $2,000, the money manager will have collected $4,000 in fee income. Thus, he will break even or make money if the bond futures contract price stays in the range of 66-74. If it moves outside that range, he will experience a net loss on the transaction.‡ Intuitively, if the call is in the money, the put will be out of the money. Since $4,000 in premium income has been collected, the money manager will lose money if the loss on either the put or the call is more than $4,000.

Benefits (Losses) to Parties in Option Contract

Market outcomes	Bank (buyer)	Money manager (writer)
Futures price is 70 or above March/70 put expires worthless	−2,000 premium	+2,000 premium
Futures price is 69 March/70 put expires +1	−2,000 premium +1,000 option −1,000	+2,000 premium −1,000 option +1,000
Futures price is 68 March /70 put expires +2	−2,000 premium +2,000 option breakeven	+2,000 premium −2,000 option breakeven
Futures price is 65 March/70 put expires +5	−2,000 premium +5,000 option +3,000	+2,000 premium −5,000 option −3,000

*It should be noted that the money manager could also have taken advantage of his interest rate expectations by buying a call option.

†It is plausible that a risk-averse bank would enter a contract which it believes had negative expected value because of its usefulness as a hedge.

‡It is not necessary to write a put and call option at the same strike price. The investor can modify the risk-return relationship by writing options with different strike prices. In each case, the maximum potential profit is the total of the premiums received. The downside break-even point is the put strike price less the total premium received. The upside break-even point is the call strike price plus the total premium received.

Appendix 2: Calculation of Margin Requirements

Margin requirements on options can best be illustrated by an example. Let us consider an investor who wishes to write a call option on thirteen-week Treasury bills on the American Stock Exchange (Amex). Margin requirements are governed by three rules:*

(1) If the option is in the money, the writer must hold a margin equal to the premium plus a fixed amount. In the case of calls on the Amex, the fixed amount is $3,500.

Example: A customer writes an uncovered thirteen-week T-bill call option with a strike price of 88. This means the bill is at a 12 percent discount (*i.e.*, the strike price for $1,000,000 face value of the bill is roughly $970,000). The market price of the bill is 90, that is, the bill is at a 10 percent discount ($975,000 for $1,000,000 face value). The option is selling at $6,250 for $1,000,000 face value of the bill. Thus, the margin requirement is:

Option premium	$6,250
Plus fixed amount	$3,500
Total	$9,750

(2) If the option is out of the money, the writer must hold a margin equal to the premium plus a fixed amount less the amount the option is out of the money.

(3) The minimum margin requirement is the option premium plus $500 per contract.

Example: In the example above, the market price of the T-bill call option falls to 85. The option is selling for $1,500. Thus, the margin requirement is:

Option premium	$1,500
Plus fixed amount	$3,500
Total	$5,000
Minus out-of-the-money amount.	−$7,500
Total	−$2,500

However, the minimum margin requirement is the option premium + $500 per contract. In this example, we have:

$1,500 option premium + $500 or $2,000.

Thus, the maintenance margin requirement is $2,000.

*Additionally, the initial deposit in a new margin account must total at least $2,000.

Appendix 3: Put-Call Parity

The text discussed the relationship between various financial factors and the call option price of new options instruments. This appendix investigates the relationship between prices on put and call options.

To gain some insight into the connection between put and call prices for equity options consider the following portfolio strategy. An investor buys a security for a price of S dollars. He finances his purchase by borrowing Ee^{-rT} dollars, promising to repay E dollars at the expiration of the option. At the same time, he buys a "European" put option for a premium of p dollars. (A European option cannot be exercised before maturity, whereas an American option can.) The initial value of this portfolio is $S + p - Ee^{-rT}$.

At the expiration of the option, the security will be worth S_1. If S_1 is less than E, the investor will exercise the option and receive the exercise price of E with which the maturing loan will be repaid. The value of the investor's portfolio at the expiration date then is zero. If S_1 is greater than E, the investor will not exercise the put option but can sell the security in the market for S_1, repay the loan, and have $S_1 - E$ dollars left over. The payoff structure of this portfolio may be summarized as follows:

Scenario	Value of put option	Value of security	Repayment of loan	Total
$S_1 < E$	$E - S_1$	S_1	$-E$	0
$S_1 \geq E$	0	S_1	$-E$	$S_1 - E$

This portfolio strategy has been selected so that its payoff structure exactly matches that from a European call option (*i.e.*, max $(0, S_1 - E)$). To avoid arbitrage opportunities, a call option must sell for a price equal to the initial price of this equivalent portfolio. Thus, the traditional put-call parity equation:

$$(1) \quad c = p + S - Ee^{-rT}$$

This equation holds for options on individual equities and options on stock indexes.

For bond options, a minor adjustment is needed to take into account coupon payments. Let G_0 be the accrued interest at the time of purchase of the option, and G_1 the accrued interest on the bond at the end of the life of the option. If the call is exercised, the buyer will receive $S_1 - E$. The security's value will be $S_1 + G_1$. If the put is exercised, the buyer will receive $E - S_1$.

Consequently, the investor must borrow $(E + G_1)e^{-rT}$ rather than Ee^{-rT}. Put-call parity can then be rewritten:

$$(2) \quad c = p + S + G_0 - (E + G_1)e^{-rT}.$$

For futures contracts, consider a portfolio which consists of writing a call, purchasing a put, and establishing a long futures position at price F. As before, all instruments have the same expiration date and the options have the same exercise price. At expiration, the payoff where F_1 is the futures price looks like:

Scenario	Sell a call	Buy a put	Buy a futures	Total
$F_1 < E$	0	$E - F_1$	$F_1 - F$	$E - F$
$F_1 \geq E$	$E - F_1$	0	$F_1 - F$	$E - F$

The initial value of this riskless position is the cost of the put less the income received from the call. Discounting the portfolio earnings at maturity and setting them equal to the initial value gives

$$(3) \quad c = p + (F - E)e^{-r_D T}.$$

The relationship between puts and calls on currency options can be derived from this. If interest rate parity holds,

$$(4) \quad F = Se^{(r_D - r_f)T},$$

where r_D is the domestic interest rate and r_f is the foreign interest rate. Arbitrage actions that establish interest rate parity can be conducted by borrowing the foreign currency, buying spot exchange, and investing the proceeds instead of purchasing a futures contract. Thus, equation (4) may be substituted into equation (3) to obtain:

$$(5) \quad c = p + Se^{-r_f T} - Ee^{-r_D T}.$$

A fixed deliverable option is essentially an option on a futures contract that expires on the date the option expires. Intuitively, a three-month call option on a six-month Treasury bill requires that a bill with six months to maturity be delivered at expiration. Purchasing a three-month futures on a six-month bill also requires that a bill with six months to maturity be delivered. Essentially, fixed deliverable options instruments are very similar to options on futures contracts. The same relationship between put and call prices holds as in the case of options on futures.

NOTES

[1] In this example, the issue used is the 10⅜ bond due 2007/12. This issue is traded on the Chicago Board Options Exchange.

[2] An option gives its purchaser the right to buy (or sell) an asset at a specific price up to a specific time but, unlike a futures or forward contract, does not *obligate* the buyer to acquire (or provide) the underlying security. Consequently, the risk distribution for an option is quite different from that for a futures contract. Whatever the price of the underlying security, an option buyer will never lose more than the premium paid. The option seller can never gain beyond the premium charged. At best, the seller will lose nothing and retain the entire premium. With a futures or forward contract, the buyer may gain or lose, depending on the market price at maturity. The lower (higher) the price of the contract at maturity, relative to the original price, the more the buyer will lose (gain) and the seller wil gain (lose).

³ It is interesting to note that, on futures contracts, both the buyer and seller are required to put up original margin requirements. This can be posted in interest-bearing form. If the market moves against them, either buyer or seller may be required to deposit variation margin to meet margin calls. These calls must be met in cash, as the other party can draw them out in cash.

⁴ The difference between fixed deliverable options and variable deliverable options is discussed more fully in Walter L. Eckardt, Jr., "An Analysis of Treasury Bond and Treasury Bill Options Premiums," a paper presented at the second annual options colloquium sponsored by the Amex, New York, N.Y., March 25–26, 1982.

⁵ See Kenneth D. Garbade and Monica M. Kaicher, "Exchange-Traded Options on Common Stock," *Quarterly Review,* Winter 1978–79, pp. 26–40.

⁶ This point can be made by considering the limit case an option on a futures contract which expires the day the futures contract is delivered. The delivery on the option would be settled at once, providing the actual security. Here no distinction exists between an option on the futures contract and an option on the physical. In reality, the options contract expires before the delivery date of the futures contract. For example, for a December option on a bond future, the option would expire in November, resulting in delivery of a December futures contract. It is unlikely that this small difference is enough to sustain two independent markets.

⁷ A Federal Reserve Bank of New York turnover study showed that for April 1983 foreign exchange turnover in the United States was $702.5 billion. Of this, $451.0 billion (or roughly, two thirds) was in spot transactions, $42.0 billion was in outright forwards, and $209.4 billion was in swaps. Foreign exchange futures turnover on the International Monetary Market is less than 10 percent of total foreign exchange turnover.

⁸ Conceptually, options on bonds could be written on a bond with particular characteristics, rather than on a particular bond. However, this would make certain option strategies, such as covered call writing, more difficult as the option would "play to a single debt issue" and the issue may change over the life of the option.

⁹ It should be noted that options on bond futures can be sold only by a CFTC-registered representative, while options on bond physicals can be sold by any registered representative. However, since there is little retail interest in the options on debt securities, this does not aid the exchange trading the options on Treasury debt securities.

¹⁰ See Fischer Black and Myron Scholes, "The Pricing of Options and Corporate Liabilities," *Journal of Political Economy,* May/June 1973.

¹¹ The Black-Scholes option pricing formula can be written as follows:

$$c = SN(d_1) - Ee^{-rT}N(d_2)$$

where
$$d_1 = (\ln(S/E) + (r + 1/2s^2)T)/s \sqrt{T}$$

and
$$d_2 = d_1 - s\sqrt{T}$$

In this formula, c is the value of the option, ln is the natural logarithm, e is the exponential, and s^2 is the instantaneous variance of the stock price. $N(\cdot)$ is the normal distribution function.

¹² The Black-Scholes formula assumes that if the stock's continuously compounded return follows a normal distribution with a constant variance, its expiration price will thus be "lognormally" distributed. While this may be a good approximation for stock indexes and currencies, it is not a good assumption for variable deliverable debt instruments. As mentioned previously, default-free bonds (other than "consols"), unlike common stock, do not have a perpetual life. As maturity approaches, a default-free bond will be valued closer to par; all other factors constant. Thus, even if interest rates remain unchanged, the passage of time alone will cause the price of a default-free bond to change. Consequently, it cannot be assumed that prices of debt instruments follow a random walk. Moreover, the variance of a bond will decline over time. A longer bond will move more in response to a 100 basis point change in interest rates than a shorter bond.

¹³ The model assumes that price movements are independent of the level of interest rates.

¹⁴ A more formal argument can be made as follows: an investor buys 100 shares of stock worth $50 per share on margin. But, instead of securing a typical margin loan, he makes an initial payment of size c, and promises $4,500 in six months. The future payment is promised on a no-recourse basis with the stock used as collateral. If the stock is worth less than $4,500 at expiration, the investor will allow the lender to claim the stock. The investor has purchased a call option with an exercise price of $45 and a time to expiration of six months, c is the premium.

If the loan were riskless, the lender would charge the investor an amount which would cover the difference between the value of the stock being delivered, S, and the present value of the future payment, Ee^{-rT} (in the example above, $4,500 is the future payment). If the loan were not riskless, the lender must charge enough to purchase an insurance premium to allow for the possibility that the stock price will be less than E dollars at expiration, leaving the lender with a loss of $E - S$. Thus, the price of the premium is the present value of the levered position in the stock plus the insurance premium, or $c = S - Ee^{-rT} + 1$, where 1 is the insurance premium. As interest rates rise, the present value of the future payment is less, hence the value of the levered position in the stock increases. Thus, the value of the call option must increase.

[15] Rational optional pricing of futures contracts takes the form:

$$c = e^{-rT} [FN(d_1) - EN(d_2)]$$

where:

$$d_1 = (\ln(F/E) + 1/2s^2T)/s\sqrt{T}$$

and

$$d_2 = d_1 - s\sqrt{T}$$

F is the price of the futures contract. This is the Black-Scholes option pricing formula given in note 11 if $F = Se^{rT}$.

[16] See, for example, George Courtadon, "The Pricing of Options on Default Free Bonds," a paper presented at a Conference on Options Pricing, Theory, and Applications, sponsored by the Salomon Brothers Center for the Study of Financial Institutions (New York University, New York, N.Y., January 18–19, 1982).

[17] See Mark B. Garman and Steven W. Kohlhagen, "Foreign Currency Option Values," unpublished working paper." (School of Business Administration, University of California at Berkeley, December 1982, for a more technical discussion. The authors have shown that the price of a call option on foreign exchange may be written as:

$$c = e^{-rT}SN(d\cdot) - e^{-r_DT}EN(d_2)$$

where:

$$d_1 = (\ln(F/E) + (r_D - r_f + 1/2s^2)T)/s\sqrt{T}$$
$$d_2 = d_1 - s\sqrt{T}$$
$$r_D = \text{domestic interest rates}, \quad r_f = \text{foreign interest rate}$$

Alternatively,

$$C = e^{-r_DT}[FN(d_1) - EN(d_2)]$$

where:

$$d_1 = [\ln(F/E) + (1/2s^2T)]/s\sqrt{T}$$
$$d_2 = d_1 - s\sqrt{T}$$

27

The Federally Sponsored Credit Agencies: An Overview

Michael J. Moran

One of the hallmarks of a sophisticated financial system is a well-developed set of financial intermediaries. In the United States, such institutions as commercial banks, savings and loan associations, insurance companies, pension funds, and investment companies promote the efficient allocation of capital by offering people financial instruments with features they could not obtain by investing directly with the ultimate users of the funds. The advantages of investing through a financial intermediary include a more desirable combination of risk and return, greater liquidity, lower transaction costs, smaller denominations for initial savings balances, and greater flexibility for subsequent additions to these balances. Borrowers and equity issuers, in turn, find a larger and more readily available pool of funds to support their spending plans. In the U.S. economy, an average of roughly 75 percent of net funds supplied and raised each year are channeled through financial intermediaries.

The federal government has established five privately owned intermediaries to channel funds to particular sectors of the economy that are deemed worthy of special support. These institutions are known collectively as the federally sponsored credit agencies:

- Federal Home Loan Banks.
- Federal Home Loan Mortgage Corporation.
- Federal National Mortgage Association.
- Farm Credit Banks.
- Student Loan Marketing Association.

The Congress established the first three intermediaries to broaden the flow of credit to the mortgage and housing markets, and the last two to provide funds to support agriculture and higher education, respectively.

From *Federal Reserve Bulletin,* June 1985, pp. 373–88.

The author is with the Federal Reserve Board's Division of Research and Statistics. Michael Maryn provided research assistance.

The sponsored agencies are expected to facilitate a more desirable outcome at times when market forces might allocate credit in ways that are not socially optimal. For example, mortgage originators and smaller commercial banks might be unable to attract sufficient deposits to meet the demands of potential home-owners and farmers—at least at interest rates that are deemed to be, in some sense, appropriate. Similarly, private lenders may be reluctant to make loans for higher education because of their long maturities or their complex servicing requirements. In other instances, lenders and borrowers in these markets may be mismatched geographically. In the first examples, the federally sponsored credit agencies can channel funds from the money and capital markets to the targeted sector; in the last example, the sponsored agencies serve to transfer funds to the place they are needed and in short supply.

Rather than lending directly to the ultimate borrowers, most of the federally sponsored credit agencies provide funds that private institutions make available to individuals and businesses. The sponsored agencies obtain funds by selling either debt or pass-through securities in the money and capital markets; they channel these funds to private lending institutions either through loan agreements or by buying the assets of the private lenders and thus providing them with funds to make new loans. With these methods, the sponsored credit agencies represent a second layer of intermediation that is built upon the financial structure in the private sector.

Many programs under the direction of the federal government serve an inter-mediary function, but two features of the federally sponsored credit agencies set them apart. First, the sponsored agencies are wholly owned by the private sector. Although they have certain unique ties with the federal government—such as board members appointed by the President and borrowing privileges from the Treasury Department—ultimately it is the stockholders or the borrowers (all private) that stand to benefit or lose from their activities. As private entities, these institutions are not subject to the appropriations process of the federal budget, nor does the Congress directly influence their financing activity or rate of growth. Second, these intermediaries borrow directly in the financial markets to raise funds, whereas other lenders under the direction of the federal government obtain their funds from the Federal Financing Bank, which, in turn, borrows from the Treasury Department. Because the sponsored agencies are privately owned, their debt securities are not guaranteed by the federal government.

One organization that frequently is associated with the federally sponsored credit agencies, but is quite different, is the Government National Mortgage Association—often referred to as GNMA, or Ginnie Mae. This organization is part of the Department of Housing and Urban Development and currently does not issue debt in the money and capital markets. The popular Ginnie Mae se-curities that trade in the marketplace are actually mortgage pass-through certifi-cates issued by mortgage originators, but Ginnie Mae guarantees the timely payment of interest and principal. This institution is not discussed further in this article.

The article next reviews the role of the federally sponsored credit agencies in the U.S. economy, including their growth over the long run and their effectiveness in channeling funds to their respective credit markets. It then discusses the financing activity of the sponsored agencies in the money and capital markets, and reviews their net income performance. The article concludes with a discussion of the future role of these intermediaries in light of some important changes unfolding in the financial system.

THE GROWTH AND CONTRIBUTION
OF THE FEDERALLY SPONSORED CREDIT AGENCIES

The simplified balance sheet for each federally sponsored agency presented in Table 1 reveals the size and nature of their activities. In general, the sponsored agencies are large participants in the U.S. financial system. The combined assets of all five sponsored agencies are about one third the size of those of the entire savings and loan industry and about one half the size of those of private pension funds. The Federal Home Loan Banks (FHLBs), the Federal National Mortgage Association (FNMA, or Fannie Mae), and the Farm Credit Banks (FCBs), taken alone, have assets much larger than those of the largest thrift institution and about the same size as those of the third-largest commercial bank. The Federal Home Loan Mortgage Corporation (FHLMC, or Freddie Mac) holds a much smaller volume of total assets than does each of the three largest sponsored agencies, but, as explained more fully later, the balance sheet understates the magnitude of its activities in the financial markets. The Student Loan Marketing Association (SLMA, or Sallie Mae) is the smallest of the federally sponsored credit agencies, but is still a substantial factor in the credit markets.

The federally sponsored credit agencies hold primarily two types of assets: loans granted to private lending institutions and loans to individuals or businesses that were purchased from private lending institutions or originated directly. The Federal Home Loan Banks issue loans (called "advances") to member savings and loan associations and mutual savings banks. These advances, which can have maturities of up to 20 years, are used by the depository institutions to meet short-term liquidity needs and to expand their asset portfolios. The Student Loan Marketing Association grants loans (called "warehousing advances") to many types of lenders, including commercial banks, thrift institutions, educational institutions, and state lending agencies. Warehousing advances must be used to maintain or expand the size of a lender's student loan portfolio. The Farm Credit Banks lend directly to individuals and businesses as well as to farm associations and cooperatives. The latter groups, in turn, either lend to agricultural and aquatic producers or provide services to the agricultural sector.

The Federal National Mortgage Association and the Federal Home Loan Mortgage Corporation provide secondary markets for mortgage loans—that is, they purchase mortgage loans from originating institutions. In addition to providing funds for loan originations, these programs have served to standardize the terms on conventional mortgage loans. Fannie Mae holds a large portion of the purchased mortgages in its portfolio, while Freddie Mac usually packages them into pass-through certificates and in effect sells them to other investors in the financial markets. Because the issuance of these pass-through securities represents the sale of the underlying mortgages, the total assets of Freddie Mac are not large, and its balance sheet thus understates its role in transferring funds from the money and capital markets to mortgage lenders. Fannie Mae also sells pass-through certificates to investors.

TABLE 1
Balance Sheets of Federally Sponsored Credit Agencies, Year-end 1984
(millions of dollars)

	Assets				Liabilities		
Agency	Loans Purchased from Private Lenders	Loans Made to Private Lenders	Other Assets	Total Assets, or Total Liabilities plus Equity	Credit Market Debt	Other Liabilities	Equity
Federal Home Loan Banks	—	74,616.0	22,376.6	96,992.6	65,085.4	23,203.2	8,704.0
Federal National Mortgage Association	84,429.5	—	3,929.3	88,358.8	83,719.5	3,431.2	1,208.1
Federal Home Loan Mortgage Corporation ...	10,008.4	—	3,144.6	13,153.0	10,185.9	2,360.5	606.6
Farm Credit Banks	—	77,089.0[1]	7,742.5	84,831.5	72,936.3	2,652.9	9,242.3
Student Loan Marketing Association	5,572.9	4,230.1	1,817.2	11,620.2	10,544.9	498.8	576.6

[1] This amount includes loans made directly to individuals and businesses.

The Student Loan Marketing Association also purchases student loans from private lenders, making it the only sponsored agency to provide both lending and secondary market facilities. Most of the loans it purchases are guaranteed either directly or indirectly by the federal government under the Guaranteed Student Loan Program.

This brief description of the federally sponsored credit agencies outlines their role only in general terms. The appendix at the end of this article provides a more complete discussion.

The Growth of the Federally Sponsored Credit Agencies

Since 1970, the combined assets of the federally sponsored credit agencies have grown at a compound annual rate of 13.5 percent. For purposes of comparison, nominal gross national product and total debt of nonfinancial sectors expanded at compound annual rates of 9.75 and 10.75 percent, respectively, over this period. As Chart 1 shows, the growth of the sponsored agencies has not been smooth. The total assets of the Farm Credit Banks, for example, trended upward during the mid-1970s and accelerated beginning in 1979, but they have shown essentially no growth in recent years. The combined assets of the three sponsored agencies in the mortgage market have alternated between rapid growth and no growth, in movements associated closely with cyclical fluctuations in the housing sector. Sallie Mae experienced its strongest growth in 1981, a period of heavy demand for student loans and the year in which it began a transition from financing itself with government loans to borrowing in the financial markets.

Farm Credit Banks.   The growth of total assets at the Farm Credit Banks since 1970 has been closely correlated with conditions in the agricultural sector. In 1972 and 1973, prices of farm commodities increased sharply, paving the way for

CHART 1
Total Assets of the Federally Sponsored
Credit Agencies

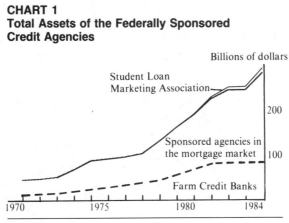

Data are for the year-end.
The sponsored agencies in the mortgage market are the Federal Home Loan Banks, the Federal Home Loan Mortgage Corporation, and the Federal National Mortgage Association.

strong growth in farm income and large gains in the value of the farmland that frequently serves as collateral for farm credit. In this environment, farmers began to take on larger volumes of debt, reflected in the upward trend in the total assets of the Farm Credit Banks. Prices of farm commodities surged again in 1978 and 1979, and in consequence farm debt accelerated.

Beginning in 1980, farm prices began to stabilize while overall prices continued to climb. The weakening in farm income caused many farmers difficulty in servicing their debts. The high levels of interest rates in the early 1980s exacerbated the problems of farmers with short-term or variable-rate debt. As expectations for farm prices and income were revised downward in the 1980s, the value of farmland began to decline, with sharp reductions realized each year from 1981 through 1984. Given the conditions confronting them in the early part of this decade, farmers were unwilling or unable to incur new debt, so the total assets of the Farm Credit Banks leveled off. (A more complete discussion of conditions in the agricultural sector is provided by Emanuel Melichar, "A Financial Perspective on Agriculture," *Federal Reserve Bulletin*, January 1984.)

Sponsored Agencies in the Mortgage Market. Over the last 14 years, the sponsored agencies serving the housing market have experienced three periods of rapid growth. The first two periods, which began in 1973 and 1978, occurred near peaks in housing and mortgage activity and at times of diminishing growth in deposits at thrift institutions (see Chart 2). This confluence of events suggests that the sponsored agencies in the mortgage market were attempting to cushion the cyclical swings in housing activity, which is heavily dependent upon thrift institutions.

On the surface, the rapid growth of the sponsored agencies in the mortgage markets in 1984 closely resembles that in earlier episodes: assets began to expand rapidly near the peak in housing activity, thus helping to cushion the fall. Last year, however, saw some important differences. First, deposit growth at thrift institutions, although volatile, tended to be at much higher levels than in previous

CHART 2
Growth of Total Deposits at Thrift Institutions, and Housing Starts

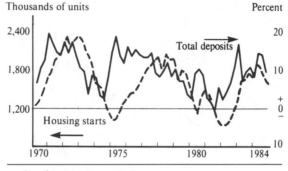

Quarterly data at annual rates.

years. Thus, arguments that the sponsored agencies were forestalling problems of credit availability may be difficult to make. Second, much of the expansion in the assets of the mortgage agencies last year represented FHLB advances to ease the liquidity problems of some financially weak institutions. Finally, a small portion of the expansion of Fannie Mae represented the acquisition of second mortgages, an asset that often supports consumer spending rather than housing activity.

Student Loan Marketing Association. The Student Loan Marketing Association experienced its most rapid rate of growth in the early 1980s: total assets increased from $2.8 billion at the end of 1980 to $9.1 billion at the end of 1983. Rising tuition costs and high levels of interest rates increased the demand for the subsidized student loans guaranteed by the federal government. The average volume of new originations in the Guaranteed Student Loan Program increased from about $2 billion in 1979 and 1980 to about $6 billion over the next three years. (Most of the loans purchased by Sallie Mae are issued under this program.) Sallie Mae's purchases were large as many private lenders elected not to hold these loans in their portfolios.

This burst in the growth of Sallie Mae's assets was associated with a shift in its method of financing. In its early years, the Sallie Mae financed its activities with loans from the Federal Financing Bank. In March 1981, however, Sallie Mae and the Treasury agreed that its level of debt at the Federal Financing Bank would not exceed $5 billion and that it could not take down new loans from this source after 1982. Sallie Mae quickly moved to its limit with the Federal Financing Bank and in 1981 issued debt in the money and capital markets for the first time to finance its rapid expansion.

Effectiveness as Financial Intermediaries

The size and growth of the federally sponsored credit agencies suggest that they are important participants in the U.S. financial system. One measure of their contributions to their specific credit markets is presented in Chart 3. This chart shows that the participation of these intermediaries has trended upward over the last 14 years; currently, they account for sizable portions of the total volume of outstanding credit in their respective markets.

CHART 3
Contributions of Federally Sponsored
Credit Agencies[1]

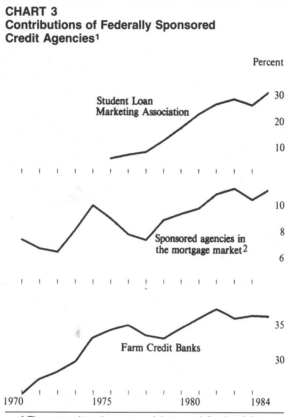

¹ The curves, based on year-end data, are defined as follows:
The top panel shows the ratio of outstanding SLMA advances and loans purchased to outstanding guaranteed student loans; the middle panel shows the ratio of outstanding FHLB advances plus total Fannie Mae and Freddie Mac mortgage assets to total residential mortgage debt outstanding; the bottom panel shows the ratio of outstanding loans from the Farm Credit Banks to total farm debt outstanding.
² This graph understates the contribution of the sponsored agencies in the mortgage market because the pass-through securities issued by Freddie Mac and Fannie Mae are not included.

Although these intermediaries maintain a substantial presence in the financial markets, their net long-run impact on the total volume of funds allocated to each sector is open to question. Changes in the behavior of other lenders and borrowers in the private sector may mean that the credit flows generated by the sponsored agencies supplant rather than supplement funds from other sources. Furthermore, even if the sponsored agencies were successful in channeling funds to a particular credit market, real economic activity in that sector might not be affected. For example, if the sponsored agencies in the mortgage market were able to increase the volume of mortgage credit, housing construction would not increase if households financed their homes with less equity and more debt than they otherwise would have or if they substituted the mortgage credit for other types of borrowing to finance the purchase of consumer goods.

The credit flows generated by the federally sponsored credit agencies may have been offset by disintermediation in the 1960s and 1970s. Commercial banks and thrift institutions frequently had to constrain their lending activity as they experienced weak or negative deposit growth when market rates rose above their interest rate ceilings. The sponsored agencies channeled funds from the money and capital markets to these private lenders to limit the number of displaced borrowers. Over time, however, this assistance may well have been partially negated because the issuance of debt securities by the federally sponsored credit agencies could itself have put further upward pressure on market rates, contributing to slower deposit inflows.

This pattern was especially prevalent in the mortgage market because thrift institutions usually suffered heavy deposit outflows when market rates increased. As Charts 1 and 2 make clear, the rapid growth in the assets of the mortgage agencies in 1973 and 1978 was associated with weak deposit growth at thrift institutions. This weakness probably was exacerbated as the heavy volume of activity by the sponsored agencies maintained upward pressure on market interest rates and thus drew funds out of thrift institutions.

Because interest-rate ceilings on nearly all types of deposit accounts now have been removed, disintermediation, per se, will not compromise the efficacy of the sponsored agencies. However, responses of borrowers and of other lenders to the changes in relative interest rates associated with the financing activities of the sponsored agencies still will influence the ultimate amount of funds allocated to each sector. At the simplest level, the issuance of debt in the capital markets and the use of the proceeds in a particular sector will lower interest rates in the targeted area relative to those in the financial markets. In such circumstances, lenders in the private sector will tend to reduce investments in the targeted area and purchase the relatively more attractive instruments in the money and capital markets. This shift will offset the credit flows provided by the federally sponsored agencies.

The sensitivity of borrowers in the targeted sectors to changes in interest rates also affects the ultimate impact of the sponsored agencies on credit flows. If individuals and businesses increase their borrowing only a little as the sponsored agencies exert downward pressure on interest rates in a particular market, the change in the volume of credit in the sector will be slight. In this case, even though the sponsored agencies may shift large amounts of funds to a particular market, the interest rate in the market would have to fall sharply to establish a new equilibrium and more private lenders will switch to other markets. Alternatively, if borrowers are very sensitive to changes in rates, they will readily absorb most of the new funds advanced by the sponsored agencies and the offsets will be slight.

The ultimate change in credit flows generated by the activity of the sponsored credit agencies is thus uncertain. The final outcome depends upon the responses of borrowers and lenders to interest rates on the targeted type of credit and on other instruments in the economy. In general, if private lenders are prompt to alter their portfolios in response to changes in relative interest rates, and if borrowers in the targeted market are insensitive to changes in interest rates, then the sponsored agencies, on balance, will have little impact. If the reverse holds—that is, if private lenders are not sensitive to interest rate changes and borrowers are— then the sponsored agencies could direct large amounts of credit to a particular sector. Whether or not a broadened flow of credit will influence the level of real economic activity in that sector depends upon the amount of debt that borrowers are willing to bear and the degree of fungibility between credit of different types.

In the mortgage market, borrowers seem highly sensitive to interest rates, so the sponsored agencies may have an important influence on credit flows. However, other lenders in this market—such as commercial banks and life insurance companies—probably would alter their portfolios quickly as relative rates changed. Thrift institutions also may now shift larger amounts of their assets out of mortgages as interest rates change because their investment powers have been expanded in recent years. The Farm Credit Banks probably will have a greater long-run effect on credit flows in their sector than will the sponsored agencies in the mortgage sector because some agricultural lenders, such as commercial banks in rural areas, are less likely to shift away from their accustomed loans to other instruments.

Sallie Mae may be expected to have an appreciable impact on the volume of student loans. The increases in the supply of funds for student lending generated by this sponsored agency will not depress interest rates because a subsidy by the federal government ties the return to lenders of guaranteed student loans to the rate on Treasury bills. Thus, as Sallie Mae expands its activity, private lenders will not have that kind of incentive to switch to other assets. Also, the liquidity that this sponsored agency provides will make lenders more willing to write student loans. Of course, Sallie Mae's activities might not expand college enrollments: students may simply substitute the government-guaranteed loans for others, or they may finance their education with more debt than they would otherwise, or they may attend a more expensive college.

THE MARKET FOR THE SECURITIES
OF THE FEDERALLY SPONSORED CREDIT AGENCIES

Federally sponsored credit agencies finance their loan programs and secondary market purchases primarily by issuing debt in the money and capital markets. These securities are not guaranteed by the federal government, but because of the ties of the sponsored agencies to the government, they are afforded certain privileges not available to most other issues:

- Exemption from the requirement to register the issue with the Securities and Exchange Commission.
- Exemption of interest income from state and local taxes (except for issues of the Federal National Mortgage Association and the Federal Home Loan Mortgage Corporation).
- Eligibility as collateral when commercial banks and thrift institutions borrow from the Federal Reserve's discount window and when thrift institutions borrow from a Federal Home Loan Bank.
- Eligibility for purchase by the Federal Reserve in open market operations.
- Eligibility as collateral for public deposits, including Treasury tax and loan accounts.
- Favorable status in the portfolios of depository institutions; for example, the shorter-term securities may be used to meet the liquidity requirements of thrift institutions belonging to the Federal Home Loan Bank System, and national banks may invest and deal in these securities without limit.

Because of these advantages, as well as the perception that the sponsored agencies are highly creditworthy, the securities are well received by a broad range of investors, including depository institutions, pension funds, insurance companies, and mutual funds. Individual investors also hold these securities, but their direct participation in the market is not great.

The sponsored agencies issue short-term securities known as "discount notes" in the money market, and they tap the longer-term markets through bonds. Those securities are sold in the marketplace with the assistance of a fiscal agent, which recommends to the sponsored agencies the offering rates on the securities and allocates the notes and bonds to securities dealers. Those dealers, in turn, distribute the securities to the public. The sponsored agencies meet the bulk of their financing needs through the issuance of discount notes and bonds, but they also have used some of the more innovative techniques that have emerged in the U.S. financial system in recent years.

Discount Notes and Bonds

Discount notes are short-term debt instruments resembling commercial paper. They have maturities ranging from overnight to 360 days, depending upon their uses. The sponsored agencies use discount notes for several purposes, such as financing short-term loans, bridging gaps that can arise between cash outflows and inflows, and delaying the issuance of longer-term debt until market conditions seem more favorable. Discount notes are offered to investors on a daily basis at interest rates that typically are 15 to 25 basis points higher than those on Treasury bills of similar maturity. At the end of 1984, the sponsored agencies had about $33 billion of discount notes outstanding, accounting for 14 percent of their credit market debt.

The sponsored agencies fill their longer-term financing needs with bonds. The Federal Home Loan Banks, the Farm Credit Banks, and the Federal National Mortgage Association offer bonds to the public each month according to a fixed schedule, and they occasionally bring to market unscheduled offerings as well. The Student Loan Marketing Association recently started to offer floating-rate notes on a monthly basis; the issuance by the Federal Home Loan Mortgage Corporation is irregular. Some of these securities have very short maturities. The Farm Credit Banks, for example, issue six- and nine-month bonds each month, and the other sponsored agencies also occasionally issue bonds with maturities under one year. Most of the longer-term securities issued by the sponsored agencies, however, are in the range of 2 to 10 years; maturities in excess of that are infrequent. Most of the sponsored agencies issue debt with maturities that approximately match those of their assets so they are not exposed to substantial interest rate risk.

The interest rates on intermediate-term bonds issued by the sponsored agencies usually are 15 to 30 basis points higher than the rate on Treasury securities of similar maturity (Chart 4). These spreads typically are narrower than those between Treasury securities and the highest-rated corporate bonds with intermediate maturities. The lower rates on the securities of the sponsored agencies result partly from their unique features and partly from the strong financial condition of their issuers. In addition, the sponsored agencies, either directly or indirectly, have lines of credit with the Treasury Department (at the discretion of its secretary) should they experience difficulty meeting their obligations. (The appendix lists the amounts of these credit lines.) Beyond these factors, some investors believe that, although there is no explicit guarantee, the federal government would not allow a sponsored agency to default on a debt issue.

CHART 4
Average Spread between Yields on Federally
Sponsored Agency Securities and on Treasury
Securities of Corresponding Maturity

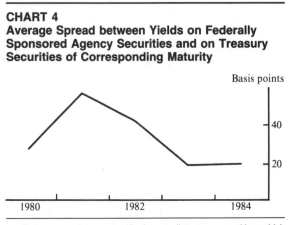

Data are yearly averages for intermediate-term securities, which
have maturities of more than one year up to five years.

Nevertheless, the confidence of investors in the quality of sponsored-agency securites was so shaken in 1981 and early 1982 that the interest-rate spreads over Treasury securities widened (Chart 4). The trigger was the weakening in the net income of the Federal National Mortgage Association (discussed below) and reports from investment analysts that the securities of Fannie Mae carried greater credit risk than previously perceived. Interest rate spreads over Treasury securities on Fannie Mae's debt averaged about 90 basis points in 1981, and some issues came to market with spreads as high as 150 basis points. The risk consciousness of investors during this period affected the other sponsored agencies, and their interest rate spreads widened some even though their financial position was sound. The concerns of investors were allayed in subsequent years as lower levels of interest rates and new strategies adopted by Fannie Mae improved its prospects for profitability. Fannie Mae securities still sell at slightly higher interest rates than do those of the other sponsored agencies, reflecting some residual investor concern and the fact that the interest income on FNMA's securities is taxable at the state and local level.

Innovative Financing

While the federally sponsored credit agencies meet the bulk of their financing needs through the traditional offerings of discount notes and bonds, they also have been involved in innovative transactions in an effort to broaden their investor base and to lower their overall interest expense.

Large current interest savings for some of the sponsored agencies have come from the issuance of long-term, zero coupon securities. These securities do not provide periodic interest payments to investors; rather, they are sold at a substantial discount from the face value that is paid at maturity. In 1984, Fannie Mae, Freddie Mac, and Sallie Mae were able to offer these securities to investors at interest rates as much as 2.5 percentage points below the rates on long-term Treasury bonds because foreign investors, especially the Japanese, were keenly interested in them. Japanese investors could avoid paying taxes on the income from foreign zero coupon securities if they sold them before maturity. The Ministry of Finance in Japan, however, does not permit its investors to hold securities that have been altered in any way, so they cannot purchase the popular zero coupon securities that are formed by stripping apart Treasury debt (although it appears that they will be permitted to purchase zero coupon securities under the Treasury's new STRIPS program). The issues of the sponsored agencies last year thus represented the highest quality zero coupon security available. Late last year, the Ministry of Finance indicated that it was reviewing the tax treatment of such securities, and in March of this year the Japanese legislature voted to subject the gains on the sale of those securities to ordinary income tax rates. The sponsored agencies ceased issuing zero coupon securities last year after the tax treatment was questioned by the Japanese government.

The sponsored agencies have made other efforts to broaden their investor base by issuing securities in foreign countries. In 1984, Fannie Mae and the Federal Home Loan Banks together issued $500 million of debt in the Eurobond market. Like many U.S. corporations, these sponsored agencies were able to issue debt denominated in dollars in foreign countries at interest rates below those in the U.S. market. Fannie Mae's Eurobond issue was sold with an interest rate that was 7 basis points higher than that on a Treasury security of comparable maturity; in the domestic market, a similar issue probably would have yielded at least 25 basis points more than a Treasury security. In subsequent trading in the secondary markets, however, the yields on these securities moved to higher levels, and since then the sponsored agencies have not attempted to issue dollar-denominated debt in foreign countries.

Yet the federally sponsored credit agencies have not avoided the foreign markets entirely. Earlier this year, Fannie Mae and Sallie Mae issued abroad securities that were denominated in Japanese yen. Like the dollar-denominated debt sold in foreign countries, these securities resulted in substantial interest savings. To protect themselves from the risks of exchange-rate fluctuations from such an issue, Sallie Mae and Fannie Mae utilized another innovative financing technique, a currency swap.

Currency swaps involve two parties that issue debt in each other's currencies, then so exchange their payment obligations that each services debt in its home currency. In the case of the recent Sallie Mae and Fannie Mae yen issues, those sponsored agencies could exchange their interest payment obligations with a Japanese firm that issued a comparable amount of debt denominated in dollars. This technique allows a borrower to raise funds in the market in which its interest expenses are lowest, regardless of the currency used in that market, without exposure to exchange-rate fluctuations.

The currency swap is similar to the interest-rate swap used extensively by Sallie Mae and to a lesser extent by Fannie Mae. An interest-rate swap is a transaction in which two parties, one with fixed-rate debt and the other with variable-rate debt, agree to exchange interest-payment obligations, thereby converting their type of payment from fixed-rate to variable-rate, or vice versa. With this type of transaction, the two parties usually find that their overall funding costs are lower than they would have been had they issued their preferred fixed- or variable-rate instrument directly. Sallie Mae, a pioneer in the technique in the United States, wished to issue variable-rate debt because most of its assets carry variable interest rates. However, it had issued so much debt of that type that investors were willing to increase their holdings only at higher rates. Sallie Mae

TABLE 2
Characteristics of Collateralized Mortgage Obligations of the Federal Home Loan Mortgage Corporation, Series A, June 1983

| | Class | | |
Characteristics	A-1	A-2	A-3
Amount sold (millions of dollars ...	215	350	435
Maximum average life (years)	3.2	8.6	20.4
Quoted yeild (percent)	10.70	11.37	11.98
Spread over yield on comparable Treasury securities (basis points)[1]	39	52	84

[1] Spread over closest Treasury constant-maturity yield on June 7, 1983.

found that it could keep its funding costs low and still be protected from interest-rate risk by issuing fixed-rate debt and engaging in an interest-rate swap. Many types of borrowers, such as savings and loan associations and nonfinancial corporations, would be interested in being a counterparty to obtain fixed-rate financing.

Perhaps the most important innovation in the sponsored-agency market is the collateralized mortgage obligation (CMO) introduced by the Federal Home Loan Mortgage Corporation. As its name implies, this security is simply a debt issue backed with mortgages or mortgage-backed securities. The unique feature introduced by Freddie Mac was the division of an issue into various classes, differing from one another in the way principal value is repaid. Table 2 presents an example. The investors in the class A-1 securities receive interest payments as well as all of the scheduled repayments and prepayments on the underlying mortgages; the investors in the other classes receive only interest payments until all the class A-1 securities are retired. Because initially the class A-1 securities receive the repayments on the underlying mortgages, their expected life is relatively short. After the class A-1 bonds are retired, the class A-2 bonds receive both interest payments and mortgage repayments while the class A-3 bonds continue to receive only interest payments. After class A-2 is retired, class A-3 receives both interest payments and mortgage repayments.

This innovation reduces (though it does not eliminate) the major disadvantage of uncertainty about maturity that is associated with mortgage pass-through securities. Because all interest and principal repayments on an underlying pool of mortgages flow through to the holders of pass-through securities, these securities will be retired earlier than expected if prepayments accelerate. Moreover, mortgage prepayments and the paydown of pass-through securities frequently increase when interest rates drop, precisely the time when investors wish to hold longer-term, fixed-rate assets. When a mortgage-related security is divided into various maturity classes, investors have a clearer expectation of when their security will be repaid.

This financing technique has been widely imitated by other issuers in the financial markets. Securities firms, for example, have issued large volumes of bonds collateralized by Ginnie Mae pass-through securities. They found that they could buy the Ginnie Mae pass-throughs in the secondary markets, package them into CMOs, and issue them at lower rates because of the enhanced certainty of maturity. These firms retained as profit the difference between the yield on the Ginnie Mae pass-through securities and the yield on the CMOs. As they began buying Ginnie Mae securities in volume, yields fell sharply: Ginnie Maes were trading 1.75 to 2.00 percentage points over Treasury securities before CMOs were introduced, but subsequently the spread narrowed to less than 1.00 percentage point.

Construction firms also have issued collateralized mortgage obligations. Many homebuilders have established finance subsidiaries in order to offer mortgage loans to potential buyers. After originating these mortgages, they frequently use them as collateral for both straight bond issues and CMOs. (These issues are referred to as "builder bonds" in the marketplace.) Savings and loan associations have also started to use this instrument as a source of funds.

FINANCIAL PERFORMANCE

For the most part, the financial performance of the federally sponsored credit agencies, as measured by their net income, has been quite good. They are able to issue debt in the financial markets at attractive rates, and because most of them do not expose themselves to substantial interest-rate risk, they have realized strong, stable earnings. The Federal Home Loan Banks, the Federal Home Loan Mortgage Corporation, the Farm Credit Banks, and the Student Loan Marketing Association carefully match the maturities of their debt liabilities and of their assets, so their positive interest rate spreads are not wiped out by interest rate fluctuations. As Table 3 shows, these sponsored agencies have consistently earned high income, as measured by the ratio of net income to average assets. For purposes of comparison, this same aftertax income measure has ranged from 0.50 to 0.60 for the commercial banking industry in the early 1980s.

The net income of the Farm Credit Banks has receded some in the last two years. Because these banks are owned by farm cooperatives, the only purpose of profits is to add to capital as total assets increase so as to maintain the same relative cushion for potential loan losses. With asset growth flat, the Farm Credit Banks could reduce earnings. Their borrowers, many of them undergoing financial strain, consequently received some interest-rate relief. Increases in loan losses and in nonperforming loans, however, also reduced profitability and limited the extent of interest-rate relief.

The Federal Home Loan Mortgage Corporation has reported remarkably strong income in the last two years. The favorable performance of Freddie Mac in 1983 and 1984 is partly the result of higher fee income. In 1981, the Federal Home Loan Mortgage Corporation introduced its "guarantor program," which led to a sharp increase in the issuance of its pass-through certificates as well as in its fees for guaranteeing these securities. (The guarantor program is explained in the appendix.) A more important factor behind this income growth has been the corporation's issuance of collateralized mortgage obligations. Freddie Mac earns as income the spread between the yields on the underlying pool of mortgages and on collateralized mortgage obligations.

Fannie Mae has experienced earnings problems because the maturities of its assets and liabilities are mismatched. In general terms, the balance sheet of this sponsored agency resembles that of a typical thrift institution: its assets are

TABLE 3
Ratio of Net Income to Average Assets of Federally Sponsored Credit Agencies (percent)

Year	Federal Home Loan Banks	Federal National Mortage Association	Federal Home Loan Mortgage Corporation	Farm Credit Banks	Student Loan Marketing Association
1978	1.30%	0.54%	0.69%	0.82%	0.78%
1979	1.29	0.34	0.86	0.86	0.50
1980	0.83	0.03	0.67	1.12	0.43
1981	0.82	−0.32	0.53	1.13	0.45
1982	1.24	−0.16	0.97	1.19	0.60
1983	0.96	0.10	2.13	0.64	0.80
1984	1.04	−0.07	2.42	0.52	0.96

concentrated in long-term, fixed-rate mortgages and they are financed primarily with shorter-term debt. As a result, Fannie Mae has experienced the same earnings difficulties as thrift institutions: in the late 1970s and early 1980s, interest expenses increased sharply as market rates moved to high levels while interest income grew much more slowly because of the long maturities of its assets. Fannie Mae's income weakened in 1979 and 1980, and it turned sharply negative in 1981 and 1982. The earnings performance improved in 1983 and 1984 as interest rates moved to lower levels, but this sponsored agency continues to be burdened with a large volume of long-term mortgages carrying relatively low yields.

The lower level of interest rates in effect over the last two years has been an important factor in easing Fannie Mae's losses, but its management also has launched an aggressive campaign to improve its long-run earnings potential. For example, fee income has increased sharply since 1981, primarily because of the issuance of a large volume of pass-through securities. Also, Fannie Mae has shifted its new asset purchases toward interest-sensitive instruments, such as adjustable-rate mortgages and second mortgages. Last year, these type of mortgages accounted for nearly 40 percent of Fannie Mae's new purchases, compared with 5 percent in 1981. Finally, as explained above, Fannie Mae has adopted some innovative financing techniques, such as zero-coupon bonds, interest-rate swaps, and debt issuance in foreign countries, to help reduce its cost of funds.

THE FUTURE ROLE OF THE FEDERALLY SPONSORED CREDIT AGENCIES

Some analysts have speculated that the role of the federally sponsored credit agencies in the economy will shrink as important structural changes in the financial system lessen the need for intervention to support the credit flows to particular sectors. As regulatory constraints are removed and as new instruments are developed, market participants in the private sector can assume a more active role in efficiently allocating credit.

Beginning in 1978, federal regulators allowed depository institutions to offer accounts with interest-rate ceilings tied to the rates on certain Treasury securities, and, in 1980, they began to dismantle the interest-rate ceilings on deposits at commercial banks and thrift institutions. Currently, nearly all categories of deposits can be offered without interest-rate limits. Thus, depository institutions have greater control over their deposit flows. Faced with large demands for credit, they can offer higher rates to depositors, thereby attracting the necessary funds; if they have exhausted their profitable lending opportunities, they can lower their deposit rates, thus discouraging their own inflows and allowing funds to flow to institutions or regions with greater credit demands. In this deregulated environment, depository institutions themselves can perform one of the important functions of the sponsored agencies—namely, transferring funds from capital-surplus areas to capital-deficient areas.

The need for the sponsored credit agencies to redistribute funds geographically also will be lessened with the erosion of the barriers to interstate banking. Recently, regulators have approved several interstate mergers involving financially weak institutions. In addition, some states have approved laws that allow out-of-state bank holding companies to acquire banks within their borders, and others are considering that step. Finally, the initiative of the private sector in moving toward interstate banking has been evident in the development of so-called nonbank banks, institutions that do not provide the full array of banking services and therefore have won approval in some cases to operate in different states. In light of these developments, the Federal Reserve Board recently advocated that the Congress establish a program to move gradually toward interstate banking.

Other recent developments are making mortgage originators less dependent on the sponsored agencies for funds. Depository institutions servicing the mortgage market now have greater direct access to the capital markets through new financial instruments. For example, savings and loan associations are holding larger amounts of mortgage-backed securities as assets, which can readily serve as collateral for new borrowing. The sponsored agencies are still important here, however, because many of these mortgage-backed securities were obtained by exchanging mortgage loans for pass-through certificates with Freddie Mac and Fannie Mae. Also, the collateralized mortgage obligation has been widely accepted by investors, and thrift institutions are beginning to issue their own mortgage-backed bonds as a source of funds. Even institutions that are not large enough to issue collateralized mortgage obligations by themselves can form consortiums to sell these securities in the financial markets. To the extent that depository institutions can tap the money and capital markets directly, the need is lessened for the federally sponsored credit agencies to channel funds to certain areas.

While these developments in financial markets narrow the distinctive role of the sponsored credit agencies, one of their unique attributes remains—namely, the implicit subsidy that their sponsored status confers in the form of lower costs. This implicit subsidy has the effect of raising borrowing costs, to some degree, both to private sectors that are not the beneficiaries of sponsored-agency activities and to the Treasury. With strong demands for credit by the federal government and heightened emphasis on resource allocation through private markets, it is not surprising that this subsidy has come under question.

Most of the attention in this debate has focused on the sponsored agencies serving the mortgage market. In public testimony and in budget proposals, the Reagan administration has advocated the complete privatization of Fannie Mae and Freddie Mac. Thus far, it has not vigorously sought to cut the ties of Fannie Mae and Freddie Mac to the government; rather, it has concentrated on developing policies that improve the competitive position of private firms servicing the secondary mortgage market. The major effort to date was the passage last year of the Secondary Mortgage Market Enhancement Act. Several provisions of this law make it easier for private firms to market mortgage-backed securities, and it limits to some extent the participation of Fannie Mae and Freddie Mac in this market.

A more recent proposal by the administration that would further alter the competitive position of all the sponsored agencies is a provision in the 1986 budget to impose one-time origination fees on their issuance of new debt and of pass-through securities. In the latest form of the proposal, the fees would be phased in beginning with 0.01 percent (1 basis point) of the amount of debt issued in 1986 and eventually increasing to 0.05 percent in 1990. The administration views the fee as a payment for special privileges that the sponsored agencies or their securities receive because of their affiliation with the federal government. Thus far, the Congress has not authorized these fees, but they remain an issue in discussions of deficit reduction measures.

CONCLUSION

The federally sponsored credit agencies were created to alter the flow of funds in cases in which, it was believed, the private markets were not allocating resources to their optimal use. For a long time, however, analysts have questioned the ability of the sponsored agencies to alter appreciably the ultimate allocation of financial capital and real resources. In a system that permits credit to flow with few impediments, private lenders and borrowers can negate the effects of the government-sponsored intermediation. As the U.S. financial system becomes less regulated, the ability of the sponsored agencies to influence the allocation of resources by serving as intermediaries may become even more dubious. If the resulting market solution to resource allocation is still viewed as suboptimal from a social point of view, some form of direct subsidy may be necessary to achieve the desired outcome.

For the time being, the sponsored agencies must be regarded as important participants in the money and capital markets. Their financial resources are substantial, they have developed expertise in their areas, and they are well established among the borrowers and lenders in the credit markets that they serve. Their activities enhance the liquidity in these markets and foster the integration of the various components of the financial system.

APPENDIX: DESCRIPTION OF THE FEDERALLY SPONSORED CREDIT AGENCIES

The appendix table summarizes the organizational characteristics of the federally sponsored credit agencies whose activities are discussed in the text. The following paragraphs examine each agency in greater detail.

The Federal Home Loan Banks

The Congress established the Federal Home Loan Bank System in 1932 to supervise federally chartered savings and loan associations and to provide a credit facility for thrift institutions. The system originally comprised only the Federal

Home Loan Bank Board, which serves primarily as a regulatory agency, and 12 regional Federal Home Loan Banks, which carry out the policies of the board and provide the credit facilities and other services for member institutions. The Federal Savings and Loan Insurance Corporation and the Federal Home Loan Mortgage Corporation were added to the system later, in 1934 and 1970 respectively.

The Federal Home Loan Banks are wholly owned by the financial institutions that join the system. The 12 banks operate individually, but they must observe guidelines established by the board. The most important activity of the banks is to provide credit to members in the form of loans (called advances). The Federal Home Loan Banks finance their advances primarily by selling debt securities in the money and capital markets and by accepting deposits from member institutions. The debt securities are sold on a consolidated basis—that is, they are the joint obligations of all 12 banks. The Federal Home Loan Banks are the only sponsored agency that issues deposit liabilities. Overnight accounts are the largest category of deposit liability at the banks, as they are used by member institutions to invest funds temporarily that otherwise might lie idle. The banks also issue demand and time deposits to their members.

Federal Home Loan Mortgage Corporation

The Federal Home Loan Mortgage Corporation also belongs to the Federal Home Loan Bank System but performs a different function than the 12 Home Loan Banks do. Freddie Mac provides a secondary market for mainly conventional mortgage loans—that is, mortgages that are not insured by the Federal Housing Administration or guaranteed by the Veterans Administration. When the corporation was established in 1970, secondary market facilities for government-insured and -guaranteed mortgages already were in place, but support for conventional home loans was lacking. Freddie Mac was created to fill this gap in the secondary market. It typically purchases mortgages from institutions originating the loans, thereby replenishing lenders' cash positions so they can write new loans.

To a small extent, the Federal Home Loan Mortgage Corporation purchases mortgage loans to hold in its portfolio. More commonly, Freddie Mac purchases mortgage loans, places them in pools, and issues pass-through certificates backed by these loans. When it issues pass-through certificates, the ownership of the underlying mortgage pool is transferred to a trustee, who distributes the cash flow from the pool to the certificate holders. Because Freddie Mac is not the owner of the pool of mortgages, these loans to not appear on its balance sheet. Thus, the $10 billion of mortgage holdings shown in Table 1 in the text greatly understates Freddie Mac's participation in the secondary market.

The volume of pass-through securities issued by Freddie Mac has increased sharply in the last three years because of the introduction of its guarantor program in 1981. Under this program, mortgage investors can exchange whole mortgage loans for FHLMC participation certificates. The interest rates on these pass-through securities are one-half percentage point below the rate on the underlying mortgage loans; the difference represents a fee to Freddie Mac for guaranteeing the pass-through security. These transactions are commonly referred to as "mortgage swaps." From 1982 to 1984, about 85 percent of the new participation certificates issued by Freddie Mac were associated with swaps. Mortgage inves-

Characteristics of Federally Sponsored Credit Agencies

Agency	Stockholders	Influence of the administration	Line of credit with Treasury	Federal tax on income of sponsored agency[1]	State and local tax on interest income of investors
Federal Home Loan Banks...............	Owned by member thrift institutions but operated by the Federal Home Loan Bank Board	President selects all 3 members of the FHLBB	$4.0 billion	No	No
Federal National Mortgage Association....	Owned entirely by private stockholders	President selects 5 of 18 board members; subject to general supervision by HUD	$2.25 billion	Yes	Yes
Federal Home Loan Mortgage Corporation	Nonvoting common stock owned by 12 FHLBs; participating preferred stock issued to member thrift institutions	Same as FHLBs	Indirect line of credit through the FHLBs	Yes[2]	Yes
Farm Credit Banks......................	Owned by farm cooperatives and credit associations	President selects 12 Board members; Secretary of Agriculture, 1	$112 million for Federal Intermediate Credit Banks; $149 million for Banks for Cooperatives; secretary may deposit $6 million in Federal Land Banks	No	No
Student Loan Marketing Association	Lenders under the Guaranteed Student Loan Program may hold voting common stock; individual investors may hold nonvoting common and preferred stock	President selects 7 of 21 Board members including the chairman	$1.0 billion[3]	Yes	No

[1] Interest on all debt of the sponsored agencies is subject to federal taxation.
[2] Effective January 1, 1985.
[3] Sallie Mae also has the authority to sell to the Federal Financing Bank securities backed by student loans.

tors engage in these transactions because the participation certificate has greater liquidity. Also, the participation certificate can serve as collateral in a repurchase agreement; thus, mortgage investors expand their borrowing capabilities by holding the Freddie Mac pass-through securities, rather than mortgage loans.

The common stock of Freddie Mac is owned by the 12 Federal Home Loan Banks. Recognizing that ultimately the thrift institutions that are members of the Federal Home Loan Bank System have a claim on its income, Freddie Mac issued $600 million of participating preferred stock to these institutions in January 1985. The distribution of this stock will be retroactive so it can boost the earnings and net worth position of thrift institutions for 1984; it also will allow a direct payment of Freddie Mac dividends to those institutions in future years.

The Federal National Mortgage Association

The Congress established the Federal National Mortgage Association in 1938 to provide a secondary market for federally underwritten mortgages. Fannie Mae was once part of the federal government, but it was separated in 1968 and now is fully owned by private investors (its shares are traded on the New York Stock Exchange). For many years Fannie Mae could deal only in mortgages underwritten by the Federal Housing Administration or guaranteed by the Veterans Administration; but in 1970, it received authority to buy and sell conventional mortgage loans, and it made its first purchase in 1972.

At the end of 1984, Fannie Mae held $84 billion in mortgages, making it the largest single investor in home loans in the country. This sponsored agency also has issued a large amount of pass-through securities, which are not reflected on its balance sheet. Most of its issuance of pass-throughs is associated with a swap program similar to that of the Federal Home Loan Mortgage Corporation.

Farm Credit Banks

The Farm Credit System has the most complex organizational structure of the five federally sponsored credit agencies. The system is divided geographically into 12 districts. Each district has a Federal Land Bank, a Federal Intermediate Credit Bank, and a Bank for Cooperatives. In addition, a Central Bank for Cooperatives participates in large loans or loans that span more than one district. These 37 banks, along with a large number of cooperative associations that own the banks, form the heart of the Farm Credit System. The Farm Credit Administration, an independent agency of the federal government, provides supervision at the national level.

The Farm Credit System is the oldest of the federally sponsored credit agencies, dating back to 1917, when the Federal Land Banks were established. The other types of Farm Credit Banks followed later: the Federal Intermediate Credit Banks in 1923, and the Banks for Cooperatives in 1933. The underlying purpose of all these banks is the same: to provide an adequate flow of credit to the agricultural sector.

The three types of Farm Credit Banks and their lending associations differ in the types of loans they make. The Federal Land Banks, through a total of about 435 land bank associations, issue primarily longer-term loans for the purchase of farms, farm equipment, or rural real estate. Most of these loans have variable interest rates. The Federal Land Banks account for about 65 percent of the total assets of the Farm Credit System. The Federal Intermediate Credit Banks advance funds to about 370 production credit associations and to other financing institutions, such as commercial banks, that make primarily short-term loans for production or operating purposes. They also write a small volume of loans for farm and rural homes and for farm-related businesses. The Federal Intermediate Credit Banks account for about 23 percent of the total assets of the Farm Credit System.

The Banks for Cooperatives make loans of all types directly to cooperative organizations providing agricultural services. The services include marketing farm products, purchasing farm supplies, or operating public utilities. As with the other

Farm Credit Banks, the Banks for Cooperatives are owned by the cooperative organizations that borrow from them.

At one time, the Federal Land Banks, the Federal Intermediate Credit Banks, and the Banks for Cooperatives each issued their own debt in the financial markets. In 1977, they issued their first consolidated debt (i.e., a security that was the joint obligation of all 37 Farm Credit Banks), and since 1979 all debt issuance has been on a consolidated basis. The Farm Credit Banks tap the short-term markets for a large proportion of their funds because most of their loans have either short terms or variable interest rates.

Student Loan Marketing Association

The Student Loan Marketing Association was created by the Congress in 1972 to provide a secondary market for student loans guaranteed by the federal government. Sallie Mae also encourages the flow of credit to higher education by providing loans to institutions, known as "warehousing advances," so they can write additional student loans.

Most of the student loans purchased by Sallie Mae are granted under the Guaranteed Student Loan Program. These loans are originated by private lending institutions (such as commercial banks, thrift institutions, and educational institutions), and they are guaranteed either directly or indirectly by the federal government. The return on the loans to the holders is adjusted quarterly and set at 3.5 percentage points above the interest rate on three-month Treasury bills (bond-equivalent basis). The federal government makes the entire interest payment while the students are in school; after graduation the students begin repaying the loans based on a fixed-interest rate stated at the outset and the federal government makes a "special allowance" payment to bring the return to 3.5 percentage points above the Treasury bill rate. Sallie Mae also purchases loans granted under other federal programs for higher education, such as the HEAL program (Health Education Assistance Loans) and the PLUS program (loans to parents of dependent undergraduate students and to independent students).

Sallie Mae is considerably smaller than other federally sponsored credit agencies, but its rate of growth over the last five years has been rapid. In addition to acquiring a large volume of new assets, Sallie Mae has broadened its array of services by offering forward purchase commitments, developing special credit plans for law and medical students, and issuing letters of credit to back student loan revenue bonds issued by state or local government agencies. In the summer of 1984, Sallie Mae acquired a savings and loan association in North Carolina to assist in providing its education-related financial services. The Congress at one time considered legislation that would prohibit this type of activity by Sallie Mae, but no legislation is currently pending.

PART FIVE

International Finance

International banking and financial markets have experienced remarkable changes in recent years. Exchange rates have been quite volatile, with the dollar rising dramatically against major currencies in the early 1980s and then declining in late 1985 following government intervention designed to reduce the exchange rate of an "overvalued" dollar. The United States experienced massive deficits in its balance of payments, financed partially by an influx of funds attracted by high real interest rates. The balance of payments position of a number of countries (e.g., the oil-exporting countries) experienced large surpluses during some years and substantial deficits during others. A number of commodity-exporting, less-developed countries amassed massive debts to the world's major banks, raising the possibility that the financial health of these banks would be endangered by defaults on their international obligations.

In the first article in this section, "A Guide to Foreign Exchange Markets," Alec Chrystal presents the basic characteristics of foreign exchange markets, including futures and options markets for currency trades. The use of the foreign exchange markets for arbitrage is discussed and illustrated, and the way in which foreign exchange traders use the market for speculation is explained. A detailed example of covered interest parity is provided.

In the second article in this section, "International Banking Facilities," Alec Chrystal discusses the growth of a new and important vehicle involved in the financing of international trade. As Chrystal points out, international banking facilities (IBF) may be considered "onshore-offshore banks." They are not a new *physical* banking facility; rather, they are a separate set of books within an already existing banking organization, usually a U.S. chartered bank. The institutional changes that made the IBFs possible in the early 1980s—permission by the Federal Reserve for the establishment of these organizations, federal legislation that exempted IBFs from the insurance coverage and assessments imposed by the FDIC, and state laws providing tax concessions—evolved from the desire to bring at least a portion of the Eurodollar market back to the United States. The success of the IBFs (by late 1983, their total assets approached $200 billion) has significantly changed the geographical pattern of international banking.

International financial markets have not only been characterized by the development of new institutions but also by the creation of new financial instruments. In "New Markets in Foreign Currency Options," Brian Gendreau discusses the development of trading in options on foreign currency futures. An option gives the holder the right (though not the obligation) to buy or sell an asset at a future date at a specified price. *Call* options allow the buyer to buy a certain amount of a foreign currency in the future at specified prices. Hence, the buyer benefits if the foreign currency increases in value. In contrast, a *put* option enables buyers to sell a certain amount of foreign currency in the future at a specified price and, hence, the holder of the option gains if the foreign currency depreciates in value. Gendreau discusses the way in which options may be used to hedge the risk of foreign currency fluctuations, both for exchange-listed options and also over-the-counter options.

Evidence on the growth of international banking, with special reference to the entry of foreign banks into the United States market and the regulatory issues that entry creates, is provided by Betsy Buttrill White in "Foreign Banking in the United States: A Regulatory and Supervisory Perspective." The existence of over 400 offices of foreign banks—located principally in New York and California—raises a number of important regulatory issues. In particular, both domestic and foreign bank regulatory agencies are and should be concerned about the soundness of foreign banks operating in the United States, a concern that requires cooperation between different regulatory agencies. Of importance also is the question of equitable treatment of foreign banks operating in the United States, compared to domestic banks, including questions of capital adequacy and allowable functions. As banks expand internationally, pressure is brought to bear upon national regulatory agencies for greater harmonization of their policies.

One of the most serious problems facing the international financial system is, of course, the potential for substantial defaults on massive quantities of debt owed by less-developed countries to major multinational banking organizations—a problem that has often been referred to as the most serious financial crisis since the 1930s. Norman Fieleke in "International Lending on Trial" reviews the causes of the crisis, the solutions that have been adopted to this point, and possible reforms that could be adopted to prevent future problems. The quantities of funds involved are massive. As shown by Fieleke, the total amount of bank loans outstanding to non-OPEC developing countries at year end 1982 exceeded $350 billion, of which more than one third was short-term in nature. While the world economic recession coupled with high interest rates certainly played a role in these financial difficulties, an important issue raised and discussed by Fieleke is the extent to which unwise lending decisions by multinational banks contributed to the problem. He also discusses the importance of developing better data sources as a basis for evaluating international credit requests.

28

A Guide to Foreign Exchange Markets

K. Alec Chrystal

The economies of the free world are becoming increasingly interdependent. U.S. exports now amount to almost 10 percent of gross national product. For both Britain and Canada, the figure currently exceeds 25 percent. Imports are about the same size. Trade of this magnitude would not be possible without the ability to buy and sell currencies. Currencies must be bought and sold because the acceptable means of payment in other countries is not the U.S. dollar. As a result, importers, exporters, travel agents, tourists, and many others with overseas business must change dollars into foreign currency or the reverse, or both.

The trading of currencies takes place in foreign exchange markets whose major function is to facilitate international trade and investment. Foreign exchange markets, however, are shrouded in mystery. One reason for this is that a considerable amount of foreign exchange market activity does not appear to be related directly to the needs of international trade and investment.

The purpose of this paper is to explain how these markets work.[1] The basics of foreign exchange will first be described. This will be followed by a discussion of some of the more important activities of market participants. Finally, there will be an introduction to the analysis of a new feature of exchange markets—currency options. The concern of this paper is with the structure and mechanics of foreign exchange markets, not with the determinants of exchange rates themselves.

THE BASICS OF FOREIGN EXCHANGE MARKETS

There is an almost bewildering variety of foreign exchange markets. Spot markets and forward markets abound in a number of currencies. In addition, there are diverse prices quoted for these currencies. This section attempts to bring order to this seeming disarray.

From *Review,* Federal Reserve Bank of St. Louis, March 1984, pp. 5–18.

K. Alec Chrystal, professor of economics-elect, University of Sheffield, England, is a visiting scholar at the Federal Reserve Bank of St. Louis. Leslie Bailis Koppel provided research assistance. The author wishes to thank Joseph Hempen, Centerre Bank, St. Louis, for his advice on this paper.

435

Spot, Forward, Bid, Ask

Virtually every major newspaper, such as *The Wall Street Journal* or the *London Financial Times,* prints a daily list of exchange rates. These are expressed either as the number of units of a particular currency that exchange for one U.S. dollar or as the number of U.S. dollars that exchange for one unit of a particular currency. Sometimes both are listed side by side (see Table 1).

For major currencies, up to four different prices typically will be quoted. One is the "spot" price. The others may be "30 days forward," "90 days forward," and "180 days forward." These may be expressed either in "European terms" (such as number of $ per £) or in "American terms" (such as number of £ per $). (See the glossary at the end of this article for further explanation.)

The spot price is what you must pay to buy currencies for immediate delivery (two working days in the interbank market; over the counter, if you buy bank notes or travelers checks). The forward prices for each currency are what you will have to pay if you sign a contract today to buy that currency on a specific future date (30 days from now, and so on). In this market, you pay for the currency when the contract matures.

Why would anyone buy and sell foreign currency forward? There are some major advantages from having such opportunities available. For example, an exporter who has receipts of foreign currency due at some future date can sell those funds forward now, thereby avoiding all risks associated with subsequent adverse exchange-rate changes. Similarly, an importer who will have to pay for a shipment of goods in foreign currency in, say, three months can buy the foreign exchange forward and, again, avoid having to bear the exchange-rate risk.

The exchange rates quoted in the financial press (e.g., those in Table 1) are not the ones individuals would get at a local bank. Unless otherwise specified, the published prices refer to those quoted by banks to other banks for currency deals in excess of $1 million. Even these prices will vary somewhat depending upon whether the bank buys or sells. The difference between the buying and selling price is sometimes known as the "bid/ask spread." The spread partly reflects the banks' costs and profit margins in transactions; however, major banks make their profits more from capital gains than from the spread.[2]

The market for bank notes and travelers checks is quite separate from the interbank foreign exchange market. For smaller currency exchanges, such as an individual going on vacation abroad might make, the spread is greater than in the interbank market. This presumably reflects the larger average costs—including the exchange-rate risks that banks face by holding bank notes in denominations too small to be sold in the interbank market—associated with these smaller exchanges. As a result, individuals generally pay a higher price for foreign exchange than those quoted in the newspapers.

An example of the range of spot exchange rates available is presented in Table 2, which shows prices for deutsche marks and sterling quoted with a one-hour period on November 28, 1983. There are two important points to notice. First, all except those in the first line are prices quoted in the interbank, or wholesale, market for transactions in excess of $1 million. The sterling prices have a bid/ask spread of only 0.1 cent (which is only about 0.07 percent of the price, or $7 on $10,000). On DM, the spread per dollars worth works out to be about half that on sterling ($4 on $10,000).[3]

Second, the prices quoted by local banks for small, or retail, transactions,

TABLE 1
Foreign Exchange Rate Quotations

Foreign Exchange

Wednesday, September 7, 1983
The New York foreign exchange selling rates below apply to trading among banks in amounts of $1 million and more, as quoted at 3 p.m. Eastern time by Bankers Trust Co. Retail transactions provide fewer units of foreign currency per dollar.

Country	U.S. $ equiv. Wed.	U.S. $ equiv. Tues.	Currency per U.S. $ Wed.	Currency per U.S. $ Tues.
Argentina (Peso)	.09652	.09652	10.36	10.36
Australia (Dollar)	.8772	.8777	1.1340	1.1393
Austria (Schilling)	.05296	.0560	18.88	17.84
Belgium (Franc)				
Commercial rate	.01851	.01855	54.01	53.90
Financial rate	.01844	.01846	54.21	54.15
Brazil (Cruzeiro)	.001459	.00149	685.	671.00
Britain (Pound)	1.4910	1.5000	.6707	.6666
30-Day Forward	1.4915	1.5004	.6704	.6664
90-Day Forward	1.4930	1.5010	.6697	.6662
180-Day Forward	1.4952	1.5028	.6688	.6654
Canada (Dollar)	.8120	.8123	1.2315	.2310
30-Day Forward	.8125	.8128	1.2307	1.2303
90-Day Forward	.8134	.8137	1.2293	1.2289
180-Day Forward	.8145	.8147	1.2277	1.2274
Chile (Official rate)	.01246	.01246	80.21	80.21
China (Yuan)	.50499	.50489	1.9802	1.9806
Colombia (Peso)	.01228	.01228	81.4	81.40
Denmark (Krone)	.10362	.10405	9.65	9.6100
Ecuador (Sucre)				
Official rate	.02082	.02082	48.03	48.03
Floating rate	.010917	.010917	91.60	91.60
Finland (Markka)	.17424	.17485	5.7390	5.7190
France (Franc)	.1238	.1238	8.0750	8.0750
30-Day Forward	.1235	.1230	8.0955	8.1300
90-Day Forward	.1224	.1223	8.1695	8.1725
180-Day Forward	.1203	.1202	8.3100	8.3150
Greece (Drachma)	.01075	.01078	93.	92.70
Hong Kong (Dollar)	.1297	.13089	7.71	7.6400
India (Rupee)	.0980	.0980	10.20	10.20
Indonesia (Rupiah)	.001015	.001015	985.	985.
Ireland (Punt)	1.1715	1.1775	.8536	.8493
Israel (Shekel)	.0173	.0173	57.80	57.80
Italy (Lira)	.000624	.0006255	1602.	1598.50
Japan (Yen)	.004072	.004067	245.55	245.85
30-Day Forward	.004083	.004079	244.88	245.15
90-Day Forward	.004107	.004102	243.48	243.75
180-Day Forward	.004147	.004142	241.10	241.39
Lebanon (Pound)	.20618	.20618	4.85	4.85
Malaysia (Ringgit)	.42462	.42489	2.3550	2.3535
Mexico (Peso)				
Floating rate	.00665	.00666	150.25	150.00
Netherlands (Guilder)	.33288	.3333	3.0040	3.000
New Zealand (Dollar)	.6497	.6505	1.5397	1.5327
Norway (Krone)	.13368	.1340	7.48	7.4625
Pakistan (Rupee)	.07518	.07518	13.30	13.30
Peru (Sol)	.0005105	.0005105	1958.89	1958.89
Philippines (Peso)	.09085	.09085	11.007	11.007
Portugal (Escudo)	.00804	.00807	124.35	123.90
Saudi Arabia (Riyal)	.28735	.28735	3.48	3.48
Singapore (Dollar)	.46609	.4664	2.1455	2.1440
South Africa (Rand)	.8870	.8900	1.1273	1.1236
South Korea (Won)	.001285	.001285	778.20	778.20
Spain (Peseta)	.00655	.00658	152.60	151.90
Sweden (Krona)	.12635	.12666	7.9140	7.8950
Switzerland (Franc)	.4596	.4591	2.1755	2.1780
30-Day Forward	.4619	.4615	216.46	2.1666
90-Day Forward	.4662	.4657	2.1449	2.1470
180-Day Forward	.4728	.4723	2.1150	2.1172
Taiwan (Dollar)	.02489	.02489	40.17	40.17
Thailand (Baht)	.043459	.043459	23.01	23.01
Uruguay (New Peso)				
Financial	.02798	.02798	35.73	35.73
Venezuela (Bolivar)				
Official rate	.23256	.23256	4.30	4.30
Floating rate	.07194	.07272	13.90	13.75
W. Germany (Mark)	.3726	.3726	2.6835	2.6835
30-Day Forward	.3740	.3741	2.6731	2.6728
90-Day Forward	.3767	.3768	2.6540	2.6538
180-Day Forward	.3808	.3808	2.6260	2.6259
SDR	1.04637	1.04903	.955685	.953625

Special Drawing Rights are based on exchange rates for the U.S., West German, British, French and Japanese currencies. Source: International Monetary Fund.
z-Not quoted.

The Dollar Spot and Forward

Sept 7	Day's spread	Close	One month	% p.a.	Three months	% p.a.
UK†	1.4860-1.4975	1.4910-1.4920	0.02-0.07c dis	−0.36	0.17-0.22dis	−0.52
Ireland†	1.1665-1.1720	1.1710-1.1720	0.36-0.30c pm	3.39	0.88-0.78 pm	2.84
Canada	1.2305-1.2320	1.2310-1.2315	0.09-0.06c pm	0.73	0.24-0.21 pm	0.73
Nethlnd.	3.0050-3.0150	3.0050-3.0070	1.12-1.02c pm	4.26	3.00-2.90 pm	3.92
Belgium	54.06-54.20	54.06-54.08	7-6c pm	1.44	14-11 pm	0.92
Denmark	9.6400-9.6800	9.6400-9.6450	2-2¹₂ore dis	−2.79	par-¹₂ dis	−0.10
W. Ger.	2.6850-2.6980	2.6865-2.6875	1.07-1.02pf pm	4.66	3.00-2.95 pm	4.42
Portugal	124.20-125.00	124.40-124.70	115-290c dis	−19.51	330-790dis	−17.98
Spain	152.40-152.70	152.50-152.60	170-220c dis	−15.33	675-775dis	−18.99
Italy	1604-1608	1605-1606	10-10¹₂lire dis	−7.65	29¹₂-31 dis	−7.53
Norway	7.4730-7.4940	7.4730-7.4780	1.90-2.20ore dis	−3.29	5.90-6.20ds	−3.23
France	8.0775-8.1225	8.0825-8.0875	2.02-2.12c dis	−3.07	9.65-9.85ds	−4.81
Sweden	7.9120-7.9265	7.9120-7.9170	0.90-1.10ore dis	−1.51	2.25-2.45ds	−1.19
Japan	245.50-246.50	245.65-245.75	0.69-0.64y pm	3.24	2.11-2.03 pm	3.36
Austria	18.89-18.95¹₂	18.89-18.90	7.50-6.70gro pm	4.50	21.00-18.50 pm	4.17
Switz.	2.1770-2.1875	2.1800-2.1810	1.10-1.05c pm	5.91	3.10-3.05 pm	5.63

†UK and Ireland are quoted in U.S. currency. Forward premiums and discounts apply to the U.S. dollar and not to the individual currency.
Belgian rate is for convertible francs. Financial franc 54.40-54.45.

Sources: *The Wall Street Journal*, September 8, 1983 (left); *London Financial Times*, September 8, 1983 (right).

which serve only as a guide and do not necessarily represent prices on actual deals, involve a much larger bid/ask spread. These retail spreads vary from bank to bank, but are related to (and larger than) the interbank rates. In some cases, they may be of the order of 4 cents or less on sterling, though the prices quoted in St. Louis involved average spreads of 8 cents on sterling. The latter represents a spread of about 5.5 percent (about $550 per $10,000 transaction). The equivalent spread for DM was 7 percent ($700 per $10,000 transaction).

The spread on forward transactions will usually be wider than on spot, es-

TABLE 2
Dollar Price of Deutsche Marks and
Sterling at Various Banks

	Deutschemark		Sterling	
	Buy	Sell	Buy	Sell
Retail				
Local (St. Louis) banks (avg.)	.3572–.3844		1.4225–1.5025	
Wholesale				
New York banks	.3681–.3683		1.4570–1.4580	
European banks (high)	.3694–.3696		1.4573–1.4583	
European banks (low)	.3677–.3678		1.4610–1.4620	
Bankers trust	.3681		1.4588	

Note: These prices were all quoted on November 28, 1983, between 2:00 p.m. and 2:45 p.m. (Central Standard Time). Prices for local banks were acquired by telephoning for their price on a $10,000 transaction. The prices quoted were reference rates and not the final price they would offer on a firm transaction. Figure for Bankers Trust is that given in the *Wall Street Journal,* November 29, 1983, as priced at 2:00 p.m. (Central Standard Time) on November 28, 1983. Other prices were taken from the Telerate information system at 2:35 p.m. New York prices were the latest available (Morgan and Citibank, respectively). European prices were the last prices quoted before close of trading in Europe by various banks. Deutschemark prices were actually quoted in American terms. The sell prices above have been rounded up. The difference between buy and sell prices for DM in the interbank market actually worked out at $0.00015.

pecially for longer maturities. For interbank trade, the closing spread on one and three months forward sterling on September 8, 1983, was 0.15 cents, while the spot spread was 0.10 cents. This is shown in the top line of the *Financial Times* report in Table 1. Of course, like the spot spread, the forward spread varies with time of day and market conditions. At times it may be as low as 0.02 cents. No information is available for the size of spread on the forward prices typically offered on small transactions, since the retail market on forward transactions is very small.

HOW DOES "THE" FOREIGN EXCHANGE MARKET OPERATE?

It is generally not possible to go to a specific building and "see" the market where prices of foreign exchange are determined. With few exceptions, the vast bulk of foreign exchange business is done over the telephone between specialist divisions of major banks. Foreign exchange dealers in each bank usually operate from one room; each dealer has several telephones and is surrounded by video screens and news tapes. Typically, each dealer specializes in one or a small number of markets (such as sterling/dollar or deutsche mark/dollar). Trades are conducted with other dealers who represent banks around the world. These dealers typically deal regularly with one another and are thus able to make firm commitments by word of mouth.

Only the head or regional offices of the larger banks actively deal in foreign exchange. The largest of these banks are known as "market makers," since they stand ready to buy or sell any of the major currencies on a more or less continuous basis. Unusually large transactions, however, will only be accommodated by market makers on more favorable terms. In such cases, foreign exchange brokers may be used as middlemen to find a taker or takers for the deal. Brokers (of which there are four major firms and a handful of smaller ones) do not trade on their own account, but specialize in setting up large foreign exchange transactions in return for a commission (typically 0.03 cents or less on the sterling spread). In April 1983, 56 percent of spot transactions by value involving banks in the United States were channeled through brokers.[4] If all interbank transactions are included, the figure rises to 59 percent.

Most small banks and local offices of major banks do not deal directly in the interbank foreign exchange market. Rather, they typically will have a credit line with a large bank or their head office. Transactions will thus involve an extra step (see Figure 1). The customer deals with a local bank, which in turn deals with a major bank or head office. The interbank foreign exchange market exists between the major banks either directly or indirectly via a broker.

FUTURES AND OPTION MARKETS FOR FOREIGN EXCHANGE

Until very recently, the interbank market was the only channel through which foreign exchange transactions took place. The past decade has produced major innovations in foreign exchange trading. On May 16, 1972, the International Money Market (IMM) opened under the auspices of the Chicago Mercantile Exchange. One novel feature of the IMM is that it provides a trading floor on which deals are struck by brokers face to face, rather than over telephone lines. The most significant difference between the IMM and the interbank market, however, is that trading on the IMM is in futures contracts for foreign exchange, the typical business being contracts for delivery on the third Wednesday of March, June, September, or December. Activity at the IMM has expanded greatly since its opening. For example, during 1972, 144,336 contracts were traded; the figure for 1981 was 6,121,932.

There is an important distinction between "forward" transactions and "futures" contracts. The former are individual agreements between two parties, say, a bank and customer. The latter is a contract traded on an organized market of a standard size and settlement date, which is resalable at the market price up to the close of trading in the contract. These organized markets are discussed more fully below.

While the major banks conduct foreign exchange deals in large denominations, the IMM trading is done in contracts of standard size which are fairly small. Examples of the standard contracts at present are £25,000; DM125,000; Canadian $100,000. These are actually smaller today than in the early days of the IMM.

Further, unlike prices on the interbank market, price movements in any single day are subject to specific limits at the IMM. For example, for sterling futures, prices are not allowed to vary more than $0.500 away from the previous day's settlement price; this limit is expanded if it is reached in the same direction for two successive days. The limit does not apply on the last day a contract is traded.

Unlike the interbank market, parties to a foreign exchange contract at the IMM

FIGURE 1
Structure of Foreign Exchange Markets

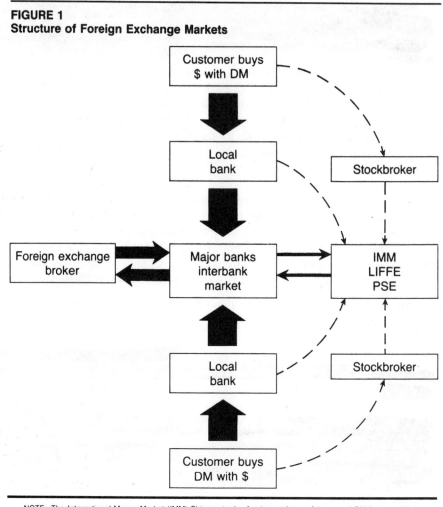

NOTE: The International Money Market (IMM) Chicago trades foreign exchange futures and DM futures options.
The London International Financial Futures Exchange (LIFFE) trades foreign exchange futures.
The Philadelphia Stock Exchange (PSE) trades foreign currency options.

typically do not know each other. Default risk, however, is minor because contracts are guaranteed by the exchange itself. To minimize the cost of this guarantee, the exchange insists upon "margin requirements" to cover fluctuations in the value of a contract. This means that an individual or firm buying a futures contract would, in effect, place a deposit equal to about 4 percent of the value of the contract.[5]

Perhaps the major limitation of the IMM from the point of view of importers or exporters is that contracts cover only eight currencies—those of Britain, Canada, West Germany, Switzerland, Japan, Mexico, France and the Netherlands—and they are specified in standard sizes for particular dates. Only by chance will these conform exactly to the needs of importers and exporters. Large firms and financial institutions will find the market useful, however, if they have a fairly continuous stream of payments and receipts in the traded foreign currencies. Although contracts have a specified standard date, they offer a fairly flexible method of avoiding exchange-rate risk because they are marketable continuously.

A major economic advantage of the IMM for nonbank customers is its low transaction cost. Though the brokerage cost of a contract will vary, a "round trip" (i.e., one buy and one sell) costs as little as $15. This is only 0.04 percent of the value of a sterling contract and less for some of the larger contracts. Of course, such costs are high compared with the interbank market, where the brokerage cost on DM 1 million would be about $6.25 (the equivalent-valued eight futures contracts would cost $60 in brokerage, taking $7.50 per single deal). They are low, however, compared with those in the retail market, where the spread may involve a cost of up to 2.5 percent or 3.0 percent per transaction.

A market similar to the IMM, the London International Financial Futures Exchange (LIFFE), opened in September 1982. On LIFFE, futures are traded in sterling, deutsche marks, Swiss francs, and yen in identical bundles to those sold on the IMM. In its first year, the foreign exchange business of LIFFE did not take off in a big way. The major provider of exchange-rate risk coverage for business continues to be the bank network. Less than 5 percent of such cover is provided by such markets as IMM and LIFFE at present.

An entirely new feature of foreign exchange markets that has arisen in the 1980s is the existence of option markets.[6] The Philadelphia Exchange was the first to introduce foreign exchange options. These are in five currencies (deutsche mark, sterling, Swiss franc, yen, and Canadian dollar). Trades are conducted in standard bundles half the size of the IMM futures contracts. The IMM introduced an options market in German marks on January 24, 1984; this market trades options on futures contracts, whereas the Philadelphia options are for spot currencies.

Futures and options prices for foreign exchange are published daily in the financial press. Table 3 shows prices for February 14, 1984, as displayed in *The Wall Street Journal* on the following day. Futures prices on the IMM are presented for five currencies (left-hand column). There are five contracts quoted for each currency: March, June, September, December, and March 1985. For each contract, opening and last settlement (settle) prices, the range over the day, the change from the previous day, the range over the life of the contract, and the number of contracts outstanding with the exchange (open interest) are listed.

Consider the March and June DM futures. March futures opened at $0.3653 per mark and closed at $0.3706 per mark; June opened at $0.3698 per mark and closed at $0.3746 per mark. Turn now to the Chicago Mercantile Exchange (IMM) futures options (center column). These are options on the futures contracts just discussed (see inset for explanation of options). Thus, the line labeled "Futures" lists the settle prices of the March and June futures as above.

Let us look at the call options. These are rights to buy DM futures at specified prices—the strike price. For example, take the call option at strike price 35. This means that one can purchase an option to buy DM 125,000 March futures up to the March settlement date for $0.3500 per mark. This option will cost 2.05 cents per mark, or $2,562.50, plus brokerage fees. The June option to buy June futures DM at $0.3500 per mark will cost 2.46 cents per mark, or $3,075.00, plus brokerage fees. The March call option at strike price $0.3900 per mark costs only 0.01 cents

TABLE 3
Futures and Options Markets

Futures Prices

Tuesday, February 14, 1984.
Open Interest Reflects Previous Trading Day.

	Open	High	Low	Settle	Change	Lifetime High	Lifetime Low	Open Interest
BRITISH POUND (IMM)—25,000 pounds; $ per pound								
Mar	1.4150	1.4400	1.4150	1.4370	+ .0170	1.6010	1.3930	17,694
June	1.4175	1.4435	1.4175	1.4395	+ .0170	1.5520	1.3950	3,251
Sept	1.4285	1.4410	1.4220	1.4410	+ .0160	1.5240	1.3980	157
Dec	1.4280	1.4435	1.4245	1.4435	+ .0160	1.4650	1.3990	75
Mar85	1.4280	1.4460	1.4270	1.4470	+ .0170	1.4625	1.4000	65
Est vol 10,651; vol Mon 1,987; open int 21,242, +78.								
CANADIAN DOLLAR (IMM)—100,000 dlrs.; $ per Can $								
Mar	.8010	.8024	.8010	.8020	....	.8169	.7979	4,033
June	.8014	.8029	.8013	.8023	....	.8168	.7983	740
Sept				.8026	....	.8147	.7988	312
Dec	.8021	.8031	.8021	.8029	....	.8040	.8021	152
Mar85	.8035	.8035	.8035	.8032	....	.8035	.8023	50
Est vol 1,087; vol Mon 535; open int 5,287, -103								
JAPANESE YEN (IMM) 12.5 million yen; $ per yen (.00)								
Mar	.4276	.4297	.4276	.4294	+ .0011	.4396	.4125	25,730
June	.4315	.4337	.4312	.4334	+ .0011	.4435	.4180	3,908
Sept	.4354	.4375	.4354	.4374	+ .0012	.4450	.4354	974
Dec	.4416	.4420	.4400	.4415	+ .0012	.4493	.4395	271
Est vol 9,133; vol Mon 3,306; open int 30,883, +534.								
SWISS FRANC (IMM)—125,000 francs; $ per franc								
Mar	.4495	.4556	.4486	.4549	+ .0047	.5230	.4470	24,164
June	.4564	.4629	.4557	.4622	+ .0051	.5045	.4536	3,165
Sept	.4632	.4692	.4632	.4688	+ .0052	.5020	.4598	153
Dec	.4705	.4780	.4705	.4747	+ .0049	.4880	.4665	71
Mar85				.4830	+ .0050	.4840	.4755	5
Est vol 30,610; vol Mon 8,466; open int 27,558, +296.								
W. GERMAN MARK (IMM)—125,000 marks; $ per mark								
Mar	.3653	.3713	.3650	.3706	+ .0036	.4100	.3537	30,974
June	.3698	.3754	.3688	.3746	+ .0037	.4002	.3568	4,911
Sept	.3743	.3790	.3743	.3780	+ .0034	.4030	.3602	362
Dec	.3780	.3825	.3780	.3825	+ .0043	.3825	.3640	204
Mar85				.3838	+ .0035	.3699	.3699	1
Est vol 30,248; vol Mon 9,045; open int 36,452, +680.								

Futures Options

Chicago Mercantile Exchange
W. GERMAN MARK—125,000 marks, cents per mark

Strike Price	Calls—Settle Mar	Calls—Settle Jun	Puts—Settle Mar	Puts—Settle Jun
34			0.01	0.01
35	2.05	2.46	0.01	0.09
36	1.11	1.66	0.06	0.25
37	0.38	1.00	0.33	0.57
38	0.10	0.54	1.00	1.02
39	0.01	0.27	....	....
Futures	3706	3746		

Estimated total vol. 2,187.
Calls: Mon vol. 180: open int. 2,416.
Puts: Mon vol. 73: open int. 1,841.

Foreign Currency Options

Philadelphia Exchange

Option & Underlying Price	Strike	Calls—Last Mar	Calls—Last Jun	Calls—Last Sep	Puts—Last Mar	Puts—Last Jun	Puts—Last Sep
12,500 British Pounds-cents per unit.							
BPound	140	3.40	r	5.70	0.40	1.85	r
143.00	145	0.70	2.40	r	3.40	r	r
50,000 Canadian Dollars-cents per unit.							
CDollar	.80	r	r	0.68	r	r	r
62,500 West German Marks-cents per unit.							
DMark	34	2.67	r	r	r	r	r
36.88	35	1.99	2.18	r	r	r	r
36.88	36	1.04	1.59	r	0.05	0.35	r
36.88	37	0.38	1.00	r	0.37	0.56	r
36.88	38	0.10	0.62	0.85	r	r	r
36.88	39	r	0.28	s	r	r	s
36.88	40	0.01	0.11	s	r	r	s
6,250,000 Japanese Yen-100ths of a cent per unit.							
JYen	42	0.95	1.49	2.04	r	r	r
42.75	43	0.30	0.90	r	0.50	0.60	r
42.75	44	0.04	0.45	0.99	r	r	r
62,500 Swiss Francs-cents per unit.							
SFranc	44	r	3.15	r	r	0.24	r
45.18	45	0.65	r	r	0.26	r	r
45.18	46	0.28	1.09	1.82	r	1.00	r
45.18	47	0.06	r	r	r	r	r
45.18	48	0.02	0.28	r	r	r	r
Total call vol.		2,271	Call open int.	37,349			
Total put vol.		799	Put open int.	26,173			

r—Not traded.　s—No option offered.　o—Old.
Last is premium (purchase price).

Source: *The Wall Street Journal*, February 15, 1984.

per mark, or $12.50. These price differences indicate that the market expects the dollar price of the mark to exceed $0.3500, but not to rise substantially above $0.3900.

Notice that when you exercise a futures call option you buy the relevant futures contract but only fulfill that futures contract at maturity. In contrast, the Philadelphia foreign currency options (right column) are options to buy foreign exchange (spot) itself, rather than futures. So, when a call option is exercised, foreign currency is obtained immediately.

The only difference in presentation of the currency option prices as compared with the futures options is that, in the former, the spot exchange rate is listed for comparison, rather than the futures price. Thus, on the Philadelphia exchange, call options on March DM 62,500 at strike price $0.3500 per mark cost 1.99 cents per mark, or $1,243.75, plus brokerage. Brokerage fees here would be of the same order as on the IMM, about $16 per transaction round trip, per contract.

We have seen that there are several different markets for foreign exchange—spot, forward, futures, options on spot, options on futures. The channels through which these markets are formed are, however, fairly straightforward (see Figure 1). The main channel is the interbank network, though for large interbank transactions, foreign exchange brokers may be used as middlemen.

FOREIGN EXCHANGE MARKET ACTIVITIES

Much foreign exchange market trading does not appear to be related to the simple basic purpose of allowing businesses to buy or sell foreign currency in order, say, to sell or purchase goods overseas. It is certainly easy to see the usefulness of the large range of foreign exchange transactions available through the interbank and organized markets (spot, forward, futures, options) to facilitate trade between nations. It is also clear that there is a useful role for foreign exchange brokers in helping to "make" the interbank market. There are several other activities, however, in foreign exchange markets that are less well understood and whose relevance is less obvious to people interested in understanding what these markets accomplish. (See the feature, "Foreign Exchange Options.")

Two major classes of activity will be discussed. First, the existence of a large number of foreign exchange markets in many locations creates opportunities to profit from "arbitrage." Second, there is implicitly a market in (foreign exchange) risk bearing. Those who wish to avoid foreign exchange risk (at a price) may do so. Those who accept the risk in expectation of profits are known as "speculators."

Triangular Arbitrage

Triangular arbitrage is the process that ensures that all exchange rates are mutually consistent. If, for example, one U.S. dollar exchanges for one Canadian dollar, and one Canadian dollar exchanges for one British pound, then the U.S. dollar/pound exchange rate should be one pound for one dollar. If it differs, then there is an opportunity for profit making. To see why this is so, suppose that you could purchase two U.S. dollars with one British pound. By first buying C$1 with U.S. $1, then purchasing £1 with C$1, and finally buying U.S. $2 with £1, you could double your money immediately. Clearly this opportunity will not last for long since it involves making large profits with certainty. The process of triangular arbitrage is exactly that of finding and exploiting profitable opportunities in such exchange-rate inconsistencies. As a result of triangular arbitrage, such inconsistencies will be eliminated rapidly. Cross rates, however, will only be roughly consistent given the bid/ask spread associated with transaction costs.

In the past, the possibility of making profits from triangular arbitrage was greater as a result of the practice of expressing exchange rates in American terms in the United States and in European terms elsewhere. The adoption of standard practice has reduced the likelihood of inconsistencies.[7] Also, in recent years, such opportunities for profit making have been greatly reduced by high-speed computerized information systems and the increased sophistication of the banks operating in the market.

Arbitrage of a slightly different kind results from price differences in different locations. This is "space" arbitrage. For example, if sterling were cheaper in London than in New York, it would be profitable to buy in London and sell in New York. Similarly, if prices in the interbank market differed from those at the IMM, it would be profitable to arbitrage between them. As a result of this activity, prices in different locations will be brought broadly into line.

Interest Arbitrage

Interest arbitrage is slightly different in nature from triangular or space arbitrage; however, the basic motive of finding and exploiting profitable opportunities still applies. There is no reason why interest rates denominated in different currencies should be equal. Interest rates are the cost of borrowing or the return to lending for a specific time. The relative price (exchange rate) of money may so change over time that the comparison of, say, a U.S. and a British interest rate requires some allowance for expected exchange-rate changes. Thus, it will be not at all

Foreign Exchange Options

An option is a contract specifying the right to buy or sell — in this case foreign exchange — within a specific period (American option) or at a specific date (European option). A call option confers the right to buy. A put option confers the right to sell. Since each of these options must have a buyer and a seller, there are four possible ways of trading a single option: buy a call, sell a call, buy a put, sell a put.

The buyer of an option has the right to undertake the contract specified but may choose not to do so if it turns out to be unprofitable. The seller of the option *must* fulfill the contract if the buyer desires. Clearly, the buyer must pay the seller some premium (the option price) for this privilege. An option that would be profitable to exercise at the current exchange rate is said to be "in the money." The price at which it is exercised is the "exercise" or "strike" price.

Consider a call option on £1000 (although options of this size are not presently available on organized exchanges, it is used to present a simple illustration of the principles involved). Suppose this costs $0.03 per pound or $30 and the exercise price is $1.50 per pound. The option expires in three months. This means that the buyer has paid $30 for the right to buy £1000 with dollars at a price of $1.50 per pound any time in the next three months. If the current spot price of sterling is, say, $1.45, the option is "out of the money" because sterling can be bought cheaper on the spot market. However, if the spot price were to rise to, say, $1.55, the option would be in the money. If sold at that time, the option buyer would get a $50 return (1000 × $0.05), which would more than cover the cost of the option ($50 − $30 = $20 profit). In contrast, a put option at the same terms would be in the money at the current spot price of $1.45, but out of the money at $1.55.

Figure 2 presents a diagrammatic illustration of how the profitability of an option depends upon the relationship between the exercise price and the current spot price.[1] Figure 2a illustrates the profit avail-

---

[1]The pricing of options has been the subject of a large theoretical literature with a major contribution being made by Black and Scholes (1973). The Black-Scholes formula has been modified for foreign exchange options by Garman and Kohlhagen (1983) [see also Giddy (1983)], but the Black-Scholes formula is complex and beyond the scope of the present paper.

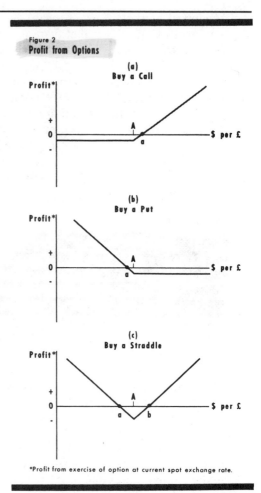

Figure 2
Profit from Options

(a)
Buy a Call

(b)
Buy a Put

(c)
Buy a Straddle

*Profit from exercise of option at current spot exchange rate.

One simple relationship which is of interest may be called "option price parity." This arises because arbitrage will ensure that the difference between a call option price (per unit) and a put option price (per unit) at the same exercise price will be equal to the present value of the difference between the exercise price and the forward exchange rate at maturity of the options (if the options are marketable, it will also hold for any date to maturity). The relationship may be expressed:

$$C - P = \frac{F - E}{1 + r},$$

when C and P are the call and put option prices at exercise price E. F is the forward exchange rate and r is the interest rate per period of the contracts. This arises because the simultaneous buying of a call and selling of a put is equivalent to buying currency forward at price E. The forward contract, however, would be paid for at the end of the period, whereas the options are transacted at the beginning. Hence, the forward contract has to be discounted back to the present.

able from buying a call option at exercise price A. At spot exchange rate A and anything lower, the option will not be exercised so the loss will equal the price of the option. At a spot exchange rate above a, the option is sufficiently in the money to more than cover its cost. Between A and a, the option is in the money but not by enough to cover cost. The profit from *selling* a call could be illustrated by reversing the + and − signs in figure 2a, or by flipping the profit line about the horizontal axis.

Figure 2b illustrates the profit from buying a put option. At spot exchange rates below a, the option with exercise price A will show a profit.

Figure 2c illustrates the profit from a simultaneous purchase of a put and call at the same exercise price. This combination will show a profit at exercise price A if the spot price goes *either* above b or below a. It is known as a "straddle." The straddle is of special interest because it makes clear the role of options as a hedge against risk. The price of a straddle can be regarded as the market valuation of the variability of the exchange rate. That is, the buyer of the straddle will show a profit if the spot price moves from some central value (the exercise price) by more than plus or minus some known percentage. The seller of the straddle accepts that risk for a lump sum. More complicated "multiple strategies" are also possible.[2]

---

[2]See Giddy (1983).

---

unusual to find interest rates denominated in dollars and interest rates denominated in, say, pounds being somewhat different. However, real returns on assets of similar quality should be the same if the exchange-rate risk is covered or hedged in the forward market. Were this not true, it would be possible to borrow in one currency and lend in another at a profit with no exchange risk.

Suppose we lend one dollar for a year in the United States at an interest rate of r_{us}. The amount accumulated at the end of the year per dollar lent will be $1 + r_{us}$ (capital plus interest). If, instead of making dollar loans, we converted them into pounds and lent them in the United Kingdom at the rate r_{uk}, the amount of pounds we would have for each original dollar at the end of the year would be $S(1 + r_{uk})$, where S is the spot exchange rate (in pounds per dollar) at the beginning of the period. At the outset, it is not known if $1 + r_{us}$ dollars is going to be worth more than $S(1 + r_{uk})$ pounds in a year's time, because the spot exchange rate in a year's time is unknown. This uncertainty can be avoided by selling the pounds forward into dollars. Then the relative value of the two loans would no longer depend on what subsequently happens to the spot exchange rate. By doing this, we end up with $\frac{S}{F}(1 + r_{uk})$ dollars per original dollar invested. This is known as the "covered," or hedged, return on pounds.

Since the covered return in our example is denominated in dollars, it can reasonably be compared with the U.S. interest rate. If these returns are very different, investors will move funds where the return is highest on a covered basis. This process is interest arbitrage. It is assumed that the assets involved are equally safe and, because the returns are covered, all exchange risk is avoided. Of course, if funds do move in large volume between assets or between financial centers, then interest rates and the exchange rates (spot and forward) will change in predictable ways. Funds will continue to flow between countries until there is no extra profit to be made from interest arbitrage. This will occur when the returns on both dollar- and sterling-denominated assets are equal, that is, when

$$(1) \qquad (1 + r_{us}) = \frac{S}{F}(1 + r_{uk})$$

This result is known as "covered interest parity." It holds more or less exactly, subject only to a margin due to transaction costs, so long as the appropriate dollar and sterling interest rates are compared.[8]

Speculation

Arbitrage in the foreign exchange markets involves little or no risk since transactions can be completed rapidly. An alternative source of profit is available from outguessing other market participants on what future exchange rates will be. This is called "speculation." Although any foreign exchange transaction that is not entirely hedged forward has a speculative element, only deliberate speculation for profit is discussed here.

Until recently, the main foreign exchange speculators were the foreign exchange departments of banks, with a lesser role being played by portfolio managers of other financial institutions and international corporations. The IMM, however, has made it much easier for individuals and smaller businesses to speculate. A high proportion of IMM transactions appears to be speculative in the sense that only about 5 percent of contracts lead to ultimate delivery of foreign exchange. This means that most of the activity involves the buying and selling of a contract *at different times* and possibly different prices prior to maturity. It is possible, however, that buying and selling of contracts before maturity would arise out of a strategy to reduce risk. So it is not possible to say that all such activity is speculative.

Speculation is important for the efficient working of foreign exchange markets. It is a form of arbitrage that occurs across time, rather than across space or between markets at the same time. Just as arbitrage increases the efficiency of markets by keeping prices consistent, so speculation increases the efficiency of forward, futures, and options markets by keeping those markets liquid. Those who wish to avoid foreign exchange risk may thereby do so in a well-developed market. Without speculators, risk avoidance in foreign exchange markets would be more difficult and, in many cases, impossible.[9]

Risk Reduction

Speculation clearly involves a shifting of risk from one party to another. For example, if a bank buys forward foreign exchange from a customer, it increases its exposure to risk while the customer reduces his. However, there is not a fixed amount of risk that has to be "shared out." Some strategies may involve a net reduction of risk all around.

As a general rule, financial institutions (or other firms), operating in a variety of currencies, will try to minimize the risk of losses due to unexpected exchange-rate changes. One simple way to do this is to ensure that assets and liabilities denominated in each operating currency are equal. This is known as "matching." For example, a bank that sells sterling forward to a customer may simultaneously buy sterling forward. In this event, the bank is exposed to zero exchange-rate risk.

Banks often use "swaps" to close gaps in the maturity structure of their assets and liabilities in a currency. This involves the simultaneous purchase and sale of a currency for *different* maturity dates. In April 1983, 33 percent of U.S. banks' foreign exchange turnover involved swaps, compared with 63 percent spot contracts and only 4 percent outright forward contracts.[10]

Covered Interest Parity: An Example

The following interest rate and exchange rate quotations are taken from the *London Financial Times* of September 8, 1983 (table 1).

Closing Exchange Rate: dollars per pound	Spot	3-Month Forward
	1.4910–1.4920	.17–.22 discount

Interest Rates: 3-Month Offer Rate	Eurosterling	Eurodollar
	$9^{13}/_{16}$	$10^{1}/_{4}$

The interest rate on the three-month eurodollar deposit is a little higher (.7 percent) than that on an eurosterling deposit. If the exchange rate remains unchanged, it would be better to hold dollars; if the exchange rate falls, the eurosterling deposit would be preferable. Suppose you decide to cover the exchange risk by selling the dollars forward into pounds. Let us compare the return to holding a sterling deposit with the return to holding a dollar deposit sold forward into sterling (assuming that you start with sterling).

Two important points need to be clarified about the above data. First, the interest rates are annualized so they are not what would actually be earned over a three-month period. For example, the three-month rate equivalent to an annual rate of $10^{1}/_{4}$ percent is 2.47 percent.

Second, the forward exchange rates need some explanation. The dollar is at a discount against sterling. This means the forward dollar buys less sterling. So we have to *add* the discount onto the spot price to get the forward price (because the price is the number of dollars per pound, not the reverse). Notice also that the discount is measured in fractions of a cent, not fractions of a dollar! So the

bid-ask spread on the forward rate would be 1.4927 – 1.4942.

Now let us see if we would do better to invest in a three-month eurosterling deposit or a three-month eurodollar deposit where the dollars to be received were sold forward into sterling. The return per £100 invested in eurosterling is £2.369 (annual interest rate of $9^{13}/_{16}$), whereas the return on a covered eurodollar deposit is

$$£2.251 = (100 \times \frac{1.4910}{1.4942} 1.0247) - 100.$$

Thus, we could not make a profit out of covered interest arbitrage. Despite the fact that dollar interest rates are higher, the discount on forward dollars in the forward market means they buy fewer forward pounds. As a result, there is no benefit to the operation. Transaction costs for most individuals would be even greater than those above as they would face a larger bid-ask spread than that quoted on the interbank market.

Consequently, there is no benefit for the typical investor from making a covered or hedged eurocurrency deposit. The return will be at least as high on a deposit in the currency in which you start and wish to end up. That is, if you have dollars and wish to end up with dollars, make a eurodollar deposit. If you have sterling and wish to end up with sterling, make a eurosterling deposit. If you have sterling and wish to end up in dollars, there is likely to be little or no difference between holding a eurosterling deposit sold forward into dollars or buying dollars spot and holding a eurodollar deposit. Of course, if you hold an "uncovered" deposit and exchange rates subsequently change, the result will be very different.

Suppose a bank has sold DM to a customer three months forward and bought the same amount of DM from a different customer six months forward. There are two ways in which the bank could achieve zero foreign exchange-risk exposure. It could either undertake two separate offsetting forward transactions; or it could set up a single swap with another bank that has the opposite mismatch of dollar/DM flows, whereby it receives DM in exchange for dollars in three months and receives back dollars in exchange for DM in six months. Once the swap is set up, the bank's net profits are protected against subsequent changes in spot exchange rates during the next six months.

Within the limits imposed by the nature of the contracts, a similar effect can be achieved by an appropriate portfolio of futures contracts on the IMM. Thus, a bank would buy and sell futures contracts so as to match closely its forward

Why Is the Dollar the "Money" of Foreign Exchange Markets?

One interesting aspect of the organization of the foreign exchange markets is that the "money" used in these markets is generally the U.S. dollar. This is generally true for spot markets and universally true for forward markets. "Cross-markets" between many currencies are very thin, and future cross markets are virtually nonexistent. For example, the bulk of foreign exchange trading between £s and cruzeiro will involve dollar-£ and dollar-cruzeiro transactions instead of direct £-cruzeiro trading. The only exception to this is the transactions involving the major Organization for Economic Cooperation and Development (OECD) currencies, especially within Europe. Of the $702.5 billion turnover in foreign exchange reported by U.S. banks in April 1983, only $1.5 billion did not involve U.S. dollars.

There are two explanations for this special role of the dollar in foreign exchange markets. Both rely upon the fact that transaction costs are likely to be lower if the dollar is used as a medium. Krugman shows that the clearing of foreign exchange markets requires some "intermediary" currency.[1] Even if ev-

ery country is in payments balance vis a vis the rest of the world, it will not necessarily be in bilateral balance with each other country. Because some currency has to be used to cover this residual finance, it is natural to choose the currency that has the lowest transaction costs. Chrystal shows there are economic reasons why cross-markets between many currencies do not exist.[2] It typically will be easier and cheaper to set up a deal in two steps via the dollar than in a single step (cruzeiro-dollar, dollar-drachma rather than cruzeiro-drachma). This is because these cross-markets, if they existed, would be fairly thin and hence relatively costly for such transactions. The two markets with the dollar, on the other hand, are well developed.

These analyses refer to the role of the dollar in the interbank market. In the development of the trading places such as the IMM in Chicago and LIFFE in London to date, it is also true that all currency futures are traded against the dollar.

---

[1] See Krugman (1980).

[2] See Chrystal (1982).

---

commitments to customers. In reality, banks will use a combination of methods to reduce foreign exchange risk.

Markets that permit banks, firms, and individuals to hedge foreign exchange risk are essential in times of fluctuating exchange rates. This is especially important for banks if they are to be able to provide efficient foreign exchange services for their customers. In the absence of markets that permit foreign exchange-risk hedging, the cost and uncertainty of international transactions would be greatly increased, and international specialization and trade would be greatly reduced.

CONCLUSION

The foreign exchange markets are complex and, for the outsider, hard to comprehend. The primary function of these markets is straightforward. It is to facilitate international transactions related to trade, travel, or investment. Foreign exchange markets can now accommodate a large range of current and forward transactions.

Given the variability of exchange rates, it is important for banks and firms operating in foreign currencies to be able to reduce exchange-rate risk whenever possible. Some risk reduction is achieved by interbank swaps, but some is also taken up by speculation. Arbitrage and speculation both increase the efficiency of spot and forward foreign exchange markets and have enabled foreign exchange markets to achieve a high level of efficiency. Without the successful operation of these markets, the obstacles to international trade and investment would be substantial and the world would be a poorer place.

GLOSSARY

American option: An option that can be exercised any time up to maturity.

American terms: An exchange rate expressed as number of currency units per dollar.

Arbitrage: The simultaneous purchase and sale of currency in separate markets for a profit arising from a price discrepancy between the markets.

Bid/ask spread: The difference between the buying (bid) and selling (ask) price.

Covered interest arbitrage: Buying a country's currency spot, investing for a period, and selling the proceeds forward in order to make a net profit due to the higher interest rate in that country. This act involves "hedging," because it guarantees a covered return without risk. The opportunities to profit in this way seldom arise because covered interest differentials are normally close to zero.

Covered interest parity: The gap between interest rates in foreign and domestic currencies will be matched by the forward exchange rate differential, such that the "covered" interest rate differential will be close to zero.

Eurodollar deposits: Bank deposits, generally bearing interest and made for a specific time period, that are denominated in dollars but are in banks outside the United States. Similarly, Eurosterling deposits would be denominated in sterling but outside the United Kingdom.

European option: An option that can be exercised only on a specified date.

European terms: An exchange rate expressed as number of dollars per currency unit.

Floating exchange rate: An exchange rate that is allowed to adjust freely to the supply of and demand for foreign exchange.

Foreign exchange speculation: The act of taking a net position in a foreign currency with the intention of making a profit from exchange-rate changes.

Forward exchange rate: The price of foreign currency for delivery at a future date agreed to by a contract today.

Futures market: A market in which contracts are traded to buy or sell a standard amount of currency in the future at a particular price.

Hedging: Or covering exchange risk, means that foreign currency is sold forward into local currency so its value is not affected by subsequent exchange-rate changes. Say an exporter knows he will be paid £10,000 in two months. He can wait until he gets the money and convert it into dollars at whatever the spot rate turns out to be. This outcome is uncertain, as the spot rate may change. Alternatively, he can sell £10,000 two months forward at today's two-month forward price. Suppose this is $1.5 per £. In two months, he will receive £10,000, fulfill his forward contract, and receive $15,000. This export contract has been hedged or covered in the forward market.

Matching: Equating assets and liabilities denominated in each currency so losses due to foreign exchange-rate changes are minimized.

Options market: A market in which contracts are traded that gives a purchaser the right but no obligation to buy (call) or to sell (put) a currency in the future at a given price.

Spot exchange rate: The price paid to exchange currencies for immediate delivery (two business days in the interbank market, or over the counter in the retail and travelers check market).

Swap: The simultaneous purchase and sale of a currency for different maturity dates that closes the gaps in the maturity structure of assets and liabilities in a currency.

NOTES

[1] For further discussion of foreign exchange markets in the United States, see Kubarych (1983). See also Dufey and Giddy (1978) and McKinnon (1979).

[2] Notice *The Wall Street Journal* quotes only a bank selling price at a particular time. The *Financial Times* quotes the bid/ask spread and the range over the day.

[3] In practice, the spread will vary during the day, depending upon market conditions. For example, the sterling spread may be as little as 0.01 cents at times and an average is about 0.05 cents. Spreads generally will be larger on less widely traded currencies.

[4] See Federal Reserve Bank of New York (1983).

[5] A bank may also insist upon minimum deposit to cover a forward contract, though there is no firm rule.

[6] For a discussion of options in commodities, see Belongia (1983).

[7] All except U.K. and Irish exchange rates are expressed in American terms. Futures and options contracts are expressed in European terms.

[8] Since there are many different interest rates, it obviously cannot hold for all of them. Where (1) does hold is if the interest rates chosen are Eurocurrency deposit rates of the same duration. In other words, if for r_{us} we take, say, the three-month Eurodollar deposit rate in Paris and for r_{uk} we take the three-month Eurosterling deposit rate in Paris, then (1) will hold just about exactly. Indeed, if we took the interest rate and exchange-rate quotes all from the same bank, it would be remarkable if (1) did not hold. Otherwise, the bank would be offering to pay you to borrow from it and lend straight back! That is, the price of borrowing would be less than the covered return on lending. A margin between borrowing and lending rates, of course, will make this even less likely so that in reality you would lose.

[9] This is not to say that all speculative activity is necessarily beneficial.

[10] See Federal Reserve Bank of New York (1983).

REFERENCES

Belongia, Michael T. "Commodity Options: A New Risk Management Tool for Agricultural Markets." *Review,* Federal Reserve Bank of St. Louis, June/July 1983, pp. 5–15.

Black, Fisher, and Myron Scholes. "The Pricing of Options and Corporate Liabilities." *Journal of Political Economy,* May/June 1973, pp. 637–54.

Chrystal, K. Alec. "On the Theory of International Money." (Paper presented to U.K. International Economics Study Group Conference, September 1982, Sussex, England). Forthcoming in J. Black and G. S. Dorrance, eds., *Problems of International Finance.* London: Macmillan, 1984.

Dufey, Gunter, and Ina H. Giddy. *The International Money Market.* Englewood Cliffs, N.J.: Prentice-Hall, 1978.

Federal Reserve Bank of New York. "Summary of Results of U.S. Foreign Exchange Market Turnover Survey Conducted in April 1983." September 8, 1983.

Garman, Mark B., and Steven W. Kohlhagen. "Foreign Currency Option Values." *Journal of International Money and Finance,* December 1983, pp. 231–37.

Giddy, Ina H. "Foreign Exchange Options." *Journal of Futures Markets,* Summer 1983, pp. 143–66.

Krugman, Paul. "Vehicle Currencies and the Structure of International Exchange." *Journal of Money, Credit and Banking,* August 1980, pp. 513–26.

Kubarych, Roger M. *Foreign Exchange Markets in the United States.* Federal Reserve Bank of New York, 1983.

McKinnon, Ronald I. *Money in International Exchange: The Convertible Currency System.* New York: Oxford University Press, 1979.

International Banking Facilities

K. Alec Chrystal

International Banking Facilities (IBFs) started operation in the United States in early December 1981. Since then, they have grown to the point where they now represent a significant part of the international banking business worldwide. The purpose of this article is to examine IBFs and to discuss their significance for international banking.

OFFSHORE BANKING

A substantial "offshore" international banking sector, often called the "Eurocurrency" market, grew up in the 1960s and 1970s. Its key characteristic is that banking business is transacted in a location outside the country in whose currency the business is denominated. Thus, Eurodollar transactions are conducted outside the United States, Eurosterling transactions are conducted outside Britain, and so on. Much of this offshore business occurs in major financial centers like London, though some business is literally in islands offshore from the United States, such as the Bahamas or Cayman Islands.

Offshore banking business is somewhat different from that conducted onshore. Though, in both cases, banks take deposits and make loans, offshore banks have virtually no checking deposit liabilities. Instead, their deposits are typically made for specific periods, yield interest, and are generally in large denominations.

Offshore banking arose as a means to avoid a variety of banking regulations. For example, offshore banks that deal in Eurodollars avoid reserve requirements on deposits, FDIC assessments, and U.S.-imposed interest-rate ceilings. The first two of these regulations increase the margin between deposit and loan rates. Avoiding these costs enables offshore banks to operate on much smaller margins. Interest ceilings, where binding, reduce the ability of banks subject to such ceilings to compete internationally for deposits.

Many "shell" bank branches in offshore centers, such as the Caymans and

From *Review,* Federal Reserve Bank of St. Louis, April 1984, pp. 5–11.

K. Alec Chrystal, professor of economics-elect, University of Sheffield, England, is a visiting scholar at the Federal Reserve Bank of St. Louis. Leslie Ballis Koppel povided research assistance.

Bahamas, exist almost solely to avoid U.S. banking regulations. Shell branches are offices that have little more than a nameplate and a telephone. They are used simply as addresses for booking transactions set up by U.S. banks, which thereby avoid domestic monetary regulations.

IBFs: ONSHORE OFFSHORE BANKS

IBFs do not represent new *physical* banking facilities; instead, they are separate sets of books within existing banking institutions—a U.S.-chartered depository institution, a U.S. branch or agency of a foreign bank, or a U.S. office of an Edge Act corporation.[1] They can only take deposits from and make loans to nonresidents of the United States, other IBFs, and their establishing entities. Moreover, IBFs are not subject to the regulations that apply to domestic banking activity; they avoid reserve requirements, interest-rate ceilings, and deposit insurance assessment. In effect, they are accorded the advantages of many offshore banking centers without the need to be physically offshore.

The Establishment of IBFs

Three regulatory or legislative changes have permitted or encouraged the establishment and growth of IBFs. First, the Federal Reserve Board changed its regulations in 1981 to permit the establishment of IBFs. Second, federal legislation enacted in late 1981 exempted IBFs from the insurance coverage and assessments imposed by the FDIC. Third, several states have granted special tax status to the operating profits from IBFs or altered other restrictions to encourage their establishment. In at least one case, Florida, IBFs are entirely exempt from local taxes.

Restrictions on IBF Activities

While IBFs may transact banking business with U.S. nonresidents on more or less the same terms as banks located offshore, they may not deal with U.S. residents at all, apart from their parent institution or other IBFs. Funds borrowed by a parent from its own IBF are subject to Eurocurrency reserve requirements, just as funds borrowed from an offshore branch would be.

Four other restrictions on IBFs are designed to ensure their separation from domestic money markets.

First, the initial maturity of deposits taken from nonbank foreign customers must be at least two working days. Overnight deposits, however, may be offered to overseas banks, other IBFs, and the parent bank. This restriction ensures that IBFs do not create a close substitute for checking accounts.

Second, the minimum transaction with an IBF by a nonbank customer is $100,000, except to withdraw interest or close an account. This effectively limits the activity of IBFs to the "wholesale" money market, in which the customers are likely to be governments, major corporations, or other international banks.[2] There is no restriction on the size of interbank transactions.

Third, IBFs are not permitted to issue negotiable instruments, such as certificates of deposit (CDs), because such instruments would be easily marketable in U.S. money markets, thereby breaking down the intended separation between IBFs and the domestic money market.

Finally, deposits and loans of IBFs must not be related to a nonresident customer's activities in the United States.[3] This regulation prevents IBFs from competing directly with domestic credit sources for finance related to domestic economic activity.

Where Are IBFs Located?

IBFs are chiefly located in the major financial centers (see Table 1). Almost half of the nearly 500 IBFs are in New York; California, Florida, and Illinois have the bulk of the rest. In terms of value of liabilities, however, the distribution is even more skewed. Of IBFs reporting monthly to the Federal Reserve (those with assets or liabilities in excess of $300 million), 77 percent of total liabilities were in New York, with California (12 percent) and Illinois (7.5 percent) a long way behind. It is notable that Florida, which has 16.5 percent of the IBFs, has only 2 percent of the liabilities of reporting banks.

While the distribution of IBFs primarily reflects the preexisting locations of international banking business, differences in tax treatment between states may have influenced the location of IBFs marginally. For example, the fact that Florida exempts IBFs from state taxes may well explain why it has the largest number of Edge Act corporation IBFs and ranks second to New York in terms of numbers of IBFs set up by U.S.- chartered banks.

Although Florida has the most advantageous tax laws possible for IBFs, it is not alone in granting them favorable tax status. Nine other states (New York, California, Illinois, Connecticut, Delaware, Maryland, Georgia, North Carolina, and Washington) and the District of Columbia have enacted special tax laws that encourage the establishment of IBFs.[4]

The reason for the favorable tax treatment for IBFs in states like Florida is not clear. There is no doubt that Florida has tried to encourage its development as an international financial center.[5] The benefits from encouragement of IBFs per se, however, are hard to see. For example, the employment gains are probably trivial. Since IBFs are merely new accounts in existing institutions, each IBF will involve *at most* the employment of a handful of people. In many cases, there may be no extra employment.

What Do IBFs Do?

The assets and liabilities of IBFs on December 30, 1981, December 29, 1982, and October 20, 1983, are recorded in Table 2; as of October 20, 1983, over 98 percent of their liabilities were dollar-denominated.

The December 30, 1981, figures largely reflect business switched from other accounts either in the parent bank or an offshore branch. Operations of the IBFs themselves are reflected more clearly in the later figures. Consider the latest available figures in the third column of Table 2. The most important aspects of these figures is the proportion of business with other banks versus the proportion with nonbank customers. On the asset side, about one sixth of total assets are "commercial and industrial loans" (Item 5a) and one ninth are loans to "foreign governments and official institutions" (Item 5c). The remainder, over 70 percent, are claims on either other IBFs, overseas banks, or an overseas branch of the parent bank. Claims on overseas banks (Items 3a and 5b) are largest, while claims on other IBFs (Item 2) and overseas offices of the parent bank (Item 1) are of broadly similar magnitude.

TABLE 1
Location of International Banking Facilities

	Total IBFs	U.S.-chartered banks[1]	Agencies and branches of foreign banks	Edge Act corporations	Liabilities of Monthly Reporting IBFs, Other than to Parent Entity		
					Amount (billions of dollars)	Percent of total reported	Number of banks reporting
TOTAL	477	144	264	69	$173.43		
New York	208	38	154	16	133.8	77%	90
California	84	16	57	11	20.1	12	27
Florida	79	27	29	27	3.3	2	8
Illinois	30	6	17	7	13.1	7.5	11
Texas	20	14	0	6			
District of Columbia	11	8	3	0			
Pennsylvania	9	7	2	0			
Washington	7	3	4	0			
Georgia	6	4	1	1			
Massachusetts	5	3	1	1	3.1	1.8	10
New Jersey	4	4	0	0	(There are too few reporting banks in other states for a data breakdown to be made available.)		
Ohio	4	4	0	0			
Connecticut	2	2	0	0			
Kentucky	2	2	0	0			
Michigan	2	2	0	0			
N. Carolina	2	2	0	0			
Rhode Island	1	1	0	0			
Virginia	1	1	0	0			

NOTE: Figures for numbers of IBFs are as of September 28, 1983. Figures for liabilities are as of October 26, 1983. Monthly reporting banks are those with assets or liabilities of at least $300 million. SOURCE: Federal Reserve Board Release G.14(518)A and Federal Reserve Board unpublished data.
[1]One savings and loan association has an IBF that is in the Florida figure.

The liability structure is even more heavily weighted toward banks. Only about 16 percent of the liabilities of IBFs (as of October 26, 1983) were due to nonbanks. Of these, one third was due to "foreign government and official institutions" (Item 10c) and two thirds were due to "other non-U.S. addresses" (Item 10d). The latter are mainly industrial and commercial firms.

The high proportion of both assets and liabilities of IBFs due to other banking institutions reinforces the conclusion that they are an integral part of the Eurodollar market. A high proportion of interbank business is characteristic of Eurocurrency business, in which there may be several interbank transactions between ultimate borrowers and ultimate lenders.[6]

An important role for interbank transactions is to provide "swaps" that reduce either exchange risk or interest-rate risk for the parties involved. Suppose, for example, an IBF has a deposit (liability) of $1 million that will be withdrawn in one month, and it has made a loan (asset) to a customer of $1 million that will be repaid in two months. There is a risk that, when the IBF comes to borrow $1 million to cover the second month of the loan, interest rates will have risen, and it will incur a loss on the entire transaction. If, however, this IBF can find a bank that has the opposite timing problem (a deposit of $1 million for two months and a loan of $1 million outstanding for one month), the two banks could arrange a swap. The second bank would loan the IBF $1 million in one month and get it back in two months (with suitable interest). The interest rate involved will be agreed on *at the*

TABLE 2
Assets and Liabilities of International Banking Facilities (millions of dollars)

	December 30, 1981	December 29, 1982	October 26, 1983
ASSETS			
1. Gross Claims on Non-U.S. Offices of Establishing Entity	$7,188	$20,125	$30,322
(1) Denominated in U.S. Dollars	6,785	19,150	29,204
(2) Denominated in Other Currencies	403	975	1,118
2. Loans and Balances Due From Other IBFs	903	16,577	26,256
3. Gross Due From:			
A. Banks in Foreign Countries	8,470	26,666	29,093
B. Foreign Governments and Official Institutions	12	276	482
4. Securities of Non-U.S. Addressees	438	1,130	1,875
5. Loans To Non-U.S. Addressees			
A. Commercial and Industrial Loans	17,081	32,808	36,753
B. Banks in Foreign Countries	11,705	30,300	32,237
C. Foreign Governments and Official Institutions	7,791	16,960	22,348
D. Other Loans	1,164	1,070	958
6. All Other Assets in IBF Accounts	880	3,839	3,262
7. Total Assets Other Than Claims on U.S. and Non-U.S. Office of Establishing Entity	49,409	132,569	156,484
(1) Denominated in U.S. Dollars (Sum of Items 2 through 6)	48,445	129,626	153,264
(2) Denominated in Other Currencies	965	2,943	3,219
8. Total Assets Other Than Claims on U.S. Offices of Establishing Entity (Sum of Items 1 and 7)	56,597	152,694	186,806
(1) Denominated in U.S. Dollars	55,229	168,776	182,469
(2) Denominated in Other Currencies	1,368	3,917	4,337
LIABILITIES			
9. Gross Liabilities Due To Non-U.S. Offices of Establishing Entity	$29,091	$56,372	$69,756
(1) Denominated in U.S. Dollars	28,779	55,114	68,535
(2) Denominated in Other Currencies	313	1,258	1,221
10. Liabilities Due To:			
A. Other IBFs	1,009	17,382	28,803
B. Banks In Foreign Countries	10,127	37,045	42,446
C. Foreign Government and Official Institutions	2,834	7,439	9,115
D. Other Non-U.S. Addressees	952	13,816	19,073
E. All Other Liabilities in IBF Accounts	336	2,756	2,170
F. Total Liabilities Other Than Due To U.S. and Non-U.S. Offices of Establishing Entity	15,686	80,080	103,674
(1) Denominated in U.S. Dollars (Sum of Items 10.A Through 10.E)	15,258	78,439	101,608
(2) Denominated in Other Currencies	428	1,641	2,066
11. Total Liabilities Other Than Due to U.S. Offices of Establishing Entity (Sum of Items 9 and 10.F)	44,777	136,452	173,430
(1) Denominated in U.S. Dollars	44,037	133,552	170,143
(2) Denominated in Other Currencies	741	2,899	3,257
RESIDUAL			
12. Net Due From (+) / Net Due To (−) U.S. Offices of Establishing Entity (Item 11 Minus Item 8)	$−11,820	$−16,242	$−13,376
(1) Denominated in U.S. Dollars	−11,193	−15,224	−12,325
(2) Denominated in Other Currencies	−627	−1,018	−1,051
Number of Reporters	56	122	146

NOTE: Unless otherwise noted, figures include only amounts denominated in U.S. dollars. This report contains data only for those entities whose IBF assets or liabilities are at least $300 million, that is, for those entities that file a monthly report of IBF accounts on form FR 2072. SOURCE: Federal Reserve Board Release G.14 (518).

beginning, so neither bank would suffer if interest rates should change in the second month.

These swap arrangements enable banks to match the maturity structure of their assets and liabilities. The existence of such swaps explains the high levels of both borrowing and lending between IBFs and overseas branches of their parent bank.[7]

THE GROWTH OF IBFs

Chart 1 shows the growth of total IBF liabilities since the end of 1981. Although the most rapid growth occurred in the first six months of their operation, IBFs have grown considerably over a period in which international banking business in general has been stagnant.[8] Within two years, they have come to be a significant part of the international money market. The liabilities of IBFs as of October 1983 (other than to parent banks) represent about 8.5 percent of gross Eurocurrency liabilities (as measured by Morgan Guaranty) or about 7.5 percent of total international banking liabilities (as measured by the Bank for International Settlements. This includes onshore bank lending).

Where did this growth come from? Has the creation of IBFs generated a large volume of new business or has business been shifted from elsewhere? The evidence is that IBF business has almost entirely been shifted from elsewhere. Terrell and Mills use regression analysis to test the hypothesis that the creation of IBFs has led to greater growth of external bank assets.[9] This hypothesis is decisively rejected.

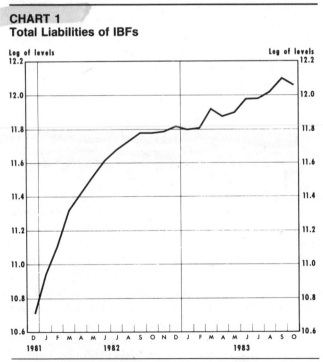

CHART 1
Total Liabilities of IBFs

Note: Liability levels were $44,777 million on December 30, 1981, and $173,140 million on October 1983. Figures exclude liabilities to parent entity.

Some evidence concerning the origins of business shifted to IBFs is available in Key.[10] It is convenient to consider separately shifts from existing institutions in the U.S. and shifts from overseas banking centers.

Shifts from Banks in the United States

Up until January 27, 1982, about $34 billion of claims on overseas residents were shifted to IBF books from other U.S. banking institutions. The bulk of this (85 percent) came from U.S. branches of foreign banks—especially Japanese and Italian. Foreign banks typically would have had a higher proportion of assets eligible for shifting to IBFs, while Japanese and Italian banks generally had not established shell branches in Caribbean offshore centers.

In the same period, shifts of liabilities (due to other parties than overseas branches of the parent bank) from books of parent entities were much smaller. These amounted to about $6 billion, of which 90 percent came from branches of foreign banks. The small shift of liabilities relative to assets was affected by several factors: the negotiable nature of some deposits (CDs); the existence of penalties for renegotiations before maturity; the delay in passing New York tax relief for IBFs until March 1981; the small proportions of short-term deposits unrelated to trade with the United States; and the availability of accounts with similar returns yet fewer restrictions as to maturity and denomination (such as repurchase agreements).

If only the domestic books of U.S.-chartered banks are considered, the shift to IBFs is extremely small. Key reports a shift of $4.3 billion (through January 27, 1982) of claims on unrelated foreigners and only $0.1 billion of liabilities to unrelated foreigners. An alternative figure for claims shifted to IBFs is obtainable by looking at the change in commercial and industrial loans to non-U.S. addresses plus loans to foreign banks (*Federal Reserve Bulletin,* table A18, for large weekly reporting banks with assets of $750 million or more). This indicates a decline of $3.3 billion in the same period.

Shifts from Other Offshore Centers

Whereas foreign banks were mainly responsible for shifts to IBFs from banks located in the United States, banks chartered in the United States were mainly responsible for shifts of business from offshore centers and other overseas banking locations. Key estimates that U.S.-chartered banks shifted about $25 billion in claims on unrelated foreigners and about $6 billion in liabilities due to unrelated foreigners (through January 27, 1982) to IBFs from overseas branches. The comparable figures for foreign banks were $5.5 billion and $9.0 billion, respectively.

This difference in the propensity to shift assets to IBFs is probably explained by the differential tax incentives of U.S. and foreign banks. U.S. banks pay taxes on worldwide income and may benefit from tax advantages of IBFs. Foreign banks may increase their tax liability to the United States by establishing an IBF instead of operating in an offshore center.

The bulk of business shifted by U.S. banks from their overseas branches has come from the Bahamas and Cayman Islands (collectively called Caribbean). In the first two months of operation of IBFs (11/30/81–1/29/82), liabilities to unrelated foreigners of branches of U.S. banks located there fell by $6.8 billion, while claims on unrelated foreigners fell by $23.3 billion. Much of this shift reflected the redundancy of shell branches, at least for business with non-U.S. residents, once IBFs were permitted.

While much of the *raison d'être* of Caribbean branches for business with foreigners has been removed by the establishment of IBFs, these branches continue to be important for business with U.S. residents. Terrell and Mills (1983) report that the proportion of the liabilities of Caribbean branches due to U.S. residents rose from less than half in mid-1981 to about 70 percent by the end of 1982. However, the attraction of offshore deposits to U.S. residents is likely to decrease as interest regulations on domestic U.S. banks are relaxed, thereby narrowing the gap between domestic and offshore deposit rates.

Based on the figures of the Bank for International Settlements, Terrell and Mills estimate that the proportion of total international banking assets and liabilities due to U.S. banks' offshore branches declined by 4 percent in the first year of IBF operation. Another 3.5 percent was lost by other overseas banking centers to IBFs.

THE SIGNIFICANCE OF IBFs FOR INTERNATIONAL BANKING

The primary significance of the experience with IBFs is that it enables us to better understand the forces that led to the growth of Eurocurrency markets. In particular, the significant decline in business in Caribbean branches following the creation of IBFs suggests that the growth of business in this area was almost entirely intended to bypass U.S. monetary regulations. Deregulation of domestic banking in the United States will presumably have further effects, since much of the remaining business in Caribbean branches of U.S. banks is with U.S. residents.

The regulatory changes that permitted the establishment of IBFs were intended to ease the burden of domestic monetary restrictions on U.S. banks in the conduct of international banking business.[11] The extent to which this aim has been achieved is probably very limited. This is because IBFs play no role in financing either activities of U.S. residents or the U.S. activities of nonresidents.

Major U.S. banks that were involved in international finance to a significant degree had already found ways around U.S. banking regulations and were not restricted in their ability to compete internationally. The fact that major U.S. banks have shifted business to IBFs from offshore centers means, of course, that there must be some benefit from having an IBF. This may result from lower transaction costs, some tax advantages, or the greater attraction, from a risk perspective, of deposits located in the United States. However, the biggest gainers among U.S. banks may be medium-sized banks that were big enough to have some international business but not big enough to have an offshore branch.[12]

Other major beneficiaries from IBFs have been the U.S. branches and agencies of foreign banks. It is no accident that well over half of all IBFs have been established by these banks. The benefit to them arises from the high proportion of their existing business that is IBF eligible—that is, the portion with nonresidents. Not the least of this would be transactions with their parent banks overseas.

CONCLUSIONS

The establishment of IBFs in the United States represents a change in the geographical pattern of international banking. It facilitates the conduct in the

United States of some business that was previously conducted offshore. It also increases the ease with which foreign banks can operate branches in the United States. The creation of IBFs, however, does not seem to have increased the total volume of international banking business. Indeed, IBFs have grown at a time when international banking growth has been at its slowest for over two decades. This growth has been largely at the expense of banking offices in other locations.

For the U.S. and world economies, however, IBFs are not of great significance. There may be efficiency gains resulting from the relaxation of U.S. regulations that led to the establishment of IBFs. But such gains are small. Interest rates in world capital markets are unlikely to have been affected. Benefits that accrue to banks located in the United States from their IBF facilities are largely offset by losses in offshore banks, though in many cases the gainers and losers are both branches of the same parent bank.

NOTES

[1] As a result of a 1919 amendment to the Federal Reserve Act initiated by Senator Walter Edge, U.S. banks are able to establish branches outside their home state. These branches must be involved only in business abroad or the finance of foreign trade. The 1978 International Banking Act allowed foreign banks to open Edge Act corporations, which accept deposits and make loans directly related to international transactions.

[2] Foreign governments are treated like overseas banks for purposes of maturity and transaction size regulations.

[3] "The Board expects that, with respect to nonbank customers located outside the United States, IBFs will accept only deposits that support the customer's operations outside the United States and will extend credit only to finance the customer's non-U.S. operations." See "Announcements" (1981), p. 562.

[4] These provisions vary from case to case. For a summary of the position in New York and California, see Key (1982).

[5] See "Florida's Baffling Unitary Tax" (1983).

[6] See Niehans and Hewson (1976) for an explanation of the intermediary function of Euromarkets. The interbank market is also discussed in Dufey and Giddy (1978), chap. 5.

[7] For a discussion of the role of swaps in foreign exchange markets, see Chrystal (1984).

[8] According to B.I.S. figures, international bank assets grew 8.8 percent in 1982 in nominal terms. This compares with figures typically in excess of 20 percent throughout the 1970s. The combined assets of overseas branches of U.S. banks declined by 0.6 percent in 1982 [see Press Release (1983)], though this partly reflects the growth of IBFs.

[9] See Terrell and Mills (1983).

[10] See Key (1982).

[11] Ibid., p. 566.

[12] It is true that the largest banks have the largest IBFs. However, the cost saving at the margin from IBFs for a bank that had, say, a Caribbean shell operation is much smaller than for a bank that had no offshore booking location.

REFERENCES

"Announcements." *Federal Reserve Bulletin,* July 1981, pp. 561–63.

Chrystal, K. Alec. "A Guide to Foreign Exchange Markets." *Review.* Federal Reserve Bank of St. Louis, March 1984, pp. 5–18.

Dufey, G., and Ian H. Giddy. *The International Money Market.* Englewood Cliffs, N.J.: Prentice-Hall, 1978.

"Florida's Baffling Unitary Tax: What Is It, Whom Does It Hurt?" *American Banker,* December 28, 1983.

Key, Sydney J. "International Banking Facilities." *Federal Reserve Bulletin,* October 1982, pp. 565–77.

Niehans, Jürg, and John Hewson. "The Euro-dollar Market and Monetary Theory." *Journal of Money, Credit and Banking,* February 1976, pp. 1–27.

Press Release. Federal Reserve Board of Governors, August 22, 1983.

Terrell, Henry S., and Rodney H. Mills. *International Banking Facilities and the Eurodollar Market.* Staff Studies no. 126, Board of Governors of the Federal Reserve System, August 1983.

30

New Markets
in Foreign Currency Options

Brian Gendreau

INTRODUCTION

In recent years, exchanges and banks have developed a variety of new financial instruments designed to give customers the option to buy or sell foreign currencies. Exchanges in Amsterdam, Montreal, and Philadelphia opened trading in standardized options on foreign currencies in late 1982. Banks responded by resurrecting an old practice of writing tailor-made foreign currency options for their customers. And in January 1984, the Chicago Mercantile Exchange opened trading in the newest instrument, an option on its deutsche mark *futures* contract.

How do these new currency options work? What do options allow traders to do that they cannot do already in foreign currency markets? Under what circumstances will they do well in the marketplace? As a first step toward examining these issues, it is important to understand exactly what options are.

WHAT ARE OPTIONS?

An option is a contract that gives its holder the right, but not the obligation, to buy or sell an asset on or before a future date at a specified price. In this regard, options differ crucially from forward and futures contracts, which are firm commitments to buy or sell an asset at a fixed price on a future date. Once forward and futures contracts are made, they must be fulfilled whether prices have moved favorably or not.[1]

An option that can be exercised only on its expiration date is called a "European option"; one that can be exercised anytime up to expiration is called an "American option." Theoretically, options can be written on any asset or com-

---

From *Business Review*, Federal Reserve Bank of Philadelphia, July/August 1984, pp. 3–12.

Brian Gendreau is an economist in the banking section of the Federal Reserve Bank of Philadelphia's Research Department. Special thanks are due to the Philadelphia Stock Exchange, the Montreal Exchange, and the Financial Options Group, Inc., for assistance in providing information used in this article. The author bears full responsibility for any errors.

modity, be it a crop, real estate, a security, or a futures contract. With foreign currency options, the underlying asset is a specified quantity of a foreign currency, say, 12,500 British pounds or 62,500 Swiss francs.

Foreign currency options, like all other options, involve two transactions. The first transaction is the purchase or sale of the *option* itself: one party buys from the other the right to exchange dollars for foreign currency in the future at a set price, known as the exercise or striking price. The person obtaining the right to make the future exchange is known as the option buyer or holder, and the person granting the right is known as the option seller or writer. To have the privilege of exchanging the currency at the price specified in the option contract, the buyer must pay the seller a fee, called a "premium."

The second transaction in an option is the future exchange of the underlying *asset:* the foreign currency. This exchange may be one of two kinds. In a *call* option, dollars may be exchanged for a specified quantity of the foreign currency; a call is thus a contract for the right to buy the foreign currency. In a *put* option, a specified quantity of the foreign currency may be exchanged for dollars; it is a contract for the right to sell the foreign currency. Because options may be bought or sold for the right to buy or sell foreign currency, four basic trading positions are possible. A market participant can:

1. Buy a call, obtaining the right to purchase the foreign currency.
2. Sell a call, standing ready to sell the foreign currency at the option buyer's discretion.
3. Buy a put, obtaining the right to sell the foreign currency.
4. Sell a put, standing ready to buy the foreign currency at the option buyer's discretion.

Each of these four positions exposes the trader to different risks and returns. Why a trader would choose to take on any of these positions may be best explained with examples, beginning with foreign currency calls.

RISKS AND REWARDS IN TRADING CURRENCY OPTIONS

Call Options.   Suppose a trader has good reason to think that the Swiss franc will rise, relative to the dollar, by more than the market expects. One way to profit from that information is to buy a call option on francs. The trader could, for example, buy a call in March giving him the right to purchase 62,500 francs at a price of $0.46 apiece in June, paying (for example) a $560 premium for the option. If the trader is correct and by March the franc rises—say to $0.48—the trader can exercise the option, buy the francs from the option writer at the exercise price, $0.46, then sell them in the spot market at $0.48 for a profit of $1,250—more than enough to cover the premium. If, instead, the franc does not rise above the option's exercise price, the trader will let the option lapse and lose the premium. In no event, however, will the buyer lose more than the $560 paid for the premium.

Put Options.   In contrast to calls, in which buyers gain from unexpected rises in the spot price, puts enable buyers to gain from unexpected *declines* in the spot price. Specifically, the buyer of a put held to expiration will profit if the price of the underlying currency falls below the exercise price by more than enough to cover the cost of the premium. If the currency price does not fall below the option's exercise price, the buyer will lose the premium.

To see how puts can be used to profit from exchange rate declines, imagine a trader who believes that the Japanese yen will drop, relative to the dollar, by more than the rest of the market expects. The trader could bet on the extra decline by paying, say, a $225 premium for a June put on 6,250,000 yen with an exercise price of $0.0042. If by June the yen falls unexpectedly, say to $0.0040, the trader will find it profitable to exercise the put and sell the yen purchased in the spot market at $0.0040 to the option seller at the exercise price of $0.0042 for a gain of $1,250, an amount that more than offsets the cost of the premium.

These examples illustrate two important features of option trading. First, the amount the option buyer stands to gain depends on the movement of the spot price of the underlying currency, relative to the option's exercise price. Second, the risks in option trading are asymmetric. The most the option buyer stands to lose is the premium, while his potential gains are limited only by the subsequent movement of the underlying currency's exchange rates. By the same token, the most the option seller can gain is the premium, though his potential losses are bounded only by the range of future exchange-rate movements.[2] In effect, the option buyer is paying the seller to take on his risk, and the premium will rise to a value that compensates the seller for assuming that risk.

In contrast to options, the upside and downside risks in trading forward and futures contracts are symmetric. The buyer of a forward contract held to maturity will lose, dollar for dollar, as much when the spot price falls below the contract price as he will gain when the spot price rises above the contract price. Options are thus likely to attract traders who wish to profit from movements of prices in one direction while limiting their losses from adverse price movements. In addition, options are likely to attract traders who wish to profit from misalignments between prices on forward or futures contracts and prices on options. Option and forward foreign exchange prices, therefore, are not independent. (See the Appendix: Put-Call Parity.)

USING OPTIONS TO HEDGE CONTINGENCIES

The asymmetries between potential gains and losses in options allow them to be used—in ways that forwards and futures cannot—to hedge *contingencies:* transactions that are not certain to materialize. Consider, for example, a U.S. firm that has submitted a competitive bid in pounds to supply communications equipment in Britain. If it wins the bid, it will receive pounds, which it will then want to convert into dollars. Until the bids are awarded, the firm is exposed to the risk of a decline in the value of the pound, which would reduce the value of the contract award if it wins the bid. The firm would like to hedge against this risk. Forward or futures contracts are not the right hedging instruments in this case, because it is not certain that the firm will actually be awarded the bid. If the firm tries to hedge the bid by selling pounds under a forward contract, and then fails to win the bid, it will be left with a forward contract but no matching business transaction in the foreign currency. The firm will have started out trying to reduce its foreign exchange risk, only to wind up with a foreign currency exposure after all.

To hedge a contingent transaction like a competitive bid a firm should use an option; in this case, it should buy a put. If the anticipated transaction does occur, the firm can exercise the option and sell the foreign currency it receives at a set price. If, instead, the transaction falls through the firm can simply let the option expire. From the firm's perspective, buying an option is like buying insurance against foreign exchange risk by paying the option seller a premium to cover its risk.

Contingent transactions are not uncommon in international finance. The terms of an investment in a foreign firm, for example, may include the acquisition of warrants to buy the firm's shares at a fixed price in the future, with payment in the foreign currency. In another case, a firm's future foreign currency requirements may hinge upon whether it decides to take advantage of an option it has obtained to purchase a foreign asset—say, the right to purchase a hotel in Bavaria. Or a firm may anticipate receiving a future award in a foreign currency depending upon the outcome of a lawsuit in a foreign court. Each of these possible, but not certain, future claims or liabilities in a foreign currency can be hedged with options. The warrants and hotel option can be covered by buying calls, and the potential receipt of a lawsuit award covered by buying a put.

THE DEMAND FOR CURRENCY OPTIONS

Despite the advantages currency options have over forward and futures contracts in some situations, no markets existed for these options until recently. An unsuccessful effort had been made to start a market for puts and calls on foreign currencies in New York in the 1920s, and U.S. banks have occasionally arranged currency options privately for customers since the 1940s. But by and large, the market for currency options was dormant until the European Options Exchange (Amsterdam), the Montreal Exchange, and the Philadelphia Stock Exchange opened trading in currency options in late 1982. Once currency option trading was established on these exchanges, banks began writing substantial quantities of currency options for customers, creating an over-the-counter market parallel to the exchange markets.

The recent demand for currency options can be attributed to two factors: increased exchange-rate volatility and the growth of international trade. Prior to 1971, exchange rates were not as variable as they are now. At the Bretton Woods conference in 1944, the industrial nations agreed to have their central banks buy and sell dollars to keep exchange-rate movements within fairly narrow bounds. As a result, traders expected little variability in exchange rates. Under these circumstances, few market participants were willing to pay for option contracts to provide protection against adverse exchange-rate movements: the costs to maintaining uncovered foreign currency positions were small, as were the fees writers could have earned by producing option coverage.

After this system of nearly fixed exchange rates collapsed in 1971, most major currencies began to float with market forces and exchange rates became more volatile. The average monthly range of fluctuations of the deutsche mark to the dollar, for example, widened from 0.44 cents over the 1959 to 1971 period to 5.66 cents between 1971 and 1982—a more than twelvefold increase. At the same time that exchange rates were becoming more variable, the volume of trade in goods and services and financial flows between nations continued to grow. The sum of exports and imports in the U.S. alone grew from $135.9 billion in 1971 to $265.7 billion in 1982 in constant (inflation-adjusted) dollars. Forward and futures contracts could have been used to hedge the lion's share of these international transactions. Some portion of foreign trade, however, is carried out under contingent contracts, for which options are the desired hedging tool. Assuming that the proportion of contingencies in international trade is constant, the combination of volatile exchange rates and growing trade meant inevitably that a market for foreign currency options to hedge those contingencies would also grow. It was to meet this expanding market that exchanges and banks began to offer options.

CREATORS OF CURRENCY OPTION MARKETS

The existence of markets is often taken for granted, but creating a market can be a costly and risky venture. Before trading can advance beyond the crudest type of barter, several obstacles must be overcome. First, someone must provide the physical facilities for bringing buyers and sellers together, whether they are open-air booths, a bank of telephones, or an elaborate computerized trading floor. Next, someone has to provide a mechanism for matching buyers' and sellers' orders at a common price. Small markets sometimes employ an auctioneer, but most markets rely on dealers or marketmakers: firms that stand ready to trade with customers, buying and selling for their own account. Standing ready to trade with customers immediately, however, is risky; the danger always exists that the next customer may be willing to buy only at a price that is less than the price the last seller received. Markets for assets that are not physically present when agreements are made to exchange must overcome yet another problem: the risk that the other party to the transaction will default. Agreements made under these circumstances are promises to trade, and trading will falter unless there is some assurance that the promises will be kept.[3] Exchanges and banks have taken different approaches to overcoming these obstacles, producing different kinds of option contracts and trading procedures.

Exchange Options.   The Amsterdam, Montreal, and Philadelphia exchanges have devoted resources to providing centralized trading floors, and have adopted the open outcry system for matching option buyers to sellers (see Executing Currency Option Trades). To open trading in currency options to a wide range of participants, the exchanges have adopted contract designs and trading safeguards that have proven successful on futures exchanges and common stock option exchanges. To begin, currency options on all three exchanges were designed as American options with standardized trading units and expiration dates (see Contract Specifications on the Amsterdam, Montreal, and Philadelphia Exchanges). Contract standardization helps to reduce the number of dimensions over which buyers and sellers must agree. Some flexibility is lost as a result, but standardization is probably necessary for contract trading in a central marketplace: matching customers with a wide range of quantity and maturity preferences would be an administrative nightmare.[4] By standardizing the contract terms, the exchanges have made it possible to trade options in a secondary market—a market in which options can be bought and sold many times before expiration. Indeed, exchange options are so readily accepted by traders that no distinction exists between new and resold options: all are traded interchangeably on the exchange floor.[5]

The greatest obstacle to achieving widespread participation in option trading is credit risk: option buyers are at risk that sellers will default when the options are exercised. To assure buyers that sellers will fulfill their contracts, the exchanges

EXECUTING CURRENCY OPTION TRADES

The way currency option trades are made is perhaps best illustrated by following a typical trade through the Philadelphia Stock Exchange; the other exchanges follow essentially similar procedures. Suppose a customer wants to buy a British pound option with a $1.45 exercise price and June expiration date at the best price available on the market. The trading process begins when the customer calls a broker who is a member of the exchange and places the order. The broker books and clocks the order, then relays it electronically to the broker's booth on the exchange trading floor. The broker's floor trader then walks over to the other pound contract traders standing near the screens on which trades are reported, and shouts out his bid of, say, 1¢. Option price bids are quoted at cents per unit of the underlying currency, and a bid of 1¢ on a 12,500 British pound contract is equal to a premium of $125.

The floor trader's bid would be answered by offers to sell from other traders, at (say) 1.25¢, 1.20¢, and 1.15¢. The offers may be coming from three kinds of traders: specialists, market-makers, or floor brokers acting as agents for other customers. *Specialists* are firms designated by the exchange to maintain orderly trading and manage the limit orders for each currency. Some customers give their brokers orders to buy or sell only when prices reach a certain limit (say, "buy at $130.00" or "sell at $150.00"), and the specialist coordinates these orders. *Market-makers* are member firms who buy and sell for their own account, and who must make a bid or offer on a customer's order if called upon to do so by the specialist. In return for standing ready to trade even when it is not always in their interest to do so, market-makers enjoy reduced margin requirements, and are able to execute trades for their own account faster than traders who must use a broker.

The floor trader takes the lowest offer—in this case 1.15¢, implying a premium of $143.75—and "matches tickets" with the selling trader, confirming the trade in pencil on printed paper slips. The buying trader hands the slips to the specialist, who staples them and gives them to an exchange employee who puts the information into the exchange's computerized reporting system. As soon as the trade is in the exchange's reporting system it is flashed onto the trading floor screens and private wire service screens. By SEC rules, the trade must be reported on the system within 90 seconds of when it occurred. The broker's floor trader then wires confirmation of the trade back to the broker, who advises his customer that the trade has been completed. If the option seller is another customer rather than a market-maker, the seller's order will have followed a similar path through the customer's broker to the exchange floor, with one difference: the seller's broker will have required a margin deposit from its customer to protect the broker, the exchange's clearing corporation, and the option buyer from default.

CONTRACT SPECIFICATIONS
ON THE AMSTERDAM, MONTREAL,
AND PHILADELPHIA EXCHANGES

The European Options Exchange (Amsterdam), the Montreal Exchange, and the Philadelphia Stock Exchange all offer trading in standardized puts and calls on foreign currencies. The following table gives the number of foreign currency units underlying each option contract offered on the three exchanges:

Currency	Trading Units		
	European Options Exchange (Amsterdam)	Montreal Exchange	Philadelphia Stock Exchange
British pounds	£5,000	£5,000	£12,500
Canadian dollars	—	CD 50,000	CD 50,000
Deutsche marks	$10,000	DM 25,000	DM 62,500
Japanese yen	—	¥ 2,500,000	¥ 6,250,000
Swiss francs	—	SF 25,000	SF 62,500
Dutch guilders	$10,000	—	—

— Indicates that the contract is not offered on that exchange.

Payment for all options on the Montreal and Philadelphia exchanges is in U.S. dollars. Payment for each of the options offered on the Amsterdam exchange, however, is in a different currency. The Amsterdam exchange offers an option on British pounds with payment in U.S. dollars, an option on U.S. dollars with payment in Dutch guilders, and an option on U.S. dollars with payment in Deutsche marks. Contracts on all three exchanges are issued with maturities of 3, 6, and 9 months, with expiration dates set in March, June, September, and December to coincide with the maturity dates of the CME's International Monetary Market's foreign currency futures contracts. Option contract sizes are also compatible with the IMM's futures contracts; the Philadelphia exchange's options, for example, are exactly one half the size of the corresponding IMM futures contracts. Making currency option contracts compatible with futures contracts facilitates cross-trading between the two kinds of instruments, encouraging trading volume growth in both markets.

restrict trading privileges to members and provide clearing corporation guarantees for their options. Exchange rules require the public to trade currency options through exchange member firms, who are liable to other members for their customers' traders. In the event that an option seller defaults, then, the seller's member firm is responsible for completing the contract with the buyer's member firm. As a result, members have an incentive to execute trades only for customers they believe are willing and able to honor their contracts. The clearing corporation guarantees, however, provide an even stronger safeguard for traders. All organized options exchanges are affiliated with a clearing corporation, a nonprofit organization of member firms that clears trades on the exchange.[6] Though customers trade options with each other through member firms on the exchange, options are legally contracts with the clearing corporation, not other customers. In effect, the clearing corporation inserts itself between the buyer and seller of every option, giving each party a contract with the clearing corporation. The clearing corporation guarantees all trades, and stands ready to assess its member firms to cover losses resulting from a default by a member firm. To protect itself from losses, the clearing corporation requires that a security deposit known as a "margin" be posted by exchange members that have sold options; the members, in turn, generally require their customers to make margin deposits with them. By providing for clearing corporation guarantees, the exchanges have created an option instrument that people can trade without worrying about each other's creditworthiness.

Options on Currency Futures.   Recently, the Chicago Mercantile Exchange (CME) introduced a new option instrument to compete with the currency options offered by exchanges and banks: an option on a foreign currency futures contract. This option contract gives the holder the right to buy or sell a futures contract for deutsche marks, rather than the marks themselves. When a buyer exercises this option, he or she receives a futures contract to buy or sell 125,00 deutsche marks on the CME's International Monetary Market at a set price. The futures contract can either be offset immediately to take the gain or can be held to maturity. Like the currency options offered on other exchanges, the CME's option has standardized delivery dates and is guaranteed by a clearing corporation.

At first glance, an option on a futures contract rather than on the underlying currency appears to be an unnecessarily cumbersome instrument. For a number of reasons, however, options on futures and currency options may be close substitutes. Futures prices and spot currency prices are so closely correlated that an option on a futures contract is for most purposes as effective a hedging instrument as an option on the currency itself. Moreover, currency futures markets are more accessible to small traders seeking to make large trades than are spot or forward foreign currency markets. In trading spot currencies with a bank, small traders typically would have to pay retail prices that are higher than the wholesale prices charged on large trades. In addition, banks are reluctant to make forward contracts that are large relative to the resources of small traders. In contrast, arranging for a large futures contract to make delivery under an option is no problem for small traders. Also, an option on a futures contract makes it easy for traders to shift between options and futures to take advantage of temporary price misalignments between the two markets. The CME hopes that its option on a futures contract will be attractive to the kinds of traders who currently trade currency options and will appeal to new groups of traders as well.

Bank Options.   The bank market for foreign currency options is composed of large U.S. banks which write options for their corporate customers. When banks write puts and calls, they are creating a market individually by buying and selling for their own account. Banks provide no trading floors for the exchange of orders; instead, they quote prices directly to customers, often by telephone. Usually, banks only sell options, and write the contracts as European options. Because the option seller is commonly a bank with whom the customer has had a long-standing relationship, the customer generally has little concern that the bank will default on the option.

Banks write currency options on an individual basis, tailoring the contracts to the specific currency, quantity, and maturity needs of each customer. Not surprisingly, no secondary market yet exists for bank options: creating a secondary market would require banks to agree to some minimal contract standardization conventions, and reaching such an agreement is likely to take some time. Banks sometimes reduce the risks they have taken in selling options, however, by buying currency options on an exchange. When banks completely offset their option sales in this way, they are acting as middlemen between their customer and the ultimate sellers of the contract. When banks choose instead not to offset options written for customers, they are acting as insurers, bearing their customers' exchange risk in return for fee income.

WHICH OPTION MARKETS WILL PROSPER?

Is the market for currency options large enough to accommodate the growing number of competitors seeking to provide traders with options? Will customers prefer some types of currency option markets to others? To the extent that differences among the option contracts offered in various markets are small, traders are likely to gravitate to the market that promises the highest trading volume. Studies of futures markets have shown that trading costs decline with volume, so a single market for any contract will provide lower cost trading than two markets that each have half as much volume.[7] This explains why each contract traded in financial futures markets has come to be traded on a single exchange, unless the exchanges have been located on different continents (with different trading hours), and there is little reason to believe that the experience with trading in foreign currency options will be different. If, on the other hand, the differences in option contracts offered in various markets are large, each contract may appeal to traders with different needs, and all marketmakers may coexist.

Differences among exchanges' options are small: the currency options traded on the Amersterdam, Montreal, and Philadelphia exchanges are fundamentally the same instruments, and it is clear that the three exchanges are competing head to head for the same kind of customers. So far, the Philadelphia Stock Exchange has generated by far the greatest trading volume: trading has expanded rapidly from an average of 394 puts and calls per day in January 1983 to over 5,778 per day in March 1984. The Philadelphia Stock Exchange has generated more trading in each of its contracts than the other two exchanges, with the exception of the Canadian dollar option, which traded in greater volume in Montreal than in

Philadelphia in every month but one in 1983. Volume on all three exchanges has picked up sharply in early 1984, reflecting in part an increase in exchange rate volatility in the first three months of the year.

Options based on currencies and the CME's option on a currency futures contract are similar enough to suggest that the CME will also be competing directly with the other exchanges. The CME's deutsche mark futures option has done well since its introduction on January 24, 1984: an average of 1,954 calls and puts were traded per day in February, 2,756 in March, and 2,332 in April 1984. Nevertheless, trading volume in Philadelphia's mark contract is still growing, indicating that for the time being both exchanges are sharing an expanding market.

While the differences among the exchanges' options are small, differences between the kinds of options offered by the exchanges and those offered by banks are large enough to suggest that they may attract different customers. The standardized and guaranteed options available on exchanges are likely to attract buyers who need options on major currencies and buyers who do not wish to incur the costs of searching out and evaluating the credit of sellers. In addition, the exchanges are likely to attract small investors: trading on exchanges is open to virtually all buyers, and to any sellers able to meet their brokers' margin requirements. The tailor-made options written by banks, on the other hand, are likely to be attractive to customers who need options in less frequently traded currencies, or who need options for maturities that differ substantially from those offered by exchanges. Bank options are also likely to attract customers who have an infrequent need for options, but make forward contracts with banks regularly.

To date, trading on the Philadelphia exchange has attracted a large number of foreign firms and individual investors, as well as U.S. and foreign banks.[8] Banks, in contrast, appear to have written options mostly for large U.S. and multinational corporations, many of whom already use the banks for their forward foreign exchange trading. These differences in customers indicate that exchange and bank options may exist side by side for some time, much as futures and forward markets for foreign exchange have coexisted during the past decade.

CONCLUSION

Since late 1982, traders have been able to use options on foreign currencies, in addition to forward and futures contracts, to manage their exchange-rate risk. These options allow traders to profit from favorable exchange rate changes while avoiding the risks of adverse movements. Because they convey the right, but not the obligation, to buy or sell a foreign currency, options can be used to hedge transactions that are not certain to occur, a task for which forward and futures contracts are not well suited.

Continued volatility in exchange rates and growth in international trade will ensure a demand for currency options. Exchange options and over-the-counter bank options are likely to coexist for some time, because they are different instruments and appeal to different customers. Many exchange options, however, are close substitutes for each other. The experience with futures markets suggests that not all exchanges' options will prosper, and that traders will increasingly give their business to the market able to offer the greatest volume and lowest cost trades.

APPENDIX

Put-Call Parity

Though options and forward contracts are distinct instruments, their prices are linked together by the actions of traders who buy and sell both instruments in search of profits. The basic trading strategy for profiting from a price difference between option and forward markets is called a *reversal*. With this strategy, a trader simultaneously buys a call and sells a put, both for the same expiration date and exercise price E. This strategy will give the trader a pattern of gains and losses that duplicates that on a forward contract to purchase the currency on that expiration date at the exercise price E. The trader will, by maturity, gain dollar-for-dollar on the call by the amount the spot price rises above E, or lose dollar-for-dollar on the put by the amount the spot price falls below E, just as he would on a forward contract. The price at which the trader has effectively purchased currency forward, however, should take into account the interest cost of borrowing the difference between the premium C paid for the call and the premium P received for the put (if C is greater than P) over the life of the contracts. Assuming the trader can borrow at an interest rate i, the price at which the trader is buying the currency forward under the reversal will be:

(1)
$$E + (C - P)(1 + i)$$

where C and P are measured per quantity of currency traded.

If the cost of obtaining the currency using this strategy is cheaper than buying it under a forward contract at the going forward rate F, the trader will, by coupling the reversal with a forward sale, earn a profit of π_r:

(2)
$$\pi_r = F - E - (C - P)(1 + i)$$

Alternatively, if the cost of buying currency under a forward contract is cheaper than obtaining it by combining puts and calls, the trader could profit by executing the mirror image trade of the reversal called a *conversion*. Here the trader would create an artificial contract to sell the currency forward by buying a put, selling a call, and investing the difference (if it is positive) between the two premiums in a money market instrument paying a rate of interest i. This strategy will, coupled with a forward purchase, produce a profit of π_c:

(3)
$$\pi_c = E + (C - P)(1 + i) - F$$

As many traders try to take advantage of price differentials between the forward and options markets, they will drive the call prices up and put prices down when executing reversals (and drive call prices down and put prices up in executing conversions) until no more profits can be made with these strategies ($\pi_r = \pi_c = 0$). This implies that in equilibrium the difference between the call and put premiums for an option at an exercise price E will be equal to the difference between the forward exchange rate F and E, discounted to the market interest rate or:

(4)
$$C - P = (F - E)/(1 + i)$$

This relationship is called *put-call parity.* How close does it come to describing the relationship we see in reported option and forward prices? A complete answer requires a careful statistical study, but a rough idea can be obtained by seing how close the put-call parity theory comes to predicting the actual price differences between puts and calls on one of the Philadelphia Stock Exchange's most active contracts on a recent date. On July 17, 1984, at 10:11 a.m., calls on the Deutsche mark contract with a \$.36 striking price and September expiration were trading for \$318.75, while puts on that contract were trading for \$631.25. These prices are the average bid-offer prices on recent trades, kindly provided by the Financial Options Group, Inc. A 2-month forward contract made on July 17th would be settled on the same date the options expired, and the average bid-offer rate on this contract posted by Citibank's New York office was \$.3555. The 2-month CD rate, taken here to be a representative interest rate, was 11.63 percent, or 1.85 percent for 2 months.

Inserting the figures for the forward rate, the exercise price, and the interest rate into the put-call parity formula gives a predicted difference between the call and put premiums of $-$ \$276.14:

$$\text{Predicted } (C - P) = [(F - E) \times 62{,}500]/(1 + i)$$

$$= [(.3555 - .36) \times 62{,}500]/(1.0185)$$

$$= -\$276.14$$

The difference between the forward price and the exercise price $(F - E)$ was multiplied by the number of Deutsche marks in the Philadelphia Stock Exchange's contract to put these prices in the same units as the premium.

The actual difference between the call and put options on July 17th was $- \$312.50$. So the parity formula used with market data gives a close prediction of what the relationship among call, put, and forward prices was on the date. Could traders have executed reversals and conversions at the time the market data were taken to profit from the price difference? The answer is no: inserting the appropriate bid and offer prices into the reversal condition formulas (equations (2) and (3)) revealed no profit opportunities. In addition, the formulas do not take brokerage costs—which are on the order of \$13 to \$16 per option—into account. At the time the market data were collected, the September Deutsche mark option with a \$.36 striking price was not mispriced relative to the forward market.

NOTES

[1] Forward and futures contracts can be fulfilled either by delivering the currency specified in the contract or by making a second, offsetting contract. Forward contracts for foreign exchange are generally made with commercial banks and can be tailored to specific customer needs. Futures contracts are similar to forward contracts, but are traded in standardized quantities with regular maturities on organized exchanges, are guaranteed by the exchanges, and generally require a security deposit (called a "margin"). See K. Alec Chrystal, "A Guide to Foreign Exchange Markets," *Review* 66, no. 3, Federal Reserve Bank of St. Louis, March 1984, pp. 5–18.

[2] Puts and calls can also be combined in a number of complex strategies to bet on price volatility, rather than on the direction of a price movement. For a discussion of these strategies in currency option markets, see Ian H. Giddy, "Foreign Exchange Options," *The Journal of Futures Markets* 3, no. 2 (1983), pp. 143–66.

[3] Sir John Hicks has called trading in markets where the goods are not present "trading in promises." See his book, *A Theory of Economic History* (Oxford: Oxford University Press, 1969), for a discussion of the crucial role of marketmakers and contract protection in the development of markets.

[4] Just imagine the difficulties involved in trying to negotiate a match between a buyer's order for a June 17 option on 145,000 deutsche marks with a striking price of 0.366 to a seller's order for an option on 112,500 marks, to expire July 2, with a striking price of 0.373.

[5] Once a secondary market exists, buyers may find it easier to sell the option to a new buyer, rather than to exercise the option and actually take delivery of (or deliver) the underlying currency. The premium on the option will always rise to reflect a difference between the spot price and the option's exercise price, and will generally exceed this amount, reflecting the probability that the spot price might deviate even further from the exercise price before the option expires. See Robert A. Jarrow and Andrew Rudd, *Option Pricing* (Homewood, Ill.: Richard D. Irwin, 1983) for a discussion of the determinants of option prices.

[6] Options on the Philadelphia Stock Exchange are cleared and guaranteed by the Options Clearing Corporation, which also clears and guarantees equity and debt options traded on the American Options Exchange, the Chicago Board Options Exchange, the Pacific Stock Exchange, and the New York Stock Exchange. Currency options on the European Options Exchange and the Montreal Exchange are cleared and guaranteed by the International Options Clearing Corporation, which is operated as a joint venture with the Vancouver Stock Exchange and Sydney Stock Exchange.

[7] See Lester G. Telser, "Why Are there Organized Futures Exchanges?" *Journal of Law and Economics* 24, no. 1 (April 1981).

[8] Subsidiaries of two bank holding companies, Bank of America and Citicorp, began serving as specialists on the floor of the Philadelphia Stock Exchange in 1984. In addition, in April 1984, the Federal Reserve Board approved an application of Fidelcor, Inc., a Pennsylvania bank holding company, to trade foreign currency options for its customers through a subsidiary.

31

Foreign Banking in the United States: A Regulatory and Supervisory Perspective

Betsy Buttrill White

The business of banking has changed substantially over the last two decades. A major aspect of this change has been the international expansion of banking operations. In the 1960s, U.S. banks moved abroad in large numbers. In the 1970s, foreign banks accelerated their expansion in this country, bringing home the effects of this change in banking.

The foreign banking presence in the United States has further stimulated competition among banks and has enhanced the international status of U.S. financial markets. But it also underscores the regulatory and supervisory issues which inevitably arise when banks move outside their home countries: What factors motivate banks to move beyond their local markets? When banks cross national boundaries, what changes in bank supervision are necessary to assure the safety and soundness of the banking system? How far does national supervisory responsibility and authority stretch? What types of regulations should apply to foreign banks in domestic markets? How do regulations affect and how are regulations affected by international banking?

INTERNATIONAL EXPANSION OF BANKING—MOTIVATING FACTORS

The evolution of international banking since the early 1960s reflects changes in the economic and regulatory environments in which banks operate. By the same token, the changing nature of banking has influenced economic activity and the nature and scope of bank regulations. This article focuses on the regulatory influence on international banking, and the impact the international expansion of this business has had on regulations and supervisory practices.[1]

During the 1960s, several factors combined to create incentives for U.S. banks to expand their overseas operations. First, the relative strength of the dollar stimulated American corporate investment abroad. Second, beginning in 1965, the

From *Quarterly Review*, Federal Reserve Bank of New York, Summer 1982.

voluntary credit restraint program imposed restrictions on lending to foreigners from domestic offices. Third, Regulation Q ceilings and reserve requirements on domestic deposits—not so onerous in low rate periods—exacted a heavy toll on domestic banking operations in the relatively high rate periods of 1966 and 1969–70.

Put another way, in the 1960s, regulation increased the cost of doing business out of domestic offices at a time when U.S. corporations and others were generating lucrative business abroad. By setting up branches in foreign countries, U.S. banks avoided the costs of these regulatory constraints. In 1960, eight U.S. banks had 102 overseas banking offices. Today, 155 Federal Reserve member banks have over 700 offices abroad.

In many respects, the rapid growth of foreign banking in this country in the 1970s is a mirror image of the U.S. banking expansion abroad. The motivations and strategies stem from the same basic factors—economics and regulations. In the 1970s, foreign corporations stepped up their investment activities in this country. Foreign banks, like their U.S. counterparts in earlier years, followed suit, setting up operations in the United States to sustain and expand the corporate relationships originally established in their home countries.

Further, the dominant role of the dollar in international finance in the 1960s and 1970s made a dollar-based operation advantageous for foreign banks doing an international business. With the emergence of New York as one of the major international financial centers of the world, foreign banks set up operations here to compete in domestic money markets as well as to provide global and around-the-clock services to their clientele.

Finally, the regulatory and political climate in the United States helped attract foreign banks here in the 1970s. Until the enactment of the International Banking Act of 1978 (IBA), branches and agencies of foreign banks were supervised and regulated only at the state level. They were not subject to Federal Reserve reserve requirements, deposit interest rate ceilings, or restrictions on interstate banking.[2]

FOREIGN BANKS IN THE UNITED STATES

Foreign banks operate in the United States through three major types of offices: agencies, branches, and subsidiaries.[3] Branches and agencies are merely extensions of the parent bank, while subsidiaries are separately capitalized banking entities. The major difference between branches and agencies is that agencies are not allowed to accept deposits from citizens or residents of the United States.[4]

The structure of foreign banking operations in this country is summarized in Table 1. At the end of 1981, the number of branches (194) and agencies (195) were about equal. However, about two fifths of foreign bank assets were held at branches and only about one fourth at agencies. The 52 foreign bank subsidiaries accounted for about one third of foreign bank assets in this country.

The organizational form chosen by foreign banks has been greatly influenced by state and federal laws. Prior to the IBA, licensing of branches and agencies was controlled at the state level. For example, California effectively prohibited entry by foreign branches. While California law explicitly permits the establishment of branches by foreign banks, it also requires that branches have Federal Deposit Insurance Corporation (FDIC) insurance. It was not until the passage of the IBA that the FDIC was authorized to insure branches of foreign banks.

TABLE 1
Foreign Banking Offices in the United States, December 1981

Location of Parent Bank	Number of Physical Offices by Ownership				
	Agencies	Branches	Subsidiaries	Total Offices	Total Assets (billions of dollars)
Japan	27	31	12	70	$88.9
Canada	20	18	10	48	23.4
United Kingdom	12	19	7	38	46.2
France	7	14	1	22	16.1
Israel	6	13	3	22	4.2
Brazil	14	6	0	20	4.0
Germany	6	14	0	20	7.3
Spain	8	6	6	20	4.0
Korea	11	5	1	17	1.9
Hong Kong	8	6	1	15	12.4
Italy	5	9	1	15	10.9
Netherlands	4	7	1	12	4.8
Mexico	10	0	1	11	3.1
Switzerland	5	6	0	11	11.1
Other Asia*	23	19	2	44	1.7
Other Latin America	13	4	3	20	7.9
Australia and New Zealand	6	7	0	13	1.3
Other Europe	3	7	2	12	5.7
Middle East and Africa	7	3	1	11	0.7
Total	195	194	52	441	255.7

U.S. Location	Number of Physical Offices by State			
	Agencies	Branches	Subsidiaries	Total Offices
New York	61	113	24	198
California	96	4	20	120
Illinois	—	36	2	38
Florida	25	—	1	26
Washington	—	10	—	10
Georgia	9	—	—	9
Oregon	—	8	—	8
All other	4	23	5	32
Total numbers	195	194	52	441
Total assets (billions of dollars)	$65.5	$107.7	$82.5	$255.7

* Excludes Middle East.

New York State law permits foreign banks to establish branches within the state, *provided* New York banks are allowed entry into the entering bank's home country. Until recently, Canadian law prohibited foreign banking operations in Canada. Consequently, Canadian banks had been limited to establishing subsidiaries and agencies in New York. Further, New York law does not allow foreign banks to operate both agencies *and* branches; the foreign bank must choose one form or the other.

The IBA authorized the Comptroller of the Currency to license federal branches and agencies, provided certain conditions are not violated. In particular, the comptroller *cannot* issue a federal license to a foreign bank to open an agency or branch in a state in which the bank already operates such an office under state law. Further, federal licenses cannot be granted to establish offices in states which generally prohibit foreign branch and agency operations. The full scope of the comptroller's authority, however, remains unclear. For example, under New York State law, foreign banks are allowed to establish branches. However, Australian banks are not allowed to establish state-licensed branches, because Australia does not allow foreign bank entry into its banking market. The comptroller granted a federal license to an Australian branch, because foreign braching, per se, is not prohibited in New York. This decision has been challenged and awaits a final ruling by the courts.

The organizational form chosen by a foreign bank can also depend on the type of business the bank expects to do. A foreign bank wishing to offer a full range of banking services in the United States would generally choose to establish or to acquire a subsidiary bank. Those seeking to conduct a wholesale lending business, in part funded in the United States, would generally need to open only branches. In states which do not allow foreign branching, some foreign banks have chosen to open both a subsidiary and an agency. The subsidiary provides a dollar deposit base while the agency, not subject to interstate branching restrictions or lending limits, affords considerable lending flexibility.[5] Foreign banks seeking to establish an investment outlet for dollar balances accumulated abroad might choose to establish only agencies here.

Foreign banking operations in this country are highly concentrated in New York, San Francisco, Los Angeles, and Chicago (Table 1). Oregon and Washington have long had a number of foreign banks—especially Canadian and Japanese. In recent years, Miami and Atlanta have experienced rapid growth of foreign banking offices. In choosing among states allowing foreign banking, foreign bankers have been influenced primarily by their choice of target markets. Consequently, such factors as the concentration of large corporate headquarters and trade flows have been important in determining the location of foreign banking offices in this country.

Although over 175 foreign banks from 39 countries operate offices in this country, the foreign presence in U.S. markets is dominated by banks from major industrial countries. Japanese, British, and Canadian banks operate over one third (156 of the total 441) of these offices (Table 1). Further, the number of banking offices understates the posiion of these banks among foreign banks in the United States. At the end of 1981, Japanese banks held one third of foreign bank assets in this country and British and Canadian banks together held over one fourth of these assets.

BANKING ACTIVITIES OF FOREIGN BANKS[6]

Most foreign banks in this country operate solely in the wholesale banking and money markets. Relatively few foreign banks actively seek retail business. In fact, a number of foreign banks discourage retail depositors by requiring relatively large minimum deposit balances. The retail banking markets—at least in large urban areas where foreign banks are located—are generally difficult for a foreign-named bank to penetrate. Moreover, establishing a retail business requires large investments in office space, computers, and personnel. Those investments typically show a profit only over a long time horizon. A good number of those foreign banks that have entered the retail market have done so through the acquisition of domestic banks with already established retail branch networks. Foreign agencies and branches are, therefore, by and large wholesale banking offices and should be analyzed separately from subsidiaries.

The target markets of foreign agencies and branches generally are determined by their parent organizations. More often than not, all U.S. agencies and branches of a given foreign bank pursue a common strategy, sometimes even guided by common management. Therefore, to analyze the business activities of a foreign bank in this country, one should look at a consolidated balance sheet of its branches and agencies, not at individual offices.[7]

The parent organization's strategy for its U.S. operations is influenced by a variety of factors. These include the parent organization's home-country banking activities and the size and scope of its worldwide banking operations. The dollar position of affiliated offices outside the United States, the areas of expertise of the bank's management staff, and home-country laws and regulations also can play a role.

The most common motivation for entering the United States is to expand existing types of business or business relationships. Most often foreign banks are seeking:

- To service the U.S. operations of corporations operating in the home country.
- To finance trade with the home country or with other countries in which the banks have offices.
- To set up a foreign exchange operation in New York.
- To operate in the U.S. money markets.
- To generate U.S. investment interest in the home country.

Some foreign banks provide a very broad range of services, while others focus on only one or two of these types of activities.

The decision to acquire or to establish a subsidiary bank in this country generally reflects the parent bank's overall U.S. or worldwide strategy. The activities of a subsidiary bank are managed separately at arm's length from the parent bank's other U.S. operations. Nevertheless, the subsidiary contributes to the scope of banking services a foreign bank can offer to its customers and, more often than not, the major activities of the subsidiary complement or supplement the services provided by other U.S. offices of the same bank.

The economic and business factors affecting foreign banking operations in the United States are common across banks. However, one factor—home-country laws, regulations, and practices—serves to distinguish the U.S. balance sheets of foreign banks from different countries. For example, Japanese banks are restricted in the number and types of foreign banking offices they may open.[8] Japanese banks do not have "shell" branches in the Caribbean as do many U.S. and other banks. Thus, Japanese agencies and branches in the United States seem to serve a somewhat broader international dollar lending role, and they have relatively more loans to non-U.S. residents than most other foreign banks. In contrast, Canadian banks book a relatively small amount of loans to nonresidents in the United States. This can be attributed, in part, to Canadian tax law, which provides an incentive to book such loans at Bahamian and Cayman branches. German bank activity in the United States is influenced by home-country regulations, which pertain to a bank's worldwide consolidated balance sheet. For example, German liquidity requirements—originally designed to protect the domestic depositor against loss—limit the degree to which asset and liability maturities can be mismatched. This, in effect, restricts the degree to which U.S. offices of German banks can extend long-term loans.

Many analysts have tried to assess foreign banking operations in the United States by looking at the balance sheets of different types of foreign banking offices. They have compared the composition and size of assets and liabilities across branches, agencies, and subsidiaries. Such an approach has several limitations. First, as discussed previously, the agencies and branches of a given foreign bank generally have the same objectives and therefore should not be analyzed separately. Second, and probably more important, the U.S. balance sheet is only one part of the whole. Foreign bank loans to U.S. residents are not always booked in this country. For example, LIBOR-priced loans are often booked at Caribbean branches, where they are funded with Eurodollar liabilities. Finally, foreign bank dollar loans to third countries may be negotiated elsewhere (e.g., at the parent bank, where management responsibility for such loans may lie) but booked in the United States where they are funded.

Table 2 presents the consolidated balance sheet of all U.S. agencies and branches of foreign banks at the end of 1981. Table 3 presents the same information for foreign bank subsidiaries. For the reasons cited, these figures, at best, present only a partial picture of foreign bank activity in this country. However, several observations can be made. First, loans to domestic nonfinancial entities which are booked at agencies and branches are not fully funded by deposits from domestic nonfinancial entities. That is, foreign banks do not appear to be raising funds in this country to lend abroad. Quite the contrary, foreign agencies and branches rely heavily on affiliates and the interbank market for funding. This suggests that many foreign agencies and branches serve primarily as investment outlets for dollar balances acquired by overseas offices.

A second observation is that foreign agencies and branches hold a relatively small amount of government and corporate securities. A review of individual branch and agency data suggests that most of the $4 billion in securities is owned by a relatively few New York City branches and agencies which have special expertise in U.S. securities markets. The reason most often given for the small holdings of government securities is their yield, which is low, relative to the funding costs faced by these banks. Further, income earned on state and local government securities, while exempt from U.S. federal taxes, is not exempt from home-country taxation.

Finally, a comparison of agency and branch balance sheets with those of subsidiaries underscores the differences in their target markets. Subsidiaries have greater retail operations and do more domestic business than do agencies and branches. This is reflected in the relatively large portion of deposits due to nonbanks. These deposits represent about 70 percent of total liabilities. Also, loans to foreigners, while only estimated, appear to be less than 5 percent of total assets. Loans to domestic nonbank entities account for about one half of total assets. In contrast, agencies and branches rely heavily on the interbank market for

---

TABLE 2
Assets and Liabilities of U.S. Agencies and Branches of Foreign Banks, December 1981

Assets	Billions of Dollars	Liabilities	Billions of Dollars
Loans to nonfinancial entities	$ 80.6	Deposits due to non-financial entities	$ 34.8
U.S. addresses	(44.2)	U.S. addresses	(26.6)
Foreign addresses	(36.4)	Foreign addresses	(8.2)
Claims on unaffiliated financial institutions*	61.7	Liabilities to unaffiliated financial institutions‡	81.0
Claims on affiliates	19.3	Liabilities to affiliates	36.5
Other assets†	7.3	Other liabilities§	20.9
Securities	4.3		
Total assets	173.2	Total liabilities	173.2

Note: see Table 3 for footnotes.

TABLE 3
Assets and Liabilities of U.S. Banks Owned by Foreigners, December 1981

Assets	Billions of Dollars	Liabilities	Billions of Dollars
Loans to nonfinancial entities	$ 47.6	Deposits due to non-financial entities	$53.8
U.S. addresses	(44.2)¶		
Foreign addresses	(3.4)¶		
Claims on financial institutions*	21.9	Liabilities to financial institutions‡	14.5
Securities	9.1	Other liabilities§	8.1
Other assets†	4.5	Capital	6.2
Allowance for possible loan loss	−0.6		
Total assets	82.5	Total liabilities and capital	82.5

Figures may not sum to totals due to rounding.

* Includes cash due from depository institutions, federal funds sold, funds loaned under repurchase agreement to banks, and loans to financial institutions.

† Includes lease-financing receivables, funds loaned under repurchase agreements to nonbanks, and "other assets" (which include income earned on loans but not collected and other claims on nonrelated parties).

‡ Includes deposits and credit balances due to banks, federal funds purchased, funds borrowed from depository institutions under repurchase agreements, other liabilities to banks for borrowed money, certified and officer's checks, traveler's checks, and letters of credit sold for cash.

§ Includes liabilities to nonbanks for borrowed money, liabilities on acceptances outstanding, funds borrowed under repurchase agreement with nondepository institutions, and "other liabilities" to nonrelated parties (which include expenses accrued and unpaid).

¶ For subsidiaries with no foreign offices or less than $100 million in assets, no breakdown between foreign and domestic loans is available. All loans reported by these banks were put in the U.S. addresses category.

funding. Two thirds of their liabilities are to financial institutions. On the asset side, loans to foreigners represent about one fifth of total assets.

U. S. REGULATIONS AND FOREIGN BANK ACTIVITY

The regulatory and legal environment in which banks operate affects the types of business banks do and the locations in which they operate. As discussed earlier, the rapid expansion of international banking over the last two decades reflects this influence. But it has also brought about changes in banking laws and regulations. In the United States, the two most recent examples of this are the enactment of the IBA and the change in federal regulations and state laws to encourage offshore banking in this country.

The growth of foreign banks in this country in the 1970s highlighted the discrepancy between the regulation of these institutions and the regulation of domestic banks at the federal level. The IBA was enacted to close this gap. This legislation set in motion a series of regulatory changes that embody the principle of *national treatment* of foreign banks operating in this country. Under national treatment, to the extent reasonably possible, foreign banks are subject to the same restrictions and have the same privileges as domestic banks. To this end, the IBA restricts the expansion of interstate deposit-taking by foreign banks, subjects foreign branches and agencies to Federal Reserve reserve requirements and interest-rate regulations, requires deposit insurance for branches engaged in retail banking, extends the restrictions on nonbank activities of the Bank Holding Company Act to foreign banks operating branches and agencies in the United States, and allows agencies and branches access to the discount window and to payment services provided by Federal Reserve banks.[9]

In providing greater equality of treatment, the IBA has also affected the business of banking for foreign bankers in this country. In this respect, perhaps the most important provision of the act was the imposition of Federal Reserve reserve requirements. As these requirements have been phased in, the reserve costs to foreign banks have increased.[10] As a result, foreign banks have found it necessary to monitor and to manage their reserve positions more closely than in the past.

Further, reserve requirements have affected the relative costs of various types of funds. For example, the 3 percent reserve requirement on jumbo certificates of deposit (CDs), effective in August of this year [1982], increases by about ⅜ percentage point the overall or "all-in" cost of CDs offered at 12 percent. Foreign bank CDs are generally priced by adding a spread to the interest rate paid by large domestic money market banks on their CDs. Consequently, foreign banks cannot adjust their CD rates (as do money-center banks) to offset the increase in reserve costs if they wish to remain competitive in issuing CDs.

Some foreign bankers claim that this has necessitated charging higher loan rates, while others assert that competition prohibits higher loan rates and that their net interest margins have suffered. In either case, the relative competitive position of foreign banks in funding and extending loans in the United States has changed. Inevitably, this will alter the future growth of their commercial lending business and may lead some banks to redirect resources to other banking activities.

In responding to the foreign bank expansion in this country, regulatory changes promulgated under the IBA generally were in the direction of greater regulatory coverage. However, the IBA also mandated a liberalization of rules governing Edge Act corporations to enable U.S. banks to compete more effectively with similar foreign-owned institutions. As a result, the Federal Reserve amended its regulations to allow Edge Act corporations to open branches nationwide and to expand their international banking services and deposit-taking ability. Keeping with the principle of national treatment, foreign banks were also permitted to own Edge corporations.

TABLE 4
Assets and Liabilities of Foreign-owned International Banking Facilities,* December 31, 1981 (in billions of dollars)

Assets and Liabilities	Country of Ownership						
	Japan	Italy	United Kingdom	Switzerland	Germany	All others	Total
Number	48	11	9	5	8	71	152
Assets:							
Loans to nonfinancial entities	12.7	1.9	2.1	0.4	0.5	3.7	21.3
Claims on unaffiliated financial institutions	6.0	2.7	2.3	1.7	0.4	2.8	16.0
Claims on affiliates	0.2	0.1	—	—	—	0.8	1.1
Securities	0.4	†	—	—	†	†	0.5
Other assets	0.3	0.1	0.1	0.1	†	0.1	0.7
Total assets/liabilities	19.7	4.8	4.5	2.2	1.0	7.5	39.6
Liabilities:							
Deposits due to nonfinancial entities	0.7	0.5	0.2	0.1	†	1.0	2.6
Liabilities to unaffiliated financial institutions	5.7	2.1	0.1	0.4	0.1	1.2	9.6
Liabilities to affiliates	6.2	0.5	1.0	1.7	0.2	2.9	12.5
Net due to establishing institution	6.9	1.1	3.0	†	0.6	2.1	13.8
Other liabilities	0.1	0.6	0.2	†	†	0.2	1.1

* These data are included in those presented in Tables 2 and 3. Figures may not sum to totals due to rounding.
† Less than $50 million.

Another reduction of U.S. regulatory restrictions stemming from the expansion of international banking was the creation of international banking facilities (IBFs). Effective December 3, 1981, depository institutions operating in the United States—both foreign and domestic—were permitted to establish IBFs for the purpose of conducting international business within this country free from interest-rate restrictions, reserve requirements, and FDIC insurance. Additionally, several states have enacted legislation that exempts IBF income from state and local taxes.[11]

The reaction to IBFs by foreign bankers seems to vary across nationalities. Japanese and Italian banks have shifted the most assets to their IBFs (Table 4). In large part, this probably reflects the fact that these banks do not operate "shell" branches in the Caribbean. Some bankers, such as the Swiss, report the appeal of U.S. country risk has led home-country customers to shift dollar deposits from third countries to IBFs. Other bankers are skeptical of the ultimate attractiveness of these facilities but have established IBFs to accommodate potential customer demand should it materialize—that is, to maintain their competitive position.

SUPERVISORY ISSUES

When banks expand beyond their home-country boundaries, the issue of supervisory responsibility cannot be ignored. The soundness of a foreign banking organization should be of concern to both the host country and the home country. Failure of such an organization could send ripple effects throughout the financial systems of both the host country and the home country. In fact, the high degree of cross-border interbank borrowing and lending leaves no banking market completely immune to the effects of a large bank failure.

The IBA authorized, for the first time, participation in the supervision of the U.S. operations of foreign banks by federal banking authorities. This included the authorization of the Federal Reserve to act as the residual supervisory agency to ensure a national overview of interstate activities of foreign banks. In exercising this authority, the Federal Reserve draws on examinations conducted by the primary federal and state bank regulatory authorities. In addition, the Federal Reserve receives annual financial information on the operations of the foreign parent banking organization.

However, effective supervision of international banks cannot be limited to unilateral efforts by domestic authorities. It requires a cooperative effort among national supervisory authorities. A major step forward in the area of supervisory cooperation was taken in 1975 with the formation at the Bank for International Settlements (BIS) of the Committee on Banking Regulations and Supervisory Practices.[12] This committee was formed by the central bank governors from the Group of Ten major industrial countries[13] and Switzerland to improve the coordination of national surveillance of international banking activities. Committee meetings provide a forum for the discussion of the key supervisory and regulatory issues by senior supervisory officials from the major industrial countries. And, perhaps more importantly, they provide an avenue for developing personal working relationships between supervisors, which facilitate rapid and effective cooperation should banks experience difficulties.

Effective supervision of international banks rests on two premises. First, national authorities must be *willing* to cooperate in monitoring the activities of the overseas operations of their own banks and the local operations of foreign banks. Second, authorities must be *capable* of supervising their banks' international business.

One of the first tasks of the committee in 1975 was to develop principles for international supervisory cooperation. In particular, guidelines were needed to ensure comprehensive and coordinated surveillance of all foreign banking offices. The general statement of the committee's views—commonly referred to as the Concordat—was endorsed by the countries represented on the committee in December 1975.

In dividing supervisory responsibility among national banking authorities, the Concordat distinguishes between the supervision of liquidity and solvency and between the supervision of foreign branches and legally separate banking subsidiaries incorporated in a foreign country. The supervision of liquidity of all foreign offices and the solvency of subsidiaries is regarded as the primary responsibility of the host-country authorities. The supervision of solvency of foreign branches is considered to be primarily in the hands of home-country authorities.

To be fully effective, the principles set forth in the Concordat need be endorsed by supervisors worldwide. Acceptance by supervisors outside the BIS member countries has spread, but no formal endorsements have been made. Further, the effectiveness of the Concordat rests on the capability of national authorities to supervise the international activities of their banks.

Fundamental to the effective implementation of the Concordat is the timely availability of information necessary to the supervisory process. In particular, worldwide consolidated financial information is needed to assess the overall soundness of a banking institution. Good progress has been made in this area by many countries, but such data are not yet available in others. The assignment of supervisory responsibility embodied in the Concordat also requires the exchange of banking information between supervisory authorities on a confidential basis. While there is agreement that such exchanges are necessary, banking secrecy laws or regulations in some countries still impede such flows of information.

While substantial progress has been made in the area of international supervisory cooperation, the increased importance of international operations of banks has raised new areas of concern to the bank supervisor. For one, the number of banks operating in the major financial centers of the world has grown to include a broad range of institutions in both size and nationality. The phenomenal growth of international money markets and payments activity has increased the interconnectedness of the world's banking system. This interconnectedness provides a ready conduit for transmitting local financial shocks throughout the system. This aspect of the market underscores the importance of ensuring that prudential market practices, internal bank control systems, and external audit and examination procedures are in place. It is largely through the proper functioning of such safeguards that the effects of the failure of a bank or one of its customers can be contained.

Another type of concern is as much political as it is financial. The prospect that governments might exert leverage over financial institutions to achieve political objectives is not new. However, the enormous volume of cross-border and cross-currency transactions effected daily in the world banking system has magnified the riskiness of such strategies. The events in Iran, Poland, and Argentina exemplify the real exposure that such international activities bring about for banking institutions—a type of risk that is very difficult to measure and control.

REGULATORY ISSUES

On the regulatory side, banking across national boundaries raises questions regarding the equitable treatment of banks in different markets. As mentioned previously, the United States has adopted the principle of national treatment. An alternative approach—one based on the principle of *reciprocity*—would afford foreign banks in the United States the same treatment that U.S. banks are given in the foreign banks' home countries. Adoption of a policy centered on national treatment affords greater potential for realizing the benefits of enhanced competition in our banking markets. It also minimizes the risk, inherent in a policy of strict reciprocity, of retaliatory actions by foreign governments to place additional restrictions on U.S. overseas banking operations.

By the same token, however, national treatment offers little basis for further advancement of U.S. banking interests abroad. For this reason, an argument can be made for introducing aspects of reciprocity into the regulatory process. For example, consideration of reciprocal treatment as a factor in the balancing test in the applications process might serve as one type of catalyst to providing more equitable treatment for U.S. as well as other foreign banks in other countries. From a broader perspective, however, any substantial relaxation of remaining restrictions on entry by foreign banks into national banking markets is more likely to be achieved through negotiations at an international level.

National treatment, in the form of the IBA, has taken us a long way toward more equitable treatment of banks operating in the United States. Nevertheless, regulatory differences from country to country continue to sustain disparities in the competitive opportunities facing banks both here and abroad. The three key areas of difference are geographic restrictions, capital requirements, and product-line restrictions.

The IBA placed foreign banks on a more equal footing with U.S. banks with respect to the limitations on interstate banking imposed by the McFadden Act and Douglas Amendment to the Bank Holding Company Act. Further, antitrust considerations continue to limit the degree to which large *intrastate* acquisitions are permitted. In effect, domestic expansion of U.S. banks is restricted. However, large foreign banks not represented in the United States are still free to expand their international operations by acquiring large U.S. banks in attractive markets. Moreover, those foreign banks having only wholesale branches are largely free to make significant acquisitions in their home state. So it follows that, unless legislative restrictions are eased, competitive considerations will continue to favor foreign banks wishing to acquire large U.S. banks—especially large troubled banks. This issue is dealt with in a limited way by legislation now pending before the Congress.[14] What is perhaps more important, from a long-run competitive position, is the fact that most large international banks enjoy nationwide banking within their home country and, as such, have access to a nationwide core deposit base. Of course, neither U.S. nor foreign banks are free to branch across state lines in this country. However, this is more limiting to the growth potential of U.S. banks than their foreign competitors, since U.S. banks are not in a position to capitalize on the full market potential of their well-established retail operations.

Another dimension of home-country regulation which has an international impact is that of capital adequacy. There is general agreement that the erosion of the capital positions experienced in recent years by most major international banks should be reversed. However, there is no international consensus on the appropriate criteria for determining the adequacy of capital—or even what constitutes capital. This should not be surprising, since U.S. bank supervisors are not in full agreement themselves on these issues. When different countries impose different degrees of stringency in assessing the capital adequacy of their banks, the impact on bank expansion plans can be significant. And banks with lower capital ratios can generally charge lower loan rates and obtain the same return as banks with higher capital requirements.

A third area in which domestic regulations affect international operations lies in restrictions on the types of activities in which banks can engage. For example, U.S. laws and regulations prohibit U.S. banks from engaging in commerce either at home or abroad. They also seek to maintain, at least within this country, a separation between investment and commercial banking. Most European countries do not require such separations. Rather, they allow banks "universal banking" capabilities. For example, a German bank can provide banking services in the United States, engage in a full range of commercial and financial activities in its home country, and through an indirect U.S. nonbank subsidiary engage in commerce here. This makes these institutions very formidable competitors of more restricted U.S. banking corporations.

Home-country regulations have not only affected the evolution of international banking but regulatory changes themselves have been influenced to an increasing degree by the multinational nature of the banking business. Banking legislation and regulation formulated before the 1960s, for good reason, focused primarily on domestic concerns and objectives. The growing importance of foreign banks in domestic markets and of banking conducted outside national regulations has necessitated a review and reevaluation of existing legal and regulatory frameworks. In the United States, the IBA was needed to fill a regulatory void created by the expansion of foreign banking activities here. And the move to allow the establishment of IBFs reflects a desire by U.S. authorities to recapture some of the banking business conducted abroad to avoid the costs of home-country regulations. The influence of foreign banking is also reflected in the 1980 revision of Canada's Bank Act and the recent liberalization of Japanese banking laws.

The restructuring of the legal and regulatory frameworks is far from complete. Domestic regulations which adversely affect banks' international competitive position are sure to come under close scrutiny, as are restrictions which apply to banks in one location but not in others. It will become increasingly difficult to sustain differences in national policy with regard to capitalization and funding practices of banks with significant international business. It will also be difficult to maintain domestic barriers separating banking from other financial services, such as investment banking activities, when both U.S. and foreign banks engage in these activities in overseas markets. These pressures for regulatory change are broadly similar to those that have characterized our dual (federal/state and commercial bank/thrift institution) approach to banking regulation.

SUMMARY

The rapid growth of international banking over the last two decades has been motivated and shaped by the interaction of economics and regulations. The development of extensive networks of foreign banks operating in domestic markets has served to initiate cooperation among national supervisors to develop comprehensive surveillance of international banking activities. Home-country legislation and regulation have been adapted to reflect the increasingly international nature of banking. Notwithstanding these changes, however, the continuing growth and evolution of the international banking system will remain a powerful force for further change in bank regulatory and supervisory practices.

NOTES

[1] In this article, *regulation* is taken to be the framework of laws and rules in which banks operate. *Supervision* refers to the enforcement of such laws and rules, especially through the oversight and examination of banks.

[2] Foreign-owned banks chartered in the United States, however, have always been subject to the same regulations as other domestic banks.

[3] Foreign banks have also established a small number of investment companies under New York State law and a large number of representative offices across the country. Investment companies are empowered to extend loans like a commercial bank and to accept credit balances but are not allowed to accept deposits. Representative offices are not allowed to conduct any banking business and serve only to disseminate information regarding parent organizations and to cultivate customer relationships. The IBA authorized foreign banks to establish Edge Act corporations as well. However, these institutions are restricted to doing international business and are not included in this analysis.

[4] Agencies are allowed to accept *credit balances* incidental to their customers' banking transactions. These funds are essentially clearing and compensating balances.

[5] Before the enactment of the IBA, foreign branches also were free from interstate restrictions.

[6] This section is based on discussions with executives at the U.S. offices of Japanese, Canadian, Swiss, French, German, and British banks and on data from the Federal Financial Institutions Examination Council's Report of Condition.

[7] As argued later, there are several factors that can distort even such a limited consolidated balance sheet, making it unrepresentative of U.S. activities.

[8] The Japanese Ministry of Finance's criteria for granting permission to open new branches were recently eased in the broad-ranging revision of Japanese banking laws, effective April 1, 1982.

[9] For a detailed description of regulatory changes resulting from the IBA, see "The International Banking Act of 1978," a report by the Board of Governors of the Federal Reserve System to the Congress, September 17, 1980. The IBA granted certain grandfather rights to foreign banks with respect to interstate banking and nonbanking operations established in the Uninted States prior to the enactment of the legislation.

[10] While some states imposed reserve requirements on foreign branch deposits, such reserves either could be held in interest-bearing form or could serve as compensating balances at correspondent banks.

[11] For a detailed description of regulatory and tax treatment of IBFs, see Sydney J. Key and Serge Bellanger, "International Banking Facilities: The Shape of Things to Come," *The World of Banking,* March–April 1982, pages 17–23.

[12] This committee is often referred to as the "Cooke Committee" after Peter Cooke of the Bank of England, its current chairman. A more complete review of the committee's history and its contributions is presented in W. Peter Cooke, "The Development of Co-operation between Bank Supervisory Authorities in the Group of Ten Countries, Luxembourg and Switzerland," a paper given at the International Conference of Banking Supervisors, Washington, D.C., September 24–25, 1981.

[13] The Group of Ten consists of Belgium (and Luxembourg), Canada, France, Germany, Italy, Japan, the Netherlands, Sweden, the United Kingdom, and the United States.

[14] In particular, under S.1720, a bank holding company could, in limited and emergency circumstances, acquire a large, closed, out-of-state bank.

32

International Lending on Trial

Norman S. Fieleke

That the world is undergoing its gravest financial crisis since the 1930s is now a commonplace. Less widely appreciated are the causes of the crisis, the remedies that are being adopted, and the measures that might be taken to forestall future crises. These are the topics surveyed in this article.

THE NATURE OF THE CRISIS

Simply put, the crisis is a widespread failure of debtors in the poorer, or "developing," countries to pay their foreign debts on schedule. While this failure was dramatized by the extension of billions of dollars in emergency credit to Mexico last August, a problem had been apparent for some time. The number of countries in arrears on international payments had risen from 15 in 1975 to 32 at the end of 1981, at which time total arrears amounted to some $6.3 billion; and the number of developing countries reported by the World Bank as obtaining debt relief rose from 6 in 1980 to 12 in each of the years 1981 and 1982.

According to the OECD (Organization for Economic Cooperation and Development), the medium and long-term indebtedness of some 158 developing countries and territories amounted to more than $625 billion at the end of 1982. World Bank data suggest that the bulk of this sum is indebtedness of public entities or is guaranteed for repayment by a public entity, but that well over $100 billion is the debt of private parties without any such guarantee. Much of this private debt is probably owed by multinational corporations operating within the developing countries.

More relevant is developing country indebtedness to commercial banks, because what might precipitate a panic would be the insolvency of major banks stemming from their inability to collect interest or principal. As can be seen from line 3 of Table 1, at the end of 1982 commercial banks and other financial institutions had about $365 billion in loans outstanding to 145 developing countries, excluding the 13 countries which belong to OPEC (Organization of Pe-

From *New England Economic Review*, Federal Reserve Bank of Boston, May–June 1983.

The author is vice president and economist, Federal Reserve Bank of Boston.

TABLE 1
Bank Lending[a] to Non-OPEC Developing Countries:
Estimated Outstanding Disbursed Amounts at Year-end,
1977–1982 (in billions of dollars, unless otherwise noted)

	1977	1980	1981	1982
1. Short-term credits	37	89	110	134[b]
2. Medium- and long-term credits	82	165	195	231
A. Officially guaranteed export credits	13	33	39	49
B. Financial loans and credits	69	132	156	182[b]
3. *Total Outstanding* (1 + 2)	119	254	305	365
(of which 4 countries[c], in percentage)	(44)	(50)	(54)	(52)

[a] International lending by commercial banks and other financial institutions, including participation of non-OECD banks in international syndicates. Data exclude bonds, shares, property, and other bank assets which are not loans. They also exclude interest payable and local-currency loans. Short-term debt covers credits with an original maturity of less than one year; an unknown amount of these short-term credits is guaranteed by governments in capital-exporting countries.
[b] Assuming some consolidation of short-term debt into medium-term debt during 1982.
[c] Argentina, Brazil, S. Korea, and Mexico.
Source: OECD, *External Debt of Developing Countries: 1982 Survey*, p. 43.

troleum Exporting Countries). Such loans comprised about 6 percent of the total assets of the lending banks. As the table indicates, a few major borrowers—Argentina, Brazil, South Korea, and Mexico—account for most of this lending. Only one of these countries—South Korea—has met its debt obligations on schedule during the past year.

A major part of the lending to developing countries is by U.S. commercial banks, whose claims on non-OPEC developing countries amounted to more than $98 billion, or 8 percent of their total assets and 149 percent of their total shareholders' capital, at the end of June, 1982 (Table 2). The major borrowers in difficulty—Argentina, Brazil, and Mexico—had loans outstanding which amounted to more than 84 percent of the capital of the lending banks. The potential threat to solvency from developing country defaults is greater for the nine largest U.S. banks, for their loans to the non-OPEC developing countries were 222 percent of their total capital, and their loans to Argentina, Brazil, and Mexico were 113 percent of their capital (Table 3).

None of the banks which has been lending to the developing countries is closing its doors or reorganizing as a result of defaults in those countries, but such upheavals are not idle fears and would surely materialize in the absence of enlightened self-interest on the part of both borrowers and lenders. Paul Volcker, chairman of the Board of Governors of the Federal Reserve System, has summarized the threat: "The situation that emerged last year was unique in its scope and potential effects. It involved several major debtors at the same time, and threatened to spread to others, weak and strong alike. It is this potential for cascading liquidity pressures, undermining the stability of the financial system, that has demanded prompt and forceful action . . . to protect the stability of the financial system as a whole and our own economy. . . . The international financial system is not separable from our domestic banking and credit system. The same institutions are involved in both markets. A shock to one would be a shock to the

TABLE 2
U.S. Bank Claims on Non-OPEC Developing Countries

| End of Period | On all Countries | | | On Argentina, Brazil, and Mexico | |
| | In Billions of Dollars | As Percent of | | In Billions of Dollars | As Percent of Total Bank Capital |
		Total Bank Assets	Total Bank Capital		
1977	46.9	6.5	115	25.8	63
1978	52.2	6.3	116	26.8	59
1979	61.8	6.1	124	29.9	60
1980	75.4	7.1	132	37.0	65
1981	92.8	8.0	148	46.7	78
June 1982	98.6	8.3	149	52.4	84

Note: data are for domestic and foreign offices of U.S. banking organizations with significant foreign banking operations. Data cover only cross-border and nonlocal currency lending.
Source: Board of Governors of the Federal Reserve System.

TABLE 3
Claims of Nine Largest U.S. Banks on Non-OPEC Developing Countries

| End of Period | On all Countries | | | On Argentina, Brazil, and Mexico | | |
| | In Billions of Dollars | As Percent of | | In Billions of Dollars | As Percent of | |
		Total Bank Assets	Total Bank Capital		Total Bank Assets	Total Bank Capital
1977	30.0	8.1	163	15.6	4.2	85
1978	33.4	7.9	176	16.4	3.9	82
1979	39.9	8.2	182	18.2	3.7	83
1980	47.9	9.0	199	22.7	4.3	95
1981	57.6	10.2	220	27.4	4.9	105
June 1982	60.3	10.6	222	30.5	5.4	113

Note: data are for domestic and foreign offices of the nine banking organizations and cover only cross-border and nonlocal currency lending.
Source: Board of Governors of the Federal Reserve System.

other. . . . We are talking about dealing with a threat to the recovery, the jobs, and the prosperity of our own country, a threat essentially without parallel in the postwar period."[1]

Because it can be very difficult, if not impossible, for creditors in one country to seize the assets of a defaulting debtor in another country, it might seem that struggling debtors would have strong incentive to repudiate their indebtedness to foreign lenders. Such is not the case, however. Private debtors who fail to honor their obligations face the prospect of a curtailment of credit and perhaps court proceedings as well. Governments which repudiated would bring upon their countries a drastic reduction in the availability of foreign credit, including credit required to finance trade flows. The trade of such nations would be further constricted by the risk that their exports might be seized in transit by foreign creditors. In addition, creditors might attach assets held abroad by repudiating governments. Thus, it is not surprising that repudiations are virtually unheard of. In fact, both borrowers and lenders have powerful incentives to avoid both repudiations and formal declarations of default and, instead, to rearrange debt repayment schedules so that neither party suffers the consequences of repudiation or its equivalent.

The unlikelihood of repudiation diminishes, but does not remove, the threat to the financial system. Creditors who do not receive timely payment from their debtors suffer an impairment of liquidity, and in extreme cases an impairment of solvency as well, whether or not the debtors repudiate. Thus, the fact that debtor governments do not repudiate—and do not go bankrupt—provides grounds for hope but not for unconcern.

It should be noted that not all developing countries are seeking to reschedule their debt. Some, including such a major borrower as South Korea, seem to be experiencing no difficulty. Still, enough countries are experiencing significant difficulties that only an ostrich would fail to perceive a general problem.

CAUSES

Although there are marked differences among the developing countries, the fact that debt rescheduling is common suggests that there is a common underlying cause or set of causal factors. The world recession is clearly one such cause. Because of stagnant or declining demand, the prices of what the non-oil-exporting developing countries sell to the rest of the world have been declining, and declining more rapidly than the less flexible prices of the items they import. In 1981, the last full year for which such data are available, export prices fell by 6 percent in relation to import prices for these countries, meaning that they would have to increase the volume of their exports by about this percentage merely in order to maintain the same inflow of goods from the rest of the world. Thus, the recession has made it more difficult for the developing countries to earn the foreign exchange needed to service their debts.

Another cause of debt repayment difficulty is the sharp rise in interest rates in 1978 and 1979 and the persistence of high rates well into 1982. The average interest cost on the medium and long-term debt of the non-OPEC developing countries rose from about 6 percent for the period 1974–1978 to more than 11 percent in 1982. This rapid rise in average interest cost occurred not only because interest rates went up but because there has been a marked decrease in the proportion of debt for which interest rates are fixed over the long term, with the result that interest rates on much outstanding debt are now frequently revised. It is estimated that the net floating-interest debt of non-OPEC, non-OECD developing countries comprised about 40 percent of their total net debt at the end of 1982, compared to only 23 percent at the end of 1978. This rise in the share of floating-interest debt reflects the effort of bank lenders to earn current market interest rates and to avoid getting locked into fixed rates of return that turn out to be well below rates later yielded in the market: bank loans (not counting export credits) now account for more than a third of the indebtedness of the non-OPEC developing countries.

The combination of declining export prices and high interest rates has made it doubly difficult for debtors in the developing countries. For example, an exporter in Brazil might well have received fewer dollars for his goods at the same time that he required more dollars to service his outstanding debt.

Fortunately for such debtors, interest rates have receded from the heights attained in 1981. Those high rates resulted from the high inflation accompanying the exorbitant oil price increases of 1979–1980 and from the ensuing anti-inflationary monetary policies adopted by some industrial countries, notably the United States. As both inflation and the restrictive policies have eased, interest rates have fallen, with significant benefits for debtors. At the end of 1982, the net floating-interest debt of non-OPEC, non-OECD developing countries was an estimated $166 billion, so every percentage point decline in interest cost represented a saving to these countries of more than $1.6 billion; and from mid-1982 to the end of the year, the relevant dollar interest rates fell by about 7 percentage points. Still, dollar interest rates remain high by historic standards, especially in relation to the declining export prices suffered by many developing nations.

While it is generally agreed that the world recession and high interest rates are important causes of the debt repayment problems of the developing countries, there is much less agreement regarding the frequent allegation that the commercial banks and the developing countries themselves have contributed heavily to the current difficulties by entering into loan agreements that were at best uneconomic, if not profligate. There is no disputing the fact that both total bank lending and net bank exposure to the non-OPEC developing countries have grown at exceptional rates in recent years. As shown by Table 1, total outstanding bank loans to these countries rose from $119 billion in 1977 to $365 billion in 1982, or 25 percent per year. For U.S. banks, total outstanding loans to these countries rose from $46.9 billion to $98.6 billion over roughly the same period, or by 18 percent per year, while for the nine largest U.S. banks the total grew from $30 billion to $60.3 billion, or 17 percent per year (Tables 2 and 3). Not only have outstanding bank loans to the non-OPEC developing countries grown very rapidly, but they have grown more rapidly than total bank assets, as illustrated by the second column of data in Tables 2 and 3.

However, to show that loan growth has been rapid is not to prove that it has been profligate. To be sure, in retrospect the managements of a number of banks no doubt wish they had been less liberal in lending to certain developing countries. Hindsight is better than foresight, especially when a recession is involved, for recessions have a way of converting seemingly sound loans into ones that any fool should have known would be unsound. On the other hand, booms do entail excesses, and many developing countries had been enjoying relatively high, if not booming, growth for some years prior to the current recession. The relevant question, then, is not whether the banks and the developing countries might now be better off if there had been less lending, but whether on the basis of the information available a few years ago they should have had the foresight to be much more conservative.

Several considerations suggest that, in general, such prescience should not have been expected. To begin, it is natural for the non-OPEC developing countries to borrow from the rest of the world; if they truly are developing economies, they will offer profitable investment opportunities for foreign lenders and will attract net capital inflows, just as the United States did during its early development. Second, for many years the losses experienced by banks on international loans have been proportionately lower than on domestic loans.

TABLE 4
Debt Indicators for Non-Oil Developing Countries, Published by the International Monetary Fund

Year	Official Reserves as Percent of Imports of Goods and Services	Long-term External Debt as Percent of:		Debt Service on Long-term External Debt as Percent of Exports of Goods and Services
		Exports of Goods and Services	Gross Domestic Product	
1973	32	89	17	14
1974	22	81	16	12
1975	19	98	18	14
1976	24	103	21	14
1977	26	105	22	14
1978	27	111	24	17
1979	23	102	23	18
1980	18	93	22	16
1981	17(16)	103(96)	24(21)	21(21)
1982	17	109	25	22

Note: reserves and debt are for end of year. Debt service consists of payments of interest and principal. Numbers in parentheses are estimates published in 1981; other data were published in 1982.
Source: International Monetary Fund, *World Economic Outlook,* 1981 and 1982.

Third, for a number of years prior to the current recession, many developing countries had compiled better records of economic growth than the industrial countries had. Fourth, widely distributed forecasts by prestigious international agencies significantly underestimated the declines in economic growth rates that were to accompany the current recession. For example, in June 1981, the IMF (International Monetary Fund) projected a growth rate of 5 percent for the non-oil developing countries for 1981, but then revised the figure downward to 2.5 percent in April 1982; similarly, at the end of 1981, the OECD projected a growth rate of 1.25 percent for the OECD countries for 1982, but then revised the figure downward to a minus 0.50 percent at the end of 1982.

Fifth, as illustrated by Table 4, not until 1982, or 1981 at the earliest, did the officially published statistics on "creditworthiness" clearly signify a distinct deterioration for the non-oil developing countries collectively.[2] To be sure, the data initially published for 1981 (in parentheses) did show that the official monetary reserves of these countries in relation to their imports of goods and services had fallen to a comparatively low level and that debt service (payments of interest and principal) had come to claim a relatively large fraction of the receipts generated by exports; but these initial data also showed long-term external debt to be well below the highest levels attained in preceding years in relation to both exports and gross domestic production.

Finally, even though bank loans outstanding to the non-OPEC developing countries continued to rise rapidly in 1981 and 1982 (Tables 1 and 2), the chart shows that the banks were not altogether oblivious to the gathering crisis, as they raised the risk premia charged on loans to Brazil, Argentina, and Mexico well before the end of 1981, and well before debt repayment problems for these countries became widely publicized. Had they taken the more severe action of refusing new loans once the crisis became apparent, they probably would have exacerbated the crisis, for reasons discussed in the next section of this article.

All of these facts suggest that the banks and the developing countries ought to be spared from blanket condemnations for failing to forestall the debt repayment problem that has materialized. On the basis of the information available as recently as two years ago [1981], there was little reason to expect a problem of the present dimensions. This is not to deny, of course, that some lenders and borrowers were less than circumspect; indeed, one of the risks faced by prudent bank lenders is that less prudent ones will follow in their wake, for once a bank has made a loan to a country it has no means of preventing the country from subsequently incurring excessive debt, thus imperiling repayment of the originally "prudent" loan.

In any event, the loans were made. Aside from the issue of whether they seem justified from the perspective of information available two or three years ago, are the loans now being put to productive uses by the developing countries? Only time will tell, and the answer will surely vary from loan to loan and country to country. Present circumstances provide a harsh test, for it is difficult to keep invested funds working productively during a recession. For the longer term, however, on the assumption that the world economy recovers, the record offers grounds for optimism. As the World Bank has noted:

> The developing countries on the whole used borrowed funds productively during the 1970s. During that decade, the middle-income countries, which include the largest borrowers from private markets among the developing economies, performed far better than the mature industrial countries. Their gross domestic investment rose by an annual average of 7.8 percent, up from an average of 7.5 percent in the 1960s. By contrast, that growth rate fell sharply in the mature industrial economies, from an average of almost 5.9 percent to 1.6 percent a year between the 1960s and 1970s. . . . The difference between investment trends helps to explain why the growth of real gross domestic product in the developing countries slowed only from an annual average of 5.8 percent in the 1960s to about 5.6 percent in the unsettled 1970s, compared with a far greater deceleration of growth in the mature industrial countries from an annual average of 5.0 percent to 3.2 percent.[3]

Certainly, it is clear from Table 5 and Figure 1 that the important "middle-income" developing countries, which include the major borrowers, Argentina, Brazil, Mexico, and South Korea, were not employing foreign funds as a substitute for their own pre-existing saving, or for the purpose of increasing their own immediate consumption, over the period from 1976 to 1980. On the contrary, their rate of domestic saving rose from 20 percent of gross domestic product in 1976 to 25 percent in 1980 (the last year for which data are available), so the funds coming in from abroad contributed to the rising rate of investment in these countries, rather than compensating for a decline in their saving. However, between 1979 and the early 1980s, there was a sharp rise in inflation in the non-oil developing countries, partly attributable to the huge oil price increases at the time, but also attributable to expansionary policies in the developing countries which received somewhat extravagant support from foreign lenders.

TABLE 5
Gross Domestic Investment and Gross Domestic Saving as Percent of Gross Domestic Product in Middle-income Developing Countries[1]

Year	Gross Domestic Investment	Gross Domestic Saving
1976	24	20
1977	25	24
1978	25	22
1979	26	25
1980	27	25

[1] Including Argentina, Brazil, Mexico, and South Korea.
Source: The World Bank, *World Development Report,* issues for 1978 through 1982.

FIGURE 1
Average Loan Rate Spreads (over London Interbank Offered Rate) Charged to Selected Borrowing Countries, First Quarter 1979– Second Quarter 1982

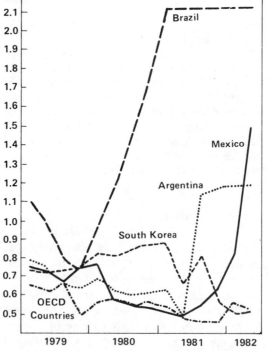

Source: *Brookings Papers on Economic Activity,* 2:1982, p. 413.

REMEDIAL MEASURES

A number of measures have been taken which should go far toward remedying the debt-repayment crisis. As inflation has subsided in the industrial countries and as monetary policy has been eased in some major countries, especially the United States, interest rates have dropped significantly and the U.S. economy seems on the verge of recovery. As noted in the preceding section, the decline in interest rates is a great boon to the debtor nations—and also, it might be observed, to their anxious creditors. Interest rates are still high in relation to the suppressed or falling export prices recorded by many of the debtors, but the widely forecast revival of U.S. economic growth, especially if accompanied by a resumption of growth in other industrial countries, would entail increased demand and higher prices for developing country exports.

Along with the policy measures taken by some industrial nations to promote economic recovery, the developing countries with major debt problems have embarked upon severe adjustment programs designed to reduce their imports and bolster their exports, thus making more foreign exchange available for the servicing of their debts. While the details of these adjustment programs vary from country to country, the programs typically include devaluation of the domestic currency in terms of foreign currencies, reduction in the growth of the domestic money supply and domestic credit and an accompanying increase in domestic interest rates, and a more restrictive fiscal policy entailing diminished government spending and higher taxation. These measures operate to reduce domestic spending on imports and to free resources for export production, which is rendered more attractive. In Argentina, Brazil, and Mexico strong emphasis has been placed on the reduction of borrowing by the government sector, and each country is committed to slashing a huge government deficit roughly in half over the course of this year alone. While in effect, such contractionary policies impose reductions in living standards already low by comparison with the industrial countries.

These adjustment measures have already borne fruit in the form of smaller trade deficits for the debtor countries, and the IMF has projected that the balance of international payments on current account for the non-oil developing countries will show a reduction in deficit of something like $20 billion in the current year [1983]. Also, the adjustment measures have helped to reassure lenders that the debtors are positioning themselves to meet their obligations, thus encouraging the lenders to cooperate by renewing loans as they come due and by sometimes extending additional credit as well. Although banks are prone to reduce their lending to a country which shows signs of debt payment difficulties, it would be counterproductive for them abruptly to terminate sizable capital flows to a debtor country and to refuse to renew outstanding loans, especially during this recessionary period, because the adjustment called for would be so harsh that few governments of debtor countries would try to impose it on their populaces. In such circumstances lenders are well advised to postpone, or reschedule, loan repayment dates, seeking payment of interest in the short run but repayment of principal only in the long run.

Both in arranging adjustment programs and the financing to support them, the IMF has played a crucial role. Banks are loathe to renew credit to a nation with a severe debt problem until the nation has undertaken an adjustment program that elicits a loan from the IMF itself, which then monitors the nation's performance. On the other hand, the IMF is reluctant to make such a loan until it is assured that the proceeds will not be used merely to repay bank creditors, rather than to support the adjustment program; indeed, in late 1982, the IMF informed the creditor banks of Argentina and Mexico that no new IMF financing for those countries would be forthcoming unless the banks also put up new money—which they did. Thus, the IMF has leverage over the policies of both the debtor and its creditors, and its role is pivotal.

Negotiations between a debtor country and its creditors concerning debt repayment are commonly conducted multilaterally—that is, with all creditors, or representatives of groups of creditors, present simultaneously at the negotiating sessions. Not only is this approach more efficient for the debtor than entering into separate debt rescheduling negotiations with each of its many creditors but the approach also facilitates uniformity of treatment of the creditors. Given the recent popularity of internationally syndicated lending, it is not uncommon for hundreds of banks to be involved in debt rescheduling negotiations. As part of the rescheduling agreement, banks usually obtain higher risk premia, or "spreads," of the sort illustrated in the chart.

As with bank loans, loans by governments and international institutions are also involved in reschedulings. Moreover, governments and international institutions have been a vital source of funding for countries confronted with debt crises. For example, during the past year the Treasury Department and the Federal Reserve System in the United States have extended several billion dollars in short-term bridging credits to Argentina, Brazil, and Mexico to help them meet their immediate liquidity requirements while adjustment and longer-term borrowing programs were being arranged. Much of this credit was extended through the Bank for International Settlements, a "central bankers' bank," which marshalled very large sums for the same borrowers from other industrial nations as well as from the United States. In addition, steps are underway to more than double the usable funds that are available to the IMF for its medium-term lending in support of adjustment programs undertaken by debtor countries.

The foregoing remedial measures are aimed chiefly at restoring the creditworthiness of the debtors in difficulty. What if, in spite of those measures, the delinquency of some debtors should undermine the liquidity of a U.S. bank? In that case, the threatened bank might turn to its central bank, the Federal Reserve System, for assistance. Provided the bank had sound collateral to pledge, it would normally be provided a loan to help it meet its own cash obligations. On the other hand, if the bank's loans to delinquent foreign debtors were deemed unrecoverable and worthless, and if writing off such loans reduced the value of the bank's assets below the level of its liabilities, the very solvency, not merely the liquidity, of the bank would then be impaired; and in such a case the bank would be obliged to close its doors unless, as commonly occurs in such instances, a takeover by another viable bank could be arranged. Bank depositors, of course, are widely insured.

PREVENTIVE MEASURES

Finding remedies for a crisis is good, but preventing it is better. What measures might be taken to forestall the development of international debt crises in the future?

The recent recession contributed substantially to the current crisis, and measures which averted major recessions would reduce the likelihood of future debt crises. Although it would be utopian to expect the immediate demise of the business cycle, it seems that the two major recessions of the past decade could easily have been avoided or at least substantially diminished. Even the most casual observation suggests that both were initiated largely by abrupt and unsustainable increases in the price charged by OPEC for its oil. As lesser increases probably would have been of greater benefit to OPEC itself, there is reason to hope that the experience will not be repeated.

Aside from measures to mitigate the business cycle, another class of possible preventive measures would be aimed at deterring uneconomic bank lending or, more precisely, at bolstering the present deterrents. These measures generally call for the collection and distribution of better information both on the creditworthiness of borrowing countries and on the loan portfolios of the lending institutions, as well as for intensified governmental supervision and regulation of the lending institutions.

As for better information on the creditworthiness of borrowing countries, the need can be illustrated by the recent confusion over the amount of Argentina's foreign debt as of the end of 1982, which was estimated at between $42 billion and $43 billion by the Economy Minister early in 1983 but then declared to be $37 billion by the governor of the Central Bank several weeks later. Other than the debtor countries themselves, sources of statistics on national indebtedness include the World Bank, the IMF, and the Bank for International Settlements. Bank lenders have expressed a need for more timely and comprehensive information than these sources now offer, and have recently established an institute to facilitate the exchange of debt statistics between commercial lenders and country borrowers. Such initiatives have the potential for providing significant social gains if it is true that loans are frequently extended—or denied—without the aid of relevant information that could be obtained at a low cost.

Data relating to the creditworthiness of a country, or to "country risk," are commonly put into the form of ratios which are used as indicators of future debt-servicing difficulties. Among such indicators are those represented in Table 4. While more timely and comprehensive information would improve the usefulness of these indicators, they would still fall short of being reliable automatic signalers of impending problems. Debt indicators resemble the leading economic indicators used to forecast business cycles in that they constitute measurement without much underlying theory that nonetheless are widely watched.

The ambiguity surrounding these indicators can easily be illustrated by reference to the oldest and most popular one, the debt-service ratio. This indicator is defined as debt-service payments (interest and principal) divided by earnings from exports of goods and services. The assumption is that, the higher the ratio, the less capacity a country has to service additional debt. In fact, a country rarely is called upon to service its foreign debt solely from current export earnings, as foreign creditors typically reinvest, rather than collect, most of scheduled principal payments and make additional investments as well if the country seems creditworthy. Moreover, a rising ratio may not signify a falling debt-servicing capacity, nor a falling ratio a rising capacity. For example, a country in outright default and paying no debt service would have the lowest possible ratio, and countries can also lower the ratio by falling into arrears. The fact is that numerous countries have had debt-service ratios of between 20 percent and 70 percent without incurring serious debt-servicing difficulties, while others have been obliged to renegotiate their debt when their ratios were well below 20 percent.

More generally, all such indicators as the debt-service ratio provide only half-truths about the capacity of a country to assume additional debt. Differences observed in these ratios between countries do not necessarily signify differences in creditworthiness, because nations differ in their relative ability to employ capital productively; moreover, any one country will differ in this respect over time. Thus, it is not surprising that neither simple nor sophisticated statistical techniques have been very successful in using such indicators to forecast debt-servicing problems; and while better statistics would assist the banks in analyzing debt-repayment prospects, equally important is the application of better analytical methods, including methods for evaluating the current and prospective quality of a country's economic management.

Another measure that might be undertaken to inhibit uneconomic bank lending would be to intensify government supervision and regulation over international lending. Indeed, at this writing this course of action is now under consideration within the United States. Moreover, in recognition of the increasing involvement of U.S. banks in foreign lending, the three federal bank regulatory agencies—the Comptroller of the Currency, the Federal Reserve System, and the Federal Deposit Insurance Corporation—adopted in 1979 a new system for evaluating the country risk to which lending banks expose themselves. Under this system, an Interagency Country Exposure Review Committee, whose members are from the three regulatory agencies, categorizes monitored countries into four main groups: those with imminent or actual debt delinquency and those categorized as weak, moderately strong, and strong. At each bank they visit, federal examiners then call to the management's attention those loans which the bank has outstanding to "weak" or "moderately strong" countries if the loans are above certain levels in relation to capital, as well as criticizing all loans to delinquent countries. The examiners also evaluate the system employed by each bank in managing its exposure to country risk.

Such examination procedures could be supplemented by more direct government restraints over international bank lending, but such discouragement of risk-taking would entail its own risks. Even the current examination procedures "could unduly inhibit international lending," according to a recent review by the U.S. General Accounting Office (GAO). The GAO reported that the current procedures had identified (as having potential debt-servicing problems) many countries which, in fact, did not incur payments arrearages during the year following their identification. A different approach from government examination or control would simply require fuller public disclosure by the banks of their country-risk exposures, on the assumption that financial market participants themselves would then discipline or inhibit excessive risk-taking by limiting the deposits or equity capital that they placed with the more venturesome banks.

In addition to the foregoing, another set of measures designed to forestall future international debt crises would aim at securing a higher proportion of equity financing for the developing countries. Unlike the interest on debt, there is no contractual requirement for dividends to be paid on equity, so the return paid by the developing countries on such capital could legitimately be sharply reduced during a recession. Moreover, the risk of financing those countries would be spread more widely beyond the banking sector. The borrowing countries themselves could promote such a development by relaxing some of the many barriers they have erected against direct and portfolio equity investment.

CONCLUSION

A widespread failure on the developing countries to pay their foreign debts on schedule has aroused anxiety that large commercial bank creditors might be driven into insolvency. However, the debt-repayment capacity of these countries is now being enhanced by several factors, including recent reductions in interest rates, the beginning of recovery from the global recession, the initiation of economic adjustment programs in the developing countries themselves, and the cooperation of their creditors and certain international institutions in extending interim financing.

The banks and the developing countries ought to be spared from blanket condemnations for failing to forestall the current debt crisis, because as recently as two years ago there was little reason for international borrowers and lenders to expect debt-repayment problems of the present magnitude. International debt crises would be less likely in the future if recession-inducing shocks, such as abrupt oil price increases, could be avoided, if more timely and comprehensive information were published on the creditworthiness of borrowing countries and on the loan portfolios of lending institutions, and if a higher share of investment in the developing countries took the form of equity financing.

NOTES

[1] Statement before the Committee on Banking, Finance and Urban Affairs, U.S. House of Representatives, February 2, 1983.

[2] Apart from the "deterioration" of 1974–1978, which the world weathered with little difficulty.

[3] The World Bank, *World Debt Tables: 1982–83 Edition*, p. ix.

PART SIX

Macroeconomic and Financial Policy

Financial institutions and markets are created to serve the public—to efficiently produce and sell financial services that meet the needs of businesses and households. Yet, it is not just the public to whom these markets and institutions must respond, not just the public that influences and evaluates their performance. *Government,* too, plays a profoundly important role in determining the kinds of financial institutions that will be allowed to operate, the services these institutions can offer, and the prices and interest rates attached to those services. Governments—federal, state, and local—also are customers of the financial system, especially in borrowing money and making payments, and in this customer role, demand an adequate supply of financial services at low cost. Even more important, however, governments represent the public interest in promoting a sound financial system in which the public's savings are managed prudently, scarce resources are utilized efficiently, and financial conditions are established that contribute to the nation's goals of full employment, low inflation, and sustainable growth in jobs and living standards. Thus, federal, state, and local governments are both customers and regulators of the nation's financial system. Their impact is felt, directly or indirectly, in every corner of that system.

While governments at all levels affect the workings of the financial system, two governmental institutions stand out, head and shoulders above the others, in influencing the performance of financial institutions and shaping financial market outcomes. These critical governmental units are the central bank—in the United States, the Federal Reserve System ("the Fed")—and the government's fiscal agent (funds collector, manager, and borrower)—in the United States, the U.S. Treasury Department. This section of the book is devoted to these two dominant governmental institutions in the nation's financial system—the Fed and the Treasury. Our purpose here is to see more clearly how these two governmental units interact with private financial institutions and the public to influence the availability and cost of financial services and the stability of the financial system.

The younger of the two, historically, is the Federal Reserve System, chartered by act of Congress in 1913. The Fed exercises great power over the financial system, especially over the growth and cost of money and credit, and it has been vested by Congress with numerous supervisory responsibilities and charged with providing several key financial services. For example, the Fed examines and supervises about 5,000 commercial banks—roughly one third of the nation's banking population—that belong to its system of member banks, and it regulates the growth of all bank holding companies—corporations that own stock in one or more commercial banks. It clears and collects most out-of-town checks and provides new currency and coin needed for the growth of commerce and industry. The Fed also acts as a safekeeping facility for securities, especially U.S. government securities owned by the public, and holds the Treasury's checking accounts through which most federal government payments are made.

Far more important, however, than any of these tasks performed daily by the Fed is its central role in carrying out government *monetary policy*—the management of the supply of money and credit in order to achieve the nation's goals of full employment, low inflation, rapid and sustainable economic growth, and a stable balance-of-payments position vis-á-vis the rest of the world. Several articles in this portion of the book describe in detail how the Fed conducts monetary policy and some of the key problems it faces in pursuit of the nation's economic goals.

First, Gordon H. Sellon, Jr., reviews the three basic instruments or tools used by the Fed to carry out monetary policy—open market operations, administration of the discount window and discount rate, and setting deposit reserve requirements. Dr. Sellon explains which units within the Federal Reserve System—the Board of Governors, the 12 Federal Reserve banks, or the Federal Open Market Committee—control each of these policy instruments and what impact each has upon the economy and financial system. The Fed's three policy tools are then linked to central bank regulation of the growth rate of the nation's money supply. Sellon points out that, while open market operations—buying and selling of government securities—remain the most important Federal Reserve policy instrument, discount-rate policy and deposit reserve requirements have become increasingly important in recent years as aids to the money-supply targeting process.

A subsequent article, prepared by R. Alton Gilbert of the Federal Reserve Bank of St. Louis, examines the method used by the Federal Reserve to control money-supply growth through targeting the growth of bank reserves. Gilbert looks at the sources of bank reserves and the factors that shape the demand for these reserves. He reviews how the Federal Reserve has altered its reserve-targeting methods in recent years, attempting first to regulate interest-rate movements, then money-supply growth, and, most recently, a combination of *both* interest rates and money growth. Gilbert explains as well the Fed's recent shift from targeting open market operations on average levels of nonborrowed reserves to targeting levels of borrowing from the Federal Reserve banks.

These two views of the Fed's policies and techniques are supplemented by the unique perspective offered by Henry C. Wallich, member of the Board of Governors—the chief administrative body within the Federal Reserve System. Dr. Wallich neatly divides the Fed's monetary control process into three *target levels*—intermediate targets (the money supply and interest rates, particularly long-term interest rates), instrumental targets (total reserves and money market interest rates), and operating targets (nonborrowed and borrowed reserves and the desired range for the Federal funds loan rate). He explains how recent innovations in financial instruments, especially the development of interest-bearing checkable deposits with variable interest rates linked to money market conditions, has forced the Fed to change its money-supply control procedures.

For many years there has been a controversy as to exactly how *fast* monetary policy works. That is, how long does it take between the time a problem develops in the economy (such as excessive inflation), the Federal Reserve recognizes the problem, manipulates its policy tools in the desired direction, and economic conditions finally respond to the Fed's actions? Until recently, the bulk of policy studies concluded that these time lags were substantial—at least six months to a year—before a significant economic impact was registered. The obvious danger with lags this long is that the Fed may actually worsen, rather than help, a deteriorating economic situation. For example, a policy of tight credit and high interest rates designed to cool off an inflationary boom might not take effect until the economy is headed into a recession, with rising unemployment contributing to the deepening of the recession.

In recent years, both theory and empirical evidence have appeared that question the long-lag hypothesis. The roots of the new theory lie in the concept of *expectations*—how the public forms its predictions of the future and how it revises them—and the notion of efficient markets. A growing body of research has been amassed suggesting that the financial markets are highly *efficient* (i.e., they react quickly, if not instantaneously, to new information relevant to security prices and interest rates). This "efficiency" is critical to monetary policy because it suggests that any change in government policy—once the public becomes convinced a true change in policy is underway—can exert a very rapid impact on the economy and financial system. There need not be long lags between policy changes and their effects on economic behavior if the public's expectations can be changed.

In a well-written article carried over from the second edition and titled "Efficient Markets, Interest Rates, and Monetary Policy," Donald J. Mullineaux explains how the relatively new theory of efficient markets can be used to explain the effects of changes in monetary policy on interest rates. Mullineaux observes that interest rates and security prices react only to *new* information. Old data on the policy moves of governmental authorities and the state of the economy have *no* effect on current rates and prices. However, if a true change in monetary policy occurs, leading to unexpected changes in the nation's money supply, the public might come to revise its expectations of future money supply growth. Interest rates will then react rapidly to this new and unexpected information, and new economic conditions may soon follow. Mullineaux points out that, because of the critical impact the public's expectations can have on the speed and effectiveness of monetary policy, the best government policy is probably one which is so stable and predictable that it avoids the generation of erratic and often damaging expectations effects.

Mullineaux's description of the rational expectations theory of government policy changes and their impact on the economy and financial system is useful background for Richard G. Sheehan's article, "Weekly Money Announcements: New Information and Its Effects." Dr. Sheehan, an economist with the Federal

Reserve Bank of St. Louis, examines the impact on the financial markets of the weekly money supply announcements made routinely by the Federal Reserve. He points out that every Thursday afternoon the Federal Reserve Board releases new figures on recent money supply growth and that market interest rates tend to react to these announcements in ways predicted by the expectations theory and the theory of efficient markets. He affirms that it is *unexpected* money-supply changes that appear to have the most substantial effects on the financial markets.

Without question, through its power to influence market expectations, money-supply growth, and interest rates, the nation's central bank—the Federal Reserve System—can exert a powerful impact on the nation's economy and financial system. But, so also does the Treasury Department have an important and sometimes overriding effect on economic and financial conditions. The Treasury exerts its policy effects through two channels: (1) *fiscal policy*—taxing and spending activities and (2) *debt management policy*—borrowing through the issue of new debt and the refunding or refinancing of outstanding government debt. Both of these forms of government economic policy share with Federal Reserve monetary policy the broad economic goals of full employment, low inflation, sustainable economic growth, and a balanced international payments position.

Both fiscal policy and debt management policy have attracted greater public and political attention in recent years, due to record-high federal budget deficits and a federal debt that has soared in response to those deficits and the effects of inflation. Many economists and financial analysts have identified some potentially (if not actually) damaging effects of such huge government deficits: (1) higher inflation accentuated by the added government demand for a scarce supply of goods and services; (2) higher or more volatile interest rates, or both, caused, in part, by increased competition between government and private borrowers for a limited supply of loanable funds; and (3) decreased private investment, which should lead eventually to lower productivity and declining national output. Whatever the merits of these arguments, the U.S. government's recent fiscal problems have stimulated a large volume of research and public comment on government budgetary activities and their impact on the economy and financial system.

The two articles that conclude this section of the book add to our knowledge and understanding of fiscal and debt-management effects on consumption and investment decisions, interest rates, and security prices. In the first of these articles, John B. Carlson and E. J. Stevens of the Federal Reserve Bank of Cleveland examine the causes of increases and decreases in the federal government's debt over the past four decades since the Second World War. They also carry out simulations of the possible growth of federal debt over the next 40 years, pointing out that future economic conditions are likely to be less favorable for reducing the nation's debt-to-GNP ratio. Carlson and Stevens suggest that control of federal expenditures and changes in tax schedules and rules may be the only certain approaches to heading off further dramatic growth in the nation's public debt. Perhaps in this way private spending can continue to grow at a rate substantial enough to lower or at least restrain the debt-to-GNP ratio and avoid such heavy reliance on foreign demand for U.S. government securities that helped to finance a significant portion of federal fund-raising efforts in the 1970s and early 1980s.

Finally, Dr. Charles E. Webster, Jr., in "The Effects of Deficits on Interest

Rates,'' examines the possible direct and indirect linkages between the size of federal budget deficits and the level of nominal (published) and real (purchasing-power-adjusted) interest rates. The conventional argument is that larger government deficits result in higher real and nominal interest rates, as added government demand for credit puts pressure on credit supplies and also engenders higher inflation. Professor Webster asks us to look more closely at this conventional wisdom and consider alternative views. He points out, for example, that government deficits need not influence the level of interest rates. Indeed, some researchers have suggested that the direction of causation may be the other way around—increased inflation forces interest rates higher which, in turn, compels the government to borrow even more to refinance its outstanding obligations. The key issues in this field clearly are unresolved; but, as Webster makes clear, a substantial volume of research is underway to find some badly needed answers.

33

The Instruments of Monetary Policy

Gordon H. Sellon, Jr.

The implementation of monetary policy by the Federal Reserve System has traditionally involved the use of three main policy instruments: open market operations, the discount rate, and reserve requirements. For many years, the use of open market operations has been the principal instrument of monetary policy. While the discount rate and reserve requirements may or may not be changed in a given year, open market operations have generally been carried out on a daily or weekly basis. As a result of the relatively infrequent use of discount rate and reserve requirement changes, discussions of monetary policy frequently understate their importance. Indeed, it has been fashionable to question whether the Federal Reserve really needs all three policy instruments.[1]

This article argues that the viewpoint claiming all three policy instruments are unnecessary is seriously out of date. The increased emphasis of the Federal Reserve on the control of inflation and the growth of money and credit has led to important changes in policy procedures and institutional arrangements that have both altered and enhanced the use of the discount rate and reserve requirements as policy instruments. A key development is the shift in Federal Reserve policy procedures from interest-rate targeting to money and reserve targeting. Most analyses of this change have focused on its broad implications for such issues as monetary control and interest rate volatility. A point that is often overlooked, however, is that this change in policy procedures directly expands the role of the discount rate and reserve requirements as policy instruments. In addition, money and reserve targeting provides a framework in which legislative changes, such as the Monetary Control Act of 1980, and regulatory actions, such as the adoption of contemporaneous reserve accounting, further enhance the scope for discount policy and reserve requirements in the monetary policy process.

In light of these developments, this article reexamines the role of the discount rate and reserve requirements. The first section provides background information

From *Economic Review*, Federal Reserve Bank of Kansas City, May 1984, pp. 3–20.

Gordon H. Sellon, Jr., is a senior economist with the economic research department at the Federal Reserve Bank of Kansas City.

ree instruments and an overview of their role in the policy process. The
.ee sections present a detailed discussion of important legislative, reg-
.atory, and policy developments that have changed the role of discount-rate
policy and reserve requirements. The final section reexamines the usefulness of
the discount rate and reserve requirements as policy instruments.

AN OVERVIEW OF THE POLICY INSTRUMENTS

Decision Making

Authority to change the three main instruments of monetary policy is divided
between the Board of Governors and the regional Federal Reserve banks. Decisions on open market operations are made by the Federal Open Market Committee (FOMC), which consists of the seven members of the Board of Governors plus
five of the 12 reserve bank presidents. Meeting eight times a year, the FOMC
makes general decisions on the course of monetary policy and transmits these
decisions in the form of a directive to the manager of the System Open Market
Account at the Federal Reserve Bank of New York. The account manager, in
consultation with the board staff and a reserve bank president, makes day-to-day
decisions on open market operations consistent with the FOMC directive.[2]

In contrast to open market operations, authority to change the discount rate
and reserve requirements does not rest with the FOMC. In the case of reserve
requirements, the Board of Governors has authority to implement regulatory
changes in the level or structure of reserve requirements within legislative guidelines determined by Congress. Discount-rate policy is somewhat more complicated. While the Board of Governors establishes regulations pertaining to the
administration of the discount window at the regional banks, discount-rate
changes are initiated by the regional reserve banks. Thus, the boards of directors
of the regional banks are required to meet at least every two weeks to recommend
a discount rate. These recommendations are then transmitted to the Board of
Governors, which has final authority to approve discount rate changes.[3]

Impact of the Policy Instruments

The three policy instruments do not affect economic activity directly but rather
work through their effects on financial markets. Thus, the policy instruments have
their initial impact on the demand for and supply of reserves held by depository
institutions. Changes in reserves then influence market interest rates and the
amount of money and credit created by financial institutions.

Reserve requirements provide the foundation of the policy process. Depository
institutions are required by law to maintain a percentage of the value of transactions accounts and certain other deposit and nondeposit liabilities in the form of
reserves. These reserves can be held either as vault cash or as deposits at Federal
Reserve banks. Because credit creation by financial institutions is based on an
expansion of deposit liabilities and deposit liabilities are backed by reserves, the
power to set reserve requirements gives the Federal Reserve important leverage
over deposit and credit creation.

While the existing level of reserve requirements serves as a constraint on
deposit and credit creation, the Federal Reserve can also undertake discretionary
changes in the level or structure of reserve requirements to tighten or ease credit

restraint. Thus, to slow the growth of money and credit, the Federal Reserve might undertake a general increase in reserve requirements on all deposit liabilities. Alternatively, reserve requirement changes can be used more selectively to influence the growth of specific types of liabilities.

The Federal Reserve can also change the supply of reserves available to financial institutions in meeting their reserve requirements. Through the purchase or sale of government securities in the open market, the Federal Reserve can directly increase or decrease the supply of reserves. Depository institutions can obtain an additional supply of reserves by borrowing from the Federal Reserve through the discount window. By regulating access to the discount window and the discount rate charged on this borrowing, the Federal Reserve controls this secondary source of reserves.

The interaction between reserve demand and supply has an important impact on market interest rates and the growth of money and credit. To the extent that the amount of reserves supplied by the Federal Reserve is greater or less than the amount demanded by financial institutions, there is greater or lesser pressure on short-term market interest rates. Changes in interest rates, in turn, provide incentives for the public to alter its demand for money and credit. Thus, through the use of open market operations, discount-rate policy, and reserve requirements, the Federal Reserve can influence interest rates, money, and credit.

Targets and Instruments of Monetary Policy

The roles that open market operations, the discount rate, and reserve requirements play in the policy process depend on the ultimate objectives of policy as well as on the procedures used to achieve these objectives. In recent years, the Federal Reserve has put increased emphasis on the goal of long-run price stability. As a means to this end, the Federal Reserve has focused on the short-run control of money growth as measured by the growth of narrow transactions-based aggregates, such as M1, and by the broader aggregates, M2 and M3.

Control of monetary growth through the use of the three policy instruments can be approached in two distinct ways. First, the policy instruments can be used in a discretionary fashion. That is, the Federal Reserve can change open market operations, the discount rate, and reserve requirements in response to excessively strong or weak money growth. For example, in an expanding economy the Federal Reserve may want to tighten policy in order to reduce money growth. A more restrictive policy can be implemented by discretionary changes in one or more of the three policy instruments. Thus, the Federal Reserve can sell securities in the open market to reduce the supply of bank reserves directly, raise the discount rate to curb banks' incentive to borrow reserves at the discount window, or raise reserve requirements to increase banks' demand for reserves and reduce potential credit expansion. All three actions tend to raise market interest rates and reduce money growth.

Second, instead of responding to excessive money growth by discretionary actions, the Federal Reserve can try to structure the system of reserve requirements and the discount mechanism to reduce the likelihood of excessive money growth. In particular, the level of reserve requirements helps determine the responsiveness of market interest rates to changes in money demand and supply. A higher level of reserve requirements tends to improve automatic monetary control by magnifying the response of interest rates to changes in money demand. For example, a given increase in the public's demand for money raises interest rates by a larger amount, the higher the level of reserve requirements. This occurs because the higher level of reserve requirements constrains the amount of money that banks can supply. At the same time, the higher interest rate tends to have a feedback effect in reducing money demand. In this case, money volatility is reduced while interest-rate volatility is increased by a higher level of reserve requirements.[4] Similarly, the structure of reserve requirements on different types of deposits and the terms of discount window borrowing may affect the volatility of money growth around its desired level. Thus, structural changes in the borrowing mechanism and reserve requirements that automatically tend to reduce the volatility of money growth may minimize the need to undertake discretionary policy actions.[5]

The following three sections examine some of the major legislative, regulatory, and operational decisions that have changed the role of discount policy and reserve requirements in the policy process. In each case, the focus is on whether the structural change strengthens or weakens the contribution of the policy instruments to discretionary and automatic monetary control. In reading the first two sections, which cover legislative and regulatory changes, it is important to recall that most of these changes occurred after the Federal Reserve adopted a reserve targeting procedure in October 1979.[6] Thus, the discussion in these two sections assumes that the Federal Reserve is using a reserve targeting procedure. This is a technical but quite important assumption that is discussed in more detail after presentation of the institutional material.

THE MONETARY CONTROL ACT OF 1980

The most important legislative development affecting the role of the policy instruments in recent years is the Depository Institutions Deregulation and Monetary Control Act of 1980. This legislation extends Federal Reserve System reserve requirements and discount window access to all depository institutions. Before the act, only those institutions choosing membership in the Federal Reserve System were subject to Federal Reserve regulations on reserve requirements. In addition, nonmember institutions were not eligible to borrow at the discount windows except in unusual circumstances. Member banks found the requirement to hold noninterest-bearing reserve balances increasingly burdensome in the high inflation, high interest-rate environment of the 1970s. Consequently, a growing number of institutions chose to relinquish their membership.[7] The loss of membership posed two problems for monetary policy. On the one hand, policymakers feared that monetary control would become increasingly complicated with a decreasing fraction of transactions deposits subject to reserve requirements. At the same time, the voluntary nature of membership severely curtailed discretionary increases in reserve requirements as a policy instrument, since institutions could withdraw from the system to avoid the higher reserve requirements.

Passage of the Monetary Control Act effectively eliminated the erosion in the reserve requirement mechanism. At the same time, however, all institutions subject to reserve requirements were granted access to Federal Reserve services, including the discount window. Since the policy implications of discount window access are potentially different from those of extended reserve requirements, it is useful to examine the two developments separately.

Extension of Reserve Requirements

Under the Monetary Control Act, all depository institutions' transactions accounts, nonpersonal time and savings deposits, and certain Eurocurrency transactions were made subject to Federal Reserve System reserve requirements.[8] Thus, reserve requirement coverage under the act is extended to nonmember banks, savings institutions, and credit unions. After a phase-in period, depository institutions are subject to a 3 percent reserve requirement on the first $28.9 million of net transactions accounts and a 12 percent reserve requirement on transactions accounts in excess of the base amount.[9] The Board of Governors is authorized to vary reserve requirements on transactions accounts in excess of the $28.9 million base in a range of 8 to 14 percent, with an additional supplemental requirement of 4 percent possible under special conditions.[10]

Reserve requirements on nontransactions liabilities were also modified. Reserve requirements against personal time and savings deposits were eliminated under the act. They were maintained on nonpersonal time deposits, however. Initially set at 3 percent, they can be varied in a range from 0 to 9 percent. The board also has the authority to determine the maturity of nonpersonal time deposits that are subject to reserve requirements. Finally, the board can set reserve requirements for certain Eurocurrency liabilities. These requirements are initially set at 3 percent, the same ratio as that for nonpersonal time and savings deposits. Table 1 provides a summary of the new system of reserve requirements and a comparison with the system in effect before the Monetary Control Act.

The new structure of reserve requirements has a number of important implications for monetary policy. Generally speaking, the structure is designed to enhance the Federal Reserve's control over the narrowly defined aggregate, M1, consisting of currency, demand deposits, and other transactions accounts. Two features of the new system work to improve M1 control.[11]

The extension of reserve requirements to transactions accounts at all depository institutions contributes to automatic control of M1. The level of reserve requirements on transactions accounts determines the degree of interest-rate pressure that occurs in response to stronger or weaker demands for transactions balances. Before the Monetary Control Act, the effective reserve requirement on transactions deposits was declining over time as banks left the Federal Reserve System and as new types of transactions accounts with lower reserve requirements were introduced. This downward trend in the level of effective reserve requirements led to a progressive reduction in automatic control of M1. Thus, passage of the act stabilized the effective reserve requirement on transactions deposits and prevented further erosion in monetary control.[12]

The new structure of reserve requirements also improves automatic control of M1 by eliminating undesired variability in money growth due to investor shifts of funds among different types of transactions and nontransactions accounts. The new system improves monetary control in three ways.

First, shifts in transactions accounts between member and nonmember institutions no longer affect M1. Under the old system, a transfer of deposits from a

TABLE 1
Reserve Requirements of Depository Institutions (percent of deposits)

Type of deposit and deposit interval	Member bank requirements before implementation of the Monetary Control Act		Type of deposit and deposit interval	Depository institution requirements after implementation of the Monetary Control Act	
	Percent	**Effective Date**		**Percent**	**Effective Date**
Net demand			**Net transaction accounts**		
$0 million-$2 million	7	12/30/76	$0-$28.9 million	3	12/29/83
$2 million-$10 million	9½	12/30/76	Over $28.9 million	12	12/29/83
$10 million-$100 million	11¾	12/30/76			
$100 million-$400 million	12¾	12/30/76	**Nonpersonal time deposits**		
Over $400 million	16¼	12/30/76	By original maturity		
			Less than 1½ years	3	10/6/83
			1½ years or more	0	10/6/83
Time and savings					
Savings	3	3/16/67			
			Eurocurrency liabilities		
			All types	3	11/13/80
Time					
$0 million-$5 million, by maturity					
30-179 days	3	3/16/67			
180 days to 4 years	2½	1/8/76			
4 years or more	1	10/30/75			
Over $5 million, by maturity					
30-179 days	6	12/12/74			
180 days to 4 years	2½	1/8/76			
4 years or more	1	10/30/75			

Source: *Federal Reserve Bulletin*, January 1984, p. A7.

member bank subject to reserve requirements to a nonmember institution would increase excess reserves in the banking system, permitting a multiple expansion of M1. Under the new system, since all transactions deposits have the same reserve requirement, regardless of institution, this type of shift does not affect excess reserves or M1.[13]

Second, in the new system of reserve requirements, all types of transactions accounts at a given institution will have the same reserve requirement. In contrast, under the old system, demand deposits had a higher reserve requirement than other transactions accounts. Thus, shifts between demand deposits and other transactions accounts will no longer affect excess reserves and potential M1 expansion.

Finally, shifts between transactions accounts included in M1 and personal time and savings deposits not included in M1 will have less impact on M1 under the new system. Under the new system, a shift from transactions deposits to personal savings deposits initially reduces M1. However, this effect is subsequently offset by a reduction in required reserves since personal savings deposits are not reservable. This reduction in required reserves permits institutions to carry out a secondary expansion of M1. Under the old system, where personal savings deposits were reservable, a similar transfer of funds released fewer required reserves. Thus, the secondary expansion of M1 would not offset as much of the initial reduction in M1.[14]

While the new structure of reserve requirements tends to enhance the Federal Reserve's ability to control M1, control over the broader aggregates, such as M2 and M3, may be weakened. The reason is that reserve requirements on many of the components of the broader aggregates have either been reduced or eliminated. This means that increased demand for these deposits by the public tends to result in a relatively small increase in required reserves and little upward pressure on market interest rates.[15]

In summary, reform of the reserve requirement system under the Monetary Control Act strengthens monetary control by improving the Federal Reserve's ability to control transactions deposits. At the same time, these reforms tend to reduce automatic control over the broader monetary aggregates. Still, the Federal Reserve retains some flexibility in setting reserve requirements on the components of the broader aggregates. As described in the next section, discretionary changes in reserve requirements on these components have been used more frequently as a policy instrument in recent years.

Extension of Discount Window Privileges

The Monetary Control Act also requires changes in discount policy. Before 1980, borrowing from the Federal Reserve was generally limited to member banks. The act broadened discount window access to all depository institutions subject to reserve requirements.

Under current discount window regulations, borrowing is divided into two categories: adjustment credit and extended credit. Adjustment credit is designed to provide institutions a short-term cushion of funds to balance unexpected outflows from reserve accounts. In contrast, extended credit provides a longer-term source of funds to institutions having strong seasonal patterns in loan demand or sustained liquidity pressures.

Broadened access to the discount window could have an adverse effect on the Federal Reserve's ability to control monetary growth. A problem could arise, for example, if newly eligible institutions tended to rely heavily on the discount window as a source of funds during a period in which the Federal Reserve was trying to restrain money and credit growth. In practice, however, two developments have minimized the problem.

First, nonmember institutions, such as savings institutions and credit unions, are expected to use special industry lenders, such as the Federal Home Loan banks and corporate central credit union facilities, before turning to the discount window. Indeed, since 1980, these institutions have undertaken relatively little borrowing under the adjustment credit program. Rather, their use of the discount window has generally been confined to borrowing under the extended credit program.

Second, borrowing that has occurred under the extended credit program has not been permitted to add to the total supply of reserves in the banking system. When borrowing occurs under the extended credit program, the Federal Reserve offsets this borrowing by subtracting an equal amount of reserves through open market operations. Thus, broadened access to the discount window under the Monetary Control Act has not had an adverse effect on monetary control.

REGULATORY DEVELOPMENTS

In addition to legislative developments affecting the role of the policy instruments, the Federal Reserve has initiated a number of regulatory changes in recent years aimed at improving the monetary control process. Three of the most significant developments are the adoption of a contemporaneous reserve accounting system, the use of reserve requirements on managed liabilities as a discretionary policy instrument, and the use of a discount rate surcharge mechanism.

Contemporaneous Reserve Accounting

From September 1968 to January 1984, financial institutions operated under a system of lagged reserve requirements (LRR). Required reserves in a given week were calculated on the basis of deposit levels two weeks earlier. This system was designed to make it easier and less costly for institutions to meet required reserves and to simplify the conduct of daily open market operations by removing the uncertainty associated with forecasting contemporaneous deposit levels.

Critics of lagged reserve accounting argued that the system impaired short-run monetary control. Because of the two-week lag between deposits and required reserves, increases in deposit growth in a particular week would not lead to an immediate increase in required reserves and so would not exert upward pressure on interest rates. Without upward pressure on interest rates, banks would have little incentive to curtail loan and deposit growth. Thus, lagged reserve accounting was seen as impairing the automatic control features of the reserve requirement mechanism.

Under the new contemporaneous reserve requirements (CRR) effective in February 1984, depository institutions that report weekly to the Federal Reserve have to maintain required reserves behind transactions deposits on an essentially contemporaneous basis. That is, these institutions compute their required reserves behind transactions deposits on the basis of average daily deposits over a two-week period that begins on a Tuesday and ends on a Monday. Reserves must then be maintained over a two-week period beginning on Thursday, two days after the start of the computation period, and ending on Wednesday, two days after the end of the computation period.[16]

Contemporaneous reserve accounting is designed to improve monetary control by speeding up the adjustment process for reserves held behind transactions deposits. Unlike the two-week lag for LRR, under CRR, from the time that an institution knows its required reserves at the end of the computation period it has only two days to adjust fully to its required reserves. The basic idea is that when faced with this shorter adjustment period, institutions will attempt to acquire reserves to support growth of transactions deposits on a more timely basis or, alternatively, will attempt to liquidate assets to reduce their required reserves. In this way, faster money growth will be translated into higher interest rates and reduced loan and credit growth on a more timely basis.

It is difficult to determine whether this change in accounting procedures will significantly improve short-run automatic monetary control. Much depends upon how institutions choose to make reserve adjustments. If they reduce required reserves by curtailing loan and deposit growth, CRR may improve monetary control. However, if institutions tend to make more frequent use of the discount window or make reserve adjustments through excess reserves or managed liabilities, CRR may not significantly improve monetary control.[17]

Reserve Requirements on Managed Liabilities

Historically, discretionary changes in reserve requirements have been used much less frequently than either open market operations or discount rate policy. At least three reasons have been advanced to explain the relatively infrequent use of reserve requirement changes. *First,* a given change in reserve requirements can be a rather blunt policy instrument. That is, an across-the-board increase in reserve requirements affects all institutions, large or small, whether or not they are contributing to a problem of excessive money and credit growth.[18] *Second,* frequent changes in reserve requirements make it difficult for banks to plan their asset and liability management decisions. *Third,* before passage of the Monetary Control Act the voluntary nature of Federal Reserve membership may have limited the use of reserve requirements as a policy instrument.

In recent years, the Federal Reserve has focused its discretionary changes in reserve requirements not on demand deposits or other transactions accounts but rather on certain managed liabilities, such as large denomination CDs and Eurodollar borrowings. This regulatory development has increased the flexibility of reserve requirements as a discretionary policy instrument by allowing the Federal Reserve to target reserve requirement changes to larger institutions that make extensive use of managed liabilities to fund credit expansion.

The focused use of reserve requirements is a response by the Federal Reserve to the rapid development and creative use of managed liabilities by banks during the 1960s and 1970s. From the banks' standpoint, an attractive feature of managed liabilities is that they are generally subject to lower reserve requirements than demand deposits. Thus, if the banking system can bring about a shift in the composition of its liabilities from demand deposits to managed liabilities, it can effectively lower reserve requirements and so extend more credit with the same supply of reserves.

While beneficial to banks, managed liabilities can pose problems for monetary policy. In a period in which the Federal Reserve is trying to restrain the growth of money and credit, extensive use of managed liabilities may permit banks to counter policy actions by expanding the amount of credit creation possible with a given amount of reserves. In addition, since increased use of managed liabilities may be associated with slower growth of demand deposits, such transactions measures of money as M1 may give a misleading impression of the tightness of monetary policy. In this way, growth in M1 may shrink at the same time that banks are expanding loans and credit.

Reserve requirements on managed liabilities affect the behavior of banks by changing the cost of these liabilities relative to other sources of funding loan expansion. By raising reserve requirements on a specific type of liability, for example, its use can be discouraged relative to other funding sources. At various times the Federal Reserve has used this instrument in three distinct ways: to control the overall level of managed liabilities, to change the composition of managed liabilities, and to change the average maturity of managed liabilities. Some examples may clarify these uses.

In October 1979, the Federal Reserve tried to reduce growth in the overall level of managed liabilities by imposing an 8 percent reserve requirement on the amount by which an institution's total managed liabilities exceeded a base period amount.[19] This action was designed to slow the expansion in bank credit financed through managed liabilities by increasing the cost of the additional use of these liabilities. Subsequently, in April 1980, this marginal reserve requirement was raised to 10 percent as part of the Credit Control Program before being reduced to 5 percent in June 1980 and 0 percent in July 1980 as credit growth slowed.

Discretionary changes in reserve requirements also have been used to affect the composition of managed liabilities. For example, in September 1969, the Federal Reserve imposed a 10 percent marginal reserve requirement on Eurodollar borrowings by U.S. banks. The reason for this action was that banks were apparently avoiding domestic credit restraint by developing overseas sources of funds. Thus, the marginal reserve requirement on foreign borrowing was designed to eliminate the cost advantage of foreign sources of funds. At other times, reserve requirements on Eurodollars have been adjusted to encourage their use. For example, in August 1978, the marginal reserve requirement on Eurodollars was lowered to encourage U.S. banks to borrow abroad and help support the foreign exchange value of the dollar.

Finally, reserve requirement changes have been used in an effort to change the maturity of particular types of managed liabilities. For example, in September 1974 and again in October 1975, the Federal Reserve established differential reserve requirements on large-denomination time deposits with different maturities. Lower reserve requirements were set on time deposits with longer maturities. The purpose of this action was to encourage banks to lengthen the maturity of their time deposits by lowering the relative cost of longer term sources of funds.

It is important to note that these examples of the use of reserve requirements on managed liabilities occurred before passage of the 1980 Monetary Control Act. Provisions of the act have reduced the flexibility of this use of reserve requirements, somewhat. For example, the act continues to permit, under ordinary circumstances, differentiated reserve requirements by personal versus nonpersonal time deposits, by maturity of nonpersonal time deposits, and by nonpersonal time deposits versus Eurocurrency liabilities. However, reserve requirements on all managed liabilities as employed in October 1979 are no longer permissible. In addition, only in extraordinary circumstances as determined by five board members and after consultation with appropriate congressional committees may reserve requirements be differentiated by types of nonpersonal time deposits or may marginal reserve requirements be imposed on selected types or on all nonpersonal time deposits.

The use of reserve requirements on managed liabilities adds to the flexibility of reserve requirements as a discretionary policy instrument. As noted in the next section, this use of reserve requirements may play a potentially valuable role in control of the broader monetary aggregates.

The Discount-Rate Surcharge

As in the case of reserve requirements, it has traditionally been difficult to target discount policy to specific size institutions. To make discount policy more flexible, in March 1980, the Federal Reserve introduced a discount rate surcharge applying to large banks that made frequent use of the discount window. The purpose of the surcharge was to prevent large banks with access to the money markets from borrowing excessively, while at the same time providing smaller banks with continued access to the discount window.

As initially structured, the discount-rate surcharge applied to banks with deposits over $500 million that borrowed for two consecutive weeks or for more than four weeks in a calendar quarter. The initial surcharge rate was 3 percent. Thus, large banks subject to the surcharge would pay the basic discount rate plus a 3 percent surcharge. The surcharge was removed in May 1980 but was reintroduced in November 1980, and it remained in effect until November 1981. During this latter period, the surcharge rate changed from 2 to 4 percent.

A discount rate surcharge can improve monetary control in two ways. *First,* the surcharge can be varied independently of the basic discount rate. Thus, the flexibility of discretionary discount rate changes is enhanced to the extent that changes in the surcharge rate can be directed at larger institutions. *Second,* the surcharge mechanism can improve the automatic nature of the monetary control system. Depending on the relationship among the federal funds rate, the basic discount rate, and the surcharge rate, large banks may have a reduced incentive to use the discount window as a source of reserves. Thus, in a period of monetary restraint, large banks subject to the surcharge may be encouraged to limit deposit and credit extension because of the higher cost of obtaining reserves through the discount window.[20]

THE CHOICE OF MONETARY POLICY TARGETS

The role that the discount rate and reserve requirements play in the policy process depends not only on institutional factors but also on the Federal Reserve's choice of policy targets. Curiously, most textbook discussions of the policy instruments place little or no emphasis on the relationship between policy targets and instruments. In contrast, this section argues that recent Federal Reserve decisions to target money and reserves, rather than interest rates, have expanded the scope to use the discount rate and reserve requirements.[21] Two issues are emphasized in this discussion: the use of a reserve approach, rather than an interest-rate approach to monetary control, and the implications of targeting several monetary aggregates.

Interest Rate versus Reserve Targeting

In October 1979, the Federal Reserve made a much-publicized change in its monetary control procedures. Until then, the Federal Reserve attempted to control monetary growth through control of short-term interest rates, specifically through control of the federal funds rate. Under this system, the FOMC chose a target interest rate that was believed to be consistent with a desired money growth rate and changed the interest-rate target only if money growth deviated significantly from its desired path. In October 1979, the Federal Reserve shifted to the use of a nonborrowed reserve target in order to control money growth. In this framework, the FOMC chooses a target path for nonborrowed reserves that is thought to be consistent with desired money growth. The nonborrowed reserve target is then maintained unless money growth deviates substantially from its desired path.[22]

The 1979 change in operating procedures was designed to improve automatic control of money growth. Under an interest rate targeting procedure, increased money demand is initially accommodated by the Federal Reserve. That is, an increased demand for money expands banks' demands for required reserves, and the Federal Reserve supplies more nonborrowed reserves to maintain the target interest rate. Under a reserves targeting procedure, in contrast, the supply of nonborrowed reserves is held constant in the face of increased demand for reserves. Thus, banks must either obtain additional reserves through the discount window or cut back loan and deposit growth to reduce their demand for required reserves.

What is the role of the policy instruments under the two operating procedures? Given the flexibility of open market operations on a daily or weekly basis, it is the principal policy instrument under either system. That is, under an interest-rate targeting procedure, open market operations are used to maintain the target interest rate in the presence of changes in reserve demand and supply. Similarly, under a nonborrowed reserves procedure, open market operations are used to maintain the target level of nonborrowed reserves. The real question, then, is whether the discount rate and reserve requirements make an independent contribution to monetary control under either system.

Under an interest-rate targeting procedure, the discount rate and reserve requirements play little part in the monetary control process. As long as open market operations are directed toward maintaining a constant interest rate, discretionary changes in the discount rate and reserve requirements have little impact on money and credit growth.[23] For example, a discount-rate increase is normally thought to increase market interest rates. Under an interest-rate target, however, open market operations routinely offset the effect of the discount rate increase by providing more nonborrowed reserves. Thus, while the discount-rate increase may reduce reserves provided through the discount window, open market operations provide an equal amount of nonborrowed reserves, leaving the total supply of reserves and interest rates unchanged.[24] Similarly, an increase in reserve requirements is normally thought to result in greater demand for reserves and upward pressure on interest rates. With an interest-rate target, however, open market operations again provide additional reserves. Since the increased demand for reserves is met by an additional supply of reserves, there is no upward pressure on interest rates or stimulus to reduce money and credit growth.[25]

Discount-rate policy and reserve requirements play a potentially more important role under reserve targeting. The reason is that, with a nonborrowed reserve target, open market operations do not automatically offset discount rate and reserve requirement changes. For example, a discount-rate increase tends to put upward pressure on market interest rates and to reduce money growth. In this instance, open market operations are directed at keeping nonborrowed reserves constant, rather than increasing nonborrowed reserves, as under the interest-rate targeting approach.

Similarly, with a nonborrowed reserve target, an increase in reserve requirements puts upward pressure on market interest rates and reduces money growth. Since open market operations are directed at maintaining a fixed supply of nonborrowed reserves, the increased demand for reserves is not accommodated as it would be under an interest-rate target. In general, then, the decision to target nonborrowed reserves opens up a greater scope for the use of discount rate policy and reserve requirements.[26]

Multiple Aggregate Targets

Since the beginning of formal monetary targeting in the mid-1970s, the Federal Reserve has set targets for a variety of monetary aggregates, ranging from transactions-based M1 to such broader aggregates as M2 and M3, as well as measures of credit or debt. The primary reason for multiple targets is the belief that no one aggregate is sufficiently reliable to be used as the exclusive focus of monetary policy. While the Federal Reserve has generally emphasized control of M1, on several occasions the behavior of M1 has been deemphasized and increased weight placed on the broader aggregates. The most recent example is the decision in late 1982 and 1983 to deemphasize M1 because of distortions in its behavior caused by deregulation and financial innovation.

Problems arise, however, in trying to control a broadly defined monetary aggregate consisting of both transactions and nontransactions components. One difficulty is that there is little automatic control of the nontransactions components. Indeed, the restructuring of reserve requirements under the Monetary Control Act and the adoption of contemporaneous reserve accounting were aimed primarily at improving control of transactions deposits. These structural changes worsen or, at best, have no effect on control of nontransactions deposits.

At the same time, the financial deregulation of recent years may have increased the difficulty of controlling the broad aggregates through the use of open market operations and discount-rate policy. As nontransactions deposits have come to pay market rates of interest, the interest sensitivity of the broader aggregates has probably declined. Thus, much larger changes in interest rates through open market operations or discount-rate policy may be required to achieve the same degree of control over these aggregates.

These considerations suggest a broader potential role for the use of reserve requirements as a policy instrument. Two different approaches to the use of reserve requirements to control the broader aggregates are possible. The first approach, discussed earlier, is the discretionary use of reserve requirement changes on certain types of managed liabilities. By using these reserve requirements to alter the relative cost of different liabilities, the Federal Reserve can directly affect the growth rates of particular components of the broader aggregates. As noted above, however, provisions of the 1980 Monetary Control Act have reduced the flexibility of this type of reserve requirement change.

A second approach to the use of reserve requirements would be to improve automatic control over the broader aggregates. One suggestion in this regard is the use of so-called shadow reserve requirements, where nonreservable components of a broad aggregate can be assigned reserve requirements in the process of computing a nonborrowed reserve target.[27] That is, growth in these deposits above a desired level would be treated as if these deposits were subject to reserve requirements. A corresponding downward adjustment in the nonborrowed reserve target would be made to offset this growth. In this way, excessive growth in these deposits would lead to upward pressure on interest rates that would tend to reduce the demand for these deposits and slow the growth of the broader aggregates.

THE ROLE OF THE POLICY INSTRUMENTS

In light of these legislative, regulatory, and policy developments, it is appropriate to reconsider the roles that the three instruments play in the monetary policy process. The thesis of this article is that these institutional developments generally enhance the importance of discount policy and reserve requirements. This position contrasts sharply with the traditional academic view that highlights the role of open market operations and deemphasizes the contribution of discount-rate policy and reserve requirements to monetary policy. The traditional view appears to be based on the observation that historically the Federal Reserve has made relatively infrequent use of discount policy and reserve requirements as policy instruments. The major difficulty with this view is a failure to recognize that the role of the policy instruments depends crucially on the Federal Reserve's choice of policy targets and that the choice of policy targets has evolved considerably in recent years.

As shown in the preceding section, the Federal Reserve's decision to target short-term interest rates or reserves is the principal determinant of the role of discount-rate policy and reserve requirements. The choice of an interest-rate targeting approach implies that short-run monetary policy can be conducted through the use of a single policy instrument. Given the administrative flexibility of open market operations, discount-rate policy and reserve requirements contribute little to monetary policy. In contrast, under a reserve targeting approach, all three instruments have an independent effect on interest rates and money growth. Thus, within this framework, legislative and regulatory actions that change the structure of discount policy and reserve requirements can make an important contribution to monetary control.

The traditional view of the policy instruments developed over a period when the Federal Reserve generally pursued an interest-rate targeting approach to monetary policy. In this context, the traditional view accurately portrayed the subsidiary role of discount-rate policy and reserve requirements. With the advent of reserve targeting, however, the traditional view clearly needs modification and more attention needs to be paid to the potential contributions of discount rate policy and reserve requirements.[28]

Role of the Policy Instruments under Reserve Targeting

While all three policy instruments are potentially important in the reserves approach to monetary control, they are not interchangeable. Each instrument has specific advantages and disadvantages that condition its use in particular situations and define its role in the policy process.

The use of open market operations continues to be the principal discretionary policy instrument under reserve targeting. Open market operations are used on a daily and weekly basis both to achieve the target level of reserves and to adjust this target in response to stronger or weaker money growth. The use of open market operations has two advantages as a discretionary policy instrument. *First,* open market operations have greater administrative flexibility than a change in discount rate policy or reserve requirements. Open market operations can be carried out on a daily basis in amounts tailored to meet existing reserve needs. Second, open market operations tend to be less subject to announcement effects. Open market operations are done frequently enough that their use is not viewed as a reliable signal of major policy changes. At the same time, however, this latter feature can turn into a disadvantage when the Federal Reserve wants to signal a policy change to financial markets.

Under a reserve targeting approach, reserve requirements can contribute to both automatic and discretionary monetary control. Reserve requirements affect the degree of automatic monetary control in two ways. First, the level of reserve requirements determines the amount of interest-rate pressure that occurs in response to faster or weaker money growth. Before the Monetary Control Act, the downward trend in effective reserve requirements on transactions deposits led to a progressive weakening in automatic monetary control. With passage of the act, the effective reserve requirement on transactions deposits was stabilized, thus contributing to automatic monetary control. At the same time, changes in the structure of reserve requirements removed unnecessary variability in the money supply due to certain types of shifts among transactions and nontransactions deposits in different depository institutions. The adoption of contemporaneous reserve accounting should also improve automatic monetary control to the extent that it accelerates the response of bank reserve demand and interest rates to faster or weaker money growth.

Reserve requirements play a less-important role as a discretionary policy instrument. A change in the overall level of reserve requirements continues to be a blunt and administratively complex policy instrument. Thus, general reserve requirement changes are likely to be infrequent under reserve targeting. With the advent of several money targets, however, selective reserve requirement changes on specific types of deposits may have become a more useful discretionary instrument. The new structure of reserve requirements is designed to improve automatic control over transactions deposits. As such, it makes little contribution to automatic control of the major nontransactions deposits included in the broader aggregates. Thus, in this framework, changes in reserve requirements on nontransactions deposits can play an important role in controlling growth in the broader aggregates.

The role of discount-rate policy under reserve targeting is more complicated than the other two instruments. In principle, discount-rate policy has implications for both automatic and discretionary monetary control. In practice, however, there is considerable controversy over whether discount policy strengthens or weakens monetary control and whether discount-rate changes are a useful discretionary instrument.

Whether discount-rate policy aids or hinders automatic monetary control depends on differing views about why institutions use the discount window. Those believing that borrowing weakens monetary control argue that banks typically use the discount window as an inexpensive source of funds for loan and credit expansion. Thus, it is argued, if the discount windows were closed or the discount rate set equal to market rates, banks would be forced to compete for a fixed supply of reserves and would limit loan and credit expansion. In contrast, those believing that the discount window improves monetary control argue that borrowing cushions the money supply from unexpected changes in the distribution of reserve demand and supply. Without a discount window, these disturbances would increase money volatility and force the Federal Reserve to take offsetting open market operations.[29]

The use of the discount rate as a discretionary instrument is also somewhat complicated. Generally speaking, under reserve targeting, discount-rate changes and open market operations have similar effects on interest rates and money growth. For example, in responding to excessive money growth, the Federal Reserve can tighten policy by using open market operations to reduce the supply of nonborrowed reserves or by increasing the discount rate to discourage banks from obtaining reserves through the discount window. There is an asymmetry to the use of discount-rate changes that is often overlooked, however. A change in the discount rate affects the supply of reserves only to the extent that it alters banks' incentive to use the discount window. If market rates are below the discount rate, banks undertake minimal discount window borrowing. In this case, discount rate changes have little effect on borrowing and so have little impact on market interest rates and money growth. Thus, this asymmetry tends to limit the usefulness of discretionary changes in the discount rate.[30]

In a situation where the discount rate is below market rates, a discount rate change may have an advantage over open market operations. Discount-rate changes tend to be more visible. That is, they may have significant effects on market interest rates by signaling changes in the direction of monetary policy. The role of these announcement effects has been the subject of controversy. Some have defended the use of discount-rate changes to signal policy changes by citing the difficulty of using open market operations to provide this information. Others have argued that the announcement effects of discount rate changes may be unreliable.[31] That is, financial markets may not receive the correct policy signal. To the extent that discount rate changes convey important information about future monetary policy, however, discount rate changes have an additional role to play in the monetary policy process.[32]

SUMMARY AND CONCLUSIONS

In recent years, a number of important legislative, regulatory, and policy developments have altered the role of the discount-rate and reserve requirements in the monetary policy process. The key development is the change in the Federal Reserve's targeting procedures. The use of a reserves approach to monetary control and the emphasis on multiple monetary targets have widened the scope for discount-rate policy and reserve requirements. Within this new policy framework, structural changes in the reserve requirement and discount mechanisms have further enhanced the role of these instruments. Thus, the traditional view that deemphasizes the contribution of the discount rate and reserve requirements should be replaced by a more balanced view of the role of the policy instruments.

NOTES

[1] Examples of this view can be found in Thomas Mayer, James Duesenberry, and Robert Aliber, *Money, Banking, and the Economy,* (New York: W. W. Norton, 1981), pp. 500–19; and Warren L. Smith, "The Instruments of General Monetary Control," in *Readings in Money, National Income, and Stabilization Policy,* 4th ed., ed. Ronald L. Teigen, (Homewood, Ill: Richard D. Irwin, 1978), pp. 190–212.

[2] A detailed discussion of FOMC decisionmaking and the role of open market operations is presented in Paul Meek, *U.S. Monetary Policy and Financial Markets,* Federal Reserve Bank of New York, 1982.

[3] The best source of information on monetary policy decisions is the *Federal Reserve Bulletin,* published monthly by the Board of Governors. Policy actions in a given year are conveniently summarized in the *Annual Report* of the Board of Governors.

4 In the case of a change in a factor affecting money supply directly, such as a shift in banks' desired holdings of excess or borrowed reserves, higher reserve requirements may reduce the volatility of both money and interest rates.

5 The distinction between discretionary and automatic monetary control can be pictured in terms of a graph showing the determination of the interest rate and quantity of money by a downward sloping money demand curve and an upward sloping money supply curve. In this framework, discretionary policy actions shift the money supply curve while automatic policy actions change the slope of the money supply curve.

6 The exception is the Federal Reserve's use of reserve requirements on managed liabilities, which dates from the late 1960s.

7 Nonmember institutions were subject to state reserve requirement regulations. Generally, these regulations were seen as less restrictive than Federal Reserve regulations.

8 The Garn-St Germain Depository Institutions Act of 1982 modifies the 1980 Monetary Control Act by providing that $2 million of reservable liabilities of each depository institution be subject to a 0 percent reserve requirement. This exemption amount is adjusted each year for the next calendar year by 80 percent of the percentage increase in total reservable liabilities of all depository institutions measured on an annual basis as of June 30. For more detail, see any issue of the *Federal Reserve Bulletin,* table 1.15, footnote 5.

9 For banks and thrift institutions that were not members of the Federal Reserve System on or after July 3, 1979, the phase-in period for the new reserve requirement structure ends September 3, 1987.

The amount of transactions deposits against which the 3 percent reserve requirement applies is modified annually by 80 percent of the percentage increase in transactions accounts held by all depository institutions determined as of June 30 each year.

10 For the conditions under which a supplemental reserve requirement may be imposed, see the *Annual Report,* Board of Governors, 1980, pp. 209–10.

11 The discussion in this section is based on a more detailed treatment in J. A. Cacy and Scott Winningham, "Reserve Requirements under the Depository Institutions Deregulation and Monetary Control Act of 1980," *Economic Review,* Federal Reserve Bank of Kansas City, September–October 1980, pp. 3–16.

12 The overall impact on the level of reserve requirements for transactions balances is complicated, since member institutions are generally subject to lower reserve requirements and nonmember institutions are subject to higher reserve requirements. The important point, however, is that without the act, reserve requirements on transactions accounts would have declined below the level established in the act.

13 This result needs to be qualified. As noted above, the first $2 million of reservable liabilities of each depository institution is subject to a 0 percent reserve requirement, while net transactions accounts are subject to a 3 percent reserve requirement on the first $28.9 million, and 12 percent on amounts in excess of the base figure. Thus, shifts of funds between institutions of different sizes will continue to affect required and excess reserves.

14 Other shifts may strengthen or weaken M1 control. For example, under the new system, shifts between assets, such as Treasury bills and time deposits, have a smaller impact on M1 because such shifts have a smaller effect on required reserves. On the other hand, deposit shifts between transactions accounts and nonpersonal time and savings deposits continue to affect M1.

15 Control of the broader aggregates is also complicated by certain deposit shifts similar to those discussed for M1. Under the new system of reserve requirements, shifts between transactions deposits and nontransactions deposits will have a larger effect on the broader aggregates because of the lower reserve requirements on the nontransactions components. For a further discussion, see Cacy and Winningham, "Reserve Requirements."

16 For a more detailed discussion of the mechanics of CRR, see R. Alton Gilbert and Michael E. Trebing, "The New System of Contemporaneous Reserve Requirements," *Review,* Federal Reserve Bank of St. Louis, December 1982, pp. 3–7.

17 A more complete treatment of this issue is found in David S. Jones, "Contemporaneous vs. Lagged Reserve Accounting: Implications for Monetary Control," *Economic Review,* Federal Reserve Bank of Kansas City, November 1981, pp. 3–19.

18 The Federal Reserve attempted to reduce this problem in 1972 by adopting a system of graduated reserve requirements based on size of deposits. This system replaced a structure in which reserve requirements depended on geographic location. Under a graduated system, reserve requirements changes can be directed at particular deposit size categories and thus at different size institutions. The new system of reserve requirements described above is a graduated system but has a smaller number of deposit size graduations than the old system.

[19] A marginal reserve requirement applies to increases in a deposit category above a base period amount. Changes in the marginal rate affect the cost of additions to the base period amount but do not force an institution to alter the base period amount.

[20] The discount rate surcharge is analyzed in more detail in Gordon H. Sellon, Jr., and Diane Seibert, "The Discount Rate: Experience Under Reserve Targeting," *Economic Review,* Federal Reserve Bank of Kansas City, November 1982, pp. 3–18.

[21] The evolution of Federal Reserve targeting procedures and its policy implications are discussed in Gordon H. Sellon, Jr., and Ronald L. Teigen, "The Choice of Short-Run Targets for Monetary Policy," Part I, *Economic Review,* Federal Reserve Bank of Kansas City, April 1981, pp. 3–16, and Part II, May 1981, pp. 3–12.

[22] A good discussion of the change in operating procedures is found in "Monetary Policy and Open Market Operations in 1979," *Quarterly Review,* Federal Reserve Bank of New York, Summer 1980, pp. 50–64.

[23] Under an interest-rate approach, discount policy can affect the amount of discount window borrowing and may have some impact on the distribution of reserves in the banking system. Similarly, reserve requirements may not affect M1 control directly but may have an impact on other aspects of bank behavior.

[24] Discount policy under interest rate and reserve targeting is analyzed in more detail in Gordon H. Sellon, Jr., "The Role of the Discount Rate in Monetary Policy: A Theoretical Analysis," *Economic Review,* Federal Reserve Bank of Kansas City, June 1980, pp. 3–15.

[25] The role of reserve requirements under different targeting procedures is discussed in Ira Kaminow, "Required Reserve Ratios, Policy Instruments, and Money Stock Control," *Journal of Monetary Economics* 3, no. 4 (October 1977), pp. 389–408.

[26] It is important to distinguish clearly the concepts of automatic and discretionary control when evaluating the impact of reserve requirement changes. With a nonborrowed reserves target, in practice, the Federal Reserve would probably cushion the immediate effect of a reserve requirement change by altering nonborrowed reserves. At the same time, however, the new reserve requirement changes the slope of the money supply function and thus affects the degree of automatic monetary control. Therefore, in practice, under a nonborrowed reserves procedure, reserve requirement changes would probably not be made to bring about immediate reserve adjustments but, rather, would be aimed at improving automatic monetary control. In contrast, with an interest-rate target, reserve requirement changes do not contribute either to discretionary or to automatic monetary control, since the form of the money supply function does not enter into the determination of the equilibrium interest rate and quantity of money.

[27] The case for the use of "shadow reserve requirements" is developed in Marcelle Arak, "Control of a Credit Aggregate," *Quarterly Review,* Federal Reserve Bank of New York, Winter 1982–83, pp. 10–15.

[28] In October 1982, the Federal Reserve decided to place less weight on M1 as a policy target because of impending innovations in the financial system. This decision required changes in the Federal Reserve's short-run operating procedures, as described by Governor Wallich in the accompanying article, "Recent Techniques of Monetary Policy." Under these revised procedures, the level of nonborrowed reserves continues to be the short-run operating target. However, changes in required reserves are accommodated by changes in nonborrowed reserves unless a decision is made to alter the degree of reserve provision. In this system, discount-rate changes have an effect on market rates similar to that under a pure nonborrowed reserves procedure, but reserve requirement changes would probably contribute little to automatic monetary control.

[29] For a discussion of these opposing views, see Sellon, "The Role of the Discount Rate in Monetary Policy," especially pp. 11–15.

[30] The impact of discount rate changes under reserve targeting is analyzed in more detail in Sellon and Seibert.

[31] A good discussion of this viewpoint is contained in Warren L. Smith, "The Instruments of General Monetary Control," pp. 199–203.

[32] A recent study suggests that discount rate changes have significant announcement effects that reinforce the basic thrust of monetary policy. See V. Vance Roley and Rick Troll, "The Impact of Discount Rate Changes on Market Interest Rates," *Economic Review,* Federal Reserve Bank of Kansas City, January 1984, pp. 27–39.

34

Operating Procedures
for Conducting Monetary Policy

R. Alton Gilbert

Within the Federal Reserve System, the body that determines the nation's monetary policy is the Federal Open Market Committee (FOMC). The FOMC meets several times each year, specifying targets for the federal funds rate and money growth over the period until the next scheduled meeting.[1] Twice each year, in February and July, the FOMC also announces its annual objectives for growth of the monetary aggregates. The committee began setting targets for the growth rates of the monetary aggregates in 1970, because of a growing recognition of the effects of money growth on total spending and inflation. The FOMC also gives some weight to the short-run stability of interest rates, expressed as ranges for the federal funds rate.

After the FOMC determines the objectives for monetary policy, the task of implementing the policy is delegated to the staff of the Open Market Desk at the Federal Reserve Bank of New York. The Open Market Desk does this by buying and selling federal government securities for the Federal Reserve System. It increases reserves of the banking system by buying additional government securities and decreases reserves by selling securities.

The FOMC's instructions to the Open Market Desk also include a procedure that it should use to implement monetary policy. This paper identifies three distinct procedures used by the Open Market Desk since 1970. The purpose of the paper is to describe the mechanics of these three operating procedures, identifying the steps followed by the Open Market Desk in determining the amount of reserves to supply through open market operations.

The first procedure, which was used in the 1970s, involved targeting on the federal funds rate; the Open Market Desk would supply the level of reserves necessary to keep the federal funds rate within ranges specified by the FOMC for periods between meetings. The next procedure, used during the three years

From *Review*, Federal Reserve Bank of St. Louis, February 1985, pp. 13–21.

R. Alton Gilbert is an assistant vice president at the Federal Reserve Bank of St. Louis. Paul G. Christopher provided research assistance.

ending in October 1982, involved targeting on levels of nonborrowed reserves (reserves other than those borrowed from Federal Reserve banks); these were based on the FOMC objectives for the money stock. This procedure allowed for wider short-run fluctuations in the federal funds rate. Under the final procedure, in effect since October 1982, the objective of the Open Market Desk in each reserve maintenance period is to keep the total of reserves borrowed by depository institutions from Federal Reserve banks near some desired level. The desired level of borrowings reflects the desired degree of reserve restraint specified by the FOMC at each meeting.

BASIC TOOL FOR EXPOSITION: SUPPLY AND DEMAND FOR RESERVES

The mechanics of the implementation of monetary policy under the three operating procedures can be described by analyzing the market for total reserves of depository institutions. These reserves include currency that depository institutions hold in their vaults and reserve balances they hold at Federal Reserve banks. Depository institutions hold reserves to facilitate their customers' transactions and to meet reserve requirements imposed by the Federal Reserve. The required reserves are based on the amount and composition of their deposit liabilities.

Because they earn no interest on reserves, there is an opportunity cost for depository institutions to hold them. The opportunity cost is identified in this paper as the federal funds rate, the interest rate that depository institutions charge each other for lending reserves.[2] If a depository institution must increase its reserves, it borrows at the federal funds rate; if it can reduce its reserves, it lends at the federal funds rate.

In the three figures used in this paper, the demand for reserves by depository institutions is drawn as a function of the federal funds rate. Reserve requirements on those deposits included in the money stock create a close relationship between the demand for money by the public and the demand for reserves by depository institutions. The demand for money is assumed to be a function of total spending in the economy and interest rates. Various influences can cause shifts in the demand curve for reserves. A change in total spending in the economy, which influences the demand for money, would cause the demand curve for reserves to shift. Shifts in the demand for reserves could also reflect changes in the random component of money demand, a change in the average reserve requirement on deposit liabilities included in the money stock or a change in the demand for excess reserves.

The factors that influence the supply of reserves can be analyzed by considering separately the determinants of borrowed and nonborrowed reserves. Nonborrowed reserves (NBR) are determined by the open market operations of the Open Market Desk.

The amount of reserves borrowed from Federal Reserve banks is influenced by the spread between the federal funds rate and the discount rate, and by the conditions set by the Federal Reserve for permitting depository institutions to borrow reserves. If the discount rate is above the federal funds rate, the amount of reserves borrowed from Federal Reserve banks tends to be relatively low and insensitive to small changes in the federal funds rate. The supply curve for reserves reflects this observation. The supply curve is drawn as a vertical line from the level of NBR (labeled N in the figures) up to the level on the vertical axis at which the federal funds rate equals the discount rate, indicated as $r_f^1 = r_d$.

The shape of the supply curve in the range in which the federal funds rate exceeds the discount rate depends on the conditions under which Federal Reserve banks permit depository institutions to borrow reserves. If the Federal Reserve did not set limits on borrowings, no institution would pay more than the discount rate to borrow reserves in the federal funds market. In that case, the relevant supply curve in the range of the horizontal axis above NBR would be horizontal at the level of the federal funds rate equal to the discount rate.

The relevant supply curve is not horizontal, however; instead, it slopes upward, like the curves in the three figures labelled S_1, S_2, and S_3. The shape of each supply curve reflects a method of nonprice rationing of borrowed reserves among depository institutions. These supply curves differ only by the amount of NBR; each curve reflects the same method of nonprice rationing of borrowed reserves.

The Federal Reserve rations borrowed reserves by setting limits on the borrowings by each depository institution. These limits are set in terms of (1) the amounts borrowed relative to the required reserves of the depository institution and (2) the frequency and duration of its borrowings. Depository institutions try to avoid exceeding these borrowing limits to ensure that they will have access to credit to cover short-term liquidity requirements. If a depository institution borrows now, it will be subjected to greater administrative pressure to limit its borrowings in the future, when the attractiveness of borrowing from the discount window might be greater. Consequently, it takes an increase in the spread between the federal funds rate and the discount rate to induce depository institutions to increase their borrowings from the discount window. The slope of each supply curve reflects this relationship between borrowings and the interest-rate spread.

The three figures in this paper illustrate short-run relationships between the supply and demand for reserves. In Figure 1, the relevant time period is a one-week reserve maintenance period.[3] The relevant time period for Figure 2 is a few weeks between FOMC meetings. For Figure 3, which illustrates the current operating procedure, the time period is a two-week reserve maintenance period. Reserve maintenance periods were lengthened from one week to two weeks in February 1984, when the Federal Reserve adopted contemporaneous reserve requirements.

Given its short-run focus, this paper does not present a complete analysis of the money-supply process under each operating procedure. The more limited purpose of this paper is to describe how open market operations are determined under each operating procedure for a given short time period. The following sections indicate how the short-run analysis of each operating procedure would fit into a more complete analysis of the money-supply process.

TARGETING ON THE FEDERAL FUNDS RATE: 1970 THROUGH SEPTEMBER 1979

The Federal Reserve attempted to control the money stock during the 1970s by confining the federal funds rate to relatively narrow ranges, specified at each FOMC meeting. The use of this procedure was based on the assumption of a stable demand function for money. (As indicated previously, money demand is assumed to be a function of interest rates and total spending in the economy. For the period of a few weeks between FOMC meetings, total spending is assumed to be independent of current policy actions.) The Federal Reserve attempted to control the money stock through its influence on interest rates by moving the public up or down its demand for money schedule.

The Statement of FOMC Objectives

At each meeting, the FOMC stated its growth objectives for the monetary aggregates as ranges from the average of the month before the meeting to the average of the month of the next scheduled meeting. For instance, on September 18, 1979, the last meeting under this operating procedure, the FOMC's objective for M1 was an annual growth rate between 3 percent and 8 percent from August through October.

At each meeting, the FOMC directed the Open Market Desk of the Federal Reserve Bank of New York to keep the federal funds rate within a range of about 50 to 100 basis points until the next meeting, and often specified an initial level for the federal funds rate within the target range. The manager of the Open Market Desk was authorized to let the federal funds rate move toward the top or bottom of the specified range if the money stock was tending to rise above or fall below that desired by the FOMC. The Open Market Desk supplied the amounts of NBR necessary to keep the federal funds rate within the target range. Occasionally, the FOMC changed the range for the federal funds rate in conference calls held between scheduled meetings if the money stock was tending to deviate substantially from its objective.[4]

The Implementation of FOMC Directives

The conduct of monetary policy under this procedure is illustrated in Figure 1. At one of its scheduled meetings, the FOMC would specify an initial level for the federal funds rate for the period immediately after the meeting (r_f^2) and a range for the rate until the next scheduled meeting ($r_u - r_l$). The Open Market Desk then would adjust NBR to keep the federal funds rate at the initial target rate immediately after the meeting and within the target range until the next meeting.[5]

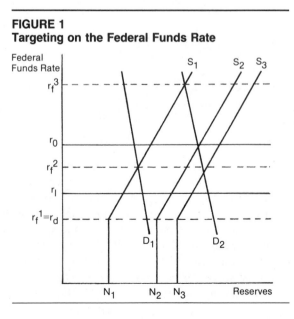

FIGURE 1
Targeting on the Federal Funds Rate

The time period for the supply and demand curves in Figure 1 is one reserve maintenance week. Lagged reserve requirements were in effect during the period in which the Open Market Desk targeted on the federal funds rate. Under lagged reserve requirements, required reserves in each maintenance week were predetermined, since they were based on deposits two weeks earlier. Consequently, the demand curves in Figure 1 are drawn relatively steep.[6] With required reserves predetermined for each period, the slope of the demand curves reflects the responsiveness of the demand for excess reserves to changes in the levels of the federal funds rate.

The demand for reserves in the first week after the FOMC meeting is denoted by the curve D_1. The Open Market Desk would supply NBR equal to N_1 to keep the federal funds rate at r_f^2. Suppose there was a large increase in the demand for reserves in the second week, represented by the shift in the demand curve from D_1 to D_2. This increase in the demand for reserves would reflect an increase in the demand for money. To accommodate the increase in the demand for reserves, the Open Market Desk would increase NBR in order to keep the federal funds rate in the target range set by the FOMC. In figure 1, the Desk would increase the supply of NBR to N, to keep the federal funds rate at r_f^2.

If, however, the money stock was tending to rise above the desired range of the FOMC, the Desk might have increased NBR to only N_2, thus allowing the federal funds rate to rise to the top of the range (r_u). Any authorization for the Open Market Desk to allow an additional rise in the federal funds rate before the next scheduled FOMC meeting would require an FOMC conference call to specify a new range for the federal funds rate.

Discussions of the advantages of this operating procedure usually emphasize how the Federal Reserve could prevent transitory fluctuations in the federal funds rate, while controlling the growth rate of the money supply over a quarter of a year or longer, periods that are relevant for stabilizing economic activity. One cause of transitory fluctuations in the federal funds rate was Open Market Desk errors in measuring NBR in the current week. The Federal Reserve had to estimate several factors that influence NBR, such as balances of the U.S. Treasury at Federal Reserve Banks and Federal Reserve float. If, however, the Federal Reserve made large errors in estimating the current level of NBR, this procedure would offset those errors automatically. For instance, if actual NBR fell below Federal Reserve estimates, the federal funds rate would tend to rise above the target rate, and the Open Market Desk would respond by buying additional securities, thus increasing NBR.

Another type of transitory effect on interest rates would be a transitory shift in the demand for total reserves. The demand for total reserves may shift for various reasons. There may be random fluctuations in the demand for money, average reserve requirements, or excess reserves. Under this procedure, the Open Market Desk would offset the effects of such transitory shifts in the demand for reserves by adjusting the level of NBR to keep the federal funds rate unchanged.

The effects of transitory shifts in the demand for total reserves are illustrated in Figure 1. The demand for reserves is illustrated by the curve D_1 in the first week after an FOMC meeting, D_2 in the second week, and D_1 again in the third week. If the Open Market Desk kept NBR at N_1 throughout the three-week period, the federal funds rate would be r_f^2 in week 1, r_f^3 in week 2, and would fall back to r_f^2 again in week 3. The Open Market Desk would avoid these fluctuations in the federal funds rate by accommodating the random fluctuations in demand for reserves. Following this policy of accommodation, NBR would be N_1 in the first week, N_3 in the second week, and N_1 again in the third week.

The Role of the Operating Procedure in the Money-Supply Process

The position of the supply curve for reserves in a given maintenance week had little effect on the quantity of reserves supplied, because required reserves in each week were based on the deposits of two weeks earlier. The position of the supply curve did influence the level of the federal funds rate. In attempting to control the money supply, the Federal Reserve relied on the influence that changes in the federal funds rate would have on other interest rates and the influence of interest rates on the quantity of money demanded in the future. Money demand was assumed to be influenced by lagged values of interest rates. A more thorough treatment of the money supply process under this operating procedure would require an analysis of the effects of policy actions over several reserve mainte- nance periods. The multiperiod analysis would include changes in the FOMC's federal funds rate objectives in response to deviations of the money stock from desired levels and the lagged effects of changes in interest rates on money demand.

The major problem with this procedure was that, in attempting to stabilize the federal funds rate, the Federal Reserve could miss its targets for the money stock for periods long enough to affect total spending in the economy. A shift in the demand for reserves may have indicated that the federal funds rate must be allowed to change if the Open Market Desk is to supply the level of reserves that is consistent with FOMC objectives for the monetary aggregates. An increase in the demand for reserves may have reflected a rise in the rate of total spending in the economy, which would cause the demand for money to rise. By targeting on a fixed level of the federal funds rate in such circumstances, the Federal Reserve may conduct a procyclical monetary policy—increasing (decreasing) the level of total reserves in response to a rise (fall) in the rate of total spending.

TARGETING ON NONBORROWED RESERVES: OCTOBER 1979 THROUGH SEPTEMBER 1982

On October 6, 1979, the FOMC abandoned the procedure of targeting on the federal funds rate in favor of an NBR operating procedure. Most of the FOMC members concluded that the degree of monetary control under the previous procedure had become unsatisfactory. They decided to adopt, instead, a pro- cedure in which the objective of open market operations was to supply the amount of reserves consistent with their objectives for money growth, while permitting larger fluctuations in the federal funds rate.[7]

The Statement of FOMC Objectives

One of the changes adopted at the meeting on October 6, 1979, involved the way the FOMC stated its objectives for the growth of the monetary aggregates for periods between scheduled meetings. The FOMC began stating its objectives as a specific percentage growth rate for each monetary aggregate from a month before the meeting to some future month. For instance, the objective for M1 adopted on October 6, 1979, was an annual growth rate of 4.50 percent from September to December 1979.

Although the FOMC continued to specify ranges for the federal funds rate, those ranges were widened significantly. For most periods, the range was 400 basis points, compared with ranges of 50 to 100 basis points under the procedure of targeting on the federal funds rate. These wide ranges on the federal funds rate played a minor role in the implementation of monetary policy under the new NBR operating procedure. In fact, on several occasions the FOMC widened its ranges between scheduled meetings, when the rate threatened to move outside the previously established limits. On other occasions, the federal funds rate was allowed to move outside its range for short time periods.[8]

The Implementation of FOMC Directives

After each FOMC meeting, the Federal Reserve staff estimated the average level of total reserves that would be necessary to support the money stock desired by the FOMC. That average level was called the "total reserve path." Estimates of the total reserve path were based on (1) FOMC objectives for M1 and M2 and (2) estimates on the average reserve requirements on deposit liabilities in M1 and M2, currency, required reserves on liabilities of depository institutions not included in M1 or M2, and excess reserves. The staff generally reestimated the total reserve path each week.

At each meeting, the FOMC made an assumption about the average level of borrowed reserves over the period until the next scheduled meeting. The FOMC's borrowings assumption was often near the average level of borrowings just before the meetings. The staff determined the level of NBR on which the Open Market Desk targeted open market operations (called the "NBR path") by subtracting the FOMC's borrowings assumption from the total reserve path.

The implementation of monetary policy under this operating procedure is illustrated in Figure 2. In contrast to the procedure illustrated in Figure 1, the Open Market Desk would not increase the level of NBR in response to an increase in the demand for reserves; it might actually *decrease* NBR to keep total reserves near its path level.[9]

Levels of total reserves and NBR on the horizontal axis refer to average levels for the weeks between FOMC meetings. The total reserve path is illustrated as $R*$. The NBR path is N_1, since the FOMC set the borrowings assumption at $R*$ minus N_1.

The demand curves for reserves represent the relationship between the federal funds rate and the average quantity of reserves demanded over a few weeks between FOMC meetings. Since the time period is a few weeks, required reserves are not predetermined but may be influenced by policy actions of the current period. A rise in the federal funds rate, for instance, might cause the quantity of money demanded to decline and, therefore, cause required reserves to decline. For these reasons, the demand curves have a flatter slope in Figure 2 than in Figure 1.

Total reserves would be at the path level $R*$ if the demand curve for reserves was D_1. From that initial position, consider the effects of an increase in the demand for reserves, illustrated by a shift in the demand curve to D_2, which resulted from an increase in the demand for money. Total reserves would rise to R_1, above the total reserve path, and the federal funds rate would rise from r_f^2 to r_f^3. Without any additional policy actions, the money stock would exceed the FOMC's objectives because total reserves would be above the path level. For a

FIGURE 2
Targeting on Nonborrowed Reserves

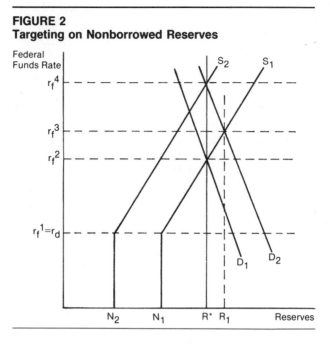

given rise in the demand for reserves, however, the amount by which the money stock would exceed the FOMC objective would be smaller under this operating procedure than if the Open Market Desk had supplied the reserves necessary to keep the federal funds rate unchanged at r_f^2.

During some periods between FOMC meetings, the Federal Reserve adjusted the level of the NBR path or the discount rate to reduce the deviations of the money stock from desired levels.[10] The Federal Reserve took those policy actions when the deviations appeared to reflect more than a transitory movement in the money demand schedule, perhaps due to a strengthening of aggregate spending.[11]

Adjustments to the NBR path or discount rate between FOMC meetings were based on projections of total reserves. After each FOMC meeting, the staff estimated the actual level of total reserves over the weeks until the next meeting, as well as the total reserve path, which was based on FOMC objectives for money growth. The estimates of total reserves were based on projections of the actual (in contrast to the desired) money stock, average reserve requirements, and excess reserves, given the existing discount rate and NBR path. A substantial deviation between the staff estimate of actual total reserves and the total reserve path indicated that additional adjustments to the discount rate or NBR path would be necessary to keep the money stock close to the FOMC objectives.

In the situation illustrated in Figure 2, the staff projects total reserves to be R_1, which is above the total reserves path (R^*). The policy action illustrated in Figure 2 is a reduction in the NBR path relative to the total reserve path (an increase in the borrowings assumption). Total reserves are constrained to be at the path level by reducing the NBR path to N_2, causing the federal funds rate to rise to r_f^4.

The Role of the Operating Procedure in the Money-Supply Process

By adopting the NBR targeting procedure, the FOMC changed the basic relationship on which the money-supply process was based. The prior procedure of targeting on the federal funds rate relied on a stable demand function for money. The second procedure of targeting on NBR relied on a relationship between reserves and the money stock. Path levels for total reserves and NBR were reestimated weekly to incorporate the most current information available on the relationship between reserves and the money stock.

TARGETING ON BORROWED RESERVES: OCTOBER 1982 TO THE PRESENT[12]

The Statement of FOMC Objectives

At a meeting in October 1982, the FOMC temporarily suspended its short-run objectives for M1. The event that precipitated the deemphasis of M1 was the maturing of a large volume of all-savers certificates in October 1982, which might have had a temporary effect on money demand. Also, movements of funds into and out of M1 were about to be affected in uncertain amounts by the scheduled introduction of a couple of monthly money market-type accounts at banks and thrift institutions. The deemphasis of M1 continued after these events, because of an observed change in the relationship between the money stock and total spending in the economy.[13]

Suspending short-run objectives for M1 made it necessary to change the operating procedure for implementing monetary policy. The procedure of targeting NBR, as described previously, gave considerable weight to the FOMC's objective for M1, since a large proportion of required reserves are against the deposit liabilities in M1. The total reserve path could not be estimated on the basis of the FOMC's objectives for M2 and M3 without an assumption or target for M1 over the intermeeting period. The FOMC has resumed the practice of specifying short-run objectives for M1 but has not directed the Open Market Desk to resume use of the procedure of targeting NBR.

In place of the NBR procedure, the Federal Reserve adopted a procedure for targeting on borrowed reserves. At each meeting, the FOMC states its objectives for open market operations in terms of degrees of reserve restraint. The directive from the FOMC to the Open Market Desk calls for more restraint, less restraint, or for the degree of reserve restraint to be unchanged. In some directives, the FOMC also states conditions for changing the degree of reserve restraint in the period before the next scheduled meeting, such as deviation of the rate of money growth from desired rates or developments in the economy.

The Open Market Desk interprets the objectives of the FOMC for the degree of reserve restraint in terms of the average level of seasonal plus adjustment borrowings over the intermeeting period.[14] More restraint would imply a higher level of borrowings and less restraint a lower level of borrowings. The Open Market Desk changes its target level for borrowings between some FOMC meetings when the conditions for changing the degree of reserve restraint specified in the latest FOMC directive do occur.

The Implementation of FOMC Directives

The amount of NBR supplied by the Open Market Desk under the current operating procedure depends on the target level for borrowed reserves and estimates of total reserves prepared by the Federal Reserve staff. The level of NBR to be supplied is determined by subtracting the target level for borrowed reserves from the staff estimate of total reserves.

The process of estimating total reserves depends on the system of reserve accounting in effect. Under lagged reserve requirements, in effect through January 1984, required reserves for each maintenance period were known by the beginning of the period. The estimate of total reserves for each period was derived by adding an estimate of excess reserves to the known level of required reserves.

Under contemporaneous reserve requirements, the reserve accounting system currently in effect, required reserves for each maintenance period are not known until after the end of the period. The staff estimates required reserves for each maintenance period, revising the estimate several times during most periods. The target levels for NBR are adjusted by the same dollar amounts as the revisions to estimates of required reserves.

The implementation of monetary policy under the current operating procedure is illustrated in Figure 3. This figure indicates that, by targeting on a given level of borrowed reserves, the Open Market Desk tends to eliminate any effect of shifts in the demand for reserves on the federal funds rate over a given reserve maintenance period.

Levels of total reserves and NBR on the horizontal axis of Figure 3 refer to average levels over a two-week reserve maintenance period. The curves that represent the demand for reserves are drawn as vertical lines in Figure 3; they are drawn as sloping downward to the right in Figures 1 and 2. This change does not

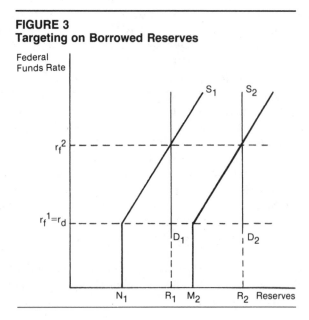

FIGURE 3
Targeting on Borrowed Reserves

imply that the demand for reserves is less interest-elastic under the procedure of targeting on borrowed reserves. The vertical demand curves reflect the way the demand for reserves is characterized under this operating procedure—that is, as a fixed amount of reserves for each maintenance period.

Early in the maintenance period, the staff estimates total reserves at the level R_1. With the target level for borrowed reserves equal to R_1 minus N_1, the Open Market Desk plans to supply NBR of N_1, which would yield an average federal funds rate of r_f^2. Suppose that, later in the period, the staff raises the estimate of total reserves to R_2. In response, the Open Market Desk raises its objective for NBR to N_2 to keep R_2 minus N_2 equal to the original target level of R_1 minus N_1. This response to a rise in the demand for reserves would keep the federal funds rate unchanged at r_f^2.

The increase in the estimate of total reserves from R_1 to R_2 may reflect a larger increase in the money stock than desired by the FOMC. If the FOMC directive calls for an increase in the degree of reserve restraint in the event of this undesired rise in the money stock, the Open Market Desk would increase its target level for borrowings. The implications of an increase in the target for borrowed reserves can be illustrated by reference to Figure 3. In response to the increase in the estimate of total reserves from R_1 to R_2, the Open Market Desk increases the supply of NBR above N_1, but not as much as N_2. In that case, the federal funds rate would rise above r_f^2. This response to an undesired rise in the money stock is similar to the response under the procedure of targeting on the federal funds rate when the Open Market Desk allowed the federal funds rate to rise to the top of its range.

The Role of the Operating Procedure in the Money-Supply Process

The current operating procedure has been described by one member of the FOMC as "an indirect method of influencing the funds rate and other short-term rates which, in turn, affect the demand for money."[15] Thus, like the procedure of targeting on the federal funds rate, the current method of controlling the money stock depends upon the influence of policy actions on interest rates and the assumption of a stable relationship between interest rates and the quantity of money demanded.

The similarity of the procedures of targeting on the federal funds rate and targeting on borrowed reserves is illustrated by examining the response of the Open Market Desk in supplying NBR to a shift in the demand for reserves. In targeting on borrowed reserves, the Open Market Desk responds to shifts in the demand for reserves in a manner similar to its response under the federal funds rate targeting procedure. The similarity is illustrated by comparing the response of the supply of NBR to a shift in demand for reserves in Figures 1 and 3. In both figures, the quantity of NBR supplied is increased in response to an increase in the demand for reserves, although the federal funds rate might be allowed to rise in response to an undesired rise in the money stock. Figure 2 indicates, in contrast, that, under the NBR targeting procedure, the Open Market Desk keeps NBR unchanged or reduces them when there is an increase in the demand for reserves that reflects an increase in the demand for money.

CONCLUSIONS

The Federal Reserve currently implements monetary policy by targeting open market operations on average levels of reserves borrowed from Federal Reserve banks. This procedure, in effect since October 1982, has some features in common with the prior two procedures used for implementing monetary policy. Like the procedure of targeting on nonborrowed reserves, in effect from October 1979 until October 1982, the official range for the federal funds rate is several hundred basis points wide. Open market operations are not conducted with the objective of keeping the federal funds rate at a specific level, as they were under the procedure of targeting on the federal funds rate used for several years prior to October 1979.

The current procedure, however, has other similarities to the procedure of targeting on the federal funds rate. There is no direct relationship between the objectives of the Federal Open Market Committee for the monetary aggregates and the supply of nonborrowed reserves, as there was under the procedure of targeting on nonborrowed reserves. Under the current procedure and that of targeting on the federal funds rate, the supply of nonborrowed reserves responds to shifts in the demand for reserves within a given reserve maintenance period in such a way that these shifts have little effect on the federal funds rate. Over longer periods, however, the federal funds rate might be allowed to move in the same direction as an undesired change in the money stock under both of those procedures.

NOTES

[1] The FOMC consists of the seven members of the Federal Reserve Board of Governors and 5 of the 12 Federal Reserve bank presidents. The chairman of the board of governors is, by tradition, chairman of the FOMC. The president of the Federal Reserve Bank of New York is a permanent member of the FOMC and, also by tradition, its vice chairman. The four remaining memberships rotate among the presidents and are held for one-year terms beginning March 1 of each year. All Federal Reserve bank presidents attend the meetings and present their views, but only those who are members of the FOMC cast votes. The FOMC currently has eight scheduled meetings each year, but may have a conference-call meeting to reevaluate monetary policy at any time.

[2] Federal funds brokers facilitate the operation of the federal funds market. These brokers receive orders from depository institutions located throughout the nation to lend or borrow reserves, and the brokers match lenders and borrowers at mutually agreeable interest rates. Most of the transactions through the federal funds market involve borrowing and lending reserves for one day. The transfers of reserves to borrowers are made the same day through wire transfer systems, including the Fed Wire of the Federal Reserve System.

[3] A reserve maintenance period is a period over which daily average reserves must equal or exceed daily average required reserves to avoid a penalty for reserve deficiency.

[4] The description of the procedure of targeting on the federal funds rate is based on Lombra and Torto (1975), Holmes and Sternlight (1977), Wallich and Keir (1979), and Lindsey (1984).

[5] In examining monetary policy actions, this paper focuses exclusively on the level of NBR. Changes in NBR through open market operations are the most frequent policy actions by the Federal Reserve. By focusing on the supply of NBR, the paper abstracts from the effects of other policy actions on the supply and demand for reserves. An increase (decrease) in the discount rate would cause the upward-sloping part of the supply curve to rise (fall). Changes in the conditions for borrowing reserves would change the slope of the supply curve in the range in which the federal funds rate exceeds the discount rate. Finally, a change in the reserve requirement ratios would cause the demand curve to shift.

[6] Under lagged reserve requirements, each maintenance period covered seven days ending each Wednesday. Required reserves for each maintenance period were based on deposit liabilities in the maintenance period two weeks earlier. Under the contemporaneous reserve requirements currently in effect, each maintenance period covers 14 days ending every other Wednesday. The required reserves of each depository institution on its checkable deposits are based on its average checkable deposits over a 14-day period ending two days before the end of the current maintenance period. See Gilbert and Trebing (1982) for a description of lagged and contemporaneous reserve requirements.

7 *Federal Reserve Bulletin,* December 1979, p. 974.

8 See Gilbert and Trebing (1981).

9 Lindsey (1982, 1983, 1984) describes how the procedure of targeting on NBR worked in practice by examining the timing of money growth relative to FOMC objectives, borrowed reserves, the federal funds rate, and the discount rate.

10 The Federal Reserve Bank of New York presents a detailed description of open market operations throughout each calendar year in the spring or summer issues of its *Quarterly Review* in the following year. Those reports indicate several occasions on which the NBR target or the discount rate were changed when the staff projected that total reserves would deviate substantially from the path levels.

11 See Lindsey (1983), p. 5.

12 This description of the procedure of targeting on borrowed reserves is based on Wallich (1984).

13 See Axilrod (1985), pp. 18–19.

14 See Wallich (1984), p. 26. Adjustment borrowings are short-term loans from Federal Reserve banks to depository institutions to aid them in adjusting their reserves to required levels. Most institutions repay their adjustment borrowings within a few days. Seasonal borrowings are longer-term loans to depository institutions that have relatively strong seasonal patterns in their loan demand or deposits. Other borrowings are called "extended credit," which is made available to institutions experiencing such severe financial difficulties that they have a hard time attracting funds from other sources. The target for borrowings under the current operating procedure is in terms of the sum of seasonal plus adjustment borrowings. Extended credit is considered a relatively fixed supply of reserves, which is not as sensitive to the spread between the federal funds rate and the discount rate as seasonal and adjustment borrowings are. Extended credit is counted as part of nonborrowed reserves for purposes of implementing monetary policy under the current operating procedure.

15 Wallich (1984), p. 22.

REFERENCES

Axilrod, Stephen H. "U.S. Monetary Policy in Recent Years: An Overview." *Federal Reserve Bulletin,* January 1985, pp. 14–24.

Gilbert, R. Alton, and Michael E. Trebing. "The FOMC in 1980: A Year of Reserve Targeting." *Review.* Federal Reserve Bank of St. Louis, August/September 1981, pp. 2–22.

———. "The New System of Contemporaneous Reserve Requirements." *Review.* Federal Reserve Bank of St. Louis, December 1982, pp. 3–7.

Holmes, Alan R., and Peter D. Sternlight. "The Implementation of Monetary Policy in 1976." *Quarterly Review,* Federal Reserve Bank of New York, Spring 1977, pp. 37–49.

Lindsey, David E. "Recent Monetary Developments and Controversies." *Brookings Papers on Economic Activity,* January 1982, pp. 245–68.

———. "Nonborrowed Reserve Targeting and Monetary Control." In *Improving Money Stock Control: Problems, Solutions, and Consequences,* Laurence H. Meyer, ed., Economic Policy Conference Series, co-sponsored by the Center for the Study of American Business at Washington University and the Federal Reserve Bank of St. Louis (Kluwer-Nijhoff, 1983), pp. 3–41.

———. "The Monetary Regime of the Federal Reserve System." Presented at a conference on Alternative Monetary Regimes, sponsored by the Ellis L. Phillips Foundation and Dartmouth College, August 22–24, 1984.

Lombra, Raymond E., and Raymond G. Torto. "The Strategy of Monetary Policy." *Economic Review,* Federal Reserve Bank of Richmond, September/October 1975, pp. 3–14.

Wallich, Henry C. "Recent Techniques of Monetary Policy." *Economic Review.* Federal Reserve Bank of Kansas City, May 1984, pp. 21–30.

Wallich, Henry C., and Peter M. Keir. "The Role of Operating Guides in U.S. Monetary Policy: A Historical Review." *Federal Reserve Bulletin,* September 1979, pp. 679–90.

35

Recent Techniques of Monetary Policy

Henry C. Wallich

Federal Reserve policies are subject to widely differing interpretations. This would probably be the case even if all members of the Federal Open Market Committee shared an identical interpretation, which is hardly plausible. If 12 people are always of the same view, 11 are dispensable. But even at the level of the techniques by which FOMC policy is implemented, there may be different views of "how monetary policy really works." In this paper I provide my own view, which may not be shared by every member of the committee and the staff, and in all details possibly by none.

Today, it seems to be widely believed that the Federal Reserve's present technique for controlling the monetary aggregates is the same as that in use prior to October 1979, before the reserve-targeting method was initiated. Observers have noted that the funds rate has moved smoothly, as was the case before October 1979, when the Federal Reserve was controlling the growth of money by influencing the quantity demanded via the funds rate and short-term interest rates generally. The policy record now speaks of "the degree of reserve restraint." Since the record began to speak of the operating instruments in these terms, there have been no sharp, sustained interest-rate movements such as were characteristic of the tight reserve-targeting procedure after October 1979. How are these observations to be interpreted?

Recent funds rate movements have indeed differed noticeably from the volatility of the period from October 1979 through the fall of 1982, after which the automatic character of the reserve-targeting method was largely modified. Changes in overall reserve positions of depository institutions since the fall of 1982 largely have reflected deliberate policy judgments, rather than an automatic response to deviations of monetary aggregates from preset target paths. Nevertheless, the Federal Reserve has not reverted entirely to the old technique. One

From *Economic Review*, Federal Reserve Bank of Kansas City, May 1984, pp. 21–30.

Henry C. Wallich is a member of the Board of Governors of the Federal Reserve System. This article is based on an address to the Midwest Finance Association at Chicago on April 5, 1984.

piece of evidence is the temporary quarter-end, statement-date pressures that still affect the funds rate. These pressures were largely absent prior to October 1979.

While short-term interest rates, and, among them, the funds rate, have reassumed some of the role they played in controlling the money supply before October 1979, a new layer of indirect control has been added to the pre-1979 procedures, employing a market mechanism. It is not the funds rate that is used as the operational instrument but a level of nonborrowed reserves derived as the difference between estimated total reserves and the desired level of borrowing at the discount window. This can also be viewed as aiming at a particular level of borrowing implemented by means of the nonborrowed-reserves path. The resulting funds rate reflecting this level of borrowing, therefore, has some input from very short-term market forces. The procedure amounts to an indirect way of influencing the funds rate and other short-term rates which, in turn, affect the demand for money. Observers may differ as to whether, given the relative frequency of nonborrowed-reserve path adjustment, this procedure is better described as targeting on the nonborrowed path or on the level of borrowing.

From the point of view of the market, where I believe these things are well understood, the focus on the level of borrowing is significant because it leads to a different interpretation of Open Market Desk operations.

The funds rate level at which the Desk enters the market to conduct open market operations does not convey the decisive message that the market tries to unravel, as it did in the days before October 1979. It is not indicative of any particular rate desired by the Desk. It is simply the rate that happens to prevail on a day when the manager believes that reserves should be added or drained in order to achieve the desired level of discount window borrowing on average for the reserve-maintenance period. The action reflects the Desk's assessment of reserve availability, rather than a desire to move the funds rate, although the action, of course, may affect the rate. Some aspects that may create a contrary impression are dealt with later in this paper.

DIRECT AND INDIRECT TARGETING

What is the advantage of pursuing indirectly a target that can also be influenced or controlled directly? Principally, it is to give greater scope to market forces. Direct action runs the risk of introducing discontinuities and rigidities. It foregoes the opportunity of benefiting from a smoothing effect of the market. Judgment errors in setting the objective of direct actions are less likely to be corrected by the input from the market. This applies primarily when "indirection" implies an interaction between a price and a quantity. It applies also, however, to the relationship of two quantities, such as when borrowed reserves or total reserves are determined by operating on nonborrowed reserves. At the same time, one must keep in mind that indirection, giving room to market forces, can introduce a degree of slippage that may interfere with attainment of the target.

The issue whether to address a target variable directly or indirectly is posed at various stages in the monetary policy transmission mechanism. At each stage, policy confronts, in simplest terms, a price and a quantity. It can determine price directly, by operations in the market, and allow quantity to be determined indirectly. Alternatively, it can determine quantity directly, with varying degrees of precision, and thereby influence price indirectly. In one or two instances, the key relation may be between two quantities, one or both of which are parts of a larger total.

For a discussion of some of the alternatives available at each stage in the transmission mechanism, the following stages are relevant, in descending order of closeness to the real sector and ascending order of controllability by the central bank:

1. Intermediate targets—the money supply and interest rates, principally long-term rates.
2. Instrumental targets—total reserves and money market rates.
3. Operating targets—nonborrowed reserves implied by borrowed reserves intentions and the funds rate range.

These layers could perhaps be structured somewhat differently and even telescoped, but they reflect the hierarchy of markets and instruments as they appear to me.

INTERMEDIATE TARGETS

At the level of intermediate targets, the policymaker confronts, in simplest terms, the relationship between money and interest rates. He can influence either one directly—money by means of a total reserves technique, relying on the money multiplier, or interest rates by buying and selling at a given rate. Alternatively, he can influence each variable indirectly—the money supply through short-term interest rates, interest rates through the money supply. It need hardly be said that this two-variable relationship functions within a general equilibrium model with many variables determined simultaneously.

Why should the policymaker prefer one intermediate target or the other, and why, having made his choice, should he prefer the direct or the indirect technique if he is given the choice only between money supply and interest rates as intermediate targets?

As for the choice of intermediate target, this presumably will depend on the policymaker's view of the transmission mechanism of monetary policy. He may believe that expenditure behavior of firms and households is driven by interest rates—in the broad sense of including all kinds of monetary and nonmonetary returns—or by the money supply, for instance, through a real balance mechanism. If he believes, as I do, that monetary policy works primarily through interest rates, he must choose between implementing his interest-rate policy directly, through market intervention, or indirectly, through the money supply. In the very short run, setting interest rates directly usually—not always—is possible for the central bank, through discount-rate and open market operations. In an extreme sense, it could do so by simply pegging a rate through unlimited purchases and sales of securities at that rate. Naturally, if the interest rate established by this technique is not consistent with a stable rate of inflation, it will have an increasingly disequilibrating effect, causing inflation to accelerate or decelerate. Inability to guess or calculate the equilibrium interest rate gives the policymaker an important reason for not trying to set it directly but instead letting the market do so.

To be sure, the policymaker also does not know what rate of money growth will generate equilibrium (constant-inflation) interest rates; but his risk of error is smaller. If he sets an inflationary rate of money growth, the long-run result will be stable, not explosive, inflation. Thus, letting the market set the interest rate for a given money-growth target is a safer way of achieving an equilibrium interest rate than trying to set it directly.

A secondary reason for choosing a money-supply target is its public information effect. Setting (and adhering to) a target informs the public that an effort is being made to control inflation. Reducing the target over time creates a desirable and persuasive expectation of secularly diminishing inflation. Setting interest rates directly would not clearly convey a sense of controlled and diminishing inflation. The role of interest rates in curbing inflation is widely misunderstood. Not a few members of the public apparently believe that, because interest enters into many prices, higher interest rates mean more inflation, which is to say that the micro effects outweigh the macro effects. Public support for a money-supply targeting policy is likely to be stronger than for an interest-rate policy, although the experience in recent years of very high interest rates under a money-supply regime may have changed that perception somewhat. In short, the advantage of influencing interest rates by targeting money is that it gives the market a chance to prevent errors that might occur if interest rates were set directly.

INSTRUMENTAL TARGETS

If it is decided to target on money, whether because the policymaker believes that money drives the economy directly, or because he believes that targeting money is a good way of indirectly targeting interest rates, which then drive the economy, again there is both a direct and an indirect technique, this time at the instrumental target level, applying to time horizons of a month or two. The central bank can target on total bank reserves which, together with the money multiplier, determine the money supply. This is a relatively direct approach, giving only limited leeway to market forces via endogenous variation in the multiplier. Slippage, of course, is still possible if control of reserves is less than perfect, or if the multiplier is unstable owing to shifts among deposit categories, changes in excess reserves, and other factors. Even given such slippage, the interaction of a relatively rigid money-supply mechanism with a demand for money that is itself stochastic probably will produce sizable variability of interest rates, at least over the short and intermediate run.

One indirect technique of controlling the money supply at the instrumental target level involves control of short-term interest rates themselves so as to evoke a level of demand for money and a resultant stock equal to the target for the money supply. Given the demand curve for money, a shift in the supply curve changes interest rates along the demand curve, as reserves are added or drained to achieve the desired rate level. The money stock, in this framework, depends on the position and shape of the money-demand curve; it is demand-determined. This approach, therefore, gives the market greater scope for infuencing the money stock. As a result, the money stock is vulnerable to error both in estimating the money-demand function and in predicting the values of arguments in that function, particularly income. Moreover, there is a substantial lag in the impact of money-market rates upon the amount of money demanded, with about half of the effect being estimated to occur within two or three months. In any event, in this process, interest rates are likely to be far less variable than under the reserves approach. The danger is that changes in money market rates will not be made quickly enough when the level consistent with the targeted money supply has been misjudged.

Another indirect technique is to target on nonborrowed reserves, which allows both short-term interest rates and the money stock to be determined in part by the public's demands for money and by the depository institutions' demands for borrowed reserves. This approach is, in a sense, a compromise between total reserves and interest rates as instrumental targets, with the outcome for interest-rate variability likely to fall between these alternative regimes.

OPERATING TARGETS

Finally, at the level of day-to-day or week-to-week operating targets, which are those the Federal Reserve can control most closely (various components of reserves, and the federal funds rate), a choice once more must be made between direct and indirect approaches to targeting reserves or the funds rate, respectively. Using total reserves as the day-to-day operating target—which the Federal Reserve has never done—would be a very direct approach, leaving little scope to the market. All kinds of slippage—especially by means of the discount window, but also through reserve carryovers—have to be avoided, or else changes in these magnitudes would have to be compensated by open market operations. These would have to be massive, since in open market operations a multiple of the initial increase, for example, in discount window borrowing would be required in order to offset further borrowing as banks sought to make up for further absorption of reserves by open market operations. Quite possibly, banks would seek to protect themselves by carrying large and variable excess reserves, thereby possibly introducing slippage between total reserves and the money supply. All this severely limits the possibility of targeting on total reserves, to say nothing of the consequences for interest-rate variability.

Targeting on nonborrowed reserves—which the Federal Reserve did after October 1979 and still does on a day-to-day basis—is a more indirect technique. The various elements of slippage in the process—discount window borrowing, reserve carryover, and, until recently, the effect of lagged reserve requirements— allow the market some leeway. Targeting on nonborrowed reserves also allows for a degree of automaticity. A deviation of the monetary aggregates from target alters required reserves. Given a constant supply of nonborrowed reserves, the deviation changes discount window borrowing and tends to alter the funds rate and other short-term rates. These rate changes—downward when the monetary aggregates are undershooting the target, and upward when they are overshooting—tend to push the money supply back toward target over time. The strength of this automatic control feature, however, is at best moderate. While this technique was in use from October 1979 to fall 1982, it had to be supplemented on occasion by discretionary action in changing the discount rate, or in raising or lowering the nonborrowed reserves path, thus reducing or increasing the need for borrowing and thereby accentuating the change in short-term rates.

A second alternative, also at the day-to-day operating level, is targeting on the funds rate. Once more, there is a choice between relatively direct and indirect techniques. The direct approach, in its extreme form, was represented by the familiar pegging operations practiced during and immediately after World War II. The Fed fixed certain rates by buying and selling (mostly buying) Treasury obligations throughout the maturity spectrum at fixed prices. A different, much less drastic approach was that employed before October 1979. A range was set for the funds rate, sometimes as narrow as one-half percent and rarely more than 1 percent. This range was subject to revision between FOMC meetings if growth in money and/or credit moved outside specified "tolerance" bounds. The Desk bought and sold securities to keep the rate within the range, or around a particular area of it, on a weekly average basis and at times on a daily basis. Reserves under this procedure became demand-determined, which made timely adjustment of the funds rate range very important.

The procedure gave some scope to market forces, in the sense that the funds rate was able to move, although only moderately, in response to such market forces as reserve supplies and bank reserve management strategies. It gave further scope to the market in the sense that control of the money supply was relatively indirect. Because demand forces were allowed so much influence on the growth of money, the procedure, in turn, yielded to a nonborrowed reserve strategy beginning in October 1979.

Since the fall of 1982, the nonborrowed reserve strategy and its automaticity have given way to a technique that allows the funds rate to be determined by the market, through the targeting of discount window borrowing from one reserve-maintenance period to the next, implemented by allowing a flexible nonborrowed reserves path. At the FOMC meeting, an intended borrowing level is set, as a policy decision. This level of borrowing is then deducted from the total of required reserves consistent with the target path for the money supply and an assumed level of excess reserves—in order to derive an initial path for nonborrowed reserves. However, during the intermeeting period, as money and reserve demands deviate from the trajectories set at the time of the FOMC meeting, the intended borrowing level is sought through appropriate adjustments to the initial nonborrowed reserves path.

The post-fall 1982 procedure differs from the post-October 1979 procedure in that, as anticipated total reserve demand diverges from initial projections, nonborrowed reserves are adjusted weekly in seeking to achieve a chosen level of borrowed reserves. In contrast, under the October 1979 procedure, borrowing was allowed to change consistent with the attainment of a nonborrowed reserves path targeted for the entire intermeeting period—although subject to technical adjustments. An assumed level of borrowing under the older procedure was set only initially at the beginning of the inter-FOMC period, but borrowing would subsequently diverge from that initial assumption reflecting unforeseen movements in the demand for money and reserves. This was the automatic feature of the technique that at times was reinforced by discretionary path changes.

The relation of the borrowing level to the funds rate, which has been one of the most familiar features of the money market, always has been relatively loose. Since a chosen level of borrowing is consistent with any of a range of values of the funds rate, current operating procedures cannot be regarded as a form of rate-pegging. Demands for discount borrowing by banks no doubt reflect market judgments about present and future deposit flows and likely reserve conditions.

Since these considerations play an important role in determining the funds rate, it is clear that the present procedure allows at least one additional degree of freedom with respect to the pre-October 1979 technique.

INTERPRETATIONS OF DESK OPERATIONS

From the point of view of the Fed watcher, the present technique offers problems of interpretation quite different from those of the pre-October 1979 procedure. Under the old procedure, the rate at which the manager entered the market was highly significant. Ordinarily, it meant that he did not want the rate to move substantially beyond that point, or even that he would like the rate to stop somewhat short of the rate at which he had entered. When the market had had an opportunity to explore the upper and lower limits of the range, it had a fairly good understanding of prevailing policy. So long as the market believed that the rate objective remained unchanged, moreover, it would help the manager stabilize the rate, believing that when it had reached one of the limits any move could only go in the other direction.

Today, the funds rate range set by the FOMC is much wider than before October 1979, typically 400 basis points. Its extremes, in fact, are rarely explored. So long as the level of borrowing is maintained, there is little reason to expect the funds rate to move strongly, at least for longer than transitory periods. The manager's entry into the market does not signify that one of the limits of the range has been reached, but that, given the borrowing target and the associated nonborrowed reserves path, reserves need to be added or drained according to Fed projections of reserve availability. In some degree, this is indicated by the fact that entry continues to occur at a set time of day instead of, as during the pre-October 1979 regime, at varying times prompted by intraday movements in the funds rate. When the reserve objective has been reached, there is no reason why the rate should not move against the intervention if that is the direction of market pressures.

Uncertainty about the reserve projections available to the Desk sometimes may create the impression that the Desk is indeed working to influence the funds rate directly, instead of seeking to influence the borrowing level. In the absence of trustworthy projections, the funds rate at times may be a more accurate indicator of reserve availability than the reserves projections. If the manager decides to act on the signal from the funds rate in assessing the volume of reserves needed, he may create the appearance that he is working to influence the rate, rather than the supply of nonborrowed reserves consistent with the intended borrowing level.

In setting the intended borrowing level, the FOMC must make an assumption about excess reserves. This can be regarded as a technical assumption, however, to be modified later by the staff implementing the directive in accordance with evidence of changes in the demand for excess reserves. Ordinarily, such changes are not large and can be reasonably well evaluated.

The degree to which the funds rate is determined more reliably by borrowed reserves or by net borrowed reserves (borrowed reserves less excess reserves) is unresolved. There are partisans of both borrowed and net borrowed reserves. Econometric work does not seem to give a decisive answer. It should be noted, however, that when the value of required reserves is known, as under lagged reserve requirements, any nonborrowed reserves target, rigorously pursued over the reserve-maintenance period, is equivalent to a net-borrowed-reserves target. Under contemporaneous reserve requirements, the same is true to the extent that required reserves can be estimated and that nonborrowed reserves are made to vary with required reserves. A word may, therefore, be appropriate at this point about the recently introduced contemporaneous reserve requirements.

CONTEMPORANEOUS RESERVE REQUIREMENTS

The shift from lagged to contemporaneous reserve requirements (CRR) reflects a phase in Federal Reserve thinking when it seemed particularly important to tighten and speed up the response of reserve conditions to deviations of M1 from its target path. Lagging required reserves by two weeks implies that, during this period, the expansion of deposits is not directly constrained by reserve availability. Banks theoretically could create deposits without limit, although it strains credulity that they would exploit this opportunity, not knowing where the reserves would come from two weeks later or what they would cost. More plausibly, the response of banks to changes in deposits and the associated changes in short-term interest rates, may be somewhat delayed by the two-week lag in the need to put up reserves. Actually, under its reserve-targeting strategy, the Federal Reserve in effect often cut the two-week lag to one by recalculating the average level of borrowing implied by a constant intermeeting average level for nonborrowed reserves as soon as incoming weekly deposit data indicated changes in future borrowing needs. This was done by lowering or raising the weekly nonborrowed reserves path, thereby producing some borrowing response one week earlier than it would have occurred otherwise. The recent move to CRR thus potentially speeds up initial responses by one week rather than two.

In any event, CRR seemed a logical complement to the automaticity of the reserve strategy. Their adoption reflected a degree of frustration stemming from the fact that the adverse features of the strategy, in the form of greater variability of interest rates, were much in evidence, while improved control over the money supply was less so. The change seemed unlikely to do harm and capable of doing some good. It implied an effort to go as far as possible in the direction of making the rigorous reserves strategy effective.

Subsequent experience with the behavior of M1 was largely responsible for making this approach less viable. Changes in operating techniques, beginning in the fall of 1982, therefore, downgraded the role of M1 and reduced the degree of automaticity. This seemed to make moot the case for CRR, at least for the duration of this policy approach. On the other hand, concern that CRR would lead to greater volatility of interest rates diminished for the same reason. What remained was a moderate potential improvement in the reserve aggregates to money-supply relation that may help reduce one element of slippage in the mechanism and that expanded the menu of feasible operating procedures for future consideration.

SOME COMMENTS ON THE AGGREGATES

A major reason for modifying the automatic reserve targeting technique has been the erratic behavior of M1 demand relative to its primary determinants. This, in turn, seems to have reflected, at least in part, the transition to a different composition for the aggregate, in the course of the rapid increase in NOW accounts and, subsequently, Super NOWs. Approximately one fourth of M1 now bears explicit interest. For the $90 billion of regular NOW accounts, this rate is not a market rate, though it is for the $40 billion of Super NOWs. It will become so, for the regular NOWs, as the minimum balance to open Super NOW accounts—which have no interest-rate ceiling—declines to $1,000 in January 1985 from the present level of $2,500 and then is entirely eliminated in January 1986. The ceiling rate on regular NOWs is close enough to the market, however, to allow small changes in market rates to produce large variations in the opportunity cost of holding regular NOW balances, so long as their rate typically remains at the present ceiling levels. For the time being, this may have made M1 more interest-elastic than before.

However, as the share of Super NOWs grows, and particularly when the minimum-balance requirement for all NOW accounts is removed, rates on the interest-bearing component of M1 increasingly will be market-related. This would reduce, perhaps substantially, the interest elasticity of this aggregate. The control of M1 through an interest-rate strategy then would function largely to the extent that interest rates influence GNP and thereby M1 demand. Of course, the possibility of controlling M1 through a total reserve strategy would remain. But, given a low M1 interest elasticity, the demand for the aggregate would not be much affected by interest-rate variations. Interest-rate volatility resulting from an effort to control M1 through total reserves, therefore, might become even more severe.

Instability in the demand function for M1 during 1982—which did not occur for the first time in that year—along with the impending introduction of MMDAs and maturing of all-savers certificates—prompted the downgrading of the aggregate as a target in 1982. The demand function seems to have stabilized somewhat in the meantime, but with altered properties. For instance, the large interest-bearing component in M1 is likely to produce more rapid growth of the entire aggregate in the future, relative to nominal income and other monetary aggregates. In past years, the difference in the growth rate between M1 on one side, and M2 and M3 on the other, averaged on the order of 3 percentage points, with cyclical variations. A secular difference of 1 to 2 percentage points now seems more likely. This smaller difference is reflected in the Federal Reserve's 1984 targets of 4 to 8 percent for M1 and 6 to 9 percent for M2 and M3. At constant rates of interest, velocity may tend to grow in the 1 to 2 percent range.

Currency also seems to have been experiencing some instability. Until very recently, its average rate of growth had risen to 10 percent or so. This would not by itself be enough to disrupt seriously the rehabilitation of M1 as a usable target. Its implications are more serious for the monetary base. With currency growing at 10 percent, setting base growth much below its 1983 average rate of almost 9 percent would mean that total reserves, which make up only 20 percent of the base, would have to decline. Reservable deposits would have to do likewise. This, in turn, would, of course, have a severe impact on M1, the deposit component of which is the principal user of reserves. Accommodating changes in the composition of M1, on the other hand (i.e., by offsetting fluctuations in the currency/deposits ratio), would be tantamount to targeting on reserves.

M2 has also undergone a change that over several years has substituted market related for regulated interest rates. The interest sensitivity of the aggregate accordingly must be presumed to have diminished. M2, in this sense, has already undergone some of the development that may be ahead for M1. Not enough time has passed, however, to provide adequate data for a test.

CAN WE SHED VELOCITY?

Recent vicissitudes of the aggregates, and prospective future changes, raise questions about the time-honored concept of velocity. The notion of a simple velocity relation between nominal income and money is so deeply embedded in the lore of money that it may seem quixotic to try to eradicate it. Nevertheless, in my view, that is what should be done. It is, after all, a primitive concept, clearly inferior to that of a demand function for money. Its calculation leaves out of account the effects of interest rates, wealth, inflation, and other arguments that may play a role in the money-demand function. Its theoretical foundations are weak, unless the demand function is connected to a velocity expression. Secularly, it should decline if money is a luxury good. Historically, since World War II, that has not been its trend, although the upward trend of interest rates and inflation during that period is partly responsible. The most appropriate way of defining velocity, by relating money to income with a lag, or without, is heuristically rather than theoretically founded.

Debates about whether or not there have been shifts in velocity, and how they should be reflected in money-supply targeting, are conducted much more meaningfully in terms of the stability of the demand function for money. Otherwise, changes in velocity that occur along a stable demand function may be confounded with changes associated with a shift in the function. Velocity may even remain stable while offsetting changes occur within the demand function. The principal loss from shedding the simple notion no doubt would be to the reputation of the economic profession, that would probably be accused once more of creating an unnecessary confusion.

36

Efficient Markets, Interest Rates, and Monetary Policy

Donald J. Mullineaux

"It is evident, then, that the rate of interest in a highly psychological phe-nomenon . . . the long-term rate of interest will depend, not only on the current policy of the monetary authority, but also on market expectations concerning its future policy . . . a monetary policy which strikes public opinion as being experimen-tal in character or easily liable to change may fail in its objective of greatly reducing the long-term rate of interest."

A well-read student of current trends in economic thinking no doubt would judge these the musings of one of today's growing number of rational-expectations theorists. Actually, though, the words were penned in 1936 by John Maynard Keynes in his classic *General Theory of Employment, Interest and Money*. This may come as a small surprise to those who credit Keynes with the proposition (or fault him with it, depending on the reader's perspective) that an increase in the supply of money will lower both short-term and long-term interest rates. To be sure, Keynes said just that: but economist par excellence that he was, qualifica-tions clearly crept into his argument.

The link between money and interest rates is, like sex, both an old issue and a hot topic. The President's economic program, which includes an assumption that the Federal Reserve will pursue gradual reductions in monetary growth over the next six years, has generated a flurry of commentary. Administration spokesmen claim that monetary deceleration will mean rapid and substantial declines in interest rates. But many economists, and pratically all the large-scale econometric models, contend that slower money growth brings on higher interest rates in the short term. Rates will fall in this traditional view only after a long period of adjustment. Since higher interest rates could have damaging effects on a recover-ing economy, the issue is more than academic.

One fairly novel approach to explaining how financial markets work—the efficient-markets view—suggests that either the administration or its critics could prove correct. A monetary slowdown can result in higher, lower, or even un-

---

From *Business Review*, Federal Reserve Bank of Philadelphia, May–June 1981.

Donald J. Mullineaux, who received his Ph.D. from Boston College, is vice president and director of research at the Federal Reserve Bank of Philadelphia. He writes on financial institutions and markets as well as on monetary theory and policy.

changed interest rates in this theory. The outcome hinges on *what's happening to expectations in financial markets*. Unlike the traditional view, the efficient-markets approach *allows for a very quick reduction* in interest rates in the face of slower money growth, though other outcomes are also possible.

The efficient-markets logic illustrates the complexities of the link between money and interest rates—an issue that policymakers can hardly ignore. The message that emerges is to avoid a monetary policy that, in Keynes's words, "strikes public opinion as being experimental in character or easily liable to change." A stable policy will be a predictable one, and where efficiency reigns, a predictable policy should lend stability to financial markets and to the economy as a whole.

THE CONVENTIONAL WISDOM: SLOWER MONEY GROWTH MEANS HIGHER RATES AND LESS ECONOMIC ACTIVITY

One of the oldest topics in monetary theory concerns the so-called transmission mechanism of monetary policy—in plain English, the way monetary policy works. Most economists agree that interest rates, especially long-term interest rates, play a center-stage role in this story. As the tale begins, in the traditional view, a deceleration in money growth induced by the Federal Reserve leads to a prompt increase in short-term interest rates. Short rates rise because people must be persuaded to slow the pace at which they build up their money holdings. Since the short-term rate (the 90-day Treasury bill rate, say) measures the interest people forgo by holding noninterest-bearing money, a sufficiently large increase in this rate should make people want to add to their money balances at a more gradual pace.

But this curtain-raiser represents only the beginning of a complicated story. Having seen that interest rates have increased, financial market participants are said to revise their outlook about the *future course* of short-term interest rates. In particular, the conventional wisdom claims that people will think that, because interest rates are higher today, they are likely to be at least somewhat higher in the near-term future. Once this happens, long-term interest rates also will increase. Why? Because long-term rates depend to some extent on what people expect to happen to future short-term rates.

Consider the following two alternatives facing Miss Marple, who has funds available to lend for a one-year period:

Strategy 1

Buy a one-year (long-term) Treasury bill yielding 12 percent.

Strategy 2

Buy a six-month (short-term) Treasury bill currently yielding 10 percent, then reinvest at maturity in another six-month bill, which she *expects* to be yielding 14 percent at the time.

If we ignore the element of risk (which arises in part because future rates are imperfectly predictable), she will be indifferent between the two strategies since each yields an average return of 12 percent over the year. But if the short-term rate expected six months from now suddenly were to increase to, say, 20 percent,

Miss Marple—and people with expectations similar to hers—would then prefer the six-month (short-term) bill: purchasing two short-term bills successively would yield an average return of 15 percent. As everyone attempted to sell off one-year bills, however, the rate on these securities would rise. In fact, it would increase until the long rate was once again approximately equal to the average of the current short rate and the expected future short rate (15 percent). Long-term rates in effect embody a forecast of future short rates.[1]

According to the standard view, then, long rates increase on the heels of decelerated money growth once people recognize that current short-term yields have risen and they consequently boost their forecasts of future rates. But rates don't change all at once; rather, it takes time for people to adjust their expectations. So long-term rates will be increasing over what might be a substantial time period following a slowdown in money growth.

The denouement to this standard transmission-mechanism story is that several kinds of spending—especially housing expenditures and business expenditures on plant and equipment—are sensitive to movements in long-term rates. Here again, people and businesses are viewed as reducing these expenditures only gradually in response to higher long-term rates, so still another time lag is introduced into the monetary policy process. Thus, slower money growth exercises a constraint on spending over a lengthy period of time, lasting at least several years.

The story has an epilogue, and economists such as Milton Friedman have strongly emphasized it.[2] As reduced spending slows economic activity, the increase in rates eventually will be reversed because of weaker demands for credit. And if the policy restraint imparts less momentum to inflation, interest rates will fall still further as lenders recognize that more slowly rising prices in the future mean each dollar they're repaid will buy more goods and services. To reflect this anticipated increase in purchasing power, they'll be satisfied with a lower rate of interest. Thus, to the extent that slower money growth means a lower rate of output or less inflation, it will bring on lower interest rates *eventually*. But according to many monetary analysts, this shift takes quite a long time. And many econometric models indicate that it will be a number of years before slower money growth leads to lower long-term rates of interest.

THE EFFICIENT-MARKETS CHALLENGE

The conventional view of the way monetary policy works pays only limited attention to the role that *information* about a policy change might play in the whole process. In particular, financial market participants are viewed as reacting mainly to information about what's happening to short-term interest rates while paying little heed to the behavior of other policy related phenomena, such as the rate of money growth. This apparent disregard for potentially useful information lies at the root of the criticism of the traditional view levied by those who believe financial markets are efficient.

Market efficiency has to do with the relation of prices to information. The market for financial assets, such as long-term bonds, is said to be efficient, for example, if the price of each bond fully reflects all the available information that might have an impact on its price. Information about the federal government's plans for future borrowing, for instance, will be reflected in current bond prices in an efficient market. If a bond's price reflects such information, so will its yield.

The argument for believing that a market is efficient flows from this fact: an inefficient market offers opportunities for above-average profits. An old economic adage says that people will move quickly to take advantage of unusual profit opportunities until they disappear. To take an example from the stock market: suppose only one person knows about tomorrow's announcement of a firm's sharply higher earnings. He can do quite well by buying that firm's stock today. But if everyone knows the announcement is coming, the stock price will have been bid up already and there won't be any unusual profit opportunity. An efficient market allows above-average profits only when relevant information isn't publicly available.[3]

A basic message of the efficient-markets approach is that only unexpected events will cause changes in interest rates, so only *new information* will have an impact on financial market yields. Past developments and even anticipated events—such as an expected large cut in government spending—already will be reflected in today's yields in financial markets.

The efficient-markets approach calls into question the traditional view of the monetary policy process, particularly its failure to distinguish anticipated from unanticipated policy shifts. Since only new information can affect yields in an efficient market, a change in the current stance of monetary policy (as reflected by the growth rate of the money supply) will affect interest rates only if the shift was not expected. An expected policy change would be factored into financial market yields *before* the shift takes place.

Interest Rates and Shifts in Money Growth: The Key Role of Expectations

Many economists argue that the interest rate on a financial asset of given maturity roughly equals the so-called real rate (the interest rate in the absence of any inflation) plus the expected rate of inflation over the asset's time horizon (the inflation premium). So if people expect inflation rates to fall in the future, they also should expect lower future short-term interest rates, because the inflation premium will fall. This anticipated reduction in future short rates should be reflected in long rates now, because long rates reflect forecasts of future short rates.

But why should people expect future inflation to be lower than today's inflation? One reason might be that they expect money growth rates to fall, since slower money growth historically has been accompanied by lower inflation rates. If people anticipate that money growth will be reduced permanently next year by five percentage points, for example, then *today's* long-term rate should be lower than if people expect no reduction in money growth. If and when money growth does so decelerate, there will be no reason for long-term rates to change, because there will be no new information in the fact that people's expectations are borne out.

But suppose people receive a piece of news that leads them to *revise* their expectations of future money growth. Suppose everyone has been expecting a steady 8 percent rate of money growth over the next 10 years. If for some reason people revise their forecasts to a permanently lower 3 percent growth rate, then long-term rates should fall quite promptly. Why? Because people now should anticipate lower inflation than before.

The notion that people can be convinced to lower their expectations about future money growth and consequently become more optimistic about the prospects for lower inflation is a major reason why administration economists believe interest rates will show a steady decline over the next four to five years. But many are skeptical of this view, especially those who subscribe to the traditional view. These traditionalists argue that monetary decelerations are almost always accompanied by at least some period of *increasing* interest rates. In fact, the efficient-markets logic itself suggests that slow-downs in money growth can be accompanied by rising rates, but only if the slower money growth *comes as a surprise* to market participants.

Money growth different from what people expected does represent new information and, therefore, should influence interest rates. In particular, an unexpected decline in money growth should mean higher rates for the very reasons stressed by the traditional view—people have to be discouraged from adding to their money holdings as rapidly as before.

One way to interpret the traditional view, then, is that it treats all shifts in money growth as unexpected, at least for a while. And, indeed, most large-scale econometric models of the economy do not attempt to differentiate between anticipated and unanticipated shifts in money growth. These models simply do not allow for revisions in anticipated money growth to have quick and direct effects on interest rates. Rather, a reduction in money growth lowers interest rates only after actual inflation begins to fall—which, the traditionalists claim, takes quite a long time.

Which view of the world is correct? If the administration's budget plan is implemented and if the Fed gradually reduces monetary growth over each of the next six years, will rates drop quickly, or will they increase, perhaps dramatically, before they begin to fall? An honest answer is: no one can say with any strong degree of confidence. We simply do not know enough about how people form expectations about monetary policy or how changes in those expectations affect interest rates. But, while the administration's interest-rate forecast may be optimistic, it is not, as some have claimed, implausible. Those who judge the rapid-rate-decline scenario totally unlikely must see no merit to the efficient-markets approach. This is an extreme position. While we lack good estimates of precisely how a particular policy package works out over time, there is a large body of evidence that says, on balance, financial markets tend to be highly efficient.

WHAT DOES THE EVIDENCE SAY ABOUT EFFICIENT MARKETS?

In a 1976 paper, William Poole had this to say about tests of the efficient-markets theory: "Numerous investigators have analyzed an enormous amount of data using many different statistical techniques, and no serious departures from the predictions of the hypothesis have been found. Thus, there is very strong evidence in favor of the hypothesis."[4] Since Poole's analysis, even more supporting evidence has accumulated, especially concerning the long-term bond market and the link between long-term rates and monetary policy actions.

Tests of financial market efficiency usually revolve around the statement that, if a market is efficient, it shouldn't be possible to explain changes in yields on the basis of any information that was publicly available *prior* to the price change: only *new* information causes prices to change. In a large number of cases, certain segments of the financial markets have been found to satisfy this condition.[5] More importantly from the perspective of students of monetary policy, several recent investigations have found that the long-term bond markets in both the United States and Canada appear to be efficient.[6] Phillips and Pippenger show, for example, that long-term rates efficiently reflect information about past inflation rates and past short-term interest rates.[7] Using a somewhat different approach, Mishkin confirms this result. And Pesando reports that changes in long-term bond rates in Canada cannot be predicted by prior changes in either interest rates or in key economic variables, such as the money supply or the unemployment rate. These studies suggest that the long-term bond market is no less efficient than the short-term debt market, the stock market, or the foreign exchange market.[8]

This evidence calls into question econometric models in the traditional view, which often violate the efficiency criterion by linking interest-rate changes to old information. But the market-efficiency studies don't offer direct support to the view that interest rates will drop rapidly if the administration's economic package, including gradual deceleration in money growth, is implemented. The reason is that none of this work examines the relationship of interest rates to *revisions in anticipated monetary policies*. Efficient-markets logic contends that a newly expected permanent deceleration in money growth should be accompanied promptly by lower interest rates. Unfortunately, no tests of this proposition have been reported in the literature to date.

But while it doesn't help predict the timing of the interest-rate outcome of this particular policy strategy, the overall evidence does embody some broad lessons for the exercise of monetary policy.

EFFICIENT MARKETS AND MONETARY POLICY

A number of important implications for the conduct of monetary policy flow from the theory of efficient markets. Perhaps the most crucial is the key role that expectations play in the process, a point that Keynes clearly recognized. To be precise, three different outcomes for long-term interest rates are possible when the Fed slows the growth of the money supply. If the shift was expected before the Fed acted, nothing should happen to financial market yields. People already would have taken account of the monetary slowdown in their decision making. But if the policy is accompanied by *revised* expectations of permanently lower money growth, then rates should fall because expectations of future inflation also should be reduced. Finally, if the deceleration in money growth is unexpected, interest rates should rise for the reasons emphasized in the traditional view.

To predict the interest-rate outcome of its policies, then, the Fed must have a good estimate of what people are anticipating. Unfortunately, this is not an easy piece of information to acquire. Yet without it, there is a serious risk that a policy will have unintended effects. Suppose policymakers reduce money growth one percentage point hoping to slow economic activity, for example. If the market had been expecting a two percentage point drop, money growth would be unexpectedly higher rather than lower. Interest rates would fall, for a while at least, and the economy would be unintentionally stimulated. One lesson of the efficient-markets approach, then, is that without a good gauge of people's expectations concerning the monetary policy outlook, the interest-rate outcome of a policy shift can't be estimated.

Policy anticipations presumably would be easier to appraise in a relatively

What is a stable monetary policy?

Stability, like motherhood and the home team, is something most people are inclined to support; the term, in other words, is a loaded one. Just what do people mean, operationally speaking, when they cite a need for a stable monetary policy?

In most instances, the phrase is used to characterize a monetary policy involving relatively infrequent changes in the longer term growth rate of the money supply. Note that the stance of policy is reflected in money growth, not some other factor such as the level of interest rates. While this is somewhat controversial, the Fed itself views the rate of money growth as the primary gauge of the thrust of policy over periods of, say, six months or more.

Also, the argument is usually made that money growth rates can fluctuate over short periods (week to week and month to month) without violating the notion of a stable policy, provided that money growth behaves smoothly over longer time periods. This means the Fed must avoid *cumulations* of short-run deviations in money growth from its longer term target in one direction or another. The case for the view that short-term changes in money growth don't reflect policy instability rests mainly on evidence suggesting these fluctuations have very little impact on economic activity.

stable environment (see What Is a Stable Monetary Policy?). To borrow again the language of Keynes, if monetary policy "strikes public opinion as . . . easily liable to change," then assessing the market's policy expectation may be next to impossible. Yet another advantage of a stable monetary policy is the prospect that policymakers would acquire more credibility concerning their intentions. Reductions in expectations of future money growth should be accompanied in efficient markets by interest-rate declines, and vice versa; but it is doubtful that public pronouncements from policymakers can have much impact on what people expect if money growth has been highly unstable.

Finally, even though the efficient-markets view suggests that interest rates might decline in the face of an unanticipated acceleration in money growth, there are reasons to doubt the wisdom of trying to exploit this link in an attempt to stimulate the economy. *First,* there is the practical problem of gauging the market's policy-related anticipations (so the Fed could do the unexpected). *Second,* some recent evidence fails to support the proposed link between unexpected money growth and long-term rates.[9] And *third,* it may not be possible for the Fed to generate unexpected shifts in money growth systematically. One school of thought, the rational-expectations view, argues that if the Fed continuously adjusts money-growth rates in attempting to smooth out fluctuations in economic activity, people will recognize this policy propensity and factor it into their forecasts of policy actions.[10] Policy-related changes in money growth, therefore, would be anticipated by financial market participants. The sum of these factors again argues for a monetary policy characterized by few, if any, changes in money growth once inflation has settled at a socially tolerable level.

In short, Keynes recognized well over 40 years ago that there are several reasons to be skeptical of what we know about the link between money and interest rates. Efficient-markets theory, rather than resolving some of that skepticism, serves mainly to offer still more outlets for Murphy's law ("If something can go wrong, it will") to work its way. In the face of all this, the best monetary policy appears to be the most predictable one, and a stable policy seems more likely to be predictable than an unstable one.

NOTES

[1] This averaging formula holds as an approximation for longer-term securities of any maturity (again, in the absence of risk). The longer the maturity, the greater the number of future short-term rates that get averaged into long rates, however.

[2] For a nontechnical discussion, see Milton Friedman, "Factors Affecting the Level of Interest Rates," Proceedings of the 1968 Conference on Savings and Residential Financing, sponsored by the U.S. Savings and Loan League (Chicago: The League, 1969), pp. 11–27.

[3] Trading on inside information (such as was alleged in recent reports of stock purchases by individuals involved in arranging corporate mergers) could yield very large profits, even in an efficient market. Trading based on this kind of information, however, generally is prohibited by law.

[4] See William Poole, "Rational Expectations in the Macro Model," *Brookings Papers on Economic Activity,* 1976:2, p. 467.

[5] For an extensive survey of the evidence, see Eugene F. Fama, "Efficient Capital Markets: A Review of Theory and Empirical Work," *Journal of Finance* 25 (May 1970), pp. 383–417.

[6] See Llad Phillips and John Pippenger, "The Term Structure of Interest Rates in the MIT-PENN-SSRC Model: Reality or Illusion?" *Journal of Money, Credit, and Banking* 11 (May 1979), pp. 151–163; James E. Pesando, "On the Efficiency of the Bond Market: Some Canadian Evidence," *Journal of Political Economy* 86 (1978), pp. 1057–76; and Frederic Mishkin, "Efficient-Markets Theory: Implications for Monetary Policy," *Brookings Papers on Economic Activity* 1978, pp. 708–52.

[7] More exactly, past interest rates don't explain long-term Treasury rates. Corporate bond rates are found to be related to past short-term rates (on commercial paper). The authors suggest the latter result may be colored by statistical problems, however.

[8] Not all the tests of market efficiency tend to be supporting, however. Some recent work suggests that prices in certain financial markets are more volatile than we should expect if markets were, in fact, efficient. Robert Shiller, for example, has recently argued that stock prices and long-term interest rates move around too much to be explained simply by the receipt of new information. See his papers: "The Volatility of Long-Term Interest Rates and Expectations Models of the Term Structure," *Journal of Political Economy* 87 (October 1979), pp. 1190–1219; and "Do Stock Prices Move Too Much to Be Justified by Subsequent Movements in Dividends?" National Bureau of Economic Research Paper No. 456. These so-called variance bounds tests represent a new approach to testing market efficiency, and the results suggest that something more than new information may be affecting behavior in financial markets. While this doesn't necessarily mean the efficient-markets view is wrong, it does imply the theory may be incomplete.

[9] See Frederic Mishkin, "Monetary Policy and Long-Term Interest Rates: An Efficient-Markets Approach," *Journal of Monetary Economics* 7 (January 1981), pp. 29–55.

[10] For a general discussion, see Donald J. Mullineaux, "On Active and Passive Monetary Policies: What Have We Learned from the Rational Expectations Debate?" *Business Review,* Federal Reserve Bank of Philadelphia, November/December 1979, pp. 11–19.

37

Weekly Money Announcements: New Information and Its Effects

Richard G. Sheehan

The consensus among economists is that monetary policy has its primary effects over relatively long time intervals—that is, quarters or years, rather than days or weeks. Financial market participants, however, devote considerable attention to the weekly money stock announcement, despite substantial "noise" in the series.[1] Moreover, some economists recently have "discovered" that an announcement of an unexpectedly large money stock increase causes interst rates and U.S. exchange rates to rise and stock prices to fall.[2]

At first glance, the weekly impacts on financial markets may seem to contradict the consensus that money has its primary effects over longer horizons. In this paper, we show why money stock announcements may have an impact on financial market variables on a daily or weekly basis, even though the principal effects of monetary policy are felt over substantially longer periods. The explanation for this apparent contradiction is the adjustment of financial markets to new information. The focus is on financial markets, since their adjustments to new information tend to be more rapid than the adjustments of other markets.[3] The paper examines three hypotheses that relate money stock surprises to financial market prices, the relationships between these hypotheses, and the existing empirical evidence that attempts to discriminate between the hypotheses.

MONEY ANNOUNCEMENTS AND MONEY EXPECTATIONS

Before examining the effects of money announcements, one must begin with an obvious observation: the money stock announcement itself does not create money. It does, however, create new information about the money stock. At the time of the announcement, the level of the money stock to be announced has already been determined. Thus, any response resulting from the announcement is

---

From *Review*, Federal Reserve Bank of St. Louis, August/September 1985, pp. 25–34.

Richard G. Sheehan is an economist at the Federal Reserve Bank of St. Louis. Larry J. DiMariano and Michael L. Durbin provided research assistance.

due to new information, rather than new money. In the following analysis, it will be important to distinguish between these two.

Announcements about the weekly money stock typically are made on Thursday afternoons at 4:30 p.m. EST; at this time, the Federal Reserve Board releases figures on the stock of money (M1) for the statement week ending 10 days earlier.[4] If changes in the money stock itself have an immediate impact on financial markets, that impact will begin to be felt almost two weeks *before* the announcement when the money stock itself changed.[5]

The evidence discussed below suggests that the money stock announcements themselves appear to influence interest rates independent of any effect that the actual money growth may have had. To explain why the money announcements— which carry only new information—may influence interest rates, one must distinguish between expected and unexpected money announcements.

Theoretical Effects of Expected and Unexpected Money Announcements

The money stock figures, when announced, are not reported in a vacuum. Financial market participants have substantial information on current and previous interest rates and previous money announcements, allowing them to form expectations about the likely amount of the money stock to be announced. Current asset prices are based in part on expected future economic conditions, including future money stocks. Observers generally believe that, if financial markets are efficient, only the unexpected component of the money stock announcement should influence financial variables. The expected component conveys information already digested by the markets and incorporated in the prices and yields of financial assets. Consequently, only surprises matter, not because they provide new money, but because they provide new information that may be useful in predicting policymakers' actions and the behavior of both real and nominal variables. The money stock announcement, to the extent that it is expected, commonly is assumed to have no impact on economic activity.[6]

THE IMPACTS OF UNANTICIPATED MONEY ANNOUNCEMENTS

There are a number of hypotheses about why money surprises influence financial market variables. The following sections compare three hypotheses and their underlying assumptions. All three hypotheses are based on the assumption that financial markets efficiently use all available information. Thus, current interest rates, exchange rates, and stock prices reflect the implications of the expected future money stocks.

The analysis of the alternative hypotheses is based on the Fisher equation, which divides the current nominal interest rate into the expected real return over the holding period of the asset and the relevant anticipated rate of inflation. The money announcement can affect market rates of interest by altering perceptions of the real rate of interest, expected inflation, or both.

Expected Liquidity Effect

Under this hypothesis, an unexpected change in the money stock that moves it away from its annual target will be followed by changes in the opposite direction to get money growth back on target.[7] The expected liquidity effect, therefore, is based on the belief that the Federal Reserve has credibility in pursuing its objectives for the money stock. The expected liquidity effect is based on financial market participants believing (1) that Federal Reserve policy is, at least in part, adhering to a long-run monetary aggregate target; (2) that it will take the necessary steps to achieve its target over a relatively short time period; and (3) that such actions will change interest rates.[8]

The impact of an unexpectedly large money stock announcement based on the expected liquidity effect is illustrated in Figure 1. The cone formed by the solid lines in Figure 1 represents the Federal Reserve's target range for money growth.[9] At any point in time, market participants know past announced money stock levels and have formed expectations about the future path of the money stock, given by the line $\dot{m}^e$ in Figure 1. The slope of this line represents financial markets' expectations of the money growth rate based on available information, including some estimate of the Fed's desired short-run growth rate.[10]

To focus on the expected liquidity effect, assume that the money stock for the week announced previously was M_a. Just before the money announcement, interest rates, exchange rates, and stock prices reflect the assumption that M_b is the money stock to be announced. Further assume that the announcement of the money stock during week t is then made and reveals that the money stock was, in fact, M_d rather than M_b.

The expected liquidity effect assumes that financial markets believe the Fed will adhere to its previous policy and will take action to return the money stock to its expected path.[11] This temporary tightening may begin even before the money announcement, since the Fed develops estimates of the money stock before its announcement. During this period, higher nominal interest rates will be expected.

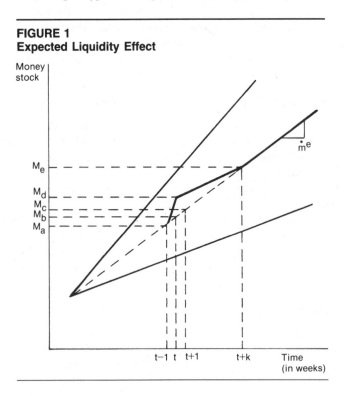

FIGURE 1
Expected Liquidity Effect

If the long-run growth rate in the money stock is assumed to remain unchanged, the rate of expected inflation should also remain unchanged. Thus, short-term real interest rates should rise as short-term nominal rates rise. Long-term rates will rise to the extent that they are an average of the current short-term rate and expected future rates.

The strength of the expected liquidity effect may vary over time.[12] A deviation of announced from expected M1 will typically have a larger effect on interest rates when market participants think the Fed is placing greater emphasis on controlling M1. Thus, the expected liquidity effect should have been stronger from October 1979 to September 1982, when the Federal Reserve targeted on nonborrowed reserves as an intermediate target.

It is not widely recognized that the expected liquidity effect also makes an assumption about the permanence of the shock underlying the unexpected change in money, assuming the Fed is not the cause of the shock. If the cause is temporary—for example, a winter snowstorm delaying check clearance—no Fed intervention is required. When the disturbance is removed, the stock of money will return to its expected growth path even without Federal Reserve intervention. A movement from M_a to M_e during week t will still be expected to yield money stock M_e in week t + k even without Fed intervention. Thus, a positive shock perceived as temporary will not result in expected monetary tightening or higher interest rates. In contrast, if the shock is perceived to be permanent, then discretionary policy action will be required to return to the expected path as discussed above.

If the change is temporary but the adjustment back to the expected path is slow, policy action may be expected. For example, if delays in processing tax refunds were an important but temporary factor in lowering money growth, the Fed might act to offset factors that would otherwise result in a temporary decline in the money stock. Thus, the expected liquidity effect is also predicated on the assumption that the cause of an unexpected money change is permanent (or of long enough duration to prompt an expectation of Federal Reserve intervention).

Inflation Premium Effect

The inflation premium hypothesis, like the expected liquidity hypothesis, focuses on market perceptions of Federal Reserve behavior in response to money surprises. In sharp contrast to the expected liquidity effect, this hypothesis assumes that the Federal Reserve will not react to offset unexpected money fluctuations.

Again assume the Federal Reserve has a target range for money growth given by the cone in Figure 2, and the dashed line represents expected money growth. The last announced value of the money stock was M_a, and M_b is the level expected to be announced in the current week. Also assume the actual announced value is M_d, yielding a positive money surprise of $M_d - M_b$.

The inflation premium effect assumes that the surprise will not be offset but that the money surprise will induce (or is the result of) changes in the Federal Reserve strategy toward less-restrictive monetary policy. Thus, the money stock is not expected to return to its former target path but is expected to move along a new path as indicated by $\dot{m}_1^e$, in Figure 2. The slope of this new path generally will be greater than that of the previous expected path, which indicates higher expected money growth and thus higher expected inflation.[13] The inflation pre-

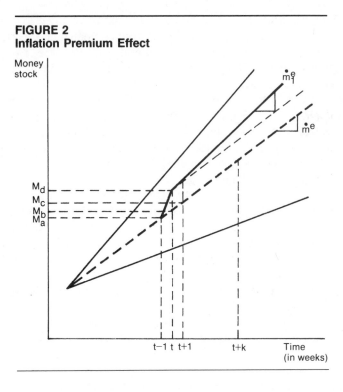

FIGURE 2
Inflation Premium Effect

mium effect predicts that the increase in expected inflation will lead to higher nominal interest rates for as long as this inflationary policy is expected to last.

A crucial assumption underlying the inflation premium effect is that an increase in the money stock, at least in part, signals an easier monetary policy stance.[14] An unexpected increase in the money stock announcement leads financial market participants to revise upward their perceptions of expected future money growth and expected inflation. What does this assumption imply about financial market participants' view of Federal Reserve policy? To the extent that the Fed has stated monetary aggregate targets, market participants must believe that those aggregates may not be the sole target of policy.

The inflation premium effect, like the expected liquidity effect, also assumes that unexpected shocks are perceived as permanent or only slowly self-correcting. If the shock were perceived as temporary, Fed intervention would be unnecessary, and money growth would return to its original expected path without Fed intervention.[15]

Money Demand Effect

A third hypothesis suggested as an explanation of positive money surprises leading to interest-rate increases focuses on money demand effects.[16] Suppose money demand depends in part on expected future output, a situation considered by Fama (1982). Since expectations about future output are unobservable, financial market participants cannot determine aggregate money demand. The money announcement then conveys information not only about money demand but also

FIGURE 3
Money Demand Effect (expected future supply and demand curves)

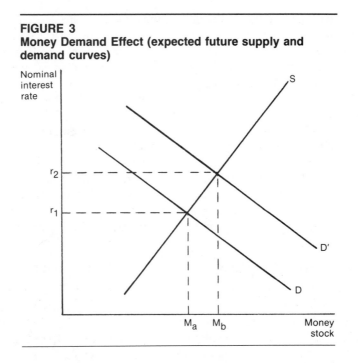

about expected future output. An increase in money demand due to an increase in expected future output is expected to persist and cause interest rates to be bid up. This effect is illustrated in Figure 3, which focuses directly on market perceptions of money supply and demand. While an increase in money demand may lead market participants to also expect an increase in money supply, it is assumed in this section that only the money demand curve has shifted. The case of money demand and supply both changing is discussed below.

Before the money stock announcement, the expected future money supply and demand curves are given by S and D, respectively. After an unexpectedly large money announcement, the future money demand curve is perceived to have shifted (permanently) from D to D'. Interest rates in the future are expected to rise to equilibrate the money market, and the expectations of higher future rates lead current rates to rise in anticipation. Note that it is the new information about the location of the present and expected future demand curves that influences interest rates. Any actual shift in the demand curve, subject to the limitations noted above, would already have had its impact felt before the announcement.[17]

Distinguishing between the Alternative Effects

The three effects described above all predict that an unexpected money stock increase will lead to higher nominal short-term interest rates. In an effort to differentiate the impacts of the expected liquidity effect, the inflation premium effect and money demand effect, some studies have examined the implications of the alternative effects on stock prices and exchange rates.[18]

Based on the expected liquidity effect, some have argued that, because the money surprise leads to higher expected interest rates, it depresses the present discounted value of future dividends, thus lowering stock prices. In addition, the expected liquidity effect predicts that, after taking into account exchange rate risk, higher expected real returns in the United States relative to, say, Germany should induce a capital inflow that will be accompanied by a rising value of the dollar vis-à-vis other currencies.

The inflation premium effect predicts that an unexpected money stock increase will lower exchange rates, as U.S. inflation increases relative to inflation in other countries. The inflation premium effect makes no prediction about the effect of an unexpected money stock increase on stock prices.[19]

In contrast, the money-demand effect implies that an unexpectedly large money announcement will increase stock prices due to the underlying increase in expected future output. The international value of the U.S. dollar may increase due to the direct impact of an increased money demand as well as the indirect effect of greater money demand leading to higher real interest rates and resulting capital inflows.[20]

COMPARING THE HYPOTHESES: SUBSTITUTES OR COMPLEMENTS?

Previous studies have advanced the three hypotheses presented above as competing theories to explain why unanticipated money announcements alter financial market variables.[21] In fact, the three effects do not necessarily compete and may be either substitutes or complements. Consider a simple example in which they are complements. As in Figures 1 and 2, the expected money stock prior to the announcement at time t was M_b, while the announced value was M_d. The expected liquidity effect again predicts a slowing of money growth from time t to t + k. Assume that this tightening is expected to be only partially successful. In terms of Figure 2, the money growth rate will be between $\dot{m}^e$ and $\dot{m}^e_f$. In this scenario, nominal interest rates will be expected to rise due to both the expected restrictive policy and higher expected inflation. Simply stated, monetary policy is expected to be tighter after the unexpected increase, but not tight enough to restore the former growth rate.

Figures 1 to 3 each focus on one monetary disturbance. There is, however, substantial noise in the weekly M1 series. Thus, temporary shifts cannot readily be distinguished from permanent shifts. Furthermore, in light of this uncertainty, which all financial market participants face, the Federal Reserve may be expected to hedge its response to fluctuations.[22] Thus, it is plausible that market participants may expect monetary policy to be tighter after an unexpected increase, but not tight enough to restore the former growth rate.

Both the expected liquidity and the inflation premium effects are based on the assumption of a permanent money market shock that may prompt Federal Reserve response. While such a shock need not originate in money demand, clearly it could. If it does, then the expected liquidity and inflation premium effects cannot be distinguished from the money demand effect.

Further complicating the analysis of the money demand effect is that it presumes a shift in money demand; but market participants are unlikely to believe money demand can shift without some Fed response based on its presumed targets. Thus, the money demand effect may imply, say, an expected liquidity effect in response. For example, assume money demand increases and the Federal Reserve is believed to be focusing exclusively on a monetary aggregate target.

The increase in money demand, ceteris paribus, will lead to increases in both the money stock and interest rates as Figure 3 demonstrates. Furthermore, the announcement of a money stock increase could lead financial market participants to expect the Fed to reduce the money supply in order to maintain its monetary aggregate target. This tightening, however, is the expected liquidity effect.

Alternately, if financial market participants believe the Federal Reserve is trying to peg nominal interest rates, the expected Fed response to a money demand increase would be very different. An increase in money demand would prompt the Fed to increase the money supply to prevent interest rates from increasing. In this scenario, the unexpected money announcements should have no effect on interest rates. Between the extremes of focusing exclusively on interest rates and focusing exclusively on a monetary aggregate, both the expected liquidity and inflation premium effects may be present.

EVALUATING THE EMPIRICAL RESULTS

The findings of previous empirical analyses of the impact of anticipated and unanticipated money announcements are summarized in Table 1. The results presented indicate considerable disagreement among previous studies.

Short-Term Interest Rates—Unexpected Changes

Most studies conclude that short-term interest rates are significantly and positively influenced by unanticipated money announcements. While this is true in both the pre- and post-October 1979 periods, the effects are substantially larger in the latter period.[23] For example, Judd (1984) finds that a 1 percent positive money surprise would increase the three-month Treasury bill rate by only 6 basis points before October 1979, but by 36 basis points after September 1979.[24] That this is true is consistent with financial markets believing that after September 1979 the Fed placed substantially more weight on short-term money stock movements in their efforts to achieve monetary aggregate targets. Apparently, the market believed the Fed's statements that its procedures were being changed. The very small estimated coefficients before October 1979 indicate that financial markets believed the Fed was less interested in short-term movements in the money stock before then.

That an unexpectedly large money announcement increases short-term nominal interest rates cannot be used as evidence to distinguish between the expected liquidity, inflation premium, and money demand effects, however. All three predict a positive relationship between the two.[25] Thus, previous research also has focused on financial market variables for which the responses to money surprises might differ. These variables include long-term interest rates, stock prices, and exchange rates.

Long-Term Interest Rates

Studies that have considered the impact of money announcements on long-term interest rates have been unanimous in concluding that neither announcement surprises nor anticipations influenced long-term rates prior to October 1979. This is again consistent with financial markets believing that the Federal Reserve was pegging interest rates before October 1979. After September 1979, with limited analysis there is some evidence that expected announcements have no impact on

TABLE 1
Summary of Empirical Results

	Pre-October 1979		Post-October 1979	
	Unexpected Money Changes	Expected Money Changes	Unexpected Money Changes	Expected Money Changes
NOMINAL INTEREST RATES				
Short-Run	+ Grossman (1981) Urich and Wachtel (1981) Roley (1982) Urich (1982) Cornell (1983a) Roley (1983) Roley and Troll (1983) Loeys (1984) Urich and Wachtel (1984) Judd (1984) Gavin and Karamouzis (1984)		+ Roley (1982) Cornell (1982) Cornell (1983a) Cornell (1983b) Shiller, et. al. (1983) Roley (1983) Roley and Troll (1983) Loeys (1984) Belongia and Kolb (1984) Urich and Wachtel (1984) Roley and Walsh (1984) Hardouvelis (1984) Judd (1984) Gavin and Karamouzis (1984) Hein (1985) Belongia and Sheehan (1985)	− Belongia and Kolb (1984) Urich and Wachtel (1984) Gavin and Karamouzis (1984) Hein (1985) Belongia and Sheehan (1985)
	0 Cornell (1983b) Roley and Walsh (1984)	0 Grossman (1981) Urich and Wachtel (1981) Urich (1982) Cornell (1983b) Roley (1983) Urich and Wachtel (1984) Roley and Walsh (1984) Gavin and Karamouzis (1984)	0 Roley and Troll (1983)	0 Cornell (1983b) Roley (1983) Roley and Walsh (1984)
Long-Run			+ Cornell (1983a) Cornell (1983b) Loeys (1984) Roley and Walsh (1984) Gavin and Karamouzis (1984)	− Gavin and Karamouzis (1984)
	0 Cornell (1983a) Cornell (1983b) Loeys (1984) Roley and Walsh (1984) Judd (1984) Gavin and Karamouzis (1984)	0 Cornell (1983b) Roley and Walsh (1984) Gavin and Karamouzis (1984)	0 Shiller, et. al. (1983) Hardouvelis (1984) Judd (1984)	0 Cornell (1983b) Roley and Walsh (1984)
STOCK PRICES	− Pearce and Roley (1983) Pearce and Roley (1985)		− Cornell (1983b) Pearce and Roley (1983) Pearce and Roley (1985)	
	0 Cornell (1983b)	0 Cornell (1983b) Pearce and Roley (1983) Pearce and Roley (1985)		0 Cornell (1983b) Pearce and Roley (1983) Pearce and Roley (1985)
EXCHANGE RATES			+ Cornell (1982) Cornell (1983b) Engel and Frankel (1984) Hardouvelis (1984) Gavin and Karamouzis (1984)	− Gavin and Karamouzis (1984)
	0 Cornell (1983b) Gavin and Karamouzis (1984)	0 Cornell (1983b) Gavin and Karamouzis (1984)		0 Cornell (1983b)

+ indicates a significant positive effect was found.
− indicates a significant negative effect was found.
0 indicates an insignificant effect.

long-term rates. Expected increases in the money stock may lead to higher inflation and higher long-term interest rates, but do not necessarily lead to higher inflation and interest rates immediately after the money announcement.

The results concerning announcement surprises are mixed. Studies that have used long-term forward rates, such as Shiller et al. (1983), Hardouvelis (1984), and Judd (1984), generally have found no significant response.[26] These findings are not consistent with the inflation-premium effect. A money surprise is apparently expected to be quickly offset by the Fed and, thus, has no effect on long-run inflation expectations. Alternately, financial market participants could simply believe that weekly money announcements, from a long-run perspective, convey little or no information useful in forecasting long-term interest rates.

Studies such as Cornell (1983a) that have used changes in actual long-term rates, which include the effects of short-term rates, have found significant effects. Whether these effects are the result of market participants' short-run expectations about current or prospective short-term interest rates or whether they truly convey information about inflation expectations has not been determined.

Stock Prices

Relatively few studies have considered the implications of money announcements on stock prices. Stock prices apparently decreased in response to positive money surprises in the post-September 1979 period. In the pre-October 1979 period, there is no consensus on whether money surprises influenced stock prices (Table 1). Expected changes had no effect on stock prices in either period.

These results are inconsistent with the money-demand effect. If the money announcement reveals an increase in money demand due to an increase in expected output, stock prices should increase.[27]

Exchange Rates

The exchange rate results presented in Table 1 indicate that neither anticipated announcements nor surprises significantly influenced exchange rates before October 1979. After September 1979, money surprises have resulted in significant appreciation of the dollar relative to some currencies, in particular the German mark and the Swiss franc. Other exchange rates, such as those relative to the British pound and the Canadian dollar, have not appreciated significantly. To date, there apparently have been no joint tests of the significance of money surprises on all exchange rates.

The evidence that exchange rates generally did not depreciate is also inconsistent with the inflation premium effect. The inflation-premium effect predicts that an unexpectedly large money announcement, associated with higher expected inflation, should lead instead to lower exchange rates.[28]

Short-Term Interest Rates—Expected Changes

Most studies also indicate that expected money announcements had no impact on short-term interest rates before October 1979. After then, Table 1 indicates a consensus that expected money announcements had significant negative effects on short-term interest rates. This result is inconsistent with any of the competing theories and the efficient-markets hypothesis.[29] Thus, either the efficient markets hypothesis is incorrect, the theories as they are currently formulated or tested are insufficiently detailed, or other factors are changing that are correlated with expected money.

It is difficult to argue that the efficient-markets hypothesis is incorrect. If it were, it would imply that profitable trading opportunities exist based only on knowledge of expected money.[30] Given that the money announcement is widely forecasted and both the forecasted and announced values are widely disseminated, it seems unreasonable to expect profitable trading opportunities to remain for long. It seems more plausible to attribute the significance of expected money either to correlation between expected money and omitted variables or to limitations in the underlying theory.[31]

CONCLUSIONS

While a number of theories have been advanced to explain why money stock announcements, particularly the component that is unexpected, influence financial market variables, this paper shows that these theories are not generally competing. For example, the expected liquidity and inflation-premium effects may be complementary depending on financial market participants' perceptions of Federal Reserve goals. Some empirical results are inconsistent with either the inflation-premium effect or the money-demand effect alone. The expected liquidity effect, by itself, can explain the responses of interest rates, exchange rates, and stock prices to unexpected money announcements. There is no reason, however, to believe that this effect, or either of the two others, operates in isolation.

NOTES

[1] That is, much of the week-to-week movements in the money stock are unrelated to any economic phenomenon. See Pierce (1981).

[2] For a sample of these results, see Cornell (1983b), Hardouvelis (1984), and Urich and Wachtel (1984).

[3] The standard assumption is that financial market prices adjust rapidly to changes in their determinants, within a span of hours or at most days, while prices in other markets tend, for a variety of reasons, to adjust more slowly. See Fama (1982).

[4] Information also is released on the monetary base for the week ending one day earlier, the components of the money stock and the monetary base, and the aggregate portfolio of weekly reporting banks.

[5] The hypothesized short-run impact on interest rates of changes in the money stock is termed the *liquidity effect*. For example, the Federal Reserve may buy government securities and, in so doing, provide currency and reserves. The convince economic agents to part with the securities in exchange for money, the Federal Reserve's purchase of securities will bid the price of securities up, thus bidding the yield down. This liquidity effect occurs as soon as the stock of money is increased. See Brown and Santoni (1983) for evidence about the existence, magnitude, and duration of the liquidity effect.

[6] See Cornell (1983b) for an explicit statement of this assumption. It should be noted, however, that more general models can be developed in which expected and unexpected announcements are both important. For example, see Belongia and Sheehan (1985b). These more general models have not been widely applied.

[7] Unexpected money deviations here refer exclusively to those as seen by financial market participants. The money announcement itself is assumed to reveal no information to the Federal Reserve. See Urich (1982).

[8] While there may be professional debate over the impact of monetary policy on the real interest rate, there is general agreement among economic textbooks that monetary policy does play a significant role. For example, see Dornbusch and Fischer (1984).

[9] Money growth in this and the following sections refers exclusively to M1 growth, since data on the M2 and M3 monetary aggregates are released only monthly. The Federal Reserve is required by Congress to state target ranges for all three monetary aggregates.

[10] To focus on the expected liquidity effect and the impact of an unexpected money shock, we temporarily abstract from the noise in the series. In fact, the actual money stock numbers on a week-to-week basis as initially released form a saw-toothed pattern with an upward trend. In a more realistic setting, expected money may also be expected to fluctuate substantially as market participants attempt to adjust their forecasts due to a host of changing economic and institutional factors.

The most common measure of expected money is the median of a survey of market expectations of money growth conducted weekly by Money Market Services, Inc. A time series forecast is infrequently used instead. Regressions of actual money changes on expected money changes indicates that about 30 percent of all money changes are expected. Thus, money changes have a large random component, but are not entirely unpredictable.

[11] The analysis in Figure 1 is presented in terms of money growth vis-à-vis its expected growth rate. Alternately, it is possible that no reaction (or a smaller reaction) would be expected until the money stock went outside of the Fed's stated target range. For example, see Roley (1983).

[12] For example, see Roley and Walsh (1984) and Gavin and Karamouzis (1984). The most important institutional change was the switch in the Federal Reserve's operating procedures for conducting monetary policy. Before October 6, 1979, the Federal Reserve primarily focused on interest rates in the short run, although there were explicit monetary aggregate targets since 1975; see Wallich and Keir (1979). From October 1979 through September 1982, to improve monetary control, the Federal Reserve adopted a policy of targeting on nonborrowed reserves in the short run. Since then, the Federal Reserve has pursued a more flexible policy, paying somewhat more attention to interest rate fluctuations than it had in the previous period, although not reverting to the pre-October 1979 regime. See Wallich (1984) and Gilbert (1985).

Institutional changes since 1977 also include changes in the money stock announcement date (switched from Thursday to Friday and back to Thursday), a change from lagged to contemporaneous reserve requirements (in February 1984), and the changes associated with financial deregulation. Any of these, in theory, could alter the informational content of the money stock announcement.

[13] If the slope along $\dot{m}_1^e$ is less than that along $\dot{m}^e$, the two paths will ultimately converge, as they are assumed to do in the analysis of the expected liquidity effect. Alternately, the growth path could have exactly the same slope, $\dot{m}_1^e = \dot{m}^e$, before and after an unexpected increase in the money stock. In this case, money growth before and after the one-week shock would be expected to be the same. The long-run money growth rate would increase only by the amount that the one-week increase had an impact on the average. Since money growth influences inflation only with a substantial lag and since a one-shot level change in the money stock is generally small in relation to, say, the year-to-year change in the money supply, a simple step up in the level of the money stock would usually have little effect on the actual or the expected inflation rate.

[14] Again, this discussion assumes financial markets believe the Fed is using a single target within the cone.

[15] This statement also abstracts from such considerations as interest-rate smoothing. For example, a temporary shock may lead to Fed intervention to smooth the adjustment to equilibrium. In addition, if the shock were temporary but led to a permanent shift in Fed policy, it could also have the effect shown in Figure 2.

[16] This effect has also been titled the real economic activity effect. See Cornell (1983b).

[17] A shift in money demand that is not due to a shift in expected future output is not necessarily associated with any change in stock prices.

One particular money demand effect that is sometimes considered separately is the reserve settlement effect. This effect existed only under lagged reserve requirements when the timing of the money announcement was such that it revealed information about current reserve demand. Consider a money stock announcement, say, on August 26, 1982. Data on the money stock were released then for the week ending August 18, 1982. But deposits for the week ending August 26, 1982, determined required reserves for the week ending September 2, 1982. When the money stock numbers were released, they may have contained incremental information on the demand for reserves.

An individual bank may know its own reserve requirements prior to the money announcement, but it has only limited information on aggregate reserves and thus on the federal funds rate expected to prevail for the remainder of the reserve settlement period. An unexpected money increase generally implies that deposits, as well as the demand for required and total reserves, are all greater than expected. The reserve settlement effect demonstrates how institutional characteristics can influence the relationship, say, between money announcements and interest rates.

[18] For example, see Cornell (1983b).

[19] See Cornell (1983b) for a more detailed explanation.

[20] It should be noted that the relationship between real interest rates and capital inflows has only recently been emphasized. See Batten and Ott (1983). Previously the emphasis would have been placed on relationships like an expected expansion leading to a rise in imports and a drop in the U.S. exchange rate.

[21] In fact, Cornell (1983b) introduces an additional theory: the risk premium hypothesis, based on increased monetary variability requiring larger risk premiums. Since neither he nor Belongia and Kolb (1984) found any evidence of its existence, it is omitted here.

[22] See Brainard (1967) for a formal model making this point.

[23] There is also substantially greater interest rate volatility in the latter period. In addition, studies that have attempted to assess the impact of money surprises have been faced with the task of sorting

out the influences of other factors, such as a change in the day of the money announcement, a discount rate surcharge, credit controls, etc. See also the institutional changes mentioned in Note 12. Most studies have simply chosen a period (or periods) for analysis and assumed that nonmoney-announcement effects were unchanging over that period. Whether this approach is valid is debatable. It should be noted, however, that most estimated equations can explain only 30 percent or less of the fluctuation in interest rates around the time of the money announcement.

[24] In general, no attempt is made here to present the magnitude of estimated coefficients, since the studies differ with respect to time periods, definitions of the dependent variable (e.g., federal funds rate versus three-month Treasury bill as the short-term interest rate), and equation specification. In addition, all the studies except Judd (1984), Loeys (1984), and Gavin and Karamouzis (1984) make no systematic study of differential effects occurring after October 1982, when the Federal Reserve deemphasized the M1 monetary aggregate.

[25] Cornell (1983b) states:

> The dramatic shift in the market response to money supply announcements after October 6 is difficult to reconcile with the expected inflation hypothesis. If the money supply announcements are providing information about future money growth, there is no obvious reason why the Fed's stated intention to control monetary aggregates should induce a positive correlation between announced innovations in money and changes in interest rates. In fact, it is more reasonable to conclude that the correlation would decline because week-to-week variation in the aggregates would no longer provide information about long-run policy.

Cornell's argument is that the expected liquidity effect predicts a greater response to money surprises pre- versus post-October 1979, while the inflation premium effect predicts no change in response. This lack of change with the inflation-premium hypothesis, however, is based on the assumption that the change in operating procedures did not alter market participants' view of the money supply process. The inflation-premium effect could also be associated with a greater response to a money surprise after October 1979 if, for example, an unexpected increase in the money stock after that date is viewed as having a greater probability of signaling monetary ease than under the previous operating procedures.

[26] Gavin and Karamouzis (1984) find the 4-year forward rate 3 years ahead is significantly influenced by money surprises, while the 23-year forward rate 7 years ahead is not.

[27] This conclusion implies only that the money demand effect by itself cannot explain all of the impacts of the money announcements.

[28] The exchange-rate results imply only that the inflation-premium effect by itself is not capable of explaining all the impacts of money announcements.

[29] After October 1979, an expected increase in the money supply would cause movement down the money-demand curve with a resulting decrease in interest rates. Market efficiency implies that this decrease in interest rates would occur immediately upon the change in expectations. Thus, if the money supply is expected to increase prior to the money announcement, interest rates would already have adjusted to this expectation prior to that announcement.

[30] To be precise, the efficient markets hypothesis would allow trading rules to exist with a positive gross return that was less than the transaction costs of making the trades.

[31] See Roley (1983) and Hein (1985) for examples of the former. A full discussion of the potential impacts of expected money is beyond the scope of this paper. For more details, see Belongia and Sheehan (1985b).

REFERENCES

Batten, Dallas S., and Mack Ott. "Five Common Myths about Floating Exchange Rates." *Review*. Federal Reserve Bank of St. Louis, November 1983, pp. 5–15.

Belongia, Michael T., and Fredric Kolb. "Risk Aversion and Weekly Money: Does the Market Expect the Fed to Offset Large Increases in M1?" *Economics Letters* 16 (1984), pp. 327–30.

Belongia, Michael T., and Richard G. Sheehan. "The Efficient Markets Hypothesis and Weekly Money: Some Contrary Evidence." Federal Reserve Bank of St. Louis, Working Paper 85–004 (1985a).

———. "On the Importance of Being Expected: Insights to the Weekly Money Puzzle." Federal Reserve Bank of St. Louis, Working Paper 85–007 (1985b).

Brainard, William C. "Uncertainty and the Effectiveness of Policy." *American Economic Review,* May 1967, pp. 411–25.

Brown, W. W., and G. J. Santoni. "Monetary Growth and the Timing of Interest Rate Movements." *Review.* Federal Reserve Bank of St. Louis, August/September 1983, pp. 16–25.

Cornell, Bradford. "Money Supply Announcements, Interest Rates, and Foreign Exchange." *Journal of International Money and Finance,* August 1982, pp. 201–08.

——. "Money Supply Announcements and Interest Rates: Another View." *Journal of Business,* January 1983a, pp. 1–23.

——. "The Money Supply Announcements Puzzle: Review and Interpretation." *American Economic Review,* September 1983b, pp. 644–57.

Dornbusch, Rudiger, and Stanley Fischer. *Macroeconomics.* New York: McGraw-Hill, 1984.

Engel, Charles, and Jeffrey Frankel. "Why Interest Rates React to Money Announcements: An Explanation from the Foreign Exchange Market." *Journal of Monetary Economics,* January 1984, pp. 31–39.

Fama, Eugene F. "Inflation, Output, and Money." *Journal of Business,* April 1982, pp. 201–32.

Gavin, William T., and Nicholas V. Karamouzis. "Monetary Policy and Real Interest Rates: New Evidence from the Money Stock Announcements." Federal Reserve Bank of Cleveland, Working Paper 8406 (December 1984).

Gilbert, R. Alton. "Operating Procedures for Conducting Monetary Policy." *Review.* Federal Reserve Bank of St. Louis, February 1985, pp. 13–21.

Grossman, Jacob. "The 'Rationality' of Money Supply Expectations and the Short-Run Response of Interest Rates to Monetary Surprises." *Journal of Money, Credit, and Banking,* November 1981, pp. 409–24.

Hafer, R. W. "The FOMC in 1983–84: Setting Policy in an Uncertain World." *Review.* Federal Reserve Bank of St. Louis, April 1985, pp. 15–37.

Hardouvelis, Gikas A. "Market Perceptions of Federal Reserve Policy and the Weekly Monetary Announcements." *Journal of Monetary Economics,* September 1984, pp. 225–40.

Hein, Scott E. "The Response of Short-Term Interest Rates to Weekly Money Announcements: A Comment." *Journal of Money, Credit, and Banking,* May 1985, pp. 264–71.

Judd, John P. "Money Supply Announcements, Forward Interest Rates and Budget Deficits." *Economic Review.* Federal Reserve Bank of San Francisco, Fall 1984, pp. 36–46.

Loeys, Jan G. "Market Perceptions of Monetary Policy and the Weekly M1 Announcements." Federal Reserve Bank of Philadelphia, Working Paper No. 84–2.

Nichols, Donald A., David H. Small, and Charles E. Webster, Jr. "Why Interest Rates Rise when an Unexpectedly Large Money Stock Is Announced." *American Economic Review,* June 1983, pp. 383–88.

Pearce, Douglas K., and V. Vance Roley. "The Reaction of Stock Prices to Unanticipated Changes in Money: A Note." *Journal of Finance,* September 1983, pp. 1323–33.

——. "Stock Prices and Economic News." *Journal of Business,* January 1985, pp. 49–67.

Pierce, David. "Trend and Noise in the Monetary Aggregates." In *New Monetary Control Procedures.* Vol. II. Federal Reserve Staff Study, Board of Governors of the Federal Reserve System. Washington, D.C., 1981.

Roley, V. Vance. "Weekly Money Supply Announcements and the Volatility of Short-Term Interest Rates." *Economic Review.* Federal Reserve Bank of Kansas City, April 1982, pp. 3–15.

————. "The Response of Short-Term Interest Rates to Weekly Money Announcements: A Note." *Journal of Money, Credit, and Banking,* August 1983, pp. 344–54.

Roley, V. Vance, and Rick Troll. "The Impact of New Economic Information on the Volatility of Short-Term Interest Rates." *Economic Review.* Federal Reserve Bank of Kansas City, February 1983, pp. 3–15.

Roley, V. Vance, and Carl E. Walsh. "Unanticipated Money and Interest Rates." *American Economic Review,* May 1984, pp. 49–54.

Shiller, Robert J.; John Y. Campbell; and Kermit L. Schoenholtz. "Forward Rates and Future Policy: Interpreting the Term Structure of Interest Rates." *Brookings Papers on Economic Activity* (1:1983), pp. 173–217.

Urich, Thomas J. "The Information Content of Weekly Money Supply Announcements." *Journal of Monetary Economics,* July 1982, pp. 73–88.

Urich, Thomas J., and Paul Wachtel. "Market Response to the Weekly Money Supply Announcements in the 1970s." *Journal of Finance,* December 1981, pp. 1063–72.

————. "The Effects of Inflation and Money Supply Announcements on Interest Rates." *Journal of Finance,* September 1984, pp. 1177–88.

Wallich, Henry C. "Recent Techniques of Monetary Policy." *Economic Review.* Federal Reserve Bank of Kansas City, May 1984, pp. 21–30.

Wallich, Henry C., and Peter M. Keir. "The Role of Operating Guides in U.S. Monetary Policy: A Historical Review." *Federal Reserve Bulletin,* September 1979, pp. 679–90.

38

The National Debt:
A Secular Perspective

John B. Carlson and E. J. Stevens

Recently, interest payments on the national debt have been growing faster than the economy (Figure 1). Since 1977, there has been an 11.5 percent average annual increase in interest payments. If this difference between growth rates were to continue unchanged until the year 2013, the federal government would be forced to borrow or tax the equivalent of the entire gross national product simply to service its existing debt.

This alarming possibility may not seem likely, because Congress and the administration are seeking deficit reductions that would slow future growth of the national debt and debt service. Unfortunately, even a large deficit reduction might not be sufficient to prevent continued cancerous growth of interest payments if the interest-rate cost of existing debt were to continuously exceed the growth rate of the economy. However, independent projections by both the Office of Management and Budget and the Congressional Budget Office have suggested that net interest payments are not likely to grow faster than the economy for very long.

Even putting aside the alarming possibility of an economic disaster 30 years from now, the fact still remains that the national debt and debt service costs have been growing very rapidly. In all but one of the past 10 years, the federal government has had to borrow not only the entire amount needed to pay the interest on the national debt, but also additional funds for noninterest expenditures. Moreover, this situation would continue for as far as the eye can see under all but the most sanguine projections discussed in this article.

This is not the first time that federal deficits have been large or that debt service needs have loomed large in federal budgets. This *Economic Review** offers two perspectives on the current federal debt situation. One is a historical view of the past 40 years, during which federal debt initially declined slightly from its wartime peak, and then began to accelerate. The other perspective is of the future, including several scenarios of what the next 40 years could be like. The frame-

From *Economic Review*, Federal Reserve Bank of Cleveland, III Q: 1985, pp. 11–24.

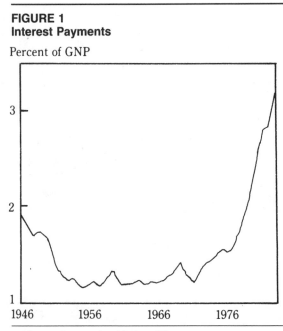

FIGURE 1
Interest Payments

Percent of GNP

Source: Congressional Budget Office.

work for looking at both the past and the future is provided by investigating the relative values of economic growth, interest rates, tax rates, and seigniorage. The analysis shows that the factors favorable to a net reduction in debt relative to GNP during the past 40 years are not likely to recur in the next 40 years. Substantial expenditure and/or tax changes are the only certain methods for preventing unprecedented peacetime levels of the national debt in the future.

I. DEBT DYNAMICS

The behavior of debt over time is complex; it involves the interaction of deficits, interest rates, and economic activity. Nevertheless, the government budget constraint provides a straightforward accounting basis for examining dynamic consequences of alternative assumptions as well as their consistency with certain expected long-run characteristics of the economy. The logic of accounting requires that the change in total outstanding government debt, D, equal the budget deficit, which is the difference between federal government expenditures, E, and total government revenues, R. This is expressed as:

$$D_t - D_{t-1} = E_t - R_t$$

Public discussion about growth of the national debt typically focuses on the budget deficit. To better appreciate the dynamic elements of deficits and debt, it is useful to break the budget deficit into two components. One is the primary deficit (or surplus), defined as the difference between noninterest outlays and total revenues. The other component is interest outlays net of recoupments from federal taxes and the Federal Reserve. Combining these two components, we have:

$$D_t - D_{t-1} = X_t + i(1 - m)(1 - b)D_{t-1}$$

where X is the primary deficit, i is the average interest rate on Treasury debt, m is the average marginal tax rate, and b is the proportion of debt held by the Federal Reserve.

This dichotomy between the primary deficit and interest payments is useful because it highlights the importance of interest payments in determining debt momentum—that is, the tendency of the debt to grow on its own. Debt momentum is to a large extent predetermined by the level of current debt and by the market rates of interest at the various times that existing debt issues were sold. Federal revenues recouped from interest payments on the debt reduce the effective interest cost and thereby retard debt's momentum. These revenues include taxes on private holders' interest income from federal debt and the portion of interest income on Federal Reserve holdings of Treasury debt (seigniorage) that is returned to the U.S. Treasury. While tax rates and Federal Reserve System holdings of Treasury debt can be altered to influence debt momentum, practical constraints limit the extent to which policymakers can change them. For example, noninflationary monetary policy clearly implies some upper limit on Federal Reserve accumulation of Treasury debt. Tax rates may be easier to change, but

---

A Primer on Government Debt

References to "the public debt" mask many details that, upon closer inspection, are qualitatively important but quantitatively small. The lion's share of $1.577 trillion dollars of the federal debt outstanding at the close of fiscal year 1984 has been issued by the Treasury to finance budget deficits and, with the exception of savings bonds, is in marketable form held by the general public. The debt would be 21 percent greater if one were to include $331 billion of outstanding interest-bearing securities issued by non-government institutions (privately owned, not federally guaranteed, but with a special relationship to the government, for example, federal intermediate credit banks). Seventy-three percent of public and agency debt outstanding in 1984 was held by the public, U.S. government accounts another 17 percent ($264 billion), and the Federal Reserve held the remaining 10 percent. Of the $1.577 trillion of federal debt, only about 11 percent was held by foreigners, and 80 percent of that was in the portfolios of foreign central banks and other official institutions. The inference that can be drawn from these calculations is that about 62 percent, or $1.0 trillion, of federal debt is directly held by domestic private owners, over 90 percent of which is in the form of marketable interest-bearing instruments and 10 percent in nonmarketable U.S. savings bonds.

Granted, a sizable federal debt exists, and most of it is willingly bought in the market and held by domestic private owners. What difference does it make whether the debt becomes larger or smaller, either absolutely or relative to the income and wealth of U.S. citizens? Three different approaches to thinking about this question can be identified, emphasizing the role of federal debt in cyclical stabilization of the economy, in meeting the portfolio needs of wealth owners, and as an alternative to taxation.

Federal debt can be a cyclical necessity. Even if the Treasury had no debt outstanding on average over a long sweep of years, debt might be issued in lean years, then retired in fat years to serve a useful public purpose. Cyclical variations in national income and output, originating from sources outside the federal budget, give rise to corresponding variation in tax receipts and inversely corresponding variations in expenditure, and thereby to federal deficits and debt outstanding. The result is a federal budget that acts as an automatic stabilizer as compared with one in which receipts were required to balance expenditures at all times. If the federal government is to act as an automatic stabilizer, then some government debt may be a cyclical necessity.[a]

Federal debt supplies a perfectly safe interest-bearing asset for private wealth owners' portfolios.[b] An increase in outstanding federal debt will make a difference to the functioning of the economy, because portfolio managers must be induced to substitute less risky federal debt for more risky private assets that directly or indirectly finance real capital. In this way, rapid growth of government debt would retard investment in new productivity-enhancing capital, thus slowing the growth rate of real income per capita.

Finally, there is the view that "we owe it to ourselves." Government can finance its operations either through taxes or through debts. The argument is that, given a level of government expenditures, the economy is essentially unaffected by the choice between these two methods of finance, because issuing debt rather than taxing to finance government expenditures implies that citizens would expect to pay future taxes necessary to service the new debt. Recognizing those increased future tax obligations, citizens would be expected to increase their saving as taxes are reduced.

---

a. The same function could be served by the Treasury accumulating holdings of private assets in fat years and reducing them in lean years.
b. "Perfectly safe," of course, within a non-revolutionary environment.

any politically acceptable policy probably could not greatly alter the *average* marginal tax rate. Nevertheless, over long periods, these factors can change.

The primary deficit (or surplus), of course, also plays a role in debt dynamics by reinforcing or offsetting debt momentum. The size of the primary deficit is directly altered by changes in the budget, such as the policy initiatives embodied in the recent Congressional Budget Resolution for 1986. The primary deficit also includes the cyclical elements of the budget deficit that arise from the effects of the business cycle on revenues and income maintenance programs. Thus, the primary deficit tends to reinforce debt momentum during economic slowdowns and to offset momentum during economic recoveries.

The magnitude of debt momentum by itself is not very instructive. What is relevant is its size relative to growth of the economy. Economic growth eases the burden of servicing debt. Additional national income and output can add to revenues and can reduce spending on social programs. The combination—sometimes called a "fiscal dividend"—can be used to make interest payments and, if sufficiently large, to pay down outstanding debt. In this sense, the burden of debt in the economy diminishes if its growth lags the growth of nominal national income. Thus, analyses concerned with economic implications of debt dynamics typically concentrate on the ratio of debt to income, measured by GNP.

Much attention has been given to the potential for runaway debt, that is, the possibility that the debt-to-GNP ratio will grow without limit. Sufficient condi-

---

Box 1   Federal Debt Dynamics

The steady-state properties of federal debt are derived from the government budget constraint, which requires that the change in total outstanding Treasury debt (including Federal Reserve holdings) be equal to the budget deficit. This is expressed as:

$$D_t - D_{t-1} = E_t - R_t,$$

where D is outstanding interest-bearing Treasury debt, E is government expenditures, and R is government revenues.[a] For simplicity, we abstract from government transfers and assume that the average marginal tax rate, m, is the same for all types of income and constant over time.

Expenditures can be divided into non-interest outlays, E' and interest payments net of taxes and adjusted for seigniorage:

$$i^a = i(1 - m)(1 - b)D_{t-1},$$

where i is the nominal interest rate on Treasury securities, and b is the proportion of Treasury debt held by the Federal Reserve. This allows separation of the budget deficit into two components—the primary deficit:

$$X_t = (E'_t - R_t),$$

and interest payments adjusted for taxes and seigniorage.[b] Thus we have:

$$D_t - D_{t-1} = X_t + i^a D_{t-1}.$$

At time t, then, the level of federal debt equals:

$$D_t = xY_t + (1 + i^a)D_{t-1},$$

where $x = X/Y$ and is assumed fixed by fiscal policy.

Assuming nominal GNP grows at trend rate g, the time path of debt-to-GNP (d) is given by:

$$d_t = x + [(1 + i^a)/(1 + g)d_{t-1}],$$

since

$$D_{t-1} = d_{t-1}[y_t/(1 + g)].$$

When the debt-to-GNP ratio is stable:

$$d_t = d_{t-1} = d^*.$$

Hence:

$$d^*[1 - (1 + i^a)/(1 + g)] = x,$$

also when i and g are small

$$(1 + i^a)/(1 + g) \simeq 1 + i^a - g,$$

and

$$d^* = x/(g - i^a).$$

The level of d_t changes when $d_0 \neq d^*$. At any subsequent time t:

$$d_t = d^* + (d_0 - d^*)(1 + i^a - g)^t.$$

It can be seen from this last equation, that if $i^a > g$, the debt-to-output ratio grows without bound. Also, it is interesting to note debt grows relative to income when:

$$d^* > d_0 \text{ and } i^a < g.$$

a. For alternative derivations of these properties, see Congress of the United States, Congressional Budget Office (February 1985), Tobin (1982), and Wallich and Cohen (1985).
b. Because interest payments are net of tax recoupments and seigniorage, government revenues here are exclusively tax receipts on nominal income.

tions for runaway debt are that: (1) there be a primary deficit and (2) the interest rate on Treasury debt net of taxes and adjusted for Federal Reserve holdings be greater than the trend growth rate of nominal GNP. Realistically, this situation could not persist, because it would ultimately require that more than all of the income generated in the economy be used to purchase annual additions to the federal debt. The structure of runaway debt conditions therefore suggests that the budget and/or economic assumptions are untenable—that somehow something must "give."

Even if the trend growth rate of nominal GNP were greater than the net interest rate, debt could still grow for a time relative to GNP. This situation arises when the primary deficit adds to the debt faster than the excess of the economic growth rate over the net interest rate subtracts. Nonetheless, this situation would not continue forever, because the algebraic value of the debt-to-GNP ratio would eventually reach a steady-state level, even if a primary deficit were allowed to persist at something like its current size. That steady-state level can be shown to be approximated by the ratio of the primary deficit (relative to GNP) to the economic growth rate/net interest-rate differential (see Box 1). There is no a priori basis, however, for thinking that the portfolio of the private sector could accommodate every possible algebraic value of the steady-state, debt-to-income ratio and still be consistent with general equilibrium in the economy. Of course, if the primary deficit were reduced sufficiently, then the debt-to-GNP ratio would fall, until a low algebraic value of the steady-state ratio were reached—again, if that were consistent with general equilibrium.

II. DEBT DYNAMICS: 1946 TO PRESENT

During World War II, enormous primary deficits caused a fivefold increase in the level of federal debt (see Box 2). Immediately after the war, the large primary deficits ceased, and the level of debt began an extended decline relative to GNP. Not until 1974 did the combined influence of primary deficits and interest rates begin to generate another sustained increase in the federal debt relative to GNP.

Figure 2 shows the absolute amount of the federal debt held in the private sector (excluding the Federal Reserve) and that same amount relative to GNP, both indexed to their 1946 levels. Although the dollar value of debt trended upward slightly until 1974, the debt-to-GNP ratio fell over the same period. This decline—from a little more than one year's output to less than one quarter's output—persisted through the Kennedy tax cut and even through the Vietnam military buildup. Reversal of the decline in the mid-1970s was initially a consequence of enlarged primary deficits resulting from the severe 1973–1975 recession, augmented by a one-time tax rebate in 1975. By the peak of the business cycle in 1979, however, at least the primary deficit had been eliminated (see Figure 3).

An important characteristic of debt dynamics during the 28-year period of declining debt ratios, was the frequent occurrence of primary surpluses that actually produced a small cumulative net primary surplus from 1946 through 1974. While many factors could account for surpluses, an important factor was the budget's response to inflation. From 1946 to 1974, the GNP deflator rose at an average annual rate of 5.5 percent but until 1972, few federal spending programs were indexed. Benefits from large entitlement programs, such as Social Security,

---

Box 2   Debt Buildup in World War II

Large deficits in the United States typically have been limited to wartime. The deficits during World War II offer the most extreme example: they averaged 25 percent of GNP. The conditions for financing those deficits were unique to wartime. Economic resources were shifted from producing consumer goods to military uses. To implement this reallocation, the federal government instituted controls, including price controls and food and gasoline rationing. Individuals accepted these controls as requirements of patriotism, if not for their own long-term interest. Although credit controls were imposed to reduce demand for housing, automobiles, and appliances, these items simply were not available, because steel, wood, and labor were diverted to the war effort.

Individuals not in military service during the war typically worked a substantial amount of overtime. While their incomes were high, there was little to spend it on. Savings rates averaged 25 percent from 1942 to 1945, compared with a peacetime average of 6 percent. Thus, while the federal debt increased five-fold during the war, the government found many willing to purchase debt at very low rates of interest. To help keep rates low, the Federal Reserve was prepared to buy government securities not purchased by individuals. But the proportion of debt monetized by the Federal Reserve did not increase sharply, because private demand was sufficient. To promote private purchases of U.S. savings bonds, the government mounted an extensive advertising campaign that appealed to the people's patriotism.

---

did not increase automatically with inflation. On the other hand, tax rates were not indexed until 1985. Revenues tended to grow proportionately more than income, as inflation placed more and more taxpayers in higher tax brackets. Thus, even a relatively low inflation rate was doubly favorable for restraining the primary deficit, because, without explicit federal action, it tended to increase revenues faster than noninterest expenditures.

Since 1974, the budget has produced a cumulative *primary* deficit of about $430 billion. This turnaround owes largely to the Economic Recovery Tax Act (ERTA) of 1981, a tax initiative that sharply reduced the rate of growth of tax revenues. Large tax cuts were instituted with the expectation that there would be subsequent spending reductions in nonmilitary programs as well as additional revenues generated by more rapid economic growth. Subsequent output growth was relatively strong and generated proportionately more revenues, but the impact of ERTA fell short of supply-sider claims that it would produce sufficient revenue growth to eliminate the deficit. Moreover, Congress did not accept all the spending cuts initially sought by the administration. Because an important feature of ERTA was to index tax rates for inflation, the imbalance is likely to persist if substantial deficit cuts are not achieved.

FIGURE 2
Federal Debt Held by Public

Percent of 1946 level

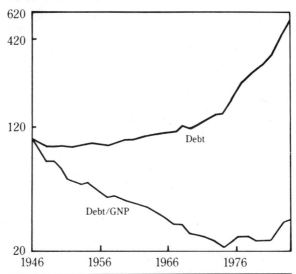

FIGURE 3
Primary and Total Deficient[a]

Percent of GNP

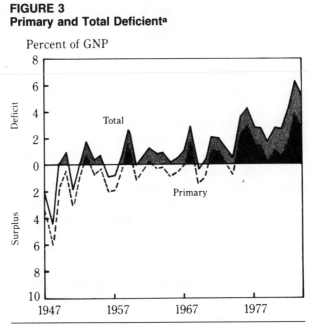

[a] Primary deficit assumes a marginal tax rate of 12 percent.

Another aspect of postwar debt dynamics was the apparent failure of interest rates to rise rapidly enough to anticipate the persistent, accelerating inflation beginning in the late 1960s. Relative price stability of the 1950s and early 1960s set a favorable tone for credit markets before the onset of more rapid inflation. Most federal debt had been auctioned at rates under 5 percent prior to 1966. When inflation began to accelerate in the late 1960s, it was apparently unanticipated. With a sizable portion of debt "locked in" at lower rates, the interest-rate cost of servicing debt adjusted only slowly to the higher rates of inflation (see Figure 4).

This inertial resistance essentially could account for the continued decline of the debt-to-GNP ratio after the mid-1960s. Figure 5 shows a rough estimate of what might have happened to the debt if inflation had been fully anticipated after 1965. It presumes that the average real interest rate would have equaled its average *ex post* rate during the low inflation period of 1954–63, and then adds actual inflation rates for periods equal to the average maturity of the debt. Multiplying interest payments on the debt by the ratio of the adjusted interest rate to the actual rate provides an approximation of debt payments and the debt-to-GNP ratio, if inflation had been fully anticipated. On this basis, debt would have stabilized relative to GNP near its mid-1960s level, rather than declining further into the mid-1970s.

Taxes are another reason that, until recently, interest-rate costs of government debt were low relative to growth in nominal GNP (see Figure 6). Estimates of the average marginal tax rate typically fall in the range of 12 percent to 25 percent. Even assuming the average marginal tax rate was only 12 percent, the annual interest-rate cost of the debt adjusted for taxes heretofore has never exceeded the five-year average growth rate of GNP. The momentum of debt growth was never augmented by interest-rate costs in excess of the longer-term nominal growth rate of the economy.

When debt was declining relative to nominal GNP, seigniorage also played an increasingly important role in slowing the momentum of debt. The monetary policy that accompanied economic growth with low inflation in the 1950s and early 1960s produced, as a byproduct, an increase in Federal Reserve holdings of Treasury securities almost proportional to the increase in nominal GNP. With debt declining relative to GNP, and Federal Reserve holdings rising proportionately with GNP, private sector holdings of the debt necessarily declined relative to GNP (see Figure 7). In fact, Federal Reserve holdings increased to almost 19 percent of all outstanding federal debt in the postwar period. This meant that by the early 1970s, seigniorage was paying roughly one-fifth of the interest cost of all debt held outside the federal government itself.

The turnaround and rapid growth of debt since 1974 has not been matched by momentum-dampening seigniorage. Disinflationary monetary policy since 1979 has constrained money growth and the seigniorage it produces. As debt has grown abruptly relative to GNP, the share held by the Federal Reserve has dropped sharply. Moreover, the Monetary Control Act of 1980 reduced overall required reserves on deposits. This, in turn, reduced the demand for monetary base (and hence, Federal Reserve holdings of debt) for a given level of nominal GNP. Thus, the effects of seigniorage, so important to debt dynamics before the 1980s, have withered.

This historical perspective emphasizes some unique conditions that influenced

FIGURE 4
Average Interest Rate on Debt and Inflation[a]

Percent

Change in deflator   Interest payments/debt

[a] Debt is adjusted for Federal Reserve holdings.
Source: Congressional Budget Office.

FIGURE 5
Actual and Hypothetical Debt (percent of GNP)

Percent of GNP

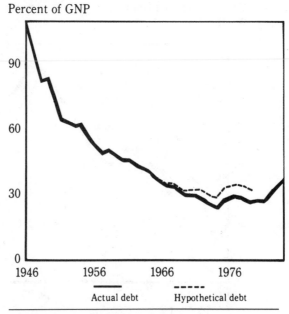

Actual debt   Hypothetical debt

Source: Congressional Budget Office

FIGURE 6
Interest Rates and GNP Growth

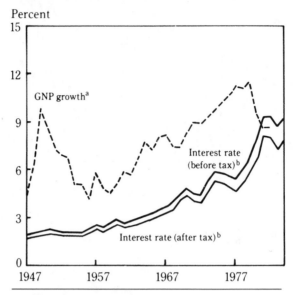

Percent

a Five year average growth rate.
b Interest payments/federal debt.
Source: Congressional Budget Office.

FIGURE 7
Federal Reserve Holdings (percent of federal debt)

Source: Congressional Budget Office.

debt dynamics in the postwar period. Of particular importance were frequent primary surpluses, low interest rates, and (relatively) high returns from seigniorage. Recreating the social and political forces leading to those same conditions is not possible. History, therefore, offers a poor basis for anticipating the future federal debt situation. But history does provide a kind of benchmark. If future debt-to-GNP levels are within the range of past experience, at least we know that these levels once proved manageable.

III. THE NEXT 40 YEARS

Long-term projections of the national debt, using the framework of primary deficits and net interest payments, rest on assumptions about the trend growth rate of nominal GNP, on the size of the primary deficit relative to GNP, on the level of interest rates, and on marginal tax rates and seigniorage. To be meaningful, a set of these assumptions must be mutually consistent with attainable future states of the economy. Lacking a generally accepted quantitative, long-run, macroeconomic model by which to generate a unique plausible set of those assumptions, we consider several different sets of assumptions to produce various debt scenarios. These scenarios should not be viewed as forecasts, but simply as potential levels of the debt-to-GNP ratio that can be compared to levels experienced over the past 40 years. Levels that fall outside the range of past experience are, ipso facto, alarming. Moreover, the projections can be examined in the context of widely accepted beliefs, or "stylized facts," about other long-run economic relationships that are thought to characterize the U.S. economy.

Table 1 contains an array of points along various steady-state paths of the debt-to-GNP ratio. Alternative values of the ratio for a common time horizon correspond to alternative assumptions about (1) the size of future primary deficits and (2) the differential between the rate of economic growth and the net rate of interest on Treasury debt. The steady-state values, based on the formula in Box 1, extend in time to horizons of 5, 10, and 40 years. A final array, based on an infinite horizon, approximates eventual steady-state values toward which the debt-to-GNP ratio tends in the very long run.

Two characteristics of these arrays are notable. *First,* the longer-run values of the debt-to-GNP ratio are clearly sensitive to what appear to be small differences in the values chosen for the assumptions. *Second,* however, the time paths of the alternative steady states are somewhat slow to distinguish themselves from one another. After five years, the debt-to-GNP ratio appears relatively unaffected by the indicated range of differences in the growth/net interest assumption; after 40 years the effect is quite significant (measured as a percent of either the low or high value), although nowhere near as substantial as in the ultimate steady state. The same pattern is evident when the effect of differences in assumed values of the primary deficit is traced. In this case, however, even the difference between the indicated high and low values at the end of five years is quite noticeable—equivalent to 10 percent of GNP.

Three paths of the debt-to-GNP ratio appear in Figure 8, corresponding to three particular sets of assumptions. The first, *scenario A,* is *not* drawn from sets of values in Table 1, but is based on our extrapolation of Congressional Budget Office (CBO) estimates that assume the July 1985 budget resolution is achieved. The CBO analysis only contained projections through 1990 and was based on two

TABLE 1
Debt-Output Ratio: Sensitivity to Changes in the Primary Deficit and Growth-Interest Differential

After 5 Years

$g - i^a$ \ x	0.5	1.0	1.5	2.0	2.5
1.5	.36	.38	.41	.43	.46
1.0	.37	.39	.42	.44	.46
0.5	.38	.40	.42	.45	.47
0.1	.38	.41	.43	.46	.48

After 10 Years

$g - i^a$ \ x	0.5	1.0	1.5	2.0	2.5
1.5	.36	.40	.45	.50	.55
1.0	.37	.42	.47	.52	.56
0.5	.39	.44	.48	.54	.59
0.1	.41	.46	.51	.56	.61

After 40 Years

$g - i^a$ \ x	0.5	1.0	1.5	2.0	2.5
1.5	.35	.50	.65	.80	.95
1.0	.41	.57	.74	.90	1.07
0.5	.47	.66	.84	1.02	1.20
0.1	.54	.74	.93	1.13	1.33

Long-Run Steady State

$g - i^a$ \ x	0.5	1.0	1.5	2.0	2.5
1.5	.3	.7	1.0	1.3	1.7
1.0	.5	1.0	1.5	2.0	2.5
0.5	1.0	2.0	3.0	4.0	5.0
0.1	5.0	10.0	15.0	20.0	25.0

Legend:
  x: Primary deficit relative to nominal GNP (percent).
  $g - i^a$: Growth-interest differential (percent).

FIGURE 8
Federal Debt

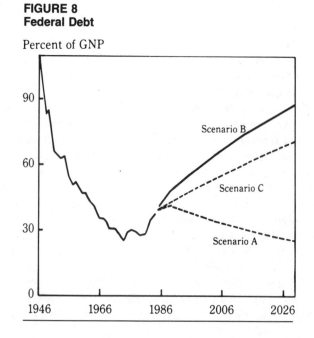

important additional assumptions: that the economy would achieve an average real growth rate of 3.4 percent and that market interest rates would decline, in part because of continuing low inflation. The projections indicate that the *primary* deficit would be eliminated by 1988, and, in the absence of any rebound in the primary deficit and of any deviation from the economic assumptions, our extrapolation shows continuing decreases in debt and interest payments as a percent of GNP over the next 40 years—a refreshing outcome indeed.

Scenario B, also examined by the CBO, assumes that *none* of the budget savings included in the July 1985 budget resolution is achieved. Again, the CBO projections only extended through 1990. Without budget cuts, the CBO projects that the primary deficit would decline from the 1984 level of 3 percent to about 1.5 percent in 1990, as the economy would approach its assumed full employment growth trend. In extrapolating, we have taken 2 percent as the value in the long run, representing an average of lower and higher values that might be achieved during future business cycles. The other CBO assumption was that, while the level of market interest rates would be slightly higher than the growth rate of nominal GNP (as has been the case for the past year), rates would nonetheless fall short of the growth rate of nominal GNP by 1.5 percent, after adjusting for the marginal tax rate on interest income and seigniorage. If the primary deficit and the growth/net interest-rate relationship were to stabilize at these average levels, our extrapolations show that the federal debt would continue to increase relative to GNP until it eventually stabilized at about one and one-third times nominal GNP (shaded values in Table 1). This result would advance only gradually, however; at the end of 40 years, the federal debt would be "only" 90 percent of a year's nominal GNP.

Scenarios A and *B* suggest a range of possible outcomes, extrapolating from medium-term projections that were based on commonly used methodology. Where in this range of outcomes the future might lie depends on the extent to which deficit reductions are achieved and maintained.

Neither of these scenarios is entirely satisfactory. The assumptions are drawn from averages of medium-term projections as proxies for long-run equilibrium values. Moreover, the projections themselves are derived from macroeconomic models and economic "rules of thumb" heavily influenced by post-World War II experience. But the unique combination of secular influences of this period—demobilization, rising inflation, and high seigniorage—is not likely to be repeated. Thus, models estimated over this period could be biased and, as argued below, biased toward a high growth-rate/interest-rate differential and a consequent underestimate of future debt growth.

Scenario C is based on assumptions that are consistent with a smaller growth-rate/interest-rate differential. Such a hypothetical case might be described as follows: Accelerating inflation beginning in the mid-1960s apparently was to some extent unanticipated. This suggests that the interest rates of this period, on average, were low relative to their "true" equilibrium values—that is, values consistent with noninflationary economic growth. This experience is unlikely to be repeated. Inflation awareness has grown with the experience of rising inflation, as well as with the experience of declining inflation. Furthermore, since 1979, the Federal Reserve has maintained a policy of disinflation. A major consequence has been that interest rates have varied more immediately and substantially to impulses arising in the real sector. This, in turn, makes it less likely that future interest rates will be "stuck" below their equilibrium levels.

The case for a smaller growth-rate/interest-rate differential seems even more plausible when one considers the productivity experience of the current expansion. Even with record levels of investment, productivity increases have been below levels for comparable stages of the cycle in the postwar period. If, in fact, trend growth of productivity is increasing around its 1970s rate of less than 1 percent, and if labor force growth were to stabilize at less than 1.5 percent, then trend output growth could be less than 2.5 percent. Moreover, as indicated in Figure 6, nominal pretax interest rates recently have exceeded the growth rate of nominal income. In fact, in the third quarter of 1985, nominal income grew at 6.7 percent, while nominal interest rates on Treasury securities averaged over 8.0 percent for a wide variety of maturities. All of this suggests that the equilibrium interest rate need not be less than the nominal growth rate, let alone the CBO assumption, which after tax is 1.5 percentage points lower.

A smaller growth-rate/interest-rate differential would produce a smaller fiscal dividend. Thus, it is likely to be associated with a higher primary deficit relative to output. It therefore seems reasonable that *consistent* assumptions would involve both a lower growth-rate/interest-rate differential and a higher primary deficit. In the context of Table 1, the potential bias of secular elements would result in assumptions toward the southeast for each time horizon.

To illustrate, consider a growth-rate/*net* interest-rate differential of 0.5 percent. While this scenario implies a pretax nominal interest rate slightly above the growth rate of nominal GNP, it would still be associated with an aftertax interest rate below the growth rate. This is not as favorable as the CBO assumption and is not as likely to be associated with the vanishing primary deficit of scenario A. Suppose that the primary deficit were reduced to 1.0 percent of GNP, roughly one third its recent level, and half the 2.0 percent of scenario B. The associated debt path appears as scenario C in Figure 8. The debt-to-GNP ratio under this alternative would rewind over the next 40 years back to a level comparable to that during the Korean War. In the longer run, the ratio would tend toward the unprecedented steady-state value of two times GNP, five times its current value.

The relevance of economic assumptions may be demonstrated in another way. How could the eventual debt-to-GNP ratio be maintained at its current 0.4 value if the growth-rate/net interest-rate differential were the 0.5 value assumed in scenario C? The primary deficit would have to be 0.2, or the equivalent of a $7.7 billion primary deficit today, roughly $110 billion less than its current value.

Useful projections—those with a semblance of future reality—should not be found to depend entirely on the precise values of their underlying assumptions. The three scenarios described here seem useful in that sense. The first, assuming prompt, substantial, and permanent deficit reduction, yields a declining debt-to-GNP ratio, with the speed of the decline depending on the size of the excess of the economic growth rate over the net interest rate. The second, extrapolating current short-run conditions into the long run, and the third, using relatively general long-run economic relationships and a sizable cut in the primary deficit, yield results quite different from the first. In either case, the debt-to-GNP ratio will slowly grow toward and might eventually exceed even the extreme values of the past.

The higher the primary deficit and the higher the net interest rate relative to the rate of economic growth, the sooner those values will be realized.

IV.   CAVEATS

Judging the usefulness of these projections also requires recognition that the assumptions might be interdependent. As noted above, less favorable economic assumptions might be associated with a higher primary deficit, reflecting a smaller fiscal dividend. The resulting debt-to-GNP ratio would be even larger than implied by the change in economic assumptions alone. Or, an assumption of greater seigniorage induced by expansionary monetary policy might produce more rapid inflation. The increase in the growth-rate/net interest-rate differential might be offset by a larger primary deficit as nominal federal spending grows relative to indexed tax receipts. The growth-rate/net interest-rate differential also might narrow as rising inflation expectations raise nominal interest rates and, perhaps, lower real economic growth. The resulting debt-to-GNP ratio could be higher than implied by increased seigniorage alone.

Bearing these possibilities in mind, what are the economic consequences of the various scenarios of the future? Are they consistent with widely held beliefs? Failure to follow through with the recent budget resolution both by actually achieving the entire deficit reduction and by extending deficit reduction beyond 1988, could mean that by early in the next century, the federal debt relative to GNP easily could exceed levels reached at the end of World War II. The challenge is to imagine how that result might be accommodated in an economic and social atmosphere less structured than the war-based economy of World War II.

An important budgetary caveat concerns the ominous debt implications of this country's commitment to Social Security, especially if demographic factors become less favorable. Recent 75-year projections published by the Social Security Administration indicate that, while the old age and survivor and disability insurance (OASDI) trust funds will continue to generate surpluses into the early part of the next century, the rate of increase of these surpluses relative to GNP will begin to decline in the 1990s. Because OASDI Trust Fund surpluses reduce the borrowing needs of the Treasury, the rapid buildup of these funds over the next 10 years is an important force in keeping the primary deficit from growing relative to GNP. If deficit reduction measures are not sufficient to reduce the primary deficit when OASDI funds generate increasing surpluses, what will happen to primary deficits and the debt when OASDI surpluses begin to decline?

Another budgetary caveat is that tax reform legislation introduces additional uncertainties. One has to do with achieving revenue neutrality. For example, the administration has presented a plan it describes as revenue-neutral, but other analyses suggest that the plan will actually reduce revenues and thereby might widen the deficit. A second uncertainty has to do with potential indirect effects of reform on net interest payments. To the extent that average marginal tax rates were to be reduced, the momentum of debt will accelerate as the after-tax interest rate rises relative to GNP growth.

Finally, a more fundamental economic caveat is that a rising debt-to-output ratio seems inconsistent with the observed constancy of the private domestic savings rate over the postwar period in the United States. This phenomenon,

FIGURE 9
Federal Share of Total Debt

Percent of GNP

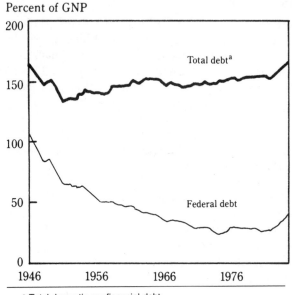

a Total domestic nonfinancial debt.
Source: Board of Governors of the Federal Reserve System,
Flow of Funds.

sometimes called "Denison's law," is akin to another empirical regularity, the relatively stable ratio of domestic nonfinancial debt (private and government) to nominal GNP (see Figure 9). An oft-cited implication of this proportionality is that a decrease in the growth of federal debt augments the growth of private (non-federal) debt relative to GNP and might enable more private domestic investment. Thus, the current concern is that federal credit demands could crowd out private credit demands and thereby stifle the private investment that is necessary to a growing economy.

Secular trends in federal and private debt from 1946 through the mid-1970s contrast strikingly with their trends over the next 40 years, according to scenarios B and C. The decline in federal debt through 1973 was met with a roughly equal rise in nonfederal debt, particularly in debt of households and businesses. This decline might have helped account for robust postwar growth, particularly in the 1960s.

Projections of a rising secular trend of federal debt imply that something must give. Either the private domestic savings rate must rise, breaking Denison's law in order to supply the extra funds required to finance higher debt-to-GNP ratios, or the nation must experience rising rates of net foreign investment, thus evading Denison's law in order to supply the extra funds. A third possibility is that investment in private capital must decline, complying with Denison's law to offset the government demand for extra funds.

So far in the current economic recovery, Denison's law has been evaded. Enlarged private and public demands for credit have been met by a record inflow of net foreign capital. This is not a cost-free consequence of a rising debt-to-GNP ratio. Growing foreign indebtedness requires growing payments out of GNP to service foreign debt. Capital investments may maintain economic growth, but the fruits of that growth will be enjoyed by the foreign investors who made it possible. Moreover, substantial adjustment costs must be paid as the capital inflow drives up the foreign exchange value of the dollar and reduces the competitive position of trade-related industries. Thus the international adjustments created by the rising debt-to-GNP ratio carry significant costs, both directly, and (potentially) indirectly through inefficiencies associated with protectionist measures.

V. CONCLUSION

Prospects for slowing growth of the national debt improved somewhat in August 1985, when Congress passed a budget resolution for fiscal year 1986. Although subsequent analysis suggests that budget savings would be less than purported, the impact on the national debt still would be significant if the resolution's budget targets were achieved. But budget resolutions are only resolutions and are frequently foresaken, particularly during periods of economic stress. The more recent congressional effort to mandate a sequence of deficit reductions leading to a balanced budget early in the next decade may be viewed as building annual legislative roadblocks in the path of the growing national debt. Whether such roadblocks could be effective can only be known when future federal budgets are known.

Uncertainty about actual federal budgets for 1986 and beyond is not the only issue troubling analysts. The reliability of deficit projections based on macroeconomic models and on rules of thumb is always tenuous. Here we have provided a secular perspective that demonstrates that future economic conditions are likely to be less favorable for constraining the debt-to-GNP ratio than they were for most of the postwar period. Whether this change is embodied in the models on which deficit and debt projections are based, is not clear.

Cutting the primary deficit remains the most certain method of preventing continuing increases in the debt-to-GNP ratio. The challenge is to look beyond annual increases to the steady advance of unprecedented peacetime levels of federal debt—and then to take the budgetary initiatives required to reverse the process.

REFERENCES

Barro, Robert J., and Chaipat Sahasakul. "Measuring the Average Marginal Tax Rate from the Individual Tax." *Journal of Business* 56, no. 4 (October 1983), pp. 419–52.

Carlson, John B. "The Debt Burden: What You Don't See," *Economic Commentary*. Federal Reserve Bank of Cleveland, May 1, 1985.

Congress of the United States, Congressional Budget Office. *The Economic and Budget Outlook: An Update, a Report to the Senate and House Committees on the Budget.* Washington, D.C.: Congressional Budget Office, August 1985.

———. *The Economic and Budget Outlook: Fiscal Years 1986–1990, a Report to the Senate and House Committees on the Budget—Part 1.* Washington, D.C.: Congressional Budget Office, February 1985.

David, Paul A., and John L. Scadding. "Private Savings: Ultrarationality, Aggregation, and 'Denison's Law,' " *Journal of Political Economy* 82, no. 2 (March/April), 1974.

de Leeuw, Frank, and Thomas M. Holloway. "Cyclical Adjustment of the Federal Budget and Federal Debt." *Survey of Current Business* 63, no. 12 (December 1983), pp. 25–40.

Executive Office of the President, Office of Management and Budget. *Budget of the United States Government, Fiscal Year 1986.* Washington, D.C.: U.S. Government Printing Office.

Friedman, Benjamin M. "The Roles of Money and Credit in Macroeconomic Analysis." *Working Paper No. 831.* National Bureau of Economic Research, December 1981.

Munnell, Alicia H. "Social Security and the Budget." *New England Economic Review.* Federal Reserve Bank of Boston, July/August 1985, pp. 5–18.

Sargent, Thomas J., and Neil Wallace. "Some Unpleasant Monetarist Arithmetic." *Quarterly Review.* Federal Reserve Bank of Minneapolis, vol. 5, no. 3 (Fall 1981), pp. 1–17.

Seater, John J. "On the Construction of Marginal Federal Personal and Social Security Tax Rates in the U.S." *Journal of Monetary Economics,* vol. 15, no. 1 (January 1985), pp. 121–35.

Tobin, James. "Discussion." *Savings and Government Policy.* Conference Series no. 25. Sponsored by the Federal Reserve Bank of Boston, October 1982, pp. 126–37.

Wallich, Henry C., and Darrel Cohen. "Perspectives on U.S. Fiscal Policy." *Kredit und Kapital* 65 (1985), pp. 109–24.

39

The Effects of Deficits on Interest Rates

Charles E. Webster, Jr.

The high interest rates of the past few years have been attributed by some analysts to deficits in the federal budget, which have increased substantially in recent years. Although some of the increase in the actual deficits has been due to declining tax revenues resulting from the recession, the deficits are expected to remain high even as the economy moves toward full employment. Moreover, based on the projected structural imbalance between the government's tax revenues and expenditures, structural budget deficits are expected to grow to unprecedented dimensions by the end of the decade.[1]

Analysts believing that growing deficits cause higher interest rates claim that huge government borrowings kept market interest rates from declining appreciably in 1981 and the first half of 1982, even as inflation was slowing and a recession was setting in. As a result of this belief, pressures have built to reduce the size of future deficits. Because much of the recently higher structural budget deficits is due to a tax cut and tax indexing provisons of the Economic Recovery Tax Act of 1981 (ERTA), much of the pressure to reduce deficits has gone into efforts to offset some of the revenue loss from ERTA. These efforts led to the passage of a $98.3 billion "revenue enhancement" bill on August 19, 1982. Since that time, market interest rates have declined substantially, which some see as confirmation of a direct relationship between the size of the deficit and the level of interest rates.

Contrary to this more popular opinion, other economists believe there is no such direct relationship between deficits and interest rates. They deny that government expenditures financed through borrowing instead of taxes have any direct implications for interest rates.

In view of these conflicting beliefs and their implications for future tax and

From *Economic Review,* Federal Reserve Bank of Kansas City, May 1983, pp. 19–28.

The author is a visiting scholar at the Federal Reserve Bank of Kansas City currently on leave from Washington University in St. Louis. The views expressed here do not necessarily represent the views of either the Federal Reserve Bank of Kansas City or the Federal Reserve System.

spending legislation, this article examines the theoretical and empirical evidence regarding the effect of budget deficits on interest rates. The first section examines conditions under which budget deficits affect interest rates. The second section assumes that the conditions for deficits to affect interest rates are met and analyzes the channels through which these effects could occur. The final section reviews the empirical evidence on whether deficit financing of government spending influences the level of interest rates.

CONDITIONS FOR BUDGET DEFICITS TO AFFECT INTEREST RATES

Budget deficits result from the government spending more than it collects in tax revenue. Deficits can be thought of as having cyclical and structural components. The cyclical component results from a decline in tax revenue during a recession. The structural component results from a structural imbalance between government spending and taxes and, therefore, persists even when the economy is operating at full employment. Many think the structural component of budget deficits have more important consequences for interest rates and other macroeconomic variables than the cyclical component. For this reason, the analysis here focuses on the effect of structural budget deficits, referred to simply as deficits.

To analyze the impact of deficits, it is useful to isolate the effects of how much the government spends from the effects of how the spending is financed. Thus, it is assumed that the amount of government spending is determined independently of whether the spending is to be financed by borrowing or by taxes.[2] By separating spending from financing effects in this way, it is possible to isolate the effects of substituting debt financing for tax financing for a given level of government spending.

Economists do not agree on whether the method of financing government spending has important consequences for interest rates and other macroeconomic variables. Some maintain that deficit financing has very different effects from tax financing.[3] Others argue that the method of financing is largely irrelevant. They maintain that whether financed by taxes or by borrowing, a given level of government spending has essentially the same effects on interest rates, income, and other macroeconomic variables. Because the proportion of government spending financed by issuing government debt is considered irrelevant for economic analysis, this hypothesis is often called the irrelevance hypothesis or the Ricardian equivalence principle after David Ricardo, a 19th century economist who first put this idea forward.[4] To determine the conditions under which deficits affect interest rates, it is useful to analyze the assumptions underlying the irrelevance hypothesis.

Assumptions of Irrelevance Hypothesis

According to the irrelevance hypothesis, deficit financing of government spending has no impact on aggregate demand or interest rates. The basic assumption underlying this result is that the private sector views government borrowing and taxes as equivalent. In other words, private spending is thought to be independent of the amount of taxes. A tax cut, for example, would not stimulate additional consumption or investment. Instead, the full amount of the resulting increase in after-tax income would be saved. The increased saving, moreover, could be invested in financial assets. Thus, the public would be willing to buy the government securities issued to finance the higher deficit without the inducement of higher yields on the securities. As a result, increased budget deficits that lead to commensurate increases in private saving have no effect on total spending or interest rates.

The reason deficits are assumed to increase private saving is that government debt is an implicit tax liability of the private sector. Interest must be paid on the debt until it is retired. Taxes must be raised to pay the interest on government debt or to retire it sometime in the future. Thus, an increase in government debt raises the private sector's future tax liabilities. The present value of these future tax liabilities, moreover, is exactly equal to the amount of the debt issued to finance the deficit. In other words, reducing taxes without reducing government spending merely transforms explicit current tax liabilities into implicit future tax liabilities. As a result, deficit financing is held to be irrelevant to private spending and, therefore, to interest rates.

Shortcomings of Irrelevance Hypothesis

Several objections have been raised to the realism of the assumptions underlying the irrelevance hypothesis.[5] One is that the private sector may not take full account of the implicit future tax liabilities corresponding to lower current tax liabilties. These future tax liabilities may be incurred, for example, by future generations instead of those benefiting directly from a current tax cut. If so, part of the increase in income from the tax cut might be spent, thereby raising aggregate demand and interest rates. Proponents of the irrelevance hypothesis point out, however, that future generations are heirs of the present generation. If people value the welfare of their heirs as highly as their own, those benefiting directly from a tax cut might still save most of it. In this case, the motive for saving is to increase bequests enough to offset the reduction in the wealth of their heirs from the higher implicit tax liabilities. In other words, intergenerational transfers could provide a motive for saving the entire amount of a tax cut, thereby preserving the validity of the irrelevance hypothesis.[6]

Another objection to the irrelevance hypothesis is that it does not take account of liquidity constraints on consumption spending. The hypothesis assumes that in deciding how much to spend in a given period, individuals base their decision on their expected lifetime income instead of on their income in that period.[7] Because of liquidity constraints, however, some people may not be able to achieve the preferred allocation of consumption over their lifetimes. Young adults, for example, often have only meager assets, even though their potential for future earnings is considerable. Unable to draw down assets or to borrow against future income, they may not be able to spend as much as they would like. As a result, an increase in disposable income resulting from a tax cut might lead such people to increase spending, even when they fully realize that lower taxes now must be offset by higher taxes sometime in the future. If a substantial number of consumers are constrained this way, the additional liquidity from a tax cut could raise total spending and interest rates.

Arguments for and against the irrelevance hypothesis cannot be resolved by economic theory alone. The arguments revolve around how people perceive government debt and the extent to which consumption spending is affected by the quidity from current income. The conditions under which deficit financing of government spending affects interest rates are clear, though. Even if only some of an increase in income resulting from a tax cut is spent, deficit financing leads to higher total spending and higher interest rates. Either of two conditions will lead to this result. First, if people do not take full account of the future tax liabilities implied by current deficits, they will perceive a current tax cut as increasing their wealth and, therefore, will increase spending. Second, if some people cannot consume what they would like because they cannot borrow against future labor income, they will use the additional liquidity provided by higher current income resulting from a tax cut to increase their spending. Under either condition, deficit financing will be accompanied by higher interest rates.[8]

CHANNELS THROUGH WHICH DEFICITS MAY AFFECT INTEREST RATES

It is assumed in this section, that the conditions are met for deficit financing of government spending to raise aggregate demand. Under this assumption, the various channels through which increased deficits would raise interest rates are analyzed. For this purpose, a distinction is made between nominal and real interest rates and between long-run and short-run effects of deficits.

Abstracting from tax rate effects, the nominal or market interest rate is equal to the real interest rate plus the expected rate of inflation.[9] To receive a given real rate of return on their investment, investors require that an inflation premium be included in the interest paid on assets to compensate for the declining purchasing power of the dollar caused by inflation. Borrowers are willing to pay this premium because they realize that the loan will be repaid in cheaper dollars. Since few financial contracts are indexed to inflation, the rate of inflation expected when a loan is made determines the inflation premium included in the nominal interest rate.

An increase in aggregate demand resulting from deficit financing of government spending could raise nominal interest rates by causing either higher real rates or an increase in inflation expectations. The magnitude of the long-run and short-run effects on those two components of nominal interest rates can be different.

Long-Run Effects

Persistent budget deficits lead to higher real interest rates in the long run. Real rates rise because the tendency for deficits to increase aggregate demand must eventually be offset to bring total real spending on goods and services into line with the capacity to produce goods and services.

To see why this happens, assume that budget deficits do not affect the economy's long-run capacity to produce.[10] For total real demand to equal the fixed supply of goods and services, greater demand for goods and services in one sector must be offset by less demand in some other sector. It is generally assumed that investment spending, expanded to include household spending on housing and consumer durables—as well as business spending on plant and equipment—is the only component of aggregate demand that is interest sensitive. Thus, the increase in consumption purchases caused by lowering taxes and issuing government debt must raise real interest rates enough to cause a commensurate reduction in investment spending.

Higher real interest rates may or may not be associated with higher nominal interest rates in the long run. If the inflation rate expected over very long periods is independent of the associated fiscal policy, nominal interest rates would increase by the amount of the increase in real interest rates. In contrast, if higher budget deficits result in expectations of permanently higher inflation, nominal interest rates would rise more than real interest rates.

Since inflationary expectations depend more on monetary policy than fiscal policy, and since monetary policy cannot keep deficits from causing higher real interest rates in the long run, it seems unlikely that expectations of long-run inflation would be affected by the magnitude of budget deficits. The increase in real rates that accompanies higher budget deficits in the long run is a real phenomenon. It is not changed by the accompanying monetary policy or other financial considerations. Thus, it seems likely that, in the long run, budget deficits would not affect inflationary expectations and, therefore, that nominal interest rates would increase by the same amount as real interest rates. The adjustment of real and nominal interest rates to the higher long-run equilibrium can be affected, however, by the short-run response of monetary policy and financial markets to budget deficits. For this reason, it is useful to analyze the alternative adjustment to long-run equilibrium under differing assumptions regarding monetary policy.[11]

Short-Run Effects

Real interest rates would adjust relatively quickly to increased budget deficits if monetary policy were unchanged. The effect of deficits on real interest rates is transmitted quickly to real spending decisions through financial markets. The increase in the demand for money associated with the increase in nominal spending caused by the deficit would result in a liquidity shortage if not offset by an increase in the supply of money by the Federal Reserve. As a result, real interest rates would rise as needed to induce the public to limit its money balances to the available supply. Looked at differently, people buying government debt issued to finance the deficit require higher real yields on government securities to compensate for the lower proportion of money balances in their portfolios.

Even without an increase in the money supply, nominal interest rates would rise temporarily more than real interest rates as a result of budget deficits. The higher aggregate demand caused by the deficits would raise the equilibrium price level. To achieve this higher price level, the rate of inflation must rise temporarily. To the extent that people anticipated the inflationary consequences of the deficits, the inflation premium in nominal interest rates would rise. Thus, nominal interest rates would rise not only because of the increase in real rates but also because of the higher expected inflation resulting from budget deficits.

The persistence of the two effects on nominal interest rates would differ, however. The increase in inflation necessary to achieve the new equilibrium price level is only temporary. The corresponding increase in the inflation premium in nominal interest rates would, therefore, also be temporary. In contrast, the increase in real interest rates would last as long as the deficit. Real interest rates would continue to increase, in fact, as the increase in the price level reduced the real value of the money stock, thereby reinforcing the scarcity of liquidity initially caused by the deficit.

Accommodative monetary policy could be used to postpone the rise in real interest rates. By increasing its purchases of government securities, the Federal Reserve could monetize part of the debt, thereby increasing the monetary base. Monetization would allow depository institutions to increase growth in the supply of money and credit, temporarily averting the liquidity shortage associated with the increase in aggregate demand resulting from budget deficits. The increased demand for money would then be accommodated by an increased supply of money, with little or no initial change in real interest rates.

Accommodative monetary policy might not prevent an immediate increase in nominal interest rates, however. More expansionary monetary policy would reinforce the expansionary effect of budget deficits on aggregate demand, leading to more upward pressure on the price level. To the extent that financial markets anticipated the associated inflation, the inflation premium in nominal interest rates would rise. Market interest rates might rise even more initially than without monetary accommodation. Moreover, unless monetary growth continued to increase indefinitely, leading ultimately to hyperinflation, growth in the real money stock would sooner or later return to the initial rate. When money growth returned to what it was initially, real interest rates would rise. Thus, the most monetary accommodation can do is postpone the increase in real rates resulting from budget deficits.

Alternatively, monetary policy might be directed toward offsetting the expansionary impact of deficits. If the Federal Reserve were committed to reducing inflation at the same time budget deficits were increasing, the increase in real interest rates would be especially pronounced. For monetary policy to be disinflationary, it must cause a net reduction in aggregate demand. Disinflationary policy, therefore, must reduce monetary growth more than enough to offset the stimulative impact of budget deficits. Because of the resulting liquidity shortage, real interest rates would increase dramatically under such a policy. The aggregate supply of money would be declining at the same time as the government was trying to induce the public to buy more government debt. Real yields would have to rise substantially to make the public willing to hold much more of its financial assets in the form of government bonds instead of money balances.

Some analysts have interpreted the high market interest rates in 1981 and early 1982 as resulting from this sort of imbalance between monetary and fiscal policy. At the same time the ERTA was leading to very large current and prospective structural budget deficits, the Federal Reserve was reducing growth of the money supply to bring down inflation. As a result, declining inflation was not matched by commensurately lower nominal interest rates. Real interest rates remained unusually high. Not until the last half of 1982 did market rates decline substantially, restoring real rates to more normal levels.

If this description of recent experience is valid, further declines in nominal interest rates can be expected to the extent that further progress is made in reducing inflation and, more importantly, expectations of future inflation. Real interest rates, however, could remain high unless the size of structural budget deficits is brought down. Monetary accommodation of the prospective deficits would, at most, be only a temporary palliative for the adverse consequences of high budget deficits.

EMPIRICAL EVIDENCE

Economists have used various empirical and statistical techniques in examining the effect of budget deficits on interest rates—unfortunately, with no consensus. Analysts have found that deficits affect both real and nominal interest rates, neither real nor nominal interest rates, and nominal but not real interest rates. The contradictory results point up the complexity of the issues and the sensitivity of empirical evidence to the choices of methodology, data, and time periods. It is useful, nevertheless, to examine the available evidence.

The empirical literature on the effect of deficits on interest rates can be divided into three main areas. One examines whether budget deficits affect aggregate demand and, therefore, real interest rates—that is, whether the irrelevance hypothesis holds. Another investigates the extent to which deficits affect nominal interest rates by raising expected inflation, as for example, by leading to higher monetary growth through monetization of government debt. The other disregards the channels of influence and focuses instead on the overall relationship of market interest rates to budget deficits. This section analyzes a representative sample of recent research in each of these areas.

Irrelevance Hypothesis

An article by Kochin in 1978 seemed to confirm the hypothesis that the method of financing government spending has no effect on total spending or interest rates.[12] If bond financing of government spending is seen as being equivalent to tax financing, consumption spending should not change when deficits increase. Kochin found that deficits and taxes have roughly the same effect on consumption spending for nondurables. He interpreted his findings as indicating that deficits do not affect total spending or interest rates.

In contrast, subsequent studies by Buiter and Tobin and by Feldstein led to the opposite conclusion.[13] Buiter and Tobin criticized both Kochin's statistical method and his theoretical framework. Using a slightly different version of Kochin's model and more recent data, they found no evidence to support the irrelevance hypothesis. However, they were not able to reject the hypothesis on a strict statistical basis.[14] Similarly, in an even more recent study, Feldstein used a different model and more sophisticated empirical techniques and found that deficits raise aggregate demand and, by implication, real interest rates. His empirical results, however, could be interpreted differently.

No definite conclusions can be drawn about whether debt financing is more expansionary than tax financing. The evidence suggests that debt financing may be somewhat more expansionary. Whether this is because people do not fully discount the implicit future tax liabilities that accompany deficits or because consumption decisions are affected by the liquidity current income affords, deficits seem to lead to higher aggregate demand and higher real interest rates. However, because the empirical evidence is mixed, no firm conclusions are warranted.[15]

Effect of Deficits on Monetization of Debt and Inflation Expectations

Several economists have tried to determine whether deficits have resulted in more expansionary monetary policy due to the Federal Reserve's monetization of debt.

Barro examined the determinants of the rate of growth of the money supply.[16] His empirical results suggest no systematic relationship between budget deficits and expected money growth. In a later study using a version of Barro's model, Hamburger and Zwick found some evidence of a positive relationship between deficits and expected money growth.[17]

Niskanen took another approach to the relationship between monetary growth and deficits. He estimated a monetary policy reaction function to explain monetary growth and found that deficits have led the Federal Reserve to increase monetary growth.[18] His results were very sensitive, however, to changes in the sample period over which the relationship was estimated. Blinder took a similar approach, but, instead of using monetary growth as the measure of Federal Reserve policy, he used the change in bank reserves relative to GNP. He also allowed for the possibility that the extent to which deficits are monetized depends on the prevailing inflation rate.[19] He found that Federal Reserve policy is slightly more expansionary when deficits are higher but that monetization of the deficit varies inversely with the rate of inflation. From this, he concluded that monetization of deficits has not caused much inflation.

Overall, empirical evidence does not confirm much effect of budget deficits on expected inflation and nominal interest rates through monetization of government debt. Although there is some evidence that past deficits were accompanied by more expansionary monetary policy, the effect was small. The relationship between monetary growth and deficits, moreover, has been estimated for periods before the October 1979 change in Federal Reserve operating procedures, a change that could have further reduced the responsiveness of monetary growth to the size of the deficit. Thus, empirical evidence does not strongly support the view that the high nominal interest rates of recent years have resulted from a belief in financial markets that the Federal Reserve will monetize some of the large budget deficits, thereby reigniting inflation.

Overall Relationship between Deficits and Interest Rates

Several analysts have tried to construct a general framework of interest-rate determination by integrating the various channels through which deficits can affect interest rates. Feldstein and Eckstein, for example, have explained interest rates by combining standard liquidity preference theory with the assumption that nominal interest rates reflect the expected rate of inflation.[20] They assumed that nominal interest rates depend on the real quantity of money, real income, inflation expectations, and government debt outstanding. Their results suggest a small but statistically significant positive effect of government debt on nominal interest rates.

Plosser has used a somewhat different approach to examine the relationship between government debt and interest rates. His approach does not require a specific model of interest rate determination but only a list of variables likely to affect interest rates.[21] Assuming that financial markets are efficient, in the sense that current yields reflect all available information, he postulated that only unexpected changes in privately held government debt, Federal Reserve holding of government debt, government purchases of goods and services, and other variables would result in changes in interest rates. His findings suggest that unexpected increases in government spending lead to an increase in interest rates but that the method of financing the higher spending has no effect. Plosser interpreted his results as indicating that the amount of government debt the public holds has little influence on interest rates, though he admitted that his results depend heavily on the method used in estimating expected values of the variables he assumed to affect interest rates.

As for other empirical evidence, results regarding a direct relationship between deficits and interest rates are inconclusive.

SUMMARY AND CONCLUSIONS

Recent large budget deficits have been accompanied by high nominal and real interest rates. Budget deficits, moreover, are expected to remain high for the foreseeable future, causing some to wonder if interest rates will sharply increase again as the economy moves toward full employment.

Theoretical and empirical evidence does not resolve whether budget deficits influence interest rates, or how. Arguments can be marshalled in support of the view that deficits do not affect interest rates at all. The assumptions underlying these arguments can be questioned, but empirical evidence does not necessarily contradict the view that budget deficits have no effect on interest rates, real or nominal. To the extent that such an impact occurs, the magnitude appears small. However, as further evidence is accumulated regarding the relationship between deficits and interest rates during a time when the size of the deficits is unprecedented and the Federal Reserve's commitment to disinflation is increasingly convincing, it may be possible to identify more precisely the magnitude and the channels of the impact of deficits on interest rates.

NOTES

[1] The structural deficit is sometimes called the high employment deficit. By measuring what the deficit would be at a high employment level of income, it removes the effect of business cycle fluctuations on tax revenues and government spending. The high employment or structural budget deficit is expected by the Office of Management and Budget to increase steadily from $154 billion in fiscal year 1983 to $306 billion in fiscal year 1988. See *Budget of the United States Government: Fiscal Year 1984,* Executive Office of the President, Office of Management and Budget, January 1983.

[2] This assumption allows an examination of whether deficit financing itself affects interest rates. Many analysts speaking of the impact of a deficit are actually talking about the impact of a deficit-financed increase in government spending. This combines the effect of government spending increases with the effect of financing of the increases by debt rather than taxes.

[3] For an overview of the impact of deficits, see V. Vance Roley, "The Financing of Federal Deficits: An Analysis of Crowding Out," *Economic Review,* Federal Reserve Bank of Kansas City, July/August 1981; Dan M. Bechter, "Budget Deficits and Supply Side Economics: A Theoretical Discussion," *Economic Review,* Federal Reserve Bank of Kansas City, June 1982; or William Buiter and James Tobin, "Debt Neutrality: A Brief Review of Doctrine and Evidence," in *Social Security versus Private Savings,* ed. G. Van Fursterberg (New York: Ballinger, 1979) for reviews of some of the economic literature on this topic.

[4] While Ricardo set forth conditions that give rise to what has become known as the Ricardian equivalence theorem that deficits do not affect interest rates, it has been questioned whether he believed that the conditions would actually be met.

[5] Several economists have investigated this issue at a theoretical level. They include Robert Barro, "Are Government Bonds Net Wealth?" *Journal of Political Economy* 82 (November/December 1974), pp. 1095-117; Paul David and John Scadding, "Private Savings: Ultrarationality, Aggregation, and Denison's Law," *Journal of Political Economy* 82, no. 2, pt. I (March/April 1974), pp. 225-49; William Buiter and James Tobin, "Debt Neutrality: A Brief Review of Doctrine and Evidence," in *Social*

Security versus Private Savings, ed. George Van Fursterberg (New York: Ballinger, 1979); and Preston Miller, "Higher Deficit Politics Lead to Higher Inflation," *Quarterly Review,* Federal Reserve Bank of Minneapolis, Winter 1983.

[6] This is not to say that the distribution of who pays cannot be affected but merely that resources cannot be shifted to the present from the future. However, a transfer of resources from current investment to current consumption can result in less future output. While the government must retire every individual piece of debt that it issues, there is no reason why it has to pay off the entire debt. Nothing in the analysis would change if, every time government-financed debt came due, it was settled by the issuance of new debt so that the government effectively never paid back any of the funds borrowed.

[7] See, for example, Walter Dolde and James Tobin, "Wealth, Liquidity, and Consumption," *Consumer Spending and Monetary Policy,* Federal Reserve Bank of Boston, 1971, p. 99–147; or Frederic Mishkin, "Illiquidity, Consumer Durable Expenditure, and Monetary Policy," *American Economic Review* 66, (September 1976), pp. 642–54.

[8] The recent discussion of the effect of Social Security on private savings centers on exactly this point—whether the reduction in savings caused by payments in the future, expected with reasonable certainty, offsets future tax liabilities of an equivalent value but uncertain incidence.

[9] Writing the nominal interest rate as the sum of the real interest rate and the inflation premium is an oversimplification that ignores, among other things, the effects of the tax system. Since nominal interest payments are taxable income to the lender and tax deductions to the borrower, to assure the lender the same rate of return in the presence of an inflation premium as in the absence of one, the nominal interest rate would have to rise by more than the inflation rate. For example, if the real rate is 3 percent and the lenders are in a 50 percent marginal tax bracket, an inflation rate of 10 percent will require that interest rates rise to 23 percent, not 13 percent.

[10] For simplicity, the economy's long-run productive capacity is assumed to be independent of budget deficits. This is somewhat unrealistic. The lower investment caused by budget deficits would probably be associated with a reduction in the economy's capacity to produce. Higher real interest rates and lower investment caused by deficits would tend eventually to reduce the private capital stock, thereby lowering the aggregate supply of goods and services. This tendency could be offset to some extent, however, by other factors. If the deficit resulted, for example, from government purchases to build roads, dams, and bridges, the effect of the reduction in the private sector's capital could be offset, at least in part, by an increase in the economy's infrastructure, with little net effect on the nation's total capital stock. Moreover, if the deficit resulted from tax cuts that increased the general willingness to work, save, and invest, then the benefits of these "supply-side effects" could counter the negative impact of high real interest rates on the nation's productive capacity.

[11] This analysis assumes that the demands for money and credit are related primarily to values of such short-run nominal variables as nominal income. If, instead, money and credit demands are functions solely of such long-run real variables as real permanent income, monetary policy would not have even a temporary effect on real interest rates or other real variables. Adjustments would be made solely on the basis of expected long-run values of the real money stock and real credit supply. The Federal Reserve could not affect perceived liquidity and, therefore, could not affect the timing or magnitude of adjustments in real interest rates or any other real variables.

[12] Lewis Kochin, "Are Future Taxes Anticipated by Consumers?" *Journal of Money, Credit, and Banking* 6 (August 1978), pp. 385–94.

[13] William Buiter and James Tobin, in *Social Security versus Private Savings;* Martin Feldstein and Otto Eckstein, "The Fundamental Determinants of the Interest Rate," *Review of Economics and Statistics* 52 (November 1970), pp. 363–75.

[14] Tobin and Buiter find that disposable income, taxes, and their own measure of the deficit are so highly correlated that the independent influence of each variable cannot be determined.

[15] Paralleling the empirical literature on deficits is the empirical literature on Social Security. See Martin Feldstein, "Perceived Wealth in Bonds and Social Security: A Comment," *Journal of Political Economy* 84 (April 1976), pp. 331–36; Martin Feldstein and Andrew Pellechio, "Social Security and Household Wealth Accumulation: New Microeconometric Evidence," *Review of Economics and Statistics,* 1979; Martin Feldstein, "Social Security, Induced Retirement, and Aggregate Capital Accumulation," *Journal of Political Economy* 82 (October/November 1974).

[16] Robert Barro, "Unanticipated Money, Output and the Price Level in the United States," *Journal of Political Economy* 86 (August 1978), pp. 549–80.

[17] Michael Hamburger and Burton Zwick, "Deficits, Money and Inflation," *Journal of Monetary Economics,* January 1981, pp. 141–50.

[18] William Niksanen, "Deficits, Government Spending, and Inflation: What Is the Evidence?" *Journal of Monetary Economics,* August 1978, pp. 591–602.

[19] Alan Blinder, "On the Monetization of Debt," National Bureau of Economic Research Working Paper 1052.

[20] Martin Feldstein, "Government Deficits and Aggregate Demand," *Journal of Monetary Economics* 9 (January 1982), pp. 1–20.

[21] See Charles Plosser, "Government Financing Decisions and Asset Returns," *Journal of Monetary Economics* 9 (May 1982), pp. 245–52.

PART SEVEN

Financial Innovation

Without question the financial markets have been a more exciting and more stressful place to work in recent years. New financial services and new variations on such traditional financial services as deposits and loans have opened up a broad (and often confusing) menu of products that financial-service firms can offer their customers, each tailored to the perceived service needs of varied segments of the population. The list of these new services is not only long but growing daily. Examples include consumer cash-management services, combined life insurance and mutual fund accounts, flexible-rate savings accounts that allow withdrawal by check, telephone, or wire transfer, securitization of loans as a way of borrowing against them, and networking of credit and debit cards to serve the customer regardless of where he or she may travel.

The *causes* of this explosive trend toward *financial-service innovation* have been discussed in earlier parts of this book. They include federal deregulation of the financial sector, intense competition among financial institutions, better-educated customers, the "invasion" of many new nonfinancial companies into financial-service markets in search of new profits and diversification, soaring operating costs, and narrowing profit margins for banks, insurance companies, and other financial firms. Moreover, rapid advances in the technology of information transfer—*technological innovation*—have eroded the old barriers of time and space, resulting in a merging of formerly distinct markets into one large competitive cauldron where the chances for survival often hinge upon who is first to reach the marketplace with new ideas.

The *consequences* of this trend toward service innovation are both positive and negative. The *positive* aspects seem to lie where economists argue they should be found—with the financial-services customer. The customer is offered a wider array of financial services, which increases the probability that he or she will find service offerings exactly responsive to a particular need. Moreover, deregulation and increased competition have encouraged financial firms to listen more carefully to their customers in designing their service menus. There are now *more* financial firms serving most local markets, so the customer is confronted with *more* supply options for essentially the same services. For example, the same or similar high-yield savings accounts may be offered by local banks, credit unions, and savings and loans, and by the local office of a national brokerage firm, insurance company, or retail store, such as Sears Roebuck.

The *negative* consequences of today's drive toward financial and technological innovation seem to lie mainly with those who work in the financial-services industry or who invest in financial firms. The development and introduction of new services and new service delivery systems sharply increases risk. Some new services and service delivery systems will turn out to be little more than "trial balloons," drifting about looking for a favorable public reception and collapsing when they find none. And, the financial institutions marketing those services may fail as well due to unrecovered costs. Indeed, failure rates of financial institutions have climbed dramatically. Among commercial banks, for example, the number of failures in recent years is the highest since the Great Depression of the 1930s.

Still, there is a positive side for financial firms as well. The trend toward creativity in new financial services and service delivery techniques increases the range of opportunity for management and employees of financial-service firms. It increases the potential rewards from successful innovation just as it increases the potential losses from unsuccessful ones. It encourages institutional adaptability and flexibility, because today's financial system puts a premium on lean and trim financial institutions and the efficient use of scarce resources.

The articles in this section begin with two excellent analyses of the financial innovation process itself. The first of these, by Alfred Broaddus, examines recent financial innovation in the United States and speculates on financial innovation in the future. Dr. Broaddus points out that financial innovation has been a continuous, though uneven, process in American history but has accelerated recently due to relatively high inflation, high interest rates, and rapid technological change that has reduced the real cost of financial transactions. Financial innovation, in Broaddus's view, has helped to bring about deregulation and, thereby, dismantled much of the elaborate financial regulatory structure that was erected during the Great Depression. He believes that in the years ahead there will be some consolidation of gains already made and a slower pace for financial innovation.

J. David Germany and John E. Morton broaden our perspective on the innovative trends discussed by Broaddus. These analysts point out that recent financial innovation has not been confined to the United States. In Canada, France, Germany, Italy, Japan, and the United Kingdom new financial assets and markets have appeared and there is also a movement afoot to let the private market play a greater role in determining the level and direction of change of interest rates on loans and securities. Competition between financial institutions, as in the United States, is continuing to intensify overseas, and financial markets everywhere are becoming increasingly internationalized. This development has forced governments and policymakers around the globe increasingly to consult and cooperate with each other in order to avoid disruption of the financial markets.

The costs of financial innovation have surfaced in many countries—greater uncertainty and risk and more complicated problems in trying to carry out monetary policy, especially where that policy is aimed at controlling monetary aggregates. It has also become more of a challenge to supervise financial markets and institutions—a problem also touched upon by Broaddus. Management of financial institutions has become more difficult and fraught with danger, due to greater volatility in interest rates and narrower profit margins.

One of the most stunningly successful of all recent financial innovations is the *interest-rate swap*. Developed first in the Eurobond market in 1981, rate swaps spread to U.S. financial markets the following year when Sallie Mae (the Student Loan Marketing Association) and ITT Financial Corporation exchanged debt-service payments on their loans. As described clearly in the article by Jan G. Loeys, interest-rate swaps permit two institutions to more closely match their assets and financing requirements, each agreeing to cover the stream of interest payments owed on the other's loans. Thus, an industrial firm or financial institution that prefers long-term borrowing at a fixed interest rate, but is prevented by a low credit rating or by other problems from borrowing cheaply in that form, may be able to find another firm that has strong long-term borrowing capability due to a high credit rating or other factors, but prefers short-term loans with flexible interest rates. These two firms simply agree to exchange all or a portion of their respective interest payments. Both wind up paying for the type of credit that each deems best and, in effect, helping each other to *hedge* against adverse interest-rate changes.

Earlier, in Part Four of the book, we looked at the problem of volatile interest rates in recent years and how one type of financial instrument—financial futures contracts—developed in the mid-1970s can be used to combat interest-rate risk. In this section of the book, we look at a more recent innovation for interest-rate hedging—options on futures contracts—which were first traded in the fall of 1982 on leading U.S. futures exchanges. G. D. Koppenhaver, senior economist at the Federal Reserve Bank of Chicago, provides us with a useful sketch of the characteristics of options contracts and how they are priced. He then considers how these contracts can be used by financial institutions in three different (but very common) problem situations. Dr. Koppenhaver points out that options can be used to generate added returns on a portfolio of financial instruments even with stable market conditions.

Another financial innovation of considerable significance is the spread of computerized electronic money systems. Automated teller ("money") machines have become commonplace in bank lobbies, drive-in windows, and other places of public convenience. Moreover, the spread of electronic money transfer systems across the United States appears to be accelerating in response to rising costs associated with the present, largely paper-based payments mechanism. Payments by wire, computer tape, and terminal now seem to be an essential innovation if we are to avoid being engulfed by the flood of transactions carried out each year through checks, money orders, and currency.

In a well-researched article, "From ATM to POS Networks: Branching, Access, and Pricing," Steven D. Felgran of the Federal Reserve Bank of Boston discusses the use of electronic payments devices at the *point of sale*. So-called POS terminals in retail stores and shopping centers permit merchants to receive an immediate transfer of funds into their deposit account from the customer's account in payment for purchases of goods and services. This transfer is usually accomplished through debit cards owned by customers and issued by financial institutions that are linked to each other through electronic networks. As Felgran observes, such payment systems can substantially reduce the resource cost of moving money between one account and another. Nevertheless, POS processing systems have run into significant hurdles that today appear at least as formidable to their future growth and expansion as technological barriers have been in the past. For one thing, many customers avoid POS terminals where possible because of the loss of checkbook float. In addition, POS systems have run into sharing problems. For example, where several financial institutions are involved, who should pay for POS equipment and maintain it? Which financial institutions should have access to such a system?

Felgran predicts that networks combining automated teller machines (ATMs) and POS terminals will continue to gain greater customer acceptance and more shared use through networking arrangements. Moreover, POS payments devices are making significant inroads among gasoline retailers and supermarkets, further reducing payments handling costs. In the future, Felgran argues, customers will be encouraged to more actively use modern payments systems due to their decreasing cost and greater convenience.

40

Financial Innovation in the United States—Background, Current Status, and Prospects

Alfred Broaddus

The purpose of this paper is to describe recent financial innovation in the United States, outline its principal implications with regard to (1) the structure and behavior of financial markets and (2) the conduct of monetary policy, and speculate on the likely character of further innovation in the near-term future. In the United States as elsewhere, financial innovation has been a continuous but uneven process, where the rate of innovation has varied substantially from one period to the next depending on a variety of circumstances. In particular, there have been a number of periods of accelerated innovation in U.S. financial history, frequently during or following periods of great social and political upheaval, such as the Civil War and the Great Depression. It seems clear in retrospect that the 1970s and early 1980s have been years of relatively rapid innovation due largely to (1) higher inflation and its impact on interest rates and (2) rapid technological progress that has significantly reduced the real costs of carrying out financial transactions. This accelerated innovation has already had a profound effect on the competitive structure and risk characteristics of American banking and financial markets, on the way these markets are regulated, and on the conduct of U.S. monetary policy. Further, while there is some reason to believe that the pace of innovation may diminish in the United States in the years immediately ahead, the full impact of the innovations that have already occurred probably has not yet been felt.

The paper is organized as follows.[1] Section I provides background information on the structure and regulation of American financial markets, with special

From *Economic Review*, Federal Reserve Bank of Richmond, January/February 1985, pp. 2–21.

This paper was delivered at the First International Symposium on Financial Development sponsored by the Korea Federation of Banks in Seoul on December 4, 1984. The views expressed in the paper are the author's and do not necessarily reflect the views of the Federal Reserve Bank of Richmond, the Federal Reserve System, or the Korea Federation of Banks.

attention to the regulation of banks and other depository institutions. Section II describes the forces that appear to underlie the accelerated rate of financial innovation in recent years. Sections III and IV discuss the impact of this innovation on financial markets and the conduct of monetary policy, respectively. Finally, Section V speculates briefly on future prospects. In view of the breadth of the topic and the purpose of the symposium for which this paper was prepared, the paper will seek to synthesize available information on recent financial innovation in the United States rather than to break new analytical ground.

I.   BACKGROUND INFORMATION ON THE STRUCTURE AND REGULATION OF U.S. FINANCIAL MARKETS

This section provides background information on the general structure of U.S. financial markets and the regulation of these markets. This perspective is essential to an understanding of the nature of recent financial innovation and the forces underlying it.

A.   Structure of U.S. Financial Markets

As is well known, the money and capital markets in the United States are among the largest and most highly developed in the world. Tables 1 and 2 provide a general idea of the size, scope and structure of these markets. Table 1 is a flow of funds table that shows total net new demands for and supplies of funds in U.S. credit markets in recent years in both dollar and percentage terms. In addition, the final column on the right side of the table shows total amounts outstanding at the end of 1983.[2] As the table indicates, total new credit flows in 1983 amounted to $515.5 billion. On the demand side, new government debt accounted for approximately 62 percent of the total, and new private debt made up the remainder. As section A2 of the table makes clear, the principal development affecting the structure of the demand for credit in the years shown has been the disproportionate growth of government debt and especially the growth of federal debt. The net increase in privately held federal debt rose from a little over 20 percent of total net demand in 1978 to almost 52 percent in 1983. Although part of this increase reflected normal cyclical developments,[3] the substantial increase in federal expenditures over the last two decades has produced a strong secular increase in the growth of federal demands for credit. Section B2 of the table shows the breakdown of the supply of funds across various categories of lenders. In 1983, commercial banks provided slightly less than 30 percent of new funds. All depository institutions (commercial banks plus thrift institutions) provided somewhat more than half of all funds.

Table 2 looks more specifically at the relative size of various classes of financial institutions using data on the stocks of financial assets held in 1983. As the data indicate, depository institutions as a group accounted for over half of the total; commercial banks held approximately a third.

Tables 1 and 2 focus on the structure of U.S. financial markets in terms of dollar flows and stocks. To appreciate fully the nature of the American financial system, however, one must take account of the institutional and geographic character of these markets. In general, financial markets are less centralized in the United States than in most other industrial countries. While New York City is clearly the financial center of the country, there are important regional market centers, including regional stock exchanges, in several other major cities. No-

TABLE 1
Demand for and Supply of Credit in U.S. Credit Markets

	1978	1979	1980	1981	1982	1983e	Amount Outstanding December 1983e
A. Net demand							
1. Annual net increases in amounts outstanding ($ billions)							
Privately held mortgages	$117.7	$113.1	$ 84.2	$ 73.7	$ 12.4	$ 67.0	$1,319.5
Corporate and foreign bonds	34.4	31.9	39.0	33.9	38.8	35.3	617.5
Total long-term private	152.1	144.9	123.2	107.6	51.1	102.3	1,937.0
Short-term business borrowing	92.2	98.0	67.6	118.6	55.5	44.9	853.5
Short-term household borrowing	52.4	49.3	9.8	35.1	23.9	49.9	575.4
Total short-term private	144.6	147.3	77.4	153.7	79.4	94.8	1,428.9
Privately held federal debt	86.5	78.6	119.5	128.9	210.9	265.9	1,504.2
Tax-exempt notes and bonds	32.5	27.8	31.9	29.2	63.6	52.6	474.7
Total government debt	119.0	106.5	151.3	158.2	274.5	318.5	1,978.9
Total	$415.7	$398.7	$351.9	$419.4	$405.0	$515.5	$5,344.8
2. Percentages[1]							
Privately held mortgages	28.3	28.4	23.9	17.6	3.1	13.0	24.7
Corporate and foreign bonds	8.3	8.0	11.1	8.1	9.6	6.8	11.6
Total long-term private	36.6	36.4	35.0	25.7	12.6	19.8	36.2
Short-term business borrowing	22.2	24.6	19.2	38.3	13.7	8.7	16.0
Short-term household borrowing	12.6	12.4	2.8	8.4	5.9	9.7	10.8
Total short-term private	34.8	36.9	22.0	36.6	19.6	18.4	26.7
Privately held federal debt	20.8	19.7	34.0	30.7	52.1	51.6	28.1
Tax-exempt notes and bonds	7.8	7.0	9.1	7.0	15.7	10.2	8.9
Total government debt	28.6	26.7	43.0	37.7	67.8	61.8	37.0
Total	100.0	100.0	100.0	100.0	100.0	100.0	100.0
B. Net supply							
1. Annual net increases in amounts outstanding ($ billions)							
Total nonbank finance	$174.5	$175.7	$152.0	$199.9	$178.5	$267.3	$2,423.2
Thrift institutions	72.8	56.7	54.9	27.2	30.6	126.2	949.5
Insurance, pensions, and endowments	72.4	62.0	68.2	72.4	91.0	109.1	998.8
Investment companies	6.6	29.3	15.9	72.4	52.3	8.0	213.2
Other nonbank finance	22.7	27.8	12.9	28.0	4.6	24.1	261.7
Commercial banks	126.1	122.2	101.8	108.9	108.5	146.3	1,600.3
Nonfinancial corporations	−0.9	7.5	−3.8	5.4	15.5	13.6	120.2
State and local governments	16.0	7.1	1.8	0.5	6.4	15.2	77.1
Foreign investors	38.0	−4.6	23.2	16.0	17.6	12.8	238.5
Residual: Households direct	61.8	90.6	76.9	88.7	78.5	60.3	885.1
Total	$415.7	$398.7	$351.9	$419.4	$405.0	$515.5	$5,344.8
2. Percentages[1]							
Total nonbank finance	42.0	44.1	43.2	47.7	44.1	51.9	45.3
Thrift institutions	17.5	14.2	15.6	6.5	7.6	24.5	17.8
Insurance, pensions, and endowments	17.4	15.6	19.4	17.3	22.5	21.2	18.7
Investment companies	1.6	7.3	4.5	17.3	12.9	1.6	4.0
Other nonbank finance	5.5	7.0	3.7	6.7	1.1	4.7	4.9
Commercial banks	30.3	30.6	28.9	26.0	26.8	28.4	29.9
Nonfinancial corporations	−0.2	1.9	−1.1	1.3	3.8	2.6	2.2
State and local governments	3.8	1.8	0.5	0.1	1.6	2.9	1.4
Foreign investors	9.1	−1.2	6.6	3.8	4.3	2.5	4.5
Residual: Households direct	14.9	22.7	21.9	21.1	19.4	11.7	16.6
Total	100.0	100.0	100.0	100.0	100.0	100.0	100.0

e Estimated.

[1] Details may not add to totals due to rounding.

Source: Kaufman, Henry, James McKeon and Steven Blitz, 1984 Prospects for Financial Markets, New York: Salomon Brothers, Inc., December 1983, p. 28.

TABLE 2
Financial Assets Held by U.S. Financial Institutions—
1983

	$ Billions	Percent of Total
Total depository institutions	$2,526.3	53.4
Commercial banks and affiliates	1,496.3	31.6
Foreign banking offices	67.7	1.4
Savings and loan associations	703.8	14.9
Mutual savings banks	169.4	3.6
Credit unions	89.1	1.9
Life insurance companies	514.4	10.9
Private pension funds	276.6	5.9
State and local government retirement funds	216.1	4.6
Finance companies	254.8	5.4
Mutual funds	54.1	1.1
Money market mutual funds	102.4	2.2
Sponsored credit agencies	236.2	5.0
Mortgage pools	244.9	5.2
Federal Reserve System	161.2	3.4
Other	141.2	3.0
Total	$4,728.2	100.0

Source: Board of Governors of the Federal Reserve System.

where is the relative decentralization of U.S. markets more apparent, however, than in the case of commercial banks.[4] As of the end of 1983 there were 14,454 insured commercial banks in the United States, of which 4,751 were national banks chartered by the federal government and the remainder were state banks chartered by the various state governments. Although several major international banking organizations are based in the United States, overall banking resources are considerably less concentrated than in most other countries. In December 1982, the 10 largest banking organizations based in the United States held only about 18 percent of total domestic deposits.

B.   The Regulation of U.S. Markets

A thorough review of the regulation of the U.S. financial system is beyond the scope of this paper.[5] The extent and intensity of regulation vary greatly across markets, from the minimal regulation of the market for U.S. government securities to the comprehensive regulation of commercial banks. It is the regulatory system applied to banks and other depository institutions that is most relevant to recent financial innovation in the United States. Therefore, the remainder of this section focuses primarily on banking regulation.

   1. Evolution of Banking Regulation in the United States.   Banking has been systematically regulated in the United States throughout the nation's history. The character of this regulatory apparatus has changed significantly from one period to the next, and it has been a major source of political controversy since the earliest days of the republic. Indeed, one of the principal political debates in the years immediately following the Revolution centered around the question of whether the federal government or the respective state governments should predominate in the regulation of banks.

This issue has never been fully resolved. The period from the Revolution until 1836 was one of constant tension. The majority of banks were chartered and supervised by the states. The federal government chartered only two banks in this period, the First Bank of the United States (1791–1811) and the Second Bank of the United States (1816–1836). These two banks, however, had branches nationwide, exercised some central banking functions, and, as a result, became principal targets for those who sought to restrict the growth of the power of the federal government.

When President Andrew Jackson vetoed the legislation that would have renewed the charter of the Second Bank, the states temporarily gained ascendancy in banking regulation. Further, between 1837 and 1860 a number of states adopted so-called free banking laws under which banks could be freely established as long as certain minimum, well-defined conditions regarding capital and collateralization of notes were met. This period has usually been regarded as an unsuccessful experiment with "laissez-faire" banking during which the absence of regulation led to abuses (by so-called wildcat banks) that demonstrated the need for greater regulation.[6] The extent of regulation began to increase gradually in the 1860s, and the federal government slowly but surely reestablished its participation with the passage of the National Banking Act in 1863 and the Federal Reserve Act in 1913.[7]

2. Foundation of the Present Regulatory System.   Although the history of banking regulation prior to the early 1930s has an important bearing on the present regulatory system, especially with regard to geographic restrictions on branching, the major force that shaped the current system was the reaction to the traumatic banking crisis that accompanied the Great Depression. Some monetary historians now attribute the crisis to the failure of the Federal Reserve System to provide adequate reserves to the banking system in the face of an international financial panic and a major worldwide economic contraction.[8] At the time, however, the upheaval was blamed mainly on (1) excessive competition in the provision of banking services and (2) speculative activity and conflicts of interest that resulted from the active participation of commercial banks in investment banking activities in the 1920s. The comprehensive banking legislation of the early 1930s, which is the foundation of the present regulatory system, was designed to correct these perceived weaknesses.

The main elements of this legislation were:

(a) Separation of Commercial and Investment Banking.   The Banking Act of 1933, known popularly as the Glass-Steagall Act, prohibited commercial banks from engaging in most underwriting and other investment banking activities. The idea was that commercial banks would invest primarily in short-term, "self-liquidating" commercial loans and other liquid assets in accordance with the real bills doctrine that was influential at the time. This effort to keep commercial banking separate from the securities industry and other commercial activities has been extended by more recent legislation, particularly the Bank Holding Company Act of 1956 and the 1970 amendments to that Act.

(b) Restrictions on the Payment of Interest on Deposits.   Banks were prohibited from paying interest on demand deposits, and the Federal Reserve was given the authority to set ceiling rates on time deposits. The Fed has regulated time deposit rates over the years through its Regulation Q.

(c) Deposit Insurance and Restrictions on Entry.   The Banking Act of 1933 established the Federal Deposit Insurance Corporation to administer a national

deposit insurance system. It set specific and generally restrictive conditions for the granting of national charters and indirectly set standards for state charters through the conditions imposed for admission to the insurance system.

(d) Maintenance of Geographic Restrictions on Branching.   The banking legislation of the 1930s left the restrictions on branching contained in the McFadden Act of 1927 unchanged. Under these restrictions, interstate branching was prohibited, and nationally chartered banks had to conform to any further restrictions imposed by state law in the states in which they operated.

The general thrust of this regulatory system is clear. Commercial banking was to be insulated from other financial and commercial activities. In order to promote stability, entry into the industry, entry into particular geographic markets, and price competition were to be severely limited. In the Hegelian dialectic, thesis generates forces producing antithesis, and the tension is eventually resolved through synthesis. In U.S. financial markets, the regulatory system established in the 1930s is the thesis, and the extensive financial innovation of recent years is the antithesis. The synthesis of these opposing forces is presently being formed.

II.   FORCES UNDERLYING RECENT FINANCIAL INNOVATION IN THE UNITED STATES

As suggested at the end of the preceding section, recent financial innovation in the United States is largely a reaction to the restrictive and essentially anti-competitive regulatory system established in the 1930s. The forces motivating this innovation have existed since the system came into being, but they have been greatly strengthened over the last 25 years by two essentially external developments: (1) accelerated technological progress in the computer and communications industries and (2) a secular increase in the rate of inflation accompanied by high and volatile interest rates. This section briefly describes these developments.

A.   Technological Advances

Technological progress in the computer and communications fields in recent years has led to a truly phenomenal reduction in the real cost of processing and transmitting data. It has been estimated that between the mid-1960s and 1980 computer processing costs declined at an average annual rate of 25 percent, and communications costs fell at a rate of 11 percent.[9] The impact of these developments has been especially great in banking and financial markets. In particular, the quantum reduction in real transactions costs has made it both feasible and profitable for banks to offer, and for business firms and households to use, sophisticated cash management techniques to reduce the proportion of liquid assets held in deposits or other instruments subject to interest rate ceilings. This same technology has made it feasible for nonbank financial institutions, such as securities firms, to offer financial products that combine their traditional investment services with transactions services that closely resemble those formerly provided exclusively by commercial banks. The Cash Management Account offered by Merrill Lynch, for example, which combines a conventional securities account with a credit line and a money market fund that has a third-party payments capability would not have been feasible in the absence of the ability to process, record and store large volumes of data relatively inexpensively. The same is true of a myriad of other cash management services now offered by both banks and other financial institutions and of the infrastructure that supports them such as electronic funds transfer systems and automated clearinghouses.

B. Inflation and Interest Rates

The technological developments described above would have had a substantial impact on cash-management practices in any event, but the incentive to develop these techniques has been greatly increased by the behavior of inflation and interest rates in the United States since roughly 1965. As indicated by Chart 1, the inflation rate was below 3 percent during most of the period between the Korean War and the mid-1960s. After 1964, the expansive fiscal and monetary policies associated with enlarged domestic social programs and the financing of the war in Vietnam and subsequently the petroleum shocks of the 1970s produced a steady if irregular increase in inflation to a peak rate exceeding 13 percent in 1980. While not particularly high by world standards, this was the highest peacetime inflation in modern American history.

The rise in inflation was accompanied by corresponding increases in the level and volatility of interest rates, which can be seen in Chart 2. Through most of the 1950s and early 1960s, the opportunity cost of holding noninterest-bearing demand deposits and savings or other time deposits subject to Regulation Q ceilings was either relatively low or nonexistent. The so-called credit crunch of 1966, however, was the first of a series of tight credit episodes during which market rates rose significantly above the Regulation Q ceilings. Initially, these episodes occasioned massive but generally temporary transfers of funds from accounts subject to the ceilings to market instruments, such as Treasury bills. This "disintermediation" of funds was both costly and disruptive. In particular, because the majority of mortgage credit in the 1960s and early 1970s was provided by savings and loan associations and other thrift institutions that derived most of their funds from time

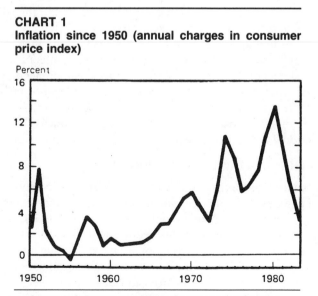

CHART 1
Inflation since 1950 (annual charges in consumer price index)

Source: U.S. Department of Labor, Bureau of Labor Statistics.

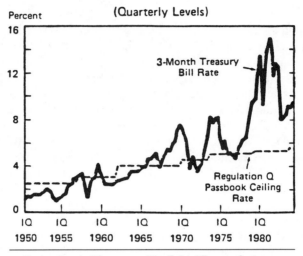

CHART 2
Interest Rates since 1950

Source: Board of Governors of the Federal Reserve System.

deposits subject to the ceilings, disintermediation led to severe periodic restrictions of the availability of credit to support residential construction. The housing and building trades lobbies are powerful political forces in the United States, and the disruption of these industries by disintermediation was an important factor leading to the reevaluation of banking regulation discussed below.

As Chart 2 shows, market interest rates have exceeded the Regulation Q passbook ceiling both substantially and continuously since the end of 1976.[10] As a result, the temporary disintermediation that characterized the period between 1965 and 1977 has been supplanted by the more comprehensive and permanent innovations described in the next section.

Aside from the higher *level* of interest rates and the incentives it has created, Chart 2 shows that the *variability* of rate movements has also increased sharply over the last decade.[11] This greater variability has increased uncertainty and risk in financial markets—particularly in markets for long-term securities. This increased interest-rate risk has created strong incentives for financial institutions to devise new financial instruments and develop new markets that make it possible for institutional and other investors to reduce their exposure to risk.

III. INNOVATION IN FINANCIAL MARKETS

The combination of forces and incentives described in Section II of this paper has produced a series of financial innovations in the United States that have become increasingly visible to the general public since the late 1950s. Rather than attempting an exhaustive inventory,[12] this section will focus on the major innovations. Special attention will be given to innovations in banking and depository markets, since these particular innovations have important implications for the conduct of monetary policy as well as the provision of financial services.[13] In addition to discussing the innovations themselves, the important movement toward the de-

TABLE 3
Major Actions to Deregulate Interest Rates on Deposits—1972–1983

Year	Action
1972	Negotiable Order of Withdrawal (NOW) accounts introduced in Massachusetts.
1973	"Wild card" experiment. Initial use of ceiling-free, small-denomination time deposits. Deposits had minimum maturity of four years. Experiment lasted four months.
1978	Introduction of six-month money market certificates with yields tied to six-month Treasury bill rate.
1979	Introduction of small saver certificates, with yields tied to U.S. Treasury securities with comparable maturities. Minimum maturity initially four years, but subsequently reduced.
1980	Passage of Depository Institutions Deregulation and Monetary Control Act.
	1. Set six-year phase out of interest rate ceilings on time deposits.
	2. Authorized NOW accounts nationwide, effective at the end of 1980.
1981	Introduction of nationwide NOW accounts.
	Introduction of ceiling-free Individual Retirement Accounts (IRAs).
1982	Introduction of several new accounts paying market rates.
	1. 91-day money market certificate.
	2. 3.5-year ceiling-free time deposit.
	3. 7–31 day time deposit.
	Passage of Garn-St Germain Act, which authorized money market deposit accounts.
1983	Nearly complete deregulation of interest rates on time deposits.
	1. Elimination of ceilings on all time deposits with original maturities exceeding 32 days.
	2. Elimination of all ceilings on time deposits with original maturities from 7 to 31 days with minimum balance of $2,500.

regulation of interest rates that is currently in progress will be summarized to date (see Table 3),[14] and the impact of these developments on the quantitative structure of depository markets will be detailed.

A. Innovation in Banking Markets

Innovation in banking and other depository markets has been proceeding at a rapid pace for at least a quarter of a century.[15] The initial developments primarily affected commercial banks and their corporate customers. By the end of the 1970s, however, it involved all depository institutions and a number of non-depository and even nonfinancial firms, and household as well as business customers.

1. The 1960s and Early 1970s: The "Cat and Mouse" Game between Banks and Regulators and Initial Steps toward Deregulation. By the late 1950s it had become apparent to most money center banks in the United States that many major corporate customers had sharpened their cash-management practices and found ways to lower their average holdings of noninterest-bearing deposits. Since these deposits were a major source of funds for these banks, it was essential that the banks react to this development, which they did with the introduction of large negotiable CDs in 1961. These CDs bore interest, although they were initially subject to the Regulation Q ceiling. The important thing about the negotiable CD was precisely that it was negotiable. Hence, when it neared maturity, it was essentially a marketable, interest-bearing liquid asset, in contrast to ordinary time deposits, which could not be transferred and could not bear interest at maturities under 30 days. The negotiable CD was a huge success in the early 1960s, and it allowed the money-center banks to regain at least temporarily much of the ground they had lost. Beyond that, the negotiable CD introduced the concept of "liability management,'' which dramatically altered the character of wholesale banking in the United States. Prior to that time, banks had depended primarily on demand deposits as their major funding source. Since banks were prohibited from paying explicit interest on these deposits, they compensated their business customers— and to a lesser degree their household customers—implicitly by providing them a variety of free services, especially payments services. The negotiable CD substituted explicit interest for implicit interest. By varying the rate of interest, banks could actively influence the volume of deposit inflows, rather than merely accepting deposits passively. Further, since negotiable CDs involved no payments services, their introduction moved banks in the direction of pure intermediation.[16] While these changes benefited banks in a number of ways, they also exposed them to the risk of unanticipated short-run swings in the cost of funds due to market forces beyond their control.

The volume of negotiable CDs grew steadily up to 1966, but the credit crunch of that year drove market rates well above the Regulation Q ceiling, and this condition persisted through most of the remainder of the decade. As a result, banks again experienced large outflows of funds and were driven to seek alternative sources not subject to the ceiling. There ensued what has been described as a ''cat and mouse'' game, in which banks would first develop either (1) a new source, such as borrowing Eurodollars from offshore affiliates, or (2) new short-term instruments, such as commercial paper issued by holding company affiliates and various forms of RP contracts. After a brief delay, the Federal Reserve would then step in, define the instrument as a deposit and subject it to the Regulation Q ceiling and to reserve requirements. In short, the 1960s illustrated the cycle of banking innovation, regulatory reaction and further innovation in an especially dynamic form.

While this process was fascinating to witness and highly profitable to the lawyers, accountants, and other specialists employed by it, it was also costly, both to individual institutions and to society as a whole in terms of its relatively inefficient use of real resources to avoid regulatory constraints. By the early 1970s, it had become apparent to financial economists and many public officials that the bank regulatory system that had been built in the 1930s was not an appropriate structure for the financial environment of the 1970s. Several events occurred in this period that were the initial steps in the deregulation process that reached its full stride in the early 1980s. *First,* in the face of continued disintermediation, the Regulation Q ceiling was lifted in 1970 for CDs over $100,000. *Second,* a Presidential Commission on Financial Structure and Regulation (the Hunt Commission) issued an important report at the end of 1971 that recommended, among other things, that all ceilings on time deposits be phased out over a five-year period and that both thrift institutions and banks be granted somewhat broader powers. Banks, in particular, would be allowed to underwrite some municipal revenue bonds and sell mutual funds.[17] *Finally,* so-called NOW (for negotiable order of withdrawal) accounts were introduced in several New England states beginning in 1972. These essentially transactions accounts were functionally equivalent to demand deposits but they bore explicit interest. NOW accounts were originally devised by thrift institutions as a means of competing more effectively with commercial banks for retail customers, but their broader significance was that they were the first financial innovation to have a direct (and beneficial) effect on ordinary retail customers as opposed to corporations and wealthy individuals.

2. 1975–1983: Accelerated Innovation, Increased Competition, and Deregulation.   As indicated in Chart 2, the sustained rise in market interest rates well above Regulation Q ceilings after 1976 greatly increased the incentive for banks to devise means to circumvent the restriction. The rise in rates also increased the opportunity cost of the noninterest-bearing reserves that banks that were members of the Federal Reserve System were required to hold, which caused many banks to drop their membership and created strong incentives to devise instruments not subject to reserve requirements. Finally, as suggested above, technological advances coupled with the relatively high profitability of banking activities created powerful incentives for nonbank institutions to enter banking markets and provide bank and quasi-bank services. These conditions ignited an explosion of financial innovation and subsequent deregulation in depository markets over the eight-year period between 1975 and 1983.

A key innovation in this period was the money market mutual fund (MMMF).[18] These funds are pools of liquid assets managed by investment companies that sell small denomination shares in the funds to the public. Although the funds are not covered by deposit insurance, they are backed fully by high-quality liquid assets, are not subject to rate ceilings or reserve requirements, and in some cases allow limited third-party transactions. Aggregate MMMF assets grew rapidly after 1976, from $3.3 billion in 1977 to $76.3 billion in 1980 to $186.9 billion in 1981. (See Chart 3.)

The growth of MMMFs put enormous competitive pressure on U.S. banks. The banks, in turn, put substantial pressure on the regulatory agencies and

---

CHART 3
Growth of Money Market Mutual Fund (MMMF) Balances in the U.S., 1973–1983

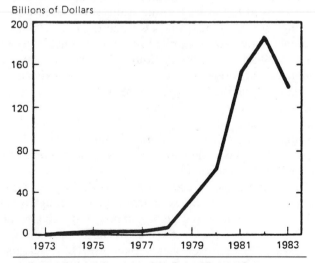

Billions of Dollars

Source: Board of Governors of the Federal Reserve System

Congress for relief. The first response to this pressure was the authorization of so-called money market certificates (MMC) by the regulatory agencies. These certificates had no third-party payment capability, but they were covered by deposit insurance, and they had a rate ceiling that floated with the six-month Treasury bill rate.

The MMCs were generally well received, but they did not significantly reduce the growth of MMMFs. Intense political pressure for further deregulation developed and culminated in the passage of the Depository Institutions Deregulation and Monetary Control Act in March 1980. This watershed legislation was the most comprehensive banking law enacted by Congress since the Banking Acts of 1933 and 1935. It has a large number of diverse provisions, but the critical ones were the following:

1. All interest-rate ceilings on time deposits were to be phased out over a six-year period.
2. NOW accounts were authorized for all banks and thrift institutions nation-wide, effective December 31, 1980. (The accounts can be offered to individuals but not to corporations.)
3. State usury laws that put ceilings on mortgage rates were to be eliminated unless a state government specifically passed a law reinstating the ceiling.
4. The restrictions on the ability of thrift institutions, such as savings and loan associations, to invest in other assets than residential mortgages were eased somewhat.
5. All depository institutions were given access to the Federal Reserve discount window and to other Fed services, but they were also subjected to Federal Reserve reserve requirements.

The importance of this legislation in the context of the historical perspective developed earlier in this article should be apparent. In particular, the lifting of interest-rate restrictions in items 1, 2, and 3 above reversed a fundamental element—and, implicitly, a fundamental premise—of the 1930s legislation: that price (i.e., interest rate) competition in banking markets is unhealthy.

The final steps in the process of deregulation to date were taken in 1982 and 1983 following passage of the Garn-St Germain Act in late 1982. Like the 1980 law, this act contained numerous detailed provisions, but the most important authorized banks and other depository institutions to offer accounts with characteristics similar to those of MMMFs. In accordance with this legislation, banks and thrifts introduced money market deposit accounts (MMDAs) in December 1982. Subsequently, so-called Super NOW accounts were introduced in January 1983. Neither of these instruments is subject to a rate ceiling. The principal difference between the two accounts is that there are no limits on the number of third-party payments transactions that can be made with a Super NOW account, while there are limits in the case of MMDA accounts. Since Super NOWs have more of the characteristics of pure transactions accounts than MMDAs, they are subject to the same reserve requirements as ordinary demand deposits and other transactions accounts. MMDAs are considered savings deposits, which are not subject to reserve requirements. Further, Super NOWs, because of their greater transactions powers, typically have lower yields than MMDAs.[19] Unlike MMMFs, both MMDAs and Super NOWs are covered by federal deposit insurance. At present, however, both instruments require a $1,000 minimum balance.

CHART 4
Comparison of the Growth of MMMFs and MMDAs

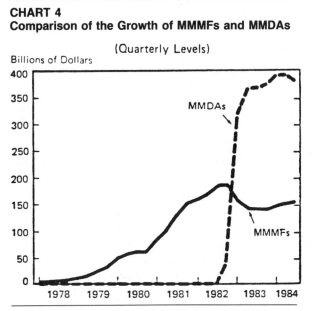

(Quarterly Levels)

Source: Board of Governors of the Federal Reserve System.

The authorization of MMDAs and Super NOWs has done much to restore the competitive position of commercial banks and thrifts in depository markets. Since most MMMFs, like MMDAs, limit the number of third-party payments the holder of an account can make, these two instruments are generally similar, and it is appropriate to compare their growth since the introduction of MMDAs. As Chart 4 shows, MMDAs grew explosively immediately following their introduction to a dollar level of approximately $350 billion, well above the peak level attained by MMMFs.[20] The level of MMMFs declined markedly in this period, and some market professionals predicted their eventual demise. The funds have made a strong effort to restore their competitive position by improving their products, however, and as the chart shows, the funds appear to be maintaining their position in 1984.

3. **The Quantitative Impact of Innovation and Deregulation on the Structure of Depository Markets.** The innovations and resulting deregulation in depository markets have had a profound impact on the structure and cost of bank and thrift liabilities. Table 4 shows the principal instruments as percentages of the total from 1959 through 1983. In 1959, noninterest-bearing demand deposits accounted for 41.1 percent of the liabilities shown in the table. Passbook savings deposits subject to a ceiling rate accounted for most of the remainder. By 1975, just prior to the accelerated deregulation of the late 1970s, the demand deposit share had declined to 19.7 percent. By 1983, the share had dropped further to 10.5 percent, and the Regulation Q ceilings had been lifted on all time deposits with the exception of passbook savings accounts. Of particular importance in the current situation, the category of "other checkable deposits" (column 3 in the table), which includes ordinary NOW accounts, Super NOWs, and other interest-bearing transactions accounts, has been rising rapidly since 1980, while the demand

TABLE 4
Principal Liabilities of Depository Institutions, Year-end 1959–1983 (percentage of total[1])

(1)	(2)	(3)	(4)	(5)	(6)	(7)	(8)	(9)	(10)
		Other			Small	Large			
	Demand	Checkable		Savings	Time	Time	Term	Term	
Year	Deposits	Deposits[2]	MMDAs	Deposits	Deposits	Deposits	RPs	Eurodollars	Total
1959	41.1	0.0	0.0	54.0	4.2	0.4	0.0	0.3	100.0
1960	39.2	0.0	0.0	55.5	4.4	0.7	0.0	0.3	100.0
1961	37.3	0.0	0.0	56.2	4.7	1.2	0.0	0.4	100.0
1962	34.6	0.0	0.0	57.0	5.9	2.0	0.0	0.5	100.0
1963	32.5	0.0	0.0	57.3	6.8	2.9	0.0	0.5	100.0
1964	31.0	0.0	0.0	57.5	7.1	3.7	0.0	0.6	100.0
1965	29.6	0.0	0.0	57.5	7.7	4.7	0.0	0.4	100.0
1966	28.8	0.0	0.0	54.1	11.8	4.9	0.0	0.4	100.0
1967	27.8	0.0	0.0	50.9	15.0	6.0	0.0	0.4	100.0
1968	27.5	0.0	0.0	47.6	17.8	6.6	0.0	0.5	100.0
1969	27.9	0.0	0.0	46.4	21.2	3.6	0.5	0.5	100.0
1970	26.5	0.0	0.0	41.5	24.2	7.2	0.3	0.3	100.0
1971	24.5	0.0	0.0	40.4	26.4	8.0	0.4	0.4	100.0
1972	23.4	0.0	0.0	38.8	28.0	8.9	0.4	0.4	100.0
1973	22.0	0.0	0.0	35.6	29.0	12.1	0.7	0.6	100.0
1974	20.9	0.0	0.0	34.0	28.9	14.5	0.8	0.8	100.0
1975	19.7	0.1	0.0	35.7	31.0	11.9	0.8	0.9	100.0
1976	18.4	0.2	0.0	37.2	32.1	9.7	1.2	1.2	100.0
1977	17.5	0.3	0.0	36.0	32.7	10.6	1.4	1.5	100.0
1978	16.7	0.6	0.0	31.7	34.4	12.9	1.8	2.1	100.0
1979	16.0	1.0	0.0	25.9	38.9	13.6	1.8	2.7	100.0
1980	15.1	1.6	0.0	22.7	41.3	14.6	2.0	2.8	100.0
1981	12.5	4.1	0.0	18.3	43.7	15.9	2.0	3.6	100.0
1982	11.7	5.0	2.1	17.6	41.7	16.0	2.0	4.0	100.0
1983	10.5	5.5	16.1	13.4	34.0	14.0	2.4	4.0	100.0

[1] Details may not add to totals due to rounding.
[2] Other Checkable Deposits includes negotiable order of withdrawal (NOW) and automatic transfer service (ATS) accounts of depository institutions, credit union share draft accounts, and demand deposits at thrift institutions.
Source: Board of Governors of the Federal Reserve System.

deposit category has been declining. This trend will almost certainly continue in the years ahead.

The changes manifested in Table 4 have obvious implications for U.S. depository institutions. First, although in the past banks and other depositories paid implicit interest in a variety of forms on demand deposits and other liabilities that did not yield explicit interest, there can be little doubt that deregulation has raised the average cost of funds for many of these institutions, especially in recent years[1]. This increase has forced the adoption of more systematic and explicit pricing policies for loans and other services and has probably reduced cross-subsidization across various categories of customers. Second, the trend toward explicit interest has increased short-run variations in the cost of funds. This has made it necessary for depository institutions, like other financial and nonfinancial firms, to "manage" interest-rate risk to a much greater extent than formerly, by either shortening loan maturities, making loan rates variable, or hedging the risk in futures markets.

4. The Present Situation: Further Increases in Competition from Nondepository

Institutions, Consolidation in the Supply of Financial Services, and the Demise of Geographic Restrictions.   While changes in the level and variability of the cost of funds have had important effects on depository institutions in recent years, the increased competition from nondepository institutions has been equally significant. In addition to the competition from MMMFs, there have been several mergers involving large investment banks and insurance companies, and some of the largest nonfinancial companies in the nation have recently added an array of additional financial service activities to their existing installment credit operations. The purpose of these consolidations is the creation of financial service conglomerates capable of providing comprehensive financial services, including banking services, to business firms and households. As an example, Sears Roebuck, the country's largest retail chain, has recently acquired a large investment bank and a large real estate finance company and linked these operations to its existing insurance, credit card, and other financial services. By offering these services through its vast chain of retail stores, Sears can reach virtually every geographic market in the United States. Merrill Lynch, American Express, and other large companies are rapidly building similar financial service conglomerates.

Although it is difficult to quantify the degree of this competition in the aggregate, some idea of the order of magnitude is conveyed by diverse statistics. At the end of 1981, the financial service subsidiaries of three large manufacturing companies (General Electric, Ford, and General Motors) held $45.8 billion of consumer installment credit, compared to the $27.7 billion held worldwide by Citicorp, the Bank of America, and Chase Manhattan. At the end of the same year, total business lending (commercial and industrial loans, commercial mortgage loans, and lease financing) by 32 nonbank companies was slightly over $100 billion, one third of the total outstanding at the 15 largest bank holding companies.[21]

In their effort to compete still more directly with banks and other depositories, a number of nonbank financial service providers have acquired commercial banks in recent years. In order to avoid being classified legally as bank holding companies and therefore subjected to banking regulation, the acquiring companies have then taken advantage of a provision in the current bank holding company law that defines a bank as an institution that both (1) offers demand deposits and (2) makes commercial loans. After the elimination of one of these two activities from the acquired bank's operations, the bank is no longer a bank in the eyes of the law, and the acquiring company is not a bank holding company. These affiliates, thus transformed, have earned the awkward designation "nonbank banks." Since nonbank banks are not banks, they are not subject to the remaining restrictions on banks, notably geographic branching restrictions. Therefore, there is no legal barrier to prevent a nonbank financial-service provider from establishing a national network of nonbank banks, which enormously increases the deposit base on which the company can draw. In the view of many observers, nonbank banks constitute a rather blatant circumvention of the Glass-Steagall Act, and they were the subject of much regulatory and legislative attention in the United States in 1984. Both houses of Congress passed bills that would have redefined a bank in such a way as to include most existing nonbank banks. For various reasons, no final bill was enacted, but the issue is almost certain to surface again in 1985.

The trend toward consolidation in the supply of financial services has not been restricted to nonbank and nondepository companies. Both banks and bank holding companies have sought to enter a variety of nonbanking industries throughout the postwar period, and their efforts have intensified in recent years.[22] Although Congress does not appear to be prepared to repeal the main provisions of the Glass-Steagall Act, an omnibus bill passed by the Senate in the summer of 1984 would have permitted bank holding companies to underwrite municipal revenue bonds and engage in several other previously proscribed activities. In addition, the Federal Reserve has approved the acquisition of discount brokerage companies (which trade but do not underwrite securities) by bank holding companies, and this action has been upheld in the federal courts.[23]

Apart from their efforts to expand into nonbanking activities, the larger bank holding companies are presently strengthening their effort to dismantle, de facto if not de jure, the remaining restrictions on geographic expansion. As noted earlier, banks and bank holding companies have not generally been permitted to carry on full banking operations across state lines. Many bank holding companies, however, operate numerous nonbank affiliates, such as consumer finance companies, in several states,[24] and, in a somewhat ironic twist, several bank holding companies have recently announced their intention to establish interstate chains of retail-oriented nonbank banks known as "consumer banks." Finally, in accordance with a provision of the bank holding company law that allows bank holding companies based in one state to operate banks in another state if the government of the second state specifically permits it, a number of states in particular regions are presently establishing or attempting to establish reciprocal regional interstate banking agreements. These agreements would permit bank holding companies based in the region to operate banks in any state in the region but would preclude entry by banks based outside the region.[25] In the absence of specific legislation halting these various developments, an acceleration of the growth of interstate banking activities appears likely in the years immediately ahead.

5. Summary. The powerful innovative forces unleashed by rising inflation and advancing technology have substantially eroded the restrictive bank regulatory structure that emerged from the Great Depression. This erosion has had three principal effects. *First,* the structure of bank funds, the average cost of these funds, and the stability of the cost of funds have all changed dramatically since 1960. These changes have greatly altered the character of banking operations in the United States. *Second,* although the legal separation of banking and other lines of commerce remains in force, the actual boundary has become increasingly blurred, due to the ability of nonbank institutions to offer depositlike products and services and the expansion of bank holding companies into nonbanking activities. *Finally,* geographic restrictions on banking operations have lost much of their force in recent years.

It is still too early to determine whether these developments have strengthened American banking markets or weakened them, and what the longer-run effect on the welfare of the general public will be. Although the overall profitability of U.S. banks is still relatively high, the current strains in the American banking and thrift industries are well known. The number of insured banks closed due to financial difficulties in 1983 (48) was the highest in any year since the 1930s. The extent to which these strains are the result of innovation and deregulation is not clear, nor is it clear how these difficulties will affect innovation and deregulation in the future. The final section of this article will speculate briefly on the prospects.

B. Other Innovations

The innovations in banking markets just described have been particularly visible to the average American citizen, and they have far-reaching implications. The same forces driving innovation in banking, however, have also produced important innovations in other financial markets. Developments in the securities markets and in mortgage markets have been especially dramatic, in the form of both new instruments and markets and changes in the character of existing instruments and markets. The common theme in nearly all of these innovations has been the effort to reduce the risk occasioned by the heightened volatility of interest rates. It would be difficult to list all of these developments, but some of the more important are the following.

1. Bond Markets.   A sizable proportion of corporate bonds issued in domestic U.S. markets currently are floating-rate bonds, and the remaining fixed-rate issues frequently have early call or put provisions. Further, the volume of zero-coupon bonds, which pay their return in the form of price appreciation, rather than coupon-interest payments, and therefore present no reinvestment risk, has grown significantly since 1980.

2. Mortgage Markets.   A majority of the residential mortgages issued in the United States at present are adjustable-rate mortgages (ARMs), which permit the lender to vary the interest rate during the term of the loan, usually on specified dates and subject to specified restrictions. Also, a large and active market for securities backed by pools of mortgages has developed, which has increased the volume of mortgage lending by insurance companies and pension funds and thus insulated the market to some extent from the difficulties currently plaguing the thrift industry as a result of the secular rise in interest rates. On balance, these innovations appear to have benefited both the residential construction industry and home buyers, since the recovery of the homebuilding sector of the economy following the 1981–82 recession was strong. There is presently considerable concern, however, that the existence of a large stock of variable-rate mortgage debt will increase the incidence of default if and when interest rates come under renewed upward pressure.

3. Futures Markets.   Trading in interest-rate futures in the United States has grown rapidly since the first market opened in 1975. There are currently markets for six instruments: mortgage-backed securities guaranteed by the Government National Mortgage Association (GNMA), U.S. Treasury bonds, U.S. Treasury bills, domestic bank CDs, Eurodollars, and U.S. Treasury notes. The existence of these markets and their increasing depth make it possible for both institutions and individuals to hedge their exposure to interest-rate movements considerably more cheaply than is possible in cash markets.[26] Because it is possible, however, for market participants motivated by a desire to speculate, rather than a desire to hedge, to engage in futures transactions with relatively small cash outlays, it is not yet clear whether the existence of futures markets has reduced or increased the overall level of risk in financial markets.

This section has focused on the impact of recent financial innovation on the structure and behavior of markets. The next section examines the implications for monetary policy.

IV.   THE EFFECT OF INNOVATION ON U.S. MONETARY POLICY

In addition to their impact on markets, innovation and deregulation have led to an intensive and extensive reexamination of the conduct of monetary policy in the United States, and this reexamination in turn has clearly affected the substance of policy actions in some recent years. This section will briefly describe the present strategy of U.S. monetary policy and then indicate some of the principal questions and operational problems that innovation and deregulation have raised regarding this strategy.

A.   The Current Strategy of U.S. Monetary Policy

The evolution of U.S. monetary policy in the postwar period has been a long and rather diffuse process. Although there has always been some attention to monetary conditions—as opposed to credit conditions—and the behavior of monetary aggregates, it is probably accurate to say that most of the emphasis in the actual conduct of policy in the 1950s and 1960s was on the effect of the Federal Reserve's policy actions on the availability and cost of credit in short-term credit markets.

Since about 1970, however, increased attention has been given to monetary conditions and, specifically, to the growth rates of various measures of the money supply. This increased focus on money, which has also developed in several other industrial countries in the same period, has resulted partly from the rise of "monetarism" to prominence in the academic literature on monetary policy in the late 1960s and early 1970s and partly from dissatisfaction with the perceived failure of credit- and interest-rate-oriented policies to deal effectively with the secular rise in inflation.

As a result of these developments, the present stated strategy of Federal Reserve policy centers around control of the monetary aggregates.[27] At the beginning of each year, the Fed establishes a target range for the growth rate of each monetary aggregate from the fourth quarter of the preceding year to the fourth quarter of the current year. It then monitors the actual growth of the aggregates in relation to the targets and acts to correct deviations from the targets unless it feels that unanticipated economic or financial developments warrant the deviation. The ultimate objective of this strategy is to contribute to the stabilization of both economic conditions in general and the behavior of prices in particular. For this reason, the strategy is often referred to as one of using monetary aggregates as "intermediate" targets of policy.

It is obvious that the successful implementation of this strategy requires a stable and predictable relationship between the monetary aggregates targeted and the ultimate objectives of monetary policy, such as the rate of growth of nominal GNP and the behavior of the price level. It is widely asserted that recent financial innovation and deregulation have weakened this relationship in the United States and made it less predictable. Further, some monetary economists believe that innovation and deregulation have reduced the ability of the Fed to control the growth of the aggregates effectively. The remainder of this section summarizes the evidence supporting these contentions.

B. Evidence of Instability in the Relationship between the Monetary Aggregates and Nominal GNP in the United States

1. Possible Downward Shifts in Money Demand, 1975 and 1980–81. The problems encountered in the conduct of U.S. monetary policy have stimulated considerable new research over the last decade on the relationship between money and GNP. Much of this research has taken the form of empirical estimation and reestimation of conventional Goldfeld-type money-demand equations or variations of these equations using the M1 aggregate, coupled with tests of the ability of the equations to predict the longer-run growth of the monetary aggregates in the out-of-sample period.[28] Table 5 reproduces a table from a recent article by Porter and Offenbacher[29] that presents empirical evidence typical of that produced by much of this research. The table shows both the annual and cumulative errors in the predicted growth of M1[30] from a standard money demand equation over the 1967–74 and 1974–81 periods, respectively. The annual growth-rate errors suggest that there may have been downward shifts in the demand for money in relation to income in 1975 and again in 1980 and 1981. Economists who believe that such shifts in fact occurred generally attribute them to financial innovation and deregulation. Improved cash-management techniques in the corporate sector are thought to be mainly responsible for the shift in 1975. More careful management in the household sector—made possible by the introduction of MMMFs—is thought to have contributed significantly to the shift in 1980 and 1981.[31]

2. The Unusual Behavior of M1 Velocity, 1982–83. A further instance of apparent instability in the relationship between M1 and nominal GNP occurred during the recession in 1982 and the recovery from that recession in 1983. In contrast to the possible downward shifts in money demand in 1975 and 1980–81, M1 grew unusually rapidly in relation to nominal GNP in the 1982–83 period. This can be depicted by charting the growth of M1 velocity (i.e., the ratio of nominal GNP to M1, as in Chart 5). As the chart makes clear, while velocity typically declines or grows more slowly in recessions than in other stages of the business cycle, the decline was much sharper in the 1981–82 recession than in any other cycle since the 1950s. Research done by the staff of the Board of Governors of the Federal Reserve suggests that the introduction of interest-bearing NOW accounts (which are included in M1 as it is presently defined) has increased the interest elasticity of M1 demand in a manner that could not have been easily predicted in advance.[32] An implication of this view is that further deregulation may also change the parameters of the M1 money-demand function in ways that cannot be anticipated. Research done at the Federal Reserve Bank of San Francisco, however, indicates that the unusual behavior of velocity in 1982 and 1983 can be explained by (1) the decline in inflation in 1982 and (2) the precipitous drop in interest rates in the third quarter of 1982 in the context of a stable money-demand function.[33]

C. Effect of the Evidence of Instability on the Recent Conduct of Monetary Policy and Policy Research

As one might expect, the evidence of possible instability in the money-GNP relationship has raised doubts regarding the feasibility of continuing to use intermediate money supply targets as a central element in the strategy of U.S. policy.

TABLE 5
Out-of-Sample Errors[1] from a Goldfeld M1 Equation for 1967:1 to 1974:2 and 1974:3 to 1981:4

Date	Cumulative Percentage Error	Annual Growth-Rate Errors	Date	Cumulative Percentage Error	Annual Growth-Rate Errors
1967:1	−0.2		1974:3	1.2	
:2	−0.3		:4	3.0	
:3	−1.0		1975:1	5.1	
:4	−1.0	−1.1	:2	5.4	
1968:1	−0.8		:3	5.9	
:2	−0.9		:4	7.6	4.8
:3	−1.5		1976:1	7.8	
:4	−1.9	−0.9	:2	7.5	
1969:1	−2.3		:3	8.2	
:2	−1.6		:4	8.6	0.9
:3	−0.5		1977:1	8.3	
:4	−0.3	1.7	:2	8.9	
1970:1	−0.1		:3	9.2	
:2	0.1		:4	8.9	0.3
:3	−0.2		1978:1	8.5	
:4	−0.1	0.2	:2	9.4	
1971:1	0.9		:3	9.9	
:2	0.8		:4	10.6	1.7
:3	0.4		1979:1	11.9	
:4	1.2	1.4	:2	11.7	
1972:1	1.7		:3	11.5	
:2	1.7		:4	11.9	1.2
:3	1.2		1980:1	12.6	
:4	0.5	−0.8	:2	16.3	
1973:1	0.2		:3	15.3	
:2	0.7		:4	14.8	2.8
:3	0.7		1981:1	18.0	
:4	0.7	1.0	:2	18.1	
1974:1	1.4		:3	20.8	
:2	2.6		:4	22.1	6.4

	1967:1 to 1974:2		1974:3 to 1981:4	
	Annualized Quarterly Growth Rates	Annual Growth Rates	Annualized Quarterly Growth Rates	Annual Growth Rates
Mean error	0.4	0.2	2.6	2.6
Root mean Square error	2.1	1.1	4.7	3.3

[1] Error is predicted value minus actual value.
  Source: Richard D. Porter and Edward K. Offenbacher, "Financial Innovation and Measurement of Monetary Aggregates," in Federal Reserve Bank of St. Louis (1984), table 3–1, pp. 53–4.

In this regard, it should be noted that much of this evidence pertains to M1. And M1, which is the narrowest of the aggregates, is intended to be a measure of transactions balances, and it has generally received more attention than the broader monetary aggregates from the general public. One of the results of the events in 1982 and 1983 just described was a temporary change in the operational emphasis of policy away from M1 in the direction of the broader measures. In particular, the Fed announced in late 1982 that it was deemphasizing M1 and

CHART 5
Four-Quarter Growth Rates of the Velocity of M1

Percent   (Quarterly)

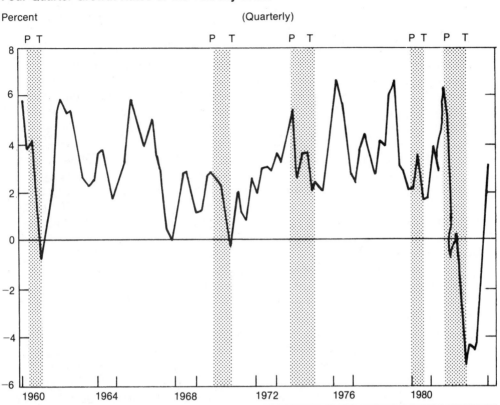

Note: shaded areas are recessions.
Source: Board of Governors of the Federal Reserve System and U.S. Department of Commerce, Bureau of Economic Analysis.

giving greater weight to M2 and M3 in its operations. Further, in 1983, the Fed established a range for the growth of a broad measure of total credit for the first time, partly in response to arguments that M1 had lost its meaning.[34] The emergence of a more normal pattern in the behavior of M1 velocity in the latter part of 1983 and the first half of 1984, however, led to the restoration of M1 to target status in July 1984.

As noted in the discussion of prospects for monetary policy in the next section of this article, the Fed has come under pressure from several quarters recently to drop its money supply targets in favor of one of several alternative strategies. To date, the Fed itself has given no indication that it is planning to take such a step. Indeed, much of the research done by the staff of the Board of Governors of the Fed in recent years has been aimed at improving the technical foundation for the continued use of a monetary aggregates strategy.

This research has taken two separate directions. *First,* an effort has been made to improve the specification of money demand equations in order to improve their performance. An example of this research is the Simpson-Porter model of money demand, which includes a so-called ratchet variable designed to capture the impact of cash-management innovations induced by the successively higher interest rate peaks in the 1970s and early 1980s.[35] Although inclusion of this variable does not eliminate the overprediction of money demand shown in Table 5, it reduces it significantly.

The *second* area of research has focused on the construction of alternative monetary aggregates known as Divisia aggregates using the theory of index numbers.[36] Conventional monetary aggregates such as M1 are simple summations of their various components with no attention given in the aggregation process to differences in the monetary services provided by the components. For example, M1 as it is currently defined, includes (1) currency and demand deposits, which pay no explicit interest but provide a wide range of transactions services, and (2) several interest-bearing accounts, such as conventional NOW accounts and Super NOW accounts, which are also partly transactions instruments, but which provide some savings services (i.e., store of value services) as well. Divisia aggregation takes account of these differences by assigning different weights to the components of an aggregate in constructing the aggregate. To be specific, the weight attached to each component is determined by the spread between the market yield paid on a nonmonetary asset, such as commercial paper, and the explicit own yield paid on the component in question. This spread is the opportunity cost of holding the component (in terms of explicit interest foregone) and is assumed to be a reasonable proxy for the rental cost of the monetary services provided by the component and, therefore, for the flow of services themselves. In this way, the highest weights are assigned to assets like currency that have the highest spreads and, therefore, presumably yield the greatest flow of monetary services.

Although Divisia aggregation would appear to be superior in principle to conventional simple-sum aggregation, empirical results using these aggregates have been mixed. In recent dynamic simulations using two money demand specifications,[37] the Divisia aggregates generally outperformed their conventional counterparts in the case of the broader aggregates, but they yielded inferior results in the case of the narrower aggregates, such as M1. For this reason, and in view of the obvious difficulties the Fed would encounter in communicating its objectives to the public if it were to substitute the Divisia aggregates for the standard aggregates in setting its monetary targets, it is unlikely that the Divisia measures will play a major operational role in the actual implementation of policy in the foreseeable future. Continued research with these measures, however, and informal monitoring of their behavior, may help the Fed avoid being misled by temporarily aberrant behavior of the conventional aggregates due to innovation and deregulation.

V. PROSPECTS AND CONCLUSIONS[38]

To this point, this article has dealt with the past and the present. This section will look to the future and speculate on how the lingering effects of the innovation that has already occurred and the effects of further innovation may influence the structure and functioning of financial markets and the conduct of monetary policy in the years ahead. Long and sometimes unhappy experience has taught the author that forecasting is the most dangerous of all the professional activities economists engage in. Accordingly, the speculative comments that follow will focus primarily on the relatively near-term future through the remainder of the 1980s.

A. Prospects for the Financial Markets and the Provision of Financial Services

As noted above, American financial institutions—especially commercial banks and thrift institutions—have come under severe pressure in recent years, due to rising competition from external sources, the impact of deregulation on the cost of funding, the apparent deterioration in the quality of some bank loan portfolios, and the increased incidence of bank failures. As a result of these developments and the concern they have stimulated both in the political arena and among regulatory agencies, the pace of deregulation slowed in 1984, and it may well remain lower in the near-term future.

The forces driving the longer-run process of innovation and deregulation, however, are still very much alive, and the process, therefore, is likely to continue in the absence of a major financial catastrophe. Several developments seem probable in the years immediately ahead. *First,* one of the measures available to deal with the current weakness of some thrift institutions and the associated risk is a more lenient stance by the regulators toward acquisitions of thrifts by bank holding companies. Such consolidations would further blur the distinctions between various categories of depository institutions. *Second,* the breakdown of the barriers to interstate banking is almost certain to continue. At the moment, it appears that the next stage of this process will take the form of regional agreements that exclude the money-center banks, but the latter can be expected to press hard for equitable access to these markets, and it is possible they will receive judicial relief under the anti-trust laws. *Finally,* the line of separation between (1) banking and (2) other financial and nonfinancial activities is likely to be eroded further as banks and nonbank institutions both seek to expand further into the other group's territory. In particular, there is a fairly high probability that legislation will be passed in the relatively near future allowing banks to underwrite municipal revenue bonds and perhaps securities backed by mortgage pools, since the potential for abuse seems minimal in these areas.

The examples just given relate to near-term prospects and are relatively narrow in scope. The larger and more important issue is: What will the structure of U.S. banking and financial markets look like in 1990? Will there be such significant further erosion of product-line barriers that banks and other companies meld into "department stores" of finance? Will small banks and other small financial institutions be swallowed up by larger institutions? It is impossible to do more than guess at the answers to these questions. Some further consolidation across product lines may occur. But many of the conflicts of interest and other risks that the Glass-Steagall Act attempted to prevent are still perceived to be real dangers, so it is unlikely that the basic legal barrier between banking and commerce will be dismantled in the foreseeable future. Perhaps more fundamentally, the microeconomics of such consolidations is not well understood at present. Specifically, the extent of joint economies in the production and consumption of diverse financial services is not known. In these circumstances, it seems likely that a substantial degree of specialization in the provision of financial services will persist, even if a further dismantling of the regulatory barriers occurs. In a similar way, since there is no clear evidence of significant economies of scale in banking, the specter of large bank holding companies absorbing most small community-oriented banks seems far-fetched, although there will probably be some reduction in the number of independent banking organizations operating in the country.

Two final comments should be made regarding the prospects for change in (1) the structure of the financial regulatory agencies and (2) the system of federal deposit insurance. Suggestions have been made for many years for changes that would simplify the currently cumbersome structure of U.S. financial regulatory agencies, which involves a mixture of federal and state agencies and the existence of several agencies with somewhat overlapping responsibilities at the federal level. The most recent formal recommendations were announced in early 1984 by the Task Group on Regulation of Financial Institutions chaired by Vice President Bush.[39] Among other things, these recommendations called for simplifying the structure at the federal level by assigning the responsibility for regulating and supervising all but the largest banking organizations to a new agency built around the present Office of the Comptroller of the Currency. Responsibility for the largest organizations would be vested in the Federal Reserve. If past experience is any guide, resistance by the affected agencies and their constituencies will prevent the early adoption of these recommendations.

Regarding the deposit insurance system, the failure of the Continental Illinois Bank and the events leading up to that failure have brought earlier recommendations for reform of the system to the attention of both the Congress and the public.[40] Many of these recommendations are for changes that would reduce the danger that the existence of deposit insurance might tempt banks to take risks they would otherwise avoid. Examples of the suggested changes are reductions in the coverage of time deposits, permitting private insurance companies to compete with government agencies in providing insurance, and permitting graduated premiums that reflect the relative risk of failure of individual institutions. Despite their logical appeal, these recommendations raise a number of questions. What criteria, for example, would be used to determine relative risk in administering graduated premiums? These kinds of questions plus the broad public support for the present insurance system make it unlikely that wholesale changes will be forthcoming at an early date unless further disruptions in banking markets force them.

B.   Prospects Regarding Monetary Policy

As pointed out in Section IV of this paper, the evidence of a reduction in the stability of the empirical relationship between the U.S. money supply and nominal GNP has caused some observers to question whether the Federal Reserve should continue to follow a strategy of using monetary aggregates as intermediate policy targets. The conventional theory of short-run economic stabilization[41] implies that if the monetary sector of the economy is less stable and predictable than other sectors—in terms of a conventional Hicksian model, the position of the LM curve is less stable and predictable than the position of the IS curve—targeting interest rates will yield a better policy performance than targeting the money supply. Against this background, some economists have concluded that innovation has in fact reduced the predictability of the money-GNP relationship to such an extent that targeting money supply growth is no longer appropriate, at least as long as significant innovation and deregulation are occurring. Several alternative targets have been suggested, including nominal GNP and real interest rates.

Others, however, favor retention of the present strategy at least for the present. They point out that the instability that has been observed in recent years has resulted from (1) concerted efforts in the 1970s to circumvent regulations in the face of high inflation and high interest rates and (2) the disruptions caused by subsequent deregulation. With the deregulation process now well advanced, future innovation may be more gradual and more predictable. Further, while innovation and deregulation may have temporarily affected the relationship between the conventional measures of money, such as M1 and the economy, they have not necessarily destabilized the monetary sector in any fundamental way. Therefore, targeting the monetary base or some other measure of high-powered money might still be feasible even if empirical problems with other monetary aggregates persisted.

A related issue that has received attention recently concerns the feasibility of monetary control if remaining interest-rate ceilings are removed. A control procedure the Fed has used frequently in the past involves the direct or indirect manipulation of short-term interest rates in order to affect the opportunity cost of holding money balances and, therefore, the demand for money. It is sometimes argued that, with interest-rate ceilings removed, yields on the components of the money supply will vary with market interest rates, thereby reducing the elasticity of money demand with respect to interest rates and increasing the change in interest rates required to produce any desired change in the growth of money. Even in a completely deregulated environment, however, explicit yields on assets providing significant monetary services are likely to vary less than market yields. Therefore, the interest elasticity of money demand—especially the demand for M1, which includes currency and other transactions instruments—may remain sufficiently high for the purposes of monetary control.

This rather technical discussion regarding intermediate targets and monetary control is important, but it is only a relatively narrow aspect of the broader public debate about monetary policy that is currently going on in the United States. The experience in recent years of historically high peace-time inflation, high and extremely volatile interest rates, two severe and protracted recessions, and wide swings in the value of the dollar in foreign exchange markets has produced demands from some quarters for far-reaching changes in the strategy of monetary policy and in the responsibilities and authority of the Federal Reserve. In particular, a small but vocal group is pressing for a return to the gold standard or some alternative commodity standard.

Although another sharp rise in interest rates or inflation or another recession might motivate the Congress to require fundamental changes in the conduct of monetary policy, the more likely outcome over the remainder of the 1980s is continuation of the present monetary aggregates strategy, coupled with an effort to change the institutional regime in which the strategy is pursued in ways that will make it more likely to succeed. Some of these changes are already in place. The Monetary Control Act of 1980 extended Federal Reserve reserve requirements to all depository institutions,[42] which reduces variations in the aggregate required reserve ratio due to shifts of deposits across classes of institutions. Further, a change in the reserve accounting mechanism in early 1984 from a lagged system to a (nearly) contemporaneous system has made it feasible for the Fed to change its procedure for controlling the monetary aggregates from one that operates through changes in short-term interest rates to one that operates through the supply of total reserves.[43] It should be emphasized, however, that, although the current strategy of U.S. policy is formally one of controlling monetary aggregates, there is considerable room within this strategy for discretionary changes in the emphasis actually given to monetary control—especially short-run monetary control—as against other objectives, such as stabilizing interest rates in particular time periods. Because it regards such flexibility as desirable, the Fed is likely to resist committing itself to a monetary control regime that significantly restricts the range of its discretionary actions in the short run.

C.   Concluding Comment

This paper has presented an overview of recent financial innovation in the United States, the deregulation it has helped to force, and some of the major effects of this process on financial institutions and markets and on monetary policy. As the discussion has indicated, these developments are extremely diverse when they are considered individually. Nonetheless, there are certain unifying themes. In broadest terms, the last 10 years have witnessed the collapse of an important part of the regulatory regime erected in the 1930s and the erosion of at least part of the philosophy of banking and financial regulation that sustained it. The forces that produced this change had been building since at least the 1950s, but they attained a certain critical mass in the 1970s that accelerated the process of change. It is, of course, possible that the process will continue at this same accelerated pace in the years immediately ahead. But it is also possible—and perhaps more likely—that the remainder of this decade will be a welcome period of consolidation characterized by a slower rate of innovation and change.

NOTES

[1] The paper is organized roughly along the lines of the framework suggested by M. A. Akhtar. See Akhtar (1984), pp. 3–25.

[2] Table 1 includes only debt instruments and therefore excludes equity funds. The net issuance of corporate stock in 1983 was $46.2 billion. Total corporate stock outstanding at the end of 1983 was $2,151.4 billion. See Kaufman, McKeon, and Blitz (1984), table 3C, p. 33.

[3] 1978 was the fourth year of the business expansion that followed the recession that ended in the first quarter of 1975. 1983 was the first year of the recovery from the recession that ended in the fourth quarter of 1982.

[4] The historical and regulatory factors that have influenced the structure of the U.S. banking industry are discussed below.

[5] For a comprehensive recent survey, see George J. Benston, "The Regulation of Financial Services," in Benston (1983B), pp. 28–63.

[6] This view of the Free Banking Era has been challenged in an important recent article by Rolnick and Weber (1983).

[7] For more detailed discussions of banking regulation in the 19th and early 20th centuries, see Thomas C. Huertas, "The Regulation of Financial Institutions: A Historical Perspective on Current Issues," in Benston (1983B). See also McCarthy (1984). The standard works on the period are Friedman and Schwartz (1963) and Hammond (1957).

[8] See Friedman and Schwartz (1963), chapter 7.

[9] See Kaufman, Mote, and Rosenblum (1983), p. 9.

[10] Ceiling rates on other time deposits subject to ceilings were scaled upward from the passbook ceiling.

[11] This heightened variability may have been due in part to changes in late 1979 in the operating procedures used by the Federal Reserve to implement monetary policy. These changes shifted the short-run operational emphasis from the Federal funds rate to various reserve aggregates. See Axilrod (1982).

[12] A comprehensive listing as of the end of 1982 can be found in Silber (1983), p. 91.

[13] The monetary policy implications are discussed in Section IV below.

[14] Table 3 lists the principal actions taken to deregulate interest rates between 1972 and 1983.

[15] Several economists have attempted to formulate theoretical models to capture the nature of the process described in this section. See in particular Ben-Horim and Silber (1977) and Kane, "Microeconomic and Macroeconomic Origins of Financial Innovation," in Federal Reserve Bank of St. Louis (1984), pp. 3–20.

[16] See Heurtes, "The Regulation of Financial Institutions," in Benston (1983B), p. 24.

[17] For an interesting retrospective on the influence of the Hunt Commission's report written by the commission's co-directors, see Almarin Phillips and Donald P. Jacobs. "Reflections on the Hunt Commission," in Benston (1983B), chap. 9.

[18] See Cook and Duffield (1979) for an extensive description and analysis of MMMFs.

[19] MMDAs permit up to six transfers per month, other than by appearing in person, but no more than three of these can be by check. In recent months, MMDA yields have exceeded Super NOW yields by approximately 2 percentage points.

[20] The considerably stronger response to MMDAs is believed to be due primarily to the insurance feature and the general public's greater familiarity with the banks and thrifts issuing MMDAs than the investment companies issuing MMMFs.

[21] See Rosenblum and Siegel (1983), chart 1B, p. 16, and table 10, p. 26.

[22] A major reason for the emergence of the bank holding company as the dominant corporate form in U.S. banking markets has been the effort to circumvent restrictions on bank entry into nonbanking activities. Both the Bank Holding Company Act of 1956 and the amendments to that act in 1970 sought to close this loophole.

[23] Space does not permit a discussion of the international activities of large U.S.-based banks. These banks are engaged in a number of nonbank activities via overseas affiliates that they are not permitted to enter in the United States. They would, therefore, be able to establish domestic operations in many of these activities rather quickly if the restrictions were lifted.

[24] As of 1981, for example, Citicorp, which is based in New York, operated 422 nonbanking offices in 40 states and the District of Columbia.

[25] A principal objective of these regional compacts appears to be to restrict entry into regional and local markets by the large money-center banks.

[26] The recent development of options markets for several financial futures contracts has significantly broadened the range of hedging strategies available to investors.

[27] The Humphrey-Hawkins Act of 1978 requires the Federal Reserve to report its objectives for the growth of the monetary and credit aggregates each year. The current formal definitions of the monetary aggregates are published each month in the notes to statistical table 1.21 in the Federal Reserve *Bulletin*.

[28] Following Goldfeld (1973), these money demand functions have the following general form:

$$\ln\frac{M^D}{P_t} = a_0 + a_1\ln(r_{1t}) + a\ln(r_{2t}) + a\ln(y_t) + a_4\ln\frac{M}{P_{t-1}}$$

where M^D = money demand.
$\quad\quad$ P = price level.
$\quad\quad r_1$ = a nominal short-term market interest rate.
$\quad\quad r_2$ = a nominal short-term regulated interest rate.
$\quad\quad$ y = real income.
For a review of much of this research, see Judd and Scadding (1982B).

[29] See Richard D. Porter and Edward K. Offenbacher, "Financial Innovations and Measurement of Monetary Aggregates," in Federal Reserve Bank of St. Louis (1984), table 3–1, pp. 53–54.

[30] The M1 series used in constructing the table was adjusted to eliminate the effects of institutional changes on this aggregate. See footnote 2 of the Porter-Offenbacher article.

[31] For specific evidence on the impact of MMMFs, see Dotsey, Englander, and Partlan (1981–82). It should be noted that, although the view that a downward shift in money demand occurred in the mid-1970s is widely held, there is much less agreement regarding the possible shift in 1980–81. For an argument that no shift occurred in the latter period, see Pierce (1982).

[32] See Brayton, Farr, and Porter (1983).

[33] See Judd (1983). See also Broaddus and Goodfriend (1984), pp. 11–14.

[34] The case for focusing on credit, rather than monetary aggregates, has been advanced especially strongly by Frank E. Morris, the president of the Federal Reserve Bank of Boston. See Morris (1982).

[35] See Simpson and Porter (1980). For a more recent example of further research on the money-demand function, see Brayton, Farr, and Porter (1983).

[36] See Barnett and Spindt (1982).

[37] See Porter and Offenbacher (1984), pp. 72–76.

[38] It should be emphasized that the somewhat speculative views presented in this section are the author's and do not necessarily reflect the views of the Federal Reserve Bank of Richmond or the Federal Reserve System.

[39] See Office of the Press Secretary to the Vice President of the United States (1984).

[40] See, for example, Benston (1983A).

[41] See Poole (1970).

[42] The requirements had previously been applied only to the minority of commercial banks that were members of the Federal Reserve System.

[43] Many monetary economists believe that control via a reserve instrument is more efficient than control through interest rates, even though there is relatively little historical experience on which to base a test of the proposition.

REFERENCES

Akhtar, M. A. *Financial Innovations and Their Implications for Monetary Policy: An International Perspective*. Basle: Bank for International Settlements, 1983.

Axilrod, Stephen H. "Monetary Aggregates and Monetary Policy in a Deregulated Financial World." In *Interest Rate Deregulation and Monetary Policy*. (Proceedings of a conference sponsored by the Federal Reserve Bank of San Francisco.) San Francisco: Federal Reserve Bank of San Francisco, 1982, pp. 1–12.

Bank for International Settlements. *Financial Innovation and Monetary Policy*. Proceedings of a meeting of central bank economists, November 9–10, 1984.

Barnett, William A., and Paul A. Spindt. *Divisia Monetary Aggregates: Compilation, Data, and Historical Behavior*. Washington, D.C.: Board of Governors of the Federal Reserve System, Staff Study no. 116, May 1982.

Ben-Horim, Moshe, and William L. Silber. "Financial Innovation: A Linear Programming Approach." *Journal of Banking and Finance* 1 (1977), pp. 277–96.

Benston, George J. "Bank Failure and Deposit Insurance." *Economic Review*. Federal Reserve Bank of Atlanta, March 1983A, pp. 4–17.

———, ed. *Financial Services: The Changing Institutions and Government Policy*. Englewood Cliffs, N.J.: Prentice-Hall, 1983B.

Brayton, Flint; Terry Farr; and Richard Porter. "Alternative Money Demand Specifications and Recent Growth of M1." Unpublished paper. Washington, D.C.: Board of Governors of the Federal Reserve System, 1983.

Broaddus, Alfred, and Marvin Goodfriend. "Base Drift and the Longer Run Growth of M1: Experience from a Decade of Monetary Targeting." *Economic Review*. Federal Reserve Bank of Richmond 70 (November/December 1984), pp. 3–14.

Cargill, Thomas F., and Gillian G. Garcia. *Financial Deregulation and Monetary Control: Historical Perspective and Impact of the 1980 Act*. Stanford, Calif.: Hoover Institution Press, 1982.

Cook, Timothy Q., and Jeremy G. Duffield. "Money Market Mutual Funds: A Reaction to Government Regulations or a Lasting Financial Innovation?" *Economic Review*. Federal Reserve Bank of Richmond 65 (July/August 1979), pp. 15–31.

———. "Short-term Investment Pools." *Economic Review*. Federal Reserve Bank of Richmond 66 (September/October 1980), pp. 3–23.

Dotsey, Michael; Steven Englander; and John C. Partlan. "Money Market Mutual Funds and Monetary Control." *Quarterly Review*. Federal Reserve Bank of New York 6 (Winter 1981–82), pp. 9–17.

Friedman, Milton, and Anna J. Schwartz. *A Monetary History of the United States, 1867–1960*. Princeton, New Jersey: Princeton University Press, 1963.

Goldfeld, Steven. "The Case of the Missing Money." *Brookings Papers on Economic Activity*. (3:1976). pp. 683–730.

———. "The Demand for Money Revisited." *Brookings Papers on Economic Activity*. (3:1973), pp. 577–638.

Gramley, Lyle E. "Financial Innovation and Monetary Policy." *Federal Reserve Bulletin* 68 (July 1982), 393–400.

Greenbaum, S. I., and C. F. Haywood. "Secular Change in the Financial Services Industry." *Journal of Money, Credit and Banking* 3 (May 1971), pp. 571–89.

Hammond, Bray. *Banks and Politics in America, from the Revolution to the Civil War*. Princeton, N.J.: Princeton University Press, 1957.

Hester, Donald D. "Panel Presentation: Alternative Intermediate Instruments of Monetary Policy." In *Interest Rate Deregulation and Monetary Policy*. Proceedings of a conference sponsored by the Federal Reserve Bank of San Francisco. San Francisco: Federal Reserve Bank of San Francisco, 1982, pp. 240–51.

Jordan, Jerry L. "Panel Presentation: Alternative Intermediate Instruments of Monetary Policy." In *Interest Rate Deregulation and Monetary Policy*. Proceedings of a conference sponsored by the Federal Reserve Bank of San Francisco. San Francisco: Federal Reserve Bank of San Francisco, 1982, pp. 215–20.

Judd, John P. "The Recent Decline in Velocity: Instability in Money Demand or Inflation?" *Economic Review*. Federal Reserve Bank of San Francisco, Spring 1983, pp. 12–19.

———, and John L. Scadding. "Financial Change and Monetary Targeting in the United States." In *Interest Rate Deregulation and Monetary Policy*. Proceedings of a conference sponsored by the Federal Reserve Bank of San Francisco, San Francisco: Federal Reserve Bank of San Francisco, 1982A, pp. 78–106.

———. "The Search for a Stable Money Demand Function: A Survey of the Post-1973 Literature." *Journal of Economic Literature* 20 (September 1982B), pp. 993–1023.

Kane, Edward J. "Accelerating Inflation, Technological Innovation and the Decreasing Effectiveness of Banking Regulation." *Journal of Finance* 36 (May 1981), 355–67.

Kaufman, Henry; James McKeon; and Steven Blitz. *1984 Prospects for Financial Markets*. New York: Salomon Brothers, December 1983.

Kaufman, George; Larry Mote; and Harvey Rosenblum. "Implications of Deregulation for Product Lines and Geographical Markets of Financial Institutions." *Journal of Bank Research* 14 (Spring 1983), pp. 8–25.

McCarthy, F. Ward, Jr. "The Evolution of the Bank Regulatory Structure: A Reappraisal." *Economic Review*. Federal Reserve Bank of Richmond 70 (March/April 1984), pp. 3–21.

Morris, Frank E. "Do the Monetary Aggregates Have a Future as Targets of Federal Reserve Policy?" *New England Economic Review*. Federal Reserve Bank of Boston (March/April 1982), pp. 5–14.

"The Nature and Implications of Financial Innovation." Report of a conference of central bankers in London, May 18–20, 1983. *Quarterly Review*. Bank of England (September 1983), pp. 358–62.

Niehans, Jurg. "Innovation in Monetary Policy: Challenge and Response." *Journal of Bank Research* 6 (March 1982), pp. 9–28.

Office of the Press Secretary to the Vice President of the United States. Press release dated January 31, 1984.

Pierce, James L. "Did Financial Innovation Hurt the Great Monetarist Experiment?" *American Economic Review* 74 (May 1980), pp. 392–96.

———. "Panel Presentation: Alternative Intermediate Instruments of Monetary Policy." In *Interest Rate Deregulation and Monetary Policy*. Proceedings of a conference sponsored by the Federal Reserve Bank of San Francisco. San Francisco: Federal Reserve Bank of San Francisco, 1982, pp. 215–20.

Poole, William. "Optimal Choice of Monetary Policy Instruments in a Simple Stochastic Macro Model." *Quarterly Journal of Economics* 84 (May 1970), pp. 197–217.

Porter, Richard D., and Edward K. Offenbacher. "Financial Innovations and Measurement of Monetary Aggregates." In *Financial Innovations: Their Impact on Monetary Policy and Financial Markets.* Proceedings of a conference held at the Federal Reserve Bank of St. Louis, October 1–2, 1982. Boston: Kluwer Nijhoff Publishing, 1984, pp. 49–98.

———; Thomas D. Simpson; and Eileen Mauskopf. "Financial Innovation and the Monetary Aggregates." *Brookings Papers on Economic Activity.* (1:1979), pp. 213–29.

Rolnick, Arthur J., and Warren E. Weber. "The Free Banking Era: New Evidence on Laissez-Faire Banking." *American Economic Review* 73 (December 1983), pp. 1080–91.

Rosenblum, Harvey, and Christine Pavel. *Financial Services in Transition: The Effects of Nonbank Competitors.* Federal Reserve Bank of Chicago, Staff Memorandum 84–1, 1984.

———, and Diane Siegel. *Competition in Financial Services: The Impact of Nonbank Entry.* Federal Reserve Bank of Chicago, Staff Study 83–1, 1983.

Roth, Howard L. "Recent Experience with M1 as a Policy Guide." *Economic Review.* Federal Reserve Bank of Kansas City 69 (March 1984), pp. 17–29.

Silber, William L., ed. *Financial Innovation.* Lexington, Mass.: D. C. Heath, 1975.

———. "The Process of Financial Innovation." *American Economic Review* 73 (May 1983), pp. 89–95.

Simpson, Thomas D. "Changes in the Financial System: Implications for Monetary Policy." *Brookings Papers on Economic Activity.* (1:1984), pp. 249–65.

———, and Patrick M. Parkinson. "Some Implications of Financial Innovations in the United States." Washington, D.C.: Board of Governors of the Federal Reserve System. Staff Studies Series no. 139, 1984.

———, and Richard D. Porter. "Some Issues Involving the Definition and Interpretation of the Monetary Aggregates." In *Controlling Monetary Aggregates III.* Proceedings of a conference sponsored by the Federal Reserve Bank of Boston, 1980, pp. 161–234.

Vrabac, Daniel J. "Recent Developments at Banks and Nonbank Depository Institutions." *Economic Review.* Federal Reserve Bank of Kansas City 68 (July/August 1983), pp. 33–45.

Wall, Larry, and Robert A. Eisenbeis. "Risk Considerations in Deregulating Bank Activities." *Economic Review.* Federal Reserve Bank of Atlanta 69 (May 1984), pp. 6–19.

Wenninger, John. "Financial Innovation—A Complex Problem Even in a Simple Framework." *Quarterly Review.* Federal Reserve Bank of New York (Summer 1984), pp. 1–8.

41

Financial Innovation and Deregulation in Foreign Industrial Countries

J. David Germany and John E. Morton

The process of financial innovation that has taken place in the United States over the past decade has also been evident in other industrial economies. Although the forms the innovations have taken have differed among countries, there have been some prominent common elements, among them the introduction of new financial assets and markets, a greater reliance upon market-determined interest rates, and increased competition among financial institutions. Changes in the regulatory environment have influenced the extent and form of financial change in individual countries, as has the increased internationalization of financial markets. Financial innovation has, in turn, had an impact on the conduct of monetary policy and the supervision and regulation of financial markets.

SOURCES OF INNOVATION

It is difficult to determine the exact source of a particular innovation in financial markets. Usually, factors have interacted with each other and with the unique regulatory and financial structure in each country. Nevertheless, several broad categories of factors are discernible. The most important are technological change, high and variable interest rates, bigger government deficits, and the growing internationalization of financial markets.

Technological change, particularly the advance in computer technology, has altered the environment of financial markets in several ways. It has made possible new types of financial assets and transactions, such as cash management or sweep accounts. More important, nearly all financial transactions have become significantly faster and cheaper, so financial institutions have incentives to furnish a wider and more competitive range of services. Finally, the increased speed and lower cost of communication have been important to the development and expansion of international markets.

From *Federal Reserve Bulletin*, October 1985, pp. 743–53.

The authors are with the board's Division of International Finance.

Technological developments alone could account for some recent financial innovations, but changes in the economic environment over the past decade have probably been of greater importance. Although the form and degree have differed in individual cases, the patterns of economic change in most of the major industrial countries have been parallel, largely because their policy responses have followed a broadly similar sequence in the wake of global economic disturbances, in particular the two periods of sharply rising oil prices in the 1970s.

The movement of average short-term interest rates and inflation rates in the major foreign industrial countries since 1970 is shown in Chart 1. Both interest and inflation rates started to move sharply higher in 1973, receded temporarily later in the decade, then surged to new peaks about 1980 before falling back again in recent years. While magnitude and timing have varied, these upsurges in interest and inflation rates have been widespread. Higher nominal and real interest rates have stimulated financial innovation by widening the gap between regulated and freely determined market interest rates. Asset holders have been motivated to economize on noninterest-bearing transactions balances and, in general, to shift out of deposits yielding below-market interest rates. Financial institutions have been forced by competitive pressures to offer market rates on deposits where regulations allowed and to push for an easing of such restrictions where they did not.

Along with a generally higher level of nominal interest rates have come periods of heightened variability of interest rates and other financial variables, such as exchange rates. These increases in variability and the resulting rise in uncertainty and risk have generated a demand for new types of financial instruments, such as loans and securities with variable rates and shorter maturities, and they have stimulated the development of financial futures and options markets as a means of managing risk.

A less-direct but often important stimulus to financial innovation has been the growth of government budget deficits, depicted in Chart 2. Rising government deficits have tended to stimulate the development of bond and other money

CHART 1
Average Inflation and Short-term Interest Rates
in Major Foreign Industrial Countries

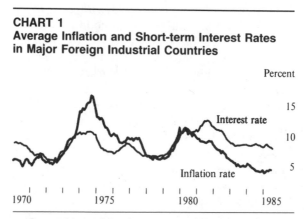

Geometric weighted averages of three-month interbank interest rates or closest equivalent and of change in consumer prices.

CHART 2
Ratio of Government Fiscal Balance
to Gross National Product, Average for Major
Foreign Industrial Countries

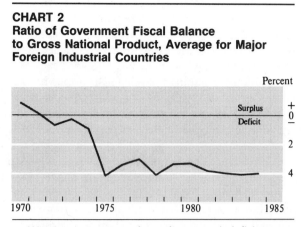

Weighted average of surpluses and deficits as a
fraction of gross national product.

markets. The greater volume of government bonds issued has deepened existing markets. Moreover, authorities have altered regulations in order to encourage the development of securities markets in which government debt instruments could be sold more easily.

The role of financial regulations in financial innovation has been complex. In the face of extensive regulation, the innovative process has often been delayed or distorted. On the other hand, avoiding regulatory restraints has been a powerful motive for financial innovation. At times, authorities have used deregulation in a deliberate attempt to liberalize financial-market structures and have thus stimulated innovation. At other times, innovations have forced authorities to alter restrictions in an effort to regain regulatory control.

Finally, the growing international openness of the industrial economies has stimulated financial innovation. This process has been operating for several decades, but its pace has quickened in recent years. As barriers to the movement of capital between countries have been lowered in the postwar period, financial flows have grown. With this growth has come increasing competition between financial institutions in different countries and the consequent development of international markets, particularly the Eurocurrency and Eurobond markets. Financial institutions within individual countries have faced increased competitive pressures from these markets. The tendency toward greater integration of, and competition among, national markets in a global system has provided opportunities for increasing efficiency and widening the scope for financial innovation.

In response to these forces for change in the economic environment over the past decade, broadly similar financial innovations have occurred in a number of countries. One important innovation, a response mainly to higher and more variable interest rates, has been the new, more-flexible financial instruments bearing market rates of interest. Recent years have seen the introduction or intensified use of negotiable certificates of deposits, money market mutual funds, money market certificates, and various interest-bearing checking accounts. Existing securities markets have grown, and new markets have come into existence. A wide variety of new types of bonds have been developed, with features including variable interest rates and inflation guarantees. Secondary bond markets have also become more numerous. New financial instruments have continued to emerge as the economic environment has evolved.

Increasing competition among financial institutions has been another important common feature of innovation. Banks have faced strong competition for deposits from near-banks and money markets and have responded both by offering improved returns on their deposits (where regulations permitted) and by pressing for financial liberalization and an easing of restrictions. On the asset as well as the liability side, competition has strengthened. Financial institutions traditionally confined to mortgage financing have moved into business lending normally dominated by commercial banks, while banks have expanded their role in the mortgage market. In consequence, as both their asset and their liability structures have grown increasingly similar, the traditional distinction between commercial banks and savings institutions has tended to break down.

EXPANDED USE OF MARKET INTEREST RATES

An important aspect of the general process of financial innovation has been the movement toward greater use of market-determined interest rates in the banking sectors of the major industrial economies. Two factors have determined the nature and extent of change in different countries. One key variable has been the degree to which banks have faced competitive pressures from other banks, nonbank financial institutions, or money markets. The second factor has been the regulatory environment.

Competitive Pressures

Table 1 provides summary information on the current banking structures in six major foreign industrial countries. Four of these countries—Canada, Germany, Italy, and the United Kingdom—currently have no limits on the payment of market rates of interest on bank deposits. Despite the absence of direct controls on interest rates, other restrictions on banks, in particular balance sheet constraints, can sometimes reduce the incentives for banks to compete actively for deposits, thus effectively holding down deposit interest rates. Both the controls of bank credit growth in Italy and the "corset" limiting the growth of banks' interest-bearing liabilities in the United Kingdom have had this effect at times over the past decade.

In the absence of regulatory restrictions on bank deposit rates, pressures for the payment of market rates have been generated by high nominal interest rates and technological change. The Canadian experience offers an example. Over the past decade, inflation and interest rates reached double-digit levels in Canada. At the same time, the spread of computer technology lowered banks' marginal costs and encouraged the expansion of certain kinds of deposits. Starting in the early 1970s, Canadian corporations employed cash-management techniques to minimize their use of zero-interest forms of demand deposits, "sweeping" all other funds into a variety of short-maturity interest-bearing deposit accounts offered by banks to meet the new needs of their corporate customers. For banks, the use of such sweep accounts had an advantage over paying interest directly on demand

TABLE 1
Current Regulatory and Competitive Conditions for Banks, Selected Foreign Industrial Countries

Country	Regulation		Competition	
	Interest rate controls	Balance sheet constraints	Other financial institutions	Nonbank financial assets
Canada	No (ceilings on certain certificate of deposit rates, 1972–75)	No	Trust and mortgage loan companies, credit unions, insurance companies	Government bonds
France..............	Yes (ceilings except for long-term, large-denomination time deposits)	Credit expansion ceilings (officially lifted 1985)	Savings banks	Government bonds, bond funds
Germany............	No	No	Life insurance companies	Small-denomination government bonds
Italy................	No	Credit expansion ceilings (officially lifted 1983)	Savings banks, special credit institutions	Treasury bills
Japan...............	Yes (regulated except for foreign currency deposits and certificates of deposit)	Window guidance (limits on bank lending)	Postal savings	Bond funds
United Kingdom......	No (not since 1975)	No (limits on growth of interest-bearing liabilities, intermittently 1973–80)	Building societies	Government-issued national savings certificates, money market funds

deposits because the short-maturity deposit accounts faced lower reserve requirements. In 1979, innovation spread to the personal sector, with the switch from monthly balances to daily balances as the basis for paying interest on savings accounts. Daily interest checking accounts became widespread in 1981.

The speed with which banks in such countries as Canada have moved to increase the use of market interest rates has depended on the degree of outside competition they face from other financial institutions, money markets, or some combination of the two. In Canada and the United Kingdom, outside competitive pressure has come mainly from other financial institutions. As described in more detail later, certain regulatory advantages have permitted both Canadian trust companies and U.K. building societies to compete strongly with banks in the struggle for deposits. This competition has often taken the form of offering new types of deposits or improved rates on existing deposits. For example, when the U.K. building societies introduced an interest-bearing checking account for small depositors, the banks were forced to respond by offering a similar account.

In other countries, money markets have competed with banks for deposits. In Italy, for example, the growth of public sector deficits in the 1970s prompted the government to offer securities with shorter maturities, variable rates, and inflation-indexed returns. Of particular importance was the growth of a broad market in small-denomination, tax-free Treasury bills, which attracted funds from bank deposits. Similarly, the sale of U.K. government national savings certificates, bearing an attractive interest rate and aimed at the small saver, offered strong competition for deposits at U.K. financial institutions.

Germany provides a good example of the way a lack of strong outside competitive pressure has allowed banks to avoid paying market rates of interest on deposits. While large depositors at German banks have been able to receive market rates of interest because of the existence of alternatives, such as the Euromark market, small depositors in general have received below-market interest rates. One reason is the relatively uncompetitive environment in which German banks operate. No variations in regulations offer competitive opportunities to near-banks in Germany, because all financial institutions performing banking functions are subject to the same reserve requirements and are generally regulated like banks. In addition, rules prohibit money market funds with checking features and certificates of deposit. Although bank deposits have competed with small-denomination, nonnegotiable, one-year government bonds sold directly to the public, in general there are relatively few alternatives to small-denomination bank deposits in Germany.

Shifting Regulatory Environment

In both France and Japan, strides have been made toward greater use of market-determined interest rates in the banking sector despite extensive regulatory controls. The process of financial innovation in both countries has been complex, as regulatory changes have mobilized new competitive pressures that in turn have spurred further changes in regulations. A feature common to the two countries has been the key role of securities markets.

Banking activity in France has been, and remains, tightly regulated. Bank deposit and lending rates are administered by the authorities. Checking accounts pay no interest, and there are severe limitations on the payment of market-determined interest rates on time and savings accounts. A system of credit ceilings was formally removed in 1985, but the growth of bank credit remains under tight administrative control. These restrictions have been reinforced by exchange controls.

In recent years, change has been introduced into the tightly controlled French system through the rapid development of the bond market. In part, this development has represented a market response to a changing economic environment, but a shift in government regulations has also played a role. The government's desire to develop the French bond market in the late 1970s arose partially from a need to finance large budget deficits. In addition, it was hoped that businesses would reduce their nearly total reliance on short-term bank loans as a source of external financing and that savers could be induced to move away from traditional outlets, such as gold and real estate. To this end, changes in laws in 1978 and 1983 greatly improved the tax incentives for both issuers and holders of bonds. Banks were encouraged to issue bonds by exempting loans financed by bond sales from credit ceilings. Most important from the standpoint of the banks, the conditions under which market-related interest rates could be paid on time deposits were severely tightened in 1981. This last change was motivated partly by a desire to stimulate the bond market, but it was aimed mainly at moderating the increase in banks' loan rates at a time when the general level of interest rates was rising.

These regulatory changes, in conjunction with high nominal interest rates, led to a fourfold increase in the size of gross and net bond issues between 1979 and 1984. Banks faced a runoff of their deposits as investors shifted into bonds, especially following the 1981 tightening of restrictions on the payment of market interest rates on time deposits. In an effort to compensate for this shift, banks started offering mutual funds invested in variable-rate and short-maturity bonds.

These bond funds grew spectacularly. By the end of 1984, their portfolios acounted for nearly one fifth of the total capitalization of French bond markets. Thus, while the ability of French banks to pay market-determined interest rates on deposits has remained severely restricted, an increasing portion of their funds has been raised at market rates because of their involvement in the bond market. This general movement will be reinforced now that banks are allowed to issue negotiable certificates of deposit.

Parallels to developments in France can be seen in Sweden, where financial innovation in a traditionally tightly regulated banking sector has also been stimulated by competition from money markets. The key event in this process was the introduction of Treasury bills in 1982. Previously, the imposition of "liquidity ratios," which required banks to hold a certain fraction of their assets in the form of government securities, had forced banks to accept new government debt issues bearing below-market interest rates. With the sharp rise in government deficits in the late 1970s, this process proved increasingly burdensome. By selling Treasury bills in the open market, the government was given direct access to the funds of nonbank investors. This relieved the pressure on banks to absorb government debt but increased competition for bank deposits.

The rapid and extensive development of the Swedish Treasury bill market has encouraged the introduction and widespread use of other short-term financial assets. The market for certificates of deposit has expanded, and a substantial commercial paper market has recently developed. Throughout this process, Swedish banks have faced competition for funds from finance companies, generally unregulated financial institutions that, unable to accept deposits, have obtained funds by offering the public a variety of financial instruments at attractive interest rates. Banks themselves have started offering depositors substantially improved terms in recent years, especially the "combination account," which pays an interest rate that varies with the size and duration of balances.

One of the most extensive changes in banking structure in recent years has taken place in Japan. Like those in France and Sweden, changes in the heavily regulated Japanese banking system have been stimulated by the development of the bond market under the pressure of rising government budget deficits. Before this process got under way in the early 1970s, Japanese financial markets were tightly controlled and segmented. Major bank deposit rates were regulated, while lending rates were tied to the Bank of Japan's discount rate. Bond markets were underdeveloped because government deficits were small and because corporations relied almost exclusively on bank loans for external financing. International transactions were tightly controlled.

About the time of the first oil shock in 1973, several changes in the economic environment began to generate pressure for financial innovation in Japan. One factor was the rise in inflation and in nominal interest rates. Another was the slowing in economic growth. As real investment fell, businesses and households started to accumulate financial assets and, in the new inflationary environment, became more interest-rate conscious and dissatisfied with regulated deposit rates. As in other industrial economies, large government budget deficits strained the traditional system of government debt finance. In Japan, a syndicate of banks and securities firms has been required to take newly issued government debt at below-market rates and hold it for a specified period before resale in the secondary market. Resistance by syndicate members to this procedure grew in the mid-1970s as net issues expanded with the government's deficits. Partly as a result of this conflict, the authorities shortened the minimum period that syndicate members were forced to hold bonds and introduced several new medium-term instruments that were sold directly at public auction at essentially market terms.

The secondary market for long-term bonds was fostered by the growth in the 1970s of the unregulated "gensaki" market, a short-term repurchase market based on long-term government bonds. In 1980, securities companies began to offer medium-term government bond funds, or "chugoku" funds, which offered rates of interest well above those on fixed-rate bank deposits. In addition to facing stiffer competition from securities companies, banks saw some of their deposits shifted to postal savings accounts, which carried higher interest rates.

In response to this competitive pressure, banks asked for, and in 1979 received, permission to issue negotiable certificates of deposit. The CD market has rapidly taken a place beside the gensaki market as a major money market in Japan. For large depositors, banks in 1985 introduced money market certificates bearing interest rates linked to CD rates. Although restrictions remain, including limits on the rates paid on savings deposits, significant deregulation in coming years is either scheduled or promised. For example, interest-rate ceilings on large-denomination time deposits are scheduled to be removed in late 1985, and liberalization for smaller deposits is to follow by 1987.

CHANGES IN FINANCIAL STRUCTURE

Although the evolution of financial structures has differed markedly across countries, a trend toward a breakdown in the segmentation of financial markets is evident. Distinctions among services offered by different financial institutions are blurring in many countries, and national markets are becoming increasingly integrated internationally. The nature and extent of these changes differ across countries, but almost everywhere competition in financial markets has intensified.

Domestic Developments

One aspect of the change in domestic financial structures has been the increasing overlap in services offered by financial institutions. For example, in Japan the introduction of bond funds by securities companies in 1980 and the granting of permission in 1984 for banks to engage in government securities trading have blurred the sharp distinctions made there between the securities business and banking. In addition, different types of Japanese banks have begun to abandon their practice of limiting their lending to particular customers at particular maturities. Specialized financial institutions in Canada and the United Kingdom have also broadened their activities, and authorities in these two countries have shown some inclination to allow the merger of specialized institutions into ones that offer a wide range of financial services. Such institutions have long existed in Germany and Switzerland, where banks may offer all banking and securities services.

An important development in Canadian financial markets has been the overlap in activities by chartered banks and near-banks, the largest of which are the trust companies. In the 1970s, the depository and lending activities of Canadian trust companies consisted primarily of offering various types of savings deposits and making mortgages. The development of interest-bearing demand deposits has, however, blurred the distinction between savings and transactions balances, inducing banks and near-banks to offer such accounts as a means of preserving their competitiveness. At first the chartered banks enjoyed a considerable advantage in offering demand deposits, because they were the sole members of the national payments system. This imbalance was addressed by the Bank Act of 1980, which permitted near-banks to join the Canadian Payments Association. In addition, near-banks remained exempt from the Bank of Canada's reserve requirements, an advantage that has made trust companies formidable competitors in the retail deposit market. Trust companies and banks have also penetrated one another's traditional lending markets: chartered banks have become a significant force in the residential mortgage market, and trust companies have moved increasingly into consumer and business loans.

The integration of Canadian financial markets has also been marked by the provision of interest-bearing accounts with check-writing privileges by securities dealers and the undertaking of discount brokerage business by some banks. Of even more importance has been the growth of financial conglomerates. This activity has typically involved trust companies and life insurance companies, some of which are provincially chartered and thus outside federal control. In response to this development, the federal government proposed in April 1985 a new form of institution: a federally incorporated holding company, which could own trust banks, insurance companies, securities companies, and other financial institutions, including a new class of wholly owned chartered banks. If adopted, the proposal would require any financial holding company owning two or more types of institutions to become federally incorporated, bringing these conglomerates under a consistent set of regulations and prudential standards. Because the current proposal would not allow existing chartered banks to form holding companies, at least until the matter is taken up in the 1990 Bank Act, the measure also would encourage the development of large broad-based competitors with the chartered banks.

Financial markets in the United Kingdom are also becoming more integrated. For the most part, the markets serviced by banks and building societies (the country's principal savings and mortgage credit institutions) during the 1970s were segmented. Because the rate of withholding tax on building society deposits was lower than the marginal tax rates on personal incomes, building societies had a substantial advantage in competing for most retail savings deposits. Moreover, building societies were effectively insulated from bank competition in mortgage lending because the Supplementary Special Deposits scheme, or "corset," limited the growth of interest-bearing bank deposits so that banks tended to restrict their lending to their prime customers. The lifting of exchange controls in October 1979, however, allowed for the potential evasion of these constraints through the use of offshore centers. The corset was abolished in June 1980, and shortly thereafter banks entered the relatively profitable mortgage market. Building societies have subsequently pressed for a broadening of their lending powers.

In addition, as discussed in an earlier section, building societies (in cooperation with banks) have introduced interest-bearing accounts with check-writing privileges to meet the growing competition for funds. In response to these pressures and in an effort to expand competition in the U.K. financial markets, the government is preparing legislation that will allow building societies to offer checking accounts directly and, subject to portfolio limitations, to hold a wider variety of assets, including real estate and unsecured personal loans. In April 1985, the government harmonized the tax treatment of interest paid on deposits in banks and building societies, and it has indicated its intention to align more closely the regulatory treatment of the two systems as building societies develop.

The most dramatic change now taking place in the U.K. financial markets is the restructuring of the principal market for equities and long-term government securities, the London Stock Exchange. In accordance with the 1983 settlement of a government-led Restrictive Practices suit, the exchange will abolish fixed commissions by the end of 1986. In addition, over the coming year it will permit the integration of brokerage and dealing functions into one securities house as well as full ownership of exchange members by outside institutions, including commercial banks. These developments have produced a rash of merger announcements involving most of the prominent members of the exchange and several outside institutions. Many of these mergers will result in broad-based financial conglomerates that can offer a full range of securities and banking services. The interest in merging has been directed largely toward participating in the restructured market for long-term government securities, or "gilt-edged" market, in which the Bank of England plans to deal directly with a set of recognized market makers. On June 17, 1985, the Bank of England announced that it had accepted 29 firms as market makers; in the present system, only 6 firms make a market in gilts, and 2 of them handle about three fourths of the business.

International Linkages

Although all market makers in the new system in the United Kingdom will be U.K. subsidiaries, a striking feature of this group is that about one half have some form of foreign affiliation. This aspect of the changes now in train at the London Stock Exchange is part of a more general trend in world markets—the growing integration of markets internationally. The trend encompasses several related developments: moves by some countries to allow foreign institutions a bigger role in domestic financial markets; the growth of international markets, such as the Eurocurrency markets; and increases in the integration of domestic markets with international markets. The trend toward the interpenetration and integration of national markets may have accelerated in recent times. Over the past year, Australia, Norway, Portugal, and Sweden have moved to ease restrictions on entry by foreign-owned banks. France has loosened its exchange controls somewhat and, in April 1985, permitted a limited reopening of the international bond market in French francs, which was closed to new issues in France four years ago. In May, the Bundesbank announced permission for foreign bank subsidiaries that are incorporated in Germany to lead manage foreign bond issues denominated in deutsche marks and authorized the issuance of variable-rate and zero-coupon bonds. The ongoing liberalization of Japanese financial markets has involved several measures to integrate them with world financial markets, including a phased reduction of restrictions on Euroyen activity.

Some of these measures represent part of a more general effort to deregulate a country's financial markets. The easing of entry by foreign banks in Australia is only one part of a broad-based series of reforms, among them the lifting of exchange controls and most interest-rate ceilings, as well as the floating of the

Australian dollar. The acceptance by the Bank of England of a large number of foreign-owned subsidiaries as recognized market makers in the restructured government securities market can be thought of as a policy to increase the capitalization, liquidity, and competition in that market. The Canadian Bank Act of 1980, which allowed entry by foreign banks as full-service banks, had the deliberate intent of increasing competition among banks. Although the act limited the market share of foreign banks to 8 percent of total bank assets, this ceiling was raised to 16 percent in June 1984.

An important aspect of the growing international integration of financial markets is the strengthening of incentives for regulators to liberalize their financial systems. For example, an increase in the desirability of maintaining a presence in foreign financial markets may reinforce pressures to grant foreign financial institutions reciprocal access. Sweden's decision, in June 1985, to allow entry by foreign banks in 1986 was motivated in part by a desire to participate in Norwegian financial markets, which had recently allowed entry by foreign banks on a selected basis. Reciprocity issues lay behind the exclusion of Japanese institutions from those foreign entities being allowed greater participation in the German and U.K. bond markets. A potential complication of reciprocity arises when foreign financial institutions that can engage in a wide range of activities at home are allowed access to a country whose own institutions are more restricted. The question is whether the foreign institutions should be subject to the same regulatory and supervisory requirements faced by their domestic counterparts or whether the powers of their domestic counterparts should be liberalized. Such questions arose in Japan when foreign banks sought permission to enter the trust business. (Nine foreign banks were granted this permission in 1985.)

Another manifestation of the international integration of financial markets has been the expansion in the listing and trading of shares of domestic companies in foreign markets. For example, between 1982 and 1984, trading in selected U.K. equities in U.S. markets grew from generally low volumes to a sizable, and in at least one case a majority, share of the total volume of transactions in these individual securities. This growth is generally ascribed to U.S. interest in U.K. equities, rather than a loss of traditional markets in London. However, the competitive threat posed by U.S. markets, combined with the possibility that a more competitive London Stock Exchange may capture a larger share of an increasingly international market for equities, almost surely made the largest members of the London exchange more favorably disposed toward reform. In turn, the prospective increase in the international competitiveness of the London exchange appears to have reinforced pressures on other exchanges to deregulate. While retaining fixed commissions, the Amsterdam Stock Exchange last year allowed members to rebate up to 75 percent of commissions charged on large bond or stock trades and will shortly eliminate the "double commission" system, in which foreign purchasers of securities have to deal with both a foreign and a Dutch broker. Recently, the Paris Bourse has agreed to eliminate fixed commissions on securities transactions.

The recent changes in German regulations governing bonds denominated in deutsche marks were also partly a response to the growth of international capital markets. Under the new procedures, the committee of leading German banks that controlled the calendar for foreign bond issues has been disbanded, and German-based subsidiaries of foreign banks have been allowed to act as lead managers for DM-denominated foreign bonds. In addition, the permitted types of DM bonds have been expanded to include floating-rate, zero-coupon, and double-currency bonds, as well as bonds linked to interest-rate swaps and currency swaps. The lengthened menu of DM-denominated assets will afford residents and nonresidents greater flexibility in meeting their financial and investment needs. To the extent that this flexibility enhances the attractiveness of DM-denominated instruments to nonresidents, these measures may indicate a shift in the attitude of German authorities toward the use of the deutsche mark as an international investment currency. This shift is partly a result of the recent strength of the dollar, which has alleviated concerns that wider international use of DM-denominated instruments would cause the deutsche mark to appreciate to an undesired level. The rise in demand for these instruments should also help to stimulate the growth of Frankfurt as an international financial center, especially as the Bundesbank has requested that the issue of foreign bonds be lead managed by German-based institutions. The secondary market in floating-rate notes, however, has tended to move outside the country because of a 0.25 percent stamp tax on certain sales of such notes in Germany. The Bundesbank has recently called for the elimination of this competitive disadvantage vis-à-vis other international financial centers.

The process of integrating Japanese financial markets with world markets has been closely connected with the liberalization of Japan's domestic financial markets. A landmark in this process was the passage in 1980 of a revised foreign exchange law, which in principle freed all international transactions from official control except in extraordinary circumstances. In practice, markets have been liberalized at varying paces, with the speed and extent of liberalization depending in part on the authorities' view of the likely impact on domestic markets. For example, following the passage of the new law, restrictions on the holding of foreign-currency deposits in Japanese banks by Japanese residents and on foreign-currency loans by Japanese banks to domestic residents were lifted promptly; however, the government continued to discourage the development of Euroyen markets and to limit access to forward markets. Lifting restrictions on these markets would in effect have given Japanese residents access to an unregulated yen market, weakening the government's control over interest rates and credit creation.

Since 1983, the Japanese Ministry of Finance and the U.S. Treasury have discussed a wide range of issues related to financial liberalization, including measures to lift the remaining capital controls on Japanese residents, to allow greater access by foreign financial institutions to Japanese financial markets, and to increase the international use of the yen. During the past one and one-half years, a broad series of measures have been introduced to offer residents and nonresidents a wider selection of yen-denominated assets for conducting international transactions, including the creation of a yen banker's acceptance market in June 1985. Measures have also been taken to broaden somewhat the access of foreign institutions to Japan's domestic markets. The relaxation of limits on forward and swap transactions by residents in April and June 1984, in conjunction with previously granted powers to hold assets denominated in foreign currencies, effectively gave Japanese financial institutions the ability to arbitrage between domestic and international yen markets. There has also been a phased reduction of restrictions on Euroyen use.

While international political pressures have played a role in stimulating liberalization, economic forces in Japan have also encouraged deregulation. The prospect of increasing amounts of seasoned long-term government debt becoming available in secondary markets, for example, was an important element in recent decisions to decontrol some short-term markets. The liberalization of access to international markets for yen was used as part of this process, sometimes as a preliminary step to the decontrol of domestic markets. The competition between Japanese banks and securities companies both in Japan and in overseas markets created pressures for the deregulation of the Euroyen bond market, especially as the development of a thriving Euroyen market would represent an important source of business for both sets of institutions. These and similar pressures can be expected to operate in the future.

IMPLICATIONS FOR ECONOMIC POLICY

Recent financial innovation and deregulation in the major industrial countries have served an important function in facilitating adjustment to changes in the economic environment. Financial systems have, in general, become more diverse and more flexible. The greater reliance upon market-determined rates of interest has tended to improve the efficiency of capital allocation, both within and between countries, as has the increase in competition among financial institutions. However, these benefits have not been costless. Changes in financial structure brought about by financial innovation have at times heightened uncertainty and risk. Financial innovation and deregulation have also tended to complicate the tasks authorities face in conducting monetary policy and in supervising financial markets.

Monetary authorities attempt to help achieve important economic goals with respect to output and inflation through control of such variables as money supplies and interest rates. Financial innovation may complicate this process in several ways: the underlying relationship between ultimate goals and policy instruments may shift; the intermediate targets of monetary policy may become more difficult to control; the measurement and interpretation of certain monetary variables may become more difficult. These problems have been evident especially in the countries that in recent years have chosen to conduct monetary policy mainly through the control of the growth of a targeted monetary aggregate.

In defining money, distinctions have traditionally been made between liquid, low-yielding transaction balances and less-liquid, higher-yielding investment assets. However, financial innovation tends to blur this distinction, as new assets appear having both payments and investment characteristics. In Canada, for example, when a policy of money-supply targeting was adopted in 1975, the aggregate chosen was M1. But innovation in bank deposit accounts eventually required a redefinition of the Canadian aggregates, including the introduction of a new aggregate, M1A, which added to M1 all daily-interest checking deposits. This new aggregate grew rapidly as M1 grew slowly or even declined. Such instability in the measures of monetary aggregates was an important element in Canada's 1982 decision to discontinue monetary targeting. Similar difficulties have arisen in France, where the rapid growth of money market funds has distorted the relationship between economic activity and the targeted M2 aggregate. It is possible in principle to redefine monetary aggregates or adjust monetary targets as financial innovation takes place; however, it takes time to establish with any confidence new relationships between the altered monetary variables and ultimate policy objectives. In any event, such redefinition may damage public perceptions of monetary policy as stable and predictable, thus impairing one of the main advantages of adopting monetary targets.

In countries that have relied on direct controls of credit or interest rates, financial innovation and the often related process of deregulation have complicated the implementation of monetary policy. Fewer key monetary variables can be controlled directly by the monetary authorities as unregulated markets and financial institutions emerge. In consequence, authorities in these countries have tended to adopt monetary policy techniques that are more market-oriented, such as open market operations, and to foresake direct quantitative controls, such as credit ceilings. In recent years the United Kingdom, France, and Italy have officially lifted the quantitative credit ceilings that had been central to monetary control.

Recent changes in the financial environment have increased the risk faced by banks and other financial institutions in several ways. The heightened variability of interest rates and other financial variables has exposed banks to greater risk, although new financial instruments and techniques have enabled banks at least partially to hedge against this exposure. In addition, the erosion of stable deposit bases paying below-market interest rates and stiffer competition from other financial institutions have created pressures on their profit margins. As the scope of activities engaged in by all financial institutions has broadened, the possibility of financial loss has increased as well. These changes have made governmental supervision and regulation of financial markets more difficult. Along with an increase in the general level of risk has come a shift in the structure of financial markets, as a growing fraction of financial transactions has moved into unregulated activities or sectors of the market. In several countries, the authorities have responded by modifying the oversight and supervision of financial markets.

Important new regulatory issues have also been raised by the increasing internationalization of financial markets. As domestic financial markets have become even more integrated into global markets, activities important to the domestic economy have passed beyond the control of domestic regulatory authorities. This problem is complicated, because attempts to tighten domestic regulations strengthen incentives for activities to move abroad, beyond the direct control of domestic authorities. The development of the Euromarkets is the most prominent example of this process. Thus, the now-global nature of issues of financial supervision and regulation has forced national authorities increasingly to consult and cooperate on such matters in a wide range of forums.

42

Interest-Rate Swaps:
A New Tool for Managing Risk

Jan G. Loeys

INTRODUCTION

Sharp movements of interest rates in recent years have created serious problems for firms in which the maturity of their assets does not match the maturity of their liabilities. For example, some financial institutions and other corporations have long-term, fixed-rate assets financed with short-term liabilities. Such firms experience an earnings squeeze whenever market interest rates rise unexpectedly, because their cost of borrowing rises faster than the yield on their assets. As a result, many firms look for ways to reduce the sensitivity—or exposure—of their earnings to interest-rate fluctuations. A recent technique that allows firms to hedge (reduce) this exposure is the "interest-rate swap." Used first in the Euro-bond market during 1981, interest-rate swaps have taken the market by storm; and now the volume of interest rate swaps in the United States alone is close to $80 billion.

Why are interest-rate swaps so popular? What are the advantages of this instrument over other hedging techniques, such as refinancing the firm's debt or purchasing interest-rate futures? The answers to these questions require first an explanation of what interest-rate swaps are and how they can be used to reduce interest-rate risk.

WHAT ARE INTEREST-RATE SWAPS?

An interest-rate swap typically involves two firms that want to change their exposure to interest-rate fluctuations in opposite directions. For example, one firm has long-term assets that yield a fixed rate of return; but it also has liabilities with interest payments that fluctuate with market rates of interest (i.e., floating-rate liabilities).[1] This firm loses when interest rates rise unexpectedly, because the

From *Business Review*, Federal Reserve Bank of Philadelphia, May/June 1985, pp. 17–25.

Jan Loeys is a senior economist in the macroeconomics section of the research department of the Federal Reserve Bank of Philadelphia. The author is indebted to Charles Gibson for helpful comments.

interest cost of its liabilities rises but the revenue from its (fixed-rate) assets remains the same. Conversely, this firm gains from an unexpected drop in interest rates. This sensitivity of a firm's net earnings to interest-rate fluctuations is the firm's *exposure to interest-rate risk*. The other firm involved in the swap faces the opposite situation: its assets yield a return that fluctuates with market rates, but the interest payments on its liabilities are fixed for a longer time. A rise in interest rates benefits this firm, because its revenues rise faster than its cost of borrowing; but a drop in market rates reduces its net earnings.

When two firms such as these have opposite interest-risk exposures, one has the makings of a swap. In a typical swap, the two firms get together—sometimes through an intermediary—and, in effect, exchange some of their interest payments. A firm with floating-rate liabilities essentially takes over some of the interest payments of a firm with fixed-rate liabilities, and in return the firm with the fixed-rate liabilities takes over some of the interest payments of the firm with floating-rate liabilities. For example, a firm that has liabilities on which the interest rate fluctuates with the three-month Treasury bill (T-bill) rate could agree to pay another firm a fixed rate of 12 percent on an agreed-upon dollar amount (principal) in exchange for a floating-rate payment of 50 basis points over the three-month T-bill rate on the same principal. *In effect,* one firm converts the interest payments on its liabilities from a floating-rate to a fixed-rate basis, and the other converts its liabilities from fixed to floating rate. (For a more detailed discussion of the mechanics of swap arrangements, see the box, How a Swap Works.) Parties to a swap agree to make *interest payments* to each other—they do not actually swap liabilities, nor do they lend money to each other. Each firm remains responsible for paying the interest and principal on its own liabilities. Therefore, swaps do not appear on a firm's balance sheet; instead, they are used to alter the exposure to interest-rate risk implied by the balance sheet.

In just a few years, interest-rate swaps have become very popular as a hedging instrument (see the box, From Zero to $80 Billion in Three Years). But why are firms using swaps, rather than other more established hedging techniques, such as purchasing interest-rate futures?

SWAPS: LONGER THAN FUTURES, BUT MORE EXPENSIVE

Futures are contracts that generate cash flows that can be used to reduce a firm's interest risk exposure. An interest-rate futures contract is an agreement to buy or sell a certain financial asset, such as a T-bill, for a specific price at a specific date in the future. During the life of the futures contract, each time the market value of the asset falls (interest rates rise), the seller in the contract makes a profit and receives cash, and the buyer takes a loss and pays cash, and vice versa if the asset's market value rises.[2]

Consider again the case of a thrift institution that has long-term, fixed-rate assets, like mortgages, that it funds with short-term liabilities, like certificates of deposit (CDs). If interest rates rise unexpectedly, this thrift will lose—it suffers reduced net earnings. But the thrift could hedge its interest-rate risk with a futures contract to deliver (sell) a CD. Then, if interest rates rise, the market value of the CD falls, and the thrift receives a cash flow. This cash inflow offsets the reduced net earnings from the higher interest cost of the thrift's short-term liabilities. When interest rates *drop,* the futures contract produces a cash outflow; but this loss is offset by a lower interest cost on the thrift's short-term liabilities. By

HOW A SWAP WORKS

The following example is based on an actual transaction that was arranged by an investment bank between a large thrift institution and a large international bank; it is representative of many swaps that have been arranged since 1982. "Thrift" has a large portfolio of fixed-rate mortgages. "Bank" has most of its dollar-denominated assets yielding a floating-rate return based on LIBOR (the London Interbank Offered Rate).

On May 10, 1983, the "Intermediary," a large investment bank, arranged a $100 million, 7-year interest rate swap between Thrift and Bank. In the swap, Thrift agreed to pay Bank a fixed rate of 11 percent per year on $100 million, every 6 months. This payment covered exactly the interest Bank had to pay on a $100 million bond it issued in the Eurodollar market. Thrift also agreed to pay Bank the 2 percent underwriting spread that Bank itself paid to issue this bond. In exchange, Bank agreed to make floating-rate payments to Thrift at 35 basis points (.35 percent) below LIBOR. Intermediary received a broker's fee of $500,000.

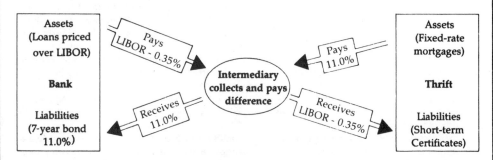

Twice a year, Intermediary (for a fee) calculates Bank's floating-rate payment by taking the average level of LIBOR for that month (Col. 2), deducting 35 basis points, dividing by 2 (because it is for *half* a year), and multiplying by $100 million (Col. 3). If this amount is larger than Thrift's fixed-rate payment (Col. 4), Bank pays Thrift the difference (Col. 5). Otherwise, Thrift pays Bank the difference (Col. 6).

[1] Date	[2] LIBOR	[3] Floating-rate payment 1/2 (LIBOR -0.35%)	[4] Fixed-rate payment 1/2 (11%)	[5] Net Payment from Bank to Thrift	[6] Net Payment from Thrift to Bank
May 1983	8.98%	—	—	—	—
Nov 1983	8.43%	$4,040,000	$5,500,000	0	$1,460,000
May 1984	11.54%	$5,595,000	$5,500,000	$95,000	0
Nov 1984	9.92%	$4,785,000	$5,500,000	0	$ 715,000
May 1985	8.44%	$4,045,000	$5,500,000	0	$1,455,000

The swap allows both Bank and Thrift to reduce their exposure to interest rate risk. Bank can now match its floating-rate assets priced off LIBOR with an interest payment based on LIBOR, while the fixed-rate interest payments on its bond issue are covered by Thrift. At the same time, Thrift can hedge part of its mortgage portfolio, from which it receives fixed interest earnings, with the fixed-rate payment it makes to Bank. However, the floating-rate payment that Thrift receives is linked to LIBOR while its cost of borrowing is more closely linked to the T-bill rate. Since LIBOR and the T-bill rate do not always move in tandem, Thrift is still exposed to fluctuations in the relation between LIBOR and the T-bill rate.

buying enough of these futures contracts, the thrift can, in principle, fully hedge its exposure to interest-rate fluctuations.

One disadvantage of futures is that they are standardized contracts that exist only with certain specific delivery dates and deliverable types of financial instruments.[3] In particular, futures are available only for delivery dates at three-month

FROM ZERO TO $80 BILLION
IN THREE YEARS

Interest rate swaps first emerged in the Eurobond market in late 1981.[a] Large international banks, which do most of their lending on a floating-rate basis, were involved in the first swaps so that they could use their fixed-rate borrowing capacity to obtain lower-cost floating-rate funds. Initially, the swapping partners consisted mainly of utilities and lower-rated industrial corporations that preferred fixed-rate financing. During 1982, the first domestic interest rate swap occurred between the Student Loan Marketing Association (Sallie Mae) and the ITT Financial Corp., with Sallie Mae making floating-rate payments to ITT. Since then, the market has grown tremendously; in 1984 about $80 billion in swap agreements were concluded.[b] Any large corporation can now use interest rate swaps as an instrument for asset-liability management.

Both investment banks and commercial banks have been active in arranging interest rate swaps. These intermediaries earn fees by bringing the different parties together, by acting as settlement agent (that is, collecting and paying the net difference in the interest payments), and by serving as guarantor of the agreement. Most intermediaries have recently gone beyond their initial role of merely bringing different parties together and function also as dealers. As a dealer, the intermediary is also the counterparty to each swap it "sells." That is, each party has an agreement only with the intermediary and is totally unaware of who might be on the other side of the swap. This arrangement allows the intermediary to sell one leg of the swap before selling the other and to work with an inventory of as yet unmatched swap agreements. The existence of dealers also facilitates an informal secondary market in swaps, where parties to a swap can sell their position to the intermediary or to another party, thereby increasing the liquidity of this instrument.

A typical swap involves a bond issue for $25 to $75 million with a 3 to 10 year maturity on one side, and a floating-rate loan on the other side. Initially, this floating rate loan was priced at a fraction over LIBOR, the London Interbank Offered Rate. Recently floating-rate loans have also been using the prime rate, the T-bill rate, or other indices of the cost of short-term borrowing.

The most common type of swap is the one described above: a dollar fixed-rate loan swapped for a dollar floating-rate loan, otherwise called the "plain-vanilla" swap. However, several variations on this basic swap have emerged in the market. One such variation is a floating-to-floating swap where parties agree to swap floating rates based on different indices. For example, a bank with assets tied to the prime rate and liabilities based on LIBOR may want to swap the interest payments on its liabilities with payments on a prime-tied, floating-rate loan. Another type of arrangement involves currency swaps such as a swap of a sterling floating-rate loan for a dollar fixed-rate loan. For firms whose assets are denominated in a different currency than are its liabilities, this type of swap may be more appropriate. Finally, rather than exchanging interest payments on liabilities, swaps can also be used to exchange yields on *assets* of different maturities or currencies.

The interest rate swap market has proven to be very flexible in adjusting its product to new customer needs. This innovativeness all but guarantees that swaps will remain a permanent feature of international capital markets.

---

[a] For more technical and institutional details on interest rate swaps, see Carl R. Beidleman, *Financial Swaps: New Strategies in Currency and Coupon Risk Management,* (Homewood, Illinois: Dow Jones-Irwin, 1985); and Boris Antl (ed.), *Swap Financing Techniques,* (London: Euromoney Publications Limited, 1983).

[b] Since there are no official reporting requirements on swaps, estimates of the size of this market vary tremendously. The amount of $80 billion, as estimated by Salomon Brothers (see *The Economist,* March 16, 1985, p. 30, Table 16), appears to be somewhere in the middle.

intervals out to about 2.5 years. This makes it impossible to hedge interest rate risk beyond 2.5 years.[4] Interest-rate swaps, in contrast, are private contracts with virtually every aspect of the agreement open to negotiation. Consequently, a swap can be tailor-made to fulfill one firm's particular needs, assuming another firm can be found to fit the other end of the contract. This flexibility allows firms to set up long-term arrangements—most swaps have a final maturity of 3 to 10 years—thereby filling the gap left by futures.

The ability to customize interest-rate swaps does not come without its disadvantages. The lack of product standardization makes it more difficult to find another party and to negotiate a mutually agreeable contract. It also costs more to close out a swap contract, if the need arises, than a futures contract position, which can be closed out readily. Apart from certain fixed costs of setting up an account with a trader and meeting regulatory requirements, the brokerage costs of initiating and eventually closing out a futures contract are 2 to 5 basis points. This is much lower than the arrangement fee of about 25 basis points that most swap brokers charge (not including additional fees for settling and guaranteeing the agreement).

Because swaps are agreements between private parties, they also have the disadvantage that one of the parties may default and thus be unable to continue the agreement. Although the other party has no principal at risk, it would again be stuck with an interest-risk exposure. It could negotiate a new swap arrangement with another firm, but the terms of that agreement would depend on current market interest rates, which may be more or less advantageous to the firm. Default risk can be reduced by requiring collateral, standby letters of credit, or a third-party guarantee—all of which are costly.[5] Futures, on the other hand, are guaranteed by the exchange in which the contracts are traded and by the funds that both parties to a futures contract must hold on margin with the exchange.

To reduce the costs stemming from the customized nature of swaps, many intermediaries have started to standardize the contract terms of swap agreements, such as the type of floating interest rate, repricing dates, and margin or collateral requirements.[6] As a result, interest-rate swaps may become similar to futures contracts, but with longer periods available for hedging.

Given a choice, firms that want to reduce their exposure to interest rate fluctuations for up to 2.5 years may be better off with interest-rate futures than with swaps, because futures are less costly to use than swaps.[7] For longer-term hedges, interest-rate swaps are a more appropriate, though relatively more expensive, hedging instrument.

SWAPS: MORE FLEXIBLE AND CHEAPER THAN REFINANCING

Rather than using such complicated instruments as swaps and futures, it may seem a lot less trouble for a firm to adjust its exposure directly by issuing liabilities (debt) with the pricing characteristics it desires. For example, a firm that has only floating-rate liabilities but now desires more fixed-rate liabilities, could buy back some of its floating-rate liabilities and issue fixed-rate liabilities, instead; that is, it could refinance some of its liabilities. However, "sellers" of interest-rate swaps claim that swaps may be less costly than refinancing for several reasons. One is that firms with lower credit ratings may have to pay relatively higher interest rates—that is, higher-quality spreads—in the fixed-rate market than in the floating-rate market. Thus, they claim, such firms should borrow in the floating-rate market and then swap, if they desire fixed-rate liabilities. Another reason is that swaps circumvent transactions costs associated with refinancing—such as legal fees, advertising, and regulatory restrictions—because swaps do not involve new borrowing; they only involve the exchange of interest payments on existing liabilities. To understand the advantages swaps can have over refinancing requires a closer look at these quality-spread differentials and transactions costs.

Quality-spread differentials.   A quality spread is the premium that a borrower with a low credit rating has to pay over a borrower with a high credit rating. For example, during 1982, when interest-rate swaps first became popular in the United States, the quality spread between Aaa and Baa rates firms in the fixed-rate corporate bond market was over 2 percentage points, a postwar high.[8] At the same time, these quality spreads were less than 1 percentage point in the floating-rate market.

To see how interest-rate swaps could exploit this apparent difference in quality spreads, consider an example typical of many of the early swaps. "Company" is a manufacturer whose assets yield a fixed rate of return. Company finances a major part of its assets by borrowing at a floating rate of 1 percentage point above the three-month T-bill rate. Company prefers to finance its assets with a fixed-rate bond issue, but, because of its low Baa credit rating, it would have to pay, say, 16 percent.

On the other side is "Bank," a large international bank, with a portfolio of commercial loans on which it charges a rate based on the three-month T-bill rate. Bank currently finances its portfolio by issuing CDs at 0.5 percentage point above the three-month T-bill rate. Given its high Aaa credit rating, it has the option of borrowing in the bond market at a fixed rate of 14 percent. Table 1 shows the different alternatives for the two firms. Note that the quality spread is 0.5 percentage point in the floating-rate market, and 2.0 percentage points in the fixed-rate market.

TABLE 1
Quality Spread Differentials

Issued by	Interest Rate on Liabilities	
	Floating Rate	**Fixed Rate**
Company (Baa)*	T-bill + 1.0%	16.0%
Bank (Aaa)*	T-bill + 0.5%	14.0%
Quality spread	0.5%	2.0%

* Credit ratings are in parentheses. Baa is the lower rating.

If each simply wanted to match maturities, Bank would borrow in the floating-rate market at 0.5 percentage point above the T-bill rate and Company would borrow in the bond market at 16.0 percent. But both borrowers could reduce their cost of borrowing if Bank borrows at a fixed rate and Company borrows at a floating rate and they swap interest payments, with Company agreeing to pay Bank, say, an additional 1 percentage point. In effect, this means that Bank borrows at a 14 percent interest rate, pays Company the T-bill rate plus 1 percentage point (Company's borrowing cost), and receives payments from Company at a 15 percent interest rate. On net, Bank makes interest payments at the T-bill rate [14% + (T-bill rate + 1%) − 15%]. On the other side of the transaction, Company in effect borrows at the T-bill rate plus 1 percentage point, pays Bank a 15 percent interest rate, and receives payments from Bank at the T-bill rate plus 1 percentage point. On net, then, Company makes interest payments at a 15 percent interest rate [(T-bill rate + 1%) + 15% − (T-bill rate + 1%)].[9] As a result, Bank effectively borrows at the T-bill rate, better than it could do by itself, and Company borrows at a fixed 15 percent, less than the 16 percent it would have to pay if it had entered the bond market on its own. The source of this reduction in borrowing costs is the difference in quality spreads between the fixed-rate and the floating-rate market. By being able to borrow at a fixed rate through Bank, Company saves more than enough over its own fixed-rate cost of borrowing to compensate Bank for Company's higher (than Bank's) cost of borrowing in the floating-rate market (0.5 percentage point).

The reduction in borrowing costs made possible by these quality-spread differentials has been a major selling point for swaps. These cost reductions may be more apparent than real, however. There is a lot of evidence that financial markets are efficient, and that pure arbitrage profits are not readily available.[10] Market efficiency suggests that the difference in quality spreads between fixed-rate and floating-rate markets—200 versus 50 basis points in the example—reflects differences in risk to lenders in these respective markets. Indeed, the quality spread that is typically quoted does not refer to debt of the same maturity. The floating-rate debt that firms use as a basis for swaps is mostly short to medium-term, while the fixed-rate debt consists of long-term bonds.[11] Debt-holders consider *short-term* debt less risky than long-term debt because they have the option not to renew the debt if the firm looks shakier than anticipated. Therefore, debt-holders require smaller quality spreads on short-term debt than on long-term debt. The possibility that debt will not be renewed, however, makes issuing short-term debt, rather than long-term debt, more risky to *equity-holders*. Issuing short-term, rather than long-term, debt, therefore, merely shifts risk from debt-holders to equity-holders.[12] A firm that considers swapping the floating-rate interest on its short-term debt for a fixed-rate interest payment as an alternative to borrowing directly long term must take into account that the lower cost of borrowing produced by the swap comes at the cost of increased risk to the firm's equity-holders.

Quality-spread differentials may seem to offer profit opportunities, and they may look like a good reason to use swaps instead of refinancing. But market efficiency suggests that true profit opportunities are likely to be short-lived at best, and that most of the time they are illusory. But there are more solid reasons why refinancing is more costly than interest-rate swaps, and they are transactions costs and other noninterest costs (as opposed to interest costs in the form of high-quality spreads).

Transactions Costs.   Refinancing can take a lot of time, while a swap can be arranged within a few days. To refinance, a firm has to buy back its outstanding liabilities, which can be expensive, or wait until these liabilities mature. Then the firm must try to convince its regular lenders to provide a different type of funds. A thrift, for example, may have to expend much time, effort, and expense to convince its depositors of short-term funds to invest instead in long-term time deposits.

If a firm's regular customers are unwilling to provide, say, fixed-rate funds, the firm can look to alternative markets, such as the domestic or the Eurodollar bond market. Bond markets, however, are costly to use. Domestic bond markets, for one, are highly regulated. To issue a new domestic bond, a firm has to register with the Securities and Exchange Commission (SEC) and meet its disclosure requirements.[13] In addition, a prospective bond issuer is well-advised to obtain a credit rating from the major rating agencies, such as Moody's, or Standard & Poor's, which requires additional expense. The actual selling of a bond issue involves other costs, such as advertising, legal fees, and an underwriting spread— that is, the difference between what the firm issuing the debt receives and the (higher) price that ultimate investors pay for the debt. This spread, which runs anywhere from 25 to 500 basis points and which averages about 80 basis points for investment-grade debt, serves as payment to the underwriter (or underwriter's syndicate) for distributing the issue to the ultimate investors, and for committing himself to buy that part of the issue that is not bought by the public at a given price.

As an alternative to the domestic bond market, a firm also can try the Eurodollar bond market. Eurodollar bonds are dollar-denominated bonds issued by international syndicates anywhere outside the United States. The Eurobond market has the advantage that it is almost totally unregulated (i.e., there are almost no registration or disclosure requirements), so issuing a bond does not take a lot of time. On the negative side, however, underwriting spreads on Eurodollar bonds are three to four times those on domestic bond issues. Also, because there are no disclosure requirements in Eurobond markets, investors are reluctant to lend to firms that do not have an excellent credit rating. Therefore, for relatively unknown firms the Eurodollar bond market is even less accessible than the domestic bond market.

The existence of interest-rate swaps makes it possible for firms to borrow in the markets in which they have a comparative advantage, rather than refinancing in markets in which they don't. These firms can then swap interest payments with firms that have a comparative advantage in another market to achieve the interest payment characteristics they desire. Comparative advantage can take the form of lower interest costs and lower transactions costs. Such lower costs can be the result of name recognition, an established retail network for issuing liabilities, government subsidies, and regulations, or other attributes associated with borrowing or lending in certain markets. For example, international banks have the name recognition that allows them to borrow in the Eurodollar market. Domestic banks and thrifts, on the other hand, have the retail network and deposit insurance that give them a comparative advantage in attracting retail savings-type deposits. Interest-rate swaps allow banks and thrifts to protect themselves against interest-rate risk without having to give up the retail (short-term) savings market in which most of them specialize.

SUMMARY

The high-interest rate volatility of recent years has induced many firms to look for ways to protect their profit margins—to hedge—against interest-rate fluctuations.

A recent and popular technique is the interest-rate swap, in which different parties *in effect* swap the interest-rate payments on each other's liabilities. An interest-rate swap typically allows a firm with floating-rate liabilities to exchange its floating-rate interest payments with another party for fixed-rate payments, thereby effectively acquiring a fixed-rate cost of borrowing.

In only a few years, interest-rate swaps have become very popular hedging instruments, because frequently they are better suited or less expensive than other hedging techniques, such as purchasing interest-rate futures or refinancing the firm's debt. Because interest-rate futures are standardized products traded on an organized market, they are inexpensive to use. But because of their standardization, they do not always meet a firm's specific requirements to hedge its interest-rate risk exposure. In particular, futures have delivery dates only out to 2.5 years, while there is no such limit for swaps. Swaps are freely negotiated agreements between private parties, and, therefore, they can be tailor-made. But this customization makes swaps more expensive to use than futures.

Interest-rate swaps can also be very useful when the high costs of entering a market as a new borrower make it too expensive for a firm to obtain directly the type of financing it needs to achieve its desired interest-risk exposure. A firm may find that attracting fixed-rate financing in the bond market, for example, is very costly because of high underwriting fees, disclosure costs, or the high risk premium that relatively unknown borrowers may have to pay. An interest-rate swap allows a firm to exchange interest flows in order to achieve the desired characteristics of its interest payments without changing the structure of its balance sheet. Interest-rate swaps are thus an indirect way of entering financial markets in situations where firms find it very costly to obtain financing directly.

NOTES

[1] There are two types of floating-rate debt: one is a short-term liability that has to be refinanced frequently; the other is a long-term liability on which the interest rate fluctuates with the interest rate of a specific market instrument.

[2] Cash flows are generated because the exchange where the contract is traded requires that both the buyer and seller in a futures contract post a certain margin. If the price of the underlying asset falls, the buyer has to deposit additional funds with the exchange to maintain the margin requirement, and the seller has his account credited by the same funds. Margins may consist of Treasury securities. For more details, see Howard Keen, Jr., "Interest Rate Futures: A Challenge for Bankers," *Business Review,* Federal Reserve Bank of Philadelphia, November/December, 1980, pp. 13–25; Mark Drabenstott and Anne O'Mara McDonley, "Futures Markets: A Primer for Financial Institutions," *Economic Review,* Federal Reserve Bank of Kansas City, November 1984, pp. 17–23; and Nancy Rothstein (ed.), *The Handbook on Financial Futures* (New York: McGraw-Hill, 1984).

[3] The four delivery dates are March, June, September, and December. The deliverable assets are Treasury bills, notes, and bonds; bank and Eurodollar CDs; sterling CDs and gilts; and Ginny Maes. However, there are no interest-rate futures on the prime rate or on the London Interbank Offered Rate (LIBOR), although many firms have their cost of borrowing tied to either of these two rates. Firms that use, say, a T-bill futures to hedge their LIBOR-based borrowing are still exposed to fluctuations in the relation between the T-bill rate and LIBOR. Swaps, though, frequently have the same problem, as it is difficult to find two firms with opposite exposure to the same market rate of interest (see the example in How a Swap Works).

[4] As a practical matter, a firm that wants to hedge as closely as possible, say, a five-year fixed-rate asset when only 2.5-year futures contracts are available, has to buy the contract with the longest available delivery date and then replace it every three months with the new 2.5 year contract. In this way, the firm can keep the delivery date of its futures contract as close to 2.5 years as possible. The firm will keep doing this until the remaining maturity of the asset reaches 2.5 years.

[5] Often the third-party guarantee is provided by the intermediary who would be required to step in and take over the obligation of the defaulting party. So far, there have been no reports of defaults on a swap agreement.

6 For more details, see "Swaps: Managing the Future," *Euromoney,* October 1984, pp. 201–21; and "Making a Market in Slightly Used Swaps," *Institutional Investor,* November 1984, pp. 77–84.

7 Firms could also use options in this case. An option is the right (rather than the commitment) to buy or sell an asset before a certain date in the future. Options are not discussed in this paper because a comparison of options with swaps is very similar to a comparison of futures with swaps. Options, like futures, are mostly standardized products, traded mostly on organized exchanges, and available only up to two years. However, certain over-the-counter options are increasingly available for longer periods.

8 Aaa and Baa are credit ratings assessed by Moody's Investors Services, Inc., a major credit-rating agency. This rating system consists of 10 grades, ranging from Aaa (highest quality), to Baa (medium quality), to Caa (poor quality), to D (default).

9 As explained in How a Swap Works (see box) only the *difference* between these two flows of payment actually changes hands. Unless the T-bill rate is above 14 percent, company pays the difference between 14 percent and the T-bill rate.

10 For a survey of the evidence, see Thomas E. Copeland and J. Fred Weston, *Financial Theory and Corporate Policy,* 2nd ed. (Reading, Mass.: Addison-Wesley, 1983).

11 The floating-rate debt that firms use as a basis for a floating-to-fixed interest-rate swap consists mostly of bank credit, commercial paper, certificates of deposits (CDs), and floating-rate notes (FRNs). More than 90 percent of commercial and industrial loans by U.S. banks are short term. Commercial paper usually has a maturity of three to six months, while most large negotiable CDs of financial institutions are for six months or less. Although FRNs have stated maturities of 7 to 15 years, almost all FRNs issued in the United States have covenants that give the holder the right to redeem the note at three-year intervals, thereby reducing the effective maturity of these FRNs to three years. Some of the FRNs that do show large quality spreads usually give the issuer the option to exchange the issue for fixed-rate debt before a certain date. Thus these last FRNs are more like fixed-rate bonds.

12 For a formal treatment of this issue, see Thomas Ho and Ronald Singer, "Bond Indenture Provisions and the Risk of Corporate Debt," *Journal of Financial Economics* (1982), pp. 375–406.

13 Under SEC rule 415, firms can shortcut the normally lengthy registration procedure by filing a single registration statement covering securities they expect to sell from time to time within two years. These firms can then sell securities "off the shelf" whenever they choose. However, this procedure is only available to the largest and most creditworthy corporations.

43

Futures Options and Their Use by Financial Intermediaries

G. D. Koppenhaver

Since the fall of 1982, futures exchanges in the United States have been allowed to trade options on futures contracts. These new option contracts give the option holder the right, but not the obligation, to buy or sell a futures contract at a specified price until a fixed future date. Currently, 25 futures option contracts are traded: 10 agricultural contracts, 5 contracts on gold and silver futures, and 10 contracts on foreign currencies, debt instruments, and stock indices. The five largest option contracts with respect to the total number of contracts outstanding are: Treasury bond futures (Chicago Board of Trade), soybean futures (Chicago Board of Trade), corn futures (Chicago Board of Trade), gold futures (Commodity Exchange), and West German Mark futures (Chicago Mercantile Exchange).[1]

At this stage in the development of futures option markets, options on financial futures dominate the trading activity. Because financial futures options represents a potentially useful method to control the risks of financial intermediary operation, this article discusses the principal aspects of financial futures options and the settings in which financial intermediaries can use them.

Specifically, this article begins with a review of the institutional features of option trading. The different types of options and their profitability at maturity are discussed, as well as the properties of option pricing. The next section considers the social value of options markets and compares option contracts with futures contracts as a risk-management tool. Futures option trading is then applied to the management of three different kinds of financial intermediary risk exposure. Information is also presented on the frequency of use of option arrangements by commercial banks in the United States. Following that, a discussion of several regulatory considerations with respect to futures options, in general, and the use of futures options by financial intermediaries, in particular, concludes the article.

From *Economic Perspectives,* Federal Reserve Bank of Chicago, January/February 1986, pp. 18–31.

The author is a senior economist at the Federal Reserve Bank of Chicago.

FEATURES OF OPTION TRADING[2]

The chief distinction between an option contract and either a futures or a forward contract lies in the obligations of the contract holder. Both futures and forward contracts obligate the buyer (long) to purchase and take delivery of the underlying instrument or commodity if the contract is held to expiration. To do otherwise is to default on the contract. The buyer of an option, however, is not legally obliged to take any further action over the life of the contract once the option has been purchased. If the option is not exercised at or prior to expiration, the option seller or writer (short) is also freed of all contractual obligations.

Depending on whether the option buyer has the right to buy or sell the underlying instrument or commodity, two different types of option contracts exist: these are calls and puts, respectively. Anyone can either buy or write either of these two option types, and for every call or put there must be both a buyer and a writer to complete the transaction.

The market price at which a call or put option contract is sold is called the "premium." It is paid by the buyer to the writer of the option in full. A complete specification of an option contract includes: the option type (call or put), the underlying instrument or commodity, the number of underlying units optioned, the expiration or maturity date of the option, the price at which the long can exercise the option rights (exercise or strike price), and the rule for exercise (either American or European). An American option can be exercised at any time after purchase; European options can only be exercised at the maturity date.

With futures options, many of the above contract specifications are standardized to facilitate contract offset. At each futures exchange, a clearing association interposes itself between the option buyer and writer to substitute the association's default risk for the default risk of the contract principal. Because of contract standardization and the operation of a clearing association, a buyer of a call option, for example, can exit the option market by writing a call on the same option contract. Therefore, an option long has three alternatives to exit the market: let the option expire unexercised, exercise the option at or prior to maturity, or sell the same option prior to maturity. A buyer of a call (put) that exercises the option receives a long (short) futures position; a seller of a call (put) that is assigned for exercise takes a short (long) futures position.

Financial futures options are traded with three expiration dates three months apart, the longest maturity being nine months forward. All are traded on a March-June-September-December cycle. Depending on the market on which the option is traded, the last option trading day is either the expiration date of the underlying futures contract or approximately three weeks prior to expiration of the futures contract. The strike or exercise prices of the options in a futures contract bracket the current price of the underlying contract at discrete intervals; as the futures price fluctuates, additional exercise prices are opened for trading by the exchange. All futures options traded in the United States can be exercised prior to maturity (American options). Each option also corresponds one-for-one with an underlying futures contract.

Table 1 shows an example of the report of the trading on the Chicago Board of Trade's Treasury bond futures option market. Option prices are reported by exercise price, option type, and maturity. Premiums in this example refer to the last futures option trade of the day. Financial futures option premiums are quoted

TABLE 1
Treasury Bond Futures Option Prices, June 24, 1985 ($100,000 face value; prices in points and 64ths of 1 percent)

Strike Price	Calls-Last Sept.	Dec.	Mar.	Puts-Last Sept.	Dec.	Mar.
72	4–00	3–57	3–51	0–30	1–24	2–21
74	2–37	2–50	2–53	0–63	2–12	3–13
76	1–31	1–55	2–02	1–53	3–20	4–20
78	0–51	1–14	1–28	3–05	4–34	5–39
80	0–24	0–48	—	4–39	6–00	—
82	0–11	0–30	—	6–25	—	8–40

Source: *The Wall Street Journal*, June 25, 1985

in one of two ways. For debt instruments and index futures options, premiums are described in points and valued in dollars. In foreign currency futures options, premiums are quoted and valued in dollars. In Table 1, for example, the premiums on the September call and the March put, both with an exercise price of 72, are $4,000 and $2,328, respectively (1 point = $1,000).

As mentioned above, once an option position has been taken, three actions are available: permit option expiration, option exercise, or option offset. To study the desirability of each of these actions, suppose an investor owns a Treasury bond futures call option with a strike price of 75 and it is the option expiration day. If the call is exercised, the investor acquires a long Treasury bond futures contract valued at $75,000. If Treasury bond futures contracts are trading for any price less than 75, exercising the call creates a loss. It would be better to let the option expire unexercised and purchase the Treasury bond futures contract directly. In general, the value of a call option is zero at expiration if the price of the underlying instrument is less than the option strike price. Therefore, the investor also does not benefit from an option offset trade (writing a call on the same option) because the premium is zero.

If the underlying Treasury bond futures price is above the call option strike price at expiration, say at 80, the investor can exercise the call option and sell Treasury bond futures at a price $5,000 greater than $75,000, the price of the long futures position acquired through the option exercise. The value of the call option at expiration is therefore equal to the difference ($5,000) between the price of the underlying futures and the option strike price; permitting the option to expire results in a lost profit opportunity.

If the option premium is trading at greater than $5,000 at expiration, the investor can offset the call position by selling or writing a call on the same option, earning the excess of the call premium over the underlying futures price less the option strike price. Similar actions by other long calls and arbitrageurs will drive the call option premium back to $5,000. If the call option premium is trading at less than $5,000 at expiration, option offset is not profitable and additional call buyers will enter the market to bid away the excess of $5,000 over the call option premium. In the end, the actions of market participants force the call option price to exactly equal the difference between the underlying futures price and the option strike price, at expiration. The same argument applies to futures put options.

If the present price of the futures contract is above (below) the strike price of the call (put) option, it is called an "in-the-money option"; if the present price of the futures contract is below (above) the strike price of the call (put) option, it is called an "out-of-the-money option." The intrinsic value of an option is the amount by which the option is in the money. Therefore, the intrinsic value of an out-of-the-money option is zero. But prior to expiration, the option premium consists of more than just its intrinsic value; it also includes a time value.

The time value of an option is the seller's compensation for the possibility that the option will be worth more at maturity than if exercised immediately. Therefore, out-of-the-money options prior to maturity trade at positive premiums, solely reflecting the option's time value. The premium rewards the option writer for the risk that the underlying futures price will change and create an in-the-money option. Of course, in-the-money options prior to maturity also have a time value; it is the difference between the option premium and the intrinsic value of the option. In sum, the most interesting question in option trading is how options are priced prior to maturity. The pricing of options has implications not only for the individual market participant but also for the social value and economic impact of these markets.

Profit diagrams show the profits at expiration from option positions as functions of the underlying instrument's price. They are a simple way to become familiar with options and option strategies, provided one considers only options with the same expiration date. Trading commissions are usually ignored to focus on the profit outcome of the option strategies. Further, you should suppose that the only instruments available to the investor are futures option puts and calls on the same futures contract and the futures contract itself. Three simple strategies are discussed: naked (uncovered) positions, hedged (covered) positions, and spread or straddle positions.

Naked positions involve only one of the three investments, taken alone. The investor can either buy or sell futures, futures call options, or futures put options. Figure 1 shows the profit diagrams for each of these actions. The trading profit is shown as a function of the different possible values of the futures price at option expiration, F_T, given that the position was established either at a futures price at time $t(t < T)$ of F_t or a futures option exercise price of S_t. In Figure 1a, increases in the futures price over F_t increase (decrease) investor profits from a long (short) futures position dollar-for-dollar as F_T exceeds F_t. The maximum loss (gain) on the long (short) futures position occurs when F_T goes to zero.

In Figure 1b, the long call yields profits similar to the long futures position if the option expires in the money ($F_T > S_t$). If it expires out of the money, however, the maximum loss from the long call is limited to the call premium, C_t. On the other hand, the maximum gain from writing a call is the same call premium; this occurs when the option expires out of the money ($F_T < S_t$). The call writer's losses are potentially unlimited if the call expires in the money. It can also be seen from this figure that the simultaneous purchase and sale of a call option at the same strike price reduces profits to zero for all values of F_T. Gains and losses for the long call are exactly matched by losses and gains for the short call. Like the futures market, the futures option market is a zero-sum game.

In Figure 1c, the long put is seen to yield profits similar to a short futures position, except that losses are now limited to the put premium, P_t. If the long put

FIGURE 1
Profit Diagrams for Naked Positions

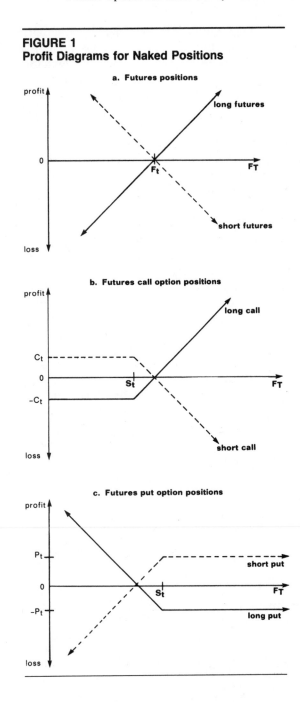

a. Futures positions

b. Futures call option positions

c. Futures put option positions

expires in the money ($F_T < S_t$), the maximum profit occurs when F_T goes to zero, and this equals the maximum profit from a short futures position less the put premium paid. The profit from a short put is at a maximum when the put expires out of the money and it equals the put premium. Although the gain is truncated when compared with a long futures position, the maximum loss from a short put is the same as for a long futures position. Finally, note that, in Figures 1b and 1c, a long option can have intrinsic value (be in the money) and still be unprofitable when exercised. This is because the amount by which the option is in the money may not cover the premium paid to the option writer. Nevertheless, the long will always want to capture an option's positive intrinsic value at expiration in order to minimize losses.

Hedged positions in this simple menu of investments involve a combination of the underlying futures contract and one or more options of the same type. The combination of investments is undertaken to manage the risks inherent in a naked position. One common hedge strategy is to write covered call options. Figure 2a shows the profit diagram for hedging a long futures position with a short call assuming, for simplicity, that the option strike price, S_t, equals the initial futures price, F_t. This hedging strategy converts all profitable futures price changes into a constant return of C_t, the call option premium. Unfavorable futures price changes are mitigated by the receipt of the call premium.

This strategy can be used to increase portfolio returns when futures prices are relatively stable or move only slightly higher. Further, notice that the profit diagram for a covered call hedge is identical to that for a short put option (see Figure 1c). This technique of fabricating put options from a covered call hedge is

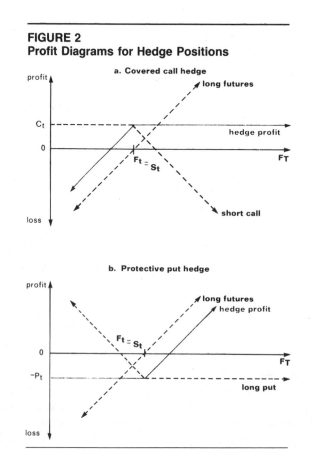

FIGURE 2
Profit Diagrams for Hedge Positions

a. Covered call hedge

b. Protective put hedge

called a "synthetic put" or "conversion." In Figure 2b, the hedge strategy is to buy protective puts. A long futures position is combined with a long put option to limit the downside risk to the price of a put option. If futures prices rise, the cost of the out-of- the-money put option can be regarded as the cost of insurance for a potential futures loss. The protective put hedge has an identical profit profile at expiration as a long call option (see Figure 1b).

In each of these simple hedging strategies, the selection of the option to be written or purchased is important in allowing the investor to capture more or less of the favorable outcomes of the underlying futures contract. In Figure 2a, for example, an investor could seek to profit from an increase in futures prices in addition to the option premium earned by writing out-of-the-money call options $(S_t > F_t)$. The premium earned on an out-of-the-money option will be smaller than C_t in Figure 2a, so the unfavorable long futures outcomes are improved less by its receipt. With this strategy constant hedge profits at expiration set in at a higher expiration price, F_T, expanding the range of futures price advances that increase portfolio returns. Similarly, out-of-the-money puts could be purchased in the protective put hedging strategy to decrease the insurance against a futures price fall and capture hedging profits at smaller F_T than in Figure 2b.

Another method of changing the risk-reward characteristics of covered hedges is to invest in fewer or more options than the number of futures contracts purchased. As fewer (more) calls are written in the covered call hedge strategy, the profit diagram in Figure 2a looks more (less) like the profit diagram for a naked long futures position and less (more) like that for a written futures put option.

Spread positions with the same three instruments involve a combination of options with different strike prices of expirations in which some options are held long and some short. A commonly used spread is called a "money" or "vertical" spread where the options have the same expiration date but different strike prices. Figure 3a and 3b illustrate the profit diagrams for two possible money spreads: a bear call spread and a bull put spread. In Figure 3a, a call option has been written with a relatively low strike price, S_t^l, earning a premium of C_t^l, and another call option has been purchased with a relatively high strike price, S_t^h, at a cost of C_t^h. This spread is termed a *bear call spread* because it shows a profit (loss) when the long futures position has unfavorable (favorable) outcomes. If both options expire out-of-the-money $(F_T < S_t^l < S_t^h)$, the maximum profit is the difference between the premium earned on the short call, C_t^l, and the cost of the long call, C_t^h. The maximum loss from the bear call spread, which occurs if both options expire in-the-money $(S_t^l < S_t^h < F_T)$, is equal to the position value at expiration $((S_t^h - F_T) - (S_t^l - F_T) = S_t^h - S_t^l)$ plus the excess of the premium received over the premium paid $(C_t^l - C_t^h)$. If $S_t^l > F_T > S_t^h$, then the long call position will expire unexercised and profits will fall with the short call position. In general, a bear call spread is profitable if futures prices fall.

Figure 3b illustrates a money spread that is profitable if futures prices rise; it is called a "bull put spread." It involves writing a put option with a high strike price and buying a put option with a low strike price. The maximum profit from a bullput spread, which occurs when both options expire out-of-the-money $(S_t^l < S_t^h < F_T)$, is equal to the excess of the premium earned over the premium paid, $P_t^h - P_t^l$. The maximum loss occurs when both put options expire in-the-money $(F_T < S_t^l < S_t^h)$. The losses from the short put are offset somewhat by the gains

FIGURE 3
Profit Diagrams for Spread Positions

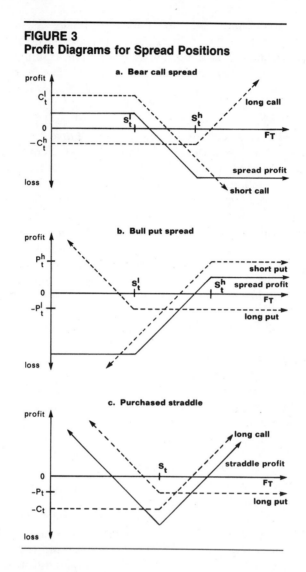

a. Bear call spread

b. Bull put spread

c. Purchased straddle

from the long put. The maximum loss is equal to $(F_T - S_t^h) - (F_T - S_t^l) = S_t^l - S_t^h$ less the premium difference, $P_t^h - P_t^l$.

Yet another type of options-only strategy is shown in Figure 3c. This combination of options involves buying both a call and a put option with the same strike price and exercise date, called a "purchased straddle." This type of strategy will be profitable in a highly volatile futures market, where the possibility exists of either a large futures price fall or a large futures price rise. Figure 3c illustrates the situation of in-the-money call options and out-of-the-money put options ($C_t > P_t$). The maximum loss from a purchased straddle ($C_t + P_t$) occurs when the futures price at expiration is at the strike price of the options. Other types of straddles can be created and it is left to the reader to draw the profit diagram for a written straddle.

SOCIAL VALUE OF OPTION MARKETS

At this point it would be useful to discuss the economic benefits of futures and option markets (derivative markets) and their effect on the allocation of resources. Perhaps the most important economic function served by derivative markets is that they provide a means to transfer risk exposure encountered in business operations or investing to those more willing to bear the risk. These markets are beneficial to society because they expand the scope of possible risk-management activities. To the extent that businesses can shed some of their risks with these contracts, resource-allocation decisions can be made with less uncertain outcomes.

Derivative markets may also reduce the overall level of risk exposure in the economy, provided hedgers willing to sell contracts are trading with hedgers willing to buy contracts. The resulting swap of risk exposure between hedgers makes each less risky. However, the risk-transfer benefits of derivative markets are lessened to the extent that cash and derivative market prices fail to move together (basis risk).

A second economic function performed by the futures and options markets deals with the forward pricing and price discovery process. Currently available information will be used by hedgers and speculators in establishing derivative contract positions; thus, market prices will reflect current and prospective demand/supply conditions in the underlying instrument. Of course, this result requires market participants to be efficient and accurate processors of information. If they are, derivative market prices could be used by nonparticipants to base transactions in "off-exchange" markets, further aiding the allocation of resources.

A third general economic function of derivative markets is to increase the liquidity of underlying cash markets. The mechanism linking cash and derivative markets is the activity of hedgers, arbitrageurs, and spreaders. For example, a bank might decide to increase its fixed-rate lending funded by variable-rate deposits when it utilizes the risk-shifting potential of derivative markets. Because of joint cash and derivative market decisions, liquidity tends to be enhanced in both markets; execution costs are reduced over transactions made without derivative markets.

There are also benefits specific to options, in general, and to futures options, in particular, that are not available with futures alone. As is obvious in Figure 1, the risk-reward trade-off for futures options is significantly different than for futures. Losses and gains can be limited, with options depending on the type of option traded; options can be used to provide insurance against unfavorable outcomes of the underlying instrument, while retaining the favorable outcomes. This is not possible with futures, because favorable (unfavorable) outcomes of the underlying instrument are generally offset by unfavorable (favorable) outcomes of the futures. This makes options a more suitable hedging device than futures for the management of quantity, as opposed to price, risks.

Quantity risks are associated with potential transactions that may or may not take place. Quantity risk tied to interest-rate movements, such as takedowns on fixed-rate loan commitments, can be hedged by purchasing financial futures options and, if the contingency underlying the quantity risk is realized, exercising them. If the contingency is not realized, the option is permitted to expire and the cost of the premium is just the cost of insurance. As Figures 2 and 3 show, options can also be used to customize the risk-reward trade-off according to the risk preferences of the investor. By creating portfolios of options and the underlying security with different strike prices and expiration dates, a whole menu of portfolio return characteristics can be offered. Options are more flexible than futures in this sense. Finally, except for naked written options, the options investor is not subject to any margin calls over the life of the option. Once the option premium is paid, the investor does not risk being forced out of a position by maintenance margin calls, as is possible in futures trading.

But what advantage is there to trading futures options instead of options on cash-market financial instruments? Currently, both options on futures and options on actuals are actively traded for the same financial instruments; both serve very similar functions in facilitating the allocation of resources. Nevertheless, there are reasons why futures options might survive this derivative market redundancy. In some cases, the volume of trade and liquidity of the underlying futures market exceeds that of the underlying actuals market. If the options are exercised, a liquid market facilitates the exit from or adjustment to the position acquired in the underlying instrument. For example, the deliverable supply of Treasury bond futures contracts is virtually limitless, unlike the deliverable supply of a specific Treasury bond issue.

Financial futures options also avoid the adjustment needed at exercise to compensate for accrued coupon or dividend payments on the underlying instrument. This is not true of options on cash Treasury bonds. Furthermore, unlike options on actuals, an exercise of a futures option does not require payment or receipt of the entire cash value of the underlying instrument implied by the option strike price. All that is needed is that the payment be the incremental futures margin to cover any gain or loss due to the difference between the current futures price and the exercise price. This reduces the capital requirement for option trading and extends the possibilities for leverage.

It may also be easier to price options on futures than options on actuals prior to expiration, because futures prices are more readily available than actuals prices. In any event, the ease with which one can speculate on either the long or the short side of futures markets, unlike most actuals markets, creates a demand for risk-limiting tools like futures options for futures participants.

THE PRICING OF FUTURES CALL OPTIONS

In 1976, Fischer Black derived a formula for calculating the theoretical price of a call option on a futures contract prior to expiration.[3] This formula shows the basic variables that a futures option investor needs to know before an estimate can be formed of what a particular option price should be. The different types of variables fall into one of three groups: variables associated with the underlying futures contract, variables associated with the option itself, and variables that are exogenous to the pricing decision. Black's formula for a futures call option is given by:

$$C_t = e^{-r\,(T-t)}[F_t \cdot N(d_1) - S_t \cdot N(d_2)]$$

where: $d_1 = [1n(F_t/S_t) + (1/2)\sigma^2(T - t)]/\sigma(T - t)^{1/2},$

and $d_2 = d_1 - \sigma(T - t)^{1/2},$

and the new notation is
   e = the exponential function,
   r = the risk-free interest rate,
$N(i)$ = the cumulative normal density function evaluated at $i = d_1, d_2,$
   ln = the logarithmic function, and
   σ = the standard deviation of the futures price.

Black derived this formula by first assuming that the futures price change can be described by a log-normal distribution with known variance, all the parameters of the capital asset pricing model are constant through time, and taxes and transaction costs are zero.[4]

Of the variables relating to the underlying futures price, the most important is the current price of the futures contract, F_t. The higher is the underlying futures price, the greater is the value of the call option, because of the greater anticipated value of the option at expiration. The volatility or variability of the underlying futures price is another variable in this group. As futures price volatility increases, so does the possibility of favorable or unfavorable outcomes for the futures investor. But for the option investor, only the in-the-money outcomes have an impact on the value of the option. Since the magnitudes of possible favorable outcomes have an impact on the value of the option. Since the magnitudes of possible favorable outcomes increase with greater futures price volatility, so does the futures call option premium.

Variables in the formula that are associated with the option itself are the option strike price and its time to maturity. Because the strike price influences the value and payoff of a call at expiration, decreasing the strike price will increase the call premium and vice versa (see Table 1). The time to maturity of a given underlying futures contract is important in futures option pricing because, as the time to expiration increases, the present value of the exercise price that could be paid at expiration decreases. Also, increasing the time to maturity increases the likelihood of favorable option outcomes during the life of the contract. Call premiums, therefore, increase as time to maturity increases.

A final variable that is assumed exogenous in Black's pricing formula is the risk-free rate of interest. An increasing interest rate decreases the present value of option profits at expiration; hence, the call premium falls as the risk-free rate rises.

Besides using Black's formula to evaluate whether a given futures option is "expensive" or "cheap," another application of the formula is to use it to derive a riskless hedge ratio.[5] A riskless hedge ratio is the ratio of the number of futures contracts that must be held per futures option to fully insulate the investor against movements in the underlying futures price. Using Black's formula, this hedge ratio, h, can be shown to be

$$h = -e^{-r(T-t)}N(d_1).$$

That is, a portfolio which includes h long futures contracts and a written futures option on the same contract leaves the value of this portfolio unchanged on net when the futures price changes. Movements in the value of the option are exactly counteracted by futures price movements and vice versa. The minus sign in the expression for h indicates that the futures and futures option are held in opposite positions, either long or short. For example, if $h = -0.5$, a change in the futures price of one point causes the value of a written futures call option to change by 0.5 points. Therefore, two call options should be written for each futures contract to leave the value of the hedged portfolio unaffected by a change in the futures price. The riskless hedge ratio changes as each of the variables discussed above changes; thus, the riskless hedge ratio must be reevaluated and adjusted frequently over the life of the hedge.

FINANCIAL INTERMEDIARIES AND FINANCIAL FUTURES OPTIONS

Having described the mechanics of futures options, we are now prepared to discuss the application of financial futures options to depository institution decision making. This section focuses on the use of futures options to either hedge or limit the risk of bank and thrift operations.

Evidence suggests that financial intermediaries have been even more reluctant to engage in option arrangements than in financial futures. Using Federal Reserve Report of Condition data, a recent study by Parkinson and Spindt shows that no more than 400 domestic commercial banks nationwide reported futures and forward market positions as of year-end 1983.[6]

Using Report of Condition data for September 1984, Table 2 shows that option arrangements are reported even less frequently by domestic commercial banks. The data on option arrangements is less than complete, since commercial banks are only required to report short call and put option arrangements.[7] Furthermore, these option positions likely include exchange-traded, over-the-counter, and personally customized option arrangements. Nevertheless, Table 2 does provide a rough idea of the extent to which commercial banks are engaged in option trading. As of this date, approximately 90 different banks reported written option arrangements, and, in this group, banks with assets greater than $1 billion tend to be the most frequent users.[8]

To highlight the potential uses of financial futures options by banks and thrifts, three different situations that a financial intermediary might face are discussed. These situations relate to the use of options in (1) a Treasury bond portfolio, (2) interest-rate risk management in the financial firm's entire balance sheet, and (3) the management of mortgage prepayment risk. For the sake of simplicity, brokerage commissions and tax considerations are not taken into account.

Bond Portfolio Protection.   Suppose that on February 15, 1985, a bond portfolio manager holds 50 Treasury bonds ($100,000 par value each) with a coupon rate of 10.75 percent and maturity of February 15, 2003. The manager seeks a strategy to protect the portfolio against rising interest rates and falling bond prices over the next three months. Further, although protecting the value of the portfolio is important, the manager would like to retain the opportunity to profit from an increase in bond prices. The current market yield on these bonds is 11.63 percent and each is worth $93,422.

To protect this value the manager decides to buy 50 June 1985 Treasury bond futures put options at a strike price of 72.[9] Since the Treasury bond futures contract is trading at 70.69 on this date, these are in-the-money puts and are priced at $2,594 each. Three months later on May 17, 1985, the market yield on the bonds

TABLE 2
Use of Option Arrangements by U.S. Banks, September 1984

	N	Frequency of Use (%)	Ratio of Options Position to Equity (%)[a]
I. Written calls:			
a. All U.S. banks	14,489	0.35	17.34[b]
			(4.25)
b. Banks with assets less than $100 million	12,139	0.21	20.63
			(NF1(6.84)
c. Banks with assets between $100 million and $500 million	1,883	0.27	36.40
			(22.34)
d. Banks with assets between $500 million and $1 billion	198	0.00	0.0
			(−)
e. Banks with assets greater than $1 billion	269	7.45	8.45
			(2.62)
II. Written puts:			
a. All U.S. banks	14,489	0.39	29.98
			(9.02)
b. Banks with assets less than $100 million	12,139	0.18	47.52
			(19.63)
c. Banks with assets between $100 million and $500 million	1,883	0.16	12.00
			(9.39)
d. Banks with assets between $500 million and $1 billion	198	1.01	3.35
			(2.20)
e. Banks with assets greater than $1 billion	269	10.78	20.37
			(8.58)

[a] For those reporting a nonzero option position.
[b] Mean with standard deviation in parentheses.

in the portfolio has fallen to 11.12 percent, instead of rising as was feared. Bonds in the portfolio are now valued at $99,835 each.[10] The cash bond portfolio has appreciated $6,413 per bond and $320,650 in total. Since the Treasury bond futures price settled at 73.88 on May 17, 1985, the put options are permitted to expire out of the money.

The net result of this protective put hedging strategy is $190,950 ($320,650 minus 50 put option premiums). In contrast, if cash bond rates had risen to 12.14 percent by May 17, 1985 (or if rates had risen by as many basis points as they actually fell), the bond portfolio would have decreased in value by a total of $40,550. If the June 1985 Treasury bond futures contract had settled at, say, 68.04, the 50 put options would be exercised at a total profit of $198,000. The net gain to the bond portfolio is $27,750 ($198,000 - $40,550 minus the cost of the purchased puts).

Asset/Liability Management.   Interest-rate futures options can be used by a financial intermediary to manage the interest-rate maturity gap in its entire balance sheet over a specific time interval in the future. To use futures options in this way, the bank or thrift must first identify the interest-rate risk exposure in its balance sheet. The maturity gap approach involves classifying all asset and liability accounts by their term to maturity or first permissible repricing, whichever comes first, and then calculating the dollar difference between assets and liabilities for subintervals in a predetermined horizon.[11] These differences or gaps represent the interest-rate risk exposure of the institution at a particular maturity subinterval.

For example, if a hypothetical bank undertook a gap analysis and found that the dollar values of assets and liabilities match at all maturities except those greater than 10 years forward and that, at maturities greater than 10 years forward, a bond investment portfolio similar to the one discussed directly above had no offsetting liabilities, then the purchase of futures put options would limit the risk of a rise in interest rates and a fall in bond prices.

In this case, managing the risk of a well-defined collection of assets (micro-risk management) also reduces the interest-rate risk exposure of the entire institution (macro-risk management). However, it is not necessarily true that a micro strategy with futures options automatically reduces an institution's entire risk exposure; one must also consider the risk-control features of cash items on the other side of the balance sheet with similar maturity or repricing characteristics. In general, a negative maturity gap (rate-sensitive liabilities exceed rate-sensitive assets) can be managed by a strategy of purchasing protective puts.

Alternatively, a financial intermediary could write futures call options to hedge the interest-rate risk exposure of a negative maturity gap. The risk-reward trade-off for a negative gap position looks very similar to the profit diagram for a long futures position (see Figure 1a). If interest rates fall and prices rise, the cost of funding fixed-rate assets declines and the profit margin widens; if rates rise and prices fall, the cost of funding fixed-rate assets increases and the profit margin narrows. Writing futures call options to hedge this risk exposure results in a profit diagram similar to Figure 2a.

For example, suppose that on March 25, 1985, a bank has funded $75 million in loans that reprice every six months with three-month Eurodollar certificates of deposit at an annual rate of 9.30 percent. If rates rise by 1 percent, the bank will have to pay an additional $187,500 to refinance the loans. To protect against a rise in funding costs, bank management decides to write June 1985 Eurodollar futures call options at a strike price of 89.50.[12] Since the June Eurodollar futures settled at 89.78 on March 25, 1985, these in-the-money calls earn a premium of $1,450 each.[13] Assuming bank management believes Eurodollar rates are more likely to fall than rise in three months, only 30 calls are written, generating $43,500 in option premiums.

Roughly three months later, on June 17, 1985, three-month Eurodollar certificates of deposit offer a 7.60 percent annual interest rate; the bank's loans can now be financed at a savings of $318,750 relative to the March 1985 rate. On this date, the June Eurodollar futures price settled at 92.44. Because the Eurodollar futures call options have matured and will therefore be exercised, the bank must pay the call buyers $7,350 ($= [92.44 - 89.50]2500$) for each option, or $220,500 in total. The net savings on the loan refunding is $141,750 ($= $318,750 + $43,500 - $220,500$).

Of course, if the bank's interest-rate risk exposure had been fully covered with 75 written calls, the net savings on the loan refunding would have been negative. Also, if Eurodollar rates had risen 1 percent instead of fallen over the three-month period, the additional $107,500 in Eurodollar funding costs would have been partially offset by the receipt of $43,500 in call premium income.

Mortgage Prepayment Protection. Financial intermediaries that extend fixed-rate mortgage loans funded by short-term liabilities (a negative maturity gap) face two different types of risk associated with interest-rate changes: if rates rise, the cost of funding these loans increases and the profit spread narrows; and if rates fall, borrowers will refinance their mortgages at lower rates and the profit spread again narrows. Therefore, when a savings and loan association, for example, makes a fixed-rate mortgage loan, it effectively writes a call option over the life of the mortgage for the borrower.[14] It will be exercised when it is in the money (i.e., whenever mortgage rates fall below the contractual rate minus any prepayment penalties or new loan origination costs). The savings and loan with a negative maturity gap can manage the risk of a rise in interest rates by either of the methods described directly above: by buying protective puts or writing calls.

To manage the risk of mortgage prepayment if rates should fall, however, the savings and loan should buy interest-rate call options. The management of this latter quantity risk is well suited to options trading.

Suppose a hypothetical savings and loan has five homogeneous mortgage loans on its books, each earning a fixed rate of 14.25 percent with 20 years to maturity on an outstanding principal of $100,000. These loans are funded with three-month certificates of deposit. On November 15, 1984, conventional mortgages yield 12.3 percent but, because the savings and loan imposes fees and charges of 2.5 percent on new loan originations, the borrowers find it unprofitable to exercise their call options. With three-month certificate of deposit rates at 9.20 percent, the savings and loan earns a 5.05 percent spread over the cost of funds, or $6,313 every quarter.

To hedge the risk of a fall in mortgage rates and mortgage prepayment, management decides to buy five March 1985 Treasury bond futures call options at a strike price of 70. This strike price roughly reflects the level to which mortgage rates must fall before the borrowers will exercise their call options (11.75 percent). On November 15, each T-bond futures call option has a premium of $851 (March 1985 Treasury bond futures = 69.78) and the total option hedge position costs $4,255. The objective of the savings and loan is, therefore, to protect its spread over the next three months.

On February 15, 1985, mortgage rates have fallen to 11.7 percent and three-month certificates of deposit earn 8.7 percent interest. The savings and loan borrowers exercise their call options to refinance at this lower rate; the savings and loan's profit spread narrows to 3 percent as a result, resulting in earnings of $3,750 every quarter. But the fall in mortgage rates also coincides with a rise in March 1985 Treasury bond futures prices. The five futures call options can be offset to return $2,109 per option, or $10,545 in total. This return exceeds the cost of the call options plus the loss in quarterly income due to prepayment and refinancing ($4,255 + $2,563 = $6,818). Of course, the hypothetical savings and loan has managed the risk of prepayment only over a three-month period and, henceforth, must deal with the lower yield on its mortgage assets.

REGULATORY CONSIDERATIONS AND CONCLUSION

One justification for this article's treatment of financial futures options as distinctly different from options to cash-market financial instruments is the jurisdictional difference in regulatory structures. In December 1981, the Commodity Futures Trading Commission (CFTC) and Securities and Exchange Commission (SEC) made an accord to clarify the jurisdictional responsibilities of the two regulators with respect to financial instrument futures and options. As a result of the accord, which was later codified in the 1982 reauthorization of the CFTC, the SEC is to regulate all options on securities, stock indices, certificates of deposit, and national exchange-traded foreign currencies. The CFTC is to regulate all futures and futures options on these same instruments, as well as an agricultural commodities.

Thus, although options on financial instrument futures and actual may have the same underlying instrument and, therefore, be highly substitutable in their economic usefulness, two different regulators oversee their trading. To the extent that there are real or philosophical differences in the way these two regulators operate, the markets in options on futures may evolve differently than the markets in options on actuals. This has implications for the long-run survival of one type of option market relative to the other. At this point in their development, it is too early to tell which is the more viable type of financial instrument option.

Another regulatory consideration related to futures options deals with the devices available to protect the financial integrity of the markets. Like other financial markets, futures and futures option markets are subject to the risk that the parties to the transaction will be unable to perform their contractual obligations and default.

Margin requirements and the daily mark-to-market provisions of futures exchange operation are important ingredients for assuring the performance of contractual obligations. Unlike equity margins, futures margins do not reflect a customer's investment in the futures position but merely the deposit of earnest money required to initiate a position and keep it open. The amount of earnest money held by the broker in the customer's account changes due to the daily mark-to-market provisions of exchange operation; as the value of a futures contract position is marked to market and effectively set to zero, all profits and losses are passed through to the respective market participants.

In contrast, futures-type margining is not required on purchases of futures options; option sellers, however, must deposit and maintain margin related to the margin on the underlying futures contract plus the option premium. Since only the futures option seller is obligated to perform over the life of the option, only short option positions are margined. However, any additional margin monies posted by the option seller are not passed through to the option buyer but are held by the seller's broker. The gains on a long put option position in a protective put strategy, for example, cannot be used to meet the maintenance margin calls on the futures position as it is marked to market. If a call option seller should fail to meet a margin call as the options move well in the money, the option seller's broker could default and the call option buyer may not be able to realize the potential profits from the long option position.[15] In sum, because the profits from a long futures option position are not settled until exercise or offset, the responsibility for financial integrity in futures option markets rests more fully on the exchange clearing associations than on margin requirements and mark-to-market provisions.

Other types of futures option regulation related specifically to financial intermediaries are imposed by the federal bank and thrift regulatory agencies. The following discussion is based just on federal bank regulations.[16] In general, the federal bank regulators disapprove of futures option trading that increases an institution's risk exposure.

The regulators are in agreement, however, that financial futures options can effectively control interest-rate risk if properly used, and that institutions should use futures options to control only the net interest-rate risk exposure in their entire balance sheet. Banks that engage in financial futures options should do so only in accordance with safe and sound banking practices. Furthermore, any trading activity should be at a level reasonably related to the bank's business activity and its capacity to fulfill the contractual obligations. Banks should evaluate their overall interest-rate risk exposure resulting from asset and liability positions to ensure that the futures option position reduces its total risk. These policy guidelines are applicable specifically to commercial banking activities and do not pertain to bank trust accounts.

Within these guidelines, some types of option positions are treated specifically by the federal bank regulators. Long-term short option contracts (i.e., those for 150 days or more) are ordinarily viewed as inappropriate for bank trading, unless special circumstances warrant. The regulators believe that such contracts are related not to the investment or business needs of the institution but primarily to the receipt of fee income or to speculating in future interest-rate movements. Moreover, Federal Reserve bank examiners are instructed to treat all naked written call option positions as per se speculative and hence inappropriate.[17] A call option is considered covered only if the underlying instrument to be hedged is deliverable against the option contract. In light of this, the above example of writing call options to manage the net interest-rate risk exposure faced by a bank with a negative maturity gap would be considered speculative behavior and contrary to policy guidelines. Because the entire balance sheet must be considered in using futures options, not just a specific instrument, the distinction employed by bank examiners in determining whether a written call is covered or naked is not economically meaningful.[18]

In conclusion, financial futures options provide financial intermediaries with another tool to manage rapidly changing interest-rate and quantity risks. The attractiveness and usefulness of financial futures options lies in their versatility; they can be used as a means to limit risk or generate additional portfolio returns even in a stable market environment. For a financial intermediary with a negative maturity gap, the purchase of futures put options allows it to limit risk associated with an increase in interest rates, and the sale of a futures call option permits it to lower the variability of its returns. Both strategies result in an institution with reduced exposure to unfavorable interest-rate changes. On the other hand, a financial intermediary with a positive maturity gap should either write futures put options or buy futures call options to decrease its interest-rate risk. The material presented here is intended as an introduction to futures option contract trading. It will have served its purpose if it helps to educate both the potential users and regulators about the economic usefulness of options on financial futures.

NOTES

[1] These four contract markets are listed in order, as of September 23, 1985.

[2] The next two sections of the article draw heavily from Robert Jarrow and Andrew Rudd, *Option Pricing* (Homewood, Ill.: Dow Jones-Irwin, 1983), chaps. 1–3. Other recent articles on financial futures options include: Laurie S. Goodman, "New Options Markets," *Quarterly Review*, Federal Reserve Bank of New York, Autumn 1983, pp. 35–47; and Michael T. Belongia and Thomas H.

Gregory, "Are Options on Treasury Bond Futures Priced Efficiently?" *Review*, Federal Reserve Bank of St. Louis, January 1981, pp. 5–13.

[3] See Fischer Black, "The Pricing of Commodity Contracts," *Journal of Financial Economics*, January/March 1976, pp. 167–79.

[4] For a discussion of the capital asset pricing model, see Michael C. Jensen, "Capital Markets: Theory and Evidence," *Bell Journal of Economics and Management Science*, Autumn 1972, pp. 357–98.

[5] Because Black's model is derived for European options, one may question whether the pricing formula given above is applicable to futures options currently traded in the United States. Merton argues, however, that any distinction between European and American options vanishes in the absence of dividends on the underlying instrument. Since futures contracts do not pay dividends (semi-annual coupons), Black's formula is applicable to futures of options. See Robert C. Merton, "The Theory of Rational Option Pricing," *Bell Journal of Economics and Management Science*, Spring 1973, pp. 141–83.

[6] See Patrick Parkinson and Paul Spindt, "The Use of Interest Rate Futures by Commercial Banks," a paper presented at the 21st annual Conference on Bank Structure and Competition, sponsored by the Federal Reserve Bank of Chicago, Chicago, May 3, 1985.

[7] This reporting requirement implicitly reveals that, if a bank holds an option arrangement instead of writing one, its maximum off-balance sheet risk exposure is limited to the option premium and, hence, does not merit monitoring. If banks attempt to use long option positions to limit or hedge their balance sheet risk exposure, as discussed in the text, it is currently impossible to tell from the call reports whether these options are used properly.

[8] A rough approximation of total put and call option usage (long and short) suggests that fewer than 180 different banks are involved, which is less than half the number of institutions reporting futures and forward contract positions.

[9] In this simple example, no adjustment is made for the difference in coupon yield and maturity of the instrument underlying the Treasury bond futures option (8 percent coupon, 20-year maturity) and the bonds in the portfolio. The Chicago Board of Trade publishes conversion factors that can be used to convert an actual issue to the hypothetical futures option bond for a match of price sensitivities.

[10] Accrued interest of $2,688 over three months is included in each of the end-of-period calculations for a cash bond.

[11] For a more detailed discussion of the maturity gap approach to measuring interest-rate risk exposure, see Elijah Brewer, "Bank Gap Management and the Use of Financial Futures," *Economic Perspectives*, Federal Reserve Bank of Chicago, March/April 1985, pp. 12–22; George G. Kaufman, "Measuring and Managing Interest Rate Risk," *Economic Perspectives*, Federal Reserve Bank of Chicago, January/February 1984, pp. 16–29; and Alden L. Toevs, "Gap Management: Managing Interest Rate Risk in Banks and Thrifts," *Economic Review*, Federal Reserve Bank of San Francisco, Spring 1983, pp. 20–35.

[12] Eurodollar futures options (International Monetary Market at the Chicago Mercantile Exchange) began trading on March 19, 1985.

[13] Eurodollar option premium quotations are based on International Monetary Market index points, where each index point (0.01) represents $25. June 1985 Eurodollar futures call options with a strike price of 89.50 were valued at 0.58 on March 25, 1985.

[14] For a discussion of the limitations of using financial futures contracts to hedge this prepayment risk, see Carl A. Batlin, "Interest Rate Risk, Prepayment Risk, and the Futures Market Hedging Strategies of Financial Intermediaries," *Journal of Futures Markets*, Summer 1983, pp. 177–84.

[15] Recently, just such an episode occurred in the gold futures option market. See articles in *Business Week*, May 27, 1985, pp. 132–34, and *The Wall Street Journal*, March 22 (p. 11) and March 25 (p. 38), 1985.

[16] Because general guidelines issued by the federal bank regulators cover option arrangements, futures contracts, and forward contracts in a single set of documents, see G. D. Koppenhaver, "Trimming the Hedges: Regulators, Banks, and Financial Futures," *Economic Perspectives*, November/December 1984, pp. 3–12, for a related discussion.

[17] See Federal Reserve Board document AD82–24 (FIS): Manual for Examination Concerning Bank and Bank Holding Company Use of Interest Rate Futures and Forward Contracts (July 26, 1982).

[18] This point was first made by Laurie S. Goodman in an unpublished paper entitled "Interest Rate Options and Financial Institutions," Federal Reserve Bank of New York, August 1982.

44

From ATM to POS Networks: Branching, Access, and Pricing

Steven D. Felgran

After years of planning and experimentation, electronic payment at the retail point of sale is now in operation in certain areas of the country. In a point-of-sale (POS) transaction, the customer uses a debit card to pay for goods or services at the retail location. An electronic network connecting the financial institutions of the customer and the merchant directly debits the customer's account and credits the merchant's account for the transaction amount. By displacing more costly paper transactions, POS payments greatly reduce the resource costs of transferring money.

To be operational, POS requires that many of a merchant's customers hold debit cards issued by financial institutions that are linked through electronic networks with the merchant's institution. POS networks are now viewed as viable because of the growth of shared automated teller machine (ATM) networks with their interbank switching capabilities and large numbers of debit cardholders.[1] Shared ATM networks allow the cardholders of one institution to carry out financial transactions at the terminals of another and can be designed to switch transactions between cardholders and merchants. Both merchants and financial institutions are aware of the efficiency of retail electronic fund transfers (EFT), but they have not determined who should pay for POS transactions.

Part I of this paper discusses the implications of a recent court case concerning whether an ATM should be considered to be a branch. A federal district court judge decided that an ATM used by the customers of a national bank to access their accounts qualifies as a branch of that bank. The U.S. Court of Appeals reversed this decision in February 1985, ruling that an ATM that has not been established (i.e., owned or rented) by a national bank is not a branch. This case is

From *New England Economic Review*, Federal Reserve Bank of Boston, May/June 1985, pp. 44–61.

Steven Felgran is an economist, Federal Reserve Bank of Boston. The author is grateful to R. Edward Ferguson for his able research assistance.

particularly interesting, not only because it clarifies the legal status of ATMs but also because it highlights the tensions between outdated laws and the realities of technological change in financial services.

Though the appeals court decision has cleared the way for continued development of ATM and POS networks, these networks will face increasingly complex access and pricing issues. Part II examines the growing trend toward greater network access by consumers as financial institutions join multiple networks and networks are consolidated. Financial institutions are willing to link their ATM networks as the marketing advantages of proprietary or unconnected networks decline. Shared ATM networks are competing with other kinds of organizations, as well as with merchants, especially oil companies and supermarkets, in developing POS networks.

Some financial institutions have recently begun to charge their customers fees for interbank ATM transactions. Part III analyzes alternative strategies, such as cost-plus pricing and incentive pricing, and discusses their proper use over time. Charging cost-plus prices in the short run may inhibit long-run growth in the demand for retail EFT, thus preventing networks from achieving economies of scale. The development of POS networks raises the additional issue of the costs and benefits enjoyed by merchants from POS transactions.

I. ARE ATMs BRANCHES?

The legality of national bank participation in shared ATM networks was recently tested in court. The case, *Independent Bankers Association of New York State* v. *Marine Midland Bank,*[2] raised the issue of whether an ATM used by a national bank's customers qualifies as a branch of that bank even if the ATM is owned by another institution. The ATM in dispute is used by Marine Midland's customers but owned by Wegmans Food Markets, Inc., and located in its store in Canandaigua, New York. Wegmans is a participating member of a shared ATM network known as HARMONEY, which is owned and operated by Marine Midland Bank.[3] In April 1984, a federal district court judge held that the use of Wegmans' ATM by Marine Midland's customers constituted unlawful branch banking and enjoined Marine Midland from using Wegmans' ATM in Canandaigua. However, in February 1985, the U.S. Court of Appeals reversed this decision, enabling shared ATM networks to continue to develop free of federal branching restrictions.

> The prevailing view has been that ATMs not established by a bank but available to the bank's customers are not branches of the bank.

The Independent Bankers Association had claimed that Wegmans' ATM was an illegal Marine Midland branch under New York banking law, which is applicable to national banks in accordance with the McFadden Act.[4] New York banking law contains a "home office protection" provision, which prohibits a bank from opening a branch in any community with a population of 50,000 or less where another bank has its principal office. The court agreed that Marine Midland may not lawfully branch in Canandaigua, because of the home office protection afforded the existing bank in that community, Canandaigua National Bank and Trust. The court had to decide whether Marine Midland had violated New York banking law by establishing its "branch" in Canandaigua through use of Wegmans' ATM.

Over the past decade, the prevailing view has been that ATMs not established by a bank but available to the bank's customers are not branches of the bank. The Office of the Comptroller of the Currency (OCC), charged with enforcement of the McFadden Act, first issued an interpretive ruling in 1974 that authorized national banks to establish off-premises customer-bank communication terminals (CBCTs) without regard to federal branching restrictions.[5] OCC's position was the CBCTs were basically means of communication, not places where banks transacted business, and were therefore not branches under the McFadden Act.

The legality of OCC's ruling was challenged by numerous parties, resulting in a major 1976 decision in *Independent Bankers Association of America* v. *Smith*.[6] This decision added to the statutory definition of a branch by concluding that "any facility that performs the traditional bank functions of receiving or disbursing funds is a 'branch' of a national bank within the meaning of Section 36(f) if (1) the facility is established (i.e., owned or rented) by the national bank, and (2) it offers the bank's customers a convenience that gives the bank a competitive advantage over other banks (national or state) that do not operate similar facilities." Accordingly, the court held that OCC's 1974 ruling was invalid and that terminals established by national banks were branches subject to federal branching restrictions.

The *Smith* decision had not been in existence long before OCC turned it on its head. In issuing regulations governing the establishment of CBCTs late in 1976, the comptroller stated that the branching restrictions of the McFadden Act did not apply to CBCTs that banks do not "own or rent" and thus have not "established."[7] Thereafter, OCC issued a series of interpretive letters along similar lines. In an advisory opinion issued in 1980, the comptroller stated that customers of national banks can use an ATM located across state lines where the ATM has been established by a bank headquartered in the other state, or by some other entity, if (1) the compensation for use is through transaction fees and (2) such use does not give national banks a competitive advantage over state banks situated in these states.[8] OCC formally adopted a regulation in 1982 that incorporated the 1976 interpretation that an ATM is not a branch of a national bank unless the bank owns or rents it.[9]

Thus, the assumption behind Wegmans' membership in the HARMONEY network was that, by sharing the use of an ATM owned and operated by Wegmans, Marine Midland would not "establish" a "branch" in Canandaigua. The district court judge, however, decided that customers of Marine Midland could perform transactions at Wegmans' ATM "with the same force and effect as if they appeared personally at a Marine Midland 'brick and mortar' branch and made the same transactions." The fact that Wegmans owned the ATM was found to be immaterial, because the machine merely provided the "vehicle" through which the bank and its customers did business. Regarding the comptroller's opinion, the district court judge termed the difference between owning or renting ATMs, and enabling customers to use ATMs through the payment of transaction fees, the "proverbial distinction without a difference." The judge also determined that permitting customers of Marine Midland to use Wegmans' ATM gave Marine Midland, a national bank, a "competitive advantage" over state banks.

For these reasons, the district court held that Wegmans' ATM was an illegal branch of Marine Midland. If this decision had been sustained, it would have meant that any ATM, regardless of who owns it and what functions it performs, would be considered a branch of any national bank whose customers share its use. If the mere use of an ATM made it a branch, a national bank would be able to use only those ATMs that were located in areas where the bank was permitted to establish a branch.

Table 1 shows the present legal status of ATMs under state laws in New England and New York. If the district court decision had been sustained, national banks would have been put at a competitive disadvantage to state banks in states such as New York where ATMs are not branches and branching is not permissible statewide. Moreover, national banks would have been barred from offering ATM access across state lines under the McFadden Act, while state banks are subject to no such prohibition.

In reversing the district court decision, the appeals court noted that the definition of "branch" is ambiguous because banking, like other industries, has changed radically since the McFadden Act was passed in 1927:

> "Brick and mortar" banking, with a single physical locus of bank-customer transactions, has been supplemented by many other forms of communication that could not have been contemplated in 1927. . . . The McFadden Act pre-dated the invention of computers as well as their application to banking through electronic funds transfer systems. Banking is no longer confined to physical transactions. . . . Furthermore, the ATM networks at issue here are not even the cutting edge of the new technology. The wave of the future includes point-of-sale terminal systems (POS) and home computer banking. . . . It would defy common sense to consider a personal computer a branch, yet home banking by computer is already available and may soon offer some of the functions performed by Wegmans' ATM.

Since technological change has rendered the language of the McFadden Act ambiguous, the appeals court based its decision on (1) legislative intent at the time the Act was passed and (2) the views of the executive agency charged with enforcing the Act. In regard to legislative intent, "the governing principle behind the McFadden Act was to strengthen national banks and achieve approximate competitive equality between the state and national banking systems." The appeals court decided that affirmation of the district court's ruling would put national banks at a competitive disadvantage for the reasons stated above.

In regard to OCC's enforcement of the McFadden Act, the appeals court decided that the district court did not accord sufficient deference to OCC's view that an ATM that is not "owned or rented" by a national bank is not a branch. A recent Supreme Court decision regarding bank ownership of a discount brokerage reaffirmed the principle that courts should defer to reasonable interpretations of

TABLE 1
Legal Status of ATMs under State Laws in New England and New York

State	Branch Status	Permissible Locations within State	Permissible Functions	Sharing within State
Connecticut	ATMs are not branches.	Statewide	Including, but not limited to, deposits, withdrawals, payments, advances, and transfers between merchants.	Mandatory sharing.[a]
Maine	Off-premises electronic facilities are not treated as branches.	Statewide	Including, but not limited to, deposits, withdrawals, advances, and transfers.	Mandatory sharing of off-premises facilities.
Massachusetts	Off-premises ATMs are "electronic branches" and may be established without complying with branching laws.	Statewide	Deposits, withdrawals, payments, advances, and transfers.	Permissive sharing, though the commissioner may order mandatory sharing.[b]
New Hampshire	Remote service units are not branches.	Statewide	Deposits, withdrawals, payments, advances, transfers, and such other services as are approved by the commissioner of banks.	Mandatory sharing.
Rhode Island	Customer-bank communication terminals are not branches.	Statewide	To the same extent as federally chartered institutions.	Permissive sharing.
Vermont	Off-premises remote electronic terminals are branches.	Statewide	Statute is silent.[c]	Statute is silent.[c]
New York	ATMs are not branches unless they are deployed in areas protected by home office laws.	Statewide, subject to home office protection	"Deposit-withdrawal activities."	Permissive sharing.

[a] Out-of-state financial institutions may not establish or use a satellite device in Connecticut without the owner's permission. The terminal must be used on a transacton fee basis and may not take deposits.

[b] A New England financial institution may establish, operate, and use electronic terminals in Massachusetts provided its home state authorizes similar activities for Massachusetts institutions. In addition, any financial institution may share or use a Massachusetts electronic terminal to perform withdrawals, advances, and check cashing, provided that the terminal was established by a Massachusetts financial institution.

[c] The Department of Banking and Insurance currently allows deposits, withdrawals, payments, advances, and transfers. Intrastate sharing of terminals has been approved. Interstate sharing has also been approved, though the terminal must be owned by a Vermont institution and the out-of-state institution is prohibited from taking deposits.

Source: *Status of ATMs under State Branching Laws*. Hearings before the Senate Committee on Banking, Housing, and Urban Affairs, 98 Cong. 2 Sess. (GPO, 1984), pp. 35–44, 202–213, Robert C. Zimmer and Theresa A. Einhorn, *The Law of Electronic Funds Transfer* (Card Services, Inc., 1978); and telephone interviews with several state banking commission offices.

statutes made by the agencies that administer those statutes.[10] In addition to the fact that OCC's interpretations appear to promote the purposes of the McFadden Act, they have been relied upon by national banks and others who have participated in shared ATM networks and would have been harmed by a reversal. The appeals court viewed congressional inaction in either overruling the comptroller's interpretations or further defining the permissible scope of national bank participation in EFT systems as lending further weight to deference to the regulatory agency.

For these reasons, the appeals court held that Marine Midland's use of Wegmans' ATM, which the bank neither owns nor rents, does not constitute the establishment and operation of a branch under the McFadden Act. The court concluded that, "given the technological promise of interstate electronic banking and the substantial steps already taken toward achieving it," only Congress and not the judiciary should decide if the momentum already developed should be stopped, particularly given the age of the statute. Clearly, Congress has no such legislation in mind.

A second issue arose in the Marine Midland case concerning whether Wegmans was engaged in banking without state authorization. The Independent Bankers Association alleged that Wegmans' ownership of the ATM constituted a banking business in violation of New York state law. The district court disagreed on the grounds that Marine Midland was doing the banking and Wegmans, at most, was "acting as an agent for a bank, and not as a banking institution itself." The appeals court did not take a stand on this issue, stating that nonbank ownership of ATMs was a matter of state law that should not have been tried in federal court.

Legislation has been proposed in Congress that would amend the McFadden Act, enabling a national bank to share "an automated device that is not established by that bank, and such automated device shall not be considered a branch of that bank. . . ."[11] This legislation was proposed to legalize national bank participation in shared ATM networks by codifying the comptroller's interpretations held invalid by the district court in the *Marine Midland* case. However, now that the district court decision has been reversed, the pressure on Congress to enact this legislation will be minimal.

II.   ACCESS ISSUES IN ATM/POS NETWORKS

Growth of Shared ATM Networks

The past few years have witnessed high rates of growth in the numbers of ATMs and ATM transactions. Of particular significance is the fact that shared ATMs have become increasingly important relative to all ATMs in the United States. As shown in Table 2, the number of shared ATMs in regional networks grew by 56 percent over 1983–84, in the process rising from 40 to 45 percent of all ATMs. The volume of ATM transactions at regional shared machines grew by 92 percent over 1983–84, rising from 25 to 38 percent of all ATM transactions. Though average transaction volume per ATM dropped by 8 percent over 1983–84 due to the relatively large number of new machines, average transaction volume per shared ATM rose by 21 percent over this period. Of the 100 million debit cards in circulation, 65 million accessed regional shared ATMs in 1984. About 9,000

TABLE 2
ATM Trends

	1982	1983	1984	Percent Change	
				1982–83	1983–84
Number of ATMs:					
Shared ATMs	11,000	16,000	25,000	+45	+56
All ATMs	31,000	40,000	55,000	+29	+38
Shared as percent of total	35	40	45		
Total monthly ATM transactions (millions):					
Shared ATMs	45	60	115	+33	+92
All ATMs	180	240	300	+33	+25
Shared as percent of total	25	25	38		
Monthly transactions per ATM					
Shared ATMs	4,100	3,800	4,600	−7	+21
All ATMs	5,800	6,000	5,500	+3	−8
Shared as percent of total	71	63	84		
Number of debit cards (millions)					
Shared	29	50	65	+72	+30
Total	60	75	100	+25	+33
Shared as percent of total	48	67	65		
Number of bank participants in shared networks	6,000	7,500	9,000	+25	+20

Note: Yearly data as of July/August of each year. Figures for shared ATMs refer to ATMs online to regional shared networks. Figures for total refer to all ATMs online to both shared and proprietary networks. Transaction volumes include both on-us and on-other transactions. All numbers are approximations.

Source: Compiled from "Bank Network News Top 50," *Bank Network News,* October 22, 1982, "Bank Network News Top 100," September 10, 1983, and "1985 EFT Network Data Book," September 25, 1984.

banks, along with uncounted numbers of thrifts and credit unions, participated in at least one of the 175 regional shared ATM networks in operation in 1984. Many of these institutions also belonged to one or more of the eight national shared ATM networks.

The relatively high growth rates exhibited by shared ATMs have not primarily been the result of the formation of new shared networks. Instead, existing shared networks have significantly expanded their terminals and transaction volumes. In addition, several major mergers and acquisitions created large regional networks, and a few new networks began operations with large numbers of online machines in place. Shared ATMs are now so prevalent in the United States that only California remains a stronghold of proprietary ATMs. Even New England now plays host to regional sharing with the recent formation of two large competing systems.

Tables A1, A2, and A3 in the Appendix provide descriptive data for the 10 largest regional shared ATM networks, the 15 largest New England shared networks, and the 8 national shared networks, respectively. These tables show the following for each network: average monthly ATM transactions (interbank and total), number of ATMs, number of access cards, geographic market area, services offered, membership, ownership, transaction fees, major costs of participation, method of settlement, national network links, and whether POS operations are in place. The regional and New England networks are listed in order of average monthly interbank ATM transactions and the national networks are listed in alphabetical order.

Expanded Sharing through Multiple Memberships

In the period since August 1983, when the Department of Justice allowed a financial institution in Texas to participate in both the MPACT and PULSE shared ATM networks, an increasing number of institutions have entered into multiple sharing arrangements. Over 25 percent of banks and thrifts that currently share their ATMs are members of two or more shared networks. Multiple memberships enable the cardholders of one network to access their accounts at ATMs connected to other networks to which their card-issuing institutions belong. If multiple sharing arrangements continue to spread, cardholder access will approach universal service.

> Providing ATM services is almost a competitive necessity for financial institutions seriously pursuing a retail business.

Multiple memberships have become increasingly popular due to changes in the competitive environment and to more liberal shared network bylaws. The environment is now such that providing ATM services is almost a competitive necessity for financial institutions seriously pursuing a retail business. Whether a financial institution decides to move beyond the mere provision of ATM services to multiple sharing depends on its competitors' strategies. If the institution's market share is threatened, it will attempt to strengthen customer relationships by improving consumer convenience. Since consumers are believed to value increased ATM access, multiple memberships are offered in markets where shared ATM coverage is high and the marketing advantages of exclusive memberships have eroded. Threats to an institution's market share come not only from local competitors but also from national banking organizations, such as Citicorp, that can provide customers with access to their accounts through memberships in regional shared ATM networks around the country and can attract deposits through mass mailing programs.

Until recently, the bylaws of many shared networks prohibited their members from participating in other networks and withheld access from members of competing networks.[12] Lately, network directors have taken a much more liberal stance towards multiple memberships as they realize that universal sharing is needed to fully implement their POS plans. POS requires that a large percentage of customers hold debit cards capable of linking their financial institutions and merchants through network arrangements. The networks that retain a role in the retail payment system will be those that enable institutions to engage in universal sharing, thus providing universal service to their cardholders.

An example of the change in sharing philosophies is provided by the two largest national ATM networks, CIRRUS and PLUS. These networks used to have exclusive membership rules that prohibited their members from participating in other national networks. However, CIRRUS has dropped its exclusivity in favor of open sharing, allowing its members to join other national networks and members of other networks to join CIRRUS, provided they can find a sponsoring institution. The lack of restrictions is best demonstrated by the fact that, in January 1985, Citicorp's subsidiary in South Dakota was sponsored into CIRRUS by Norwest Corporation, in spite of Citicorp's position as a competitor of various CIRRUS proprietary members, such as Manufacturers Hanover in New York and Citicorp's operation of a competing national shared ATM network, CITISHARE. PLUS has also relaxed its membership rules and recently announced that its members can open their ATMs to cardholders from the rival CIRRUS network.

> Consolidation will occur as the efficiency of direct linkage outweighs the marketing advantages of multiple memberships.

Efficiency through Direct Linkage

The more liberal sharing policies of ATM networks are setting the stage for consolidation or direct links among these networks. Direct links are the logical next step after multiple memberships, since they enable financial institutions in different networks to be interconnected through network switches. Processing ATM transactions through direct links resembles check processing, in that both are performed by all financial institutions for each other. Direct links have the great advantage over multiple memberships of being a more efficient way to structure organizational and interchange arrangements. Consolidation will occur as the efficiency of direct linkage outweighs the marketing advantages of memberships in multiple unconnected networks.

Consolidation is already evident in the form of mergers among some regional ATM networks to create "super regional" systems. For example, MOST and NETWORK EXCHANGE in the Washington, D.C., area have merged; MONEY STATION consists of four shared networks and one bank network in Ohio; MAC has gone online to its franchisee in Pittsburgh; and Mellon Bank-owned CASH-STREAM now includes the former GEORGE network due to Mellon's acquisition of Girard Bank. In the greater New York region, the New York Cash Exchange (NYCE) was recently formed out of the networks of such major banks as Chemical, Manufacturers Hanover, Marine Midland, Bank of New York, and Barclays Bank (but not Citicorp, which chose not to join even though membership is open). In New England, regional networks including VEC, TX, and POCKETBANK are forming the CASH NETWORK, though they will retain their individual logos.

Discussions reportedly are underway that may lead to the consolidation of some of the national ATM networks with the major credit card companies.[13] In particular, CIRRUS, PLUS, and NATIONET are separately engaged in discussions with Visa and MasterCard concerning the development of communications systems for direct-debit POS transactions. These talks have been prompted by several considerations, including, *first,* the growing realization that multiple net-works, each with its own communications system, are redundant in a POS environment. *Second,* the networks want to develop a unified service mark for debit transactions similar to the Visa and MasterCard logos, which have become the ubiquitous signs of credit card acceptance. *Third,* the networks want to keep control of POS payments in the hands of banks and out of the hands of both credit card and nonbank organizations. The networks are aware of the role nonbanks see themselves playing in retail payments, as evidenced by the fact that about 15 to 20 percent of ATM shipments in 1984 went to nonbank organizations.

Consolidation of the shared ATM networks makes economic sense and will take place as the market signals the need for universal service. Consolidation will not cause the payment system to be controlled by one huge public utility or financial institutions to stop competing. To the contrary, just as the major credit cards are widely accepted yet compete, financial institutions will continue to do battle for customers. However, as consolidation occurs, the locus of competition will shift from the provision of electronic payment services to the nature and pricing of these services. Cooperation will occur over the "backroom" switching and clearing operations needed to achieve universal service. The market will determine the extent to which institutions engage in sharing, based on the declin-ing marketing advantages of ATMs versus the growing cost savings of rationaliz-ing EFT operations.

Growth of POS Networks

Given the diffusion of ATM technology, the links established through shared networks, and the massive number of debit cards in circulation, it is widely believed that electronic payment at the retail point of sale may soon be possible in many areas of the country. Retail payments via POS terminals allow customers and merchants to transfer funds instantaneously between their accounts. Shared ATM networks are taking the lead in moving POS from the experimental phase it has been in for several years to a commercial financial service in the near future. It is estimated that about 25 regional shared ATM networks will operate commercial POS services by year-end 1985, even though most did not until recently have a single POS terminal. The number of POS terminals in commercial operation will grow from about 2,200 at year-end 1984 to about 10 times that by year-end 1985.[14]

The network interchange setup among banks, merchants, and customers is essentially the same for POS as for ATM transactions. In the usual setup, the merchant is sponsored into a network by a member bank, which then handles all of the merchant's POS transactions. As shown in Figure 1, the merchant's POS terminals are accessible both by customers who hold debit cards issued by the merchant's bank and by customers of other banks belonging to connected net-works. Whenever a POS terminal is used, the processor of the merchant's bank examines the transaction to see whether the customer has an account with that bank. The processor keeps "on-us" transactions by directing them to the bank's computer, and sends "on-other" transactions to its network switch. This switch then routes the transactions to the customer's institution either directly or through another switch, depending on network arrangements.

The network usually has no direct contact with the merchants sponsored by

FIGURE 1
POS Network Interchange

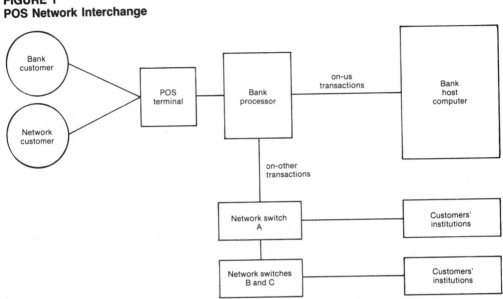

member banks. POS terminal ownership, services offered, and prices charged are negotiated between merchants and their member banks. Network interchange fees are usually lower for POS than for ATM transactions, because POS systems are less expensive to operate and maintain.

Though shared ATM networks are at the forefront of POS development, some non-ATM and nonbank organizations are also getting involved. For example, the INTERLINK network in California was organized specifically for POS by the state's five largest banks, which do not share ATMs. INTERLINK POS terminals at gasoline stations, supermarkets, and other retail locations will be operational in the first half of 1985. Mobil Oil has organized its own national POS interchange system and Exxon Oil is issuing customers its own debit cards in a pilot program. Some oil companies with their own POS systems are signing up banks and bank-owned networks as participants and processing transactions through the auto-mated clearinghouse (ACH), an electronic parallel of the check-collection system. Financial institutions can use the ACH network to settle ATM-POS transactions directly among themselves, at prices below those charged by ATM networks.

Oil companies and supermarkets appear to be the retailers most interested in the new payments technology. Motivated by the need to reduce check, credit card, and cash handling costs in their high-volume, low-margin businesses, gas-oline retailers and supermarkets are initiating POS discussions with banks and networks. Some gasoline retailers are also motivated by the extra sales that they believe POS generates. For example, Mobil Oil, which offers customers paying by debit card the same discount that is given to cash customers, has reported that a high percentage of debit card sales have come from new customers.[15]

TABLE 3
Selected POS Systems

Market	Network/Bank	Number of Terminals	Average Monthly Transactions	Significant Merchants	Establishments
California	Crocker National Bank	729	102,000	Mobil Oil	700
	First Interstate Bank			Arco	29
Florida	HONOR	988	14,000	7-Eleven	375
				Mobil Oil	230
				Publix Suuper Markets	10
Iowa	ITS, Inc.	308	72,800	Hy-Vee Food Stores	17
				Dahl's Foods	9
Ohio	INSTANET/Ameritrust	275	4,000	Gas Town	25
				Gray's Drug Stores	17
Pennsylvania	CASHSTREAM	52	16,260	PA State Liquor Stores	29
				Gulf	15
				Amoco	6
Texas	MAC	50	7,500	Sunoco	50
	MPACT	322	3,500	Mobil Oil	230
				The Shoe Box	13
Washington, D.C., and suburbs	MOST CASH FLOW/Sovran	60	17,000	Mobil Oil	60
Wisconsin	TYME	49	20,000	Pick 'n Save Foods	3

At this time, less interest in POS exists among department and specialty store retailers. However, many banks that specialize in serving merchants that accept credit cards plan to interest these merchants in direct debit POS systems. The merchants being approached first are those equipped with electronic terminals capable of authorizing and processing credit card transactions. Table 3 shows selected POS systems in operation, by market area.

III. PRICING ISSUES IN ATM/POS NETWORKS

Consumer Interchange Fees

The financial services industry is currently debating whether consumers should be charged directly for ATM-POS transactions. The vast majority of financial institutions eventually will charge their customers directly for all kinds of electronic and paper transactions. Some institutions have already begun to charge for ATM interchange transactions, those performed at terminals established by other institutions. Amid much controversy, these institutions have claimed that it is reasonable to pass along all or part of network interchange fees plus direct costs in the form of consumer interchange fees.

The practice of charging customers for interchange transactions started with banks in the PULSE network in Texas, and it has spread to members of other networks, including HONOR in Florida, MOST in the Washington, D.C., area, AVAIL in Georgia, CASHSTREAM in Pennsylvania, and the national CIRRUS network. The consumer interchange fees are set by the individual network members and vary within and among networks. For example, the HONOR network's 55¢ withdrawal fee has prompted a range of consumer interchange fees set by members, such as 25¢ charged by NCNB National Bank, 50¢ charged by Southeast Bank, and 75¢ charged by Barnett Banks.[16] The particular fee charged depends not only on the network interchange fee and other costs, such as paperwork and communication lines, but also on marketing considerations.

Markets with consumer interchange fees tend to have relatively high numbers of off-premises ATMs, often owned by merchants or other nonbanks that issue few or no debit cards and hope to profit from fees paid by the card-issuing banks. Such banks, particularly those with large numbers of cardholders and on-premises ATMs, are net payers of network interchange fees and are more likely to assess consumer interchange fees. For example, banks in the HONOR network (mentioned above) assess consumer fees in part because of the many interchange transactions performed at ATMs owned by fellow HONOR member, Publix Super Markets. Clearly, consumer fees have been set to avoid short-run losses, though they may inhibit the development of the universal service required for POS.

Not surprisingly, ATM networks disapprove of consumer interchange fees, but they are reluctant to enforce any pricing discipline for fear of incurring an antitrust violation. Merchants feel that these fees are unfairly taxing use of their terminals at a time when they are trying to displace their check-cashing services with retail EFT.

Incentive versus Cost-Plus Pricing

Whether consumer interchange fees actually inhibit the development of retail EFT depends on the extent of the public's demand. A part of the public is currently interested in ATM access, though the amount demanded is small in comparison to its long-run potential. Nevertheless, the fact that part of the public desires ATM access enables card-issuing institutions to charge for ATM services. The institutions charge prices that cover all of their variable costs and some of their fixed costs while contributing to profits. This pricing strategy may inhibit the long-run growth in demand for ATM and POS services. The public, now just learning about retail EFT, is expected to substitute electronic for paper transactions in the future. At the same time, the costs of providing retail EFT are much higher now than they will be once large volumes and operational efficiencies are realized. Institutions that intend to aim for this demand/supply situation in the long run may wish to set relatively low incentive prices now. Such prices will induce demand growth and result in economies of scale.

These ideas are illustrated in Figure 2. The average cost curve, LAC, shows that costs per transaction decline as the quantity of retail EFT provided by a financial institution increases over a range. The small size of the short-run demand curve, D_s, indicates that a limited demand for the institution's supply of retail EFT exists. The institution can compare this demand to its relatively high short-run costs and set a price of P_s or more to cover those costs. However, this strategy takes account neither of the reduction in costs per transaction as use of EFT increases nor of the potentially large long-run demand, D_L. Thus, a short-run incentive price, such as P_L, might be a better choice to encourage the growth of EFT. In determining price, the institution should consider changes in demand and supply as the public becomes familiar with EFT and the tradeoff between short-run and long-run profits.

Evidence exists that consumer interchange fees have already lowered rates of growth in interchange volumes. Some networks whose members have begun to

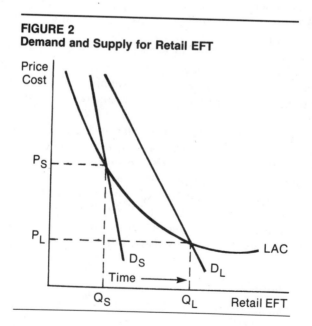

FIGURE 2
Demand and Supply for Retail EFT

charge customers for interbank transactions have experienced declines in growth rates, though these declines appear to be temporary. Customers who face sufficiently high on-other fees and no on-us fees will tend to revert to their own institution's ATMs for routine transactions. In addition to charging, some institutions have chosen to install more of their own ATMs in off-premises locations to lure their customers away from "foreign" machines and increase their own interchange revenues. These activities are clearly inefficient because they prevent institutions from achieving economies of scale through sharing. It makes much more economic sense to share ATMs and charge customers once demand has been firmly established.

To obtain the desired growth in demand for retail EFT, incentive pricing must reflect not only the low long-run processing costs of electronic transactions but also their small size relative to the production and processing costs of paper transactions. The resource costs of the different payment instruments now amount to approximately 68¢ per check and 34¢ per automated clearinghouse transaction.[17] Though checks cost at least twice as much to produce and process as EFT, most banks do not assess a per-item check fee unless a customer's balance has fallen below some minimum, while many assess an ATM interchange fee regardless of the customer's balance. More banks may want to introduce "differential pricing" of EFT and checks to reflect the relatively low long-run costs of ATM-POS transactions and induce greater volumes. For example, banks might charge greater per-item fees for checks than for EFT, regardless of minimum balances and on-us or on-other transactions. Any premiums earned through check fees could help to subsidize EFT incentive prices.

POS Pricing Strategies

The development of POS networks introduces another complication into pricing: the role of merchants in the fee structure. Merchants now pay their banks for check processing and sell credit card receipts at a discount. However, merchants who own ATMs receive network interchange fees as do other terminal owners. Should merchants who own POS terminals pay or be paid?

In the usual POS setup, merchants who own POS terminals have no direct contact with a network. Instead, all POS transactions are handled through the bank that sponsors the merchant into the network. The issue of POS pricing, then, boils down to an arrangement between the merchant and his bank over transaction fees and discounts. At issue are the merchant's and the bank's relative benefits and costs of POS, and their relative degrees of market power.

In regard to benefits and costs, it is widely believed that full POS implementation will benefit merchants more than banks. Besides the savings in the costs of processing EFT, merchants will benefit from increased customer convenience, reduced check-out time, reduced float, and the displacement of check-cashing services and bad check risks. Though merchants may eventually achieve these benefits, they might be charged incentive prices in the short run to encourage them to invest in POS terminals and network connections, POS fees could be so structured in accordance with long-run costs that retailers view debit cards as preferable to cash, checks, or credit cards. Financial institutions might consider subsidizing merchants' POS fees to solidify the long-run market for POS services.

These institutions would gain not only the cost savings of EFT but also the competitive advantages of being at the forefront of the new technology.

Banks that currently offer POS services are divided over whether to charge merchants transaction fees. The banks that do not charge intend to wait until volumes build and processing costs come down before assessing fees. The banks that do charge are often those that not only process transactions but also equip merchants with POS terminals. In many cases, the relative degrees of market power held by merchants and banks will determine the existence and size of POS fees.

In the final analysis, the public will pay for POS regardless of the institutional pricing and interchange arrangements. Before setting POS fees for consumers, institutions should determine the expected demand for POS and should charge in accordance with the anticipated low long-run costs of POS transactions.

CONCLUSION

Widespread participation in shared networks is necessary for electronic payment at the retail point of sale to operate efficiently. Networks will increasingly be shared as the cost savings of network linkages become more important and the marketing advantages of proprietary or unconnected networks diminish. Financial institutions will cooperate over network interchange arrangements to avoid redundancy and gain economies of scale. As universal service to the public becomes feasible, merchants may find it in their interest to invest in POS facilities. Currently, POS is being initiated by gasoline retailers and supermarkets, which see immediate advantages in reduced check, credit card, and cash-handling costs.

As network sharing increases, electronic terminals will no longer be viewed by financial institutions as extensions of their competitive identities. The maintenance of customer relationships will cause institutions to offer increasingly accessible methods of retail EFT. Banks and thrifts will compete by differentiating their EFT prices and services, which will be determined given their market shares, marketing strategies, and long-run profit goals. Thus, even though cooperation will increase to accommodate universal service, competition among financial institutions will be retained.

Regardless of whether electronic terminals are viewed at any particular moment as branches, competitive entities, or multi-user utilities, the public will eventually bear the costs of transactions of these terminals. Financial institutions will begin to charge their customers for transactions as the marketing advantages of merely possessing their own terminals subside due to sharing. Since the demand for retail EFT is still relatively small, institutions may wish to charge incentive prices to induce the growth of long-run demand. These prices would reflect the low long-run costs of retail EFT, both in absolute terms and relative to paper transactions. Though all sorts of conflicts over access and pricing have arisen among financial institutions, merchants, and networks, all participants share the need to create widespread public acceptance of retail EFT through intelligent long-run pricing strategies.

NOTES

1 For background on ATMs, see Steven D. Felgran, "Shared ATM Networks: Market Structure and Public Policy," *New England Economic Review,* January/February 1984.

2 *Independent Bankers Association of New York State* v. *Marine Midland Bank,* 583 F.Supp. 1042 (W.D.N.Y., April 6, 1984), appeal nos. 84–7424, 84–7448 (2d Cir., Feb. 27, 1985).

3 The use of a HARMONEY debit card enables Marine Midland's customers to access their accounts using Wegmans' ATM to make deposits or withdrawals, inquire about balances, or obtain cash advances. Wegmans retains ownership of the ATM and is responsible for loading the machine with cash. Wegmans has no access to the secured container in which deposits are automatically placed and is not responsible for any discrepancy between the amount displayed on the transaction slip and the amount actually deposited. Marine Midland is responsible for emptying the deposit container each day. When a customer uses the ATM for a withdrawal, the ATM dispenses cash provided by Wegmans, but only after electronic approval has been received through the computer network from Marine Midland. Once a transaction is approved by Marine Midland, the customer's account is debited and Wegmans' account is credited. Wegmans' account is also credited with a transaction fee paid by Marine Midland for each transaction made by one of its customers through Wegmans' ATM.

4 Section 36(c) of the McFadden Act authorizes a national bank to establish branches only within the state where its principal office is located; and then only to the extent that state banks are expressly permitted to do so under state law. Section 36(f) provides that a "branch" is any bank office at which "deposits are received, or checks paid, or money lent." 12 U.S.C. 36.

5 39 Fed. Reg. 44.416 (Dec. 24, 1974); 12 C.F.R. Section 7,7491 (1975).

6 534 F.2d 921 (D.C. Cir.), cert. denied, 429 U.S. 862 (1976).

7 41 Fed. Reg. 48,333 (Nov. 3, 1976).

8 Letter No. 153, July 7, 1980, Fed. Banking Law Reporter (CCH 1981–82 Transfer Binder) para. 85,234.

9 12 C.F.R. Section 5.31(b) (1984).

10 *Securities Industry Association* v. *Board of Governors of the Federal Reserve System,* 104 S.Ct. 3003, 3009 (1984).

11 *Banking Convenience Act of 1985,* S. 206 and H.R. 688, 99 Cong. 1 Sess. See also *Status of ATM's under State Branching Laws*, Hearings before the Senate Committee on Banking, Housing, and Ubran Affairs, 98 Cong. 2 Sess. (Government Printing Office, 1984).

12 In contrast, shared ATM networks established by bank holding companies, which must be approved by the Federal Reserve Board, must have open sharing policies towards their own members and potential entrants. To date, the board has approved six applications by bank holding companies to establish joint ventures to operate EFT systems: Interstate Financial Corporation (GREEN MACHINE), June 14, 1983; Atlantic Bancorporation et al. (HONOR), July 12, 1983; Centerre Bancorporation et al. (MONETARY TRANSFER SYSTEM), July 13, 1983; CB&T Bancshares et al. (AVAIL), June 25, 1984; First National Cincinnati Corporation et al. (MONEY STATION), October 15, 1984; and Barclays Bank PLC and Barclays Bank International LTD et al. (NYCE), December 11, 1984.

13 "Consolidation of Retail Funds Networks Pushed," *American Banker,* January 14, 1985, pp. 1, 9; "Why the National Networks are Huddling," *Bank Network News,* January 25, 1985.

14 Author's estimates based on telephone interviews.

15 "Mobil, Citing a Good Start, Revs Up Its Point-of-Sale Plans; 2,500 Service Stations Will Have the System by Midsummer," *American Banker,* January 4, 1985, p. 3; "Mobil Sees Promise in Debit Cards," *Payment Systems Newsletter,* March 18, 1985, pp. 1, 6, 7.

16 "A Battle Over Network Interchange Fees," *Bank Network News,* December 11, 1984; "Levying Fees for Use of ATMs Spreads to Florida from Texas," *American Banker,* February 14, 1985, pp. 1, 14.

17 The numbers cited are the sums of unit production and processing costs to the payor, payee, bank, and Federal Reserve, calculated from 1983 data. When *user* costs, including the costs of float, are calculated, this relationship changes to 15¢ per check and 33¢ per ACH transaction. See David Burras Humphrey, "The U.S. Payments System: Costs, Pricing, Competition and Risk," *Monograph Series in Finance and Economics,* Salomon Brothers Center for the Study of Financial Institutions at the Graduate School of Business Administration of New York University, monograph 1984–½, p. 14.

APPENDIX   SHARED ATM NETWORKS—DESCRIPTIVE DATA

TABLE A1
Ten Largest Regional Shared ATM Networks

Network[a]	Average Monthly ATM Transactions (millions)		Number of ATMs	Number of Access Cards (millions)	Market Area	Services Offered[b]					Membership	Ownership
	Interbank	Total				Withdrawals	Deposits	Transfers	Cash Advances	Payments		
MPACT	3.2	6.1	1,200	2.2	New Mexico Oklahoma Texas	X	X	X	X	X	430 banks 50 thrifts 20 credit unions	MCorp, Dallas
MAC	3.0	5.5	957	2.8	Delaware New Jersey Pennsylvania	X	X	X	X	X	200 financial institutions	Philadelphia National Bank
PULSE	1.9	8.6	3,100	5.2	Louisiana Oklahoma Texas	X		X	X		1,180 banks 59 thrifts 75 credit unions 54 processors	Members
TYME	1.7	1.9	575	1.8	Illinois Michigan Wisconsin	X	X	X	X	X	328 banks 54 thrifts 61 credit unions	Members
HONOR	1.6	8.5	2,001	4.0	Florida	X		X	X	X	295 financial institutions 34 processors	9 members
INSTANET	1.6	4.0	500	2.0	Indiana Kentucky Ohio West Virginia	X	X	X	X		80 banks 17 thrifts 25 credit unions	Ameritrust Co., Cleveland
AVAIL	1.0	8.0	825	2.0	Georgia	X			X		59 banks 26 thrifts 27 credit unions	12 members
THE EXCHANGE	1.0	1.6	525	2.0	Idaho Montana Oregon Washington British Columbia	X	X	X	X	X	50 banks 25 thrifts 100 credit unions	30 members
ITS, Inc.	1.0	4.0	578	0.8	Illinois Iowa Missouri Nebraska South Dakota	X	X	X			565 banks 22 thrifts 320 credit unions	Members
MAGIC LINE	0.8	5.5	2,250	3.0	Michigan	X	X	X	X		130 banks 11 thrifts 81 credit unions	10 members

[a] NYCE (New York Cash Exchange) will probably become one of the top regional shared ATM networks in 1985. NYCE is owned by eight depository institutions in New York and Connecticut.
[b] Subject to state laws and regulations.
[c] Fee based on volume.
Source: survey conducted by the author, March 1985.

TABLE A1 *(concluded)*

Interbank Transaction Fees (cents)				Major Costs of Participation	Method of Settlement	National Network Affiliation	POS Operations
	Total	ATM Owner Share	Network Share				
Withdrawal	60	40	20	$1,500 to $10,000 initial fee based on asset size. Series of monthly account-based fees.	Single corre- spondent	CIRRUS CITISHARE EXPRESS CASH PLUS	Yes
Deposit	125	120	5				
Bal. inquiry	30	25	5	$30 per $1 million in assets initial fee. $200 per ATM monthly fee.	Single corre- spondent		Yes
Withdrawal[c]	30–55	25	5–30				
Deposit[c]	55–80	50	5–30				
Bal. inquiry[c]	5–30	0	5–30	Texas banks: $1,000 and $500 per ATM initial fees. Non-Texas banks: $200 annual fee. Processors: $8,000 to $10,000 hook-up fee. Monthly fee of $760.	Corre- spondent banks	None	No
Withdrawal	74	65	9				
Bal. inquiry	49	40	9				
Withdrawal	50	39	11	$80 per $1 million in retail depos- its and $200 per ATM initial fees.	Federal Reserve	NATIONET	Yes
Deposit	50	39	11				
Withdrawal	55	40	15	Financial institutions: $50 per $1 million in deposits initial fee with a $4,000 minimum. $20 per $1 million in deposits annual fee with a $2,000 minimum. Processors: $20,000 initial fee. $5,000 annual fee.	Single corre- spondent	None	Yes
Bal. inquiry	35	20	15				
Withdrawal	45	25	20	$7,500 initial fee. $500 quarterly marketing fee.	Single corre- spondent	CIRRUS	Yes
Deposit	65	45	20				
Bal. inquiry	20	0	20				
Withdrawal	55	40	15	Chartered funding members: origi- nal capital contribution. Participating members: initial and annual fees based on deposit size.	Federal Reserve	None	No
Bal. inquiry	35	15	20				
Withdrawal	55	30	25	$6,000 and $250 per ATM initial fees. $600 monthly fee.	Single corre- spondent	EXPRESS CASH NATIONET THE EXCHANGE	No
Deposit	55	30	25				
Bal. inquiry	55	30	25				
Withdrawal	29	16	13	$300 per $1 million in deposits initial fee. Other fees based on services provided.	Federal Reserve	CIRRUS NATIONET	Yes
Deposit	74	61	13				
Bal. inquiry	29	16	13				
Withdrawal	85	60	25	$30 per $1 million in assets initial fee. $5 per $1 million in assets annual fee.	Federal Reserve	NATIONET	No
Deposit	85	60	25				

TABLE A2
Fifteen Largest New England Shared ATM Networks

Network[a]	Average Monthly ATM Transactions (thousands)		Number of ATMs	Number of Access Cards (thousands)	Market area	Services Offered[b]					Membership	Ownership
	Interbank	Total				Withdrawals	Deposits	Transfers	Cash Advances	Payments		
YANKEE 24	250	4,080	609	1,100	Connecticut	X	X	X	X		25 banks 43 thrifts 15 credit unions	Members
MONEC	173	1,150	585	811	New England Maryland New York	X	X	X	X	X	160 financial institutions	Bank of Boston
X-PRESS 24	100	5,000	614	1,000	Massachusetts New Hampshire	X	X	X	X	X	17 banks 13 thrifts 5 credit unions	BayBanks, Inc.
INSTACARD	98	160	90	250	Maine	X	X	X		X	8 banks 16 thrifts 15 credit unions	Maine National Bank, Portland
ACTION NETWORK	80[c]	800[c]	350	300	Massachusetts	X		X	X		15 banks 12 credit unions	Shawmut Corp., Boston
TX	70	600	185	520	Massachusetts	X	X	X	X		1 bank 76 thrifts 19 credit unions	40 members and ADP
MONEY SUPPLY	60	60	135	1,500	Massachusetts New Hampshire	X					195 financial institutions	Bank of Boston and BayBanks, Inc.
POCKETBANK	60	250	100	130	New Hampshire	X	X	X	X	X	29 banks 8 thrifts 2 credit unions	7 members
ACCESS	29	170	21	51	Vermont	X	X	X	X	X	5 banks 2 credit unions	The Howard Bank, Burlington
BARNY/ MULTICARD 24	16	808	180	450	Connecticut	X	X	X	X	X	7 banks 17 thrifts 5 credit unions	Connecticut Bank & Trust, Hartford
BANCPORT	15	500	130	180	Connecticut	X	X	X		X	2 banks 2 thrifts 2 credit unions	Connecticut National Bank, Hartford
VISA BANKING CENTER	8	115	60	165	Massachusetts	X	X	X	X	X	4 banks 39 thrifts	State Street Bank & Trust Co., Boston
REDI-CASH	7	124	53	90	Massachusetts	X	X	X		X	5 thrifts	Members
CITYTELLER 24	5	100	52	25	Connecticut	X	X	X	X	X	1 bank 1 thrift 4 credit unions	Citytrust, Bridgeport
VEC[c]	4	4	73	863	Massachusetts	X	X		X		57 financial institutions	9 members

[a] POCKETBANK, TX, and VEC will be linking to form CASH NETWORK, though each will retain its own logo. The financial institutions involved will be sharing both on-premises and off-premises ATMs, and expect to be operational in early 1985.

[b] Subject to state laws and regulations.

[c] Data from "1985 EFT Network Data Book," *Bank Network News*, September 25, 1984, p. 20.

TABLE A2   *(concluded)*

Interbank Transaction Fees (cents)				Major Costs of Participation	Method of Settlement	National Network Affiliation	POS Operations
	Total	ATM Owner Share	Network Share				
Withdrawal	50	32	18	$5,000 initial fee. $35 per ATM monthly fee.	Federal Reserve	None	Early 1986
Deposit	80	62	18				
Bal. inquiry	50	32	18	$7,500 initial fee.	Single corre-spondent	PLUS	Pilot
Withdrawal	60	40	20				
Deposit	85	65	20				
Bal. inquiry	60	40	20	$6,500 and $1,000 per ATM initial fees. $250 monthly fee.	Single corre-spondent	CIRRUS	No
Withdrawal	50	35	15				
Deposit	50	35	15				
Bal. inquiry	50	35	15	Initial fee based on asset size with a $5,000 minimum.	Single corre-spondent	Committed to PLUS	No
Withdrawal	60	40	20				
Deposit	60	40	20				
Bal. inquiry	60	40	20				
Withdrawal	60	50	10	$1,500 initial fee. Hookup fee based on type of connection. $150 monthly fee.	Single corre-spondent	None	Within year
Bal. inquiry	40	30	10				
Withdrawal	40	25	15	$2,500 initial fee. $1,000 annual marketing fee. $275 monthly fee.	ACH/ Federal Reserve	None	No
Deposit	90	75	15				
Bal. inquiry	35	20	15				
Withdrawal[d]	42–50	0	42–50	Initial and annual fees based on asset size.	Two corre-spondents	None	No
Bal. inquiry[d]	42–50	0	42–50				
Withdrawal	60	50	10	$6,000 initial fee. $2,000 annual fee. $.0.05 per card monthly advertising fee.	Single corre-spondent	Plan to connect with CIRRUS	No
Bal. inquiry	30	20	10				
Withdrawal	31.5	15	16.5	$4,900 initial fee. $100 annual fee. Monthly fee of $1 per account with newly issued cards.	Single corre-spondent	Plan to connect with PLUS and VISA ATM NETWORK	No
Deposit	31.5	15	16.5				
Bal. inquiry	2.5	0	2.5				
Withdrawal	60	50	10	$5,000 initial fee if ATM owner; $2,500 initial fee if card issuer. $200 per ATM and $0.05 per card on file monthly fees.	Single corre-spondent	None	No
Deposit	85	75	10				
Bal. inquiry	20	10	10				
Withdrawal	25	0	25	$2,500 annual fee.	Single corre-spondent	CIRRUS	No
Deposit	75	0	75				
Bal. inquiry	15	0	15				
Withdrawal	70	50	20	$1,500 initial fee. $0.04 per card and $100 monthly fees.	Single corre-spondent	VISA ATM NETWORK	No
Deposit	95	75	20				
Bal. inquiry	20	0	20				
No network charges among members.				Annual licensing fee based on asset size.	Between institutions	None	No
Withdrawal	75	0	75	None	Between institutions	EXPRESS CASH	No
Withdrawal	70	35	35	$100 to $500 monthly fee based on asset size.	Single corre-spondent	None	No
Deposit	70	35	35				

[d] Fee based on volume.

[e] The VEC network also processes approximately 320,000 check verifications monthly, and in addition to its 73 terminals that handle banking transactions, includes 41 terminals that process only check verifications. 363,000 supermarket courtesy cards can also access the network for this function.

Source: survey conducted by the author, March 1985.

TABLE A3
National Shared ATM Networks

Network	Average Monthly ATM Interbank Transactions	Number of ATMs	Number of Access Cards (millions)	Market Area	Services Offered[a]						Membership	Ownership
					Withdrawals	Deposits	Transfers	Cash Advances	Payments	Travelers Checks		
CIRRUS	400,000	6,600	20.0	46 states	X			X			2,000 financial institutions 15 regional networks	14 principal members
CITISHARE	n.a.	2,500	11.0	22 states	X			X	X		6 regional networks	Citicorp
EXPRESS CASH	n.a.	2,405	2.1	31 states	X			X	X		500 financial institutions 9 regional networks	American Express Co.
MASTERTELLER	n.a.	800	4.0	14 states	X			X			424 financial institutions 4 regional networks	MasterCard International
NATIONET	500	1,695	12.0	14 states British Columbia	X			X	X		2,500 financial institutions 15 regional networks	15 regional networks
PLUS	530,000	4,400	45.0	47 states	X			X	X		1,380 financial institutions	35 proprietary members
THE EXCHANGE	300,000	3,400	3.7	34 states and D.C. British Columbia	X	X	X	X	X		776 financial institutions	Members
VISA ATM NETWORK	n.a.	2,633	33.0	26 states and D.C. Australia Puerto Rico Spain	X			X	X		300 financial institutions	Visa International

n.a. = not available.
[a] Subject to state laws and regulations.
Source: survey conducted by the author, March 1985.

TABLE A3 *(concluded)*

| Transaction Fees (cents) | | | | | |
Total	ATM Owner Share	Network Share	Major Costs of Participation	Method of Settlement	National Network Link
Withdrawal 75 / Balance inquiry 50	50 / 25	25 / 25	Principal member: n.a. Associate member: $50,000 initial fee. $2,500 monthly fee. Corresponding member: fees determined by franchising principal or associate member.	Single correspondent	None
Withdrawal 65 / Balance inquiry 40	40 / 15	25 / 25	None.	Single correspondent	MASTERTELLER VISA ATM NETWORK Credit and debit cards issued from Citibank, South Dakota have access to CIRRUS THE EXCHANGE
Withdrawal — Fee varies			None.	American Express card: Federal Reserve: Bank card: settlement account at each regional network	
Withdrawal 83	75	8	None. Service is an extension of MasterCard membership.	Nonbank third party: MasterCard International Federal Reserve	CITISHARE
Withdrawal 70 / Balance inquiry 55	55 / 40	15 / 15	Equity owner: initial costs of a $5,000 stock purchase and $25,000 participation fee. Nonequity member: $5,000 initial fee, $5,000 connection fee, and a $5,000 service fee per year for three years.		None
Withdrawal 75 / Balance inquiry 40	50 / 15	25 / 25	Proprietary member: $200,000 initial fee. Quarterly assessment for operating costs. Sponsored member: $500 initial fee. $50 monthly administrative fee. Other fees are negotiated with sponsoring institution. Processing member: $50,000 initial fee.	Single correspondent	VISA ATM NETWORK
Determined by participants in each state.			Monthly fee based on cards issued.	Single correspondent	EXPRESS CASH
Withdrawal 75	75	0	None. Service is an extension of Visa membership.	Nonbank third party: Visa International	PLUS CITISHARE

International transactions: $1.75 plus 0.33% of transaction value to the ATM owner.

13 -16, 28

27

8 -12, 1 -7